LAW, BUSINESS, AND SOCIETY

Sixth Edition

LAW, BUSINESS, AND SOCIETY

Sixth Edition

Tony McAdams
University of Northern Iowa

Contributing Authors

James Freeman
University of Kentucky

Laura P. Hartman
DePaul University

Boston   Burr Ridge, IL   Dubuque, IA   Madison, WI   New York   San Francisco   St. Louis
Bangkok   Bogotá   Caracas   Lisbon   London   Madrid
Mexico City   Milan   New Delhi   Seoul   Singapore   Sydney   Taipei   Toronto

McGraw-Hill Higher Education

*A Division of The **McGraw-Hill** Companies*

LAW, BUSINESS, AND SOCIETY
Published by Irwin/McGraw-Hill, an imprint of The McGraw-Hill Companies, Inc. 1221
Avenue of the Americas, New York, NY, 10020. Copyright © 2001, 1998, 1995, 1992,
1989, 1986, by The McGraw-Hill Companies, Inc. All rights reserved. No part of this
publication may be reproduced or distributed in any form or by any means, or stored in a
data base or retrieval system, without the prior written consent of The McGraw-Hill
Companies, Inc., including, but not limited to, in any network or other electronic storage
or transmission, or broadcast for distance learning.
Some ancillaries, including electronic and print components, may not be available
to customers outside the United States.

This book is printed on acid-free paper.

1 2 3 4 5 6 7 8 9 0 DOC/DOC 0 9 8 7 6 5 4 3 2 1 0

ISBN 0-07-231401-X

Senior vice president and editorial director: *Robin J. Zwettler*
Sponsoring editor: *Andy Winston*
Editorial assistant: *Sara E. Strand*
Marketing manager: *Brad Shultz*
Project manager: *Laura Griffin*
Production associate: *Gina Hangos*
Senior designer: *Kiera Cunningham*
Supplement coordinator: *Carol A. Bielski*
Media technology producer: *Barb Block*
Compositor: *Interactive Composition Corporation*
Typeface: *10/12 Times Roman*
Printer: *R. R. Donnelley & Sons Company*
Cover image: "Woman Seated on an Armchair"
                  © 2000 Estate of Pablo Picasso/
                  Artist Rights Society (ARS), New York.

Library of Congress Cataloging-in-Publication Data

McAdams, Tony.
    Law, business, and society / Tony McAdams contributing authors, James Freeman,
  Laura P. Hartman.— 6th ed.
        p. cm. – (Irwin/McGraw-Hill legal studies in business series)
    Includes bibliographical references and index.
    ISBN 0-07-231401-X
    1. Business enterprises–Law and legislation–United States.   2. Trade regulation–United States.
  3. Business ethics–United States.   4. Industries–Social aspects–United States.
  I. Freeman, James, 1950.   II. Hartman, Laura Pincus.   III. Title.   IV. Series.

KF1355.M28 2000
346.73'065–dc21   00-027291

www.mhhe.com

Brief Contents

Contents

Preface

A New Direction. Trying to keep pace with the electronic revolution, we have added a variety of cyberlaw materials to this sixth edition. The most notable addition is Chapter 18, Internet Law and Ethics. Jurisdiction, privacy, freedom of speech, contracts, intellectual property, and tax policy are among the topics we address in that new chapter. Furthermore, we have closed each chapter with one or more Internet Exercises, we have provided occasional computer-related materials in other chapters, and we have provided some 200 selected Web sites throughout the text.

OVERVIEW

This text is directed to courses at both the upper-division undergraduate and masters levels in the legal environment of business and government and business, as well as business and society. To date, authors of textbooks in these areas have often relied on a single discipline (for example, law, economics, or management) as the foundation for their efforts. In this text, we take an interdisciplinary approach, utilizing elements of law, political economy, international business, ethics, social responsibility, and management. This large task necessarily requires certain trade-offs, but we hope the product will more accurately embrace the fullness of the business environment.

We want to emphasize at the outset that our primary goal is to produce an interesting reading experience. Naturally, accuracy and reasonable comprehensiveness cannot be sacrificed. Our feeling, however, is that a law text can be both intellectually and emotionally engaging without sacrificing substantive ends. To meet our objective we have given extensive attention to read-

ings, provocative quotes, and factual details (surveys, data, and anecdotes) that add flesh to the bones of legal theory.

The book is divided into five parts as follows:

Part I—Business and Society. We do not begin with the law. Rather, in Chapter 1 (Capitalism and the Role of Government), Chapter 2 (Business Ethics), and Chapter 3 (The Corporation and Public Policy: Expanding Responsibilities), we hope to establish the influences that determine the character of our legal system.

Part I should meet the following goals: (*a*) enhance student awareness of the many societal influences on business, (*b*) establish the business context from which government regulation arose, and (*c*) explore the roles of the free market, government intervention, and individual and corporate ethics in controlling business behavior.

The student must understand not merely the law but the law in context. What forces have provoked government intervention in business? What alternatives to our current "mixed economy" might prove healthy? These considerations help the students respond to one of the critical questions of the day: To what extent, if any, *should* we regulate business?

Part II—Introduction to Law. Chapter 4 (The American Legal System) and Chapter 5 (Constitutional Law and the Bill of Rights) survey the foundations of our legal system. Here, we set out the "nuts and bolts" of law, combining cases, readings, and narrative. Then, with Chapter 6 (International Ethics and Law), we examine business and public policy in the global context.

Part III—Trade Regulation and Antitrust. Chapter 7 (Government Regulation of Business: An Introduction) is a bit of a departure from the approach of many texts in that significant attention is directed to state and local regulations. Chapter 8 (Administrative Agencies and the Regulatory Process), Chapter 9 (Business Organizations and Securities Regulation), Chapter 10 (Antitrust Law—Monopolies and Mergers), and Chapter 11 (Antitrust Law—Restraints of Trade) survey the heart of government regulation of business.

Part IV—Employer–Employee Relations. Chapter 12 (Employment Law I: Protecting the Employee), Chapter 13 (Employment Law II: Discrimination), and Chapter 14 (Employment Law III: Labor–Management Relations) are intended not only to survey the law in those areas, but also to introduce some of the sensitive and provocative social issues that have led to today's extensive government intervention in the employment relationship.

Part V—Business and Selected Social Issues. Three of the closing chapters of this book—Chapter 15 (Consumer Protection), Chapter 16 (Product Liability), and Chapter 17 (Environmental Protection)—emphasize the dramatic expansion of the public's demands on the business community, while Chapter 18 (Internet Law and Ethics) surveys some cyberlaw problems.

ACCREDITATION

Our text conforms to the undergraduate and MBA "Perspectives" portion of the American Assembly of Collegiate Schools of Business (AACSB) curriculum standards for accreditation:

Standard: Both undergraduate and MBA curricula should provide an understanding of perspectives that form the context for business. Coverage should include:

- Ethical and global issues,
- The influence of political, social, legal and regulatory, environmental, and technological issues, and
- The impact of demographic diversity on organizations.

Two chapters are devoted exclusively to ethics materials, while ethics themes emerge throughout the book. At the same time, law and economics clearly must remain central ingredients in meeting our goal of explaining the business and social context in which

government regulation arose. The chapter on employment discrimination should be quite helpful in aiding students' understanding of the "demographic diversity" topic.

Furthermore, as required by the rapidly changing nature of commerce and as recommended by the AACSB, the text devotes extensive attention to issues arising from international business. Various topics throughout the text (for example, comparative economic systems, the Foreign Corrupt Practices Act, and global pollution) afford the student a sense of the worldwide implications of American business practice, and Chapter 6 is entirely devoted to international themes.

PHILOSOPHY

As noted, our primary goal is to provoke student thought. To that end, heavy emphasis is placed on analysis. The questions asked are considered more important than the answers. The student is acquainted with existing policy in the various areas not merely for the purposes of understanding and retention but also to provoke inquiry as to the desirability of those policies. Then, where appropriate, an effort is made to explore with the student the desired managerial role in shaping and responding to governmental policy.

Our book takes a strong public policy orientation. Part I of the text is, as explained, a necessary foundation on which the student can build a logical understanding of the regulatory process, but the business and society themes don't stop there. In virtually every chapter, we look beyond the law itself to other environmental forces. For example, in the antitrust chapters economic philosophy is of great importance. Antitrust is explored as a matter of national social policy. We argue that antitrust has a good deal to do with the direction of American life generally. Law is at the heart of the fair employment practices section, but materials from management, sociology, economics, and the like are used to treat fair employment as an issue of social policy rather than as a series of narrower technical legal disputes. These kinds of approaches characterize most chapters as we attempt to examine the various problems in the whole and, to some degree, from a managerial view point. Having said all this, it should be understood that the law remains the bulky core of the book.

KEY FEATURES/DEPARTURES

Journalistic and scholarly readings seek to give the book a stimulating, real-world quality.

Ethics and social responsibility are at the heart of the text rather than an afterthought to meet accreditation standards.

International issues receive extensive attention.

Law cases are of a length sufficient to clearly express the essence of the decision while challenging the reader's intellect.

The law is studied in the economic, social, and political context from which it springs.

Attention is given to critics of business values and the American legal system.

Approximately 200 selected websites have been added to the 6th edition, and each chapter includes at least one Internet Exercise.

Perhaps the key pedagogical tactic in the book is the emphasis on questions rather than on answers.

INSTRUCTOR'S MANUAL

A package of supplementary materials is included in the instructor's manual. Those materials include (*a*) chapter outlines, (*b*) general advice regarding the goals and purposes of the chapters, (*c*) summaries of the law cases, (*d*) answers for the questions raised in the text, and (*e*) a test bank.

COMPUTERIZED TEST BANK

This version of the Test Bank includes all of the material in the printed version with added flexibility. Instructors can add, remove, modify, and shuffle questions according to their preference and teaching style.

BOOK WEBSITE

This site, located at **www.mhhe.com/mcadams**, truly enriches the text. In addition to offering instructors a downloadable version of the Instructor's Manual and Test Bank, it also contains additional cases, readings, and supporting text for the benefit of both instructors and students.

 Look for this icon denoting topics that receive further treatment on the site.

ACKNOWLEDGMENTS

Completion of the sixth edition of this book depended, in significant part, on the hard work of others.

The authors are pleased to acknowledge the contributions of these good people: Craig Beytien, publisher, Andy Winston, sponsoring editor, Laura Griffin, project manager, and Sara Strand, editorial assistant.

Brooke Kelderman, undergraduate business student at the University of Northern Iowa, displayed unusual competence and patience in helping prepare the sixth edition of this book. The authors also thank the 35 reviewers from past editions, and the following professors who reviewed portions of the text and otherwise provided valuable guidance for this edition: Steven Abraham, SUNY–Oswego; Thomas R. Berry, Floyd College; Martha A. Broderick, University of Maine; Yvonne Brown, Nova Southeastern University; Frank Cavico, Nova Southeastern University; Susan Denbo, Rider College; George Generas, Jr., University of Hartford; Ishaq Ghanayem, Lincoln University; Ilene Goldberg, Rider University; Marc Hall, Auburn University; Charles Hartmann, Wright State University; Doug Hess, Oakland City University; Harvey S. James, Jr., University of Hartford; Marc Lampe, University of San Diego; Chad Lewis, Everett Community College; Susan M. Lowe, Golden Gate University; Toni MacDonald, Oakland City University; Henry E. Mallue, Jr., College of William and Mary; Greg K. McCann, Stetson University; Robert F. O'Neil, University of San Diego; Cliff Olson,

Southern Adventist University; Mark W. Peacock, Milligan College; John C. Quinn, University of South Dakota; Gregory S. Richardson, Pfeiffer University; Patricia Rinke, St. Mary College; Ira Sprotzer, Rider College; Ann C. Wendt, Wright State University; James P. West, Moravian College.

SUGGESTIONS

The authors welcome comments and criticism from all readers.

Tony McAdams

Business and Society

Chapter 1

Capitalism and the Role of Government

Part One—Introduction

Are you a capitalist? If so, what role, if any, should the law play in your business life? How much government does America need? These themes, examining the relationship between government and business in America, are the core of this text. Since the fall of the Soviet Union and the general decline of Communist influence, free market reasoning has dominated worldwide economic discourse.

> Are you a capitalist?

Indeed, former U.S. State Department policy planner Francis Fukuyama has argued that capitalism and Western democracy have so thoroughly proven their worth that the capitalism/collectivism debate is over.[1]

On the other hand, distinguished management scholar Henry Mintzberg says we have misunderstood the lesson of the ascendance of capitalism:

"Capitalism has triumphed." That was the pat conclusion reached in the West as, one by one, the communist regimes of Eastern Europe began to fall. It has become such an article of faith that we have become blind to its effects. Those effects are highly negative—indeed, dangerous—because the conclusion itself is wrong.

* * * * *

Capitalism did not triumph at all; balance did. We in the West have been living in balanced societies with strong private sectors, strong public sectors, and great strength in the sectors in between. The countries under communism were totally out of balance. In those countries, the state controlled an enormous proportion of all organized activity. There was little or no countervailing force.

The belief that capitalism has triumphed is now throwing the societies of the West out of balance, especially the United Kingdom and the United States. That the imbalance will favor private rather than state ownership will not help society.[2]

* * * * *

Warp-Speed Capitalism.   Whether a victory for capitalism (Fukuyama) or for balance (Mintzberg), the new global, technologically based economy is leading us in directions we can only dimly foresee. Does that uncertain future call for strengthened government controls, or are we wisest to let the market sort out our lives on a case-by-case basis? As scholar Robert Heilbroner notes, we are in an era of "warp-speed capitalism,"[3] fired by unprecedented faith in market-based decision making, but Heilbroner also wonders whether the great strength of global, capitalist markets won't, perhaps paradoxically, require stronger government rules. The increasing complexity of capitalist economies, growing business power, and the "globalization" of the economy may combine to generate new rules even as the market rushes forward. In their recent book, *The Commanding Heights—The Battle Between Government and the Marketplace That Is Remaking the Modern World,* analysts Daniel Yergin and Joseph Stanislaw point, for example, to the global financial markets where pressure for new government rules seems likely to increase because of fear that a miscalculation or two in one corner of the world may threaten the economic health of all.[4] In a sense, we have witnessed a quiet revolution as the market has soared and governments have faltered, but Yergin and Stanislaw wonder whether the market can provide all that we expect of it, including the following:

- Prosperity.
- Social fairness.
- Environmental protection.
- Preservation of strong national identities.
- Methods for coping with demographic change.[5]

The ongoing, global struggle between markets and governments provides the context in which American business operates.

The volatility of that struggle was dramatically underscored in December 1999 when angry riots broke out at the Seattle meeting of the World Trade Organization (WTO). Representatives from 135 nations met to reduce trade barriers and coordinate the global economy. Some 35,000 protesters responded with street demonstrations and violence unseen in the United States since the Vietnam War era. Critics see the WTO as little more than an undemocratic pawn of giant transnational corporations while those corporations and the United States argue that a worldwide free market is the surest path to prosperity and peace for all. As suggested by the following article, the protesters worry that the WTO, in its pursuit of free trade and global capitalism, will give scant attention to the environment, genetically engineered foods, sweatshops, labor unions, and human rights, generally. [For a more detailed discussion of globalization, see Chapter 3.]

THOUSANDS HEAD WEST FOR "PROTEST OF THE CENTURY": WORLD TRADE MEETING BECOMES LIGHTNING ROD FOR VARIOUS CAUSES

Nita Lelyveld

SEATTLE—Tom Wilson, 54, has spent years fighting the multinationals that have moved in to mine copper and gold in his native Wisconsin. This week, he used up his frequent-flyer miles to fight what he sees as a rising tide of corporate globalism by coming to protest the World Trade Organization.

"What we're seeing is a control of world power by corporations," said the white-haired Mr. Wilson wearing a yellow poncho with the words "Seattle '99, Protest of the Century."

On his hood was a pin: "Mean Corporations Suck." He lifted his poncho to show the words on his T-shirt: "Not for sale."

Around Mr. Wilson in the street, cordoned off by police in riot gear, stood several hundred other protesters. They, too, had made their way to Seattle—to lobby for Tibetan freedom, for the safety of sea turtles, for the end of slave labor, for boycotts against companies that use sweatshops, for a dozen other causes that suddenly seemed joined under one banner.

Dan Steinberg, 28, of San Francisco said the WTO had become a lightning rod. The trade organization touches on all the protesters' issues when it meets in closed sessions and makes decisions in the name of free trade that lower environmental and economic and social justice standards worldwide, Mr. Steinberg said.

"The WTO subverts democracy by declaring democratically achieved laws—such as restrictions on child labor—as being trade barriers," he said. "The organization is run by big businesses. And if we don't stop them, they will control the world."

Protesters said the stores that were damaged with graffiti—names like Banana Republic and NikeTown—were targeted because they represent the new global economy, made up of large chains, dependent on cheap, foreign labor.

Questions

1. Are corporations a threat to world welfare or the only way to general peace and prosperity? Explain.
2. Should you decline to shop at global chains like Banana Republic and Nike? Explain.

[For arguments in support of globalization, see **http://www.iccwbo.org/home/menu_case_for_the_global_economy.asp**]

[For a critique of globalization, see **http://www.oneworld.org/guides/globalisation/index.html**]

Our Purpose. Thus, the ongoing global struggle between government intervention and free markets, between corporations and their critics, provides the unstable context in which

American business operates. Within that context, then, the purpose of this book is to ask two questions:

1. What is the proper role of business in American and global society?
2. How much, if any, government regulation of business is necessary to secure that role?

Markets and Governments?   In the United States, we certainly cannot understand our system of laws without a firm appreciation for the principles of capitalism from which those laws spring. We chose a capitalist, democratic approach to life. Other cultures have placed less faith in the market and more in government planning. The legal systems in those countries reflect a preference for greater central authority.

In this chapter, we will explore the full range of the economic spectrum, moving from a laissez-faire, free market approach on the extreme right, to a brief reminder of command economy principles on the far left, but the bulk of our attention will rest where the world is at this moment—that is, we will examine the notion of the *mixed economy.*

The free market approach assumes that we can operate our business structure and our society at large free of all but the most basic legal mechanisms such as contract and criminal law. The wisdom of the market—our individual judgments, in combination with our individual consciences—would serve to "regulate" American life. Government regulatory agencies, occupational licensure, zoning restrictions, antitrust law, and all but the most basic government services (perhaps limited to the police, the courts, and the army) would be unnecessary.

On the other hand, the collectivist alternatives (communism, socialism, and their variations) assume that the business community and society at large require expansive government intervention. Individual judgment would be supplemented with or largely supplanted by the collective will.

As noted, today's debate is no longer about capitalism versus communism but about the mixed economy—that is, about what form of capitalism best serves the world's needs. At the moment, the center of the struggle lies in the U.S., Japanese, and European versions of capitalism, but that will surely change as China's remarkable economic transformation so vividly reminds us. Capitalism has shown itself to be the stronger vehicle for productivity, efficiency, and personal freedom. Is it the stronger vehicle for building a sense of community, for improving the standard of living of all citizens, and for coping with the uncertainties of the future? Should we embrace the Japanese practice of close cooperation between government and business? Or the European model of capitalism with its heavy overlay of welfare programs? Or America's firmer commitment to market principles? Or some amalgam of the three? Or will a new direction emerge? Indeed, at this writing, the Japanese are moving guardedly toward a less-managed market system, and the Europeans are making tough decisions about welfare.

Law.   Finally, this chapter should be read as a foundation for the study of law that follows. Once a society settles on some broad political and economic principles, it pours a thin veneer or many heavy coats (depending on the system chosen) of social control on that foundation to implement the goals of the larger system. The law serves as a primary method of social control. So, to understand the law, we need to understand its roots in political economy.

Questions—Part One

1. Former Secretary of Labor, Robert Reich, speculates about five possible scenarios for the 21st century. Which do you think is the more likely direction? Explain.

   a. History is ending in bureaucratic corporatism . . . Key decisions are shifting away from elected politicians and legislative bodies toward multinational bureaucracies (such as the G-7) and global corporations unaccountable to any single population.

   b. History alternates between periods of central control and chaos, and we are again entering the latter. The 40-year interval of superpower stability is giving way to tribal fragmentation and warfare with ethnic tensions flaring over Eastern Europe and the former Soviet Union, the Asian subcontinent, and even within advanced industrial nations . . .

   c. History is ending in cultural authoritarianism. Societies like Japan and Germany, which reward group loyalty and investment, are gaining economic power over societies organized around individual liberty and personal consumption. Meanwhile, much of the Third World is succumbing to Islamic fundamentalism.

   d. History is ending in liberal democracy and individual liberty. Modern economies depend on educated work forces, which in turn are demanding rights and freedoms that only liberal democracies can provide (look at Latin America).

   e. All of the above.[6]

2. In 1999, *The Wall Street Journal* asked leading economists, executives, and others whether capitalism's triumph over socialism is, in fact, complete, or whether challenges remain. What challenges threaten capitalism in the next millennium? See Paul Hofheinz, "What Now?" *The Wall Street Journal,* September 27, 1999, p. R25.

Part Two—Capitalism

Capitalism in Theory—Ayn Rand

Capitalism was built on a sound intellectual footing and was stimulated by the promise of unprecedented general welfare. These forces, in combination with America's natural resources and an astonishingly courageous and hardy population, led to the development of a powerful economic machine. But that machine, in the view of many Americans, ran out of control for a time. The era of the Robber Barons and abuses associated with them brought widespread popular sentiment for governmental restraints on capitalism. Thus, as is discussed in subsequent chapters, America's substantially free market economy was, in increasing increments, placed under government regulation. And despite the striking rhetoric and significant deregulation strides of the current free market era, America remains a nation of big government.

Our purpose now is to reconsider the merits of a purer form of capitalism. Did we turn too hastily from the market? Should we further shed our governmental role in economic affairs and restore our faith in the Invisible Hand? Can we, in large measure, do without regulation by law? Will a genuinely unfettered market better serve our needs than our current amalgam of business restrained by government? To answer these questions, we need a firm understanding of capitalism in a pure form, which has almost entirely slipped from view. The controversial philosopher and novelist Ayn Rand was an uncompromising advocate of free market principles. She believed the necessary categories of government were only three in number: the police, the armed services, and the law courts. Via her philosophy of Objectivism, Rand argued that the practice of free market principles is necessary to the pursuit of a rational, moral life. Rand's viewpoint has been the subject of vigorous criticism. Its merits are for the reader to assess, but it is fair to say that she was among America's most ardent and articulate apostles of a genuine free market.

MAN'S RIGHTS

Ayn Rand

If one wishes to advocate a free society—that is, capitalism—one must realize that its indispensable foundation is the principle of individual rights. If one wishes to uphold individual rights, one must realize that capitalism is the only system that can uphold and protect them.

"Rights" are a moral concept—the concept that provides a logical transition from the principles guiding an individual's actions to the principles guiding his relationship with others—the concept that preserves and protects individual morality in a social context—the link between the moral code of a man and the legal code of a society, between ethics and politics. *Individual rights are the means of subordinating society to moral law.*

Every political system is based on some code of ethics. The dominant ethics of mankind's history were variants of the altruist-collectivist doctrine which subordinated the individual to some higher authority. Consequently, most political systems were variants of the same statist tyranny.

* * * * *

Under all such systems, morality was a code applicable to the individual, but not to society. Society was placed *outside* the moral law, and the inculcation of self-sacrificial devotion to social duty was regarded as the main purpose of ethics in man's earthly existence.

Since there is no such entity as "society," since society is only a number of individual men, this meant, in practice, that the rulers of society were exempt from moral law; subject only to traditional rituals, they held total power and exacted blind obedience—on the implicit principle of: "The good is that which is good for society, and the ruler's edicts are its voice on earth."

This was true of all statist systems, under all variants of the altruist-collectivist ethics, mystical or social. As witness: the theocracy of Egypt, with the Pharaoh as an embodied god—the unlimited majority rule or *democracy* of Athens—the welfare state run by the Emperors of Rome—the Inquisition of the late Middle Ages—the absolute monarchy of France—the welfare state of Bismarck's Prussia—the gas chambers of Nazi Germany—the slaughter house of the Soviet Union.

All these political systems were expressions of the altruist-collectivist ethics—and their common characteristic is the fact that society stood above the moral law . . . Thus, politically, all these systems were variants of an *amoral* society.

The most profoundly revolutionary achievement of the United States of America was *the subordination of society to moral law.*

The principle of man's individual rights represented the extension of morality into the social system—as a limitation on the power of the state . . . The United States was the first *moral* society in history.

All previous systems had regarded man as a sacrificial means to the ends of others, and society as an end in itself. The United States regarded man as an end in himself, and society as a means to the peaceful, orderly, *voluntary* coexistence of individuals. All previous systems had held that man's life belongs to society, that society can dispose of him in any way it pleases, and that any freedom he enjoys is his only by favor, by the *permission* of society, which may be revoked at any time. The United States held that man's life is his by *right,* that a right is the property of an individual, that society as such has no rights, and that the only moral purpose of a government is the protection of individual rights.

A "right" is a moral principle defining and sanctioning a man's freedom of action in a social context. There is only *one* fundamental right (all the others are its consequences or corollaries): a man's right to his own life . . .

America's inner contradiction was the altruist-collectivist ethics. Altruism is incompatible with freedom, with capitalism, and with individual rights . . .

It was the concept of individual rights that had given birth to a free society. It was with the destruction of individual rights that the destruction of freedom had to begin.

A collectivist tyranny dare not enslave a country by an outright confiscation of its values, material or moral. It has to be done by a process of internal corruption . . . The process entails such a growth of newly promulgated "rights" that people do not notice the fact that the meaning of the concept is being reversed . . .

The Democratic Party platform of 1960 summarizes the switch boldly and explicitly. It declares that a democratic administration "will reaffirm the economic bill of rights which Franklin Roosevelt wrote into our national conscience 16 years ago."

Bear clearly in mind the meaning of the concept of *"rights"* when you read the list which that platform offers:

1. The right to a useful and remunerative job in the industries or shops or farms or mines of the nation.
2. The right to earn enough to provide adequate food and clothing and recreation.
3. The right of every farmer to raise and sell his products at a return which will give him and his family a decent living.
4. The right of every businessman, large and small, to trade in an atmosphere of freedom from unfair competition and domination by monopolies at home and abroad.
5. The right of every family to a decent home.
6. The right to adequate medical care and the opportunity to achieve and enjoy good health.
7. The right to adequate protection from the economic fears of old age, sickness, accidents, and unemployment.
8. The right to a good education.

A single question added to each of the above eight clauses would make the issue clear: *At whose expense?*

Jobs, food, clothing, recreation (!), homes, medical care, education, etc., do not grow in nature. These are man-made values—goods and services produced by men. *Who* is to provide them?

If some men are entitled *by right* to the products of the work of others, it means that those others are deprived of rights and condemned to slave labor.

* * * * *

Observe, in this context, the intellectual precision of the Founding Fathers: they spoke of the right to *the pursuit* of happiness—*not* of the right to happiness. It means that a man has the right to take the actions he deems necessary to achieve his happiness; it does *not* mean that others must make him happy . . .

Property rights and the right of free trade are man's only "economic rights" (they are, in fact, *political* rights)—and there can be no such thing as "an *economic* bill of rights" . . .

And while people are clamoring about "economic rights," the concept of political rights is vanishing . . .

Such is the state of one of today's most crucial issues: *political* rights versus "*economic* rights." It's either-or. One destroys the other. But there are, in fact, no "economic rights," no "collective rights," no "public-interest rights." The term *individual rights* is a redundancy: there is no other kind of rights and no one else to possess them.

Those who advocate laissez-faire capitalism are the only advocates of man's rights.

In 1999 an ad was placed in Ivy League college newspapers offering $50,000 for ovarian eggs from women with minimum credentials of a combined SAT score of 1400 and a height of 5 feet, 10 inches. Similarly, an Internet site now auctions eggs from models and actresses.

a. Does capitalism encourage us to treat people as products?
b. Are people, in fact, products? Explain.

Capitalism in Practice—"Privatization" in America and Abroad

Around the globe, from Russia to Eastern Europe and from the United Kingdom to Southeast Asia, expanded faith in the free market was the singular economic message of the 1980s and 1990s. The basic point to recognize is the free market argument that virtually all services now performed by government may be more efficiently and more equitably "managed" by the impersonal forces of the market.

Most commonly, privatization follows two patterns: (1) contracting out where government, in effect, turns over a portion of its duties, such as garbage collection, to a private firm; and (2) the sale of public assets, such as an airport, to a private purchaser. Contracting with private firms to provide public services has become widespread in the United States and includes activities such as golf course operations, tree trimming, building maintenance, and computer services. A survey of 120 municipalities in 1997 found that 54 percent contracted with private firms for garbage service, an increase from 30 percent in 1987. Some 73 percent hired private firms for janitorial work, an increase from 52 percent in 1987.[7]

Privatization is now a commonplace of American life. More than 30 states have turned over portions of their welfare systems to private companies.[8] An entire federal agency, the Office of Personnel Management, has been converted to a for-profit firm owned by its former federal employees. The company does background checks on job applicants for the federal government, casinos, and others, and in the first 15 months of privatization, saved taxpayers about $20 million.[9] Some states are now experimenting with privately funded highways and so-called congestion pricing. In crowded Orange County, California, drivers pay as much as $2.75 per trip to take a privately funded and operated, 10-mile stretch of highway rather than suffer the frustrations of the public road.[10] The idea is that traffic jams are caused by not requiring drivers to pay for the costs (delays) they impose on others. The market-based solution, then, is to charge for driving where congestion is a problem. Experts, note, however, that the Orange County toll road is one of the few successes in privately financed transportation,[11] and critics worry about creating fast-moving "Lexus lanes" for rich people.

> **Critics worry about creating fast-moving "Lexus lanes" for rich people.**

Author Joan Didion referred to our highways as America's only communion. Would it be a social/ethical wrong to adopt widespread "congestion fees" and privately operated toll roads that would permit those with money to avoid the democracy of the highways?

Prisons.   Getting tough on crime is a centerpiece of current social policy in America such that, in 1999, 2.0 million Americans were behind bars, but the cost of housing our booming prison population has forced many states and communities to look at private-sector alternatives to public jails.[12] Private jails housed about 11,000 inmates nationally in 1989, but that number rose to more than 132,000 by 1998.[13] A number of studies show that private prisons can be operated about 10 to 15 percent cheaper than those in the public sector.[14] Of course, part of that saving is the result of paying employees substantially smaller salaries than those in the public sector. Furthermore, critics point to serious security lapses in some privately operated prisons, and they worry that rehabilitation efforts will be shortchanged in the drive for profits.

Schools.   Is capitalism the answer to poor school performance? Can the competitive power of the market reform America's struggling public school systems? The idea was unthinkable a few decades ago, but some increasingly frustrated parents and school boards are considering a free market "fix." As yet only a small number of schools are experimenting with free market approaches such as open enrollment (students attend the school of their choice regardless of their place of residence), charter schools (funded by taxes, but freed of much government oversight), and vouchers (students "spend" their taxpayer-provided dollars on the school of their choice). Whether those strategies, if widely adopted, will significantly improve American education is simply unknown at this point. Critics are concerned, not only that privatization will not improve academic performance, but that market-based schools will undermine the ideals of common experience, community, and joint responsibility that have been hallmarks of public education. They fear a balkanized school system and society with increasingly deep divisions between races and socioeconomic classes.

Question

1. What concerns would you raise about converting public schools to private businesses?

[For an extensive database favorable to privatization, see **http://www.privatization.org/**]

Privatization Abroad. Capitalism has swept the globe. The results have not always been happy as evidenced most vividly by Russia's thus-far catastrophic transformation of its economy from state ownership to private sector domination. Elsewhere the news has been generally favorable. New Zealand has

Capitalism has swept the globe.

made perhaps the most adventuresome commitment to privatization by imposing competition on former monopolies in electricity, telecommunications, and transportation. Postal rates, in the now private system, have fallen and next-day deliveries are up dramatically. New Zealand Electric cut its staff by 71 percent and doubled its profits.[15] While the government share of the gross domestic product remains at 36 percent and the government still owns big sectors of the economy, the progress is so remarkable that *The Economist* now considers New Zealand's economy to be the freest in the world.[16] Even in China, where the central government remains the final word, privatization is gradually bringing free market competition to the economy. In 1999, the Chinese government announced that the nation's biggest refinery, China National Petroleum Corp., would be opened to private investors in a deal that was expected to raise some $10 billion.[17]

[For information on privatization abroad, see **http://www.adamsmith.org.uk/policy/ publications/world-privatization.htm**]

Privatization in Sum. Studies indicate that contracting out services reduces costs by 10 to 20 percent.[18] Privatization supporters also point to improved managerial skills and increased expertise when turning government services over to private sector specialists. Critics, however, argue that those savings result simply from paying substandard wages and cutting corners on quality. Professor Jonathan Goodrich lists these primary concerns regarding privatization:

- Unemployment of government workers.
- Lower quality of services.
- Government loss of control and accountability.
- Excessive government payments for private sector work.
- Corruption and scandal.[19]

In 1998, *The Wall Street Journal* reported that "the early stirrings of backlash against the market are in sight."[20] While the most obvious concern lies with profit-seeking hospitals and cost-cutting "managed" health care, many Americans share broader worries about how far the free market should reach. Daniel Yergin and Joseph Stanislaw in their book, *The Commanding Heights,* point particularly to the market's uncertainties:

> Americans are willing to tolerate more insecurity than people in other industrial nations, but there are still limits to how much insecurity they will accept. Elections and opinion polls demonstrate that while the public does not want government to extend its reach, neither does it want this rich country to abandon its American-style safety net.[21]

Questions—Part Two

1. *a.* Should we turn the U.S. Postal Service over to the private sector? Explain.
   b. Which segments of society would be harmed most by that move? Explain.
2. From the capitalist viewpoint, why is the private ownership of property necessary to the preservation of freedom?
3. Ayn Rand argued: "Altruism is incompatible with freedom, with capitalism, and with individual rights."
   a. Define altruism.
   b. Explain why Rand rejected altruism.
4. In describing life in aggressively commercialized Hong Kong, Alvin Rabushka praised the "single-minded pursuit of making money" and the "emphasis on the material things in life." Rabushka admitted to finding "Hong Kong's economic hustle and bustle more interesting, entertaining, and liberating than its lack of high opera, music, and drama."
   a. Although it is often criticized in America, is materialism the most certain and most interesting path to personal happiness? Explain.
   b. Would "sophisticated" culture (such as opera and drama) substantially disappear in America without government support? Explain.
   c. If so, how may we justify that support? If not, how may we justify that support?
5. Assume the federal government removed itself from the purchase and maintenance of its parks.
   a. Left to the private sector, what sorts of parks would develop under the profit incentive?
   b. Would Yellowstone, for example, survive in substantially its present state? Explain.
   c. How can it be argued that the federal parks are an unethical, undemocratic expropriation of private resources?
6. Assume the abolition of the federal Food and Drug Administration. How would the free market protect the citizenry from dangerous food and drug products?
7. Should education be returned to the free market? Explain. How would poor Americans finance a private-sector education?
8. Scholar Amitai Etzioni argues that America must choose between rededication to economic growth and emphasis on a quality-of-life society (slower growth, emphasis on

ecology, concern for safety, harmony with oneself and others). He argues that the monetary costs and the social-psychic strains of pursuing these two divergent courses exceed America's resources, both physical and emotional.

   a. Do you agree with Etzioni? Explain.

   b. Which path would you choose? Explain.

   c. Will the market support the quality-of-life approach? Explain.

9. Puritan leaders felt concern over the morality of merchants selling goods for "more than their worth." That concern was particularly grave when the goods were scarce or in great demand.

   a. Should our society develop an ethic wherein goods are to be sold only "for what they are worth"? Explain.

   b. Can a seller make an accurate determination of worth? Explain.

   c. Does a product's worth differ from the price that product will bring in the marketplace? Explain.

   d. Personalize the inquiry: Assume you seek to sell your Ford auto for $5,000. Assume you know of several identical Fords in a similar state of repair that can be purchased for $4,500. Assume you find a buyer at $5,000. Will you unilaterally lower your price or direct the purchaser to the other autos? Explain.

   e. If not, have you acted justly? Explain.

10. Critics of our capitalist system contend that ability and effort often are less responsible for one's success than "unearned" factors such as family background, social class, luck, and willingness to cheat. Do you agree? Explain.

11. Commentator Irving Kristol asked whether it was "just" for Ray Kroc (now deceased, formerly of McDonald's) to have made so much money by merely figuring out a new way to sell hamburgers. He concluded that capitalism says it is just because he sold a good product; people want it; it is fair.

   a. Do you agree with Kristol? Explain.

   b. Does contemporary American capitalism offer excessive rewards to those clever enough to build near-term paper profits (lawyers, accountants, financial analysts) through mergers, tax write-offs, and the like while diverting scarce resources from long-term productive ventures (such as new product development or more efficient production processes)? Explain.

   c. If so, is capitalism fatally flawed? Explain.

12. Professor Robert E. Lane argued that the person who is motivated by needs for affiliation, rather than by needs for achievement, does less well in the market. Such a person is not rewarded so well as autonomous, achievement-oriented people.

   a. Is Lane correct? Explain.

   b. Is capitalism, in the long run, destructive of societal welfare in that achievement is better rewarded than affiliation? Explain.

13. Make the argument that the federal highway program, although well-intentioned, was merely one in a series of federal interventions that distorted the market, leading, in this instance, to the long-term decline of inner cities.

14. How would poor people be cared for in a free market society?

15. "Kevin Mattson, a researcher at Rutgers University, fears the gated community, where people shut themselves off from public life. The privatization of everything including garbage service, he said, disassociates people from contributing to the public good and from their responsibility to other people."

    Do you agree? Explain. See Lisa Rathke, "School Choice Experts Discuss Impact of Choice," *Associated Press State & Local Wire,* February 8, 1999.

Part Three—Collectivism

The term *collectivism* embraces various economic philosophies on the left of the political-economic spectrum; principally, communism and socialism. Capitalism is characterized by economic individualism. Communism and the various styles of socialism feature economic cooperation.

COMMUNISM

While China, Cuba, North Korea, and a few other nations continue to practice Communism, the balance of the world has clearly rejected *Marxist-Leninist* totalitarianism, and even China, as noted above, is gradually, but aggressively, embracing important elements of free market thought. Despite the decline of Communism, we need to briefly remind ourselves of some fundamental Marxist principles because, as *The Wall Street Journal* reminded us a few years ago, "His Shadow Persists: Marx Can't Be Ignored. In His Critique of Capitalism the Great Analyst Helped to Shape Today's Agenda."[22] Lenin, not Marx, created the Communist dictatorship in Russia. Lenin and the other Communist totalitarians, most notably Stalin and Mao, cannot be defended. However, Marx, along with Freud and Einstein, are among the thinkers who have most profoundly shaped the 20th century. For our purposes, Marx's central message concerns the severe abuses that can accompany unrestrained capitalism. Marx was particularly concerned about the growing imbalance between rich and poor. Moreover, he felt that the pursuit of wealth and self-interest would erode society's moral core. More broadly, Marx built an economic interpretation of history, arguing that "the mode of production in material life determines the general character of the social, political and spiritual processes of life."[23]

[For an introduction to Communist thought, see **http://www.maths.tcd.ie/~belle/comm.html**]

SOCIALISM

Communism appears to have run its course philosophically. However, the problems that generated its appeal—poverty, oppression, political inequality, and so on—remain. Hence, the world continues to look to government intervention. The question is: How much? We will briefly remind ourselves of the *socialist* response to that question. Socialists reject communist totalitarianism and embrace democracy while calling for aggressive government intervention to correct economic and social ills. Historically, socialism has been associated with democratic governments and peaceful change while communism has been characterized by totalitarianism and violent revolution.

Socialists aim to retain the benefits of industrialism while abolishing the social costs often accompanying the free market. Nationalization is limited to only the most vital industries, such as steel, coal mining, power generation, and transportation. While nationalization may be relatively uncommon, the government is likely to be directly involved in regulating growth, inflation, and unemployment. In the contemporary Western world, Austria, Norway, Denmark, Sweden, South Africa, and France are among the nations where socialist principles have assumed a significant presence. Now those nations are increasingly embracing free markets, although socialist concerns and principles remain influential worldwide.

Socialist Goals

A critical distinction between socialists and capitalists is that the former believe a society's broad directions should be carefully planned rather than left to what some take to be the whimsy of the market. Furthermore, socialists are convinced that problems of market failure (inadequate information, monopoly, externalities, public goods, and so on—see Chapter 7) mean that the free market is simply incapable of meeting the needs of all segments of society. The socialist agenda includes these elements:[24]

1. Liberty.   To the capitalist, socialism appears to harshly restrain individual freedom. To the socialist, the freedoms of capitalism are largely an illusion, accessible only to the prosperous and powerful.

2. Social Welfare.   Socialists reserve much of their concern for the condition of the lower class—poverty, exploitation, cultural deprivation, and so on. Socialists feel that the economy must be directed toward the general interest rather than left free to multiply the welfare of successful capitalists. Hence, socialists advocate income supports, free education, free health care, generous sick pay, family planning, and so on, to correct the wrongs of capitalism.

3. Fulfilling Work.   Socialists object to the harshness of working life where a large segment of society is chained to degrading labor.

> Socialists seek a communitarian approach to life

4. Community.   Socialists seek a communitarian approach to life where the excessive individualism of capitalism is muted by a concern for the welfare of all.

5. Equality.   Class distinctions are anathema to the collectivist. All humans are equally meritorious, and distinctions among them are inherently unjust.

6. Rationality.   Socialists fear the "irrationality" of a society based upon competition and unrestrained pursuit of industrial growth.

The following account of a recent visit by some Santa Clara University professors to a coffee plantation in Guatemala reminds us why collectivists fear unrestrained capitalism while finding great strength in community.

FINCA LA VICTORIA

James Reites and Don Dodson

We stand in a circle, our attention focused on Julio César Archilla as he tells us the heart-breaking story of his community—the campesinos of Finca Los Cerros, a large coffee plantation in the southwestern highlands of Guatemala. As two of his young children look on, he explains how 88 families stood up to the finca owner's decision to throw them off the land where they had lived and worked for generations.

The trouble at Finca Los Cerros began in 1995, when the workers started organizing. Before they created the union, they had earned 12.50 quetzales ($2.10) a day; afterward, their pay was increased to 15.50 quetzales a day. The workers thought they had won a major concession when they were told they could take a vacation—a right they had never had before. But in April 1995 when 10 men returned from their vacations, they no longer had jobs.

When the people complained to the local magistrate, the situation escalated. The *finca* owner tried to evict the workers, cutting off electricity and sending his servants to pull up banana and papaya trees. Thirteen people starved to death, 11 of them children. At one point, the women of the community surrounded the owner's men and held them for two weeks.

The impasse was broken when the bishop of San Marcos, Alvaro Ramazzini (himself under death threats for supporting the *campesinos*), successfully negotiated a settlement that allowed the 88 families to move to new land—land that, for the first time in their lives, they would own.

That the parcel is not large enough to sustain them and that access to drinking water is extremely difficult do not diminish their pride. "We are very happy because we have succeeded with this struggle," the leader of the women tells us. "We are joyful because we have some-place to go—*our* place."

While we talk, we watch men and boys dismantle the simple sheds where they had lived at Finca Los Cerros and carry them, piece by piece, to their new land. There, they will make a clearing for a dirt floor and reconstruct their dwellings, albeit without roofs, because they are not allowed to take the corrugated tin that had covered their former homes.

Julio is full of plans for the new *finca*. He wants to raise money for a pump to get water from a nearby stream, and he even hopes some organization will donate enough for the families to purchase another piece of land for cash crops. He also speaks proudly of plans to build a school, a church, and a community center on the new land, pointing out the location of each.

"The *campesinos* are down underneath your shoe," says Julio, stamping his foot. "We care for ourselves be-cause, if we don't, there are people out there who are bigger who will eat us up. We, as *campesinos*, have to group together to contradict that."

Source: Markkula Center for Applied Ethics, Santa Clara University. © 1996 Markkula Center for Applied Ethics. Reprinted by permission. [http://www.scu.edu/Ethics/]

China—Coping with Capitalism.   China provides a helpful example of the relentless demands of the free market. An acceleration of free market reforms in 1997 led to widespread unemployment, shrinking welfare benefits, and, by 1999, an economy that was actually deflating. Nonetheless, the Communists in charge of China vigorously affirmed their commitment to the market in 1999 by altering China's constitution to treat the private sector as "an important component" of the "socialist market economy," rather than the "supplement" it had formerly been. The change in language merely reflects the reality of contemporary Chinese practice where a 1997 Gallup survey showed the most commonly held attitude toward life was "Work hard and get rich" (56 percent) and the least popular was "Never think of yourself; give everything in service to society" (3 percent).[25] China remains a Communist nation, but the state's role in economics is steadily receding as the people enthusiastically embrace the market.

"Work hard and get rich"

> HARBIN, China—Zhang Hongwei drives a black Mercedes-Benz sedan, collects frequent-flier miles on United Airlines and works out of a marble-and-glass office tower in this northeastern capital.
>
> What's most outstanding about Zhang Hongwei, though, is that he doesn't stand out in today's reformist China. Thousands of private businessmen have bicycle-to-Benz tales to tell. Together they have quietly . . . turned this last major redoubt of communism, statistically speaking, into a capitalist state.[26]
>
> [For a general database on China, see **http://china.com/**]

Questions

1. Does a rise in crime inevitably accompany the movement from collectivism to capitalism? Explain.
2. Does the rise of capitalism mean the decline of the strong sense of community, mutual support, and group solidarity that have characterized Chinese culture over the centuries? Explain.

Part Four—Middle Ground? A Mixed Economy (The Third Way)

Communism has failed. Socialist principles, to the extent that they call for central planning, bloated bureaucracies, and restraints on personal freedom, are discredited. An era has passed, but the shape of the future is unclear. Some middle ground in free market and welfare state principles seems to be the next step, but the appropriate mixture is proving elusive. For years, the Scandinavian states of Sweden, Norway, and Denmark practiced their market socialism or social democracy with such success that it was labeled a "third way" between the harsher extremes of capitalism and communism. Their welfare states provided healthy economic growth with cradle to grave social care for all in a system emphasizing the collective welfare over individual preferences. Scholar Robert Livingston described Germany's similar approach:

The *social* aspects have always been as important—perhaps more important—than the profit motive. Not only is the social-welfare net essential, not only does a "social partnership" exist between employers and the employed . . . but more broadly the economic system rests upon an implicit social contract, in which employers, the employed (through their unions), the government and, less clearly, the Central Bank are all partners.[27]

WELFARE

Now at the turn of the century, that dream of social justice funded by cooperative capitalism is struggling in Europe. Economic growth has been sluggish and unemployment in much of Western Europe is at 10 percent or higher (compared with approximately 4.3 percent in the United States in 1999). Sweden, among others, has been successful in turning the economic corner by imposing spending ceilings and raising taxes, but in Germany, the clear leader of the European economy, the continuing conflict between welfare goals and the harsh demands of the international market has yet to be resolved. Worldwide competitive pressure is forcing German businesses to consider moving across borders to escape Germany's high taxes and restrictive work rules. At the same time, Germany has introduced competitiveness to former monopolies in telecommunications, mail, and energy so that economists expect some renewed vigor in the German economy.

SOCIAL JUSTICE

America dominates the globe, and yet, for many Americans and many, many more observers around the world, America remains flawed—perhaps fatally—by what those critics take to be a winner-take-all, cowboy mentality that allows the rich to get richer while the disadvantaged slide further behind. The following excerpt from a 1993 University of Minnesota forum on "The Challenge of Social Justice in the Global Economy" describes those perceived shortcomings in the American Way.

SOCIAL JUSTICE

Kay Miller

Americans have long prized individualism—that frontier mentality of the lone cowboy taming the frontier . . . The unspoken assumption in the myth of the rugged individualist is that people who are poor, sick or unemployed have somehow brought it on themselves.

Americans don't use the term "social justice" very much, columnist William Pfaff noted. When one conference participant suggested Americans already have purchased all the social justice they really wanted, a murmur of agreement rippled through an auditorium packed with scholars, public officials, policy wonks and concerned corporate types.

* * * * *

"We can't underestimate the ideology—and I use the word advisedly—which has dominated (U.S.) public life [for many years] that the market solves all problems: that God acts through the market," Pfaff said.

*   *   *   *   *

For some time, American disagreement over how much our government should do has been disguised by a rough balance between economic growth and the cost of social programs. But mounting global competition now is undermining that equation, said former Vice President Walter Mondale:

"We have something like 38 (to) 40 million Americans who work around the clock. They're not on welfare. They're not asking for anybody to help them. And when you get all done, their life is such that they could never go to a movie. They can never go out for a meal. They can never afford a baby sitter. They can never take a vacation where money's involved."

And if they get sick, they're in real trouble. Retirement looks bleak. And they've passed the aspirations of limitation on to their children.

Americans seem to have lost the feeling that we're all in this together.

Douglas Fraser, former president of the United Auto Workers, remembers coming to this country as a boy and living in a neighborhood populated by immigrants. "Maybe misery loves company, but there was a feeling of unity and solidarity in those days among those people," Fraser said.

Source: *Waterloo–Cedar Falls Courier,* February 28, 1993, p. E1. Reprinted with permission of the *Star Tribune,* Minneapolis–St. Paul.

Questions—Parts Three and Four

1. Taxes in the United States are much lower than those of our chief European competitors and slightly lower than those in Japan, and yet we think we are overtaxed. Why? Are we greedy? Explain.

2. According to the article "Social Justice," Americans tend to believe that "God acts through the market" while Europeans are more likely to see a God-given command to "help one's fellow citizens."
   a. Which characterization corresponds most closely to your own view of life? Explain.
   b. How do you explain the pronounced difference in philosophical directions between Europeans and Americans?

3. Americans feel a great deal of faith in the free market. Explain some of the weaknesses in the market. That is, where is the free market likely to fail?

4. Writing in *Dissent,* Joanne Barkan says, "[A]lmost all Swedes view poverty, extreme inequalities of wealth, and the degradation that comes with unemployment as unacceptable."[28]
   a. Do you agree with the Swedes? Explain.
   b. Why are Americans more tolerant of those conditions than are the Swedes?

5. In the late 1970s, correspondent R. W. Apple of the *New York Times* reported that Sweden had willfully pursued a policy of economic leveling:

   As a result almost every family living near the sea has a boat, but almost all are small boats. A large percentage of families have summer houses, but none of them rivals the villas of the Riviera or the stately manor houses of Britain. Virtually no one has servants.

Even among the handful of people who might be able to afford it, conspicuous consumption is frowned upon. There are fewer than 25 Rolls Royces in Sweden.[29]

a. Is that Swedish approach preferable to the extreme conspicuous consumption permitted—and even encouraged—in this country? Explain.

b. Is the opportunity to garner luxuries necessary to the successful operation of the American system? Explain.

c. Does our system generate guilt among those who enjoy its fruits in quantities well beyond the norm? Explain.

6. a. Should an American citizen's primary duty be to her- or himself or to all other members of society? Explain.

b. Should all humans be regarded as of equal value and thus equally worthy of our individual support? Explain.

c. Can social harmony be achieved in a nation whose citizens fail to regard the state as a "superfamily"? Explain.

7. a. In your view, is an individual's possession of extravagant wealth a moral wrong?

b. Would economic justice require that we treat "being rich" as a social wrong? Explain.

See George Scialabba, "Asking the Right Questions," *Dissent,* Spring 1988, p. 114.

8. Philosopher Thomas Hobbes said that "The value or worth of a man, as of all other things, [is] his price . . ." Do you agree with Hobbes that the worth of all things in our lives is best measured by the market? Explain.

See James B. Rule, "Markets, in Their Place," *Dissent,* Winter 1998, pp. 29, 30.

9. In Sweden, spanking children is a violation of the law.

a. What reasoning supports that legislation?

b. Would such legislation help reduce violence in America? Explain.

10. Eskimos, among other cultures, regarded all natural resources as free or common goods to be used but never possessed by any individual or group. What arguments may be raised to justify our notion of private ownership of natural resources?

Part Five—America's Economic Future: Where Are We Going?

Michael Douglas, as Gordon Gekko in the movie, *Wall Street*: "Greed is good! Greed is right! Greed works! Greed will save the USA!"

The combined wealth ($135 billion) of the world's three richest families (Microsoft's Bill Gates; the Walton family, owners of WalMart; and the Sultan of Brunei) is greater than the annual income of 600 million people in the least developed countries, according to a United Nations report, and a "grotesque" gap between the rich and poor is widening.

Source: Charlotte Denny and Victoria Brittain, "UN Attacks Growing Gulf Between Rich and Poor," *The Guardian,* July 12, 1999, p. 14.

We have inspected the entire economic continuum. We know that communism has been discredited. Hence, the far left has little to offer. President Reagan and, to a lesser extent, Presidents Bush and Clinton gave us a 20-year view of the virtues and demerits of greater faith in the free market. Should we heed Reagan's call to place our faith in largely unrestrained capitalism, or do we need to move our present *mixed economy* a bit closer to the welfare state model, which itself is under great pressure? Or must a new model emerge? In sum, how much government do we need?

At the turn of century, Americans are enjoying a remarkable economic boom that may prove to be the most prosperous era in our history. Not surprisingly, that economic boom has been accompanied by a general decline in many familiar social ills, such as crime and unemployment. According to the United Nations' annual report on the overall quality of life in 174 nations, the United States in 1999 ranked third in the world behind Canada (1) and Norway (2) and ahead of Japan (4), Belgium (5), Sweden, Australia, the Netherlands, Iceland, and Britain.[30] Sierra Leone and Niger ranked at the bottom of the list.[31] In 1998, the UN also ranked the nations according to the gap in the quality of life between men and women, and the United States ranked sixth on that list with Canada again ranking first.[32]

the United States in 1999 ranked third in the world

Americans' own assessment of the quality of national life is similarly optimistic, according to the 1999 annual report by the bipartisan National Commission on Civic Renewal, which looks at such factors as crime rates, family stability, and political participation to assess the nation's civic health. After the Commission's Index of National Civic Health dropped more than 20 percent from 1984 to 1994 (largely because of escalating crime), the study found that the Index rebounded dramatically through 1997 based on favorable data including falling levels of crime, divorce, and illegitimate births.[33] Consider some of that data:

- For the seventh consecutive year, crime in the United States fell sharply in 1998,[34] and in 1997 the nation's murder rate fell to its lowest rate since 1967.[35]
- Unemployment in early 1999 stood at 4.3 percent; just above the rate that economists have historically considered to represent full employment.[36]
- Drunk driving arrests fell almost 20 percent from 1986 to 1997.[37]
- By many important measures, American children are thriving: The number of children committing and falling victim to crime dropped steadily from 1993 to 1998; sophomores and seniors smoking cigarette fell by about 10 percent from 1997 to 1998 following years of consistent increases; teen girls are having fewer babies.[38]
- Infant mortality (deaths from birth to age 1), while still exceeding rates in most industrial nations, fell from 10.1 per thousand births in 1987 to 7.1 in 1997.[39]

Unease

Despite all of the good news, public opinion polls show that many Americans are not comfortable with contemporary life. A 1999 national survey of likely voters found America headed down "the wrong track" by a 51 to 36 margin, and a June 1999 Fox poll showed a nine-point drop from March 1999 in adult Americans thinking the country is headed in the right direction.[40] The biggest concerns appear to be a perceived decline in moral values and in civility.[41] Is capitalism in some way to blame for those problems? Most Americans probably think not, but critics contend that capitalism's winner-take-all attitude, materialism, and selfishness inevitably corrode our moral standards. (We will examine those free market/morality themes further in Chapters 2 and 3.)

Thus, while we are making good progress, Americans understand that serious problems remain. For example:

> A record 2.0 million Americans were in prisons and jails in 1999

- As noted, a record 2.0 million Americans were in prisons and jails in 1999 at a cost to states alone of perhaps $30 billion annually.[42] As a result of felony convictions, 13 percent of black males cannot vote in elections.[43] Only Russia holds more prisoners than America.
- While births to teens have declined, as noted above, teenage pregnancy in the United States is twice as high as in Canada and England and nine times as high as in Japan.[44]
- Continuing a 30-year rise, more than 5 percent of American children live in homes headed by their grandparents.[45]

Economic Injustice?

Critics of contemporary capitalism attribute those continuing problems and others like them at least partially to the free market itself. While the market may be the best decision maker we can currently conceive of, the critics argue that it is faulty; especially in the sense that many are left behind while great wealth and comfort accrue to a relative few. Let's look at those concerns.

Poverty.   In 1999, over 13 percent of Americans lived beneath the government's official poverty line (about $17,000 for a family of four) despite the nation's extraordinary economic expansion.[46] According to a 1999 Census Bureau report, about one-fifth of Americans (about 49 million) in 1995 lived in a home where at least one basic need, such as rent, utilities, food, or health care, could not be met.[47] About 4.8 percent of the population reported not having enough to eat.[48] Of course, the later 1990s saw an economic expansion that probably reduced that suffering. We should also note another Census Bureau report indicating that poverty is usually a transitory condition with most people escaping poverty within a few months.[49] Only 5 percent of the nation's population remained poor over the full 24 months of the study.[50] [For data on United States poverty, see **http://www.census.gov/hhes/www/poverty.html**]

> About 4.8 percent of the population reported not having enough to eat.

Conditions internationally are much more difficult than those in the United States. A 1999 United Nations report found half of the world's 6 billion people "mired in poverty, trying to eke out a living on $3 a day or less."[51] Nearly one-sixth of the world's people cannot read or write.[52] The market has brought extraordinary comfort to most Americans. Can it do the same for the 3 billion poor? Wealthy financier and philanthropist George Soros, who understands the market and has profited greatly from it, believes there are "collective interests that don't find expression in market values."[53] That is, the market cannot, he thinks, solve all of our problems. Author Nadine Gordimer, winner of the Nobel Prize, argues that the market most values consumption, but consumption by the rich, she says, will not eradicate the world's poverty:

> It will not be achieved . . . through worldwide shopping on the Internet. In our century consumption has grown unprecedentedly . . . But the spending and devouring spree, far from widely benefiting the poor, has undermined the truly human prospects for globalization: sustainable human development for all.[54]

In 1999, President Clinton toured some of America's most economically depressed regions, including the Lakota Sioux's Pine Ridge Indian Reservation in South Dakota. He was the first president in 60 years to visit any reservation. Pine Ridge is home to descendants of the great chiefs, Crazy Horse and Red Cloud, and it is the site of the Wounded Knee Massacre of 1890 that ended the Indian Wars. *Seattle Times* reporter, Alex Tizon, described what Clinton saw:

> The Lakota Sioux were the last to fall, and in many ways, they have remained fallen ever since. Nearly 40,000 people live on this rolling, barren swatch of land that the U.S. Census Bureau has labeled as the poorest place in the country for the past two decades. The per-capita income hovers at $11,000, unemployment soars to 85 percent, and the average home houses 17 people. Life expectancy for Sioux men is 56 years—for Sioux women, 66—the lowest anywhere in this hemisphere except Haiti.

Source: Alex Tizon, "President Clinton's Poverty Tour—Nation's Poorest Play Host to President," *Seattle Times,* July 8, 1999, p. A1.

[For pictures and more information about the Lakota Sioux, see **http://www.lakota.org/**]

The Gap.   As *The Sacramento Bee* characterized it, the United States is the richest industrial nation, but it is also the poorest;[55] that is, the United States has the highest levels of both wealth and poverty among the industrial nations. Extravagant wealth, side by side with punishing poverty, is perhaps the greatest disappointment and injustice, from the critics' point of view, in the great, global victory of the free market. Harvard economist Richard B. Freeman wonders whether the United States is headed toward an "apartheid economy"—"one in which the wealthy and powerful prosper while the less well-off struggle."[56] Considerable data support his concern. A family at the 90th percentile in income in the early 1970s earned about 6 times that of a family at the 10th percentile, but by the 1990s that ratio had reached 8 to 1.[57] Similarly, the top 1 percent of households in the United States now have more wealth than the bottom 95 percent combined.[58] The same phenomenon is manifest on the job where, in 1998, CEOs of America's 365 largest corporations earned 419 times the pay of the average blue-collar worker.[59] CEO raises in 1998 averaged 36 percent versus 3.9 percent for white-collar workers and 2.7 for blue-collar.[60] Should we care about these vast and apparently growing gaps in income and wealth? Commentator Dan Seligman says we shouldn't be troubled since the number of poor is really all that matters; not the gap between the poor and the rich.[61] Furthermore, the 1999 Heritage Foundation/*Wall Street Journal* Index of Economic Freedom demonstrates

> Harvard economist Richard B. Freeman wonders whether the United States is headed toward an "apartheid economy"

that the greater the degree of freedom in an economy the better off are the people at *all* income levels, and the income gap is smallest in countries with the freest economies.[62] Under the Index, the United States is considered one of the world's 10 "free" economies. Nonetheless, ethicist William Sundstrom argues, among other things, that fairness does matter very much, that the income we receive should bear some reasonable relationship to what we "deserve," and that democracy may not be able to tolerate too much social stratification.[63]

Scholar Edward Luttwak's 1999 book, *Turbo-Capitalism,*[64] analyzes the risks in our zealous commitment to rapidly changing (turbo) capitalism. A *New York Times* book review summarizes Luttwak's views:

> Luttwak identifies several distinct but interconnected perils. Turbo-capitalism produces efficiency but also insecurity and uniformity. It "generates new wealth from all the resources released by the competition-powered destruction of inefficient practices, firms, and entire industries . . . Also destroyed, of course, are the secure jobs of employees they once sheltered." Unemployment may be down in the United States, Luttwak argues, but wage inequalities are extreme; worldwide, meanwhile, unemployment is rising. In traditional societies, turbo-capitalism sweeps away reciprocal social arrangements, leaves small economies at the mercy of distant speculative whims, and subordinates all other values and goals to those of the marketplace.
>
> By intensifying economic insecurity, turbo-capitalism generates fears that are transformed into social backlashes. Luttwak traces everything, from intensified lock-'em-up attitudes on crime to a new puritanism about smoking, sex, and seat belts, to displaced economic insecurities.
>
> Why do ordinary people in the United States, the home of turbo-capitalism, sit still for the gross extremes of inequality and the destruction of security? Luttwak blames American Calvinism. The winners are convinced of their virtue and the losers suspect their economic failure must be their own fault. "Living in a country that so greatly respects and admires high-earning winners, losers find it hard to preserve their self-esteem."[65]

Question

1. Why does Luttwak blame Calvinism for Americans' toleration of the inequality and insecurity of contemporary capitalism?

The Wall Street Journal, in 1998, reported on emerging doubts about our seemingly absolute commitment to the free market:

> "What I'm concerned about is the idolatry of the market," says conservative intellectual William Bennett, a former education secretary and author of the *The Book of Virtues.* He worries particularly that the market for popular music and movies with sexual or violent content has a corrosive effect. "Unbridled capitalism . . . may not be a problem for production and for expansion of the economic pie, but it's a problem for human beings. It's a problem for . . . the realm of values and human relationships."

Source: David Wessel and John Harwood, "Capitalism Is Giddy with Triumph; Is It Possible to Overdo It? *The Wall Street Journal,* May 14, 1998, p. A1.

Questions

1. *a.* What does Bennett mean by "the idolatry of the market?"
   b. Do you have any doubts about the market and your role in it? Explain.
2. *a.* In what sense do we have a market in "values and human relationships"?
   b. What does Bennett mean about the corrosive effect of popular culture?
   c. Can we have a free market in economic affairs without harming our social values and relationships? Explain.

BEYOND IDEOLOGY

The data above confirm that serious problems remain in America even though the wisdom of the capitalist approach is almost universally conceded. Arguably, the problem, in brief, is expressed by a 20-year-old Cuban student and Communist organizer: "Capitalism is more efficient . . . But it is not more fair."[66] Perhaps, then, the answer to progress for *all* is to be found somewhere beyond the capitalist-collectivist debate.

We began this chapter with Francis Fukuyama's interesting suggestion that we are at the end of ideological history, by which he meant that Western liberal democracy has vanquished fascism and communism and shown itself to be the clearly superior means of ordering human affairs. As we conclude this chapter, we should consider the possibility that our hopes for a better future simply can't be found in the current debate about the proper balance of market forces and government intervention. As journalist Clarence Page says:

> "Capitalism is more efficient . . . But it is not more fair."

> We need a new definition of civil society which answers the unanswerable questions posed by both the market forces and the governmental ones, as to how we can have a society that fills us up again and makes us feel that we are part of something bigger than ourselves.[67]

Questions—Part Five

1. *a.* Do you agree that the current preoccupation with the free market-government intervention debate is too narrow to embrace the needs of genuine reform in contemporary life? Explain.
   b. Do we need reform? Explain.
2. Journalist Lauren Soth says, "Let's challenge the sacred goals of economic growth, greater output of goods and services, greater productivity."[68] How could we have a better life if we were to diminish our attention to those seemingly central requirements?
3. Scholars William Halal and Alexander Nikitin contend that

   > [F]reedom always entails a price, and the price that Americans pay is the lack of a sense of community. The competitive stress, absence of social support, and sheer meaningless of American life seem to be a major underlying cause for a variety of crippling social disorders that run rampant in the United States, such as crime, illiteracy, drug use, violence, and other social problems that are among the highest in the modern world.[69]

   a. Do you agree with Halal and Nikitin that America lacks a "sense of community"? Explain.

  b. Is American life "meaningless"? Explain.

INTERNET EXERCISE

Using the oneworld web page on globalization and world trade [**http://www.oneworld.org/ guides/trade/front.shtml**], explain oneworld's primary concerns about world trade in light of increasing globalization.

CHAPTER QUESTIONS

1. *a.* Is Francis Fukuyama correct in arguing that we are witnessing the end of ideology? Explain.

   b. Fukuyama also argues that the end of ideology will mean the replacement of politics with economics, resulting in "a very sad time," because the great political questions about how to shape a better world will be replaced by the cultural banality that is one of the products of capitalist society's preoccupation with material goods. Explain what Fukuyama means. Is he correct?

2. Commenting in *Newsweek,* economist Robert Samuelson said, "The . . . pervasive problem of capitalist economies is that almost no one fully trusts capitalists."[70] Do you agree? Why?

3. Dartmouth English professor Noel Perrin laments the explosive growth of the world population, which amounts to about 2 million additional persons per week. In 1987, the world population was 5 billion, and at the turn of the century the total is about 6 billion. Perrin says, "Why not stem the population explosion by paying women not to have babies?"[71] He proposes government payments to each fertile woman each year commencing with $500 at puberty and rising by $100 for each year thereafter so long as the woman does not give birth. That total would reach nearly $100,000 by age 53, but he compares that with, for example, the nearly $200,000 cost of bringing up one abandoned child in New York City. In sum, he argues that the plan would be less expensive than our current welfare program.

   a. Would you support Professor Perrin's market-based approach to birth control? Explain.

   b. Do you consider such a program immoral? Explain.

4. "America's real problem," says former Council of Economic Advisers Chairman Herbert Stein, a conservative Republican, is that it has "serious deficiencies that one would not expect in so rich a country . . . the public is saying that even though we are very rich, we have too much crime, too much homelessness, too much illiteracy and ignorance."[72]

   a. Do you agree? Explain.

   b. How do you account for our problems?

   c. Do we need a greater measure of government intervention in order to correct those problems? Explain.

5. *a.* Noted economist Lester Thurow argues that the economic demands of the market are destroying the traditional two-parent, nuclear family. Explain his argument.

   b. Child development authority Benjamin Spock likewise blames capitalism for the "destruction of the American family," but his reasoning differs from Thurow's:

   > The overriding problem is excessive competition and our glorification of it. It may contribute to our rapid technological advancement, but it has done so at a great price. We are taught to be rugged individualists, and we are obsessed with getting ahead. The family gets lost in this intense struggle. In a healthy society, family should come first, community second, and our outside jobs third. In this country, it is the other way around.[73]

   1. Comment.
   2. If Spock is correct, how did we reach this condition?

6. Some Nike shareholders, in 1998, called for linking compensation for CEO Phil Knight and other executives more closely to wages being paid in Nike's contract factories in Asia. Knight made $1.7 million in salary alone in 1997, and according to one shareholder, Knight earned 5,273 times the annual pay of the average worker in Nike shoe factories while executive pay in Japan, according to that shareholder, is 16 times that of the average worker and about 21 times that of the average worker in Germany.[74] How would you vote on that shareholder proposal? Explain.

7. We often read that many college professors actively criticize capitalism and support welfare state principles.
   a. Has that been your experience? Explain.
   b. If that assessment is accurate, how do you account for the leftist inclinations among intellectuals?

8. As noted in the readings, privatization is enjoying immense popularity.
   a. Make the arguments for and against turning our prisons and jails over to private enterprise.
   b. Would you favor a penal system operated for profit? Explain.

9. If we are fundamentally selfish, must we embrace capitalism as the most accurate and, therefore, most efficient expression of human nature? Explain.

10. Economist and jurist Richard Posner has suggested a free market in babies. Given that "production costs" are relatively low and the value of babies to childless people is high, Posner observed the possibilities for mutually beneficial transactions.
    a. Explain some of the advantages and disadvantages of a market in babies.
    b. Would you favor the legalization of the sale of babies? Explain.

11. Is capitalism a necessary condition for successful democracy? Or, put another way, in a democracy will increasing state control necessarily result in the destruction of that democracy? Explain.

12. Richard Falk argues for "some sense of global identity." Does capitalism enhance or impede the development of a world community? Explain.

13. Socialist Michael Harrington argued for life "freed of the curse of money":

    > [A]s long as access to goods and pleasures is rationed according to the possession of money, there is a pervasive venality, an invitation to miserliness and hostility to one's neighbor.[75]

    Should we strive to make more and more goods and services "free"? Raise the competing arguments.

14. The great intellect Adolph Berle once said: "A day may come when national glory and prestige, perhaps even national safety, are best established by a country's being the most beautiful, the best socially organized, or culturally the most advanced in the world."[76]
    a. Is government intervention necessary to achieving Berle's goal? Explain.
    b. If faced with a choice, would most Americans opt for Berle's model or for a nation preeminent in consumer goods, sports, and general comfort? Explain.

15. Edward Luttwak, in his book, *Turbo Capitalism,* says it is dangerous for the United States to export its mostly unregulated capitalism around the world because many other nations do not have firmly in place two central forces that balance capitalist power in the United States.
    a. What are those two forces?
    b. Do you agree with Luttwak that many other nations are not ready to fully embrace our free market system? Explain.

16. Benjamin Barber, writing in *The Atlantic,* sees two possible political futures, which he labels the "forces of Jihad" and the "forces of McWorld":

    > The first is a retribalization of large swaths of humankind by war and bloodshed . . . culture is pitted against culture, people against people, tribe against tribe—a Jihad in the name of a hundred narrowly conceived faiths against every kind of interdependence . . . The second is being borne in on us by the onrush of economic and ecological forces that demand integration and uniformity and that mesmerize the world with fast music, fast computers, and fast food—with MTV, Macintosh, and McDonald's pressing nations into one comercially homogeneous global network: One McWorld tied together by technology, ecology, communications, and commerce.[77]

    a. Do either of these scenarios make sense to you? Explain.
    b. Which would you prefer? Explain.

17. Critics argue that socialism requires a uniformity, a "sameness" that would destroy the individuality Americans prize.
    a. Are Americans notably independent and individualistic? Explain.
    b. Explore the argument that socialism would actually enhance meaningful individualism.

18. Hilda Scott wrote a book to which she affixed the provocative title, *Does Socialism Liberate Women?*

a. Answer her question. Explain.

b. Are minority oppression and oppression of women inevitable by-products of capitalism? Explain.

19. In Wisconsin, members of the Old Order Amish religion declined to formally educate their children beyond the eighth grade. The U.S. Supreme Court held that their First Amendment right to freedom of religion was violated by the Wisconsin compulsory education statute, which required school attendance until the age of 16. Chief Justice Burger explained:

> [T]hey object to the high school, and higher education generally, because the values they teach are in marked variance with Amish values and the Amish way of life; they view secondary school education as an impermissible exposure of their children to a "worldly" influence in conflict with their beliefs. The high school tends to emphasize intellectual and scientific accomplishments, selfdistinction, competitiveness, worldly success, and social life with other students. Amish society emphasizes informal learning-through-doing; a life of "goodness," rather than a life of intellect; wisdom, rather than technical knowledge; community welfare, rather than competition; and separation from, rather than integration with, contemporary worldly society.[78]

a. Have the Amish taken the course we should all follow? Explain.

b. Could we do so? Explain.

20. Distinguished economist Gary Becker argues for a free market approach to America's immigration difficulties:

> In a market economy, the way to deal with excess demand for a product or service is to raise the price. This reduces the demand and stimulates the supply. I

suggest that the United States adopt a similar approach to help solve its immigration problems. Under my proposal, anyone willing to pay a specified price could enter the United States immediately.[79]

Comment on this view.

21. Management scholars Rabindra Kanungo and Jay Conger remark that " 'Altruism' is a word rarely associated with the world of business," but they ask: "Does altruism have a place in our business lives? And does it make good economic sense?"[80] Answer their questions.

22. George C. Lodge and Ezra Vogel edited a book entitled *Ideology and National Competitiveness: An Analysis of Nine Countries,* in which they compared the industrial policies of those nine nations.[81] Lodge and Vogel argue that the success of Japan and several Southeast Asian nations in the international market is at least partially attributable to those nations' communitarian approaches to life. On the other hand, they argue that the emphasis on individualism in the United States has harmed our ability to be internationally competitive. Do you agree with Lodge and Vogel? Explain. See Professor Jeffrey A. Hart's review of the book (*Business Horizons* 30, no. 6, November/December 1987, p. 83).

23. In 1994, *Reader's Digest* commissioned a scientific poll of 1,053 Americans to ask, among others, the following questions:

a. Is it better to ensure that each individual has as much opportunity as possible, even if that means some people enjoy far more success than others, rather than to ensure equality of income?

b. Which is the bigger threat to America's future—big business, big labor, or big government?[82]

Answer those questions. Explain.

NOTES

1. Francis Fukuyama, "Are We at the End of History?" *Fortune,* January 15, 1990, p. 75.

2. Henry Mintzberg, "Managing Government—Governing Management," *Harvard Business Review* 74, no. 3 (May–June 1996), p. 75.

3. Robert Heilbroner, "Warp-Speed Capitalism," *Los Angeles Times Book Review,* February 8, 1998, p. 5.

4. Daniel Yergin and Joseph Stanislaw, *The Commanding Heights—The Battle Between Government and the*

Marketplace That Is Remaking the Modern World (New York: Simon & Schuster, 1998).

5. Kenneth Minogue, "Market Values," *The Wall Street Journal,* January 27, 1998, p. A20.

6. Robert Reich, "Is Liberal Democracy the Hallmark of Our Era?" *The Wall Street Journal,* February 6, 1992, p. A12.

7. David Wessel and John Harwood, "Capitalism Is Giddy with Triumph; Is It Possible to Overdo It?" *The Wall Street Journal,* May 14, 1998, p. A1.

8. Richard Wolf, "Public Aid Going Private in Many States," *USA Today,* August 3, 1998, p. 3A.

9. David Wessel, "A Government Agency Becomes a Company," *The Wall Street Journal,* May 14, 1998, p. A10.

10. Kim Clark, "How to Make Traffic Jams a Thing of the Past," *Fortune,* March 31, 1997, p. 34.

11. Wessel and Harwood, "Capitalism Is Giddy," p. A1.

12. Ted Strickland, "Private Prisons: The Bottom Line," *Washington Post,* June 13, 1999, p. B01.

13. Ibid.

14. William Petroski, "Private Prisons," *Des Moines Register,* January 10, 1999, p. 1G.

15. Martin Wooster, "Lessons from Liberated Kiwis," *American Enterprise,* March–April, 1997, p. 90.

16. Ibid.

17. "China Dusts Off Its Aborted Privatisation Programme," *Financial Times,* July 1, 1999, p. 32.

18. David Wessel, "The American Way?" *The Wall Street Journal,* October 2, 1995, p. R8.

19. Jonathan N. Goodrich, "Privatization in America," *Business Horizons* 31, no.1 (January–February 1988), pp. 11–16.

20. Wessel and Harwood, "Capitalism Is Giddy," p. A1.

21. Ibid.

22. Henry Myers, "His Statues Topple, His Shadow Persists: Marx Can't Be Ignored," *The Wall Street Journal,* November 25, 1991, p. A1.

23. Ibid.

24. Elements of this list are drawn from Agnes Heller and Ferenc Feher, "Does Socialism Have a Future?" *Dissent,* Summer 1989, p. 371.

25. James A. Dorn, "The Death of Communism in China," *Journal of Commerce,* March 5, 1999, p. 5A.

26. Joseph Kahn, "Spreading Capitalism, New Entrepreneurs Are Remaking China," *The Wall Street Journal,* July 20, 1995, p. A1.

27. Robert Livingstone, "A Social-Conscience Driven Economy," *The Wall Street Journal,* February 19, 1992, p. A19.

28. Joanne Barkan, "Not Yet in Paradise, But . . . ," *Dissent,* Spring 1989, pp. 147, 150.

29. R.W. Apple, Jr., "Swedes Feel They're Lumped Together in 'National Blandness,'" *Lexington Leader,* July 26, 1978, p. A15.

30. Leo Rennert, "Report: Globalization Creates Increase in Economic Inequity," *Sacramento Bee,* July 12, 1999, p. A5.

31. Ibid.

32. Leo Rennert, "U.S. Ranked Richest—and Poorest— Industrial Nation," *Sacramento Bee,* September 9, 1998, p. A9.

33. Morton Kondracke, "Public Mood Not What Doomsayers Say," *Waterloo–Cedar Falls Courier,* May 7, 1999, p. A6.

34. "Another Drop in Crime," *New York Times,* May 23, 1999, sec. 4, p. 2.

35. Marlene Cimons, "Study Finds Murder Rate at 30-Year Low," *Los Angeles Times,* January 3, 1999, p. A14.

36. Kimberly Blanton, "U.S. Economy Creates 268,000 Jobs in June," *Boston Globe,* July 3, 1999, p. F1.

37. Stephen Fuzesi, "Drunk Driving Arrests Dropping," *Los Angeles Times,* June 14, 1999, p. A6.

38. *Washington Post,* "American Children Thriving, Study Says," *Waterloo–Cedar Falls Courier,* July 9, 1999, p. A1.

39. Philip Hilts, "Nation is Falling Short of Health Goals for 2000," *New York Times,* June 11, 1999, p. A30.

40. Kondracke, "Public Mood," p. A6.

41. Ibid.

42. Jesse Katz, "America Marches Two Millionth Prisoner Behind Bars," *Waterloo–Cedar Falls Courier*, February 20, 2000, p. F1.

43. "Study Finds 13% of Black Men Can't Vote," *Los Angeles Times,* October 23, 1998, p. A17.

44. Jane Brody, "More Young Teens Having Sex," *Denver Rocky Mountain News,* September 27, 1998, p. 6F.

45. Steve Fuzesi, "Child-Rearing by Grandparents on the Rise, Census Bureau Says," *Los Angeles Times,* July 1, 1999, p. A11.

46. "Clinton's Overdue Trip to Help Nation's Poor," *San Francisco Chronicle,* July 7, 1999, p. A18.

47. Sri Ramakrishnan, "Study Details Impact of Poverty in U.S.," *Washington Post,* July 9, 1999, p. E01.

48. Ibid.

49. "Poverty Not Chronic, Study Says," *Atlanta Journal and Constitution,* August 10, 1998, p. 10A.

50. Ibid.

51. Stella Danker, "Half of Mankind Live in Poverty," *Straits Times,* July 8, 1999, p. 7.

52. Barbara Crossette, "UNICEF Study Predicts 16% World Illiteracy Rate Will Increase," *New York Times,* December 9, 1998, p. A11.

53. Nadine Gordimer, "The World's Haves Are Duty-Bound to Help the Have-Nots," *Sacramento Bee,* February 8, 1999, p. B5.

54. Ibid.

55. Rennert, "U.S. Ranked Richest," p. A9.

56. Richard B. Freeman, "Toward an Apartheid Economy?" *Harvard Business Review* 74, no. 5 (September–October 1996), p. 114.

57. William A. Sundstrom, "The Income Gap," *Issues in Ethics,* Fall 1998, p. 13.

58. Ellen Goodman, "Garish CEO 'Wages' on Money Tree," *Des Moines Register,* April 18, 1999, p. 3AA.

59. Special Report, "Executive Pay," *Business Week,* April 19, 1999, p. 72.

60. Ibid.

61. Dan Seligman, "Gap-osis," *Forbes,* August 25, 1997, p. 74.

62. Bryan T. Johnson, Kim R. Holmes, and Melanie Kirkpatrick, "Freedom Is the Surest Path to Prosperity," *The Wall Street Journal,* December 1, 1998, p. A22.

63. Sundstrom, "The Income Gap," p. 13.

64. Edward Luttwak, *Turbo-Capitalism* (New York: HarperCollins, 1999).

65. Robert Kuttner, "Running with the Bulls," *New York Times,* February 28, 1999, sec. 7, p. 20.

66. Associated Press, "A Threat to Castro," *Des Moines Register,* August 30, 1994, p. 8A.

67. Clarence Page, "First Couple Leaves Us Stranded," *Des Moines Register,* May 29, 1993, p. 9A.

68. Lauren Soth, "Seek Better Care of People and Earth," *Des Moines Register*, April 24, 1993, p. 5A.

69. William Halal and Alexander Nikitin, "One World," *The Futurist* 24, no. 6 (November–December 1990), p. 9.

70. Robert Samuelson, "Economics Made Easy," *Newsweek,* November 27, 1989, p. 64.

71. Noel Perrin, "A Nonbearing Account," *Newsweek,* April 2, 1990, pp. 10, 11.

72. Karen Pennar, "The Free Market Has Triumphed, But What About the Losers?" *Business Week,* September 25, 1989, p. 178.

73. Carla McClain, "Dr. Spock: Restore the Family," *Des Moines Register,* November 7, 1993, p. 3E.

74. Associated Press, "Nike Rejects Proposal to Tie Executive Pay to Factory Wages," *Waterloo–Cedar Falls Courier,* August 24, 1998, p. B5.

75. Michael Harrington, "Why We Need Socialism in America," *Dissent,* May–June 1970, pp. 240, 286.

76. Adolph Berle, *Power* (New York: Harcourt Brace Jovanovich, 1969), pp. 258–59.

77. Benjamin Barber, "Jihad v. McWorld," *The Atlantic* 269, no. 3 (March 1992), p. 53.

78 *Wisconsin* v. *Yoder,* 406 U.S. 205 (1972).

79. Gary Becker, "Why Not Let Immigrants Pay for Speedy Entry?" *Business Week,* March 2, 1987, p.20.

80. Rabindra Kanungo and Jay Conger, "Promoting Altruism as a Corporate Goal," *The Academy of Management Executive* 8, no. 3 (August 1993), p. 37.

81. George C. Lodge and Ezra Vogel, *Ideology and National Competitiveness: An Analysis of Nine Countries* (Boston: Harvard Business School, 1987).

82. Everett C. Ladd, "Generation Gap? What Generation Gap?," *The Wall Street Journal,* December 9, 1994, p. A12.

Business Ethics

Vice is a monster of so frightful mien,
As, to be hated, needs but to be seen;
Yet seen too oft, familiar with her face,
We first endure, then pity, then embrace.

Alexander Pope

Part One—Foundations of Ethical Theory

Chapter 1 explored the capitalism-collectivism economic continuum to remind the reader of the fundamentals of political economy and to encourage some judgment about the degree of government intervention necessary to achieve a desirable relationship between business and the balance of society. That is, might we rely on the market alone to "regulate" the course of business, or must we interpose some degree of government regulation?

Chapter 2 introduces self-regulation as a technique for achieving a more desirable role for business in society. To what extent can we rely on the ethical quality, the morality, of the businessperson and the business organization to govern the path of commerce? If we felt full faith in the free market and the ethical quality of individuals and companies, regulation by law would be reduced at least to those minimums suggested in Chapter 1 by Ayn Rand.

INTRODUCTION TO ETHICS

No effort will be made to *teach ethics*. The purpose here is not to improve the reader's "ethical quotient." Rather, the goal is to sensitize the reader to the ethical component of business life. Some sense of the ethical climate of business—some glimpse of the specific ethical problems facing the businessperson—should be useful in assessing the role of ethics in business decision making and in evaluating the utility of ethics as a "regulator" of business behavior. The three cases that follow illustrate the complexity of ethical analysis. Case 1, "Destroy All Girls," raises, among others, the question of whether a business should invoke its own values and conscience in deciding which merchandise to sell or leave that decision to the customer. Case 2, "Deans' Quiz," presents the dilemma of bending the rules a little in order to achieve a greater overall good. Case 3, "A Mill Owner's Compassion," addresses the familiar business problem of short-term profits versus long-term community welfare from the personal perspective of an owner. [For an extensive ethics database, see **http://www.scu.edu/Ethics/**]

CASE 1: DESTROY ALL GIRLS

Galyan's Trading Co. is a Plainfield, Indiana, subsidiary of The Limited, Inc. A Galyan's customer in Minnesota complained when she saw a slogan on a Galyan's shirt saying, "Destroy all girls." How would you respond if you were the Galyan's CEO? The Associated Press details the company's decision:

> A maker of in-line skating equipment thought it could attract aggressive young male buyers with a simple slogan: "Destroy all girls."
>
> An offended retailer came up with an equally forceful response—ending all sales.
>
> Galyan's Trading Co. announced Monday it sent back the fall line of T-shirts, sweatshirts, pants, and boxer shorts made by Senate, a private company based in Huntington

Beach, Calif. The slogan was carried on the apparel's laundry-instruction tags.

> Galyan's said it also is returning Senate's wheels, bearings, and other skating gear carried at its nine sporting goods stores in Indiana, Ohio, Minnesota, and Kansas.
>
> Senate said the slogan was not meant to be taken literally.
>
> "The tag was supposed to say, 'Kill your parents,' but some people thought that was too extreme. Go figure," said Arlo Eisenberg, one of the five partners who founded Senate three years ago.

Source: Associated Press, "Clothing Line with 'Destroy All Girls,' Slogan on Tags Is Pulled by Retailer," *Waterloo–Cedar Falls Courier*, May 20, 1997, p. B6.

Questions

1. In your opinion, was Galyan's making a principled decision, a practical decision, or both?
2. Should retailers leave moral judgments about products to the customers? Explain.
3. If the product were a video, book, or compact disc with the same "destroy all girls" message, should the retailer remove it from the shelves? Explain.

CASE 2: DEANS' QUIZ

The Wall Street Journal recently reported the results of a scholarly survey of 291 business-school deans:

> Here's a pop quiz for business-school deans: Would you admit a clearly unqualified student to your school just because the candidate's family donated $1 million? Forty-eight percent of the 291 deans . . . answered yes.

How would you respond to some of the other questions asked of the deans:

1. What if the potential student's father was just a friend and not a donor?

2. Would it be ethical for a dean to remove an honor code violation from a student's record in exchange for a $1 million donation to the school?
3. Would it be ethical for a dean to personally accept a $500,000 bequest that was meant for the school but was mistakenly willed to the dean?

Source: Gordon Fairclough, "For Business-School Deans, Ethics Appear to Come in Shades of Green," *The Wall Street Journal*, August 10, 1998, p. A8.

CASE 3: A MILL OWNER'S COMPASSION RESCUES THOUSANDS OF JOBS AFTER DEVASTATING FIRE

Richard Lorant
Associated Press

METHUEN, MA.—As he watched Malden Mills burn, Michael Lavallee was sure the factory where he had worked for 25 years was being reduced, building by building, to a memory. "We just kept staring at the place, saying, 'It's over. It's done. It's gone,'" said Lavallee, an engineer.

* * * * *

The next morning, [mill owner Aaron] Feuerstein vowed to rebuild Malden Mills Industries without layoffs, embarking on a road that would lift him to national prominence as a symbol of corporate compassion in a seemingly heartless era.

At Malden Mills, Feuerstein appears to be succeeding in his effort to rebuild after the Dec. 11, 1995, fire that threatened 3,100 high-paying manufacturing jobs in this economically depressed region north of Boston. The blaze injured 33 people, 8 of them severely. Six have not yet returned to work, and at least one will never work again.

Feuerstein has said everything about his Jewish upbringing and his 50-year history in the local business told him to rebuild. "It was the right thing to do and there's a moral imperative to do it, irrespective of the consequences," Feuerstein said.

The new plant is scheduled to open in February. Filled with shining machinery, it was designed to boost production of the mill's patented Polartec fabric, which has become the fleece of choice for manufacturers of name-brand winter clothes. All Malden Mills' employees received full pay and benefits for three months after the fire. Since then, 85 percent have returned to work on makeshift production lines located in once and future warehouses. About 400 workers remain idle—a shortcoming Feuerstein regards as a failure—but he pledges to restore those jobs "come hell or high water" within two years.

Feuerstein has spent more than $300 million to build the new plant, replace lost machinery, and cover business losses. Insurers have paid half that amount so far.

The rest has come from bank loans and from his family's savings.

After falling off because of the fire, production of Polartec and Polarfleece is back to previous levels. "Unquestionably, in the long run, it will pay dividends," he said.

But, while Feuerstein defends his decision to rebuild as a good business move, it originated in the old-fashioned way his family has run the mill since it was founded by his grandfather in 1906. Despite its technical innovations, Malden Mills is in some ways a throwback to the days when a mill was like an extended family, with the owner at its head. Almost all of the many mills in the area have closed, following cheap labor to the South and then overseas.

Whole families in the immigrant-filled neighborhoods of Methuen and nearby Lawrence see the mills as their tickets into the middle class. If their $11-an-hour jobs were to disappear, many would end up with lower-paying service jobs.

If the fire provided Feuerstein with a challenge of the magnitude few business owners face, he also had two key advantages that helped him take the high road and stand by his workers. First, Malden Mills was a profitable company offering a patented product, Polartec, that had carved out a $3 billion market and a loyal customer base. Second, as a privately held company, Malden Mills Industries was free of the pressure to produce short-term profits and satisfy Wall Street analysts faced by publicly traded businesses.

"He's still pretty lonely, but the idea has appeal," said Michael Useem, a professor at the University of Pennsylvania's Wharton School. "The thinking is: employees can be seen as an ultimate competitive advantage. If you treat them well, they'll pay you back in really hard work later on."

Source: Richard Lorant, Associated Press. Reprinted in *Chicago Tribune*, December 10, 1996, p. 8. Reprinted by permission.

Afterword

Aaron Feuerstein became something of an overnight national hero by protecting his workers. His Polartec products have since sold very well, but other parts of the company have faltered with losses reportedly reaching some $37 million over two years. Ironically, the losses forced Feuerstein, in 1998, to close Malden's velvet upholstery unit and lay off about 300 employees.[1] Feuerstein, however, may have inspired others. A 1999 fire did $4.5 million in damage at the Titan Homes factory in Utica, New York, but when workers went to pick up what they assumed would be their final paychecks they were told they were being retained with full pay and benefits. Titan general manager, Jack Ireton-Hewitt said, "Not only is it the right, responsible thing to do, it's also good business."[2]

Questions

1. *a.* Are we in the midst of a "heartless" era as the author suggests? Explain.
   b. Are you "heartless"? Explain.
2. Malden Mills owner Aaron Feuerstein said that rebuilding and protecting his workers was the "right thing" to do.
   a. How did he reach that conclusion?
   b. How do you identify the "right thing" when faced with an ethical dilemma?
3. If you were a successful entrepreneur with the flexibility of Aaron Feuerstein, would you operate your business like "an extended family"? Explain.
4. Will the ethical manager of a publicly traded company ignore the short-term pressure of the stock market and do "the right thing" as Feuerstein did with his privately held company? Explain.

The Ethics Officer Association and the Ethical Leadership Group sampled a cross-section of workers at large companies nationwide. How would you respond?

1. "Is it wrong to use company e-mail for personal reasons?"
2. "Is it wrong to play computer games on office equipment during the workday?"
3. "Is it OK to take a $100 holiday food basket?"
4. "Due to on-the-job pressure, have you ever abused or lied about sick days?"

Source: *"The Wall Street Journal* Workplace-Ethics Quiz," *The Wall Street Journal,* October 21, 1999, p. B1.

ETHICS THEORIES

Volumes of literature are devoted in general terms to the question of defining ethics. We cannot hope to advance that discussion here. Ethics, of course, involves judgments as to good and bad, right and wrong, and what ought to be. Business ethics refers to the measurement of business behavior based on standards of right and wrong, rather than relying entirely on principles of accounting and management. (In this discussion, morals will be treated as synonymous with ethics. Distinctions certainly are drawn between the two, but those distinctions are not vital for our purposes.)

Finding and following the moral course is not easy for any of us, but the difficulty may be particularly acute for the businessperson. The bottom line is necessarily unforgiving. Hence, the pressure to produce is intense and the temptation to cheat may be very great. Although the law provides useful guideposts for minimum comportment, no clear moral guidelines have emerged. Therefore, when the businessperson is faced with a difficult decision, a common tactic is simply to do what he or she takes to be correct at any given moment. Indeed, in one survey of ethical views in business, 50 percent of the respondents indicated that the word *ethical* meant "what my feelings tell me is right."[3]

Philosophers have provided powerful intellectual support for that approach. Existentialists, led by the famed Jean-Paul Sartre, believe standards of conduct cannot be rationally justified and no actions are inherently right or wrong. Thus, each person may reach his or her own choice about ethical principles. That view finds its roots in the notion that humans are only what we will ourselves to be. If God does not exist, there can be no human nature, because there is no one to conceive that nature.

In Sartre's famous interpretation, existence precedes essence. First humans exist; then we individually define what we are—our essence. Therefore, each of us is

Existence precedes essence

free, with no rules to turn to for guidance. Just as we all choose our own natures, so must we choose our own ethical precepts. Moral responsibility belongs to each of us individually.

Universal Truths?

Have we then no rules or universal standards by which to distinguish right from wrong? Have we no absolutes? Philosophers seek to provide guidance beyond the uncertainties of ethical relativism. We will survey two ethical perspectives, teleology and deontology, which form the core of ethical analysis. Before proceeding to those theories, we will note the important role of religion in ethics and take a brief look at two additional formulations—libertarianism and virtue ethics—that have been increasingly influential in contemporary moral analysis.

1. Religion.   Judeo–Christian beliefs, the Moslem faith, Confucianism, Buddhism, and so on, are powerful ethical voices in contemporary life. They often feature efforts such as the Golden Rule to build absolute and universal standards. Scholarly studies indicate that most American managers believe in the Golden Rule and take it to be their most meaningful moral guidepost. From a religious point of view, the deity's laws are absolutes that must shape the whole of one's life, including work. Faith, rather than reason, intuition, or secular knowledge, provides the foundation for a moral life built on religion.

2. Libertarianism.   Contemporary philosopher Robert Nozick has built an ethical theory rooted in the notion of personal liberty. For him, morality springs from the maximization of personal freedom. Justice and fairness, right and wrong are measured not by equality of results (e.g., wealth) for all, but from ensuring equal opportunity for all to engage in informed choices about their own welfare. Hence, Nozick takes essentially a free market stance toward ethics.

3. Virtue Ethics.   In recent years, an increasing number of philosophers have argued that the key to good ethics lies not in rules, rights, and responsibilities but in the classic notion of character. As Plato and Aristotle argued, our attention should be given to strategies for encouraging desirable character traits such as honesty, fairness, compassion, and generosity. Aristotle believed that virtue could be taught much as any other skill. Virtue ethics applauds the person who is motivated to do the right thing and who cultivates that motivation in daily conduct. A part of the argument is that such persons are more morally reliable than those who simply follow the rules but fail to inspect, strengthen, and preserve their own personal virtues.

Teleology or Deontology—An Overview

Teleological ethical systems emphasize the end, the product, the consequences of a decision. The morality of a decision is determined by measuring the probable outcome. A morally correct decision is one that produces the greatest good. The teleological approach calls for reaching moral decisions by weighing the nonmoral consequences of an action. For the teleologist, the end is primary.

To the deontologist, principle is primary and consequence is secondary or even irrelevant. Maximizing right rather than good is the deontological standard. The deontologist might well refuse to lie even if doing so would maximize good. *Deontology,* derived from the Greek word meaning *duty,* is directed toward what ought to be, toward what is right. Relationships among people are important because they give rise to duties. A father may be morally committed to saving his son from a burning building, rather than saving another person who might well do more total good for society. Similarly, deontology considers motives. For example, why a crime was committed may be more important than the actual consequences of the crime.

The distinction here is critical. Are we to guide our behavior in terms of rational evaluations of the consequences of our acts, or are we to shape our conduct in terms of duty and principle—that which ought to be? Let's take a closer look at *utilitarianism,* the principal teleological ethical theory, and *formalism,* the principal deontological ethical theory.

Teleology

Utilitarianism.   In reaching an ethical decision, good is to be weighed against evil. A decision that maximizes the ratio of good over evil for all those concerned is the ethical course. Jeremy Bentham (1748–1832) and John Stuart Mill (1806–1873) were the chief intellectual forces in the development of utilitarianism. Their views and those of other utilitarian philosophers were not entirely consistent. As a result, at least two branches of utilitarianism have developed. According to *act-utilitarianism,* one's goal is to identify the consequences of a particular act to determine whether it is right or wrong. *Rule-utilitarianism* requires one to adhere to all the rules of conduct by which society reaps the greatest value. Thus, the rule-utilitarian may be forced to shun a particular act that would result in greater immediate good (punishing a guilty person whose constitutional rights have been violated) in favor of upholding a broader rule that results in the greater total good over time (maintaining constitutional principles by freeing the guilty person). In sum, the principle to be followed for the utilitarian is the greatest good for the greatest number. [For an extensive database exploring utilitarianism, see **http://www.hedweb.com/philsoph/utillink.htm**]

Deontology

Formalism.   The German philosopher Immanuel Kant (1724–1804) developed perhaps the most persuasive and fully articulated vision of ethics as measured not by consequences (teleology) but by the rightness of rules. In this formalistic view of ethics, the rightness of an act depends little (or, in Kant's view, not at all) on the results of the act. Kant believed in the key moral concept of "the good will." The moral person is a person of goodwill, and that person renders ethical decisions based on what is right, regardless of the consequences of the decision. Moral worth springs from one's decision to discharge one's duty. Thus, the student who refuses to cheat on exams is morally worthy if his or her decision springs from duty, but morally unworthy if the decision is merely one born of self-interest, such as fear of being caught.

How does the person of goodwill know what is right? Here, Kant propounded the *categorical imperative,* the notion that every person should act on only those principles that he or she, as a rational person, would prescribe as universal laws to be applied to the whole of humankind. A moral rule is "categorical" rather than "hypothetical" in that its prescriptive force is independent of its consequences. The rule guides us independent of the ends we seek. Kant believed that every rational creature can act according to his or her categorical imperative because all such persons have "autonomous, self-legislating wills" that permit them to formulate and act on their own systems of rules. To Kant, what is right for one is right for all, and each of us can discover that "right" by exercising our rational faculties.

USING UTILITARIANISM AND FORMALISM: LAYOFFS

Obviously, ethical theory does not provide magic answers to life's most difficult questions. However, those theories are useful in identifying and sorting the issues that lead to better decision making. Look back to Aaron Feuerstein and Malden Mills. In aiding his workers, Feuerstein said: "It was the right thing to do and there's a moral imperative to do it, irrespective of the consequences." Was Feuerstein employing utilitarian or formalist reasoning? In your view, was he correct to say that the consequences, in this instance, did not matter?

In the summer of 1996, *The Wall Street Journal* raised the question: "Are Layoffs Moral?"[4] Feuerstein apparently did not think so, but finances later forced him to shed workers. Should we establish a universal, formalist rule forbidding layoffs of all hard-working employees, or should we rely on utilitarian reasoning to answer the *Journal* question?

"Are layoffs moral?"

Commenting on Feuerstein's approach to his employee's needs, Wharton School professor Michael Useem said, "The thinking is: employees can be seen as an ultimate competitive advantage. If you treat them well, they'll pay you back in really hard work later on." Was Useem expressing formalist or utilitarian reasoning? In a 1986 pastoral letter, the United States Catholic bishops said "every economic decision and institution must be judged in light of whether it protects or undermines the dignity of the human person."[5] Does the thinking paraphrased by Useem undermine that dignity and as such require rejection under either utilitarian or formalist reasoning?

Columnist Joe Fitzgerald recently pointed to Aaron Feuerstein's concern for his workers and contrasted it with the layoffs that often accompany mergers:

> Feuerstein's loyalty to his workers captured national attention because it was water in a barren land, which is what corporate America is fast becoming as conscience gives way to the bottom line in hell-bent pursuit of the Almighty Dollar.
>
> Take this morning's Federal Reserve Bank hearing on the March merger of BankBoston and Fleet Financial Group, ostensibly to ponder whether their marriage will adversely affect the community.
>
> Why not ask those 5,000 workers who were thrown to the wolves how the quality of their lives was affected when they were told to hit the bricks?
>
> Why not ask how it felt to realize they were nothing more than cannon fodder to bank honchos Chad Gifford and Terrence Murray, who had the effrontery to swap high-fives as if they'd just accomplished something noble rather than the consummation of a deal that wreaked so much personal havoc?
>
> They were jubilant because their new institution will boast a solvency of $180 billion, but no matter how they explain it, it's still blood money.

Aside from personal goals, why might honorable, well-meaning managers properly feel that a merger, costing 5,000 jobs, was the "right thing to do?"

Source: Joe Fitzgerald, "Big Business Gleefully Gobbles Up People's Lives," *Boston Herald,* July 7, 1999, p. O24.

Questions—Part One

1. Think about ethical dilemmas in your own life.
   a. Do you find yourself turning primarily to teleological or deontological reasoning to resolve those problems? Or neither? Explain.
   b. Have you developed any systematic means of addressing ethical issues? Explain.
2. Do you think that philosophers' analyses of ethics, as we have briefly explored them in this text, can be of value in your future professional life? Explain.
3. Some commentators decry what they take to be a growing sense of moral uncertainty in America. *U.S. News & World Report* explains:

   > Perhaps more important, heterogeneous 20th-century America has grown cautious about making value judgments. "[There is] a growing degree of cynicism and sophistication in our

society," says Jody Powell, former press secretary to Jimmy Carter, "a sense that all things are relative and that nothing is absolutely right or wrong." When a New York City student last year turned in a purse she had found—complete with $1,000 in cash—not a single school official would congratulate her on her virtue. As her teacher explained, "If I come from a position of what is right and wrong, then I am not their counselor." The apparent translation: We no longer believe in black and white, only shades of gray.[6]

Is moral relativism a threat to the nation's moral health? Explain.

Part Two—Managerial Ethics: Evidence and Analysis

AMERICA'S MORAL CLIMATE

Ironically, America's remarkable prosperity and unprecedented world power have not brought peace to the nation's soul. As *The Wall Street Journal* headlined in 1999, "Americans Decry Moral Decline."[7] From dramatic tragedies like the killings at Colorado's Columbine High, to drug use, to graphic sex and violence in popular culture, to the predictable "lack of respect" for authority and elders, Americans at the turn of the century are deeply troubled by growing signs of what many take to be a decaying society. A 1998 survey found 44 percent of the public blaming our social and economic problems on "moral decline" while 43 percent cited "financial pressures and strains on the family."[8] A focus group sponsored by *The Wall Street Journal,* discussing these moral themes, pointed particularly to a breakdown in family routines:

> "Americans Decry Moral Decline"

"It used to be, you came home from school, and an hour and a half later you all sat down and ate dinner. Then you watched one show on TV and did your homework," says Nancy Thompson, a middle-aged telephone operator . . . "There's none of that today. It's all haphazard."[9]

At the same time, much of the objective evidence contradicts Americans' dire sentiments. In 1999, *The Des Moines Register* asked: "Immoral Americans? Take another look. By almost every measure, the behavior of Americans is improving":

- Teen sexual activity in the United States fell by 11 percent from 1991 to 1997.
- Cocaine and marijuana use has fallen by almost half since 1980.
- Welfare case loads have dropped by nearly 40 percent since 1993.
- The crime rate has fallen by one-third since the mid-1980s and burglaries are down by half in many inner cities.[10]

Teens Worse Than Ever?

Regardless of the good news about sexual activity, drug use, and the like, most adults and, perhaps surprisingly, most teens are convinced that young people today are in something like a moral freefall. Seventy-one percent of adults, according to a 1999 survey, think

young people today are in
something like a moral freefall

teenagers are irresponsible, rude, or wild and more than half think today's youths will make America a worse place or will have little impact on the nation's future.[11] Interestingly, teens have even less faith in themselves, with fewer than one-third thinking they will make America a better place.[12] Regrettably, teen misconduct, as self-reported in a 1998 Josephson Institute of Ethics survey of 10,000 10th, 11th, and 12th graders, tends to confirm the general fears:

- 46 percent say they have stolen something from a store (up from 39 percent in 1996).
- 70 percent say they have cheated on an exam (up from 64 percent in 1996).
- 92 percent say they have lied to a parent (up from 85 percent in 1996). And 78 percent say they have lied to a parent two or more times (up from 73 percent in 1996).[13] [For the Josephson Institute of Ethics, see **http://www.jiethics.org/**]

College Students

Ninety-five percent of 3,000 undergraduate business students polled in 31 universities admit they had cheated in high school or college, although only 1 to 2 percent admit having done so "frequently."[14] Professor Joseph Patrick, co-author of the study, attributes the cheating to "the academic welfare mentality." "Business-school students feel morally entitled to get what they need to do well in business."[15] The survey gave female students higher ethical marks than males and concluded that business students see themselves as less ethical than their parents. A female accounting student at the University of Dayton noted: "When you get to college, you don't follow the same rules your parents laid down for you. But we're just taking a break. We'll likely get back to [the rules] later."[16]

The survey gave female
students higher ethical marks
than males

UCLA's annual survey of the nation's college freshmen finds: "New freshmen are almost twice as likely to identify being 'well off financially' as a very important objective than developing 'a philosophy of life.' That's essentially a reversal from three decades ago."

a. Are you conscientiously seeking "a philosophy of life?"
b. Are you more committed to making money or to finding a philosophy of life?
c. Does it matter? Explain.

Source: Mary Beth Marklein, "Taking the Pulse of America's Freshmen," *USA Today,* January 25, 1999, p. 6D.

Business Practice

A Gallup Poll of consumers and CEOs of large companies, published in 1995, found that 44 percent of the CEOs believed business ethics had improved in recent years while 56 percent of consumers felt business ethics had declined. Similarly, 64 percent of CEOs saw their organizations as "highly ethical" while only 27 percent of employees shared that judgment.[17] Another recent nationwide survey of 4,035 employees at all levels across a variety of industries likewise raises serious questions about ethics in the business community:

> Ninety-seven percent of the employees surveyed said good ethics are good business. But responses to other questions indicated that many employees don't think that their companies agree. Two-thirds of the respondents said that ethical conduct isn't rewarded in American business. Eighty-two percent believe that managers generally choose bigger profits over "doing what's right." One-fourth said that their companies ignore ethics to achieve business goals. One-third reported that their superiors had pressured them to violate company rules.[18]

Four in 10 workers report that they knew of ethical or legal violations at their company in the previous two years.[19] The most frequently observed lapses and the percentage of employees observing those wrongs included:

Wrong	Percentage
Sexual harassment	19
Lying on reports/records	16
Conflict of interest	15
Stealing/theft	15
Lying to supervisor	15
Bias (race, age, etc.)	15[20]

[For ethics links and other business ethics materials, see **www.depaul.edu/ethics**]

WHY DO SOME MANAGERS CHEAT?

Moral Development

Scholars argue that some individuals are better "educated" to make ethical judgments than are others. Psychologist Lawrence Kohlberg built and empirically tested a comprehensive theory of moral development in which he claimed that moral judgment evolves and improves primarily as a function of age and education.

Kohlberg, via interviews with children as they aged, was able to identify moral development as movement through distinct stages, with the later stages being improvements on the earlier ones.

Kohlberg identified six universal stages grouped into three levels.

1. **Preconventional Level:**
   Stage 1: Obey rules to avoid punishment.
   Stage 2: Follow rules only if it is in own interest, but let others do the same. Conform to secure rewards.

2. Conventional Level:
   Stage 3: Conform to meet the expectations of others. Please others. Adhere to stereo-
           typical images.
   Stage 4: Doing right is one's duty. Obey the law. Uphold the social order.
3. Postconventional or Principled Level:
   Stage 5: Current laws and values are relative. Laws and duty are obeyed on rational
           calculations to serve the greatest number.
   Stage 6: Follow self-chosen universal ethical principles. In the event of conflicts,
           principles override laws.[21]

At Level 3, the individual is able to reach independent moral judgments that may or may
not be in conformity with conventional societal wisdom. Thus, the Level 2 manager might
refrain from sexual harassment because it constitutes a violation of company policy and the
law. A manager at Level 3 might reach the same conclusion, but his or her decision would
have been based on independently defined, universal principles of justice.

Kohlberg found that many adults never pass beyond Level 2. Consequently, if Kohlberg
was correct, many managers may behave unethically simply because they have not reached
the upper stages of moral maturity.

Kohlberg's model is based on very extensive longitudinal and cross-cultural studies over a
period of more than three decades. For example, one set of Chicago-area boys was interviewed at 3-year intervals for a period of 20 years. Thus, the stages of moral growth exhibit
"definite empirical characteristics" such that Kohlberg was able to claim that his model had
been scientifically validated.[22] While many critics remain, the evidence, in sum, is supportive
of Kohlberg's general proposition. [For more information about Kohlberg's theory of moral
development, see **http://snycorva.cortland.edu/~ANDERSMD/KOHL/content. HTML**]

Feminine Voice?   One of those lines of criticism requires a brief inspection. Carol
Gilligan, a colleague of Kohlberg, contends that our conceptions of morality are, in substantial part, gender-based.[23] She claims that men typically approach morality as a function of
justice, impartiality, and rights (the ethic of justice) while women are more likely to build a
morality based on care, support, and responsiveness (the ethic of care). Men, she says, tend
to take an impersonal, universal view of morality as contrasted with the feminine "voice" that
rises more commonly from relationships and concern for the specific needs of others.
Gilligan then criticizes Kohlberg because his highest stages, 5 and 6, are structured in terms
of the male approach to morality while the feminine voice falls at stage 3. Further, Kohlberg's
initial experimental subjects were limited to young males. The result, in Gilligan's view, is
that women are underscored. Of course, a danger in the ethic of care is that it might be interpreted to restore and legitimize the stereotype of women as care-giving subordinates not
deserving of moral autonomy.[24] [For an organization of young business leaders committed
to "responsible management practice," see **http://www.net-impact.org/**]

Organizational Forces

The businessperson's individual moral stance obviously plays a role in workplace
wrongs, but a considerable body of evidence suggests that forces external to the

> Fifty-six percent of those surveyed felt some pressure to act unethically or illegally

individual are also quite influential. A 1997 survey directed to a cross-section of over 1,300 American workers examined the question of "workplace pressure" as a factor in on-the-job wrongs. Fifty-six percent of those surveyed felt some pressure to act unethically or illegally, and 48 percent admitted they had done so in the past year in order to meet job demands.[25] Workers cited a number of factors that contributed to the pressure felt at work. The leading factors and the percentage of workers citing them included balancing work and family (52 percent), poor leadership (51), poor internal communications (51), work hours/work load (51), lack of management support (48), little or no recognition of achievements (46), need to meet company goals (e.g., sales) (46), company politics (44), personal financial worries (41), and insufficient resources (40).[26] Despite acknowledging the stress and pressure of the workplace, only 15 percent agreed that "ethical dilemmas are an unavoidable consequence of business and cannot be reduced."[27]

The pressure to produce is, of course, very great for those at the bottom of the power structure, but it often does not go away with advancement. Thirty recent graduates of the Harvard MBA program agreed to in-depth interviews about their on-the-job ethics experiences. One of the interesting conclusions from the interviews was the degree to which those younger subordinates understood and empathized with the pressure felt by their primarily middle-manager bosses:

> I really feel for people who are middle management, with a wife and four kids, under financial strain . . . You see it happen all the time, that people are indicted for fraud or larceny. You can empathize with their situation. The world is changing fast. And a lot of people have been blindsided by it—so they've done things that they don't like. I can't say that will never happen to me. It's easy for me as a single person . . . but when you're desperate, you're desperate.

> [My boss] was not willfully unethical. It was the pressure of the time . . . I have no idea what pressures were on him to drive the project. It probably wasn't [his] initiative to fudge the numbers. There may have been a good intention at some point in the organization. But as it got filtered through the organization, it changed. Some executive may have said, "This is an interesting project." Unfortunately this got translated as, "The vice president really wants this project." This sort of thing can happen a lot. Things start on high. As they go down they are filtered, modified. What was a positive comment several levels above becomes "do this or die" several levels down.[28]

> [My boss] was not willfully unethical. It was the pressure of the time

The Boss

Consistent with the experience of the Harvard MBAs, substantial scholarly evidence[29] supports the notion that bosses are crucial in setting the ethical climate in an organization. The article that follows, an excerpt from Thomas O'Boyle's book, *At Any Cost: Jack Welch, General Electric, and the Pursuit of Profit,*[30] examines many alleged illegalities and ethical lapses at General Electric. Much of the blame for that alleged wrongdoing is placed with Jack Welch, long-time General Electric CEO. [For extensive data on GE and more than 1,500 other corporations, see Hoover's Online at **http://www.hoovers.com**]

PROFIT AT ANY COST

Thomas F. O'Boyle

Helen Winebrenner vomited for hours afterward. "It must have been the nurse in me to check for a pulse," she recalls. But it was obvious from the state of the corpse that none would be found. She had discovered here husband's body in their bedroom, where he had shot himself in the head, using the shotgun he bought to go deer hunting with his son. Ivan Winebrenner was 39 years old. Two days earlier, on June 10, 1993, he had received his termination notice from General Electric.

He was one of about 200 workers to whom GE gave "lack of work" notices that day, at the Erie Works plant on the shores of Lake Erie, where GE had made locomotives since 1910. This division was on a roll, recording its best profits. The jobs were eliminated as part of GE's strategy of buying locomotive parts rather than making them in-house. Two days after Winebrenner's death, co-worker Anthony Victor Torelli also killed himself. He is said to have gone into the plant with a loaded gun, looking for his foreman, before turning the gun on himself. There have been additional suicides since.

"The numbers cause managers to do things that would be seen as totally inhuman in any other context," says Sheldon Potter, an engineering supervisor at Erie. He quit his management job rather than continue the tyranny. He still carries a laminated card in his wallet, with GE's "Beliefs" on one side—such as Belief One: "People, working together, are the source of our strength."

The truth is, more than 300,000 people have lost their jobs in Jack Welch's 17-year tenure as CEO at GE, earning him the nickname "Neutron Jack"—for the bomb that destroys people but leaves buildings intact. Long before most chief executives had heard of corporate restructuring, Welch was practicing it. He took the reins of GE in 1981. By the end of 1982, the 404,000 employees that Welch had taken command of had been chopped by 35,000, and just one year later another 37,000 were gone. In the context of the early 1980s, these actions were extraordinary, because they were taken not to curtail losses but to enhance profitability. In that, they presaged a change in philosophy that would become the prevailing attitude of the 1990s.

The layoffs were part of Welch's transformation of a once-great research and manufacturing company, which he through gut-wrenching upheaval turned into a financial services firm. He closed or sold 98 plants in the U.S., 43 percent of the 228 it operated in 1980. Rather than reinvesting heavily to exploit the company's historic skills, he chose to quit business after business because the money to be made lending money or producing television shows was greater than the Edisonian mission of *making things*. In the process a great research institution was diminished. The company Thomas Edison began today generates more revenue from selling insurance, lending money, servicing residential mortgages, managing credit cards, and other financial activities than it does from its five largest manufacturing businesses *combined*. Financial services, 8 percent of corporate earnings in 1980, generates about 40 percent today.

For most businesspeople, such moves have made Welch America's premier corporate changemaster, the wunderkind of Big Business. His methods are extrolled in business schools, praised by the media, and copied by others. GE under Welch is the world's most profitable and most valuable company, bringing investors 22 consecutive years of dividend increases—with a 1,155 percent increase in share value from 1982 to 1997. In the summer of 1997, GE became the first corporation to be valued at over $200 billion, up from $57 billion a decade earlier. By July 1998 its shares had risen another $100 billion.

Welch has many strengths, to be sure. At the same time, his way of doing business carries a heavy penalty, not necessarily for him or stockholders, but for the people who do his bidding and for government and society, which must often clean up his mess.

General Electric has compiled an ethical record during Welch's tenure that speaks for itself in both the severity of the miscues and the scope of the offenses:

- In one of Wall Street's biggest scandals of the 1990s, GE's Kidder, Peabody securities firm lost $1 billion before the remains were sold to Paine Webber in 1994. The SEC subsequently sanctioned three of Kidder's former senior bond executives.
- *Dateline NBC,* the signature newsmagazine of GE's TV network, rigged GM pickup trucks with rockets so they would explode for viewers, which caused GM to sue NBC for libel. (GM dropped the suit after *Dateline* issued an on-air apology.)
- GE's Aircraft Engine division pled guilty in 1992 to stealing $42 million from Uncle Sam and diverting the money to an Israeli general to win orders for jet engines.
- The same division paid $7.2 million to the federal government in 1995 to settle a whistleblower lawsuit brought by a young GE engineer who had charged his company with selling to the U.S. Air Force jet engines that didn't comply with contract terms.
- GE was involved in more instances of Pentagon fraud (before it sold its arms business in 1993) than any other military contractor, with 15 criminal convictions and civil judgments between 1985 and 1992— more than double the offenses at Teledyne, which came in second.

In addition, GE has been the defendant in many lawsuits during the Welch era. Among the more noteworthy allegations are these:

- Kidder, Peabody was sued by the Equal Employment Opportunity Commission and accused of illegally forcing out 17 investment bankers because of age—to that date, the largest age-discrimination case ever filed by the feds against a Wall Street brokerage house.
- GE's nuclear businesses were the object of several lawsuits based on alleged retaliation against employees who sought to expose illegal and unsafe practices at nuclear facilities.
- GE's synthetic diamond business and the De Beers cartel were indicted, along with two executives, in

February 1994 for conspiring to fix prices, capping a two-year Justice Department probe that led to a lawsuit which was later dismissed.

- The Massachusetts attorney general is investigating allegations that GE covered up internal memos that might have revealed the presence of banned chemicals on residential property in Pittsfield; 18 homeowners have sued the company for damages from diminished property values.

Why hasn't there been a more candid examination of GE's ethical problem? Because the man at the top doesn't think there is one, and directors, who have profited enormously, no doubt concur. When Welch took over GE, it ranked 11th among American corporations in the total value of its stock. He made it number one. GE now earns more profit in a single quarter than it did the entire year before Welch took over, and most people would argue that's the bottom line for judging a CEO's performance.

But it surely is no coincidence that criminality within GE hit its apex at the very time it was most profit driven and treating its employees with the most egregious disregard. Certainly greed has also contributed to the lawlessness, and there was plenty of that to go around in the latter half of the 1980s. But the common element in all GE's transgressions is the business credo championed by Welch. He's intimidating, tough, and unrelenting in his pursuit of ever higher profits, as are the people who report to him. It's a company managed by threat and intimidation rather than encouragement. "People at GE don't go off to work every morning. They go off to war," says one former battle-weary executive. The constant pressure to "get the numbers" has led, inevitably, to aberrant behavior.

Consider the 108-count indictment returned against General Electric by a federal grand jury in Philadelphia on March 26, 1985, the day Welch's company became the first major defense contractor to be indicted on charges of defrauding the government on a defense contract. The indictment stemmed from work GE had done at its Space Systems division in Valley Forge, Pa. (now owned by Martin Marietta), which made parts for

Minuteman nuclear missiles. GE managers there allegedly doctored time cards submitted by hourly workers. The alleged fraud began after a top executive at Fairfield headquarters warned Philadelphia managers that "heads would roll" if they did not stop cost overruns. The solution they came up with was to charge $800,000 of the Minuteman work to a phony project to be reimbursed by the Pentagon under a separate contract. "The managers feared for their jobs," Ed Zittlau, the assistant U.S. attorney who prosecuted the case, told the *Washington Post.*

A similar case occurred at Aircraft Engines, where machinist foreman John Gravitt in 1982 stood up during a training session and told 30 colleagues that the company was ripping off Uncle Sam. "The time cards going into supervisors' offices aren't the same ones coming out," he said. Following his later dismissal, Gravitt filed a lawsuit against GE, disclosing he had been pressured by superiors to coax subordinates to doctor their time cards. He said he was summoned to his boss' office for "the 'GE real world speech'—that cheating was something we had to do to keep our jobs." He decided to alert senior management, slipping into the office on weekends to photocopy altered time cards, and in June 1983 he delivered the evidence to the division president. That same day he was dismissed.

The pressure to make the numbers was systemic at GE. Consider, for another example, the way GE treated its suppliers. Through the 1980s GE had championed a concept called "partnering," in which a select few suppliers got the lion's share of the business. But by 1993, the new program was "Target 10," demanding that suppliers cut prices 10 percent each year. In some instances 10 percent was more than the suppliers made, but the choice was clear: give up your profit margin, or lose GE's business. "One minute it was 'partnering,' the next minute it was, 'We'll break your kneecaps if you don't give us what we want,'" said one supplier.

A company known for paternalism had turned to cannibalism. It wasn't that way prior to Welch. In 1978, then-CEO Reg Jones said the "spirit of General Electric" had three elements: innovation, moral integrity, and loyalty. In Welch's era, innovation came to mean financial gamesmanship. Rather than being known for "moral integrity," GE was infamous in law enforcement circles as a recidivist. And loyalty was openly ridiculed, replaced with purposeful insecurity.

People had once joined GE right out of college and worked there for 40 years. But "'loyal' became a bad word" to Welch, said one executive. The very word *loyalty* was expunged from GE's lexicon and excised from press releases, in something akin to the Cultural Revolution under Mao; people at corporate headquarters in Fairfield, Conn., referred to it as the "campaign against loyalty."

As GE chemist Mark Markovitz summed it up, "All Welch understands is increasing profits. That, and getting rid of people, is what he considers a vision." The ethos under Welch became a tyranny of numbers. The employees who once felt valued and protected now felt as if Welch regarded them as the enemy. And, in a sense, he did.

One of the most egregious examples was that of Vera English—a nuclear power plant whistle-blower similar to Karen Silkwood, who was portrayed by Meryl Streep in the film *Silkwood.* Her case—*English* v. *General Electric Co.*—eventually made its way to the Supreme Court. The unanimous victory English won there set an important precedent, but didn't improve her lot one iota. English lost her job, her savings, her security, her home, and, for a time, nearly her mind.

English's job had been to monitor fuel quality, and when uranium did not conform, to send it for reprocessing. That meant costly delays. When management stepped up its pressure for higher productivity, English began to suspect colleagues were falsifying data. When she complained, other supervisors ridiculed her.

She became the victim of harassment, vandalism, and intimidation. The first incident took place in August 1980, when her home was ransacked. Although the case was never solved, English believes the vandals were fellow employees seeking to intimidate her. The incident was the first of 14 that New Hanover County Police investigated between 1980 and 1988, including burglaries, vandalism, obscene phone calls, and, in one instance, gunfire.

The treatment she received from her bosses at GE was not much better. Fired from her job in July 1984, English initiated an eight-year legal battle, in which an administrative law judge ruled that management had used a trumped-up charge as "pretext for getting rid of an employee who would not stop reporting violations to the Nuclear Regulatory Commission." The judge ordered reinstatement and payment of $70,000, but the company had the decision overturned on procedural grounds. The NRC also sided with English (though four and a half years after the event). But all GE ever paid for wrongfully terminating English was $24,000.

More than anything, the case provided insight into the cannabilistic character of GE under Welch. Though both the NCR and the court concluded GE was in the wrong, management still fought to win, no matter that their foe was a widowed grandmother. Had GE accepted the initial ruling, they would have saved the company a legal bill of $1 million. But GE fought on in a blizzard of motions, in the end, GE management convincing themselves *they* were doing the right thing by meting out punishment against an adversary who deserved what she got.

It was one among many cases that marked a clear decline in values within the GE society. In the revolution Welch had worked, earnings became the Holy Grail of every manager's existence. And that in turn led GE managers into ethical lapses. As the 1990s would unfold, those lapses would become more frequent and celebrated.

Welch at one point recognized the problem and tried to correct it. In 1989, he pushed through a performance evaluation system in which executives would be graded on how they supported six GE values. "Live within both the spirit and letter of the law," was one; "teamwork depends on trust, mutual understanding, and the shared belief that the individual will be treated fairly in any environment" was another.

The problem was these lofty goals were at odds with a repeated insistence to get the numbers. And so the ethical scandals went on. In 1992 there was Infact's Oscar-winning portrayal of GE's weapons-related activities, with its exhortation to boycott GE. In 1993 came the rigged truck crash on *Dateline* at NBC. And in 1994 there was the diamond caper, which created a huge wave of bad publicity.

The biggest and most costly scandal of all began to unfold in the spring of 1994, involving GE's Kidder, Peabody securities firm. It began with accusations leveled by the firm against a 36-year-old bond trader named Orlando Joseph Jett, and would cost GE $1.2 billion in 1994, before Kidder was liquidated and its remains sold to rival PaineWebber. The entire dizzying implosion occurred in the space of just six months, one of the most sudden and catastrophic failures in the history of Wall Street.

Through a glitch in Kidder's internal computer system, Jett was able to hide $350 million in faked profits in bond trades over several years, before any superior became suspicious. When the lid blew off, the GE mantra was Jett did it, Jett did it, Jett did it. But only a few months before, Jett (whom colleagues had dubbed the "human piranha" for his voraciousness in pursuing profits) had been held up at GE's annual management retreat as a model employee. Welch had sanctioned the recognition of Jett as Kidder, Peabody's 1993 "Man of the Year," while approving the $9 million bonus he received just months before the scandal broke. Welch had failed to ask one elementary question: How could Jett have possibly achieved trading profits of $150 million in 1993 from swapping bonds with the Federal Reserve, one of the world's lowest-margin markets, when the previous full-year earnings had been only $20 million?

The truth is, it was not Joseph Jett but the imperative to achieve profits at any cost that ruined Kidder. As GE's own inquiry into the Jett affair concluded, it was Jett's enormous contributions to the bottom line that made his superiors reluctant to ask questions. "As his profitability increased," the report observed, "skepticism about Jett's activities was often dismissed or unspoken." Rather than questioning Jett, his superiors promoted him, and allowed him to keep a private, and separate, accounting system. Even *Fortune* magazine, which had done more than any other publication to elevate Welch to management sainthood, proclaimed, "Like it or not, the scandals at Kidder, Peabody were brought on by GE's management."

The Jett affair, it turned out, was the least of Kidder's troubles. In the months that followed Jett's unraveling, other Kidder traders were dimissed for trading irregularities. And a growling bear market in mortgage-backed bonds made it difficult to finance Kidder's huge mortgage inventory, for which it could find no buyers. Losses for the year through September, excluding the Jett writeoff, were $400 million. By October Kidder had been sold.

The board should not have been surprised. When GE purchased Kidder, Peabody in 1986, one board member had demurred, objecting that Kidder was involved in the financing of hostile takeovers, an unsavory business GE should avoid. The board sided with Welch, but the director's objection proved prescient—for Kidder did indeed turn out to be quite dirty, and a horrendous mistake.

But all that was forgotten. Although GE's shares lost value in 1994, directors rewarded Welch handsomely for his handling of the Kidder crisis, increasing his 1994 salary and bonus 8 percent, to $4.35 million, and conferring stock rights on an additional 320,000 shares (adding to a treasure chest of unexercised options worth $107 million at the end of 1996). In the process, the board's compensation committee praised Welch's "drive to reinforce a culture of integrity."

Welch Defended.   The book review that follows questions the fairness of Thomas O'Boyle's attack on Welch and GE.

"COST" MAKES WHIPPING BOY OF ITS SUBJECT

Charles Stein

The first hint of trouble in Thomas O'Boyle's book comes on the very first page. In his author's note, he points out that the subject of his book, Jack Welch, chairman of General Electric Co., refused to cooperate with the project. But not to worry, O'Boyle tells the reader: "I have done everything in my power to write a balanced and fair account."

And the check is in the mail.

"At Any Cost" is actually a remarkably one-sided book about Welch's tenure at GE. To call it a hatchet job would be too kind. Ax murder would be closer to the mark. O'Boyle has made Welch the poster boy for modern capitalism and all the ills that accompany it: downsizing, deal-making, ethical violations, pollution. If the book had come out a few months later, O'Boyle probably would have blamed Welch for the Asian financial crisis and the collapse of the ruble.

When Jack Welch took over GE in 1981, he inherited a slow-moving, bureaucratic company. Its old-line manufacturing businesses were under intense pressure from rivals both in this country and abroad. Welch rolled up his sleeves and went to work. He chopped the work forces of traditional businesses—light bulbs, power systems, and appliances—because he recognized that in a global economy only low-cost producers can survive. At the same time he moved GE into service businesses like entertainment and finance that promised greater growth and higher returns. Welch didn't invent the forces of modern capitalism. He anticipated them. And he put his company in a position to profit from them.

The numbers speak for themselves. Between 1982 and 1997 GE's stock price rose 1,155 percent. The company's earnings have grown at a steady 10 to 1 percent clip per year. Bill Gates may be America's best known corporate leader, but in business circles, Jack Welch is probably more admired. Gates has achieved great success by doing one thing well. Welch has created winners in at least half a dozen separate fields.

Thomas O'Boyle isn't impressed. He dismisses Welch's foray into finance—probably his greatest triumph—in a few paragraphs. The money business may be profitable, but to O'Boyle it is nothing more than "glitz," "financial engineering," and "gamesmanship." The author has practically nothing to say about GE's accomplishments in aircraft engines or medical devices because they don't fit his central thesis: that under Welch, GE has abandoned all research, technology, and manufacturing.

O'Boyle has plenty to say about the problems of the Welch years. Unfortunately he frequently blows them out of all proportion. He calls the failure of a new GE refrigerator in the 1980s "one of the greatest fiascoes in modern engineering." Was it really? The author spends a full 50 pages describing the government's attempt to prosecute GE for price fixing in the industrial diamond business. Yet at the very end of this tedious account we learn that the courts threw out the case. So why are we reading so much about it?

O'Boyle does raise some legitimate issues. More than 100,000 GE jobs have been axed under Welch, in a series of downsizings that have devastated old industrial towns like Pittsfield [Mass.] and Schenectady, N.Y. Did Welch need to be so hard-nosed? Could the transformation of GE have been accomplished in a more humane way?

It is also fair to ask how much blame Welch should bear for some of the ethical lapses that have happened on his watch, especially in the defense business. While Welch has never told his employees to break the law, the high-pressure culture he has created may have encouraged some of his underlings to cross the line in pursuit of greater profits. As O'Boyle puts it, "Some clearly felt that cheating was the only way to deliver the numbers needed to protect their jobs."

In the business press, Jack Welch receives very different treatment. Over the past 17 years, he has probably been on more magazine covers than Cindy Crawford. The accompanying articles are nearly always fawning. He is inevitably praised for his acumen. His words are treated like pronouncements from on high.

Someday, a book will come along that provides a balanced account of Jack Welch. Suffice to say, this isn't it.

Source: Republished with permission of the *Boston Globe*. "Cost Makes Whipping Boy of Its Subject," Charles Stein, November 10, 1998; permission conveyed through Copyright Clearance Center.

Questions

1. *a.* After reading these materials, do you regard Welch as a capitalist hero or villain or something of both? Explain.
   b. Do you see yourself as most likely to resist the pressures of the market, the corporate culture, and your bosses or will you bend your standards? Explain.
2. A *New York Times* review of *At Any Cost* says: "This account would be more convincing . . . if O'Boyle had displayed equal resolve at getting both sides of the story. Generally, he doesn't. O'Boyle seems more interested in depicting Welch and G.E. as actors in a 'vast American morality play: in which the chief villain is the short-term fixation of American business.'"[31]
   a. Is the market the real villain in this story?
   b. If so, are we, then, to blame for buying GE appliances and watching NBC television? Explain.

3. Downsizing and mergers at GE and most other major American corporations have resulted in millions of lost jobs. Sociologist Richard Sennett, in his 1998 book, *The Corrosion of Character: The Personal Consequences of Work in the New Capitalism,*[32] argues that the near disappearance of lifetime employment with one firm and the consequent movement from firm to firm will reduce our opportunities to build strong character. As he says: "Horace writes that the character of a man depends on his connections to the world." Since those connections are now constantly in flux for so many of us, Sennett is concerned that we have no foundation for building enduring character. Our work lives become "illegible," leaving us unable to construct a meaningful life narrative—which is a cornerstone of character development.[33]

   a. Do you think your character will be at risk if your career consists of moves from job to job?
   b. Have you thought about your "life narrative" to this point? Explain.
   c. How has your life narrative influenced your character development?

Questions—Part Two

1. Does a corporation have a conscience? Explain. See Kenneth Goodpaster and John B. Matthews, Jr., "Can a Corporation Have a Conscience?" *Harvard Business Review,* January–February 1982, p. 136.
2. Saul Gellerman, dean of the University of Dallas Graduate School of Management, speculated about why managers who are normally good, decent people would occasionally engage in unethical conduct. Gellerman attributes the problem in part to four rationalizations. For example, he believes managers often "rationalize" their wrongdoing by convincing themselves that they will not be caught. Identify other rationalizations that permit good managers to do bad deeds. See Saul Gellerman, "Why 'Good' Managers Make Bad Ethical Choices," *Harvard Business Review,* July–August 1986, p. 85.
3. Business schools are giving increasing attention to ethics. Will that attention make a difference in the ethical quality of actual business practice? Professor David Vogel put the issue this way in a commentary in *The Wall Street Journal* entitled "Could an Ethics Course Have Kept Ivan [Boesky] from Going Bad?":

   > Before we set about reforming the nation's business through its business schools, we might want to reflect more carefully on the relationship between these two institutions. Does anyone believe that if Mr. Levine or Mr. Siegel [inside traders] had been exposed to a few lectures, or even a course, on business ethics they would have been better able to resist the temptation to benefit financially from insider information?[34]

   What value, if any, is likely to be derived from the study of ethics in business schools?
4. As explained earlier, psychologist Lawrence Kohlberg developed a theory of moral development holding that humans proceed through six stages before reaching moral maturity. Kohlberg built his theory from the interviewees' responses to a series of moral dilemmas. For example (stated briefly), should you steal drugs if doing so is the only way to save your spouse's life?
   a. Is Kohlberg's theory consistent with your own view of moral development? Explain.
   b. Rank your moral development using Kohlberg's scale.

       c. Carol Gilligan has argued that men and women have differing moral languages. Gilligan suggests women make moral decisions based on responsibility and caring, whereas moral decision making for males is founded in rules and justice. Comment.

       d. Many men continue to have negative attitudes toward women as managers/executives. Would you expect to find lower levels of moral development in those men? Explain.

Part Three—Business Ethics in Practice

INTRODUCTION: ETHICS CODES

Having established a general ethical foundation, we now turn to the pragmatics of dealing with specific ethical problems. As noted, when questioned regarding the forces that contribute to unethical decision making in working life, managers point to the behavior of their superiors and the nature of company policy regarding wrongdoing. Hence, we assume that the organization committed to ethical quality can institute some structures and procedures to encourage decency. Codes of conduct are a common corporate ethics tool. The codes vary from generalized value statements and credos to detailed discussions of ethical policy. The value statements and credos normally refer, in brief, generalized terms, to the culture of the company and to the company's responsibilities to its various stakeholders (employees, community, shareholders, et al.). The Johnson & Johnson Credo, on page 54, is the most frequently cited corporate ethics statement. Ethics codes are more detailed, specific expressions of company expectations. They address such topics as relations with the United States government, matters of personal character, product safety, environmental affairs, customer/supplier relations, and political contributions. They vary in length from brief booklets to Boeing's 50-page-plus manual.[35] Recent surveys indicate that more than 90 percent of large American companies have some form of ethics code.[36]

    At the turn of the century, ethics codes have become something of a growth industry with a number of trade and political organizations around the world working toward codes of ethical practice in business. In 1999, the European Union adopted a new code of ethical business practices addressing such problems as employees' working conditions and environmental protection. Failure to comply will risk loss of EU funds. Likewise in 1999, the United States announced initial steps on a new, voluntary code of "best practices" to fight bribery and kickbacks around the world, and a number of industrial nations agreed to a code of conduct that, among other things, protects shareholder rights and encourages "active cooperation" between businesses and their "stakeholders," including workers and suppliers. The code, developed by the Organization for Economic Cooperation and Development, is a response to the Asian and Russian financial crises of the late '90s and is expected to serve as a standard for ethical and sound corporate governance in developing nations.[37] In 1995, the United States adopted its own "Model Business Principles" providing guidelines for international commerce in such areas as bribery, workplace safety, collective bargaining, freedom of expression, and the environment. The United States, according to

Undersecretary of State Stuart Eizenstat, views business corruption as a barrier to world-wide prosperity:

> There are really very few things that are more threatening to the spread of democracy and free-market reform and to the restoration of confidence in the financial system than failure to deal with corruption.[38]

Finally, in 1999, the United Nations Development Program upped the stakes significantly by calling for international codes to counteract what are seen as the negative effects of business globalization in areas such as environmental protection, fair trade, and labor practices:

> **Multinationals are too dominant in the world economy**

> Multinationals are too dominant in the world economy for voluntary codes to be enough, the report says . . . "The new rules of globalisation—and the players writing them—focus on integrating global markets, neglecting the needs of people that markets cannot meet. The process is concentrating power and marginalising the poor, both countries and people.

> The report cites an ever-widening income gap between the world's richest and poorest: In 1960, 20 percent of the world's population living in the richest countries had 30 times the income of the poorest 20 percent. By 1997, the richest were 74 times richer.[39]

[For information on global corporate governance and citizenship, see **http://www.conference-board.org/**]

Do They Work?   The important question, of course, is whether the codes are effective. Much of the evidence suggests that a code standing alone is of little value. The Ethics Resource Center's National Business Ethics Survey found that only 19 percent of employees frequently find a code useful in making business decisions.[40] With an accompanying ethics office and mandatory training, respondents finding the full program useful totaled 42 percent.[41] In code-only companies, 38 percent of respondents indicated that they report the misconduct they see, while in companies with full programs (office, training, and code), reporting of observed wrongdoing increases to 56 percent.[42] So aggressive, thorough ethics programs appear to provide some dividends. Workers often remain skeptical, however, as indicated by the responses of the 30 young Harvard MBAs mentioned earlier:

> The young managers were dubious about ethics programs for several reasons. The programs failed to address the issues commonly faced by young managers, other people in the organization paid no attention to them, and the principles espoused in the codes and programs seemed inconsistent with "what the company was all about."[43]

According to business ethics consultant and Harvard Divinity School graduate, Steve Priest: "Most codes of conduct stink." "They're written for lawyers, by lawyers, and just tell people, 'Don't break the law.'"

Source: Michael J. McCarthy, "An Ex-Divinity Student Works on Searching the Corporate Soul," *The Wall Street Journal,* June 18, 1999, p. B1.

[For the Codes of Ethics Online Project and its large database of ethics codes, see **http:// 216.47.152.67/codes/**]

[For the Ethics Resource Center, see **http://www.ethics.org/index. html**]

Our Credo

We believe our first responsibility is to the doctors, nurses and patients,
to mothers and fathers and all others who use our products and services.
In meeting their needs everything we do must be of high quality.
We must constantly strive to reduce our costs
in order to maintain reasonable prices.

We are responsible to our employees,
the men and women who work with us throughout the world.
Everyone must be considered as an individual.
We must respect their dignity and recognize their merit.
They must have a sense of security in their jobs.
Compensation must be fair and adequate,
and working conditions clean, orderly and safe.
We must be mindful of ways to help our employees fulfill
their family responsibilities.
Employees must feel free to make suggestions and complaints.
There must be equal opportunity for employment, development
and advancement for those qualified.
We must provide competent management,
and their actions must be just and ethical.

We are responsible to the communities in which we live and work
and to the world community as well.
We must be good citizens—support good works and charities
and bear our fair share of taxes.
We must encourage civic improvements and better health and education.
We must maintain in good order
the property we are privileged to use,
protecting the environment and natural resources.

Our final responsibility is to our stockholders.
Business must make a sound profit.
We must experiment with new ideas.
Research must be carried on, innovative programs developed
and mistakes paid for.
New equipment must be purchased, new facilities provided
and new products launched.
Reserves must be created to provide for adverse times.
When we operate according to these principles,
the stockholders should realize a fair return.

Reprinted with permission of Johnson & Johnson.

BRIBERY ABROAD

As explained above, strategies for curbing corrupt business practices around the world have become a matter of urgency in this era of closely entwined stock markets and financial institutions. What was once merely a Western standard of ethical business practice has now become, the American business community believes, a necessity for the entire global economy, but that new expectation raises complex ethical dilemmas for America's multinational businesses. In many cultures, the payment of bribes—*baksheesh* (Middle East), *mordida* (South America), or *dash* (Africa)—is accepted as necessary and, in some cases, a lawful way of doing business. American firms and officers wishing to succeed abroad have faced great pressure to engage in practices that are, of course, illegal and unethical

$16 million in hidden payments

in the American culture. For example, in 1999, two subsidiaries of Litton Industries pleaded guilty in federal court to making more than $16 million in hidden payments to secure nearly $200 million in defense business from Taiwan and Greece.[44] Litton will pay $18.5 million in fines and other penalties for fraud and other violations. Litton was not charged under the primary statutory weapon against bribery abroad, the Foreign Corrupt Practices Act.[45] In fact, FCPA prosecutions have totaled fewer than 50, but the act does seem to serve as a strong deterrent to misconduct.

The FCPA was enacted in 1977 in response to disclosure of widespread bribery by American firms, including government officials at the highest levels. In brief, the FCPA, as amended in 1998, provides that United States nationals and businesses acting anywhere in the world as well as foreign nationals and companies acting in the United States are engaging in criminal conduct if they offer or provide bribes to foreign officials to obtain "any improper advantage." FCPA accounting standards eliminate "slush funds" and other devices useful in facilitating bribes. The act does not forbid "grease" payments to foreign officials or political parties where the purpose of the payments is "to expedite or to secure the performance of a routine governmental action,"[46] such as processing papers (e.g., visas), providing police protection, and securing phone service. And those accused may offer the affirmative defense that the alleged payoff was lawful in the host country or was a normal, reasonable business expenditure directed to specific marketing and contract performance activities. Criminal penalties include fines of up to $2 million for companies, while individuals may be fined $100,000 and imprisoned for as long as five years if they either participate in a violation, know of a violation, or are "aware of the high probability of the existence" of a bribery situation "unless the person actually believes that such circumstance does not exist."[47] That is, corporations and individuals cannot use "head-in-sand" tactics to avoid knowledge of wrongdoing. [For a detailed explanation of the antibribery provisions of the FCPA, see **http://www.tradecompass.com/library/legal/antibri.htm**]

Controversy

The FCPA has been controversial from the outset. Some businesspeople see it as a blessing both because it is an honorable attempt at a firm moral stance and because it is often useful

for an American businessperson abroad to say, "No, our laws forbid me from doing that."
On the other hand, some have seen the act as damaging to our competitiveness. Now other
nations are recognizing that corruption is a great risk to the global economy. Once believing that bribery aided the poor, most industrial countries are now moving toward the zero
tolerance view held by the United States, recognizing that the money mainly goes to the
well-connected and that bribery is inefficient, harmful to democratic institutions, and a
threat to the stability of the world financial system. As of this writing in 1999, 12 nations,
including the United States, have begun enforcing the OECD Convention on Combating
Bribery which is much like the FCPA and requires significant criminal penalties for bribery
of foreign officials. At least 22 other nations have signed the Convention and are moving
toward enforcement, and other countries around the world are expected to do so. The

> German firms have legally
> spent an estimated $3 billion
> per year in bribes

United States strongly encouraged the Convention in recognition of our
immense financial interest in a level playing field and in sound worldwide
financial practices. A recent State Department study found over $24 bil-
lion in lost contracts for United States firms over a five-year period in the
international arena where bribes allegedly influenced the outcome.[48] German firms have legally spent an estimated $3 billion per year in bribes[49] although the new
Convention is expected to change that practice. The Convention, likewise, discourages (but
does not forbid) the tax deductions that many nations permit for bribes. The United States
is also one of 25 North and South American countries signing an Inter-American Convention similar to the OECD Convention, but the United States has yet to implement the Inter-
American treaty.

A 1999 World Bank survey shows that bribery is a routine cost of doing business in most of
Eastern Europe. Some examples:

	Percentage of Firms that Must Bribe Frequently	*Average Bribe as a Percentage of Annual Revenue*
Azerbaijan	59.3%	6.6%
Romania	50.9	4.0
Poland	32.7	2.5
Russia	29.2	4.1
Croatia	7.7	2.1

Source: John Reed and Erik Portanger, "Bribery, Corruption Are Rampant in Eastern
Europe, Survey Finds," *The Wall Street Journal*, November 9, 1999, p. A21.

United States Corruption?   While the United States has been the clear world leader in
encouraging anticorruption efforts, we should not be unduly prideful. Indeed, the United
States ranks only 17th in the world on Transparency International's 1998 Corruption Per-

alleged bribes paid to attract the 2002 Winter Olympics to Salt Lake City

ception Index.[50] Denmark tops the list and most of Western Europe as well as Canada are viewed as less corrupt than the United States. (The Index does not measure corruption, but rather combines the results of a number of surveys measuring the *perception* of corruption from the view of the public and international business.) Of course, corruption may simply receive much greater scrutiny and public exposure in the United States as exemplified by the worldwide publicity associated with the multimillion dollars in alleged bribes paid to attract the 2002 Winter Olympics to Salt Lake City. [For the Transparency International website, see **http://www.transparency.de/**]

Bribery in Practice. Naturally, corruption is most threatening in poorer nations, especially those in Africa and those experiencing the current turmoil of moving toward capitalism in China and Russia. A 1997 investigation by Chinese authorities found that each of McDonald's 38 outlets in Beijing was subjected to 31 separate fees for such purposes as river dredging and flower displays, with only two of the fees having any clear legal justification.[51] In Russia, bribery is simply a way of life.

Questions

1. To some, the FCPA and the Convention on Combating Bribery are merely further evidence of American paternalism or imperialism. What do they mean?
2. America ranks 17th in the 1998 Corruption Perception Index, about the same ranking as in infant mortality. Journalist Martin Dyckman says that every nation ahead of us in the Corruption Index is also ahead of us in preventing infant deaths.[52] Everyone, Dyckman explains, also has a national health care system. Do you see any relationship between our comparatively poor showing in the Corruption Index and our comparatively poor showing in infant mortality? Explain.
3. Carl Kaufmann of Du Pont raised the following bribery issue. As the head of a multinational corporation, you learn that one of your plant managers has been arrested in a distant republic. His alleged crime is that goods found in your warehouse lack the proper customs stamp and papers. But the truth is more complicated. For years, *grease* has been a way of life in this country's bureaucracy, and your plant manager has been paying gratuities to the customs officers. But he knows it is against home office policy, and so he stops. Their inspection follows. The price for dropping all charges: $18,000.
   a. Would you pay up? Or let your man be put in jail? Explain.
   b. Which alternative is more ethical?[53] Explain.
4. Your employer, as you see it, is taking advantage of poor, powerless production workers in an overseas subsidiary located in a country where jobs are in short supply. You are a mid-level manager in the home office.
   a. Do you have any responsibility vis à vis the situation abroad?
   b. What should you do? Explain.

BUSINESS/WHITE-COLLAR CRIME

At this writing in 1999, three former executives with Archer Daniels Midland (the giant food processor), one of them the son of the former ADM chairman, Dwayne Andreas, have been sentenced to prison for conspiring to fix prices in the $600 million, worldwide lysine market (see Chapter 12). On the other side of the globe Nick Leeson walked out of a Singapore prison after serving more than three years for securities fraud. Leeson had fraudulently hidden more than $1.4 billion in trading losses at Barings Bank, which collapsed when the losses came to light. These are but two examples of extravagantly expensive white-collar crime. While precise data are not available, the white-collar crime bill in the United States is estimated at perhaps $400 *billion* dollars annually.[54] A recent study by the Association of Certified Fraud Examiners found that the average organization loses about 6 percent of its total annual revenue to employee fraud and abuse.[55] Fraud perpetrated by managers resulted in losses 16 times greater than that of nonmanagerial personnel.[56]

Businesses themselves are victims of billions of dollars annually in employee theft, shoplifting, and so on, but here we are concerned about crimes committed by corporations and their managers such as those at ADM and Barings. Those crimes take many forms including fraud, antitrust wrongs, bribes, pollution, food and drugs violations, tax evasion, and conspiracy. White-collar crime is very difficult to detect and difficult to prosecute, but a major conviction can be quite influential because of the message it sends. An interesting recent example involved more than 25 former American Honda executives who, in the mid-1990s, were either convicted or pleaded guilty to criminal charges for extracting bribes from "dirty dealers" here in the United States who made payments to secure additional dealerships and a steady flow of new cars at a time when the cars were scarce.[57] Dealers who failed to pay bribes claim they did not receive the desirable cars needed to remain competitive. Following the criminal case, 1,800 Honda dealers joined together in a class action to bring bribery claims under civil Racketeer Influenced and Corrupt Organizations Act (RICO) laws (see Chapter 10). That suit was settled in 1998 for just under $330 million.[58] The RICO lawsuit alleged not only that Honda executives conspired to secure the bribes, but also that others at the highest level knew of the bribes and ignored them.[59] The bribes to Honda executives reportedly included Hong Kong shopping sprees, cash approaching $1 million, and children's college tuition.

> more than 25 former American Honda executives were either convicted or pleaded guilty to criminal charges for extracting bribes from "dirty dealers"

Punishment.   Anger over corporate crime has been magnified for many years by the widespread sense that business criminals often are not meaningfully punished. In order to achieve greater predictability and consistency in punishments for both white-collar and street crime, Congress, in 1987, authorized *federal sentencing guidelines* for individuals, followed in 1991 with guidelines for organizations. The guidelines, which are binding on federal judges, were developed by the U.S. Sentencing Commission.

The guidelines for individuals use a grid to categorize and rank over 2,000 federal crimes based on their seriousness. Additional factors such as the criminal history of the offender and specific characteristics of the offense (e.g., was a gun used?) are also given weight. By plotting the crime on the grid according to its seriousness and the additional factors, the judge determines the range of sentence that must be imposed (e.g., 21–27 months). The judge has latitude to depart from the prescribed range based on such considerations as community involvement, but must provide a written justification for doing so.

The organizational guidelines permit fines, which can reach hundreds of millions of dollars. A base fine is computed according to the seriousness of the offense and the money gained or lost as a consequence of the crime. That fine may then be raised or lowered according to a culpability score. That score can be lowered if the corporation has an effective program for preventing and detecting violations, but the corporation can be placed on probation if an effective compliance program is not in place. The guidelines, both individual and corporate, have been vigorously criticized.

Federal Guidelines for Preventing Corporate Crime

Under the Federal Guidelines for Sentencing, companies can accrue credits against potential penalties by showing they have complied with the following crime prevention steps, among others:

- Firms must establish crime prevention standards and procedures for employees and agents. Large companies must have written programs.
- High-level employees with substantial responsibility must be assigned to enforce standards.
- Companies must take steps to prevent employees with an apparent propensity to engage in criminal activity from exercising discretionary authority.
- Companies must communicate anticrime standards to all employees and agents either in writing or through training programs.
- The anticrime program must include strategies to prevent and detect crimes. Hotlines must be set up and whistle-blowers must be protected from reprisals.[60]

Guidelines Successful?   Experts question the wisdom and success of the guidelines, but prosecution of corporations has increased significantly in recent years with the number of organizations sentenced more than doubling (from 108 to 220) from 1994–95 to 1997.[61] Those numbers remain small, but penalties are increasing in size, and experts note a trend toward substantial criminal penalties for large, public companies.[62] In 1999, both Sears Roebuck and Banker's Trust paid $60 million fines in criminal fraud cases,[63] and in 1996 Japan's Daiwa Bank was fined $340 million and banished from the United States for covering up securities trading losses and for its lack of a meaningful compliance program as encouraged by the sentencing guidelines.[64] Critics question the fairness of prosecuting large, publicly held companies where much of the penalty falls on innocent stockholders,[65] but the guidelines clearly encourage those prosecutions.

> Japan's Daiwa Bank was fined $340 million and banished from the United States

In addition to formal penalties for criminal wrongs, we would expect the market to punish wrongdoers through adverse publicity, increased costs of doing business, or both.

Recent scholarly evidence offers support for that supposition. A 1997 study compared 68 *Fortune* 300 firms convicted of wrongdoing with 194 unconvicted firms and found that those convicted of crimes experienced significantly lower return on assets and lower sales growth.[66] The study does not, however, prove that a causal relationship exists between the convictions and the subsequent declines in financial performance.

Corporate Compliance

I. Advice

The sentencing guidelines and recent court decisions have made it apparent that corporations must now develop effective internal compliance programs to avoid serious criminal and civil penalties. Experts suggest the following ingredients for a legally sound internal compliance plan:

1. Set out standards and procedures in a code of conduct.
2. Designate a high-level executive who is responsible for oversight.
3. Avoid delegating substantial discretionary managerial authority to those with a history of questionable conduct.
4. Carefully communicate the plan to employees and agents.
5. Monitor the program to assure compliance is being achieved.
6. Consistently enforce the program with appropriate discipline.
7. Periodically reassess and modify the program.

   Source: Bruce E. Yannett and Leigh R. Schachter, "Corporate Compliance Programs: No Longer a Luxury," *White-Collar Crime Reporter* 13, no. 9 (October 1999), p. 1.

II. In Practice

After admitting it had paid a $1 million bribe to an Egyptian lawmaker for help in selling aircraft in that country, Lockheed Martin agreed in 1995 to pay a nearly $25 million criminal fine. Since then Lockheed has developed computer programs for employees to engage in step-by-step training on ethics and legal compliance. The programs also track alleged wrongdoing inside the company; recording, for example, that 217 employees were fired for ethics violations between 1995 and 1999. Likewise all employees, including the CEO, must play the company's ethics game, The Ethics Challenge, at least once annually.

   Source: Michael J. McCarthy, "How One Firm Tracks Ethics Electronically," *The Wall Street Journal*, October 21, 1999, p. B1.

WHISTLE-BLOWING

Today, employees seem increasingly inclined to follow the dictates of conscience in speaking out—publicly, if necessary—against wrongdoing by their employers. Historically, complaints were taken to management and resolved there. "Going public" was considered an act of disloyalty. Americans continue to maintain a strong tradition against "squealing." Indeed, management has good reason to discourage irresponsible, precipitous whistle-

| Americans continue to maintain a strong tradition against "squealing" |

blowing that might disclose legitimate trade secrets, cause unnecessary conflict among employees, unfairly tarnish the company image, and so on.

However, increased respect for whistle-blowing has provoked expanded legislative and judicial protection for whistle-blowers. Congress and President Bush agreed on the Whistleblower Protection Act of 1989, which, in brief, makes it easier for federal employees to get their jobs back if they have been demoted or fired after revealing mismanagement. More than 20 other federal laws provide some form of whistle-blower protection and most apply to both public and private employees.

Many states now also have whistle-blower protection statutes for public-sector employees. Some of those also offer protection to private-sector employees discharged for complaining about a company action believed to violate a law or regulation. In some instances, those state whistle-blower laws apply only if the employee first gave management a chance to resolve the alleged difficulty.

Finally, some court decisions have afforded protection to whistle-blowers by denying employers the right to fire *at-will* employees (those not working under contract) because of their decision to blow the whistle. Traditionally, at-will employees could be fired for any reason (see Chapter 12), but courts have begun to restrict that right, particularly when the firing is deemed to violate public policy (as in the case of a legitimate whistle-blowing complaint). [For a law firm dedicated to representing whistle-blowers as well as the stories of some of those whistle-blowers, see **http://www.whistleblowers.com/**]

Retribution.   Despite legal protections, whistle-blowers often pay a high price for exercising their consciences. Henry Boisvert was a testing supervisor for FMC Corp., the manufacturer of the Bradley Fighting Vehicle, a troop carrier. Boisvert had written a report criticizing the ability of the Bradley to "swim" across rivers and lakes, as it was designed to do. Boisvert then refused to sign his name on a report that he did not believe to be accurate. Boisvert was fired in 1986.[67] The Army bought at least 9,000 Bradleys for as much as $1.5 million each, and the Army defends the vehicle.[68] Boisvert sued for wrongful termination and won a $200,000 judgment, but the real news came in 1998 when he won a $125 million jury verdict against FMC under the federal False Claims Act, which rewards those who report wrongdoing by federal contractors. The judge reduced the jury verdict leaving the total award at $87.14 million, of which Boisvert will receive 25–30 percent if the victory holds up on appeal.[69]

The Wall Street Journal columnist Hal Lancaster interviewed some whistle-blowers and all said they would "do it again," despite the tribulations. Some, such as Boisvert, claim whistle-blowing cost them their jobs. Others suffer only mild discomforts. Lancaster advises whistle-blowers to (1) document your claims, (2) talk to a lawyer, and (3) plan for the worst.[70]

Questions

1. Why is the role of "squealer" or whistle-blower so repugnant to many Americans?
2. How would you feel about a classmate who blew the whistle on you for cheating on an examination? Would you report cheating by a classmate if it came to your attention? Explain.

In 1997, a British priest, the Reverend John Papworth, reportedly suggested that shoplifting is not a sin—as long as the victim is a big supermarket. In a radio interview, Reverend Papworth then explained: "With these institutions, all you are confronted with are these boardroom barons . . . plotting how to take the maximum amount of money out of people's pockets for the minimum in return." Papworth said he did not mean to encourage shoplifting, although "if people wander in and wander out without paying for the stuff I think it is a perfectly comprehensible action."

Do you feel any sympathy for Papworth's position?

Source: Associated Press, "Thou Shalt Not Steal, Except . . . ," *Des Moines Register,* March 16, 1997, p. 8A.

INTERNET EXERCISES

1. Using the [**www.Gallup.com**] database (Gallup Poll), summarize the American public's views about the seriousness of violence in movies, video games, television, and recorded music, and explain whom the public identifies as responsible for restricting children from violent entertainment.
2. Using the [**http://www.whistleblowers.com/**] database, summarize the story of whistle-blower Robert Wityczak.

CHAPTER QUESTIONS

1. Can the realistic businessperson expect to be both ethical and successful? Explain.
2. Resolve this ethical dilemma posed by Carl Kaufmann of Du Pont:[71]

   Assume that federal health investigators are pursuing a report that one of your manufacturing plants has a higher-than-average incidence of cancer among its employees. The plant happens to keep excellent medical records on all its employees, stretching back for decades, which might help identify the source of the problem. The government demands the files. But if the company turns them over, it might be accused of violating the privacy of all those workers who had submitted to private medical exams. The company offers an abstract of the records, but the government insists on the complete files, with employee names. Then the company tries to obtain releases from all the workers, but some of them refuse. If you give the

   records to the feds, the company has broken its commitment of confidentiality. What would you do?

3. Among your classmates, would you expect to find a difference between males and females in the incidence of cheating? Explain.
4. *a.* In her book, *Lying,* Sissela Bok argues that lying by professionals is commonplace. For example, she takes the position that prescribing placebos for experimental purposes is a lie and immoral. Do you agree with her position? Explain.
   b. Is the use of an unmarked police car an immoral deception? Explain.
   c. One study estimates that Americans average 200 lies per day if one includes "white lies" and inaccurate excuses. On balance, do you believe Americans approve of lying? Explain.
5. "Tonight Show" host Jay Leno performed in commercials encouraging his audience to "eat your body weight in Doritos."[72] He says that he turned down

alcohol ads at twice the money. "I don't drink . . . And I don't like to sell it. You don't see dead teenagers on the highway with bags of Doritos scattered around them."[73]

    a.   Are you in agreement with the moral distinction that Leno draws between encouraging the consumption of alcohol and encouraging the consumption of Doritos? Explain.

    b.   Given the influence of television and of "stars," is all television advertising by celebrities inherently unethical? Explain.

6.   The following quote and questions are drawn from Leonard Lewin's "Ethical Aptitude Test."

    As with other goods and services, the medical care available to the rich is superior to that available to the poor. The difference is most conspicuous in the application of new and expensive lifesaving techniques.[74]

    a.   Is ability to pay an acceptable way to allocate such services? Explain.

    b.   If not, how should such services be apportioned?

    c.   Many lifesaving drugs can be tested effectively only on human beings. But often, subjects are exposed to such dangers that only those who feel they have nothing to lose willingly participate. Are there any circumstances in which it would be right to conduct such tests without ensuring that the persons tested clearly understood the risks they were taking? Explain.

    d.   How much in dollars is the average human life worth?

7.   Aaron Burr said, "All things are moral to great men." Regardless of your personal point of view, defend Burr's position.

8.   A pharmacist in Lexington, Kentucky, refused to stock over-the-counter weight reducers. His reasons were (1) the active ingredient is the same as that in nasal decongestants; (2) he feared their side effects, such as high blood pressure; and (3) he felt weight reduction should be achieved via self-discipline.[75] Assume the pharmacist manages the store for a group of owners who have given him complete authority about the products stocked. Was his decision ethical? Explain.

9.   When *Business and Society Review* surveyed the presidents of 500 large U.S. companies, 51 responded with their reactions to hypothetical moral dilemmas. One question was:

    Assume that you are president of a firm which provides a substantial portion of the market of one of your suppliers. You find out that this supplier discriminates illegally against minorities, although no legal action has been taken. Assume further that this supplier gives you the best price for the material you require, but that the field is competitive. Do you feel that it is proper to use your economic power over this supplier to make him stop discriminating?[76]

Respond to this question.

10.   The insider trading scandals of the 1980s seemed to involve an unexpectedly high percentage of younger professionals rather than Wall Street veterans. Do younger people operate with less stringent ethical guidelines than their older counterparts? Explain.

11.   We are in the midst of a period of unprecedented concern regarding the ethical quality of the nation. However, to many observers our problems are no more serious now than has always been the case. Robert Bartley, editor of *The Wall Street Journal,* comments:

    No, we do not live in an age of moral collapse. We more nearly live in an age of moral zealotry. We are applying to ourselves, or at least to our public and private leaders, standards of ethics never before expected of ordinary mortals.[77]

Are we asking too much of ourselves? Explain.

12.   In general, does the American value system favor "cheaters" who win in life's various competitions over virtuous individuals who "lose" with regularity? Explain.

13.   If you were an executive about to hire a new manager, which of the following qualities would you consider most important/least important: verbal skills, honesty/integrity, enthusiasm, appearance, sense of humor? Explain.

14.   In general, do smaller firms have higher ethical standards than larger firms? Explain.

15.   *a.*   Rank the following occupations as to your perception of their ethical quality: businesspersons, lawyers, doctors, teachers, farmers, engineers, carpenters, librarians, scientists, professional athletes, letter carriers, secretaries, journalists.

    b.   In general, do you find educated professionals to be more ethical than skilled but generally less-educated laborers? Explain.

    c.   Can you justify accepting an occupation that is not at or near the top of your ethical ranking?

Explain how your ranking affects your career choices.

16. Can businesspeople successfully guide their conduct by the Golden Rule?

17. Comment on the following quotes from Albert Z. Carr:

[M]ost bluffing in business might be regarded simply as game strategy—much like bluffing in poker, which does not reflect on the morality of the bluffer.

I quoted Henry Taylor, the British statesman who pointed out that "falsehood ceases to be falsehood when it is understood on all sides that the truth is not expected to be spoken"—an exact description of bluffing in poker, diplomacy, and business.

* * * * *

[T]he ethics of business are game ethics, different from the ethics of religion.

* * * * *

An executive's family life can easily be dislocated if he fails to make a sharp distinction between the ethical systems of the home and the office—or if his wife does not grasp that distinction.[78]

18. Anthropology professor Lionel Tiger has argued for the creation of "moral quality circles" to help improve business conduct. Tiger notes that:

[O]ur species evolved in small groups of perhaps 25 to 200 hunters and gatherers, groups in which there was no place to hide. Over 200,000 generations or so we evolved great face-to-face sensitivity and a lively skill for "whites-of-their-eyes" assessments of others.

* * * * *

These ancient but still-lively emotions can be tied into the nature of organizational life to help overcome the all-too-evident capacity of large groups to yield to "if you want to get along, go along." My hunch is that moral laxity emerges when members of such groups receive little or no dignified opportunity to define their moral views on practical matters without the risk of endangering their occupational health.[79]

Our moral systems sprang from that small-group context; but today, with complex industry replacing hunter-gatherers, those moral systems no longer correspond to contemporary needs. Tiger goes on to argue that we have a kind of "gene for morality" and that most of us have a rather clear sense of right and wrong. Given these conditions, he proposes the moral quality circle, in which workers would discuss the ethical implications of their duties and of the company's conduct in much the same manner that quality circles are now used to improve productivity and reliability. Do you see any value in Tiger's proposal? Explain.

19. Assume that you are working as manager of women's clothing in a large department store. You observe that the manager of equivalent rank to you in men's clothing is performing poorly in that she arrives late for work, she keeps her records ineptly, and she is rude to customers. However, her work has no direct impact on your department.

   a. Do you have any responsibility either to help her or to report her poor performance? Explain.

   b. If the store as a whole performs poorly, but you have performed well, do you bear any degree of personal responsibility for the store's failure when you confined your efforts exclusively to your own department even though you witnessed mismanagement in other departments? Explain.

20. We are often confronted with questions about the boundaries of our personal responsibilities.

   a. How much money, if any, must you give to satisfy your moral responsibility in the event of a famine in a foreign country? Explain.

   b. Would your responsibility be greater if the famine were in America? Explain.

NOTES

1. Steve Bailey and Steve Syre, "For Malden Mills, A Painful Fight Back," *Boston Globe,* August 11, 1998, p. C1.

2. Associated Press, "Jobs That Wouldn't Die," *New York Times,* January 31, 1999, sec. 3, p. 4.

3. Raymond Baumhart, *Ethics in Business* (New York: Holt, Rinehart & Winston, 1968), p. 10.

4. Timothy D. Schellhardt, "Are Layoffs Moral? One Firm's Answer: You Ask, We'll Sue," *The Wall Street Journal,* August 1, 1996, p. A1.

5. Ibid.

6. Merril McLoughlin, Jeffrey L. Sheler, and Gordon Witkin, "A Nation of Liars?" *U.S. News & World Report,* February 23, 1987, pp. 54–55. Copyright, 1987, *U.S. News & World Report.*

7. Albert R. Hunt and Bernard Wysocki, Jr., "Americans Decry Moral Decline," *The Wall Street Journal,* June 24, 1999, p. A9.

8. Albert R. Hunt, "Respondents Split on Blaming Morals or Economics for Ills," *The Wall Street Journal,* March 5, 1998, p. A14.

9. Hunt and Wysocki, "Americans Decry," p. A9.

10. "Immoral Americans?" *Des Moines Register,* February 23, 1999, p. 8A.

11. Staff Reporter, "Teens, Survey Finds, Are Seen Negatively By Most Americans," *The Wall Street Journal,* May 3, 1999, p. B9.

12. Ibid.

13. Patricia Edmonds, "America's Escalating Honesty Crisis," *USA Weekend,* October 16–18, 1998, p. 15.

14. Lee Berton, "Business Students Hope to Cheat and Prosper, New Study Shows," *The Wall Street Journal,* April 25, 1995, p. B1.

15. Ibid.

16. Ibid.

17. Gene Laczniak, Marvin Berkowitz, Russell Brooker, and James Hale, "The Ethics of Business: Improving or Deteriorating?" *Business Horizons* 38, no. 1 (January–February 1995), p. 39.

18. Shaun O'Malley, "Ethical Cultures—Corporate and Personal," *Ethics Journal,* Winter 1995, p. 9.

19. Anne R. Carey and Grant Jennings, "Ethics Lapses in the Workplace," *USA Today,* May 11, 1998, p. 1B.

20. Ibid.

21. For an elaboration of Kohlberg's stages, see, e.g., W. D. Boyce and L. C. Jensen, *Moral Reasoning* (Lincoln, NE: University of Nebraska Press, 1978), pp. 98–109.

22. Lawrence Kohlberg, "The Cognitive-Developmental Approach to Moral Education," *Phi Delta Kappan* 56 (June 1975), p. 670.

23. Carol Gilligan, "In a Different Voice: Women's Conceptions of Self and Morality," *Harvard Educational Review* 47, no. 4 (November 1977), p. 481. And see, e.g., C. Gilligan, *In a Different Voice* (Cambridge, MA: Harvard University Press, 1982); L. Blum, "Gilligan and Kohlberg: Implications for Moral Theory," *Ethics* 98, no. 3 (April 1988), p. 472; and O. Flanagan and K. Jackson, "Justice, Care and Gender: The Kohlberg-Gilligan Debate Revisited," *Ethics* 97, no. 3 (April 1987), p. 622.

24. For an overview of the justice versus care debate, see Grace Clement, *Care, Autonomy, and Justice* (Boulder, CO: Westview Press, 1996).

25. Edward S. Petry, Amanda E. Mujica, and Dianne M. Vickery, "Sources and Consequences of Workplace Pressure: Increasing the Risk of Unethical and Illegal Business Practices," *Business and Society Review* 99 (1998), pp. 25–30.

26. Ibid.

27. Ibid.

28. Joseph L. Badaracco, Jr., and Allen P. Webb, "Business Ethics: A View from the Trenches," *California Management Review* 37, no. 2 (Winter 1995), pp. 8, 12.

29. See, e.g., Barry Posner and Warren Schmidt, "Values and the American Manager: An Update," *California Management Review* 26, no. 3 (Spring 1984), p. 202.

30. Thomas O'Boyle, *At Any Cost: Jack Welch, General Electric, and the Pursuit of Profit.* (New York: Knopf, 1998).

31. Roger Lowenstein, "A Long Way From the Light Bulb," *New York Times,* November 15, 1998, sec. 7, p. 58.

32. Richard Sennett, *The Corrosion of Character: The Personal Consequences of Work in the New Capitalism* (New York: Norton, 1998).

33. This question is drawn from Paul Rosenberg, "Life's Getting Harder to 'Read,'" *Des Moines Register,* November 8, 1998, p. 1Q.

34. David Vogel, "Could an Ethics Course Have Kept Ivan from Going Bad?" *The Wall Street Journal,* April 27, 1987, p. 18.

35. Patrick E. Murphy, "Corporate Ethics Statements: Current Status and Future Prospects," *Journal of Business Ethics* 14, no. 9 (September 1995), p. 727.

36. Ibid.

37. Paul Lewis, "Corporate Conduct Code Is Proposed for Third World Nations," *New York Times,* April 29, 1999, p. A7.

38. Glenn R. Simpson, "Rev. Sullivan, Apartheid Foe, Helps U.S. Write Anticorruption Code for Business," *The Wall Street Journal,* February 17, 1999, p. B2.

39. Andrew Balls and Quentin Peel, "Call for Rules on Global Integration," *Financial Times,* July 12, 1999, p. 4.

40. "A Little Knowledge . . ." *Ethics Today* 2, no. 1 (Spring 1997), p. 6.

41. Ibid.

42. Ibid.

43. Badaracco and Webb, "A View from the Trenches," pp. 8, 14.

44. David Rosenzweig, "2 Litton Firms Plead Guilty on Foreign Deals," *Los Angeles Times,* July 1, 1999, p. A3.

45. Ibid.

46. 15 U.S.C. 78dd–1(b),–2(b) (1982), as amended by 1988 Trade Act 5003(a), (c).

47. Foreign Corrupt Practices Act Amendments of 1988, 15 U.S.C. 78dd–1 A (f) (2) (A) (B).

48. "Bribes Cost U.S. Firms $24B in Contracts," *Ottawa Citizen,* July 1, 1999, p. D4.

49. Richard Bray, "Stiff Penalties for Doing 'Business as Usual'" *Ottawa Citizen,* April 8, 1999, p. D14.

50. Martin Dyckman, "Taking a Reading on Corruption Around the World," *St. Petersburg Times,* October 11, 1998, p. 3D.

51. Peter Montagnon, "Public Turning Against the Use of Bribery," *Financial Times,* October 14, 1998, p. 7.

52. Dyckman, "Taking a Reading," p. 3D.

53. Carl Kaufmann, "A Five-Part Quiz on Corporate Ethics," *Washington Post,* July 1, 1979, pp. C–1, C–4.

54. Josh Martin, "An HR Guide to White-Collar Crime," *HR Focus* 75, no. 9 (September 1998), p. 1.

55. Ibid.

56. Ibid.

57. Michael Baylson and Melissa Maxman, "Honda Settles Class Action Aspect of Dealership RICO Litigation for Record 329 Million," *Civil RICO Report* 14, no. 13 (November 25, 1998).

58. Associated Press, "Judge OKs Big Settlement in Lawsuit Against Honda," *Buffalo News,* October 31, 1998, p. 7A.

59. Ibid.

60. Arthur Hayes, "Businesses Are Slow to Respond to Corporate Sentencing Rules," *The Wall Street Journal,* November 1, 1991, pp. B1, B7.

61. Joseph Savage, Jr., and Thomas Hughes, "Corporate Criminal Liability Goes Mainstream," *Business Crimes Bulletin* 6, no. 5 (June 1999), p. 1.

62. Ibid.

63. Ibid.

64. Dove Izraeli and Mark S. Schwartz, "What Can We Learn from the U.S. Federal Sentencing Guidelines for Organizational Ethics?" *Journal of Business Ethics* 17 (July 1998), p. 1045.

65. Savage and Hughes, "Corporate Criminal Liability," p. 1.

66. Melissa S. Baucus and David A. Baucus, "Paying the Piper: An Empirical Examination of Longer-Term Financial Consequences of Illegal Corporate Behavior," *Academy of Management Journal* 40, no. 1 (February 1997), p. 129.

67. Lee Gomes, "A Whistle-Blower Finds Jackpot at the End of His Quest," *The Wall Street Journal,* April 27, 1998, p. B1.

68. Ibid.

69. "Verdicts: The Big Numbers of 1998," *National Law Journal,* February 22, 1999, p. C10.

70. Hal Lancaster, "Workers Who Blow the Whistle on Bosses Often Pay a High Price," *The Wall Street Journal,* July 18, 1995, p. B1.

71. Kaufmann, "Five-Part Quiz," p. C–4.

72. "Short Takes," *The Des Moines Register,* February 5, 1990, p. 2T.

73. Ibid.

74. Leonard C. Lewin, "Ethical Aptitude Test," *Harper's,* October 1976, p. 21.

75. Reported on WKYT TV, Channel 27, "Evening News," Lexington, Kentucky, May 12, 1980.

76. "Business Executives and Moral Dilemmas," *Business and Society Review,* no. 13 (Spring 1975), p. 51.

77. Robert Bartley, "Business Ethics and the Ethics Business," *The Wall Street Journal,* May 18, 1987, p. 18.

78. Albert A. Carr, "Is Business Bluffing Ethical?" *Harvard Business Review* 46, no. 1 (January–February 1968), pp. 143–52.

79. Lionel Tiger, "Stone Age Provides Model for Instilling Business Ethics," *The Wall Street Journal,* January 11, 1988, p. 22.

Chapter 3

The Corporation and Public Policy: Expanding Responsibilities

INTRODUCTION

The bulk of this book is devoted to the law regulating business conduct, but before turning in that direction we need to remind the reader of the context—the environment—in which the law developed. Therefore, a major purpose of this chapter is to raise some critical issues regarding the business community's relationship to the larger society. Should we "free" business from government intervention to achieve greater productivity and profit? Should business play a larger role in politics, education, and other public-sector activities? Should business assume greater responsibilities in correcting societal ills? The reader is expected to use this chapter to make a tentative assessment of the very large question: What is the proper role of business in society? Only after acquiring some preliminary grasp of that issue can one logically and fruitfully turn to various "control devices" (such as law) as a means of enforcing that proper role.

The second major goal of this chapter is to alert the reader to some of the primary criticisms raised against the corporate community. The successful businessperson and the good citizen must understand and intelligently evaluate the objections of those who criticize the role of the corporation in contemporary life. Of course, government regulation is, in part, a response to those criticisms. (A detailed investigation of the forces generating government intervention is offered in Chapter 7.)

Finally, this chapter is designed to introduce what has come to be known as corporate public policy. Tomorrow's leaders must understand the interdependent relationship between business and the larger society. They must understand the public policy issues that have emerged from that relationship, and they must build the skills necessary to successfully manage that relationship. In the 1960s, the public began to demand more of business than simply producing products and services. We began to expect the business community to make a broad contribution to general societal welfare—to become a corporate citizen with all of the responsibilities that corporate wealth and power suggest. Those new demands led to the evolutionary development of public policy. We will examine that evolution in four parts: (1) criticisms of corporate America, (2) the emergence of the expectation of *corporate social responsibility,* (3) the move in recent years toward the process labeled *corporate public policy,* and (4) the examination of some specific business and society issues.

Part One—Corporate Power and Corporate Critics

Corporate critics have long argued that the public interest has not been well served by America's big corporations. We recognize that colossal size and the economies of scale that accompany it have been critical to American competitiveness in today's unforgiving global market. At the same time, that very size, the critics say, permits continuing abuse of the American public. Of course, we recognize that big companies are a fixture of the American landscape. However, a reminder of the specifics may be useful.

In 1998 General Motors, though it continued to struggle in many ways, was America's most prodigious enterprise as measured by sales revenue for the third year in a row (see Table 3.1). According to *Fortune* magazine, GM's 1998 sales topped $161 billion, down nearly 10 percent from 1997. GM employed 594,000 workers, down from

> Wal-Mart now is America's leading corporate employer with 910,000 workers

over 700,000 in 1995. Wal-Mart now is America's leading corporate employer with 910,000 workers.[1] GM, in 1998, also topped *Fortune's* Global 500, based again on revenues.[2] GM's tenure at the top appears to have ended, however, following governmental approval of the Exxon/Mobil merger. The combined company generates annual sales of about $204 billion.[3] Furthermore, if we look at companies ranked by market value, GM is already well down *Business Week's* Global 1,000 list, which is topped by Microsoft at $407.22 billion.[4]

Measured by market value in 1999, 34 of the top 50 global firms and 62 of the top 100 are American.[5] On the other hand, only 2 of the world's 10 largest banks, ranked by assets, are American (Citigroup, number 4, and BankAmerica, number 6).[6] Of most interest, perhaps, is the relative decline of the Japanese banks, 2 of which are in the top 10[7] as compared to the early and mid-1990s when 8 of the top 10 banks were Japanese. Three of the

TABLE 3.1   The World's Largest Corporations

Corporation	Country	Sales Revenue (in billions)
1. General Motors	U.S.	$161.3
2. DaimlerChrysler	Germany	$154.6
3. Ford Motor	U.S.	$144.4
4. Wal-Mart Stores	U.S.	$139.2
5. Mitsui	Japan	$109.4
6. Itochu	Japan	$108.7
7. Mitsubishi	Japan	$107.2
8. Exxon	U.S.	$100.7
9. General Electric	U.S.	$100.5
10. Toyota Motor	Japan	$ 99.7

Source: Jeremy Kahn, "The Global 500," *Fortune,* August 2, 1999, p. 144.

largest Japanese banks, in 1999, announced merger plans that will create the world's largest bank, as measured by assets.

The extraordinary wealth of America's corporate institutions is such that they tower over most of the countries of the world in economic might. If we compare corporate sales with gross national products, General Motors annually ranks around the 25th largest *anything* in the world. Indeed, GM's annual sales are larger than the gross domestic products of, for example, Thailand or Norway.[8] Approximately 50 of the 100 largest economies in the world are corporations, and the 300 largest global corporations hold one-quarter of the entire globe's productive assets.[9] Corporate wealth and power are similarly concentrated in the United States where the revenues of the top 500 corporations equal about 60 percent of America's total economic output.[10] (Do you see any risk in corporations holding greater economic muscle than many of the nations of the world? Certainly the danger in these numbers is transparent to the critics—too much power in too few hands.) [For further detail on global corporate power, see **http://www.uaw.org/solidarity/9610/11_2.html**]

> General Motors annually ranks around the 25th largest *anything* in the world

The critics' concerns seem to be shared by many Americans. In a 1999 Gallup Poll, only 30 percent of Americans expressed "a great deal" or "quite a lot" of confidence in big business. Highly rated institutions were the military (68 percent), organized religion (58 percent), the police (57 percent), the presidency (49 percent), and the Supreme Court (49 percent). Big business did rank ahead of a few institutions, including organized labor (28 percent) and health maintenance organizations (HMOs—17 percent).[11]

THE CORPORATE STATE

Historically, the foundation of the critics' argument has been that giant companies hold monopoly power, permitting them to secure "excess profits" at the expense of the consumer. Considerable evidence supported that view,[12] but it has been rendered somewhat passé in this era of fierce international economic competition with the giants of Japan, Germany, and the balance of the world. Further, many of America's old-line titans (GM, IBM, Sears, and so on) are struggling to retain their strength, suggesting that bigness is not a guarantor of success in the contemporary market.

A litany of societal ills—pollution, discrimination, white-collar crime, misleading advertising—has long been laid at the corporate doorstep. Now the subject of intense governmental, public, and internal corporate scrutiny, those problems, while yet very real, seem no longer attributable to mere corporate size and/or malevolence. The bulk of this book is devoted to the governmental/corporate/public attack on those serious social ills. However, the critics say, those specific ills are only symptomatic of a more encompassing malady. Basically, the concern is that America has committed its *soul* to business values in a way that is progressively undermining our national well-being. We will briefly examine that argument in order to have it in mind as we proceed through our more detailed study of corporate social responsibility and government regulation of business.

> America has committed its *soul* to business values

America's Soul?

Generally, the critics contend the power of the business community has become so encompassing that virtually all dimensions of American life have absorbed elements of the business ethic. Values commonly associated with businesspersons (competition, profit seeking, reliance on technology, faith in growth) have overwhelmed traditional humanist values (cooperation, individual dignity, human rights, meaningful service to society). In the name of efficiency and productivity, the warmth, decency, and value of life have been debased. We engage in meaningless work in an artificial culture. Objects dominate our existence. We operate as replaceable cogs in a vast, bureaucratic machine. Our natural environment is shredded in the pursuit of progress. Indeed, we lose ourselves, the critics argue. Charles Reich, former Yale University law professor, addressed the loss of self in his influential book of the Vietnam War era, *The Greening of America:*

> Objects dominate our existence

> Of all of the forms of impoverishment that can be seen or felt in America, loss of self, or death in life, is surely the most devastating . . . Beginning with school, if not before, an individual is systematically stripped of his imagination, his creativity, his heritage, his dreams, and his personal uniqueness, in order to style him into a productive unit for a mass, technological society. Instinct, feeling, and spontaneity are repressed by overwhelming forces. As the individual is drawn into the meritocracy, his working life is split from his home life, and both suffer from a lack of wholeness. Eventually, people virtually become their professions, roles, or occupations, and are henceforth strangers to themselves.[13]

Some interesting empirical evidence supports Reich's view that we have become hollow men and women dominated by the demands of big institutions. The Harris Alienation Index shows a generally steady rise in Americans' feelings of powerlessness from 1966 when the index stood at 29 to the 1995 poll in which the index stood at 67, its all-time high.[14] Alienation, as defined in the survey, includes feelings of economic inequity (the rich get richer, the poor get poorer), feelings of disdain about the people in power, and feelings of powerlessness (being left out and not counting for much).

Dario Del Degan's letter to a Toronto, Canada, newspaper attributes part of the blame for the 1999 student deaths at Columbine High School in Colorado to us, in that our society gives more value to money than to fairness and equality:

> The massacre at Columbine High is, in part, the responsibility of all of us who have replaced intrinsic human values with dollar signs. The capitalist mentality that governs North America endorses the exploitation of people and resources. Omnipresent in our psyches is our position within the widening gap of the haves and the have-nots. The erosion of education . . . further illustrates the corporate elite's desire to replace thinkers with a collective of clock-punchers. The alienation felt by Harris and Klebold is felt by many marginalized individuals throughout North America.

Source: Cheryl Hnatiuk, "Letter of the Day," *Toronto Star,* April 30, 1999.

Questions

1. Management theorist John Nirenberg:

> In a world where democracy is breaking out in some of the unlikeliest places and in a world now committed to the idea of liberty, it is sadly ironic that Americans have so thoroughly surrendered themselves to corporate tyranny.
>
> How have we come to accept so thoroughly the sacrifice of over half of our waking consciousness to the god of earning a living without the slightest thought to the propriety of the relationships in the workplace and the fact that we must surrender ourselves to an impersonal bureaucracy that defies our influence? How have we so completely surrendered ourselves to the rule of the dollar and the powers of an unelected, often unaccountable boss?[15]

   a. Do you agree with Nirenberg? Explain.
   b. Answer Nirenberg's questions.

Politics.   We can elaborate on the case of the corporate critics by directing our attention to some areas of special concern. We will begin with politics, where critics charge that superior resources enable the business community to unfairly slant the electoral and law-making processes in favor of corporate interests.

In recent years, the corporate community has taken a more direct and vigorous role in the political process. As a result, corporate critics are increasingly concerned that the financial weight of big business will prove so influential that our pluralist, democratic approach to governance may be significantly distorted. Today, money is central to the task of acquiring elective office. And following election, dollars to finance lobbying on Capitol Hill can be critical in shaping congressional opinion.

Corporate funds cannot lawfully be expended for federal campaign contributions. However, corporations (as well as labor unions, special interest groups, and others) can lawfully establish *political action committees* (PACs) to solicit and disburse voluntary campaign contributions. That is, corporations can solicit contributions from employees, shareholders, and others. That money is then put in a fund, carefully segregated from general corporate accounts, and is disbursed by the PAC in support of a federal election campaign.

Big Money.   Obviously, for many years the checkbook has dominated politics at the national level, but the 1998 midterm congressional election set a new spending record at over $1 billion.[16] *USA Today* noted our first billion-dollar congressional class:

> the 1998 midterm congressional election set a new spending record at over $1 billion

> The new Congress . . . has got to be some of the best politicians money can buy. Special interests wanting to bend government policy in their favor certainly paid enough to get them elected.[17]

The article that follows summarizes the role of "soft money" (unregulated) contributions, largely by big corporations, in the 1998 federal election.

MONEY WINS FRIENDS, INFLUENCES ELECTIONS

Stephanie Cook and Pierre Marcoux
Courier/Medill News Service

Companies helped the national political parties amass $180.1 million in soft money contributions in the 1998 election, money that industry executives say supports party agendas, get-out-the-vote compaigns or specific pieces of legislation.

But the understanding on Capitol Hill is that many of those companies were vying for political clout—even though soft money can't be used to elect federal candidates.

"(Soft money donations are) intended to win friends and influence people," said Larry Makinson, executive director at the Center for Responsive Politics in Washington. "Pressure (to donate) can come from members of Congress."

Because soft-money contributions aren't regulated by federal election laws, companies are not limited in their donations, which can be appealing, he said. Soft money, however, is supposed to be used only to support party-building activities, such as advertising or administrative costs, or encouraging people to vote.

Companies make the donations often because they are asked to make them, and they tend to donate more heavily to Republican party committees, Makinson said. Executives probably feel that if they don't contribute, it might be held against them, he added.

"Almost every corporation who gives big money has a list of (policy) items" they are interested in, he said, such as financial or telecommunications policies. "It's difficult (for politicians) to ignore the biggest donors."

Companies usually give to both parties, but tend to donate more to the one they favor. By contributing to both, they are covering their bases and trying to avoid becoming a "target" for the other party.

MCI WorldCom Corp., for example, gave $630,815 in the 1997–98 election cycle, making it one of the top 10 organizational donors, according to a Medill News Service analysis of Federal Election Committee reports filed through Oct. 15.

It gave $370,250 to Republicans and $260,565 to Democrats from January 1997 to October 1998. The company gave to both parties in order to gain support for its views on telecommunications, said spokesperson Claire Hassett.

"Ultimately, these are funds that support candidates," Hassett said. "And ultimately, there are candidates in both parties that support our goals."

MCI wants to open local telecommunication markets to competitors and let consumers choose their provider. And because these policies are clearly defined and well known by both parties, Hassett is confident that all donations to committees will go for activities or candidates supporting these views.

"We trust that it does" go to the appropriate candidates, she said.

Tobacco companies like Philip Morris Inc. lead in making soft money donations, giving more to Republicans, Makinson said.

Phillip Morris gave $2.2 million in the last election cycle, making it the largest corporate contributor. It gave $1.8 million to Republican committees and $417,823 to Democrats.

Phillip Morris gave to both parties because it tends to support all congressional candidates who have similar views on issues important to the company, said spokesperson Richmond Temple.

"Phillip Morris is an active participant in the political process, and we express our views on issues that affect our three main products: food, tobacco, and beer," Temple said. "We do so in the hope of getting fair government."

* * * * *

Eli Lilly & Co. of Indianapolis, a major pharmaceutical manufacturer whose products include Prozac, did not donate with particular legislation in mind, said spokesman Edward West. The company gave $273,350 to Republicans and $113,706 to Democrats in the last election cycle.

West said the company made soft-money contributions to both parties because it supported two-party debate, voter registration, and get-out-the vote campaigns.

"We think the political process is healthy when there's debate," West said.

In 1996 it donated $300,000 to Republicans and $190,000 went to Democrats, he said.

West said the company tends to give more to Republican committees because they support "positions and policies that foster a free-market system . . . but this is not limited to the Republican side."

Teachers' unions gave a total of $1 million in the 1997–1998 election cycle. The American Federation of Teachers gave the most, $713,400 that went entirely to Democratic committees, and ranked in the top 10 of organization contributors. While it tends to give mostly to Democrats, it has contributed to both parties, explained AFT spokesman Darrell Capwell. The union supports candidates who favor public education and oppose voucher initiatives, which would allow parents to use goverment money to send their children to private schools, Capwell said.

Source: Waterloo–Cedar Falls Courier, December 6, 1998, p. A1. Reprinted by permission.

Reform?   National politicians have for years agreed that campaign reform is necessary, and for years they have been unwilling to act. Arizona Senator John McCain, 2000 presidential candidate and outspoken advocate of campaign finance reform, raised some eyebrows in 1999 by accepting $10,000 in contributions from AT&T executives shortly after introducing legislation to remove Federal Communications Commission authority to approve telecommunications mergers. At the time, AT&T was awaiting FCC review of its purchase of the cable company, MediaOne. Senator McCain indicated that he wanted to eliminate dual Justice Department and FCC authority over such mergers.[18] Adding uncertainty to the reform effort was the Supreme Court's 1999 decision to review a First Amendment challenge to the current limits on campaign contributions. [For an overview of concerns about campaign financing and reform concepts, see **http://lwv.org/~lwvus/cfrcon.html**]

Lobbying.   Those who criticize corporate influence on the legislative process are not concerned with PACs and soft money alone. Sophisticated and expensive lobbying is a staple of the business community's efforts to implement its legislative agenda. Lobbying is defended as an efficient method of better acquainting busy politicians with the subtleties of the diverse issues they must address. Of course, lobbying is not confined to the "big spenders" of the business community—witness the many influential consumer and environmental interest groups. Washington lobbying has become an enormous industry, spending nearly $702 million to influence Congress and the federal agencies in just the last half of 1998, an astounding total of nearly $4 million dollars a day.[19] In the past few years Congress has passed rules requiring registration of lobbyists, greater disclosure of their activities, and limiting or banishing gifts from lobbyists to politicians, but the impact of those rules seems negligible.

Microsoft surprised most observers in 1999 by lobbying Congress to slash Justice Department funding even as that Department continued its pursuit of antitrust charges against Microsoft. At the same time, Microsoft urged charities and others indebted to Microsoft to join that lobbying campaign. The *Washington Post* commented:

> The effort by Microsoft to get the proposed budget of the Justice Department's antitrust division slashed fits a comical caricature of the thuggish company that Microsoft's enemies believe the software giant to be. It would be comical, that is, except that the effort was real. Microsoft's lobbyists sought to knock $9 million out of the division's budget request even as a federal judge ponders the merits of the department's antitrust case against the company. The effort appears to have largely failed; the conference committee has settled on a figure closer to the administration's request than to the lower figure approved by the House of Representatives that Microsoft was pushing . . .
>
> The company is, to be sure, entitled to defend itself in the litigation as vigorously as it sees fit. Indeed, the issues in the Microsoft case are far more complicated than Microsoft's foes like to acknowledge. But for the defendant in an antitrust action to make its conflict with the government into an appropriations vendetta demeans the very real issues the government has raised in the case and the court system that has been asked to adjudicate those issues. A law enforcement agency should not be threatened with punishment for seeking vigorously to enforce its vision of the law.

Source: Editorial, "Microsoft's Bad Lobbying," *Washington Post,* October 24, 1999, p. B06.

Buy Votes?   In the end, does all of the money buy votes? In most cases, probably not, but it certainly buys access and returned phone calls, and the evidence suggests that, in most cases, it does buy elections. The Center for Responsive Politics, a nonpartisan research organization, reports that in 94 percent of the 1998 midterm congressional elections, the candidate who spent the most money won the race.[20] Furthermore, while we cannot say that politicians sell their votes, we do have considerable evidence that money influences voting patterns. For example, an analysis by the Campaign for Tobacco-Free Kids found that members of Congress who took money from tobacco companies were three times more likely to vote against a bill to fight cigarette sales to minors.[21] Of course, contributions are most likely to go to those who are predisposed to favor the tobacco industry position. A recent academic study found that "PAC contributions are negatively related to new firm entry in manufacturing industries."[22] Basically the research argues that existing firms use contributions to create political barriers to entry (laws, rules, and enforcement practices) by new competitors. Though the research does not establish a causal relationship between PAC contributions and difficulty of entry, "the results suggest that corporate PACs may play a role in inhibiting new entry to an industry."[23] [For the Center for Responsive Politics and its extensive database on money in politics, see **http://www.opensecrets.org/home/index.asp**]

> in 94 percent of the 1998 midterm congressional elections, the candidate who spent the most money won the race

Questions

1. *USA Today,* in 1997, called for campaign finance reforms, including the possibility of public funding:

   > If all this cash would produce the best government money can buy, the money would be well spent. But those promoting their own narrow agendas, not the public interest, are doing most of the buying.
   >
   > Two states—Maine and Vermont—have voted to try something better. Private money will be limited, discouraged, or barred. Instead, the public, as a whole, provides a central campaign fund. Other states are considering similar reform.
   >
   > To get good government, we may have to pick up the tab. Better us than big spenders trying to buy the kind of government most beneficial to them.[24]

   a. Do you agree that public funding may be necessary to assure a fair election process? Explain.
   b. Now assume you are arguing for campaign finance reform from a free market point of view. What changes would you advocate?

2. Then-Defense Secretary William Perry repeatedly told Congress that the Pentagon did not want more B-2 Stealth bombers than the 20 planes already delivered or on order. Nonetheless, in 1995, Congress agreed to spend nearly one-half billion dollars more on the bombers. Explain why Congress would approve weapons not wanted by the Pentagon.

3. Richard Goodwin, aide to former President John F. Kennedy, speaks out on PACs:

   > Morally the system is bribery. It is not criminal only because those who make the laws are themselves accomplices. Government is for sale. But the bids are sealed, and the prices are very high.
   >
   > There is an easy way out: Eliminate PACs. We should place a rigorous ceiling on all congressional campaigns, allocate public funds to finance campaigns, and require television stations—the most costly component of modern political campaigns—to give a specified amount of air time to candidates.[25]

   a. Should we forbid PACs? Explain.
   b. Would such action be constitutionally permissible? Explain.

Too Much Business?

We can see, then, that the business community's influence in America's political life is enormous, but the critics' concerns only begin there. The corporation is arguably the central institution in contemporary America. In every dimension of American life, business values are increasingly pervasive. To those who criticize the corporation, that near-blanket adoption of the business ethic signals a dangerous distortion of the nation's priorities. In an editorial, the *Des Moines Register* commented that commercials have become so interwoven with our total existence that they cannot effectively be "separated out":

The insinuation of commercials into American life is everywhere. On Saturday mornings, the cartoon character the kids are watching may be for sale at the toy store. On prime-time shows and in movies, the brand-name product that is used as a stage prop probably isn't there by accident.

No one seems to mind. In an ad-saturated society, people willingly pay a premium price for a shirt that is adorned with an advertising logo. By choice, people wear commercial messages.

It's the triumph of hucksterism in America.[26]

Judge for yourself as we take a quick glimpse at several areas of concern.

Schools.   In the face of nationwide alarm about elementary and secondary education, the corporate community has played an increasingly aggressive role in supporting and reforming our schools. And considerable good may come from that corporate pressure and assistance as evidenced by a Rand study that concluded that a day-to-day business commitment was the primary reason for faster reform progress in Texas and North Carolina than in other states.[27] Critics, however, are concerned that cash-short schools become vulnerable to corporate marketing strategies and the disproportionate influence of business values. Consider the Colorado Springs, Colorado, schools, which were the first to accept corporate advertising:

> At Palmer High, Burger King and Sprite advertise on the sides of school buses. Norwest, Cub Foods, and Mountain Dew have posters in school hallways. Next fall, there will be a new scoreboard on the football field with a Pepsi logo on it. For most students, the ads seem to have become just part of the environment. "It doesn't offend me, but it's sort of stupid," says Lauren Kinnee, a junior. "They're ugly."
>
> What does Palmer get out of all this? In the 1996–97 school year, the school district took in $145,000, of which it paid 30% to the marketing firm that helped sell the ads. Each of the 53 schools in the district got a percentage of what was left, amounting to a few thousand dollars for Palmer.[28]

Since 1989, Channel One has supplied educational programming and television sets to schools. The 12-minute programs include two minutes of advertising for Reebok, Mountain Dew, and others.[29] Corporations often give educational equipment and learning materials to schools, some of which is clearly valuable and some of which is "barely disguised corporate propaganda, such as environmental videos from oil companies or nutritional information on chocolate from candy makers."[30] [For the Channel One news, see **http://www.channelone.com/news/**]

Anxious to keep the valuable assistance, some school officials appear to have become promoters of the corporate sponsors:

> Last September in Colorado Springs, Colo., a school district official sent a memo to principals, exhorting them to crank up sales of Coke products to meet a quota or risk losing revenue. Signing the letter "The Coke Dude," he urged schools to consider allowing students to drink Coca-Cola's juices and teas—if not soft drinks—in classrooms.[31]

The San Francisco school board, on the other hand, declared their children "not for sale," and, in 1999, approved a policy limiting ads and paid endorsements in the schools and

The San Francisco school board, declared their children "not for sale"

forbidding districtwide, exclusive contracts for soft drinks and snack foods.[32] The stakes for that kind of commercial-light environment are high. For example, one Ohio school district of 2,600 students is expected to earn $700,000 in benefits over a 10-year period after choosing Pepsi over Coke for an exclusive contract.[33]

From kindergarten through graduate school, the "business mentality" is ever-present. Students and their parents call for a "quick fix" of skills (such as accounting, management, and marketing) as a replacement for occupationally ambiguous disciplines such as history, literature, and philosophy. The bargain has been struck. Education is consumed much like any other product, and the student hopes to proceed into the Corporate State, but did that student buy a good life or an empty existence? Charles Reich offers his opinion:

> The process by which man is deprived of his self begins with his institutionalized training in public school for a place in the machinery of the State. The object of the training is not merely to teach him how to perform some specific function; it is to make him become that function, to see and judge himself and others in terms of functions, and to abandon any aspect of self, thinking, questioning, feeling, loving, that has no utility for either production or consumption in the Corporate State. The training for the role of consumer is just as important as the training for a job, and at least equally significant for loss of self.[34]

The famed surf city, Huntington Beach, California, has named Coke its "official city beverage" giving the bottler exclusive rights to place its logo and vending machines on all city property. Pepsi can still be sold on private property in the city. Coke will pay $300,000 annually as well as $300,000 to repair one of the city's parks each year of the contract. The result is that the city will be able to paint its buildings for the first time in two years. Huntington Beach hopes to reach similar arrangements with a credit card company, an airline, and others.

Source: Martin Kasindorf, "For One City, Coke Is It, Officially," *USA Today,* February 25, 1999, p. 3A.

Culture.   Does America possess a cultural life? For decades, the concern was that so-called "high" culture—classical music, opera, ballet, and the like—would give way to rock and roll, television, and video games. Now that battle is over; Americans (and the world) have clearly voted for "South Park" and the like. Interestingly, corporations are among the last big advocates of traditional culture. While the federal government's National Endowment for the Arts spent less than $100 million in 1997, corporate support for the arts was estimated at well over $1 billion.[35] Government and business have become partners of a sort in aiding the arts, especially in that the business contributions are tax deductible. But the other side of the corporate cultural coin is illustrated by the Walt Disney Company. Journalist Mitchell Landsberg explains,

Americans (and the world) have clearly voted for "South Park"

These days, it seems we're all living in Disney's America.

   With its purchase of ABC, the company founded by Walter Elias Disney in 1923 deepened its claim on the American psyche, from Main Street to Tomorrowland. It would be hard to name another company that has ever exercised such influence on American culture. It would be hard to find another company so widely admired—even loved—by Americans.[36]

To critics such as Yale University Professor Harold Bloom, the expanding power of Disney threatens the remaining shreds of America's cultural life:

"At the end of this road lies cultural homogenization of the most ghastly kind," Bloom told *The Philadelphia Inquirer* after the Disney-ABC deal was announced. "It's a disaster."[37]

Bloom and others believe Disney's version of culture is now so powerful that other messages simply cannot be heard.

   Diana Green, editor of a guide to children's toys and media, summarizes her concerns about Disney's cultural influence as a double-edged sword:

On one side, she says, are the cheerful Disney characters "whistling while they work, 'doing the right thing' and things will work out." That's OK, she says, because "no child can get along without hope." On the other side, however, Green says, "Disney has embraced the big 'M'—materialism. Better for Disney to move more to help children develop as full human beings and not just consume, consume, consume."[38]

Questions

1. *a.* What does Harold Bloom mean about Disney producing "cultural homogenization of the most ghastly kind"?
    b. Does Disney possess too much influence over America's cultural life? Explain.
    c. Would we better off if Disney's values were yet more dominant? Explain.
    d. Would America be a better nation if we all cared more about Beethoven than Tarzan or Pocahantas? Explain.

In 1998 the Reverend Robert Schuller, builder of the Crystal Cathedral church complex in Garden Grove, California, and popularizer of drive-in churches, announced that he intends to add a food court to his church along with an exhibition hall honoring the great "Christian capitalists." Benjamin J. Hubbard, chair of comparative religion at California State University, Fullerton, criticized Schuller's blending of faith and convenience: "It smacks of the mall mentality gone crazy." "You shop for religion and then swing by the food court."

   Source: *Los Angeles Times,* "Schuller Adding Food Court to Complex," *Waterloo–Cedar Falls Courier,* September 8, 1998, p. A4.

Sports.   Major League Baseball, in 1999, announced consideration of plans to sell one-inch square advertising spaces on players' sleeves.[39] Baltimore Orioles star Albert Belle said he was not opposed to the plan, but "I guess we'd be like walking billboards, huh? . . .

Isn't everybody making enough (money already)?"[40] Of course, advertising on uniforms is hardly an innovation. Nike seems to have mastered the strategy with swooshes showing up wherever a television camera might point. Penn State University, for example, agreed to the Nike swoosh for its football uniforms even though its longtime coach, Joe Paterno, had never permitted the players' names or the school sports logo to appear on the uniforms. Sports commentator Roger Thurow criticized Penn State's decision: ". . . For $2.6 million over three years, the Penn State athletic department sold not only its soles but a bit of its soul, too."[41] But as Florida State University athletic director, Dave Hart, reminded us: "Everytime I say this publicly, I can see people cringe: Athletics is a business. But it is."[42]

One sports fan was moved to write a letter to the editor:

> We would be a healthier society if professional sports did not exist. The love of money, or greed, takes all the fun out of sports, demeans the integrity of the games, corrupts the athletes and belittles the fans . . . Pure amateurism puts sports in proper perspective . . . The love of money is slowly, subtly destroying sports and America.[43]

The Salt Lake City Olympic bribery scandal of 1999 and thereafter brings into clearer focus the risks of converting sports to a business enterprise. International Olympic Committee members, who vote on the location of the Games, received at least $1.2 million in gifts, cash, travel, and other incentives from organizers of the 2002 Salt Lake City, Utah, Winter Games.[44] At this writing, six IOC members have resigned, the IOC has promised reforms, and various investigations are continuing. Of course, a great deal of money is required to produce the Olympic spectacles, but the lure of that money and the now overwhelming influence of commercial values seems to be staining the Olympic tradition. The following article explains how Nike, in effect, created a 1998 Winter Olympic team for its advertising purposes.

KENYAN SKIERS NIKE PRODUCTS?

Associated Press

One of the feel-good stories of the Nagano Olympics began two years ago with a brainstorm at Nike's marketing department: What if we transform a couple of Kenyan runners into cross-country skiers?

Now Nike's backing of the two athletes may have backfired, with some accusing the company of going too far to put its swoosh on a good story.

"These are not athletes clearing hurdles to reach their Olympic dream," wrote Detroit News columnist Bob Wojnowski. "These are marketing pawns financed by well-heeled publicity-seekers."

Details of Nike's involvement began to emerge even before one of the great photo moments of the game—Kenyan cross-country skier Philip Boit crossing the finish line dead last in the 10-kilometer race Thursday and being embraced by the gold medal winner from Norway.

Nike, which had its signature swoosh on Boit's hat, collar and sweater, hatched the idea two years ago to send Kenyan distance runners Boit and Henry Bitok to Finland to learn cross-country skiing.

They would be like the celebrated Jamaican bobsled team at the Calgary Games in 1988.

Nike paid for their move and spent a reported $200,000 for their lodging and a Finnish coach. The athletes even got custom ski uniforms, courtesy of the company.

Nike spokeswoman Martha Benson said Nike has financially backed Kenyan runners since 1991 and the move into cross-country skiing came out of a series of meetings between Nike and Kenyan running officials.

Steve Miller, a senior Nike executive in Japan, conceded that less idealistic goals also figured into the company's support.

"People forget, we are a business, and part of our objective as a business is to get attention," he said.

Source: *Des Moines Register,* February 14, 1998, p. 4S. Courtesy of the Associated Press.

Question

1. In the future, will "amateur" athletes compete for corporations, for example, Team Nike, rather than universities or nations?

The New York City Museum of Modern Art, in 1999, previewed the "architecture of the next century" with images of 26 homes of the future. Architecture writer Peter Whoriskey, reviewed the exhibit:

> What's scary is what has happened to the idea of home. In the exhibit's designs, the forces of business have invaded the domestic refuge. Home and office have become one, a union enabled by the electronic "freedom" to work at home. In some instances, it's hard to tell, for example, whether a home is in fact a home, or just a corporate office where people happen to sleep over.

a. Do you think the house of the future will be as much a place of work as a home?

b. If so, should we be concerned about that development? Explain. See Peter Whoriskey, "Brave New House," *Miami Herald,* August 1, 1999, p. 5M.

Globalization

All of the critics' concerns about the domination of American life by big corporations and business values are now being applied equally to the entire globe. With the fall of the Soviet Union and the triumph of capitalism, the world has come to understand that free markets are simply more efficient than government rules. As a result, national boundaries are receding in importance, technology is shrinking the world, transportation costs are declining, multinational companies are treating the world as one big market, less-developed countries are trying to improve living standards by connecting to that market, financial assets flow freely and almost instantaneously from one side of the globe to the other, and the world becomes one highly greased, interconnected mass market. A lot of good news emerges from globalization: less-developed countries have the opportunity to raise their standard of living, the benefits of competition and efficiency (better products at lower prices) reach more people, and as one Canadian journalist expresses it, the world is now at our door:

> I can buy Paris- or New York-designed garments at Philippines or Indonesian prices at what amounts to my local corner store. Where strong coffee was unobtainable a dozen years ago, I now have four espresso-equipped cafes within three blocks. In my small town, I can have delivered to my door *Le Monde,* the *Asian Wall Street Journal* and *Izvestia.* After coming home in my Swedish car, I can watch on my Japanese TV set the BBC news at 1800 hours, news from Paris at 1900 and news from Brussels at 2200 hours.[45]

Fears.   America is enjoying unprecedented prosperity and, from our view, globalization simply looks like the welcome spread of capitalist values to the entire world. Not surprisingly, however, many people are alarmed. They see a world rapidly coming under the thumb of America, and more particularly, America's giant, multinational corporations. Capital, technology, goods, and services can be moved rapidly throughout the world aided by the new free trade arrangements such as the North American Free Trade Agreement, the World Trade Organization, the European Union, and so on. These free trade mechanisms, in the critics' view, have essentially nullified the regulatory power of national governments and left corporations free to do largely as they wish. They see a world ruled by corporate interests with the following results:

> They see a world rapidly coming under the thumb of America

- The rich get richer and the poor fall further behind.
- Whole eco-systems, such as the Amazon Basin, are despoiled for profit-seeking purposes.
- Rural cultures are displaced and an urban migration follows.
- Financial instability, like the Asian financial crisis of the late 1990s, is inevitable.
- Labor is exploited to satisfy market demands.
- Consumerism swells and traditional values are submerged.

[For the World Trade Association, see **http://www.wto.org**]

An Assessment.   Are the critics correct that America's multinational corporations and our thorough commitment to business values are a threat to the well-being of the world? Certainly markets are imperfect. Many economists concede that financial instability, in the short term at least, is likely to accompany globalization.[46] And we don't yet have any meaningful global mechanism for dealing with the monopoly concerns that American antitrust laws address. (See Chapters 10 and 11.) Furthermore, the developed nations, led by the United States, clearly are complicit in some degree of labor exploitation, and we clearly do consume more than our "fair" share of the world's dwindling supply of fish, forests, clean air, and other resources. In general then, while markets are clearly more efficient than rules, we still must doubt whether largely unrestrained markets produce increased fairness. A 1999 United Nations report finds globalization, for the present at least, compounding the gap between rich and poor.[47] The report points to 60 nations that are actually worse off today than in 1980, and it worries whether the gap will continue to grow as technology's force increases.[48] The report notes that the United States has more computers than the balance of the world combined and that 80 percent of the world's websites are in English.[49] Of course, some of that rich-poor gap must be attributed to corruption and mismanagement, but moral sensitivity and our own interests require that we reflect a bit on the world's sharp division between haves and have nots. As journalist Lawrence Connor put it:

> [U]nless we find a way to spread the wealth and educate the backward countries on how to deal with globalization, the world will be faced with revolts, rampant crime and terrorism, especially from the economically deprived who link up with those feeling culturally deprived—groups like Osama bin Laden's followers in Afghanistan and the fanatics who bombed the World Trade Center in 1993.[50]

Cultural Imperialism? While embracing Nike, Disney, and The Gap, much of the world holds decidedly ambiguous feelings about America. Part of that uncertainty springs from a deep discomfort about America as the "world's policeman" accompanied by a realization that only America is presently equipped to occupy that role. That military unease serves as an uncomfortable backdrop to the, in some ways, larger conflict over culture and values. Not only does globalization threaten to overwhelm the world's resources, but also many nations now worry that their own national identities, their sense of cultural uniqueness, will be consumed by America's business-driven values. The article that follows describes those worries from the author's Canadian perspective.

COMMODITY VERSUS CULTURE: BATTLE LINES DRAWN

Hilary Mackenzie

Sneakers, blue jeans, burgers, Hollywood blockbusters—cultural icons of our times? Or, cultural imperialism? It is the fault line that is characteristic of the globalization of world culture.

To many, globalization is synonymous with Nike, Levi's, and MTV. It crowns the United States the king of pop culture. It lauds Walt Disney the new Goethe of our times.

It pits the United States against Canada. Or for that matter Hollywood Inc. & Madison Ave. vs. The World.

"There is a fundamental difference of view in Canada and the U.S. as to what culture is," said Anne McCaskill, a trade consultant who has fought on the frontlines in the culture war, "and how important culture is to any individual country."

Americans tend to see culture as the fine arts—art galleries, theatre, ballet, opera. Everything else—television, films, music, magazines—is pop culture. It's business. It's entertainment.

American officials argue that these are "commodities" and can, indeed should, be traded like other commodities in a free and open marketplace where market forces determine who wins, who loses.

They Just Don't Get It

What the United States has always misunderstood, or conveniently denied, McCaskill said, is that countries like Canada, that don't have the economic clout, let alone the political heft of the United States, have to keep vigil over their own channels of communication, preserve their own cultural identity and own their cultural production.

"It's not part of the U.S. experience," McCaskill said, "They don't have to worry about their identity being overwhelmed by anybody else in the world. Nobody else is big enough to overwhelm them."

"They just don't get it," she said, laughing.

The fact they don't get it is not entirely divorced from the fact that the single biggest export industry of the United States is the entertainment industry, based in California and New York.

Not surprisingly the home states of Hollywood Inc., and Madison Ave., are political heavyweights. They drive the export engine that fuels the hot-as-a-piston U.S. economy in the future.

Politically incorrect as it may seem, Canada is irrelevant to this global assault. By all accounts—from mind-numbing stats like newsstand space devoted to *Cosmo* and *Hustler, Time* and *Newsweek* or hours logged to Lethal Weapon and the Corrupter—the United States has already trumped the Canadian market.

*   *   *   *   *

Americans are looking far beyond their "best friend" and "biggest trading partner," to the north, as deputy U.S. Trade Representative Richard Fisher reassuredly called Canada.

They have their sights set on China, Europe, and Japan. Markets where they don't yet sell 50 percent of their magazines or flog their three Kleenex-box movies like *Saving Private Ryan* and *Schindler's List*.

"They don't want other countries to get wacky Canadian notions about the importance of being able to retain an independent identity," McCaskill said.

In fact, argues author Salman Rushdie, the globalizing power of U.S. culture is opposed "by an improbable alliance that includes everyone from cultural relativist liberals to hard-line fundamentalists, with all manner of pluralists and individualists, to say nothing of flag-waving nationalists and splintering sectarians, in between."

Cultural imperialism has evoked such flights of oratory that globalization is the Darwinian equivalent of the survival of the fittest at the expense of cultural diversity. It has inflamed a veritable attack on "the world's precious localness: the Indianness of India, the Frenchness of France," Rushdie said.

*   *   *   *   *

At its core the debate is about cultural policy, how countries individually and as an international community view the importance of cultural diversity and the means to nurture an independent identity in our brave new world of globalization. It is about how to ensure that globalization doesn't lead to a loss of cultural diversity, a loss of independent identity.

Even President Bill Clinton acknowledged that globalization "ain't worth it if we lose the human face of the international community."

"The U.S. should do more than heed these warnings; it should recognize that strong cultures are in America's self-interest," wrote Jeffrey Garten, dean of the Yale School of Management, a former investment banker and undersecretary of commerce for international trade in the first Clinton administration.

"If societies feel under assault, insecurities will be magnified, leading to policy paralysis, strident nationalism and anti-Americanism," Garten added.

Arguing that the spread of U.S. culture cannot, nor should be, stopped because of satellites and the Internet, Garten proposed that corporate America and the administration's trade hawks encourage cultural diversity around the globe.

The Time Warners and PepsiCo Incs of the United States "could fund native entrepreneurs wishing to create local cultural industries." In a pithy come-on to the administration, Garten declared that Washington's push for open markets is viewed abroad as a Trojan horse for the likes of Walt Disney Co. and Cable News Network, which will dominate foreign lifestyles and values.

"The Clinton administration could reverse current trade policy and permit temporary quotas and subsidies abroad to preserve certain local cultural industries, such as film and TV," he argued.

Others are less charitable. "What you define as culture is beyond believability," argued David DeRosa, adjunct professor of finance at the Yale School of Management, in an incredulous tone. "Advertising in magazines . . .?"

France, he noted, got snooty about Euro Disney. But "no one car-jacked a Parisian and dragged them to Euro Disney." Ditto CNN. "No one in the world is sitting in

Stanley Kubrick's *Clockwork Orange* strapped into a chair with his eyelids forced open wathcing CNN."

"There's an element of paranoia about this," DeRosa suggested. "No one is forcing anyone to read *Time* magazine," he said, his voice rising. "I don't think it's culture. I think it's protectionism vs. the free market. We Americans can't make you read anything or watch anything."

"If the French want to go to Euro Disney and Canadians want to read *Time,* it's the people's culture. I can't imagine the U.S. declaring a Ministry of Culture" he added speaking of Canadian heritage. "It's paranoid."

"The idea of national cultural identity smacks of paranoia. I wonder how many take it seriously?"

"If you tell me you don't like Mickey Mouse and you don't like violence—what do you want?" DeRosa asked in an exasperated tone as a reporter tried to fathom cultural differences. "Don't go to Disney Land or watch a Schwarzenegger movie. If you don't like those magazines (*Time.* etc.) don't buy 'em."

Source: *Montreal Gazette,* March 16, 1999, p. B1. Courtesy of *Southam News.*

Questions

1. What is cultural imperialism?
2. Are you most in agreement with Jeffrey Garten's view of cultural imperialism or that of David DeRosa? Explain.
3. Why should nations worry about the loss of their traditional cultures?
4. Does cultural diversity matter to the welfare of the world?
5. In what way is globalization a threat to worldwide consumers' rights?

[See the Corporate Watch website for an extensive database of concerns about globalization: **http://www.corpwatch.org**]

Questions—Part One

1. Journalist Eric Liu complained, in early 1999, about the conversion of public spaces (parks, streets, schools, stadiums) to advertising "vessels":

   Rollerblade now hawks its wares in Central Park under the banner "The Official Skate of New York City Parks." Buses in Boston and other cities don't just carry ad placards anymore; some of them have been turned into rolling billboards . . . [W]e haven't yet draped Mount Rushmore with a Nike "swoosh." But things are heading in that general direction.

   You might say at this point, "What's the big deal? America is commercialized—get over it!" And I admit my views may sound a bit old-fashioned. But this isn't a matter of priggishness or nostalgia. Public spaces matter . . .[51]

   Why should we be concerned about the "commercialization" of public spaces?

2. According to *The Wall Street Journal,* "[S]hopping can be all things to all people. It can alleviate loneliness and dispel boredom; it can be a sport and can be imbued with the thrill of the hunt; it can provide escape, fulfill fantasies, relieve depression."[52]

   a. Is shopping an American addiction that requires treatment in the manner of alcoholism, for example? Explain.

   b. Does shopping fill a void of some sort in our lives? If so, how was that void created? Or was it always there?

   c. If you reduced shopping in your life to that which is required to meet only the necessities, how would you use the time that would then be available to you?

   d. Are shopping malls replacing the family in American life? Explain.

   e. Even if shopping has assumed excessive importance in our lives, is the business community in any way to blame for that condition? Explain.

3. Tom Bratz, in a *Newsweek* commentary, spoofed America's willingness to make a buck in any way possible. He argued that we need to be more aggressive in our efforts to balance the federal budget. His suggestion: advertising.

   > The first step would be to name the official products of various government agencies. The Ford Probe is an obvious choice as the official automobile of the Department of Justice . . . Next would come the subtle placement of various products at televised events—When the president addresses the nation from the Oval Office, what could possibly look more natural than a Big Mac and some french fries sitting on his desk? . . . Then we'd start to have corporate sponsors for all government functions. We'd no longer have a State of the Union Address; it would be the Miller Lite State of the Union Address . . .[53]

   Comment.

4. Bob Ortega, reporter for *The Wall Street Journal:*

   > To denizens of the counterculture, Wal-Mart stands for everything they dislike about American society—mindless consumerism, paved landscapes and homogenization of community identity.
   >
   > "We've lost a sense of taste, of refinement—we're destroying our culture and replacing it with . . . Wal-Mart," says Allan B. Wolf [an Ohio high school teacher].[54]

   Is Wal-Mart a threat to America's long-term well-being? Explain.

5. a. Has your education been designed primarily to prepare you for a utilitarian role as a producer and/or consumer in the Corporate State? Explain.

   b. Is business America's dominant art form? Explain.

6. *USA Today:*

   > The national parks are cash-strapped and desperate. Since 1983, visits have risen 30 percent, while the National Park Service's operating budget, adjusted for inflation, has shrunk 20 percent. The repair backlog for roads, trails, campsites and so forth exceeds $4 billion . . . Interior Secretary Bruce Babbitt has been exploring alternative sources, including a plan before Congress to sell official park system sponsorships for as much as $10 million a pop. In exchange, sponsors would be licensed to use a special logo in their advertising and would receive "limited" in-park recognition by the Park Service.[55]

   a. What public policy risks, if any, would accompany a government decision to allow corporate sponsorships of our national parks?

   b. How would you vote on such a proposal? Explain.

7. David Gil, professor of social policy at Brandeis University, "called for the dismantling of corporations that have destroyed 'self-directed work' and for the return of resources to the people for their own direction 'in human-sized communities where people can come together and jointly determine their economic way of life.'"[56]

    a. Does our economic way of life reflect the will of the people? Explain.

    b. Is the corporate form destructive of the quality of the work experience? Explain.

    c. Is Gil's proposal workable? Explain.

8. In *Time* magazine, commentator Walter Shapiro wonders "Why We've Failed to Ruin Thanksgiving":

   > Americans have grown inured to crass commercialism, with corporate sponsorship profaning everything from bowl games to the Bill of Rights. But somehow Thanksgiving has resisted the blandishments of an age of avarice. How the greeting-card sharpies and the flower-power florists must lament a national holiday in which they are doomed to play a minor role.[57]

    a. On balance, is the "commercialization" of most holidays a good or bad development? Explain.

    b. Who is to blame for the conversion of holidays to commercial feasts? Explain.

9. In your judgment, does either of the following quotes accurately express the current American attitude toward the accumulation of money? Explain.

   Myron Magnet of *Fortune:*

   > Money, money, money is the incantation of today. Bewitched by an epidemic of money enchantment, Americans in the 80s wriggle in a St. Vitus' dance of materialism unseen since the Gilded Age or the Roaring 20s. Under the blazing sun of money, all other values shine palely. And the M&A decade acclaims but one breed of hero: He's the honcho with the condo and the limo and the Miró and lots of dough.[58]

   Michael Novak of the American Enterprise Institute:

   > The vast majority of Americans choose what they want to do, and they don't choose merely to seek wealth. Most of the people I know seek the work that satisfies them most completely. Of course a sliver of people want money, money, money, but I think they're only a small number.[59]

10. *a.* Do Americans *trust* the business community? Explain.

    b. Does it matter? Explain.

11. In 1980, Ted Peters, an associate professor of systematic theology at the Pacific Lutheran Seminary and the Graduate Theological Union, asked:

    > How will the advancing postindustrial culture influence the course of religion? It is my forecast that religion will become increasingly treated as a consumer item.
    >
    > Because our economy produces so much wealth, we are free to consume and consume beyond the point of satisfaction. There is a limit to what we can consume in the way of material goods—new homes, new cars, new electronic gadgets, new brands of beer, new restaurants, and so on. So we go beyond material wants to consume new personal

experiences—such as broader travel, exotic vacations, continuing education, exciting conventions, psychotherapy, and sky diving.

What will come next and is already on the horizon is the consumption of spiritual experiences—personal growth cults, drug-induced ecstasy, world-traveling gurus, training in mystical meditation to make you feel better, etc. Once aware of this trend, religious entrepreneurs and mainline denominations alike will take to pandering their wares, advertising how much spiritual realities "can do to you." It will be subtle, and it will be cloaked in the noble language of personal growth, but nevertheless the pressure will be on between now and the year 2000 to treat religious experience as a commodity for consumption.[60]

   a.   Now at the turn of the century, is Peters's forecast coming true? Explain.
   b.   Is marketing necessary to the survival and growth of religion? Explain.
   c.   Is marketing a threat to the legitimacy and value of religion? Explain.
12. In 1992, 1,600 faculty, staff, and students at Clifton Middle School in Houston, Texas, each received a $70 pair of K-Swiss sneakers from the manufacturer and Foot Locker. The shoes were first prize in a stay-in-school video contest.[61] The use of corporate sponsors and merchandise prizes in education contests has exploded in recent years. Critics say the students are being taught to be more materialistic and to value education, not for its intrinsic satisfactions, but for its commercial rewards. However, the adviser for the Houston students says that such prizes can attract students who otherwise would not participate, and some of them then discover the satisfactions of education. In your view, do these prizes corrupt or enhance education? Explain.
13. In 1993, a scholarly book, *The Concept of Honest Poverty,* attacking Japan's money-centered society, became a huge best-seller (600,000 copies sold in eight months). The author, Koki Nakano, explained his thesis:

   However rich Japan becomes, it will never get the respect of the world. To earn respect, we need dignity, chivalry and the philosophy of honest poverty. Our image is that of a country that's good at making things but has no culture. Foreigners say Japanese lack character and dignity, and think of us just as people with money.[62]

   a.   What does he mean by "honest poverty"?
   b.   Do we honor honest poverty in America? Explain.
   c.   Do you admire the Japanese? Explain.
   d.   Aren't rich people highly respected in America? Explain.
   e.   Why is American culture so widely admired?
   f.   In the end, is culture more important to the fate of a nation than wealth? Explain.
14. Do you think allegiance to the company will become more important than allegiance to the state? Is that a desirable direction? Raise the arguments on both sides of the latter question.
15. As expressed in *Business Week,* "Increasingly, the corporation will take over the role of the mother, supplying day-care facilities where children can be tended around the clock."[63] How do you feel about the corporation as mother? Explain.

Part Two—Corporate Social Responsibility

INTRODUCTION

As illustrated in Chapter 2 and in Part 1 of this chapter, the business community has been the subject of intense criticism. Journalist Daniel Seligman put it this way:

> A standard view of the American corporation . . . is that it is an efficient deliverer of goods and services, yet also a wellspring of social injustice. Driven by a narrow calculus of profits, it is oblivious to the common good. And so, the litany goes, it degrades the environment, promotes unsafe products, skimps on workplace safety and (current indictment No. 1) lays off workers who have given it years of service.[64]

That broadly shared perception of business misdeeds or indifference, in conjunction with the growing influence of business values throughout American life, has led in recent decades to the development of the notion of *corporate social responsibility*. The issue is as follows: Must business decision making include consideration not merely of the welfare of the firm but of society as a whole? For most contemporary readers, the answer is self-evident—of course business bears a social responsibility. Business has enjoyed a central and favored role in American life. As such, it must assume a measure of the burden for the welfare of the total society. Problems like those mentioned above by Seligman require the full strength of the nation, including the vast resources of business. Indeed, businesspeople themselves now generally endorse business responsibility to help solve society's problems.

Americans are cynical about the business community's concern for their workers. In a 1997 Gallup Poll, Americans were asked: "In general, do you think most businesses in the United States today are only concerned with profits and not concerned with the economic interests of their workers, or do you think most businesses do take into account the economic interests of their workers while still trying to make a reasonable profit? Sixty-five percent said "profits only" with 32 percent citing "workers' interests."

Source: George Gallup, Jr., *The Gallup Poll* (Wilmington, Delaware: Scholarly Resources, Inc., 1997), p. 137.

A New Ideology

The ascendance of the social responsibility concept represents one of the most striking ideological shifts in American history. From the colonial period until roughly 1950, business was expected to concentrate on one goal—the production and distribution of the best products at the lowest possible prices. Of course, social responsibility arguments were raised, but business was largely exempt from any affirmative duty for the resolution of social problems. Rendered practical perhaps by increasing prosperity, the public, led by business scholars and critics, began in the 1950s to consider a larger role for corporate America. Now as we enter the 21st century, the role of business in society has been radically altered. Profit seeking remains central and essential, but for most businesspersons, the rather unwieldy ingredient of social responsibility must be added to the equation.

WHAT IS SOCIAL RESPONSIBILITY?

The sweeping notion of corporate social responsibility is not readily reduced to a brief definition, but Davis and Blomstrom some years ago captured the core ingredients: "The idea of social responsibility is that decision makers are obligated to take actions which protect and improve the welfare of society as a whole along with their own interests."[65] More broadly, the social role of business can be thought of as an ideological continuum, corresponding roughly to the familiar American political spectrum of conservative/Republican views on the right, moderates in the middle, and liberal/Democrats on the left. Figure 3.1 depicts that continuum and is best understood by reading "backwards" from right to left. On the right side of the spectrum lies the free market view where *profit maximization* is considered the best measure of social responsibility. Across the middle lies a viewpoint that is commonly thought of as the *long-term, company interest* where profits are the first consideration, but where satisfied workers, customers, and community members are also of importance, within some reasonable limits, in order to secure the firm's long-term survival. On the left side of the spectrum lies what we are labeling the *welfare maximization* view where social goals are paramount and running a business solely for profit would be considered misguided or even unethical. Here businesses would act, so far as possible, in the interests of all affected parties (shareholders, employees, customers, and so on) not because company interests require it, but because it is the morally correct thing to do. At the same time, the welfare maximizing company would not allow itself to fail financially in order to meet social goals.[66] Of course, few firms would fit tidily and persistently in any one of these three categories. Rather, most exhibit all three behaviors at different times and under differing circumstances, but most also develop some general behavioral pattern. Let's examine the continuum in a bit more detail. [For the Corporate Social Responsibility home page, see **http://www.elca.org/dcs/Corp.html**]

FIGURE 3.1   The Social Responsibility Continuum

Welfare Maximization (Good Deeds + Profit)	*Long-Term* *Company Interest* (Profit + Good Deeds)	*Profit Maximization* (Profit)

Profit Maximization.   Here the dominant concern lies in maximizing shareholders' interests. Those shareholders, after all, are the owners of the firm. They are taking the financial risk. Hence, from a profit maximization point of view, the only responsible and moral course of behavior is to reap the highest return possible, within the law. Nobel–prize-winning economist Milton Friedman is the most prominent advocate of the profit maximization view:

> the only responsible and moral course of behavior is to reap the highest return possible

> [In a free economy] there is one and only one social responsibility of business—to use its resources and engage in activities designed to increase its profits, so long as it stays within the rules of the game, which is to say, engages in open and free competition, without deception or fraud.[67]

Friedman, employing free market reasoning, believes the firm that maximizes its profits is necessarily maximizing its contribution to society. He asks how managers can know what the public interest is. He also argues that any dilution of the profit-maximizing mode—such as charitable contributions—is a misuse of the stockholders' resources. The individual stockholder, he contends, should dispose of assets according to her or his own wishes.

Herbert Stein, former chair of the President's Council of Economic Advisors, shares Friedman's doubts about the idea of social responsibility, but Stein's concerns are of a more pragmatic nature. He argues that business is simply ill suited for solving social problems:

> Efficiency in maximizing the nation's product . . . is not the only objective of life. But it is the one that private corporations are best qualified to serve. I don't want to be a purist about this. I don't object to corporations contributing to the United Givers Fund . . . But to rely on corporations' responsibility to solve major social problems—other than the problem of how to put our people and other resources to work most efficiently—would be a wasteful diversion from their most important function. Our other objectives can be better served in other ways, by individuals and other institutions.[68]

Long-Term, Company Interest.   Across the broad middle ground of our social responsibility continuum lie those firms, doubtless the great majority, who believe that a strong bottom line, in many cases, requires considerations beyond the immediate, short-run, profit-maximizing interests of the firm. In a sense, these managers are merely taking a longer-term view of profit maximization. They recognize the imperative of a strong return on the shareholder's investment, but they also believe that achieving that return may require heightened sensitivity to the welfare of employees, consumers, and the community. Furthermore, they often embrace the view that socially responsible behavior, within reasonable bounds, is simply the "right thing" to do.

Welfare Maximization.   Here we find a point of view, probably practiced by a rather slender band of firms, whose explicit mission is to subordinate profit seeking to the needs of the total community of stakeholders. While profit is necessary to maintain the enterprise, these managers' first consideration is the well-being of employees, customers, community, and the like. For these managers, profits do not accurately and adequately measure a firm's contribution to society. Thus, they are measuring their performance primarily by additional standards such as employee satisfaction, working conditions, product quality, environmental citizenship, philanthropy, and so on.

FIGURE 3.2 The Social Responsibility Pyramid

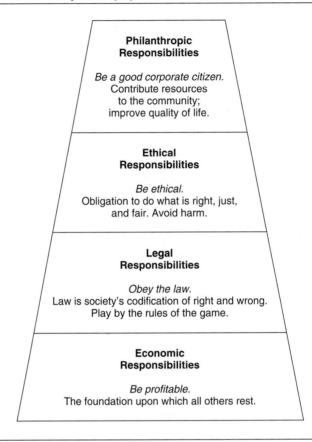

**Philanthropic
Responsibilities**

Be a good corporate citizen.
Contribute resources
to the community;
improve quality of life.

**Ethical
Responsibilities**

Be ethical.
Obligation to do what is right, just,
and fair. Avoid harm.

**Legal
Responsibilities**

Obey the law.
Law is society's codification of right and wrong.
Play by the rules of the game.

**Economic
Responsibilities**

Be profitable.
The foundation upon which all others rest.

Source: Archie B. Carroll, "The Pyramid of Corporate Social Responsibility: Toward the Moral Management of Organiza-tional Stakeholders." Reprinted from *Business Horizons* 34, no. 4 (July–August 1991), pp. 39, 42. Copyright 1991 by the Foundation for the School of Business at Indiana University: Used with permission.

Social Responsibility Pyramid.   Another way of visualizing socially responsible business practice, developed by Archie Carroll, is depicted in Figure 3.2. Social responsibility, or "corporate citizenship" as Professor Carroll sometimes labels it, necessarily begins with making a profit in a lawful fashion, but simultaneously the socially responsible firm moves beyond the minimum demands of economics and law to find the ethical course of action—the behavior best suited to the demands of virtue and moral principle. In striving for profitable, lawful, ethical conduct, that company may also choose to engage in philanthropic (charitable) efforts (money, time, facilities, programs) to build a better community. [For a "comprehensive, worldwide information resource on corporate social responsibility," see **http://www.bsr.org/resourcecenter/index.html**]

Social Responsibility in Practice

Obviously, we have no shortage of social problems to which corporate attention can usefully be directed, and much of the corporate community is directly investing its resources in addressing those problems. Consider *Business Ethics* magazine's 1998 ethics award winners:

- **SmithKline Beecham.** The global drug company was recognized for its "$1 billion commitment to eradicating lymphatic filariasis," a tropical disease that is the world's second-largest cause of disability.[69]
- **Wainwright Bank & Trust Co.** The relatively small, young Boston bank actively practices a "model of inclusion [where] employees, customers and communities have an equal place at the table alongside stockholders." "The bank's progressive agenda includes a commitment to affordable housing, community development, women's rights, and the gay and lesbian community."[70]
- **S.C. Johnson.** For 60 years, the household products company (which produces Johnson Wax) has engaged in sustainable development in Brazil to meet the company's needs while preserving resources for the future.[71]

The article that follows describes one of the firms most prominent in the social responsibility movement, Ben & Jerry's ice cream company. Over the years, Ben & Jerry's company policy has, for example, provided an entrepreneurial fund to encourage new businesses and paid workers' regular salaries when they do community volunteer work. Interestingly, business conditions in recent years have forced Ben & Jerry's to move from being what we have characterized as a welfare-maximizing organization to something much nearer the long-term, company interest middle ground. [At this writing in early 2000, the British-Dutch conglomerate, Unilever, has agreed to acquire Ben & Jerry's.]

BEN & JERRY'S TASTE IRONY

Mary Lamey

There aren't many business big shots known to millions simply by their first names. Even Bill, the world's most powerful computer geek, has to tag on a "Gates" when he gets on the phone.

Ben Cohen and Jerry Greenfield have no such problem. The laid-back pair behind the Ben & Jerry's ice cream empire are on a first-name basis with anyone who has ever had a lick of Chunky Monkey or Chubby Hubby.

*   *   *   *   *

The story of how the boyhood friends parlayed $12,000 and a fledgling Burlington, Vermont ice cream shop into a $200-million-a-year business has become part of legend. Equally well-known is their commitment to donating 7.5 per cent of the company's pretax profits to social causes. Ben and Jerry support small business, sustainable development, and the family farm.

"Their message makes perfect sense. If you give to your community, it will come back to you," said Morrie

Baker, owner of three B&J franchises in Montreal. Baker yesterday handed out cheques totaling $5,400 to the Children's Wish Foundation and the YM-YMHA.

Like Vanilla and Chocolate

Cohen and Greenfield continue to preach the gospel of profitability and social responsibility, two concepts they say go together as well as vanilla and chocolate. Their talk last night was expected to draw between 500 and 600 listeners.

"It isn't a hard message to sell, especially if you bring ice cream along," Greenfield said with a smile. (When it comes to the division of labour, Greenfield does most of the business talking. Asked what his end of the bargain is, the slightly more hippie-looking Cohen said, "I'm the colour.")

The company's growth has not been painless, Greenfield acknowledged. A well-publicized essay contest to find a new chief executive officer resulted in the hiring and, 18 months later, the departure of Robert Holland, Jr.

A union-drive at the company's St. Albans, Vt., plant, which management opposed vigorously, and the hiring of Perry Odak, formerly of U.S. Repeating Arms, a gun manufacturer, as Ben & Jerry's chief executive have garnered headlines. Odak has held the post for two years and recently signed a contract extension, Greenfield said.

These things are at odds with the ice cream guys' do-good image. Greenfield said he understood that the press enjoyed the "irony" of such controversies.

In the end, Ben & Jerry's is a pro-union company, he said. The fight was over whether 21 maintenance workers could vote to unionize, or whether the vote should include all the plant's employees. The Labour Department ruled in favour of the maintenance workers who are currently bargaining their first contract.

As for Odak, he has a long history of activism and support for progressive causes, Greenfield said.

The new chief executive has helped the company fix production and distribution problems and claw its way back to profitability. Ben & Jerry's recently reported a 20 percent jump in net sales, to $50 million U.S., with net profit of $1.2 million. More than 85 percent of its sales are made through grocery stores. The company has about 5 percent of retail ice cream sales in the U.S.

There were a few years in the middle of the decade when consumers turned away from high-fat treats like premium ice cream., but the trend has reversed itself. Today, the company can chart the decline in sales of its no-fat sorbets and the leveling off in demand for frozen yogurt. Ice cream sales are skyrocketing, Greenfield said.

"Let's face it, that other stuff just doesn't taste as good."

Both continue to consume their own product. Greenfield describes himself as a "recreational" ice cream eater, who favours Phish Food (chewy chocolate with caramel and marshmallow swirls and fish-shaped bits of fudge). Cohen is "more of a critical eater," who regularly chows on Cherry Garcia (vanilla with chocolate chunks and cherries).

Source: *Montreal Gazette*, June 10, 1999, p. C1. Courtesy of the *Montreal Gazette*. [For the Ben & Jerry's home page, see **http://www.benjerry.com/**]

Question

1. In your view, is the primary purpose of management to maximize shareholder wealth? Explain.

But Is Corporate Responsibility Good Business?

The evidence is mixed, but generally supportive of the idea that the market rewards good conduct and punishes bad conduct. A 1999 review of the sound, scholarly work to date found 33 studies showing a positive relationship between socially responsible behavior and favorable financial performance, while 5 studies found a negative relationship and 14 found no effect or were inconclusive. The authors conclude that "the vast majority of studies support the idea that, at the very least, good social performance does not lead to poor financial performance," but the key question of whether good social performance produces good financial performance is "not yet resolved."[72] More specifically, another review of 27 studies found very convincing statistical evidence that the stock market punishes firms caught in illegal or socially irresponsible behavior by reducing shareholder wealth, at least in the short term.[73] On the more positive side, a 1998 study found that businesses that avow a commitment to ethical practice in their annual report to shareholders turn out to have higher financial performances than those that do not indicate that commitment.[74]

Question

1. What do you think about the wisdom of social responsibility? Build a list of the arguments for and against social responsibility for business.

Part Three—Corporate Public Policy

MANAGING SOCIAL RESPONSIBILITY

As the principle of social responsibility has become increasingly acceptable to the corporate community, the nature of the debate has shifted to identifying the new duties and assessing whether the corporation is meeting those duties. Many corporations, particularly those of great size, are confronting the practical notion of how best to manage the firm's response to social issues. Corporations are increasingly considering what scholars have labeled the *stakeholder model* of social responsibility. Under that model, the corporation identifies all of those groups (stockholders, customers, employees, communities, governments, unions, schools, and the like) that have a relationship with the firm and that may benefit from the relationship or be burdened by it. These are groups with a "stake" in the activities of the corporation. Of course, we have wide divisions of opinion about how expansive the list of stakeholders should be and, once identified, we have wide divisions of opinion about the extent of the corporation's duties toward those stakeholders. Certainly, scholarly advocates of the stakeholder approach see it as a redefinition of the nature of the corporation. Simply maximizing the interests of the primary stakeholders, the shareholders, would not, from the advocates' point of view, satisfy the corporation's social duties. [For an overview of stakeholder research, see **http://www.mgmt.utoronto.ca/~stake/**]

PUBLIC POLICY

Hence, in recent years, we have witnessed the evolution of *corporate public policy,* wherein business takes a more activist stance in addressing contemporary social issues. Public policy refers to the process by which the total society identifies and manages its problems and goals. The corporate public policy approach calls for the business community to recognize that it should play a part in establishing and accomplishing the larger public policy agenda. Hence, business, rather than taking a responsive role, must be an active player in social themes. Business now must be closely attuned not merely to market signals but to government signals and to the larger society's preferences. All of this, of course, requires the contemporary manager to learn about a much broader range of issues than was the case historically. Profit now rests not merely in providing the best product or service at the lowest price, but in understanding and dealing with the very complex interplay between the corporation, government, and society. Thus, today's socially responsible firm is likely to be ever more involved in identifying and attempting to manage social issues. To do so, many corporations have now built the public policy process into their management structure and systems.

> Business now must be closely attuned not merely to market signals but to government signals

Results.   Measuring the success of social responsibility performance is very difficult. Recently, however, a public-interest group, the Council on Economic Priorities, has developed the first global standard, SA8000 (social accountability 8000), that measures companies' social and environmental records.[75] SGS-ICS, an independent Swiss certification agency will, accredit companies that meet the SA8000 standards in the areas of child labor, forced labor, health and safety, freedom of association, discrimination, disciplinary practices, working hours, compensation, and management systems.[76]

"Today's consumers care about more than price and quality," said Jeff Horner, SGS-ICS corporate director. "They want to know the items they buy are not made by children, by companies paying slave wages or by organizations with little regard for their employees' health and safety. We will be auditing interested companies to identify who does and who does not deserve the SA8000 mark."[77]

Part Four—Business and Society Issues

Managing the volatile business and society interface is demanding. The materials that follow raise three contemporary social responsibility issues—layoffs as a management strategy, domestic-partner insurance, and student protests against sweatshops—that are presently causing headaches for corporate leaders who must produce a profit but who also must conform to society's expectations for responsible conduct. Note that issues like these often generate calls for new laws and/or regulations. Thus, these three themes raise the question of where a company's social responsibility lies, but they also call into play the larger theme of this book: Can the business community successfully regulate itself, or must government intervene?

SOCIAL RESPONSIBILITY?

"Chainsaw" Al and Layoffs

"Downsizing" may have been the dominant corporate strategy of the 90s. Nearly 30 percent of United States workers lost their jobs from 1990 to 1995 due to cuts or shutdowns.[78] In Chapter 2, we looked at Malden Mills, whose owner, Aaron Feuerstein, tried to retain all his employees despite a devastating fire. Here we introduce "Chainsaw" Al Dunlap, whose approach to management contrasts sharply with Feuerstein's. As you read this account, think about whether Dunlap is a "socially responsible" manager.

> "Downsizing" may have been the dominant corporate strategy of the 90s

HE ARGUES LEAN REQUIRES "MEAN"

Noam M. M. Neusner

The latest "My Way" opus from corporate America comes from Al Dunlap, a West Point alumnus with a New Jersey accent who lives in Boca Raton [Florida] with his wife, Judy, two German Shepherds, and an art menagerie of predatory animals.

He also has a collection of nicknames from "Chainsaw" to "Rambo in Pinstripes" and "Darth Vader," earned in a career on the corporate front lines.

In *Mean Business,* his book released last month, the 59-year-old Dunlap does more than tell a personal story. He philosophizes on the future of corporate America and offers his own prescription to fix it.

"Whether you like it or not, it can't be ignored," he declared in a recent interview. "It's just like me."

True enough. Dunlap is unapologetically brash and controversial.

He's also rich. And what has made him rich is a simple idea, applied to four companies he has led during his career: Take an existing company that is losing money, cut costs, and make it profitable.

When he starts, Dunlap buys huge stakes of company stock, betting his hard-nosed management will increase its market value, which, not coincidentally, is his sole measure of a company's performance. He

delights in bucking the recent trend toward bashing corporations for cutting jobs to make money for shareholders. At Scott Paper Co., where he worked less than two years, Dunlap made about $100 million by the time his "Dunlapping" was complete.

Some grumble he made that money on the backs of fired employees. He axed about 35 percent of the work force, closed facilities including the posh headquarters in Philadelphia (which had a pond stocked with company-owned geese) and ultimately consummated a sale to rival Kimberly-Clark Corp.

The deal helped company shareholders, who saw total value of their stock go from $2.5 billion to $9.4 billion. In late July, he tackled yet another project that trades on his reputation around Wall Street.

Sunbeam Corp., the appliance company based in Fort Lauderdale, has struggled mightily for years. With Dunlap announced as chief executive, company stock soared 49 percent in one day. Basically, he made the company worth $495 million more just by joining.

Dunlap got in on those profits, too, buying $3 million of Sunbeam stock before the announcement. He skirted insider trading rules by buying directly from the company's treasury stock, which means essentially both the buyer and seller had the same inside information.

Dunlap hardly has started wielding the knife on Sunbeam, but he is bullish on the company's future despite its troubled past.

"A lot of these companies have a great name and some great products," he said. "But there isn't a great company in the world that can't be killed by bad management."

Critics warn it won't be that simple to fix Sunbeam. And there are plenty of critics.

In *Mean Business,* Dunlap takes on such sacred cows as consultants, affirmative action, boards of directors, fancy corporate digs, CEO pay critics, and anyone who says businesses should serve society's best interests.

He reiterates his own vision comes down to one thing: shareholders [sic].

"They own the company. They take all the risks," he said in the interview. "No one has given a shareholder their money back."

Yes, others concede, but does that vision really improve a company?

Dunlap is "an 80s-style liquidator dressed up for the 90s as an angry white guy," columnist Thomas Petzinger, Jr., wrote recently in *The Wall Street Journal.* "He may be good at what he does, but don't confuse it with the harder and more meaningful job of managing."

Going for the long-term, some management theorists contend, means taking a harder look at what a business does well, who makes that happen, and encouraging those operations. People like Dunlap "go after the low-hanging fruit," said consultant Jeff Garner. Firing people derails long-term success because layoffs destroy worker trust.

And the critics don't just take on Dunlap's gospel. They also question his record.

A critical profile of his work at Scott in *Business Week's* January edition argued that, along with the fat, Dunlap cut much muscle. Also, former executives quoted anonymously in the magazine said the cuts weren't even Dunlap's idea; some of the executives who departed soon after his arrival had planned to leave anyway.

Dunlap called that report "trash."

"If CEOs had done their job, I would never have existed," he said. "In every case, I've gone into a job where they've done miserably."

At Sunbeam, if there were any doubts about the authenticity of his methods, he has put some to rest already. In his first month, he forced out or fired at least a half-dozen executives.

* * * * *

If unconventionality is his reputation, Dunlap regales in it. In *Mean Business,* he recalls the time he stormed out of a corporate restroom, throwing rolls of toilet paper down the hall, because his hosts had stocked the competition's product.

And he points with great pride to the plain talk of the book, which has the audacity, in an age of multisyllabic business theories, to boil down his wisdom into four rules.

That simplicity has led some critics to say he has been lucky.

"If I was this lucky this consistently, I should go to Las Vegas," he snorted in response. "I'd make a lot more money."

Source: *The Tampa Tribune,* September 8, 1996, Business and Finance Section, p. 1. © 1996 The Tampa Tribune Co. Reprinted by permission.

Afterword I

The Wall Street Journal reported that "Chainsaw Al" believed the challenge facing him at Sunbeam required a new strategy. He did not apologize for his job-cutting approach, but he said that growth was his goal at Sunbeam. Dunlap's message. "You can't make money just firing people. Mickey Mouse can do that."[79]

Afterword II

Dunlap announced dismissals for 6,400 Sunbeam workers, but before the plan could be implemented, Dunlap himself was fired after a 1998 first quarter loss of $45 million, amid allegations that Dunlap had earlier overstated earnings.[80] Job cuts, in the end, were expected to total about 2,300.[81] Dunlap is suing Sunbeam claiming he is owed $5.25 million in unpaid salary, and in 1999 a judge ordered Sunbeam to pay $1.4 million to Dunlap and his former vice-chairman for their legal fees in defending against the inflated earnings charges.[82]

Questions

1. *a.* Based on this reading, how would you characterize Dunlap's view of social responsibility?
   b. Do you share his view? Explain.
2. In 1999, Bob Thompson sold his road building firm for $422 million. Then he divided $128 million among his 550 workers, more than 80 of whom became millionaires. Thompson explained his generosity by saying, "I wanted to go out a winner, and I wanted to go out doing the right thing."[83]
   a. Which management strategy, Dunlap's layoffs or Thompson's bonuses, is the more socially responsible? Explain.
   b. Could Dunlap, in managing publicly traded companies owned by their shareholders, practice the same kind of generosity to employees that Thompson followed in distributing money that was literally his own? Explain.
   c. Stanford professor Jeffrey Pfeffer reflecting on the bonus strategy: "It's how you look at your work force . . . When I look at you, do I see a cost or do I see you as the only thing that separates me from my competition?"[84] Comment.
   d. Do you agree with Thompson that he did the "right thing"? Explain.
3. In the reading, consultant Jeff Garner says layoffs destroy worker trust. Is worker trust a critical ingredient in socially responsible management? Explain.
4. Al Dunlap: "Corporate charity exists so CEOs can collect awards, plaques and honors, so they can sit on a dais and be adored. This is not what the shareholder is paying them a million bucks a year—plus stock options and bonuses—to do!"[85] Comment.
5. Based on the reading, do you admire Dunlap? Explain.

Domestic Partner Insurance Coverage

The article that follows discusses giant NationsBank's decision to extend health care coverage to the full-range of "family members," including same-sex domestic partners. San Francisco, under its Equal Benefits Ordinance, requires companies doing business with the city to extend health benefits to its workers' partners (homosexual and heterosexual) who live in the city. That ordinance has been challenged in court and by Congress, but at this writing in 1999, the state of California is considering similar legislation for all state and some city employees.

NATIONSBANK OFFERS BENEFITS TO WIDER FAMILY

Teresa Burney

In one word that nearly got lost in Monday's big bank merger, NationsBank Corp. CEO Hugh McColl, Jr., made a promise that could have a big impact on NationsBank's 100,000 employees and their families.

"Yes," he said, NationsBank will do what merger partner BankAmerica Corp. already does—make health insurance available to employee family members who have never before been covered.

In addition to the spouses and children who traditionally are covered, NationsBank employees will be able to insure domestic partners, parents, grandparents, siblings, or adult children.

The practice of insuring the domestic partners of employees, regardless of marital status or whether they are the same sex, is becoming more common as companies seek to add benefits that will attract the best workers.

Many companies have expanded the benefits despite criticism from social conservatives who view benefits for gay couples as undercutting the traditional family.

But the idea of allowing employees to add other family members who share the same household to the company health insurance plan is extremely rare, say human resource experts.

And the thought of NationsBank, headquartered deep in the Bible Belt, offering such liberal benefits is one more example to indicate there will be a merger of cultures as well as assets between the Charlotte, N.C.-based NationsBank and the San Francisco-based BankAmerica.

"It helps attract more employees, and you have to be competitive in getting the best employees and we think this is the best way to do this," said NationsBank spokesman George Owen.

Todd Martinez-Padilla Simmons, local chairman of the Human Rights Task Force of Florida, applauded the change.

"I know that every gay and lesbian employee of NationsBank is going to feel great when they go to work tomorrow morning—more loyal to their employers and they'll appreciate the environment that they are working in," Simmons said.

"It's pretty rare that you see someone look at the whole picture as it speaks to the changing roles of family and different home structures," he said.

In fact, a recent study by Hewitt Associates, an Illinois consulting firm, shows that about 10 percent of the companies surveyed offer health insurance to employees' domestic partners. Some large companies, including Disney, offer the benefit.

But extending the coverage opportunity to other family members is so rare that Hewitt has never bothered to survey the phenomenon, said Monica Gallagher, a Hewitt spokeswoman.

BankAmerica started offering what it calls "expanded family benefits" in January 1997, in the wake of the city of San Francisco's edict that it would not do business with any company that failed to offer health-care benefits to the domestic partners of employees.

But the company had been discussing the benefit for some time, said BankAmerica spokesman Dennis Wyss.

"What this benefit was all about is an acknowledgement by the company that the family may include parents, siblings, and domestic partners who have a significant relationship with the employee," Wyss said.

Under BankAmerica's plan, the employees can insure themselves, their children and one other adult. The other adult can be a spouse, a domestic partner with whom they have been in a "committed relationship" for at least six months, or adult children, siblings, parents, or grandparents under 65 years old who qualify as dependents as defined by the Internal Revenue Service.

Wyss said that the program made its homosexual employees happy, but it also benefited others who have family members that lack health insurance.

There are an estimated 3 million uninsured Americans ages 55 to 64.

"Anecdotally, we heard from a lot of boomers with aging parents" who needed insurance, Wyss said.

Wyss would not give the costs of expanding medical coverage at BankAmerica. "I can tell you that it's not a significant cost increase," he said.

And, whatever it costs, it bought the company something in return, Wyss said.

"It's a competitive world out there in terms of getting good employees, and we felt it would make us more of an employer of choice," he said.

Source: *St. Petersburg Times,* April 17, 1998, p. 1E, Reprinted by permission.

Questions

1. *a.* How does NationsBank decide when an unmarried couple is engaged in a relationship that justifies insurance coverage for the employee's partner?
   b. What "marriage equivalency" standards would you set, or would you decline to offer such coverage if you were in charge? Explain.
2. In your view, is offering both same-sex and heterosexual domestic partner coverage evidence of socially responsible behavior by a corporation? Explain.
3. List the issues that you would consider if you were a CEO deciding whether to extend health insurance to the same-sex partners of your employees.
4. Christopher Mossey in a letter to *The Wall Street Journal:* "Your Oct. 11 In Marketing to Gays, Lesbians Are Often Left Out, raises a provocative question about the direction of the gay advocacy movement: Must gay men and lesbians be 'recognized' by the marketing departments of large corporations? The comments in the article by Kate Kendell, executive director of the National Center for Lesbian Rights, suggest that it is a social responsibility of corporations to pitch products to gay people."

   In your judgment, do corporations have a social responsibility to "recognize" and practice targeted marketing towards gays and lesbians? Explain. See Christopher Mossey, "Marketing to Gays: Why Is It Needed?" *The Wall Street Journal,* October 29, 1999, p. A19.

College Students and Sweatshops

Nike announced that it was lifting its monthly minimum wage in Indonesia from $29.66 to $31.44

In early 1999, Nike announced that it was lifting its monthly minimum wage in Indonesia from $29.66 to $31.44. That wage, along with housing and other allowances, guarantees that no Indonesian Nike employee will earn less than $39.39 monthly. The country's minimum wage was expected, at this writing, to rise to $27.41 monthly.[86] The article that follows reports on an increasingly zealous student movement to put pressure on American companies doing business with sweatshops. (Chapters 5, 6, and 12 also address sweatshops and related issues.)

NIKE ON THE RUN AS SIT-INS SPREAD ACROSS THE U.S.

Larry Elliott

Thirty years after American campuses erupted in opposition to the Vietnam war, student protest is back in fashion in the United States in a campaign against the use of sweatshops by big business.

Nike rather than Nixon is the target of the new generation of protesters—often the sons and daughters of the 60s campaigners. They are taking direct action in an attempt to stop their colleges buying sportswear made by workers on poverty wages in developing countries.

Corporations and universities have been taken by surprise as long-forgotten symbols of dissent—the takeover and the sit-in—have been revived by students on 100 campuses acting in coalition with U.S. unions fighting for better pay and working conditions.

Sweatshops were virtually eliminated in the U.S. between the 30s and the 70s as President Franklin Roosevelt's New Deal legislation led to a crackdown on unscrupulous employers.

But globalisation has led to a new wave of exploitation in factories in the Caribbean, Latin America, and Asia. Imports account for 60 percent of the U.S. market in clothing and footwear—up from 4 percent in the early 60s—and provide hefty profits for U.S. multinationals.

One of the most lucrative markets for clothing firms has been in sweatshirts and other sportswear adorned with U.S. university logos. Students are putting pressure on their administrators to make sure tough codes of conduct are drawn up to guarantee that goods are made under decent conditions and that workers get a living wage.

Direct action has been taken at the Universities of Wisconsin, Duke, Michigan, and Georgetown, while a four-day sit-in at the the University of North Carolina ended with college authorities bowing to the pressure and agreeing to more stringent guidelines.

"University administrators should keep in mind that any code created, adopted, or administered over the heads of students will be met with severe public criticism at many campuses," says United Students Against Sweatshops (USAS), the umbrella body representing the protesters.

"We will not allow our universities to profit from the sweat of inhumane conditions and the suffering of worker mistreatment."

Under their contract with the clothing firms, universities get a share of the retail price of sports apparel. Students want to include labour rights in these contracts and ensure that monitoring of factories is systematic and independent, rather than carried out by financial auditors with close links to the manufacturers.

The big multinationals have started to take notice of the campaign. Nike, which has spent most of the 90s trying to fend off accusations that it has exploited cheap labour in Southeast Asia, has said it will make public a list of its overseas plants.

One reason for corporate concern is the effect bad publicity has on the bottom line: profit.

James Jacobsen, incoming chairman of the American Apparel Manufacturers' Association, warned executives in the clothing industry that the "ongoing controversy about overseas sweatshops was causing anxiety on Wall Street."

Ginny Coughlin, a USAS campaign organiser, said students had recognised that corporate power was "out of control."

She said the Clinton administration had tried to set up joint monitoring of sweatshops by business and unions, but that the government's failure to give the deal teeth meant corporations wielded all the power.

"Tiny steps forward that cover up the real problem do not help us, and the real problem is the power of corporations to do whatever they want, wherever they want to whoever they want."

Source: Larry Elliott, *London Guardian,* June 25, 1999, p. 16. Courtesy of the *London Guardian.* [For information about the United Students Against Sweatshops and related links, see **http://www.asm.wisc.edu/usas/**]

Questions

1. *a.* Do you, as a student, have a responsibility to protest if your college logo appears on sportswear made in low wage sweatshops? Explain.
    b. Do you think a united student movement would have the power to force change in apparel manufacturers' labor policies? If so, should that power be exercised? If not, do corporations hold too much power in American life? Explain.
    c. Have you ever inquired about the manufacturing source of a product you were considering, or have you declined, as a matter of principle, to buy certain garments or other items because you believe the manufacturer engages in unfair labor practices? Explain.
2. *a.* Are the corporate critics trying to impose American values on the balance of the world? Explain.
    b. Is this campaign to police international suppliers unfair to the average American consumer? Explain.
3. Should American companies refuse to do business in countries:
    a. That do not practice democracy?
    b. That routinely practice discrimination?
    c. That tolerate or even encourage the abuse of children? Explain.

INTERNET EXERCISES

1. Many critics, activists, international scholars, and others are concerned that the economic "globalization" of recent years will serve corporate/governmental interests at the expense of Third World citizens and the global natural environment. Using the Corporate Watch website [**http://www.corpwatch.org/**] explain those concerns in more detail.
2. Using the website Opensecrets.org., find the latest campaign finance data for your congressperson or one of your senators. While there, perhaps you will want to take a look at the personal financial condition of those same politicians. See [**http://www.opensecrets.org/home/index.asp**]

CHAPTER QUESTIONS

1. *a.* In general, do you think employers are more concerned with profits or with delivering quality goods and services? Explain.
    b. Which *should* they be more concerned about? Explain.
    c. Are you most concerned about receiving a quality education or earning a degree? Explain.
2. Scholar Denis Goulet argued that we will find no facile resolution to the conflict between the values of a just society and the sharply opposing values of successful corporations.

a. Do you agree that the values of a just society oppose those of successful corporations? Explain.
b. Can a solution be found? Explain.

3. Bristol-Myers Squibb introduced Nutrament as an energy and fitness drink but that approach failed. Then Squibb noticed that Nutrament was popular among some ethnic groups. The company began to advertise heavily to inner-city residents, treating the drink as a "well-balanced meal replacement." The drink is welcomed by junkies and crackheads who have difficulty eating solid food. Nutrament is also rumored to fend off the "shakes"

that trouble drug users. Independent studies, however, show that the drink, which does contain vitamins and minerals, is loaded with sugar. One 12-ounce can contains the same amount of sugar as 10 Oreo cookies. Nutrament sales have been increasing at double-digit rates.[87]

Is Bristol-Myers Squibb wrong to encourage inner-city residents to drink Nutrament? Explain.

4. In criticizing General Motors, Ralph Nader is reported to have said:

> Someday we'll have a legal system that will criminally indict the president of General Motors for these outrageous crimes. But not as long as this country is populated by people who fritter away their citizenship by watching TV, playing bridge and Mah-Jongg, and just generally being slobs.[88]

  a. Is the citizenry generally unconcerned about unethical corporate conduct? Explain.
  b. To the extent that corporations engage in misdeeds, does the fault really lie with the corporate community or with society at large?

5. Journalist Michael Kinsley expresses some serious reservations about corporate social responsibility:

> In particular, I am not impressed by corporate charity and cultural benefaction, which amount to executives playing Medici with other people's money. You wouldn't know, from the lavish parties corporate officers throw for themselves whenever they fund an art exhibit or a PBS series, that it's not costing them a penny. The shareholders, who aren't invited, pick up the tab.[89]

Comment on Kinsley's statement.

6. The Pennsylvania garment maker, AND1, developed a line of T-shirts directed to young males and adorned with sayings such as "Your game is as ugly as your girl," and "You like that move? So does your girl." A feminist group complained that the shirts "put down" girls and implied that "girls are the property of boys." In 1999, the J.C. Penney Co., which was selling the shirts, withdrew them after the complaints.[90] Was Penney's decision the socially responsible course of action, or did Penney's cave in to "politically correct" pressure? Or did Penney's simply make a wise business move? Explain.

7. *USA Today:*

> The friendly folks at Ford have outfitted their 18.9-foot Excursion, which debuted Friday, with a "blocker beam," a kind of under-the-bumper bumper designed for collisions. That's nice of them. If the biggest sports utility vehicle of all time, chugging along at 10 miles per gallon of gas, rams a Toyota compact with a Sierra Club bumper sticker, the latter won't get decapitated.
>
> The Excursion, big enough to hold nine finger-wagging environmentalists and 44 gallons of their gas, is earning piles of scorn half a year before going on sale. Among other no-nos, it is so big that federal fuel-economy standards for cars and small trucks don't apply.[91]

  a. Are giant cars a social wrong?
  b. If so, who is to blame, the manufacturers or us?
  c. If not, how do we justify those vehicles in the face of the economic struggles of most of the world's citizens? Explain.

8. In actual practice, do you think most companies operate primarily with the goal of maximizing shareholder wealth or with the goal of maximizing stakeholder welfare? Explain.

9. In 1992, the rapper Ice-T released a song entitled "Cop Killer" as part of his album, "Body Count."

> Then-President Bush labeled the rap "sick" as a glorification of killing law enforcement officers. Some music retail chains removed "Body Count" from their shelves. However, Time Warner continued to distribute the album. Ice-T eventually decided to remove "Cop Killer" from the album.

  a. Was Time Warner socially irresponsible in its decision to market the album while it included the "Cop Killer" tune?
  b. Defend Time Warner.
  c. Assume the rap had said "fag killer," or "black killer," or "Jew killer," or "woman killer." Explain what you would have done had you been in charge of Time Warner and Ice-T included one of those raps on his album.
  d. Rap and heavy metal music often degrade women and glorify sexual violence. Do you decline to purchase music of that character? Explain.

10. The Institute for Transportation and Policy Development (a nonprofit organization addressing Third World needs) argues for the use of bicycles rather than autos in the Third World:

> The oil and automobile companies, having already made Americans auto-dependent, are targeting Asia, Latin America, and Africa for future growth, aided by

large loans from the World Bank and other international funding sources. Many developing countries, by repeating our mistakes, are deep in debt and often spend half of their foreign exchange earnings to pay for oil and cars that fail to meet the basic mobility needs of the majority.[92]

a. Have the oil and auto companies *made* Americans auto-dependent? Explain.

b. Should the socially responsible auto or oil company discourage the purchase of autos in Third World nations? Explain.

c. On balance, if we could somehow turn back the technology clock, would the United States be a better place to live had we not so thoroughly embraced the automobile to meet our transportation needs? Explain.

11. a. Are you a "socially conscious" consumer in the sense that your buying habits are influenced by your perception of a firm's stance on social issues?

b. Should you be? Explain.

c. If we were able to successfully rate firms according to a social responsibility index, and if most or all Americans were guided in their buying, investing, and employment decisions by that index, would ours be a better society? Explain.

12. You are the sole owner of a neighborhood drugstore that stocks various brands of toothpaste. Assume that scientific testing has established that one brand is clearly superior to all others in preventing tooth decay.

a. Would you remove from the shelves all brands except the one judged best in decay prevention? Explain.

b. What alternative measures could you take?

c. Should the toothpaste manufacturers be required to reveal all available data regarding the effectiveness of their products? Explain.

13. IBP, the world's largest fresh beef and pork processor, brought 1,300 jobs and a $23 million payroll to the town of Columbus Junction, Iowa (population 1,400), when it reopened and expanded a Rath Packing Co. plant. The plant "saved" the local economy. Because the company could not meet its labor needs locally, IBP recruited in "the nation's most desperate pockets of unemployment."[93] Many of those people came to Columbus Junction with little in the way of resources. (At the time, IBP's blue-collar wages began at $6 per hour.) The result was social upheaval for the community.

The police chief estimated that crime rose 400 percent after IBP arrived. In the fall of 1989 alone, junior high and high school pupil turnover was 25 percent. Many of the new recruits and their children could not speak English.[94]

a. What responsibility, if any, does IBP have to help Columbus Junction deal with its changed circumstances? Explain.

b. Higher wages would attract additional local employees. Should IBP be expected to increase its wage scale in order to reduce its reliance on recruiting the urban unemployed? Explain.

c. Defend IBP.

14. *The Wall Street Journal:*

TAMPA, Fla.—A lip-licking lizard leers from an ad in the liquor section adjacent to the Albertson's supermarket here. "Ask Me About My Tooters!" the ad says.

Tooters Lingo Liqueurs are potent, single-serve cocktails made from vodka, tequila, and other liquors. With such frat-boy names as Yellin Melon Balls, Bamama Hama and Blu-Dacious Kamikaze, they come in a "Party Pack" that looks like something from chemistry class. Thirty foil-sealed test tubes sit on a cardboard rack, and each contains a single shot of fruit-colored liquid, with a hefty alcohol content of 15%. Albertson's sells the 750-milliliter Party Pack for $12.99.[95]

Activists against underage drinking are outraged by products they believe to be targeted to young people. They point to products like Flugel, the label of which features a bug-eyed pink duck and the expression, "It's dynamite." As one critic said, "There aren't a lot of adults that relate to frogs or lizards in advertising, and I don't think mature adults are the ones choosing to use Jell-O shots."[96] Do you consider these marketing practices socially irresponsible? Explain

15. Approximately $10 million is expended annually for alcohol ads in college newspapers. Many millions more are expended in other youth-oriented publications such as *National Lampoon* and *Rolling Stone*. The beer industry sponsors many campus athletic contests. And brewers have established promotional relationships with rock bands. Is beer and liquor advertising directed to the youth market unethical? Explain.

16. Starbucks Coffee Co. has adopted guidelines designed to improve working conditions at its foreign coffee suppliers. Among other things, the guidelines call for the suppliers to pay wages and benefits that at least

"address the basic needs of workers and their families."[97]

   a. As you interpret the guideline, what must those suppliers do to meet Starbucks' expectations?

   b. In your opinion, are guidelines of this kind of any practical value? Explain.

17. In 1999, when President Clinton advocated a plan to "save Social Security" that would have involved the government buying up about 4 percent of the stock market, the Reverend Jesse Jackson remarked: "I think he should not invest in gun manufacturers, and shouldn't invest in liquor companies, and shouldn't invest in tobacco companies."[98] When you invest in the stock market will you avoid the product lines Jackson singles out? Explain.

18. In 1992, Congress passed a bill that prevented Hornell Brewing Co. from using the brand name Crazy Horse (a Sioux Indian chief) for one of its malt liquors. Native Americans and others objected to the brand name as offensive to Indian dignity and history and argued that the liquor was targeted to Native Americans. How would you have voted on the bill? Explain.

19. Former General Motors vice president John Z. DeLorean wrote in his book, *On a Clear Day You Can See General Motors:*

> It seemed to me then, and still does now, that the system of American business often produces wrong, immoral, and irresponsible decisions, even though the personal morality of the people running the business is often above reproach. The system has a different morality as a group than the people do as individuals, which permits it willfully to produce ineffective or dangerous products, deal dictatorially and often unfairly with suppliers, pay bribes for business, abrogate the rights of employment, or tamper with the democratic process of government through illegal political contributions.[99]

   a. How can the corporate "group" possess values at odds with those of the individual managers?

   b. Is DeLorean merely offering a convenient rationalization for corporate misdeeds? Explain.

   c. Realistically, can one expect to preserve individual values when employed in a corporate group? Explain.

20. Do you agree or disagree with the following statements? Explain.

   a. "Social responsibility is good business only if it is also good public relations and/or preempts government interference."

   b. "The social responsibility debate is the result of the attempt of liberal intellectuals to make a moral issue of business behavior."

   c. "'Profit' is really a somewhat ineffective measure of business's social effectiveness."

   d. "The social responsibility of business is to 'stick to business.'"[100]

21. The Worldwatch Institute says that the richest one-fifth of the planet, the "consumer class," is ruining the planet because of excessive consumption that leads to environmental harm such as acid rain and greenhouse gases. Worldwatch recommends longer vacations in place of higher wages.[101]

   a. Do American consumer practices amount to abuse of the lesser-developed world?

   b. Would lesser wages and longer vacations be a good prescription for what ails America and the world? Explain.

22. Increasingly, we are treating education as a product and students as consumers. Do you see any problems in that trend? Explain.

NOTES

1. Nelson D. Schwartz, "A Tale of Two Economies," *Fortune,* April 26, 1999, p. 198.

2. Jeremy Kahn, "The Global 5 Hundred," *Fortune,* August 2, 1999, p. 144.

3. Allen R. Myerson, "Exxon and Mobil Announce $80 Billion Deal to Create World's Largest Company," *New York Times,* December 2, 1998, p. A1.

4. Joseph Weber, "Call It the Net Effect," *Business Week,* July 12, 1999, p. 50.

5. Ibid.

6. "The Biggest Banks in the World," *The Wall Street Journal*, March 11, 1999, p. A6.

7. Ibid.

8. Judith Miller, "Globalization Widens Rich-Poor Gap, U.N. Report Says," *New York Times,* July 13, 1999, p. A8.

9. "Facts from the Corporate Planet: Ecology and Politics in the Age of Globalization," Corporate Watch website,

[**http://www.corpwatch.org/trac/feature/
planet/fact_1.html**], citing Joshua Karliner, *The
Corporate Planet* (San Francisco: Sierra Club
Books, 1997).

10. Ibid.

11. Leslie McAneny, "Military on Top, HMOs Last in Public
Confidence Poll," Gallup News Service, July 14, 1999,
[**http://www.gallup.com/poll/releases/ pr990714.asp**].

12. Peter Asch, *Industrial Organization and Antitrust
Policy* (New York: John Wiley & Sons, 1983),
p. 162.

13. Charles Reich, *The Greening of America* (New York:
Bantam Books, 1970), pp. 7–8.

14. Staff, "Alienation Index—Trend Since 1966,"
Louisville Courier-Journal, January 15, 1996, p. 1.

15. John Nirenberg, *The Living Organization* (Homewood,
IL: Business One Irwin, 1993), p. 65.

16. Julia Malone, "Groups' Donations Fueled Races
Nationwide," *Atlanta Journal and Constitution,*
November 5, 1998, p. 4K.

17. Editorial, "Public Financing Best Antidote to Special-
Interest Voting Meddling," *USA Today,* December 1,
1998, p. 14A.

18. Editorial, "An Inch on Campaign Finance," *Washington
Post,* July 21, 1999, p. A20.

19. Deirdre Sheshgreen and Bill Lambrecht, "Lobbying Is
the Sport Everyone Likes to Play," *St. Louis Post-
Dispatch,* May 16, 1999, p. A7.

20. Malone, "Groups' Donations," p. 4K.

21. Associated Press, "Study Shows Influence of Tobacco
Contributions," *Waterloo–Cedar Falls Courier,*
September 2, 1997, p. C6.

22. Thomas J. Dean, Maria Vryza, and Gerald E. Fryxell,
"Do Corporate PACs Restrict Competition?" *Business
& Society* 37, no. 2 (June 1998), pp. 135, 149.

23. Ibid.

24. Editorial, "Best Government Money Can Buy? Sadly,
No," *USA Today,* August 22, 1997, p. 11A.

25. Richard N. Goodwin, "PACs Gobbling Up Congress,"
Waterloo–Courier, December 17, 1985, p. A4.

26. Editorial, "Triumph of Hucksterism," *Des Moines
Register,* May 29, 1989, p. 8A.

27. Editorial, "Business Leaders' New Tack Poses
Challenge to Public Schools," *USA Today,* February 25,
1999, p. 14A.

28. Pat Wechsler, "This Lesson Is Brought to You By . . ."
Business Week, June 30, 1997, pp. 68, 69.

29. Deeann Glamser, "This Class Brought to You By . . . ,"
USA Today, January 3, 1997, p. 3A.

30. Wechsler, "This Lesson Is Brought," pp. 68, 69.

31. *Los Angeles Times,* "San Francisco Takes Stand Against
Campus Commerce," *Waterloo–Cedar Falls Courier,*
July 16, 1999, p. A9.

32. Ibid.

33. Ibid.

34. Reich, *Greening of America,* pp. 141–42.

35. Associated Press, "Companies Emerge as Art
Benefactors," *Waterloo–Cedar Falls Courier,*
December 26, 1997, p. D5.

36. Mitchell Landsberg, "Disney's Expansions Show It's
Not a Small World After All," *Waterloo–Cedar Falls
Courier,* August 9, 1995, p. B1.

37. Ibid.

38. Jeff Rowe, "Some Fear Growing Disney Influence,"
Waterloo–Cedar Falls Courier, June 2, 1996, p. F5.

39. Hal Bodley, "Baseball Considers Ads on Uniforms,"
USA Today, April 1, 1999, p. 1C.

40. Ibid.

41. Roger Thurow, "Shoe Companies, Tongues Out, Buy
Up College Teams Wholesale," *The Wall Street
Journal,* November 17, 1995, p. B10.

42. Ibid.

43. Paul Whiteley, Sr., "Fan Fears Greed Is Ruining
Sports," *Des Moines Register,* August 27, 1995, p. 9D.

44. John Powers, "IOC Begins Purge," *Boston Globe,*
March 18, 1999, p. D1.

45. Kristian Palda, "How to Enjoy Globalization in One
Easy Lesson," *Ottawa Citizen,* May 7, 1998, p. A15.

46. Robert J. Samuelson, "Globalization's Downside,"
Washington Post, December 17, 1997, p. A25.

47. Judith Miller, "Globalization Widens Rich-Poor Gap,"
p. A8.

48. Ibid.

49. Ibid.

50. Lawrence S. Connor, "Surviving in the Global
Economy," *Indianapolis Star,* June 9, 1999, p. A15.

51. Eric Liu, "Remember When Public Space Didn't
Carry Brand Names?" *USA Today,* March 25, 1999,
p. 15A.

52. Betsy Morris, "As a Favored Pastime, Shopping Ranks High with Most Americans," *The Wall Street Journal,* July 30, 1987, pp. 1, 13.

53. Tom Bratz, "Your Ad Here," *Newsweek,* February 5, 1996, p. 12.

54. Bob Ortega, "Aging Activists Turn, Turn, Turn Attention to Wal-Mart Protests," *The Wall Street Journal,* October 11, 1994, p. A1.

55. Editorial, "Businesses Can Help Parks," *USA Today,* September 19, 1996, p. 13A.

56. *University of Iowa Spectator,* March 1980, p. 4.

57. Walter Shapiro, "Why We've Failed to Ruin Thanksgiving," *Time,* November 27, 1989, p. 94.

58. Myron Magnet, "The Money Society," *Fortune,* July 6, 1987, p. 26.

59. Forum,"Is There Virtue in Profit?" *Harper's Magazine,* December 1986, pp. 37, 42.

60. Ted Peters, "The Future of Religion in a Post-Industrial Society," *The Futurist,* October 1980, pp. 20, 22.

61. Ann de Rouffignac, "School Contests Help Concerns Promote Brands," *The Wall Street Journal,* July 3, 1992, p. B1.

62. Richard Holman, "Book Captures Japan's New Mood," *The Wall Street Journal,* May 6, 1993, p. A11.

63. "More Leisure in an Increasingly Electronic Society," *Business Week,* September 3, 1979, pp. 208, 212.

64. Daniel Seligman, "Helping the Shareholder Helps the Society," *The Wall Street Journal*, June 21, 1996, p. A12.

65. Keith Davis and Robert L. Blomstrom, *Business and Society: Environment and Responsibility,* 3rd ed. (New York: McGraw-Hill, 1975), p. 6.

66. This social responsibility continuum is drawn, in part, from Debra Schleef, "Empty Ethics and Reasonable Responsibility: Vocabularies of Motive Among Law and Business Students," *Law and Social Inquiry* 22 (Summer 1997), p. 619.

67. Milton Friedman, *Capitalism and Freedom* (Chicago: University of Chicago Press, 1962), p. 133.

68. Herbert Stein, "Corporate America, Mind Your Own Business," *The Wall Street Journal,* July 15, 1996, p. A10.

69. Jan Leschly, "SmithKline Beecham Tries to Improve Public Health," *Minneapolis Star Tribune,* November 30, 1998, p. 3D.

70. Robert Glassman, "Wainwright Bank Finds Social Investment Pays," *Minneapolis Star Tribune,* November 30, 1998, p. 3D.

71. William D. Perez, "Ethics Go Hand-in-Hand with Growth and Success," *Minneapolis Star Tribune,* November 30, 1998, p. 3D.

72. Ronald Roman, Sefa Hayibor, and Bradley Agle, "The Relationship Between Social and Financial Performance," *Business & Society* 38, no. 1 (March 1999), pp. 109, 121.

73. Jeff Frooman, "Socially Irresponsible and Illegal Behavior and Shareholder Wealth," *Business & Society* 36, no. 3 (September 1997), p. 221.

74. Curtis C. Verschoor, "A Study of the Link Between a Corporation's Financial Performance and Its Commitment to Ethics," *Journal of Business Ethics* 17 (1998), p. 1509.

75. Simon Buckby, "Global Standard for Business Ethics Launched," *Financial Times,* June 11, 1998, p. 10.

76. Ibid.

77. Ibid.

78. Associated Press, "Fearful Workers Fretting About Future," *Des Moines Register,* December 25, 1996, p. 8S.

79. Joann Lublin and Oscar Suris, "'Chainsaw Al' Now Aspires to Be 'Al the Builder,'" *The Wall Street Journal,* April 9, 1997, p. B1.

80. Associated Press, "Sunbeam Fires Chairman 'Chain Saw' Al Dunlap," *Waterloo–Cedar Falls Courier,* June 15, 1998, p. B7.

81. Rick Babson, "Ex-Sunbeam Chief 'Chain Saw' Al Got the Ax He Deserved," *Kansas City Star,* August 26, 1998, p. B3.

82. *New York Times,* "Sunbeam Owes Dunlap Fees, Judge Rules," *Miami Herald,* June 25, 1999, p. C8.

83. Associated Press, "Boss Rewards Workers' Loyalty—Shares $128 Million," *Cedar Falls-Waterloo–Cedar Falls Courier,* September 12, 1999, p. B1.

84. Greg Miller, "Extreme Generosity Shocks Firm's Employees, Analysts," *Des Moines Register,* December 18, 1996, p. 1A.

85. Noam Neusner, "He Argues Lean Requires 'Mean,'" *Tampa Tribune,* September 8, 1996, Business & Finance section, p. 1.

86. Staff, "Nike to Increase Wages for Indonesian Workers," *Seattle Times,* March 23, 1999, p. C2.

87. Suein Hwang, "Nutrament, Debunked as a 'Fitness' Drink, Is Reborn in the Slums," *The Wall Street Journal,* November 2, 1994, p. 1.

88. Charles McCarry, *Citizen Nader* (New York: Saturday Review Press, 1972), p. 301.

89. Michael Kinsley, "Companies as Citizens: Should They Have a Conscience?" *The Wall Street Journal,* February 19, 1987, p. 29.

90. "Penney Hears Protests, Agrees to Trash T-Shirts," *Des Moines Register,* July 6, 1999, p. 2A.

91. Editorial, "King of the Road," *USA Today,* March 1, 1999, p. 14A.

92. Michael Replogle, Fund-Raising Letter for Institute for Transportation and Policy Development, 1990.

93. Dennis Farney, "A Town in Iowa Finds Big New Packing Plant Destroys Its Old Calm," *The Wall Street Journal,* April 3, 1990, p. A1.

94. Ibid.

95. Alejandro Bodipo-Memba, "'Shooter' and Other Alcoholic Novelties Face Scrutiny," *The Wall Street Journal,* April 14, 1999, p. B1.

96. Ibid.

97. G. Pascal Zachary, "Starbucks Asks Foreign Suppliers to Improve Working Conditions," *The Wall Street Journal,* October 23, 1995, p. B4.

98. Editorial, "The Rubin-Jackson Raid," *The Wall Street Journal,* February 1, 1999, p. A20.

99. John Z. DeLorean with J. Patrick Wright, "Bottom-Line Fever at General Motors" (excerpted from *On a Clear Day You Can See General Motors*), *The Washington Monthly,* January 1980, pp. 26–27.

100. Steven N. Brenner and Earl A. Molander, "Is the Ethics of Business Changing?" *Harvard Business Review* 55, no. 1 (January–February 1977), p. 68.

101. Associated Press, "Study: Consumerism, Malls Ruining Planet," *Des Moines Register,* July 26, 1992, p. 2A.

Introduction to Law

Chapter 4

The American Legal System

INTRODUCTION

Presumably, we can agree that some business practices have unfavorable consequences for society. Thus, the issue becomes: What should be done, if anything, to change those consequences? The fundamental options in the United States have been threefold: let the market "regulate" the behavior; leave the problem to the individual decision maker's own ethical dictates; or pass a law. Market regulation was discussed in Chapter 1. Self-regulation through ethics was explored in Chapters 2 and 3. This chapter, then, begins the discussion of the legal regulation of business with a brief outline of the American legal system and how it functions.

This chapter will also introduce a fourth alternative for addressing business/society conflicts. This alternative looks at conflict resolution processes such as negotiation, mediation, and arbitration that do not resort to the legal system. Although these alternatives are not new, they have been receiving much more attention in recent years.

Before turning to our detailed examination of the technical dimensions of the law, we should remind ourselves of the central purpose of our legal system—the pursuit of justice. As you read this chapter, ask yourself repeatedly: "Does this rule (this procedure, this case) contribute to the search for justice?"

Justice

A 1998 American Bar Association poll demonstrates the American public's mixed feelings about our ability to achieve justice:

- Only 30 percent of the respondents were "extremely or very confident" in the United States justice system, while 27 percent were no more than "slightly confident" in the system.
- Half the respondents gave the United States Supreme Court a high confidence rating—higher than any other institution or profession measured in the survey.
- Only 14 percent of the respondents gave lawyers a high confidence rating, slightly lower than Congress, but above the media.

- Slightly more than half the respondents believed courts treat men and women alike, while 39 percent said the courts treat all racial and ethnic groups alike. Only a third of the respondents said they think the justice system treats rich and poor alike.
- This country's justice system is the best in the world, said 80 percent of the respondents . . . Nevertheless, 51 percent of the respondents said the justice system needs a complete overhaul and that the country would be better off with fewer lawyers.[1] [For a daily update of legal news, see **http://www.lawnewsnet.com**]

Reasons. Why do many Americans doubt the fairness of our legal system? Plausible contributors include the impact of money on the process, racism, enormous civil damage awards, high-profile trials like O. J. Simpson's, and procedural imperfections, such as delays, in the justice system itself. Perhaps more influential, however, is a pattern of rising expectations among Americans. Stanford Law School professor Lawrence Friedman argues that Americans in previous centuries commonly did not receive justice in life and thus did not expect justice from the legal system.

> They didn't have modern medicines. Women died in childbirth. Men were often carried off by cholera and other diseases. There was no federal deposit insurance, locusts could eat your crop, and if you were injured you didn't expect to collect money . . . So if fate screwed you, you were screwed.[2]

Now we have an active government, private insurance, superb medical care, and high technology. As a result, Friedman explains, "people expect that if something bad happens to them, someone else is going to pay."[3] A 1994 American Bar Association survey resoundingly supports Friedman's theory. Ninety-one percent of the respondents believe that injuries caused by the negligence of others should be compensated and 39 percent believe that *every* injury should be compensated.[4]

Law and the Market. Justice is critical to our individual sense of well-being and to the survival of democracy itself, but for the purposes of this textbook, we should remind ourselves of the crucial role of a reliable legal system in fostering and maintaining capitalism and our method of commerce. The following law review excerpt explains:

THE IMPORTANCE OF LAW TO THE PRIVATE ENTERPRISE SYSTEM

Deb Ballam

Nobel economist Frederich von Hayek describes the theoretical importance of law to private enterprise. According to Hayek, law that secures property rights in modern society is prerequisite to private enterprise. Without the order of law enforcing private property ownership and facilitating the transfer of property rights, business enterprise in a complex, heterogeneous culture is simply infeasible.

The importance of law to the conduct of private enterprise is evident in economic developments in the former Soviet Union and the Republic of China. In moving from state-controlled to private enterprise, these countries have faced substantial difficulties arising from lack of a legal system that would secure property ownership and the contractual transfer of property rights. Reports from Russia indicate continuing economic turmoil due largely to the absence of adequate legal institutions and the absence of social experience in observing legal rules securing the marketplace. Not law, but extortion, intimidation, and violence today control much private enterprise in Russia . . .

In contrast to the economy of the former Soviet Union, China's economy has grown steadily in recent years. Minxin Pei, a political scientist at Princeton University, explains law's contribution to that growth: "Legal reform has become one of the most important institutional changes in China since the late 1970s . . . Within China, the changing legal institutions have begun to play an increasingly important role in governing economic activities, resolving civil disputes, enforcing law and order, and setting the boundaries between the power of the state and the autonomy of society." Dr. Pei reports that the number of lawyers in China grew threefold between 1986 and 1996 and that the number of commercial disputes adjudicated by the courts grew from about 15,000 annually in the early 1980s to some 1.5 million annually in the mid-1990s . . .

Of course, the importance of law to private enterprise goes far beyond its initial support as an institutional framework guaranteeing ownership rights. As the market system grows more complex both nationally and internationally, the legal recognition of promise keeping becomes increasingly significant in facilitating business. A condition for emerging economies entering international trade is learning how to keep promises to strangers, and whether enforced through litigation or arbitration, promise keeping in business requires the ordering presence of contract law.

In a democracy, law is important to business for another reason quite separate from its function in establishing ownership rights and facilitating promise keeping necessary to their transfer: it provides the formal expression of democratic social will. That expression implicates private enterprise in a plethora of ways, including regulation of the environment, employment laws, securities regulation, consumer protection statutes, and product liability. As contemporary society becomes increasingly diverse, law grows, not diminishes, in its importance to private enterprise, and in spite of valid concerns about the impact of law on efficiency, future business managers will need to know more, not less, about how law affects business operations. No evidence suggests any other conclusion.

Source: "The Importance of Law to the Private Enterprise System," Deb Ballam from the American Legal Studies in Business Task Force Report by O. Lee Reed. *American Business Law Journal* 36, no. 1 (Fall 1998), p. ix. Reprinted by permission.

Questions

1. *a.* Do you expect to see greater reliance on law as our society becomes increasingly complex?
   b. Can you think of any meaningful substitutes for law as we now practice it? Explain.
2. At this writing in 1999 Harvard Law School expects to introduce its first course in animal rights. The elective class is designed to discuss whether legal rights should be extended beyond humans. Scientific evidence indicates that some animals, especially chimps, have much higher intelligence than we had assumed. Other law schools already offer such courses. Does justice require that we consider legal rights for animals, or would animal rights further reduce our faith in the legal system? Explain.
3. States appoint and pay for public defenders to represent poor people charged with crimes. In Connecticut, each public defender is responsible for up to 1,000 clients annually. Nearly every state pays public defenders less than the $58 per hour needed, on

the average, to maintain a profitable law practice. The result is that public defenders cannot invest the necessary time in these cases and the defenders are often young and inexperienced.[5] Should we spend substantially more in public money to elevate the quality of repesentation accorded to indigent criminal defendants? Explain.

4. Sociologist Franz Schurmann says:

> No issue so suggests the existence of a dual justice system in America as the composition of its prison population. Those being fed into the prison system are overwhelmingly young, poor or dark skinned. They are the people without rights, who are, in effect, its modern, legal slaves.[6]

    a. In your opinion, is ours a dual justice system? Explain.

    b. Are the young, poor, and dark skinned of our prisons the equivalent of slaves? Explain.

5. Bernard McCummings was shot in the back and paralyzed from the waist down while he was robbing and beating a 72-year-old man in a subway station. McCummings was shot by a plainclothes police officer. McCummings pleaded guilty to robbery and served 32 months in prison. McCummings brought a civil action for his injuries. At trial, the officer testified that he shot when McCummings lunged at him. McCummings testified that he was running away when he was shot. Some corroborating evidence supported McCummings's testimony, and McCummings won a $4.3 million negligence judgment. New York's highest court upheld the jury's judgment for McCummings, saying the officer "did not exercise that degree of care which would reasonably be required of a police officer under similar circumstances."

    On the other hand, dissenting high court justice Bellacosa said the decision was an "inversion of justice." He went on to say, "The instant case approaches the surreal zone. It involves split-second decisions by public safety employees made in the most dangerous and volatile circumstances."

    In your judgment, was justice achieved in this case? Explain. See *McCummings* v. *New York City Transit Authority,* 619 N.E. 2d 664 (NY 1993); cert. den. *New York City Transit Authority* v. *McCummings,* 62 *Law Week* 3375 (1993).

Part One—Legal Foundations

OBJECTIVES OF THE LAW

Law is shaped by social forces. Values, history, ideas, and goals all help shape a society's legal system. The diverse character of American society leads inevitably to differences of opinion regarding the proper direction for our legal system. However, some broad goals can be identified.

1. Maintain Order.   The law is instrumental in imposing necessary structure on America's diverse and rapidly changing society. With stop signs, zoning ordinances, marriage licenses, homicide statutes, and the like, the legal system seeks to prevent harm by enforcing established codes of conduct. Immediate self-interest is often muted in favor of long-term general welfare. The problem then becomes one of how far to go in seeking to preserve a valuable but potentially oppressive commodity. Should the law require all motorcyclists to wear helmets? Or all businesses to close on Sunday?

2. Resolve Conflict.   Because society cannot and would not wish to impose rules on all dimensions of human conduct, a system for solving differences is required. An effort is made to substitute enlightened dispute resolution for the barbarism that might otherwise attend inevitable differences of opinion. With the law of contracts, for example, we have developed a sophisticated, generally accepted, and largely successful system for both imposing order and resolving conflict.

Consider the 1998 case of 10-year-old Samantha Frazer, who sought to divorce her mother. Samantha said her mother did not care for her or love her. From age 6 to 10, Samantha's mother, troubled by drug problems, had allegedly abandoned her daughter and Samantha had moved through four foster homes. Delaware's state Division of Family Services asked for termination of Samantha's mother's parental rights. A judge denied that request and Samantha asked the state Supreme Court to accord her legal *standing* (explained later in the chapter) to appeal that decision on her own behalf instead of leaving that authority to Family Services case workers or other state appointees. In a striking ruling, the Supreme Court granted Samantha's request, but in an equally striking development, Samantha decided that she wanted to move back with her mother.[7] Samantha's victory is one of a very small number of cases where children have been accorded the authority, the standing, to go to court on their own behalf. The decision is a good example of our legal system struggling to maintain order and resolve new varieties of conflicts born of stunning societal change. Should children be able to bring lawsuits on their own? Will this decision lead to frivolous claims by other children?

3. Preserve Dominant Values.   Americans have reached general accord regarding many values and beliefs, and the law has been put to work in preserving those standards. For example, in the Bill of Rights we have set out those fundamental freedoms that must be protected to preserve the character of the nation. Of course, in many instances societal opinion is divided. What happens when no clear consensus emerges about an issue? What if the issue involves a conflict between two cherished values? Freedom of speech is central to a meaningful life, but what if that speech consists of anti-Semitic parades and demonstrations organized by the Ku Klux Klan?

4. Guarantee Freedom.   That Americans are free and wish to remain so is the nation's most revered social value. It is, in a sense, a subset of the third goal in this list, but because of its preeminence, it properly stands alone. The problem, of course, is that freedom must be limited. Drawing the line often gives rise to severe societal conflict.

In general, you are free to do as you like so long as you do not violate the rights of others. But what are those rights? Do I have a right to smoke-free air, or do you have a right to smoke wherever you wish? Even if the rights of others are not directly violated, personal freedom is limited. The so-called victimless crimes—vagrancy, gambling, pornography, prostitution—are examples of instances where the law retards freedom in the absence of immediate injury to the rights of others. Should each citizen be free to do as he or she likes so long as harm does not befall others? Or does pornography, for example, inevitably give rise to societal harm?

5. Preserve Justice.   In sum, justice, as we have noted, is the goal of the American legal system. Professor Franz Schurmann traces a bit of the evolution of the notion of justice.

> Since ancient times, great sprawling empires with many diverse peoples were held together not only by armies but by common systems of justice. The first such system was that of the Babylonian ruler Hammurabi at the end of the third millennium B.C. While most Americans would view his rigid "eye for an eye and tooth for a tooth" with horror, in his time it represented a great step forward for humankind. It announced that Babylon would treat all its subjects according to the same system of justice.

*   *   *   *   *

> Rome, as a republic and then an empire, inspired America's founding fathers. Rome's grandeur lasted a millennium. If the "great American experiment" is to last well into the next century, history indicates that, besides strength, it will need justice—the guarantee that every member of the polity will be treated fairly and equitably.

*   *   *   *   *

> Roman law took a long time evolving but reached its fullest development when Rome became a great empire ruling over a vast human diversity. After it started freeing its slaves, its core practical principle became encapsulated in the phrase *suum cuique,* "to each his own," meaning that everyone has a legitimate place in the realm and a right to expect fair and equal treatment from the state.[8]

More than any other, the issue of justice should be at the forefront of all legal studies. The *Graff* case that follows depicts the legal system struggling to determine where justice lies. That is, even if the system is fair, some questions are so difficult that justice, at least in the sense of finding the truth, may remain elusive. [For help with legal research on the Internet, see **http://www.virtualchase.com**]

The Case Law: Locating and Analyzing

To prepare for *Graff,* the first law case in this text, a bit of practical guidance may be useful. The study of law is founded largely on the analysis of judicial opinion. Except for the federal level and a few states, trial court decisions are filed locally for public inspection rather than being published. Appellate opinions, on the other hand, are generally published in volumes called *reports.* State court opinions are found in the reports of that state, as well as a regional reporter published by West Publishing Company that divides the United States into units, such as South Eastern (S.E.) and Pacific (P.).

Within the appropriate reporter, the cases are arranged in a workable fashion and are *cited* by case name, volume, reporter name, and page number. For example, *Royce Graff, Debra Graff, Bobby Hausmon and Betty Hausmon* v. *Brett Beard and Dorothy Beard,*

858 S.W.2d 918 (Texas S.Ct. 1993) means that the opinion will be found in volume 858 of the South Western Reporter, 2d series, at page 918 and that the decision was reached in 1993 by the Texas Supreme Court. Federal court decisions are found in several reporters, including the *Federal Reporter* and the *United States Supreme Court Reports*. [For a broad database of law topics, see **http://www.findlaw.com** or see **http://www.yahoo.com/law**]

Briefing the Case

Most law students find the preparation of *case briefs* (outlines or digests) to be helpful in mastering the complexities of the law. A brief should evolve into the form that best suits the individual student's needs. The following approach should be a useful starting point.

1. Parties   Identify the plaintiff and the defendant.
2. Facts   Summarize only those facts critical to the outcome of the case.
3. Procedure   Who brought the appeal? What was the outcome in the lower court(s)?
4. Issue   Note the central question or questions on which the case turns.
5. Holding   How did the Court resolve the issues? Who won?
6. Reasoning   Explain the logic that supported the Court's decision.

ROYCE GRAFF, DEBRA GRAFF, BOBBY HAUSMON AND BETTY HAUSMON v. BRETT BEARD AND DOROTHY BEARD
858 S.W.2d 918 (Texas S.Ct. 1993)

Justice John Cornyn

We are asked in this case to impose a common-law duty on a social host who makes alcohol available to an intoxicated adult guest who the host knows will be driving . . .

Houston Moos consumed alcohol at a party hosted by the Graffs and Hausmons, and allegedly left in his vehicle in an intoxicated condition. En route from the party, Moos collided with a motorcycle, injuring Brett Beard. Beard sued both Moos and his hosts for his injuries. The trial court ultimately dismissed Beard's claims against the hosts for failure to state a cause of action. An en banc divided court of appeals reversed the trial court's judgment and remanded the case, holding for the first time in Texas jurisprudence that social hosts may be liable to third parties for the acts of their intoxicated adult guests.

Under the court of appeals's standard, a social host violates a legal duty to third parties when the host makes an alcoholic beverage available to an adult guest who the host knows is intoxicated and will be driving. In practical effect, this duty is twofold. The first aspect of the host's duty is to prevent guests who will be driving from becoming intoxicated. If the host fails to do so, however, a second aspect of the duty comes into play—the host must prevent the intoxicated guest from driving.

The legislatures in most states, including Texas, have enacted dram shop laws that impose a statutory duty to third parties on commercial providers under specified circumstances. We have recently held that when the legislature enacted the Texas dram shop statute it also imposed a duty on the provider that extends to the patron himself. Because the dram shop statute applies only to commercial providers, however, it does not govern the duty asserted in this case.

We think it significant in appraising Beard's request to recognize common-law social host liability that the legislature has considered and declined to create such a duty. A version of the bill that eventually became our dram shop statute provided for social host liability. Although that version passed the Senate, the House rejected it. The Senate-House conference committee deleted social host liability from the bill the legislature eventually enacted.

The highest courts in only four states have done what we are asked to do today: judicially impose a duty to third parties on social hosts who make alcohol available to adult guests. In two of these states, California and Iowa, the legislatures subsequently abrogated the judicially created duty. Neither of the two remaining jurisdictions, Massachusetts and New Jersey, had dram shop statutes when their courts acted. Rather, their courts first imposed a common-law duty to third parties on commercial establishments and then extended the duty to social hosts.

*   *   *   *   *

Deciding whether to impose a new common-law duty involves complex considerations of public policy. We have said that these considerations include "'social, economic, and political questions,' and their application to the particular facts at hand." Among other factors, we consider the extent of the risk involved, "the foreseeability and likelihood of injury weighed against the social utility of the actor's conduct, the magnitude of the burden of guarding against the injury, and the consequences of placing the burden on the defendant." We have also emphasized other factors. For example, questions of duty have turned on whether one party has superior knowledge of the risk, and whether a right to control the actor whose conduct precipitated the harm exists.

Following our decisions in *Seagrams* and *Otis Engineering Corp.,* we deem it appropriate to focus on two tacit assumptions underlying the holding of the court of appeals: that the social host can reasonably know of the guest's alcohol consumption and possible intoxication, and possesses the right to control the conduct of the guest. Under Texas law, in the absence of a relationship between the parties giving rise to the right of control, one person is under no legal duty to control the conduct of another, even if there exists the practical ability to do so.

*   *   *   *   *

Instead of focusing on the host's right of control over the guest, the court of appeals conditioned a social host's duty on the host's "exclusive control" of the alcohol supply. The court defined "exclusive control," however, as nothing more than a degree of control "greater than that of the guest user." Under the court's definition, at a barbecue, a wedding reception, a backyard picnic, a pachanga, a Bar Mitzvah—or a variety of other common social settings—the host would always have exclusive control over the alcohol supply because the host chooses whether alcohol will be provided and the manner in which it will be provided. The duty imposed by the court of appeals would apparently attach in any social setting in which alcohol is available regardless of the host's right to control the guest. Thus, as a practical matter, the host has but one choice—whether to make alcohol available to guests at all.

But should the host venture to make alcohol available to adult guests, the court of appeals's standard would allow the host to avoid liability by cutting off the guest's access to alcohol at some point before the guest becomes intoxicated. Implicit in that standard is the assumption that the reasonably careful host can accurately determine how much alcohol guests have consumed and when they have approached their limit. We believe, though, that it is far from clear that a social host can reliably recognize a guest's level of intoxication. First, it is unlikely that a host can be expected to know how much alcohol, if any, a guest has consumed before the guest arrives on the host's premises. Second, in many social settings, the total number of guests present may practically inhibit the host from discovering a guest's approaching intoxication. Third, the condition may be apparent in some people but certainly not in all . . .

*   *   *   *   *

This brings us to the second aspect of the duty implicit in the court of appeals's standard: that should the guest become intoxicated, the host must prevent the guest from driving. Unlike the court of appeals, however, we cannot assume that guests will respond to a host's attempts, verbal or physical, to prevent the guests from driving. Nor is it clear to us precisely what affirmative actions would discharge the host's duty under the court of appeals's standard. Would a simple request not to drive suffice? Or is more required? Is the host required to physically restrain the guests, take their car keys, or disable their vehicles? The problems inherent in this aspect of the court of appeals' holding are obvious.

*   *   *   *   *

Ideally, guests will drink responsibly, and hosts will monitor their social functions to reduce the likelihood of intoxication. Once a guest becomes impaired by alcohol to the point at which he becomes a threat to himself and others, we would hope that the host can persuade the guest to take public transportation, stay on the premises, or be transported home by an unimpaired driver. But we know that too often reality conflicts with ideal behavior. And, given the ultimate power of guests to control their own alcohol consumption and the absence of any legal right of the host to control the guest, we find the arguments for shifting legal responsibility from the guest to the host, who merely makes alcohol available at social gatherings, unconvincing. As the common law has long recognized, the imbiber maintains the ultimate power and thus the obligation to control his own behavior: to decide to drink or not to drink, to drive or not to drive. We therefore conclude that the common law's focus should remain on the drinker as the person primarily responsible for his own behavior and best able to avoid the foreseeable risks of that behavior.

We accordingly reverse the judgment of the court of appeals and render judgment that Beard take nothing.

Dissenting Opinion—Justice Gammage joined by Justice Doggett

I respectfully dissent. The majority errs in holding that the legislature must "create" the duty for social hosts not to send intoxicated guests driving in our streets to maim and kill. Logic, legal experience and this court's own earlier decisions dictate a contrary result. The legislature may enact a statute that creates a duty. But the legislature's failure to act does not "un-create" an existing duty. A duty created by the common law continues to exist unless and until the legislature changes it, and such an existing common law duty applies to the defendants here.

The majority confuses issues of proof with issues of whether to recognize the tort duty. The majority is concerned that the social host might not be able to persuade or control his intoxicated guest to keep him or her from driving. The host, however, clearly does control whether alcohol is being served, and in what quantities and form. The answer to the "duty" question is that the host should not let the driving guest have the alcohol in intoxicating quantities. If the guest becomes inebriated, however, just as with any other dangerous situation one helps create, the host has the duty to make every reasonable effort to keep the dangerously intoxicated guest from driving. If

the guest resists those efforts, then there is a question for the factfinder to resolve whether the host's efforts were all that reasonably could be done under the circumstances.

The majority expresses concern that "the reasonably careful host" may not be able to detect when some guests are intoxicated. If that is so, then the factfinder should have no difficulty determining that the host did not serve them while they were "obviously intoxicated." The majority further asserts, without citation to authority, that the "guest . . . is in a far better position to know the amount of alcohol he has consumed" than the host.

This assertion defies common sense, because from personal observation we know that most persons, as they become intoxicated, along with losing their dexterity and responsive mental faculties, gradually become less and less cognizant of how much they've had and how badly intoxicated they are. Even if the host is also intoxicated, as a third party viewing the guest, the host is probably in a better position to evaluate the guest's intoxication. Intoxicated guests need someone to tell them not to drive . . .

If circumstances do not permit the social host to adequately monitor and control the quantity of alcoholic beverages a guest consumes, the host still retains absolute control over whether alcoholic beverages should be served at all . . .

* * * * *

. . . All culpable parties should be liable—the social host who knowingly intoxicated the guest and the guest who drunkenly caused the accident. I am persuaded that both should be liable to the extent of their responsibility for the accident. The television commercial says, "Friends don't let friends drive drunk." That is sound public policy. But today the majority says, "Intoxicate your friends and send them out upon the public streets and highways to drive drunk. Don't worry; you won't be liable." That is, in the kindest term I can muster, unsound policy.

Questions

1. Who won this case and why?
2. What do the dissenting justices mean by saying "the majority confuses issues of proof with issues of whether to recognize the tort duty"?
3. In your judgment, does the Texas Supreme Court decision represent a just result? Explain.

[For the National Center for State Courts, see **http://www.ncsc.dni.us/**]

CLASSIFICATIONS OF LAW

Some elementary distinctions will make the role of law clearer.

Substantive and Procedural Law.   *Substantive laws* create, define, and regulate legal rights and obligations. Thus, for example, the Sherman Act forbids restraints of trade. By judicial interpretation, price-fixing between competitors is a restraint of trade.

Procedural law embraces the systems and methods available to enforce the rights specified in the substantive law. So, procedural law includes the judicial system and the rules by which it operates. Questions of where to hear a case, what evidence to admit, and which decisions can be appealed fall within the procedural domain.

Law by Judicial Decision and Law by Enactment.   In general, American rules of law are promulgated by court decisions (*case law*) or via enactments by constitutional assemblies, legislatures, administrative agencies, chief executives, and local government authorities. Enactments include constitutions, statutes, treaties, administrative rules, executive orders, and local ordinances.

Case Law (Judicial Decisions).   Our case law has its roots in the early English king's courts, where rules of law gradually developed out of a series of individual dispute resolutions. That body of law was imported to America and is known as the *common law.* (This term may be confusing because it is frequently used to designate not just the law imported from England of old but also all judge-made or case law.)

The development of English common law rules and American judicial decisions into a just, ordered package is attributable in large measure to reliance on the doctrine of *stare decisis* (let the decision stand). That is, judges endeavor to follow the precedents established by previous decisions. Following precedent, however, is not mandatory.

As societal beliefs change, so does the law. For example, a Supreme Court decision approving racially separate but equal education was eventually overruled by a Supreme Court decision mandating integrated schools. However, the principle of stare decisis is generally adhered to because of its beneficial effect. It offers the wisdom of the past and enhances efficiency by eliminating the need for resolving every case as though it were the first of its kind. Stare decisis affords stability and predictability to the law. It promotes justice by, for example, reducing "judge-shopping" and neutralizing judges' personal prejudices.

Statutes (Enactments).   Here our primary concern is with the laws that have been adopted by the many legislative bodies—Congress, the state legislatures, city councils, and the like. These enactments are labeled *statutory law.* Some areas of law, such as torts, continue to be governed primarily by common law rules, but the direction of American law lies largely in the hands of legislators. Of course, legislators are not free of constraints. Federal legislation cannot conflict with the U.S. Constitution, and state legislation cannot violate either federal law or the constitutions of that state and the nation.

Law and Equity.   Following the Norman conquest of England in 1066, a system of king's courts was established in which the king's representatives settled disputes. Those representatives were empowered to provide remedies of land, money, or personal property. The king's courts became known as *courts of law,* and the remedies were labeled *remedies of law.* Some litigants, however, sought compensation other than the three provided. They took their pleas to the king.

Typically, the chancellor, an aide to the king, would hear these petitions and, guided by the standard of fairness, could grant a remedy (such as an injunction or specific performance) specifically appropriate to the case. The chancellors' decisions accumulated over time such that a new body of remedies—and with it a new court system, known as *courts of equity*—evolved. Both court systems were adopted in the United States following the American Revolution, but today actions at law and equity are typically heard in the same court.

Public Law and Private Law.   *Public law* deals with the relationship between government and the citizens. Constitutional, criminal, and administrative law (relating to such bodies as the Federal Trade Commission) fall in the public law category. *Private law* regulates the legal relationship between individuals. Contracts, agency, and commercial paper are traditional business law topics in the private category.

Civil Law and Criminal Law.   The legislature or other lawmaking body normally specifies that new legislation is either *civil* or *criminal* or both. Broadly, all legislation not specifically labeled criminal law falls in the civil law category. *Civil law* addresses the legal rights and duties arising among individuals, organizations such as corporations, and governments. Thus, for example, a person might sue a company raising a civil law claim of breach of contract. The *criminal law,* on the other hand, involves wrongs against the general welfare as formulated in specific criminal statutes. Murder and theft are, of course, criminal wrongs because society has forbidden those acts in specific legislative enactments. Hence, wearing one's hat backwards would be a crime if such a statute were enacted and if that statute met constitutional requirements.

Crimes.   Crimes are of three kinds. In general, *felonies* are more serious crimes, such as murder, rape, and robbery. They are typically punishable by death or by imprisonment in a federal or state penitentiary for more than one year. In general, *misdemeanors* are less serious crimes, such as petty theft, disorderly conduct, and traffic offenses. They are typically punishable by fine or by imprisonment for no more than one year. *Treason* is the special situation in which one levies war against the United States or gives aid and comfort to its enemies.

Elements of a Crime.   In a broad sense, crimes consist of two elements: (1) a wrongful act or omission (*actus reus*) and (2) evil intent (*mens rea*). Thus, an individual who pockets a ball-point pen and leaves the store without paying for it may be charged with petty theft. The accused may defend, however, by arguing that he or she merely absentmindedly and unintentionally slipped the pen in a pocket after picking it off the shelf to consider its merits. Intent is a state of mind, so the jury or judge must reach a determination from the objective facts as to what the accused's state of mind must have been.

Criminal Procedure.   In general, criminal procedure is structured as follows: For more complex, arguably more serious, crimes the process begins with the prosecuting officials bringing their charges before a grand jury or magistrate to determine whether the charges have sufficient merit to justify a trial. If so, an *indictment* or *information* is issued, charging the accused with specific crimes. (Grand juries issue indictments; magistrates issue informations.) In those instances where action by a grand jury or magistrate is not required, cases are initiated by the issuance of a warrant by a judge, based on a showing of probable cause that the individual has committed or will commit a crime. Where necessity demands, arrests may be made without a warrant, but the legality of the arrest will be tested by probable cause standards.

After indictment or arrest, the individual is brought before the court for arraignment, where the charges are read and a plea is entered. If the individual pleads not guilty, he or she will go to trial, where guilt must be established *beyond a reasonable doubt.* (In a civil trial, the plaintiff must meet the lesser standard of *a preponderance of the evidence.*) In a criminal trial, the burden of proof is on the state. The defendant is, of course, presumed innocent. He or she is entitled to a jury trial but many choose to have the case decided by the judge alone. If found guilty, the defendant can, among other possibilities, seek a new trial or appeal errors in the prosecution. If found innocent, the defendant may, if necessary, invoke the doctrine of *double jeopardy* under which a person cannot be prosecuted twice in the same tribunal for the same criminal offense. [For an extensive criminal justice database, see **http://www.ncjrs.org**]

Put Them in Jail?

America's prison and jail population in 2000 reached 2.0 million, a lamentable landmark, to be sure.[9] The incarceration rate in the United States is second only to Russia and is 6 to 10 times that of other industrial nations.[10] Nearly one in every 150 Americans is in jail or prison.[11] Paradoxically, the United States crime rate has been falling since 1994. The reason, then, for the increased numbers behind bars is primarily the trend in the 1990s of "getting tough on crime," which has kept inmates behind bars for longer periods of time than in the past.[12] The bill for sustaining each inmate averages about $20,000 annually, not including the expense of building jails and prisons.[13] While housing all of those prisoners is a very expensive proposition, studies show that keeping the bad guys off the streets can make sense in that an estimated 7 percent of the criminals are responsible for perhaps two-thirds of all violent crime.[14] And according to United States Bureau of Justice statistics, 52 percent of the increase in the male prison population from 1990 to 1997 consisted of those violent offenders.[15] Of course, drug crimes, particularly at the state level, have played a big role in the increase in prisoners.[16]

Juveniles.   We now routinely imprison children in the same manner as adults. As a society we have become so terrified by crime and so frustrated with our inability to deal with it that we have begun treating violent juvenile criminals as adults. The article that follows details one such case and raises some of the competing considerations in deciding whether children who have committed terrible crimes should spend much or all of a lifetime behind bars.

PAYING AN ADULT PRICE FOR CRIME

Stephanie Simon

MILWAUKEE—Her head is down. Her fingers are worrying a hole in the Formica tabletop.

She talks mainly in sullen monotones: Yes. No. Dunno. But this one thing, La'Tasha Armstead will say. It seems to seep out of her and fill the tiny interview room with confused despair.

"I feel scared," she says.

Her fingers pick, pick. Her head sags lower.

La'Tasha, 15, is headed to prison today, to serve a life term. For a murder she committed when she was 13. She was tried as an adult. She was sentenced as an adult. She is one of the youngest homicide suspects ever seen in U.S. criminal courts.

Should we care?

Her crime was gruesome. She and her 17-year-old boyfriend, James, wanted a car, a red Chevrolet Cavalier. So they plotted to kill the middle-aged nurse who owned it.

They persuaded the nurse, Charlotte Brown, a mother of five who was caring for La'Tasha's disabled grandma, to take the two of them for a ride. La'Tasha, in the front seat, dropped a Walkman to distract Brown. Then James, in the back, wrapped a telephone cord around Brown's neck. At the end, La'Tasha slashed at the nurse's throat with a steak knife, cutting superficial wounds. La'Tasha then drove to a vacant lot—James was shaking too much to steer—and together they dumped the body.

James was sentenced to life in prison. He'll be eligible for parole in 101 years.

And La'Tasha? How much time should she serve?

Would the answer be the same if she were 20? If she were 10?

La'Tasha will find out today in court when, if ever, she'll be eligible for parole. By law, the earliest would be 2010. Or she may never get out.

A decade ago, La'Tasha surely would have been tried as a juvenile. A judge, not a jury, would have heard her case. She would have served her time in a juvenile facility emphasizing education and counseling. And she would have gone free when she turned 18, or maybe 21.

But America has grown wary of juvenile courts.

And so tens of thousands of adolescents—not old enough to vote, not old enough to drink, but old enough to commit heinous crimes—land in the adult court system each year. Most aren't killers. They're drug dealers and burglars, armed assailants and thugs. Many have long rap sheets. They're 14, 15, even 11 or 12.

So many kids are in the adult penal system—as the country marks the 100th anniversary of the first juvenile court—criminologist Freda Adler of Rutgers University calls it "one of the most important issues we'll face in the new millennium."

La'Tasha isn't really sure if she's a kid or a grown-up. "A kid," she says, not convincingly.

She is 15 now, having spent the past two years in juvenile detention while her attorneys fought in vain to move her out of adult court. Even at 13, however, she had experienced more than many grown-ups. As her grandma, Emily Armstead, put it: "She didn't have a Norman Rockwell–type background."

By age 13, La'Tasha had been raped by several neighborhood boys. She had at least one miscarriage. She had tried, painfully and with ferocious love, to get her drug-addled mom to go straight. Since her father was in prison for killing one of her 10 half-siblings, La'Tasha raised her little sister. She also washed her disabled grandma's swollen legs, even carried her to the bathroom.

But all that responsibility shoved her way couldn't change the calendar. She bore adult burdens. Yet she was still 13.

She was pregnant again at age 13—her son was born in juvenile detention. She didn't know how to put on a bra.

She liked to lick sugary Kool-Aid mix. She called her mother "Mommy-Pie." She jumped rope. But she also helped plan a murder.

When she was on trial, La'Tasha had firm ideas about her own defense, just like an adult. These were her suggestions: Her lawyers should stop questioning the witnesses, lest they annoy the judge. She should wear ripped jeans to court, because there was no rule saying she had to dress up. And during the pivotal cross-examination of her boyfriend, her lawyers should ask the following questions: Do you still love La'Tasha? Do you still think she's pretty? Are you sleeping with anyone else?

Defense attorney Robin Shellow, who has built an impassioned career helping juveniles, points to La'Tasha's proposed defense strategy as proof kids do not belong in adult court.

On one level, La'Tasha surely could follow basic trial proceedings—although she did ask, on the eve of her testimony, "What does the jury do again?" But on a more fundamental level, Shellow contends, teens can't process the gravity and complexity of a criminal court case.

To be sure, many adult offenders are equally unsuited to aid their defense. And, as proponents of tougher sentencing point out, kids who plot a crime can't be dismissed as tender innocents.

Still, some researchers believe children do not have the cognitive abilities to navigate the adult penal system.

In juvenile court, social workers are on hand to help young defendants. And lawyers on both sides—as well as the judge—are used to deciphering kidspeak. Plus, since the stakes are much lower, everyone involved is more likely to cooperate in figuring out what's best for the child. Adult court tends to be rushed and adversarial. Offenders constantly must weigh pros and cons of various actions, from accepting a plea bargain to testifying in their own defense.

Most kids under 13 can't perform such tricky mental reckoning, according to psychologist Laurence Steinberg, who has been studying such issues for the MacArthur Foundation Research Network. Kids over 16, however, do about as well as the average adult.

It's the 13- to 16-year-olds that are hardest to peg; their skills vary by education, temperament and maturity. "We're trying to understand where to draw the line between childhood and adulthood," Steinberg said. "We really don't know."

Under Wisconsin law, any child at least 10 years old goes to adult court automatically if charged with first-degree intentional homicide.

"They obviously understand enough to commit the crime," reasons state Rep. Bonnie Ladwig, who helped write the law. Adult processing, she said, is therefore appropriate. "Much better than giving a slap on the wrist and putting (the offender) back on the street."

Legislators around the nation agree.

Over the past decade, nearly every state passed laws directing more—and younger—juveniles into adult court.

In Wisconsin, young defendants in adult court receive a hearing at which a judge weighs their prior record, maturity and potential for rehabilitation, among other criteria. La'Tasha received such an evaluation when she appealed to be transferred to juvenile court. But judge after judge rebuffed her, all the way to the Wisconsin Supreme Court.

And that, prosecutor Mark Williams argues, was as it should be.

"This case was so horrific," Williams said, "that anything less than what we did I think would diminish the severity of the offense."

Williams says La'Tasha should be in adult court because she masterminded a crime so awful she poses a threat to society—a threat a few years in a juvenile facility would not defuse.

La'Tasha may go to the Taychedah Correctional Facility, the women's prison in Fond du Lac, this afternoon. Or she may first spend a few years behind bars in a prison for serious juvenile offenders. The timing is up to corrections officials.

La'Tasha, in any case, is terrified.

She heard girls get raped at Taychedah. She worries she won't get a daily phone call. She wonders what she'll do all day in her cell. In juvenile detention she goes to school, plays cards, watches movies. She doubts they'll let her study music at Taychedah. She doubts they'll show "The Nutty Professor."

Source: *Los Angeles Times,* August 6, 1999, p. A1. Reprinted by permission.

Afterword

A Wisconsin Circuit Court judge subsequently ruled that La'Tasha would be eligible for parole in 15 years—at age 30.

Questions—Part One

1. *a.* Would you treat La'Tasha as an adult for criminal justice purposes?
    b. In your judgment, does the threat of adult punishment serve as a deterrent to youthful crime? Explain.
2. Iowa, a state particularly troubled by methamphetamine abuse, imposed a new criminal penalty in 1999 providing that sales of meth to minors or producing the drug with that intent would lead to a 99-year prison term, and a second offense would bring life without parole. What concerns would you raise about that stern new law?
3. In 1999, Denmark legalized prostitution.
    a. Should the United States do the same?
    b. Should we remove criminal penalties from all of the so-called victimless crimes including vagrancy, pornography, and gambling? Should we regulate those practices in any way? Explain.
4. *The Wall Street Journal* commenting on the criminal justice system in Japan:

    > [D]espite its image of dealing tough justice, Japan's legal system is surprisingly lenient, geared toward reinstating most suspects into the cultural mainstream. Many who are arrested for minor crimes are let off the hook before indictment if they show remorse, legal experts say. And those who are indicted tend to get much lighter sentences if they confess, show remorse, compensate victims, and demonstrate that they have a strong family to return to.
    >
    > That gives a big incentive for an indicted suspect to cooperate with prosecutors and use the trial as a stage for shows of contrition. That may explain why 60% of those convicted and sentenced to prison terms last year had their sentences suspended.[17]

    Should American judges and prosecutors adopt the lenient Japanese response to crime? Explain.
5. What steps would you advocate to reduce crime in America?
6. A Rhode Island man pleaded guilty to child molestation. As an alternative to imprisonment and as a condition of his probation, the judge ordered him to purchase a newspaper ad displaying his picture, identifying himself as a sex offender, and encouraging others to seek assistance. A number of courts across the country have required apologies or other forms of humiliation in criminal cases.
    a. What objections would a defendant's lawyer raise to that method of punishment?
    b. Would you impose a "humiliation sentence" were you the judge in a case like that in Rhode Island? Explain.

Part Two—The Judicial Process

Most disputes are settled without resort to litigation, but when agreement cannot be reached, we can turn to the courts—a highly technical and sophisticated dispute resolution mechanism.

STATE COURT SYSTEMS

While state court systems vary substantially, a general pattern can be summarized. As shown in Figure 4.1, at the base of the court pyramid in most states is a *trial court of general jurisdiction,* commonly labeled a *district court* or a *superior court.* It is here that most trials—both civil and criminal—arising out of state law would be heard, but certain classes of cases are reserved to courts of limited subject matter jurisdiction or to various state administrative agencies (such as the state public utilities commission and the workers' compensation board). Family, small claims, juvenile, and traffic courts are examples of trial courts with limited jurisdiction. At the top of the judicial pyramid in all states is a court of appeals, ordinarily labeled the *supreme court.* A number of states also provide for an intermediate court of appeals located in the hierarchy between the trial courts and the highest appeals court.

FIGURE 4.1   State and Federal Court Systems

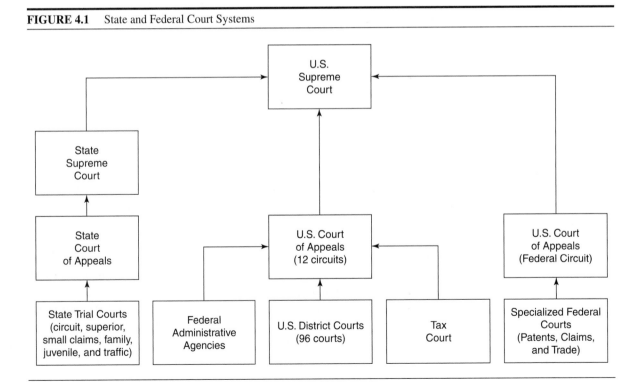

FEDERAL COURT SYSTEM

District Courts

The district courts provide the foundation of the federal judicial system. The Constitution provides for a Supreme Court and such inferior courts as Congress shall authorize. Pursuant to that authority, Congress has established at least one district court for each state and territory. These are trial courts where witnesses are heard and questions of law and fact are resolved. More populous areas with heavier case loads have additional district courts. As circumstances demand, Congress adds courts at the district level. Most federal cases begin in the district courts or in a federal administrative agency (such as the Federal Communications Commission). Congress has also provided for several courts of limited jurisdiction, including a Tax Court and a U.S. Claims Court.

[For access to all federal court websites, see the Federal Judicial Center at **http://www.fjc.gov/**]

Court of Appeals

Congress has divided the United States geographically into 11 judicial circuits and the District of Columbia and has established a court of appeals for each. Those courts hear appeals from the district courts within their circuit and review decisions and enforce orders of the various federal administrative agencies.

In 1982, Congress created the U.S. Court of Appeals for the Federal Circuit. That court hears, among others, all patent appeals and all appeals from the U.S. Claims Court (monetary claims against the United States).

Some judges and scholars argue that our appeals process is now so overburdened that we have, in effect, a two-level justice system where routine cases such as individual disability claims get brief attention and only complex cases of broader significance such as civil rights claims and antitrust problems are accorded full and careful review. As Professor Thomas Baker expressed it, "[A]ppeals today are processed in a kind of assembly line and the judges are not paying enough attention to individual cases, because they can't."[18]

Supreme Court

The Supreme Court consists of nine justices appointed for life by the president and confirmed by the Senate. In limited instances, the Supreme Court serves as an original or trial court. However, almost all of the Supreme Court's work consists of reviewing lower court decisions, principally from the courts of appeal and from state high courts. Virtually all parties seeking Supreme Court review must petition the Court for a *writ of certiorari,* which commands the lower court to forward the trial records to the Court.

Decisions regarding those petitions are entirely discretionary with the Court. Typically it will hear those cases that will assist in resolving conflicting courts of appeal decisions, as well as those that raise questions of special significance about the Constitution or the national welfare. However, as the following analysis by *USA Today* reveals, the current Supreme Court is hearing only a limited number of cases as it moves sharply away from the judicial activism that has often marked the Court's philosophy in the modern era.

COURT'S INACTION ALLOWS CONFUSION

Tony Mauro

WASHINGTON—At the Supreme Court, silence speaks volumes. With increasing frequency and impact, the nation's highest court is steering clear of many of the nation's hottest controversies.

School vouchers. Campaign financing. Affirmative action. Gay rights. The right to bear arms. Partial-birth abortion. The legal landscape is strewn with issues in which parties have gone to the Supreme Court in hopes of a final word, only to have the court decline to hear their appeals.

A *USA Today* study of the court's docket finds that the current justices, in exercising their nearly unique power to refuse to consider cases put before them, are making fundamental changes in the court's role in American life.

"More than any court in the nation's history, this Supreme Court has decided it isn't our rabbi or priest; it isn't the place to go for answers to every question," says University of Chicago law professor Cass Sunstein.

Not only is the court issuing fewer signed opinions— 93 last term, compared with 170 in 1981—but as the number of cases brought before the court has grown, the chances that the court will pluck out any one case for review has plummeted.

Petitions today are five times more likely to be denied review by the Supreme Court than they were 20 years ago . . .

As a result, critics say, the Supreme Court is risking one of its core functions as the nation's highest court: bringing a measure of consistency to the law, so that legal rules on issues ranging from affirmative action to parochial school aid are the same nationwide.

* * * * *

The court's trend runs the gamut of the issues. A *USA Today* analysis of the cases filed between July 1,

1996, and July 1, 1998, finds that on subjects ranging from housing to trademarks, agriculture to nuclear energy, the court rejects 95% or more of the cases brought before it.

Why the Court's Stepping Back

Many factors are behind the silence at the Supreme Court.

The current court is keen on stepping back from the limelight to let the elected branches of government settle hot debates. "It's better to let the people decide," Justice Antonin Scalia has said more than once.

* * * * *

University of Chicago's Sunstein approves of the court's new view of itself, but adds, "I can understand the frustration of some people who think that the law is a mess."

"The court today is not a liberal or a conservative court, it is a court court, deciding narrowly, not broadly. They know that sometimes they don't know how to settle things, and that other institutions ought to settle them instead," says Sunstein. "There are a lot of virtues in a minimalist court."

Scalia, intellectual leader of the court's conservative wing, was asked after a speech two years ago why the court did not decide hot issues more definitively. "My colleagues and I don't know what John Q. Public thinks," he replied. On issues such as abortion or the right to die, he added, "Why would you leave that to nine lawyers, for heaven's sake?"

* * * * *

Source: *USA Today,* December 23, 1998, p. 1A. Reprinted by permission.

Questions

1. Must the Supreme Court resolve burning social issues such as abortion or the right to die, or are we best to leave those issues to other institutions and the market to resolve slowly over time? Explain.
2. If an issue such as affirmative action is not directly addressed by the Supreme Court, will it, nonetheless, find resolution over time? Explain.

Here are some Associated Press picks of "unusual or significant" laws going into effect in the summer of 1999:

- Louisiana requires students in kindergarten through fifth grades to address teachers with courtesy titles such as "sir" or "ma'am."
- Tennessee and Indiana require parental consent for body piercing of young people.
- Vermont allows needle exchange programs for the first time.
- South Carolina legalizes interracial marriages.

Source: *Waterloo–Cedar Falls Courier,* June 30, 1999, p. A1.

JURISDICTION

A plaintiff may not simply proceed to trial at the court of his or her preference. The plaintiff must go to a court with *jurisdiction*—that is, a court with the necessary power and authority to hear the dispute. The court must have jurisdiction over both the subject matter and the persons (or, in some instances, the property) involved in the case.

Subject-Matter Jurisdiction

Subject-matter jurisdiction imposes bounds on the classes of cases a court may hear. The legislation or constitution creating the court will normally specify that court's jurisdictional authority. For example, state courts of general jurisdiction may hear most types of cases, but a criminal court or probate court is limited in the subject matter it may hear.

The outer bounds of federal jurisdiction are specified in the Constitution, while Congress has further particularized that issue by statute. Essentially, the federal district courts may hear two types of cases: (1) those involving a federal question and (2) those involving diversity of citizenship and more than $75,000.

Federal question jurisdiction exists in any suit where the plaintiff's claim is based on the U.S. Constitution, a U.S. treaty, or a federal statute. Thus, litigants can bring to the federal courts cases involving, for example, the federal antitrust statutes, federal criminal laws, constitutional issues such as freedom of the press, and federal tax questions. Federal question jurisdiction does not require an amount in controversy exceeding $75,000. Further, federal and state courts have *concurrent jurisdiction* for some federal questions. Thus, some federal question cases are decided in state courts applying federal law. Congress has accorded the federal courts exclusive jurisdiction over certain subjects, including federal criminal laws, bankruptcy, and copyrights. Under *diversity jurisdiction,* federal district courts may hear cases involving more than $75,000 where the plaintiff(s) and the defendant(s) are citizens of different states. (Corporations are treated as citizens both of their state of incorporation and the state in which their principal place of business is located.) Diversity cases may also be heard in state courts, but plaintiffs frequently prefer to bring their actions in federal courts. The quality of the federal judiciary is generally believed to be superior to that of the states, and the federal courts are considered less likely to be influenced by local bias. Federal court action may also have procedural advantages, such as greater capacity to secure witnesses' testimony.

Personal Jurisdiction

Judicial authority over the person is known as *in personam jurisdiction.* In general, a state court's powers are limited to the bounds of the state. While the matter is fraught with complexities, it is fair to say that state court jurisdiction can be established in three ways: (1) When the defendant is a resident of the state, a summons may be served at that residence. (2) When the defendant is not a resident, a summons may be personally served should he or she be physically present in the state. (3) All states have legislated "long-arm" statutes that allow a court to secure jurisdiction against an out-of-state party where the defendant has committed a tort in the state or where the defendant is conducting business in the state. Hence, in an auto accident in Iowa involving both an Iowa resident and an Illinois resident, the Iowan may sue in Iowa and achieve service of process over the Illinois defendant as a consequence of the jurisdictional authority afforded by the long-arm statute.

A state court may also acquire jurisdiction via an *in rem action.* In that instance the defendant may be a nonresident, but his or her property, which must be the subject of the suit, must be located within the state.

The following case illustrates some of the issues arising from a jurisdictional dispute involving Minnesota's long-arm statute.

SHERBURNE COUNTY SOCIAL SERVICES v. KENNEDY
409 N.W.2d 907 (Minn. App. 1987)

Judge Randall

Appellant Kevin Kennedy appeals the trial court's denial of his motion to dismiss this paternity action. Kennedy's motion asserted that the court lacked personal jurisdiction over him because he is a resident of Montana, and because there are insufficient contacts with the State of Minnesota concerning the issue before the court.

Facts

Appellant, while a resident of Minnesota, engaged in consensual intercourse with Jean Pouliot, a Minnesota resident, on July 30, 1983. Thereafter appellant moved to Montana and still resides there. In November 1983, over the Thanksgiving holiday and between November 20 and November 26, Pouliot and a friend visited appellant at his Montana home. Pouliot and appellant engaged in intercourse approximately two or three times during this visit.

On September 5, 1984, Pouliot gave birth to a son. The County of Sherburne subsequently brought this action in Minnesota to determine paternity, to assign responsibility for medical expenses relative to the birth, and to set child support. Appellant did not answer, but moved to dismiss based on lack of personal jurisdiction. The trial court denied the motion.

Issue

Did the trial court properly deny appellant's motion to dismiss, finding Minnesota had personal jurisdiction over him?

Analysis

Minnesota served appellant under the long-arm statute, Minn.Stat. § 543.19 (1984). Appellant argues he has insufficient minimum contacts with Minnesota for this state to exercise personal jurisdiction over him. He claims that his July 30, 1983, act of intercourse with Pouliot is insufficient basis to assert personal jurisdiction over him because the child was not conceived then, and he has no other Minnesota based contacts. He contends that if he is the father, the act of intercourse leading to conception must have occurred during Pouliot's visit to Montana in November 1983. Pouliot gave birth thirteen months and one week after the intercourse in Minnesota, and approximately nine and one half months after the intercourse in Montana.

Before Minnesota courts can exercise long-arm jurisdiction over nonresidents, two tests must be met: (1) the long-arm statute, Minn.Stat. § 543.19, must be satisfied, and (2) plaintiff must show minimum contacts between defendant and his state such that asserting jurisdiction does not offend due process. *Howells* v. *McKibben,* 281 N.W.2d 154, *State* v. *Hartling,* 360 N.W.2d 439.

Long-Arm Statute

Minnesota's long-arm statute permits a court of this state having subject matter jurisdiction to exercise personal jurisdiction over a nonresident individual if that individual:

Commits any act outside Minnesota causing injury or property damage in Minnesota. Paternity is a tort cause of action, within the scope of § 543.19.

In *Howells* the supreme court found that, even though conception may have occurred in Wisconsin, the "injury" to the plaintiff occurred in Minnesota. The court defined "injury" as the mother's physical and emotional suffering caused by having to raise the child alone, the resulting medical expenses, and those expenses incident to raising the child. Here, although conception occurred outside Minnesota, the birth is inside Minnesota. For the purposes of appellate review, the first part of the long-arm statute has been satisfied. We now turn to whether or not the burden placed on the appellant by being brought under the state's jurisdiction would violate fairness and substantial justice.

Minimum Contacts

Appellant argues he does not have sufficient minimum contacts with Minnesota to be compelled to defend a paternity suit here.

Due process, the basis of the minimum contact test, is served only where there exists a "sufficient nexus between Minnesota and defendant so that it is both fair and reasonable to require defense of the action in this state." *Howells,* 281 N.W.2d at 157. The pertinent factors to be considered are:

1. the quantity of defendant's contacts with the state;
2. the nature and quality of the contacts;
3. the connection of the cause of action with those contacts;
4. the interest of the state in providing a forum; and
5. convenience to the parties.

A. Quantity of Appellant's Contacts with Minnesota Appellant formerly lived in Minnesota. One isolated sexual incident with Pouliot occurred here. Appellant's contacts with Pouliot in Minnesota are minimal. If medical science is to be believed, their act of intercourse on July 30, 1983, did not result in the September 5, 1984, birth. "When the quantity of contacts is minimal, the nature and quality become dispositive." *Hartling,* 360 N.W.2d at 441.

B. Nature and Quality of the Contacts Appellant argues the quality of contacts between him and Pouliot does not support exercise of personal jurisdiction over him, because the act that resulted in her pregnancy, if he is the father, did not occur in Minnesota. Respondent argues appellant knew he was having intercourse in Montana with a Minnesota resident who would eventually return to Minnesota, and thus, jurisdiction in Minnesota is proper.

*   *   *   *   *

Pouliot concedes that there was one isolated act of sexual intercourse in Minnesota in July 1983. Thereafter she voluntarily traveled to Montana in November 1983, and engaged in sexual intercourse there with appellant. Pouliot does not dispute that if appellant is the father, the act of intercourse leading to conception took place in November 1983 in Montana. Appellant's contacts with Minnesota are minimal, and the limited quality and quantity of contacts in Minnesota are dissimilar enough that *Hartling* is not controlling on this issue.

C. Source and Connection of the Cause of Action with those Contacts Appellant argues this element has not been proved because Pouliot did not have a continuing relationship with appellant, her contacts with him were isolated incidents, and the couple had more contacts in Montana than in Minnesota. Since we accept the parties' statements that the sexual contact that led to the cause of action, if appellant is the father, arose in Montana, appellant prevails on this element.

D. Interest of Minnesota in Providing a Forum In *West American Insurance Co.* v. *Westin, Inc.,* 337 N.W.2d 676 (Minn. 1983), the Minnesota Supreme Court noted the critical focus in any jurisdictional analysis must be on "the relationship among the defendant, the forum, and the litigation" . . . This tripartite relationship is defined by the defendant's contacts with the forum *state,* not by the defendant's contacts with *residents* of the forum.

Here appellant has no contacts with the forum state, other than the allegation he has fathered the child of a Minnesota resident.

E. Relative Convenience of the Parties In *West American,* the Minnesota Supreme Court held, "this

factor is irrelevant unless the defendant also has, as a threshold matter, sufficient contacts with the forum state." Appellant argues that since the element of "sufficient contacts" has not been met, convenience is not dispositive. We agree, and do not decide this case on relative convenience. We note the availability of legal redress in the State of Montana for Sherburne County and Pouliot under the Uniform Reciprocal Enforcement of Support Act.

We hold appellant's contacts with Minnesota are insufficient to require him to come to Minnesota to defend this paternity action.

Reversed.

Questions

1. Which facts allowed the Minnesota Court of Appeals to conclude that the Minnesota long-arm statute had been satisfied?
2. Why did the court decide in favor of the appellant and putative father, Kevin Kennedy?
3. The Robinsons filed a product liability suit in an Oklahoma state court to recover for injuries sustained in an automobile accident in Oklahoma. The auto had been purchased in New York from the defendant, World-Wide Volkswagen Corp. Oklahoma's long-arm statute was used in an attempt to secure jurisdiction over the defendant. World-Wide conducted no business in Oklahoma. Nor did it solicit business there.
   a. Build an argument to support the claim of jurisdiction for the Oklahoma court.
   b. Decide. See *World-Wide Volkswagen Corp.* v. *Woodson,* 100 S.Ct. 559 (1980).
4. Burger King conducts a franchise, fast-food operation from its Miami, Florida, headquarters. John Rudzewicz and a partner, both residents of Michigan, secured a Burger King franchise in Michigan. Subsequently, the franchisees allegedly fell behind in payments, and after negotiations failed, Burger King ordered the franchisees to vacate the premises. They declined to do so, and continued to operate the franchise. Burger King brought suit in a federal district court in Florida. The defendant franchisees argued that the Florida court did not have personal jurisdiction over them because they were Michigan residents and because the claim did not arise in Florida.

However, the district court found the defendants to be subject to the Florida long-arm statute, which extends jurisdiction to "[a]ny person, whether or not a citizen or resident of this state" who, "[b]reach[es] a contract in this state by failing to perform acts required by the contract to be performed in this state." The franchise contract provided for governance of the relationship by Florida law. Policy was set in Miami, although day-to-day supervision was managed through various district offices. The case ultimately reached the U.S. Supreme Court.

a. What constitutional argument would you raise on behalf of the defendant franchisees?

b. Decide. See *Burger King Corp.* v. *Rudzewicz,* 471 U.S. 462 (1985).

VENUE

Once jurisdictional authority; that is, the power to hear the case, is established, the proper *venue* (geographic location within the court system) for the case comes into question. Ordinarily, a case will be heard by the court geographically closest to the incident or property in question or to where the parties reside. Thus, a lawsuit springing from a crime ordinarily would be filed in the county where the crime took place. Sometimes pretrial publicity or other factors may cause one of the parties to seek a *change of venue* on the grounds that a fair trial is impossible in the original location. The following case displays the confusion that often emerges as parties seek venues best suited to their tactical advantage. This case is particularly complicated because of the high stakes and the number of plaintiff/ nations and defendant/tobacco companies involved. The judge resolves the case with both common sense and extraordinary wit. [For the International Court of Justice, see **http://www.icj-cij.org/icjwww/icj002.htm**]

REPUBLIC OF BOLIVIA v. PHILIP MORRIS COMPANIES
39 F. Supp. 2d 1008 (S.D. Tex. Galveston Div. 1999)

Judge Kent

Plaintiff, the Republic of Bolivia, brings this action to recover from numerous tobacco companies various health care costs it allegedly incurred in treating illnesses its residents suffered as a result of tobacco use. This action was originally filed in the District Court of Brazoria County, Texas, 239th Judicial District, and removed to this Court on February 19, 1999, by certain Defendants alleging jurisdiction under 28 U.S.C. § 1331 and 28 U.S.C. § 1332. For the following reasons, the Court exercises its authority and discretion pursuant to 28 U.S.C. § 1404(a) to **TRANSFER** this case to the United States District Court for the District of Columbia.

This is one of at least six similar actions brought by foreign governments in various courts throughout the United States. The governments of Guatemala, Panama, Nicaragua, Thailand, Venezuela, and Bolivia have filed suit in the geographically diverse locales of

Washington, D.C., Puerto Rico, Texas, Louisiana, and Florida, in both state and federal courts. Why none of these countries seems to have a court system their own governments have confidence in is a mystery to this Court. Moreover, given the tremendous number of United States jurisdictions encompassing fascinating and exotic places, the Court can hardly imagine why the Republic of Bolivia elected to file suit in the veritable hinterlands of Brazoria County, Texas. The Court seriously doubts whether Brazoria County has ever seen a live Bolivian . . . even on the Discovery Channel. Though only here by removal, this humble Court by the sea is certainly flattered by what must be the worldwide renown of rural Texas courts for dispensing justice with unparalleled fairness and alacrity, apparently in common discussion even on the mountain peaks of Bolivia! Still, the Court would be remiss in accepting an obligation for which it truly does not have the necessary resources. Only one judge presides in the Galveston Division—which currently has before it over seven hundred cases and annual civil filings exceeding such number—and that judge is presently burdened with a significant personal situation which diminishes its ability to always give the attention it would like to all of its daunting docket obligations, despite genuinely heroic efforts to do so. And, while Galveston is indeed an international seaport, the capacity of this Court to address the complex and sophisticated issues of international law and foreign relations presented by this case is dwarfed by that of its esteemed colleagues in the District of Columbia who deftly address such awesome tasks as a matter of course. Indeed, this Court, while doing its very best to address the more prosaic matters routinely before it, cannot think of a Bench better versed and more capable of handling precisely this type of case, which requires a high level of expertise in international matters. In fact, proceedings brought by the Republic of Guatemala are currently well underway in that Court in a related action, and there is a request now before the Judicial Panel on Multidistrict Litigation to transfer to the United States District Court for the District of Columbia all six tobacco actions brought by foreign governments, ostensibly for consolidated treatment. Such a Bench, well-populated with genuinely renowned intellects, can certainly better bear and share the burden of multidistrict litigation than this single judge division, where the judge moves his lips when he reads . . . .

Regardless of, and having nothing to do with, the outcome of Defendants' request for transfer and consolidation, it is the Court's opinion that the District of Columbia, located in this Nation's capital, is a much more logical venue for the parties and witnesses in this action because, among other things, Plaintiff has an embassy in Washington, D.C., and thus a physical presence and governmental representatives there, whereas there isn't even a Bolivian restaurant anywhere near here! Although the jurisdication of this Court boasts no similar foreign offices, a somewhat dated globe is within its possession. While the Court does not therefrom profess to understand all of the political subtleties of the geographical transmogrifications ongoing in Eastern Europe, the Court is virtually certain that Bolivia is not within the four counties over which this Court presides, even though the words Bolivia and *Brazoria* are a lot alike and caused some real, initial confusion until the Court conferred with its law clerks. Thus, it is readily apparent, even from an outdated globe such as that possessed by this Court, that Bolivia, a hemisphere away, ain't in south-central Texas, and that, at the very least, the District of Columbia is a more appropriate venue (though Bolivia isn't located there either). Furthermore, as this Judicial District bears no significant relationship to any of the matters at issue, and the judge of this Court simply loves cigars, the Plaintiff can be expected to suffer neither harm nor prejudice by a transfer to Washington, D.C., a Bench better able to rise to the smoky challenges presented by this case, despite the alleged and historic presence there of countless "smoke-filled" rooms. Consequently, pursuant to 28 U.S.C. § 1404(a), for the convenience of parties and witnesses, and in the interest of justice, this case is hereby **TRANSFERRED** to the United States District Court for the District of Columbia.

SO ORDERED.

Questions

1. Why did the Texas District Court rule that Bolivia's case should be moved to the District of Columbia District Court?
2. Why did the Court treat this case with such an amused, mocking tone?

STANDING TO SUE

Resorting to the courts is frequently an undesirable method of problem solving. Therefore, all who wish to bring a claim before a court may not be permitted to do so. To receive the court's attention, the litigant must demonstrate that she or he has *standing to sue.* That is, the person must show that her or his interest in the outcome of the controversy is sufficiently direct and substantial as to justify the court's consideration. The litigant must show that she or he personally is suffering, or will be suffering, injury. Mere interest in the problem at hand is insufficient to grant standing to sue.

THE CIVIL TRIAL PROCESS

Civil procedure varies by jurisdiction. The following generalizations merely typify the process. (See Figure 4.2.) [For a vast "catalogue" of law on the Internet, see **http://www.catalaw.com/**]

Pleadings

Pleadings are the documents by which each party sets his or her initial case before the court. A civil action begins when the plaintiff files his or her first pleading, which is labeled a *complaint.* The complaint specifies (1) the parties to the suit, (2) evidence as to the court's jurisdiction in the case, (3) a statement of the facts, and (4) a prayer for relief (a remedy).

FIGURE 4.2   Stages of a Lawsuit

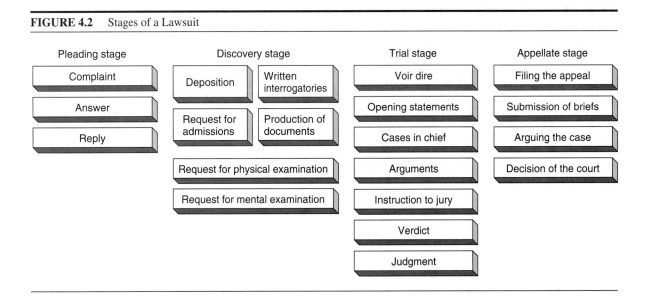

The complaint is filed with the clerk of court and a *summons* is issued, directing the defendant to appear in court to answer the claims alleged against him or her. A sheriff or some other official attempts to personally deliver the summons to the defendant. If personal delivery cannot be achieved, the summons may be left with a responsible party at the defendant's residence. Failing that, other modes of delivery are permissible, including a mailing. Publication of a notice in a newspaper will, in some instances, constitute good service of process. Ordinarily, a copy of the complaint accompanies the summons, so the defendant is apprised of the nature of the claim.

The defendant has several options. He or she may do nothing, but failure to respond may result in a default judgment in favor of the plaintiff. The defendant may choose to respond by filing a *demurrer* or a *motion to dismiss,* the essence of which is to argue that even if the plaintiff's recitation of the facts is accurate, a claim on which relief can be granted has not been stated. For example, a student may file suit objecting to a teacher's "bizarre" manner of dress; but, barring unusual circumstances, the student could not, as a matter of law, successfully challenge the teacher's costume.

Alternatively, the defendant may file with the court an initial pleading, called an *answer,* wherein the defendant enters a denial by setting out his or her version of the facts and law, or in which the defendant simply concedes the validity of the plaintiff's position. The answer may also contain an *affirmative defense* that would bar the plaintiff's claim. For example, the defendant might assert the statute of limitations or the statute of frauds. The defendant's answer might include a counterclaim or cross-claim. A *counterclaim* is the defendant's assertion of a claim of action against the plaintiff. A *cross-claim* is the defendant's assertion of a claim of action against a codefendant. In some states, these would be labeled *cross-complaints.* In the event of a counterclaim or the assertion of new facts in the answer, the plaintiff will respond with a *reply.* The complaint, answer, reply, and their components are the pleadings that serve to give notice, to clarify the issues, and to limit the dimensions of the litigation.

Motions

As necessary during and after the filing of the pleadings, either party may file motions with the court. For example, a party may move to clarify a pleading or to strike a portion deemed unnecessary. Of special importance is a motion for a judgment on the pleadings or a motion for summary judgment. In a *motion for a judgment on the pleadings,* either party simply asks the judge to reach a decision based on the information in the pleadings. However, the judge will do so only if the defendant's answer constitutes an admission of the accuracy of the plaintiff's claim, or if the plaintiff's claim clearly has no foundation in law.

In a *motion for a summary judgment,* the party filing the motion is claiming that no facts are in dispute. Therefore, the judge may make a ruling about the law without taking the case to trial. In a summary judgment hearing, the court can look beyond the pleadings to hear evidence from affidavits, depositions, and so on. These motions serve to avoid the time and expense of trial.

Discovery

Justice is the goal of the legal system. Information is central to reaching a just result. *Discovery* is the primary information-gathering stage in the trial process. Discovery (1) preserves the testimony of witnesses who may not be available for trial, (2) reduces the likelihood of perjury, (3) aids in defining and narrowing the facts and issues, (4) promotes pretrial settlements, (5) increases the likelihood of concluding the case with a summary judgment, and (6) helps prevent surprises at the trial.

In general, five discovery techniques are provided.

1. *Depositions.* A party or a witness may be required to appear before a court officer to give recorded, sworn testimony in response to questions raised by the attorneys for both sides of the controversy. Testimony is much like that at trial. *Depositions* are particularly helpful in trial preparation.
2. *Interrogatories.* Written questions calling for written answers signed under oath may be required. Unlike depositions, *interrogatories* may only be directed to parties, and they can call for information outside the party's personal knowledge, requiring the party to peruse her or his records.
3. *Discovery of documents and property.* Either party may request access to documents, as well as real and personal property, for the purpose of inspection relevant to the trial.
4. *Physical and mental examinations.* When the physical and/or mental state of a party is at issue, the court may be asked to enter an order calling for an examination. Good cause must be shown, and the court must be satisfied that the need for information outweighs the party's constitutional right to privacy.
5. *Admissions.* Either party may make written requests of the other, seeking an *admission* as to the truth of a specified issue of fact or law. If the receiving party agrees to or fails to deny the truth of the admission, that issue of fact or law is conclusively established for trial purposes. For example, in a suit alleging a defective transmission in a recently purchased automobile, the auto dealer might be asked to agree that the auto was sold under a warranty and that the warranty included the transmission.

Because of widespread concerns about delays and expenses associated with litigation, the federal rules governing trials were changed to, among other things, limit interrogatories and depositions and require the parties to confer and develop a discovery plan and discuss settlement possibilities. In a similar search for improved efficiency and effectiveness in federal trial practice, the American Bar Association in 1998 adopted recommended guidelines for such innovations as allowing jurors themselves, under some circumstances, to ask questions of witnesses and providing criteria for courts to consider when deciding whether to televise trials.

Pretrial Conference

Either party may request, and many courts require, a pretrial meeting involving the attorneys, the judge, and occasionally the parties. Usually following discovery, the conference is designed to plan the course of the trial in the interests of efficiency and justice. The participants seek to define and narrow the issues through informal discussion. The parties also attempt to settle the dispute in advance of trial. If no settlement is reached, a trial date is set.

The Judge and Jury

The federal Constitution and most state constitutions provide for the right to a jury trial in a civil case (excepting equity actions). Some states place dollar minimums on that guaranty. At the federal level and in most states, unless one of the parties requests a jury, the judge alone will hear the case and decide all questions of law and fact. If the case is tried before a jury, that body will resolve questions of fact.

Jurors are selected from a jury pool composed of a cross section of the community. A panel is drawn from that pool. The individuals in that panel are questioned by the judge, by the attorneys, or by all to determine if any individual is prejudiced about the case such that he or she could not reach an objective decision on the merits. The questioning process is called *voir dire.*

From an attorney's point of view, jury selection is often not so much a matter of finding jurors without bias as it is a matter of identifying those jurors who are most likely to reach a decision favorable to one's client. To that end, elaborate mechanisms and strategies have been employed—particularly in criminal trials—to identify desirable jurors. For example, sophisticated, computer-assisted surveys of the trial community have been conducted to develop objective evidence by which to identify jurors who would not admit to racial prejudice but whose "profile" suggests the likelihood of such prejudice. A few attorneys have taken the rather exotic tactic of employing body language experts to watch potential jurors during *voir dire* for those mannerisms said to reveal their inner views.

After questioning, the attorneys may *challenge for cause,* arguing to the judge that the individual cannot exercise the necessary objectivity of judgment. Attorneys are also afforded a limited number of *peremptory challenges,* by which the attorney can have a potential juror dismissed without the judge's concurrence and without offering a reason. However, peremptory challenges may not be used to reject jurors on the basis of race or gender.

Jury selection and the jury system are the subject of considerable debate in the legal community. Are juries necessary to a just system? How small can a jury be and still fulfill its duty? Is the jury process too slow and expensive? Should very long and complex cases, such as those in the antitrust area, be heard only by judges?

The Trial

The trial begins with the opening statement by the attorney having the burden of proof. Then the opposing attorney offers his or her statement. Each is expected to outline what he or she intends to prove. The plaintiff then presents evidence, which may include both testimony and physical evidence, such as documents and photos, called *exhibits.*

The attorney secures testimony from his or her own witness via questioning labeled *direct examination.* After the plaintiff's attorney completes direct examination of the plaintiff's own witness, the defense attorney may question that witness in a process labeled *cross-examination. Redirect* and *re-cross* may then follow, and the plaintiff's remaining witnesses go through the same process. The plaintiff's attorney then summarizes the testimony and the exhibits and "rests" his or her case.

At this stage, the defense may make a motion for a *judgment as a matter of law,* arguing, in essence, that the plaintiff has offered insufficient evidence to justify relief, so time and expense may be saved by terminating the trial. Understandably, the judge considers the motion in the light most favorable to the plaintiff. Such motions ordinarily fail, and the trial goes forward with the defendant's presentation of evidence.

At the completion of the defendant's case, both parties may be permitted to offer *rebuttal* evidence, and either party may move for a directed verdict. Barring a directed verdict, the case goes forward, with each party making a *closing argument.* When the trial is by jury, the judge must instruct the jurors as to the law to be applied to the case. The attorneys often submit to the judge their views of the proper instructions. Because the law lacks the clarity that laypersons often attribute to it, framing the instructions is a difficult task, frequently resulting in an appeal to a higher court. Finally, the verdict of the jury is rendered and a judgment is entered by the court.

For the first time ever, 8 of the 10 largest jury verdicts in a year (1998) topped $100 million. Altogether those 10 judgments totaled $2.8 billion. Most probably will be reduced on appeal, but as lawyer and tort-reform advocate Victor Schwartz observed, "Now you can have a $50 million award and it is not even in the newspaper." Legal experts attribute the increasing size of verdicts to juries' awareness of the publicity that comes with big awards and growing anger with the business community.

Source: Associated Press, "10 Biggest Jury Awards Total $3 Billion," *Des Moines Register,* January 9, 1999, p. 8S.

Post-Trial Motions

The losing party may seek a *judgment notwithstanding the verdict (judgment n.o.v)* on the grounds that in light of the controlling law, insufficient evidence was offered to permit the jury to decide as it did. Such motions are rarely granted. The judge is also empowered to enter a judgment n.o.v on his or her own initiative.

Either party may also move for a new trial. The winning party might do so on the grounds that the remedy provided was inferior to that warranted by the evidence. The losing party commonly claims an error of law to support a motion for a new trial. Other possible grounds for a new trial include jury misconduct or new evidence.

Appeals

After the judgment is rendered, either party may appeal the decision to a higher court. The winner may do so if he or she feels the remedy is inadequate. Ordinarily, of course, the losing party brings the appeal. The appealing party is the *appellant* or the *petitioner,* while the other party is the *appellee* or *respondent.* The appeals court does not try the case again. In theory, at least, its consideration is limited to mistakes of law at the trial level. For example, the appellant will argue that a jury instruction was erroneous or that the judge erred in failing to grant a motion to strike testimony alleged to have been prejudicial. The appeals court does not hear new evidence. It bases its decision on the trial record, materials filed by the opposing attorneys, and oral arguments.

The appellate court announces its judgment and ordinarily explains that decision in an accompanying document labeled an *opinion.* (Most of the cases in this text are appellate court opinions.) If no error is found, the lower court decision is *affirmed.* In finding prejudicial error, the appellate court may simply *reverse* (overrule) the lower court. Or, the judgment may be to *reverse and remand,* wherein the lower court is overruled and the trial court must try the case again in accordance with the law as articulated in the appeals court opinion. After the decision of the intermediate appellate court, a further appeal may be directed to the highest court of the jurisdiction. Most of those petitions are denied.

Experts.   In this highly technological and scientific era, one of the biggest dilemmas facing judges and juries is the weight to give to expert testimony. Very often, in cases such as medical malpractice and product liability (see Chapter 16), the testimony of experts is decisive to the outcome, but that testimony varies wildly in its reliability and credibility. The automobile accident case that follows involves the admissibility of expert testimony by a tire failure analyst.

KUMHO TIRE COMPANY v. PATRICK CARMICHAEL
119 S.Ct. 1167 (1999)

Justice Breyer

In *Daubert* v. *Merrell Dow Pharmaceuticals, Inc.,* 509 U.S. 579 (1993), this Court focused upon the admissibility of scientific expert testimony. It pointed out that such testimony is admissible only if it is both relevant and reliable. And it held that the Federal Rules of Evidence "assign to the trial judge the task of ensuring that an expert's testimony both rests on a reliable foundation and is relevant to the task at hand." . . . This case requires us to decide how *Daubert* applies to the testimony of engineers and other experts who are not scientists. . . .

I

On July 6, 1993, the right rear tire of a minivan driven by Patrick Carmichael blew out. In the accident that followed, one of the passengers died, and others were severely injured. In October 1993, the Carmichaels brought this diversity suit against the tire's maker and its distributor, whom we refer to collectively as Kumho Tire, claiming that the tire was defective. The plaintiffs rested their case in significant part upon deposition testimony provided by an expert in tire failure analysis, Dennis Carlson, Jr., who intended to testify in support of their conclusion.

* * * * *

Carlson's testimony accepted certain background facts about the tire in question. He assumed that before the blowout the tire had traveled far. (The tire was made in 1988 and had been installed some time before the Carmichaels bought the used minivan in March 1993; the Carmichaels had driven the van approximately 7,000 additional miles in the two months they had owned it.) Carlson noted that the tire's tread depth, which was 11/32 of an inch when new, had been worn down to depths that ranged from 3/32 of an inch along some parts of the tire, to nothing at all along others. He conceded that the tire tread had at least two punctures which had been inadequately repaired.

Despite the tire's age and history, Carlson concluded that a defect in its manufacture or design caused the blowout. He rested this conclusion in part upon three premises which, for present purposes, we must assume are not in dispute: First, a tire's carcass should stay bound to the inner side of the tread for a significant period of time after its tread depth has worn away. Second, the tread of the tire at issue had separated from its inner steel-belted carcass prior to the accident. Third, this "separation" caused the blowout.

Carlson's conclusion that a defect caused the separation, however, rested upon certain other propositions, several of which the defendants strongly dispute. First, Carlson said that if a separation is *not* caused by a certain kind of tire misuse called "overdeflection" (which consists of underinflating the tire or causing it to carry too much weight, thereby generating heat that can undo the chemical tread/carcass bond), then, ordinarily, its cause is a tire defect. Second, he said that if a tire has been subject to sufficient overdeflection to cause a separation, it should reveal certain physical symptoms. These symptoms include (a) tread wear on the tire's shoulder that is greater than the tread wear along the tire's center, (b) signs of a "bead groove," where the beads have been pushed too hard against the bead seat on the inside of the tire's rim, (c) sidewalls of the tire with

physical signs of deterioration, such as discoloration, and/or (d) marks on the tire's rim flange. Third, Carlson said that where he does not find *at least two* of the four physical signs just mentioned (and presumably where there is no reason to suspect a less common cause of separation), he concludes that a manufacturing or design defect caused the separation.

Carlson added that he had inspected the tire in question. He conceded that the tire to a limited degree showed greater wear on the shoulder than in the center, some signs of "bead groove," some discoloration, a few marks on the rim flange, and inadequately filled puncture holes (which can also cause heat that might lead to separation). But, in each instance, he testified that the symptoms were not significant, and he explained why he believed that they did not reveal overdeflection. . . .

Carlson concluded that the tire did not bear at least two of the four overdeflection symptoms, nor was there any less obvious cause of separation; and since neither overdeflection nor the punctures caused the blowout, a defect must have done so.

Kumho Tire moved the District Court to exclude Carlson's testimony on the ground that his methodology failed Rule 702's reliability requirement. The court agreed with Kumho that it should act as a *Daubert*-type reliability "gatekeeper," even though one might consider Carlson's testimony as "technical," rather than "scientific." The court then examined Carlson's methodology in light of the reliability-related factors that *Daubert* mentioned, such as a theory's testability, whether it "has been a subject of peer review or publication," the "known or potential rate of error," and the "degree of acceptance . . . within the relevant scientific community." The District Court found that all those factors argued against the reliability of Carlson's methods, and it granted the motion to exclude the testimony.

* * * * *

The Eleventh Circuit reversed. . . . We granted certiorari . . . .

II

In *Daubert,* this Court held that Federal Rule of Evidence 702 imposes a special obligation upon a trial judge to "ensure that any and all scientific testimony . . . is not only relevant, but reliable." The initial question before us is whether this basic gatekeeping obligation applies only to "scientific" testimony or to all expert testimony. We, like the parties, believe that it applies to all expert testimony.

For one thing, Rule 702 itself says:

If scientific, technical, or other specialized knowledge will assist the trier of fact to understand the evidence or to determine a fact in issue, a witness qualified as an expert by knowledge, skill, experience, training, or education, may testify thereto in the form of an opinion or otherwise.

This language makes no relevant distinction between "scientific" knowledge and "technical" or "other specialized" knowledge. It makes clear that any such knowledge might become the subject of expert testimony . . .

Neither is the evidentiary rationale that underlay the Court's basic *Daubert* "gatekeeping" determination limited to "scientific" knowledge . . .

Finally, it would prove difficult, if not impossible, for judges to administer evidentiary rules under which a gatekeeping obligation depended upon a distinction between "scientific" knowledge and "technical" or "other specialized" knowledge. There is no clear line that divides the one from the others . . .

III

We further explain the way in which a trial judge "may" consider *Daubert*'s factors by applying these considerations to the case at hand. The District Court did not doubt Carlson's qualifications, which included a masters degree in mechanical engineering, 10 years' work at Michelin America, Inc., and testimony as a tire failure consultant in other tort cases. Rather, it excluded the testimony because, despite those qualifications, it initially doubted, and then found unreliable, "the methodology employed by the expert in analyzing the data obtained in the visual inspection, and the scientific basis, if any, for such an analysis." After examining the transcript in "some detail," and after considering respondents' defense of Carlson's methodology, the District Court determined that Carlson's testimony was not reliable. It fell outside the range where experts might reasonably differ. . . . In our view, the doubts that triggered the District Court's initial inquiry here were reasonable, as was the court's ultimate conclusion. . . .

We have found no indication in the record that other experts in the industry use Carlson's two-factor test or that tire experts such as Carlson normally make the very fine distinctions about, say, the symmetry of comparatively greater shoulder tread wear that were necessary, on Carlson's own theory, to support his conclusions. Nor, despite the prevalence of tire testing, does anyone refer to any articles or papers that validate Carlson's approach . . .

In sum, Rule 702 grants the district judge the discretionary authority, reviewable for its abuse, to determine reliability in light of the particular facts and circumstances of the particular case. The District Court did not abuse its discretionary authority in this case.

Reversed.

Questions

1. What is the "basic gatekeeping operation" that judges must fulfill according to the *Kumho* decision?
2. Why did the Supreme Court in *Kumho* rule that the "gatekeeping obligation" applies to all expert testimony rather than being limited to scientific testimony?
3. Why did the District Court and the Supreme Court agree that Carlson's testimony should be excluded?
4. Why are the *Kumho* and *Daubert* decisions considered significant victories for the business community?

Class Actions

Several thousand holiday travelers were stuck on planes for up to 11 hours at the Detroit Metropolitan Airport during a 1999 New Year's blizzard. In many cases, the Northwest Airlines passengers were without food, drink, or functioning toilets. Such situations are rarely litigated or are settled in small claims court, but in this instance the passengers have bound together in a *class action* against the airline claiming false imprisonment, infliction of emotional distress, and breach of contract.[19] A class action allows a group of individuals to sue or be sued in one judicial proceeding, provided they are "similarly situated"; that is, their claims or the claims against them arise out of similar or closely related grievances. The class action thus permits lawsuits that might otherwise be impractical due to the number of people involved or the small amount of each claim. The class action is also expedient; many potential causes of action can be disposed of in one suit.

Class actions have been highly controversial in recent years. Defendant companies see them as frivolous, expensive efforts by greedy lawyers who are creating classes where none had existed. Public interest lawyers argue that claimants often recover little while their lawyers secure enormous fees. The Supreme Court handed consumers what appears to be a significant victory in a 1999 decision which sets strict standards before courts can approve class-action settlements that apply on a mandatory basis to all plaintiffs.[20] In essence, the Court was concerned that judges sometimes approve settlements without independent investigations of what the defendants can actually afford to pay. The case involved asbestos-related health claims against Fibreboard, an Owens Corning subsidiary. Under the plan approved by a federal judge, Fibreboard's insurers would have paid about $1.54 billion to the 186,000 plaintiffs, but Fibreboard would have paid only $500,000, despite its $235 million net worth.[21]

Questions—Part Two

1. What are the purposes and uses of the concept of jurisdiction? Why do we limit the courts to which a claim can be taken?
2. Law cases often read like soap operas while they reveal important truths. A woman and man, each married to others, had engaged in a long-term love affair. The woman's husband died, and she pleaded with her paramour to leave his New York home to visit her in Florida. She affirmed her love for the man. They made arrangements to meet in Miami, but on his arrival at the airport he was served a summons informing him that he was being sued. His Florida "lover" sought $500,000 for money allegedly loaned to him and for seduction inspired by a promise of marriage.
    a.   Does the Florida court have proper jurisdiction over him?
    b.   What if he had voluntarily come to Florida on vacation? See *Wyman* v. *Newhouse,* 93 F.2d 313 (2d Cir. 1937).
3. Only two people interviewed by the *Washington Post* in a nationwide poll of 1,005 persons could name all nine members of the U.S. Supreme Court.

    While only 9 percent of those polled could name the chief justice of the United States (William Rehnquist), 54 percent could name the judge on TV's "The People's Court" (Joseph Wapner).[22]
    a.   The Supreme Court intentionally operates in relative obscurity. Should we be concerned that Judge Wapner is much better known than are members of the Supreme Court? Explain.
    b.   Why are we more interested in judges as entertainers than judges as shapers of American life?
    c.   Should the Supreme Court televise its proceedings? Explain.

4.   *a.*   Would a prosecutor who is seeking a conviction against a black male for armed robbery prefer to try the case before an all-white jury; that is, do the demographics of the jury significantly influence the outcome of a case? Explain.

b.   Could that prosecutor legally exclude blacks and women from the jury by use of peremptory challenges? Explain.

5.   In your opinion, is our criminal justice system racist? Explain.

Part Three—Criticisms and Alternatives

CRITICISMS

To many Americans, our system of justice is neither systematic nor just. A big portion of that concern is the view that we are awash in lawyers.

Too Many Lawyers and Lawsuits?

In 1991, then–Vice President Dan Quayle asked whether "America really needs 70 percent of the world's lawyers"[23] In fact, most countries do not collect reliable data regarding lawyer numbers, and definitions about what actually constitutes a lawyer vary widely. Nonetheless, the theme generated enormous, generally favorable, publicity. So in 1999, then-presidential candidate Quayle again attacked what he called the "legal aristocracy."[24] As journalist Sam Stanton remarked in commenting on the Quayle speech: "Pity the poor lawyers. After centuries of harassment and torment, the insults just keep coming."[25] [For a database of lawyer jokes, see **http://dir.yahoo.com/Entertainment/Humor/Jokes/Lawyer_Jokes/**]

Much of the frustration with lawyers comes, of course, with the thick fog of laws that seems to meet us at every turn. As columnist Chuck Green argues:

The problem with letting the lawyers write the rules is that there are too many lawyers and they write too many rules . . . [The rules are] supposed to create litigation . . . No matter what the rule is, lawyers will say the new rules are wrong. So then they will change them again, only to complain that the new rules are wrong. As long as the rules keep changing, there are no rules. And when you think about it, that's a full-employment plan for attorneys.[26]

The book review that follows elaborates on Green's "too many rules" thesis.

RULES 'LUNACIES' TIE US UP IN LEGAL KNOTS

Bill Leonard

Four years ago, bricks were added to the official list of toxic materials. After all, said the Occupational Safety and Health Administration, if you sawed a brick in half, you could release a small amount of silica. Therefore a warning had to accompany every pallet of bricks sent to a construction site. It carefully defined a brick as "a hard ceramic body . . . with no odor" and listed its boiling point.

In 1994, OSHA relented and decided that bricks aren't poisonous, after all. That left just 600,000 items on OSHA's list of toxics.

Three years ago, Chicago's transportation commissioner found that water was leaking into an old railroad tunnel under the Chicago River downtown. He told engineers to fix it. They estimated the cost at $10,000; a contractor offered to fix it for $75,000. The commissioner, following bureaucratic policy, put the job up for bids, a process requiring weeks. The Chicago River, following the law of gravity, didn't wait. It broke through the tunnel, wrecked wiring, and flooded basements, doing $1 billion in damage.

The state of Georgia offers wide-ranging services for austistic children in its special-education program. But the parents of an autistic rural Georgia child weren't satisfied. The courts ordered the local school district to pay for sending the child to the school the parents chose—in Tokyo.

These anecdotes aren't gleaned from some radical rewrite of "Alice in Wonderland." They happened—in a nation where bureaucracy has gone berserk. They're among examples that author Philip Howard, a New York lawyer, has strung together in "The Death of Common Sense" to show that legal lunacy is reducing a nation of laws to a nation tied in legal knots.

Nothing to Chance

It began in the 1960s, Howard argues, when social engineers decided—with the help of Congress—that writing more and more laws could protect consumers, producers, workers, minorities, the young, the aged, the disabled.

* * * * *

In hopes of leaving nothing to chance, New York specified that day-care center operators must fill out a 68-page, single-spaced checklist. (Also, New York felt it necessary to specify that day-care teachers must "comfort a child when in distress.")

Elsewhere in New York:

- A deputy commissioner of the New York City Human Rights Commission took his 2-year-old to the movies, but was barred lest the chatter keep others from

enjoying the film. Daddy complained; the commission ruled it age discrimination.

- A student attacked a security guard. The assault was witnessed by another guard, a teacher, and a dean. But the student's suspension was rejected; there was no student witness . . .

In Rhode Island, a disabled man made a crusade of finding violations of the Americans With Disabilities Act, forcing schools and public buildings to be modified with special doorknobs, lowered light switches, etc. He forced a school to move its dance to a different building; the first choice lacked a wheelchair ramp. He has filed more than 2,000 complaints, costing millions.

Howard makes little mention of any good that regulation may have accomplished. His purpose is to show the folly of replacing common sense with a binding bundle of bureaucratic rules whose purpose is to micromanage every inch of our lives and livelihood (and keep the armies of attorneys, paper shufflers, and supernumeraries endlessly employed). Some contractors, he said, won't bid on government jobs, or else they add 30 percent or so to their bid, because paperwork on government contracts is so mountainous. The feds let $200 billion in contracts yearly; 30 percent would mean $60 billion down the tube to satisfy the petty rules.

Racial Issues

If the most ludicrous examples of regulation gone mad are in the areas of workplace safety, the stickiest—and most disturbing—are in efforts to erase racism from the workplace. Writes Howard:

"There is a rash of litigation over 'compelled self-defamation.'

"Before you struggle too hard trying to figure out how people can defame themselves, here is the reasoning: It is because a negative job evaluation might have to be disclosed to a potential new employer. That, at least, has one cure: Tell all workers they're wonderful.

"But being too nice is also illegal: The Equal Employment Opportunity Commission is now investigating companies that give unduly rosy reviews of women and blacks. The theory, not illogical, is that false praise impedes self-improvement.

"Employers rarely give [references] any longer, because there is a potential lawsuit in any message, whether a negative reference (which can be construed as an act of discrimination or defamation) or a glowing report ('So why didn't you promote me? It must be discrimination')."

It's possible to dismiss Howard's thesis as a blatant attempt to smear all regulation through listing of worst-case anecdotes that bury worthwhile efforts. But to ignore the thesis is also dangerous. The waste caused by runaway regulation is a fact of bureaucratic life.

Source: Taken from a book review of *The Death of Common Sense: How Law Is Suffocating America* by Philip K. Howard. *The Des Moines Register,* March 26, 1995, p. 4C. Copyright 1995, reprinted with permission by the *Des Moines Register.*

On the Other Hand

Lawyers are reviled as indecent sharks driven by greed, but very many, in fact, seek simply to do justice. More than half of the law students participating in a 1998 survey reported that they want to work for a small firm or in the public sector rather than taking corporate or large-firm jobs that typically pay much more.[27] Among practicing lawyers who are happy with their choice of professions, 28 percent said the main reason they like their work is the opportunity to help people.[28]

Furthermore, we should not forget that our legal system has been vital in building America. We are the envy of the oppressed people of the world in our efforts to maximize freedom, fairness, and democracy for all. Laws and lawyers are central to economic efficiency. Lawyers devise the rules, processes, and structures that permit capitalism to operate effectively. Indeed, many of the rapidly developing nations of the world now recognize that an efficient legal system is a prerequisite to economic progress. The Cultural Revolution virtually eliminated lawyers from China, but today China's lawyers number about 100,000 and many more are needed. Indeed, in 1998 President Clinton and Chinese President Jiang Zemin announced a cooperative "rule of law initiative" in order to improve Chinese legal institutions. The aim, broadly, is to provide the stability required for successful capitalism. As columnist Anthony Lewis observed, "[L]aw . . . meets the fundamental human desire for both freedom and order."[29] The following article shows how the introduction of the rule of law is changing life in China. [For a large database of public international law, see **http://www.law.ecel.uwa.edu.au/intlaw/**]

DEVELOPING A CAPITALIST TASTE
FOR LITIGATION

James Harding

Just as Qian Yuan was leaving Watson's, a pharmacy on one of Shanghai's busiest shopping streets, the store alarm went off.

The 19-year-old university student was taken down to the basement and searched for shoplifting. She was scanned with a portable electronic detector. Then, much to her embarrassment, she says, the female security guard asked her to unzip her trousers, twice. On both occasions, nothing was found.

The incident might have remained nothing more than a personal humiliation, but Ms. Qian decided to take Watson's to court.

Last September, she sued the store, which is owned by the Hong Kong–based company Hutchison Whampoa in which the magnate Li Ka-shing has a substantial stake, demanding compensation for her mental anguish. She said she was "picking up the legal weapon to demand justice and safeguard her human dignity."

The district court found resoundingly in Ms. Qian's favour—Watson's was ordered to place an apology in Shanghai's most popular daily newspaper and pay damages of Rmb 250,000 ($30,000), equivalent to roughly 20 years' pay for an average Shanghai worker.

Ms. Qian is one of a growing breed of litigants in China. Where once disputes were handled by an official, adjudicated by a neighbourhood Party committee or, simply and frequently, left unresolved, these days more and more Chinese people are turning to the courts.

And handsome pay-outs for personal injury, emotional distress, and mental anguish are turning the business of accidents into something of a legal industry. When misfortune strikes, many Chinese people now call a lawyer.

Zhang Yuqi, a former Shanghai policeman-turned-attorney, says he was inundated with requests for representation after he secured a Rmb 130,000 compensation last year for a client who walked into a glass wall at a department store in which foreigners had invested.

"Ordinary people have tended to solve their problems between themselves. Average consumers do not know how they can protect their legal rights through the courts. But, things are changing. They are beginning to realise how the law can help them," he says.

The signs that Chinese people are starting to show a litigious streak may suggest that a Communist-run country is moving towards a rule-based society. But the cases themselves illustrate how very far China has to go—they have exposed a patchy set of legal statutes and an often arbitrary court system.

*   *   *   *   *

The scale of the award for Ms. Qian created something of a stir in Shanghai, simply because the size of the compensation payment seemed astronomical to ordinary people. But, the government seemed to consider the level of damages a mark of progress.

"Greater contact with other countries since the reforms and opening up began, has made the Chinese understand the importance of reparations," an official report explained.

More modest damages underestimated the extent of the victim's suffering and "did not teach others a lesson." Lawyers, too, have naturally been in favour of higher compensation payments, as they tend to be paid on a percentage of the final award.

*   *   *   *   *

Last month, the [Qian] case took a puzzling turn. Watson's appealed. The store has maintained that Ms. Qian was never body-searched. The Shanghai No. 2 Intermediate People's Court still judged that Watson's had violated the human dignity of Ms. Qian, but decided the award was too high. Instead of damages of Rmb 250,000, the sum was reduced to Rmb 10,000.

*   *   *   *   *

The speculation has been that pressure—either from other foreign retailers or domestic political interests eager not to displease Watson's chief owner, the powerful Li Ka-shing—was brought to bear on the Shanghai courts.

Indeed, a spokeswoman for Hutchison Whampoa, which owns the shop, acknowledges that there was "a lot of pressure from retail people. It was not just a Watson's issue. It became a supermarket operator issue." But, she says, Hutchison left the Shanghai division of Watson's to handle the case. Certainly, she says, Mr. Li was not involved.

Whatever the background to the revised verdict, it has left many people perplexed. Like many other areas of the law in China, the rules governing personal injury and emotional distress awards are a collage of statutes, regulations, and directives that sometimes overlap, sometimes contradict, and often leave large areas blank. "There is not a very clear basis in China's Civil Law for emotional compensation for personal injuries," says Mr. Zhang.

Indeed, the experiences of the eager new band of Chinese litigants suggests that recourse to the rule of law in China by no means guarantees a transparent, level, and fair hearing.

Source: Courtesy of *Financial Times* (London), February 26, 1999, p. 18.

Questions

1. List some of the services performed by lawyers and the legal system that are necessary to an efficient free market.
2. Do you see it as a sign of progress that China is encouraging the growth of its legal infrastructure? Explain.
3. *a.* In your opinion, why do lawyers in America have such an unfavorable image?
   b. Is that image deserved? Explain.

The results of a 1999 poll of 1,002 lawyers (489 blacks and 477 whites) regarding perceptions of racism in our justice system:

How much racial bias exists in our justice system? "Very much," answered more than half (52.4 percent) of the black lawyers in a new poll. "Very little," said about a third (29.6 percent) of the white lawyers, with more than half (55.7 percent) of the whites saying, "some."

Source: Poll conducted by the American Bar Association and the *National Bar Association Magazine*. Published in *Parade*, March 7, 1999, p. 25.

Reform: Judicial Efficiency

Governments, businesses, lawyers, judges—all are frustrated with the expense and inefficiency of our overburdened judicial system. Some small businesses are now buying legal services insurance or prepaid legal services for a flat monthly fee.

Some cities have taken novel approaches to adjudication such as business courts that hear only commercial claims, thus allowing jurists to become very efficient handling contract problems, shareholder claims, and the like. Chicago now turns minor city code cases over to its system of administrative law officers who are independent contactors hired by the city to quickly, efficiently, and fairly dispose of about 350,000 cases annually, ranging from traffic tickets to building code violations. Their decisions have the force of law and can be appealed to the state courts. The hearing officers, many of whom also practice law, are paid $45 per hour. They achieve a steady income stream, the city disposes of its caseload quickly leaving more serious matters to the conventional judiciary, and citizens spend 30 minutes or less resolving the city's civil complaint against them.[30] The Chicago system is a variation on the small claims courts that have long proven effective in settling minor disputes.

Small Claims Courts.   Suppose you move out of your apartment and your landlord refuses to return your $500 damage deposit even though the rooms are spotless? Hiring a lawyer doesn't make good financial sense and is beyond your means anyway, but a small claims court may provide an effective solution. Small businesses have been particularly satisfied with the small claims courts as an efficient device for collecting unpaid bills without the expense of bill collectors and lawyers. The article that follows outlines the primary features of the small claims process.

13 THINGS YOU SHOULD KNOW ABOUT SMALL CLAIMS COURT

Ralph Warner

1. How Much Can I Sue For?

In most states, about $2,500. But the limit is set by state law and ranges from $500 to $10,000.

2. How Much Does It Cost to Sue?

Generally, the filing fee is $10 to $50. (New York City offers a surprising bargain: just $5.84 to file.) If you win, you can add the filing fee to the amount the defendant owes you.

3. What Kinds of Cases Can Be Taken to Small Claims Court?

Small Claims Courts exist primarily to resolve small monetary disputes. Lawsuits involving contracts, security deposits, personal injuries, and warranties are common in Small Claims Courts.

In a few states, Small Claims Courts handle some other types of disputes, such as evictions. You cannot use Small Claims Court to file a divorce, guardianship, name change, or bankruptcy, or to ask for an emergency court order. A few states also limit or prohibit suits for libel, slander or false arrest.

*   *   *   *   *

4. Is Small Claims Court Paperwork Complicated?

No. In most states, starting a case requires only filling out a one-page form stating your grievance in fairly general terms. In some states, such as California, courts make small claims legal advisors available to provide free help. Both filing your court papers and delivering them to the other party can often be done by mail.

5. Will the Court Help Me Settle a Case Without Going to Trial?

Many Small Claims Courts now refer people to community- or court-based mediation programs. A mediator is a neutral person who is trained to help you arrive at a settlement. Mediation works best where the parties want to stay on good terms, as is generally the case with neighbors or small business associates. If mediation doesn't work, you can still go to court.

6. Are There Time Limits on When I Can Sue?

All states have "statutes of limitation," which limit the time for suing after an event occurs or, in some instances, is discovered. These rules apply in all courts, including small claims.

You almost always have at least one year, measured from the event, to sue. More often, you'll have much longer. For example, in many states, the deadline is two years for the breach of an oral contract and four years when a written contract is broken.

*   *   *   *   *

7. Where Should I File My Small Claims Lawsuit?

If the other party lives or does business in your state, you'll usually sue in the small claims district closest to their residence or headquarters. In some instances, you may need to sue in the district where a contract was signed or a personal injury (such as an auto accident) occurred.

As a general rule, if a defendant has no contact with your state, you'll have to sue in the state where the defendant lives or operates a business. It may not be worth the trouble.

8. If I Win, Am I Guaranteed Payment?

Unfortunately, winning a lawsuit and getting paid are cows with very different spots. You, not the court, will have to see that you get paid.

Don't bother suing a person or business that is "judgment proof"—that is, without money or assets and unlikely to acquire any in the foreseeable future. If you are suing an individual, it should be reasonably easy to collect if the person has a steady job, bank account, real estate, or investments. Keep in mind that court judgments are good for at least 10 years in many states and can usually be renewed. A person with no assets now could inherit money, win the lottery, get a good job, or have another personal economic turnaround sometime down the road.

9. If I'm Sued in Small Claims Court, but the Other Party Is Really at Fault, Can I Countersue?

In most states, you can countersue if your claim arises out of the same event or transaction.

* * * * *

10. Can I Hire a Lawyer to Represent Me?

In most states, you can be represented by a lawyer, but some states . . . don't allow them. However, hiring a lawyer is rarely cost-efficient . . . Happily, several studies show that people who represent themselves in Small Claims Cases usually do just as well as those who hire a lawyer.

11. What Should I Do to Prepare My Small Claims Case?

It's usually not what you say, but what you bring with you to court to back up your story, that determines whether you'll win or lose. The judge has no idea who you are or whether your spoken testimony is reliable. And your opponent is likely to claim that the true story is extremely different from your version.

Your chances of winning will go way up if you carefully collect and prepare your evidence. Depending on the case, you may want to bring eyewitnesses, photographs, bills, receipts, canceled checks, letters from experts, advertisements, written leases, or contracts.

12. What's the Best Way to Present My Case to the Judge?

Realize that the judge is busy and has heard dozens of stories like yours. To keep the judge's attention, get to the point fast by first describing the actual event that gave rise to your claim. Immediately follow up by stating how much money you are requesting. For example, "Your Honor, my car was damaged on January 10, when the defendant ran a red light at Rose and Hyacinth Streets in Saginaw and hit my front fender. I have a canceled check to show it cost $427 to fix the fender."

Then it's time to double back and tell the judge the events that led up to your loss. For example, you might explain that you were driving within the speed limit, entered the intersection when the light was green, and did your best to avoid the other car.

* * * * *

13. Should I Bring Witnesses to Testify in Person?

If possible, bring your key witnesses to court. If you can't, most judges will accept a memo or letter.

Source: *NOLO News*, Fall 1995. © 1995 *NOLO News*, Reprinted by permission.

[For Practical advice on legal problems, see **http://www.nolo.com**]

ALTERNATIVE DISPUTE RESOLUTION (ADR)

Businesses, in particular, are increasingly looking outside the judicial system for dispute resolution strategies.

In 1995, McGraw-Hill CEO Joseph Dionne instructed his legal department to begin developing a formal, in-house *alternative dispute resolution* mechanism. He was looking for a quick, inexpensive way of settling internal problems, but he wanted to be sure that employees left the process feeling that they had been treated fairly. Later that year McGraw-Hill initiated its Fast and Impartial Resolution (FAIR) program for its more than 15,000 employees in 35 locations across the United States:

> The three-step program is voluntary, and starts with bringing in a supervisor or human resource representative to resolve a dispute. If that does not work, it moves to mediation with a neutral third party. If mediation is fruitless, the third step is binding arbitration with a written decision. The company pays the mediation and arbitration costs.[31]

What Is ADR?

Of course, any form of *negotiation and settlement* would constitute an alternative to litigation, but *mediation* and *arbitration* are the most prominent of the alternatives to formal, full-blown litigation. Given the expense, frustrations, and exploding numbers of lawsuits, we are seeing increasing imagination in building other ADR options including *private trials* and *mini-trials.*

Mediation

Mediation introduces a neutral third party into the resolution process. Ideally, the parties devise their own solution, with the mediator as a facilitator, not a decision maker. Even if the mediator does propose a solution, it will be in the nature of a compromise, not a determination of right and wrong. The bottom line is that only the disputing parties can adopt any particular outcome. The mediator may aid the parties in a number of ways, such as opening up communication between them.

Arbitration

Arbitration is a process in which a neutral third party is given the power to determine a binding resolution of the dispute. Depending on the situation, the resolution may be either a compromise solution or a determination of the rights of the parties and a win/lose solution. Even in the latter case, however, it may be quicker and less costly than a trial, and the arbitrator may be an expert in the subject area of the dispute instead of a generalist, as a judge would be. It is procedurally more formal than mediation, with the presentation of proofs and arguments by the parties, but less formal than court adjudication. The arbitrator's decision is legally binding, although in some cases, such as labor disputes, it may be appealed to a court.

Private Trials

A number of states now permit private trials, sometimes labeled "rent-a-judge," where the litigants agree on that approach. Normally a third party such as a mediation firm makes the

| "rent-a-judge" | necessary arrangements including hiring a retired judge as well as jurors to hear the case. The proceedings are conducted much as in a courtroom. |

Since the parties are paying, however, the dispute comes to trial more quickly, the process normally moves along more rapidly, and the proceeding may be conducted in private. Normally, the parties agree in advance that the decision will be binding. Appeals to the formal judicial system are provided for in some states. Critics question the fairness of the private system and wonder if it will further erode faith in public trials, but the time and money saved can be quite substantial.

Mini-Trials

In recent years, some corporations have agreed to settle their disputes by holding informal hearings that clarify the facts and the issues that would emerge if the dispute were litigated. In the mini-trial, each organization presents its version of the case to a panel of senior executives from each organization. The trial is presided over by a neutral third party who may be called upon for an opinion as to what would happen were the case to be litigated. That opinion has no binding force. The executives then meet to attempt to negotiate a settlement. The neutral third party sometimes facilitates that discussion. Mini-trials are voluntary and nonbinding, but if an agreement is reached, the parties can formalize it by entering a settlement contract.

Uses of ADR

ADR mechanisms are employed in a variety of roles across many industries and businesses. Almost all union contracts have some arbitration procedure. Many auto companies use ADR to resolve warranty claims as well as disputes with dealers. Consumer complaints are sometimes settled by arbitration sponsored by the Better Business Bureaus. Brokerage firms as well as some banks and insurance companies require customers to arbitrate disputes over their accounts. Approximately 100 nations are parties to the New York Convention agreeing to uphold international arbitration awards. [For information on international ADR, see **www.internationaladr.org**]

As the following *New York Times* excerpt demonstrates, ADR now commonly plays a role in settling very expensive, high-profile disputes.

> The great Times Square sign battle ended when an arbitrator ruled that Nasdaq, the electronic stock market, could erect the largest video screen in the world on the new Conde Nast skyscraper in Times Square despite objections from S.I. Newhouse, Jr., the magazine publishing tycoon.
>
> After months of delays, Frank G. Zarb, chief executive of Nasdaq's parent, can now get on with building the 8-story, 14,000-square-foot sign that will wrap around the cylinder that forms the northeast corner of 4 Times Square, at Broadway and 43d Street. Mr. Zarb is hoping that the $25 million sign, which is roughly the size of three basketball courts, will give Nasdaq a dazzling public profile at the so-called crossroads of the world.
>
> Mr. Newhouse, whose Conde Nast company publishes *The New Yorker, Vanity Fair, Allure,* and 14 other magazines, is moving into the 48-story office tower and did not want a huge blinking sign outside his windows.[32]

The article that follows describes alternate dispute resolution in practice in San Francisco.

THE PEACEMAKERS

Peter Sinton

When former San Francisco Superior Court Judge Daniel Weinstein left the bench a decade ago for a new career in alternative dispute resolution, he said a lot of people didn't know the difference between mediation and meditation.

Today they do. And Weinstein is at the top of his new profession after successfully mediating settlements worth a total of about $1 billion last year. They included the $187.5 million settlement of the giant class-action lawsuit against Bank of America over its handling of California municipal bond funds.

Mediation and arbitration are on the rise as courts become increasingly clogged and companies, government agencies, and families realize they can save time, money, and their nerves by reaching a settlement outside the courtroom.

State and federal courts in Northern California now require that parties to civil litigation first go through some type of alternative dispute resolution or ADR.

And many companies stipulate in contracts that if a disagreement arises, customers or business partners must agree to mediation or arbitration.

A study by Cornell University and Pricewaterhouse-Coopers two years ago found that 88 percent of the top 1,000 U.S. companies have used mediation, where parties try to reach a compromise through an independent agent. Seventy-nine percent used arbitration, where parties agree to present their cases to a private judge or panel and live by the decision.

Taking advantage of this trend, a growing number of judges and lawyers with an entrepreneurial spirit are starting or joining mediation firms.

Weinstein exemplifies the new breed of legal negotiator. For the past decade, he has been a lead mediator for JAMS/Endispute, one of the nation's leading ADR firms. More than 90 percent of the cases he has mediated have been settled out of court.

* * * * *

Weinstein decided to leave the bench in 1989, when the courts were backed up with asbestos cases and plaintiffs and defendants were looking for a quicker way out.

"Everyone wanted a new product—a different way to get cases resolved quickly," he said.

* * * * *

One of Weinstein's biggest mediations has been the BofA case. There, the state of California and nearly 300 municipal agencies charged that between 1977 and 1992, the bank diverted to its own account hundreds of millions of dollars of unclaimed bond payments.

Weinstein said all sides "were getting exhausted by the gargantuan size of the litigation and the prospects that gathering data, trial, and appeals would go on for years." In addition, NationsBank recently had agreed to buy BofA and wanted a clean slate.

Weinstein was chosen because he was acceptable to all sides in the dispute. These included the defendant, Bank of America; plaintiffs, the state of California and the city of San Francisco, which represented thousands of municipal bond issuers; and former BofA employee Pat Stull, who filed the class-action suit.

While Weinstein dealt with the legal issues, two other independent and unbiased experts approved by all sides were hired to analyze the numbers: University of California at Berkeley Economics Professor Daniel McFadden and UC Davis Management Professor Michael Maher.

McFadden said Weinstein explained that "the first job in mediation is to get the parties to change their thinking from I'm right, you're wrong'" to an understanding of the other side's position and the odds of losing.

After the two professors spent about a week gathering and evaluating evidence, Weinstein figured it could take two or three months of mediation to reach a settlement. Instead, he was able to resolve the dispute after two long days last November.

The first day was for presentations, which involved so many experts and attorneys from all sides that they needed a conference room at the Union Square Hyatt. The next day, Weinstein put the different parties in separate rooms at JAMS/Endispute's 11th floor offices in Embarcadero Center No. 2 and shuttled between them.

"Weinstein was helpful on several levels," said San Francisco Chief Trial Deputy Pat Mahoney, who attended the marathon sessions with City Attorney Louise Renne. "He brought in independent experts for the complex analysis of damages. He understood the issues and the interests of each party. And he had a sense of humor, which created an environment where mediation could move forward."

For example, at about 6 P.M. on the second day, with the parties still far apart on a dollar settlement, Mahoney recalls that Weinstein referred to himself as "a rug merchant" and he would be happy to convey any price although he doubted it was the best price to make a sale.

Around 11 P.M., with Renne missing a San Francisco opera performance for the higher financial drama, the $187.5 million deal with BofA, the state and cities was struck.

McFadden came away impressed not only with Weinstein's skill of "humoring, cajoling, and bullying" the participants but also the mediation process. "It promotes truth finding by giving each party an opportunity to gain perspective on the merits of its own case and obviously avoids the risks of trial judgments," he said.

But to be successful, McFadden observes certain necessary preconditions. Namely, each side needs to be predisposed to settle and have sufficient data so neutral experts can evaluate the strengths and weaknesses.

* * * * *

In addition to BofA, Weinstein has handled consumer class-action cases involving credit cards and life insurance; personal injury and medical claims cases including contaminated blood products; and environmental cases such as current contamination claims at San Francisco International Airport.

He also has mediated intellectual property cases involving Apple, Motorola, Intel, and Hewlett-Packard.

But you don't have to be a big company to benefit from ADR. The nation's oldest and largest ADR firm, the American Arbitration Association, has about 18,000 part-time mediators and arbitrators who dealt with 95,000 cases last year.

For mediation cases, the filing fee is $150 per party, and the hourly charge is $190 to $450 an hour, according to Stephen Van Liere, regional vice president of AAA's San Francisco office. For arbitration, the filing fee is $500 for settlements up to $10,000. The fee is $7,000 for cases involving $1 million to $5 million.

At JAMS/Endispute, which has about 30 retired judges and five lawyers in its San Francisco office, the hourly rate is $300 to $600. The daily charge ranges from $2,500 to $7,500 depending on the case and the seniority of the mediators.

Source: *San Francisco Chronicle*, May 5, 1999, p. B1. Reprinted by permission.

ADR Assessed

A 1996 study put the median cost of mediation at $2,750, and of arbitration at $11,800 with the median duration of mediation at 1 day, compared to 60 days for arbitration.[33] Ordinarily, of course, ADR costs less and is resolved more quickly than litigation. ADR is less formal and less adversarial than the judicial process. Further, the parties have more control over the proceedings in that they can choose the facilitator, they can choose when and where the dispute will be heard, and they can keep the dispute private if they wish.

Despite those strengths, alternative dispute resolution is not without its own problems. In situations involving new or complex problems, litigation may be preferable. In situations where the arbitration or other ADR method is paid for by one of the parties (ordinarily, a company), can we feel confident the process will be fair to all? ADR does not provide precedent of any kind for future disputes. Further, lawyers are troubled that ADR, when mandatory, deprives plaintiffs of their Seventh Amendment right to a jury trial.

Critics consider ADR to be particularly threatening in those now-common situations where employment contracts mandate arbitration as the method for settling job discrimination. In 1991, the United States Supreme Court allowed arbitration of employment cases in the securities industry and by extension other industries as well.[34] Many members of Congress and the Equal Employment Opportunity Commission continue to oppose mandatory arbitration as a condition of employment. (For further discussion of the use of arbitration in employment, see Chapters 13 and 14.)

As with all other dimensions of our lives, the Internet is beginning to play a role in dispute resolution. Cyber$ettle.com went on-line late in 1998 and less than a year later had been involved in settling hundreds of cases, mostly personal injury claims involving slip-and-fall injuries and fender benders. The parties log on to Cyber$ettle and type in a sum they are willing to settle for. The computer compares the bids, round by round, and automatically settles the case if the bids fall within $5,000 or 30 percent of each other. Basically, the idea is that in many controversies one side is willing to offer what the other will accept, but neither knows of their common ground.

Source: Ann Davis, "For Dueling Lawyers, the Internet Is Unlikely Referee," *The Wall Street Journal,* May 12, 1999, p. B1.

Questions—Part Three

1. Is an arbitration clause as a condition of employment a fair method of alternate dispute resolution, if entered knowingly and voluntarily? Explain.
2. In an effort to reduce legal expenses, some major banks and other businesses follow policies providing that all customer complaints will be subject to arbitration. Is mandatory arbitration fair to consumers? Explain.
3. Economist Stephen Magee argues that one way to strengthen the American economy would be to close the law schools:

   Every time you turn out one law school graduate you've got a 40-year problem on your hands, he says. These guys run around and generate a lot of spurious conflict. They're like heat-seeking missiles.[35]

INTERNET EXERCISE

Go to the "Hands-On Practice" page of the Virtual Chase website [**http://www.virtualchase.com/govdoc/handson.shtml**] and answer one of the sample questions.

CHAPTER QUESTIONS

1. Steven Levitt and John Donohue, two highly respected American scholars, have produced a study, not published at this writing, indicating that the 1973 *Roe* v. *Wade* Supreme Court decision legalizing abortion had the unexpected effect of reducing crime. The decline in crime rates during the early 1990s comes roughly 20 years after the *Roe* decision. Children who would have been born absent abortions would have been reaching their peak criminal years of 18 to 24. The young adults who would have been at greatest risk of criminal activity, unwanted children in difficult socioeconomic circumstances, according to the study, were aborted at disproportionateiy high rates. Every 10 percent increase in abortion led, according to the analysis, to about a 1 percent drop in later crime. Statistically speaking, the decline in crime exceeded that which would have been expected simply because fewer children were born. Further, the study shows that the five states that legalized abortion before the 1973 *Roe* decision all saw reduced crime rates in advance of the balance of the nation. Levitt has been careful to say, "In no sense do our results condone the wanton use of abortion as a method of birth control."[36]
   a. Do those study results "make sense" to you?
   b. Could birth control and abortion be better justified if sound scientific evidence over time were to show that reduced crime would follow? Explain.

2. Professor and criminal justice expert Morgan O. Reynolds argues that sterner punishment has led to reduced crime in the United States:

   This reflects a broader pattern: As our crime rates have fallen, serious crime rates in England have risen substantially, as a recent study from the U.S. Bureau of Justice Statistics found. For example, victim surveys show that:

   • The English robbery rate was about half the U.S. rate in 1981, but was 40% higher than America's in 1995.

   • The English assault rate was slightly higher than America's in 1981, but more than double by 1995.
   • The English burglary rate was half America's in 1981, but nearly double by 1995.

   Why these dramatic increases in English crime rates, while Americans' lives and property grew safer? The obvious explanation has been too often downplayed or ignored: The U.S. has instituted tougher, more predictable punishment for crime. The study's authors attribute the trends they note to the increasing conviction rates and longer sentences meted out in the U.S., vs. the decreasing conviction rates and softer sentences in England and Wales. English conviction rates for rape, burglary, assault, and auto theft have plunged by half or more since 1981, while the likelihood of serving prison time for committing a serious violent crime or a burglary has increased sustantially in the U.S.[37]

   a. Do you agree that harsher and more certain punishment will reduce criminal behavior?
   b. Do "root causes" such as being born out of wedlock affect criminal behavior? Explain.

3. Murderers, rapists and other felons are now unable to lawfully buy guns in the United States. Should that policy be extended to those who commit misdemeanors, such as petty theft and drunken driving, on the theory that they are more likely to commit additional crimes? Explain.

4. As of mid-1999, President Clinton had appointed more women and blacks to the United States district and appeals courts than did Presidents Reagan and Bush combined. Assuming the candidates are otherwise well qualified, in your view, is added diversity on the federal bench an important goal? Explain.

5. A question directed to "The Law," a column in *USA Weekend:* "I've heard that plaintiffs in small claims

courts often don't see the money that's awarded to them. Is this true? How does the court ensure that the money gets paid?"[38] Answer those questions.

6. A letter to *The Wall Street Journal:*

> The problems with our legal system go much deeper than irresponsible plaintiffs, amoral lawyers, and inept juries. The trouble is, our system of checks and balances has been corrupted; 100 percent of the executive, 100 percent of the judicial, and 43 percent of the legislative branches have been taken over by one group—lawyers.
>
> The Constitution charges Congress to ordain and establish the courts. It is no wonder it has created a system that maximizes the incomes of its own kind. The system is rigged to drag out cases that are billed by the hour, or to find moochers and looters willing to bring huge civil suits against productive citizens and corporations in front of dumbed-down juries.[39]

Do you agree? Explain.

7. Are the flaws in our legal system of such magnitude that respect for the law is threatened? Explain.

8. According to Warren Avis, founder of Avis Rent-a-Car:

> We've reached a point in this country where, in many instances, power has become more important than justice—not a matter of who is right, but of who has the most money, time, and the largest battery of lawyers to drag a case through the courts.[40]

   a. Should the rich be entitled to better legal representation, just as they have access to better food, better medical care, better education, and so on? Explain.
   b. Should we employ a nationwide legal services program sufficient to guarantee competent legal aid to all? Explain.

9. As discussed in the readings, peremptory challenges may not constitutionally be used to exclude a potential juror from a trial on racial or gender grounds.
   a. Must a criminal jury reflect the ethnic or racial diversity of the community? Explain. See *Powers* v. *Ohio,* 111 S.Ct. 1364 (1991).
   b. Could potential jurors lawfully be rejected on the basis of their place of residence? Explain. See *U.S.* v. *Bishop,* 959 F.2d 820 (1992).

10. French journalist Alain Clement offered a partial explanation for Americans' increasing reliance on lawsuits to resolve conflicts:

> Diverse causes explain the growth of the contentious mood in America. One could be called the devaluing of the future. In 1911, the Russian political scientist Moise Ostrgorski wrote: "Confident of the future, Americans manifest a remarkable endurance to an unhappy present, a submissive patience that is willing to bargain about not only civic rights, but even the rights of man."[41]

   a. What does Clement mean?
   b. How do you explain our increased reliance on litigation?

11. Maintenance of our adversary system of justice sometimes compels lawyers to engage in practices that some consider unethical. Anne Strick relates one such situation.

> Once upon a time, Williston, called by a colleague "one of the most distinguished and conscientious lawyers I or any man have ever known," was defending a client in a civil suit. In the course of the trial, Williston discovered in his client's letter file material potentially damaging to the man's case. The opposition failed to demand the file; nor did Williston offer it. His client won. But, recounts Williston in his autobiography, the judge in announcing his decision made clear that his ruling was based in part on his belief in one critical fact: a fact Williston, through a letter from the file in his possession, knew to be unfounded.
>
> Did Williston, that "most conscientious lawyer," speak up? Did he correct the Court's unfounded belief, the better to serve both truth and justice? He did not.
>
> "Though," he wrote, "I had in front of me a letter which showed his [Honor's] error," Williston kept silent. Nor did he question the propriety of his behavior. For, said he, the lawyer "is not only not obliged to disclose unfavorable evidence, but it is a violation of his duty to his client if he does so."[42]

   a. Did Williston act properly? Explain.
   b. Should we turn to more cooperative, less combative, approaches to dispute resolution? Explain.

12. On July 5, 1884, four sailors were cast away from their ship in a storm 1,600 miles from the Cape of Good Hope. Their lifeboat contained neither water nor much

food. On the 20th day of their ordeal, Dudley and Stevens, without the assistance or agreement of Brooks, cut the throat of the fourth sailor, a 17- or 18-year-old boy. They had not eaten since day 12. Water had been available only occasionally. At the time of the death, the men were probably about 1,000 miles from land. Prior to his death, the boy was lying helplessly in the bottom of the boat. The three surviving sailors ate the boy's remains for four days, at which point they were rescued by a passing boat. They were in a seriously weakened condition.

    a. Were Dudley and Stevens guilty of murder? Explain.

    b. Should Brooks have been charged with a crime for eating the boy's flesh? Explain. See *The Queen* v. *Dudley and Stephens,* 14 Queen's Bench Division 273 (1884).

13. Tompkins was a citizen of Pennsylvania. While walking on a railroad footpath in that state, he was struck by an object protruding from a passing freight train owned by the Erie Railroad Company, a New York corporation. Tompkins, by virtue of diversity of citizenship, filed a negligence suit against Erie in a New York federal court. Erie argued for the application of Pennsylvania common law, in which case Tompkins would have been treated as a trespasser. Tompkins argued that the absence of a Pennsylvania statute addressing the topic meant that federal common law had to be applied to the case. Should the court apply the relevant Pennsylvania state law, or should the federal court be free to exercise its independent judgment about what the common law of the state is or should be? See *Erie Railroad* v. *Tompkins,* 304 U.S. 64 (1938).

14. As noted in the readings, China is rapidly training lawyers and moving toward a more Western approach to judicial systems. The following quote describes China's historic view of dispute resolution.

> Most Chinese persons engage in a large variety of economic and social activities and resolve disputes involved in those activities without coming in contact with the formal legal system. As in Japan, litigation in a court of law is not considered a normal way to resolve a dispute. Custom and extrajudicial dispute settling mechanisms are utilized not only by private parties but by public entities. Decisions declaring someone right and someone wrong are not a desirable goal. Settlements and compromises are preferable. Even in court, Chinese litigants generally do not obtain a clear defeat or victory.[43]

In your view, would China be better off in the contemporary world to retain its traditional means of conflict settlement or should it continue its turn toward Western-style litigation? Explain.

15. As explained in the readings, alternate dispute resolution offers many advantages in resolving business conflicts. However, some cases do not lend themselves well to ADR. Can you list some of the considerations a company should evaluate in deciding between ADR and litigation? See Campbell Killefer, "Some Disputes Still Deserve Their Day in Court," *The Wall Street Journal,* October 12, 1992, p. A10.

16. University of Chicago law professor Richard Epstein points out how quickly Americans turn to legal remedies rather than relying on informal social customs (negotiation, neighborhood groups, simply accepting small losses and disturbances rather than fighting about them) to resolve conflicts. In your view, why are social customs increasingly ineffective in settling disputes in this country?

17. Judicial reform advocates often argue that the United Sates should adopt the English rule providing that the winner in a lawsuit is entitled to recover its reasonable litigation expenses from the loser.

    a. In brief, what are the strengths and weaknesses of the English rule?

    b. Would you favor it? Explain. See Herbert Kritzer, "Searching for Winners in the Loser Pays Rule," *ABA Journal,* November 1992, p. 55.

18. In deciding wether to confirm a president's nominee for the Supreme Court, policy analyst Terry Eastland suggests that senators ask, among others, the following question: "[I]f there is an injustice in society, and Congress or the states have failed to act, should the Supreme Court fill the void?" Answer Eastland's question. See Terry Eastland, "What Republicans Should Ask the Supreme Court Nominee," *The Wall Street Journal,* April 14, 1993, p. A15.

NOTES

1. James Podgers, "Message Bearers Wanted," *ABA Journal* 85 (April 1999), p. 89.

2. Steven Keeva, "Demanding More Justice," *ABA Journal* 80 (August 1994), pp. 46, 47.

3. Ibid.

4. Ibid.

5. Dennis Cauchon, "Indigents' Lawyers: Low Pay Hurts Justice," *USA Today,* February 3, 1999, p. 6A.

6. Franz Schurmann, "Justice for All Is a Fragile Ideal," *Des Moines Register,* April 25, 1993, p. 1C.

7. Associated Press, "Girl Reconciles with Estranged Mother," *Waterloo–Cedar Falls Courier,* June 30, 1998, p. A2.

8. Schurmann, "Justice for All," p. 1C.

9. Jesse Katz "America Marches Two Millionth Prisoner Behind Bars," *Waterloo–Cedar Falls Courier,* February 20, 2000, p. F1.

10. "Incarceration Rate No Cause for Panic," *Atlanta Journal and Constitution,* August 4, 1998, p. 8A.

11. Editorial, "Filling the Nation's Prisons . . . " *St. Louis Post-Dispatch,* March 22, 1999, p. B6.

12. "More Prison Cells and Less Crime," *Tampa Tribune,* August 5, 1998, p. 8.

13. "Filling the Nation's Prisons," p. B6.

14. "More Prison Cells and Less Crime," p. 8.

15. "Incarceration Rate No Cause for Panic," p. 8A.

16. Mark Tran, "U.S. Jail Population Hits Record 1.8 M," *London Guardian,* March 16, 1999, p. 13.

17. Norihiko Shirouzu, "Japan Conviction Rate Dazzles, Deceives," *The Wall Street Journal,* December 19, 1995, p. A12.

18. William Glaberson, "Judges Say Workload Cheats Appeal Cases," *Des Moines Register,* March 14, 1999, p. 1A.

19. Susan Carey, "Class-Action Status Is Granted to Suits Against Northwest over Blizzard Delay," *The Wall Street Journal,* June 21, 1999, p. B14.

20. *Ortiz* v. *Fibreboard Corporation,* 119 S.Ct. 2295 (1999).

21. Robert Greenberger, "High Court Rejects Asbestos-Related Settlement," *The Wall Street Journal,* June 24, 1999, p. A3.

22. Editorial, "The Anonymous Justices," *Des Moines Register,* July 18, 1989, p. 6A.

23. Stan Darden, "Quayle Debates with ABA Head over Legal Reform," United Press International, August 13, 1991, Finance section.

24. Sam Stanton, "Lawyer-Bashing Jokes Are Jurisimprudence," *San Diego Union-Tribune*, July 8, 1999, p. E-1.

25. Ibid.

26. Chuck Green, "Lawyers Prosper as Laws Multiply," *Denver Post,* June 24, 1998, p. B-01.

27. Martha Neil, "Noble Ambitions Drive Law Students: Survey," *Chicago Daily Law Bulletin,* October 21, 1998, p. 1.

28. Ibid.

29. Anthony Lewis, "Rule of Law to Play Growing Role in China," *Houston Chronicle,* July 7, 1998, p. A18.

30. John Flynn Rooney, "Administrative Hearings Process Takes Load Off Courts," *Chicago Daily Law Bulletin,* January 29, 1999, p. 1.

31. Dominic Bencivenga, "Fair Play in the ADR Arena," *HR Magazine* 41, no. 1 (January 1996), p. 51.

32. Charles Bagli, "Nasdaq Wins Battle to Build Huge Video Sign," *New York Times,* August 4, 1999, p. B3.

33. F. Peter Phillips, "Five Good Reasons to Mediate Employment Disputes," *HRFOCUS,* December 1998, p. S8.

34. *Gilmer* v. *Interstate/Johnson Lane Corporation,* 111 S.Ct. 1647 (1991).

35. "An Economist Out to Be Sued," *Los Angeles Times,* October 8, 1990, p. D1.

36. See, e.g., Karen Brandon, "Legal Abortion Cut Criminals, Scholars Claim," *Des Moines Register,* August 8, 1999, p. 1A, and Abraham McLaughlin,

"A Jarring Theory for Drop in US Crime," *Christian Science Monitor,* August 11, 1999, p. 1.

37. Morgan O. Reynolds, "Europe Surpasses America—in Crime," *The Wall Street Journal,* October 16, 1998, p. A14.

38. Steven J. Vite letter to Roger Cossack and Greta Van Susteren, "Q & A, The Law," *USA Weekend,* May 9–11, 1997, p. 8.

39. Darrell Dusina, "Lawyers, Everywhere," *The Wall Street Journal,* November 23, 1998, p. A23.

40. Warren Avis, "Court Before Justice," *New York Times,* July 21, 1978, p. 25.

41. Alain Clement, "Judges, Lawyers Are the Ruling Class in U.S. Society," *Washington Post,* August 22, 1980, p. A25.

42. Anne Strick, *Injustice for All* (New York: Penguin Books, 1978), p. 123.

43. Percy Luney, "Traditions and Foreign Influences: Systems of Law in China and Japan," *Law and Contemporary Problems* 52 (Spring 1989), pp. 129, 136.

Chapter 5

Constitutional Law and the Bill of Rights

We the people of the United States, in order to form a more perfect union, establish justice, insure domestic tranquility, provide for the common defense, promote the general welfare, and secure the blessings of liberty to ourselves and our posterity, do ordain and establish this Constitution for the United States of America.

The Preamble to our Constitution, the words that open this chapter, summarizes the "Founding Fathers'" lofty goals for America. The idealism embodied in the Preamble is both inspiring and touching. In reading it, we should reflect on the dream of America and the Constitution's role in molding and protecting that entirely new image of a nation. That we continue to be guided, more than 200 years later, by those rather few words is testimony to the brilliance and wisdom of its creators and to our determination to build a free, democratic, just society. Our Constitution is a remarkable document, so powerful in its ideas and images that it has reshaped the world.

CREATING A CONSTITUTION

You may recall that the Constitution grew out of the Articles of Confederation as enacted by Congress in 1778. The Articles contemplated a "firm league of friendship," but each state was to maintain its "sovereignty, freedom and independence." The Articles soon proved faulty.

Seven years of war had nearly bankrupted the colonies, and both credit and currency were almost worthless. The supposedly united states quarreled fiercely over economic resources, such as oyster-harvesting rights in Chesapeake Bay, and Congress had no real power to keep the peace.[1]

Thus, as described in the following article, the Constitutional Convention began in Philadelphia on May 25, 1787. [For a database of many nations' Constitutions, see **http://www.uni-wuerzburg.de/law**]

HOW THE DEED WAS DONE

Otto Friedrich

Actually the 55 delegates who concocted that remarkable Constitution over the course of a long, hot summer had no real mandate to do what they did. They had gathered only to consider some possible improvements in the Articles of Confederation . . . Neither Congress nor anyone else had authorized the delegates to invent a whole new political system.

* * * * *

[T]he basic issue was the comparative voting strengths of large states and small. Most of the big states demanded a powerful national government; the small ones feared coercion and insisted on states' rights. And neither side put much trust in the other.

* * * * *

As with many battles that have long since been won, it is hard now to realize how near the delegates came to failure, an event that might have led to the breakdown of the fledgling confederation, even to the reappearance of European forces eager to recapture their lost lands.

* * * * *

It took 60 ballots before the convention could agree on how to pick a president. It voted five times to have the president appointed by Congress and voted once against that. It voted repeatedly on whether a president could be impeached and how long his term should be and whether he must be native born.

The delegates also avoided settling some things, like the future of slavery.

* * * * *

With the coming of September, the framers could finally see the beginning of the end. The Pennsylvania state legislature had reconvened, and it needed the chamber where the Constitutional Convention was meeting. The dwindling collection of delegates, a dozen of whom had already gone home for one reason or another, picked a five-man Committee of Style and Arrangement to undertake the actual writing of the Constitution.

Although they were not supposed to change the substance of what the convention had so far decided, it was hardly accidental that all five were strong-government advocates, and that one of them was [James] Madison [of Virginia].

When the committee presented its constitution on September 12, the delegates eagerly began trying to change things all over again, in ways large and small. [George] Mason of Virginia declared for the first time that summer that there should be a bill of rights. He was voted down by 10 states to none.

The changing continued right up to the scheduled closing day, September 17, but then it was finally time to sign. Three of the delegates present still had objections and refused, among them Virginia's Governor [Edmund] Randolph. The rest, however, generally subscribed to [Benjamin] Franklin's [of Pennsylvania] declaration that although he too still had doubts and reservations, "I consent, sir, to this Constitution because I expect not better."

Still ahead lay nine months of bitter debate before the necessary nine states ratified what had been written that summer in Philadelphia. Ahead lay the creation of the Bill of Rights.

Source: *Time*, July 6, 1987, pp. 58–61. Copyright 1987 Time Inc. Reprinted by permission.

STRUCTURE AND PURPOSE

The Constitution is reprinted for you in Appendix A. Now take a moment to review its structure and purposes.

The Preamble identifies certain goals for our society, such as unity (among the various states), justice, domestic tranquility (peace), defense from outsiders, an increasing general welfare, and liberty. Article I sets up Congress and enumerates its powers. Article I, Section 8, Clause 3 is particularly important because it gives Congress the power to regulate commerce (the Commerce Clause). Article II sets up the executive branch, headed by the president, while Article III establishes the court system. Articles IV and VI, as well as the Fourteenth Amendment, address the relationship between the federal government and the states. Article VI provides in Clause 2 (the Supremacy Clause) for the supremacy of federal law over state law. Article V provides for amendments to the Constitution. The first 10 amendments, known as the Bill of Rights, were ratified by the states and put into effect in 1791. The remaining 16 amendments (Eleven through Twenty-six) were adopted at various times from 1798 through 1971.

From this review we can see that the Constitution serves a number of broad roles:

1. It establishes a national government.
2. It controls the relationship between the national government and the government of the states.
3. It defines and preserves personal liberty.
4. It contains provisions to enable the government to perpetuate itself.[2]

Recall that the Constitution was enacted to protect the citizenry from the government. The Constitution does not protect the citizenry from purely private concentrations of power, such as large corporations. In fact, corporations themselves are often entitled to the protections of the Constitution.

In establishing a national government, the Constitution sets up three branches and provides mechanisms for them to check and balance each other.

Federalism

Another role of the Constitution is to balance the central federal authority with dispersed state power. As established by the Constitution, the federal government holds only those powers granted to it by the states. The people via the states hold all of those powers not expressly denied them by the Constitution. The division of power between the federal government and the states is a key battleground for our ongoing liberal-conservative cultural and political war. Conservatives generally favor bringing power as close to the people as possible, while liberals are skeptical of local biases and favor a more unified national approach to many domestic issues. The Supreme Court, under the conservative leadership of Chief Justice William Rehnquist, has revisited the federalism debate and squarely supported

> Conservatives generally favor bringing power as close to the people as possible

states' rights principles in several recent decisions. The most vivid of those decisions, in 1999, held that state employees in Maine could not sue the state of Maine for monetary damages in its courts for Maine's failure to pay them overtime wages as required by the federal Fair Labor Standards Act (see chapter 12).[3] The 5–4 decision was based on the principle of "sovereign immunity" (that the state cannot be sued if it does not want to be) which does not appear in the Constitution, but which the majority found in legal history and the silence of the framers on the issue. Thus, the Court ruled that Congress, in writing at least some new laws, cannot constitutionally authorize individuals' suits for money damages against states in state courts. Since the Supreme Court in 1996 ruled that individuals cannot sue states in federal courts for violations of a variety of federal laws, individuals wronged by their states now have significantly reduced options. Some states might simply choose to waive their immunity. Some state statutes, for example, in the civil rights area, provide protection equivalent to or greater than that of federal law. Injunctions or civil fines may still be sought in state courts. Finally, the federal government can sue in state courts on behalf of workers like those in Maine, but whether it will wish to do so in most cases is unclear.

At this writing in 1999, the Supreme Court has agreed to look at three more federalism cases including a dispute involving the right of some University of Florida professors to sue the state of Florida for money damages in that state's courts for alleged violations of the federal Age Discrimination in Employment Act. That decision will clarify whether the Supreme Court is engaged in a major "counterrevolution" against decades of expansion of federal power or whether these states' rights decision represent a more limited balancing of state and federal power. Stanford Law School dean, Kathleen Sullivan, notes that nothing in the decisions to date restricts the right of the federal government to regulate the states, though the decisions do generally expect the federal government to enforce its own regulations rather than turn to individual suits in the state courts for enforcement action.[4] On the other hand, University of Southern California law professor Erwin Chemerinsky sees bigger consequences:

> This is a radical change in American government. It says the states can violate federal law with impunity, and nowhere can they be sued for damages in a federal or state court. Imagine if a state lab dumps toxic waste into someone's back yard in violation of the federal environmental laws. This says the homeowners cannot sue the states for their damages.[5]

A 1998 national poll shows that American teenagers are much more knowledgeable about pop culture than about the United States Constitution. More teens:

- Can name three of the Three Stooges than can name the three branches of government (59 percent to 41 percent).
- Know the Fresh Prince of Bel-Air than know the Chief Justice of the Supreme Court (94.7 percent to 2.2 percent).
- Know that the musical group Hanson is made up of three brothers than know how many members are in the United States Senate (81 percent to 21 percent).

(Continued)

> Mayor Edward Rendell of Philadelphia called the results "alarming," and said: "The Constitution doesn't work by itself. It depends on active, informed citizens . . ."
>
> Source: National Constitution Center [**http://www.constitutioncenter.org/**]

The Constitution, the Bill of Rights, and Business

The Constitution and, in particular, the Commerce Clause (Article 1, Section 8, Clause 3) profoundly shape the practice of American business. Indeed, in some important ways, the Constitution is a commercial document reflecting the economic interests of the framers. We will defer discussion of the Commerce Clause until Chapter 7. In this chapter, we will devote our attention primarily to the Bill of Rights. When we think of the Bill of Rights, corporations ordinarily do not come to mind. Extensive litigation in recent years, however, serves notice that the relationship between the corporate "person" and the fundamental freedoms is both important and unclear.

The Bill of Rights protects our personal freedoms (speech, religion, and the like) from encroachment by the federal government. Furthermore, the Supreme Court has interpreted the Due Process Clause of the Fourteenth Amendment, which is directed at the states, to absorb or incorporate those fundamental liberties and protect them against intrusion by state governments as well.

THE FIRST AMENDMENT

> Congress shall make no law respecting an establishment of religion, or prohibiting the free exercise thereof; or abridging the freedom of speech, or the press; or the right of the people peaceably to assemble, and to petition the Government for a redress of grievances.

These few words constitute one of the most powerful and noble utterances in history. The freedoms guaranteed in the First Amendment reflect the basic beliefs of American life. Much of the magnificence that we often associate with America is embodied in the protections of the First Amendment. After 200 years, it remains a source of wonder that our vast bureaucratic system and our approximately 270 million independent citizens continue to rely on that sentence as a cornerstone of our way of life.

1. Freedom of Religion

The First Amendment forbids (1) the establishment of an official state religion (the Establishment Clause), and (2) undue state interference with religious practice (the Free Exercise Clause). Government may neither encourage nor discourage the practice of religion generally, nor may it give preference to one religion over another. Broadly, the idea of the First Amendment is to maintain a separation between church and state. However, the precise boundary of that separation has become one of the more contentious social issues in contemporary life. [For the Freedom Forum database on the First Amendment, see **http://www.freedomforum.org/**]

City Hall?   Separation of church and state has been a core ingredient in American constitutional policy since the inception of the nation, but drawing the line between the two, in practice, remains a source of often bitter dispute more than 200 years later. Four thousand residents of the Manhattan, Kansas, area signed a petition to continue displaying the Ten Commandments just outside city hall. However, in 1999 after 40 years on the spot, the five-foot-high granite stone was removed by city officials following legal action by the American Civil Liberties Union and others.[6] In a similar vein, Jersey City, New Jersey, used public money to place a creche, a menorah, and a Christmas tree in front of City Hall. That display was challenged in court, and the City lost on separation of church and state grounds,[7] at which point the City added plastic figures of Santa Claus, Frosty the Snowman, a red sled, and Kwanzaa symbols on the tree along with signs indicating the display was one of several through the year designed to celebrate cultural and ethnic diversity. The United States Third Circuit Court of Appeals, finding no unconstitutional "establishment" or endorsement of religion in the blending of religious and secular symbols, allowed the display to stand.[8]

Schools?   These public spaces disputes are reflective of the frustrating but necessary debate under our constitutional system about where to draw the church/state dividing line. That line is most frequently tested in our public school classrooms where clear rules are few.

> May a state constitutionally require all public schools to set aside "a brief period of quiet reflection . . ."

- May a state constitutionally require all public schools to set aside "a brief period of quiet reflection . . . not intended to be conducted as a religious service or exercise?" Yes, according to the 11th Circuit Court of Appeals, ruling on a challenge to a Georgia statute.[9]
- May a public school board constitutionally allow a private religious group to place Bibles on unattended tables in the schools' halls one day per year so the students can take those Bibles if they so choose? Yes, according to the Fourth Circuit Court of Appeals, ruling on a challenge to a West Virginia school district's policy.[10]
- May a public school constitutionally provide for a student-selected, student-given "brief invocation or message" before a football game "to solemnize the event, to promote good sportsmanship and student safety, and to establish the appropriate environment for the competition?" No, according to a three-judge panel of the Fifth United States Circuit Court of Appeals, ruling on a challenge to a Santa Fe, Texas, school policy.[11]

Legal decisions regarding religion in the schools are inconsistent and confusing. The Supreme Court has not provided guidance recently. In 1999, the United States House of Representatives weighed in by passing legislation that would allow states to individually decide whether their public schools will be permitted to display the Ten Commandments. The article that follows details some of the competing reasoning on the question of the constitutionality of prayers at high school graduations.

FEW CLEAR ANSWERS ON
COMMENCEMENT PRAYERS

Washington Post

WASHINGTON—Of the many church-state issues debated by religious leaders and politicians, none is trickier than whether prayer should be allowed at public high school graduations.

Last month, emotions erupted in a Calvert County, Md., community after the principal of Northern High School asked a senior girl to delete references to God in an invocation she volunteered to give at graduation ceremonies. When she delivered a "reflection" in place of a prayer and asked for 30 seconds of silence, many in the audience of 4,000 began reciting aloud the Lord's Prayer.

The audience's prayerful outburst in turn angered another senior, who stormed out of the building in protest—and then was not allowed back in to receive his diploma. The American Civil Liberties Union of Maryland is representing the male student and investigating to see whether his rights were violated.

In Florida and Idaho, appellate judges recently said they will rehear cases about students who were invited to speak at graduation and prayed during their presentations. In Idaho, the ruling to be reviewed said it was all right for students being honored at commencement to pray during their speeches; in Florida, the court had said it was not all right for students selected by their peers to pray during speeches.

Specialists in First Amendment rights attribute the "murkiness" in the school prayer debate to too few definitive court rulings and to misunderstandings about what the law allows.

The most common misconception is that the U.S. Supreme Court has banned all prayer in school, said Charles C. Haynes, editor of "Finding Common Ground: A First Amendment Guide to Religion and Public Education," published by the First Amendment Center at Vanderbilt University.

The Supreme Court has ruled against state-sponsored or state-organized prayer, meaning school officials cannot organize, mandate or participate in student religious activities, including prayer. But students are free to pray alone or in groups—for example, around a flagpole before the beginning of school—as long as they do not pressure other students to attend, he said.

Student-led graduation prayers are another matter. Federal appeals courts have issued conflicting opinions, Haynes said. But most courts that have ruled on the matter consider a graduation crowd to be a captive audience and any prayers before a captive audience to be unconstitutional.

If officials are unclear about what laws apply to their school, the best approach—until a direct U.S. Supreme Court ruling on the issue—is to refuse to allow student prayers at graduation, Haynes said. "It's a reasonable way to go," he said.

But Jay Alan Sekulow, chief counsel for the American Center for Law and Justice in Virginia Beach, Va., argues that the Supreme Court has left open the possibility of student-initiated, student-led prayer. In *Lee* v. *Weisman* (1992), the court "held only that . . . school officials (cannot) invite clergy to give prayers at commencement," Sekulow writes in the center's guide "Students' Rights and the Public Schools."

In an interview, Sekulow said students who have been given the opportunity to speak because of their high academic standing or leadership should be allowed to pray or say whatever they want in their speeches. To avoid charges of censorship on religion or any other subject, school officials should not read speeches in advance, he said.

Other legal minds interpret *Lee* v. *Weisman* differently. "School officials are neither required nor permitted to include a student-led prayer in a formal graduation ceremony, even if a majority of students vote to endorse the prayer," Maryland Attorney General J. Joseph Curran Jr. (D) wrote in a 1993 opinion about religion in public schools.

Also in 1993, the ACLU successfully challenged a Loudoun County, Va., school district plan to include student-led prayers at graduation exercises.

Haynes says the legal battles over graduation prayer are "counterproductive" and advises religious groups to hold voluntary baccalaureate services near the time of graduation. In that setting, he said, "you can have all the sermons and prayers you want."

Source: Copyright 1999 *The Washington Post.* Reprinted with permission.

Questions

1. *a.* What do the courts mean by a "captive audience?"
    b. What is its legal significance in these school-prayer situations?
2. In the case of the Santa Fe, Texas, football prayer, the court also reviewed the school's policy for graduation prayers. That policy allows the senior class to vote on whether to include prayers in the graduation ceremony. If the vote is "yes" the students elect willing students to deliver a nonsectarian, nonproselytizing invocation and benediction. The Court found that policy constitutional. How did the court distinguish the impermissible football policy from the permissible graduation policy?

A 1999 Gallup/CNN/*USA Today* poll found widespread support for religion in the schools:

* 70 percent favor allowing daily spoken prayers.
* 74 percent favor allowing schools to display the Ten Commandments.
* 83 percent favor allowing students to say prayers as an official part of commencement.

Source: The Gallup Organization [**http://www.gallup.com/poll/releases/pr990709.asp**]

[For an examination of the First Amendment and religion, see
http://www.freedomforum.org/religion/]

2. Freedom of Speech

Freedom of speech is the primary guarantor of the American approach to life. Not only is it indispensable to democracy and personal dignity, but Americans believe that the free expression of ideas is the most likely path to the best ideas. We believe in a marketplace of ideas just as we believe in a marketplace of goods.

Freedom of speech is not absolute. Clearly, we cannot freely make slanderous statements about others, publicly utter obscenities at will, speak "fighting words" that are likely to produce a clear and present danger of violence, or yell "Fire" in a crowded theater. At the same

> *Hustler Magazine* publisher Larry Flynt: "If the First Amendment will protect a scumbag like me, then it will protect all of you. Because I am the worst."

time, in general, the state cannot tell us what we can say; that is, the state cannot, for the most part, regulate the *content* of our speech. On the other hand, the state does have greater authority to regulate the *context* of that speech; that is, the state may be able to restrict where, when, and how we say certain things if that regulation is necessary to preserve compelling state interests. We have broad free speech rights in so-called *public forums* such as downtown business districts, parks, college campuses, and public plazas. Even in those places, however, the state may need to impose reasonable time and place regulations. Thus, while the Ku Klux Klan clearly can express hatred for black people (the content of the message), the state may restrict where and when those expressions are made (the context of the message) if necessary for the public safety. [For the Freedom Forum at Vanderbilt University database on the First Amendment and speech, see **http://www.freedomforum.org/speech**]

Of course, we have no constitutional right to freedom of speech on the private property of another, such as our place of employment. What about the enclosed shopping malls that are so much a part of our lives—are they public forums where we are substantially free to speak as we wish? At least seven state high courts have reached that conclusion,[12] but in a 1999 decision the Minnesota Supreme Court ruled that the giant Mall of America is private property for speech purposes.[13] In that case, protesters inside the mall peacefully distributed leaflets and carried signs urging shoppers to boycott Macy's because it sells fur coats. Some of the protesters were arrested for trespassing after refusing to leave the Mall. The Minnesota Supreme Court ruled that easy public accessibility to the Mall did not convert it from a private to a public space.

Sometimes, the question becomes one of what constitutes speech. The First Amendment clearly extends to expression in forms other than actual verbiage or writing. In a leading case in this area, the Supreme Court extended First Amendment protection to the wearing of black armbands to high school as a protest against the Vietnam War where no evidence of disruption was presented.[14] Does panhandling (begging) on a public street constitute speech? [See *Loper* v. *New York City Police Dept.,* 802 F. Supp. 1029 (S.D.N.Y. 1992).]

Speech Codes.   In recent years, First Amendment controversies have become routine. Among the most highly publicized episodes have been those involving university speech codes. In efforts to stop on-campus expressions of bigotry, hundreds of colleges and universities have established rules that forbid certain specified classes of expression. For example, Stanford University amended its student code to provide that

> Speech and other expression constitutes harassment by personal vilification if it is intended to insult or stigmatize an individual or a small number of individuals on the basis of their sex, race, color, handicap, religion, sexual orientation, or national and ethnic origin; is addressed directly to the individual or individuals whom it insults or stigmatizes; and makes use of insulting or "fighting" words or non-verbal symbols.

Now those codes demanding so-called politically correct speech appear to be receding in the face of public pressure and court decisions. The Stanford speech code as well as others around the nation have been struck down as violations of the First Amendment and other constitutional provisions. The University of Wisconsin student speech code was ruled unconstitutional in 1991, but in 1999 the University engaged in a careful debate about the wisdom of its faculty speech code, as the *New York Times* explained:

> The issue that gray February day was one of delicate balance: how to assure the freedom to discourse on Hitler's "Mein Kampf," as one participant put it, but not to use the word "Jew" as a verb, to lecture on sexuality but not to refer to female students as "babes."
>
> The debate—over a faculty speech code—filled the pale blue faculty senate room in Bascom Hall with passion. It was the latest round in a dispute that began on the lakeside campus of the University of Wisconsin nearly two years ago but had been simmering, in some fashion, for generations. A plaque on the building's entrance celebrates freedom of inquiry—the "fearless sifting and winnowing by which alone the truth can be found"—installed after the 1894 exoneration of an economics professor accused of teaching socialism and other "dangerous ideas."
>
> The question on the floor—and it is being mulled on hundreds of campuses across the country, from the University of California to Bowdoin College in Maine—was how to promote such "fearless sifting" while still creating a welcoming environment for groups that have historically felt slighted at American universities. For while robust intellectual inquiry is a self-stated goal of every university, so too is creating a diverse and tolerant nation.
>
> Student and faculty codes punish, sometimes through suspension, expulsion or firing, words or deeds that create an environment perceived as hostile. Backers say codes insure that minorities and other vulnerable groups will not be mistreated.[15]

By a narrow margin, the Wisconsin faculty voted in 1999 to eliminate its speech code.[16] Of course, the hurtful, purposeless insults and harassments addressed by the codes continue. Many First Amendment scholars believe the correct antidote to hate speech is simply more speech; that is, they place their faith in the marketplace of ideas rather than in rules, however well intended. [For an outline of the law of speech codes as well as an examination of the pros and cons of the codes, see **http://www.fac.org/publicat/warwords/warofwrd.htm**] [For a strong critique of campus "political correctness" see **www.shadowuniv.com**]

Matthew Shepard, a gay student at the University of Wyoming, was abducted and beaten to death in 1998, allegedly in part because of his homosexuality. James Byrd, Jr., a black man, died after being tied to a pickup and dragged three miles along a rural Texas road. The three white men accused of killing Byrd were allegedly motivated, at least in part, by racial hatred. Forty states and the federal government have *hate crimes* legislation that increases penalties or otherwise singles out crimes motivated by race, color, religion, or national origin. The federal government does not offer hate crime protection for gays; 19 states do so. A 1999 Gallup Poll finds that 7 out of 10 Americans favor hate crimes legislation at the state level.

Do you support hate crimes laws for serious wrongs to African Americans? To gays? Explain.

Source: The Gallup Organization. [**http://www.gallup.com/poll/releases/pr990407.asp**]

Student Fees.   University decisions in spending student fee money are now being subjected to First Amendment challenges. The Supreme Court in 1999 agreed to review[17] a seventh Circuit Court of Appeals decision supporting three University of Wisconsin students who argued that their First Amendment rights were violated by using portions of their student fees to fund political and ideological activities.[18] The student plaintiffs objected to their fee money going to groups, among others, that support abortion rights and gay rights. The Court noted that its ruling does not affect student funding for nonpolitical and nonideological uses such the student union or the health center.

> The student plaintiffs objected to their fee money going to groups, among others, that support abortion rights and gay rights

In the Workplace?   David Howard, an aide to District of Columbia mayor Anthony Williams, resigned in 1999 following rumors that he had used a racial epithet in conversation with his staff. Howard, a white man, used the word *niggardly* (which means stingy and does not carry any racist connotation) in talking about carefully managing city money. Following a great deal of adverse publicity, the mayor decided to rehire Howard.[19] While the D.C. mayor and others may have shown poor judgment and, in some cases, inadequate knowledge of the English language, we know that words can be destructive weapons. Hence, in some instances, the First Amendment does not shield us from punishment when our words hurt others. At the same time, we want to allow a maximum range of expression. The precedent-setting California case that follows examines the still largely unexplored and potentially explosive conflict between laws forbidding harassment in the workplace and freedom of speech.

AGUILAR v. AVIS RENT A CAR SYSTEM
1999 Cal. Lexis 4850 (1999)

Chief Justice George

A jury found that defendants had engaged in employment discrimination, in part by permitting plaintiffs to be the target of racial epithets repeatedly spoken by a fellow employee. In addition to awarding damages, the trial court issued an injunction prohibiting the offending employee from using such epithets in the future. Defendants argue that such an injunction constitutes a prior restraint that violates their constitutional right to freedom of speech.

I

Seventeen Latino employees of Avis Rent A Car System, Inc., sued Avis and 10 named individuals, alleging causes of action for employment discrimination violation of the [California] Fair Employment and Housing Act (FEHA).

The complaint alleged that plaintiffs were employed by Avis as "drivers," at its San Francisco Airport facility, to move Avis vehicles among parking lots and from one airport location to another. Defendant John Lawrence was "the service station manager at the SFO Avis location and was authorized to direct and control the drivers." The complaint alleged that Lawrence "verbally harassed [plaintiffs] constantly. He routinely called *only* the Latino drivers 'motherf_____' and other derogatory names, and continually demeaned them on the basis of their race, national origin and lack of English language skills." Defendant Kathy Black was alleged to have conducted a discriminatory investigation into the suspected theft of a calculator from a rental vehicle, detaining and questioning only Latino employees. In the course of this inquiry, a police officer was summoned and plaintiffs were told that the Immigration and Naturalization Service would be called if they did not cooperate. The calculator was found the following day, and Black apologized to plaintiffs.

*   *   *   *   *

On December 15, 1994, a hearing was held to consider plaintiffs' request for injunctive relief.

Defendants argued there was no evidence of ongoing harm, nor any danger of ongoing harm, and the court responded; "Well, there was evidence presented sufficient for the jury to find that . . . as to four plaintiffs who were working there, all of whom had a common characteristic, that is, that they were Latinos or members of Hispanic Latino racial ancestry, Lawrence had engaged in acts of harassment so continual and severe as to alter the working conditions for those people there, because that was the statutory test; Secondly, that Avis knew or should have known of that harassment. It may be that the bringing of the action at the Department of Fair Employment and Housing and the action here had a chilling effect on the harassment. But I want to make sure that that chilling effect survives the end of this process."

The court further stated during the hearing: "Well, the court is making a finding of fact based on evidence observed during the trial, that based on the evidence showing harassment and discrimination to the extent already commented on by Mr. Lawrence, there's a substantial likelihood based on his actions that he will do so in the future unless restrained."

On February 14, 1995, the court entered judgment awarding damages against Avis in the amount of $15,000 each to Hernandez, Lazo, Ramirez, Reyes, and Serrano, and damages against Avis and Lawrence jointly and severally in the amount of $25,000 each to Mojica, Peraza, and Recinos. The court also issued an injunction that stated as follows: "Defendant John Lawrence shall cease and desist from using any derogatory racial or ethnic epithets directed at, or descriptive of, Hispanic/Latino employees of Avis Rent A Car System, Inc., and shall further refrain from any uninvited intentional touching of said Hispanic/Latino employees, as long as he is employed by Avis Rent A Car System, Inc.

in California. Defendant Avis Rent A Car System, Inc. shall cease and desist from allowing defendant John Lawrence to commit any of the acts described in [the above quoted paragraph], under circumstances in which it knew or should have known of such acts; and shall further not investigate or permit investigations regarding breaches of its employment rules or practices when such investigations are limited to subjects or targets who are Hispanic/Latino employees of said defendant, unless the circumstances are such that no employees other than Hispanic/Latinos are reasonably subjects or targets of such investigation(s)."

The injunction further ordered Avis to post certain notices advising employees to report any instances of discriminatory or harassing conduct by Avis or its employees and to "publish a policy statement in English and Spanish delineating employee rights and manager responsibilities with regard to employee complaints of racial or national origin harassment or discrimination . . . "

Defendants appealed "from the mandatory and prohibitory injunction portion of the Judgment," . . .

The Court of Appeal concluded "that to the extent the injunction prohibits Lawrence from continuing to use racist epithets in the workplace it is constitutionally sound, but to the extent it reaches beyond the workplace it improperly exceeds the scope of the FEHA violation sought to be prevented and must be modified accordingly." . . . Plaintiffs have not challenged the Court of Appeal's restriction of the terms of the injunction, but Avis and Lawrence sought review of the court's decision, arguing that the injunction, even as limited by the Court of Appeal, constitutes an improper prior restraint of freedom of expression. We granted review to address this question.

*   *   *   *   *

II

One form of employment discrimination is harassment on the basis of race or national origin. [FEHA] Section 12940, subdivision (h)(1), states that it is unlawful: "For an employer . . . or any other person, because of race . . . [or] national origin . . . to harass an employee or applicant. Harassment of an employee or applicant by an employee other than an agent, or supervisor shall be unlawful if the entity, or its agents or supervisors, knows or should have known of this conduct and fails to take immediate and appropriate corrective action." California Code of Regulations defines harassment to include "verbal harassment, e.g., epithets, derogatory comments or slurs on a basis enumerated in the Act[.]"

Verbal harassment in the workplace also may constitute employment discrimination under Title VII of the Civil Rights Act of 1964, the federal counterpart of the FEHA.

Of course, not every utterance of a racial slur in the workplace violates the FEHA or Title VII. . . . For sexual harassment to be actionable, it must be sufficiently severe or pervasive 'to alter the conditions of [the victim's] employment and create an abusive working environment.' . . .

California courts have adopted the same standard in evaluating claims under the FEHA.

In the present case, Avis and Lawrence do not contest the validity of that portion of the judgment awarding monetary damages against them. They concede that the jury's findings that they violated the FEHA are supported by substantial evidence and they do not claim that the damage award violates the First Amendment. For purposes of this case, therefore, it is established that Lawrence's conduct created a hostile or abusive work environment for plaintiffs on the basis of race, and that Avis properly was held liable for knowingly failing to prevent this misconduct by Lawrence.

III

Avis and Lawrence challenge only that portion of the judgment awarding injunctive relief. It is beyond question that, in general, both the Department of Fair Employment and Housing and courts enforcing the FEHA are empowered not only to redress past instances of employment discrimination, but to prevent a recurrence of such misconduct.

*   *   *   *   *

IV

Avis and Lawrence claim that the injunction is invalid because it is a prior restraint that violates their rights to free speech guaranteed by the First Amendment to the federal Constitution, and article I, section 2, of the California Constitution. We first consider defendants' claims under the federal Constitution.

A

The First Amendment to the United States Constitution states: "Congress shall make no law . . . abridging the freedom of speech . . ." This fundamental right to free speech applies to the states through the Fourteenth Amendment's due process clause.

Although stated in broad terms, the right to free speech is not absolute. Many crimes can consist solely of spoken words, such as soliciting a bribe, perjury, or making a terrorist threat. As we stated in *In re M.S.* "The state may penalize threats, even those consisting of pure speech, provided the relevant statute singles out for punishment threats falling outside the scope of First Amendment protection." In this context, the goal of the First Amendment is to protect expression that engages in some fashion in public dialogue, that is, "communication in which the participants seek to persuade, or are persuaded; communication which is about changing or maintaining beliefs, or taking or refusing to take action on the basis of one's beliefs . . ." Civil wrongs also may consist solely of spoken words, such as slander and intentional infliction of emotional distress. "Acts of invidious discrimination in the distribution of publicly available goods, services, and other advantages cause unique evils that government has a compelling interest to prevent—wholly apart from the point of view such conduct may transmit. Accordingly, like violence or other types of potentially expressive activities that produce special harms distinct from their communicative impact, such practices are entitled to no constitutional protection."

This reasoning applies equally when spoken words, either alone or in conjunction with conduct, amount to employment discrimination. As already noted, the United States Supreme Court has held that the use of racial epithets that is sufficiently severe or pervasive constitutes "employment discrimination" in violation of Title VII and these decisions are at least implicitly inconsistent with any suggestion that speech of this nature is constitutionally protected. Furthermore, in *R.A.V. v. St. Paul*, the high court made this point explicit in discussing certain circumstances in which spoken words are not constitutionally protected, stating: "Since words can in some circumstances violate laws directed not against speech but against conduct (a law against treason, for example, is violated by telling the enemy the Nation's defense secrets) . . . speech can be swept up incidentally within the reach of a statue directed at conduct rather than speech. Thus, for example, sexually derogatory 'fighting words,' among other words, may produce a violation of Title VII's general prohibition against sexual discrimination in employment practices."

*   *   *   *   *

Defendants contend that, although it is proper to punish a defendant after the fact for a violation of the FEHA based upon spoken words, the trial court's injunction against the use of future epithets is an invalid prior restraint of speech. Under well-established law, however, the injunction at issue is not an invalid prior restraint, because the order was issued only after the jury determined that defendants had engaged in employment discrimination, and the order simply precluded defendants from continuing their unlawful activity.

* * * * *

In *Pittsburgh Press Co.* v. *Human Rel. Comm'n.,* the United States Supreme Court upheld an order prohibiting a newspaper from publishing advertisements in a manner that would constitute employment discrimination. The city ordinance at issue in that case proscribed discrimination in employment in a manner similar to the FEHA and had been interpreted to forbid newspapers from carrying "help wanted" advertisements in gender-designated columns under captions such as "Male Help Wanted" and "Female Help Wanted." Observing that the ordinance made sexual discrimination in employment illegal, the high court held that the First Amendment did not protect such illegal conduct, stating: "We have no doubt that a newspaper constitutionally could be forbidden to publish a want ad proposing a sale of narcotics or soliciting prostitutes." The high court concluded: "Any First Amendment interest which might be served by advertising an ordinary commercial proposal and which might arguably outweigh the governmental interest supporting the regulation is altogether absent when the commercial activity itself is illegal and the restriction on advertising is incidental to a valid limitation on economic activity."

[H]igh court decisions recognize that once a court has found that a specific pattern of speech is unlawful, an injunctive order prohibiting the repetition, perpetuation, or continuation of that practice is not a prohibited "prior restraint" of speech . . . The injunction at issue is based upon a continuing course of repetitive speech that has been judicially determined to violate the FEHA. Thus, prohibiting Avis and Lawrence from continuing to violate the FEHA does not violate their First Amendment rights.

Affirmed.

Dissent: Justice Mosk

The plurality conclude that a remedial injunction under the Fair Employment and Housing Act (FEHA), banning a list of derogatory words from use in the workplace, is a permissible remedy for employment discrimination by defendants John Lawrence and Avis Rent A Car System, Inc. I disagree. Among our most cherished constitutional principles is that speech—even if offensive—should be protected unless, and until, it produces a demonstrable harmful effect.

Both the First Amendment of the United States Constitution and the California Constitution restrict the use of content-based prior restraints on speech. The order at issue here—enjoining any future use in the workplace of specified words—constitutes just such a prior restraint. It impermissibly restricts speech based on the mere assumption that these words will inevitably create a hostile and abusive work environment amounting to employment discrimination. Nor is this injunction salvaged by labeling it a restraint on *conduct* rather than *speech.*

* * * * *

I

The crux of the lead opinion is that the injunction forbidding the use of a list of words does not amount to a prior restraint so long as it was issued after a jury determination of past employment discrimination. It endorses the formulation of amicus curiae American Civil Liberties Union of Northern California that speech was properly enjoined here because "a fair judicial process has determined that a repetitive pattern of speech is unprotected." I am unpersuaded.

"The term 'prior restraint' is used 'to describe administrative and judicial orders *forbidding* certain communications when issued in advance of the time that such communications are to occur.' Temporary restraining orders and permanent injunctions—*i.e.,* court orders that actually forbid speech activities—are classic examples of prior restraints." The injunction here falls squarely within that definition. It was not transformed into something acceptable simply because it was issued after a judicial finding of past employment discrimination.

According to the Chief Justice, the injunction passes constitutional muster because it simply precludes defendants from continuing their unlawful activity. It does more than that. It directly targets otherwise protected speech, forbidding *any* future use of a list of offensive words in the workplace—even outside the presence of plaintiffs and even if welcome or overtly permitted. Although the lead opinion insists that it would prohibit an illegal course of *conduct,* in fact it regulates *speech* on the basis of expressive content. . . .

I am not persuaded that a judicial finding that employees were previously subjected to verbal harassment in violation of FEHA could justify a prior restraint on expression not amounting to "fighting words."

Questions

1. Summarize the majority reasoning in the *Aguilar* case.
2. Explain Justice Mosk's dissenting opinion.
3. Concurring opinions not reprinted in the text added to Chief Justice George's reasoning in support of the constitutionality of the injunction. What arguments could be made to add strength to George's opinion?
4. Michelle Alexander, an attorney with the American Civil Liberties Union: "The U.S. Supreme Court has made clear that speech that is protected on the sidewalk isn't protected at work."20 Explain why we might restrict speech at work that is permissible on the sidewalk.
5. T.W., a minor, was suspended from school for three days after he drew a picture of a Confederate flag on a piece of paper. The Kansas school, Derby Unified, suspended T.W. because it believed he had violated the district's "Racial Harassment or Intimidation" policy, which prohibits students from possessing at school "any written material, either printed or in their own handwriting, that is racially divisive or creates ill will or hatred." Confederate flags were included in a list of prohibited items. The Court found that Derby Unified had a history of racial harassment. Were T.W.'s First Amendment rights violated? Explain. See *West* v. *Derby Unified School District # 260,* 23 F. Supp. 2d 1223 (1998).
6. The United States Supreme Court and lower federal courts have repeatedly ruled that burning the American flag is speech protected by the First Amendment. At this writing Congress is considering a flag protection amendment to the Constitution that would allow Congress and the states to make flag burning illegal. A 1999 Gallup Poll found 63 percent of Americans favoring that amendment. How would you vote? Explain. [See The Gallup Organization at **http://www.gallup.com/poll/releases/ pr990706.asp**]
7. Timothy Boomer's canoe hit a rock in Michigan's Rifle River, and he fell in. A passing mother and her young children heard Boomer cuss repeatedly (they said) or once or twice (his lawyer said). A 102-year-old Michigan law forbids swearing in front of children. Boomer was ticketed and tried.
    a. Did Boomer violate the statute?
    b. Does the First Amendment protect Boomer's outburst? Explain.

Free Speech in Cyberspace?   The sometimes bewildering world of computer-based communications technology is raising social problems previously unknown. Not surprisingly, the legal system must now play referee in the new world of cyberspace. Our legislators and judges must construct new rules for living in the age of the Internet.

In 1998, Congress and the President approved the Child Online Protection Act (COPA), which requires commercial Web sites to ensure that children do not reach material deemed "harmful to minors." Access to that material was to be limited to those with credit cards or those who completed an age-verification process. A federal district court judge in 1999, however, found COPA violative of free speech and other constitutional rights and blocked its enforcement.[21] The Justice Department is appealing the decision at this writing. The COPA followed a 1996 law, the Communications Decency Act (CDA), which made Internet transmission of smut a crime punishable by two years in prison and a $250,000 fine. Well-settled First Amendment law offers at least some protection to "indecent" speech while "obscenity" is expression so objectionable that it is not protected. The case that follows examines the CDA and outlines the law governing Internet transmission of indecent and obscene materials.

RENO v. AMERICAN CIVIL LIBERTIES UNION
521 U.S. 844 (1997)

Justice Stevens

Facts

The Communications Decency Act (CDA) of 1996 was challenged in court by a group of businesses, libraries, educational societies, and others including the American Civil Liberties Union. The plaintiffs sought a preliminary injunction barring enforcement of portions of the Act which prohibited the distribution to minors of "indecent" or "patently offensive" materials through interactive computer networks. In brief, the statute makes it a crime to initiate the transmission, by a telecommunications device, of a communication which is obscene or indecent, knowing that the recipient of the communication is under 18 years of age, and the same for a communication that "in context, depicts or describes, in terms patently offensive as measured by contemporary community standards, sexual or excretory activities or organs." A three-judge panel of the federal district court granted the injunction as to "indecency," but expressly preserved the government's right to act against Internet obscenity or child pornography. The government appealed to the Supreme Court.

I. Sexually Explicit Material

Sexually explicit material on the Internet includes text, pictures, and chat and "extends from the modestly titillating to the hardest-core." These files are created, named, and posted in the same manner as material that is not sexually explicit and may be accessed either deliberately or unintentionally during the course of an imprecise search. "Once a provider posts its content on the Internet, it cannot prevent that content from entering any community." Thus, for example

> When the UCR/California Museum of Photography posts to its Web site nudes by Edward Weston and Robert Mapplethorpe to announce that its new exhibit will travel to Baltimore and New York City, those images are available not only in Los Angeles, Baltimore, and New York City, but also in Cincinnati, Mobile, or Beijing—wherever Internet users live. Similarly, the safer sex instructions that Critical Path posts to its Web site, written in street language so that the teenage receiver can understand them, are available not just in Philadelphia, but also in Provo and Prague.

Some of the communications over the Internet that originate in foreign countries are also sexually explicit.

Though such material is widely available, users seldom encounter such content accidentally. "A document's title or a description of the document will usually appear before the document itself . . . Almost all sexually explicit images are preceded by warnings." Unlike communications received by radio or television, "the receipt of information on the Internet requires a series of affirmative steps more deliberate and directed than merely turning a dial. A child requires some sophistication and some ability to read to retrieve material and thereby to use the Internet unattended . . ." Systems have been developed to help parents control the material that may be available on a home computer with Internet access . . . "Although parental control software currently can screen for certain suggestive words or for known sexually explicit sites, it cannot now screen for sexually explicit images." Nevertheless, the evidence indicates that "a reasonably effective method by which parents can prevent their children from accessing sexually explicit and other material which parents may believe is inappropriate for their children will soon be available."

*   *   *   *   *

V. [II.–IV. Omitted]

[S]ome of our cases have recognized special justifications for regulation of the broadcast media . . . In these cases, the Court relied on the history of extensive government regulation of the broadcast medium, the scarcity of available frequencies at its inception, and its "invasive" nature.

Those factors are not present in cyberspace. Neither before nor after the enactment of the CDA have the vast democratic fora of the Internet been subject to the type of government supervision and regulation that has attended the broadcast industry. Moreover, the Internet is not as "invasive" as radio or television.

Finally, unlike the conditions that prevailed when Congress first authorized regulation of the broadcast spectrum, the Internet can hardly be considered a "scarce" expressive commodity. It provides relatively unlimited, low-cost capacity for communication of all kinds.

* * * * *

VI

[T]he many ambiguities concerning the scope of [CDA] coverage render it problematic for purposes of the First Amendment. For instance, each of the two parts of the CDA uses a different linguistic form. The first uses the word "indecent," while the second speaks of material that "in context, depicts or describes, in terms patently offensive as measured by contemporary community standards, sexual or excretory activities or organs." Given the absence of a definition of either term, this difference in language will provoke uncertainty among speakers about how the two standards relate to each other and just what they mean. Could a speaker confidently assume that a serious discussion about birth control practices, homosexuality, . . . or the consequences of prison rape would not violate the CDA? This uncertainty undermines the likelihood that the CDA has been carefully tailored to the congressional goal of protecting minors from potentially harmful materials.

The vagueness of the CDA is a matter of special concern for two reasons. First, the CDA is a content-based regulation of speech. The vagueness of such a regulation raises special First Amendment concerns because of its obvious chilling effect on free speech . . . Second, the CDA is a criminal statute. The severity of criminal sanctions may well cause speakers to remain silent rather than communicate even arguably unlawful words, ideas, and images . . .

* * * * *

VII

We are persuaded that the CDA lacks the precision that the First Amendment requires when a statute regulates the content of speech. In order to deny minors access to potentially harmful speech, the CDA effectively sup-presses a large amount of speech that adults have a constitutional right to receive and to address to one another. That burden on adult speech is unacceptable if less restrictive alternatives would be at least as effective in achieving the legitimate purpose that the statute was enacted to serve.

In evaluating the free speech rights of adults, we have made it perfectly clear that "sexual expression which is indecent but not obscene is protected by the First Amendment . . . "

It is true that we have repeatedly recognized the governmental interest in protecting children from harmful materials. But that interest does not justify an unnecessarily broad suppression of speech addressed to adults. As we have explained, the government may not "reduc[e] the adult population . . . to . . . only what is fit for children."

* * * * *

The breadth of the CDA's coverage is wholly unprecedented . . . [T]he scope of the CDA is not limited to commercial speech or commercial entities. Its open-ended prohibitions embrace all nonprofit entities and individuals posting indecent messages or displaying them on their own computers in the presence of minors. The general, undefined terms "indecent" and "patently offensive" cover large amounts of nonpornographic material with serious educational or other value. Moreover, the "community standards" criterion as applied to the Internet means that any communication available to a nation-wide audience will be judged by the standards of the community most likely to be offended by the message. The regulated subject matter . . . may . . . extend to discussions about prison rape or safe sexual practices, artistic images that include nude subjects, and arguably the card catalogue of the Carnegie Library.

* * * * *

Under the CDA, a parent allowing her 17-year-old to use the family computer to obtain information on the Internet that she, in her parental judgment, deems appropriate could face a lengthy prison term. Similarly, a parent who sent his 17-year-old college freshman information on birth control via e-mail could be incarcerated even though neither he, his child, nor anyone in their home community, found the material "indecent" or "patently offensive," if the college town's community thought otherwise.

The breadth of this content-based restriction of speech imposes an especially heavy burden on the

Government to explain why a less restrictive provision would not be as effective as the CDA. It has not done so . . . [W]e are persuaded that the CDA is not narrowly tailored if that requirement has any meaning at all.

* * * * *

We agree with the District Court's conclusion that the CDA places an unacceptably heavy burden on protected speech . . .

Affirmed.

Afterword

Decisions subsequent to Reno have struck down other portions of the CDA, but in 1999 the Supreme Court affirmed the constitutionality of one interesting element of the Act. That portion of the CDA makes it a crime to transmit a "communication which is obscene, lewd, lascivious, filthy or indecent with intent to annoy, abuse, threaten or harass another person." The provision applies to all e-mail messages, even those between friends. A federal court of appeals affirmed the constitutionality of the provision interpreting it to apply only to obscene messages. The Supreme Court affirmed that ruling. [See *ApolloMEDIA Corp.* v. *Reno,* 119 S.Ct. 1450 (1999)].

For further information about the CDA, see the American Civil Liberties Union Web site [**http://www.aclu.org/**] or the Center for Democracy and Technology Web site [**http:// www.cdt.org/**].

Questions

1. *a.* List the legal issues that were central to the Court's decision in *Reno.*

   b. What practical considerations were influential in the Court's decision?

2. *a.* Did the Court decide to treat the Internet more like a newspaper or more like television? Explain.

   b. Which direction do you think is best? Explain.

3. Prior to the Supreme Court ruling in *Reno,* Cathy Cleaver of the Family Research Council had called for the court to "reverse the radical lower court ruling which gave Bob Guccione the right to give his *Penthouse* magazine to our children on the Internet."[22] Comment.

4. An Oregon federal jury in 1999 handed down an award of $107 million in damages to Planned Parenthood, which sued antiabortion activists who provided material to a Web site known as the "Nuremberg Files."[23] The site, which appeared to drip blood, listed doctors, their photos, addresses, and other information about them, and labeled them "Baby Killers." The site included "Wanted" posters for the abortion providers who were labeled "Guilty of Crimes Against Humanity." When one of the doctors was killed, a line was drawn through his name. The jury found the defendants/activists were liable for threatening violence. Along with the fine, the court issued an injunction against further publication of the materials on the Nuremberg Web site if done with an "intent to harm."

   a. In your opinion, did the jury reach a good decision on the substance of the case?

   b. On appeal, should the decision be struck down as a violation of the First Amendment? Explain.

Commercial Speech.   Governments sometimes seek to regulate the public communications (e.g., liquor ads or the location of billboards) of profit-seeking, private-sector organizations. In 1942, the Supreme Court held that *commercial speech* was not entitled to the protection of the First Amendment.[24] Today, however, the Supreme Court's general position is that the First Amendment shields commercial speech but to a lesser degree than political, not-for-profit expression. Hence, governments may yet impose reasonable restrictions on commercial speech where those restrictions are necessary for the public welfare. The case that follows examines the reasonableness of a government restraint on commercial speech using the four-part *Central Hudson* test, which is the Court's primary measure of the constitutionality of commercial speech restraints.

GREATER NEW ORLEANS BROADCASTING ASSOCIATION v. UNITED STATES
119 S.Ct. 1923 (1999)

Justice Stevens

Federal law prohibits some, but by no means all, broadcast advertising of lotteries and casino gambling. In *United States* v. *Edge Broadcasting Co.,* 509 U.S. 418 (1993), we upheld the constitutionality of 18 U.S.C. 1304 as applied to broadcast advertising of Virginia's lottery by a radio station located in North Carolina, where no such lottery was authorized. Today we hold that 1304 may not be applied to advertisements of private casino gambling that are broadcast by radio or television stations located in Louisiana, where such gambling is legal.

*   *   *   *   *

II

Petitioners are an association of Louisiana broadcasters and its members who operate FCC-licensed radio and television stations in the New Orleans metropolitan area. But for the threat of sanctions pursuant to 1304, petitioners would broadcast promotional advertisements for gaming available at private, for-profit casinos that are lawful and regulated in both Louisiana and neighboring Mississippi. According to an FCC official, however, "under appropriate conditions, some broadcast signals from Louisiana broadcasting stations may be heard in neighboring states including Texas and Arkansas," where private casino gambling is unlawful.

Petitioners brought this action against the United States and the FCC praying for a declaration that 1304 and the FCC's regulation violate the First Amendment as applied to them, and for an injunction preventing enforcement of the statute and the rule against them.

[T]he District Court ruled in favor of the Government. The Court . . . concluded that the restrictions at issue adequately advanced the Government's "substantial interest (1) in protecting the interest of nonlottery states and (2) in reducing participation in gambling and thereby minimizing the social costs associated therewith." The Court pointed out that federal law does not prohibit the broadcast of all information about casinos, such as advertising that promotes a casino's amenities rather than its "gaming aspects," and observed that advertising for state-authorized casinos in Louisiana and Mississippi was actually "abundant."

A divided panel of the Court of Appeals for the Fifth Circuit agreed with the District Court . . .

The majority relied heavily on our decision in *Posadas de Puerto Rico Associates* v. *Tourism Co. of P.R.,* 478 U.S. 328 (1986) and endorsed the theory that, because gambling is in a category of "vice activity" that can be banned altogether, "advertising of gambling can lay no greater claim on constitutional protection than the underlying activity." . . .

III

In a number of cases involving restrictions on speech that is "commercial" in nature, we have employed *Central Hudson's* four-part test to resolve First Amendment challenges:

"At the outset, we must determine whether the expression is protected by the First Amendment. For commercial speech to come within that provision, it at least must concern lawful activity and not be misleading. Next, we ask whether the asserted governmental interest is substantial. If both inquiries yield positive answers, we must determine whether the regulation directly advances the governmental interest asserted, and whether it is not more extensive than is necessary to serve that interest."

* * * * *

IV

All parties to this case agree that the messages petitioners wish to broadcast constitute commercial speech, and that these broadcasts would satisfy the first part of the *Central Hudson* test: Their content is not misleading and concerns lawful activities, *i.e.,* private casino gambling in Louisiana and Mississippi. As well, the proposed commercial messages would convey information—whether taken favorably or unfavorably by the audience—about an activity that is the subject of intense public debate in many communities. In addition, petitioners' broadcasts presumably would disseminate accurate information as to the operation of market competitors, such as pay-out ratios, which can benefit listeners by informing their consumption choices and fostering price competition. Thus, even if the broadcasters' interest in conveying these messages is entirely pecuniary, the interests of, and benefit to, the audience may be broader.

The second part of the *Central Hudson* test asks whether the asserted governmental interest served by the speech restriction is substantial. The Solicitor General identifies two such interests: (1) reducing the social costs associated with "gambling" or "casino gambling," and (2) assisting States that "restrict gambling" or "prohibit casino gambling" within their own borders. Underlying Congress' statutory scheme, the Solicitor General contends, is the judgment that gambling contributes to corruption and organized crime; underwrites bribery, narcotics trafficking, and other illegal conduct; imposes a regressive tax on the poor; and "offers a false but sometimes irresistible hope of financial advancement." With respect to casino gambling, the Solicitor General states that many of the associated social costs stem from "pathological" or "compulsive" gambling by approximately 3 million Americans, whose behavior is primarily associated with "continuous play" games, such as slot machines. He also observes that compulsive gambling has grown along with the expansion

of legalized gambling nationwide, leading to billions of dollars in economic costs; injury and loss to these gamblers as well as their families, communities, and government; and street, white-collar, and organized crime.

We can accept the characterization of these two interests as "substantial," but that conclusion is by no means self-evident. No one seriously doubts that the Federal Government may assert a legitimate and substantial interest in alleviating the societal ills recited above, or in assisting like-minded States to do the same. But in the judgment of both the Congress and many state legislatures, the social costs that support the suppression of gambling are offset, and sometimes outweighed, by countervailing policy considerations, primarily in the form of economic benefits. Despite its awareness of the potential social costs, Congress has not only sanctioned casino gambling for Indian tribes through tribal-state compacts, but has enacted other statues that reflect approval of state legislation that authorizes a host of public and private gambling activities. That Congress has generally exempted state-run lotteries and casinos from federal gambling legislation reflects a decision to defer to, and even promote, differing gambling policies in different States. . . .

Of course, it is not our function to weigh the policy arguments on either side of the nationwide debate over whether and to what extent casino and other forms of gambling should be legalized . . . But we cannot ignore Congress' unwillingness to adopt a single national policy that consistently endorses either interest asserted by the Solicitor General. Even though the Government has identified substantial interests, when we consider both their quality and the information sought to be suppressed, the crosscurrents in the scope and application of 1304 become more difficult for the Government to defend.

* * * * *

V

The third part of the *Central Hudson* test asks whether the speech restriction directly and materially advances the asserted governmental interest. "This burden is not satisfied by mere speculation or conjecture; rather, a governmental body seeking to sustain a restriction on commercial speech must demonstrate that the harms it recites are real and that its restriction will in fact alleviate them to a material degree." Consequently, "the regulation may not be sustained if it provides only ineffective or remote support for the government's purpose." . . .

The fourth part of the test complements the direct-advancement inquiry of the third, asking whether the speech restriction is not more extensive than necessary to serve the interests that support it. The Government is not required to employ the least restrictive means conceivable, but it must demonstrate narrow tailoring of the challenged regulation to the asserted interest . . . On the whole, then, the challenged regulation should indicate that its proponent 'carefully calculated' the costs and benefits associated with the burden on speech imposed by its prohibition."

As applied to petitioners' case, 1304 cannot satisfy these standards. With regard to the first asserted interest—alleviating the social costs of casino gambling by limiting demand—the Government contends that its broadcasting restrictions directly advance that interest because "promotional" broadcast advertising concerning casino gambling increases demand for such gambling, which in turn increases the amount of casino gambling that produces those social costs. Additionally, the Government believes that compulsive gamblers are especially susceptible to the pervasiveness and potency of broadcast advertising. Assuming the accuracy of this causal chain, it does not necessarily follow that the Government's speech ban has directly and materially furthered the asserted interest. While it is no doubt fair to assume that more advertising would have some impact on overall demand for gambling, it is also reasonable to assume that much of that advertising would merely channel gamblers to one casino rather than another. More important, any measure of the effectiveness of the Government's attempt to minimize the social costs of gambling cannot ignore Congress' simultaneous encouragement of tribal casino gambling, which may well be growing at a rate exceeding any increase in gambling or compulsive gambling that private casino advertising could produce. And, as the Court of Appeals recognized, the Government fails to "connect casino gambling and compulsive gambling with broadcast advertising for casinos"—let alone broadcast advertising for non-Indian commercial casinos.

We need not resolve the question whether any lack of evidence in the record fails to satisfy the standard of proof under *Central Hudson,* however, because the flaw in the Government's case is more fundamental: The operation of 1304 and its attendant regulatory regime is so

pierced by exemptions and inconsistencies that the Government cannot hope to exonerate it. Under current law, a broadcaster may not carry advertising about privately operated commercial casino gambling, regardless of the location of the station or the casino. On the other hand, advertisements for tribal casino gambling authorized by state compacts . . . are subject to no such broadcast ban, even if the broadcaster is located in or broadcasts to a jurisdiction with the strictest of antigambling policies. Government-operated, nonprofit, and "occasional and ancillary" commercial casinos are likewise exempt.

From what we can gather, the Government is committed to prohibiting accurate product information, not commercial enticements of all kinds, and then only when conveyed over certain forms of media and for certain types of gambling—indeed, for only certain brands of *casino* gambling—and despite the fact that messages about the availability of such gambling are being conveyed over the airwaves by other speakers.

Even putting aside the broadcast exemptions for arguably distinguishable sorts of gambling that might also give rise to social costs about which the Federal Government is concerned—such as state lotteries and parimutuel betting on horse and dog races, the Government presents no convincing reason for pegging its speech ban to the identity of the owners or operators of the advertised casinos. The Government cites revenue needs of States and tribes that conduct casino gambling, and notes that net revenues generated by the tribal casinos are dedicated to the welfare of the tribes and their members. Yet the Government admits that tribal casinos offer precisely the same types of gambling as private casinos. Further, the Solicitor General does not maintain that government-operated casino gaming is any different, that States cannot derive revenue from taxing private casinos, or that any one class of casino operators is likely to advertise in a meaningfully distinct manner than the others. The Government's suggestion that Indian casinos are too isolated to warrant attention is belied by a quick review of tribal geography and the Government's own evidence regarding the financial success of tribal gaming.

* * * * *

The second interest asserted by the Government—the derivative goal of "assisting" States with policies that disfavor private casinos—adds little to its case . . .

The Government argues that petitioners' speech about private casino gambling should be prohibited in Louisiana because, "under appropriate conditions," citizens in neighboring States like Arkansas and Texas (which hosts tribal but not private commercial casino gambling) might hear it and make rash or costly decisions. To be sure, in order to achieve a broader objective such regulations may incidentally, even deliberately, restrict a certain amount of speech not thought to contribute significantly to the dangers with which the Government is concerned. But Congress' choice here was neither a rough approximation of efficacy, nor a reasonable accommodation of competing State and private interests. Rather, the regulation distinguishes among the indistinct, permitting a variety of speech that poses the same risks the Government purports to fear, while banning messages unlikely to cause any harm at all. Considering the manner in which 1304 and its exceptions operate and the scope of the speech it proscribes, the Government's second asserted interest provides no more convincing basis for upholding the regulation than the first.

VI

Accordingly, respondents cannot overcome the presumption that the speaker and the audience, not the Government, should be left to assess the value of accurate and nonmisleading information about lawful conduct. Had the Federal Government adopted a more coherent policy, or accommodated the rights of speakers in States that have legalized the underlying conduct, this might be a different case. But under current federal law, as applied to petitioners and the messages that they wish to convey, the broadcast prohibition in 18 U.S.C. 1304 violates the First Amendment.

Reversed.

Questions

1.
   a. The Supreme Court applied the four-part *Central Hudson* test to the *New Orleans* case. Explain the Court's conclusion and reasoning regarding parts 1 and 2 of that test.
   b. Now do the same for parts 3 and 4 of the test.
2. Based on the *New Orleans* decision, do you think that broadcasters in states where nontribal gambling is illegal may now lawfully air ads promoting casino gambling? Explain.

3. First Amendment considerations aside, in your judgment, should the government protect us from gambling temptations by limiting advertising? Explain.
4. Two Rhode Island statutes prohibited all price advertising on liquor in the state, except for price tags and signs within a store itself which were not visible on the street. The state sought to reduce alcohol consumption. Two licensed liquor dealers challenged the statutes' constitutionality.
   a. How would you rule on that challenge? Explain.
   b. Why would the elimination of price advertising arguably contribute to reduced alcohol consumption? See *44 Liquormart, Inc.* v. *Rhode Island,* 116 S.Ct. 1495 (1996).
5.
   a. How would you rule on the First Amendment constitutionality of federal laws and rules forbidding brewers to put alcohol content levels on beer labels? Explain.
   b. Why would the government ban that alcohol-content labeling? See *Rubin* v. *Coors Brewing Co.,* 115 S.Ct. 1585 (1995).
6. Hornell Brewing Co. marketed a malt liquor labeled Crazy Horse. The name brought protests on the grounds that it amounted to targeting Native Americans and because it was considered disrespectful to the memory of the highly regarded Sioux leader. Responding to that criticism, Congress attached a rider to an appropriations bill that forbade the use of the name Crazy Horse on an alcoholic beverage label. Hornell then challenged the constitutionality of the federal law.
   a. What is the nature of that challenge?
   b. How would you rule on it? Explain, See *Hornell Brewing Co.* v. *Nicholas Brady,* 819 F. Supp. 1227 (E.D.N.Y. 1993), and Laura Bird, "Makers of a Brew Called 'Crazy Horse' . . . ," *The Wall Street Journal,* April 14, 1993, p. B8.
7. A U.S. statute forbade the mailing of unsolicited advertisements for contraceptives. Youngs, which sold contraceptives, mailed contraceptive ads to the public at large. The ads included information regarding the public health benefits of contraceptives (e.g., family planning and prevention of venereal disease).
   a. Do the ads constitute commercial speech? Explain.

b. Does the government have a "substantial interest" in preventing the mailings where the statute shields citizens from material that they are likely to find offensive and where the statute helps parents control their children's access to birth control information? Explain. See *Bolger* v. *Youngs Drug Products Corp.*, 463 U.S. 60 (1983).

8. The Township of Willingboro prohibited the posting of real estate "For Sale" or "Sold" signs. The town's purposes were to promote racial integration and to retard the flight of white homeowners. Is the Willingboro action constitutionally permissible? See *Linmark Associates, Inc.* v. *Willingboro,* 431 U.S. 85 (1977).

THE FOURTH AMENDMENT

In an increasingly complex and interdependent society, the right of the individual to be free of unjustified governmental intrusions; that is, to a reasonable degree of privacy, has taken on new significance. The Fourth Amendment provides that:

> [T]he right of the people to be secure in their persons, houses, papers, and effects, against unreasonable searches and seizures, shall not be violated, and no Warrants shall issue, but upon probable cause.

Some constitutional limitations on the police powers of government officials are a necessity. However, the boundaries of freedom from unreasonable search and seizure are the subject of continuing dispute. The police are under great pressure to cope with America's crime problems, but they must do so within the confines of the Constitution, which is designed to protect us all—including criminals—from the power of an unfair, overreaching government.

Certainly, the most controversial dimension of Fourth Amendment interpretation is the *exclusionary rule,* which provides that, as a matter of due process, no evidence secured in violation of the Fourth Amendment may be admitted as evidence in a court of law. As ultimately applied to all courts by the 1961 U.S. Supreme Court decision in *Mapp* v. *Ohio,*[25] we can see that the exclusionary rule, while a very effective device for discouraging illegal searches, seizures, and arrests, also, from time to time, has the effect of freeing guilty criminals.

Drugs

Of course, search and seizure rules are often at issue in the government's efforts to stop illegal drug distribution. In general, a search warrant issued by a judge is necessary to comply with the Constitution in making a narcotics search. However, a warrantless search is permissible where reasonable, as in association with an arrest or where probable cause exists to believe a drug-related crime has been committed but circumstances make securing a warrant impracticable. Incident to an arrest, a search may lawfully include the person, a car, and the immediate vicinity of the arrest. Further, a police officer may lawfully secure drugs that have been abandoned or that are in plain view even though a warrant has not been obtained.

1. Traffic Stops.   Consider this recent episode:

[The] case began with a routine police stop on an empty stretch of Interstate 25 in Natrona County in central Wyoming on July 23, 1995. Just after midnight, Highway Patrol Officer Delane Baldwin pulled over a car driven by David Young of Casper, Wyo., for speeding and because a brake light was out.

As Baldwin asked Young for his driver's license and registration, he noticed a syringe in the driver's pocket. Baldwin told Young and two women passengers to get out of the car.

After searching Young and the two women for drugs, Baldwin then began to look through the car. In the back seat, he found a purse in which he discovered a wallet-sized bag with two syringes and a vial containing diluted methamphetamine.

Baldwin then arrested the bag's owner, Sandra Houghton, also of Casper, and charged her with possession of a controlled substance.[26]

Young had admitted to using the syringe to take drugs, but he was never charged with a crime because tests of the syringe revealed no trace of drugs. The case reached the United States Supreme Court in 1999 where the justices, in a 6–3 ruling, held that the officer had not violated Houghton's Fourth Amendment rights.[27] Broadly, the Court found that "the police can search a passenger's belongings when they have probable cause to believe that a car contains contraband even where there is no basis for suspecting the passenger of any criminal conduct."[28] The ruling did not extend to the body or clothing of the passenger.

On the other hand, the Supreme Court, in a unanimous 1999 decision, struck down an Iowa statute that allowed police to conduct a full search during a routine traffic stop where they issued a ticket instead of making an arrest.[29] A police officer stopped Patrick Knowles for speeding in Newton, Iowa, and issued a ticket. Then without consent or probable cause, the officer searched the car and found marijuana and a "pot pipe." Knowles thought the search violated his Fourth Amendment rights and the United States Supreme Court agreed, saying that the traditional reasons for permitting a search incident to arrest—preserving evidence and disarming suspects—are not present to a sufficient extent in a traffic citation case.[30] [For an analysis of another recent Supreme Court traffic stop case, see **http://www.fbi.gov/leb/nov965.txt**]

> Then without consent or probable cause, the officer searched the car and found marijuana and a "pot pipe"

2. Testing Students.   The Rush County, Indiana, Schools in 1996 adopted a program prohibiting students from participating in extracurricular activities or driving to school unless the student consented to random, unannounced, urinalysis exams for drugs. The Seventh Circuit United States Court of Appeals ruled that the program was constitutionally permissible,[31] and the United States Supreme Court declined to review the matter.[32] In December 1997, James Willis was suspended from Anderson (Indiana) Community High School for fighting with a fellow student. Upon his return to school and pursuant to school policy, Willis was informed that he would be required to provide a urine sample for testing even though school officials conceded they had no evidence that he had been using drugs or alcohol. Willis filed suit challenging the school testing policy as a violation of the

Fourth Amendment. The United States Seventh Circuit Court of Appeals agreed with Willis holding, in essence, that the drug test before reinstatement requirement was unconstitutional unless students are individually suspected of drug or alcohol use.[33] The Supreme Court then declined to review that ruling.[34]

These decisions suggest that the Supreme Court will need to revisit the drug testing issue. In 1995, the Court had ruled that the Vernonia, Oregon, school policy of requiring all athletes to submit to drug tests at the beginning of each season and randomly thereafter was constitutional. The majority in the 6–3 ruling reasoned that school athletes have a reduced expectation of privacy, that the loss of privacy was modest in light of other physical exams and vaccinations undertaken by students, that students give up their expectation of privacy by using communal locker rooms, and that the state's power over schoolchildren permits control that could not be exercised over adults.[35]

As these cases suggest, the key inquiries in search and seizure cases often are these:

1. Did the individual subjected to the search have a reasonable expectation of privacy?
2. Did the authorities have probable cause to conduct their search?

Questions

1. *a.* Are the Rush County, Anderson Community, and Vernonia decisions inconsistent? Explain.
   b. Which of the three drug testing policies do you favor, if any? Explain.

[For the story of the ACLU challenge to student drug testing, see **http://www.aclu.org/news/1999/no81899a.html**]

2. *a.* Can the police lawfully search an individual's garbage once it has been placed at the curb for disposal? In a recent case, a Connecticut resident, Paul DeFusco, was convicted of drug trafficking based on evidence found in his home. The police conducted the home search with a warrant secured on the basis of an informant's information as well as evidence (some short cut straws, glassine baggies, and prescription bottles) turned up in sifting through DeFusco's garbage.
   b. Explain the central issue in this case. See *State of Connecticut* v. *Paul DeFusco,* 620 A.2d 746 (Conn. S.Ct. 1993).
3. An informant told the police that a man, whom the informant described, was selling narcotics from the trunk of his car at a particular location. Police drove there, saw the car, and later stopped the car and arrested the driver who matched the informant's description. An officer opened the car's trunk, saw a brown bag, opened it, and found glassine bags of heroin. The car was then driven to police quarters where another warrantless search of the trunk produced a leather pouch containing money. At trial, may the heroin and cash lawfully be introduced as evidence? Explain. See *United States* v. *Ross,* 456 U.S. 798 (1982).

Business Searches

We have looked at Fourth Amendment search and seizure law in the context where it probably receives the most attention—drug cases—but now we need to examine that same Fourth Amendment protection as applied in a much less colorful venue—business practice. The government tries to protect us from business hazards such as pollution, defective products, and unsafe workplaces and business crimes such as fraud and bribery. In order to do so, the government often wants to enter company buildings, observe working conditions, and examine company books. But for urgent circumstances, we know our homes are protected from searches in the absence of a warrant. Can the same be said for a place of business? The Supreme Court has answered that question:

> The Warrant Clause of the Fourth Amendment protects commercial buildings as well as private homes. To hold otherwise would belie the origin of that Amendment, and the American colonial experience . . . "[T]he Fourth Amendment's commands grew in large measure out of the colonists' experience with the writs of assistance . . . [that] granted sweeping power to customs officials and other agents of the king to search at large for smuggled goods." . . . Against this background, it is untenable that the ban on warrantless searches was not intended to shield places of business as well as of residence.[36]

The importance of search and seizure law to businesses is well illustrated by the 1999 search of Coca-Cola offices in four European nations. Officials from the European Commission appeared unannounced and asked for and received access to company files. The searches appear to have been part of an ongoing inquiry into whether Coke has abused its dominant market position. The inquiry was precipitated by a complaint from Pepsi Cola.[37]

The following case involves a challenge to the constitutionality of a warrant to search a business for evidence of fraud and other crimes.

U.S. v. GAWRYSIAK
972 F. Supp. 853 (D.N.J. 1997)

Judge Simandle

This matter is before the court upon the pretrial motion of defendant Edmund Danzig to suppress evidence obtained during a search conducted on October 24, 1996, at his business premises. Defendant Danzig has been charged in an indictment with one count of wire fraud, in violation of 18 U.S.C. § 1343 . . .

Factual Background

On October 18, 1996, agents from the Federal Bureau of Investigation ("FBI") obtained a warrant to search the business premises of defendant Danzig in Sarasota, Florida. The warrant was issued by United States

Magistrate Judge Mark A. Pizzo of the Middle District of Florida, in Tampa, on the basis of a 24-page affidavit filed with the court by Special Agent Lynn Billings of the FBI.

By its terms, the warrant imposed four primary limitations on what items could be seized from defendant Danzig's place of business. First, the agents were only permitted to seize evidence of violations of the following federal criminal statutes: 18 U.S.C. § 371 (conspiracy), 18 U.S.C. § 1343 (wire fraud), 18 U.S.C. § 1621 (perjury), and 18 U.S.C. § 1623 (false declarations). Second, the warrant encompassed evidence concerning crimes committed by Edmund Danzig, Patrick Gawrysiak, Thomas Fox and their co-conspirators only. Third, the warrant only encompassed evidence of these crimes committed by those individuals between 1992 and 1995. Fourth, the warrant explained that the evidence to be seized had to pertain to one of sixteen enumerated persons or entities, such as "Edmund R. Danzig," "Terra Ceia Ventures, Inc.," or "Jonathan Bowers." . . .

The affidavit submitted to Magistrate Judge Pizzo, subscribed by Special Agent Lynn M. Billings, gave the details of pervasive fraud investigations being conducted by the FBI's Special Agent Wadsworth in New Jersey and Special Agent Lynn Williams in Virginia targeting Patrick Gawrysiak and identifying Danzig as a co-conspirator. Gawrysiak, using the alias Gray, claimed to be the principal of Great American Raceways International, Inc. ("GARI"), which issued forged GARI bonds falsely claimed to be backed by U.S. Treasury bonds. Danzig was described as President of Terra Ceia Ventures, Inc., a financially troubled company which had undertaken a real estate development project on Terra Ceia Island, Florida, for which Danzig and Gawrysiak sought interim financing ("bridge financing") . . .

The affidavit laid out the contours of four known frauds allegedly involving Danzig occurring between 1992 and January 1996, which were:

1. A scheme involving misappropriation of at least $250,000 as "loans" from Moors & Cabot brokerage accounts by Thomas Fox to Edmund Danzig in 1992 and 1993;
2. A scheme involving a $60,000 loan from Jonathan Bowers in 1993 for bridge financing for the Terra Ceia project, in which Danzig allegedly falsely represented to Bowers that a $100,000 GARI bond secured repayment of Bowers' note when in fact Danzig knew the GARI bonds to be worthless;

3. A scheme to gain a $1 million loan from Citizen's Bank to be collateralized by Gawrysiak's forged GARI bonds in May and June 1993;
4. A scheme to falsely represent to victim Paul Maillis that Danzig had $40 million in financing, and that Maillis' loan to Danzig would be backed by the worthless GARI bonds.

The affidavit supporting the warrant also attached numerous exhibits as examples of the forgeries and misrepresentations mentioned in the affidavit.

* * * * *

The affidavit demonstrated that evidence of Danzig's culpability for these schemes was likely to be found at his office, as well as evidence implicating others in these crimes even if Danzig is himself innocent.

The affidavit is too detail-rich to fully recount here. It adequately tied together the various accomplices, victims, and other actors into a highly articulated demonstration of a pattern of fraud . . .

On October 24, 1996, FBI agents executed the search, seizing from defendant's place of work approximately five boxes of various materials as well as copies of defendant's computer files.

In moving to suppress the seized items, defendant Danzig alleges primarily that: (1) the search warrant issued by Judge Pizzo was overbroad and therefore invalid; and (2) the law enforcement agents conducting the search acted in bad faith and with the intent to seize items beyond the scope of the warrant.

* * * * *

[FBI agent] Wadsworth testified that before commencing the search, the other five agents participating in the search met with him to discuss how to conduct the search at the Sarasota FBI at 8:00 A.M. The meeting lasted approximately 30 minutes. Agent Billings gave a presentation about the search plan and made the warrant available to the others. For part of that time, Agent Wadsworth described to the other agents the type of fraudulent schemes believed to be involved in this case. . . .

According to Agent Wadsworth, the agents also reviewed the "Search Plan" that had been drafted by Agent Billings. The Search Plan set forth the background of the government's investigation of defendants Gawrysiak and Danzig, and described the responsibilities of each of the six agents participating in the search.

* * * * *

Agent Wadsworth further testified that the agents used substantial care during the search itself. The premises before, during, and after the search were photographed by Special Agent Blake. Also, because of concern that defendant Danzig's files might contain privileged attorney/client information, Agent Huff, who is also an attorney, was assigned the responsibility of functioning as a "Chinese Wall" during the search and seizure to ensure that the other agents would not come in contact with such potentially privileged documents. . . .

According to Agent Wadsworth, out of approximately 200 boxes of documents in defendant Danzig's office, only five boxes of documents were ultimately seized. The parties agree, however, that the agents seized approximately half of the documents in the office that pertained to the time period of 1992 through 1995. The government explains this substantial 50% ratio by arguing that within that time period, defendant Danzig's business affairs were pervaded by fraud.

Mr. Danzig was allowed to be present during the search. Afterward, the FBI furnished a detailed inventory of all documents taken, along with copies of same; defendant has pointed to no document that is beyond the scope permitted by the warrant, nor has defendant indicated that any seized document is within a privilege.

I find the testimony of Special Agent Wadsworth to have been credible and candid. His testimony was comprehensive, convincing, and essentially unrebutted. He described a careful and deliberate investigation of wide-ranging wire and mail fraud schemes in New Jersey, Virginia, and Florida . . .

Discussion

Defendant's contentions in support of his motion to suppress may be grouped into two general areas of inquiry: (1) whether Magistrate Pizzo issued a valid warrant that was sufficiently particularized and not a "general warrant"; and (2) whether the government's search team acted in good faith and properly executed the warrant.

I. The Validity of the Warrant Issued by Judge Pizzo

A. Whether the Warrant Was a "General Warrant"
One of the primary arguments made by defendant on this motion is that the warrant to search defendant's premises was so overbroad as to constitute an impermissible "general warrant."

The prohibition against general warrants stems directly from the text of the Fourth Amendment to the Constitution, which requires that all warrants describe "particularly . . . the place to be searched, and the persons or things to be seized." As interpreted by the Supreme Court, this language prohibits a "'general, exploratory rummaging in a person's belongings.'"

*　*　*　*　*

In this case, the warrant imposed four significant limitations that channeled the discretion of the searching FBI agents and provided the particularized description required by the Constitution. First, the warrant provided that the agents were only permitted to seize evidence of violations of the federal criminal statutes concerning conspiracy, wire fraud, perjury, and false declarations. . . . Second, the warrant encompassed only crimes committed by Edmund Danzig, Patrick Gawrysiak, Thomas Fox, by the entities under their control . . .

Third, the warrant encompassed only the enumerated crimes committed by those individuals between 1992 and 1995. Fourth, the warrant provided that the evidence to be seized had to pertain to one of the sixteen persons or entities listed in Attachment B to the warrant . . .

Because of these limitations, this was not a warrant that provided the searching agents with unbridled discretion to rummage through defendant's possessions in search of any evidence of criminal activity. That conclusion is confirmed by the small percentage of documents actually seized from defendant's premises, indicating that the warrant did have limits that could be and were applied by the agents conducting the search.

The scope of this warrant was indeed relatively broad. Broad phrasing in a warrant, however, does not necessarily render the warrant invalid. The court concludes that the breadth of the warrant in this case was justified by evidence before Judge Pizzo indicating that defendant Danzig's business operations were substantially pervaded by fraud during the time period in question.

*　*　*　*　*

B. Whether Magistrate Judge Pizzo had Probable Cause to Issue the Warrant
Defendant also contends that the affidavit offered in support of the warrant did not provide probable cause concerning certain portions of the warrant.

*　*　*　*　*

In this case, the government has easily demonstrated that Judge Pizzo had probable cause to issue the warrant authorizing the search of defendant Danzig's premises. The affidavit and appendix of documents filed in support of the warrant provides significant detail concerning how each of the sixteen entities/persons listed in Attachment B materially relates to the fraudulent schemes allegedly carried out by Gawrysiak and Danzig between 1992 and 1995. There was ample reason to believe that evidence concerning these crimes would be found in these premises at this time. The affidavit provides more than a substantial basis for Judge Pizzo's conclusion that probable cause to believe that evidence of these frauds would be found in Danzig's office existed in this case.

*   *   *   *   *

[The Court's discussion of the conduct of the agent's in carrying out the search is omitted.] [The defendant's motion to suppress is denied.]

Questions

1. What reasoning and evidence allowed the Court to conclude that the warrant in *Gawrysiak* was sufficiently particularized as to meet constitutional requirements?
2. What reasoning and evidence supported the *Gawrysiak* court's conclusion that the magistrate had probable cause to issue the warrant?
3. Joseph Burger owned and operated an automobile junkyard where, among other things, he dismantled autos and sold the parts. A New York statute permitted police to conduct warrantless inspections of auto junkyards. Without objection by Burger, police conducted a warrantless inspection of his business. The inspection revealed stolen vehicles and stolen parts. Burger was charged with possession of stolen property. In court, Burger moved to suppress the evidence arising from the search on the grounds that the New York statute under which the search was conducted was unconstitutional.
    a. Does the statute violate the Fourth Amendment's prohibition of unreasonable searches and seizures? Explain.
    b. Why do many states, including New York, explicitly permit the warrantless inspection of automobile junkyards? See *New York* v. *Joseph Burger,* 482 U.S. 691 (1987).
4. Occupational Safety and Health Administration (OSHA) inspectors received permission from the Army Corps of Engineers to inspect a federal construction site where an accident had occurred. The contractor declined consent, but OSHA secured a federal district court order allowing inspection. OSHA found some obvious violations, but others were apparent only after initial observations led to follow-up interviews with employees and closer looks at equipment. The contractor objected to the search on Fourth Amendment grounds.
    a. Explain the nature of that objection.
    b. Decide the case. See *National Engineering & Contracting Co.* v. *Occupational Safety and Health Administration,* 928 F.2d 762 (1991).

Recently, Fourth Amendment issues have been prominent in cases involving drug testing and searching of employees. For a discussion of those issues, turn to Chapter 13.

THE FIFTH AND FOURTEENTH AMENDMENTS

Takings

The Fifth Amendment prohibits the taking of private property for a public purpose without just compensation to the owner. Thus, the Fifth Amendment imposes bounds on the eminent domain process commonly used by governments to condemn property for such projects as new highways. For a discussion of Takings law, turn to Chapter 7.

Privileges and Immunities

In a big surprise to the legal community, the Supreme Court, in 1999, revived a Fourteenth Amendment clause relied on only once by the Court in 130 years. The clause provides that "No state shall make or enforce any law which shall abridge the privileges or immunities of citizens of the United States . . ." The issue arose from California's effort to limit welfare payments to new residents. The California plan provided that new arrivals from states paying lesser benefits would, for the first year, receive welfare payments equal to the amount that would have been paid by the former state. The Supreme Court struck down the California plan since it abridged one of the privileges or immunities shared by all Americans; that is, the right to travel.[38] The Court ruled that the newly arrived citizen enjoys the same privileges and immunities as every other citizen of the state. The future of the privileges and immunities clause is unclear, but it could restrict states' economic regulations such as occupational licensure and interstate barriers to practicing law since those rules arguably would give the state's citizens fewer rights (the right to make an honest living) than citizens in other states or would discriminate against outsiders.[39]

Due Process

The *Due Process* Clauses of both the Fifth Amendment (applying to the federal government) and the Fourteenth Amendment (applying to the states) forbid the government to deprive citizens of life, liberty, or property without due process of law.

Substantive Due Process.   Laws that arbitrarily and unfairly infringe on fundamental personal rights and liberties such as privacy, voting, and the various freedoms specified in the Bill of Rights may be challenged on due process grounds. Basically, the purpose of the law must be so compelling as to outweigh the intrusion on personal liberty or the law will be struck down. For example, the U.S. Supreme Court ruled that a Connecticut statute forbidding the use of contraceptives violated the constitutional right to privacy (although the word *privacy* itself does not appear in the U.S. Constitution).[40] By judicial interpretation, the Fourteenth Amendment Due Process Clause "absorbs" the fundamental liberties of the *federal* Constitution and prohibits *state* laws (in this case, the Connecticut contraceptive ban) that abridge those fundamental liberties such as privacy.

Procedural Due Process.   Basically, procedural due process means that the government must provide *notice* and a *fair hearing* before taking an action affecting a citizen's life, liberty, or property. A fair hearing might require, among others, the right to present evidence, the right to a decision maker free of bias, and the right to appeal. However, the precise nature of procedural due process depends on the situation. A murder trial requires meticulous attention to procedural fairness; an administrative hearing to appeal a housing officer's decision to banish a student from a dormitory, while required to meet minimal constitutional standards, can be more forgiving in its procedural niceties.

Punitive Damages

The most contentious and highly publicized due process issue of recent years involves the ongoing debate about whether *punitive damages* are sometimes so large as to violate fundamental fairness. The Supreme Court in 1996 addressed the issue in the now-famous *BMW* v. *Gore* case.[41] Gore purchased a new BMW and was not told that the car had been repainted due to some minor predelivery damage. BMW's corporate policy was to advise dealers only of those predelivery repairs that exceeded 3 percent of the car's suggested retail price. Gore learned of the repainting and sued claiming he was a victim of fraud. The Alabama jury awarded Gore $4,000 in compensatory damages and $4 million in punitive damages. The $4 million award was reduced to $2 million by the Alabama Supreme Court, but BMW took the case to the United States Supreme Court which found the award "grossly excessive" in relation to the state's legitimate interest in punishing and deterring wrongful conduct. The Court employed a three-factor test to determine that the award was grossly excessive and thus violative of the Due Process Clause: (1) The degree of reprehensibility of the defendant's conduct, (2) the ratio between the plaintiff's compensatory damages and the punitive damages, and (3) a comparison between the punitive damage award and the penalties that the state could impose for similar misconduct. By all three standards, the award was so extreme as to violate BMW's due process rights. In 1997, the Alabama Supreme Court cut Gore's award to $50,000 and told him he could accept that amount or proceed with a new trial.

> The Alabama jury awarded Gore $4,000 in compensatory damages and $4 million in punitive damages

$4.9 Billion! The punitive damages question has drawn national attention again with a remarkable $4.9 billion, 1999 judgment against General Motors. A California jury awarded $4.8 billion in punitive damages and $107 million in compensatory damages to six people who were severely burned when their Chevrolet Malibu was struck in the rear and burst into flames. (The story is described in greater detail in Chapter 16.) The punitive award was reduced to $1.09 billion by the trial judge who said that amount was warranted because General Motors designed the fuel tank with profits rather than safety in mind. The case is on appeal at this writing.

Ralph Estes, director of the Stakeholder Alliance, applauded the big jury verdict in the Malibu case:

> How much does it take to make General Motors "get it"? Its revenue is greater than the gross domestic product of some not-so-small countries, like Norway, Egypt, South Africa, Poland, Chile, Saudi Arabia. It can flick away even a billion-dollar fine like it might a gnat—a billion dollars would, after all, amount to only only-half of one percent of GM's annual revenue.

* * * * *

> The purpose of the corporate system has been perverted, from originally serving the broader public interest to now exploiting the public for narrow private gains. We'll continue to have exploding automobiles, unsafe workplaces, sweatshops, toxic pollution and waste until corporations are made to put the public interest over private profit.

Apologists for large corporations like General Motors and Ford should stop trying to block a legal system that strives to bring about a nominal degree of corporate accountability, and start trying to restore a responsible corporate system, one in which each corporation repays the substantial benefits conveyed in its charter by first serving the public that provides that charter. If companies do that well, gains to stockholders will follow—without risking customers' lives.[42]

Question

Do you agree with Estes? Explain.

Equal Protection

The Fourteenth Amendment provides that no state shall "deny to any person within its jurisdiction the equal protection of the laws." The Due Process Clause of the Fifth Amendment has been interpreted to provide that same protection from the federal government. Fundamentally, these provisions forbid a government from treating one person differently than another where there is no rational basis for doing so. In short, the equal protection provisions forbid discrimination by the government. (See Chapter 3 for greater details.)

Gay Marriage?   The Vermont Supreme Court made headlines across America in late 1999 when it ruled that gay and lesbian couples in that state have been denied equal protection of the law under the Vermont constitution and are entitled to the same legal benefits and protections as heterosexual couples.[43] The Court did not legalize gay marriages, but it did instruct the state legislature to find a way to extend equal protection under the law to gay couples. The state legislature could make same-gender marriages lawful in Vermont, but the more likely possibility is that Vermont will provide some sort of domestic partner status to guarantee gay rights. The decision is the first in the United States by a Supreme Court to directly rule that gay couples have been the victims of discrimination. Since the decision was based on the Vermont constitution it cannot be appealed to the United States Supreme Court.

The Vermont high court ruling was based on the common benefits clause of the Vermont constitution, which provides "That government is, or ought to be, instituted for the common benefit, protection and security of the people, nation or community, and not for the particular emolument or advantage of any single person, family or set of persons, who are a part only of that community." A number of states, having similar constitutional provisions, presumably will soon need to address the same issues.

Hawaii, rather famously, brought the matter to the larger public attention in the 1990s when the state Supreme Court ruled that the state's failure to recognize gay marriages amounted to discrimination. Since that ruling, gay couples in Hawaii have acquired certain rights to property, family leave, and other opportunities previously available only to heterosexual couples. The Hawaiian constitution, however, was amended in 1998 to forbid gay marriages, and the state Supreme Court in 1999 at least temporarily closed the door on the issue by saying that the amendment legally precluded gay marriages in Hawaii. The nine-year battle in Hawaii was closely watched in part because gay activists and others argued that the federal Constitution's Full Faith and Credit Clause (Article IV, Section 1), which broadly commands each state to recognize the court rulings and laws of all other states, would permit gay couples to come to Hawaii to be married and then return home expecting their states to recognize the legal validity of their union. Many states, however, have historically declined to fully accept the marriage laws of other states. At this writing, California voters are expected to approve a March 2000 ballot initiative limiting marriage to opposite-gender couples. The article that follows describes some of the questions that will emerge across America in light of the Vermont Supreme Court decision.

RULING WILL STIR STATES ON SAME-SEX MARRIAGES

Stacy A. Teicher

A groundbreaking court decision that imparts all the benefits of marriage to gay couples—short of the marriage certificate itself—is expected to touch off a state-by-state reassessment of what constitutes wedlock in society today.

The Dec. 20 decision in Vermont is the first by a state supreme court to say that unions between homosexuals should be afforded the same benefits and protections that married heterosexual couples enjoy.

The Vermont court did not order the legislature to allow same-sex marriage, but it left the door open for the state to establish another way to give homosexuals all the rights of married couples. Still, the ruling is being celebrated by gay-rights groups across the U.S. as the fruition of a 20-year push for government sanction of gay partnerships.

Those who have watched America wrestle with the issue of same-sex marriage over the past several years say the Vermont ruling is likely to affect the political, legal, and moral debates in other states. Its obvious impact, they say, is in removing a barrier to gay marriage.

"The fact that the court says you have to give the same benefits . . . is going to blur the distinction between being married and being a same-sex couple," says Robert Volk, a law professor at Boston University.

Current law points to an America deeply divided over whether and how to recognize homosexual unions. Domestic partnerships are already acknowledged in several states and many cities, most often to extend health-insurance benefits.

But as recently as 1996, Congress enacted the Defense of Marriage Act, which defines marriage for federal purposes as a union between one man and one woman.

Action in the States

About 30 states have passed similar laws, although some legal analysts say these statutes may be vulnerable to a court challenge under the U.S. Constitution if one state refuses to recognize a marriage sanctioned by another. If, for example, Vermont lawmakers opt to permit gay marriage—as some predict they will—a couple who marries there and then moves to another state may attempt to assert its rights by, say, filing a joint tax return.

Such a case, though, is probably years away. "Over the next five years, things will happen legislatively, state by state," says Michael Wald, a law professor at Stanford University in Palo Alto, Calif.

The Vermont ruling "could possibly be duplicated" elsewhere, adds Mr. Volk. Its basis is a "common benefits" clause in the state constitution—one that is similar to provisions in a number of other state constitutions, he says.

Indeed, the ruling concluded that acknowledging gay couples who "seek nothing more, nor less, than legal protection and security for their avowed commitment to an intimate and lasting human relationship is simply, when all is said and done, a recognition of our common humanity."

For gay-rights attorney Beatrice Dohrn of the Lamba Legal Defense and Education Fund in New York, reading those words made the hairs on the back of her neck stand up. She says she'd become a bit jaded in her years of activism, but here "the court is coming out and saying that . . . there is no greater reason to support heterosexuals than to support gay couples . . . It's a sea change."

Other state courts may indeed look to the Vermont decision as gay couples bring claims for a more comprehensive set of rights. In the Vermont case, *Baker* v. *State,* the three gay couples who brought the suit pointed to more than 300 state protections married couples enjoy, including the right to visit each other in a hospital and inherit from each other without a will.

Back in Vermont

While some are basking in the symbolic magnitude of this week's ruling, questions remain about its practical ramifications.

Vermont lawmakers may decide to establish a domestic-partnership registry, but gay-rights activists wonder if that will meet the court's requirements. They hope that civil marriage laws will be extended.

Supporters of the traditional definition of marriage say they're pleased the high court did not require an outright recognition of same-sex marriage. But they also see the equal-rights decision as inappropriate judicial activism.

"We don't believe a court has the authority to order people to subsidize immorality," says Robert Knight, senior director of cultural studies at the Family Research Council in Washington. He urges the Vermont legislature to defy the order, or pass a constitutional amendment, as Hawaii did last year. The state should "specifically mandate marital benefits for marital relationships only," he says.

If Vermont allows gay couples to be married, observers predict some degree of magnet effect.

"It will be like people flying to Reno to get divorced in the 1950s," says Kenneth Sherrill, a political scientist at the City University of New York's Hunter College. In addition to those in-and-out trips, he says, some couples would also want to move there permanently.

Source: This article first appeared in *The Christian Science Monitor* on December 22, 1999. Reprinted by permission. © Copyright 1999. The Christian Science Publishing Society. All rights reserved.

Questions

1.
   a. List some of the legal and financial benefits that United States couples secure upon marriage.
   b. Should American law extend our conception of spouse to include same-sex couples?
   c. Should that interpretation be further extended to allow marriage between same-sex couples? Explain.
2. If the Vermont legislature were to legalize same-sex marriages would you see the law as a threat to the family relationship in that state and in this country? Explain.
3. Describe the steps taken by some American corporations to respond to the benefit needs of their homosexual employees.
4.
   a. How would you express the central issue facing the Vermont Supreme Court in the gay rights case?
   b. What role, if any, should religious values have played in the Vermont Supreme Court decision?

INTERNET EXERCISES

1. Prepare a brief essay outlining some of the many ways in which socialism is a constitutionally mandated ingredient of life in China. [See **http://www.uni-wuerzburg.de/law**]
2. Read the American Civil Liberties Union's 1999 complaint filed in federal court for the Western District of Oklahoma challenging school drug testing. [See **http://www.aclu.org/news/1999/no81899a.html**]. Explain the ACLU's objections.

CHAPTER QUESTIONS

1. Fifty-three percent of Americans responding to a 1999 poll thought the press has too much freedom in the United States.[44] The poll further found that most Americans celebrate the First Amendment, but feel uncomfortable with some of the public speech that is protected by the Amendment.
    a. List some of those forms of speech that are protected but are troubling to many Americans.
    b. How do you feel about First Amendment protection for those forms of speech? Explain.

2. A homeless man, Richard Kreimer, frequented the Morristown, New Jersey, public library. Testimony indicated that he spent much of his time staring at other patrons or following them around the library. Testimony also indicated that he was unkempt and his extreme body odor made the reading room unusable to some in his presence. The library barred the man for his violation of library rules requiring civil behavior, reasonable personal hygiene, and actual use of the library (rather than simply loitering there). Mr. Kreimer, with the assistance of the American Civil Liberties Union and others, filed suit claiming a violation of, among others, his First Amendment rights.
    a. How can Mr. Kreimer claim that his freedom of expression rights were violated by the library rules?
    b. Decide the case. See *Kreimer* v. *Bureau of Police for Town of Morristown,* 958 F.2d 1242 (3d Cir. 1992).

3. Several city ordinances in Arkansas made it illegal for "any person to place a handbill or advertisement on any other person's vehicle parked on public property within city limits." Church members contested the constitutionality of the ordinances, which prevented them from lawfully placing religious handbills on parked cars. Decide. Explain. See *Krantz* v. *City of Fort Smith,* 160 F.3d 1214 (8th Cir. 1998).

4. The Georgia Outdoor Advertising Control Act, in essence, prohibits any off-premises outdoor advertising of commercial establishments where nudity is exhibited. Cafe Erotica lawfully provides food and adult entertainment including nude dancing, and advertises those services on billboards. Cafe Erotica challenged the constitutionality of the Advertising Control Act. Decide. Explain. See *Georgia* v. *Cafe Erotica,* 507 S.E.2d 732 (Ga. S. Ct. 1998).

5. Colorado School of Law Professor Pierre Schlag, summarizing the central theme raised by Ronald K. L. Collins and David M. Skover in their book *The Death of Discourse:*

    > Stated most broadly, the predicament is this: with the perfection of communications technology, the refinement of capitalist rationality, and the intensification of market-created desire, the resulting culture is one that renders its own ostensible steering mechanism—namely, reasoned discourse—impossible. This broad scale rendition of the predicament is quite bleak, for there is no exit; everyone is included. We are all living in a culture that is, quite literally, doing itself in, mindlessly devoting itself to frivolous self-amusement: the unbridled pursuit of thrills, chills, titillations, fun, and ultimately, death.[45]

    Do you agree with the argument that reasoned discourse is now impossible in our culture of advanced communications and obsessive, market-induced desire for pleasure? Explain.

6. The Labor Department conducts regular investigations of business records to ensure compliance with the wages and hours provisions (e.g., higher pay for overtime) of the Fair Labor Standards Act. When a compliance officer sought to inspect certain financial records at the Lone Steer restaurant/motel in Steele, North Dakota, the restaurant declined his admittance

until the government detailed the scope of the investigation. Not receiving a satisfactory response, the Lone Steer demanded a search warrant prior to inspection. As provided for under the FLSA, the government secured an administrative subpoena, which, unlike a search warrant, does not require judicial approval. Once again, Lone Steer denied admission. The government then filed suit. Decide. Explain. See *Donovan* v. *Lone Steer,* 464 U.S. 408 (1984).

7. This chapter noted a number of decisions affording protection to commercial speech. Why are corporations unlikely to begin using their vast resources to speak out on the wide range of public issues from abortion to organized prayer in schools to the death penalty? Explain.

8. The California Public Utilities Commission ordered a regulated private utility, Pacific Gas and Electric Company, to include in its billing envelopes the comments of a rate reform group with whose views the company disagreed. The company appealed, claiming its First Amendment rights were violated. Decide. Explain. See *Pacific Gas and Electric Company* v. *Public Utilities Commission of California* 106 S.Ct. 903 (1986).

9. Restaurant owner Smith reads of studies suggesting that women typically work more diligently than men. He decides therefore to hire only women for his new restaurant. He runs an employment ad in the local newspaper and includes the language, "Only women need apply." Smith is challenged in court on the grounds that the ad violates Title VII of the Civil Rights Act of 1964, which forbids discrimination in employment on the basis of race, religion, color, sex, or national origin. Smith loses the lawsuit, but he appeals the decision on constitutional grounds.
    a. What constitutional law argument might be raised in Smith's behalf?
    b. Decide. Explain. See *Pittsburgh Press* v. *Human Relations Commission,* 413 U.S. 376 (1973) for a relevant decision.

10. Tanner and others sought to distribute handbills in the interior mall of the Lloyd Corporation shopping center. The literature concerned an anti-Vietnam War meeting. Lloyd Corporation had a strict rule forbidding handbilling. When security guards terminated distributions within the center, Tanner et al. claimed a violation of their First Amendment rights. Both the district court and the Court of Appeals found a violation of constitutional rights. The decision was appealed to the U.S. Supreme Court. Decide. Explain. See *Lloyd Corporation* v. *Tanner,* 407 U.S. 551 (1972).

11. Philip Zauderer, an Ohio attorney, ran a newspaper ad promising a full refund of legal fees if clients accused of drunk driving were convicted. He later ran an ad soliciting clients who believed themselves to have been harmed by the Dalkon Shield intrauterine contraceptive. That ad included a line drawing of the device as well as a promise that "[i]f there is no recovery, no legal fees are owed by our clients." The Office of Disciplinary Counsel of the Supreme Court of Ohio charged that Zauderer violated several provisions of the Disciplinary Rules of the Ohio Code of Professional Responsibility, including:
    i. The drunk-driving ad was deceptive because it purported to allow a contingent fee arrangement in a criminal case when that payment method was explicitly forbidden by Ohio rules.
    ii. The Dalkon Shield ad failed to disclose the fact that clients might be liable for *litigation costs* (rather than legal fees) and, therefore, was deceptive.
    iii. The Dalkon Shield ad violated rules forbidding the use of illustrations in ads.
    iv. The Dalkon Shield ad violated rules forbidding "soliciting or accepting legal employment through advertisements containing information or advice regarding a specific legal problem."

Zauderer was found to have violated the Ohio Disciplinary Rules, and a public reprimand was issued. He took his case to the U.S. Supreme Court.
    a. What constitutional claim should be raised on behalf of Zauderer?
    b. Decide. Explain. See *Zauderer* v. *Office of Disciplinary Counsel of the Supreme Court of Ohio,* 471 U.S. 626 (1985).

12. American Bar Association rules seek to discourage lawyers from aggressive pursuit of clients in an "ambulance-chasing" fashion. In-person solicitation of clients is entirely forbidden. General mass mailings not directed to individuals known to be in need of legal assistance are permissible under the bar's guidelines. Some attorneys have used targeted mailings to potential clients known to be facing legal difficulties. For example, attorneys have offered their legal assistance via express mail messages to families whose relatives have been killed or injured in crashes or other disasters. ABA rules discourage targeted advertising, and many states have followed the ABA's advice by adopting

guidelines restraining that type of advertising by lawyers.

A Kentucky lawyer sought to mail letters to individuals against whom home foreclosure proceedings had been instituted. He offered "free information on how you can keep your home." Kentucky rules forbade targeted mailings. The attorney claimed a First Amendment violation. How would you rule? Explain. See *Shapero* v. *Kentucky Bar Association,* 486 U.S. 466 (1988).

13. A California sales and use tax of 6 percent on all personal property sales was applied to the distribution of religious materials by religious organizations. The Jimmy Swaggart Ministries challenged the tax on constitutional grounds.
    a. What constitutional issue was raised by the plaintiff?
    b. Decide. Explain. See *Jimmy Swaggart Ministries* v. *Board of Equalization of California,* 493 U.S. 378 (1990).

14. Southwest Texas State University adopted a rule that restricted the distribution of commercial newspapers on its campus to specified locations, newspaper boxes, or subscriptions. The *Hays County Guardian* sued, claiming interference with its First Amendment rights.
    a. How does the University defend its position?
    b. Decide.
    c. Would the result be different if Southwest Texas were a private college? Explain. See *Hays County Guardian* v. *Supple,* 969 F.2d 111 (5th Cir. 1992); cert. den. 113 S.Ct. 1067 (1993).

15. J. R.'s Kitty Kat Lounge in South Bend, Indiana, featured young women dancers who progressively removed their clothing until they were performing in the nude. Public nudity is banned by statute in Indiana. On the strength of that statute, the city tried to close the Kitty Kat Lounge. The dancing was not obscene as a matter of law. As the judge saw it, the issue was "whether nonobscene nude dancing of the barroom variety, performed as entertainment, is expression and thus entitled to protection under the First Amendment." How would you rule? Explain. See *Barnes* v. *Glen Theatre,* 111 S.Ct. 2456 (1991).

16. In recent years, Congress and various state legislatures and municipalities have considered legislation designed to make pornographers pay damages to sexual abuse victims. For example, the Pornography Victims' Compensation act of 1991, a federal proposal that was not approved, would have permitted those who believe

their attackers were spurred on by obscene material to sue producers, distributors, and sellers of that material.
    a. How would you vote on such legislation? Explain.
    b. Would you favor extending such legislation to sexually explicit movies or to television violence? Explain.
    c. Could we lawfully ban all material that "subordinates or degrades" women in that such material would constitute a form of sex discrimination? Explain. For a related decision, see *American Booksellers Ass'n* v. *Hudnut,* 771 F.2d 323 (1985); aff'd 475 U.S. 1001 (1986). Also see *Regina* v. *Butler,* 89 D.L.R. 4th 449 (S.Ct. of Canada, 1992).

17. The sons of a murder victim brought a wrongful death/negligence action against a magazine, *Soldier of Fortune,* alleging that it had published an ad creating an unreasonable risk of violent crime. A former police officer had placed the ad offering his services as a bodyguard under the heading, "Gun for Hire." The ad resulted in the officer being hired to kill the plaintiffs' father. The ad included the phrases "professional mercenary," "very private," and a statement indicating that "all jobs" would be considered, but it also included a list of legitimate jobs that involved the use of a gun. The plaintiffs won the negligence action and were awarded a $4.3 million judgment. *Soldier of Fortune* appealed on First Amendment grounds. Decide. See *Braun* v. *Soldier of Fortune Magazine, Inc.,* 968 F.2d 1110 (11th Cir. 1992); cert. den. 113 S.Ct. 1028 (1993).

18. As you have read, "hate speech," that is, racist, sexist, homophobic remarks, is generally protected by the First Amendment. Commercial speech, often in the form of intellectually empty, symbol- and emotion-laden advertisements, is similarly protected. The Madisonian idea of the First Amendment was to protect serious political discourse. Now the First Amendment seems often to protect hate speech and commercial babble. In a 1996 book review and commentary, lawyer Paul Reidinger raises the concern that we may have "too much" free speech. Reidinger says, "The question these days is not whether government threatens free speech, but whether free speech threatens us . . . [T]here is a tidal wave of fetid speech washing over the American landscape." Has the marketplace of ideas failed? See Paul Reidinger, "Weighing Cost of Free Speech," *ABA Journal* 82 (January 1996), p. 88.

NOTES

1. Otto Friedrich, "How the Deed Was Done," *Time,* July 6, 1987, p. 59.

2. Jerre Williams, *Constitutional Analysis in a Nutshell* (St. Paul, MN: West Publishing, 1979), p. 33.

3. *Alden* v. *Maine,* 119 S.Ct. 2240 (1999).

4. Kathleen Sullivan, "Federal Power, Undimmed," *New York Times,* June 27, 1999, sec. 4, p. 17.

5. News Services, "In 3 Decisions, Divided Court Strengthens States' Rights," *Minneapolis Star Tribune,* June 24, 1999, p. 17A.

6. John Bacon, "Ten Commandments," *USA Today,* April 29, 1999, p. 3A.

7. *ACLU of New Jersey* v. *Schundler,* 931 F. Supp. 1180 (D.N.J. 1995).

8. *American Civil Liberties Union of New Jersey* v. *Schundler,* 168 F.3d 92 (1999).

9. *Brown* v. *Gwinnett County School District,* 112 F.3d 1464 (11th Cir. 1997).

10. *Peck* v. *Upshur County Board of Education,* 155 F.3d 274 (4th Cir. 1998).

11. *Jane Doe* v. *Santa Fe Independent School District,* 168 F.3d 806 (5th Cir. 1999).

12. Deborah Jacobs, "Free Speech in Malls, The New Town Squares," *St. Louis Post-Dispatch,* November 13, 1998, p. C17.

13. *Minnesota* v. *Wicklund,* 589 N.W. 2d 793 (S.Ct. Minn. 1999).

14. *Tinker* v. *Des Moines School District,* 393 U.S. 503 (1969).

15. Ethan Bronner, "Big Brother Is Listening," *New York Times,* April 4, 1999, sec. 4A, p. 23.

16. Editorial, "A Speech Code Dies," *The Wall Street Journal,* July 16, 1999, p. A14.

17. *Board of Regents of University of Wisconsin* v. *Southworth,* 119 S.Ct. 1332 (1999).

18. *Southworth* v. *Grebe,* 151 F.3d 717 (1998).

19. Associated Press, "Use of the Word 'Niggardly' Won't Cost D.C. Man His Job," *Waterloo-Cedar Falls Courier,* February 4, 1999, p. A2.

20. Greg Mitchell, "Ca. Supreme Court Upholds Hate-Speech Gag," *Legal Intelligencer,* August 4, 1999, p. 4.

21. *American Civil Liberties Union* v. *Reno,* 31 F. Supp. 2d 473 (1999).

22. Editorial, "Freedom in Cyberspace," *San Francisco Examiner,* December 15, 1996, p. C-20.

23. See, e.g., James C. Goodale, "Can Planned Parenthood Silence a Pro-Life Web Site?" *New Jersey Law Journal,* May 10, 1999, p. 37, and Elizabeth Amon, "Anti-Abortionists Liable for Threats," *National Law Journal,* February 15, 1999, p. A8.

24. *Valentine* v. *Chrestensen,* 316 U.S. 52 (1942).

25. 367 U.S. 643.

26. Mark Helm, "Court Expands Power of Police to Search Cars," *Des Moines Register,* April 6, 1999, p. 3A.

27. *Wyoming* v. *Sandra Houghton,* 119 S.Ct. 1297 (1999).

28. David Cole, "Fourth Amendment Takes Another Beating," *Fulton County Daily Report,* July 15, 1999.

29. *Patrick Knowles* v. *Iowa,* 119 S.Ct. 485 (1998).

30. Charles F. Williams, "Red and Blue Light Specials," *ABA Journal* 85 (January 1999), p. 36.

31. *Todd* v. *Rush County Schools,* 133 F.3d 984 (7th Cir. 1998).

32. *Todd* v. *Rush County Schools,* 119 S.Ct. 68 (1998).

33. *Willis* v. *Anderson Community Schools,* 158 F.3d 415 (7th Cir. 1998).

34. *Anderson Community Schools* v. *Willis,* 119 S.Ct. 1254 (1999).

35. *Vernonia School Dist.* v. *Acton,* 115 S.Ct. 2386 (1995).

36. *Marshall* v. *Barlow's,* 436 U.S. 307 (1978).

37. Constance Hays, "Regulators Seize Documents from Coca-Cola in Europe," *New York Times,* July 22, 1999, p. C3.

38. *Saenz* v. *Doe and Doe,* 119 S.Ct. 1518 (1999).

39. Thomas E. Baker, "Traveling Back in Time: Privileges and Immunities Clause Unearthed to Strike Down State Welfare Law," *Legal Times,* July 12, 1999, p. S24.

40. *Griswold* v. *Connecticut,* 381 U.S. 479 (1965).

41. *BMW* v. *Gore,* 517 U.S. 559 (1996).

42. Ralph Estes, "Punitive Damages Remind Big Companies Not to Sin," *Houston Chronicle,* July 22, 1999, p. A35.

43. *Baker* v. *State,* 1999 Vt. LEXIS 406.

44. Associated Press, "Americans Say Press Is Too Free," *Waterloo-Cedar Falls Courier,* July 4, 1999, p. A2.

45. Pierre Schlag, "This Could Be Your Culture—Junk Speech in a Time of Decadence," *Harvard Law Review* 109, no. 7 (1996), p. 1801.

Chapter 6

International Ethics and Law

INTRODUCTION

The preceding chapters have addressed general concepts of ethics and American law. As companies today expand, not only within their domestic borders but many times across continents and seas, an understanding of ethics and law across borders is critical. Unless a firm continues to meet the demands of worldwide constituents (clients, customers, consumers), it may be left behind without the means to effectively challenge its competitors. By globalizing, firms have more efficient access to resources, reduce tariffs paid, and take advantage of the geographical area that provides the best return for the firm's investment. And companies are not alone in this effort to globalize; they are supported by their governments, which have entered into agreements with other countries in order to facilitate the process. For instance, in the fall of 1993, Canada, the United States, and Mexico joined in the North American Free Trade Agreement (NAFTA), which opened the trade borders of North America, allowing easier access and growth opportunities for affected firms.

But what are the implications of this expansion around the globe? To what laws are companies subject if they cannot even determine what is their "home" country? As firms become companies of the world, rather than of one nation, conflicts that might otherwise have been easily settled are now legal quagmires.

THE INTERNATIONAL ENVIRONMENT

Since Adam Smith, many have argued that it is axiomatic that a decrease in trade barriers between any number of countries will stimulate the world economy, not simply those of the countries involved in the specific trade agreement. Accordingly, the NAFTA was successful in the U.S. Congress because the legislators believed that a stimulation of the Mexican and Canadian economies would lead to a boost in the American economy. At the same time, during the national debate on the NAFTA, labor leaders contended that, with a lowering of trade barriers, U.S. firms would immediately take advantage of lower-cost labor locations in Mexico and thus sacrifice American jobs. This, however, is seen by some as a short-term setback to the American economy in trade for long-term gains by the creation of more robust markets for American goods.

201

[For an overview of NAFTA, see **www.nafta.net**] [But also see "NAFTA Stumbles Short of Expectations," **www.latinolink.com/nafecon.html**]. [For information on Canada/Mexico trade in light of NAFTA, see **www.embamexcan.com/bilateral.html** and **www.embamexcan.com/trade.html**].

The desire to reach some common legal ground in international business is not a recent development. United States commercial treaties, negotiated as early as 1778, regulated shipping and trading rights and rules between individuals of different countries. However, with the advent of the multinational enterprise, these early international treaties have become outmoded. With new agreements come new concerns.

As the NAFTA debate shows, countervailing forces are at work in the global economy. On the one hand, consider the practically unprecedented expansion of world trade through agreements such as the NAFTA; the General Agreement on Tariffs and Trade (GATT), which is now regulated by the World Trade Organization (WTO); the MERCOSUR Common Market (created by Argentina, Brazil, Paraguay, and Uruguay); and the East African Community (created by Kenya, Tanzania, and Uganda), among others. These alliances represent not only legislative victories but also resistance to a growing isolationist tendency in the United States and elsewhere.

For example, despite the support of every living president in the United States, as well as Nobel Prize–winning economists, almost half of the American public opposed the NAFTA. The alliance, which expands trade across the North American continent, was passed in Congress by only a slight margin. In addition, after years of negotiation, many tariff barriers have been reduced across the globe. Most notably in late 1999, the United States and the People's Republic of China reached an understanding that is expected to significantly decrease Chinese duties on American goods while expediting China's admission to the World Trade Organization. [For the WTO, see **www.wto.org**]

Finally, there is a clear indication of a shift toward a more uniform concept of international justice. War criminals, brutal totalitarian leaders, and those who have contributed to crimes against humanity around the world are gradually being brought to justice by the unified and consistent efforts of nations on a global scale. This is a remarkable happening since, up to now, many in their situation have easily escaped justice by "forum shopping"—finding a geopolitical haven sympathetic to their deeds.

Countervailing Forces.   While the world is finding common ground in important respects, other forces are, in effect, limiting the globalization of world business. First, while the European Union's original aims have been supported by the successful issuance of the Euro, its value relative to the dollar has been disappointing to Europeans. Financial and immigration concerns, as well as power struggles, have characterized the debate on this topic, slowing efforts at trade expansion. Second, the former Soviet Union is experiencing chaos and has uncovered corruption at the highest levels, undermining confidence in that economy and frustrating former Russian leader Boris Yeltsin's original timeline for reform and a free market economy. Yeltsin had to deal with the election of a number of right-wing legislators who opposed the swiftness and direction of his reforms. Consequently, he was forced to decelerate the privatization process, which in turn accelerated inflation and removed the nation, for a time, from international trading. Finally, while China has its inflation as well as its growth rate under relative control, it too has seen a real erosion of foreign investor confidence. Both China and Russia are therefore "capital-starved"—Russia because of its corruption and China because of fears of a continued totalitarian atmosphere and the inefficiency of the Chinese communist bureaucracy.

Also limiting globalization efforts is the continued obstinacy of several governments that are either completely totalitarian, such as Indonesia, or simply highly corrupt, such as Mexico. One unfortunate example of this limitation is the disappointing results of NAFTA, which has been held back by distrust among trading partners fueled by reports of corruption at the very top of the Mexican government.

THE INTERCULTURAL ENVIRONMENT: ETHICS ACROSS INTERNATIONAL BORDERS

Social Responsibility to Host Country

Where a firm is involved in business abroad, does that firm have social duties to the host country beyond those required by the market and the law of that country? This issue has arisen most recently in connection with the environment. For instance, are firms that engage in business that may result in a depletion of the rain forests responsible for protecting the forests, even where there are no laws that require them to do so?

Power companies AES Corporation and New England Electric System evidently believed that they were responsible. When they learned that the carbon dioxide emissions from fossil-fueled power plants in the United States were dangerous to trees in the rain forests, they engaged in a voluntary program to replant the forest with new trees in order to offset the effects of their industry.[1] On the other hand, Chiquita, Dole, and Del Monte have all been cited as companies that have engaged in harmful practices. These companies have expanded their banana plantations in Central and South America, increasing the amount of pesticides used in those areas, which has then led to extreme deforestation.

Substandard Working Conditions.   The question of a firm's responsibilities to the labor forces of a host country has been in the press a great deal lately. Under the moniker "sweatshops," some foreign operations or suppliers of organizations have been chastised for allowing working conditions to prevail that Western cultures would consider substandard. Publicly denounced but often privately supported, sweatshops pose a host of commercial, economic, ethical, political, and social questions. Do businesses owe a social responsibility to the host country to improve their labor conditions? Do business realities require sweatshops? Are there economic and ethical justifications for sweatshops—at least sometimes? Do sweatshop practices harm local communities in developing and developed countries? Are evolutionary improvements of sweatshop working conditions possible? Can governments, businesses, labor, consumers, and social organizations bring about these changes? [See Chapter 12 for other sweatshop issues.]

According to the U.S. General Accounting Office, a place of work with "an employer that violates more than one federal or state labor, industrial homework, occupational safety and health, workers' compensation, or industry registration law" is a sweatshop.[2] Other groups are concerned about labor rights. The AFL-CIO Union of Needletrades, Industrial and Textile Employees defines a sweatshop as a place of employment with "systematic violation of one or more fundamental workers' rights that have been codified in international and U.S. law."[3] Some would say that a variety of substandard labor practices needs to be present before a place of employment can be called a sweatshop. Others, such as the Interfaith Center on Corporate Responsibility, require only a single questionable practice: "[though] a factory may be clean, well-organized and harassment free, unless its workers are paid a sustainable living wage, it's still a sweatshop."[4]

Recently various statutes have been passed to address sweatshop issues. In 1997, President Clinton signed a bill that prohibited the import of any product made with child slave or bonded child labor. While apparently a victory for sweatshop opponents, enforcement appears practically impossible since these same groups estimate that the United States imports more than $100 million of goods each year made under child slave or bonded-child labor conditions.[5] Other challenges remain as well. The U.S. Council for International Business (USCIB) has expressed concerns that codes that are imposed by external sources (as opposed to internally created corporate codes of conduct) are "unacceptable to the business community, are unworkable, and would be ineffective in resolving labor and environmental problems."[6] The USCIB contends that compliance with the demands of numerous codes of conduct imposed on multinational enterprises is unrealistic and argues that "the preponderance of the business community rejects the notion that companies can be held responsible for the overall behavior and policies of their subcontractors and suppliers throughout the supply chain."[7]

Free market economists believe that sweatshops are necessary and beneficial; sweatshops improve global well-being; consumers in global markets pay less for the products they buy; and the economies of developing countries improve because their export sectors expand. Sweatshops have been an element of every developed country's transformation from an agrarian society to an urban-based, highly industrialized economy. If poor countries want to develop, the economists argue, a sweatshop stage is necessary:

> When Harvard University economist Jeffrey D. Sachs was recently asked whether there were too many sweatshops in poor nations, he replied that his concern was "not that there are too many sweatshops, but that there are too few."
>
> Many other economists are also coming to recognize that low-wage plants overseas making clothing and shoes for export to America and other industrialized-world markets are actually providing an important service to their workers. These plants are a necessary first step toward prosperity in developing countries.
>
> Sachs says these types of jobs eventually led to prosperity in Hong Kong and Singapore and are what is now needed in Africa to facilitate the transition to increased prosperity from today's backbreaking rural poverty in many areas.
>
> Within a generation, apparel-assembling and similar jobs in Hong Kong, Singapore, South Korea and Taiwan took national incomes from about 10 percent of that of the U.S. to 40 percent.[8]

Nike.   The article that follows describes the significant progress the Nike Corporation has made in dealing with the highly publicized, substandard working conditions in its shoe suppliers' Vietnamese factories.

NIKE'S IMAGE PROBLEM

Julie Schmit

BIEN HOA, Vietnam—When 200 workers making Nike shoes here were told recently that they would have to work a Sunday, they balked.

They demanded the customary double-time pay. The Korean-owned factory, which Nike pays to make its shoes, wanted the workers to simply take a different day off during the week.

In the past, the scene could have been explosive. This was, after all, the same factory in which 40 Vietnamese workers were forced in 1996 to kneel with their hands in the air as punishment for poor performance. In 1997, 56 Vietnamese workers making Nike shoes at a Taiwanese-owned plant were forced to run around a factory in the stifling heat because they didn't wear regulation shoes. Twelve fainted. In other Vietnam factories, workers had been slapped with shoes or ordered to lick factory floors.

This time, trouble was muted. Nike's own managers, located in Vietnam near the plant, demanded that the Tae Kwang Vina factory pay double time and give the workers another day off. They then banned Sunday work at the five Vietnam factories that make Nike shoes but are Korean- or Taiwanese-owned.

What a difference a global outcry over working conditions can make.

It has been more than two years since reports of atrocious working conditions in Nike's subcontractor plants in Vietnam set off huge waves of consumer, investor and labor-rights protests. Today, while the plants are hardly inspiring places to work, they are better than they were. What's more, Nike's experience has sent a warning to other companies who hire overseas contractors: Ignoring poor working conditions is not acceptable.

"People now know that if they don't accept that responsibility, they may not have consumers in the next century," says Dusty Kidd, Nike's head of global labor practices in Beaverton, Ore.

This is not to say all is rosy in the Vietnam factories, which employ 35,000 and account for 12% of Nike's shoe production. *USA Today,* escorted by plant management, recently toured two factories in Vietnam and, separately, interviewed workers in their homes.

Managers still sometimes swear and yell, said the workers, most of whom are women in their early 20s. Last year, a Korean manager dragged a worker by her collar after she squeezed him as she rushed out the factory door. (He was fined $300 and had to apologize.) In parts of the plants, workers endure excessive heat and noise.

Six days a week, for eight or more hours a day, they sit on stools hunched over sewing machines or assembly lines. They rarely lift their heads. Supervisors stand nearby, sometimes at their shoulders. In one plant, some managers banned talking until last year.

On average, the workers make $47 a month—about what Reebok's Vietnam-based subcontractor pays—but less than half of what other foreign companies pay their least skilled factory workers in Vietnam, a recent survey shows. Tong Thi Hanh, 21, a four-year Nike shoe-making employee, makes $54 a month and dreams of owning a television and refrigerator.

That may take awhile. In Vietnam, shoe workers toil about 20 minutes just to buy an egg, estimates the Interfaith Center on Corporate Responsibility.

Still, the workers interviewed agreed: "Things are much better than before," says Pham Thi Loan, 25, a four-year employee. She used to cower around a Korean manager who snapped the bra straps of workers as he addressed them. That doesn't happen anymore.

What changed? Nike's attitude for starters. When it came under attack, "it shut the doors," says Brian Quinn, Vietnam coordinator for the Harvard Institute of International Development. Nike bristled at charges that it was exploiting workers, because it believed that its shoes were being made under some of the best conditions in the industry, Kidd says.

Yet, with more than a 40% market share and with basketball superstar Michael Jordan as its lead pitchman, it presented a big target. In one year, Nike paid Jordan as much (about $25 million) to pitch the shoes as its subcontractors paid 35,000 Vietnamese to make them.

Finally in May 1998, at a headline-making press conference, Nike CEO Philip Knight admitted that the brand had become "synonymous with slave wages and arbitrary abuse"—and he pledged to do something about it.

And Nike has.

"It is leading the way in grappling with these very complicated and controversial issues," says Steve Koenig, president of the Informed Investors Group in Seattle and a member of the Interfaith Center.

The Vietnam plants have seen improvements in terms of:

- **Cleaner air.** In 1994, Nike started removing petroleum-based compounds, which can cause skin and respiratory ailments, from glues, primers and cleansers.
- **Tougher rules.** In 1997, Nike banned its subcontractors from seeking exemptions to Vietnam's minimum wage, which one plant was doing. It also banned "training wages," which were about 70% of a worker's full wage and could be easily abused.
- **More oversight.** Three years ago, Nike didn't have anybody specifically working on labor issues. Now, it has 28 people. Three years ago, Nike's on-site production manager in each plant wasn't required to monitor conditions, Now, 20% of his or her time is devoted to doing so.

    Nike also now requires higher standards of factories that supply shoe pieces to the subcontractors. In June, Nike canceled an order from one Vietnam plant because it still used benzene, a carcinogen.
- **Better communication.** When Nike's Korean and Taiwanese subcontractors moved into Vietnam in 1995, they brought expatriate managers. They didn't know the Vietnamese culture or language. They also didn't bother to learn. Only one of five plants offered a Vietnamese language course. Today, they all do. Korean and Taiwanese managers "now know what is acceptable and what is not," says Quinn. At least 10 managers have been fired in recent years for poor behavior, Kidd says. (The one who made the workers run around the plant was sentenced by a local court to six months in prison.)
- **Some independent monitoring.** In December, Nike let environmental researcher Dara O'Rourke into one of the Vietnam plants. He applauded Nike's cleaner air but said some workers were still overexposed to some hazardous chemicals, heat and noise. Letting O'Rourke in was "an astounding transformation for a company that once . . . limited factory access to people they thought would write favorable reports," says Medea Benjamin, co-director of the San Francisco-based human rights group Global Exchange.

But Benjamin says Nike has yet to tackle its biggest shortcoming: wages. Activists claim a livable wage is not assured.

*   *   *   *   *

Nike maintains that its wages are driven by the market and are better than those paid by Vietnamese-owned shoe factories.

At the Hunsan shoe company in Ho Chi Minh City, for instance, 500 employees work 66 to 77 hours a week for an average monthly wage of $45, says President Thai Van Hung.

"We have to pay Michael Jordan . . . what the market dictates because he sells shoes for us. We pay workers this amount because that's the market," says Chris Helzer, Nike's manager of corporate responsibility in Vietnam.

Despite the wage complaints, every worker interviewed was grateful to have a job in a country where unemployment is pushing 20%. Vu Thi Hong, 21, dropped out of school in the ninth grade to help support her family. Her mother and two younger brothers depend on her $54-a-month salary. She lives in a shoe-box-sized apartment with her cousin.

For four years, she has glued the bottom parts of Nike shoes to the upper parts. She would like a different job, but she sees no prospects. For now, her job provides her with an annual income that is more than twice the per capita income in Vietnam, where most people still work on farms.

Nguyen Thi Hue, 33, a mother of two, has spent four years sewing Nike shoes together. It is her first job off the farm. Does she like it? "I have no choice," she says.

But one thing has made it more tolerable: "We used to be scared. We are not now."

Source: *USA Today,* October 4, 1999, p. 1B. Reprinted by permission.

Questions

1.   *a.* Has Nike fulfilled its social responsibility by paying its employees whatever the market requires?

    b. Was it wrong to pay Michael Jordan as much for one year as a Nike pitchman as 35,000 factory workers were paid for one year of their labor? Explain.

2. If you were the vice president for business strategy for a large retailing firm, how would you choose your global suppliers?

3. Do you think that a Code of Vendor Conduct is appropriate for all types of firms who purchase resources from other companies? Which firms would find this type of document more useful than others? How would you propose to enforce your Code of Vendor Conduct?

4. What types of labor standards would you impose on suppliers from other countries, if any?

[For sweatshop websites, see Sweatshop Watch:

http://www.sweatshopwatch.org/
UNITE: **http://www.uniteunion.org/sweatshops**
Human Rights Watch: **http://www.hrw.org/**
Global Exchange: **http://www.globalexchange.org**
International Labour Organization: **http://www.ilo.org**]

Social Responsibility to Home Country?

Notwithstanding a potential responsibility to the countries in which a firm does business, does that firm have any special obligation to its home country? A social responsibility to a home country might necessitate imposing the values of one's home country throughout the world. The United States exports its values structure in a variety of ways including through the extraterritorial application of its laws. When the United States Supreme Court declared that antidiscrimination provisions of United States statutes such as Title VII of the Civil Rights Act of 1964 did not apply extraterritorially,[9] Congress reversed the decision with its 1991 Amendments to Title VII. Accordingly, American firms that do not maintain certain Title VII standards abroad will be subject to liability in their home country. Though it extended the reach of provisions of the Civil Rights Act, the U.S. Congress has yet to extend extraterritorially the Fair Labor Standards Act, which regulates minimum age and maximum hours, or the Occupational Safety and Health Act, which establishes standards for safe workplaces.

U.S. Executive Branch Actions to Encourage "American Values" throughout the World. In 1995, the Department of Commerce introduced the Model Business Principles.[10] The principles established a set of guidelines for American businesses with worldwide operations. Specifically, the principles encouraged all businesses "to adopt and implement voluntary codes of conduct for doing business around the world" that cover at least the following areas:

1. Provision of a safe and healthy workplace.
2. Fair employment practices, including avoidance of child and forced labor and avoidance of discrimination based on race, gender, national origin, or religious

beliefs; and respect for the right of association and the right to organize and bargain collectively.

3. Responsible environmental protection and environmental practices.
4. Compliance with U.S. and local laws promoting good business practices, including laws prohibiting illicit payments and ensuring fair competition.
5. Maintenance, through leadership of all levels, of a corporate culture that respects free expression consistent with legitimate business concerns, and that does not condone political coercion in the workplace; that encourages good corporate citizenship and makes a positive contribution to the communities in which the company operates; and where ethical conduct is recognized, valued, and exemplified by all employees.[11]

[For more on the Model Business Principles, see **http://www.ita.doc.gov/bgp/model.html**]

In 1998, President Clinton initiated the White House Apparel Industry Partnership (AIP) to draft labor standards for factories and factory suppliers of the participating firms, and to develop a manner by which to better inform consumers of the conditions under which their purchases were created. This latter objective was included in response to critics' concerns that consumers are not the appropriate means by which to establish market demand in this arena, given their lack of complete information. The voluntary partnership was comprised of clothing and shoe manufacturers, trade unions, and consumer and human rights organizations. After eight months of deliberation, the partnership ceremoniously unveiled its Workplace Code of Conduct and Principles of Monitoring.[12] The code was formulated by some members of the partnership, but not all, since some members chose to secede as a result of ideological conflicts, including the garment workers union UNITE and the Interfaith Center on Corporate Responsibility. These groups contended that the proposal included serious shortcomings in its attention to living wages, hours worked, overtime pay, and the right to organize.[13]

[Copies of the code and principles can be found at **http://www.dol.gov/dol/esa/public/ nosweat/partnership/report.htm;** UNITE Statement on the White House Apparel Industry Partnerships, **http://www.sweatshopwatch.org/swatch/headlines/1998/ aip_nov98.html#UNITE;** "Sweatshop Watch's Response to the White House Apparel Industry Partnership Agreement," *Corporate Watch Web Site,* **http://www.igc.org/trac/ feature/sweatshops/swatch.html**]

THE CAUX ROUND TABLE
PRINCIPLES FOR BUSINESS

Joe Skelly

The Caux Round Table was established 10 years ago to bring together global corporate leaders for the purpose of reducing trade tensions. Created in 1994, the principles form an international code of ethical conduct for global firms and were created through collaboration with business leaders in Europe, Japan, and the United States.

These principles are rooted in two basic ideals: *kyosei* and human dignity. The Japanese concept of *kyosei* means living and working together for the common good—enabling cooperation and mutual prosperity to coexist with healthy and fair competition. Human dignity refers to the sacredness or value of each person as an end, not simply as a means to the fulfillment of others' purposes or even majority prescription.

*   *   *   *   *

Section 2. General Principles

Principle 1. The responsibilities of business: beyond shareholders to stakeholders.

Principle 2. The economic and social impact of business: toward innovation, justice, and world community.

Principle 3. Business behavior: beyond the letter of law toward a spirit of trust.

Principle 4. Respect for rules.

Principle 5. Support for multilateral trade.

Principle 6. Respect for the environment.

Principle 7. Avoidance of illicit operations.

Source: Reprinted by permission from *Business Ethics*, P.O. Box 8439, Minneapolis, MN 55408. (612) 879-0695. [For the Caux website, see **www.cauxroundtable.org**]

The Foreign Corrupt Practices Act (FCPA)

Consider the problem of bribery and other forms of corruption in certain countries. Some in those countries may contend that there is nothing wrong with bribery, while other nations criticize it greatly. How would you define bribery? What is the main problem with it? For years, U.S. firms have tackled this problem in their own and other countries. On a governmental scale, Congress has attempted to respond harshly to corruption in other governments and to support U.S. firms that do not participate in foreign corruption.

As we saw in Chapter 2, the FCPA prohibits United States companies and some joint ventures from making certain payments or gifts to government officials for the purpose of influencing business decisions. While the FCPA appears to be well motivated, some critics argue that it is inappropriate for the United States to unilaterally try to impose its sense of morality on others via foreign trade. In addition, others argue that the FCPA unduly restricts American companies operating abroad and prevents them from effectively competing with other firms.

[To see how one firm addresses the corruption issue, see **www.ingersoll-rand.com/general/coc10.htm**]

FOUNDATIONS OF INTERNATIONAL LAW

Having briefly examined some international ethics themes, we now turn our attention to problems of global law.

A firm with manufacturing plants in Argentina and Thailand, and corporate headquarters in Bangkok, enters into a contract with a French firm to distribute its products produced in the Argentinean plant. The French firm is not satisfied with the quality of the products being sent. What law would apply to this situation? Argentinean? Thai? French? The answer to this question is not simple, even for seasoned lawyers; yet the firms involved will be greatly affected by the decision since contract law varies from country to country.

The source of law applicable to an international issue depends on the issue involved. In general, private parties are free to form agreements in whatever manner they wish. The parties to the agreement can determine, for instance, which nation's law shall govern the contract, where disagreements in connection with the contract shall be settled, and even in which language the transactions shall be made. This is considered *private law*. Whenever the parties to a transaction are from different jurisdictions and are involved in a lawsuit, the court will look to the agreement of the parties to resolve these issues. Otherwise, where the contract is silent as to the choice of law, jurisdiction, and other questions, the court must decide. Generally, the choice of law rule of the jurisdiction in which the transaction occurred is applied. If the transaction is done by mail, as are many international trade negotiations, most often the law of the jurisdiction of the seller's place of business applies. Recall, however, that the parties to the contract may always reach an agreement on the law to be applied.

Public law, on the other hand, includes those rules of each nation that regulate the contractual agreement between the parties—for instance, import and export taxes, packaging requirements, and safety standards. In addition, public law regulates the relationships between nations.

Public law derives from a number of sources. The most familiar source of public law is a *treaty* or *convention* (a contract between nations). For example, the United States, Canada, and Mexico have the NAFTA, a convention regarding free trade between those countries. Public law is also found in *international custom* or *generally accepted principles of law.* These terms refer to those practices that are commonly accepted as appropriate business or commercial practices between nations. For instance, sovereign immunity is an accepted principle of international law. A custom is derived from consistent behavior over time that is accepted as binding by the countries that engage in that behavior. [For current news and updates on many dimensions of international business law, see **http://www.lawnews.net/papers**]

The Development of Customs.   One might better understand the concept of custom if it is analogized to the law of sales in the United States. For years, merchants would follow certain accepted customs or principles in connection with the sale of goods. These customs or manners of dealing between merchants were later codified in the Uniform Commercial Code (UCC) that regulates the sale of goods and has certain provisions specifically related to the sale of goods between merchants. In this way, customs or practices traditionally followed by merchants have become accepted principles of law.

On the other hand, in the international legal arena, customary practices are not stagnant; the development of custom as a guide for behavior or decision making is in a constant state of evolution. For instance, in connection with personal privacy or information flow between countries, the custom has been that personal information moves freely between countries in order to encourage the free flow of information in the business world. However, recently the European Union began to examine the potential for invasions of privacy and has now proposed minimum standards that must be maintained by a country receiving information from an EU country.

Two factors are used to determine whether a custom exists: (1) consistency and repetition of the action or decision and (2) recognition by nations that this custom is binding. The first merely holds that the action or decision must be accepted by a number of nations for a time long enough to establish uniformity of application. The second dictates that the custom be accepted as binding by nations observing it. If the custom is accepted as merely persuasive, it does not rise to the level of a generally accepted principle of law. Through persistent objections, any nation may ensure that certain customs are not applied to cases in which it is involved.

Courts seldom agree as to what constitutes customary law. In fact, the International Court of Justice has warned against imposing the customs of one country on another. In one case, *Fisheries Jurisdiction, United Kingdom and Northern Ireland* v. *Iceland,* the court considered the claim that it was "customary" international law that a country had exclusive fishing rights for 12 miles from its shore. In discussing the requirements for establishing a practice as a custom, the court stated: "Uniformity is good only when it is convenient, that is to say when it simplifies the task at hand; it is bad when it results from an artificial assimilation of dissimilar cases. The nature of international society does not merely make it difficult to develop rules of international law of general application, it sometimes makes them undesirable."

Courts.   As evidenced by the *Fisheries* case, public international law is also found in *judicial decisions.* The only court that is devoted entirely to hearing cases of public law is the aforementioned International Court of Justice (ICJ) in the United Nations. The ICJ is made up of 15 judges from 15 different member countries. The ICJ may issue two types of decisions depending on its jurisdiction. The court has *advisory jurisdiction* where the United Nations asks the court for an opinion on a matter of international law. These opinions do not bind any party. The ICJ may also have *contentious jurisdiction.* This exists only where two or more nations (not individual parties) have consented to the jurisdiction of the court and have requested an opinion. In this case, the opinion would be considered binding on the parties involved. The court, however, is not bound by its own earlier decisions as precedent. [For the International Court of Justice, see **www.icj-cij.org**]

The article that follows illustrates the interpretation of international law by an American court.

U.S. COURTS HANDLE
INTERNATIONAL LAW

Steven P. Garmisa

Tom Beanal—a member of an Indonesian tribe called the Amungme—filed a lawsuit in Louisiana accusing two U.S. corporations of violating international law.

A subsidiary of the American corporations operates a gigantic open-pit mine in Irian Jaya, Indonesia.

According to Beanal, the American corporations are guilty of (1) human rights violations, (2) "cultural genocide" and (3) pollution.

A law that permits foreigners to sue in U.S. courts for alleged violations of international law might sound like something cooked up by stoned hippies who stumbled into law school. But Beanal relied on one of the first laws enacted by Congress—the Alien Tort Statute.

This 1789 law says that aliens can sue in federal court for wrongful conduct "committed in violation of the law of nations."

When warlord Radovan Karadzic was in Manhattan in 1993, for example, he was sued for violating international law. Muslim and Croat citizens of Bosnia-Herzegovina accused Karadzic of commanding troops that used mass rape, torture and summary executions in a campaign of genocide. Federal appellate judges ruled the Alien Tort Statute can be used in suing Karadzic for genocide and war crimes.

With Beanal's case, U.S. District Judge Stanwood R. Duval Jr. had to decide whether the "facts" alleged in the complaint would, if true, add up to violations of international law.

Here is what Beanal alleges: The defendants (Freeport McMoRan Inc. and Freeport-McMoRan Copper & Gold Inc.) are Delaware corporations that are headquartered in New Orleans. Through a subsidiary they operate an open-pit copper, gold and silver mine in Irian Jaya.

Security guards employed by the subsidiary allegedly arrested, detained, tortured and murdered members of the Amungme tribe and destroyed their property. The American corporations allegedly committed "cultural genocide" on the tribe. And mining operations allegedly destroyed the rain forest and polluted the water where the Amungme live.

The McMoRan companies argued they couldn't be sued for violating international law because Beanal didn't claim they acted under authority of the Indonesian government.

Some evil acts don't violate international law unless they are performed by someone acting with government authority, Duval explained. If a home invader tortures a victim to find out where money is hidden, the crime doesn't violate international law. But when government officials arrest and torture political enemies, there's a violation of international law.

Other atrocities violate international law even if the defendants acted on their own and no government was involved. Genocide, hijacking, war crimes and piracy violate international law even if the defendants aren't acting with official authority, Duval recounted.

One of the problems with the complaint filed by Beanal is that "cultural genocide" doesn't violate international law. The Geneva Convention on Genocide defines genocide as acts that are intended to destroy a national, ethnic, racial or religious group.

Genocide doesn't include international destruction of a "culture," Duval decided. Yet some of the things alleged by Beanal—such as arbitrary arrest, torture and summary execution—could add up to genocide if these acts were specifically intended to destroy the Amungme tribe.

With the other alleged human rights violations, the alleged "facts" didn't add up to a violation of International Law because Beanal didn't claim the American corporations acted under the auspices of the Indonesian government. And Duval decided that the alleged "environmental torts" aren't offenses under international law. So Duval threw out the complaint. But the judge gave Beanal a chance to file an amended claim.

Source: *Chicago Sun-Times*, September 24, 1997, Section; Finance, p. 64.

Questions

1. Why might some think that a law permitting foreigners to sue in U.S. courts for international law violations is zany?
2. Do you think that "cultural genocide" such as that depicted by Beanal in this particular case should constitute a violation of international law? Does this strike you as arbitrary?

Comity

The unique aspect of public international law is that countries are generally not subject to law in the international arena unless they consent to such jurisdiction. For instance, a country is not bound by a treaty unless that country has signed the treaty. A country is not bound by international custom unless it has traditionally participated in that custom. And prior judicial decisions are only persuasive where a country is persuaded by and accepts these decisions as precedent. In fact, perhaps the most critical element in understanding international law is understanding that it is not actually "law" in the way that we generally consider law. Countries are not bound to abide by it except through "comity." *Comity* is the concept that countries *should* abide by international custom, treaties, and other sources of international direction because that is the civil way to engage in relationships. Nations must respect each other and respect some basic principles of dealing in order to have effective relationships.

It may be helpful to analogize the concept of comity to deontological ethical theory: the view of ethical reasoning that suggests there are certain universal principles of a civilized society to which all involved should adhere. This type of reasoning assumes that there are certain acts that are right and certain acts that are wrong, no matter where you are or where you are from. The belief that countries *should* abide by international agreements would be a universal principle that is arguably right according to comity, no matter what situation is proposed.

Although some believe that the origins of law are in religion and its commandments, others have argued that, instead, law derives from a natural tendency to prevent chaos. International law is that attempt to prevent chaos in the international marketplace through the application of universal principles, and comity is the means by which it is encouraged.

REGULATION OF INTERNATIONAL TRADE

As explained above, there is no such thing as one body of international law per se that regulates international contracts and trade. Instead, contracts between firms in different countries may be subject to the laws of one country or the other, depending on (1) whether it is a sales contract subject to the UN Convention on the International Sale of Goods (CISG, discussed on page 227), (2) whether the contract itself stipulates the applicable law and forum in which a dispute will be heard, and (3) the rules regarding conflict of laws in each jurisdiction.

On the other hand, many countries have domestic laws that regulate business conducted within their borders or by their domestic firms outside of its borders. These laws govern the areas of employment-related activities and discrimination, product liability, intellectual property, antitrust and trade practices, and import taxes, to name a few.

The concept of extraterritorial application of national laws, that is, application of those laws beyond the borders of the country imposing them, may pose ethical dilemmas. For instance, if the culture of one country holds that it is unethical for a woman to work, the extraterritorial application of America's antidiscrimination laws may pose an ethical dilemma to an American manager in that foreign country. Does the manager abide by American law or abide by the business ethics of that foreign country? The same may be true in connection with the abhorrence of bribes in American business. If an American firm is operating in another country where a bribe is required, does the manager break American law and pay the bribe or follow American business ethics but risk financial failure? [For an extensive international trade law database, see **http://lexmercatoria.net/**]

Employment–Related Regulations

When the U.S. Congress passed the Civil Rights Act of 1991, it expressly provided for *extraterritorial* application of Title VII's antidiscrimination provisions. In doing so, Congress extended American firms' liability for discrimination against their employees to situations that occur outside of the United States. For instance, if a firm conducts operations in Saudi Arabia, where women are not expected to hold certain management positions, that firm is still held to Title VII's prohibition against gender discrimination. Extraterritorial application of Title VII is considered essential since over 5 million Americans work abroad. However, compliance with American civil rights laws is not required where doing so would violate the host country's laws.

Female Managers

Six percent of North American managers serving abroad are female, up from 3 percent in 1987, estimates Nancy Adler, professor of management at McGill University in Montreal. In the process they are overturning myths, such as the one that they are hindered by prejudice in other countries. Prof. Adler says many more of the female managers she surveyed for a new book found their sex an advantage: Being such a minority, they are "highly visible."

Source: Labor Letter, *The Wall Street Journal,* September 20, 1994, p. A1.

Other U.S. employment-related statutes also survive the trip across borders and oceans. For instance, the Occupational Safety and Health Act and the Employee Retirement Income Security Act do not distinguish between workers for American firms who work in the United States and those who work in other parts of the world. Moreover, labor regulations of other countries may differ to a large extent from those in the United States, and an American firm doing business in that country may be responsible for complying with these regulations. For instance, Italy requires that employees receive the benefit of the government pension plan, a staff medical plan, a relocation allowance, insurance coverage to reimburse medical expenses, and scholarships to the staff's children. In Spain, companies with more than 100 workers must have a committee in charge of all matters relating to health and safety at work, and all employees are statutorily entitled to an appropriate health and safety policy at work.

One of the few internationally applied, employment-related laws is the European Works Council Directive, implemented in 1996 by 17 European nations. This directive provides that any multinational firm with at least 1,000 workers in the countries covered by the directive must comply with its regulations. The regulations include an employee voice in company deliberations, prior consultation with works councils over a wide range of employment issues, and specific rules of engagement for negotiations that are similar to the United States' National Labor Relations Act (see Chapter 14). Firms operating in other countries are also subject to the individual employment laws of those countries. The following article highlights some of the intricacies of dealing with those laws.

EMPLOYMENT CONTRACTS: IN WRITING OR NOT?

Alan Chesters

One of the marked differences of the employment process between the United States and most European countries is the extent of written communication between the company and the employee regarding applicable terms and conditions of employment.

In the United States, written correspondence normally will be limited to a short offer letter noting time, place and initial compensation for the new hire. In Europe, however, employers frequently provide a detailed statement of particulars, often accompanied by further generic statements of policy.

The origin of this difference can be traced back to the basic legal systems. The United States, the United Kingdom and Ireland operate under *common law,* meaning there's an assumption that contracts made between two equally independent contractors may resolve disputes through the courts. The rest of Europe operates under *Roman law,* which regulates through statutory general principle relationships between different types of citizens, such as employers and employees.

Thus, the United States has no single body of employment law, and regulations are made at federal, state and local levels. There's no requirement for written statements of detail in an employment contract—although such statements are becoming more common in contracts for senior managers, fixed-term contracts and contracts with unusual terms and conditions. In these cases, special attention typically is paid to compensation and benefits, confidentiality, noncompetition and termination rights and circumstances.

The European Union (EU) on the other hand, has a *European directive* requiring employers to provide written proof of a contract of employment—giving the details of terms and conditions within two months of starting work. There are exceptions for employees who are temporary (less than a month) and part-time (less than eight hours a day).

How employers must comply varies among European countries. We'll take a close look at four of these countries.

The United Kingdom Requires a Written Statement

Strictly speaking, the following applies to England and Wales, as Scotland and Northern Ireland have different legal systems. But the provisions relating to employment contracts are basically the same for all four regions.

The United Kingdom derives its employment law from three sources: common law (as in the United States), statute law and EU directives. Until the 1960s, individual employment law was governed, as in the

States, by the law of contract. Since then, there has been much statute- and EU-driven legislation, and in the area of written contracts, the law now requires all employers to issue a written statement covering:

1. Name of employer and employee.
2. Date when employment began.
3. Rights to any continuation of previous employment rights.
4. The rate of pay and method of calculating remuneration.
5. The pay periods.
6. Hours of work.
7. Vacation entitlement.
8. Sickness pay schemes.
9. Pension scheme.
10. Place of work.
11. Job title.
12. Disciplinary rules.
13. Grievance procedure.
14. Notice period.

Some of these may be covered by reference to a collective agreement or general policy statement.

In Germany, Oral Contracts Are the Official Word

Perhaps surprisingly, there's no legal requirement to provide a written contract of employment in Germany. Oral agreements are as legally binding as written agreements. The EU directive requires written particulars to be supplied, but this isn't regarded as a legal contract.

Contractual rights in Germany arise from the Civil Code and many subsequent legislative regulations—all of which are being integrated into the new Labour Law Code. As a result, legal provisions on minimum notice, hours of work, wages, vacations, maternity/paternity rights, works council (or consultative body) rights, confidentiality provisions, equal pay, sickness pay, invention rights and noncompetition duties apply automatically whether written or not.

In addition, many terms and conditions are regulated by collective agreement (excluding managerial employees), and these are deemed to form part of the employment contract. Despite the lack of legal require-ment, it's the custom and practice to provide a written contract of employment specifying the particular provisions in relation to the above list as it provides a firmer basis for the resolution of disputes than oral agreements.

Prudence Calls for Written Records in Italy

Similarly, in Italy there's no legal requirement for a written contract of employment but, even more so than in Germany, prudence dictates that written particulars are desirable in the complex, and at times confusing, legal structure in Italy.

Contracts of employment in Italy are governed by:

- The Constitution and some specific regulations.
- Statutes, particularly the Civil Code.
- Regulations by authorities other than the Parliament and the Government.
- Custom and practice.
- Corporate rules determined by collective bargaining.

It's normal, in establishing both parties' interests, that the contract is "indefinite," (or without a prescribed end date) and should provide written details of the following:

1. Start date.
2. Probationary period.
3. Working hours.
4. Category of employment and duties.
5. Job description.
6. Place of work.
7. Basic salary.
8. Noncompete clause.

In addition, collective bargains often require that written statements of the main terms and conditions of employment are provided—and this will apply equally to managers (*dirigenti*) who have their own collective agreement between FNDAI, the industrial management, or FNDAC, the commercial management, and the employers.

Contracts Are the Law in France

France requires a written contract of employment to be given to an employee within two months of commencing work. The contract must set out the identity of the parties, the place of work, the title of the employee or the type of job or job description, the date of commencement, vacation period, notice period, basic salary, dates of payment, hours of work and relevant collective agreement.

The contract, whether based on a collective agreement or not, operates within the Labour Code, which itself defines minimum notice periods, limits on working hours, minimum wages, vacations, maternity/ paternity rights, confidentiality and noncompete duties, and sickness provisions.

The provisions applying to other European countries have similar variations but usually require, either by law or prudence, the provision of a reasonably extensive written contract of employment. The use of references to standard provisions in collective agreements, often nationally based, can limit the length of the employment contract in a number of countries. But rarely do these apply to senior management. In fact, the trend toward written contracts for senior managers in the United States is following the established practice in Europe.

Each country in Europe will be different. Therefore, it's important to obtain appropriate advice when initiating the contract to ensure that you're fulfilling the legal requirements and prudent management practice in that particular country.

Source: *Global Workforce*, 2, no. 2, April 1997, pp. 12–13.

Questions

1. If you were general counsel for a multinational firm, would you recommend one standard contract for all employees worldwide or different contracts depending on the country in which the worker is performing her or his duties?
2. What are some of the advantages and disadvantages of each option in question one?
3. What is the source of the disparity between the different countries' protection of workers?

Declaration on the Elimination of Violence against Women

Concerned that violence against women is an obstacle to the achievement of equality, development, and peace, as recognized in the Nairobi Forward-Looking Strategies for the Advancement of Women, in which a set of measures to combat violence against women was recommended, and to the full implementation of the Convention on the Elimination of All Forms of Discrimination Against Women . . .

[We] solemnly proclaim the following Declaration on the Elimination of Violence Against Women and urge that every effort be made so that it becomes generally known and respected:

*   *   *   *   *

Article 3

Women are entitled to the equal enjoyment and protection of all human rights and fundamental freedoms in the political, social, cultural, civil, or any other field. These rights include, inter alia:

a. The right to life.
b. The right to equality.
c. The right to liberty and security of person.

(Continued)

---

    d. The right to equal protection under the law.
    e. The right to be free from all forms of discrimination.
    f. The right to the highest standard attainable of physical and mental health.
    g. The right to just and favorable conditions of work.
    h. The right not to be subjected to torture, or other cruel, inhuman, or degrading treatment or punishment.

    Source: UN General Assembly Resolution 48/104, February 23, 1994.

Questions

1.   *a.* How are these rights different, if at all, from the rights afforded under the American Bill of Rights?
    b. Why do you think they might be slightly different?
2. Do you notice any right that should be included, in your opinion, but is not?

Intellectual Property Regulation

Intellectual property generally refers to copyrights, patents, and trademarks—as opposed to real property, which encompasses land or real estate, and personal property, which refers to all other tangible items.

Trademarks.   A *trademark* is what identifies a product, whether it is the trade name, the packaging, the logo, or other distinguishing mark. When the law protects a trademark, it grants to the holder of the mark a limited monopoly: No one else may use that mark without the holder's permission. Under section 526 of the Tariff Act of 1930, it is unlawful to import goods bearing a trademark that has been registered with the Patent Office and that is "owned by a citizen of, or by a corporation or association . . . organized within the United States" without the permission of the mark holder.

   This provision regulates the importation of goods that would infringe on a trademark holder's rights in the United States. But what about an American company that wants to obtain trademark protection in other countries? Each country has distinct trademark regulations and different levels of protection offered marks registered in other countries.

Paris Convention.   In 1883, several countries entered into an agreement called the International Convention for the Protection of Intellectual Property, which was revised in 1971. At least 98 countries, including the United States, are parties to the agreement, now called the Paris Convention. In short, according to the Paris Convention, member countries ensure trademark protection to marks registered in other member countries. The Convention also provides for *national treatment* requiring that any individual claiming infringement will have the same protections as would a national of that country. A member country may not favor its own nationals as against foreigners. The Madrid Agreement, established after the Paris Convention, attempts to create an international trademark system. If a holder registers a trademark with the World Intellectual Property Organization in Switzerland, that mark is protected in all member countries requested by the holder. The United States has yet to adopt the Madrid Agreement.

Inventions. A *patent* is a monopoly on a product, process, or device where the item or process claimed is an innovation, unique and inventive, and useful. The Paris Convention refers to patents as well as trademarks; however, it does not establish a worldwide network of protection. Instead, it requires that member countries follow simplified procedures for registration. The most important provision provides the *right of priority,* which grants the first person to obtain a patent in any member country priority over other individuals seeking to register the same patent. In addition, since a patent must be original to be registered in any country, many countries hold that patents previously awarded in other countries automatically preclude additional patent registration. The European Patent Convention was established in 1978 in order to create an international registration procedure for patents. Individuals who obtain patents through the European Patent Office have valid patents in each member country.

Authors/Artists. A *copyright* is a government grant giving the copyright holder exclusive control over the reproduction of a literary, musical, or artistic work. Most developed nations provide copyright protection within their borders, but many also belong to international copyright protection pacts. The Berne Convention of 1886 and the Universal Copyright Convention (UCC) of 1952 both provide a measure of international protection against the unauthorized reproduction of one's original books, photos, drawings, movies, and the like. Copyright protection extends for a period provided by national law. For example, in the United States, the copyright spans the author's life plus 50 years. The United States is a party to the UCC and the Berne Convention.

Broadly, we should recognize that we have not succeeded in establishing a solid international system of protection for intellectual property. The following case offers a prime example of the interplay between the United States offer of trademark protection through the Lanham Act and the global protection offered through the Paris Convention.

PIAGGIO & C.S.p.A. v. SCOOTERWORKS USA, INC., ET AL.
1999 U.S. Dist. LEXIS 13296 (N.D. IL 1999)

George M. Marovich

Plaintiff Piaggio & C.S.p.A. ("Piaggio") has filed this action against Defendants Scooterworks USA, Inc. ("Scooterworks"), Vesparts International, L.L.C. ("Vesparts") and Philip S. McCaleb ("McCaleb"), alleging trademark and copyright infringement. For the reasons set forth below, Scooterworks' and Vesparts' motion is granted in part and denied in part, and McCaleb's motion is denied.

Background

Piaggio is an Italian corporation with its principal place of business in Pontedera, Italy. Scooterworks is an Illinois corporation with its principal place of business in Chicago, Illinois. Vesparts is a Nevada corporation with its principal place of business in Chicago, Illinois. McCaleb is an officer, president and co-shareholder, together with his wife, of Scooterworks. He is also an officer, president, and shareholder of Vesparts.

Piaggio is engaged in the business of manufacturing, distributing, and selling motor scooters, motorcycles, mopeds, and light transport vehicles, as well as related parts and accessories, throughout the world, including the United States. Piaggio owns the common law rights and registration for . . . the "PIAGGIO Trademarks." Piaggio has used, for over 50 years, the PIAGGIO Trademarks on and in connection with the distribution, marketing, and sale of motorized vehicles.

In 1948, Piaggio introduced a new line of motorized scooters under trademarks using the term VESPA ("VESPA scooters"). VESPA scooters have been in continuous production since their introduction. Piaggio owns the common law rights and registration of the word mark VESPA, VESPA with Design, and other Piaggio trademarks containing the term VESPA (the "VESPA Trademarks"). Piaggio has always used its VESPA Trademarks on and in connection with the distribution, marketing, and sale of VESPA scooters, with over 16 million units produced and sold in over 150 countries, including the United States, and it has had exclusive use of the VESPA Trademarks in connection with the sale of its motor scooters.

Piaggio also owns a family of VESPA trademarks registered under Italian law. The word mark VESPA, the VESPA logo, and other Piaggio trademarks containing the term VESPA are extremely well known in Italy.

Piaggio continuously utilized VESPA trademarks on and in connection with the manufacture, distribution, and sale of VESPA scooters in the United States up through approximately 1987, at which time, for various reasons, Piaggio "temporarily suspended" sales of its VESPA scooters in the United States. Nonetheless, Piaggio has continued to aggressively market and distribute VESPA scooters all over the world and to sell parts and promote its marks in the United States. Piaggio plans to resume VESPA scooter sales in the United States within the next 12 months.

McCaleb, Scooterworks, and Vesparts are in the business of selling replacement parts and accessories for VESPA scooters, as well as other goods and services of interest to fans of VESPA scooters. Beginning in approximately 1992, McCaleb attempted, but was unsuccessful, to establish some type of business relationship between Piaggio and McCaleb's start-up business, Scooterworks.

In 1995, without Piaggio's prior approval, Scooterworks filed an application with the United States Patent and Trade Office ("PTO") to register a VESPA mark for use in connection with the sale of key chains, posters, clothes, labels, models, and related goods. The PTO refused to register Scooterworks' application because the trademark in the application was deemed identical to trademarks previously registered by Piaggio. Thereafter, Piaggio applied to register the same trademark, based upon an assignment from Scooterworks to Piaggio of Scooterworks' rights in its prior application, and was approved.

In January 1996, Piaggio and Scooterworks entered into a License Agreement dated January 4, 1996. Pursuant to the License Agreement, Piaggio gave Scooterworks the exclusive right to produce and market in the United States under the VESPA Trademark, models of VESPA scooters, for a two-year period. Throughout 1996, Scooterworks attempted to secure from Piaggio a broader agreement providing for exclusive rights to distribute the VESPA scooter and related parts under the VESPA trademark. However, no definite agreement was ever reached and negotiations were abandoned in January 1997.

Piaggio claims that Defendants have improperly used Piaggio's PIAGGIO and VESPA Trademarks in several ways. For example, Piaggio alleges that McCaleb and Scooterworks, on their Web site and in the free catalog offered through their Web site, "repeatedly assert and imply they have an exclusive arrangement with Piaggio to import and distribute authentic VESPA replacement parts in the United States" and display the VESPA and PIAGGIO Trademarks in such a manner as "to imply that Scooterworks is sponsored, supervised, endorsed or otherwise connected with Piaggio." However, Piaggio alleges, McCaleb and Scooterworks are not sponsored, supervised or endorsed by Piaggio but that their only connection to Piaggio is that Scooterworks markets and sells replacement parts and accessories for VESPA scooters. Piaggio also alleges that McCaleb and Scooterworks "wrongfully offer miniature VESPA motor scooters for sale" and "repeatedly misuse VESPA Trademarks by using VESPA as a generic name of a product rather than as a brand name for scooters." Piaggio asserts that although it has requested that Defendants cease their willful and wrongful acts, Defendants have refused to cooperate with Piaggio and continue in their improper and infringing activities.

On November 24, 1998, Piaggio filed its Complaint in this Court asserting 13 claims: trademark infringement, false designation, unfair competition and anti-dilution under the Lanham Act, 15 U.S.C. § 1051, et seq.; trademark infringement and unfair competition under the International Convention for the Protection of Industrial Property of March 20, 1883, 21 U.S.T. 1583, as amended (the "Paris Convention"); trademark infringement, unfair competition, violation of the Uniform Deceptive Trade Practices Act and anti-dilution under Illinois state law; breach of contract; copyright infringement and declaratory judgment. On January 27, 1999, Scooterworks filed a counterclaim seeking, inter alia, to cancel Piaggio's federal trademark registrations.

* * * * *

II. Paris Convention Claims— Counts IV and V (I omitted)

In Counts IV and V of the Complaint, Piaggio alleges claims under Articles 6 bis and 10 bis, respectively, of the Paris Convention. The Paris Convention, to which both the United States and Italy are signatories, is an international agreement which prohibits, among other things, unfair competition. Scooterworks argues that Counts IV and V should be dismissed because (1) the Paris Convention is not a self-executing treaty and there is no private right of action under the Paris Convention, and (2) even if there was a private right of action, such claims are duplicative of those asserted under the Lanham Act. This Court finds that Section 44 of the Lanham Act implements the Paris Convention but that the Paris Convention does not provide a relief distinct from that of the Lanham Act. Accordingly, Scooterworks' motion to dismiss Counts IV and V is granted.

The Lanham Act, which prohibits specific types of unfair competition, provides in section 44(b):

> Any person whose country of origin is a party to any convention or treaty relating to trademarks . . . to

which the United States is also a party . . . shall be entitled to the benefits of this section under the conditions expressed herein to the extent necessary to give effect to any provisions of such convention [or] treaty . . . in addition to the rights to which any owner of a mark is otherwise entitled by this chapter.

Section 44(h) of the Lanham Act extends to foreign citizens such as Piaggio "effective protections against unfair competition, and the remedies provided in this chapter for infringement of marks . . . so far as they may be appropriate in repressing acts of unfair competition."

Piaggio argues that it has pleaded acts of unfair competition over and above those acts which constitute unfair competition under the Lanham Act, and thus, its Paris Convention claims are not duplicative and should not be dismissed. However, this Court agrees with the reasoning of the courts that hold that "subsections 44(b) and 44(h) [of the Lanham Act] work together to provide foreign nationals with rights under United States law which are coextensive with the substantive provisions of the treaty involved." . . . In other words, "the Paris Convention does not provide substantive rights in the United States, [instead] Section 44 [of the Lanham Act] merely extends existing Lanham Act and state law protections to foreign nationals conducting business in the United States." . . .

Therefore, as the Court finds that the Paris Convention does not create a separate and distinct cause of action than that already available under the Lanham Act, Counts IV and V are duplicative and, accordingly, are dismissed.

Questions

1. Should it have mattered to the disposition of the case that Scooterworks filed an application with the United States PTO without Piaggio's prior approval to register a VESPA mark for use in connection with the sale of paraphernalia?
2. If the Lanham Act implements the Paris Convention through its section 44, but offers no new relief, why would anyone bring a claim under the Paris Convention if she or he already has a claim under the Lanham Act?

Imports

The General Agreement on Tariffs and Trade (GATT), now governed by the World Trade Organization (WTO), regulates import duties among signatory countries in order to reduce barriers to trade and to ensure fair treatment. Without the WTO, it is argued, countries with stronger markets would be able to wrestle better deals on imports than would other countries. In addition, countries with strong market economies could use the threat of higher import taxes as a bargaining chip in other negotiations. There are several important components of the WTO that affect decisions about where a company may conduct operations and to which country that company may export its products.

In order to promote fair trading practices, the WTO prohibits two practices in its member countries. The first is called *dumping*. Dumping occurs where a manufacturer sells its goods in a foreign country for less than their normal value. If this practice causes or threatens material injury to a domestic or established foreign manufacturer in the foreign country, the act is prohibited. The price is considered less than normal value if it is less than the price charged in the producer's home country. A firm may want to dump its goods in a foreign market for two reasons. First its home market may be saturated and cannot support any further supply. Second, in an effort to establish itself and perhaps drive other firms out of the market, the firm may sell its goods in a foreign market at a price below other competitors and support that price with higher prices in its home country. In this way, its competitors may be forced from the market, and the producer may then raise prices to the normal level or above. [For the United States International Trade Administration Anti-Dumping page, see **http:www.ita.doc.gov/import_admin/records/**]

The WTO also prohibits the payment of *unfair subsidies* by governments. This occurs where a government, in an effort to encourage growth in a certain industry, offers subsidies to producers in that industry. The producers are therefore able to sell their goods at a price lower than the prices of its worldwide competitors. Subsidies are considered unfair where they are used by the governments to promote export trade that harms another country. Where unfair subsidization or dumping has been found to occur in the United States, the U.S. Department of Commerce may impose *countervailing duties* on those products in an amount sufficient to counteract the effect of the subsidy or the decreased price.

International trade barriers are discussed during trade "rounds" in which a number of countries negotiate duties and other agreements. One negotiation principle is called *"most favored nation" (MFN) status*. If the United States has MFN status with France, the United States has the right to the lowest applicable tariff on its goods imported by France. If France negotiates a lower tariff with Korea, the United States is entitled to a reduction in its tariff rates as well. In fact, all nations having MFN status with France would be entitled to that lower tariff rate. A second negotiating principle is called *national treatment*. This concept dictates that, once goods have been imported into a country, they must be treated as if they were domestic goods. Consequently, the only place where a tariff may be felt is at the border. [For an overview of WTO/GATT, see **www.wto.org/wto/dispute/**]

Import Duties.   The tariff treatment that the United States imposes on an imported product often depends on such considerations as whether the product was made with American raw materials and whether the product was actually fabricated abroad or whether it was simply assembled abroad using American-made components. The case that follows examines the question of the appropriate duty for a very specific Nike sneaker.

NISSHO IWAI AMERICAN CORPORATION AND NIKE, INC. v. UNITED STATES
143 F.3d 1470 (Fed. Cir. 1998)

Judge Lourie

[Nissho Iwai American Corporation and Nike, Inc. (collectively "Nike") appeal from the judgment of the United States Court of International Trade. That court held that Nike shoes would be taxed at a rate of 20% rather than the 6% rate that Nike sought. In rejecting the importers' arguments, the court determined that the footwear at issue could not be classified under certain subheadings, dutiable at 6%, which expressly exclude footwear containing "a foxing or foxing-like band." The Court of International Trade interpreted the tariff term "foxing-like band" as applying to athletic shoes having an externally visible band applied or molded at the sole and overlapping the upper.]

*   *   *   *   *

Background

The athletic footwear at issue, imported in the late 1980s and early 1990s, are constructed with a "foot frame mid-sole" sandwiched between the outer sole and the upper of the shoes. At various points around the perimeter of the shoes, portions of the outer sole and the mid-sole overlap the upper to create a "wavy" band that substantially encircles the shoes. The outer sole overlaps the upper at the toe and arch of the shoes. The remaining overlap originates at the mid-sole.

Nike claims that the footwear should have been classified under either of two subheadings, 6402.91.40 and 6402.99.15, both of which expressly exclude "footwear having a foxing or a foxing-like band applied or molded at the sole and overlapping the upper." A "foxing" is a band of material, such as rubber, applied to the shoe or

boot, as in a Converse All Star (R), that overlaps and bonds the sole to the upper. It is undisputed that the athletic shoes at issue do not have a "foxing"; however, the United States Customs Service found that they had bands which were "foxing-like." Accordingly, it found each shoe to be within the exception and thus classifiable only in one of the three basket provisions (depending on the features of the particular shoe), each encompassing a variation of "footwear with outer soles and uppers of rubber or plastics" not otherwise classified.

In the Court of International Trade, Nike again argued that its shoes did not have a "foxing-like band" within the meaning of the tariff provisions, asserting that only shoes resembling the "traditional sneaker or tennis shoe" could have a "foxing-like band." Nike argued that the term does not apply to athletic shoes, such as the imports in question, that contain a visible mid-sole. The Court of International Trade was unpersuaded and held that the existence or nonexistence of a mid-sole was irrelevant to the "foxing-like band" issue. On summary judgment, the court concluded that the wavy overlap created by the combined overlapping portions of the outer sole and mid-sole constituted a "foxing-like band" within the meaning of the tariff provisions. Nike appealed to this court.

Discussion

We review the Court of International Trade's grant of summary judgment "for correctness as a matter of law, deciding de novo the proper interpretation of the governing statute and regulations as well as whether genuine issues of material fact exist." Determining the proper scope of a classification in the Harmonized Tariff Schedule of the United States ("HTSUS") is an issue of statutory interpretation and thus a question of law.

Determining whether a particular imported item falls within the scope of the various classifications as properly construed is a question of fact. Because the nature and use of the imported athletic shoes are not in dispute in this case, the resolution of this appeal turns on the determination of the proper scope of the relevant classifications. The specific issue before us is whether the "foxing-like band" exclusion in the tariff provisions applies to athletic shoes in which part of the "band" overlapping the upper is formed by a mid-sole rather than exclusively by the outer sole. We hold that it does.

Nike asserts once again that the term "foxing-like band" is applicable only to shoes resembling the traditional sneaker or tennis shoe and thus argues that the exception cannot apply to the modern day athletic shoe containing a mid-sole. According to Nike, athletic shoes that do not closely resemble the traditional sneaker cannot have a "foxing-like" band. Nike has not argued that the wavy band on its shoes is visually dissimilar to the band formed by a traditional foxing so as to be outside the exception.

The tariff provisions in question do not expressly identify the type of shoe that possesses a foxing-like band. Subheading 6402.91.40, for example, encompasses "footwear with outer soles and uppers of rubber or plastics" and having "uppers of which over 90 percent of the external surface area . . . is rubber or plastics except (1) footwear having a foxing or foxing-like band applied or molded at the sole and overlapping the upper." On its face, the exception applies to any footwear otherwise within the subheading that has a foxing or foxing-like band so applied or molded. The applicability of the exception thus depends on undefined language. All that is clear is that the exception is not expressly limited to footwear resembling a traditional sneaker having a foxing or foxing-like band. It is undisputed that the term "foxing-like," unlike the term "foxing," has no common and commercial meaning. Thus, there is no relevant industry practice on which to rely. Instead, congressional intent must be gleaned from the statutory language itself and, given its ambiguity, the legislative history.

Seeking support from the legislative history, Nike relies on the following single paragraph of the Tariff Classification Study (TCS), published by the United States

Tariff Commission in 1960, which discusses the origins of the "foxing-like band" language in the Tariff Schedules of the United States (TSUS), the predecessor to the HTSUS:

> The parenthetical exception "except footwear having foxing or a foxing-like band applied or molded at the upper" in item 700.55 is designed to insure classification in item 700.60 [the basket provision] of a style of imported shoes with plastic coated uppers having the general outward appearance of the traditional "sneaker" or tennis shoe.

Nike argues that this statement in the TCS clearly limits the exception to shoes bearing a close resemblance to the traditional sneaker that existed in the early 1960s and does not apply to modern day athletic shoes. Specifically, Nike asserts that the term "foxing-like" was meant to encompass only an injection molded shoe prevalent in the 1960s that did not use a foxing, but that was nonetheless nearly indistinguishable from the typical 1960s sneaker containing a foxing. Nike places significant emphasis on the TCS's use of the phrase "traditional sneaker," arguing that such a phrase does not encompass the broader category "athletic footwear."

Nike further argues that its position is supported by Customs' own guidelines published in Treasury Decision 83–116, which quotes the TCS's statement that the exception applies to shoes having the general outward appearance of the traditional sneaker or tennis shoe. Additionally, Nike asserts that Customs has permitted numerous athletic shoes to enter the United States without classifying them as possessing a "foxing-like band." None of Nike's arguments is persuasive.

An examination of the entire discussion in the TCS regarding the "foxing-like band" language places the cited paragraph in context and undermines Nike's arguments. The TCS, which was produced contemporaneously with the introduction of the term in question into the TSUS, is indicative of legislative intent . . . The TCS discusses the history leading up to the current footwear classifications and describes the problems associated with the previous classification scheme:

> [Under the old scheme,] the three original statutory provisions have been made into 24 separate rate descriptions. The complete dependence of the original provisions for footwear on the component-

material-of-chief-value principle of classification is, in itself, potentially a breeder of anomalous results. The various actions by which such provisions have been subdivided into 24 separate rate descriptions have not only introduced additional complexities and ambiguities, but they have also intensified the problems incident to the use of the component-material-of-chief-value principle for footwear classifications . . .

The TCS explains that the previous tariff provisions were ineffective at levying higher duties on footwear competing with domestic manufacturers.

In recent years, however, there have been imports of footwear which have the appearance and are in fact of a kind made by the domestic rubber footwear industry, but which by some relatively minor change in construction, have avoided classification for duty purposes under the tariff provision [with the higher duties].

According to the TCS, the addition of a general category of footwear with an exception for footwear with a "foxing or foxing-like band" simplified and replaced the then-existing complex web of tariff provisions. By distinguishing shoes based on the presence of a foxing or foxing-like band, the current tariff provisions prevented importers from avoiding high duties by a slight alteration of the composition of the shoes. The newly introduced general category was intended to encompass imported footwear that did not compete directly with domestic manufacturers. The "foxing or foxing-like band" exception was inserted to capture footwear that did compete with the domestic footwear industry.

* * * * *

The TCS then states, in the paragraph quoted by Nike, that if the athletic footwear has a visible band formed by the sole overlapping the upper (such that it resembles the traditional sneaker or tennis shoe), it falls within the exclusion.

The TCS describes some of the types of rubber-soled footwear intended to be encompassed within the general provision: thonged sandals, a rubber-soled shoe having an upper made of vinyl-coated fabric, molded plastic shoes, and certain women's dress shoes. However, shoes with the "general outward appearance of the traditional sneaker or tennis shoe" which were produced by the domestic footwear industry at that time were intended to fall within the exception and be dutiable at a higher rate. The TCS states that the shoes competing with the domestic rubber-soled footwear industry included "such types as tennis oxfords worn for exercise, recreation, and ordinary footwear in mild weather; lace-to-lace shoes, commonly called basketball shoes, but used also for other sports and gymnastics; and specialties designed for leisure, beach, and streetwear." Accordingly, the legislative history indicates that the exception applied to the broad range of rubber-soled footwear manufactured by the domestic industry. As indicated in the quoted passages, these shoes included sneakers, tennis shoes, basketball shoes, and similar footwear having a visible band formed by the sole overlapping the upper, i.e., having a resemblance to the foxing of the traditional sneaker or tennis shoe.

* * * * *

The relevant inquiry is not whether the shoes are similar to the traditional sneaker or tennis shoe, but whether the band is similar to the foxing found on the traditional sneaker or tennis shoe, i.e., whether the band is "foxing-like." Accordingly, the Court of International Trade properly discounted the relevance of Nike's evidentiary submissions professing to demonstrate that shoes with a footframe mid-sole do not appear like or similar to traditional sneakers. For example, the hypothesis tested in Nike's consumer survey, "that specific shoes are, or are not, seen as looking 'like' shoes which are accepted as prototypes of shoes constructed using 'foxing'," fails to address the critical question: whether the band on the shoes appears "foxing-like." Notwithstanding Nike's protestations, this analysis does not sweep all athletic shoes into the exception. Rather, the exception encompasses only those athletic shoes with a visible "foxing-like band" overlapping the upper. Thus, as Nike notes, many "joggers" and "running shoes" which do not possess any overlap from sole to upper fall outside the exception. We have considered Nike's other arguments and find them to be unpersuasive.

* * * * *

Conclusion

The Court of International Trade did not err in determining that the imported athletic shoes, which have a band formed by the outer sole and mid-sole overlapping the upper, are properly within the exception "footwear having a foxing or a foxing-like band applied or molded at the sole and overlapping the upper." Accordingly, the court did not err in classifying the imported shoes in the basket provisions under subheadings 6402.91.80, 6402.91.90, and 6402.99.90.

Questions

1. Why does the United States impose import duties?
2. Isn't it a little difficult to believe that court and attorney time is taken up discussing whether a sneaker has a "foxing?" What is the real question at issue here?

3. Were you persuaded by Nike's argument? Do you believe that Nike believed its argument or simply wanted to pay a lower tax rate? Can you think of a more persuasive argument?
4. *Web-based question:* Compare the prices of Nike shoes in any online store to shoes without foxing. Do you think the diffference in price is due, in part, to import duties?

[For the United States Customs Service, see **www.customs.ustreas.gov**]

Exports

While imports are regulated in order to protect American businesses, exports by these businesses may also be regulated. Export regulation serves several purposes, articulated in the Export Administration Act of 1979, which states the following:

It is the policy of the United States to use export controls only after full consideration of the impact on the economy of the United States and only to the extent necessary

a. to restrict the export of goods and technology that would make a significant contribution to the military potential of any other country . . . which could prove detrimental to the national security of the United States;

b. to restrict the export of goods and technology where necessary to further significantly the foreign policy of the United States or to fulfill its declared international obligations; and

c. to restrict the export of goods where necessary to protect the domestic economy from the excessive drain of scarce materials and to reduce the serious inflationary impact of foreign demand.

Under the act, anyone wishing to export any type of goods or technology from the United States to a foreign country must obtain a license. Violations of the licensing requirement may bring imprisonment of up to 10 years and/or fines of up to $250,000, or five times the value of the export or $1 million, whichever is higher.

Two types of licenses are available, *general* or *validated* licenses. The shipper is responsible for determining which type is required. A commodity control list is published that specifies which goods are controlled and for which countries a validated license is required. Otherwise, a general license is available if no specific export license is required. To obtain a general license, the shipper must merely fill out a declaration form at the time of shipping. A validated license is required when a firm exports certain goods or technology to specified controlled countries. Firms must apply for the license at the Office of Export Administration in the Department of Commerce prior to shipping.

In determining whether to award a license, the Department of Commerce will look to several factors, including the type and amount of the exported good, the importing country, the good's use or purpose, the unrestricted availability of the same or comparable item in the importing country, and the intended market in the importing country. [For the Bureau of Export Administration, see **www.bxa.doc.gov**]

DOING BUSINESS IN A FOREIGN COUNTRY

UN Convention on Contracts for the International Sale of Goods

There is no such thing as one body of international law per se that regulates international contracts and trade. Instead, contracts between firms in different countries may be subject to the laws of one country or the other, depending on (1) whether it is a sales contract subject to the UN Convention on Contracts for the International Sale of Goods (CISG), (2) whether the contract itself stipulates the applicable law and forum in which a dispute will be heard, and (3) the rules regarding conflict of laws in each jurisdiction. Consequently, a business owner may actually decide to market a good in one country over another simply because of that country's laws relating to the particular good or commercial contracts in general. [For the Pace University CISG database, see **cisgw3.law.pace.edu/**]

In 1988, 10 nations signed and became bound by the UN Convention on Contracts for the International Sale of Goods. As of 1999, 53 nations had signed it. The CISG applies to contracts between parties of countries that have signed the convention and provides uniform rules for the sale of goods.

The CISG contains rules regarding the interpretation of contracts and negotiations and the form of contracts. Many obligations of the parties are enunciated by the CISG. For instance, the seller is required to deliver the goods and any documents relating to the goods, as well as to make sure that the goods are in conformance with the contract terms. The buyer, on the other hand, is required to pay the contract price and to accept delivery of the goods. The CISG, however, does not answer all questions that may arise in the course of a transaction. For instance, questions of a contract's validity are left to national law. Under American law, an enforceable contract requires four elements:

- *Capacity* to enter the contract.
- *Offer* and *acceptance* of the terms of the contract.
- *Consideration* for the promises in the contract.
- *Legality of purpose* of the contract.

Capacity refers to the parties' ability to understand the nature and consequences of the contract. For example, an individual who is under the influence of alcohol might not have capacity to enter into a contract. The offer and acceptance must evidence a "meeting of the minds" between the parties; that is, there must be a mutual understanding regarding the terms of the contract. Consideration means that something of value (whether monetary or otherwise) has passed between the parties. For example, one party agrees to pay money, and the other party agrees to deliver the goods requested. Countries that are not based in the common law, but instead in civil law systems, do not require consideration for a contract. The final element requires that the contract's purpose be legal. For instance, under American law, if a company agreed to pay money to import certain goods to a country where those goods are not allowed, that agreement would not be enforceable.

Generally, once a contract has been created, it is enforceable according to its terms by all parties to the contract. The following case highlights the *commercial impracticability* defense to a contract, where one party may rescind or modify a contract on the basis that performance of the contract's terms is not impossible, but commercially impracticable.

TRANSATLANTIC FINANCING CORPORATION v. UNITED STATES
363 F.2d 312 (D.C. Cir. 1966)

Judge Skelly Wright

[In 1956, Transatlantic Financing, a steamship operator, contracted with the United States to ship wheat from Texas to Iran. Six days after the ship left port for Iran, the Egyptian government was at war with Israel and blocked the Suez Canal to shipping. The steamer therefore was forced to sail around the Cape of Good Hope. Transatlantic accordingly sued the United States for its added expenses as a result of this change of circumstances. Transatlantic contended that it had contracted only to travel the "usual and customary" route to Iran and that the United States had received a greater benefit than that for which it contracted. The district court held for the United States; Transatlantic appealed.]

Transatlantic's claim is based on the following train of argument. The charter was a contract for a voyage from a Gulf port to Iran. Admiralty principles and practices, especially stemming from the doctrine of deviation, require us to [infer] into the contract the term that the voyage was to be performed by the 'usual and customary' route. The usual and customary route from Texas to Iran was, at the time of contract, via Suez, so the contract was for a voyage from Texas to Iran via Suez. When Suez was closed this contract became impossible to perform. Consequently, appellant's argument continues, when Transatlantic delivered the cargo by going around the Cape of Good Hope, in compliance with the Govern-

ment's demand under claim of right, it conferred a benefit upon the United States for which it should be paid on quantum meruit.

The contract in this case does not expressly condition performance upon availability of the Suez route. Nor does it specify 'via Suez' or, on the other hand, 'via Suez or Cape of Good Hope.' Nor are there provisions in the contract from which we may properly [infer] that the continued availability of Suez was a condition of performance. Nor is there anything in custom or trade usage, or in the surrounding circumstances generally, which would support our constructing a condition of performance. The numerous cases requiring performance around the Cape when Suez was closed indicate that the Cape route is generally regarded as an alternative means of performance. So the implied expectation that the route would be via Suez is hardly adequate proof of an allocation to the promisee of the risk of closure. In some cases, even an express expectation may not amount to a condition of performance. The doctrine of deviation supports our assumption that parties normally expect performance by the usual and customary route, but it adds nothing beyond this that is probative of an allocation of the risk.

If anything, the circumstances surrounding this contract indicate that the risk of the Canal's closure may be deemed to have been allocated to Transatlantic. We know or may safely assume that the parties were aware, as were most commercial men with interest affected by the Suez situation, that the Canal might become a dangerous area. No doubt the tension affected freight rates, and it is arguable that the risk of closure became part of the dickered terms. We do not deem the risk of closure so allocated, however. Foreseeability or even recognition of a risk does not necessarily prove its allocation. Parties to a contract are not always able to provide for all the possibilities of which they are aware, sometimes because they cannot agree, often simply because they are too busy. Moreover, that some abnormal risk was contemplated is probative but does not necessarily establish an allocation of the risk of the contingency which actually occurs. In this case, for example, nationalization by Egypt of the Canal Corporation and formation of the Suez Users Group did not necessarily indicate that the Canal would be blocked even if a confrontation resulted. The surrounding circumstances do indicate, however, a willingness by Transatlantic to assume abnormal risks, and this fact should legitimately cause us to judge the impracticability of performance by an alternative route in stricter terms than we would were the contingency unforeseen.

We turn then to the question whether occurrence of the contingency rendered performance commercially impracticable under the circumstances of this case. The goods shipped were not subject to harm from the longer, less temperate Southern route. The vessel and crew were fit to proceed around the Cape. Transatlantic was no less able than the United States to purchase insurance to cover the contingency's occurrence. If anything, it is more reasonable to expect owner-operators of vessels to insure against the hazards of war. They are in the best position to calculate the cost of performance by alternative routes (and therefore to estimate the amount of insurance required), and are undoubtedly sensitive to international troubles which uniquely affect the demand

for and cost of their services. The only factor operating here in appellant's favor is the added expense, allegedly $43,972.00 above and beyond the contract price of $305,842.92, of extending a 10,000-mile voyage by approximately 3,000 miles. While it may be an overstatement to say that increased cost and difficulty of performance never constitute impracticability, to justify relief there must be more of a variation between expected cost and the cost of performing by an available alternative than is present in this case, where the promisor can legitimately be presumed to have accepted some degree of abnormal risk, and where impracticability is urged on the basis of added expense alone.

We conclude, therefore, as have most other courts considering related issues arising out of the Suez closure, that performance of this contract was not rendered legally impossible.

Affirmed.

Questions

1. Would there be a different result in this case if the shipment had been tomatoes as opposed to wheat? Explain.
2. Would there be a different result in this case if the United States and Transatlantic agreed by contract that shipment was to arrive in Iran within a period of time that was only possible if the shipper used the canal route? Explain.
3. What do you think it would take for a court to render a contract commercially impracticable? In this case, the shipper was forced to spend almost $44,000 more than it had expected to spend in performing the $305,000 contract. What if the added cost had amounted to $100,000? Would you be persuaded that the contract was then commercially impracticable? What if the closing of the canal doubled the price of the contract? Explain.

Different Forms of Global Business Expansion

Multinational Enterprise (MNE). The term *multinational enterprise* traditionally refers to a company that conducts business in more than one country. Any of the following operations, except for a direct contract with a foreign purchaser, may qualify a company as an MNE.

Direct Contract.   A firm may expand its business across territorial borders using a variety of methods. The most simplified, from a contractual perspective, occurs where a firm in one country enters into an agreement with a firm or individual in another country. Using the example of sales, a firm might decide to sell its product to a purchaser in another country through a basic contractual agreement. This is called a *direct sale* to a foreign purchaser. In this situation, the parties agree on the terms of the sale and record them in the contract.

Where the contract is silent as to a term of the sale, the law that will apply in connection with the missing term will be the law specified in the contract or, where none is specified, the applicable law will depend on the country in which the court is located. Some courts will apply the *vesting of rights doctrine,* where the applicable law is the law of the jurisdiction in which the rights in the contract vested. Other courts may apply the *most significant relationship doctrine,* where the applicable law is that of the jurisdiction that has the most significant relationship to the contract and the parties. Finally, some courts will apply the *governmental interest doctrine,* where the court will apply the law either of its own jurisdiction or of the jurisdiction that has the greatest interest in the outcome of the issue.

One of the most complicated issues pertaining to direct sales is that of *payment*. The seller should and usually does require an *irrevocable letter of credit,* which the buyer obtains from a bank after paying that amount to the bank (or securing that amount of credit). The bank then promises to pay the seller the amount of the contract after conforming goods have been shipped. The "irrevocable" component is that the bank may not revoke the letter of credit without the consent of both the buyer and the seller. In this way, the seller is protected because the buyer already has come up with adequate funds for the purchase, confirmed by a bank. The buyer is protected because the funds are not turned over to the seller until it has been determined that the goods conform to the contract. It is important to the buyer, however, that the letter of credit be specific as to the conformance of the goods, as the bank will only ensure that the goods conform to the letter of credit and not to the contract itself.

Foreign Representation.   A second type of foreign expansion is a sale through a representative in the foreign country, whether it is through a distributor, agent, or other type of representative. In this way, the firm has some representation in the foreign country and, depending on the type of representation, someone with experience dealing with that country's customs and regulations. A firm may decide to sell through an *agent*—that is, it hires an individual who will remain permanently in the foreign country, negotiate contracts, and assist in the performance of the contracts. The agent would be compensated on a commission basis. On the other hand, the firm may act through a *representative,* who may solicit and take orders but, unlike an agent, may not enter into contracts on behalf of the firm. *Distributors* purchase the goods from the seller, then negotiate sales to foreign purchasers on their own behalf. In doing so, a distributor may be more likely to invest resources to develop the foreign market for the good.

It is important to note that *exclusive dealing* agreements with a distributor, where the distributor agrees to sell only the goods of one manufacturer and the manufacturer agrees to sell only to that distributor in that area, generally are not allowed in many countries. While the antitrust laws of the United States are more lax in this area, foreign antitrust laws such as those in the European Union consider this a restrictive practice that unreasonably restrains trade.

Export trading companies are firms that specialize in acting as the intermediary between business and purchasers in foreign countries. The firm will take title to the good being sold and then proceed to complete the sale in the foreign country. *Export management companies,* on the other hand, merely manage the sale but do not take title to the goods; consequently they do not share in any of the risk associated with the sale.

Joint Venture.   Foreign expansion may also occur through an agreement of a *joint venture* between two or more parties. This type of agreement is usually for one or several specific projects and is in effect for a specified period of time. For instance, several Japanese automobile manufacturers have entered into joint ventures with American firms in order to manufacture some or all of certain models in America. Mitsubishi entered into a joint venture with Chrysler Corporation in connection with the Eclipse and Eagle Talon models. In this way, companies such as Mitsubishi can market certain models by claiming that they were made in America, using American parts and labor.

Branch Office or Subsidiary.   A branch office is a wholly owned extension of a corporate entity in a foreign country. A subsidiary is a separate corporation formed in a foreign country and owned in whole or in part by the parent company. For example, an Indian paper company may open a branch office in London in order to market and sell its products. That office would be a mere extension of the offices established already in India. On the other hand, the Indian firm may create a separate subsidiary to handle its British orders, which might then have an office in London. A subsidiary or branch office relationship may also come about through an acquisition of an existing firm in the foreign country.

The primary difference between branch offices and subsidiaries comes into play with the question of liability. In most situations where a subsidiary is sued, the parent company is not liable. To the contrary, however, the liabilities of a branch office immediately become the liabilities of the main office. In addition, the income of a branch office is considered income to the parent firm and must be reported on that firm's income tax return. Income to a subsidiary remains on the balance sheet of the subsidiary. On the other hand, there is a benefit to opening a branch office. The branch office is considered by all dealing with it as merely an arm of the parent firm. In this respect, loans and insurance may be easier to obtain for a branch, as opposed to a subsidiary.

Licensing.   Where a company has no interest in commencing operations in a foreign country but instead merely wants to have its product or name on the market there, the company may decide to license the rights to the name or to manufacturing the product to another company. For instance, assume an American firm owns the rights to the name "Wash 'n Dry" car-wash service. This firm manufactures and operates car-washing machines for instant washes. A firm in Italy may license the right to use the name, product, and process in Italy in exchange for a royalty fee and would then be responsible for all aspects of the business operation.

The benefit to this type of relationship is that the licensor (holder of the right) has the opportunity to enter the foreign market, while the licensee assumes all of the obligations of running the business. In addition, the foreign government may be more hospitable to a domestic company's operations than a foreign firm's. On the other hand, it is critical in a licensing situation that the license contract be particular as to the quality of the good produced or service provided. Imagine the problems that could arise where a firm licenses the right to use its name on something that is of a much lower quality than the original good.

Franchising.   In a franchise agreement, the franchisee pays the franchisor for a license to use trademarks, formulas, and other trade secrets. The difference between a franchising agreement and a licensing contract is that a franchise agreement may be made up of a number of licensing arrangements, as well as other obligations. For instance, in a typical franchise agreement for a fast-food franchise, the franchisor will license to the franchisee the right to use its trademark, name, logo, recipes, menus, and other recognized resources. The agreement may also include a commitment from the franchisor to lease a space for the franchisee, or to provide advertising or training; or it may include a commitment from the franchisee to comply not only with quality standards but also with hours of operation, marketing, and sales programs.

FOREIGN BUSINESSES IN THE UNITED STATES

Foreign firms may wish to establish operations in the United States because Americans are more inclined to buy goods made in this country. As we have seen, foreign car companies have built manufacturing plants in the United States and consequently have used as a marketing theme the fact that many of their cars sold in the United States are now also made in the United States. On the other hand, doing business in the United States brings with it the requirement that these foreign businesses comply with U.S. laws and regulations. As a result of a growing foreign trade deficit in the United States, the U.S. government has been more diligent in enforcing regulations against unfair trade practices of foreign businesses. The Department of Justice has been actively enforcing antidumping and countervailing duty laws, as well as requiring that certain countries (e.g., Japan) open their markets to U.S. exports where that country engages in voluminous exports to the United States.

RESTRICTIONS ON INTERNATIONAL DISPUTE RESOLUTION

As we have seen to this point, international ethical/legal relationships are highly complex. Disputes are inevitable. Resolution of these international disputes often faces several roadblocks. First, as mentioned above, the interpretation of contract terms, the language of the contract, the law applicable to the resolution of the conflict, and the appropriate jurisdiction in which to resolve the dispute all raise dilemmas that are not easily dismissed. Moreover, two doctrines, accepted as general principles of international law, also pose quandaries to the courts and barriers to judicial enforcement of rights: the *act of state doctrine* and the *doctrine of sovereign immunity*.

Act of State Doctrine

It is generally accepted that a country has absolute rule over what occurs within its borders. Consequently, the act of state doctrine holds that a judge in one country does not have the authority to examine or challenge the acts of another country within that country's borders. For instance, an American court may not declare the acts of the British government invalid, because it is presumed that the foreign country acted legally within its own territory.

One area that has caused a great deal of dispute in connection with the act of state doctrine is *expropriation*. Expropriation is the taking by a national government of property and/or rights of a foreign firm within its borders. The United States contends that international law dictates that an individual or firm be compensated for the taking by the government. Not all governments agree with this statement of law. On the other hand, where a government expropriates property or rights without offering just compensation, the foreign government of the firm affected may retaliate economically or otherwise.

Doctrine of Sovereign Immunity

The doctrine of sovereign immunity is based on the concept that "the king can do no wrong." In other words, if the king makes the rules, how could the king ever be wrong? As Chief Justice Marshall explained in *The Schooner Exchange* v. *McFaddon*,[14] "The jurisdiction of the nation within its own territory is necessarily exclusive and absolute. It is susceptible of no limitation not imposed by itself, deriving validity from an external source would imply a diminution of its sovereignty to the extent of the restriction, and an investment of that sovereignty to the same extent in that power which could impose such restriction."

The doctrine has been codified in the United States by the Foreign Sovereign Immunities Act of 1976 (FSIA), which provides that foreign countries may not be sued in American courts, subject to several exceptions. Accordingly, it would not be possible for a U.S. citizen to sue Britain in the U.S. courts. A foreign country may be sued in American courts if the claim falls into one of the following FSIA exceptions:

1. The foreign countries have waived their immunity (i.e., they have consented to be sued in another country's courts). Or
2. The legal action is based on a *commercial activity* by the foreign country in the United States or outside the United States but having a direct effect in the United States.

Therefore, a country that conducts a commercial activity in a foreign country may not hide behind sovereign immunity if sued, while a country acting on its own behalf and not for a commercial purpose would be able to avail itself of the protection. This "restrictive theory of immunity" is to be contrasted with the policies of some countries, which contend that immunity is absolute—no exceptions exist.

The following cases examines sovereign immunity.

DOE v. UNOCAL CORP.
963 F. Supp. 880; (C.D. Ca. 1997)

Judge Paez

[Doe plaintiffs are farmers from the Tenasserim region of Burma. They brought a class action against defendants Unocal Corp. ("Unocal"), Total S.A. ("Total"), the Myanmar Oil and Gas Enterprise ("MOGE"), the State Law and Order Restoration Council ("SLORC"), and individuals John Imle, President of Unocal, and Roger C. Beach, Chairman and Chief Executive Officer of Unocal. According to plaintiffs' complaint, SLORC is a military junta that seized control in Burma in 1988, and MOGE is a state-owned company controlled by SLORC that produces and sells energy products. Plaintiffs seek relief for alleged international human rights violations perpetrated by defendants in furtherance of defendants Unocal, Total, and MOGE's joint venture, the Yadana gas pipeline project.

Plaintiffs allege that defendants, through the SLORC military, intelligence and/or police forces, have used and continue to use violence and intimidation to relocate whole villages, enslave farmers living in the area of the proposed pipeline, and steal farmers' property for the benefit of the pipeline. Plaintiffs allege defendants' conduct has caused plaintiffs to suffer death of family members, assault, rape and other torture, forced labor, and the loss of their homes and property, in violation of state law, federal law, and customary international law.]

*   *   *   *   *

A. Foreign Sovereign Immunities Act

*   *   *   *   *

Here, plaintiffs do not dispute that SLORC and MOGE are foreign sovereigns. Accordingly, defendants have established a prima facie case under the FSIA, and SLORC and MOGE are presumptively entitled to sovereign immunity. . . Plaintiffs request an opportunity to engage in jurisdictional discovery; however, as the following discussion demonstrates, plaintiffs' allegations regarding SLORC and MOGE's human rights violations perpetrated in connection with the Yadana gas pipeline project are insufficient to invoke the commercial activity exception. Consequently, there is no need for jurisdictional discovery to resolve Unocal's motion to dismiss plaintiffs' claims against SLORC and MOGE.

Plaintiffs contend that the FSIA's commercial activity exception exposes SLORC and MOGE to suit in the United States courts. "Under international law, states are not immune from jurisdiction of foreign courts insofar as their commercial activities are concerned[.]"

*   *   *   *   *

Plaintiffs contend that SLORC and MOGE are not entitled to immunity because this case falls within clauses two and three of the commercial activity exception.

Clause two applies only to claims that are based upon acts performed in the United States. "A plaintiff's claim is 'based upon' those activities that are elements of the claim that would entitle the plaintiff to relief." Here, plaintiffs' human rights claims are based upon acts of SLORC and MOGE allegedly committed in Burma, not upon acts allegedly performed in the United States. While the commercial negotiations and decision making that allegedly occurred in the United States may suffice to establish that defendants were joint actors, they are not "elements" of plaintiffs' claims against the foreign state defendants. Thus, clause two does not apply to plaintiffs' claims against SLORC and MOGE.

Although plaintiffs' claims initially appear to fall within the statutory language of clause three of the exception because they are based on acts outside the United States (human rights violations allegedly committed by SLORC and MOGE) in connection with commercial activity of the foreign state outside the United States (the installation of the Yadana pipeline), controlling authority precludes such an interpretation.

The FSIA defines "commercial activity" as

either a regular course of commercial conduct or a particular commercial transaction or act. The commercial character of an activity shall be determined by reference to the nature of the course of conduct or particular transaction or act, rather than by reference to its purpose.

The Supreme Court has elaborated upon the meaning of "commercial activity," relying on the meaning "generally attached to that term under the 'restrictive' theory [of foreign sovereign immunity] at the time the statute was enacted." Thus, "when a foreign government acts, not as regulator of a market, but in the manner of a private player within it, the foreign sovereign's actions are 'commercial' within the meaning of the FSIA." Instead of asking whether the foreign state is seeking to profit from its activities, "the issue is whether the particular actions that the foreign state performs (whatever the motive behind them) are the type of actions by which a private party engages in 'trade and traffic or commerce.'" In essence, "a state engages in commercial activity under the restrictive theory where it exercises only those powers that can also be exercised by private citizens, as distinct from those powers peculiar to sovereigns."

In *Nelson,* the Supreme Court concluded that Saudi Arabia's wrongful arrest, imprisonment and torture of a United States citizen working at a Saudi hospital could not be considered commercial in nature for purposes of clause one of the commercial activity exception. The *Nelson* court held that such conduct

> boils down to abuse of the power of its police by the Saudi Government, and however monstrous such abuse undoubtedly may be, a foreign state's exercise of the power of its police has long been understood for purposes of the restrictive theory as peculiarly sovereign in nature . . . Exercise of the powers of police and penal officers is not the sort of action by which private parties can engage in commerce.

Here, SLORC and MOGE engaged in commerce in the same manner as a private citizen might do when they allegedly entered into the Yadana gas pipeline project. In addition, they engaged in the acts upon which the claims are based "in connection with" that commercial activity. Nonetheless, SLORC and MOGE's alleged violations of plaintiffs' human rights, allegedly committed in connection with the Yadana gas pipeline project, do not fall within the ambit of the commercial activity exception to the FSIA, as it has been interpreted by the Supreme Court and the Ninth Circuit. Plaintiffs claim that defendants, through the SLORC military, in-

telligence and/or police forces, have used and continue to use violence and intimidation to relocate whole villages, enslave farmers living in the area of the proposed pipeline, and steal farmers' property for the benefit of the pipeline. Because plaintiffs essentially allege that SLORC and MOGE abused their police power, the foreign sovereign defendants' acts that form the basis of plaintiffs' claims are "peculiarly sovereign in nature" and do not come within the commercial activity exception to the FSIA.

*   *   *   *   *

Moreover, . . . plaintiffs cannot demonstrate that SLORC and MOGE's alleged acts of torture and expropriation have a direct effect in the United States within the meaning of the FSIA. "An effect is 'direct' for purposes of the commercial activity exception if it follows as an 'immediate consequence' of the defendant's activity." Plaintiffs contend that (1) the use of forced labor and forced relocation, allegedly obtained by recourse to battery, rape, killing and other forms of torture, (2) reduced the cost of the Yadana pipeline project and decreased defendants' labor and operational costs, which (3) provided defendants with an unfair competitive advantage in the United States gas market. However,

> mere financial loss by a person—individual or corporate—in the U.S. is not, in itself, sufficient to constitute a 'direct effect.' Rather, courts often look to the place where legally significant acts giving rise to the claim occurred in determining the place where a direct effect may be said to be located.

The legally significant acts giving rise to plaintiffs' claims occurred in Burma, not in the United States. Accordingly, plaintiffs cannot satisfy the direct effects requirement of the commercial activity exception, and SLORC and MOGE are entitled to sovereign immunity from plaintiffs' suit.

Questions

1. Why do you believe that the plaintiffs chose to litigate this dispute in the U.S. courts?
2. Whether or not you agree with the impact of the court's decision, are you persuaded by its legal analysis? Where were the plaintiffs' strongest arguments?
3. How do you feel about the end result of the decision?

Arbitration

In light of the difficulty of obtaining jurisdiction and the choice of laws, language, and forum issues, parties to an international contract may prefer to insert a clause that calls for international arbitration in case of a dispute. Arbitration is a nonjudicial means to settle a conflict where the parties agree to a hearing in front of a third party who will issue a binding award decision. (See Chapter 4.) The arbitration clause will specify the identity of the third party (or the association from which the parties will seek a third party), the place of arbitration and, in many cases, the laws that will apply.

While arbitration is considered binding on the parties who consent to it, there are times when a losing party may opt not to satisfy the award to the other party. In that case, the successful party must petition a court of law to enforce the award. In that regard, the United Nations Convention on the Recognition and Enforcement of Foreign Arbitral Awards, signed by 120 countries as of 1998,[15] provides that the successful party obtain possession of the property of the losing party located in any signatory country for the purpose of satisfying the debt.

The following case illustrates the problems that may arise in collecting an award, even where an arbitration clause apparently is clear.

IN THE MATTER OF THE ARBITRATION BETWEEN SEVEN SEAS SHIPPING (UK) LTD v. TONDO LIMITADA, ON BEHALF OF THE REPUBLIC OF ANGOLA
1999 U.S. Dist. Lexis 9574 (S.D.N.Y. 1999)

District Judge Denise Cote

Seven Seas Shipping Ltd., owner of a yacht named Mitsa, is a British corporation with its principal place of business in Berkshire, England. The respondent, Tando Limitada is organized and existing under the laws of Angola, with its principal place of business in Luanda, Angola. On September 25, 1996, the two entered into a charter party agreement in which Tando chartered the Mitsa to carry wheat from Houston, Texas, to Lobito, Luanda, and Namibe, Angola.

The Mitsa was loaded and ready to depart at Houston, Texas, on October 10, 1996, but because a letter of credit for payment that was required under the governing charter party was not in order, the vessel was not allowed to proceed to the loading berth. The problem was not remedied by Tando until October 24, 1996. After the wheat cargo arrived and was discharged in Angola, Seven Seas presented Tando with invoices of alleged detention damages at the loading port in Houston, and demurrage incurred in discharging at the three Angolan ports, for the total amount of $138,312.47. In response, Tando claimed that the detention charges only amounted to $62,840.

As a result of disputes over the detention costs, pursuant to their agreement, Seven Seas sought to arbitrate. The matter was considered by the arbitrators and on January 27, 1999, Seven Seas was awarded

$95,603.28 for damages and Tando was ordered to pay the full amount of the arbitration fees, which totaled $5,425. Seven Seas now requests an order confirming the award as a judgment of the Court in the amount of $101,078.28 with interest at the rate of 7.75% until entry of judgment. Tando has not responded to Seven Seas' motion.

Discussion

1. The Standard

Whether to recognize and enforce an arbitration award is governed in the first instance in this case by the Convention on the Recognition and Enforcement of Foreign Arbitral Awards. The Convention requires contracting states such as the United States,

> to recognize an agreement in writing under which the parties undertake to submit to arbitration all or any differences which have arisen or which may arise between them in respect of a defined legal relationship, whether contractual or not, concerning a subject matter capable of settlement by arbitration.

The Second Circuit has recently held that

> any commercial arbitral agreement, unless it is between two United States citizens, involves property located in the United States, and has no reasonable relationship with one or more foreign states, falls under the Convention.

Here, clause 44(a) of the [agreement] indicates that there is an agreement in writing to arbitrate all disputes that arise out of a commercial contractual relationship. According to the clause, all disputes are to be arbitrated in New York and are subject to United States law. Both parties are foreign corporations with their principal places of business outside of the United States. The agreement is, therefore, governed by the Convention.

The confirmation of an arbitration award is a summary proceeding that converts a final arbitration award into a judgment of the court. A court shall confirm an arbitration award made under the Convention "unless it finds one of the grounds for refusal or deferral of recognition or enforcement of the award specified in the said Convention." The Court may refuse recognition and enforcement of an award "at the request of the party against whom it is invoked, only if that party furnishes to the competent authority" proof of the existence of any one of five circumstances. Because Tando has not contested Seven Seas' motion in this case, none of these grounds for refusal is relevant. Under the Convention, Article V(2), the Court may refuse to recognize an award upon its own finding that:

1. the subject matter of the difference is not capable of settlement by arbitration under the law of the country where recognition is sought;
2. the recognition or enforcement of the award would be contrary to the public policy of that country.

2. Subject Matter Capable of Settlement by Arbitration

The Federal Arbitration Act governs arbitration in the United States and "reflects a legislative recognition of the 'desirability of arbitration as an alternative to the complications of litigation.'" Section 2 of the FAA provides, in relevant part:

> an agreement in writing to submit to arbitration an existing controversy . . . shall be valid, irrevocable, and enforceable, save upon such grounds as exist at law or in equity for the revocation of any contract.

This proceeding seeks confirmation of an arbitration award pursuant to the written agreement of the parties to arbitrate any controversy between them. This Court is not aware of any grounds for the revocation of this contract, and finds that the disputed subject matter is, therefore, capable of resolution by arbitration under the laws of the United States.

3. Contrary to Public Policy

The United States, as a signatory of the Convention, is in agreement with the central policy statement of the Convention, which is

> to encourage the recognition and enforcement of commercial arbitration agreements in international contracts and to unify the standards by which agreements to arbitrate are observed and arbitral awards are enforced in the signatory countries.

This statement evidences a strong public policy in support of arbitration proceedings and enforcement of arbitration awards. A court should find that enforcement is contrary to public policy only where enforcement would violate our "most basic notions of morality and justice." No understanding of the facts before this Court supports the notion that enforcement of this arbitration award would violate our basic notions of morality and justice. Instead, the confirmation of this award is quite consistent with the stated policy of the United States, and other signatories of the Convention, to encourage the resolution of commercial disputes by arbitration.

Conclusion

For the reasons stated above, Seven Seas' motion is granted. The arbitral award is confirmed and the Clerk of Court shall enter judgment in the amount of $101.078.28 with interest at the rate of 7.75% per annum from February 25, 1999 [thirty days after the date of the arbitration award, during which time Tando had an opportunity to satisfy the award without interest accruing] to the date of entry of the judgment.

INTERNET EXERCISE

Identify a multinational firm that conducts business with suppliers in developing countries. Find its code of vendor conduct on the Web and evaluate the areas of enforcement that might prove to be the most difficult.

CHAPTER QUESTIONS

1. Nigeria contracted to purchase large quantities of cement from Portland Cement in order to support its rapidly expanding infrastructure. Nigeria overpurchased the cement and the country's harbors became clogged with ships waiting to unload. Imports of other goods ground to a halt as well. Nigeria consequently repudiated its contracts with those shippers, who then filed suits to enforce the contracts. Nigeria responded that it is immune from prosecution in connection with these contracts under the Foreign Sovereign Immunities Act, claiming that its contracts were governmental and not of a commercial nature. What should be the result? See *Texas Trading and Milling Corp.* v. *Federal Republic of Nigeria,* 647 F.2d 300 (2d Cir. 1981).

2. Original Appalachian Artworks (OAA) is the manufacturer and license holder of Cabbage Patch Kids Dolls. Granada Electronics imported and distributed Cabbage Patch Kids dolls to the United States that were made in Spain by Jesmar under a license from OAA. Jesmar's license permitted manufacture and distribution of the dolls in Spain, the Canary Islands, Andorra, and Ceuta Melilla. Under the license, Jesmar agreed not to make, sell, or authorize any sale of the dolls outside its licensed territory and to sell only to those purchasers who would agree not to use or resell the licensed products outside the territory as well. Jesmar's argument that Granada's sales do not constitute "gray market" sales is that OAA's dolls sold in the United States have English-language adoption papers, birth certificates, and instructions while Granada's dolls come equipped with Spanish-language adoption papers, birth certificates, and instructions. In addition, Granada argues that the role of trademark law is to prevent an infringer from passing off its goods as being those of another. Such is not the case here. Are these sales prohibited? Explain. See *Orig. Appalachian Artworks* v. *Granada Electronics,* 816 F.2d 68 (2d Cir. 1987).

3. What are the relative advantages and disadvantages of each form of doing business in a foreign country? Why would a firm choose one form over another?

4. Assume that you are interested in importing silk blouses from Bangkok to France. What facts might persuade you

to enter into an agency agreement with a Thai blouse manufacturer rather than a distributorship and vice versa?

5. Prior to 1941, Kalmich owned a business in Yugoslavia. In 1941, the Nazis confiscated his property as a result of Kalmich's Jewish heritage and faith. Bruno purchased the business from the Nazis in 1942 without knowledge of the potential unlawful conversion. Kalmich contends that, as the confiscation was in violation of well-defined principles of international law prior to the German occupation, the transfer to Bruno was ineffective. Kalmich seeks to apply a 1946 Yugoslavian law called "Law Concerning the Treatment of Property Taken Away from the Owner." That law provides that where property is taken from its owners, the owner may bring an action against "responsible persons" for recovery. Does the act of state doctrine apply here? If not, what should be the result in an American court? Explain. See *Kalmich* v. *Bruno,* 450 F. Supp. 227 (N.D.IL 1978).

6. Bandes owned and managed 73 percent of the shares of Industria Nacional de Clavos y Alambres (INCA), a Nicaraguan corporation. In 1978, INCA paid $460,000 to Harlow & Jones, Inc. (H & J), a U.S. company, for steel billets. However, the events of the Nicaraguan civil war prevented INCA from taking delivery of the goods after they had been paid for and caused Bandes to flee the country. Decree no. 10, enacted by the new Nicaraguan government, gave the state the right to intervene in any business that had been abandoned. In 1979, the Nicaraguan government confiscated the shares held by others in the company and stripped Bandes of all power to represent INCA. In February 1980, the government issued another decree stating that all individuals who lost rights under the prior decree no. 10 must appear in Nicaragua within 10 days to contest the taking; otherwise, the property would belong to the state with no further right to contest. Bandes did not appear because his act of abandonment would have been considered a crime under the decree, but he later filed suit in the U.S. district courts seeking to get back from H & J the money INCA had paid to it, which Bandes believed he was rightly due.

   Does the act of state doctrine apply here? Are the acts of the Nicaraguan government in line with U.S. law and policies? Does it make a difference that the funds sought by Bandes are located in the United States? Explain. See *Bandes* v. *Harlow & Jones, Inc.,* 852 F.2d 661 (1988).

7. Lee Bun entered Hong Kong illegally by boat from China. He sought to claim refugee status on the basis that he had been involved in political protests in China and feared persecution if he returned. After judicial review of deportation orders was dismissed, Lee Bun claimed that he had been denied the right to a fair hearing, guaranteed by the Geneva Convention. The Department of Immigration responded that, while Britain had ratified the Convention, it had not been extended to Hong Kong and was not, therefore, part of the law of Hong Kong. What arguments could Lee Bun make in his favor supporting the application of the Geneva Convention to his right to a fair hearing? See *Lee Bun* v. *Dir. of Immigration,* 2 HKLR 466 (1990).

8. Zedan received a telephone call from a Saudi Arabian organization offering him an engineering position at a construction project in Saudi Arabia. The Ministry of Communications, an agency of the government, guaranteed payment to Zedan for any work he performed there, whether for the government or for a nonsovereign third party. After three years, Zedan left the country without being fully paid. After he returned to the United States, he filed an action in federal court seeking to enforce the Ministry's guarantee. The Ministry argued that it was protected under the Foreign Sovereign Immunities Act. Was Zedan's recruitment in the United States a commercial activity as required by the act? Did this action have a direct effect in the United States as required by the act? Explain. See *Zedan* v. *Kingdom of Saudi Arabia,* 849 F.2d 1511 (1988).

9. Dubai and Sharjah were Arab territories under the protection of Great Britain since 1892 but without clearly defined boundaries. The extent of territory the ruler of each controlled in each of these areas depended on which tribes offered him allegiance. Since the tribes were nomadic and moved around a great deal, the areas controlled by each ruler were indefinite. At the territories' request, Britain intervened in the 1950s, awarding certain lands to one or the other territory. However, uncertainty and dissatisfaction continued, notwithstanding the fact that the parties had requested that Britain arbitrate the boundaries. A compromise between the parties was signed in 1976 that provided for continued arbitration regarding the boundary dispute. One of the recurring issues was the choice of law to be applied as, unfortunately, no applicable law had been specified. Dubai argued that international law governed, which would dictate that equity reign, whereas Sharjah argued that the federal law of the United Arab Emirates applied, which would have given greater weight to allegiance of the tribes. What should be the result here? How would you arrive at a decision regarding the

delineation of territory? What factors are important to your decision? See *Dubai-Sharjah Border Arbitration, International Court of Justice, Court of Arbitration,* October 19, 1981.

10. In 1954, Italy filed a petition with the International Court of Justice based on a 1951 war reparations declaration made by America, Britain, and France. The declaration concerned the removal of certain Albanian gold from Italy in 1943 by German authorities (who then turned over the gold to Albania). The issue that concerned Italy at this hearing was whether the gold was in fact property of Italy or Albania at the end of World War II. In fact, Italy was not asking the court to order Albania to return the gold but to order the United States, Britain, and France to make reparations to Italy under the declaration. Just to complicate matters, the court was also asked to decide whether, if the gold was found to be Italy's, it should still be given to Britain in settlement of a prior judgment by Britain against Albania. Britain argued that its claim for the gold from Albania had priority over Italy's claim to the gold. Notwithstanding these truly complex matters, however, the first concern of the court was whether it had jurisdiction over all of the parties. Which parties to this action must have consented to the action in order for the court to finally decide the issues presented to it and enforce a judgment? See *Monetary Gold Removed From Rome, I.C.J. Reports 1954,* p. 19.

11. *a.* Emma is employed as an operations manager for a large midwestern manufacturing firm and has worked at the firm for 10 years. She is aware that there is an opening for someone with her abilities at the company's plant in the Middle East. The firm does not offer her the position, claiming that women are not treated well as managers in that area and that she would not have the respect that she deserves in that position. They are concerned that she, therefore, would not be able to adequately perform her functions. Emma is upset and considers filing a complaint with the EEOC (Equal Employment Opportunity Commission). What guidance would you offer to her?

   b. Consider a slight change to the above scenario. Emma is the assistant operations manager for the Middle East plant and resides in that area. She is told that if she wants a higher position, she should either move back to the States or consider a different company. The firm cites the reasons mentioned above for this conclusion. Does Emma have rights under Title VII?

12. Camel Manufacturing imported nylon tents to the United States. The tents held nine people and weighed over 30 pounds. The tents' floors ranged from 8 feet by 10 feet to 10 feet by 14 feet. The tents were to be used as shelter during camping. The importer categorized the goods as "sports equipment," which carried a 10 percent import duty, while the U.S. Customs Service considered the tents "textile articles not specifically provided for," with a duty of $.25 per pound plus 15 percent import duty. The importer appealed the decision. What should be the result? Explain. See *Camel Manufacturing Co.* v. *United States,* 686 F.Supp. 912 (C.I.T. 1988).

NOTES

1. Desda Moss, "Report: Companies Help Rain Forests Breathe a Little Easier," *USA Today,* September 15, 1993, p. 5A.

2. **http://www.sweatshopwatch.org/swatch/industry/**

3. **http://www.uniteunion.org/sweatshops/whatis/ infosheet.html**

4. Ruth Rosenbaum, David Schilling, "In Sweatshops, Wages Are the Issue" (May 1997).

5. Pamela Varley, *The Sweatshop Quandary: Corporate Responsibility on the Global Frontier* (Washington, DC: Investor Responsibility Research Center, 1998), p. 406.

6. PRNewswire, *USCIB Rejects Efforts to Impose and Monitor Standardized Codes on Multinational Corporations* (Dec. 21, 1998).

7. Ibid.

8. Allen R. Myerson, "In Principle, a Case for More 'Sweatshops,'" *New York Times,* June 22, 1997, Sec. 4, p. 5.

9. *EEOC* v. *Arabian American Oil Co.* 499 U.S. 244 (1991).

10. See a copy of the principles at **http://www.ita.doc.gov/bgp/model.html**. For information on the implementation of the principles

within various federal departments, see Bureau of Democracy, Human Rights and Labor, Dept. of State, *Promoting the Model Business Principles,* (Washington, DC: Department of State, Publication 10486, released June 1997), **http://www.state.gov/www/global/ human_rights/business_principles.html**.

11. Ibid.

12. Copies of the code and principles can be found at **http://www.dol.gov/dol/esa/public/nosweat/ partnership/report.htm**. See also **http://www.natlconsumersleague.org/aipagree.html**; Michael Shellenberger, "White House Sweatshop Agreement Announced," *Global Exchange* **(http://www.globalexchange.org/ economy/ corporations/sweatshops/pr110498.html)**; see also Dow Jones Newswire, "White House Signs Pact Covering Overseas Plants," *Global Exchange,* November 5, 1998 **(http://www.globalexchange.org/ economy/corporations/sweatshops/dj110598.html)**.

13. Steven Greenhouse, "Groups Reach Agreement for Curtailing Sweatshops," and "Plan to Curtail Sweatshops Rejected by Union," *New York Times,* Nov. 5, 1998, (electronic version); Steven Greenhouse, "Two More Unions Reject Agreement for Curtailing Sweatshops," *New York Times,* Nov. 6, 1998, (electronic version); UNITE Statement on the White House Apparel Industry Partnership, **http://www.sweatshopwatch.org/ swatch/headlines/1998/aip nov98.html#UNITE**; "Sweatshop Watch's Response to the White House Apparel Industry Partnership Agreement," *Corporate Watch Web Site,* **http://www.igc.org/trac/feature/ sweatshops/swatch.html**.

14. 11 U.S. (7 Cranch) 116 (1812).

15. "Legal Instruments for International Trade," *International Trade Forum* 3 (1998), pp. 20–21.

Trade Regulation and Antitrust

Chapter 7

Government Regulation of Business: An Introduction

INTRODUCTION

Chapter 1 raised the issue of the proper balance between the free market and government. Chapter 2 addressed the utility of individual and corporate ethics as self-regulatory mechanisms for governing the behavior of the corporate community. Chapter 3 continued our exploration of the proper role of business in society. Chapters 4, 5, and 6 offered a brief overview of the justice system. Chapters 7 and 8 introduce the general idea of government regulation of business.

Thereafter, the text is devoted to a series of more specific legal and ethical topics including antitrust, employment law, and the Internet. Throughout that investigation, keep in mind the issues of the introductory chapters. What is the proper role of business in society? Has business abused the public trust? If so, is government the answer to the problem? Or might we rely on self-regulation (ethics and social responsibility) and market "regulation"? What is the proper blend of these "control" devices as well as others left unexplored (e.g., custom)?

The phrase *mixed economy* is commonly applied to the contemporary American system. In pursuing the greatest good for the greatest number, America has turned to the government to ameliorate the injustices and discomforts of contemporary life. Market "regulation" and self-regulation have been supplemented by government intervention.

Government regulation pervades our lives. Government directly controls certain dimensions of the economy, such as the public utilities, although that hold is weakening. Government indirectly intervenes across the spectrum of the economy in matters as diverse as child labor and zoning restrictions; and, in the larger sense of national economic policy, the government engages in antitrust activity designed to preserve our conception of a free, efficient marketplace. To the proponents of government intervention, the successes are evident: cleaner air, safer cars, fewer useless drugs, more jobs for minorities, safer workplaces, and so on. To the critics, many government regulatory efforts either did not achieve their purpose or did so at a cost exceeding the benefits. The late 1970s and the 1980s were marked by increasingly insistent calls from virtually all segments of society to retard the reach of government. Indeed, significant deregulation has been effected and, after a quiet period in the early 1990s, regulatory reform at the turn of the century remains important to both the president and Congress. Nonetheless, government remains an enormous force in shaping business strategy and practice.

WHY REGULATION?

Market Failure

In theory, government intervention in a free enterprise economy would be justified only when the market is unable to maximize the public interest—that is, in instances of market failure.

Market failure is attributed to certain inherent imperfections in the market itself.

Imperfect Information.   Can the consumer choose the best pain reliever in the absence of complete information about the virtues of the competing products? An efficient free market presumes reasoned decisions about production and consumption. Reasoned decisions require adequate information. Because we cannot have perfect information and often will not have adequate information, the government, it is argued, may impose regulations either to improve the available information or to diminish the unfavorable effect of inadequate information. Hence we have, for example, labeling mandates for consumer goods, licensure requirements for many occupations, and health standards for the processing and sale of goods.

Monopoly.   Of course, the government intervenes to thwart anticompetitive monopolies and oligopolies throughout the marketplace. (That process is addressed in Chapter 10.) Of immediate interest here is the so-called natural monopoly. Telephone and electrical services are classic examples of a decline in per unit production costs as the firm becomes larger. Thus, a single large firm is more efficient than several small ones, and a natural monopoly results. In such situations, the government has commonly intervened (in the form of public service commissions) to preserve the efficiencies of the large firm while preventing that firm from taking unfair advantage of the consumer. (We should note that natural monopoly theory is under increasing challenge from free market economists, and government has, of course, substantially deregulated the telephone industry and is gradually doing the same with electric utilities.)

Externalities.   When all the costs and/or benefits of a good or service are not fully internalized or absorbed, those costs or benefits fall elsewhere as what economists have labeled *externalities, neighborhood effects,* or *spillovers.* Pollution is a characteristic example of a negative externality. The environment is used without charge as an ingredient in the production process (commonly as a receptacle for waste). Consequently, the product is underpriced. The producer and consumer do not pay the full social cost of the product, so those remaining costs are thrust on parties external to the transaction. Government regulation is sometimes considered necessary to place the full cost burden on those who generated it, which in turn is expected to result in less wasteful use of resources. Positive externalities are those in which a producer confers benefits not required by the market. An example of such a positive externality is a business firm that, through no direct market compulsion, landscapes its grounds and develops a sculpture garden to contribute to the aesthetic quality of its neighborhood. Positive externalities ordinarily are not the subject of regulation.

Public Goods.   Some goods and services cannot be provided through the pricing system because we have no method for excluding those who choose not to pay. For such *public goods,* the added cost of benefiting one person is zero or nearly so, and, in any case, no one can effectively be denied the benefits of the activity. National defense, insect eradication, and pollution control are examples of this phenomenon. Presumably most individuals would refuse to voluntarily pay for what others would receive free. Thus, in the absence of government regulations, public goods would not be produced in adequate quantities. [For an argument that government should sometimes intervene even if the market has not failed, see **http://plsc.uark.edu/book/books/budget/marketfail/market.htm**]

Two months following the April 1999 killings at Columbine High School in Colorado, *USA Weekend* polled Americans about whether we should create government rules to curb violence involving children. The results:

- 89 percent favor some restrictions on gun ownership; 19 percent believe most gun ownership should be banned while 9 percent believe guns should be unregulated.
- 59 percent favor restricting violence in movies and music.
- 67 percent favor regulating violence in video games and on TV.
- 64 percent favor regulating violence on the Internet and in music videos.
- a majority opposes regulating books.

In your judgment, has the market failed such that we need to impose restrictions on commerce in guns, movies, music, and the like? Explain.

Source: Gregg Easterbrook, "*USA Weekend's* Third Annual America's Poll," *USA Weekend,* July 2–4, 1999, p. 6.

Philosophy and Politics

The correction of market failure could explain the full range of government regulation of business, but an alternative or perhaps supplemental explanation lies in the political process. Three general arguments have emerged.

1. One view is that regulation is considered necessary for the protection and general welfare of the public. We find the government engaging in regulatory efforts designed to achieve a more equitable distribution of income and wealth. Many believe government intervention in the market is necessary to stabilize the economy, thus curbing the problems of recession, inflation, and unemployment. Affirmative action programs seek to compensate for the racism and sexism of the past. We even find the government protecting us from ourselves, both for our benefit and for the well-being of the larger society. For example, cigarette advertising is banned on television, and seatbelts are required in many states.

2. Another view is that regulation is developed at the behest of industry and is operated primarily for the benefit of industry. Here, the various subsidies and tax advantages afforded to business might be cited. In numerous instances, government regulation has been effective in reducing or entirely eliminating the entry of competitors. Antitrust law has been instrumental in sheltering small businesses. Government regulation has also permitted legalized price-fixing in some industries. Of course, it may be that although regulation is often initiated primarily for the public welfare, industry eventually "captures" the regulatory process and ensures its continuation for the benefit of the industry. Some corporations seek government standards so they can do what is best for society without being undercut by their less socially responsible competitors. Both public and business interests have been influential in generating government intervention in the marketplace.

3. Finally, bureaucrats who perform government regulation are themselves a powerful force in maintaining and expanding that regulation.

THE CONSTITUTIONAL FOUNDATION OF BUSINESS REGULATION

The Commerce Clause of the U.S. Constitution broadly specifies the power accorded to the federal government to regulate business activity. Article I, Section 8 of the Constitution provides that: "The Congress shall have the power . . . To regulate Commerce with foreign Nations, and among the several States, and with the Indian Tribes . . ." State authority to regulate commerce resides in the police power reserved to the states by the Constitution. *Police power* refers to the right of the state governments to promote the public health, safety, morals, and general welfare by regulating persons and property within each state's jurisdiction. The states have, in turn, delegated portions of the police power to local government units. [For a brief explanation of each portion of the Constitution, see **http://majoritywhip.house.gov/constitution/View/viewmenu.htm**]

Supremacy Clause

Sometimes state or local law conflicts with federal law. Such situations are resolved by the *Supremacy Clause* of the Constitution, which provides that "This Constitution and the Laws of the United States . . . shall be the Supreme Law of the Land."

Ours is a *federalist* form of government wherein we divide authority among federal, state, and local units of government. Conflicts between the preferences of each level are inevitable. However, the Supremacy Clause, as interpreted by the Supreme Court, establishes that, in the event of an irreconcilable conflict, federal law will prevail and the state/local law will be ruled unconstitutional. Were it not so, we would have great difficulty in achieving a unified national policy on any issue.

At the same time, the Supreme Court affirmed the states' strong role in our dual system of government by announcing that "it will read federal law to preempt state governmental functions only if Congress plainly states its intent to do so."[1]

Commerce Clause

The Commerce Clause, as interpreted by the judiciary, affords Congress exclusive jurisdiction over foreign commerce. States and localities, nevertheless, sometimes seek in various ways to regulate foreign commerce. For example, a state may seek, directly or indirectly, to impose a tax on foreign goods that compete with those locally grown or manufactured. Such efforts violate the Commerce Clause.

Federal control over interstate commerce was designed to create a free market throughout the United States, wherein goods would move among the states, unencumbered by state and local tariffs and duties. Not surprisingly, that profoundly sensible policy has been the source of extensive conflict and litigation. As with foreign commerce, the states and localities have tried to influence the course of interstate commerce, often to favor local economic interests. The judiciary has not been sympathetic with those efforts. Indeed, judicial decisions have dramatically expanded the reach of the federal government. Even intrastate activities having an effect on interstate commerce have been subject to federal regulation. In *Wickard* v. *Filburn,* the Supreme Court, in interpreting a federal statute regulating the production and sale of wheat, found that 23 acres of homegrown and largely home-consumed wheat affected interstate commerce and that it was subject to federal regulation.[2] (As a small test of the mind, you may wish to deduce the economic reasoning that supported the Court's position.) Clearly, the federal lawmakers with the approval of the judiciary have expanded the power of the central government at the expense of states and localities. The argument goes that expansion has been necessary to maximize the general good, which might otherwise be thwarted by economic self-interest or prejudice in specific states and localities. Then in 1995 and 1996, the Supreme Court appeared to begin to rethink the federal government's sweeping authority under the Commerce Clause.

New Direction?   Perhaps reflecting the current conservative tide, the Supreme Court's 1995 *Lopez* decision surprised most observers by striking a blow for states' rights. In 1990, the federal government approved the Gun-Free School Zones Act, which forbade "any individual knowingly to possess a firearm at a place that [he] knows . . . is a school zone."[3]

> A 12th-grade San Antonio, Texas, student carried an unloaded, concealed gun into his high school

A 12th-grade San Antonio, Texas, student carried an unloaded, concealed gun into his high school and was charged with violating the act. His case reached the Supreme Court, where he claimed and the Court agreed that Congress did not have the constitutional authority to regulate the matter. By a 5–4 vote the Court held that Congress exceeded its powers by defining the possession of a gun as economic activity that, through repetition elsewhere, would have a substantial effect on interstate commerce.[4]

Lopez clearly expects Congress to look closely before regulating intrastate activities to see whether they, in fact, have a *substantial effect* on interstate commerce. If not, the federal government lacks the constitutional authority to act. The Court, in substance, said that the federal government was trying to regulate a *local* matter, a subject left by the Constitution to local or state government. The decision upset no existing precedents, but it clearly signaled the Court's willingness to examine congressional power over our lives; power that has expanded essentially without question since the New Deal of the 1930s.

In 1999, the Fourth Circuit Federal Court of Appeals, in *Brzonkala* v. *Virginia Polytechnic Institute*[5] ruled that the federal Violence Against Women Act (VAWA) is unconstitutional. The Court, following the *Lopez* reasoning, held that Congress had exceeded its Commerce Clause authority in passing the law that allows sexual assault victims to sue in federal court for damages, thus converting a traditionally local matter into a federal issue. The case involved a woman, Brzonkala, who claimed she was raped by two football players, Morrison and Crawford, when all three were students at VPI. The Court explained:

> Brzonkala alleges that soon after she met Morrison and Crawford, the two defendants pinned her down on a bed in her dormitory and forcibly raped her. Afterwards, Morrison told Brzonkala, "You better not have any f* * *ing diseases." And, subsequently, Morrison announced publicly in the dormitory's dining hall, "I like to get girls drunk and f* * * the s* * * out of them."[6]

After Brzonkala complained to the University, Morrison was found guilty of abusive conduct by the VPI judicial committee and was to be suspended for one year, but that suspension was subsequently lifted.[7] Brzonkala then sued for damages in federal court, which led eventually to the Court of Appeals decision. In passing VAWA, Congress held hearings and developed "a huge record"[8] on the aggregate economic impact of violence against women including driving up medical costs and discouraging women from traveling and from holding jobs, but the federal court ruled that the necessary *substantial effect* had not been established. Perhaps as an indication of the increasing politicization of the judiciary, it is interesting to note that the 7–4 *Brzonkala* vote was by straight party line—those voting to strike down VAWA had all been appointed by Republican presidents and the four dissenters all had been appointed by Democrats.[9] The Supreme Court has agreed to review *Brzonkala*. [For the federal Violence Against Women Office, see **http://www.usdoj.gov/vawo/**] [For an executive summary of VAWA, see **http://www.usdoj.gov/vawo/cycle.htm**]

Soon after the *Brzonkala* decision, a New York federal district court upheld the constitutionality of VAWA, finding that Congress, in passing the law, had shown that gender-based acts of violence signficantly affect interstate commerce.[10] That case involved allegations of sexual harassment against the Syracuse University tennis coach. Since *Lopez,* other "noneconomic" federal laws such as a statute protecting access to abortion clinics and another enforcing the interstate collection of child support, have, for the most part, withstood constitutional challenge.[11] Thus, considerable uncertainty marks the Commerce Clause dispute, but regardless of the current debate, Congress's power to regulate intrastate activities that have a substantial effect on interstate commerce is unchanged. The following classic decision illustrates the importance of Commerce Clause reasoning in shaping contemporary American life; in this case Congress used its Commerce Clause authority to open public accommodations (hotels, restaurants, and the like) to all persons.

HEART OF ATLANTA MOTEL v. UNITED STATES
379 U.S. 241 (1964)

Justice Clark

This is a declaratory judgment action, attacking the constitutionality of Title II of the Civil Rights Act of 1964 . . . [The lower court found for the United States.]

1. The Factual Background and Contentions of the Parties

. . . Appellant owns and operates the Heart of Atlanta Motel, which has 216 rooms available to transient guests. The motel is located on Courtland Street, two blocks from downtown Peachtree Street. It is readily accessible to interstate highways 75 and 85 and state highways 23 and 41. Appellant solicits patronage from outside the State of Georgia through various national advertising media, including magazines of national circulation; it maintains over 50 billboards and highway signs within the state, soliciting patronage for the motel; it accepts convention trade from outside Georgia and approximately 75 percent of its registered guests are from out of state. Prior to passage of the act the motel had followed a practice of refusing to rent rooms to Negroes, and it alleged that it intended to continue to do so. In an effort to perpetuate that policy this suit was filed.

The appellant contends that Congress in passing this act exceeded its power to regulate commerce under [Article I] of the Constitution of the United States . . .

The appellees counter that the unavailability to Negroes of adequate accommodations interferes significantly with interstate travel, and that Congress, under the Commerce Clause, has power to remove such obstructions and restraints . . .

[A]ppellees proved the refusal of the motel to accept Negro transients after the passage of the act. The district court sustained the constitutionality of the sections of the act under attack and issued a permanent injunction . . . It restrained the appellant from "[r]efusing to accept Negroes as guests in the motel by reason of their race or color" and from "[m]aking any distinction whatever upon the basis of race or color in the availability of the goods, services, facilities, privileges, advantages, or accommodations offered or made available to the guests of the motel, or to the general public, within or upon any of the premises of the Heart of Atlanta Motel, Inc."

2. The History of the Act

. . . The act as finally adopted was most comprehensive, undertaking to prevent through peaceful and voluntary settlement discrimination in voting, as well as in places of accommodation and public facilities, federally secured programs, and in employment. Since Title II is the only portion under attack here, we confine our consideration to those public accommodation provisions.

3. Title II of the Act

This Title is divided into seven sections beginning with § 201(a) which provides that:

"All persons shall be entitled to the full and equal enjoyment of the goods, services, facilities, privileges, advantages, and accommodations of any place of public accommodation, as defined in this section, without discrimination or segregation on the ground of race, color, religion, or national origin."

4. Application of Title II to Heart of Atlanta Motel

It is admitted that the operation of the motel brings it within the provisions of § 201(a) of the act and that appellant refused to provide lodging for transient Negroes because of their race or color and that it intends to continue that policy unless restrained.

The sole question posed is, therefore, the constitutionality of the Civil Rights Act of 1964 as applied to these facts . . .

[Part 5 omitted.]

6. The Basis of Congressional Action

While the act as adopted carried no congressional findings the record of its passage through each house is replete with evidence of the burdens that discrimination by race or color places upon interstate commerce . . . This testimony included the fact that our people have become increasingly mobile with millions of people of all races traveling from state to state; that Negroes in particular have been the subject of discrimination in transient accommodations, having to travel great distances to secure the same; that often they have been unable to obtain accommodations and have had to call upon friends to put them up overnight, and that these conditions have become so acute as to require the listing of available lodging for Negroes in a special guidebook which was itself "dramatic testimony to the difficulties" Negroes encounter in travel. These exclusionary practices were found to be nationwide, the Under Secretary of Commerce testifying that there is "no question that this discrimination in the North still exists to a large degree" and in the West and Midwest as well. This testimony indicated a qualitative as well as quantitative effect on interstate travel by Negroes. The former was the obvious impairment of the Negro traveler's pleasure and convenience that resulted when he continually was uncertain of finding lodging. As for the latter, there was evidence that this uncertainty stemming from racial discrimination had the effect of discouraging travel on the part of a substantial portion of the Negro community. This was the conclusion not only of the Under Secretary of Commerce but also of the Administrator of the Federal Aviation Agency, who wrote the Chairman of the Senate Commerce Committee that it was his "belief that air commerce is adversely affected by the denial to a substantial segment of the traveling public of adequate and desegregated public accommodations." We shall not burden this opinion with further details since the voluminous testimony presents overwhelming evidence that discrimination by hotels and motels impedes interstate travel.

7. The Power of Congress over Interstate Travel

The power of Congress to deal with these obstructions depends on the meaning of the Commerce Clause.

* * * * *

In short, the determinative test of the exercise of power by the Congress under the Commerce Clause is simply whether the activity sought to be regulated is "commerce which concerns more States than one" and has a real and substantial relation to the national interest. Let us now turn to this facet of the problem.

* * * * *

The same interest in protecting interstate commerce which led Congress to deal with segregation in interstate carriers and the white-slave traffic has prompted it to extend the exercise of its power to gambling, to criminal enterprises, to deceptive practices in the sale of products, to fraudulent security transactions, and to racial discrimination by owners and managers of terminal restaurants . . .

That Congress was legislating against moral wrongs in many of these areas rendered its enactments no less valid. In framing Title II of this act Congress was also dealing with what it considered a moral problem. But that fact does not detract from the overwhelming evidence of the disruptive effect the racial discrimination has had on commercial intercourse. It was this burden which empowered Congress to enact appropriate legislation, and, given this basis for the exercise of its power, Congress was not restricted by the fact that the particular obstruction to interstate commerce with which it was dealing was also deemed a moral and social wrong.

It is said that the operation of the motel here is of a purely local character. But, assuming this to be true, "[i]f it is interstate commerce that feels the pinch, it does not matter how local the operation which applies the squeeze."

* * * * *

Thus the power of Congress to promote interstate commerce also includes the power to regulate the local incidents thereof, including local activities in both the states of origin and destination, which might have a substantial and harmful effect upon that commerce. One need only examine the evidence which we have discussed above to see that Congress may—as it has—prohibit racial discrimination by motels serving travelers, however "local" their operations may appear.

* * * * *

The only questions are (1) whether Congress had a rational basis for finding that racial discrimination by motels affected commerce, and (2) if it had such a basis, whether the means it selected to eliminate that evil are reasonable and appropriate. If they are, appellant has no "right" to select its guests as it sees fit, free from governmental regulation.

* * * * *

It is doubtful if in the long run appellant will suffer economic loss as a result of the act. Experience is to the contrary where discrimination is completely obliterated as to all public accommodations. But whether this be true or not is of no consequence since this Court has specifically held that the fact that a "member of the class which is regulated may suffer economic losses not shared by others . . . has never been a barrier" to such legislation . . .

We, therefore, conclude that the action of the Congress in the adoption of the act as applied here to a motel which concededly serves interstate travelers is within the power granted it by the Commerce Clause of the Constitution, as interpreted by this Court for 140 years . . .

Affirmed.

Questions

1. In your judgment, does the Commerce Clause afford the federal government the authority to regulate a local business like the Heart of Atlanta motel? Explain.
2. Should the federal government regulate local business to further the cause of racial equity? Explain.
3. What arguments were offered by the government to establish that the Heart of Atlanta racial policy affected interstate commerce? Are you persuaded by those arguments? Explain.
4. What test did the Court articulate to determine when Congress has the power to pass legislation based on the Commerce Clause?
5. Ollie's Barbecue, a neighborhood restaurant in Birmingham, Alabama, discriminated against black customers. McClung brought suit to test the application of the public accommodations section of the Civil Rights Act of 1964 to his restaurant. In the suit, the government offered no evidence to show that the restaurant ever had served interstate customers or that it was likely to do so. Decide the case. See *Katzenbach* v. *McClung,* 379 U.S. 294 (1964).
6. Juan Paul Robertson was charged with various narcotics offenses and with violating the federal Racketeer Influenced and Corrupt Organizations Act (RICO) by investing the proceeds from his unlawful activities in an Alaskan gold mine. He paid for some mining equipment in Los Angeles and had it shipped to Alaska. He hired seven out-of-state employees to work in the Alaskan mine. Most of the resulting gold was sold in Alaska, although Robertson transported $30,000 in gold out of the state. He was convicted on the RICO charge, but appealed claiming that the gold mine was not engaged in or affecting interstate commerce. Was Robertson's gold mine engaged in or affecting interstate commerce? Explain. See *United States* v. *Juan Paul Robertson,* 115 S.Ct. 1732 (1995).
7. In the San Antonio case (*Lopez*) in which a 12th-grade student brought a concealed gun to school, how would you argue that the possession of a gun in a school zone substantially affects interstate commerce?

STATE AND LOCAL REGULATION OF INTERSTATE COMMERCE

As noted, the states via their constitutional police power have the authority to regulate commerce within their jurisdictions for the purpose of maintaining the general welfare. That is, in order to assist in maintaining the public health, safety, and morals, states must be able to control persons and property within their jurisdictional authority. However, we have seen that the Commerce Clause, as interpreted, accords the federal government broad authority over commerce. As explained, the federal government has exclusive authority over foreign commerce. Purely intrastate commerce, having no significant effect on interstate commerce, is within the exclusive regulatory jurisdiction of the states. Of course, commerce purely intrastate in nature is uncommon. The confusion arises in the middle ground of interstate commerce where regulation by the federal government or state governments or both may be permissible. While federal government regulation of interstate commerce is pervasive, it is not exclusive.

So here we are concerned with commerce that is clearly interstate in nature, but which is being subjected to state and/or local regulation. The concern, then, is whether that regulation is unconstitutional because it (1) discriminates against interstate commerce or (2) unduly burdens interstate commerce such that the burden imposed clearly exceeds the local benefits. In the *Waste Management* case that follows, the Sixth Circuit Court of Appeals asks whether Nashville, Tennessee, is discriminating against interstate commerce and, if so, whether other means exist by which Nashville can achieve its goals.

WASTE MANAGEMENT, INC. v. METROPOLITAN GOVERNMENT
130 F.3d 731 (6th Cir. 1997) [Certiorari Denied, 118 S.Ct. 1560 (1998)]

Circuit Judge Alan E. Norris

Plaintiff, Waste Management, Inc. of Tennessee ("WMIT"), appeals the district court's denial of its motion for relief from enforcement of a flow control regulation . . . [T]he flow control regulation [was] enacted by defendant, Metropolitan Government of Nashville and Davidson County ("Metro") . . .

I

Defendant Metro is the local governing authority of Nashville and Davidson County, Tennessee. Between January 1991 and May 1994, defendant promulgated ordinances and regulations governing the disposal of solid waste generated within its boundaries. [T]he flow control regulation ("flow control provisions") requires that all persons collecting, hauling, or removing waste from Metro be licensed; that the waste be disposed of only at sites approved by Metro; and that all residential waste collected within Metro be disposed of at a waste-to-energy facility owned by Metro and operated by the Nashville Thermal Transfer Corp. ("NTTC"). NTTC supplies power to buildings in downtown Nashville with the energy it generates by burning solid waste. The amended regulation does not require that nonresidential waste collected within Metro be disposed of at NTTC, unless that facility has not received the 6,300 tons of solid waste per week it needs to operate.

* * * * *

Plaintiff is one of several waste collectors licensed to collect and dispose of waste within the boundaries of Metro, but it is the only collector which actually operates a waste disposal facility in Metro. The other licensed collectors include Browning–Ferris Industries of Tennessee, Inc. ("BFI") and Sanifill . . .

[P]laintiff . . . alleg[es] that the flow control and waste disposal fee provisions violate the Commerce Clause of the United States Constitution . . .

The district court . . . did not enjoin enforcement of the flow control provisions . . . [Waste Management appealed.]

II

Commerce Clause

The United States Constitution expressly authorizes Congress to "regulate Commerce with foreign Nations, and among the several States," and "the 'negative' or 'dormant' aspect of the Commerce Clause prohibits the States from 'advanc[ing] their own commercial interests by curtailing the *movement of articles of commerce,* either into or out of the state.'" The negative Commerce Clause also limits the actions of municipalities such as Metro, where such actions "burden interstate commerce or impede its free flow." *C & A Carbone, Inc.* v. *Clarkstown,* 511 U.S. 383 (1994).

In deciding if a particular law violates the negative Commerce Clause, a court must first "determine whether [the law] 'regulates evenhandedly with only incidental effects on interstate commerce, or discriminates against interstate commerce.'" A law that discriminates against interstate commerce treats in-state and out-of-state interests differently, benefitting the former and burdening the latter.

If a law discriminates against interstate commerce, it is "virtually *per se* invalid," unless "the municipality can demonstrate, under rigorous scrutiny, that it has no other means to advance a legitimate local interest." On the other hand, "nondiscriminatory regulations that have only incidental effects on interstate commerce are valid unless 'the burden imposed on such commerce is clearly excessive in relation to the putative local benefits.'"

Flow Control Provisions

Plaintiff argues that the district court erred in ruling that defendant's flow control provisions do not violate the Commerce Clause. The court held that the provisions are nondiscriminatory, with incidental effects on interstate commerce, and that the burden they impose is not clearly excessive in relation to their putative local benefits. It distinguished this case from *Carbone* on the grounds that the provisions at issue here do not totally exclude disposal of waste outside of Metro, or create or result in a monopoly for NTTC. Rather, the court reasoned, plaintiff can still dispose of nonresidential waste at facilities other than NTTC that are located outside of Metro or even outside of Tennessee.

Before the court concluded that defendant's flow control provisions do not discriminate against interstate commerce, it proceeded as if they do discriminate. In considering whether defendant had any other means of advancing a legitimate local interest, the court again distinguished these provisions from those at issue in *Carbone,* on the ground that they do not just generate revenues, which would not be a legitimate local interest justifying such discrimination. They also "implicate[ ] significant public environmental interests," such as ensuring that a proportion of solid waste collected within Metro's boundaries is used as fuel, and enabling Metro to comply with Tennessee's Solid Waste Management Act of 1991, which requires municipalities to reduce by twenty-five percent the volume of solid waste disposed of in landfills and incinerators in Tennessee.

In *Carbone,* the Supreme Court stated that the flow control ordinance at issue there "hoard[ed] solid waste, and the demand to get rid of it, for the benefit of the preferred processing facility." The provisions at issue in this case do the same, even though they do not require that all waste be sent to NTTC. They require that all *residential* waste be sent to NTTC, thereby preventing plaintiff from disposing of such waste at a cheaper facility, and threatening the well-being of plaintiff's own dump sites. In *Wyoming* v. *Oklahoma,* 502 U.S. 437 (1992), the Supreme Court observed that "[t]he volume of commerce affected measures only the *extent* of the discrimination; it is of no relevance to the determination whether a State has discriminated against interstate commerce." As we read *Wyoming,* plaintiff's ability to send some waste to facilities other than NTTC goes to the extent of the discrimination, not whether there was discrimination in the first place.

Having determined that defendant's flow control provisions do in fact discriminate against interstate commerce, we must now decide whether "the municipality [has] demonstrate[d], under rigorous scrutiny, that it has no other means to advance a legitimate local interest." Although defendant may have cited two legitimate local interests, there are other means of advancing such interests, like charging competitive tipping fees for waste disposed of at NTTC. Moreover, Metro concedes that it could secure a flow of waste to NTTC by increasing its collections either directly or by contract, "but this could not be done without legislation and some further time for preparation." Because defendant's flow control provisions are facially discriminatory, and because there are other means of advancing the legitimate local interests cited, these provisions cannot satisfy the rigorous scrutiny to which such laws are subjected under the Commerce Clause. We hold, therefore, that the district court erred in refusing to enjoin their enforcement.

* * * * *

Reversed.

Questions

1.
    a. Was Nashville found to be discriminating against interstate commerce? Explain.
    b. Did Nashville have other reasonable means by which to achieve its goals? Explain.

2. What was Nashville's motive in creating the flow control regulation?

3. An Indiana statute prohibited the practice of backhauling municipal waste. Indiana was trying to prevent truckers from hauling trash on the homeward-bound leg of a trip after having delivered other goods on the outbound leg. On its face, the statute applied evenly to intrastate and interstate carriers. Most in-state waste was hauled in dedicated garbage trucks (those used exclusively for garbage). The Indiana statute was challenged by two companies engaged in brokering waste disposal.

   a. What constitutional challenge was raised by the plaintiffs?

   b. What defense was raised by Indiana?

   c. Decide.

   See *Government Suppliers Consolidating Service and Jack Castenova* v. *Evan Bayh and Kathy Prosser,* 975 F.2d 1267 (1992); cert. den. 113 S.Ct. 977 (1993).

4. North Dakota rules require those bringing liquor into the state to file a monthly report, and out-of-state distillers selling to federal enclaves (military bases, in this instance) must label each item indicating that it is for consumption only within the enclave. The United States challenged those rules after sellers said they would discontinue dealing with the military bases or they would raise their prices in order to meet the cost of dealing with the two rules.

   a. What are the constitutional foundations of the federal government's challenge?

   b. What were the state's reasons for adopting the rules?

   c. Decide. Explain. See *North Dakota* v. *United States,* 495 U.S. 423 (1990).

5. Premium Standard Farms, a large Missouri hog-raising operation, was pumping manure through a two-mile-long pipe into Iowa to be spread on a farm whose operator sought the manure for fertilizer. Iowa citizens objected and asked Attorney General Tom Miller to act. Can the Iowa Attorney General stop the pumping? Explain.

Federalism and Free Trade

America's political structure is built on the federalist principle of a careful balance of power between the local, state, and federal governments. We believe in maximizing local control. We believe those closest to a problem are best situated to understand and address it. Nonetheless, we also recognize that we cannot have a meaningful nation with all the benefits of that status without substantial central control. As we saw in the Nashville waste case, localities and states may pass rules to meet their needs but the nation's needs, as expressed in the Constitution, may be undermined. If lawful, each state would be racing to erect protectionist trade barriers to benefit its citizens while burdening commerce from other states and localities. The Commerce Clause is the legal standard that prevents that kind of fracturing of the United States. Still, ample protectionism remains. Some of it, of course, is necessary. We cannot, for example, simply move from one state to another to practice law or sell real estate. Each state sets up its own licensing rules to protect the welfare of its citizens. Of course, those rules also restrict competition.

James V. Koch, president of Old Dominion University, recently pointed to state barriers to a free market in higher education. ODU offers the nation's largest fully accredited program in televised, interactive distance learning. Most states, however, "forbid institutions of higher eduation not headquartered within their borders from offering courses and degree programs to their citizens without prior permission."[12] Thus, ODU must comply with time-consuming, expensive regulatory permission processes in order to bring their product (education) to the full national market. From each state's point of view, of course, citizens expect to be protected from shoddy products and services so regulation is necessary.

Globalism and Free Trade

Those protectionist tendencies that we see among our 50 states are much more pronounced around the globe as nations try to erect facially reasonable, and often well-meaning, rules, which have the effect (sometimes intended) of protecting national interests at the expense of open markets. The United States engages in an ongoing international crusade to break down trade barriers, and, in most cases, we have practiced what we preach. Overall, our import tariffs are among the lowest in the world. At the same time, when it suits our political and pecuniary needs, we too practice protectionism. Journalist James Cox provides some examples:

> Trade experts say tariffs and other protectionism make the economy less efficient and force consumers to pay higher prices and taxes to subsidize jobs.
>
> • Stiff U.S. tariffs on imported ball bearings, for instance, have shielded jobs in domestic manufacturing. But Americans pay $438,356 for every job saved, according to research by economists Gary Hufbauer and Kimberly Elliott. In other industries, protectionism has been even more costly: $758,678 per job in softwood lumber; $933,628 in luggage making; and more than $1 million in benzenoid chemical manufacturing, by the economists' calculations. Overall, they reckon, protectionism costs the U.S. economy more than $70 billion a year, or 0.8% of gross domestic product.
> • Japanese and European airlines aren't allowed to land in a U.S. city, pick up paying passengers and fly to another U.S. destination. But U.S. carriers can take on new passengers in Japan and Europe and whisk them to other Asian and European destinations.
> • Quotas. The U.S. puts ceilings on foreign sugar, peanuts, and dairy products. After foreign tobacco producers hit their quotas, additional shipments face 350% tariffs.[13]

[For a database on streamlining government rules, see **http://www.tabd.com/index1.html**]

Questions

1. Journalist Max Frankel, writing in the *New York Times,* argues that the next century's "Great Revolution" will be the "collapse of nationhood."[14] He says that collapse will be powered largely by technology and the global financial market.
   - *a.* Explain what Frankel means.
   - *b.* Do you agree? Explain.
   - *c.* Frankel quotes finance experts, George Shultz, William Simon, and Walter Wriston, who said: "The gold standard has been replaced by the information standard, an iron discipline that no government can evade." . . . "No country can hide."[15] What do they mean?

2.   *a.*   Can you envision a time when all of the nations of the world are able to agree on the elimination of regulatory barriers? Explain.

   b.   Would you favor that development? Explain.

3.   The U.S. Congress has passed laws effectively imposing rather uniform federal standards on a number of areas of business practice, including securities trading, civil rights, and copyrights. Now, businesses are lobbying Congress requesting uniformity in other areas in order to avoid the costs and frustrations of dealing with a patchwork of state laws.

   a.   What areas of law might benefit from greater uniformity across the states? Explain.

   b.   Make the arguments for and against greater uniformity in those areas. See Edward Felsenthal, "Firms Ask Congress to Pass Uniform Rules," *The Wall Street Journal,* May 10, 1993, p. B5.

SUMMARY OF STATE AND LOCAL REGULATIONS

We hear so much about federal rules governing business that we perhaps fail to take note of the vast array of state and local regulations that also play an important role in business practice. Indeed, as encouraged by the 1994 Workforce Reduction Act, the number of executive branch federal employees has actually declined from 2.2 million in 1993 to 1.9 million in 1996 while state and local government employees increased by 22 percent between 1985 and 1995.[16]

We need to remember that this upward spiral at the state and local level, however lamentable in some ways, often springs from our demands for a better life, including improvements in education, health care, infrastructure, and so on. Furthermore, the states and localities serve the important civic purpose of bringing government close to the people.

Just as state and local employee rolls have grown, so have the rules that some of those employees enforce. Many of those rules are designed to regulate business behavior. Those regulations fall into three broad categories: (1) controlling entry into business, (2) regulating competition, and (3) preventing consumer fraud.

The states are primarily responsible for regulating the insurance industry and are heavily involved in regulating banking, securities, and liquor sales. Many businesses and professions—from funeral preparation to barbering to the practice of medicine—require a license from the state. Public utilities (e.g., gas, electricity, and sewage disposal) are the subject of extensive regulation governing entry, rates, customer service, and virtually the fullness of the companies' activities. All states have some form of public service commission charged with regulating utilities in the public interest. Many states seek to directly enhance competition via antitrust legislation. Many states have passed laws forbidding usury, false advertising, stock fraud, and other practices harmful to the consumer. Furthermore, Congress pushes federal activities such as welfare and highway safety rules back to the states, suggesting that state government growth is unlikely to abate. [For the "largest Internet compilation" of state government materials, see **http://www.hg.org/hg.html**]

Licensure.   Local regulation is much less economically significant than state regulation. Local government intervention in business typically involves various licensure requirements. For example, businesses like bars and theaters are often required to obtain a local permit to operate. Similarly, some 10 percent of America's jobs (practicing medicine and law, building construction, electrical work, and so on) can be occupied only by those who have successfully secured licensure from state and/or local authorities. Licensure is to protect the public from unsafe, unhealthy, and substandard goods and services, but critics contend that the presumed benefits of licensure are exceeded by its costs in increased prices, decreased services, and administrative overhead. Rules governing taxi, van, and limousine services are good examples of these competing views. Las Vegas, for example, has had no new taxicab entrants in its tightly regulated market in the past quarter century.[17] Likewise, according to *The Wall Street Journal,* "only three small new limousine operators have been approved in Las Vegas in the past 20 years."[18] Regulators point to the importance of safe, clean, timely taxi service to make a good impression on visitors, but the *Journal* points to the power of political forces:

> Las Vegas is one of the premier convention centers on the planet and many of its 25 million annual visitors hire limousines or taxicabs. But the market is almost as closed as the one for first-class mail. In 1997, Nevada's wealthy Bell family pushed through the state legislature a law that enshrines its dominance of the limousine market. The law created the Transportation Services Authority and ordered that any vehicle "in passenger service must be impounded by the authority if a certificate of public convenience and necessity" hasn't been issued . . .[19]

Rules and the New Business. Dealing with government regulations is an important part of starting and successfully operating a new business. The article that follows gives us a sense of the "red tape" facing the budding entrepreneur in Houston, Texas, not a city known for tight government oversight.

SMALL BUSINESS; BUREAUCRACY; UNRAVELING THE RED TAPE

Rebecca Mowbray

When Teresa Byrne-Dodge started *My Table* magazine five years ago, she knew a periodicals permit was essential for cheaper second-class mailing.

But every time she talked to the post office, she seemed to get a different answer about how to qualify. Wading through pages and pages of arcane language in the postal rule books didn't help much.

"I was always worried that I would make some little error somewhere and hundreds of hours of work and all of those advertisers who've paid to be in there would be wasted," Byrne-Dodge said. "You feel like you're just swimming through all these regulations."

Last year—four years after she began publishing—Byrne-Dodge discovered that a sales and use tax permit could have saved her hundreds of dollars on each bimonthly printing.

Entire departments of government from Houston to Austin to Washington are built around issuing permits to businesses. Every business—whether it handles food or hazardous materials, sells goods or services, or is constructing a new building for itself—needs at least a few permits to operate legally.

The City of Houston's One Stop Business Center is a good place for small business owners to begin.

"They can contact us and we'll give them a list of the different permits and licenses they'll need," said manager Neal Polansky.

In addition, regulatory agencies offer help on the permits they require, and some Houston small business owners say communication and customer service have improved at many agencies. Many departments now have publications, 800-numbers and Web sites to guide business owners through the permit process. Increasingly, these agencies also have forms that can be downloaded from the Internet, saving time and parking fees.

Faced with the specter of obtaining all the permits necessary to open a restaurant, the owners of Masraff's, a new restaurant, decided to hire a private company to fill out the restaurant's forms and stand in line. "Without the help of others there's no way a small company can do it on your own," Tony Masraff said.

Wade Hudson built his entire business—Hudson License Service—around the axioms that permits are confusing, and that entrepreneurs don't have the time, patience, or knowledge to get them.

"We do the legwork for people applying for licenses. Most of them prefer paying a service to do the legwork than to drive all over town," said Hudson, who will fetch alcohol, cigarette, lottery ticket, and food stamp selling licenses for about $450.

Permit service firms fill out many forms every day, are on a first-name basis with permitting agents, and have learned how to phrase responses on the forms so they're less likely to get sent back.

Every business has specialized permitting needs, but there are some filings common to almost all businesses.

DBA.   Any business that's doing business under a name different from that of its owner needs a DBA, or "doing business as" certificate. A DBA is not a legal claim to the name, but a public declaration linking the business name with its owner for consumer protection purposes.

Without a DBA, a business owner can't open a company bank account or apply for the other licenses necessary to do business. That's why reserving a company name in all counties where the company will be operating is generally the first step in business.

The DBA generally costs less than $13, depending on how many people are listed as principals in the business and whether the application has been notarized. The DBA is valid for 10 years.

State taxes.   Any business selling taxable items or providing a taxable service has to get a sales tax permit from the Texas comptroller's office. Operating without a sales tax permit could cost a business owner $500 each day. The office of the comptroller can also help a business determine whether it needs to post a sales tax bond or pay a franchise tax.

Federal taxes.   Entrepreneurs can open the business using a Social Security number as a taxpayer identification number for the Internal Revenue Service, but once the business hires an employee, or files pension or excise tax returns, the IRS requires an employer identification number.

Property inventory.   All businesses must file a list of all business assets with the Harris County Appraisal District by April 15 of each year so the county can determine local property taxes. Anything that's a movable, tangible asset—inventory, raw materials, leasehold improvements, machinery, office equipment, furniture, and vehicles—must be on the list, as well as when the items were acquired and their cost.

Beyond these essential filings, there are more specialized permits, licenses, and registrations that vary with the type of business.

A business in a newly remodeled building might need a certificate of occupancy, a permit for a sign, a permit to reserve waste water capacity, and an inspection for compliance with fire and air quality regulations. If the business is a restaurant that serves alcohol, it would need a food handler's permit and an alcoholic beverage license, among others.

Sometimes these requirements are not always obvious. There are registrations for holding a laser beam show, storing corpses, handling eggs or shellfish, operating a car wash or a tanning salon, and manufacturing antifreeze.

But as Richard Pignetti discovered, applying for permits is one thing, and getting approval for them is another.

Opening day of Pignetti's restaurant came and went three times as he wrangled with permit inspectors about whether his remodeled building fulfilled requirements.

Three months and $20,000 later, Pignetti's finally opened after satisfying city building inspectors. "It varies from inspector to inspector how loose or tight they're going to be," Pignetti said, "You're pretty much at their mercy."

Source: *Houston Chronicle,* March 21, 1999, Business Section, p. 4. Reprinted by permission.

Afterword

Frustrating though they may be, regulations and the government officials who make them are obviously a necessary ingredient in contemporary life, and a new study of state government suggests that those officials, in general, do their jobs well. The two-year study at Syracuse University concluded that, based on management effectiveness rather than policy or political philosophy, 28 states received good or excellent ratings for their oversight of finances, planning, human resources, and the like.[20]

Questions

1. The city government in Cedar Falls, Iowa, home of the University of Northern Iowa, declined to renew the liquor license of a local bar after 58 of 100 "bar checks" over a period of nearly two years found minors drinking illegally. One hundred and seventy four alcohol-related tickets were issued over that period.[21]
   a. Could the free market satisfactorily protect the public from the various risks associated with excessive drinking by college-aged students, or are rules necessary?
   b. Would you vote to renew this bar's liquor license? Explain.
2. As you see it, why are many state and local governments growing rapidly?
3. In general, do we rely too much on government in the United States? Explain.
4. Two Dallas, Texas, ordinances were challenged in court. One gave the police very broad authority to deny licenses to "adult" businesses such as bookstores. The other, which was directed at prostitution, barred motel owners from renting rooms for fewer than 10 hours.
   a. What challenges would you raise against these ordinances?
   b. How would you rule? Explain. See *FW/PBS Inc* v. *City of Dallas,* 493 U.S. 215 (1990).
5. The city of Pomona, California, passed an ordinance requiring, among other things, that businesses having on-premises signs in foreign alphabetical characters must devote one-half of the space in those signs to English alphabetical characters. The city took the position that the ordinance was necessary in case of emergencies. The ordinance was challenged in court.
   a. What constitutional challenges would you raise against the ordinance?
   b. How would you rule? Explain. See *Asian American Business Group* v. *Pomona,* 716 F. Supp. 1328 (C.D. Cal. 1989).
6. The city of Los Angeles, California, enacted an ordinance that created a dress code for cab drivers and imposed fines for violations. For example, tank tops and cutoff pants are forbidden. In addition, being rude to passengers can also lead to fines.
   a. By what constitutional authority does Los Angeles instruct cab drivers regarding dress and behavior?
   b. Do you favor the ordinance? Explain.

TAKINGS

At local, state, and federal levels, government bodies have been increasingly willing in recent decades to take private property for public use without the owner's consent—a procedure called *eminent domain.* If the state wants to build a road, or a dam, or an airport, for example, a property owner ordinarily cannot stop the *taking* of the required land, assuming a necessary and proper public purpose. The Fifth Amendment, however, provides that private property shall not be "taken for public use, without just compensation." Therefore, the government can take the land, but the owner must be paid.

Now, what happens when the government does not *take* the property but rather, under its police power, simply *regulates* it in a manner that deprives that property of some or all of its economic usefulness? For example, without providing *just compensation,* can the state lawfully limit the amount a landlord can charge for rent in an effort to preserve housing for low-income citizens? Or can a state forbid roadside billboards? Or can the government reduce logging in a timber area inhabited by an endangered species—for example, spotted owls?

These *regulatory takings* normally do not require government compensation because to do so would severely impair the state's ability to govern in an orderly manner. Nonetheless, in recent years, the courts have been more aggressive about requiring just compensation for some regulatory takings. Three broad classes of such takings have emerged in court decisions. [For an "introduction to the takings issue," see **http://www.envpoly.org/takings/**]

> the South Carolina Coastal Commission passed erosion rules having the effect of preventing David Lucas from building any permanent structure on his $975,000 beachfront lots

1. Total Takings. If a governmental body acts in a way that takes *all of the economic value* of a property or permanently physically invades the property, the taking requires just compensation unless the government is preventing a nuisance or the regulation was permissible under property law at the time of the purchase of the property. When the South Carolina Coastal Commission passed erosion rules having the effect of preventing David Lucas from building any permanent structure on his $975,000 beachfront lots, Lucas sued claiming a Fifth Amendment violation. The United States Supreme Court, in 1992, agreed with Lucas and held that a taking requiring just compensation had occurred because the state had deprived Lucas of *all* economically beneficial use of the property and the property did not fall in one of the two exceptions.[22]

2. Exaction/Mitigation. A second class of regulatory takings involves situations where the government allows land development only if the owner dedicates some property interest (called an *exaction*) or money to the government (called a *mitigation* or *impact fee.* Thus, if you are developing land for housing, the city government might require that you devote a portion of that land to parks. Or you might be required to pay a fee to help the city meet the recreational needs of the citizens your development will be housing. The Supreme Court dealt with just such a case in *Dolan* v. *Tigard,* a 1994 decision.[23] Florence Dolan, owner of a plumbing and electrical supply store in Tigard, Oregon, applied for a city permit to nearly double the size of her store and to pave her parking lot. Concerned with increased traffic and water runoff due to the proposed expansion, the city granted the permit, subject to a pair of conditions: (1) Dolan was to dedicate the portion of her property that lay within the 100-year floodplain to the city to improve drainage for the creek that ran along her property, and (2) she was to dedicate an additional 15-foot strip of her land adjacent to the floodplain for use as a bicycle path/walkway to relieve traffic congestion. Dolan sought a variance from the requirements, but her petition was denied. She sued and her case eventually reached the United States Supreme Court. The Court set out a two-part test for these exaction cases. Government can compel a dedication of private property to public use where it can show two factors. The first is a nexus or relationship between the government's legitimate purpose (flood and traffic control in *Dolan*) and the condition imposed (the land Dolan was to dedicate to public purposes). Second, if step 1 is established, then the government must show a "rough proportionality" between the burden imposed (the land given over to public use) and the impact of the development (increased water runoff and increased traffic).[24] The Supreme Court, in a firm defense of private property rights, ruled that Tigard had failed to meet those standards, and Dolan won the case.

Supreme Court decisions, like *Dolan,* often have an immediate and practical impact. The City Council in Peachtree City, Georgia, had required the Peachtree City United Methodist Church to set aside 25 acres of green space as one of 11 conditions for approving the Church's site plan for building a new church complex on 63 acres. The 25 acres had no designated use in the site plan because the land was to be developed over a 20- to 50-year period. Neighbors, however, were concerned about the "unknown," noise, traffic, and the like. The Church challenged the 25-acre requirement, and the city attorney advised that the green space requirement was an unconstitutional taking of private property without just compensation. The City Council agreed, and the 25-acre exaction was withdrawn in 1999.[25]

3. Partial Takings.   Many, perhaps most, takings problems are neither total takings nor exactions, but rather fall into a case-by-case analysis that depends greatly upon the facts in each instance. The primary considerations in these cases are threefold:

1. The importance of the government interest (health, safety, etc.) that generated the regulation.
2. The economic effect on the landowner.
3. The landowner's legitimate, investment-backed expectations at the time of purchase.

Broadly here, the Court is simply asking whether the regulation goes "too far" in burdening the property owner. That is, should the property owner bear the costs of the regulation or should those costs be borne by the public by paying compensation to the property owner in exchange for the value (a public beach, a park, an unobstructed view, or whatever) derived from the regulation.[26]

> Bloomington, Indiana, the home of Indiana University, limited the occupancy of dwellings in certain neighborhoods to a maximum of three unrelated adults

Maximum Occupancy.   The case that follows deals with a problem close to many students' lives. Here Bloomington, Indiana, the home of Indiana University, limited the occupancy of dwellings in certain neighborhoods to a maximum of three unrelated adults. One rental property owner challenged that law as an unconstitutional taking, and the Indiana Supreme Court applied elements of the total and partial takings analyses.

BOARD OF ZONING APPEALS, BLOOMINGTON, INDIANA v. LEISZ
702 N.E.2d (Ind. S.Ct. 1998)

Justice Boehm

Factual and Procedural Background

Effective June 8, 1985, Bloomington passed a zoning ordinance that limited the occupancy of dwellings in certain neighborhoods to a maximum of three unrelated adults per unit. Among the affected properties were two that had been continuously rented to more than three unrelated adults prior to 1985. At the time Bloomington adopted the zoning ordinance it also enacted a grandfathering provision that permitted owners of properties that became nonconforming uses under the zoning ordinance to preserve their lawful nonconforming use status if they registered it by October 1, 1985. Notice of the zoning ordinance and grandfathering provision was published in the local newspaper during the summer of 1985. Notice of both was also mailed to all owners of rental property registered under a separate housing ordinance that required the registration of rental properties in order to facilitate their inspection for compliance with health and safety regulations. Because the two properties involved in this case were not registered under the housing ordinance, the then owners were not given mailed notice of the zoning change. Whether for that reason or otherwise, they did not register the nonconforming use.

Jack and Barbara Leisz purchased the properties in 1989. In 1993, the City of Bloomington notified the Leiszs that their properties were in violation of the 1985 zoning ordinance. The Leiszs requested an administrative ruling that their properties were exempt from the ordinance as pre-existing lawful nonconforming uses. This request was denied by the planning director, and the Leiszs appealed to the Board of Zoning Appeals (BZA), which affirmed. The Leiszs sought review in the trial court, which initially affirmed BZA's decision, but then reversed that decision in ruling on the Leiszs' motion to correct error. The Court of Appeals affirmed the trial court. We granted BZA's petition to transfer.

I. The Takings Issue

. . . In their brief to the Court of Appeals, the Leiszs argued that "any ordinance which bans an existing lawful use within a zoned area is unconstitutional as a taking of property without due process of law and as an unreasonable exercise of police power." Due process is a term found in both the Fifth and Fourteenth Amendments to the federal constitution. In addition to the provisions found in both the Fifth and Fourteenth Amendments prohibiting depriving a person of property "without due process of law," the Fifth Amendment includes a prohibition against taking private property for public use without just compensation. This in turn has been held applicable to the states by reason of the Fourteenth Amendment. We conclude that the claims presented turn on whether the forfeiture of the Leiszs' nonconforming use due to the failure to register it violated these provisions of the federal constitution.

A. The Federal Takings Clause

"While property may be regulated to a certain extent, if regulation goes too far it will be recognized as a taking." *Pennsylvania Coal Co.* v. *Mahon,* 260 U.S. 393 (1922). Mahon "is generally regarded as the seed from which all modern regulatory taking cases have grown." Seventy years after *Mahon,* however, the Supreme Court acknowledged that the decision "offered little insight into when, and under what circumstances, a given regulation would be seen as going "too far" for purposes of the Fifth Amendment." *Lucas* v. *South Carolina Coastal Council,* 505 U.S. 1003. Indeed, the Court has "generally eschewed any set formula for determining how far is too far, preferring to engage in . . . essentially ad hoc, factual inquiries." "Although no precise rule determines when property has been taken, the question necessarily requires a weighing of private and public interests." *Agins* v. *City of Tiburon,* 447 U.S. 255, (1980). As an overarching concern, the Court has stated that the Takings Clause is "designed to bar Government from forcing some people alone to bear public burdens which, in all fairness and justice, should be borne by the public as a whole[.]" *Penn Cent. Transp. Co.* v. *City of New York,* 438 U.S. 104.

The Court has identified two discrete categories of regulations that violate the Takings Clause regardless of the legitimate state interest advanced. The first consists of regulations that compel a property owner to suffer a physical invasion, no matter how minute, of his property. The second category concerns regulations that deny "all economically beneficial or productive use of the land."

A zoning ordinance that provides for the forfeiture of unregistered nonconforming uses does not fall into either of these prohibited categories. The forfeiture involved no physical invasion of the Leiszs' property. It merely limits the use of their rental property to three unrelated adults instead of four, five, or more. Second, the ordinance does not deny the Leiszs all economically beneficial or productive use of their land. Rather, it denies them at most 25% to 40% of the rental income that they might otherwise receive.

1. Legitimate state interest.   Even if there is no per se taking, the Fifth Amendment is violated when a land-use regulation "does not substantially advance legitimate state interests[.]" Prior Supreme Court cases "have not elaborated on the standards for determining what constitutes a 'legitimate state interest,'" but have upheld "a broad range of governmental purposes and regulations," including scenic zoning, landmark preservation, and residential zoning.

The purpose of the registration requirement, according to the BZA, was to establish an administrative process for making a one-time determination of preexisting status that protects both the owner and the zoning authority from later lengthy disputes and extensive proof problems related to the validity of a nonconforming use. The landowners make a qualified concession in this regard: "The Leiszs concede that the city may require a grandfather registration form to be filled out by lawful, preexisting, nonconforming use and that record-keeping is useful for the BZA, and protects against problems of proof." Thus, the Leiszs do not attack the registration requirement itself, but rather challenge only its forfeiture penalty.

In upholding a provision similar to Bloomington's, the Court of Civil Appeals of Texas noted that the purpose of this registration ordinance is to provide [the City] with sufficient knowledge of the nature and extent of nonconforming uses claimed within the City so that the City can consider these nonconforming uses in planning and can monitor their abandonment. Without a registration scheme it would be impossible for [the City] to begin to implement the plan for the fair and reasonable return of the property to the character of the surrounding neighborhood.

* * * * *

The very real problem associated with proving the existence of a nonconforming use several years in the past is highlighted by this case. The Leiszs offered affidavits and copies of old leases listing the names of four or five individuals living in the rentals when the ordinance was enacted. However, the BZA found this insufficient to prove uninterrupted occupancy by more than three adults since 1985. Moreover, one of the purposes of any city's zoning regulations is to promote the orderly, responsible, and beneficial development and growth of its city. This would be very difficult—if not impossible—without some mechanism to monitor nonconforming uses.

Although they concede the value of requiring registration of nonconforming uses, the Leiszs seem to suggest that there should be no penalty for noncompliance. The forfeiture provision, however, is a necessary part of the registration requirement. By its very nature, registration requires that a deadline be set. In this case, the June 8, 1985, ordinance required registration of nonconforming uses by October 1, 1985. Allowing nonconforming uses to continue indefinitely after the expiration of the registration deadline would make the entire registration requirement an exercise in futility. In sum, we conclude that the registration requirement, including the forfeiture sanction, substantially advances a legitimate state interest.

2. Economic considerations.   The U.S. Supreme Court has identified three factors of "particular significance" to an ad hoc takings inquiry: (1) "the economic impact of the regulation on the claimant," (2) "the extent to which the regulation has interfered with distinct investment-backed expectations," and (3) "the character of the governmental action." Under the current zoning ordinance, the Leiszs may continue to use their two properties as rental units. Due to the failure of the prior owners to register their nonconforming use, however, they are restricted to renting the units to a maximum of three unrelated adults. Their property continues to have an economically viable use, even if it is somewhat diminished.

When a regulation is, as in this case, "reasonably related to the promotion of the general welfare," the Supreme Court has "uniformly rejected the proposition that diminution in property value, standing alone, can establish a 'taking[.]'" Although a valid consideration, the diminution of the value of the Leiszs' rentals is not the only consideration. Even if it is a fair measure of "the economic impact of the regulation" prong of *Penn Central,* other factors are equally relevant to the takings issue under the facts of this case. In particular, the forfeiture of the Leiszs nonconforming use caused no interference with their reasonable investment-based expectations. Both the ordinance and the prior owners' failure to register were matters of public record at the time the Leiszs bought their property. Property owners are charged with knowledge of ordinances that affect their property.

* * * * *

The registration requirement takes nothing from the landowner. Rather, it merely requires the filing of a form by a designated date. Noncompliance with the regulation, not the regulation itself, results in the forfeiture of a vested property right. The power to protect the property interest rests solely with the landowner.

* * * * *

We conclude that the forfeiture of the Leiszs' nonconforming use due to its nonregistration is not a taking under the Fifth and Fourteenth Amendments. The ordinance at issue serves important public purposes. Any diminution in the economic value of the Leiszs'

property is the direct result of their predecessors' failure to comply with a reasonable registration requirement. Under these facts, the forfeiture of the Leiszs' nonconforming use in no way offends notions of "fairness and justice."

Reversed.

Questions

1. *a.* What is a grandfather clause?
    b. What is its significance in this case?
2. Why did the Court rule for the city?
3. In your view, is it "fair" that cities often establish maximum occupancy rules for neighborhoods near colleges and universities? Explain.
4. Marilyn and James Nollan applied for a permit to replace their beachfront home with a larger structure. The California Coastal Commission agreed on the condition that the Nollans grant an easement on their beach that would allow the public to cross that property and thus facilitate movement between the public beaches that lay on both sides of the Nollan beach. The Nollans sued, claiming a violation of the Takings Clause. Decide. Explain. See *Nollan* v. *California Coastal Commission,* 483 U.S. 825 (1987).
5. Alarmed by a decline in low-rent housing, New York City passed a law placing a moratorium on the conversion or demolition of hotels and "single-room occupancy" buildings while requiring owners to rehabilitate those properties so that each unit was habitable. The idea was to involve developers in the effort to increase housing for the aged, ill, and poor. Property owners sued, contending the law constituted an unlawful taking in violation of the Fifth Amendment. Decide. Explain. See *Seawall Associates* v. *City of New York,* 542 N.E.2d 1059 (1989), 492 U.S. 935 (1989).

Takings Activism. In keeping with the generally conservative political tone of the 80s and 90s, the Takings Clause has acquired new visibility. Property rights activists, politicians, and jurists have sought to raise the Takings Clause to a level of influence and visibility more like the First Amendment rights of speech, religion, press, and assembly. The general idea is to diminish government authority and elevate individual power. The movement has raised interesting and novel claims, but has met with mixed success. The aforementioned *Lucas* and

Dolan cases were clear victories for property rights activists, but nothing like a trend rolling back government power over property has emerged. The Supreme Court did take a potentially important step for the activists in 1999 by ruling that regulatory takings claimants have a right to a jury trial against local governments.[27] Thus, developers who are blocked by local land-use laws may be able to find sympathy from jurors who are less predictable than judges.

Reflecting the mixed judicial response to the takings initiative, the Supreme Court in 1996 strengthened government hands in confiscating property that is linked to a crime. In this instance, Tina Bennis sued when Wayne County (Detroit), Michigan, authorities took the car she jointly owned with her husband after police arrested him for receiving oral sex from a prostitute while parked in the car. A 1925 anti-nuisance law permitted the seizure, but Tina Bennis claimed it amounted to an unconstitutional taking since she was an innocent half owner of the 1977 Pontiac for which the couple had paid $600. By a 5–4 vote, the Court upheld the government's right to take the car and thus confirmed police power to seize property connected to a crime.[28]

Thus far, Exxon and its subsidiary, SeaRiver Maritime, have had no success in a takings action regarding the giant oil tanker, SeaRiver Mediterranean, formerly known as the Exxon *Valdez.* You will remember the 1989 oil spill in Alaska's Prince William Sound where 11 million gallons of crude oil poured out of the Valdez into Alaskan waters. Since that time the *Valdez* has been used in the Mediterranean because of a congressional ban on use of the ship in Alaska. SeaRiver/Exxon claims the ban amounts to a taking because the *Valdez* can, as a practical matter, be used only in Mediterranean Sea routes rather than the more profitable Alaskan route for which it was custom designed. An Alaskan judge rejected the takings claim in 1998, and SeaRiver/Exxon is appealing at this writing.[29]

Government restraints on property development are not merely a modern imposition, as we learn from the following description of a zoning law in the Byzantine Empire:

> Next came the first zoning law for the beach. Coastal vistas were so cherished, and the competition for them so keen, that by the sixth century the Emperor Justinian the Great was compelled to pass an ordinance barring construction within one hundred feet of the shore to protect sea views.

Source: Lena Lencek and Gideon Bosker, *The Beach: The History of Paradise on Earth* (New York: Penguin Group, 1998), p. 31.

TOO MUCH REGULATION?

The dominant public policy debate of the 1980s and 1990s was the question of how much government we need in America. We have seen that state and local governments, in particular, have expanded rapidly and are imposing or seeking to impose a wide array of new rules on the business community. Our natural and perhaps correct reaction is to call for a reduction in government intervention. However, we need a balanced view of that critical issue.

Turn now to a "real-life" situation where new rules have been proposed or imposed. Your task is to evaluate this situation and make a judgment: Should the government intervene?

Body Piercing

Many states are now imposing licensing requirements and other rules on businesses that provide body piercing services.

STATES TAKE STAB AT REGULATING TEEN BODY PIERCING

Karen Thomas

From navel jewels to dainty eyebrow rings and chunky tongue studs, body piercing is no longer a rebellious badge of honor reserved for incorrigible punks.

For today's teens, the multipierced look has become as mainstream as hanging out at the mall and using invisible zit cream, forcing parents to take a hard look at the burgeoning industry.

As family doctors have peered unfazed past bejeweled tongues to peek at young patients' tonsils, school nurses are examining more infected navels and tongues, and dentists are treating more chipped teeth caused by tongue jewelry.

No one knows how common body-piercing infections are in the largely unregulated industry, but lawmakers nationwide have heard an earful from those concerned about its safety.

Body-piercing regulations "are becoming more of an issue because it has become so accessible in recent years," said Stephanie Wilson of the National Conference of State Legislatures (NCSL).

Piercing can take place in a doctor's office, but more often, teens doubt Mom and Dad will share their enthusiasm for body adornment and have the piercing done at T-shirt factories, music festivals, head shops, tattoo parlors or at-home "salons," where lawn chairs serve as the operating table.

More states are moving to restrict body piercing. Ten states now regulate the profession, and Indiana, Florida and Texas are the most recent to enact laws, according to the NCSL.

Illinois and Oklahoma, both poised to pass laws in the coming weeks, are among several more states, including New York, Michigan and South Carolina, that have introduced body-piercing bills this year.

In 1998, the Iowa House approved proposed legislation requiring minors to have a parent's permission before they undergo body piercing to adorn parts of their body—other than ear lobes—with jewelry. The parental consent requirement was part of a bill that, for health and safety reasons, would have established state regulation of body-piercing establishments.

The bill did not pass the Senate, however, and was not reintroduced this year.

Typically, the body-piercing laws and proposals require licenses and training and regulate how instruments and facilities are sterilized. Fines range from $50 to $5,000; some include jail time. While many states require written parental permission, several laws stipulate that parents must be present when a minor is pierced.

New legislation is getting stronger, with harsher penalties for piercers who don't get parental permission before taking on an underage client, Wilson says. "Just taking the word of someone isn't good enough anymore. You have to have checked ID."

Most experts point out that teenagers' bodies change rapidly, thus a spurt of growth could make the piercings unattractive.

Source: Gannett News Service, *Des Moines Register*, July 12, 1999, p. 5M. Copyright 1999, *USA Today*. Reprinted with permission. [For Oregon's body piercing rules, see **http://www.hdlp.hr.state.or.us/bphome.htm**]

Questions

1. Illinois' body piercing statute requires liability insurance, licensing, training, and health inspections, and parents are to accompany minors. Do each of those requirements seem appropriate to you? Explain.
2. *a.* Can we rely on the market in this situation involving children? Explain.
    b. Has the market failed? Explain.
3. Should the federal government regulate body piercing? Explain.
4. Why do businesses sometimes welcome or even encourage government regulations?

INTERNET EXERCISE

Explain the purposes and goals of the Trans Atlantic Business Dialogue using the Web site **http://www.tabd.com/index1.html**

CHAPTER QUESTIONS

1. In 1999, Matthew Hale, a law school graduate, was denied a license to practice law in Illinois because Hale is an avowed racist and the leader of a white supremacist group. A state panel assessed the character and general fitness of all those who had passed the Bar exam and graduated from law school and decided that Hale's active racism disqualified him. Illinois is one of 32 states with character and fitness standards. Hale has appealed on First Amendment grounds, among others. Should Hale be excluded from the practice of law, or should we let the market decide his fitness? Explain.

2. In Alabama, selling or distributing "any obscene material or any device designed or marketed as useful primarily for the stimulation of human genital organs" is a misdemeanor punishable by as much as one year in jail and a $10,000 fine. The law was challenged as overly broad and a violation of due process. Does the state have a constitutional right to banish "sex toys" from its populace? Explain. See *Williams* v. *Pryor,* 41 F. Supp. 2d 1257 (N.D. Ala. 1999).

3. In 1999, New York City began enforcing a law that allows the police to immediately impound the cars of *accused* drunk drivers. Those who measure 0.1 or more on a breath test or who decline to give a reading lose their cars on the spot and cannot get them back without going to civil court.
    a. Is the policy constitutional?
    b. Is it a good idea? Explain.

4. City officials in Machesney Park, Illinois, in 1999 required nine-year-old Gregory Webb to tear down his makeshift tree house on the grounds that it was a nuisance. Webb had built the structure from lawn chairs, leftover carpet, and a pet carrier, among other objects. The city was criticized for its decision.
    a. Why would a city choose to exercise its police power over nuisances in this seemingly trivial case?
    b. What would you do if you were the city planning and zoning director and thus responsible for the situation?

5. Iowa's Farmland Preservation Act of 1982 created Agricultural Area Designations and made the property within them immune from nuisance suits. Farmers still had to obey environmental regulations, but they could not be sued for the odors, noise, and dust that often accompany farming. In 1994, a number of Iowa farmers applied to their County Board of Supervisors for establishment of an agricultural area of about 1,000 acres on which they intended to build a large hog-raising operation. The application was approved, but neighbors challenged it in court.
    a. What constitutional claims were raised on behalf of the plaintiffs?
    b. How would you rule on the case? Explain. See *Bormann* v. *Girres,* 584 N.W.2d 309

(Ia. S.Ct. 1998); cert. denied *Girres* v. *Bormann,* 119 S.Ct. 1096 (1999).

6. Culver City, California, had charged Richard K. Ehrlich a special $280,000 recreation fee and a $32,000 community art fee in return for changes in the city's land use plan permitting construction of condominiums on property previously designated for private recreational use. Ehrlich had operated a failed tennis and sports club on the land. Ehrlich challenged the fees on constitutional grounds.

   a. What claim(s) did he raise?

   b. Decide. Explain. See *Ehrlich* v. *City of Culver City,* 911 P.2d 429 (1996).

7. Notwithstanding the deregulation efforts of recent years, the clear trend in the United States over the past 50 years has been that of increased government regulation of business. How do you explain that trend?

8. Define: Positive and negative externalities. Public goods.

9. As a safety measure, Arizona enacted a statute that limited the length of passenger trains to 14 cars and freight trains to 70 cars. Trains of those lengths and greater were common throughout the United States. The Southern Pacific Railroad challenged the Arizona statute.

   a. What was the legal foundation of the Southern Pacific claim?

   b. Decide the case. Explain. See *Southern Pacific Railroad* v. *Arizona,* 325 U.S. 761(1945).

10. Many large American cities closely regulate cab service and severely restrict the number of cabs that may lawfully serve the community.

   a. Why would cities choose to limit a useful service for its citizens that also provides much-needed jobs?

   b. Who is harmed by these regulations? Explain. See Allen Randolph, "New York Taxi Policy Is a Lemon," *The Wall Street Journal,* March 17, 1992, p. A14.

11. Taalib-Dan Abdul Uqdah owned and operated Cornrows & Co., a hair-braiding salon in Washington, D.C. The D.C. Board of Cosmetology pursued Uqdah for years because he and his 10 employees had not secured cosmetology licenses. At one point, Uqdah was fined $1,000 and ordered to close unless he and his employees went to school for nine months. The schooling would have cost about $5,000 per person and did not teach the natural African techniques that were Uqdah's practice. Uqdah's business did not use chemicals.

   a. Why was the Washington, D.C., board imposing the license requirement on Uqdah?

   b. Should it have done so? Explain. See Editorial, "Forgotten Civil Rights," *The Wall Street Journal,* August 14, 1992, p. A12, and Editorial, "Barring Entry," *The Wall Street Journal,* December 23, 1992, p. A8.

12. A *Journal of the American Medical Association* study indicates that a state-mandated drinking age of 21 has been quite successful in reducing auto deaths among drivers aged 19 and 20. The study of Tennessee drivers found that single-vehicle night-time crash deaths in that age group fell by 38 percent after Tennessee changed its drinking age from 19 to 21.[30]

   a. What constitutional authority allows the states to regulate the age at which one may lawfully consume alcoholic beverages?

   b. Were the power yours, at what age would you allow drinking? Explain.

13. Richard Moe, president of the National Trust for Historic Preservation:

   Drive down any highway leading into any town in the country, and what do you see? Fast-food outlets, office parks, and shopping malls rising out of vast barren plains of asphalt. Residential subdivisions spreading like inkblots obliterating forests and farms in their relentless march across the landscape . . . You see the graveyard of livability. You see communities drowning in a destructive, soulless, ugly mess called sprawl.[31]

   Moe's solution:

   What's needed is action by state governments to develop growth-management legislation with teeth in it, legislation that requires local government to develop rational strategies for using already developed land more efficiently [and] to make thoughtful choices about new development . . .[32]

   a. Do you agree with Moe's characterization of America's urban sprawl? Explain.

   b. If so, do you agree that more state and local regulation is the key to correcting the problem? Explain.

   c. If not, how do you defend the unsightliness of that sprawl?

14. In recent years, hundreds of local communities have banished or limited billboards on the grounds that they constitute traffic hazards and are unsightly. Many of the communities permit phase-out periods of five years or so

for existing billboards, and they allow the billboards to be relocated.

   a. What constitutional questions are raised by these policies?

   b. Are these policies lawful? Explain. See Arthur Hayes, "Signs of Battles over Billboards Are Easy to See," *The Wall Street Journal,* March 23, 1993, p. B1.

15. Columnist George Will, in 1997, observed that the federal government is trying to shrink, that the "balance of financial, as well as intellectual, resources is tilting to the states," and that the United States Supreme Court has steered away from judicial activism.[33] In the late 20th century, power seems to be leaving the federal government. Will then cites Justice Charles Fried of the Massachusetts Supreme Court who says that the return of power to the states will not be without costs:

   Our economy of allegiance simply is not infinitely expandable. If we become more Virginian or Georgian, surely we will also feel more remote, less responsible for the poor of Kentucky or of the ghettos of Chicago. If we become more Virginian, we would be less American.[34]

   a. Make the argument that our political culture will be improved by this transfer of power.

   b. Do you approve of this transfer of power back to the states? Explain.

16. A provision of the Airline Deregulation Act of 1978 prohibits states from enforcing any law "relating to rates, routes, or services" of any air carrier. In 1987, the National Association of Attorneys General (representing all 50 states) passed guidelines designed to regulate fare advertisements in order to prevent deception. A specific concern was ads that displayed reduced fares in large print, with taxes and add-ons in small print. Several airlines filed suit to block the guidelines.

   a. What constitutional argument did they raise?

   b. Decide. Explain. See *Morales* v. *Trans World Airlines,* 112 S.Ct. 2031 (1992).

17. Alabama's legislature imposed a higher tax on out-of-state insurance companies than on in-state firms. Out-of-state companies could reduce, but not eliminate, the differential by investing in Alabama.

   a. What constitutional objection was raised by the out-of-state firms?

   b. What defense was raised by the state?

   c. Decide. Explain. See *Metropolitan Life Ins. Co.* v. *Ward,* 470 U.S. 869 (1985).

18. The Pennsylvania legislature passed legislation requiring all trucks over a specified weight to display an identification marker and pay a $25 annual fee for that marker. Trucks registered in Pennsylvania were exempted from the marker on the grounds that the $25 would be treated as a part of the general state vehicle registration fee. Later, the Pennsylvania legislature reduced the $25 fee to $5 and imposed a $36-per-axle fee on all trucks over a specified weight. At the same time, the legislature reduced the fee for registering trucks (of the specified weight class) in Pennsylvania by the amount of the axle tax. The American Trucking Associations challenged the Pennsylvania laws.

   a. Identify the central constitutional issue in this case.

   b. Decide the case. Explain. See *American Trucking Associations, Inc.* v. *Scheiner,* 483 U.S. 266 (1987).

19. Overall, which level of government (local, state, or federal) do you consider the more trustworthy? Explain.

20. In the interest of safety, an Iowa statute prohibited the use of 65-foot double-trailer trucks within its borders. Scientific studies revealed that 65-foot doubles were as safe as 55-foot singles (permissible under Iowa law). The State of Iowa argued that the statute promoted safety and reduced road wear by diverting much truck traffic to other states. Consolidated Freightways challenged the statute. Decide. See *Raymond Kassel et al.* v. *Consolidated Freightways Corporation of Delaware,* 101 S.Ct. 1309 (1981).

NOTES

1. "Federalism—Clear Congressional Mandate Required to Preempt State Law," *Harvard Law Review* 105, no. 1 (November 1991), p. 196.

2. 317 U.S. 111 (1942).

3. 18 U.S.C. 922(q) (1) (A).

4. *United States* v. *Lopez,* 115 S.Ct. 1624 (1995).

5. 169 F.3d 820 (4th Cir. 1999).

6. Ibid., p. 827.

7. Ibid., p. 908.

8. Marcia Coyle, "High Court to Decide Key Powers Case," *National Law Journal,* March 22, 1999, p. A7.

9. Stuart Taylor, "Power Struggle Among the Branches," *New York Law Journal,* March 15, 1999, p. 2.

10. *Ericson* v. *Syracuse University,* 45 F. Supp. 2d 344 (1999).

11. Coyle, "High Court to Decide," p. A7.

12. James V. Koch, "Protectionism in Higher Education," *Boston Globe,* April 27, 1999, p. C4.

13. James Cox, "Not Quite Land of Free Trade," *USA Today,* May 6, 1999, p. 1B.

14. Max Frankel, "The Next Great Story," *New York Times,* March 15, 1998, sec. 6, p. 30.

15. Ibid.

16. "Work Force Facts," *Washington Post,* September 2, 1996, p. A21.

17. Editorial, "Rigged Rides," *The Wall Street Journal,* March 16, 1999, p. A26.

18. Ibid.

19. Ibid.

20. Richard Wolf, "Report: Cooperation Is Key to Running States Well," *USA Today,* February 1, 1999, p. 6A.

21. Jennifer Jacobs, "Judge Backs City's Refusal to Renew Bar's License," *Waterloo-Cedar Falls Courier,* November 22, 1998, p. C3.

22. *Lucas* v. *So. Carolina Coastal Commission,* 112 S.Ct. 2886 (1992).

23. *Dolan* v. *City of Tigard,* 114 S.Ct. 2309 (1994).

24. Frank A. Vickory and Barry A. Diskin, "Advances in Private Property Protection Rights: The States in the Vanguard," *American Business Law Journal* 34, no. 4 (Summer 1997), p. 561.

25. Wayne Snow, "Church Wins Site-Plan Battle," *Atlanta Journal and Constitution,* August 12, 1999, p. 3JM.

26. See Vickory and Diskin, "Advances in Private Property," p. 561, and David L. Callies, "Regulatory Takings and the Supreme Court," *Stetson Law Review* 28 (Winter 1999), p. 523.

27. *City of Monterey* v. *Del Monte Dunes,* 119 S.Ct. 1624 (1999).

28. *Bennis* v. *Michigan,* 116 S.Ct. 994 (1996).

29. See Thomas Kupper, "Ex-Exxon Valdez Eyes Alaska," *San Diego Union-Tribune,* March 15, 1999, p. B2.

30. Associated Press, "Raising Drinking Age Does Cut Traffic Fatalities, Study Finds," *Des Moines Register,* December 23, 1988, p. 4T.

31. Richard Moe, "Mindless Madness Called Sprawl," *Des Moines Register,* January 19, 1997, p. 1C.

32. Ibid.

33. George Will, "Clinton's Terms May Leave No Footprints," *Des Moines Register,* January 19, 1997, p. 2C.

34. Ibid.

Chapter 8

Administrative Agencies and the Regulatory Process

This chapter is divided into four parts. Parts One through Three discuss the nature and duties of the many federal agencies. Part Four evaluates the strengths and weaknesses of the federal regulatory process.

Part One—Introduction to Administrative Agencies[1]

The materials that follow raise the central themes in this chapter: (1) our lives arguably suffer from excessive government regulation, but (2) some regulation is necessary in an increasingly complex society; therefore, (3) where do we draw the line?

The excerpt that follows illustrates some rules that businesses routinely encounter and explains something of the role of administrative agencies in addressing those rules.

MENU FOR SUCCESS

Jill Schachner Chanen

It is the kind of matter that hardly any lawyer would consider unusual: A client has just purchased a piece of land in a rapidly developing area of the city on which to build a restaurant and bar overlooking the adjacent waterfront. The client asks you to handle the entire deal, and you quickly agree.

But as the project progresses, it becomes apparent that this is no ordinary deal. The land is in the middle of a former manufacturing corridor and is still zoned for industrial uses. To make matters worse, the city is

rationing liquor licenses, and the area where your client wants to open his business has reached its quota.

Matters for the courts to decide? Not really. More likely, the road to resolution will lead through the fields of administrative law . . .

Encountering the often quirky and occasionally political ways of government agencies that control zoning, environmental permits and liquor licenses is enough to make some lawyers throw up their hands in frustration . . .

And practitioners may have little choice but to become more familiar with administrative law. By all indications, and despite promises by elected officials to shrink government bureaucracy at all levels, it continues to expand.

For practitioners, this means an increasing likelihood of encountering administrative issues and proceedings . . .

"There is no way to avoid it," says Ronald Cass, dean of Boston University School of Law. "The government has become such a pervasive regulator of so many areas of the economy."

At every level, government enacts legislation creating programs, benefits and policies. Agencies are created to carry out the mandates of these statutes. Administrative law, says Cass, is the civil procedure that agencies establish to tell people how to obtain benefits, participate in programs, defend themselves against charges of violating rules and regulations, and seek government authorization to engage in certain activities.

* * * * *

Consider everything a lawyer could encounter—from zoning to business permits to employee injuries to immigration to retirement—in something so simple as a restaurant.

The Right Zone

The restaurants and bars opening in that old warehouse and manufacturing area are already making it a "hot"

entertainment district. To get in on the action, though, will take a zoning change for land with a very limited industrial use and a dynamite water view.

License to Drink

A slew of business licenses and permits—each administered by a different agency—are usually necessary for any business. For a restaurant, the biggest trophy may be the liquor license.

The Pain of Employee Injuries

One reality of business is that employees inevitably get hurt on the job. At a restaurant, a chef burns a hand, a waiter slips on a stray tomato, a flying cork pops a bartender in the eye. All of that brings another administrative agency into the mix—the state workers' compensation system.

Border Bureaucracies

Even local restaurants can be global concerns. When the strategy is to have chefs from around the world prepare their native cuisines, someone will have to cruise the federal bureaucracies for authorization for them to enter and work in the United States.

* * * * *

Source: *ABA JOURNAL,* October 1998, p. 49. Reprinted by permission.

On the Other Hand.   As Jill Chanen explains, we run into government rules at every turn, and the administrative law system that helps us deal with those laws is often complex, frustrating, and expensive. Nonetheless, journalists James Flansburg and Vermont Royster argue that government is vital to civilized life.

James Flansburg:

If it weren't for government:
Where would you send your kids to school?
How would you choose a bank and be sure that your money wouldn't disappear?
What would stop someone from building a slaughterhouse next door to your house?
Who would take care of the streets?

To whom would you appeal if someone with a double-barrelled, 12-gauge shotgun moved into your house and told you to leave? How would you prove that you and not that person owned that house? Government keeps the records you'd need.[2]

Vermont Royster:

If I hesitate to join the hue for deregulation, even when much of the regulation is misguided, it's because I shudder at the thought of a wholly deregulated society. I prefer knowing my pharmacist has to be licensed and that somebody checks on him; so also with the butcher so that I have some assurance his scale registers a true measure.

As a matter of fact, regulation to protect consumers is almost as old as civilization itself. Tourists to the ruins of Pompeii see an early version of the bureau of weights and measures, a place where the townsfolk could go to be sure they weren't cheated by the local tradesmen. Unfortunately, a little larceny is too common in the human species.

So regulation in some form or other is one of the prices we pay for our complex civilization. And the more complicated society becomes, the more need for some watching over its many parts.[3]

Question

1. Does the government intrude excessively in your life? Explain.

THE AGENCIES

That branch of the law governing the administrative operations of government is *administrative law.* The Federal Administrative Procedure Act defines an *agency* as any government unit other than the legislature and the courts. Thus, administrative law technically addresses the entire executive branch of government. Our attention, however, will be directed to the prominent regulatory agencies (Federal Trade Commission, Federal Communications Commission, Securities and Exchange Commission, etc.) rather than the various executive departments (Agriculture, Defense, etc.) and nonregulatory welfare agencies (Social Security Administration, Veterans Administration, and the Public Health Service). Although our fundamental concern lies at the federal level, administrative law principles are fully applicable to the conduct of state and local governments. At the local level, planning and zoning boards and property tax assessments appeals boards are examples of administrative agencies. At the state level, one might cite public utility commissions and the various state licensure boards for law, medicine, architecture, and the like. [For a "one-stop shopping point" for federal government information on the World Wide Web, see **http://www.access.gpo.gov/su_docs**]

History

Congress established the Interstate Commerce Commission (ICC), the first federal regulatory agency, in 1887 for the purpose of regulating railroad routes and rates. The Food and Drug Administration (FDA—1907) and the Federal Trade Commission (FTC—1914) followed, but federal regulation became pervasive only in response to the Great Depression of the 1930s. Congress created the Securities and Exchange Commission (SEC), the Federal Communications Commission (FCC), the Civil Aeronautics Board (CAB), and the National Labor Relations Board (NLRB), among others, as a response to the widely shared belief that the stock market crash and the Depression were evidence of the failure of the free market.

The next major burst of regulatory activity arrived in the 1960s and 1970s when Congress created such agencies as the Equal Employment Opportunity Commission (EEOC—1965), the Environmental Protection Agency (EPA—1970), the Occupational Safety and Health Administration (OSHA—1970), and the Consumer Product Safety Commission (CPSC—1972).

Note that the work of most of the early agencies was directed to controlling entire industries such as transportation or communications and that the primary purpose of most of those agencies was to address economic concerns. Then with the arrival of the prosperity and social turbulence of the 1960s and 1970s, Congress built a rather massive array of new agencies directed not to economic issues but to social reform in such areas as discrimination, the environment, job safety, and product safety.

As we explore later in the chapter, the free market enthusiasm of the 1980s resulted in strenuous efforts to deregulate the economy and reduce the influence of the federal agencies and the government generally. Now, at the turn of the century, we appear to be in a period of respect for the free market, tempered by concern that some government oversight remains vital to the general welfare. Federal government downsizing and further deregulation are quite likely, but the federal regulatory agencies will continue to be influential institutions directly affecting virtually every corner of American life.

Creating the Agencies

The so-called independent agencies (e.g., FTC, FCC, NLRB, and SEC) are created by Congress via statutes labeled *enabling legislation*. For example, the FTC is empowered to pursue unfair trade practices by the authority of its enabling legislation, a portion of which follows:

Federal Trade Commission Act (excerpts)

Section 1: A commission is created and established, to be known as the Federal Trade Commission, which shall be composed of five commissioners, who shall be appointed by the President, by and with the advice and consent of the Senate . . .

Section 5: Unfair methods of competition in or affecting commerce, and unfair or deceptive acts or practices in or affecting commerce, are hereby declared unlawful.[4]

In creating an agency, Congress delegates a portion of its authority to that body. Congress acknowledges the existence of a problem and recognizes that it is not the appropriate body to address the specific elements of that problem—hence, the agency. The president, ordinarily with the advice and consent of the senate, appoints the administrator or the several commissioners who direct each agency's affairs. Commissioners are appointed in staggered terms, typically of seven years' duration. The appointment of commissioners for most of the independent agencies must reflect an approximate political balance between the two major parties.

In effect, Congress has created a fourth branch of government. Recognizing that it possesses neither the time nor the expertise to handle problems arising from nuclear power, product safety, racial discrimination, labor unions, and much more, Congress wisely established "minigovernments" with the necessary technical resources and day-to-day authority to address those problems.

The president likewise delegates authority by creating so-called executive agencies. Those agencies (e.g., Department of Commerce, Department of Labor, Department of Justice, and Department of State) are, in most instances, headed by cabinet officers who serve at the behest of the president and may be removed at will.

Agency Duties

The authority of the federal regulatory agencies falls broadly into three categories.

1. Control of Supply.   Some agencies control entry into certain economic activities. The Federal Communications Commission grants radio and television licenses. The Food and Drug Administration decides which drugs may enter the American market. The Securities and Exchange Commission (see Chapter 9) acts as a gatekeeper, preventing the entry of new securities into the marketplace until certain standards are met. The general feeling in these areas and others like them is that the market alone cannot adequately protect the public interest.

2. Control of Rates.   Historically, those federal agencies charged with regulating utilities and carriers (Federal Energy Regulatory Commission, ICC, and CAB) set the prices to be charged for the services offered within their jurisdictions. For example, the consumer facing an interstate change of address found little value in comparison shopping for the least expensive furniture mover because the rates, regulated by the Interstate Commerce Commission, were virtually identical. Government rate setting remains important at the state level. However, at the federal level, the deregulation movement resulted in the elimination of the CAB and the ICC (although some ICC functions and personnel were shifted to the newly created Surface Transportation Board) and a general decline in agency rate-setting. That is, the federal government decided to reduce or eliminate its authority in decisions such as the price of airline tickets, cable TV rates, and long-distance telephone rates.

3. Control of Conduct.
   (a) Information.   A major element of government regulation is simply requiring information. Agencies commonly compel companies to disclose consumer information that would otherwise remain private. For example, warning labels may be mandated.
   (b) Standards.   Where simply requiring information is deemed inadequate to the public need, the government may establish minimum standards that the private sector must meet. For example, a ladder might be required to safely hold at least a specified weight, or workers might lawfully be exposed to only a specified maximum level of radiation.

(c) Product Banishments.   In those unusual instances where information alone is deemed inadequate to protect the public, products can be banned from the market. The Consumer Product Safety Commission banned the flame retardant Tris (used in children's sleepwear) because of evidence of the product's cancer-causing properties.

Questions—Part One

1. The phrase *government regulation* embraces many functions. Define it.
2. Is the federal regulatory process limited in its goals to the correction of market failures? Should it be so limited? Explain.
3. In 1975, Scholar James Q. Wilson said, "All democratic regimes tend to shift resources from the private to the public sector and to enlarge the size of the administrative component of government."[5]
    a. Is Wilson correct? Explain.
    b. Given the striking economic and political changes around the world, would he say the same today? Explain.
4. Scholar George Stigler asked, "What benefits can a state provide to an industry?"[6] Answer Stigler's inquiry.
5. Does the real origin of government regulation of business lie in the citizen's fear? That is, do the people consider the market too risky and, therefore, opt for a system that affords them some protection from economic loss? Explain.
6. Have we reason for concern because the federal agencies have become a fourth branch of government not directly accountable to the public via the electoral process? Explain.

Part Two—Summary of the Administrative Process

As we have noted, the administrative agencies act as minigovernments, performing quasi-executive, quasi-legislative (rule-making), and quasi-judicial (adjudicatory) roles broadly involving control of supply, rates, and conduct in large segments of American life. Let's look now at how those agencies undertake their business.

OPERATING THE AGENCIES

Executive Functions

The basic executive duty of the various agencies is to implement the policy provided for in the enabling legislation and in the agencies' own rules and regulations. A large part of agency activity consists of performing mundane, repetitive tasks that are necessary for a smoothly operating society but that do not merit the day-to-day attention of Congress or the courts. Thus, agencies enter into contracts, lease federal lands, register securities offerings, award grants, resolve tax disputes, settle workers' compensation claims, administer government benefits to the citizenry, and so on. Some agencies, such as the Food and Drug Administration, are charged with protecting the public by engaging in inspections and testing. Most agencies offer informal advice, both in response to requests and on their own initiative, to explain agency policy and positions. For example, each year, the Federal Trade Commission receives many inquiries regarding the legal sufficiency of warning labels on various potentially dangerous products. Supervisory duties, including most notably the active and close attention given to the banking industry, are a further illustration of agency executive duties.

Of course, a big part of the agencies' executive duties is the protection of the public in one way or another by ensuring compliance with laws and regulations. Therefore, most agencies spend a great deal of time conducting inspections and investigations and collecting information. For example, the Occupational Safety and Health Administration regularly checks businesses for safety hazards.

Similarly, in June 1996, the FAA temporarily shut down the operations of the low-fare air carrier, ValuJet. The FAA is responsible for airline safety and, after a careful inspection of ValuJet systems, the Agency found a number of areas of noncompliance and concluded that ValuJet had failed to demonstrate that it had an effective maintenance control system. The airline was under close scrutiny following the loss of 110 lives in the May 11, 1996, Florida Everglades crash of ValuJet Flight 592. [For the FAA Web site, see **http://www.faa.gov**]

Legislative Functions

The agencies create *rules* that, in effect, are laws. These rules provide the details necessary to carry out the intentions of the enabling legislation. In day-to-day business practice, the rules are likely to be much more important than the original congressional legislation. The Occupational Safety and Health Act calls for a safe and healthy workplace, but the rules necessary for interpreting and enforcing that general mandate come, not from Congress, but from OSHA.

Rules.   Agencies enact three types of rules: (1) procedural rules, (2) interpretive rules, and (3) legislative rules. *Procedural rules* delineate the agency's internal operating structure and methods. *Interpretive rules* offer the agency's view of the meaning of those statutes for which the agency has administrative responsibility. The agency seeks to clarify for interested parties the meaning of congressional statutory language that is often very broadly drawn. Interpretive rules do not have the force of law, but they are important expressions of opinion as to what the governing legislation requires. Internal Revenue Service regulations are an example of interpretive rules. *Legislative rules* are policy expressions having the effect of law. The agency is exercising the law-making function delegated to it by the legislature. Federal Trade Commission rules providing for a cooling-off period of three business days within which the buyer may cancel door-to-door sales the FCC approved new rules requiring at least three hours of network educational television per week for children

contracts are an example of agency lawmaking that significantly affects business behavior.

In 1996, the FCC approved new rules requiring at least three hours of network educational television per week for children. The programming must be specifically designed to meet children's cognitive, social, and emotional needs; must be regularly scheduled; and must air between 7 A.M. and 10 P.M. (In your view, should we leave children's television viewing habits up to parents?)

In 1999, the FCC announced a number of changes in its rules governing ownership of television stations. Basically, the new rules will allow owners to buy more stations or in other ways combine with other stations to expand their businesses. The television industry has wanted the new authority for some time as it seeks ways to compete with new rivals such as cable TV, satellite TV, and the Internet. The commission felt that the old rules, designed to prevent consolidation of power and programming in a limited number of companies, were inappropriate to the current marketplace. [For the FCC Web site, see **http://www.fcc.gov**]

Some of the New FCC Television Ownership Rules

- Broadcasters may acquire a second TV station in one market if that station has failed or is struggling.
- Broadcasters may own two TV stations in markets where at least eight TV stations are operated by different owners.
- Broadcasters who own one or two TV stations in a market may also own up to six or seven radio stations in the same market.

Source: Kathy Chen and Martin Peers, "FCC Relaxes Its Rules on TV Station Ownership," *The Wall Street Journal,* August 6, 1999, p. A3.

The Rule-Making Process.   The Administrative Procedure Act provides for both *informal* and *formal* rule-making processes for legislative rules. Under both approaches, the process begins with the publication of a Notice of Proposed Rule Making in the *Federal Register* (a daily publication of all federal rules, regulations, and orders). Thereafter, in the case of informal rule making, the agency must permit written comments on the proposal and may hold open hearings. Having received public comments, the agency either discontinues the process or prepares the final rule.

In the case of formal rule making, after providing notice, the agency must hold a public hearing that must be conducted with most of the procedural safeguards of a trial, where all interested parties may call witnesses, challenge the agency evidence, and so on. The agency decision must be based on the formal record only.

Final agency rules are published in the *Federal Register* and later compiled in the *Code of Federal Regulations*. The following table explains the process.

Agency Rule-Making Process	
Informal Agency Rule Making (legislative in character)	*Formal Agency Rule Making (legislative/judicial in character)*
Public notice in *Federal Register*	Public notice in *Federal Register*
Public comment (informal)	Public comment (formal)
Final rule in *Federal Register*	Final rule in *Federal Register*

Challenging an Agency Rule.   The enormous importance of the agency rule-making process and of the agencies themselves is well illustrated by the continuing battle between the FCC and various state utility regulators and communication giants over who has rule-making authority in America's local telephone markets. The landmark federal Telecommunications Act of 1996 was designed to open communications to market competition freeing the telephone, television, and computer industries from laws that had prevented them from competing against each other. Among the deregulation initiatives in the far-reaching bill were provisions to ease entry to the local phone business controlled by GTE, US West, Bell Atlantic, and others. The FCC wrote rules providing for how the local monopolies would be forced to share their networks, including prices for access to those local networks. FCC authority over that changeover process was challenged both by the incumbent local providers and by state utility regulators. In 1999, however, the Supreme Court interpreted the Telecommunications Act to give the FCC general authority over the implementation of the act.[7] Thus, the FCC is firmly in charge of opening local phone service to the power of the market.

> The FCC wrote rules providing for how the local monopolies would be forced to share their networks

Judicial Functions

Although informal procedures such as settlements are preferred, agencies commonly must turn to judicial proceedings to enforce agency rules. The National Labor Relations Board may hold a hearing to determine if an employee was wrongfully dismissed for engaging in protected union activities. The Federal Communications Commission may decide whether to remove a radio license because of a failure to serve the public interest. The Federal Trade Commission may judge whether a particular ad is misleading. Adjudicatory administrative hearings are equal in significance and much superior in numbers to all federal court trials each year.

Rule Making or Adjudication?   Many issues facing agencies could properly be resolved in either the rule-making or the adjudicatory format. The distinction between the two cannot be drawn vividly. Characteristically, however, an adjudication addresses specific parties involved in a specific present or past dispute. Rule making ordinarily involves standards to be applied to the future conduct of a class of unspecified parties. The rule-making/adjudication decision is discretionary with the agency (subject to judicial review) and is based on the nature of the issue and fairness to the parties. Regardless, the agencies are, in effect, "making law" either by setting a judicial-like precedent in the case of an adjudication or by passing a rule that has authority much like a law.

Administrative Hearing.   Typically, after an investigation, a violation of a statute and/or rule may be alleged. Affected parties are notified. An effort is made to reach a settlement via a *consent order,* in which the party being investigated agrees to steps suitable to the agency but under which the respondent makes no admission of guilt (thus retarding the likelihood of subsequent civil liability). Federal law also encourages the use of alternate dispute resolution methods such as arbitration.

ALJ.   Failing a settlement, the parties proceed much as in a civil trial. Ordinarily, the case is heard by an *administrative law judge (ALJ).* The respondent may be represented by counsel. Parties have the right to present their cases, cross-examine, file motions, raise objections, and so on. However, they do not have the right to a jury trial. The ALJ decides all questions of law and fact and then issues a decision (*order*). In general, that decision is final unless appealed to the agency/commission. After exhausting opportunities for review within the agency, appeal may be taken to the federal court system.

CONTROLLING THE AGENCIES

As noted, agency influence in business practice and in American life generally is enormous. However, none of these agencies and their thousands of employees are directly accountable to the people, and all of them operate under necessarily broad grants of power. What is to keep them from abusing their discretion? Just as with our constitutional system generally, certain checks and balances are in place to constrain agency conduct while allowing the latitude necessary to achieve effectiveness.

Executive Constraints

As noted, the president appoints the top administrators for the various agencies, thus significantly influencing the conservative/liberal slant of the agency. Further, the president obviously has great influence in the budget process. Recent presidents, particularly Ronald Reagan, have sought to extend executive influence over the regulatory process via the Office of Management and Budget (OMB). The Clinton Administration has initiated its own regulatory reforms following the general path laid out by President Reagan. *Executive (presidential) Order* 12866, issued in 1993, directs major regulations to the OMB for review and oversight and requires each agency to submit an annual regulatory plan to the OMB. The order also requires cost-benefit analyses for major regulations, although various exceptions have depreciated the rule's impact. In general, new regulations are to be adopted "only if they are required by law, necessary to correct market failures, or otherwise called for by compelling public need."[8] In effect, the executive branch OMB has become something of a funnel through which all significant new regulations must pass. The executive branch has also ordered a variety of changes in environmental, health, safety, and other regulations directed toward the business community. Reduced paperwork and increased compliance flexibility along with fewer fines are among the goals of those changes. Small businesses are expected to benefit most.

Congressional Constraints

Congress creates and can dissolve the agencies. Congress controls agency budgets and thus can encourage or discourage particular agency action. Broadly, Congress oversees agency action, and agencies often check with Congress before major initiatives are undertaken. Congress can directly intervene by amending the enabling legislation or by passing laws that require agencies to take specific directions. In 1996, Congress and the president approved new legislation giving Congress 60 session days in which to review proposed agency rules, and, if it wishes, override those rules before they become effective.

Judicial Review

Agency rules and orders may be challenged in court, and the threat of judicial review is probably the chief constraint on agency power. The sheer bulk of agency activities, however, means only a very small portion of those activities will receive judicial scrutiny. Indeed, many appeals of agency actions may be denied on technical grounds (as when the appealing party does not have standing to sue). Assuming those procedural hurdles are scaled and review is granted, the question becomes that of the scope of judicial review. Which issues will the court consider? Historically, the courts have taken a rather narrow approach to judicial review. Two commonsense considerations support that restrained judicial stance. The first is deference to the presumed expertise of the administrative agencies. The jurists, being generalists in the field of law, have been reluctant to overrule the judgment of specialists specifically chosen to regulate within their area of expertise. Second, very crowded judicial calendars act as a natural brake on activist judicial review. For those reasons, judges have traditionally disposed of administrative law cases in an expeditious manner, by readily sustaining the judgment of the agency. Of course, the courts have overruled the agencies when appropriate, and of late we can see evidence of a firmer judicial role.

Not surprisingly, judicial review of agency decisions raises a variety of technical, esoteric issues of law. The nature of those issues depends, in part, on whether the court is reviewing an agency's rule-making function or its adjudicatory function. Cases turn on questions like these:

1. Does the legislature's delegation of authority meet constitutional requirements?
2. Has the agency exceeded the authority granted by the enabling legislation?
3. Has the appealing party exhausted all the available administrative remedies?
4. Are the agency's findings of fact supported by substantial evidence in the record as a whole?

These issues are close to the heart of the administrative law practitioner, but their exploration is not necessary to the layperson's understanding of the larger regulatory process. The case that follows will be our only consideration of the formalities of judicial review. This appeal from a Federal Communications Commission adjudication sheds some light on the agency regulatory process and judicial review; but, much more importantly, the case raises fundamental questions regarding freedom of speech in a technologically advanced society.

F.C.C. v. PACIFICA FOUNDATION
98 S.Ct. 3026 (1978)

Justice Stevens

This case requires that we decide whether the Federal Communications Commission has any power to regulate a radio broadcast that is indecent but not obscene.

A satiric humorist named George Carlin recorded a 12-minute monologue entitled "Filthy Words" before a live audience in a California theater. He began by referring to his thoughts about "the words you can't say on the public, ah, airwaves, um, the ones you definitely wouldn't say, ever." He proceeded to list those words and repeat them over and over again in a variety of colloquialisms. The transcript of the recording . . . indicates frequent laughter from the audience.

At about 2 o'clock in the afternoon on Tuesday, October 30, 1973, a New York radio station, owned by respondent Pacifica Foundation, broadcast the "Filthy Words" monologue. A few weeks later a man, who stated that he had heard the broadcast while driving with his young son, wrote a letter complaining to the commission. He stated that, although he could perhaps understand the "record's being sold for private use, I certainly cannot understand the broadcast of same over the air that, supposedly, you control."

The complaint was forwarded to the station for comment. In its response, Pacifica explained that the monologue had been played during a program about contemporary society's attitude toward language and that, immediately before its broadcast, listeners had been advised that it included "sensitive language which might be regarded as offensive to some." Pacifica characterized George Carlin as a "significant social satirist" who "like Twain and Sahl before him, examines the language of ordinary people . . . Carlin is not mouthing obscenities; he is merely using words to satirize as harmless and essentially silly our attitudes toward those words." Pacifica stated that it was not aware of any other complaints about the broadcast.

On February 21, 1975, the commission issued a declaratory order granting the complaint and holding that Pacifica "could have been the subject of administrative sanctions." . . . The commission did not impose formal sanctions, but it did state that the order would be "associated with the station's license file, and in the event that subsequent complaints are received, the commission will then decide whether it should utilize any of the available sanctions it has been granted by Congress."

* * * * *

[T]he commission concluded that certain words depicted sexual and excretory activities in a patently offensive manner, noted that they "were broadcast at a time when children were undoubtedly in the audiences (i.e., in the early afternoon)" and that the prerecorded language, with these offensive words "repeated over and over," was "deliberately broadcast." . . .

In summary, the commission stated: "We therefore hold that the language as broadcast was indecent and prohibited." . . .

The United States Court of Appeals for the District of Columbia Circuit reversed, with each of the three judges on the panel writing separately . . .

Judge Tamm concluded that the order represented censorship and was expressly prohibited by ¶ 326 of the Communications Act. Alternatively, Judge Tamm read the commission opinion as the functional equivalent of a rule and concluded that it was "overbroad." . . .

Chief Judge Bazelon's concurrence rested on the Constitution. He was persuaded that ¶ 326's prohibition against censorship is inapplicable to broadcasts forbidden by ¶ 1464 (prohibiting "obscene, indecent, or profane language by means of radio communications"). However, he concluded that ¶ 1464 must be narrowly construed to cover only language that is obscene or otherwise unprotected by the First Amendment . . .

Judge Leventhal, in dissent, stated that the only issue was whether the commission could regulate the language "as broadcast." . . .

Emphasizing the interest in protecting children, not only from exposure to indecent language, but also from exposure to the idea that such language has official approval, . . . he concluded that the commission had correctly condemned the daytime broadcast as indecent.

Having granted the commission's petition for certiorari, . . . we must decide: (1) whether the scope of judicial review encompasses more than the commission's determination that the monologue was indecent "as broadcast"; (2) whether the commission's order was a form of censorship forbidden by ¶ 326; (3) whether the broadcast was indecent within the meaning of ¶ 1464; and (4) whether the order violates the First Amendment of the United States Constitution.

(I)

The general statements in the commission's memorandum opinion do not change the character of its order. Its action was an adjudication . . . It did not purport to engage in formal rule making or in the promulgation of any regulations. The order "was issued in a specific factual context"; questions concerning possible action in other contexts were expressly reserved for the future. The specific holding was carefully confined to the monologue "as broadcast." . . .

(II)

The relevant statutory questions are whether the commission's action is forbidden "censorship" within the meaning of ¶ 326 and whether speech that concededly is not obscene may be restricted as "indecent" under the authority of ¶ 1464 . . .

*　*　*　*　*

The prohibition against censorship unequivocally denies the commission any power to edit proposed broadcasts in advance and to excise material considered inappropriate for the airwaves. The prohibition, however, has never been construed to deny the commission the power to review the content of completed broadcasts in the performance of its regulatory duties.

*　*　*　*　*

Entirely apart from the fact that the subsequent review of program content is not the sort of censorship at which the statute was directed, its history makes it perfectly clear that it was not intended to limit the commission's power to regulate the broadcast of obscene, indecent, or profane language. A single section of the [Radio Act of 1927] is the source of both the anticensorship provision and the commission's authority to impose sanctions for the broadcast of indecent or obscene language. Quite plainly, Congress intended to give meaning to both provisions. Respect for that intent requires that the censorship language be read as inapplicable to the prohibition on broadcasting obscene, indecent, or profane language.

We conclude, therefore, that ¶ 326 does not limit the commission's authority to impose sanctions on licensees who engage in obscene, indecent, or profane broadcasting.

(III)

The only other statutory question presented by this case is whether the afternoon broadcast of the "Filthy Words" monologue was indecent within the meaning of ¶ 1464 . . .

The commission identified several words that referred to excretory or sexual activities or organs, stated that the repetitive, deliberate use of those words in an afternoon broadcast when children are in the audience was patently offensive and held that the broadcast was indecent. Pacifica takes issue with the commission's definition of indecency, but does not dispute the commission's preliminary determination that each of the components of its definition was present. Specifically, Pacifica does not quarrel with the conclusion that this afternoon broadcast was patently offensive. Pacifica's claim that the broadcast was not indecent within the meaning of the statute rests entirely on the absence of prurient appeal.

The plain language of the statute does not support Pacifica's argument. The words "obscene, indecent, or profane" are written in the disjunctive, implying that each has a separate meaning. Prurient appeal is an element of the obscene, but the normal definition of "indecent" merely refers to nonconformance with accepted standards of morality.

*　*　*　*　*

Because neither our prior decisions nor the language or history of ¶ 1464 supports the conclusion that prurient appeal is an essential component of indecent language, we reject Pacifica's construction of the statute. When that construction is put to one side, there is no basis for disagreeing with the commission's conclusion that indecent language was used in this broadcast.

(IV)

Pacifica makes two constitutional attacks on the commission's order. First, it argues that the commission's construction of the statutory language broadly encompasses so much constitutionally protected speech that reversal is required even if Pacifica's broadcast of the "Filthy Words" monologue is not itself protected by the First Amendment. Second, Pacifica argues that inasmuch as the recording is not obscene, the Constitution forbids any abridgement of the right to broadcast it on the radio.

A

The first argument fails because our review is limited to the question of whether the commission has the authority to proscribe this particular broadcast. As the commission itself emphasized, its order was "issued in a specific factual context." . . .

That approach is appropriate for courts as well as the commission when regulation of indecency is at stake, for indecency is largely a function of context—it cannot be adequately judged in the abstract.

* * * * *

It is true that the commission's order may lead some broadcasters to censor themselves. At most, however, the commission's definition of indecency will deter only the broadcasting of patently offensive references to excretory and sexual organs and activities. While some of these references may be protected, they surely lie at the periphery of First Amendment concern . . .

B

When the issue is narrowed to the facts of this case, the question is whether the First Amendment denies government any power to restrict the public broadcast of indecent language in any circumstances. For if the government has any such power, this was an appropriate occasion for its exercise.

The words of the Carlin monologue are unquestionably "speech" within the meaning of the First Amendment. It is equally clear that the commission's objections to the broadcast were based in part on its content. The order must therefore fall if, as Pacifica argues, the First Amendment prohibits all governmental regulation that depends on the content of speech. Our past cases demonstrate, however, that no such absolute rule is mandated by the Constitution.

The classic exposition of the proposition that both the content and the context of speech are critical elements of First Amendment analysis is Mr. Justice Holmes's statement . . .

We admit that in many places and in ordinary times the defendants in saying all that was said in the circular would have been within their constitutional rights. But the character of every act depends upon the circumstances in which it was done . . . The most stringent protection of free speech would not protect a man in falsely shouting fire in a theater and causing a panic. It does not even protect a man from an injunction against uttering words that may have all the effect of force . . . The question in every case is whether the words used are used in such circumstances and are of such a nature as to create a clear and present danger that they will bring about the substantive evils that Congress has a right to prevent.

Other distinctions based on content have been approved . . . The government may forbid speech calculated to provoke a fight . . . It may pay heed to the "commonsense differences between commercial speech and other varieties." . . . It may treat libels against private citizens more severely than libels against public officials . . . Obscenity may be wholly prohibited . . .

The question in this case is whether a broadcast of patently offensive words dealing with sex and excretion may be regulated because of its content. Obscene materials have been denied the protection of the First Amendment because their content is so offensive to contemporary moral standards . . . But the fact that society may find speech offensive is not a sufficient reason for suppressing it. Indeed, if it is the speaker's opinion that gives offense, that consequence is a reason for according it constitutional protection. For it is a central tenet of the First Amendment that the government must remain neutral in the marketplace of ideas. If there were any reason to believe that the commission's characterization of the Carlin monologue as offensive could be traced to its political content—or even to the fact that it satirized contemporary attitudes about four-letter words—First Amendment protection might be required. But that is simply not this case. These words offend for the same reasons that obscenity offends . . .

* * * * *

In this case it is undisputed that the content of Pacifica's broadcast was "vulgar," "offensive," and "shocking." Because content of that character is not entitled to absolute constitutional protection under all circumstances, we must consider its context in order to determine whether the commission's action was constitutionally permissible.

C

We have long recognized that each medium of expression presents special First Amendment problems . . . And of all forms of communication, it is broadcasting that has received the most limited First Amendment protection . . . The reasons for [that distinction] are complex, but two have relevance to the present case. First, the broadcast media have established a uniquely pervasive presence in the lives of all Americans. Patently offensive, indecent material presented over the airwaves confronts the citizen, not only in public, but also in the privacy of the home, whether the individual's right to be left alone plainly outweighs the First Amendment rights of an intruder . . . Because the broadcast audience is constantly tuning in and out, prior warnings cannot completely protect the listener or viewer from unexpected program content . . .

Second, broadcasting is uniquely accessible to children, even those too young to read . . .

It is appropriate, in conclusion, to emphasize the narrowness of our holding. This case does not involve a two-way radio conversation between a cab driver and a dispatcher, or a telecast of an Elizabethan comedy. We have not decided that an occasional expletive in either setting would justify any sanction or, indeed, that this broadcast would justify a criminal prosecution. The commission's decision rested entirely on a nuisance rationale under which context is all-important. The concept requires consideration of a host of variables. The time of day was emphasized by the commission. The content of the program in which the language is used will also affect the composition of the audience, and differences between radio, television, and perhaps closed-circuit transmissions, may also be relevant . . .

The judgment of the court of appeals is reversed.

[Omitted is the appendix containing a transcript of the "Filthy Words" monologue.]

Afterword

The George Carlin case, in a sense, lives on more than two decades after it was heard. Its most recent spasm was a Supreme Court decision[10] declining to review a 7–4 federal appeals court decision in the *Action for Children's Television case*,[11] which ordered the current 10 P.M. to 6 A.M. "safe harbor" for indecent radio and television programming. The tortured history of the government's regulation of indecency is illuminating. All was well for a few years after the Carlin case until broadcasters began pushing the boundaries by talking about sex without using the seven dirty words; then Geraldo and Sally Jessy and other talk show hosts began to intimately examine topics like cross-dressing, and complaints began to clutter the FCC mailbox.

In 1987, the FCC wrote new rules to expand its conception of indecency to include describing sexual topics in a "patently offensive way." Those rules were struck down in 1989 by a federal court of appeals, which ordered a safe harbor during which adults would be able to hear or see indecent programming. Congress responded by legislating a 24-hour ban on indecent programming. That law was struck down by the appeals court in 1991. Congress passed a second law in 1992 allowing a midnight to 6 A.M. safe harbor and the FCC established conforming regulations.[12] Those rules were challenged in the *Action for Children's Television* case, mentioned above, and the appeals court set the current 10 P.M. to 6 A.M. safe harbor. [For an overview of indecency in broadcasting litigation, including links to George Carlin and Howard Stern Web sites, see **http://www.cba.uni.edu/decencyl**]

Questions

1. a. Why was the question of whether the FCC's decision constituted adjudication or rule making significant to the subsequent judicial appeals?
   b. Explain the Supreme Court's resolution of that issue.
2. Why is the two-letter word *or* critical to the outcome of this case?
3. Why was the FCC's action not considered censorship?
4. Would the Court's ruling in the *Action for Children's Television* (see Afterword that follows) decision affect television shows that include profane language and nudity if they were telecast outside the safe harbor? Explain.
5. This continuing First Amendment struggle is well illustrated by the FCC's pursuit of radio shock jock

Howard Stern. From 1988 through 1994, the FCC proposed nearly $2 million in fines for Stern's employer, Infinity Broadcasting. Stern's 6 to 11 morning program held the number one rating in both New York City and Los Angeles. For an extended period of time, much of Stern's programming was devoted to sexual matters. He and celebrities discussed sexual fantasies, he invited women to disrobe in his studio, and he described the process over the radio. He talked at length about masturbation and "spewing evil gunk all over everybody"; he discussed anal intercourse and rectal bleeding and remarked that two of his critics might be stranded at sea and "be forced to drink their own urine."

Responding to the FCC decision, columnist James Kilpatrick said: "By any standard known to the law, the broadcasts were in fact indecent, and the fine was appropriate to the offense."[9]

    a. Do you agree?

    b. Do you see any risk to society in curbing Stern's speech?

6. Employ free market reasoning to examine the FCC's indecency stance.

Part Three—An Example: The Food and Drug Administration

Having achieved an overview of the agency *procedures,* we turn now to the *substance,* the actual business, of one of the more prominent agencies.

The Food and Drug Administration, a division of the Department of Health and Human Services, is responsible for protecting the public from dangerous processed food (except meat and poultry), seafood, drugs, and cosmetics and for ensuring the effectiveness of drugs. Our inquiry will be limited largely to those situations in which the FDA governs the entry of new products into the market and in which the agency recalls products from the market that fail to meet government standards (on grounds of mislabeling, subpotency, etc.). [For the FDA Web site, see **http://www.fda.gov**]

HISTORY OF THE FDA

Today's FDA had its roots in the Bureau of Chemistry in the Department of Agriculture beginning in the 1880s. Consumer abuse of a magnitude that would today generate outrage was commonplace around the turn of the century. For example, adulterated, dangerous, worthless, sometimes habit-forming patent medicines, sold as miracle cures, constituted a significant health hazard. The muckraking literature of the day (e.g., Upton Sinclair's *The Jungle,* an exposé of unsanitary conditions in the meat-packing industry) and the increasing support of the American Medical Association and various industry trade associations led Congress in 1906 to approve the Food and Drug Act. In essence, the act prohibited the adulteration and misbranding of foods and drugs under federal jurisdiction. The legislation had been encouraged by the colorful tactics of Dr. Harvey Wiley, head of the Bureau of Chemistry, who formed what he called a "poison squad"—a group of 12 volunteers who ate meals laced with common preservatives of the era (borax, boric acid, formaldehyde, sulfurous acids, and others)—and then submitted the results to Congress.[13]

Weaknesses in the 1906 law generated appeals for further legislation. In 1937, a drug manufacturer released a new sulfa drug without benefit of toxicity tests. The first 40 gallons of "Elixir Sulfanilamide-Massengill" caused more than 100 deaths before its removal from the market.[14] Soon thereafter, Congress approved the Food, Drug, and Cosmetics Act of 1938, which, among other requirements, prevented the marketing of new drugs until their safety was established and authorized the new FDA to remove from the market drugs found to be hazardous.

The final major piece of legislation investing the FDA with its current authority was the 1962 Kefauver Drug Amendments Act, which, among other provisions, required the effectiveness of a drug to be established by "substantial evidence" before it could lawfully be marketed. Interestingly, passage of the Kefauver Act was likewise secured by a major scandal. Many pregnant women in Europe and Canada who had used the sedative thalidomide gave birth to children with deformed or missing limbs. The drug had been limited to experimental use in the United States. Although the Kefauver Amendment would have had no impact on the thalidomide product, the publicity surrounding that horror was instrumental in passage of the act.

FDA DUTIES

The Food and Drug Administration is arguably the nation's most ubiquitous regulatory agency, with regulatory authority over more than $1 trillion worth of consumer products annually. They range from tongue depressors and x-ray machines to drugs, vaccines, home pregnancy tests, and artificial sweeteners.[15]

With such a vast and influential domain, we should not be surprised that the FDA has been both aggressively adding to its long list of regulations in order to add to public safety while also trying to enhance its efficiency in improving new drugs. A partial list of recent FDA business will suggest the agency's importance.

Sunscreen.   Concerned that consumers have been misled, the FDA in 1999 banned the words *sunblock* and *waterproof,* among others, from sunscreen labels. The agency also required SPF testing and other measures to improve consumer safety in using all over-the-counter sunscreens.[16]

Labels.   According to new FDA guidelines issued in 1999 some 100,000 cold remedies, aspirins, and other over-the-counter drugs must, by 2001, display labels following a strict format specifying the drug's ingredients, uses, warnings, and directions. As the *Washington Post* put it: "Today's drug label is often an illegible glob of tiny type that makes hunting for information difficult."[17]

> Today's drug label is often an illegible glob

Inadvertent Deaths.   Most Americans would doubtless be surprised to learn that mistakes in consumption of *prescription* drugs is one of the six leading causes of death in the

United States, with some 100,000 people dying annually from known allergic reactions, dosage mistakes, drug interactions, and like problems.[18] In response, the FDA in 1999 began an initiative with drug companies, the American Medical Association, and others to protect patients. The initiative proposes a variety of strategies including measures to avoid medication errors, a computer upgrade to more quickly circulate news of unexpected drug reactions, clearer warnings to consumers on new drugs, and an international agreement designed to more quickly identify global drug reaction trends.

Stud Pill.   We can see that the FDA has been aggressive in recent years in addressing consumer safety, but the agency's oversight is not unlimited, and we continue to count on market forces as our primary line of defense against dangerous food, drugs, and cosmetics. For example, the now-huge business of dietary supplements gets very little attention. (Dietary supplements for weight gain, weight loss, depression alleviation, sexual energy, and much more range from the familiar St. John's Wort and DHEA to the obscure milk thistle.) Indeed, in 1994 Congress approved the Dietary Supplement Health and Education Act, which in fact reduced already relaxed FDA oversight with the purpose of making dietary supplements more readily available to the public.[19] If safety data is inadequate, the FDA can stop the marketing of diet supplements, but in general, the supplements can be introduced to the market without being reviewed by the FDA for either safety or effectiveness.

While we applaud the freedom and efficiency of limited or nonexistent government oversight, some risks should be considered. In the case of dietary supplements, *The Wall Street Journal* reported on a Minnesota Web-based entrepreneur who began selling "The Stud Pill for Men," the androstenedione diet supplement popularized by home-run star Mark McGuire.[20] The Web business has gone well, aided by advertising claiming that the product is "safe," "proven," and "FDA legal" although the *Journal* reports that no studies have confirmed the safety of andro and the FDA, of course, has not approved or even formally reviewed the supplement.[21] Such claims must be substantiated by evidence under Federal Trade Commission rules. The FDA, as of early 1999, had received no reports of adverse reactions to andro.[22]

> *The Wall Street Journal* reported on a Minnesota Web-based entrepreneur who began selling "The Stud Pill for Men," the androstenedione diet supplement popularized by home-run star Mark McGuire

Drug Approval

Health supplements, sunscreens, and the like are objects of FDA concern, but the giant agency's primary work and most contentious responsibility lies in reviewing prescription drugs for safety and effectiveness. The agency has been widely criticized for being too slow and bureaucratic in testing drugs and medical devices, but that pressure resulted in reducing the approval process time from an average of about 30 months in 1992 to 15 months in 1997.[23] Nonetheless, free market advocates and others believe the process needs further reform in order to get more drugs to the market more quickly. Without reform, one critic says, "fewer drugs will be developed, market competition will erode, and prices to patients will increase."[24]

But criticism abounds on the other side of the debate especially since 5 drugs had to be withdrawn from the market in an 18-month period during the late 1990s because of side effects that had not been discovered, or had not been considered worrisome during the FDA review.[25] That withdrawal rate nearly equals the number that had been withdrawn in the previous 10 years, causing critics to question whether the FDA's fast-track approval process is giving attention to speed at the expense of safety.[26] Thirteen-year FDA pharmacologist Elizabeth Barbehenn told the Associated Press that she decided to leave the agency in 1998 because of frustration with pressure to ignore safety concerns: "The message was that 'one should be approving things, not questioning problems that arise, and . . . give the drug company the benefit of the doubt.'"[27]

> 5 drugs had to be withdrawn from the market in an 18-month period

---

The FDA decided in 1997 to let prescription drug companies advertise on television. The results of this piece of deregulation?

1. Ads have encouraged Americans to make use of the best, new medicines.
2. Americans are consuming more medicine.
3. The average price of prescriptions climbed 40 percent to over $37 in five years during a period when inflation was running at 15 percent. Schering-Plough, for example, spent $97 million in 7 months to promote the allergy drug, Claritin. [Of course, television advertising costs are only one reason for increased prices, and in the long term, the ads may drive some prices down.]

Source: *Los Angeles Times,* "TV Pharmaceutical Ads Raise Consumer Interest, Costs," *Waterloo-Cedar Falls Courier,* November 28, 1999, p. B1.

Tobacco.   Despite the great controversy over FDA drug-approval practices, the bigger issue in recent years, perhaps the biggest in FDA history, is the question of whether the FDA has the power to regulate tobacco products because of nicotine's addictive and harmful properties. The tobacco death toll is about 100,000 Americans annually, and the FDA has boldly claimed authority to regulate even though Congress has never explicitly given it that power.

> The tobacco death toll is about 100,000 Americans annually

The FDA argues that nicotine is a "drug" and that tobacco products are "devices" to deliver nicotine to the body. In 1996, the FDA created new rules designed to prevent tobacco companies from advertising and promoting their product to young people, but those rules were struck down in court on First Amendment grounds. The larger question of whether the FDA has the power to regulate tobacco went to the United States Supreme Court, and in early 2000, the Court ruled by a 5–4 vote that only Congress has that authority.

In *FDA* v. *Brown & Williamson* (2000 U.S. LEXIS 2195) Justice Sandra Day O'Conner, writing for the "conservative" majority in the case, said that Congress had "clearly precluded" the FDA from asserting jurisdiction over tobacco products. Congress had done so by rejecting bills that would have provided that authority, and for years the FDA had said it did not have the power to regulate tobacco. Further, the majority concluded, if the FDA had authority to regulate cigarettes it would have to remove them from the market since the agency has concluded they are unsafe and have no therapeutic value. However, Congress has "foreclosed a ban on such products," preferring to set up a regulatory scheme of labeling and advertising rules. Thus a ban would conflict with congressional intent, but the failure to impose a ban would violate FDA duties. Consequently, the majority concluded, Congress cannot have intended the FDA to have the authority to regulate tobacco products.

The FDA has the statutory authority to regulate articles (other than food) intended to affect the structure or any function of the body. The four-person dissent, in *Brown & Williamson,* argued that evidence recently brought to the surface from tobacco files demonstrated that tobacco products clearly fit within the FDA's definition of a drug and that the companies "intended" the drug to "affect" the body. Indeed, the new evidence was a primary motivator in the FDA's decision to claim the power to regulate tobacco products.

What Now?   Clearly, the tobacco ball has bounced back to the congressional court. What Congress will do is anybody's guess. Congress could write its own rules; it could instruct the FDA to do so; or it could do nothing. Philip Morris, the largest of the United States tobacco manufacturers, has indicated that it would favor congressional rules over things like youth marketing and warnings so long as tobacco is not declared a drug. Of course, cigarette manufacturers are under great financial pressure from their long battle in the courts. (See Chapter 16 for more details.)

Some analysts believe the tobacco companies will now turn to Congress to regulate tobacco in exchange for the right to sell the "safe" cigarettes that they expect to market in the future. The tobacco companies also would likely seek from Congress some kind of cap on losses they may sustain from continuing litigation by smokers. [For the FDA "Children and Tobacco" home page, see **http://www.fda.gov/opacom/campaigns/tobacco.html**]

Questions

1. If Congress, at some point, gives the FDA authority over tobacco, what steps might we expect the agency to take short of an outright ban on tobacco products?
2. Comment on the following statement in a letter to the editor: "Evidence produced in congressional hearings and courtrooms has conclusively established that the tobacco industry's record is permeated with deceit regarding the dangers of smoking. Regulation of this irresponsible, amoral industry is essential."[28]

Questions—Part Three

1. How does the FDA's careful drug review process arguably result in increased drug development abroad?
2. Because of new FDA rules, fresh-squeezed juice producers, in 1998, had to begin putting warnings on their products saying: "Warning. This product has not been

pasteurized and therefore may contain harmful bacteria that can cause serious illness in children, the elderly, and persons with weakened immune systems." The FDA imposed the new rule in response to the death of a child and 66 illnesses in a 1996 episode involving unpasteurized apple juice tainted with E. coli bacteria. Fresh juice represents about 2 percent of all juice consumption in the United States and has been responsible for 339 reported illnesses between 1993 and 1996. The juice is produced by about 1,070 operators, most of whom are small and independent.[29] In a cost/benefit sense, was the FDA, in your judgment, wise to impose the new rule on fresh juice? Explain.

3.   *a.*   Does advertising significantly influence the smoking behavior of adolescents? Explain.

        b.   If so, are the FDA and President Clinton correct in their efforts to curb childhood smoking? Explain.

        c.   Do you think tobacco advertising is intentionally directed toward children? Explain.

4. Jane King sued Collagen Corporation, claiming that she developed autoimmune disease after using Zyderm, a medical device inserted under the skin to smooth wrinkles. She raised various claims, including negligence in manufacturing. The device had been approved for distribution by the FDA and, according to a federal appeals court, was the subject of "extensive regulation." The court ruled that the FDA approval preempted the plaintiff's claims.

        a.   Legal issues aside, was the decision in the best interests of the American public? Explain the competing public policy considerations.

        b.   Why didn't the plaintiff sue the FDA for approving a product that subsequently proved to be dangerous?

        c.   In a concurring opinion, two of the judges said, "Perfection is impossible and a few individuals may be denied full protection at the cost of benefiting the rest." What do they mean? As a matter of public policy and morality, how do you feel about their position? Explain. See *King* v. *Collagen*, 983 F.2d 1130, 1138 (1993).

5. Oraflex, an arthritis drug manufactured by Eli Lilly & Co., was denied access to the American market in 1980. It was subsequently admitted to the British market. Later, the FDA reversed its position and permitted the sale of Oraflex in the United States. After reports of many illnesses and a number of deaths apparently linked to the drug, Lilly removed it from the market. In a subsequent congressional investigation, the acting director of the FDA testified that Lilly had submitted data revealing various side effects from Oraflex, but the FDA did not look at the data, and Lilly failed to bring the data directly to the attention of the FDA.[30]

        a.   Should all new drug applicants be required to explicitly identify all hazards known to be associated with their products? Explain.

        b.   Should cigarette manufacturers be required to reveal all the evidence in their possession regarding the health hazards associated with their products? Explain.

        c.   In either of the cases explored in (*a*) and (*b*), should producers be required not merely to reveal known hazards but to advertise that information broadly? Explain.

Part Four—The Federal Regulatory Process Evaluated

Free market advocates seek to reduce government, while others favor a constrained market where the government plays an important role in preventing and correcting market failure. The economic signature of the late 1980s and 1990s was the stunning ascendance of market economics in Eastern Europe, the former Soviet Union, Great Britain, and China. (See Chapter 1.) At the same time, the Reagan administration worked to sharply reduce the regulatory role of the federal government in American life. The Bush and Clinton administrations moved back toward the center on the question of government intervention. Against that historical backdrop, the argument continues—should the government be more or less involved in American business? The principal criticisms of the regulatory process follow. [For a database exploring worldwide regulatory reform, see **http://www.oecd.org/puma/ regref/index.htm**]

CRITICISMS

Excessive Regulation

In brief, the argument of excessive regulation is that government rules reduce business efficiency, curb freedom, and unjustly redistribute resources. Consider some of the more specific costs.

Total Bill. Recent estimates put the total cost of federal government regulation at about $2,800 per person, per year.[31] Each American spends more than 40 workdays just to pay his or her share of the total cost of federal regulations.[32]

Another revealing way of looking at regulatory expense is that small businesses (fewer than 500 employees) spend about $5,000 annually per employee in meeting federal regulatory, paperwork, and tax compliance requirements, according to the Small Business Administration, while big companies spend about $3,400 per employee.[33] Small and medium-sized businesses generate about two-thirds of all new jobs.[34] (Note that these figures do not reflect the benefits derived from those regulations.)

Paper and Personnel. In 1970 the Code of Federal Regulations, an annual listing of all executive agency regulations published in the *Federal Register,* totaled 54,834 pages, a figure that rose to 132,112 pages by 1996.[35] On the other hand, total federal employment fell from 3.1 million in 1990 to 2.8 million in 1997,[36] while full-time civilian employment outside of the Pentagon and the Post Office in 1998 totaled 1,106,000, a decline of 62,000 from 1990.[37]

Growth. Economist Robert Hahn reminds us that direct costs are only the most visible regulatory "tax":

> The measurable costs of regulation pale against the distortions that sap the economy's dynamism. The public never sees the factories that weren't built, the new products that didn't appear, or the entrepreneurial idea that drowned in a cumbersome regulatory process.[38]

Indeed, some estimates place the regulatory cost to the economy in unrealized growth at $500 billion annually.[39]

Summary.   In addition to the expense of the regulations, the business community's primary complaints can be summarized as follows:

1. Overlap and conflict among agencies.
2. Overextension of agency authority, not merely in setting goals but in dictating how those goals are to be met.
3. Adversarial attitudes toward business.
4. Agency delay in issuing required permits, rules, and standards.
5. Escalating reporting requirements.
6. Federal agencies claim duties that the business community believes are best left to states and localities.

Insufficient Regulation

Our society is changing, complex, and, in many ways, troubled. Consequently, calls for new government regulations and more money for existing regulatory efforts are routine. For example, aren't most Americans pleased that the Federal Communications Commission issued rules helping to keep telemarketers at a distance? Advocates of increased regulation point to the many successes of government intervention: legal equality for minorities and women; prevention of the sale of dangerous food and drugs; the Auto Safety Act; child labor laws; increasingly safe workplaces; cleaner air; and on and on. Furthermore, if we do reduce regulations increased lawsuits are likely to follow:

Regulation Out, Lawsuits In

Public policy problems like smoking by children, the flood of handguns, and sweatshop labor once might have been fought with new laws. But with "regulation" a bad word, the fight today has moved from Congress to court. That's the observation of former secretary of labor Robert Reich, in a *USA Today* article published Feb. 11. "Regulating U.S. industry through lawsuits isn't the most efficient way of doing the job," he wrote, but it's "better than not regulating at all."[40]

Perhaps we actually need more rules in selected dimensions of American life?

Excessive Industry Influence

The industries to be regulated were often instrumental in spawning the various federal agencies. Noted economist George Stigler summarized the argument: "[R]egulation is acquired by the industry and is designed and operated primarily for its benefit."[41] Stigler further argued that, where possible, firms will encourage government regulations restricting entry (licensing), thus limiting competition: "Every industry or occupation that has enough political power to utilize the state will seek to control entry."[42]

As evidence of industry influence in agency affairs, critics argue that agency employees who leave federal service frequently turn to jobs in the industry they were formerly charged with regulating. Similarly, agency recruits are often drawn from the industry being regulated. Industry influence over the regulatory process is considerable. Industry expertise is invaluable, and the industry voice should be heard. The question is one of the "volume" of the voice.

Underrepresentation of Public Opinion

Agency critics also charge that the diffuse voice of public opinion does not receive the attention accorded the pleas of special interests. Public sentiment, being largely unorganized, often is greatly underrepresented in regulatory matters, while well-financed, skillfully organized special interests carry political weight far beyond the numbers they represent.

Bureaucratic Processes

The mechanics of agency conduct are frequently assailed. Allegations of inefficiency, incompetence, and arbitrariness are commonplace. The pace of work is said to be slow, and enforcement of policy often appears weak and ineffectual.

DEREGULATION

In response to those criticisms, both Democrats and Republicans, beginning in the late 1970s, began to reduce the quantity of federal regulatory intervention. The deregulation movement primarily consisted of shrinking the federal bureaucracy, eliminating as many government rules as possible, and expediting the process of complying with those rules that could not be removed.

In those cases where a government role continued to be considered necessary, the deregulation advocates argued for applying free market incentives and reasoning to the achievement of regulatory goals. Thus, rather than forbidding undesirable conduct (such as pollution and industrial accidents), the government might impose a tax on those behaviors society wants to discourage. In effect, a business would purchase the right to engage in conduct society considers injurious or inefficient. Similarly, rather than rationing portions of the radio spectrum or the right to land at airports at peak times, the government might auction those rights to the highest bidder. Market incentives would (1) encourage companies to use cost-effective compliance means and (2) raise the price of dangerous

---

Auto air bags eventually will save 3,000 lives a year, federal regulators now say—far fewer than the 9,000 to 13,500 forecasts used to justify today's requirements that all new cars and trucks have dual air bags.

Source: *USA Today,* "Regulators Cut Estimate of Lives Saved by Air Bags," *Des Moines Register,* December 12, 1996, p. 9A.

TABLE 8.1   Alternative Ways to Reduce the Risk of Death

	Regulatory Burden Per Life Saved	Certified No. of Lives Saved	No. of Lives Lost*	Actual Lives Lost	Alternative Use of Regulatory Burden	Cost Per Life Saved	Claimed No. of Lives Saved	Actual Lives Saved
DES Cattle feed ban	$178,000,000	1	24	23	Cervical cancer screening	$62,411	2,852	2,828
Asbestos ban	$110,700,000	1	15	14	Breast cancer screening	$199,715	554	539
Coke ovens occupational exposure limit	$83,400,000	1	11	10	Lung cancer screening	$174,751	477	466
Arsenic standards for glass plants	$192,000,000	1	26	25	Kidney dialysis	$499,288	385	359
Cover/move (active) uranium mill tailings	$71,600,000	1	10	9	Colo-rectal cancer blood tests	$24,964	2,868	2,858

*Calculated by dividing regulatory burden per life saved by $7.5 million.

Source: Angela Antonelli, "Alternative Ways to Reduce the Risk of Death." [**http://www.heritage.org/issues/96/regs_t3.gif**]

products, thus discouraging their use. However, monitoring difficulties, particularly in the case of pollution, render the taxing or auction methods inexact at best. Some object to the idea of allowing businesses to engage in undesirable conduct or highly prized conduct merely because they have the resources to pay for those privileges.

Similarly, cost-benefit analysis would be applied to all regulations. Regulations would be imposed only if added benefits equaled or exceeded added costs. Table 8.1, from 1998, shows that very large regulatory costs can be imposed without commensurate benefits or even with a net loss of lives. Indeed, influential scholar, Cass Sunstein, argues that we have moved to a "cost-benefit state" to replace the New Deal regulatory approach where big government was broadly embraced with little concern for the cost-benefit equation.[43] Sunstein, however, favors a "soft" form of cost-benefit calculation where qualitative considerations that cannot be carefully measured should nonetheless be considered, especially in health and environmental regulations.[44]

FURTHER DEREGULATION OR REREGULATION?

The United States remains the least regulated of all the industrialized nations. Central planning, direct government investment, and social welfare regulation greatly exceeding our own are represented in varying proportions among all other advanced economies. Highly regarded economist Lester Thurow reminds us that America's economic performance has improved since the onset of the intensive government intervention of the New Deal.[45] Government regulation in America normally arises not from ideology but from actual problems.[46] America is not committed to government regulation as a matter of political policy. Rather, regulation in this country has, in many instances, resulted from an honorable effort to correct evident wrongs. Much-maligned agencies such as the EPA, OSHA, and the FDA were not born of a desire for big government and central planning. Pollution, industrial accidents, and dangerous food and drugs were clearly the impetus for the creation of those agencies.

Less Government?

We turn now to the central inquiry: Should we further deregulate the American economy? Some argue for more regulations. Others favor exclusive reliance on the free market. Most fall somewhere between. In recent years, we have engaged in a national debate about the proper measure of government regulation of business.

Is deregulation desirable? In the 1990s, the American public did not display much zeal for further deregulation. Virtually everyone favors reducing paperwork, eliminating red tape, and getting bureaucrats off our backs, but when addressing specific issues such as auto safety, banking, job health and safety, the environment, and the stock market, few Americans want less regulation. Most either favor the current balance or prefer greater government intervention. Thus, deregulation in health and safety measures, in particular, does not seem to have great political support, but Congress continues to seek rule reduction and restraint in economic activities, as Congress and President Clinton vividly demonstrated in late 1999, by approving the Financial Services Modernization Act, which deregulated the financial services industry. For more than 20 years, industry lobbyists and politicians had sought repeal of the Depression-inspired Glass-Steagall Act which had erected barriers between banks, securities firms, and insurance companies in the belief that risky securities speculation by banks had contributed to the 1929 Crash. The new law removes those barriers and is expected to produce a retailing environment in financial services where "financial supermarkets," big one-stop "department stores," will offer loans, insurance, and investments under one roof while smaller "boutiques" will serve more specialized needs.

> bigger banks generally charge higher fees than do smaller ones

Critics argue that the open market in financial services will result in a merger boom leading to a small number of financial giants who will hold excessive power, charge higher prices, and assume such enormous financial significance that we could not let them fail; that is, public money would be used to bail them out should bankruptcy be threatened. Supporters argue that the change will promote new products, increase competitiveness, and lower prices. Studies to date, however, indicate that bigger banks generally charge higher fees than do smaller ones. The new approach may, in fact, not produce dramatic change of any kind since banks, securities firms, and insurance companies have long since found various ways around the old rules and presumably have already tapped some of the more desirable opportunities. Nonetheless, the bill represents a dramatic affirmation of faith in the free market.

The Financial Services Modernization Act did provide some specific protections for those not satisfied that the market is the best solution to all problems:

- Commercial firms, such as General Motors, cannot buy financial services firms.
- Consumers, worried about their privacy, can, by written request, forbid financial companies from sharing their personal data with telemarketers and others outside the corporate

group, although all of the firms within that group can legally exchange information about customers. Critics say the privacy protection is riddled with exceptions that make abuse likely.

- Banks wishing to expand into new financial activities must have a satisfactory record of making loans to low-income and minority communities.

[For Minnesota Senator Paul Wellstone's critique of the Financial Services Modernization Act, see **http://www.senate.gov/~wellstone/What_s_New/Financeflr.htm**]

Telecommunications.   The Telecommunications Act of 1996 represents a resounding vote of confidence in deregulation and free market thinking and already is altering the course of commerce and culture in America and, inevitably, around the world. The legislation evidences our faith in a substantially free market as the best means of addressing the coming global telecommunications revolution. The bill's core provisions include the following:

- *Competition*—Frees the telephone, television, and computer industries from laws that had prevented them from competing in each other's businesses.
- *Expansion*—Allows television companies to own stations reaching up to 35 percent of viewers (had been a 25 percent maximum).
- *Cable TV*—Immediately deregulated rates for customers of small systems; deregulated all rates by 1999 (or sooner if competition was present in the market); makes it harder for cable customers to contest rates with the FCC.
- *Long-distance phone service*—Allows the seven regional Bell companies (Baby Bells) to provide long-distance service.
- *Local phone service*—Preempts state and local laws, thus easing entry for big competitors such as AT&T, MCI, and cable TV companies.
- *Sex/violence issues*—Makes it a crime for online computer services or users to transmit indecent material over the Internet without restricting minors' access. Mandates TV manufacturers to include V-chips in new sets, which allow customers to automatically block objectionable programming.
- *Guaranteed phone service*—Guarantees phone service everywhere, but lets states and the FCC decide how to pay for it.[47]

Pros and Cons.   Supporters of the bill expect dramatic new product breakthroughs, many new jobs, U.S. worldwide telecommunications superiority, expanded consumer choice, and lower prices. Critics think the bill is essentially a prescription for consolidation and monopoly in the telecommunications industry. They envision more jobs lost than gained, shrinking consumer choices, and higher rates. Arguably, new technologies such as powerful satellites and compression of movies over phone lines will reduce the threat of consolidation and monopoly. The measures to curb children's access to sex and violence are being tested in court, largely on First Amendment grounds (see Chapter 5).

A 1999 report by two consumer interest groups was highly critical of the early impact of the Telecom law.

Sweeping changes in federal telecommunications laws enacted three years ago have hurt all but the wealthiest cable and telephone customers, according to a study released Wednesday by two consumer groups.

The Consumers Union and Consumer Federation of America say the law has not yet led to more competition within the cable and phone industries or lower prices for consumers.

Instead, cable prices have soared 21% during that time and in-state long-distance prices have risen 10%. Local phone and interstate long-distance fees remained stagnant.[48]

Other analysts, however, urge patience with the new law arguing that cable competition is beginning to emerge and that the pending entry of AT&T into the local phone market will enhance competition.[49] [For favorable views and information on telecom deregulation, see **http://www.telecompolicy.net/dereg/**]

Electricity.   Soon you will be able to shop for cheaper electricity. Or perhaps you are already able to do so, depending on where you live. The electricity industry is the next big deregulation target in America. Nearly half the states have approved, in principle, the process of reducing the governmental role in electricity sales and rate setting. The eventual result is expected to be a relatively open market where consumers can shop for electricity providers much as they now can for telephone service. Of course, state governments will maintain policy-making oversight and will continue to set many rules for the foreseeable future. At this writing in 1999, the predicted reduction in utility rates has yet to be realized in California, Massachusetts, Pennsylvania, Rhode Island, and New Jersey, the states that have actually implemented deregulation. The nature of the industry that will ultimately emerge is simply unknown at this point, but the change is dramatic. For decades public utilities were thought to be natural monopolies where optimum efficiency resided in a single firm serving a market area. [For an overview of the electric deregulation story, see **http://www.stateline.org/**]

Deregulation Assessed: The Good News

Deregulation to date seems to be a clear success although some rough spots are evident. Scholars Robert Crandall and Jerry Ellig have identified the following "patterns" in the deregulation of trucking, railroads, airlines, telecommunications, and natural gas:

- *Lower prices.* Adjusted for inflation, prices in the five industries fell between 28 and 57 percent in the decade after the deregulation . . .
- *More innovation.* After deregulation, airlines developed "hub-and-spoke" routing systems, enabling them to operate more efficiently. Deregulation allowed truckers and railroads to develop "intermodal" transport systems where trucks are shipped by rail for long distances. Intermodal systems are so efficient that 28 percent of America's trucks now spend some time on a railroad.
- *More business.* Falling prices ensure more demand for products. Natural gas consumption increased 21 percent in the first decade after deregulation. Falling trucking costs were a major reason United Parcel Service doubled in size between 1980 and 1995. The number of airline flights nearly doubled after a decade of deregulation.

- *Improved lives.* Airline deregulation allowed the rise of low-cost airlines such as Southwest, making airline tickets affordable for people who would otherwise have to spend hours on a bus. Telephone deregulation lowered long-distance rates, allowing more people to spend more time talking to distant friends and relatives. Natural gas deregulation dramatically reduced the cost of heating homes.[50]

As *Business Week* observed:

> Deregulation dramatically increased the flexibility and responsiveness of U.S. corporations in a period of rapid technological and competitive change. Indeed, by making it easier to shift capacity where it is needed, deregulation deserves some of the credit for the current low rate of inflation.[51]

Deregulation Assessed: The Bad News

Deregulation has not been a painless process. Initially, while the market was adjusting to the new approach, bankruptcies were common in the airline and trucking industries. Similarly, critics place part of the blame for huge losses in the savings and loan debacle of the late 1980s and early 1990s on weakened government oversight. Currently, perhaps the biggest deregulation fear is that monopolies will emerge in some industries. The airlines are an area of particular concern in that many hubs are dominated by one carrier, leading to very high business fares and a sense that passengers are being treated poorly. Likewise, dramatically increased concentration in the telecom industry (five giants are expected to remain following the current merger binge) has renewed fears of abuse in that sector. Specifically, cable television rates have risen 7 percent annually over the past three years, thus far exceeding the overall inflation rate.[52] Of course, deregulation assumes the market will bring new competitors and new technologies such that quality will rise and prices will fall in time.

> cable television rates have risen 7 percent annually over the past three years

Deregulation problems are likewise evident in the aforementioned electrical power industry. According to some users, the hybrid electricity market with its reduced but certainly not eliminated rules has so far brought reduced service, sometimes soaring costs, reduced investment in new power plants,[53] and only modestly reduced rates for big users and slight savings or actual increases for small users.[54] Of course, those results involve only a handful of states and a few years of experience, and the long-run prospects appear bright after an interim period of volatility.

Fears about electricity deregulation are symptomatic of larger, long-term fears about reducing government oversight throughout our lives. "A recent U.S. Department of Agriculture study suggested that deregulation (of electricity) would force higher rates in at least 19 states, many of them largely rural."[55] Will the market fairly serve small towns, poor people, the elderly, and others disadvantaged in a variety of ways? As one commentator put it, "Can the 'little guy' afford deregulation?"[56]

What does deregulation say about our vision of America's future? Government intervention was often designed, in part, to provide some shelter to groups, locales, and industries that likely would suffer in an open market. We guaranteed plane and bus service to smaller communities and profits to some carriers. We subsidized rural phone service with funds from larger markets. These strategies arguably were useful in preserving small-town, rural life and in providing a cushion for economically disadvantaged Americans. Of course, from a free market perspective, those efforts actually harmed those they were designed to benefit and imposed a penalty on all others.

Deregulation in Japan?   While we have made a bold commitment to deregulation in the economic arena, our trading rivals in Japan remain skeptical. The Japanese government recognizes the need for opening Japanese markets and systems, and is some taking steps in that direction, but the people are unsure.

The Japanese are divided about the need to open their economy, according to a study by a Japanese think-tank.

More than 35 percent of those polled said they were "fairly close" to the opinion that society should be governed by regulations to preserve national well-being, rather than eliminating rules to encourage private initiative. About 28 per cent said they would favour movement toward a nonregulated society.

The results of a report by the Dentsu Institute for Human Studies suggest the country's slow progress on deregulation reflects the fact the Japanese people "prefer a regulated society, supported by the government, a big government," said Shinji Fukukawa, who helped compile the report.

Source: Alexandra Harney, "Japan Split on Whether to Open Economy," *Financial Times Limited,* July 12, 1999, Asia-Pacific section, p. 6.

Questions

1. *a.*   Why are the Japanese reluctant to embrace deregulation?
    b.   Can Japan maintain its regulated, orderly economic system and still remain competitive in the open, global market? Explain.
2. *a.*   Has deregulation affected your life? Explain.
    b.   Do you *trust* the free market? The government? Both? Neither? Explain.
    c.   On balance, has business deregulation been a good direction for America? Explain.
3. The *Des Moines Register* recently advocated a free market approach to cable television, labeling it a "nonessential activity." Should the government be involved in regulating only those products and services that we cannot do without? Explain.

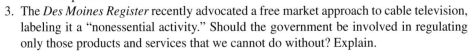

INTERNET EXERCISE

Using the Public Citizen Web site [**htpp://www.citizen.org/**] build a list of critics' concerns about electricity deregulation.

CHAPTER QUESTIONS

1. *a.* Do you think smoking would significantly decline in the United States if we forbade all advertising of tobacco products (assuming First Amendment requirements could be satisfied)? Explain.
   b. Why would we expect total health care costs to rise if we all stopped smoking?
2. Do you expect deregulation of cable television to lead to lower rates? Explain.
3. A 1999 study concludes that African-American youths, especially those between 18 and 29, are 50 percent less likely to wear seat belts than whites or Hispanics. The report estimated that regular use of seat belts by all African Americans would save 1,300 lives per year, prevent 26,000 injuries, and reduce societal costs by $2.6 billion.[58] According to the National Highway Transportation Safety Commission, if all Americans wore seat belts regularly, we would save 10,000 lives, 200,000 injuries, and $20 billion annually.[59] Should Congress require seat belt use? Explain.
4. In 1995, Congress repealed the nationwide 55 miles per hour speed limit.
   a. List some of the competing considerations in making that decision.
   b. Do higher speed limits result in increased highway deaths and injuries? Explain.
5. Former Secretary of Labor Robert Reich: "The era of big government may be over, but the era of regulation through litigation has just begun."[60] Explain what Reich meant.
6. The Federal Communications Commission received a pair of complaints from viewers about allegedly indecent television and radio programming. In one case, a Seattle television station showed graphic scenes in a sex-education class. In another, a St. Louis radio station broadcast a reading of a *Playboy* interview with Jessica Hahn, who alleged that she was raped by evangelist Jim Bakker. Sheep sounds were played in the background during the reading.

   Does either case violate the indecency standards for broadcasting as you understand them? Explain. [See Daniel Pearl, "Hot Career of the Future: Indecency Screener," *The Wall Street Journal,* July 13, 1995, p. B1.]
7. Transportation deregulation has resulted in an immediate loss of service to some smaller communities. Some of that loss has been compensated for with the entry of smaller, independent firms.

   a. Has deregulation endangered small-town America? Explain.
   b. Should we apply free market principles to the postal service, thus, among other consequences, compelling those in small and remote communities to pay the full cost of service rather than the "subsidized" cost now paid? Explain.
8. The expense of government regulation is not limited to the direct cost of administering the various agencies. Explain and offer examples of the other expenses produced by regulation.
9. To the extent the federal government achieves deregulation, what substitutes will citizens find for protection?
10. Pulitzer Prize–winning author and presidential advisor, Arthur Schlesinger:

    The assault on the national government is represented as a disinterested movement to "return" power to the people. But the withdrawal of the national government does not transfer power to the people. It transfers power to the historical rival of the national government and the prime cause of its enlargement—the great corporate interests.[61]

    a. Using 19th- and 20th-century American economic history, explain Schlesinger's claim that corporate interests are the primary cause of big government.
    b. Do you agree with Schlesinger that we continue to need big government to counteract corporate interests and achieve fairness for all in American life? Explain.
11. Make the argument that increasing government rules and jobs leads to decreasing private-sector businesses and jobs.
12. *a.* How might a student such as yourself usefully employ cost-benefit reasoning to improve your academic performance?
    b. Do you do so? Explain.
13. A study by Professor Andrew Chalk of Southern Methodist University concluded, in effect, that the free market is more effective than the rules of the Federal Aviation Administration in ensuring air safety.[62] Assume the role of Professor Chalk. Explain the market mechanisms that have been influential in building our present impressive safety record in air travel.
14. Joseph Stiglitz, the chief White House economist, at the time, argued in 1996 that "a huge economic literature"

supports his view that "appropriately circumscribed government programs can lead to a higher-growth economy."[63] How can government programs stimulate the economy rather than act as a drag on it?

15. A major issue facing the Federal Aviation Administration is congestion in the airways caused by too many planes seeking to take off or land at peak times at high-demand airports. How might we solve that problem while maintaining reasonable service?

16. In calculating the costs and benefits of a new rule, make the argument that added regulation normally slows the economy and leads to increased deaths.

17. Many politicians and scholars have called for widespread adoption of "sunset" policies wherein laws, regulations, and government agencies would be reviewed periodically and would cease to exist if justification for their continuing role could not be established. The federal government and some states have made limited use of sunset provisions. A primary justification for sunset policies is a phenomenon sometimes labeled "legal obsolescence," a term describing the reduced usefulness of a statute, regulation, or agency. Explain how it is that laws, regulations, and agencies can become obsolete.

NOTES

1. The organizational structure of Parts One and Two of this chapter owes a great deal to the suggestions of Professor Cynthia Srstka, Augustana College (South Dakota).

2. James Flansburg, "The Cost of Civilization," *Des Moines Register,* October 27, 1996, p. 3C.

3. Vermont Royster, "'Regulation' Isn't a Dirty Word," *The Wall Street Journal,* September 9, 1987, p. 30.

4. 15 U.S.C. 41, 45(a)(1), 1914.

5. James Q. Wilson, "The Rise of the Bureaucratic State," *The Public Interest* 41 (Fall 1975), as quoted in *Perspectives on the Administrative Process,* ed. Robert L. Rabin (Boston: Little, Brown, 1979), pp. 16, 33.

6. George Stigler, "The Theory of Economic Regulation," *Bell Journal of Economics and Management Science* 2 (Spring 1971), p. 3.

7. *AT&T Corporation* v. *Iowa Utilities Board,* 119 S. Ct. 721 (1999).

8. Jonathan B. Baker, "'Continuous' Regulatory Reform at the Federal Trade Commission," *Administrative Law Review* 49, no. 4 (Fall 1997), pp. 859, 862.

9. James Kilpatrick, "Indecent Radio Broadcasts Deserve Fine," *Des Moines Register,* December 27, 1992, p. 3C.

10. *Action for Children's Television* v. *Federal Communications Commission,* 116 S. Ct. 701 (1996).

11. *Action for Children's Television* v. *FCC,* 58 F.3d 654 (1995).

12. This historical overview of the indecency issue is drawn from Edmund Andrews, "Court Upholds a Ban on 'Indecent' Broadcast Programming," *New York Times,* July 1, 1995, sec. 1, p. 7.

13. Jerry Mashaw, "Regulation, Logic, and Ideology," *Regulation,* November–December 1979, p. 48.

14. Ibid.

15. Henry I. Miller, "Failed FDA Reform," *Regulation* 21, no. 3 (Summer 1998), p. 24.

16. "FDA Finalizes Rules for Sunscreen Goods, Bans Certain Words," *The Wall Street Journal,* May 24, 1999, p. A18.

17. *Washington Post,* "FDA Issues New Guidelines for Drug Labels," *Waterloo-Cedar Falls Courier,* March 11, 1999, p. A1.

18. *Los Angeles Times,* "FDA to Unveil Plan Today to Avoid Inadvertent Drug-Related Deaths," *Waterloo-Cedar Falls Courier,* May 10, 1999, p. A1.

19. Rochelle Sharpe, "One Effect of a Law on Diet Supplements Is Leaner Regulation," *The Wall Street Journal,* January 27, 1999, p. A1.

20. Ibid.

21. Ibid.

22. Ibid.

23. Doug Levy, "FDA Role Key in New Drug Direction," *USA Today,* November 24, 1998, p. 17A.

24. Miller, "Failed FDA Reform," p. 24.

25. Thomas G. Donlan, "Reducing Risk," *Barron's,* May 10, 1999, p. 47.

26. Associated Press, "Critics Question FDA Safety Net," *Des Moines Register,* July 11, 1998, p. 6S.

27. Ibid.

28. Edward L. Koven, "Tobacco Must Be Regulated," *National Law Journal,* May 31, 1999, p. A21.

29. Eleena De Lisser, "FDA Is Putting the Squeeze on Makers of Fresh Juice," *The Wall Street Journal,* September 22, 1998, p. B2.

30. "Congress Wondering How Oraflex Was Approved," *Waterloo Courier,* August 4, 1982, p. B1.

31. "Key Regulatory Facts & Figures," at **http://www.regulation.org/keyfacts.html.**

32. Ibid.

33. Ibid.

34. Ibid.

35. Ibid.

36. Associated Press/Amy Kranz, "Fewer Working, More Complaining," *Waterloo-Cedar Falls Courier,* January 19, 1999, p. A7.

37. David Wessel and Christopher Georges, "In March to a Surplus, Government Changed in Many Small Ways," *The Wall Street Journal,* February 3, 1998, p. A1.

38. Louis Richman, "Bringing Reason to Regulation," *Fortune,* October 19, 1992, p. 94.

39. Miles Pomper, "Rush to Change Federal Safety Regulations Worries Some," *Waterloo Courier,* January 17, 1995, p. A1.

40. "Company Watch," *Business Ethics,* March–April 1999, p. 5.

41. Stigler, "Theory of Economic Regulation," p. 3 as cited in *The Politics of Regulation,* ed. James Q. Wilson (New York: Basic Books, 1980), p. 358.

42. Ibid., p. 5.

43. Thomas O. Garrity, "A Cost-Benefit State," *Administrative Law Review* 50, no. 1 (Winter 1998), p. 7.

44. Ibid.

45. Lester Thurow, *"The Zero-Sum Society* (New York: Penguin Books, 1980), p. 140.

46. Ibid., p. 136.

47. Drawn from Associated Press, *Des Moines Register,* and *The Wall Street Journal* reports.

48. David Lieberman, "Study: Telecom Laws Need Fixing," *USA Today,* February 4, 1999, p. 2B.

49. Ibid.

50. Martin Wooster, "The Benefits of Deregulation," *The American Enterprise,* September–October 1997, p. 87.

51. Editorial, "Deregulation Is Great, But . . ." *Business Week,* April 5, 1999, p. 130.

52. Ibid.

53. Josh P. Hamilton, "Electricity Deregulation Creates Power Struggle," *Chicago Sun-Times,* August 22, 1999, p. 49.

54. Nancy Rivera Brooks, "Power Rates Slow to Cool," *Los Angeles Times,* August 29, 1999, p. C1.

55. Jake Thompson, "Johanns Wary of Electricity Deregulation," *Omaha World-Herald,* June 30, 1999, p. 18.

56. Nancy Lange, "Can the 'Little Guy' Afford Deregulation?" *Des Moines Register,* February 8, 1999, p. 7A.

57. John M. Coyne, "Hang Up, America!" *USA Today,* March 31, 1999, p. 14A.

58. R. J. King, "U.S. Seat Belt Law Is Urged: Report: Hundreds of Lives Would Be Saved, Especially Among African Americans," *Detroit News,* July 20, 1999, p. B4.

59. Ibid.

60. Robert B. Reich, "Regulation Is Out, Litigation Is In," *USA Today,* February 11, 1999, p. 15A.

61. Arthur Schlesinger, Jr., "In Defense of Government," *The Wall Street Journal,* June 7, 1995, p. A14.

62. Andrew Chalk, "Market Outperforms FAA as Air Safety Enforcer," *The Wall Street Journal,* September 1, 1987, p. 26.

63. Bob Davis, "In Presidential Race, the Key Question Is, 'What Causes Growth?'" *The Wall Street Journal,* September 27, 1996, p. A1.

Chapter 9

Business Organizations and Securities Regulation

Part One—Business Organizations

CHOOSING AND CREATING A STRUCTURE

The success of a business, from a one-person start-up to a giant corporation, depends in good part on understanding the law governing the structure and operation of that organization. Whether you take a job as a management trainee in a big company or decide immediately to build your own business, you need to be familiar with the legal structures, principally sole proprietorships, partnerships, corporations, and, increasingly, limited liability companies, that have been developed for doing business and the rules that have emerged for operating those structures.

In general, smaller businesses with few employees and little likelihood of dramatic expansion (and accompanying capital needs) may be best suited for a *sole proprietorship*. A *partnership* may be more suitable if greater capital is required and a group of individuals want to pool their various resources and skills. As capital requirements, complexity, and the diversified nature of the operation increase, a *corporation* may be the best form to take. Recently, most state legislatures have been willing to carve out new, hybrid forms, labeled *limited liability companies,* which combine some of the advantages of partnerships and corporations. The accompanying Table 9.1 summarizes the advantages and disadvantages of four of the principal forms of organizing a business.

When determining which legal form a business will adopt, most thoughtful promoters focus on five factors: cost, continuity, control, liability, and taxes. The order of importance of these considerations will vary from business to business, but all five certainly merit serious analysis. *Cost* reflects the initial and subsequent expenses (direct and indirect) associated with a particular form of organization. *Continuity* refers to the consequences of an owner dying or otherwise withdrawing from participation in the firm, or a new owner joining the business. *Control* focuses on who will set firm policy and run the business. *Liability* concerns what assets of the owners may be used to pay firm debts; tax considerations are based on maximizing the share of corporate resources available to the owner and

TABLE 9.1   Comparing Principal Business Forms

Form	Primary Advantages	Primary Disadvantages
Sole proprietorship	Easily and inexpensively created and operated. Owner independence in decision making. All profits to owner. Profits taxed as personal income.	Capital accumulation limited to resources of proprietor. Owner personally liable for debts of business. Terminates on death or withdrawal of proprietor.
General partnership	Allows pooling of individuals' talents and resources. Easily organized and operated. Taxes paid on partners' personal returns.	Partners personally liable for business debts. Terminates on death or withdrawal of partner. Shared management authority (may also be an advantage, depending upon circumstances).
Corporation	Investors' risk of loss limited to capital invested. Effective structure for raising capital. Easy transferability of shares. Separate legal entity that can own property, enter contracts, and sue or be sued. Can have perpetual life.	Double taxation: corporate income taxes and individual income taxes on distributed dividends. May be expensive to create. States often require variety of reports.
Limited liability company (LLC)	Limited liability in the manner of corporations. Taxed in the manner of partnerships. Separate legal entity that can hold property, enter contracts, and sue or be sued. Easily dissolved.	Must conform to state LLC statute. Terminates on death or withdrawal of member (barring unanimous vote to continue). Not yet available in all states. Some lingering questions about tax treatment as partnership.

minimizing those due the government. [For general information on business organizations, see **http://www.poznaklaw.com/home.html**]

Sole Proprietorships

> The least complex and most common form of business organization in the United States is a sole proprietorship

The least complex and most common form of business organization in the United States is a sole proprietorship, a situation in which one person, the owner, is in fact the business.

Cost.   Few, if any, legal forms are required for organization. A sole proprietorship is not a separate legal entity. Any lawsuit against the business would be directed to its owner, although the business probably would be mentioned.

Continuity.   A sole proprietorship terminates upon the death or withdrawal of the owner.

Control.   A sole proprietorship offers enormous independence of operation. All decisions and directions lie with the owner and all profits return to the owner.

Liability.   The biggest problem is that the owner is personally responsible for all losses and liabilities (as contrasted with the *limited liability* features of some other business organizations). Thus, if your sole proprietorship's liabilities exceeded its assets, you, as the owner, might be forced to pay your business debts with your personal assets.

Taxes.   Taxes are levied at the owner's personal tax rate, so they would often be lower in a corporate structure, for example.

Sole proprietorships are desirable in that they are easily and inexpensively created, they provide the owner great flexibility and independence, all profits go to the owner, and tax treatment would normally be more advantageous than that offered by the corporate form. Thus, if you were entering business on your own—particularly a relatively small, uncomplicated enterprise—a sole proprietorship might make good sense. Of course, it also carries the personal liability and termination disadvantages noted above; and perhaps a bigger problem is that in a sole proprietorship you would have no way of raising capital beyond your own assets and any loans you can secure. [The U.S. Chamber of Commerce provides small business information at **http://www.uschamber.org/**]

Partnerships

A partnership can be defined as two or more persons carrying on as co-owners of a business for profit. A group of persons who agree to form a partnership or who act like partners have done just that—created a partnership. Normally, no written agreement, filings at the courthouse, or other legal notice must be given in advance for a legal partnership to exist. Of course, a written partnership agreement is advisable to set forth rights and responsibilities and to limit confusion. Furthermore, the partners' agreement, whether written or oral, can be changed at any time with their consent.

In those situations in which a partnership is formed without the partners agreeing to the terms under which it will operate, state laws supply the operating conditions for the partnership. Most jurisdictions have, in essence, adopted the *Uniform Partnership Act of 1914 (UPA),* which sets forth a traditional allocation of powers and responsibilities for partnerships. Some of its provisions are:

1. All partners share equally in partnership profits and losses.
2. All partners are expected to devote their full time and energies to partnership business, without compensation, and to act in the best interests of the partnership at all times.
3. An agreement made by any partner may bind the entire partnership to the terms of the agreement.

4. Unanimous consent is necessary to admit a new partner.
5. The partnership can be terminated at any time for any reason by any partner.

A partnership is free to tailor the provisions of its agreement to the particular needs of the partners. Many times, profits and losses are not shared equally, or one partner receives a salary in addition to his or her share of profits, but such variances from the UPA must be spelled out and agreed to. Failure to do so automatically triggers the UPA's provisions and may have costly and perhaps fatal consequences when disputes arise. [Some states have now adopted the Revised Uniform Partnership Act. For the text and history of that revision, see **http://www.law.upenn.edu/bll/ulc/fnact99/1990s/upa97fa.htm**]

Cost.   The costs in establishing a partnership are minimal. Normally, state law imposes no legal requirements, other than obtaining local business licenses and permission to operate under the proposed partnership name.

Continuity.   Continuity is a problem for many partnerships that were not set up to last for a fixed period of time. Every time a partner leaves for any reason (e.g., death, insanity, voluntary or involuntary withdrawal, or personal bankruptcy) or a new partner joins, the partnership must be legally dissolved and a new one created. While under most circumstances the partnership continues to operate during the process, dissolution requires all firm creditors to be notified and appropriate arrangements made. The value of the partnership must be determined, and the withdrawing partner must be given his or her appropriate share. If the partners cannot reach an agreement, the dissatisfied partner may be able to force the partnership to sell all of its assets and give each partner his or her appropriate share. From a business point of view, it can be disastrous if partnership assets must be sold quickly to pay off a withdrawing partner. A good partnership agreement can reduce these problems.

Control.   Control in a partnership is relatively simple. Either each partner has an equal say in partnership policy, or the partnership agreement sets forth an alternative scheme under which some partners have a greater voice than others. On most issues, unless otherwise agreed to by the partners, a majority vote is necessary to approve a course of action.

Liability.   Liability is often the issue that forces promoters to choose the corporate form over a partnership. All members of a partnership are personally liable to the full extent of their assets for all partnership debts. If, for instance, the partnership were to lose money and be unable to pay a bank loan on time, or if a partnership employee were to cause environmental damage, the partners might be forced to sell their stocks, bonds, and other personal possessions to meet the demands of various creditors. If the business is likely to be sued regularly or face catastrophic losses from accidents or other tort liability, a partnership probably would not be appropriate. On the other hand, if the partners are judgment proof (i.e., have no unencumbered assets) or the risks they face are insurable, the penalty associated with the unlimited personal liability for partnership debts is largely illusory.

Taxes.   Taxation is the reason many small businesses are established as partnerships. Partnerships merely serve as conduits for profits flowing from the business directly to the partners. The partners then report partnership profits or losses on their tax returns and pay the appropriate taxes at the ordinary personal income tax rate. The partnership itself merely reports the amount of income to appropriate taxing agencies and does not actually pay any income tax. Many states levy a yearly tax against the authorized shares of corporations chartered in their states. Partnerships typically escape such taxes. [For daily business news, see **http://www.money.com/**]

Corporations

Partnerships and sole proprietorships make economic sense for people who are essentially selling their own and their partners' labor, expertise, or experience (e.g., three doctors, eight attorneys, or five computer repairers). Businesses that utilize many different factors in production, need large amounts of capital, and expect to continue unabated after the founding owners have departed often find partnerships unwieldy and economically unfeasible. For these businesses, organizing as a corporation may be more appropriate.

Creation.   Broadly, the creation of a corporation involves two phases: (1) organization and (2) incorporation. During the organization phase, prior to the legal emergence of the new business, the *promoter* of the corporation typically develops an idea, raises capital, enters contracts, and so forth to get the idea off the ground. The promoter is liable for those contracts (such as lawyer fees, money borrowed, and equipment purchased) at least until the corporation adopts the contracts. If the corporation never comes into being or it declines to assume the promoter's liabilities, those liabilities normally remain with the promoter.

   In the incorporation phase, the new business achieves legal status. Requirements vary from state to state, but normally the process is initiated by filing the articles of incorporation with the secretary of state. The articles must include the name of the corporation, the number of authorized shares to be issued, the address of the corporation's initial registered office, the name of the initial registered agent, and the names and addresses of the *incorporators.* Other information such as the purpose and duration of the corporation and the corporation's initial capitalization may also be included in the articles. Once the articles of incorporation are filed and the necessary fees are paid, the secretary of state, in many states, issues a *certificate of incorporation,* also labeled a *charter.*

   For a promoter, a particularly important decision in creating a new corporation lies in deciding which state should be its legal home. A corporation doing most of its business in one state is likely to save money by incorporating in that state. Corporations engaged in interstate business should consider a variety of factors in deciding about the state of incorporation, including (1) the differences in taxes and fees among the states; (2) the degree of management decision-making discretion permitted under the statutes and court decisions of the state (e.g., state law is often a decisive factor in the success of corporate mergers and takeovers); and (3) the record-keeping requirements of the state. Delaware is a particularly popular choice for incorporation because of its low fees and favorable legal climate.

Cost.   The cost of setting up a corporation is often higher than that associated with a partnership. Obtaining a charter typically requires an attorney and the completion of numerous forms and procedures dictated by the state. Taxes and license fees often have to be paid. The corporation must also undertake similar obligations in other states in which it plans to do business. After the corporation is chartered, it must file regular reports with the state, pay taxes and fees, maintain an agent for service of process, and generally comply with the state's corporate laws. This might require election of a board of directors, regular audits, shareholder meetings, and any number of items thought necessary by the state to ensure the corporation is run fairly for the benefit of all shareholders. [For business forms of all kinds, see **http://www.lectlaw.com/formb.htm**]

Continuity.   As long as all state requirements are met, a corporation may enjoy a perpetual existence, thus eliminating continuity problems (such as those occurring in a partnership when an important partner decides to withdraw at an inopportune time). Ownership of stock in a corporation does not connote a personal, fiduciary duty like that existing between partners, who must always act in the best interests of the partnership, even if it is not personally advantageous. Shares typically may be transferred freely to anyone without corporate approval, and the corporation is usually under no obligation to buy back the shares of a disgruntled or departing shareholder. Likewise, on the death of a shareholder, the shares simply transfer to his or her heirs, and the corporate structure remains unchanged.

Control.   Control is usually much easier to maintain in a corporation than in a partnership. Shares of stock are often sold to widely diverse groups of people who have no connection with each other and no interest in being involved in corporate dealings. For publicly traded companies, large blocks of shares are controlled by banks, mutual funds, or insurance companies, which tend to vote for the continuation of current management except in the most unusual situations. The groups that control major corporations often own or control very small percentages of the company's stock but are able to maintain their positions as board members or top corporate officers. Corporations sometimes issue nonvoting as well as *voting stock*. This *nonvoting stock* participates in firm profits and dividends but does not vote at shareholder meetings. Through this technique, existing owners can raise additional capital for the firm without risking loss of control.

Liability.   Shareholder liability is much more limited than partner liability. Because a corporation is a separate entity, it can sue and be sued. Corporate debts are

> Because a corporation is a separate entity, it can sue and be sued

the sole obligations of the corporation and must be paid from corporate assets. In other words, a party aggrieved by an action of a corporation (e.g., an unpaid debt or an automobile accident), but unable to recoup adequate damages from the corporation cannot expect to recover its losses from the personal assets of the individual shareholders. Except in the most egregious or unusual circumstances, shareholders' losses are limited to their original investment in the corporation (limited liability).

This inability of creditors to use personal shareholder assets to satisfy corporate debts or obligations is often a powerful incentive to incorporate. By incorporating, a person starting a small business can rest at night with the assurance that a business reverse will not cause the owner's automobiles, jewelry, and so on to be sold to pay corporate debts.

Taxes.   The issue of taxation presents the major drawback for choosing a corporate existence. Because a corporation is a separate economic entity, it is also a separate taxable entity. As such, corporations must pay a corporate income tax to the federal government as well as to most states in which they conduct business. Joint state and federal income taxes can approach 40 percent of profits. Furthermore, an individual receiving dividends from a corporation must pay income tax on the dividends to state and federal authorities. Thus, corporate profits are said to be subject to double taxation—first when the corporation reports a profit, and later when those profits are distributed to owners in the form of dividends.

Hybrid Organizations

Because corporations and general partnerships have various shortcomings, businesses have sought alternatives. State legislatures and Congress have responded by authorizing four other forms of organization: limited partnerships, limited liability partnerships, Sub S corporations, and limited liability companies.

Limited Partnerships.   A *limited partnership* is like a partnership in many respects: It is not a taxable entity, and all losses or gains are passed through to the partners. The principal difference is that there are two classes of partners. One class, typically investors, is referred to as limited partners. They are not allowed to participate in management decision making, but they are granted limited liability so that their maximum liability in case of failure is their original investment in the project. The other class, typically the promoters, is referred to as general partners. They manage the business and are personally liable for all losses. A corporation can be the general partner in many instances, thus offering the actual general partners (the owners of the corporation) the equivalent of limited liability. Limited partnerships are particularly suitable for (1) raising capital for single-project alliances among diverse groups of investors (e.g., developing an office building or shopping mall) and (2) sheltering other income from taxation.

In a limited partnership, the shares or interests of the limited partners may be sold or transferred freely. Death, bankruptcy, insanity, and so on have no effect on the partnership. The general partners, on the other hand, are subject to roughly the same restrictions as in a regular partnership. However, provision is usually made in the limited partnership agreement for an alternate general partner so that the project can continue unabated should a general partner be forced to withdraw. Limited partnerships are often more complicated than corporations to form. Failure to comply with all the requirements may subject the limited partners to unlimited liability just as if they were general partners.

Limited Liability Partnerships (LLPs).   In the early and mid-1990s many states passed legislation permitting the creation of a new business form, the *limited liability partnership.* That new structure is largely a response to increasing liability concerns in professional partnerships such as those for accountants and lawyers. LLPs are created according to the terms of the state enabling legislation. Normally the partners must register with the state; pay a fee; include some language such as "limited" in their partnership name, thus indicating LLP status; and maintain sufficient professional liability insurance.

Broadly, the point of an LLP is to allow those who want to operate in a partnership framework to enjoy some of the benefits of limited liability. LLP legislation eliminates a partner's personal liability for another partner's mistakes, misconduct, negligence, and wrongful acts. That is, a partner's liability for the negligence or malpractice of another partner is limited to the partnership's assets. On the other hand, LLP status leaves the partnership itself fully liable for partners' malpractice and negligence; partners remain liable for their own torts, supervising partners may be liable for the wrongdoing of subordinates, and partnerships retain liability for all other debts such as loans.

Sub S Corporations.   Some business projects call for the formation of a *Sub S corporation.* This creation of federal tax law allows, in certain situations, an incorporated business to escape most corporate income tax. The owners of the business then have the best of both worlds—limited liability without double taxation. To qualify, a corporation must have no more than 35 shareholders and meet other Internal Revenue Code requirements.

Limited Liability Companies (LLCs).   Most states have now passed statutes authorizing what are known as *limited liability companies,* structures designed to combine the tax advantages of a partnership with the operating advantages of a corporation. Because of a 1988 IRS ruling, LLCs retain the limited liability of corporations but are treated as partnerships for tax purposes and thus do not pay federal income tax. Rather, LLC members are taxed on profits and losses as part of their individual federal tax returns. An LLC is created by filing articles of organization with the secretary of state.

Typically, an LLC will operate according to an agreement among the members. An LLC operates like a corporation as a separate entity and may sue, be sued, enter contracts, hold property, and so on. An LLC may be managed by the members themselves or by a management team agreed upon by the members. LLC members have no personal liability for LLC obligations. Ordinarily, LLCs may be easily dissolved by death, bankruptcy, or retirement of any member, among other things, although the remaining members can continue to operate the business by their unanimous agreement. In many states, LLCs are limited by statute to a lifetime of 30 years.

Advantages.   LLCs have considerable advantages over other business forms. LLCs tend to be easier to create than limited partnerships and have no restrictions on the maximum number of investors, as do Sub S corporations. Furthermore, unlike a limited partnership, in which the general partners have unlimited liability, an LLC protects its members from personal liability, except for fraud. Currently, tax consequences sometimes make it difficult for existing, profitable businesses to become LLCs, but new businesses do not face that issue. [For more on limited liability companies, see **http://www.llc-usa.com/**]

Franchises

In building a new business, some may seek to reduce the risk of failure by engaging in a *franchise* agreement. A franchise is essentially a distribution system in which the *franchisor* (e.g., McDonald's) holds a trade name, trade mark, copyright, or the like and uses it to build a national system and image. The *franchisee,* on the other hand, pays a fee to the franchisor and has the right to use the franchisor's name and business system to sell goods or services. Legally, a franchise may operate as a partnership, corporation, or other business organization structure.

The franchisee benefits from the experience, name exposure, and goodwill of the franchisor, and the franchisor finds benefits in shifting investment risk to franchisees and in adding the zeal and initiative of those franchisees. Franchisees are in a subordinate role in these arrangements and sometimes have been abused. As a result, most states as well as the Federal Trade Commission have instituted rules requiring franchisors to extensively disclose their operating requirements and protecting franchisees from arbitrary franchisor decisions, especially those involving termination of the franchise agreement. [For many links to business law topics generally, see **http://www.business.gov/**]

OPERATING A PARTNERSHIP

Having examined the primary options in structuring your new business, let's turn now to a closer look at partnership law and the actual operation of a partnership.

A critical initial step lies in providing for the partners' rights and obligations. If those are not specified in the partnership agreement, the general provisions of the UPA will control. The controlling principle is that the partners owe each other and the partnership the utmost in good faith and loyalty. Theirs is a *fiduciary* relationship and, as such, a variety of rights and duties emerge.

Management Authority.   Broadly, each partner acts as a general manager for the enterprise. Absent an understanding to the contrary, each shares equally in decision making. Normally, the majority rules, but special decisions such as admitting a new partner or changing the nature of the business require unanimous consent.

Partners always have right of access to the books and the right to copy them, and under the UPA, they can demand a formal *accounting* in which, if need be, a court will supervise a review of the partnership records and books. This situation might arise, for example, when one of the partners has been wrongfully excluded from partnership business. Finally, each partner has the right to assign her or his partnership interest to another. The *assignee* is entitled to a share of the profits but does not become a partner without consent of the other partners.

Management Obligations.   Each partner has a variety of duties that are to be fullfilled within the spirit of the fiduciary relationship including:

> What happens if you have entered an accounting partnership with some old pals from school, but you decide to serve some clients on your own outside the partnership framework?

1. A general duty to serve the partnership.
2. A duty to reveal information pertinent to the operation of the partnership.
3. A duty to exercise reasonable skill and prudence.
4. A duty to maintain confidentiality.
5. A duty to pay other partners for expenditures made on behalf of the partnership and for liabilities other partners incurred while working for the partnership.
6. A duty not to exceed the authority granted by the partnership.

A partner's duties extend beyond the six listed here. For example, what happens if you have entered an accounting partnership with some old pals from school, but you decide to serve some clients on your own outside the partnership framework? In fact, you have a duty not to compete against the partnership. Have you done so? The case that follows examines the complexities of the duty not to compete.

VEALE v. ROSE
657 S.W.2d 834 (Texas Ct. of App. 1983)

Chief Justice Nye

Facts

Paul Veale, Sr., Paul Veale, Jr., Gary Gibson, James Parker, and Larry Rose were partners in an accounting firm. The written partnership agreement listed the general duties of the partners and expressly recognized that Veale, Sr., and Rose had other business commitments. All the partners could pursue other business so long as those activities did not conflict with the partnership practice or materially interfere with the partners' duties. While a partner with Veale et al., Rose performed accounting work for Right Away Foods and Ed Payne and, in both instances, was personally compensated for that work. Rose's partners claimed that he owed them a share of that compensation in that he had competed with the firm in violation of the partnership agreement. The jury concluded that Rose had not competed with the partnership. The partners appealed.

* * * * *

The partnership agreement between Rose and the appellants provided in part:

> Except with the expressed approval of the other partners as to each specific instance, no partner shall perform any public accounting services or engage in the practice of public accounting other than for and on behalf of this partnership.

Partners may be said to occupy a fiduciary relationship toward one another which requires of them the utmost degree of good faith and honesty in dealing with one another. Breaches of a partner's duty not to compete with the partnership are compensable at law by awarding to the injured partners their proportionate shares of the profits wrongfully acquired by the offending partner.

It is undisputed that while a partner of Paul G. Veale and Company, Rose rendered accounting services for Right Away Foods for which he billed and received payment personally. It is also undisputed that the partnership did not share in the proceeds of these private billings. It was established that Rose was an officer and shareholder in Right Away, but that the compensation Rose received for his accounting services was not received in that capacity. There was some testimony from which the jury could have inferred that the work which Rose did for Right Away Foods for which he was paid (personally) was of a type which did not require the services of a CPA. However, Rose himself admitted as such on his letterhead. He also admitted that there was no reason why he could not have rendered the same services to Right Away Foods as a partner in the accounting firm. At least one of the other partners, Parker, testified that he knew of other public accounting firms which performed the types of services in question. In fact, in regard to services in connection with mergers and acquisitions, he indicated that he was unaware of any required forms that are not prepared by public accounting firms. The preponderance of all of the evidence clearly establishes that Rose had, in fact, performed accounting services for Right Away Foods while a partner of Paul G. Veale and Company, in competition with the partnership. The jury's answer in this respect was in error.

The record reveals that Rose also admitted that he performed accounting services for various enterprises owned by Mr. Ed Payne during his tenure as a partner at Veale for which he billed and received payment personally. There is no question that those services were public accounting services. His later testimony that he performed these services, in effect, after hours, or in addition to his duties to the partnership, is of no value in light of the obligations imposed by the partnership agreement and by the common understanding of the term "competition."

Reversed and remanded

Questions

1.
   a. Why was Rose's work for Right Away Foods and Payne considered a violation of the partnership agreement?
   b. Does a partner not have "after hours" time, the time that Rose says he used in working for Payne?

2. Could Rose operate a gas station, for instance, without violating the partnership agreement?

Third Parties and the Partnership

Technically, a partnership produces a *principal–agent* relationship, the partnership being the principal, the partners the agents. Therefore, each partner's interactions with third parties (people outside the partnership) can have important implications for the partnership. Broadly, those implications can be discussed in the context of contracts, torts, and crimes.

Contracts. Where a partner had *actual or apparent authority* to enter a contract, the partnership becomes responsible for that contract. Under the Uniform Partnership Act, partners have *joint liability* for the contractual obligations of the partnership. Thus, for a third party to successfully sue a partnership on a breach of contract claim, each of the partners must be joined to the suit. Otherwise, neither the individual partners nor the partnership can be held responsible.

Torts. Ordinarily, where a *tort* is committed in the scope of partnership business, the partnership and the partners are *jointly and severally liable* for the harm to third parties. That means the injured party may sue all of the partners jointly or one or more of the partners severally for the entire amount. The partner who was actually responsible for the tort is required to *indemnify* the partners and partnership for whatever damages they may have paid. Normally, the partnership is not responsible for the intentional torts of partners.

Crimes.   In general, partners are not liable for the criminal conduct of their copartners. Unless partners participate in a crime or authorize it, they do not manifest the intent that is required for the finding of criminal conduct. Historically, a partnership itself could not be liable for a crime because it was not considered to be a legal entity; however, many states have passed legislation treating partnerships as persons in the eyes of the law, thus opening them to the possibility of being responsible for criminal conduct when a partner commits a crime.

Ethics Questions

As noted, partnerships are now sometimes held criminally liable. The same can be the case for corporations. Philosopher Peter French argues that corporations are more than "legal persons," they are "moral persons" with all the moral responsibilities and duties that attend personhood. More specifically, he says that corporations have an internal decision-making system that permits them to form the intent that is necessary to hold persons responsible for criminal conduct.

Questions

> Is a partnership a moral person whom we should hold morally responsible in the event of criminal conduct?

1. Could we say the same of a partnership?
2. Is a partnership a moral person whom we should hold morally responsible in the event of criminal conduct?
3. Should we differentiate between the moral responsibilities of partnerships and corporations?
4. Can a partnership commit manslaughter or murder? Explain.

Termination

The termination of a partnership consists of two steps: dissolution and winding up. *Dissolution* occurs when a partner, due to death, bankruptcy, retirement, and so forth, ceases to be a part of the conduct of the partnership's business. *Winding up* involves the collection and distribution of the partnership's assets; that is, the liquidation of the partnership's assets.

Dissolution.   The terms of a wisely prepared partnership agreement can dictate the course of action in a business. For example, the agreement might provide that the partnership would continue for 10 years or until $500,000 in assets had been accumulated or until any party chose to withdraw. On the other hand, regardless of what the agreement says, a partnership can be dissolved at any time if the partners concur. Alternatively, any partner could unilaterally withdraw from the partnership even if doing so would violate the partnership agreement. The withdrawing partner remains entitled to his or her share of the value of the partnership minus any damages caused.

If the partnership agreement includes an expulsion clause and other partners, if any, agree, a partner can be expelled based upon negligence, poor productivity, or even incompatibility.

In the absence of an expulsion clause, a court order would be required. Broadly, the court would require evidence that the party to be expelled is incapable of performance (e.g., adjudicated insanity), is guilty of misconduct, or is rendering the partnership commercially impractical. Normally, something more concrete than a mere allegation of laziness, for example, would be necessary.

Since a deceased or retired partner can no longer carry out the business, a dissolution has occurred, but often it is only technical in nature (see "Continuation" below). A partnership is also dissolved when a partner is declared bankrupt or when it becomes unlawful for the partnership or a partner to continue in business (as where the partners own a bar, the liquor license is issued to the partnership, and one of the partners commits a crime that disqualifies him from eligibility for a liquor license). In most cases, upon dissolution all affected third parties must be notified.

Winding Up.   During winding up, the partnership's assets are liquidated, debts are paid, accounts are collected, and all other business is completed. The proceeds from the liquidation are then distributed according to the following order:

1. Claims of creditors who are not members of the partnership.
2. Claims of creditors who are themselves partners (that is, partners who loaned money to the partnership).
3. Claims of partners who had made contributions to the partnership's working capital.
4. Profits to the partners.

If the partnership has suffered a loss, each partner must bear the loss according to the terms of their agreement or, if no agreement, in the same ratio as profit sharing.

Continuation.   Following dissolution, the partners may want to capitalize on accrued goodwill and continue the partnership rather than proceeding to termination. The partnership agreement or a separate agreement may provide continuation rules including methods for settling accounts. If not, the process continues according to the UPA. Most commonly when a partner has died or retired, the remaining partners must expeditiously settle with the estate or the departing partner in an amount equal to the value of that partner's interest in the partnership. Then bookkeeping changes are entered, and a new partnership emerges.

OPERATING A CORPORATION

Directors

The *shareholders,* the owners of the corporation, elect the members of the *board of directors.* Directors who are employees of the corporation, usually officers, are *inside directors.* Boards also commonly include so-called *outside directors* who have no employment relationship with the corporation and are chosen for the board because of their expertise, influence, and other reasons. Ordinarily, the board—especially in larger firms—does not directly engage in the day-to-day management of the corporation. Rather, it appoints *officers* (discussed below) for that purpose. Broadly, the directors are responsible for setting corporate policy and, so far as possible, ensuring the success and integrity of the operation. Consequently, they may establish a strategic plan, confer with top management, monitor the CEO, and so forth. They are also responsible for such critical decisions as issuing stock, setting dividends, removing officers, and amending bylaws. Typically, the directors establish committees, from among their number, to more efficiently manage the corporation's affairs. For example, a compensation committee would review and set pay, stock options, and the like for top officers, and an executive committee would act for the board when it is not in session.

Officers

The Model Business Corporation Act (MBCA) requires that a corporation include at least one officer who is responsible for those duties that would normally fall to a corporate secretary. Officers ordinarily are appointed by the board in accord with the bylaws. They are responsible for carrying out the policies mandated by the board and for overseeing the day-to-day business of the corporation.

Unlike directors, officers are agents of the corporation and are subject to agency law, which means that the corporation is bound by the actions of its officers when they are acting within the scope of their authority. Broadly, officers have *express authority* as conferred by the bylaws or by the board of directors, and *implied authority* that allows those actions reasonably necessary to accomplish their express duties. Normally, the officers have no personal liability on contracts properly entered on behalf of the corporation, but both directors and officers are liable for their own torts and crimes even if committed on behalf of the corporation.

Duties of Directors and Officers

The MBCA, state legislatures, and the courts have built an array of expectations for those who govern corporations. Broadly, directors and officers have a fiduciary duty to the corporation requiring them generally to operate with due care and loyalty.

Due Care.   Directors and officers must operate prudently and honestly. Failure to do so makes them liable for losses to the corporation. The general standard of *due care and diligence* requires that officers and directors act in good faith and in the manner that a reasonably prudent person, similarly situated, would employ.

Perhaps you aspire someday to be an officer or director in a corporation. In that role, you would seek to build that business. Suppose in making that effort you made a bad decision; perhaps you purchased a smaller company that proved not to be a wise investment or you allowed a subordinate a great deal of latitude in operating part of the business, and he or she hurt company performance. Have you violated the duty of due care and diligence?

The courts and the framers of the MBCA have recognized the uncertainties and risks involved in corporate decision making, and they have understood that most of us would not want to occupy roles of authority if we were subject to liability for every error. As a result, the *business judgment rule* was developed. It protects officers and directors from second-guessing in the courts so long as those officers and directors have acted in a reasonably prudent manner, that is, no bad faith, fraud, or breach of duty was involved. Bad judgment, in and of itself, would not hold a director or officer liable for a decision. That liability is possible, however. The Delaware Supreme Court, in the very influential 1985 *Van Gorkom* case, held directors liable for approving a corporate acquisition at $55 per share when they did so after a meeting of only two hours with little evidence offered and little effort made to establish the market value of the company. Thus, the directors had failed to satisfy the standards of the business judgment rule.[1] The famous case that follows demonstrates the deference the courts have shown to the judgment of officers and directors.

SHLENSKY v. WRIGLEY
237 N.E.2d 776 (Ill. App. Ct. 1968)

Justice Sullivan

Facts

Plaintiff Shlensky, a minority stockholder in the Chicago Cubs major league baseball team, sued the corporation's directors on the grounds of mismanagement and negligence because of their refusal to install lights at Wrigley Field, then the only major league stadium without lights. One of the defendant directors, Philip K. Wrigley, owner of 80 percent of the stock, allegedly objected to lights because of his personal opinion that "baseball is a 'daytime sport' and that the installation of lights and night baseball games will have a deteriorating effect upon the surrounding neighborhood." Allegedly, Wrigley also said that he was not interested in whether the Cubs would benefit financially from lights. Allegedly, the other members of the board of directors deferred to Wrigley on this matter and allowed him to dominate the board.

Shlensky claimed that lights would maximize attendance and revenue. The Cubs, in the years 1961–65, lost money from direct baseball operations. Shlensky attributed those losses to poor attendance and argued that without lights the losses would continue. Shlensky's evidence indicated that the Cubs drew greater attendance on the road than at home and that Chicago White Sox night games during the week drew better than the Cubs' daytime games. Shlensky sought damages and an order requiring the installation of lights and the scheduling of night games. He lost at the trial level and appealed to the Illinois Appellate Court.

* * * * *

The question on appeal is whether plaintiff's amended complaint states a cause of action. It is plaintiff's position that fraud, illegality, and conflict of interest are not the only bases for a stockholder's derivative action against the directors. Contrariwise, defendants argue that the courts will not step in and interfere with honest business judgment of the directors unless there is a showing of fraud, illegality, or conflict of interest.

The cases in this area are numerous . . . However, the courts have pronounced certain ground rules . . . The court in *Wheeler* v. *The Pullman Iron & Steel Co.,* said:

It is, however, fundamental in the law of corporations that the majority of its stockholders shall control the policy of the corporation, and regulate and govern the lawful exercise of its franchise and business . . . Every one purchasing or subscribing for stock in a corporation impliedly agrees that he will be bound by the acts and proceedings done or sanctioned by a majority of the shareholders, or by the agents of the corporation duly chosen by such majority, within the scope of the powers conferred by the charter, and courts of equity will not undertake to control the policy or business methods of a corporation, although it may be seen that a wiser policy might be adopted and the business more successful if other methods were pursued. The majority of shares of its stock, or the agents by the holders thereof lawfully chosen, must be permitted to control the business of the corporation in their discretion, when not in violation of its charter or some public law, or corruptly and fraudulently subversive of the rights and interests of the corporation or of a shareholder.

* * * * *

Plaintiff in the instant case argues that the directors are acting for reasons unrelated to the financial interest and welfare of the Cubs. However, we are not satisfied that the motives assigned to Philip K. Wrigley, and through him to the other directors, are contrary to the best interests of the corporation and the stockholders. For example, it appears to us that the effect on the surrounding neighborhood might well be considered by a director who was considering the patrons who would or would not attend the games if the park were in a poor neighborhood. Furthermore, the long-run interest of the corporation in its property value at Wrigley Field might demand all efforts to keep the neighborhood from deteriorating. By these thoughts we do not mean to say that we have decided that the decision of the directors was a correct one. That is beyond our jurisdiction and ability. We are merely saying that the decision is one properly before directors and the motives alleged in the amended complaint showed no fraud, illegality, or conflict of interest in their making of that decision.

While all the courts do not insist that one or more of the three elements must be present for a stockholder's derivative action to lie, nevertheless we feel that unless the conduct of the defendants at least borders on one of the elements, the courts should not interfere. The trial court in the instant case acted properly in dismissing plaintiff's amended complaint.

We feel that plaintiff's amended complaint was also defective in failing to allege damage to the corporation . . . There is no allegation that the night games played by the other nineteen teams enhanced their financial position or that the profits, if any, of those teams were directly related to the number of night games scheduled. There is an allegation that the installation of lights and scheduling of night games in Wrigley Field would have resulted in large amounts of additional revenues and incomes from increased attendance and related sources of income. Further, the cost of installation of lights, funds for which are allegedly readily available by financing, would be more than offset and recaptured by increased revenues. However, no allegation is made that there will be a net benefit to the corporation from such action, considering all increased costs.

Plaintiff claims that the losses of defendant corporation are due to poor attendance at home games. However, it appears from the amended complaint, taken as a whole, that factors other than attendance affect the net earnings or losses. For example, in 1962, attendance at home and road games decreased appreciably as compared with 1961, and yet the loss from direct baseball operation and of the whole corporation was considerably less.

The record shows that plaintiff did not feel he could allege that the increased revenues would be sufficient to cure the corporate deficit. The only cost plaintiff was at all concerned with was that of installation of lights. No mention was made of operation and maintenance of the lights or other possible increases in operating costs of night games, and we cannot speculate as to what other factors might influence the increase or decrease of profits if the Cubs were to play night home games.

* * * * *

Finally, we do not agree with plaintiff's contention that failure to follow the example of the other major league clubs in scheduling night games constituted negligence. Plaintiff made no allegation that these teams' night schedules were profitable or that the purpose for which night baseball had been undertaken was fulfilled. Furthermore, it cannot be said that directors, even those of corporations that are losing money, must follow the lead of the other corporations in the field. Directors are elected for their business capabilities and judgment and the courts cannot require them to forgo their judgment because of the decisions of directors of other companies. Courts may not decide these questions in the absence of a clear showing of dereliction of duty on the part of the specific directors and mere failure to "follow the crowd" is not such a dereliction.

Affirmed.

Afterword—Duty of Care

The aforementioned *Van Gorkom* decision and an increasing reluctance by insurance companies to insure officers and directors caused some worried outside directors to leave corporate boards. As a result, some states have changed their duty of care standard such that proof of *intentional misconduct* or *gross negligence* would be required to establish a breach.

Questions

1. What was the issue in the Chicago Cubs case?
2. The Chicago Cubs added lights in 1988. How is it that the board of directors was meeting its duty of due

care in the 1960s by not erecting lights and was also meeting its duty of care in the 1980s by doing so?

3. As noted below, some states have changed their laws to offer more protection to corporate directors by requiring a showing, broadly, of intentional misconduct or gross negligence. Do you favor that move toward enhanced protection? Explain.

4. Charles Pritchard, Sr., was CEO and director of Pritchard & Baird Intermediaries Corporation. His wife, Lillian, and his two sons, Charles, Jr., and William, also served on the board of directors. Pritchard & Baird was a successful company although Pritchard, Sr., had engaged in questionable business practices. Charles, Jr., and William began running the company in the late 1960s. Charles, Sr.,

died in 1973. Lillian was never involved in oversight of the corporation. Charles, Jr., and William drained the corporation of over $12 million in what were labeled "shareholder loans" that were never repaid. The corporation went bankrupt. Lillian died in 1978. Creditors of the bankrupt firm sued Lillian's personal estate seeking $10 million and claiming that she was negligent in performing her directorial duties. It was argued that Lillian had been "a simple housewife who served as a director as an accommodation to her husband and sons." Decide this case. Explain.

[See *Francis* v. *United Jersey Bank,* 432 A.2d 814 (N.J.S.Ct. 1981).]

Liability. Both the corporation itself and its employees are potentially liable for the torts and crimes committed by those employees while conducting corporate business. Under the doctrine of *respondeat superior* the corporation itself is ordinarily responsible for torts committed by its employees so long as the acts in question were performed in the *scope of employment.* Of course, directors, officers, and employees will also bear personal liability for their torts and crimes committed within the scope of employment. However, directors and officers are often indemnified for the cost of any civil or criminal litigation against them; that is, the company chooses to pay attorney fees, settlement costs, judgments, and so forth. Indeed, under the MBCA, directors, officers, and employees must be indemnified when they are fully successful in their litigation. Many corporations purchase liability insurance to cover the litigation costs of directors and officers. The justification for these protective measures is to encourage able people to serve as directors and officers. [For current business news, see **http://www.cnnfn.com/**]

Shareholders

Most of us think of shares of corporate stock as investment vehicles, but remember that the purchase of a share makes us an owner of a portion of that company. With that ownership comes certain rights and responsibilities that are broadly outlined in state law and the articles of incorporation. Shares take a variety of forms, but the most common classes are labeled *preferred* and *common shares.* A fundamental difference between the two is that preferred shareholders ordinarily have first claim to dividends and assets upon dissolution (see below). A *dividend,* typically paid in cash or stock, is a distribution of corporate profits to shareholders. Dividends are paid by order of the board of directors and need not be paid each year or on a regular basis. Decisions regarding the payment of dividends are protected by the business judgment rule, although shareholders have occasionally been successful in suing to require a dividend payment.

Shareholder Duties.   Broadly, shareholders fulfill three important roles: (1) electing and removing directors, (2) amending the articles of incorporation, and (3) voting on fundamental changes such as mergers with other corporations or selling most of the corporation's assets.

Voting.   Shareholder duties are accomplished largely through annual and special meetings. The former are used to conduct ongoing shareholder business, including the election of directors and changes in the articles of incorporation. Special meetings may be needed to accomplish urgent business that cannot wait until the next annual meeting. In most cases, only holders of common stocks have voting rights, which normally consist of one vote per share (labeled *straight voting*). To strengthen minority shareholders' voices on the board of directors, *cumulative voting* is either permitted or required in many states. Each shareholder is entitled to one vote times the number of shares held times the number of directors to be elected. Thus, if you own 100 shares in a company and three directors are to be elected, you could cast all of your 300 votes for one candidate or you could split your votes as you wish.

As a practical matter, most shareholders, at least in large corporations, do not attend corporate meetings. Rather, they direct another person, via a written authorization labeled a *proxy,* to vote their shares. Often proxies are arranged by management, which writes to shareholders asking them to authorize a particular director or other designated party to serve as the shareholders' proxy. That approach aids management in its efforts to control the direction of the corporation.

Shareholder Rights.   Given a legitimate purpose, shareholders have the right to inspect the corporation's books and records. In most states, if provided for by the articles of incorporation, a shareholder may have a *preemptive right* to buy a fraction of any new shares issued equal to the fraction of existing shares held by that shareholder. The idea here is to protect existing shareholders if new shares are issued at a price less than the current market price (thus diluting the value of the existing shares) and to permit shareholders to maintain the degree of control in voting and the like that they enjoyed prior to the issuance of the new shares.

Shareholders also have the right to sue the corporation. They may do so individually or as part of a class action with other shareholders when they believe they have been wronged by the corporation (e.g., a dividend was declared but not paid). The most important form of shareholder litigation is the *derivative suit* when the corporation has been wronged either by outsiders or insiders (directors, officers, managers), but the directors refuse to act. Here shareholders are allowed to sue on behalf of the corporation and any recovery ordinarily goes to the corporation. The *Shlensky* case that we looked at earlier, in which the Chicago Cubs board of directors was sued for failing to install lights at Wrigley Field, is an example of a derivative action.

Shareholder Liability.   As mentioned, a great virtue of the corporate form is the idea of limited liability, meaning that in the event of corporate failure the financial responsibility lies with the corporation and the investors' losses are limited to the amount invested in the corporation. Investors' personal assets cannot be reached. Some exceptions, however, can be of importance. For example, the business may never have been properly incorporated, or its stock may have been sold for inadequate consideration (*watered stock*). But the most important exception to the limited liability doctrine is the notion of *piercing the corporate veil;* that is, under some circumstances, the shareholders can be held personally liable when the corporation is unable to pay its obligations. For instance, the corporate veil of limited liability can be pierced if a business is started with so little capital that it is obvious to the courts that the sole purpose of incorporating was for the shareholders to escape liability for their actions.

Suppose a corporation with little or no capital was established to supply propane gas to civic arenas, theaters, and so on. This business kept no insurance, had no assets, and would have nothing to lose should a tank explode, killing or injuring numerous people. Although its owners might think themselves to be insulated from liability and the corporation to be *judgment proof,* a court might pierce the corporate veil and hold the owners personally liable on the theory that the gross undercapitalization of their business so abused the corporate privileges granted them in their charter that they should be denied limited liability.

Dissolution.   Theoretically, a corporation can "live" forever, but it need not do so. *Dissolution,* that is, the termination of a corporation's legal existence, can occur both voluntarily and involuntarily. Normally, a voluntary dissolution transpires either because the incorporators failed to get the corporation underway or because it proved to be unprofitable in its operation. Articles of dissolution are filed with the state, and the state in turn issues a certificate of dissolution, officially signaling the end of the corporation.

The state can involuntarily dissolve a corporation under some circumstances, including failure to meet administrative requirements such as filing forms or paying taxes. Shareholders can file suit seeking the involuntary dissolution of a corporation under circumstances of gross mismanagement, deadlock that is preventing the corporation from acting, or oppression of minority shareholders by those in control.

Winding Up.   Normally, in a voluntary dissolution the directors act as trustees and are responsible for completing contracts, liquidating corporate assets, and distributing the proceeds to creditors and shareholders. A court-appointed receiver takes care of the winding-up duties in an involuntary dissolution. [For the American Bar Association's business law website, see **http://www.abanet.org/buslaw/efss/home.html**]

Questions—Part One

1. Partners Carroll and Fulton operated C&F Trucking. Carroll spent $4,600 of his personal money to buy a trailer for C&F Trucking. Both the sales invoice and the certificate of title for the trailer listed C&F Trucking as the owner. Fulton filed for bankruptcy and claimed the trailer among his assets. Does the trailer belong to the partnership or to Carroll? Explain. [See *In Re Fulton,* 43 B.R. 273 (M.D. Tenn. 1984).]

2. Mr. and Mrs. Patel, owners of the City Center Motel in Eureka, California, formed a partnership with their son, Raj, under which all three parties owned and operated the

motel. However, the real estate records were not changed, so the recorded ownership remained in the parents' names. The partnership agreement included a clause according Raj the right to approve before the property could be sold. Mr. and Mrs. Patel then sold the motel without telling Raj and without notifying the buyers of Raj's right of refusal. Raj learned of the deal and refused to sell. The buyers sought a court order compelling the sale. Decide. Explain. [See *Patel* v. *Patel,* 260 Cal. Rptr. 255 (Cal. Ct. App. 1989).]

3. Stephen Vrabel and a companion were drinking in the Acri Cafe in Youngstown, Ohio, in 1947. Without provocation, Michael Acri shot Vrabel and his companion. Vrabel was seriously injured, and his friend died. Michael Acri and his wife owned the Cafe. Michael had a history of mental problems from the time of his marriage to Florence in 1931 through 1946 when they separated. Florence claimed that Michael had beaten her, but he had never acted violently toward others prior to the shootings. During their years together, Florence played a limited role in operating the cafe, and following their separation Michael had exclusive control of the operations. Vrabel sued Florence Acri and won a court order for $7,500. Florence appealed. Decide. Explain. [See *Vrabel* v. *Acri,* 103 N.E.2d 564 (Ohio S.Ct. 1952).]

4. James Cates and others formed two partnerships to sell insurance. The partnerships contracted with insurance providers including Lloyds of London and ITT Life Insurance. Cates sued Lloyds and ITT alleging, among other things, failure to pay claims promptly. The partnerships were dissolved, but during the winding-up process, Cates died. His wife then intervened in his lawsuit against Lloyds and ITT saying that, as Cates' heir, she was entitled to an interest in partnership assets, including a share of any damages that might be awarded in the lawsuit. ITT and Lloyds won at trial. Mrs. Cates appealed. Decide. Explain. [See *Cates* v. *International Telephone and Telegraph Corp.,* 756 F.2d 1161 (5th Cir. 1985).]

5. Sylvester and Balvik formed an electrical contracting partnership. They then decided to incorporate. Each was a director, officer, and employee of the new corporation. Sylvester had 70 percent of the voting stock and Balvik 30 percent. They quarreled, and Balvik was fired, allegedly for poor performance. Balvik sought a dissolution of the corporation on the grounds that he was the victim of "oppression" and had been squeezed out. Decide. Explain. [See *Balvik* v. *Sylvester,* 411 N.W.2d 383 (N.D. 1987).]

6. Morad, Thomson, and Coupounas were shareholders in Bio-Lab, Inc., of Birmingham, Alabama. Morad and Thomson were also officers and directors. After some disputes, Morad and Thomson incorporated and operated Med-Lab, Inc., a competing business in Tuscaloosa, Alabama. Morad served as president of both companies. Coupounas filed a derivative suit on behalf of Bio-Lab claiming that Morad and Thomson, through Med-Lab, had taken a corporate opportunity that belonged to Bio-Lab. The trial court found for Coupounas. Morad and Thomson appealed. Decide. Explain. [See *Morad* v. *Coupounas,* 361 So.2d 6 (Ala. S.Ct. 1978).]

7. In 1971, Koch and Dahlbeck incorporated Viking Construction, Inc., to develop real estate. Viking was initially capitalized with $3,000, and Dahlbeck extended a $7,000 loan to the corporation. Viking began developing two Omaha, Nebraska, subdivisions with 65 lots and a total value of $430,000. Business went well for four years and then declined sharply. Dahlbeck and Koch initially received $15,000 annual salaries from

Viking, but as sales declined the salaries declined and finally stopped entirely. Viking's initial capitalization of $3,000 was never expanded. Throughout its existence, Viking's average liabilities exceeded its average assets. In 1978 Viking began to liquidate and transferred all of its $11,000 in net worth to Dahlbeck to satisfy his loans to Viking. Viking dissolved in 1980, but still owed money to various creditors, including a $16,000 debt to J. L. Brock Builders. Brock sued Dahlbeck personally. Should Brock be able to pierce Viking's corporate veil and reach Dahlbeck's personal assets? Explain. [See *J. L. Brock Builders, Inc.* v. *Dahlbeck,* 391 N.W.2d 110 (Neb. S.Ct. 1986).]

8. In 1969, upon learning that Honeywell, Inc., was manufacturing antipersonnel fragmentation bombs for use in the Vietnam War, Pillsbury bought shares in Honeywell. Pillsbury testified that his motivation for buying the shares was to lobby Honeywell management and stockholders in order to convince Honeywell to stop producing munitions. Pillsbury sought to inspect Honeywell's shareholder ledgers and all corporate records dealing with weapons and munitions manufacture. Must Honeywell open its records to its shareholder, Pillsbury? Explain. [See *State Ex Rel. Pillsbury* v. *Honeywell, Inc.,* 191 N.W.2d 406 (Minn. S.Ct. 1971).]

9. Art Modell owned 80 percent of the stock of the Cleveland Stadium Corporation (CSC) and 53 percent of the stock of the Cleveland Browns pro football team. Modell was president of CSC and served on the board of directors of the Browns. Several other Browns board members also served on the CSC board. In 1982 the Browns' board voted to buy all of the CSC stock for $6 million. Robert Gries, a Browns board member, and his business, Gries Sports Enterprises, Inc., owned 43 percent of the Browns. CSC had been appraised at no more than $2 million, and Gries objected to the purchase on the grounds that the Browns' debt load was unnecessarily increased and that Modell unfairly benefited from the purchase. The other Browns directors outvoted Gries, so he filed a derivative suit seeking to rescind the CSC purchase. In addition to Modell and Gries, the Browns' board consisted of Modell's wife, three Browns employees, and Richard Cole. Decide Gries's claim. Explain. [See *Gries Sports Enterprises, Inc.* v. *Cleveland Browns Football Co.,* 496 N.E.2d 959 (Ohio S.Ct. 1986).]

10. In 1968, the Democratic National Committee ran up a phone bill of $1.5 million. Shareholders in American Telephone & Telegraph sued AT&T and its directors, claiming the company had not made a good faith effort to collect and thus had, in effect, made a political contribution to the Democratic party, an illegal contribution under federal law. The lower court cited the business judgment rule and dismissed the claim. The shareholders appealed. Decide. Explain. [See *Miller* v. *American Telephone & Telegraph Co.,* 507 F.2d 759 (3d Cir. 1974).]

11. According to *The Wall Street Journal,* courts have pierced the corporate veil fewer than 150 times in the past 10 years. What are the ramifications for business if piercing the corporate veil becomes more common?

12. *a.* Why are partnerships not taxable entities for income tax purposes, yet corporations are taxable? Does this distinction make sense? Explain.

    b. What would be the ramifications of taxing corporations at much lower rates or not taxing them at all?

13. *a.* Why does federal law allow Sub S corporations? Do they serve any useful purpose? Explain.
    b. Do limited partnerships serve any useful purpose? Explain.

Part Two—Securities Regulation

In 1995, Netscape Communications Corporation, maker of software for browsing the World Wide Web, went public; that is, in an effort to raise capital, the company began selling shares to the public through what is known as an *initial public offering (IPO).* In one of the most riotous entries in stock market history, 13.8 million shares traded hands the first day, giving the then 15-month-old company a market value of $1.9 billion even though it had not yet turned a profit. The stock opened the day at $28.00 per share and at times that first day rose as high as $74.75 before closing at $58.25.

Netscape's Internet browsing software, Navigator, was created by Marc Andreessen and fellow graduate students at the University of Illinois. Silicon Graphics founder James Clark persuaded Andreessen and his team to leave school and start the new company with funding from Clark and other investors.

Source: Julie Pitta, "Investors Get Caught Up in the Netscape," *Los Angeles Times,* August 10, 1995, p. D1.

INTRODUCTION TO FEDERAL AND STATE SECURITIES LAWS

The *Securities Act of 1933* regulates the initial issuance to the public of *new, nonexempt* securities and prohibits their sale until they have been properly registered with the *Securities and Exchange Commission (SEC).* The act requires issuers of new stocks to make extensive disclosures about operational and financial matters and bars fraudulent and deceptive practices. The *Securities Exchange Act of 1934* controls the resale of securities on the *secondary market* through exchanges and brokers. The 1934 act requires issuers of publicly traded securities to make regular reports to their shareholders. It established the SEC and set standards for the industry, including requiring the registration of brokers and dealers and prohibiting deceptive practices. Many other federal laws and SEC rules regulate the securities markets, but our primary concern will be with the 1933 and 1934 acts. [For the SEC home page and EDGAR, the automated system for public-company document filings with the SEC, see **http://www.sec.gov/**]

The Securities and Exchange Commission.   The SEC administers the various federal securities statutes. The agency creates specific rules and regulations to implement those general statutory guidelines. The SEC has primary responsibility for investigating securities law violations and securing compliance with the law. The SEC also serves in a judicial capacity in that administrative law judges hold hearings to determine whether securities laws have been violated. If so, the SEC can issue *cease and desist orders,* instructing the defendant to stop its violations, and it can impose civil fines. The SEC does not have the authority to impose criminal penalties, although it can ask the Justice Department to do so.

State Laws.   Some states turned to protective securities legislation even before the 1933 and 1934 federal statutes were enacted. State *blue sky laws* are based on the theory that a state has a duty to protect its citizens from unwise, fraudulent, or excessively speculative investments. Most states have adopted the Uniform Securities Act of 1956 as drafted by the National Conference of Commissioners on Uniform State Laws, but many of those states have amended the act so that blue sky laws differ somewhat from state to state. In general, the blue sky laws provide for registration of securities, registration of brokers, and various measures to prevent fraud.

Self-Regulation.   The SEC is the primary federal agency responsible for regulating the securities industry, but it cannot do the entire job itself. The securities industry has been a leader in building self-regulation programs. The New York Stock Exchange (NYSE) and the National Association of Securities Dealers (NASD), with SEC oversight, "police" the securities markets. [For the NYSE and the NASD, see **www.nyse.com** and **www.nasdr.com**]

TOPLESS BAR GOES PUBLIC

Rick's Cabaret, the posh Houston topless bar . . . , now is publicly traded on the Nasdaq Small Cap Market.

Club owner Robert Watters achieved his dream of taking Rick's public on October 13, 1995. The stock opened at $3 a share, and proceeds of the offering totaled $5.6 million. The stock closed at $3.81.

Nasdaq at first denied Watters' request to be traded, but Watters appealed and won the chance to put his company's name on the exchange.

"We took a long, hard look at Rick's because of the nature of the business," Nasdaq spokesman Mark Beauchamp said. "We concluded it was a legitimate, licensed business that met listing requirements."

The money flowing into Rick's coffers will go toward expansion of Watter's nightlife interests.

Source: Associated Press, *Des Moines Register,* November 24, 1995, p. 6S.

Question

1. As a matter of ethics, did Nasdaq make the proper decision in listing Rick's Cabaret? Explain.

What is a Security?

The Securities Act of 1933 defines a security as:

> any note, stock, treasury stock, bond, debenture, evidence of indebtedness, certificate of interest or participation in any profit-sharing agreement, collateral-trust certificate, preorganizational certificate or subscription, transferable share, investment contract, voting-trust certificate, certificate of

deposit for a security, fractional undivided interest in oil, gas, or other mineral rights, or, in general, any interest or instrument commonly known as a "security," or any certificate of interest or participation in, temporary or interim certificate for, receipt for, guarantee of, or warrant or right to subscribe to or purchase, any of the foregoing.

Any instrument called a *bond, stock debenture, share,* and so on will almost certainly be considered a security. Often, disputes over the applicability of securities laws involve attempts by promoters to raise money for various schemes in which investors pool their money with the expectation of future returns, but no pieces of paper that look like securities are involved. The securities laws, of course, do not apply to transactions not involving securities; therefore, an understanding of just what a security is becomes quite important. Scotch whiskey receipts, citrus groves with management contracts, and restaurant properties are a few examples of deals that have been held to be securities. In *S.E.C. v. Howey,*[2] the United States Supreme Court established the broad test for determining when a transaction involves a security: the *investment of money* in a *common enterprise* with the *expectation of profits generated by the efforts of others.* The article that follows demonstrates the application of the *Howey* reasoning to the protection of investors from risky movie investments.

STATE ORDERS FIRMS TO REMOVE ONLINE INVESTMENT PITCHES

Jeffrey Gettleman

[California] state officials have ordered more than a dozen entertainment companies to remove unauthorized investment solicitations from the Internet.

"Some of these companies essentially said they were making the next 'Titanic,'" said Bill McDonald, enforcement director of the Department of Corporations. "Those kind of representations are fraudulent, because entertainment projects are very risky."

The companies failed to register with state officials and the Securities and Exchange Commission, McDonald said. They also failed to publish the required investment prospectus detailing risks to investors.

One company promised investors huge returns for investing in a low-budget horror film titled "Video Pirates From Mars." Another sought money to produce a "mystical romance" with the working title of "Beverly Hills Love Story," state officials said.

Dynamo Bunny Productions of Valley Village tried to raise $75,000 to finish a movie called "Miamsa,"

"a hilarious dark comedy about romance and recovery from a man's point of view," the website says. For $150, producer Ryan Effner offered investors a signed script and a special mention in the film credits.

Effner said he didn't think that was an illegal offering because he was selling something: the script and the credit.

State officials, however, said the value of Effner's script is based on the success of the movie. And since risk is a factor, the sale of the scripts should have been registered as a security.

The orders cap a month-long sweep in which state investigators posed as potential investors, joined chat rooms, and downloaded thousands of entertainment-related websites looking for unauthorized investment solicitations.

Source: *Los Angeles Times,* July 29, 1999, p. B6. Reprinted by permission.

Questions

1. Do these movie deals appear to meet the *Howey* test for what constitutes a security? Explain.
2. Why do we care whether a particular enterprise should be classified as a security?
3. Fifty-seven residents of Co-op City, a cooperative housing project in New York City, purchased contracts labeled *stocks* that permitted them to acquire apartments. Should those stocks be treated as securities for the purpose of applying federal law when the tenants bought the stocks not for investment, but to secure living space, and when stocks did not give dividend rights, could not appreciate in value, and were not negotiable? Explain. [See *United Housing Foundation, Inc.,* v. *Forman,* 421 U.S. 837 (1975).]

Ethics Question

Since the risk involved in movie making is generally well known, at least among active investors, should the state involve itself in protecting people who imprudently invest in movie ventures?

RAISING MONEY/SELLING SECURITIES: THE 1933 ACT

Businesses rarely begin with an *initial public offering (IPO).* Rather, they are built step by step with other financing strategies until some reach the point at which an IPO is desirable. Often, inventors and other small business developers initially scramble for resources. They may rely on sweat equity; their own, probably limited funds; family loans; government aid, such as Small Business Administration (SBA)–backed loans; bank loans; and other sources. Start-ups or growth also may be funded by individual, private investors who are simply looking for ways to make money. These "angels" are estimated to provide tens of billions of dollars in risk capital each year. Particularly promising new businesses may be able to secure capital from *venture capital funds,* which are partnerships, corporations, investment banks and other organizations designed to make money by investing in new, growing and often risky enterprises. However, few businesses are so fortunate. Even if they secure the necessary initial funding and have some success, they likely will never reach the financial heights necessary to mount an IPO. Rather, the next stage in capital formation for those who are beginning to prosper and want to grow often would be to issue some form of *exempt security.* [For information on government aid to start-ups, see **http://www.sbaonline.sba.gov/**]

Exemptions

The 1933 act provides that every securities offering, unless exempt, must be registered with the SEC prior to sale. The legal, accounting, and professional fees involved in registering a *nonexempt* security can be very large, as are the printing and underwriting costs. Mistakes, along with delays in getting approval from regulatory bodies, can generate enormous expense. The cost of floating a $10 million initial public offering can easily exceed $1 million. Further, if the issuer is successful in bringing the new security to the market, heavy additional expenses are encountered each year thereafter. Annual audits, SEC reports, and quarterly financial reports must be prepared and distributed. Shareholder meetings must be held. Few entrepreneurs can expect to be so well favored as those offering some of the extraordinarily promising new technology stocks, such as Netscape, for example. Hence, your most promising strategy in building your business and looking for money—particularly if you are seeking a relatively small sum—may be to qualify your security for one of the registration exemptions provided by the law. Broadly, the law offers two kinds of exemptions from the 1993 act's registration requirements: *securities exemptions* and *transaction exemptions*. Note that these exemptions apply to registration requirements but do not provide protection from the liability/antifraud provisions of the law.

Securities Exemptions.   Securities exempt from registration include those issued or guaranteed by federal, state, or local governments, as well as those of banks and savings and loans, charitable and religious institutions, and common carriers such as motor carriers and railroads (for certain types of offerings). Most insurance and annuity contracts are similarly exempt.

Transaction Exemptions.   Transactions in securities that are exempt from registration requirements take three primary forms: private placements, intrastate offerings, and small issues.

Private Placements.   These are securities sold without a public offering, thus excusing them from registration requirements. *Private placement* sales generally may be made to an unlimited number of *accredited investors* (institutional investors such as banks and pension funds, wealthy individuals, larger businesses, and upper-level insiders of the issuer). Private placements may be sold to no more than 35 nonaccredited investors, and those investors must either be financially sophisticated themselves or be represented by those who are sophisticated about investment matters. No general public selling of private placement securities is permitted. Broadly, all private placement purchasers must either receive or have access to all the information necessary to make an informed decision. The general theory of private placement law is that sophisticated investors do not need extensive government protection.

Intrastate Offerings.   *Intrastate offerings* are those sold only in a single state to residents of that state. Even if this requirement is met, the issuer must demonstrate that 80 percent of its business (revenues, assets, and so on) and 80 percent of the proceeds from the issue are to be used in that state. This exemption is designed to aid purely local business people in obtaining funds without meeting costly SEC registration requirements.

Small Issues.   Congress has been concerned about easing access to capital for small businesses. To lower costs for *small issues,* the SEC has provided a variety of exemptions from registration requirements for securities offerings not exceeding $1 to $5 million, depending on the exemption.

Although an issue may qualify for a total or partial exemption from SEC rules, state blue sky laws may not offer the same exemptions. In that case, issuers would still have to comply with those states' laws. [For a general securities law database, see **http://www.law.uc.edu/CCL/**]

Registration Requirements

Blue Sky Laws.   Most states require registration of securities issued or traded in that state. In many states, registration requirements specify disclosure of certain information and operate on the premise that informed investors can digest that information and substantially protect themselves. In those states, securities meeting federal registration requirements can routinely fulfill the state's requirements. Other states believe that more activist intervention is required to protect investors. In those states the securities regulator must be convinced that the issue actually has investment merit and is likely to produce a reasonable return.

The 1933 Act.   Unlike state protective statutes, the Securities Act of 1933 is not concerned with the value or speculative nature of an issue; rather, it focuses on full disclosure of all the material facts. Before an offering can be sold, a detailed *registration statement* must be submitted to the SEC. The statement will include audited financial records, a description of the business, an overview of the management of the firm, and other information necessary for the SEC to determine that the registration contains all the data investors need to evaluate the security. Additionally, a *prospectus* must be given to every person to whom the security is offered for sale. The prospectus, which contains much the same information as the registration statement, is the primary sales document for the offering and is designed to disclose the information necessary for an offeree to make an informed decision.

Some lawyers think the SEC has been behaving like a cranky professor since instituting its "plain English" rules in late 1998. Prospectuses must now be free of legalese, jargon, and unnecessarily long sentences, and they must be displayed in a readable format:

The recent IPO for **MarketWatch.com** was a smash, soaring 470% on its opening day.

But by one important measure, the filing initially didn't pass muster when it first landed at the Securities and Exchange Commission last year.

Why? It got an F for, ahem, writing style.

"These sentences are too long, complex and legalistic to be understandable on first reading," wrote an SEC examiner reviewing the Web company's filing for an initial public stock offering. In another passage, the examiner wrote, "We don't understand the purpose of the third paragraph. Is this a risk or an explanation?"

Source: Bridget O'Brian, "Paper Chase: SEC Is Tough Grader," *The Wall Street Journal,* July 6, 1999, p. C1. [For SEC advice on plain English compliance, see **http://www.sec.gov/offices/corpfin/cfslb7a.htm**]

The Registration Process

The 1933 act divides the IPO registration process into well-defined periods with strict rules for each.

Prefiling Period.   This is the time before the registration is filed. All offers to buy or sell the security are forbidden prior to registration. Publicity designed to condition the market, to encourage interest in the new issue or having that effect, is forbidden during the prefiling period.

Waiting Period.   This is the time between the filing and the declaration by the SEC that the registration is effective. Technically, the registration is effective 20 days after receipt by the SEC. However, if the SEC review discloses deficiencies, the issuer receives a new 20-day period in which to make changes. Although the SEC cannot reject an offering based on its perception of the likelihood of the offering's success, it can lengthen the approval process and increase accompanying expenses; thus, offerings the SEC deems undesirable or misleading become practically impossible to market.

During this period, sales are not permitted, but the new issue can be publicized by a preliminary prospectus called a *red herring* and by a *tombstone ad.* A red herring summarizes the information in the registration statement and specifies that both sales and offers to buy must await registration approval. A tombstone ad is limited to setting forth what is being offered, when it is available, and from whom a prospectus may be obtained. The tombstone ad must specify that it does not constitute an offer to sell.

Thus, the general point of the waiting period is to allow buyers to calmly reflect on the wisdom of buying the new issue while it is being scrutinized by the SEC. Of course, many do not do so. Instead, they may rely on their brokers, their own intuition, or other evidence, but they will have received a prospectus. Thus, the SEC does not protect investors from their own foolishness, but it does ensure that all have access to adequate information.

Post-Effective Period.   This is the period after the SEC has declared the registration to be effective. Once the registration is effective, sales may begin; but a final prospectus must accompany or precede delivery of the security. Normally, the IPO issuer and underwriter are expected to sell out the issue as soon as possible; however, under a procedure labeled a *shelf registration,* large, reliable issuers may file a registration with the SEC and hold the securities "on the shelf" to await more favorable market conditions before selling. This approach offers considerable cost savings in the registration process. [For SEC filings and financial analysis since 1994, see **http://www.tenkwizard.com/**]

LIABILITY AND REMEDIES: THE 1933 ACT

Defects, both intentional and negligent, in the registration process can lead to significant penalties under the 1933 act. Criminal liability may be imposed for willful violations of the act. The act also imposes civil liability for all material misstatements, misleading data, or omissions in the prospectus and other registration material filed with the SEC. Quite simply, anyone who purchases an initial public offering that is subject to registration requirements and contains errors, omissions, or misleading statements or for which no registration material is filed may be able to recover damages in an amount up to the original purchase price for all money lost as a result of the investment. No proof of reliance and causation is necessary.[3]

Due Diligence

The primary defense to a false registration claim is to establish *due diligence,* which, over-simplified, means that the party being sued was not guilty of negligence. All defendants except the issuer can employ the due diligence defense. The precise standards of the due diligence defense depend on the role of the defendant in the registration process and the portion of the registration statement that is faulty. In general, one displays due diligence by conducting a reasonable investigation to establish reasonable grounds to believe and, in fact, believing that the registration statement is both true and free of material omissions. The famous case that follows illustrates the application of the due diligence defense to alleged violations of the Securities Act of 1933.

ESCOTT v. BARCHRIS CONSTRUCTION CORP.
283 F. Supp. 643 (S.D.N.Y. 1968)

Facts

BarChris constructed bowling "centers" consisting of bowling alleys and, often, restaurants and bars. Business boomed with the introduction of automatic pin setters in 1952. In 1961, BarChris decided to raise money by selling debentures. A registration statement was filed with the SEC. However, by 1962 the bowling industry was saturated, new orders declined, and existing customers were unable to pay. BarChris itself went bankrupt in 1962 and was unable to make its interest payments on the debentures. Escott and others who had bought debentures sued BarChris, its officers, directors, auditors, the debenture underwriters, and others under Section 11 of the Securities Act of 1933. They claimed that BarChris's registration statement contained significant errors regarding sales, assets, liabilities, and so on.

*   *   *   *   *

District Judge McLean

I turn . . . to the question of whether defendants have proved their due diligence defenses. The position of each defendant will be separately considered.

Russo

Russo was, to all intents and purposes, the chief executive officer of BarChris. He was a member of the executive committee. He was familiar with all aspects of the business . . .

It was Russo who arranged for the temporary increase in BarChris's cash in banks on December 31, 1960, a transaction which borders on the fraudulent. He was thoroughly aware of BarChris's stringent financial condition in May 1961. He had personally advanced large sums to BarChris of which $175,000 remained unpaid as of May 16.

In short, Russo knew all the relevant facts. He could not have believed that there were no untrue statements or material omissions in the prospectus. Russo has no due diligence defenses.

* * * * *

Trilling

Trilling . . . was BarChris's controller. He signed the registration statement in that capacity, although he was not a director . . .

Trilling was not a member of the executive committee. He was a comparatively minor figure in BarChris. The description of BarChris's "management" on page 9 of the prospectus does not mention him . . .

Trilling may well have been unaware of several of the inaccuracies in the prospectus. But he must have known of some of them. As a financial officer, he was familiar with BarChris's finances and with its books of account. He knew that part of the cash on deposit on December 31, 1960 had been procured temporarily by Russo for window-dressing purposes. He knew that BarChris was operating Capitol Lanes in 1960. He should have known, although perhaps through carelessness he did not know at the time, that BarChris's contingent liability on Type B lease transactions was greater than the prospectus stated. In the light of these facts, I cannot find that Trilling believed the entire prospectus to be true.

But even if he did, he still did not establish his due diligence defenses. He did not prove that as to the parts of the prospectus expertised by Peat, Marwick he had no reasonable ground to believe that it was untrue. He also failed to prove, as to the parts of the prospectus not expertised by Peat, Marwick, that he made a reasonable investigation which afforded him a reasonable ground to believe that it was true. As far as appears, he made no investigation. He did what was asked of him and assumed that others would properly take care of supplying accurate data as to the other aspects of the company's business. This would have been well enough but for the fact that he signed the registration statement. As a signer, he could not avoid responsibility by leaving it up to others to make it accurate. Trilling did not sustain the burden of proving his due diligence defenses.

* * * * *

Auslander

Auslander was an "outside" director, i.e., one who was not an officer of BarChris. He was chairman of the board of Valley Stream National Bank in Valley Stream, Long Island . . .

In February and early March 1961, before accepting Vitolo's invitation, Auslander made some investigation of BarChris. He obtained Dun & Bradstreet reports which contained sales and earnings figures for periods earlier than December 31, 1960. He caused inquiry to be made of certain of BarChris's banks and was advised that they regarded BarChris favorably.

* * * * *

Auslander was elected a director on April 17, 1961. The registration statement in its original form had already been filed, of course without his signature. On May 10, 1961, he signed a signature page for the first amendment to the registration statement which was filed on May 11, 1961. This was a separate sheet without any document attached. Auslander did not know that it was a signature page for a registration statement. He vaguely understood that it was something "for the SEC."

Auslander attended a meeting of BarChris's directors on May 15, 1961. At that meeting he, along with the other directors, signed the signature sheet for the second amendment which constituted the registration statement in its final form. Again, this was only a separate sheet without any document attached. Auslander never saw a copy of the registration statement in its final form.

At the May 15 directors' meeting, however, Auslander did realize that what he was signing was a signature sheet to a registration statement. This was the first time that he had appreciated that fact. A copy of the registration statement in its earlier form as amended on May 11, 1961, was passed around at the meeting. Auslander glanced at it briefly. He did not read it thoroughly.

* * * * *

In considering Auslander's due diligence defenses, a distinction is to be drawn between the expertised and nonexpertised portions of the prospectus. As to the former, Auslander knew that Peat, Marwick had audited the 1960 figures. He believed them to be correct because he had confidence in Peat, Marwick. He had no reasonable ground to believe otherwise.

As to the nonexpertised portions, however, Auslander is in a different position. He seems to have been under the impression that Peat, Marwick was responsible for all the figures. This impression was not correct, as he would have realized if he had read the prospectus carefully. Auslander made no investigation of the accuracy of the prospectus. He relied on the assurance of Vitolo and Russo, and upon the information he had received in answer to his inquiries back in February and early March. These inquiries were general ones, in the nature of a credit check. The information which he received in answer to them was also general . . .

It is true that Auslander became a director on the eve of the financing. He had little opportunity to familiarize himself with the company's affairs. The question is whether, under such circumstances, Auslander did enough to establish his due diligence defense with respect to the nonexpertised portions of the prospectus.

* * * * *

Section 11 imposes liability in the first instance upon a director, no matter how new he is. He is presumed to know his responsibility when he becomes a director. He can escape liability only by using that reasonable care to investigate the facts which a prudent man would employ in the management of his own property. In my opinion, a prudent man would not act in an important matter without any knowledge of the relevant facts, in sole reliance upon representations of persons who are comparative strangers and upon general information which does not purport to cover the particular case. To say that such minimal conduct measures up to the statutory standard would, to all intents and purposes, absolve new directors from responsibility merely because they are new.

I find and conclude that Auslander has not established his due diligence defense with respect to the misstatements and omissions in those portions of the prospectus other than the audited 1960 figures.

* * * * *

Peat, Marwick

The part of the registration statement purporting to be made upon the authority of Peat, Marwick as an expert was . . . the 1960 figures . . . [T]he question is whether . . . Peat, Marwick . . . had reasonable ground to believe and did believe that the 1960 figures were true and that no material fact had been omitted from the registration statement which should have been included in order to make the 1960 figures not misleading.

* * * * *

The 1960 Audit

Peat, Marwick's work was in general charge of a member of the firm, Cummings, and more immediately in charge of Peat, Marwick's manager, Logan. Most of the actual work was performed by a senior accountant, Berardi . . .

Berardi was then about thirty years old. He was not yet a C.P.A. He had had no previous experience with the bowling industry. This was his first job as a senior accountant. He could hardly have been given a more difficult assignment.

* * * * *

Capitol Lanes

First and foremost is Berardi's failure to discover that Capitol Lanes had not been sold. This error affected both the sales figure and the liability side of the balance sheet.

* * * * *

Berardi testified that he inquired of Russo about Capitol Lanes and that Russo told him that Capitol Lanes, Inc. was going to operate an alley some day but as yet it had no alley. Berardi testified that he understood that the alley had not been built and that he believed that the rental payments were on vacant land.

I am not satisfied with this testimony. If Berardi did hold this belief, he should not have held it. The entries as to insurance and as to "operation of alley" should have alerted him to the fact that an alley existed. He should have made further inquiry on the subject. It is apparent that Berardi did not understand this transaction.

* * * * *

The S-1 Review

The purpose of reviewing events subsequent to the date of a certified balance sheet (referred to as an S-1 review when made with reference to a registration statement) is to ascertain whether any material change has occurred in the company's financial position which should be disclosed in order to prevent the balance sheet figures from being misleading. It does not amount to a complete audit.

* * * * *

Berardi made the S-1 review in May 1961. He devoted a little over two days to it, a total of $20\frac{1}{2}$ hours. He did not discover any of the errors or omissions pertaining to the state of affairs in 1961 . . . The question is whether, despite his failure to find out anything, his investigation was reasonable within the meaning of the statute.

What Berardi did was to look at a consolidating trial balance as of March 31, 1961, which had been prepared by BarChris, compare it with the audited December 31, 1960, figures, discuss with Trilling certain unfavorable developments which the comparison disclosed, and read certain minutes. He did not examine any "important financial records" other than the trial balance . . .

In substance, . . . Berardi . . . asked questions, he got answers which he considered satisfactory, and he did nothing to verify them.

* * * * *

Berardi had no conception of how tight the cash position was. He did not discover that BarChris was holding up checks in substantial amounts because there was no money in the bank to cover them. He did not know of the loan from Manufacturers Trust Company or of the officers' loans. Since he never read the prospectus, he was not even aware that there had ever been any problem about loans from officers.

* * * * *

There had been a material change for the worse in BarChris's financial position. That change was sufficiently serious so that the failure to disclose it made the 1960 figures misleading. Berardi did not discover it. As far as results were concerned, his S-I review was useless.

* * * * *

Here again, the burden of proof is on Peat, Marwick. I conclude that Peat, Marwick has not established its due diligence defense.

* * * * *

[Judgment for Escott and other debenture buyers]

Questions

1. Why was the Court willing to find the director, Auslander, liable even though he was "new" to the corporation and "had little opportunity to familiarize himself with the company's affairs"?
2. What is an S-1 review?
3. In March 1976, Holiday Inn filed a registration statement with the SEC with respect to the issuance of public stock. In reliance on the prospectus published on March 23, Straus bought 100 shares of Holiday Inn stock. The value of Straus's stock declined, and she sued Holiday Inn under Section 11 of the 1933 act, claiming that the prospectus contained misleading statements and omissions in that it failed to disclose a decline in profits. Specifically, Straus argued that Holiday Inn suffered a financial decline in the first two months of 1976 as compared with the first two months of 1975 and that Holiday Inn was aware of that decline on March 23. She said that if Holiday Inn's foreign currency translation losses (due to a decline in the value of the dollar) were excluded, Holiday Inn suffered a seven-cents-per-share decline in profits for the first two months of 1976 as compared to the first two months of 1975 and that the decline should have been disclosed in the prospectus. Including the translation losses as provided for under generally accepted accounting principles resulted in a one-cent-per-share decline in profits for January–February 1976 as compared to January–February 1975. Did Holiday Inn violate Section 11? Explain. [See *Straus* v. *Holiday Inn,* 460 F. Supp. 729 (S.D.N.Y. 1978).]
4. Rule 144a allows approximately 4,000 large institutions to trade privately placed securities that may not be offered to or traded by small (or many) individual investors.
   a. As these securities make up approximately 35 percent of all recent offerings, what problems does the rule cause small investors?
   b. Is the volume of private placements likely to rise or fall? Explain.
   c. What regulatory lessons can be derived from the fact that investors are willing to commit billions of dollars to investments that may not have complied with all the requirements of SEC rules?
   d. Are SEC rules counterproductive in some situations? List some examples of this problem.

REGULATING THE RESALE OF SECURITIES: THE 1934 ACT

The subsequent *resale* of securities after an IPO—buying and selling of shares on the open market—is regulated by the 1934 Securities Exchange Act. Thus, the 1933 act has, in the main, a one-time impact commanding detailed registration requirements as securities pass from the issuer to the market; whereas the 1934 act is primarily directed to all trading subsequent to that IPO stage and requires all securities issuers to engage in regular information disclosures. Indeed, the general purpose of the 1934 act is to ensure the steady flow of reliable information to investors. [For an extensive securities law database, see **http://www.seclaw.com**]

Disclosure

The 1934 act regulates many aspects of the financial dealings of publicly held companies. Any company with more than $10 million in assets and 500 shareholders is subject to some provisions of the act as are any businesses that recently sold securities to the public or issued a class of securities traded on a national securities exchange. All companies required to register with the SEC must file regular reports. Not only does the prompt dissemination of information limit the possibilities for insider trading, but it also allows the financial markets to operate more efficiently. To the extent that information is public, the financial markets can process that information so that stock prices reflect that new data.

In addition, the 1934 act sets up the SEC and gives markets like the New York Stock Exchange some power of self-regulation to be exercised with SEC oversight. Furthermore, the SEC is authorized to regulate the extension of credit used to buy securities, trading by members of the exchanges, and manipulative practices by members. It may also suspend trading of securities if necessary. The SEC also regulates brokers and dealers, municipal securities dealers, and others dealing in securities information. The SEC also has the power to establish accounting rules for listed securities that ordinarily is accomplished by deferring to the expertise of the Financial Accounting Standards Board (FASB).

Day-to-Day Oversight

Besides registration and submission of various reports, publicly held companies are regulated concerning their recordkeeping, repurchases of securities, proxy solicitations, director changes, corrupt foreign practices, and many other areas of day-to-day activities. Increasingly, shareholders are putting pressure on corporations to meet various social goals

> Cracker Barrel shareholders wanted the company to bar discrimination against gays

such as reducing employment discrimination. In 1992, Cracker Barrel shareholders wanted the company to bar discrimination against gays. Cracker Barrel refused to include the proposal in its proxy statement so that it could be voted on by all shareholders. The SEC supported Cracker Barrel, saying the proposal dealt with matters of "ordinary business," which companies are not obliged to put to a vote. However, in 1998 the SEC changed positions and decided companies can no longer automatically bar votes on shareholder proposals in "social concern" areas such as affirmative action, sweat shops, and discrimination.

On-line Trading

Traditional stockbrokers are reeling a bit from the new and very aggressive competition from on-line brokers. In early 2000, the traditional brokers complained to the Federal Trade Commission that on-line brokers are making unrealistic promises of quick money and unfairly discrediting the full-service brokers.[4] Those complaints are symptoms of broader concerns about the need for some government oversight in the highly volatile on-line market. From 1996 to 1999, on-line trades grew from fewer than 100,000 per day to more than 500,000.[5] An area of particular concern is labeled *suitability*. Under federal securities rules, brokers have a general responsibility to ensure that their clients' investments are suitable for their financial experience, means, and goals. On-line brokers argue that they have no suitability responsibilities since they often only fill orders, but increasingly the on-line firms are taking steps that amount to recommendations. Of course, an excessive government response could cripple the efficiency virtues of the Internet.

The SEC took its first enforcement action against an online firm in 1999 when Datek Online Brokerage Services Corp. was censured and fined for allegedly using its customers' cash to pay some of its expenses.[6] Then in early 2000, a securities industry arbitration panel ordered Ameritrade to pay Laei Desmond, a medical student, $40,000 for allowing him to make risky investments that were unsuitable for his circumstances.[7]

Day Trading.   A particular concern of regulators is the minute-by-minute stock trading that has become increasingly feasible with the quick and relatively inexpensive on-line trading. These so-called *day traders* often hold stocks for hours or even minutes seeking profits on tiny shifts in prices. In 1999, SEC chair Arthur Levitt Jr. told the United States Senate that an investigation of day trading had uncovered many marketing lies and bad loan policies with companies that provide the computers linking day traders to Wall Street.[8] Levitt compared day trading with gambling and said that 80 percent of the companies investigated engaged in "questionable marketing practices" while half the firms allowed traders to borrow too much money for trading purposes.[9] Nonetheless, in late 1999, the New York Stock Exchange and the National Association of Securities Dealers voted to increase the amount of money that investors can borrow to buy stocks while requiring day traders to keep at least $25,000 in cash and securities in their accounts at all times (up from the general requirement of $2,000). The SEC is considering that proposed change in rules.[10]

Stock Market Reform.   Electronic commerce is rewiring the way securities are traded and threatening Wall Street's longstanding dominance. Globalization and the Internet are moving stock trading toward a 24-hour schedule, and huge numbers of small investors are entering the markets through online trading and electronic communications networks (ECNs). ECNs are automated stock trading systems, such as Island ECN and Instinet, which have been trading extensively in Nasdaq-issued stocks, and offer commission costs that are a fraction of those demanded in the traditional markets. ECNs directly match buyers and sellers, thus eliminating the need to go through brokers and New York Stock Exchange (NYSE) middlemen. They have emerged in recent years as important competitors for the established stock markets. The ECNs have not been allowed to trade all stocks on the Intermarket Trading System (ITS), which links the New York Stock Exchange, regional exchanges, and NASDAQ (a computerized network of dealers) in an electronic order-routing system, but the SEC, seeking more efficient markets, voted in December 1999 to expand the ITS to all NYSE-listed stocks, which will in time give all trading firms full access to Big Board stocks. The ITS ensures that the best price offered by a dealer anywhere in the country will be honored by every United States market.

By summer 2000, Nasdaq expects to have in place a system electronically linking the ECNs and the big market makers such as Merrill Lynch. Likewise, the NYSE is currently developing electronic trading. Those electronic systems will allow investors to easily see the best buy and sell prices. [For the NASDAQ Stock Market, see **http://www. nasdaq.com**]

Rule 390.   Recognizing the new world of stock trading, the New York Stock Exchange is adjusting its trading rules. In December 1999, the NYSE voted to repeal its Rule 390, which had forbade trading certain stocks anywhere but on the Big Board. With full implementation of the 390 repeal, the big brokerage houses and the ECNs will be able to trade in those stocks without going through the NYSE or regional exchanges. Rule 390 is considered anticompetitive, and its repeal will amount to a significant deregulation of America's stock market system.

Self-Regulation.   Both the NYSE and the NASDAQ Stock Market expect in 2000 to move from their longtime structure as membership associations into investor-owned, for-profit enterprises. The 1934 act was designed with the expectation that Wall Street would police itself with the SEC providing oversight. Thus, a big question facing the SEC at this writing is whether it will need to assert more direct regulatory oversight or whether self-regulation can remain viable in the approaching for-profit environment.

Competition.   In the long run, the SEC hopes to build a national market probably consisting, not of a single exchange, but of a rather small number of competing exchanges all electronically linked so that all price quotes could be seen by all investors. Thus, market forces should make stock trading more competitive. Transactions would be faster and cheaper and investors could secure the most desirable prices; that is, the highest possible price when selling and the lowest possible price when buying. Critics of the proposed changes fear either excessive concentration or excessive fragmentation. If we move toward one or a few markets, competition may be reduced, but excessive fragmentation (numerous markets) could lead to price wars that might drain capital from the markets, leading to higher risks for investors.

> In the long run, the SEC hopes to build a national market

TENDER OFFERS

In the 1980s, takeovers became a primary weapon in big business strategy as colorful figures like corporate raider T. Boone Pickens captured front-page attention with their bold and often hostile attempts to buy out desirable targets. Commonly, a takeover is accomplished via a *tender offer*, which is a public bid to the shareholders of the target firm offering to buy shares at a specified price for a defined period of time. A tender offer thus goes past management and directly to the shareholders. When management objects, the takeover is considered hostile. The Williams Act, an amendment to the Securities Act of 1934, regulates all tender offers and forbids various unfair practices in connection with those offers.

SEC Takeover Rules

When one company attempts to take over another, SEC rules can often be crucial. All tender offers must be registered with the SEC. Furthermore, certain disclosure rules are triggered when groups purchase more than 5 percent of a company's outstanding stock.

Takeover Defenses

In recent years, as hostile takeover attempts have become more frequent, many strategies have been developed to limit their success. Typically, management uses state requirements to slow down or eliminate the possibility of a hostile takeover. Takeover candidates use their political clout to convince legislators of the harmful effects a takeover could have for the state in which the business is incorporated or has a major presence. Such economic issues as plant closings, wholesale transfers, or moving the headquarters often strike a responsive chord. From the standpoint of investors, regulators, and raiders, such tactics are troublesome, and they may turn to SEC standards to advance their cause.

Bidders for a company can rely on amendments to the 1934 act to get more information about a target company and to shorten the period of time during which shareholders can decide whether to accept the offer. These amendments also have placed additional restrictions on a company's ability to use state law to fend off a takeover. For instance, in the Mobil-Marathon takeover battle, the *lockout defense* was rejected by the courts. In this maneuver, the target's board opposed a "totally inadequate" offer by giving another friendly corporation (*white knight*) the right to purchase 10 million authorized but unissued shares and a contingent option to purchase a major oil field in the event of a hostile takeover. The purpose of this transaction was to make the takeover candidate more expensive and financially unattractive to the raider. The court held this practice to be manipulative in that it set an artificial ceiling on what the shareholders could expect to receive should the company or its assets be sold. In effect, the shareholders were being harmed in order to keep the company from being sold and to keep existing management in power.

Other Defenses.   Additional defensive strategies include selling large blocks of stock to employees, issuing much new debt, attempting to take over the hostile bidder, requiring that the same sale or exchange terms be offered to all shareholders, mandating that the board or a supermajority of all shareholders must approve takeover bids, selling off the most attractive corporate assets, finding another purchaser, or buying out the bidder at a profit (*greenmail*). Clearly, some of these techniques are more desirable than others from the standpoint of the target, and many, such as taking on substantial new debt or selling off attractive corporate assets (*scorched earth defense*), can seriously damage the long-run prospects of the business.

SECURITIES FRAUD

Section 10(b) of the 1934 act and SEC Rule 10b-5 [implementing the policy Congress established in section 10(b)] are the principal securities law antifraud weapons. Rule 10b-5 prohibits misstatements or omissions of material fact. Although the precise boundaries are not fully clear, the plaintiff ordinarily must show (1) the misstatement or omission was *material,* that is, it was likely to affect the price of the security; (2) the defendant acted with *scienter,* that is, the fraud was intentional or, according to many courts, the product of gross recklessness; or (3) the plaintiff *relied on* the defendant's fraud. [For a powerful database on Securities Fraud, see **http://securities.stanford.edu/about/caveat.html**]

   In an interesting example of the influence of free market financial reasoning on the law, some courts have adopted the *fraud-on-the-market theory* allowing investors to demonstrate reliance merely by showing they bought shares and in so doing assumed the integrity of the price set by the market. The fraud-on-the-market hypothesis is that in an open and developed securities market the price of a stock will reflect all of the available material information about that stock. The market absorbs all of that material information and transforms it into the market price. Thus, when buying stock one automatically relies on its price as an accurate measure of its value given the available information.

For every interesting, efficient, potentially profitable investment, some enterprising person thinks of an equally interesting, almost always profitable, but fraudulent form of that same investment. Promising "fabulous returns," the Ostrich Group, Inc., sold contracts for the sale and boarding of breeding pairs of ostriches to investors. The SEC charged the four Ostrich Group principals with civil fraud for allegedly using most of the money on personal expenses rather than for buying and boarding ostriches. "They told investors they had 247 breeder ostriches when in fact they only had 2 breeders and maybe 20 chicks," said Joel Kornfeld, the senior SEC trial attorney on the case. The Ostrich Group owners were ordered to repay nearly $2 million plus interest.

   Source: Bloomberg News, "O.C. Man to Repay Ostrich Farm Investors," *Los Angeles Times,* June 4, 1999, p. C7.

Fraud Limits

In December 1995, Congress overrode President Clinton's veto to enact the Private Securities Litigation Reform Act, which is designed to stop groundless fraud claims, especially class actions, by angry investors whose stock purchases went awry. Critics say the bill provides too much protection for the investment community and effectively closes the courthouse door for many wronged investors. The bill, which imposes substantial limitations on private fraud actions under the 1933 and 1934 acts, will be clarified by judicial interpretation, but its primary ingredients include significant protections for the financial community:

- It creates a safe harbor from legal liability for forward-looking statements about company prospects. Those forecasts must, however, be accompanied by warnings about risks. This provision allows companies to more safely publicize earnings and new product projections.
- It requires a plaintiff's fraud pleading (the complaint initiating the case) to include facts showing that the defendant intentionally engaged in misleading behavior. Failure to provide that proof would prevent moving to the discovery stage of a trial, in which the plaintiff can search for damaging evidence.
- It protects accountants and securities underwriters whose clients have engaged in fraud. The bill abolishes *joint and several liability* for those secondary defendants who audited the books or did the underwriting for a firm that engaged in fraud but subsequently went broke. Traditionally, under joint and several liability each participant in a tortious act like fraud can be held fully liable for damages, which made the deep pockets of the secondary defendants particularly desirable and vulnerable. Now, with very limited exceptions, those accountants and underwriters can be liable only for the portion of the harm they actually caused as well as a 50 percent premium in cases where the principal defendant is insolvent.
- It gives the SEC authority to sue those who aid and abet the commission of fraud. Private investors do not have that power.

The States?   The 1995 Reform Act spurred lawyers to take their securities fraud cases to state courts to avoid the new federal standards. Congress was, therefore, inspired to pass the Securities Litigation Uniform Standards Act of 1998, which requires securities fraud class action cases involving nationally traded securities to be tried in federal courts under federal law. A big motivation for both laws was to protect start-up companies and their notoriously volatile stock prices from being abusively sued merely because their share prices plummet. Further, companies can now safely make candid disclosures to investors. Individuals and classes of 50 and fewer can still sue in state courts, but the financial incentives for doing so are diminished when the class is small. Of course, other routes to remedies remain. [For two securities class action designated Internet sites, see **http://securities.milberg.com/** and **http://securities.stanford.edu**]

Ethics Question

> Is it fair to substantially deprive defrauded investors of the deep pockets of large public accounting firms?

Accounting firms paid an estimated $1.6 billion in fraud claims arising out of the 1980s savings and loan crisis, in large part because the savings and loan operations audited by the accounting firms often were insolvent. As noted, the Private Securities Litigation Reform Act permits liability only for the portion of the fraud that is directly attributable to the responsible accountants. Is it fair to substantially deprive defrauded investors of the deep pockets of large public accounting firms? Explain.

RICO

The 1970 Racketeer Influenced and Corrupt Organizations Act (*RICO*), which was originally designed to stop organized crime activities, has often been used to pursue securities fraud. However, the 1995 Private Securities Litigation Reform Act (discussed above) amends RICO to explicitly preclude its use for securities fraud claims except where a criminal fraud conviction has been obtained. Clearly, the point of the amendment was to force plaintiffs to use the securities laws rather than RICO (with its appealing treble damages provision), although the precise implications of the amendment will not be clear until tested in court.[11] [For a RICO summary, see **http://www.lectlaw.com/files/cri18.htm**]

Insider Trading

The use of inside information for financial profit in securities transactions is called *insider trading* and might be subject to civil, criminal, and regulatory liability. Congress and the SEC have taken the position that fairness as well as confidence in our securities markets requires that insiders be forbidden from trading on information not available to the general public. Various laws forbid insider trading, but it is most commonly pursued as a form of fraud in violation of Section 10(b) of the 1934 act and SEC Rule 10b-5 which is a clarification of Section 10(b). Unfortunately, we have no official definition of insider trading. Further, we have a great debate about who should be treated as an insider. Much of the world only tepidly restricts insider trading and wonders why we in America find it so troublesome. Many critics argue that much insider trading is actually beneficial and the problem, if there is one, should be left to the market. Nonetheless, after a period of relative quiet, we have recently seen a significant increase in SEC insider investigations. Much of the activity appears to be triggered by the recent wave of mergers and acquisitions that provides insiders with privileged information about impending deals and presents a very big temptation to trade (illegally) on that information.

The Law.   The philosophical debate aside, once a person is determined to have inside information the rules on insider trading appear to be very simple—anyone who has access to nonpublic information of a material nature (such as a recent oil strike, results of a major lawsuit, huge earnings increases, an impending takeover bid) must (1) refrain from trading in the stock and from telling friends, relatives, and others to trade in the stock or (2) release the information to the public, wait a reasonable period of time, and then trade as desired.

Not surprisingly, the simplicity of those rules turns out to be deceptive. In practice, insider trading is an area of enormous uncertainty, as evidenced by the following discussion of short-swing profits, Rule 10b-5, and temporary insiders. [For a detailed explanation of the law of insider trading, see **http://encyclo.findlaw.com/lit/5650art.htm**]

Short-Swing Profits

One of the earliest SEC concerns was that insiders would use access to financial reports and other data to buy (or sell) shares just prior to releasing positive (negative) information about the company and then almost immediately sell (or buy) back the shares at a profit when the market price of the stock had responded to this new information. In an attempt to limit the ability of major participants in corporate affairs to gain a short-term economic advantage due to their early access to earnings reports and other inside, nonpublic information that might cause a change in stock prices when made public, the 1934 act prohibits officers, directors, and 10 percent beneficial owners of a corporation from receiving *short-swing profits*. These are any profits made on company stock held for less than six months. Any such profits must be returned to the company whether or not inside information was used to secure that profit.

Rule 10b–5

The prohibition against short-swing profits leaves open the possibility that an *insider* could still profit by buying (selling) shares just prior to the release of positive (negative) information but then refraining from trading for at least six months. While the trade would not trigger the short-swing profits provision, it would still be insider trading under Rule 10b-5, and the insider could be prosecuted. Although the short-swing profits restriction spells out exactly who is an insider and what transactions are forbidden, the persons and behavior covered by Rule 10b-5 can be much less clear. In recent years, the question of who is an insider under Rule 10b-5 and the conditions under which someone can be held liable for dealing in insider information have been in a state of flux. Clearly, corporate officers, directors, and attorneys may have access to inside information; but so could brokers, analysts, printers, and journalists.

Selective Disclosure.   Companies often disclose important inside information to securities analysts and large investors before providing that information to the general public. In late 1999, the SEC proposed a new rule that would require a company to issue a press release or otherwise inform the general public of market-moving information at the same time that information is made available to select audiences. The SEC has noted a great deal of "unusual trading" following selective disclosures leading the agency to believe that the practice reduces investor confidence and is simply unfair to those not receiving the early notices. Critics of the proposed rule, on the other hand, think it will restrict the flow of useful information.

Temporary Insiders and Outsiders

Insider trading is rooted, generally, in the notion of breach of *fiduciary duty;* that is, insiders should not seek to profit in ways that violate their responsibilities to the firm and its shareholders. That same responsibility can also extend to those who are not technically insiders, but nonetheless are in possession of inside information. Temporary insiders such as consultants, accountants, engineers, and lawyers would breach their fiduciary duty if they traded personally on information they acquired in their inside work or if they tipped others.

Outsiders are all those people who might indirectly receive inside information. Although the subject of great controversy, recent court decisions have increasingly found some outsiders to be guilty of insider trading. That guilt springs generally from two theories: the tipper/tippee theory and the misappropriation theory.

Tipper/Tippee Theory.   A *tipper* (one who conveys inside information to another) violates the law if (1) the tip is used in trading, (2) the tip constitutes a breach of the tipper's fiduciary duty, and (3) the tipper receives a personal benefit of some kind from the disclosure. The recipient of that information (the *tippee*) even though an outsider— commonly a friend or relative—likewise may not lawfully trade on inside information if he or she knew or should have known that the tipper was violating a fiduciary duty in disclosing the information.

James J. McDermott, former investment banking CEO, and "porn" actress, Kathryn B. "Marylin Star" Gannon, were indicted in late 1999 for allegedly engaging in illegal inside trading. McDermott is accused of giving nonpublic information about at least six pending bank mergers to Ms. Gannon, allegedly his mistress at the time, who then allegedly traded on the information to earn at least $88,000. Ms. Gannon supplemented her income with a Marylin Star "love doll," which was sold over the Internet for $69.99.

Source: Sandra Sugawara, "Banker, Porn Actress Charged with Insider Stock Trading," *Washington Post,* December 22, 1999, p. A1.

Misappropriation Theory.   Outsiders may also be guilty of violating Rule 10b-5 if they wrongfully secure material, nonpublic information and tip or trade on it for personal gain—this is known as *misappropriation.* The outsider might be a lawyer, an underwriter, a printer who distributes SEC-required documents, or even a therapist. In effect, the outsider has stolen the information. In doing so, if the outsider has breached a fiduciary duty

> In an unusually egregious breach of trust, a California psychotherapist used information secured in an August 1994 therapy session

to the source of the information, a misappropriation claim may be raised. In an unusually egregious breach of trust, a California psychotherapist used information secured in an August 1994 therapy session and employed it to earn trading profits (with a partner) of over $177,000. The psychotherapist, a veteran of 35 years in practice, was engaging in marriage counseling with an executive who mentioned that his employer, Lockheed, was approaching a major financial deal. The therapist immediately traded on that information and profited when Lockheed and Martin Marietta merged a few days after the counseling session. In 1995, the therapist pleaded guilty to one criminal count of insider trading and settled SEC civil charges for $110,000. As a matter of law, the therapist misappropriated the information that he had received in confidence, thus breaching his fiduciary relationship with the executive.[12]

In the *O'Hagan* case that follows, the Supreme Court addressed the misappropriation theory.

UNITED STATES v. O'HAGAN
521 U.S. 642 (1997)

Justice Ginsburg

I

Respondent James Herman O'Hagan was a partner in the law firm of Dorsey & Whitney in Minneapolis, Minnesota. In July 1988, Grand Metropolitan PLC (Grand Met), a company based in London, England, retained Dorsey & Whitney as local counsel to represent Grand Met regarding a potential tender offer for the common stock of the Pillsbury Company, headquartered in Minneapolis. Both Grand Met and Dorsey & Whitney took precautions to protect the confidentiality of Grand Met's tender offer plans. O'Hagan did no work on the Grand Met representation. Dorsey & Whitney withdrew from representing Grand Met on September 9, 1988. Less than a month later, on October 4, 1988, Grand Met publicly announced its tender offer for Pillsbury stock.

On August 18, 1988, while Dorsey & Whitney was still representing Grand Met, O'Hagan began purchasing call options for Pillsbury stock. Each option gave him the right to purchase 100 shares of Pillsbury stock by a specified date in September 1988. Later in August and in September, O'Hagan made additional purchases of Pillsbury call options. By the end of September, he

owned 2,500 unexpired Pillsbury options, apparently more than any other individual investor. O'Hagan also purchased, in September 1988, some 5,000 shares of Pillsbury common stock, at a price just under $39 per share. When Grand Met announced its tender offer in October, the price of Pillsbury stock rose to nearly $60 per share. O'Hagan then sold his Pillsbury call options and common stock, making a profit of more than $4.3 million.

The Securities and Exchange Commission (SEC or Commission) initiated an investigation into O'Hagan's transactions, culminating in a 57-count indictment. The indictment alleged that O'Hagan defrauded his law firm and its client, Grand Met, by using for his own trading purposes material, nonpublic information regarding Grand Met's planned tender offer. According to the indictment, O'Hagan used the profits he gained through this trading to conceal his previous embezzlement and conversion of unrelated client trust funds. O'Hagan was charged with 17 counts of securities fraud, in violation of § 10(b) of the Securities Exchange Act of 1934 (Exchange Act) and SEC Rule 10b-5. A jury convicted

O'Hagan, and he was sentenced to a 41-month term of imprisonment.

* * * * *

A divided panel of the Court of Appeals for the Eighth Circuit reversed all of O'Hagan's convictions. Liability under § 10(b) and Rule 10b-5, the Eighth Circuit held, may not be grounded on the "misappropriation theory" of securities fraud on which the prosecution relied . . .

II

We address first the Court of Appeals' reversal of O'Hagan's convictions § 10(b) and Rule 10b-5.

* * * * *

A

Under the "traditional" or "classical theory" of insider trading liability, § 10(b) and Rule 10b-5 are violated when a corporate insider trades in the securities of his corporation on the basis of material, nonpublic information. Trading on such information qualifies as a "deceptive device" under § 10(b), we have affirmed, because "a relationship of trust and confidence [exists] between the shareholders of a corporation and those insiders who have obtained confidential information by reason of their position with that corporation." That relationship, we recognized, "gives rise to a duty to disclose [or to abstain from trading] because of the 'necessity of preventing a corporate insider from . . . taking unfair advantage of . . . uninformed . . . stockholders.'" The classical theory applies not only to officers, directors, and other permanent insiders of a corporation, but also to attorneys, accountants, consultants, and others who temporarily become fiduciaries of a corporation.

The "misappropriation theory" holds that a person commits fraud "in connection with" a securities transaction, and thereby violates § 10(b) and Rule 10b-5 when he misappropriates confidential information for securities trading purposes, in breach of a duty owed to the source of the information. Under this theory, a fiduciary's undisclosed, self-serving use of a principal's information to purchase or sell securities, in breach of a duty of loyalty and confidentiality, defrauds the principal of the exclusive use of that information.

The two theories are complementary, each addressing efforts to capitalize on nonpublic information through the purchase or sale of securities. The classical theory targets a corporate insider's breach of duty to shareholders with whom the insider transacts; the misappropriation theory outlaws trading on the basis of nonpublic information by a corporate "outsider" in breach of a duty owed not to a trading party, but to the source of the information. The misappropriation theory is thus designed to "protect the integrity of the securities markets against abuses by 'outsiders' to a corporation who have access to confidential information that will affect the corporation's security price when revealed, but who owe no fiduciary or other duty to that corporation's shareholders."

In this case, the indictment alleged that O'Hagan, in breach of a duty of trust and confidence he owed to his law firm, Dorsey & Whitney, and to its client, Grand Met, traded on the basis of nonpublic information regarding Grand Met's planned tender offer for Pillsbury common stock. This conduct, the Government charged, constituted a fraudulent device in connection with the purchase and sale of securities.

B

[M]isappropriation, as just defined, satisfies § 10(b)'s requirement that chargeable conduct involve a "deceptive device or contrivance" used "in connection with" the purchase or sale of securities. [M]isappropriators deal in deception. A fiduciary who "[pretends] loyalty to the principal while secretly converting the principal's information for personal gain," "dupes" or defrauds the principal . . . A company's confidential information qualifies as property to which the company has a right of exclusive use. The undisclosed misappropriation of such information, in violation of a fiduciary duty, constitutes fraud akin to embezzlement . . . Deception through nondisclosure is central to . . . the misappropriation theory . . . 10(b) is not an all-purpose breach of fiduciary duty ban; rather, it trains on conduct involving manipulation or deception. [F]ull disclosure forecloses liability under the misappropriation theory: [I]f the fiduciary discloses to the source that he plans to trade on the nonpublic information, there is no "deceptive device" and thus no § 10(b) violation . . .

We turn next to the § 10(b) requirement that the misappropriator's deceptive use of information be "in connection with the purchase or sale of [a] security." This element is satisfied because the fiduciary's fraud is consummated, not when the fiduciary gains the confidential information, but when, without disclosure to his principal, he uses the information to purchase or sell securities. The securities transaction and the breach of duty thus coincide. This is so even though the person or entity defrauded is not the other party to the trade, but is, instead, the source of the nonpublic information. A misappropriator who trades on the basis of material, nonpublic information, in short, gains his advantageous market position through deception; he deceives the source of the information and simultaneously harms members of the investing public.

* * * * *

The misappropriation theory comports with § 10(b)'s language, which requires deception "in connection with the purchase or sale of any security," not deception of an identifiable purchaser or seller. The theory is also well-tuned to an animating purpose of the Exchange Act: to insure honest securities markets and thereby promote investor confidence. Although informational disparity is inevitable in the securities markets, investors likely would hesitate to venture their capital in a market where trading based on misappropriated nonpublic information is unchecked by law.

* * * * *

[I]t makes scant sense to hold a lawyer like O'Hagan a § 10(b) violator if he works for a law firm representing the target of a tender offer, but not if he works for a law firm representing the bidder. The text of the statute requires no such result. The misappropriation at issue here was properly made the subject of a § 10(b) charge because it meets the statutory requirement that there be "deceptive" conduct "in connection with" securities transactions.

C

The Court of Appeals rejected the misappropriation theory primarily on two grounds. First, as the Eighth Circuit comprehended the theory, it requires neither misrepresentation nor nondisclosure. As we just explained, however, deceptive nondisclosure is essential to the § 10(b) liability at issue. Concretely, in this case, "it [was O'Hagan's] failure to disclose his personal trading to Grand Met and Dorsey, in breach of his duty to do so, that made his conduct 'deceptive' within the meaning of [§]10(b)."

Second and "more obvious," the Court of Appeals said, the misappropriation theory is not moored to § 10(b)'s requirement that "the fraud be 'in connection with the purchase or sale of any security." According to the Eighth Circuit, three of our decisions reveal that § 10(b)

liability cannot be predicated on a duty owed to the source of nonpublic information . . . We read the statute and our precedent differently, and note again that § 10(b) refers to "the purchase or sale of any security," not to identifiable purchasers or sellers of securities.

* * * * *

Vital to our decision that criminal liability may be sustained under the misappropriation theory, we emphasize, are two sturdy safeguards Congress has provided regarding scienter. To establish a criminal violation of Rule 10b-5, the Government must prove that a person "willfully" violated the provision. Furthermore, a defendant may not be imprisoned for violating Rule 10b-5 if he proves that he had no knowledge of the rule . . .

The Eighth Circuit erred in holding that the misappropriation theory is inconsistent with § 10(b).

[Reversed and remanded.]

Afterword

O'Hagan officially endorses the misappropriation theory, but difficult problems remain. At this writing in early 2000, both the courts and the SEC are grappling with two misappropriation-related issues:

1. If other requirements are met, can an inside trading case succeed where the insider was merely *aware* of the inside information or must she have *used* the information?
2. Is a fiduciary relationship *presumed* to exist when inside information is provided by a spouse, parent, child, or sibling of the receiver of the information?

Questions

1. Explain the Court's decision that misappropriation is the proper subject of a § 10(b) charge.
2. What public policy consideration weighed heavily in the Court's decision?
3. In 1998, a university researcher was accused of telling a group of California physicians about disappointing results of late-stage testing on an experimental drug to treat hepatitis B. The doctors allegedly then profited by, among other strategies, selling stocks in the two drug companies that were developing and marketing the drug. Do those sales constitute unlawful inside trading? Explain.

INTERNET EXERCISE

Using [**www.securitieslaw.com/**] answer the following questions:

1. What duties are owed by stockbrokers and brokerage firms to customers?
2. How does a customer know when he or she has been defrauded?

CHAPTER QUESTIONS

1. Today the SEC, the stock exchanges, and the states share regulatory authority over securities transactions. Would both the securities traders and the public be better served by having one independent regulatory agency with authority over the entire industry? Explain.
2. Do we need closer SEC oversight of investment-related Internet chat rooms? Explain.
3. Your broker recommends buying stock in a little-known company. The broker appears to have had access to inside information, but you do not ask any questions. Can you legally buy stock in that company? Explain.
4. Define (*a*) security, (*b*) private placements, (*c*) blue sky laws, (*d*) fraud, (*e*) short-swing profits, (*f*) tender offers, (*g*) registration, and (*h*) prospectus.
5. Discuss the exemptions available for certain types of securities.
6. Explain how federal securities laws attempt to make provisions for small businesses.
7. Ivan Landreth and his sons owned all of the stock in a lumber business they operated in Tonasket, Washington. The owners offered the stock for sale. During that time a fire severely damaged the business, but the owners made assurances of rebuilding and modernization. The stock was sold to Dennis and Bolten, and a new organization, Landreth Timber Company, was formed with the senior Landreth remaining as a consultant on the side. The new firm was unsuccessful and was sold at a loss. The Landreth Timber Company then filed suit against Ivan Landreth and his son seeking rescission of the first sale, alleging, among other arguments, that Landreth and sons had widely offered and then sold their stock without registering it as required by the Securities Act of 1933. The district court acknowledged that *stocks* fit within the definition of a *security,* and that the stock in question "possessed all of the characteristics of conventional stock." However, it held that the federal securities laws do not apply to the sale of 100 percent of the stock of a closely held corporation. Here, the district court found that the purchasers had not entered into the sale with the expectation of earnings secured via the labor of others. Managerial control resided with the purchasers. Thus, the sale was a commercial venture rather than a typical investment. The Court of Appeals affirmed, and the case reached the Supreme Court. Decide. See *Landreth Timber Co.* v. *Landreth,* 471 U.S. 681 (1985).
8. For two years, representatives of Basic Incorporated and Combustion Engineering, Inc., had engaged in various meetings and conversations regarding the possibility of a merger. During that time, Basic issued three public statements indicating that no merger talks were in progress. Then, in 1978 the two firms merged. Some Basic shareholders had sold their stock between the first public denial of merger talks and the time when the merger was announced. Those stockholders filed a class action claiming Basic had made false and misleading statements in violation of Section 10(b) of the 1934 Securities Act and SEC Rule 10b-5. The plaintiff stockholders claimed they had suffered injury by selling their stocks at prices artificially depressed by the allegedly false statements. They argued that they would not have sold their stocks had they been truthfully informed of the merger talks. The trial court, in finding for Basic, took the position that preliminary merger discussions are immaterial. But the lower court certified (approved) the stockholders' class action, saying that reliance by the plaintiffs on Basic's statements could be presumed (and thus reliance need not be proved by each plaintiff in turn). In certifying the class action, the lower court embraced the efficient-market theory or the fraud-on-the-market theory. The court of appeals agreed with the lower court's class action certification based on

efficient-market reasoning, but the appeals court reversed the immateriality finding regarding preliminary discussions. The case went to the Supreme Court.

    a. Explain the efficient-market theory and its role in this case.

    b. Decide the materiality issue. Explain.

See *Basic, Inc.* v. *Max L. Levinson,* 485 U.S. 224 (1988).

9. Christopher Farrell commented in *Business Week* regarding the 1987 stock market crash, which resulted in an immediate 23 percent "devaluation of corporate America":

> Economists will argue for years over what caused the crash of 1987. But it's already clear that the October 19 cataclysm marks the failure of the most pervasive belief in economics today: an unquestioning faith in the wisdom of free markets.

Do you agree? Explain. See "Where Was the Invisible Hand?" *Business Week,* April 18, 1988, p. 65.

10. This chapter addresses insider trading and other suspect practices in the securities markets. Commentator George Will thinks those, and similar problems, as popularized in the movie *Wall Street,* are "draining capitalism of its legitimacy":

> A moral vulnerability of capitalism today is the belief that too much wealth is allocated capriciously, not only by the randomness of luck but by morally tainted short-cuts around a level playing field for all competitors. The legitimacy of the economic order depends on a consensus that, on balance, rewards are rationally related to the social value of the effort involved.

Do you agree? Explain. See "Capitalist Flaws Should Worry GOP," *Des Moines Register,* December 30, 1987, p. 6A.

11. From a free market point of view, restraints on insider trading do not make a great deal of sense.

    a. Explain that view.

    b. Do you agree with the free market position? Explain.

NOTES

1. *Smith* v. *Van Gorkom,* 488 A.2d 858 (Del. S.Ct. 1985).

2. *Securities & Exchange Commission* v. *W. J. Howey Co.,* 328 U.S. 293 (1946).

3. In 1995 the Supreme Court ruled that liability for omissions or misstatements under section 12(2) of the 1933 act is limited in its reach to the initial public offering and thus does not apply to later purchases of that stock. See *Gustafson* v. *Alloyd Company,* 115 S.Ct. 1061 (1995).

4. Associated Press, "On-line Ads by Brokerages Draw Complaint," *Waterloo–Cedar Falls Courier,* February 1, 2000, p. B5.

5. Gretchen Morgenson, "Regulators See Need for Rules of the Road for Online Trading Firms," *New York Times,* November 23, 1999, sec. C, p. 1.

6. Associated Press, "SEC Fines, Censures On-Line Brokerage; Settlement Is 1st Action Taken by US Against Net Trading Firm," *Boston Globe,* May 19, 1999, p. D2.

7. Rebecca Buckman, "Student Awarded $40,000 from Firm in Trading Case," *The Wall Street Journal,* January 17, 2000, sec C, p. 16.

8. Ianthe Jeanne Dugan, "Day-Trading Firms Faulted," *Washington Post,* September 17, 1999, p. E1.

9. Ibid.

10. Ianthe Jeanne Dugan, "New Rules Proposed for Day Traders," *Washington Post,* December 11, 1999, p. E1.

11. See "Congress Passes Bill Removing Securities Fraud from RICO's List of Predicate Acts," *Civil RICO Report* 11, no. 16 (February 5, 1996).

12. Ralph Vartabedian, "Therapist Pleads Guilty to Insider Lockheed Deal," *The Wall Street Journal,* December 14, 1995, p. D1.

Chapter 10

Antitrust Law—Monopolies and Mergers

INTRODUCTION

The Microsoft *monopoly* case has given Americans a valuable lesson in the obscure law of antitrust. In April 2000, United States District Court Judge Thomas Penfield Jackson ruled that Microsoft is a monopoly that maintained its power by anti-competitive means. Judge Jackson concluded that Microsoft controlled 95 percent of the Intel-compatible operating systems market, that no viable alternative was available to consumers, and that potential competitors faced high barriers to entry. That control of the market, the Judge concluded, allowed Microsoft to engage in anticompetitive behavior including:

- Attempting to monopolize the browser market.
- Using its market power in Windows to persuade IBM, Compaq, and others to favor Microsoft products over those of its competitors.
- Hampering innovation in software by demonstrating to potential competitors that it would use the fullness of its monopoly resources to combat entry.
- Tying its Internet Explorer to Windows 98 thus making it more difficult for consumers to make their own choice of browsers (e.g., Netscape's Navigator).

At this writing, the federal government has recommended dividing Microsoft into a pair of companies; one in operating systems, the other in application software. Judge Jackson will decide on a remedy with a settlement or an appeal likely to follow. Regardless, the central policy questions raised by the Microsoft battle will not be answered in the courts alone.

"Americans by 49 percent to 41 percent disagree with Judge Thomas Penfield Jackson's finding that Microsoft is a monopoly. And by 52 percent to 29 percent they don't think Microsoft should be broken up. 'We don't use polls to enforce the law,' responds one federal official."

Source: Ronald G. Shafer, "People's Court," *The Wall Street Journal*, December 17, 1999, p. A1.

Power.   The big civic virtue of the Microsoft battle has been the opportunity and the responsibility for all of us to think about the appropriateness of government intervention in business practice. More broadly yet, we have been obliged to think about what we want America to be and what role the law should play in securing that ideal. This chapter is designed to explore those same themes. Antitrust law is remote from our daily lives, but by thinking about the Microsoft case and other, less publicized decisions we can learn the rudiments of that law while thinking carefully about how much faith we want to place in the free market. The article that follows condemns the increasing concentration of wealth and power in the hands of a small number of corporate giants and wealthy individuals.

PERSPECTIVE ON ANTITRUST:
KEEP AN EYE ON THE MONOPOLISTS

Jeff Gates

Like Br'er Rabbit tossed into the briar patch, Bill Gates must be laughing at his predicament in the Microsoft antitrust case, particularly the mindlessly narrow scope of suggested remedies. Who could blame him? Both the Justice Department and U.S. District Judge Thomas Penfield Jackson missed the point of antitrust.

It should come as no surprise in these market-myopic times that the case turned on the narrow issue of competition. Yet that confuses the means with the end. The trust-busters of the 1890s had no idea how markets would be dominated a century later. That wasn't the issue. The target was not the monopoly but the monopolists—the economic royalists with their kingly prerogatives—and the keen dangers they pose to democracy. That's why they urged that monopolies be broken up and their forbidden fruits dispersed.

Jefferson and Madison were similarly insistent. They warned about monarchical tendencies in the marketplace and the impossibility of maintaining a robust democracy alongside an economic oligarchy. Yet that's what today's market-obsessed perspective has wrought. The financial wealth of the top 1% of Americans now exceeds the combined net worth of the bottom 95%, according to New York University economist Edward Wolff. Gates' wealth alone exceeds the net worth of the bottom 45%. The personal assets of Microsoft co-founders Paul Allen and Gates plus Berkshire Hathaway's Warren Buffet exceed the combined gross domestic products of the world's 41 poorest countries, with their 550 million citizens. So much for being a beacon of hope for democracy.

*   *   *   *   *

It's easy to pick on Gates. But he's just the most visible tip of this nation's plutocratic iceberg. The wealth of the Forbes 400 richest Americans grew by an average $940 million each over the past two years (topping a combined $1 trillion). That's while the modest net worth of the bottom 40% shrunk by 80% between 1983 and 1995. For the well-to-do, that's an average increase in wealth of $1.3 million per day. Eighty-six percent of stock market gains between 1989 and 1997 were harvested by the top 10% of households, while fully 42% flowed to the topmost 1%.

Over the past three years, we've seen $3.7 trillion in mergers in the United States alone, topped by this week's $163.4-billion blending of America Online and Time Warner. Monday saw Time Warner Vice Chairman

Ted Turner's net worth jump by $2.53 billion. That's more than the entire value of Turner Broadcasting System prior to its 1996 merger with Time Warner.

Why would we allow our 400 richest citizens to monopolize assets equivalent to one-eighth of the GDP? Meanwhile, as of 1997, the median household financial wealth (net worth less home equity) totaled $11,700, $1,300 less than in 1989. So now we've allowed unfettered markets to undermine not only democracy but our fiscal well-being as well, leaving 76 million baby boomers with votes yet virtually no assets, a certain formula for a politically fractious future.

Microsoft must be forced to divest its key components, including breaking up the operating system division into several firms. It's tempting to impose a conduct remedy akin to saying: Go out and sin no more. Or to simplistically order a spinoff of its operating system division. That's about what I'd expect from today's market-obsessives. Yet the only remedy consistent with antitrust's market-taming intention is a structural one that not only breaks up the monopoly but also reallocates wealth from the monopolists' ill-gotten gains.

In civil antitrust suits, the law allows highly punitive treble damages. Instead, Microsoft could be ordered to sell off its components for one-third their appraised value. Major shareholders could be required to accept in payment a non-interest-bearing note, with the principal paid solely from future sales generated by those independent operations.

In truth, that may be too generous, as it would allow the monopolists to retain a huge component of their loot along with the ability to recover the balance to the extent that the successor companies can succeed in a genuinely competitive market. Yet any more traditional bust-up will further reward the offending parties, while conduct remedies are even worse.

Contrary to the misplaced focus of the current debate, antitrust isn't just about monopolizing markets. Never was. It's about redressing the antidemocratic results that accompany abuse of the market. To address only the means while leaving intact the gains mocks the very rationale for antitrust.

Microsoft's breakup should include financed-stakes that foster widespread ownership of this market-dominant behemoth. Preferred stakes should be reserved not only for employees and independent contractors but also for those employed by suppliers, distributors and even those customers and competitors who make up the web of this company's much-abused market relationships.

Source: *Los Angeles Times,* January 12, 2000; Metro, Part B; p. 7. Reprinted by permission. [For more on Jeff Gates and his view of free enterprise, see **www.sharedcapitalism.org**]

Questions

1. *a.* Do you see increasing concentration of wealth and power as a threat to America's long-term welfare? Explain.
   b. If that concentration is a concern, is antitrust law the best remedy?
2. *a.* Jeff Gates, in the foregoing article, says antitrust is about "redressing the antidemocratic results that accompany abuse of the market." Explain what he means.
   b. Do you favor Gates's plea for "shared capitalism?" Explain.
3. Does the Microsoft case stand simply for the view that bigness is bad? Explain.
4. Critics have argued that technology is eliminating the imperfections of the market, making antitrust law enforcement obsolete in this high-tech era.
   a. Explain that argument.
   b. Now build the argument that high-tech industries may actually be especially susceptible to antitrust problems because of the need to maintain the compatibility of equipment (like the dominance of the VHS format in the video business).

ANTITRUST—EARLY GOALS

Antitrust, perhaps more than any other branch of the law, is a product of changing political and economic tides. Historically, antitrust law sought, broadly expressed, to maintain an approach to life where every American, at least in theory, had the opportunity to reach the top. More specifically, antitrust advocates were concerned about the following issues:

1. *The preservation of competition.* Antitrust law was designed to provide free, open markets permitting the virtues of capitalism to be fully expressed. The belief was (and continues to be) that competition would bring the best products and services at the lowest possible prices.
2. *The preservation of democracy.* Many businesses in competition meant that none of them could corner economic, political, or social power.
3. *The preservation of small businesses, or more generally, the preservation of the American Dream.* Antitrust was designed to preserve the opportunity for the "little people" to compete with the giants.
4. At least for a segment of society, antitrust laws were *an expression of political radicalism.* Those laws were meant to be tools for reshaping America to meet the needs of all of the people, rather than those of big business.

During President Ronald Reagan's tenure, a free market mentality dominated, and reliance on antitrust law declined. While the federal government continued to avidly pursue collusion between competitors and certain other antitrust violations, the prevailing temperament was that the market would function most effectively in the absence of government intervention.

Antitrust Resurgent

Today in the federal courts, conservative Reagan/Bush judges remain powerful, and antitrust, while important in ensuring a competitive economy, is certainly not being used aggressively as a lever for social change. The political and sociological concerns noted above, while not abandoned, have taken a back seat to efficiency considerations and to rather pragmatic, case-by-case consideration of the economic facts. Nonetheless, recent developments, including the *Microsoft* case, demonstrate that antitrust is playing a dramatically reinvigorated role in American economic policy. (Of course, a change to a Republican presidency in the 2000 elections would likely diminish immediate attention to antitrust.)

Do not misunderstand. The government is not routinely intervening in the market. Nor do these signals suggest any rejection of the general idea of deregulation. What we are seeing is a more centrist role for antitrust where, in appropriate cases, the legal system will be employed to deal with market imperfections. [For an extensive overview of the Federal Justice Department's Antitrust Division, see **http://www.usdoj.gov/atr/index.html**]

Part One—The Foundation of Antitrust Law

ANTITRUST STATUTES

A brief look at the various antitrust statutes will place them in historical context.

Sherman Antitrust Act, 1890

Section 1 of the Sherman Antitrust Act forbids restraints of trade, and Section 2 forbids monopolization, attempts to monopolize, and conspiracies to monopolize. Two types of enforcement options are available to the federal government:

1. Violation of the Sherman Act opens participants to criminal penalties. The maximum corporate fine is $10 million per violation, while individuals may be fined $350,000 and/or imprisoned for three years. Sherman Act violations are classified as felonies.
2. Injunctive relief is provided under the civil law. The government or a private party may secure a court order preventing continuing violations of the act and affording appropriate relief (such as dissolution or divestiture).

Perhaps the most important remedy is available to private parties. An individual or organization harmed by a violation of the act may bring a civil action seeking three times the damages (treble damages) actually sustained. Thus, the victim is compensated, and the wrongdoer is punished.

Clayton Act, 1914

Sherman forbade the continued practice of specified anticompetitive conduct, but it did not forbid conduct that was *likely to lead to* anticompetitive behavior. Furthermore, many felt that judicial interpretations of Sherman had seriously weakened that legislation: hence, the 1914 approval of the Clayton Act. The Clayton Act forbids price discrimination, exclusive dealing, tying arrangements, requirements contracts, mergers restraining commerce or tending to create a monopoly, and interlocking directorates.

Civil enforcement of the Clayton Act is similar to the Sherman Act in that the government may sue for injunctive relief, and private parties may seek treble damages. Injunctive relief was also extended to private parties under both the Clayton and Sherman Acts. In general, criminal law remedies are not available under the Clayton Act.

Federal Trade Commission Act (FTC)

The Federal Trade Commission Act created a powerful, independent agency designed to devote its full attention to the elimination of anticompetitive practices in American commerce. The FTC proceeds under the Sherman Act, the Clayton Act, and Section 5 of the FTC Act itself, which declares unlawful "unfair methods of competition" and "unfair or deceptive acts or practices in or affecting commerce." The commission's primary enforcement device is the cease and desist order, but fines may be imposed. The agency's action is subject to judicial review under the principles articulated in Chapter 8. [For the FTC home page, see **http://www.ftc.gov/**]

FEDERAL ANTITRUST LAW AND OTHER REGULATORY SYSTEMS

State Law

Most states, through legislation and judicial decisions, have developed their own antitrust laws. Relying on that legislation, 19 states and the District of Columbia joined the federal government in the Microsoft case. The states' action lent weight and additional resources to the case and increased the potential penalties. The Microsoft action is the latest instance of a much more aggressive state role in antitrust enforcement in recent years.

Patents, Copyrights, and Trademarks

Each of these devices constitutes a limited, government-granted monopoly. As such, they are in direct conflict with the general thrust of antitrust law. However, each device serves to protect—and thus encourage—commercial creativity and development. The resulting antitrust problem is essentially that of limiting the patent, copyright, or trademark holder to the narrow terms of its privilege.

Law of Other Nations

Part Four of this chapter addresses international antitrust issues.

Part Two—Monopoly

The *Microsoft* case amply illustrates the continuing power of monopoly law in business practice, but the message had earlier been vividly articulated when Intel, the computer chip giant, agreed in 1999 to settle Federal Trade Commission charges. In brief, the government argued that Intel's monopoly market power was so strong that it forced companies to reveal design secrets in order to buy chips from Intel and to be granted the Intel technical data necessary to produce products compatible with the Intel chips. The power of the government's case was in some decline in that Intel's share of microprocessors slipped from 85 percent in 1997 to 76 percent in 1998.[1] Intel and Microsoft are important cases because they directly address market concentration and misconduct in the booming high-technology market. Similar market concentration in more mature industries would probably be much less worrisome to government regulators. [For the American Bar Association Antitrust section, see **http://www.abanet.org/antitrust**]

Principal Monopoly Legislation: Sherman Act, Section 2.

> Every person who shall monopolize, or attempt to monopolize, or combine or conspire with any other person or persons, to monopolize any part of the trade or commerce among the several States, or with foreign nations, shall be deemed guilty of a felony punishable by a fine.

Throughout the two antitrust chapters, 10 and 11, the principal legislation is identified, but understand that most, if not all, antitrust violations are subject to more than one piece of legislation. In particular, Section 5 of the Federal Trade Commission Act is arguably applicable to all antitrust violations.

From an economic viewpoint, a *monopoly* is a situation in which one firm holds the power to control prices and/or exclude competition in a particular market. The general test for monopolization is

1. The possession of monopoly power in the relevant market.
2. The willful acquisition or maintenance of that power, as distinguished from growth or development as a consequence of a superior product, business acumen, or historic accident.[2]

Thus, the critical inquiries are the percentage of the market held by the alleged monopolist and the behavior that produced and maintained that market share. The Sherman Act does not, as interpreted, punish efficient companies who legitimately earn and maintain large market shares.

Indeed, many economists now argue that market concentration should no longer be a major consideration in antitrust analysis because concentration, alone, often is not an accurate predictor of reduced competition and higher profits. High market concentration actually promotes competition, at least in some cases, while a fragmented market of many little firms may produce higher prices. (Imagine a retail food market of lots of little, corner grocery stores and no supermarkets.) Nonetheless, the federal government continues to rely strongly on market concentration data *(structure)* in combination with evidence of actual behavior *(conduct)* to identify anticompetitive situations. Market share alone is highly unlikely to lead to antitrust action, but a high market share acquired and/or maintained via abusive conduct (as alleged in *Microsoft*) is the sort of situation the Justice Department and/or the Federal Trade Commission is likely to attack.

Oligopoly.   A few firms sharing monopoly power is an *oligopoly,* a market structure that may also violate antitrust laws. Market reality, however, suggests that oligopolies may be a natural product of the contemporary global market. In many markets three to five firms are dominant: Beverages (Coke, 44.5 percent of the market, Pepsi, 31.4 percent, Cadbury Schweppes, 14.4 percent), cars (GM, 29.3 percent, Ford, 24.9 percent, Chrysler, 16.1 percent), and music (PolyGram, 24.5 percent, Warner, 18.2 percent, Sony, 16.6 percent, EMI, 12.9 percent, BMG, 12.2 percent).[3] Managers are often more comfortable in an oligopoly than in a monopoly because a little competition keeps them sharp and keeps the government at bay while allowing managers to retain substantial control. As explained above, oligopolies may also promote greater competition than would result from a fragmented market. Still, oligopolies raise the threat of collusion, which can lead to price fixing and other anticompetitive conduct.

Questions

1. *a.* Should the United States government challenge the Coke/Pepsi shared market dominance?
   b. In your experience are Coke and Pepsi vigorous competitors?
   c. Is the soft drink market one where new products can readily gain entry? Explain.

MONOPOLIZATION ANALYSIS

Although the case law is not a model of clarity, a rather straightforward framework for monopoly analysis has emerged:

1. Define the relevant *product market.*
2. Define the relevant *geographic market.*
3. Compute the defendant's *market power.*
4. Assess the defendant's *intent.*
5. Raise any available *defenses.*

1. Product Market

Here, the court seeks, effectively, to draw a circle that encompasses categories of goods in which the defendant's products or services compete and that excludes those not in the same competitive arena. The fundamental test is that of interchangeability, as determined primarily by the price, use, and quality of the product in question.

An analysis of cross elasticity of demand is a key ingredient in defining the product market. Assume that two products, X and Y, appear to be competitors. Assume that the price of X doubled and Y's sales volume was unchanged. What does that tell us about whether X and Y are, in fact, in the same product market?

Defining the product market is really the process we all go through in routine purchasing decisions. Let us assume that you feel a rather undefined hunger for salty snack food. You proceed to the nearby convenience store. Many options confront you, but for simplicity, let's confine them to chips, nuts, and popcorn. Of course, each of those food types is composed of variations. As you sort through the choices—corn chips, cheese curls, Spanish peanuts, rippled potato chips, and so on—you employ the criteria of price, use, and quality in focusing your decision. In so doing, you are defining the product market for "salty junk food." Products closely matched in price, use, and quality are interchangeable, and thus competitors, and thus in the same product market. But, for example, an imported salty cheese at \$10 per quarter pound presumably is not in the same product market as salted sunflower seeds.

Expressed as a matter of elasticity, the critical question becomes something like the following: If the price of potato chips, for example, falls by 10 percent, does the sales volume of salted nuts likewise fall? If so, we have a strong indication that potato chips and salted nuts lie in the same product market and thus are competitors.

2. Geographic Market

Once the product market has been defined, we still must determine where the product can be purchased. The judicial decisions to date offer no definitive explanation of the geographic market concept. A working definition might be "any section of the country where the product is sold in commercially significant quantities." From an economic perspective, the geographic market is defined by elasticity. If prices rise or supplies are reduced within the geographic area in question (e.g., New England) and demand remains steady, will products from other areas enter the market in quantity sufficient to affect price and/or supply? If so, the geographic market must be broadened to embrace those new sources of supply. If not, the geographic market is not larger than the area in question (New England). Perhaps a better approach is to read the cases and recognize that each geographic market must simply be identified in terms of its unique economic properties.

3. Market Power

Market Share.   We have no firm guidelines as to what percentage of the market must be controlled to give rise to a monopoly. In the *Alcoa* case, Judge Hand found a monopoly where Alcoa had 90 percent of the virgin ingot aluminum market.[4] In *U.S.* v. *United Shoe Machinery Corporation,*[5] a 75 percent share of the shoe machinery market was a monopoly share, but a 50 percent share in some supply markets was not large enough to constitute a monopoly. The Fifth Circuit Court of Appeals once indicated that "something more than 50 percent of the market is a prerequisite to a finding of monopoly."[6] The complexity of the market share decision is well illustrated by a recent federal appeals court ruling that freed Kodak from a pair of decades-old government restraints on its marketing practices. The government had imposed those restraints and sought to retain them because of Kodak's market dominance. Kodak continued to control 70 percent of the domestic film market, but the appeals court felt that Kodak's 36 percent global share did not represent market power and that foreign competition would restrain Kodak's ability to raise prices.[7]

Additional Factors.   Market share alone cannot be determinative of monopoly power. The courts are interested in other features of the market, including *barriers to entry,* the strength of the competition, *economies of scale,* trends in the market, and pricing patterns. The point of these inquiries is to determine whether the market in question remains competitive even though one firm has a large market share. Why are the courts interested in barriers to entry?

4. Intent

Assuming the market share is of threatening proportions, the next test element is proof of an intent to monopolize. A monopoly finding requires both a showing of monopoly power and evidence of the willful acquisition or maintenance of that power. A showing of intent does not demand, for example, an internal memo, setting out a plan to acquire monopoly power. Rather, a showing of purposeful or deliberate acts that are predatory or unfair (such as price-fixing) will normally suffice to establish the requisite intent.

5. Defenses

The defendant may yet prevail if the evidence demonstrates that the monopoly was "*thrust upon*" the firm, rather than that the firm affirmatively sought its monopoly posture. The thrust-upon defense had its genesis in Judge Learned Hand's opinion in the aforementioned *Alcoa* case, where that most aptly named jurist suggested the Sherman Act would not be violated if monopoly power were innocently acquired via superior skill, foresight, or industry or by failure of the competition as a consequence of changes in costs or consumer preference. Depending on the circumstances, other defenses (such as possession of a patent, for example) may be persuasive.

ATTEMPTED MONOPOLIZATION

The Sherman Act forbids attempts to monopolize as well as monopoly itself. In the 1993 *Spectrum Sports* decision,[8] the Supreme Court set out its three-part test for attempted monopolization: (1) that the defendant has engaged in predatory or anticompetitive conduct with (2) a specific intent to monopolize and (3) a dangerous probability of achieving monopoly power.[9] The Court made it clear that part (3) of the test requires proof of the relevant market and evidence that the defendant had a "realistic probability" of achieving monopoly power in that market. A showing of unfair or predatory conduct alone will not suffice to establish the dangerous probability.

MONOPOLY CASE

The *Syufy* case that follows reflects what is probably the dominant "ideological" view among federal court judges. The decision embodies the free market philosophy of the Reagan/Bush administrations and their judicial appointees, and it suggests an increasing judicial acceptance of the position that what might be considered monopoly market shares may be earned and maintained legitimately—particularly where competition may easily enter the market.

The case is also notable because Judge Kozinski, in the spirit of the facts, managed to insert the names of nearly 200 movies in his 25-page opinion (only a small portion of which is reprinted here).

U.S. v. SYUFY ENTERPRISES
903 F.2d 659 (9th Cir. 1990)

Circuit Judge Kozinski

Suspect that giant film distributors like Columbia, Paramount, and Twentieth Century–Fox had fallen prey to Raymond Syufy, the canny operator of a chain of Las Vegas, Nevada, movie theaters, the United States Department of Justice brought this civil antitrust action to force Syufy to disgorge the theaters he had purchased in 1982–84 from his former competitors. The case is unusual in a number of respects: The Department of Justice concedes that moviegoers in Las Vegas suffered no direct injury as a result of the allegedly illegal transactions; nor does the record reflect complaints from Syufy's bought-out competitors, as the sales were made at fair prices and not precipitated by any monkey business; and the supposedly oppressed movie companies have weighed in on Syufy's side. The Justice Department nevertheless remains intent on rescuing this platoon of Goliaths from a single David.

After extensive discovery and an eight-and-a-half day trial, the learned district judge entered comprehensive findings of fact and conclusions of law, holding for Syufy. He found, *inter alia,* that Syufy's actions did not injure competition because there are no barriers to entry—others could and did enter the market—and that Syufy therefore did not have the power to control prices or exclude the competition . . .

Facts

Gone are the days when a movie ticket cost a dime, popcorn a nickel, and theaters had a single screen: This is the age of the multiplex. With more than 300 new films released every year—each potentially the next *Batman* or *E.T.*—many successful theaters today run a different film on each of their 6, 12, or 18 screens . . .

Raymond Syufy understood the formula well. In 1981, he entered the Las Vegas market with a splash by opening a six-screen theater. Newly constructed and luxuriously furnished, it put existing facilities to shame. Syufy's entry into the Las Vegas market caused a stir, precipitating a titanic bidding war. Soon, theaters in Las Vegas

were paying some of the highest license fees in the nation, while distributors sat back and watched the easy money roll in.

It is the nature of free enterprise that fierce, no-holds-barred competition will drive out the least effective participants in the market, providing the most efficient allocation of productive resources. And so it was in the Las Vegas movie market in 1982. After a hard-fought battle among several contenders, Syufy gained the upper hand. Two of his rivals, Mann Theatres and Plitt Theatres, saw their future as rocky and decided to sell out to Syufy. While Mann and Plitt are major exhibitors nationwide, neither had a large presence in Las Vegas. Mann operated two indoor theaters with a total of three screens; Plitt operated a single theater with three screens. Things were relatively quiet until September 1984; in September, Syufy entered into earnest negotiations with Cragin Industries, his largest remaining competitor. Cragin sold out to Syufy midway through October, leaving Roberts Company, a small exhibitor of mostly second-run films, as Syufy's only competitor for first-run films in Las Vegas.

It is these three transactions—Syufy's purchases of the Mann, Plitt, and Cragin theaters—that the Justice Department claims amount to antitrust violations. As government counsel explained at oral argument, the thrust of its case is that "you may not get monopoly power by buying out your competitors." . . .

Discussion

*   *   *   *   *

[O]f significance is the government's concession that Syufy was only a monopsonist, not a monopolist. Thus, the government argues that Syufy had market power, but that it exercised this power only against suppliers (film distributors), not against its consumers (moviegoers). This is consistent with the record, which demonstrates that Syufy always treated moviegoers fairly: The movie tickets, popcorn, nuts, and the Seven-Ups cost about the same in Las Vegas as in other, comparable markets. While it is theoretically possible to have a middleman who is a monopolist upstream but not downstream, this is a somewhat counterintuitive scenario. Why, if he truly had significant market power, would Raymond Syufy have chosen to take advantage of the big movie distributors while giving a fair shake to ordinary people? And why do the distributors, the alleged victims of the monopolization scheme, think that Raymond Syufy is the best thing that ever happened to the Las Vegas movie market?

The answers to these questions are significant because, like all antitrust cases, this one must make economic sense . . . Keeping in mind that competition, not government intervention, is the touchstone of a healthy, vigorous economy, we proceed to examine whether the district court erred in concluding that Syufy does not, in fact, hold monopoly power. There is universal agreement that monopoly power is the power to exclude competition or control prices . . . The district court determined that Syufy possessed neither power. As the government's case stands or falls with these propositions, the parties have devoted much of their analysis to these findings. So do we.

1. Power to Exclude Competition

It is true, of course, that when Syufy acquired Mann's, Plitt's, and Cragin's theaters he temporarily diminished the number of competitors in the Las Vegas first-run film market. But this does not necessarily indicate foul play; many legitimate market arrangements diminish the number of competitors . . . If there are no significant barriers to entry, however, eliminating competitors will not enable the survivors to reap a monopoly profit; any attempt to raise prices above the competitive level will lure into the market new competitors able and willing to offer their commercial goods or personal services for less . . .

* * * * *

The district court . . . found that there were no barriers to entry in the Las Vegas movie market . . . Our review of the record discloses that the district court's finding is amply supported by the record.

* * * * *

Immediately after Syufy bought out the last of his three competitors in October 1984, he was riding high, having captured 100 percent of the first-run film market

in Las Vegas. But this utopia proved to be only a mirage. That same month, a major movie distributor, Orion, stopped doing business with Syufy, sending all of its first-run films to Roberts Company, a dark-horse competitor previously relegated to the second-run market. Roberts Company took this as an invitation to step into the major league and, against all odds, began giving Syufy serious competition in the first-run market. Fighting fire with fire, Roberts opened three multiplexes within a 13-month period, each having six or more screens. By December 1986, Roberts was operating 28 screens, trading places with Syufy, who had only 23. At the same time, Roberts was displaying a healthy portion of all first-run films. In fact, Roberts got exclusive exhibition rights to many of its films, meaning that Syufy could not show them at all.

By the end of 1987, Roberts was showing a larger percentage of first-run films than was the Redrock multiplex at the time Syufy bought it. Roberts then sold its theaters to United Artists, the largest theater chain in the country, and Syufy continued losing ground. It all boils down to this: Syufy's acquisitions did not short-circuit the operation of the natural market forces; Las Vegas's first-run film market was more competitive when this case came to trial than before Syufy bought out Mann, Plitt, and Cragin.

The Justice Department correctly points out that Syufy still has a large market share, but attributes far too much importance to this fact. In evaluating monopoly power, it is not market share that counts, but the ability to *maintain* market share . . . Syufy seems unable to do this. In 1985, Syufy managed to lock up exclusive exhibition rights to 91 percent of all the first-run films in Las Vegas. By the first quarter of 1988, that percentage had fallen to 39 percent; United Artists had exclusive rights to another 25 percent, with the remaining 36 percent being played on both Syufy and UA screens.

Syufy's share of box office receipts also dropped off, albeit less precipitously. In 1985, Syufy raked in 93 percent of the gross box office from first-run films in Las Vegas. By the first quarter of 1988, that figure had fallen to 75 percent. The government insists that 75 percent is still a large number, and we are hard-pressed to disagree; but that's not the point. The antitrust laws do not require that rivals compete in a dead heat, only that neither is unfairly kept from doing his personal best. Accordingly, the government would do better to plot these points on a graph and observe the pattern they form than to focus narrowly on Syufy's market share at a particular time. The numbers reveal that Roberts/UA has steadily been eating away at Syufy's market share: In two and a half years, Syufy's percentage of exclusive exhibition rights dropped 52 percent and its percentage of box office receipts dropped 18 percent. During the same period, Roberts/UA's newly opened theaters evolved from absolute beginners, barely staying alive, into a big business.

* * * * *

Confronted with this record and the district court's clear findings, the government trots out a shopworn argument we had thought long abandoned: that efficient, aggressive competition is itself a structural barrier to entry. According to the government, competitors will be deterred from entering the market because they could not hope to turn a profit competing against Syufy . . .

The notion that the supplier of a good or service can monopolize the market simply by being efficient reached high tide in the law 44 years ago in Judge Learned Hand's opinion in *United States* v. *Aluminum Co. of Am.,* 148 F.2d 416 (2d Cir. 1945). In the intervening decades the wisdom of this notion has been questioned by just about everyone who has taken a close look at it . . .

* * * * *

The Supreme Court has distanced itself from the *Alcoa* legacy, taking care to distinguish unlawful monopoly power from "growth or development as a consequence of a superior product, business acumen, or historic accident."

* * * * *

2. Power to Control Prices

The crux of the Justice Department's case is that Syufy, top gun in the Las Vegas movie market, had the power to push around Hollywood's biggest players, dictating to them what prices they could charge for their movies. The district court found otherwise. This finding too has substantial support in the record.

Perhaps the most telling evidence of Syufy's inability to set prices came from movie distributors, Syufy's supposed victims. At the trial, distributors uniformly proclaimed their satisfaction with the way the Las Vegas first-run film market operates; none complained about the license fees paid by Syufy . . . Particularly damaging to the government's case was the testimony of the

former head of distribution for MGM/UA that his company "never had any difficulty . . . in acquiring the terms that we thought were reasonable," . . . explaining that the license fees Syufy paid "were comparable or better than any place in the United States. And in most cases better." . . .

The documentary evidence bears out this testimony. Syufy has at all times paid license fees far in excess of the national average, even higher than those paid by exhibitors in Los Angeles, the Mecca of Moviedom. In fact, Syufy paid a higher percentage of his gross receipts to distributors in 1987 and 1988 than he did during the intensely competitive period just before he acquired Cragin's Redrock.

While successful, Syufy is in no position to put the squeeze on distributors . . .

* * * * *

It is a tribute to the state of competition in America that the Antitrust Division of the Department of Justice has found no worthier target than this paper tiger on which to expend limited taxpayer resources. Yet we cannot help but wonder whether bringing a lawsuit like this, and pursuing it doggedly through 27 months of pretrial proceedings, about two weeks of trial and now the full distance on appeal, really serves the interests of free competition.

* * * * *

Affirmed.

District Judge Quackenbush concurring

I concur in the result reached in Parts 1 and 2 of the opinion . . .

I do not agree with those portions of Parts 1 and 2 which state that if there are no significant barriers to entry, there can be no monopoly as a matter of law . . .

* * * * *

If the opinion stands for the proposition that a finding of lack of barriers to entry *mandates* a finding of lack of monopoly power, then I disagree with the opinion. While I agree that the issue of monopoly power often depends heavily upon market share and barriers to entry, the analysis should also include consideration of the extent of the alleged monopolist's market share, the ability to maintain that share, the power to control prices, and capability of excluding competitors, and the intent of the alleged monopolist, along with the existence of barriers to entry.

Questions

1. At one point, Syufy held 100 percent of the first-run market. Why was Syufy not a monopolist?
2. Is this decision rooted more in structural (market share) or conduct (e.g., predatory pricing) considerations? Explain.
3. What role did the issue of Syufy's intent to monopolize play in this case? Explain.
4. Assume we have historical data showing that when the price of rolled steel has increased, the sales volume of rolled aluminum has remained constant. What, if anything, does that fact tell us about the product market for rolled steel?
5. Define the product market for championship boxing matches. See *United States* v. *International Boxing Club of New York, Inc.*, 358 U.S. 242 (1959).
6. Adidas provides cash, sporting goods, and the like to universities in exchange for various promotional rights, including the team's or coach's agreement to wear Adidas clothing in athletic activities.

National Collegiate Athletic Association (NCAA) rules limit the amount of advertising that may appear on a uniform being used in competition. Adidas sued the NCAA claiming, among other things, that the advertising restrictions constitute an attempted monopoly by the NCAA. In pursuing its monopoly claim, Adidas defined the relevant market as "the market for the sale of NCAA Promotional Rights." The NCAA responded by saying that a market consisting solely of the sale of promotional rights by NCAA member institutions (colleges and universities) on athletic apparel used in intercollegiate activity is not a plausible relevant market.

    a. Define the relevant product market from the NCAA point of view.

    b. How would the Court decide where the product market actually lies? See *Adidas America, Inc* v. *NCAA,* 64 F. Supp. 2d 1097 (1999).

Questions—Parts One and Two

1. A federal district court found IBM guilty of unlawful monopolization in a portion of the computer industry. IBM manufactured and distributed both central processing units (CPUs) and various peripheral devices (PDs), including magnetic tape drives and printers. Telex manufactured PDs compatible with IBM's CPUs, but not with the CPUs of other manufacturers. It was established at trial that relatively inexpensive interfaces could be used to make Telex PDs compatible with the CPUs of manufacturers other than IBM, and at a relatively modest cost Telex could produce PDs compatible with CPUs other than those of IBM. The district court concluded that the relevant product market was PDs compatible with IBM CPUs and that IBM controlled at least 80 percent of that market. Given IBM's monopoly power, the district court also found IBM guilty of predatory behavior. For example, in response to competition from Telex and others, IBM lowered its leasing fees for PDs and offered more desirable leasing terms. Similarly, IBM reduced the sales prices of its PDs. In setting those prices, IBM considered the ability or inability of its competitors to respond to those prices. At the reduced prices, IBM achieved a 20 percent profit margin and increased its market share.

    Was the district court correct? Explain. See *Telex Corporation* v. *IBM Corporation,* 510 F.2d 894 (10th Cir. 1975), cert. denied, 423 U.S. 802 (1975).

2. *a.* A traditional concern about monopolies is that a lack of competition discourages efficiency and innovation. Argue that monopolies may actually *encourage* innovation.

   b. Even if monopolies do not discourage invention, we have firm economic grounds for opposing monopolies. Explain.

3. Real estate developer Ernest Coleman built an apartment complex in Stilwell, Oklahoma (population 2,700), and ordered electric service from an out-of-town utility, Ozark Electric. Stilwell officials said they would deny him city water and sewer service if he did not buy his electricity from the city-owned utility service. Since he could not buy water or sewer service elsewhere, Coleman decided to switch to Stilwell's utility.

   In 1996, the federal Justice Department sued Stilwell. Explain the federal government's complaint and decide the case. See Bryan Gruley, "Little Town Becomes First Municipality Sued by U.S. for Antitrust," *The Wall Street Journal,* June 3, 1996, p. A1.

4. Historically, perhaps the most important interpretation of the Sherman Act's proscription of monopolization was Judge Learned Hand's opinion in the *Alcoa* case. After finding that Alcoa controlled 90 percent of the aluminum ingot market, Hand had to determine whether Alcoa possessed a general intent to monopolize. Hand concluded that Alcoa's market dominance could have resulted only from a "persistent determination" to maintain control [148 F.2d 416, 431 (2d Cir. 1945)].

   > It was not inevitable that it should always anticipate increases in the demand for ingots and be prepared to supply them. Nothing compelled it to keep doubling and redoubling its capacity before others entered the field. It insists that it never excluded competitors; but we can think of no more effective exclusion than progressively to embrace each new opportunity as it opened, and to face every newcomer with new capacity already geared into a great organization.

   Comment on Judge Hand's remarks.

5. Is a monopolist who makes only a "fair" profit in violation of the law? Explain.

6. May a monopolist lawfully increase its market share, assuming it does so without recourse to predatory or exclusionary tactics? Explain. Should it be able to do so? Explain.

7. The U.S. government sued Du Pont, claiming a monopolization of the cellophane market. Du Pont produced almost 75 percent of the cellophane sold in the United States. Cellophane constituted less than 20 percent of the "flexible packaging materials" market. The lower court found "[g]reat sensitivity of customers in the flexible packaging markets to price or quality changes."

   a. What is the relevant product market?

   b. Who wins the case? Explain. See *United States* v. *E.I. du Pont de Nemours & Co.,* 351 U.S. 377 (1956).

8. The National Football League was organized in 1920. During the 1960 season, it had 14 teams located in 13 cities—Chicago (two teams), Cleveland, New York, Philadelphia, Pittsburgh, Washington, Baltimore, Detroit, Los Angeles, San Francisco, Green Bay, Dallas, and Minneapolis. The rival American Football League commenced play in 1960 with eight teams in eight cities—Boston, Buffalo, Houston, New York, Dallas, Denver, Los Angeles, and Oakland.

In its first season, the AFL was successful in competing for outstanding players and in acquiring a desirable television contract. "[R]epresentatives of the American League declared that the League's success was unprecedented." Nevertheless, the AFL sued the NFL, claiming monopolization. A central issue in the case was that of the geographic market. The AFL characterized the market as those 17 cities either having an NFL franchise or seriously considered for a franchise. The NFL saw the market as nationwide.

Define the geographic market in this case. Explain. See *American Football League* v. *National Football League,* 323 F.2d 124 (4th Cir. 1963).

Taking Control (Passenger Market Share at Greater Pittsburgh International Airport)

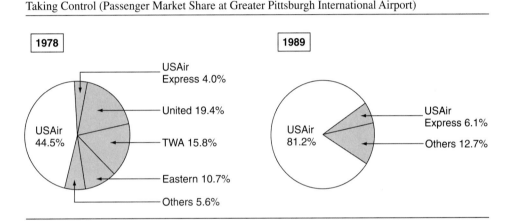

Source: Allegheny, PA, County Department of Aviation. Published in Asra Q. Nomani and Paul M. Barrett, "Control of Major Airports by Carriers Is Focus of Justice Department Inquiry," *The Wall Street Journal,* June 18, 1990, p. A3. Reprinted by permission of *The Wall Street Journal.* © 1990 Dow Jones & Company, Inc. All Rights Reserved Worldwide.

9. Consider the accompanying table, which depicts airline market shares at the Pittsburgh Airport. Do these figures suggest that USAir is a monopolist in that market? Explain.

10. Several smaller airlines sued the two giants, United and American, claiming that the two violated the Sherman Act through their computerized reservation systems (CRSs). The heart of the plaintiffs' position was that United and American were monopolists who violated the law by denying other airlines reasonable access to their CRSs. American and United had the largest CRSs, but other airlines also maintained CRSs. Neither had blocked any other airline's access to its CRS, but they had charged fees (in American's case, $1.75 per booking to the airline that secured a passenger through American's CRS). United and American each controlled about 12 to 14 percent of the total air transportation market. According to the court, the plaintiffs were "unhappy" about United and American's ability to extract booking fees from them for the use of the CRSs. The U.S. Ninth Circuit Court of Appeals ruled for the defendants and the Supreme Court declined to review this case.

    a. Explain why the plaintiffs felt wronged by American and United.

    b. Explain the defendants's argument that they could not successfully charge "excessive" prices for the use of the CRSs. See *Alaska Airlines* v. *United Airlines,* 948 F.2d 536 (9th Cir. 1991), cert. den., 112 S.Ct. 1603 (1992).

11. A principal fear about monopoly power is that it can lead to *predatory pricing,* where large firms price their goods below cost in order to drive their competition out of the market, then raise those prices to monopoly levels.

    a. As a matter of economics, explain why predatory pricing of that nature is quite unlikely.

    b. On the other hand, as a matter of economics, explain how predatory pricing might be successful where a monopolist operates in several markets and sells below cost in one or two of them.

12. Nintendo of America is a Redmond, Washington, subsidiary of Nintendo of Kyoto, Japan, the world's largest manufacturer of video games. Both were sued by a rival game maker, Atari, on the grounds, among others, that Nintendo monopolized the home video game business in the United States. At times, Nintendo controlled 90 percent of the relevant market. Evidence introduced at trial showed that Nintendo was able to maintain its prices for more than four years while other consumer electronics prices were falling. According to Atari's translation of the minutes, a Nintendo board meeting included an open discussion of its "monopoly" position. Atari claimed that Nintendo maintained its market dominance by requiring game makers to give Nintendo an exclusive two-year license for their games. Atari had suffered severe financial reverses, but Nintendo's evidence suggested that those problems were caused by Atari's own missteps.

    Is Nintendo a monopolist? Explain. See *Atari Corp.* v. *Nintendo Co. Ltd. and Nintendo of Am., Inc.,* no. C-89–0824-FMS (N.D. Cal. May 1, 1992).

Part Three—Mergers

> we are in the midst of the greatest merger boom in business history

At the turn of the century, we are in the midst of the greatest merger boom in business history. In February 2000, after months of battling, two European giants combined in the largest takeover in history, valued at over $180 billion. The British mobile phone firm, Vodafone, bought Mannesmann, a German telecom and engineering company, to create the world's fourth-largest corporation behind Microsoft, General Electric, and Cisco. That deal exceeded the previous record for size held briefly by Time Warner, the world's number one media and entertainment company, and America Online, the world's leading Internet service provider, which combined in a merger valued at $156 billion. Those combinations, in turn, exceeded in size the MCI Worldcom and Sprint merger of late 1999 valued at $114 billion which, in turn, surpassed the $80 billion Exxon–Mobil combination. This spiral of records reflects the dramatic transformation of business practice in a world being remade by technology. (The Exxon–Mobil merger has largely achieved regulatory approval, but the others are in the midst of government review at this writing.)

The Numbers. Through mid-December 1999, United States firms had been involved in 8,802 mergers for the year, worth a record $1.36 trillion. Those figures represent a more than 15 percent increase in mergers from 1998 and an 11 percent increase in total value.[10] More dramatically, those 1999 mergers approximately doubled the value of the total mergers only three years earlier in 1996 ($659 billion).[11]

Why? The continuing merger boom is fueled, in part, by conventional reasons including cutting costs, increasing market share to enjoy the competitive advantages of size, responding to technological change, and generally enhancing efficiency. At the same time, the primary force in the merger boom doubtless rests in the blossoming of the global economy. The Mobil Exxon merger illustrates the power of the worldwide market, as explained in the following excerpt from a *Washington Post* commentary:

> At first glance, it doesn't make sense: Why would Mobil Corp., a huge and profitable oil company that has been around for 88 years, agree to be acquired by its biggest rival, Exxon Corp.? . . .
>
> The answer, according to oil industry analysts, is that Mobil opted to self-destruct because it had run out of good alternatives. . . .
>
> The story of Mobil's demise as an independent company offers a harsh lesson in the economics of the global marketplace. It's not possible any more to be a comfortable laggard—getting the business equivalent of a "gentlemen's C." If you aren't one of the top two or three companies these days, you're dead.[12]

Another Why? Perhaps a yet more interesting question is why the United States government has been much more cooperative about some big mergers than was the case historically. Big oil was once under the intense scrutiny of federal regulators, but the climate for colossal combinations like Exxon Mobil has clearly changed. Why? George Washington University law professor, William Kovacic, cites three potent forces:

> One is a growing awareness in the federal antitrust agencies and Congress that international economic developments dictate adjustments in antitrust policy . . . Antitrust officials realize more keenly how international competition impels even the largest firms to cut costs and improve productivity . . .
>
> The second phenomenon is a change in analytical perspective that attaches less importance to structural industry conditions in determining competitive vigor. Since 1982, the federal horizontal merger guidelines have de-emphasized concentration data and given more weight to qualitative factors that afford a fuller basis for deciding whether increased concentration will enable the merging parties to exercise market power . . .
>
> The third shift is the increased tendency of antitrust agencies to entertain remedies that treat specific competitive concerns . . . [House of Representatives hearings] suggested that Exxon and Mobil can gain approval from federal antitrust regulators for their deal with a suitable package of divestitures.[13] [Gas stations, a refinery, and pipelines are expected to be sold.]

Understand, however, that the government, as explained below, continues to closely evaluate major mergers and frequently blocks or requires alterations in those deals. [For a summary of FTC Chairman Robert Pitofsky's 1998 Congressional testimony regarding the current merger wave, see **http://www.ftc.gov/opa/1998/9806/chairtes.htm**]

Merger Virtues

Of course, mergers often should be approved because they can have clearly beneficial effects. Some of the potential virtues of mergers include:

1. Mergers permit the replacement of inefficient management, and the threat of replacement disciplines managers to be more productive.
2. Mergers may permit stronger competition with formerly larger rivals.
3. Mergers may improve credit access.
4. Mergers may produce efficiencies and economies of scale. For example, the Exxon Mobil deal will save about $3.8 billion annually, but about 16,000 jobs (15 percent of the combined workforce) will be cut.[14]
5. Mergers frequently offer a pool of liquid assets for use in expansion and in innovation.
6. Very often, mergers offer tax advantages.
7. Growth by merger is often less expensive than internal growth.
8. Mergers help to satisy the personal ambitions and needs of management.

Managers.   For American bosses, this deal-making fever has profound professional and personal consequences. Job security appears to have evaporated. On the other hand, rapid change means striking new opportunities. In this volatile managerial setting, experts now say that personal, managerial conditions have become a major factor in merger negotiations. *The Wall Street Journal* explains:

> Job security appears to have evaporated

> Amid the record boom in mergers, it hasn't necessarily been a financial or strategic matter. Often, it is who gets to run the show—or who gets the last word on a new name and headquarters of the new firm.[15]

Scholars Mathew Hayward and Donald Hambrick measured a variation on this theme with their study of "CEO hubris" (exaggerated self-confidence). Hayward and Hambrick were interested in why acquiring firms often pay much more than market value in making acquisitions. They hypothesized that some CEOs are so convinced of their own excellence that they are sure the acquisition will pay off once they are in charge. In order to measure CEO hubris, Hayward and Hambrick constructed an index based on (1) recent organizational success, (2) media attention from major newspapers, and (3) self-importance as measured by high pay in comparison with the next highest subordinate. After studying acquisitions in the late 1980s and early 1990s, the authors showed that those three factors accurately predicted the size of the acquisition premium (amount the sale price exceeded the acquired firm's market value). They also found that acquisition premiums increased by an average of 4.8 percent for each highly favorable article about the acquiring firm's CEO. The result? On average, shareholder wealth declined for the acquiring firms.[16]

Merger Problems

Naturally, some acquisitions prove to have been sensible; some do not, but analysts generally agree that the merger wave of the 1990s has been based more nearly on strategic fundamentals than was the conglomerate merger wave of the 1960s, when big firms were simply slapped together, and the junk-bond-fueled mergers of the 1980s, when mergers often made little strategic sense. Despite the wiser motivations for today's mergers, the empirical evidence of success, as recently summarized by *The Wall Street Journal,* is not encouraging:

> Mark Sirower analyzed 168 deals made between 1979 and 1990 and concluded that two-thirds of them destroyed shareholder value . . . Similarly, in 1995, *Business Week* magazine and Mercer Management Consulting studied 150 deals struck between 1990 and 1995 and found that about half produced negative returns to shareholders . . . A third study, by PriceWaterhouseCoopers LLP for *CFO* magazine, looked at deals between 1994 and June 1997. It found that the average acquirer's stock was 3.7 percent lower than its industry peer group a year later.[17]

Financial reverses are, of course, the key fear about the latest merger boom, but other important concerns should be noted:

1. Too much power is being concentrated in too few hands threatening our economic well-being and undermining genuine democracy.
2. A particular merger, while not threatening in and of itself, may trigger a merger movement among industry competitors.
3. Higher market concentration may lead to higher prices for consumers and lower prices for suppliers.
4. Innovation may be harmed as smaller companies grow into larger, more bureaucratic structures.
5. Some companies have become so large that they significantly shape global affairs.
6. Some companies may have become so large that we cannot allow them to fail.[18]

Consumers pay nearly $30 a year more on average for checking accounts at big banks than at small ones . . . the U.S. Public Interest Research Group said . . . "Merger mania (among banks) is making the fee-gouging banks even bigger," said Ed Mierzwinski, the group's consumer program director. "Fewer and fewer banks mean consumers face fewer choices, less competition and even higher fees."

Source: Associated Press, "Survey: Consumers Pay More at Big Banks," *Waterloo–Cedar Falls Courier,* July 31, 1997, p. B8.

Questions

1. How was the current merger wave encouraged by the stock market boom of the late 1990s?

2. From a free market perspective, why should we be untroubled by the Exxon Mobil merger?
3. Mergers are often generated by the prospect of cost savings and the opportunity to simply buy a customer base. Thus bigger is often better. But the young entrepreneurs whose start-up companies have been so influential in the growth of America's high-tech economy point to two other qualities that will determine business success in the "new" economy. What are those two factors, and why are they so important? See Alan W. Webber, "Mergers Get Headlines, But Young Start-Ups Keep Pace," *USA Today,* December 2, 1998, p. 25A.

INTRODUCTION TO MERGER LAW

We turn now to the law that governs merger activity in the United States. Mergers are addressed by the Sherman Act, Section 1, but the Clayton Act, Section 7, is the primary legislative directive in merger law:

> That no person engaged in commerce shall acquire the whole or any part of the stock or the assets of another person engaged also in commerce where the effect of such acquisition may be substantially to lessen competition, or to tend to create a monopoly.

Technically, a *merger* involves the union of two or more enterprises wherein the property of all is transferred to the one remaining firm. However, antitrust law embraces all those situations wherein previously independent business entities are united—whether by acquisition of stock, purchase of physical assets, creation of holding companies, consolidation, or merger.

Mergers fall, somewhat awkwardly, into three categories:

1. A *horizontal merger* involves firms that are in direct competition and occupy the same product and geographic markets. A merger of two vodka producers in the same geographic market would clearly fall in the horizontal category. Would the merger of a vodka producer and a gin producer constitute a horizontal merger?
2. A *vertical merger* involves two or more firms at different levels of the same channel of distribution, such as a furniture manufacturer and a fabric supplier.
3. A *conglomerate merger* involves firms dealing in unrelated products. Thus, the conglomerate category embraces all mergers that are neither horizontal nor vertical. An example of such a merger would be the acquisition of a pet food manufacturer by a book publisher. (Conglomerate mergers currently receive little attention from the government, and we will not be examining them further.)

Premerger. Under the 1976 Hart-Scott-Rodino Antitrust Improvements Act (HSR), corporate mergers and acquisitions valued at $15 million or more must be reported to the Federal Trade Commission and the Justice Department if one of the companies has sales or assets of at least $100 million and the other has sales or assets of $10 million. The parties must allow a specified waiting period of 15 to 30 days (depending on the nature of the acquisition) to pass before completing the merger. The merging firms are also required to provide documentation about the merger's impact on competition. Thus, the government is afforded time and information to determine whether to challenge the merger in court. In 1999, the New York investment firm, Blackstone Capital Partners II Merchant Banking Fund L.P., agreed to pay the maximum civil penalty of $2.8 million for violating HSR. Blackstone certified the truth and completeness of information submitted to the government regarding a deal to buy an Indiana firm, Prime Succession, when it "knew or should have known" that the facts submitted were "materially deficient." In the first payment of its kind under Hart-Scott-Rodino, the Fund general partner also agreed to pay $50,000 to settle the matter.[19]

Negotiation.   The Supreme Court has not issued a substantive merger decision since 1974, but enforcement remains vigorous. Federal regulators, however, now prefer to negotiate disputes rather than litigate them. Deals are worked out. Often, as with Exxon Mobil, divestitures are required where competition is threatened. [For an overview of merger law and policy, see **http://www.antitrust.org/mergers.htm**]

Criticisms.   Not surprisingly, the federal government's active oversight of mergers has led to loud complaints. Hart-Scott-Rodino is widely criticized because, to many observers, HSR gives the federal government near veto power over mergers. If merger partners do not agree to government demands, the government can sue; a long, expensive process for both sides. As noted, litigation is unusual, but the process of investigating a proposed merger and working out an arrangement suitable to both sides often takes so long that, in effect, the government can compel submission to its expectations, the critics allege.

When passed, HSR affected only about 150 mergers a year. By 1999, however, the law reached nearly 5,000 transactions, which caused Congress to consider a bill to raise the cutoff to $35 million and to reduce the government's power to demand documents from the merger partners.

Adding to the complexity of the merger review process is the increasing activism of state regulators and those in other countries. Because states can prosecute mergers under federal law yet the states are not bound by federal settlement decisions, merger partners must reach agreements with all affected states. They must do the same with other nations; some 40 foreign countries were expected to review the Exxon Mobil merger.[20]

Furthermore, as this book was going to press in early 2000, the Federal Trade Commission was signaling an increased willingness to litigate some cases.[21] While divestitures and other negotiated settlements will remain the preferred strategies, the FTC now seems inclined to take a tougher course with mergers that threaten the public interest. FTC studies indicate that in most cases divestitures work to maintain competition, but where that result seems unlikely or where the market would be difficult to monitor, the FTC now seems more likely to sue. The federal Justice Department probably will take a similar stance.

HORIZONTAL ANALYSIS

Of course, horizontal mergers raise the risk of anticompetitive effects because former competitors are joined together. The analysis is outlined in the FTC/Justice Department 1992 horizontal merger guidelines, which focus primarily on a pair of concerns:

1. *Collusion.* Will the merger facilitate cooperation such that the parties might fix prices, reduce output, reduce quality, or otherwise coordinate their activities rather than competing against each other?
2. *Unilateral effects.* Will the merger allow a firm to unilaterally raise prices, restrict output or control innovation?

Normally, unilateral effects arise with differentiated products (those which accomplish the same functional purpose, but which are viewed by consumers as being different) that significantly restrain each other prior to the merger. The worry is that after the merger that constraint will be gone and the merged company may be able to raise prices. Even if other substitutes are available, the consumer may be more likely to buy the product perceived to be the closer substitute. Thus, unilateral effects arise from submarkets within a larger product category. The *Staples* case set out later in this chapter relies, in part, on unilateral effects reasoning. That reasoning has been applied to such product categories as beer, color film, toilet tissue, and facial tissue. For example, in evaluating the merger of paper products manufacturers, Scott and Kimberly-Clark, the Justice Department found that Scott's facial tissue brand, Scotties, and Kimberly-Clark's facial tissue brand, Kleenex, had significantly constrained each other's prices prior to the merger and that the merger would, therefore, allow unilateral and profitable price increases for both Scotties and Kleenex. In response, Kimberly-Clark agreed to divest itself of Scott's facial tissue brands.[22]

Market Power.   Broadly, the guidelines are designed to identify mergers that may result in market power, defined as the ability of a seller "profitably to maintain prices above competitive levels for a significant period of time." The guidelines set out a five-step methodology for analyzing horizontal mergers:

1. Market definition.
2. Measurement of market concentration.
3. Identification of likely anticompetitive effects.
4. Liklihood of future entrants to the market.
5. Appraisal of efficiencies and other possible defenses.

Market.   The market will be defined as the smallest product and geographic market in which a hypothetical monopolist could raise prices a "small but significant and nontransitory" amount (usually set at 5 percent) above current prices.[23]

Market Concentration.   The Herfindahl–Hirschman Index (HHI) is employed to measure market concentration. Notwithstanding the formidable-sounding title, the index is computed quite easily. The market share of each firm in a market is squared and the results are summed. Thus, if five companies each had 20 percent of a market, the index for that market would be 2,000. The HHI is useful because it measures both concentration and dispersion of market share between big and small firms. If 10 firms each have 10 percent of the market, the resulting HHI is 1,000. The larger the HHI, the more concentrated the market. The new guidelines establish "safe harbors" for mergers that are considered unlikely to produce anticompetitive effects. Hence, a postmerger HHI of 1,000 or less ordinarily would not be challenged.

On the other hand, postmerger concentration of more than 1,800 accompanied by a change in the HHI above 50 (from the premerger HHI) is potentially threatening. That threat can be overcome by showing that market harm is unlikely, which could be established by reference to such other factors in the guidelines as adverse effects, ease of entry, efficiencies, and so on. In the middle ground involving postmerger HHI figures of 1,000 to 1,800 accompanied by changes in the HHI above 100, the guidelines find that the potential for competitive concerns depends on the analysis of the other factors. To illustrate, consider again a market composed of five companies, each with 20 percent of the market. If two of them merge, the HHI would rise from 2,000 to 2,800, and the merger would be presumed threatening pending consideration of the other factors in the guidelines. Thus, the government's new guidelines reject the older notion of market size *alone* as a threat to the welfare of the economy.

Anticompetitive Effects. Although the guidelines provide highly complex instructions about conditions likely to raise adverse competitive effects, the basic point is that the government is worried that the merger may permit cartel-like behavior in the merged firm's market.

Ease of Entry. The idea here is that the newly merged firm cannot arbitrarily raise prices or otherwise abuse the market if entry by competitors is timely, likely, and sufficient, since those new competitors will force the existing firms to charge competitive prices and otherwise conform to the discipline of the market.

Defenses. An otherwise unacceptable merger may be saved by certain defenses. Most prominent among them are the failing company doctrine and efficiencies. The failing company doctrine permits a merger in order to preserve the assets of a firm that would otherwise be lost to the market. Efficiencies include such desirable economic results as economies of scale or reduced transportation costs as a result of the merger. The FTC adopted new efficiency guidelines in 1997, recognizing that "mergers have the potential to generate significant efficiencies by permitting a better utilization of existing assets, enabling the combined firm to achieve lower costs in producing a given quality and quantity than either firm could have achieved without the proposed transaction."

VERTICAL ANALYSIS

A vertical merger typically involves an alliance between a supplier and a purchaser. The primary resulting threat to competition is labeled market foreclosure. As illustrated in Figure 10.1, a vertical merger may deny a source of supply to a purchaser or an outlet for sale to a seller, thus potentially threatening competition in violation of the Clayton Act. The government would then look closely at that foreclosure to determine whether it actually does have an anticompetitive effect. In addition to foreclosing sources of supply or outlets for sale, the government may be concerned about other anticompetitive effects such as raising rivals' costs, raising barriers to entry, increasing access to competitively sensitive

---

FIGURE 10.1 Vertical Merger

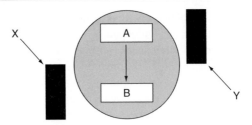

Wherein: A supplies B. A and B merge. X (A's competitor) had traditionally sold to B and Y (B's competitor) had traditionally purchased from A. How then do we decide the legality of such a merger?

---

information, encouraging discrimination in access to products and services, enhancing opportunities for collusion among vertically integrated companies, and reducing incentives for innovation.

The government has raised a number of vertical merger challenges in recent years, but all have been resolved through consent agreements so we have no recent evidence about how courts will treat the vertical concerns noted above. Certainly, the government has not changed its generally lenient attitude toward vertical mergers, but under some conditions they will be challenged. For example, in 1999, the FTC raised objections to Barnes & Noble's proposed $600 million acquisition of the Ingram Book Group. Barnes & Noble is the nation's number one book retailer while Ingram is the nation's largest book wholesaler. Facing a probable challenge from the FTC, the merger was dropped. The FTC had raised three primary reservations about the deal:

1. Small bookstores argued that their just-in-time needs for book delivery might be compromised if their primary supplier, Ingram, was owned by their biggest competitor, Barnes & Noble.
2. The merger might have discouraged new entrants to the Internet bookselling market because a start-up Internet retailer might need to count on Ingram as a supplier while Ingram would be controlled by Barnes & Noble, one of the two biggest Internet book sellers.
3. Reflecting a particular concern for any vertical merger that also exhibits horizontal ingredients, the FTC noted that Barnes & Noble has its own wholesale unit that competes with Ingram. The merger might have dampened competition between the two.[24] [For FTC chairman Robert Pitofsky's explanation of current federal vertical merger policy, see **http://www.ftc.gov/speeches/pitofsky/fordham7.htm**]

HORIZONTAL MERGER CASE

The Staples/Office Depot horizontal merger litigation that follows illustrates the complex factual and legal issues that must be examined in a strategically pivotal alliance like that proposed between the two office supply giants.

FEDERAL TRADE COMMISSION v. STAPLES, INC. AND OFFICE DEPOT, INC.
970 F.Supp. 1066 (D.D.C. 1997)

Judge Hogan

Background

*   *   *   *   *

Staples is the second largest office superstore chain in the United States with approximately 550 retail stores located in 28 states and the District of Columbia, primarily in the Northeast and California. In 1996 Staples' revenues from those stores were approximately $4 billion through all operations. Office Depot, the largest office superstore chain, operates over 500 retail office supply superstores that are located in 38 states and the District of Columbia, primarily in the South and Midwest. Office Depot's 1996 sales were approximately $6.1 billion. OfficeMax, Inc., is the only other office supply superstore firm in the United States.

On September 4, 1996, defendants Staples and Office Depot . . . entered into an "Agreement and Plan of Merger" whereby . . . Office Depot would become a wholly-owned subsidiary of Staples . . . Pursuant to the Hart-Scott-Rodino Improvements Act of 1976, Staples and Office Depot filed a Premerger Notification and Report Form with the FTC and Department of Justice on October 2, 1996. This was followed by a seven month investigation by the FTC. The FTC issued a Second Request for Information on November 1, 1996, to both Staples and Office Depot. The Commission further initiated a second Second Request on January 10, 1997. In addition to the hundreds of boxes of documents produced to the FTC during this time, the FTC took depositions of 18 Staples and Office Depot officers and employees . . .

On March 10, 1997, the Commission voted 4–1 to challenge the merger . . . Following this vote, the defendants and the FTC staff negotiated a consent decree that would have authorized the merger to proceed on the condition that Staples and Office Depot sell 63 stores to OfficeMax. However, the Commission voted 3–2 to reject the proposed consent decree on April 4, 1997. The FTC then filed this suit on April 9, 1997, seeking a temporary restraining order and preliminary injunction against the merger . . .

I. Discussion

Analysis of the likely competitive effects of a merger requires determinations of (1) the "line of commerce" or product market in which to assess the transaction, (2) the "section of the country" or geographic market in which to assess the transaction, and (3) the transaction's probable effect on competition in the product and geographic markets.

II. The Geographic Market

One of the few issues about which the parties to this case do not disagree is that metropolitan areas are the appropriate geographic markets for analyzing the competitive effects of the proposed merger. In its first amended complaint, the FTC identified forty-two such metropolitan areas as well as future areas which could suffer anticompetitive effects from the proposed merger. Defendants have not challenged the FTC's geographic market definition in this proceeding. Therefore, the Court will accept the relevant geographic markets identified by the Commission.

III. The Relevant Product Market

*   *   *   *   *

The Commission defines the relevant product market as "the sale of consumable office supplies through office superstores," with "consumable" meaning products that consumers buy recurrently, i.e., items which "get used up" or discarded. For example, under the Commission's definition, "consumable office supplies" would not include capital goods such as computers, fax machines, and other business machines or office furniture, but does include such products as paper, pens, file folders, post-it notes, computer disks, and toner cartridges. The defendants characterize the FTC's product market definition as "contrived" with no basis in law or fact, and counter that the appropriate product market within which to assess the likely competitive consequences of a Staples–Office Depot combination is simply the overall sale of office products, of which a combined Staples–Office Depot accounted for 5.5% of total sales in North America in 1996.

* * * * *

The general rule when determining a relevant product market is that "[t]he outer boundaries of a product market are determined by the reasonable interchangeability of use [by consumers] or the cross-elasticity of demand between the product itself and substitutes for it." Interchangeability of use and cross-elasticity of demand look to the availability of substitute commodities, i.e. whether there are other products offered to consumers which are similar in character or use to the product or products in question . . .

[T]he Commission has argued that a slight but significant increase in Staples–Office Depot's prices will not cause a considerable number of Staples–Office Depot's customers to purchase consumable office supplies from other non-superstore alternatives such as Wal–Mart, Best Buy, Quill, or Viking. On the other hand, the Commission has argued that an increase in price by Staples would result in consumers turning to another office superstore especially Office Depot, if the consumers had that option. Therefore, the Commission concludes that the sale of consumable office supplies by office supply superstores is the appropriate relevant product market in this case, and products sold by competitors such as Wal-Mart, Best Buy, Viking, Quill, and others should be excluded.

The Court recognizes that it is difficult to overcome the first blush or initial gut reaction of many people to the definition of the relevant product market as the sale of consumable office supplies through office supply superstores. The products in question are undeniably the same no matter who sells them, and no one denies that many different types of retailers sell these products. After all, a combined Staples–Office Depot would only have a 5.5% share of the overall market in consumable office supplies. Therefore, it is logical to conclude that, of course, all these retailers compete, and that if a combined Staples–Office Depot raised prices

after the merger, or at least did not lower them as much as they would have as separate companies, that consumers, with such a plethora of options, would shop elsewhere.

The Court acknowledges that there is, in fact, a broad market encompassing the sale of consumable office supplies by all sellers of such supplies, and that those sellers must, at some level, compete with one another. However, the mere fact that a firm may be termed a competitor in the overall marketplace does not necessarily require that it be included in the relevant product market for antitrust purposes. The Supreme Court has recognized that within a broad market, "well-defined submarkets may exist which, in themselves, constitute product markets for antitrust purposes."

* * * * *

[In defining the submarket] the FTC focused on what it termed the "pricing evidence." . . . First, the FTC presented evidence comparing Staples' prices in geographic markets where Staples is the only office superstore, to markets where Staples competes with Office Depot or OfficeMax, or both. Based on the FTC's calculations, in markets where Staples faces no office superstore competition at all, something which was termed a one firm market during the hearing, prices are 13% higher than in three firm markets where it competes with both Office Depot and OfficeMax.

* * * * *

This evidence suggests that office superstore prices are affected primarily by other office superstores and not by non-superstore competitors such as mass merchandisers like Wal–Mart, K mart, or Target, wholesale clubs such as BJ's, Sam's, and Price Costco, computer or electronic stores such as Computer City and Best Buy, independent retail office supply stores, mail order firms like Quill and Viking, and contract stationers.

* * * * *

In addition, Staples' own pricing information shows that warehouse clubs have very little effect on Staples' prices.

* * * * *

There is similar evidence with respect to the defendants' behavior when faced with entry of another competitor. The evidence shows that the defendants change their price zones when faced with entry of another superstore, but do not do so for other retailers.

* * * * *

Despite the high degree of functional interchangeability between consumable office supplies sold by the office superstores and other retailers of office supplies, the evidence presented by the Commission shows that even where Staples and Office Depot charge higher prices, certain consumers do not go elsewhere for their supplies. This further demonstrates that the sale of office supplies by non-superstore retailers are not responsive to the higher prices charged by Staples and Office Depot in the one firm markets. This indicates a low cross-elasticity of demand between the consumable office supplies sold by superstores and those sold by other sellers.

* * * * *

The Court has observed that office supply superstores look far different from other sellers of office supplies. Office supply superstores are high volume, discount office supply chain stores averaging in excess of 20,000 square feet, with over 11,000 of those square feet devoted to traditional office supplies, and carrying over 5,000 SKUs of consumable office supplies in addition to computers, office furniture, and other nonconsumables. In contrast, stores such as K mart devote approximately 210 square feet to the sale of approximately 250 SKUs of consumable office supplies. Kinko's devotes approximately 50 square feet to the sale of 150 SKUs. Target sells only 400 SKUs. Both Sam's Club and Computer City each sell approximately 200 SKUs.

In addition to the differences in SKU numbers and variety, the superstores are different from many other sellers of office supplies due to the type of customer they target and attract. The superstores' customer base overwhelmingly consists of small businesses with fewer than 20 employees and consumers with home offices. In contrast, mail order customers are typically mid-sized companies with more than 20 employees . . .

* * * * *

Based on the Court's observations, the Court finds that the unique combination of size, selection, depth and breadth of inventory offered by the superstores distinguishes them from other retailers

* * * * *

While it is clear to the Court that Staples and Office Depot do not ignore sellers such as warehouse clubs, Best Buy, or Wal–Mart, the evidence clearly shows that Staples and Office Depot each consider the other superstores as the primary competition.

* * * * *

For the reasons set forth in the above analysis, the Court finds that the sale of consumable office supplies through office supply superstores is the appropriate relevant product market for purposes of considering the possible anticompetitive effects of the proposed merger between Staples and Office Depot.

* * * * *

IV. Probable Effect on Competition

After accepting the Commission's definition of the relevant product market, the Court next must consider the probable effect of a merger between Staples and Office Depot in the geographic markets previously identified. One way to do this is to examine the concentration statistics and HHIs within the geographic markets. If the relevant product market is defined as the sale of consumable office supplies through office supply superstores, the HHIs in many of the geographic markets are at problematic levels even before the merger. Currently, the least concentrated market is that of Grand Rapids–Muskegon–Holland, Michigan, with an HHI of 3,597, while the most concentrated is Washington, D.C. with an HHI of 6,944. In contrast, after a merger of Staples and Office Depot, the least concentrated area would be Kalamazoo–Battle Creek, Michigan, with an HHI of 5,003, and many areas would have HHIs of 10,000. The average increase in HHI caused by the merger would be 2,715 points. The concentration statistics show that a merged Staples–Office Depot would have a dominant market share in 42 geographic markets across the country. The combined shares of Staples and Office Depot in the office superstore market would be 100% in 15 metropolitan areas. It is in these markets the post-merger HHI would be 10,000. In 27 other metropolitan areas, where the number of office superstore competitors would drop from three to two, the postmerger market shares would range from 45% to 94%, with postmerger HHIs ranging from 5,003 to 9,049. Even the lowest of these HHIs indicates a "highly concentrated" market.

* * * * *

The HHI calculations and market concentration evidence, however, are not the only indications that a merger between Staples and Office Depot may substantially lessen competition. Much of the evidence already discussed with respect to defining the relevant product market also indicates that the merger would likely have an anticompetitive effect. The evidence of the defendants' own current pricing practices, for example, shows that an office superstore chain facing no competition from other superstores has the ability to profitably raise prices for consumable office supplies above competitive levels. The fact that Staples and Office Depot both charge higher prices where they face no superstore competition demonstrates that an office superstore can raise prices above competitive levels. The evidence also shows that defendants also change their price zones when faced with entry of another office superstore, but do not do so for other retailers.

* * * * *

V. Entry Into the Market

"The existence and significance of barriers to entry are frequently, of course, crucial considerations in a rebuttal analysis . . .

* * * * *

The Commission offered Office 1 as a specific example of the difficulty of entering the office superstore arena. Office 1 opened its first two stores in 1991. By the end of 1994, Office 1 had 17 stores, and grew to 35 stores operating in 11 Midwestern states as of October 11, 1996. As of that date, Office 1 was the fourth largest office supply superstore chain in the United States. Unfortunately, also as of that date, Office 1 filed for Chapter 11 bankruptcy protection. Brad Zenner, President of Office 1, testified through declaration, that Office 1 failed because it was severely undercapitalized in comparison with the industry leaders, Staples, Office Depot,

and OfficeMax. In addition, Mr. Zenner testified that when the three leaders ultimately expanded into the smaller markets where Office 1 stores were located, they seriously undercut Office 1's retail prices and profit margins. Because Office 1 lacked the capitalization of the three leaders and lacked the economies of scale enjoyed by those competitors, Office 1 could not remain profitable.

For the reasons discussed above, the Court finds it extremely unlikely that a new office superstore will enter the market and thereby avert the anticompetitive effects from Staples' acquisition of Office Depot.

* * * * *

VI. Efficiencies

* * * * *

First, the Court notes that the cost savings estimate of $4,947 billion over five years which was submitted to the Court exceeds by almost 500% the figures presented to the two Boards of Directors in September 1996, when the Boards approved the transaction. The cost savings claims submitted to the Court are also substantially greater than those represented in the defendants' Joint Proxy Statement/Prospectus "reflecting the best currently available estimate of management," and filed with the Securities and Exchange Commission on January 23, 1997 . . .

* * * * *

[T]he Court cannot find that the defendants have rebutted the presumption that the merger will substantially lessen competition . . .

VII. The Equities

There are two types of equities which the Court must consider, private equities and public equities. In this case, the private equities include the interests of the shareholders and employees of Staples and Office Depot. The public equities are the interests of the public, either in having the merger go through or in preventing the merger . . .

After examining the evidence in this case, the Court finds that in light of the public equities advanced by the plaintiff, the equities, both public and private, set forth by the defendants are insufficient to overcome the presumption in favor of granting a preliminary injunction.

* * * * *

Both the plaintiff as well as the defendants introduced evidence regarding the combined company's postmerger plans, including the consolidation of warehouse and supply facilities in order to integrate the two distribution systems, the closing of 40 to 70 Office Depot and Staples stores, changing the name of the Office Depot stores, negotiating new contracts with manufacturers and suppliers, and, lastly, the consolidation of management which is likely to lead to the loss of employment for many of Office Depot's key personnel. As a result, the Court finds that it is extremely unlikely, if the Court denied the plaintiff's motion and the merger were to go through, that the merger could be effectively undone and the companies divided if the agency later found that the merger violated the antitrust laws . . .

More importantly, in addition to the practical difficulties in undoing the merger, consumers would be at risk of serious anticompetitive harm in the interim. Without an injunction, consumers in the 42 geographic markets where superstore competition would be eliminated or significantly reduced face the prospect of higher prices than they would have absent the merger.

* * * * *

Turning finally to the private equities, the defendants have argued that the principal private equity at stake in this case is the loss to Office Depot shareholders who will likely lose a substantial portion of their investments if the merger is enjoined. The Court certainly agrees that Office Depot shareholders may be harmed, at least in the short term, if the Court granted the plaintiff's motion and enjoined the merger. This private equity alone, however, does not suffice to justify denial of a preliminary injunction.

* * * * *

Conclusion

* * * * *

[T]he Court finds that the Commission has shown a likelihood that it will succeed in proving, after a full administrative trial on the merits, that the effect of the proposed merger between Staples and Office Depot "may be substantially to lessen competition" in violation of Section 7 of the Clayton Act . . . The FTC's motion for a preliminary injunction shall be granted.

Afterword

Citing the time and money involved in battling the federal government, Staples and Office Depot officially called off their proposed merger days after Judge Hogan's decision.

Staples CEO Thomas Stemberg was interviewed following the *FTC* v. *Staples* battle.

Q: Should a company expect to be treated fairly by staff members of the antitrust regulators?
A: I do believe that the people in these agencies are well-intentioned and are trying to do the right thing for the consumer. As one who has spent the last decade or more of his business career fighting cartels and trying to induce pro-competitive activity in the marketplace,

(*Continued*)

their goals are very much the same as ours, which is to give the consumer the best deal possible. The antitrust regulators are some of the hardest working people I have even seen. They are extremely dedicated, and if you aren't prepared to go 15 rounds, you're picking a bad fight. Some of the mergers that are out there today that they are contesting, I'd be contesting if I were them, too.

Source: Del Jones, "Today's Issue: Some Lessons Learned in an Antitrust Fight," *USA Today,* March 30, 1998, p. 5B.

Questions

1. *a.* What "general rule" did the Staples court employ in determining the relevant product market?
   b. What evidence supported the use of the "office supply superstore submarket" as the relevant product market?
2. *a.* What evidence supported the FTC's claim that the merger would lead to anticompetitive effects?
   b. In weighing the "public and private equities," why did the Court come down on the side of the government?
3. Analysts have argued that in the Staples case the government was less worried about market shares than about the price impact of the merger were it to be approved. Explain what those analysts mean.
4. The United States sued to block the proposed merger of two nonprofit hospitals in Rockford, Illinois, a city of 140,000 people. The two hospitals were the largest in the community with a combined market share estimated at 64 to 72 percent. If approved, the merger would have resulted in an estimated market share of 90 percent for the three largest hospitals in Rockford. The hospitals argued that the geographic market should not be limited to Rockford and parts of nearby counties as defined by the lower court judge, but should include a ten-county area of northern Illinois and southern Wisconsin centered on Rockford. That area included a number of smaller, rural hospitals. Ninety percent of hospitalized Rockford residents were hospitalized in Rockford itself. How would you rule on the legality of the merger? Explain. See U.S. v. Rockford Memorial Corp., 898 F. 2d 1278 (7th Cir. 1990).
5. In 1958, Pabst Brewing Company acquired Blatz Brewing Company. Pabst was America's 10th-largest brewer, while Blatz was the 18th largest. After the merger, Pabst had 4.49 percent of the nationwide beer market and was the fifth-largest brewer. In the regional market of Wisconsin, Michigan, and Illinois, the merger gave Pabst 11.32 percent of the sales. After the merger, Pabst led beer sales in Wisconsin with 23.95 percent of that statewide market. The beer market was becoming increasingly concentrated, with the total number of brewers declining from 206 to 162 during the years 1957 to

1961. In *United States* v. *Pabst Brewing Co.*, 384 U.S. 546 (1966), the Supreme Court found the merger violated the Clayton Act, Section 7. The Court did not choose among the three geographic market configurations, saying that the crucial inquiry is whether a merger may substantially lessen competition anywhere in the United States. Thus, the Court held that, under these facts, a 4.49 percent share of the market was too large.

Respected scholar and jurist Richard Posner labeled the Pabst decision an "atrocity" and the product of a "fit of nonsense" on the part of the Supreme Court.25 What economic arguments would support Posner's colorful complaint?

6. In the period 1917–19, Du Pont acquired 23 percent of the stock in the then-fledgling General Motors Corporation. By 1947, Du Pont supplied 68 percent of GM's automotive finish needs and 38 percent of its fabric needs. In 1955, General Motors ranked first in sales and second in assets among all U.S. industrial corporations, while accounting for approximately two-fifths of the nation's annual automobile sales. In 1949, the Justice Department challenged Du Pont's 1917–19 acquisitions of GM stock.

   a. Why did the government challenge Du Pont's acquisition?

   b. May an acquisition be properly challenged 30 years after the fact, as in Du Pont?

   c. Given your general understanding of finishes and fabrics, how would you defend DuPont?

   d. Decide. Explain. See *United States* v. *E. I. du Pont de Nemours & Co.*, 353 U.S. 586 (1957).

Part Four—American Antitrust Laws and the International Market

America's commercial market embraces the entire globe. Antitrust questions can become extremely complex in transactions involving multiple companies, in multiple nations, where those transactions are potentially governed by U.S. and foreign antitrust laws. U.S. antitrust laws are, of course, applicable to foreign firms doing business here. The Sherman, Clayton, and FTC acts, among others, are all potentially applicable to American business abroad. [For a brief overview of Canadian antitrust law, see **http://www.smithlyons.ca/dbic/com_anti.htm**]

Sherman Act

The Sherman Act applies to the conduct of American business abroad when that business has a direct effect on American commerce. That the business was conducted entirely abroad or that the agreement was entered into in another nation does not excuse an American firm from the reach of the Sherman Act (assuming American courts can achieve the necessary jurisdiction).

Clayton Act

Section 7 of the Clayton Act is clearly applicable to acquisitions combining domestic and foreign firms and is potentially applicable to acquisitions not involving American firms if the effect would be harmful to competition in the American market.

Federal Trade Commission Act

As noted earlier, the FTC shares antitrust enforcement authority with the Justice Department, and Section 5 of the act strengthens Clayton 7.

Enforcement

The complexity and uncertainty of the antitrust laws can be particularly daunting in the international arena. However, the Justice Department has provided a mechanism for achieving greater clarity. Under its Business Review Procedure, the Justice Department will prepare a statement of its likely response to a proposed transaction so that the parties will have advance notice of the government's antitrust stance.

FOREIGN ANTITRUST LAWS

The United States historically has taken a much more aggressive attitude toward antitrust policy and enforcement than have the nations of Western Europe and Japan. Indeed, those nations generally regard cooperative economic arrangements and concentrations of industrial power as necessary and desirable components of economic success. Of course, Japan and the European Union historically have practiced economic policies involving government quite directly in regulating and "managing" commercial practice for the general good.

Now we are seeing more active antitrust policies around the globe.

• The *European Union* maintains a set of competition rules that roughly parallel our treatment of antitrust problems. Like Sherman Section 1, the EU rules forbid concerted practices that harm competition. Abuse of market dominance (monopoly) is also forbidden, and in that instance, the EU law appears to be more aggressive than ours because, to be considered threatening, a market share in the EU need not be so large as what we would require for a challenge here in the United States.[26] Further, the EU rules are more aggressive than ours in the sense that charging "excessive" prices is considered abusive and may be attacked under the antitrust laws.

Mergers in the EU are regulated like those in the United States, with premerger notification requirements and the European Commission to review those proposed mergers. Broadly, Commission review is limited to cases with EU implications (rather than those limited to one nation). Judicial review is available via the European Court of Justice. In its first 12 months, the Commission reviewed 50 mergers and disapproved one while negotiating adjustments in several others.[27] The chief concern is that one firm will secure market dominance as a consequence of a merger. In addition to the EU antitrust rules, each nation can continue to enforce its own national laws in those cases not exhibiting EU implications.

EU policy toward mergers was well illustrated by regulators' 1999 clearance of Ford Motor Co.'s $6.45 billion purchase of the passenger car division of the Swedish manufacturer, Volvo. In approving the deal, the European Commission noted that the company's European market share will not exceed 15 percent; competition from GM, BMW, and others is strong; and the merger was not expected to increase entry barriers.[28] [For an extensive database on EU merger law, see **http://europa.eu.int/en/comm/dg04/ dg4home.htm**]

• *Germany* revised its antitrust laws in 1999 to harmonize them with EU policies. The German/EU approach reflects greater concerns about market concentration than the comparable American stance. For example, Germany specifies market shares that are (rebuttably) presumed to constitute actionable market dominance:

One company has a market share of at least one-third of the relevant market.

Up to three companies have a market share of at least 50 percent of the relevant market.

Up to five companies have a market share of at least two-thirds of the relevant market.[29]

• In 1999, *Japan* amended its Antimonopoly Act to require foreign companies with large sales volumes in Japan to report mergers to Japan's Fair Trade Commission.[30]

• *Israel* and the United States, in 1999, reached an agreement to cooperate on antitrust enforcement, much like similar American arrangements with Canada and the European Union. Basically, the agreement provides for notice of antitrust actions that will affect the other nation.[31]

ANTITRUST AND GLOBAL COMPETITIVENESS

Antitrust law figures prominently in American trade policy. In keeping with the globalization movement, United States antitrust policy encourages free and open markets around the globe. Thus, where international price fixing and other restraints of trade unlawfully interfere with American commercial interests, our antitrust laws are increasingly playing a role.

Extraterritoriality.   Our most controversial expression of antitrust in trade policy was the Justice Department decision, announced in 1992, to more broadly apply American antitrust law abroad. The general idea is to sue foreign firms that violate United States antitrust laws even when the anticompetitive actions take place entirely overseas (extraterritorial application). In practice, the Justice Department files suit in United States courts against foreign companies operating in the United States, where those foreign companies are taking action abroad that (1) harms competition in the United States, or (2) limits

American access to markets in other nations. Those lawsuits are permissible under United States law only where the conduct abroad has a "direct, substantial, and reasonably foreseeable" effect on the United States domestic market, United States imports, or United States exports.

Criminal Extraterritoriality.   Initially, extraterritorial application of American antitrust law was employed in civil cases, but in a striking development, the federal First Circuit Court of Appeals in 1997 ruled that United States criminal antitrust laws apply to foreign companies even if the entirety of the criminal behavior took place abroad so long as the criminal activity was intended to have and, in fact, did have substantial effects in the United States.[32]

That potentially far-reaching decision arose from an antitrust action in which the United States brought criminal price fixing charges against Nippon Paper Industries of Japan. The Justice Department claimed that Nippon had conspired with other Japanese manufacturers to fix prices in the fax paper market thus violating the Sherman Act. The First Circuit decision, affirmed the Justice Department's right to bring the charges, but when the case went to trial the jury deadlocked and a federal district court judge then threw out the charges, ruling that the government had failed to prove its case. While some paper prices did rise, others remained the same, and yet others actually fell. Thus, the government failed to prove that the conspiracy had a "substantial effect" in the United States.[33] The decision was a particularly stern blow to the government in that, at the time of the decision in 1999, some 20 to 30 grand juries in the United States were investigating international cartels.

> The United States brought criminal price fixing charges against Nippon Paper Industries of Japan

Questions—Parts Three and Four

1. Poplar Bluff is a city of 17,000 people in southeastern Missouri. Sikeston and Cape Girardeau, Missouri, both towns with populations of over 40,000, are 40 and 60 miles away from Poplar Bluff. Tenet Healthcare owns Lucy Lee Hospital in Poplar Bluff and proposed to buy Doctors' Regional Medical Center, also in Poplar Bluff. Both hospitals are profitable, but both are underutilized and have had trouble attracting specialists. The Federal Trade Commission filed suit to block the acquisition. The key question involved definition of the geographic market. The FTC proposed a relevant geographic market that essentially matched the service area: a 50-mile radius of downtown Poplar Bluff. Ninety percent of the two hospitals' patients come from that area. Four other hospitals are in that area. The merged hospital would have 84 percent of the patients in that geographic market. Tenet argues that the geographic market should encompass a 65-mile radius from downtown Poplar Bluff. That area includes 16 hospitals. How should the Court of Appeals decide where the geographic market lies? See *FTC* v. *Tenet Health Care Corp.,* 186 F.3d 1045 (8th Cir. 1999).
2. Staples CEO Thomas Stemberg was asked, based on his experience, "which mergers will be contested and which ones will sail through?" How do you think the government decides which mergers to challenge? See Del Jones, "Today's Issue: Some Lessons Learned in an Antitrust Fight," *USA Today,* March 30, 1998, p. 5B.

3. A major concern with horizontal mergers is the increased potential for collusion. List those structural conditions that would encourage coordinated interaction between competitors.

4. Critics are concerned that increasing mergers, especially those involving media firms, threaten democracy.

    a. Explain that argument.

    b. Do you agree? Explain.

5. Among the various stakeholder groups, list the likely losers in the current merger boom.

6.   *a.* In your judgment, must we nudge Japan more vigorously than we have to date by bringing antitrust litigation in American courts to challenge business practices in Japan? Explain.

    b. If we do so, could Japan then legitimately raise challenges in Japanese courts using Japanese law against American business practices such as "Buy American" programs or a community that declined to buy Toyota autos for its municipal police force? See Editorial, "Barr vs. Consumers," *The Wall Street Journal,* March 3, 1992, p. A12.

7. In 1986 distinguished economist William Shepherd argued:

> It may not be too late to turn back from this road to serfdom by reviving the case for antitrust, but the odds aren't favorable. More probably, antitrust will continue to sink.[34]

    a. What did Shepherd mean about "this road to serfdom?"

    b. In reading this chapter, do you think antitrust has been revived? Explain.

    c. Is bigness bad, or is it necessary in today's global economy? Explain.

8. Antitrust attorney Joel Davidow says that four policy measures have been critical to the success of formerly socialist nations that are moving to a market economy: privatization, restructuring, deregulation, and adoption of competition legislation (antitrust). Now almost all of the industrial nations of the world, including former Soviet states Russia, Poland, Hungary, and Bulgaria, are taking all of these measures.

    a. Why is antitrust law important to the success of the new market economies in these formerly collectivist nations?

    b. Is antitrust of importance to developing nations such as India, Argentina, and Brazil? Explain. See Joel Davidow, "The Relevance of Antimonopoly Policy for Developing Countries," *The Antitrust Bulletin* 37, no. 1 (Spring 1992), p. 277.

9. Is the influence of big business so persuasive that it nullifies the effective enforcement of the antitrust laws? Explain.

10. Antitrust authorities must address a critical and empirically difficult policy problem: Does seller concentration in a market ordinarily result in increased prices? That is, in a particular market, are fewer firms with larger shares likely to produce higher prices than would be the case with a more fragmented market? Free market theorists are generally untroubled by concentration. What do you think? Explain.

11. The Federal Trade Commission in 1996 forced an adjustment in a merger in the gene therapy market that is expected to reach $1 billion in value by 2001:

> In a striking extension of antitrust enforcement into the laboratory, the government forced Swiss drug giants Ciba-Geigy AG and Sandoz AG to license to rivals critical technology in order to prevent a market monopoly that doesn't yet exist.

The Federal Trade Commission's conditions for letting the two manufacturers merge—thus creating the world's second-largest drug maker, Novartis AG—are intended to prevent the new company from dominating gene-therapy research, a promising technology that could one day treat certain cancers and genetic diseases but is still years from the marketplace.[35]

    a.   Explain what the FTC forced Novartis to do.

    b.   Why did the FTC impose that requirement on Novartis?

12. The Justice Department has traditionally been reluctant to accept economies of scale as a defense to an otherwise unlawful merger. Why?

13. How can a merger benefit society?

14. Which economic considerations support the view that unilateral growth is preferable to growth by merger?

15. Excel, a division of Cargill, was the second-largest firm in the beef-packing market. It sought to acquire Spencer Pack, a division of Land-O-Lakes, and the third-largest beef packer. After the acquisition, Excel would have remained second ranked in the business, but its market share would have been only slightly smaller than that of the leader, IBP. Monfort, the nation's fifth-largest beef packer, sought an injunction to block the acquisition, claiming a violation of Clayton Section 7. In effect, Monfort claimed the merger would result in a dangerous concentration of economic power in the beef-packing market, with the result that Excel would pay more for cattle and charge less for its processed beef, thus placing its competitors in a destructive and illegal price–cost squeeze. Monfort claimed Excel's initial losses in this arrangement would be covered by its wealthy parent, Cargill. Then, when the competition was driven from the market, Monfort claimed, Excel would raise its processed beef prices to supracompetitive levels. Among other defenses, Excel averred that the heavy losses Monfort claimed were merely the product of intense competition, a condition that would not constitute a violation of the antitrust laws. The district court found for Monfort and the appeals court, considering the cost–price squeeze a form of predatory pricing, affirmed. Excel appealed to the Supreme Court. Decide. Explain. See *Cargill, Inc.* v. *Monfort of Colorado, Inc.,* 479 U.S. 104 (1986).

INTERNET EXERCISE

Assistant United States Attorney General for Antitrust, Joel Klein, testified in 1998 before the United States Senate regarding Justice Department policy toward mergers. Answer the following questions using Klein's testimony at [**http://judiciary.senate.gov/joelk616.htm**]

a. Explain the Justice Department's view of the role of size, in and of itself, in determining whether a merger threatens competition.

b. Explain why the government decided to challenge mergers involving Primestar, Raytheon, and Northrop Grumman.

NOTES

1. John R. Wilke, Dean Takahashi, and Keith Perine, "Accord Lets Intel Avoid Trial and a Beating Such as Microsoft Is Taking," *The Wall Street Journal,* March 9, 1999, p. A1.

2. *United States* v. *Grinnell,* 384 U.S. 563, 570-1 (1966).

3. G. Pascal Zachary, "Let's Play Oligopoly," *The Wall Street Journal,* March 8, 1999, p. B1.

4. U.S. v. *Aluminum Company of America,* 148 F.2d 416 (2d Cir. 1945).

5. 110 F. Supp. 295 (Mass. 1953), aff'd per curium, 347 U.S. 521 (1954).

6. *Cliff Food Stores, Inc.* v. *Kroger Co.,* 417 F.2d 203, 207 n. 2 (5th Cir. 1969).

7. For a journalistic account, see Wendy Bounds, "Court Ruling Backs Kodak on Two Decrees," *The Wall Street Journal,* August 7, 1995, p. A9.

8. *Spectrum Sports, Inc.* v. *Shirley McQuillan,* 122 L. Ed. 2d 247 (1993).

9. Ibid., p. 257.

10. Debora Vrana, "Market Savvy," *Los Angeles Times,* December 16, 1999, p. C4.

11. "U.S. Mergers Set Record," *Des Moines Register,* January 1, 2000, p. 8S.

12. David Ignatius, "Mobil's Suicide," *Washington Post,* January 10, 1999, p. C7.

13. William Kovacic, "Can Exxon Mobilize?" *Fulton County Daily Report,* April 13, 1999.

14. David Koenig, "Oil Merger to Cost 16,000 Jobs," *Montreal Gazette,* December 16, 1999, p. C4.

15. Steven Lipin, "In Many Merger Deals, Ego and Pride Play Big Roles in Which Way Talks Go," *The Wall Street Journal,* August 22, 1996, p. C1.

16. Mathew Hayward and Donald Hambrick, "Explaining the Premiums Paid for Large Acquisitions: Evidence of CEO Hubris," *Administrative Science Quarterly* 42 (1997), p. 103.

17. Steven Rattner, "Mergers: Windfalls or Pitfalls?" *The Wall Street Journal*, October 11, 1999, p. A22.

18. See Michael J. Mandel, "All These Mergers Are Great, But . . . ," *Business Week,* October 18, 1999, p. 48, and Jeffrey Garten, "Megamergers are a Clear and Present Danger," *Business Week,* January 25, 1999, p. 28.

19. "FTC Fines Firm for Violations of Antitrust Rules," *The Wall Street Journal,* March 31, 1999, p. A4.

20. William Kovacic, "Can Exxon Mobilize?"

21. John R. Wilke, "FTC Weighs Stricter Policy on Mergers," *The Wall Street Journal,* January 12, 2000, p. A3.

22. Note, "Analyzing Differentiated-Product Mergers: The Relevance of Structural Analysis," *Harvard Law Review* 111 (June 1998), p. 2420.

23. Wayne D. Collins and Steven C. Sunshine, "Rigor and Sophistry in the New Merger Guidelines," *The American Enterprise* 4, no. 2 (March–April 1993), p. 61.

24. Stephen Labaton and Doreen Carvajal, "Book Retailer Ends Bid for Wholesaler," *New York Times,* June 3, 1999, sec. C, p. 1.

25. Richard Posner, *Antitrust Law* (Chicago: The University of Chicago Press, 1976), p. 130.

26. Margot Horspool and Valentine Korah, "Competition," *Antitrust Bulletin* 37, no. 2 (Summer 1992), p. 337.

27. Ibid., p. 343.

28. Associated Press, "EU Clears Ford Buyout of Volvo Car Division," *Waterloo–Cedar Falls Courier,* March 29, 1999, p. C5.

29. Carsten Gromotke, "What the New German Antitrust Law Means for International Businesses," *New York Law Journal,* February 18, 1999, p. 1.

30. John R. Schmertz, Jr., "Japan Amends Anti-Monopoly Act," *International Law Update* 5, no. 3 (March 1999), Section: Competition.

31. "U.S. and Israel Sign Antitrust Cooperation Agreement," *International Enforcement Law Reporter* 15, no. 5 (May 1999), Section VIII: Anti-Trust Enforcement Cooperation.

32. *U.S.* v. *Nippon Paper Industries Co., Ltd.,* 109 F.3d 1 (1st Cir. 1997); cert. den. *Nippon Paper Industries Co., Ltd.* v. *United States,* 522 U.S. 1044 (1998).

33. *U.S.* v. *Nippon Paper Industries Co., Ltd.,* 62 F. Supp. 2d 173 (D. Mass. 1999).

34. William G. Shepherd, "Bust the Reagan Trustbusters," *Fortune,* August 4, 1986, pp. 225, 227.

35. John R. Wilke, "U.S. Forces New Drug Giant to Share Genetic Research," *The Wall Street Journal,* December 18, 1996, p. B4.

Chapter 11

Antitrust Law—Restraints of Trade

INTRODUCTION

Not surprisingly, the big government–free market debate that has dominated American politics in recent years also plays an important role in antitrust policy. The "Chicago School," with its advocacy of free market theory, has been successful in reshaping antitrust analysis. Efficiency has become the goal and cornerstone of the new view of antitrust. For this reason and others, the merits of "bigness" have become more broadly acknowledged. Nonetheless, dramatic Supreme Court reversals of "old" antitrust law have been the exception, and recent decisions such as the *Microsoft* ruling (see Chapter 10), suggest an increasing interest in looking at the specific facts, marketing practices, costs, and benefits of each case rather than relying unreservedly on free market reasoning.

Mistrust of the business community and doubts about the free market as a complete cure for our problems presumably will continue to compete with the undeniable intellectual power of efficient markets thinking. Justification for the mistrust and doubts has been abundant in recent years as colossal global price-fixing scandals have been uncovered and punished by American antitrust authorities. In May 1999, the Justice Department secured a record-setting criminal fine of more than $750 million from three international vitamin manufacturers, F. Hoffman La Roche & Co. of Switzerland, BASF AG of Germany, and Rhone-Poulenc SA of France. While hardly household names, the three companies control about 80 percent of the world market for the leading vitamins, including A, C, and E. The Justice Department claimed that the companies colluded to fix worldwide prices in meetings around the world:

> the Justice Department secured a record-setting criminal fine of more than $750 million

According to the Justice Department, vitamin makers developed an elaborate set of rules and enforcement agreements to ensure prices and market allocations were fixed and stayed that way. Top managers allegedly would gather yearly to haggle over which company would be allowed to sell how much of each particular vitamin. A maker of vitamin C, for instance, would be granted a certain percent of the market. This so-called top-shot meeting would also establish price increases for the coming year.

A few months later, global marketing heads would meet to approve the "budget." Then at a third meeting, other executives would gather to make certain that all participants were sticking to the cartel's rules. The companies, according to Justice, tried to hide their activities by burning any paper documenting the conspiracy.[1]

The criminal fine was only the beginning. Six vitamin industry giants (those noted above as well as three from Japan) agreed later in 1999 to a $1.1 billion settlement of civil price-fixing claims based on overcharges to about 1,000 corporate buyers of bulk vitamins used as supplements in everything from peanut butter to animal feed. Three United States executives and two from Canada have also pleaded guilty to price-fixing charges while other criminal and civil charges are yet expected in the vast conspiracy. [For many of the settlement documents in the vitamin civil case, see **http://www.dcd.uscourts.gov/99ms197d.pdf**]

The importance of government attention to these price fixers is evident not only in the vitamin scandal but in the recent criminal and civil pursuit of food processing giant, Archer Daniels Midland, and competitors who fixed prices in the lysine and citric acid markets. ADM paid a then-record $100 million fine and in 1998 three of ADM's top executives, including the son of chairman Dwayne O. Andreas, were found guilty of criminal price-fixing charges. The younger Andreas was sentenced to two years in federal prison and fined $350,000. [For an update on ADM's continuing price-fixing problems and its response to those problems, see **http://www.herald-review.com/03/adm0711-9.html**]

The article that follows describes the prosecution of the vitamin conspiracy in Canada.

5 VITAMIN MAKERS FINED HEAVILY IN CANADA FOR PRICE FIXING PLOT

Barry Brown

Five international pharmaceutical companies that supply most of the bulk vitamins used in Canadian food as supplements have been slapped with the largest corporate fine in Canadian history—$61 million (U.S. funds)—after pleading guilty to price fixing.

The five—F. Hoffman-La Roche of Switzerland, BASF AG of Germany, Rhone-Poulenc SA of France and two Japanese companies, Eisai and Danchi Pharmaceutical—admitted they plotted to divide up the Canadian market and fix prices above competitive levels for nearly a decade.

The five companies—and others still under investigation—rigged the price of a range of vitamins that are used in milk, bread, orange juice, cereals, and animal feed.

The companies recorded Canadian sales of more than $460 million (U.S.) during their 1990–1999 marketing conspiracy when prices were pushed up by as much as 30 percent over competitive levels.

Dan McTeague, a consumer advocate and member of Parliament for the Liberal Party, said the global plot to fix vitamin prices fell apart after a lengthy grand jury investigation in Texas earlier this year pushed the companies into admitting their collusion.

Canadian prosecutor Martin Low said the companies' top executives would hold annual meetings in Switzerland to divide up the global vitamin market.

To reduce the fines they faced in Canada, Low said, the executives traveled to Ottawa this spring to confess their crimes and offer evidence of their wrongdoing.

But the fines were small by U.S. standards. After plea bargaining in the U.S., Hoffman-La Roche was hit with a $500 million fine, BASF $225 million and other conspirators $65 million.

By contrast, La Roche received a fine of $33 million (U.S.) in Canada, while BASF paid about $12.5 million (U.S.), followed by Rhone-Poulenc at $12.6 million (U.S.) and the two Japanese companies, which were fined about $1.5 million (U.S.) each.

Along with those fines, Roche also pleaded guilty to a separate scheme with Archer Daniels Midland to fix the market for citric acid and paid an additional fine of $2 million (U.S.) following ADM's penalty of $11 million (U.S.), which it paid last year.

While the fines close the door on most of the government's actions against the companies, Low said eight class-action lawsuits still are pending.

Source: *Buffalo News,* September 26, 1999, p. 6A. Reprinted by permission of the copyright holder, Barry Brown.

Questions

1. La Roche's fines, though record-setting, were only a fraction of the company's $110 billion market capitalization. Should antitrust fines be large enough to cause actual harm to the financial well-being of the wrongdoers? Explain.
2. Chairman Dwayne Andreas apologized for ADM's price-fixing episode, but the apology appears to have been directed primarily to shareholders. Would an Andreas apology to the American public be of any value? Explain.

Part One—Horizontal Restraints

RULE OF REASON

Not surprisingly, our legal system casts a particularly unyielding eye on horizontal restraints of trade. After all, cooperation among those who should be competitors nullifies much of the virtue of the market system. The various horizontal restraints are governed by Section 1 of the Sherman Act, which forbids contracts, combinations, or conspiracies in restraint of trade. The statute was, of course, broadly drawn to embrace the many possibilities that arise in American commerce. Therefore, the courts were left to determine what Congress meant by the phrase *restraint of trade*. In the *Standard Oil*[2] decision of 1911, the U.S. Supreme Court articulated what has come to be known as the *Rule of Reason*. In essence, the Court said that the Sherman Act forbids only *unreasonable* restraints of trade. The reasonableness of a restraint of trade is largely determined by balancing the pro- and anticompetitive effects of the situation in question. Thus, the plaintiff must prove the existence of an anticompetitive agreement or conduct and also prove that, on balance, the agreement or conduct is harmful to competition. [For an antitrust overview, see **http://www.law.cornell.edu/topics/antitrust.html**]

PER SE VIOLATIONS

Some antitrust violations such as horizontal price fixing are perceived to be so injurious to competition that their mere existence constitutes unlawful conduct. Plaintiffs must prove that the violation in question occurred, but they need not prove that the violation caused, or is likely to cause, competitive harm. Such violations are simply unlawful on their face.

However, in recent years, the use of the *per se* doctrine has declined. The economics-based notions of efficiency and consumer welfare are increasingly causing jurists to insist on a showing of the defendant's economic abuse before finding an antitrust violation.[3] [For the Federal Trade Commission antitrust division, see **http://www.ftc.gov/ftc/antitrust.htm**]

HORIZONTAL PRICE-FIXING

Principal legislation: Sherman Act, Section 1.

> Every contract, combination in the form of trust or otherwise, or conspiracy, in restraint of trade or commerce, among the several States, or with foreign nations, is hereby declared to be illegal.

Competitors may not lawfully agree on prices. The principle is simple and fundamental to an efficient, fair marketplace. Establishing the presence of an unlawful price-fixing arrangement, on the other hand, ordinarily is anything but simple.

Proof

The major dilemma in price fixing and all other Sherman Act Section 1 violations is the measure of proof that satisfies the requirement of a contract, combination, or conspiracy. Evidence of collusion arises in a variety of ways. Broadly, a showing of cooperative action amounting to an agreement must be established. In general, that showing may be developed by any of the following four methods of proof:

1. *Agreement with direct evidence.* In the easiest case, the government can produce direct evidence such as writings or testimony from participants proving the existence of collusion.
2. *Agreement without direct evidence.* Here, the defendants directly but covertly agree, and circumstantial evidence such as company behavior must be employed to draw an inference of collusion.
3. *Agreement based on a tacit understanding.* In this situation, no direct exchange of assurances occurs, but the parties employ tactics that act as surrogates for direct assurances and thus "tell" each other that they are, in fact, in agreement.
4. *Agreement based on mutual observation.* These defendants have simply observed each others' pricing behavior over time, and they are able therefore to anticipate each other's future conduct and act accordingly without any direct collusion but with results akin to those that would have resulted from a direct agreement.[4]

Parallel Conduct. An unlawful conspiracy is to be distinguished from independent but parallel business behavior by competitors. So-called *conscious parallelism* is fully lawful because the competitors have not agreed either explicitly or by implication to follow the same course of action. Rather, their business judgment has led each to independently follow parallel paths.

Contemporary Cases. Obviously, price-fixing undermines the effectiveness of the market so prosecutors have been aggressive in attacking those conspiracies. Among those attacks are the following:

- **Federal—Nasdaq.** In 1998, the biggest names in the securities world, while denying wrongdoing, agreed to pay $1.03 billion to settle charges of a price-rigging scheme for stocks listed on the Nasdaq market. The payment was the largest antitrust settlement in United States history.[5] [For more on the Nasdaq case, see **http://www.antitrust.org/cases/pricefixing.html#nasdaq**]
- **International—SGL.** Of course, price fixing is not confined to the United States. Like the vitamin and ADM episodes, SGL Carbon AG, a German maker of graphite electrodes, agreed in 1999 to pay a $135 million fine and plead guilty to United States price-fixing charges.[6] Interestingly, China's government actually encourages price fixing by industry associations in products ranging from sugar to autos. The government fears price slashing: "China's economy is still immature," says Men Xiaowei, of the State Economic and Trade Commission. "Chaotic price competition will ruin industries unless we guide it."[7]

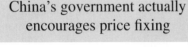

China's government actually encourages price fixing

- **The States—Abbott.** In 1996, Abbott Laboratories agreed to pay $32.5 million to settle claims in 17 states alleging that Abbott had conspired to fix prices in the infant formula market.[8]

Questions

1. Should immature markets such as those in China be officially protected by price-fixing arrangements? Explain.
2. *a.* Why does the government settle so many of its antitrust cases rather than taking them to court for a full review of the issues?
   b. What does the government lose when it settles rather than litigating?

A Reasonable Restraint of Trade?

Historically, a contract, combination, or conspiracy among competitors (like that among the vitamin producers) that reduced or eliminated price competition was an unreasonable *restraint of trade* and per se unlawful. Thus, an inquiry into the reasonableness of the price or proof of a harmful effect was unnecessary. Recent decisions, however, such as the *Law* case below, demonstrate that the judiciary is questioning the *per se rule* in some instances of horizontal price fixing. [For a price-fixing database, see **http://www.antitrust.org/price.htm**]

LAW v. NATIONAL COLLEGIATE ATHLETIC ASSOCIATION
134 F.3d 1010 (10th Cir. 1998)
[Cert. Den., 119 S.Ct. 65 (1998)]

Circuit Judge Ebel

Defendant-Appellant the National Collegiate Association ("NCAA") promulgated a rule limiting annual compensation of certain Division I entry-level coaches to $16,000. Basketball coaches affected by the rule filed a class action challenging the restriction under Section 1 of the Sherman Antitrust Act. The district court granted summary judgment on the issue of liability to the coaches and issued a permanent injunction restraining the NCAA from promulgating this or any other rules embodying similar compensation restrictions. The NCAA now appeals.

I. Background

During the 1980s, the NCAA became concerned over the steadily rising costs of maintaining competitive athletic programs, especially in light of the requirements imposed by Title IX of the 1972 Education Amendments Act to increase support for women's athletic programs. The NCAA observed that some college presidents had to close academic departments, fire tenured faculty, and reduce the numbr of sports offered to students due to economic constraints. At the same time, many institutions felt pressure to "keep up with the Joneses" by increasing spending on recruiting talented players and coaches and on other aspects of their sports programs in order to remain competitive with rival schools. In addition, a report commissioned by the NCAA known as the "Raiborn Report" found that in 1985 42% of NCAA Division I schools reported deficits in their overall athletic program budgets, with the deficit averaging $824,000 per school.

In January of 1989, the NCAA established a Cost Reduction Committee (the "Committee") to consider means and strategies for reducing the costs of intercollegiate athletics "without disturbing the competitive balance" among NCAA member institutions. In his initial letter to Committee members, the Chairman of the Committee thanked participants for joining "this gigantic attempt to save intercollegiate athletics from itself." It was felt that only a collaborative effort could reduce costs effectively while maintaining a level playing field because individual schools could not afford to make unilateral spending cuts in sports programs for fear that doing so would unduly hamstring that school's ability to compete against other institutions that spent more money on athletics.

The Committee proposed an array of recommendations to amend the NCAA's bylaws, including proposed Bylaw 11.6.4 that would limit Division I basketball coaching staffs to four members—one head coach, two assistant coaches, and one entry-level coach called a "restricted-earnings coach."

A second proposed rule restricted compensation of restricted-earnings coaches in all Division I sports other than football to a total of $12,000 for the academic year and $4,000 for the summer months (the "REC Rule" for restricted-earnings coaches).

* * * * *

In this case, plaintiffs–appellees were restricted-earnings men's basketball coaches at NCAA Division I institutions in the academic year 1992–93. They challenged the REC Rule's limitation on compensation under section 1 of the Sherman Antitrust Act, as an unlawful "contract, combination . . . or conspiracy, in restraint of trade."

On January 5, 1996, the district court permanently enjoined the NCAA from enforcing or attempting to enforce any restricted-earnings coach salary limitations against the named plaintiffs, and it further enjoined the NCAA from "reenacting the compensation limitations embodied in [the REC Rule]." The NCAA appeals the permanent injunction.

* * * * *

[Part II omitted.]

III. Rule of Reason Analysis

Section 1 of the Sherman Act provides, "Every contract, combination in the form of trust or otherwise, or conspiracy, in restraint of trade or commerce among the several States, or with foreign nations, is hereby declared to be illegal." Because nearly every contract that binds the parties to an agreed course of conduct "is a restraint of trade" of some sort, the Supreme Court has limited the restrictions contained in section 1 to bar only "unreasonable restraints of trade." To prevail on a section 1 claim under the Sherman Act, the coaches needed to prove that the NCAA (1) participated in an agreement that (2) unreasonably restrained trade in the relevant market. The NCAA does not dispute that the REC Rule resulted from an agreement among its members. However, the NCAA does contest the district court's finding that on the record before it, there was no genuine dispute of fact that the REC Rule is an unreasonable restraint of trade.

Two analytical approaches are used to determine whether a defendant's conduct unreasonably restrains trade: the *per se* rule and the rule of reason. The *per se* rule condemns practices that "are entirely void of redeeming competitive rationales." Once a practice is identified as illegal *per se,* a court need not examine the practice's impact on the market or the procompetitive justifications for the practice advanced by a defendant before finding a violation of antitrust law. Rule of reason analysis, on the other hand, requires an analysis of the restraint's effect on competition. A rule of reason analysis first requires a determination of whether the challenged restraint has a substantially adverse effect on competition. The inquiry then shifts to an evaluation of whether the procompetitive virtues of the alleged wrongful conduct justifies the otherwise anticompetitive impacts. The district court applied the rule of reason standard to its analysis of the REC Rule.

Horizontal price-fixing is normally a practice condemned as illegal *per se.* By agreeing to limit the price which NCAA members may pay for the services of restricted-earnings coaches, the REC Rule fixes the cost of one of the component items used by NCAA members to produce the product of Division I basketball. As a result, the REC Rule constitutes the type of naked horizontal agreement among competitive purchasers to fix prices usually found to be illegal *per se.*

* * * * *

However, the Supreme Court recognized that certain products require horizontal restraints, including horizontal price-fixing, in order to exist at all.

The Supreme Court in *NCAA* v. *Board of Regents* departed from the general treatment given to horizontal price-fixing agreements by refusing to apply a *per se* rule and instead adopting a rule of reason approach in reviewing an NCAA plan for televising college football that involved both limits on output and price-fixing.

* * * * *

The "product" made available by the NCAA in this case is college basketball; the horizontal restraints necessary for the product to exist include rules such as those forbidding payments to athletes and those requiring that athletes attend class, etc. Because some horizontal restraints serve the procompetitive purpose of making college sports available, the Supreme Court subjected even the price and output restrictions at issue in *Board of Regents* to a rule of reason analysis.

* * * * *

Board of Regents concluded that because horizontal agreements are necessary for sports competition, all horizontal agreements among NCAA members, even those as egregious as price-fixing, should be subject to a rule of reason analysis.

The Supreme Court has made it clear that the *per se* rule is a "demanding" standard that should be applied only in clear-cut cases. As a result, courts consistently have analyzed challenged conduct under the rule of reason when dealing with an industry in which some horizontal restraints are necessary for the availability of a product, even if such restraints involve horizontal price-fixing agreements. Thus, we apply the rule of reason approach in this case.

Courts have imposed a consistent structure on rule of reason analysis by casting it in terms of shifting burdens of proof. Under this approach, the plaintiff bears the initial burden of showing that an agreement had a substantially adverse effect on competition. If the plaintiff meets this burden, the burden shifts to the defendant to come forward with evidence of the procompetitive virtues of the alleged wrongful conduct. If the defendant is able to demonstrate procompetitive effects, the plaintiff then must prove that the challenged conduct is not reasonably necessary to achieve the legitimate objectives or that those objectives can be achieved in a substantially less restrictive manner. Ultimately, if these steps are met, the harms and benefits must be weighed against each other in order to judge whether the challenged behavior is, on balance, reasonable.

A. Anticompetitive Effect

We first review whether the coaches in this case demonstrated anticompetitive effect so conclusively that summary judgment on the issue was appropriate. A plaintiff may establish anticompetitive effect indirectly by proving that the defendant possessed the requisite market power within a defined market or directly by showing actual anticompetitive effects, such as control over output or price.

The NCAA argues that the district court erred by failing to define the relevant market and by failing to find that the NCAA possesses power in that market. The NCAA urges that the relevant market in this case is the entire market for men's basketball coaching services, and it presented evidence demonstrating that positions as restricted-earnings basketball coaches make up, at most, 8 percent of that market. Thus, the NCAA argues it has at least created a genuine issue of material fact about whether it possesses market power and that summary judgment was therefore inappropriate.

The NCAA misapprehends the purpose in antitrust law of market definition . . . No "proof of market power" is required where the very purpose and effect of a horizontal agreement is to fix prices so as to make them unresponsive to a competitive marketplace. Thus, where a practice has obvious anticompetitive effects—as does price fixing—there is no need to prove that the defendant possesses market power. Rather, the court is justified in proceeding directly to the question of whether the procompetitive justifications advanced for the restraint outweigh the anticompetitive effects under a "quick look" rule of reason.

We find it appropriate to adopt such a quick look rule of reason in this case. Under a quick look rule of reason analysis, anticompetitive effect is established, even without a determination of the relevant market, where the plaintiff shows that a horizontal agreement to fix prices exists, that the agreement is effective, and that the price set by such an agreement is more favorable to the defendant than otherwise would have resulted from the operation of market forces. Under this standard, the undisputed evidence supports a finding of anticompetitive effect. The NCAA adopted the REC Rule to reduce the high cost of part-time coaches' salaries, over $60,000 annually in some cases, by limiting compensation to entry-level coaches to $16,000 per year. The NCAA does not dispute that the cost-reduction has effectively reduced restricted-earnings coaches' salaries. Because the REC Rule was successful in artificially lowering the price of coaching services, no further evidence or analysis is required to find market power to set prices.

* * * * *

B. Procompetitive Rationales

Under a rule of reason analysis, an agreement to restrain trade may still survive scrutiny under section 1 if the procompetitive benefits of the restraint justify the anticompetitive effects.

In *Board of Regents* the Supreme Court recognized that certain horizontal restraints, such as the conditions of the contest and the eligibility of participants, are justifiable under the antitrust laws because they are necessary to create the product of competitive college sports. Thus, the only legitimate rationales that we will recognize in support of the REC Rule are those necessary to produce competitive intercollegiate sports. The NCAA advanced three justifications for the salary limits: retaining entry-level coaching positions; reducing costs; and maintaining competitive equity. We address each of them in turn.

1. Retention of Entry–Level Positions

The NCAA argues that the plan serves the procompetitive goal of retaining an entry-level coaching position. The NCAA asserts that the plan will allow younger, less experienced coaches entry into Division I coaching positions.

* * * * *

The NCAA did not present any evidence showing that restricted-earnings positions have been filled by entry-level applicants or that the rules will be effective over time in accomplishing this goal. Nothing in the record suggests that the salary limits for restricted-earnings coaches will be effective at creating entry-level positions.

2. Cost Reduction

The NCAA next advances the justification that the plan will cut costs. However, cost-cutting by itself is not a valid procompetitive justification. If it were, any group of competing buyers could agree on maximum prices. Lower prices cannot justify a cartel's control of prices charged by suppliers, because the cartel ultimately robs the suppliers of the normal fruits of their enterprises. Further, setting maximum prices reduces the incentive among suppliers to improve their products. Likewise, in our case, coaches have less incentive to improve their performance if their salaries are capped.

The NCAA adopted the REC Rule because without it competition would lead to higher prices. The REC Rule was proposed as a way to prevent Division I schools from engaging in behavior the association termed "keeping up with the Joneses," i.e., competing. However, the NCAA cannot argue that competition for coaches is an evil because the Sherman Act "precludes inquiry into the question whether competition is good or bad."

While increasing output, creating operating efficiencies, making a new product available, enhancing product or service quality, and widening consumer choice have been accepted by courts as justifications for otherwise anticompetitive agreements, mere profitability or cost savings have not qualified as a defense under the antitrust laws.

The NCAA argues that reducing costs can be considered a procompetitive justification because doing so is necessary to maintain the existence of competitive intercollegiate sports.

*   *   *   *   *

We are dubious that the goal of cost reductions can serve as a legally sufficient justification for a buyers' agreement to fix prices even if such cost reductions are necessary to save inefficient or unsuccessful competitors from failure. Nevertheless, we need not consider whether cost reductions may have been required to "save" intercollegiate athletics and whether such an objective served as a legitimate procompetitive end because the NCAA presents no evidence that limits on restricted-earning coaches' salaries would be successful in reducing deficits, let alone that such reductions were necessary to save college basketball. Moreover, the REC Rule does not equalize the overall amount of money Division I schools are permitted to spend on their basketball programs. There is no reason to think that the money saved by a school on the salary of a restricted-earnings coach will not be put into another aspect of the school's basketball program, such as equipment or even another coach's salary, thereby increasing inequity in that area.

3. Maintaining Competitiveness

We note that the NCAA must be able to ensure some competitive equity between member institutions in order to produce a marketable product. The NCAA asserts that the REC Rule will help to maintain competitive equity by preventing wealthier schools from placing a more experienced, higher-priced coach in the position of restricted-earnings coach.

While the REC Rule will equalize the salaries paid to entry-level coaches in Division I schools, it is not clear that the REC Rule will equalize the experience level of such coaches. Nowhere does the NCAA prove that the salary restrictions enhance competition, level an uneven playing field, or reduce coaching inequities. Rather, the NCAA only presented evidence that the cost reductions would be achieved in such a way so as to maintain without "significantly altering," "adversely affecting," or "disturbing" the existing competitive balance. The undisputed record reveals that the REC Rule is nothing more than a cost-cutting measure and shows that the only consideration the NCAA gave to competitive balance was simply to structure the rule so as not to exacerbate competitive imbalance. Thus, on its face, the REC Rule is not directed towards competitive balance.

Affirmed.

Afterword

A 1999 Supreme Court decision in the *California Dental Association* price-fixing case appeared to hold that the "quick-look" analysis, noted in *Law,* is appropriate only when the restraint at issue is clearly anticompetitive.[9] Similarly, in 1999, the Federal Trade Commission and Department of Justice affirmed the importance of considering likely efficiencies (rather than routinely finding per se violations) in their jointly issued draft of "Antitrust Guidelines for Collaborations Among Competitors." In today's economy, competitors often want to engage in joint ventures to share increasingly expensive research and development costs, to expand into overseas markets, to achieve production efficiencies, and so on. Broadly, the guidelines call for reasoning like that for horizontal mergers (see Chapter 10) to determine whether those collaborations are likely to be anticompetitive. The guidelines do not have the force of law, but courts and industry rely upon them as persuasive expressions of the government's view of antitrust law.[10]

Questions

1. Under the quick look *Rule of Reason* analysis, how is anticompetitive effect established?
2. Outline the rule of reason analysis employed by the *Law* court.
3. According to the *Law* court, when is the rule of reason the appropriate analytical tool in a horizontal restraint of trade case?
4. Why did the NCAA lose the *Law* case?
5. Assume two drugstores, located across the street from each other and each involved in interstate commerce, agree to exchange, on a monthly basis, a list of prices charged for all nonprescription medications. Is that arrangement lawful in the absence of any further cooperation? Explain.
6. As common sense and the cases reveal, sharing of price information among competitors can facilitate anticompetitive collusion, but how might that sharing facilitate competition?
7. Justify the use of per se rulings.
8. The gasoline dealers association in a community reaches an agreement providing that (1) both major brands and independents will not give trading stamps or other premiums and (2) majors agree not to advertise their prices except on the pumps.
   a. What is the purpose of the arrangement?
   b. What violation of law might be alleged? Decide the case. Explain. See *U.S.* v. *Gasoline Retailers Association,* 285 F.2d 688 (1961).
9. Assume that 10 real estate firms operate in the city of Gotham. Further assume that each charges a 7 percent commission on all residential sales.
   a. Does that uniformity of prices in and of itself constitute price-fixing? Explain.
   b. Assume we have evidence that the firms agreed to set the 7 percent level. What defense would be raised against a price-fixing charge?
   c. Would that defense succeed? Explain. See *McLain* v. *Real Estate Board of New Orleans, Inc.,* 444 U.S. 232 (1980).

REFUSAL TO DEAL

Principal legislation: Sherman Act, Section 1.

A *group boycott* is an instance of concerted action in which a collectivity of traders jointly refuses to deal with another trader or traders. Typically, the purpose of such an arrangement is to remove or "police" a competitor. The per se rule is applied to group boycotts involving horizontal agreements among direct competitors. All other boycotts are to be subjected to the Rule of Reason analysis.

The potential anticompetitive effect of group boycotts was illustrated by a 1998 Federal Trade Commission settlement of antitrust charges against 25 northwestern United States car dealers. The FTC alleged that the dealers had threatened to boycott their supplier, Chrysler, unless it reduced the number of vehicles being allocated to a competing car dealer, Dave Smith Motors of Kellogg, Idaho. The alleged boycott reflected the striking influence of our emerging computer-based economy in that Dave Smith Motors had developed a highly successful Internet dealership that offered preset, online prices for its Chrysler vehicles. Since Chrysler's new car allocations are based on sales volume, the other dealers claimed that Dave Smith Motors' multistate sales and resulting high volume gave it an unfair advantage. The group of 25 dealers did not admit any wrongdoing, but the settlement prohibits them from engaging in or threatening any boycott of any car manufacturer or consumer.[11]

Per Se. In *Klor's* v. *Broadway-Hale Stores, Inc.,*[12] the Supreme Court applied the per se rule to boycotts. Klor's, Inc., operated a retail store on Mission Street, San Francisco, California. Broadway-Hale Stores, Inc., a chain of department stores, operated one of its stores next door. The two stores competed in the sale of radios, television sets, refrigerators, and other household appliances.

Klor's filed suit against Broadway-Hale and 10 appliance manufacturers and made the following allegations: George Klor started an appliance store some years before 1952. Klor's was as well equipped as Broadway-Hale to handle all brands of appliances. Nevertheless, manufacturers and distributors of such well-known brands as General Electric, RCA, Admiral, Zenith, Emerson, and others conspired among themselves and with Broadway-Hale either not to sell to Klor's or to sell to it only at discriminatory prices and highly unfavorable terms. Broadway-Hale used its "monopolistic" buying power to bring about this situation.

Broadway-Hale submitted unchallenged affidavits showing there were hundreds of other household appliance retailers, some within a few blocks of Klor's, who sold many competing brands of appliances, including those the defendants refused to sell to Klor's.

The Court found a group boycott in violation of the Sherman Act in that the combination deprived Klor's of the opportunity to buy appliances in the open market, thus driving Klor's out of business in the retail market for those appliances.

Questions

1. Sears, issuer of the Discover credit card, acquired a savings and loan, MountainWest. Sears then sought to issue a low-interest, "Prime Option" Visa card through Mountain West. However, a Visa bylaw barred membership by "any applicant which is issuing, directly or indirectly, Discover cards or American Express cards, or any other cards deemed competitive by the board of directors." Hence, Visa, a joint venture, refused MountainWest's application for membership. MountainWest then filed suit claiming a violation of the Sherman Act by Visa. Visa responded by saying that the Sherman Act should not apply to a joint venture that, in effect, simply refuses to share its property. And Visa noted that Sears, with its Discover card, is a direct competitor and one of the largest issuers of credit cards in the United States.
   a. What charge(s) would you raise on behalf of Sears?
   b. Defend Visa.
   c. Decide. Explain. See *SCFL ILC Inc. d/b/a Mountainwest Financial* v. *Visa U.S.A. Inc.,* 819 F. Supp. 956 (DC Utah, 1993).
2. Baptist Eye Institute, a group of nonspecialized ophthalmologists in Jacksonville, Florida, controlling approximately 15 percent of the referral market, sent nearly all of

their retina cases to the Florida Retina Institute. Is BEI engaging in an unlawful group boycott against plaintiff Retina Associates, a retina care provider in competition with the Florida Retina Institute? Explain. See *Retina Associates P.A.* v. *Southern Baptist Hospital of Florida Inc.,* 105 F.3d 1376 (11th Cir. 1997).

3. Discon, a telephone salvage company, sold services to MECo, a subsidiary of NYNEX, a phone company for the New York/New England area. MECo switched from Discon to AT&T Technologies, a Discon competitor, and paid a higher price to AT&T than it had paid to Discon. Discon claimed that the buyer and NYNEX then received a rebate from AT&T at the end of the year. Discon argued that NYNEX was able to pass on its higher costs to its customers because NYNEX was a part of a regulated phone market. Discon claimed that NYNEX, its subsidiaries and AT&T were engaging in a group boycott in violation of the Sherman Act in order to drive Discon out of the market. Decide. Explain. See *NYNEX Corp.* v. *Discon, Inc.,* 119 S.Ct. 493 (1998).

Part Two—Vertical Restraints

We have been studying unfair trade practices by competitors, that is, horizontal restraints of trade. Now we turn our attention to antitrust violations on the vertical axis: that is, restraints involving two or more members of a supply chain (e.g., a manufacturer and a retailer of that manufacturer's products).

Toys

Government concern about vertical restraints has increased in recent years as vividly evidenced by the Federal Trade Commission's controversial complaint against toy retailing giant, Toys "R" Us. Basically, the FTC alleges that Toys "R" Us used its market power, beginning in 1989, to force toy manufacturers to reduce sales to discount clubs/warehouses. The government claims Toys "R" Us secured agreements from manufacturers that "they would not sell the same toys to the clubs that were purchased by Toys "R" Us; that similar toys sold to the clubs would be repackaged with added features to create 'club specials' that were more expensive than merchandise at Toys "R" Us; and that manufacturers would notify the retailer before selling to the clubs to eliminate any 'competitive conflict.'"[13]

Toys "R" Us denies any anticompetitive behavior, and experts, at this writing, are somewhat puzzled by the FTC allegations in that the 20 percent market share held by Toys "R" Us is well beneath the level normally considered sufficient to provide anticompetitive market power. Further, in recent years, Toys "R" Us has experienced weakened earnings and strengthened competition from Wal-Mart and others.[14]

The FTC claim is in the federal courts at this writing, but Toys "R" Us elected to settle a class action brought by 44 states on grounds similar to those raised by the FTC. While admitting no wrongdoing, Toys "R" Us agreed to pay $40.5 million in cash and toys for persuading toy manufacturers like Mattel to refuse to sell specified toys, such as Barbie Dream House, to some discount chains.[15]

Normally companies not holding monopoly power can unilaterally refuse to deal with others and can lawfully insist on exclusive dealing arrangements. Such arrangements are common. Victoria's Secret, for example, has the sole right to sell the Miracle Bra, and The Sharper Image catalog and retail chain specializes in exclusive upscale products. Since the upscale Sharper Image cannot compete with discounters on price, exclusive arrangements are critical to the company's marketing success.[16] The FTC Toys "R" Us initiative may help to clarify the limits, if any, on these marketing strategies. [For the Toys "R" Us antitrust litigation page, see **http://www.toysettlement.com/info.html**]

RESALE PRICE MAINTENANCE/VERTICAL TERRITORIAL AND CUSTOMER RESTRAINTS

Principal legislation: Sherman Act, Section 1; Federal Trade Commission Act, Section 5.

Manufacturers and distributors often seek to specify the price at which their customers may resell their products. Having sold its product, why should a manufacturer or distributor seek to influence the price at which the product is resold? The primary reasons are threefold: (1) by establishing a minimum price, the product's reputation for quality may be enhanced, (2) resale price maintenance policy seeks to prevent discount stores from undercutting regular retail outlets, and (3) to prevent *free riders*. (Why does the manufacturer or distributor prefer its products to be sold in traditional retail stores rather than in discount enterprises?) [For a database of vertical restraints law, see **http://www.antitrust.org/vertical.htm**]

Colgate Doctrine

An *agreement* between a seller and its buyer, fixing the price at which the buyer may resell the product, is a per se violation. However, under the Supreme Court's 1919 *Colgate* decision,[17] sellers may lawfully engage in resale price maintenance if they do nothing more than specify prices at which their products are to be sold and unilaterally refuse to deal with anyone who does not adhere to those prices. Now some legal experts believe *Colgate's* safe harbor for sellers has been abandoned by many courts.[18]

Nonprice Restraints

In addition to price restraints, manufacturers commonly wish to impose restrictions on where and to whom their product may be resold. Those restrictions typically afford an exclusive sales territory to a distributor. Similarly, manufacturers may prevent distributors from selling to some classes of customers (e.g., a distributor might be forbidden to sell to an unfranchised retailer). Of course, such arrangements necessarily retard or eliminate intrabrand competition. Because price and service competition among dealers in the same brand ordinarily is of benefit to the consumer, the courts have frequently struck down such arrangements. Still, those territorial and customer allocations also have merits. The *GTE Sylvania* case[19] enunciated those virtues and established the position that vertical restrictions are to be judged on a case-by-case basis, balancing interbrand and intrabrand competitive effects while recognizing that interbrand competition is the primary concern of antitrust law. Thus the Rule of Reason is to be applied to vertical territorial and customer restraints.

At this point, the student will want to understand the critical distinction between horizontal and vertical restraints. The former, in general, are per se unlawful. The latter are to be resolved under the Rule of Reason unless an agreement on prices is involved. As explained above, *horizontal* restrictions are those arising from an agreement among the *competitors* themselves, while *vertical* restrictions ordinarily are those imposed on *buyers* by their *suppliers*. The *Business Electronics Corporation (B.E.C.)* case that follows offers a summary of the Supreme Court's analysis of both vertical price and nonprice restraints and it demonstrates the difficulty of proving resale price maintenance.

BUSINESS ELECTRONICS CORPORATION v. SHARP ELECTRONICS CORPORATION
485 U.S. 717(1988)

Justice Scalia

Petitioner Business Electronics Corporation seeks review of a decision of the United States Court of Appeals for the Fifth Circuit holding that a vertical restraint is per se illegal under § 1 of the Sherman Act, only if there is an express or implied agreement to set resale prices at some level. We granted certiorari to resolve a conflict in the Courts of Appeals regarding the proper dividing line between the rule that vertical price restraints are illegal per se and the rule that vertical nonprice restraints are to be judged under the rule of reason.

I

In 1968, petitioner became the exclusive retailer in the Houston, Texas, area of electronic calculators manufactured by respondent Sharp Electronics Corporation. In 1972, respondent appointed Gilbert Hartwell as a second retailer in the Houston area. During the relevant period, electronic calculators were primarily sold to business customers for prices up to $1,000. While much of the evidence in this case was conflicting—in particular, concerning whether petitioner was "free riding" on Hartwell's provision of presale educational and promotional services by providing inadequate services itself—a few facts are undisputed. Respondent published a list of suggested minimum retail prices, but its written dealership agreements with petitioner and Hartwell did not obligate either to observe them, or to charge any other specific price. Petitioner's retail prices were often below respondent's suggested retail prices and generally below Hartwell's retail prices, even though Hartwell too sometimes priced below respondent's suggested retail prices. Hartwell complained to respondent on a number of occasions about petitioner's prices. In June 1973, Hartwell gave respondent the ultimatum that Hartwell would terminate his dealership unless respondent ended its relationship with petitioner within 30 days. Respondent terminated petitioner's dealership in July 1973.

Petitioner brought suit in the United States District Court for the Southern District of Texas, alleging that respondent and Hartwell had conspired to terminate petitioner and that such conspiracy was illegal per se under § 1 of the Sherman Act. The case was tried to a jury. The district court submitted a liability interrogatory to the jury

404 Part III Trade Regulation and Antitrust

that asked whether "there was an agreement or understanding between Sharp Electronics Corporation and Hartwell to terminate Business Electronics as a Sharp dealer because of Business Electronics's price cutting." The district court instructed the jury at length about this question:

> The Sherman Act is violated when a seller enters into an agreement or understanding with one of its dealers to terminate another dealer because of the other dealer's price cutting. Plaintiff contends that Sharp terminated Business Electronics in furtherance of Hartwell's desire to eliminate Business Electronics as a price-cutting rival.
>
> If you find that there was an agreement between Sharp and Hartwell to terminate Business Electronics because of Business Electronics's price cutting, you should answer yes to Question Number 1.

* * * * *

> A combination, agreement, or understanding to terminate a dealer because of his price cutting unreasonably restrains trade and cannot be justified for any reason. Therefore, even though the combination, agreement, or understanding may have been formed or engaged in . . . to eliminate any alleged evils of price cutting, it is still unlawful.
>
> If a dealer demands that a manufacturer terminate a price-cutting dealer, and the manufacturer agrees to do so, the agreement is illegal if the manufacturer's purpose is to eliminate the price cutting.

The jury answered Question 1 affirmatively and awarded $600,000 in damages . . .

* * * * *

The Fifth Circuit reversed . . .

II

A

Section 1 of the Sherman Act provides that "[e]very contract, combination in the form of trust or otherwise, or conspiracy, in restraint of trade or commerce among the several States, or with foreign nations, is declared to be illegal." Since the earliest decisions of this Court interpreting this provision, we have recognized that it was intended to prohibit only unreasonable restraints of trade. Ordinarily, whether particular concerted action violates § 1 of the Sherman Act is determined through case-by-case application of the so-called rule of reason . . . Certain categories of agreements, however, have been held to be per se illegal, dispensing with the need for case-by-case evaluation . . .

* * * * *

Although vertical agreements on resale prices have been illegal per se since *Dr. Miles Medical Co.* v. *John. D. Park & Sons Co.,* we have recognized that the scope of per se illegality should be narrow in the context of vertical restraints. In *Continental T.V. Inc.* v. *GTE Sylvania Inc.* we refused to extend per se illegality to vertical nonprice restraints, specifically to a manufacturer's termination of one dealer pursuant to an exclusive territory agreement with another. We noted that especially in the vertical restraint context "departure from the rule-of-reason standard must be based on demonstrable economic effect rather than . . . upon formalistic line drawing." We concluded that vertical nonprice restraints had not been shown to have such a "pernicious effect on competition" and to be so "lack[ing][in] . . . redeeming value" as to justify per se illegality. Rather, we found, they had real potential to stimulate interbrand competition, "the primary concern of antitrust law":

> [N]ew manufacturers and manufacturers entering new markets can use the restrictions in order to induce competent and aggressive retailers to make the kind of investment of capital and labor that is often required in the distribution of products unknown to the consumer. Established manufacturers can use them to induce retailers to engage in promotional activities or to provide service and repair facilities necessary to the efficient marketing of their products. Service and repair are vital for many products . . . The availability and quality of such services affect a manufacturer's goodwill and the competitiveness of his product. Because of market imperfections such as the so-called free-rider effect, these services might not be provided by retailers in a purely competitive situation, despite the fact that each retailer's benefit would be greater if all provided the services than if none did.

Moreover we observed that a rule of per se illegality for vertical nonprice restraints was not needed or effective to protect *intra*brand competition. First, so long as interbrand competition existed, that would provide a "significant check" on any attempt to exploit intrabrand market power. In fact, in order to meet that interbrand competition, a manufacturer's dominant incentive is to lower resale prices. Second, the per se illegality of vertical restraints would create a perverse incentive for manufacturers to integrate vertically into distribution, an outcome hardly conducive to fostering the creation and maintenance of small businesses.

* * * * *

Our approach to the question presented in the present case is guided by the premises of *GTE Sylvania:* that there is a presumption in favor of a rule-of-reason standard; that departure from that standard must be justified by demonstrable economic effect, such as the facilitation of cartelizing, rather than formalistic distinctions; that interbrand competition is the primary concern of the antitrust laws; and that rules in this area should be formulated with a view towards protecting the doctrine of *GTE Sylvania.* These premises lead us to conclude that the line drawn by the Fifth Circuit is the most appropriate one.

There has been no showing here that an agreement between a manufacturer and a dealer to terminate a "price cutter," without a further agreement on the price or price levels to be charged by the remaining dealer, almost always tends to restrict competition and reduce output. Any assistance to cartelizing that such an agreement might provide cannot be distinguished from the sort of minimal assistance that might be provided by vertical nonprice agreements like the exclusive territory agreement in *GTE Sylvania,* and is insufficient to justify a per se rule. Cartels are neither easy to form nor easy to maintain . . .

The District Court's rule on the scope of per se illegality for vertical restraints would threaten to dismantle the doctrine of *GTE Sylvania.* Any agreement between a manufacturer and a dealer to terminate another dealer who happens to have charged lower prices can be alleged to have been directed against the terminated dealer's "price cutting." In the vast majority of cases, it will be extremely difficult for the manufacturer to convince a jury that its motivation was to ensure adequate services, since price cutting and some measure of service cutting usually go hand in hand. Accordingly, a manufacturer that agrees to give one dealer an exclusive territory and terminates another dealer pursuant to that agreement, or even a manufacturer that agrees with one dealer to terminate another for failure to provide contractually obligated services, exposes itself to the highly plausible claim that its real motivation was to terminate a price cutter. Moreover, even vertical restraints that do not result in dealer termination, such as the initial granting of an exclusive territory or the requirement that certain services be provided, can be attacked as designed to allow existing dealers to charge higher prices. Manufacturers would be likely to forgo legitimate and competitively useful conduct rather than risk treble damages and perhaps even criminal penalties.

We cannot avoid this difficulty by invalidating as illegal per se only those agreements imposing vertical restraints that contain the word "price," or that affect the "prices" charged by dealers. Such formalism was explicitly rejected in *GTE Sylvania.* As the above discussion indicates, all vertical restraints, including the exclusive territory agreement held not to be per se illegal in *GTE Sylvania,* have the potential to allow dealers to increase "prices" and can be characterized as intended to achieve just that. In fact, vertical nonprice restraints only accomplish the benefits identified in *GTE Sylvania* because they reduce intrabrand price competition to the point where the dealer's profit margin permits provision of the desired services. As we described it in *Monsanto:* "The manufacturer often will want to ensure that its distributors earn sufficient profit to pay for programs such as hiring and training additional salesmen or demonstrating the technical features of the product, and will want to see that 'free-riders' do not interfere."

* * * * *

. . . Petitioner has provided no support for the proposition that vertical price agreements generally underlie agreements to terminate a price cutter. That proposition is simply incompatible with the conclusion of *GTE Sylvania* and *Monsanto* that manufacturers are often motivated by a legitimate desire to have dealers provide services, combined with the reality that price cutting is frequently made possible by "free riding" on the services provided by other dealers. The district court's per se rule would therefore discourage conduct recognized by *GTE Sylvania* and *Monsanto* as beneficial to consumers.

* * * * *

Affirmed.

Afterword

In 1997 the United States Supreme Court ruled that vertical *maximum* price fixing is to be analyzed under the rule of reason.[20] Thus, a supplier now may lawfully specify a price beyond which the buyer may not resell the product in question so long as the arrangement does not harm competition. The decision overruled a 1968 Supreme Court decision that had treated vertical maximum price-fixing as a per se antitrust violation.[21] The ruling emerged from a deal between an Illinois gasoline supplier, State Oil, and a gasoline dealer in suburban Chicago, Barkat Khan. State Oil specified that Khan could sell gasoline at whatever price he liked, but if that price was higher than State Oil's suggested retail price, the excess was to be returned to State Oil. Among the practical implications of the decision is the possibility that manufacturers may impose maximum resale prices on high demand items such as some Porsches or Poké-mon collectables.[22]

Questions

1. Summarize the essence of the *B.E.C.* holding.
2. What practical effects would you expect the *B.E.C.* decision to have on the behavior of *(a)* manufacturers and *(b)* discounters?
3.   *a.* What is the *Colgate* doctrine?
     b. Is the *Colgate* doctrine a practical, workable standard of conduct? Explain.
4. Assume a manufacturer communicates to its distributors a "suggested retail price" for its product. Further assume the distributors individually decide to follow that suggestion.
     a. Does that conduct violate the law? Explain.
     b. Would it matter whether the product is heavily advertised? Explain.
     c. What is fair-trade pricing?
     d. What is its current status?
5. In *Continental T.V., Inc.,* v. *GTE Sylvania Inc.,* 433 U.S. 36 (1977), the Supreme Court took the position that interbrand, rather than intrabrand, agreements must be the primary concern of antitrust law.
     a. Why does the Court take that view?
     b. Is the Court correct? Explain.
6. The *GTE* decision distinguished vertical "nonprice" restrictions (such as location clauses) from vertical price restrictions (resale price maintenance). Make the argument that the Court's distinction was not meaningful.
7. What is the "free-rider" problem that frequently concerns the courts in cases involving vertical territorial restraints?
8. Assume a manufacturer assigns an "area of primary responsibility" to a distributor. The distributor's sales are not confined to that area, but he or she must devote his or her best efforts to that area, and failure to do so may result in termination of the distributorship. Is that arrangement lawful? Explain.
9. In 1977, Michelin failed to renew its dealership agreement with the Donald B. Rice Tire Company of Frederick, Maryland. After seven years with Michelin, approximately 80 percent of Rice's business was derived from wholesaling the tires to smaller authorized and unauthorized dealers. Other authorized dealers complained to Michelin of Rice's wholesale business. In an effort to assume primary wholesaling responsibility, Michelin chose not to renew its relationship with Rice. Rice contended that the nonrenewal was a consequence of its refusal to comply with Michelin's customer and territorial restraints, and Rice filed an antitrust action on that basis. Michelin argued that it was a new entrant into a concentrated market, and as such, restraints on intrabrand competition were necessary to induce retailers to carry Michelin tires. However, the court found frequent shortages of Michelin tires. Michelin also argued that nonrenewal was "necessary to prevent free riding by retailers on the services provided by other dealers."

   Rice had not advertised in a quantity commensurate with his sales volume. He sold to unauthorized dealers who were not bound to do any advertising and could thus reap benefits of advertising by authorized dealers. Michelin wanted to encourage point-of-sales services and the offering of specialized services but feared authorized dealers would not invest the necessary expenditures because of their fear of being underpriced by unauthorized dealers. Decide the case. See *Donald B. Rice Tire Company Inc.* v. *Michelin Corporation,* 483 F. Supp. 750 (D. Md. 1980), 638 F.2d 15 (1981), cert. den., 454 U.S. 864 (1981).

TYING ARRANGEMENTS

Principal legislation: Clayton Act, Section 3; Sherman Act, Sections 1 and 2; Federal Trade Commission Act, Section 5.

> Clayton Act, Section 3. That it shall be unlawful for any person engaged in commerce, in the course of such commerce, to lease or make a sale or contract for sale of goods . . . or other commodities . . . or fix a price charged therefore, or discount from or rebate upon, such price, on the condition, agreement, or understanding that the lessee or purchaser thereof shall not use or deal in the goods . . . or other commodities of a competitor or competitors of the lessor or seller, where the effect of such lease, sale, or contract for sale or such condition, agreement, or understanding may be to substantially lessen competition or tend to create a monopoly in any line of commerce.

The typical tying arrangement permits a customer to lease or buy a desired product (the tying product) only if she or he also leases or buys another product (the tied product). Of course, such an arrangement may harm consumers, but the primary antitrust concerns are twofold: (1) A party who already enjoys market power over the tying product is able to extend that power into the tied product market; and (2) competitors in the tied product market are foreclosed from equal access to that market.

In brief, proof of the following conditions constitutes a per se violation:

1. The existence of separate products. (That is, two products are present rather than one product consisting of two or more components, or two entirely separate products that happen to be elements in a single transaction.)
2. A requirement that the purchase of one of the products (the tying product) is conditioned on the purchase of another product (the tied product).
3. Market power in the tying product.
4. Substantial commerce in the tied product is affected. (Some courts require a substantial *anticompetitive* effect in the tied product market.)

While the courts have clearly looked with disfavor on tying agreements, certain conditions do justify such arrangements. For example, a tying agreement is more likely to be acceptable when employed by a new competitor seeking entry against established sellers. [How would you defend a computer lessor who required its lessee to use only the tabulating cards supplied by the lessor? See *IBM* v. *U.S.,* 298 U.S. 131 (1936).]

The case that follows illustrates the application of tying concerns to the vast franchising sector of the American economy.

> European Union antitrust policy regarding vertical restraints of trade has recently embraced more free market, "Chicago School" thinking: "Minimum resale price maintenance is banned, but suggested retail prices are OK. And there is a market share threshold for application of the vertical regulations on exclusive dealing and tying." Steven P. Reynolds, "EU Vertical Restraints Policy—A New Regulation and New Approach," *Law and Policy Related to Vertical Restraints* [**http://www.antitrust.org/law/vertical.html**]

QUEEN CITY PIZZA, INC. v. DOMINO'S PIZZA, INC.
124 F.3d 430 (3d Cir. 1997) [Cert. Denied *Baughans, Inc.* v. *Domino's Pizza*, 523 U.S. 1059 (1998)]

Circuit Judge Scirica

I. Facts and Procedural History

A

Domino's Pizza, Inc. is a fast-food service company that sells pizza through a national network of over 4,200 stores. Domino's Pizza owns and operates approximately 700 of these stores. Independent franchisees own and operate the remaining 3,500. Domino's Pizza, Inc. is the second largest pizza company in the United States, with revenues in excess of $1.8 billion per year.

Under the franchise agreement, the franchisee receives the right to sell pizza under the "Domino's" name and format. In return, Domino's Pizza receives franchise fees and royalties.

The essence of a successful nationwide fast-food chain is product uniformity and consistency. Uniformity benefits franchisees because customers can purchase pizza from any Domino's store and be certain the pizza will taste exactly like the Domino's pizza with which they are familiar. This means that individual franchisees need not build up their own good will. Uniformity also benefits the franchisor. It ensures the brand name will continue to attract and hold customers, increasing franchise fees and royalties.

For these reasons, section 12.2 of the Domino's Pizza standard franchise agreement requires that all pizza ingredients, beverages, and packaging materials used by a Domino's franchisee conform to the standards set by Domino's Pizza, Inc. Section 12.2 also provides that Domino's Pizza, Inc. "may in our sole discretion require that ingredients, supplies and materials used in the preparation, packaging, and delivery of pizza be purchased exclusively from us or from approved suppliers or distributors." Domino's Pizza reserves the right "to impose reasonable limitations on the number of approved suppliers or distributors of any product." To enforce these rights, Domino's Pizza, Inc. retains the power to inspect franchisee stores and to test materials and ingredients. Section 12.2 is subject to a reasonableness clause providing that Domino's Pizza, Inc. must "exercise reasonable judgment with respect to all determinations to be made by us under the terms of this Agreement."

Under the standard franchise agreement, Domino's Pizza, Inc. sells approximately 90 percent of the $500 million in ingredients and supplies used by Domino's franchisees. These sales, worth some $450 million per year, form a significant part of Domino's Pizza, Inc.'s profits. Franchisees purchase only 10 percent of their ingredients and supplies from outside sources. With the exception of fresh dough, Domino's Pizza, Inc. does not manufacture the products it sells to franchisees. Instead, it purchases these products from approved suppliers and then resells them to the franchisees at a markup.

B

The plaintiffs in this case are eleven Domino's franchisees and the International Franchise Advisory Council, Inc. ("IFAC"), a Michigan corporation consisting of approximately 40 percent of the Domino's franchisees in the United States, formed to promote their common interests.

* * * * *

[The lower court dismissed the plaintiffs' antitrust complaints. We turn now to the Appeals Court's analysis of the relevant product market—Ed.]

Plaintiffs suggest the "ingredients, supplies, materials, and distribution services used by and in the operation of Domino's pizza stores" constitutes a relevant market for antitrust purposes. We disagree.

As we have noted, the outer boundaries of a relevant market are determined by reasonable interchangeability of use.

Here, the dough, tomato sauce, and paper cups that meet Domino's Pizza, Inc. standards and are used by

Domino's stores are interchangeable with dough, sauce and cups available from other suppliers and used by other pizza companies. Indeed, it is the availability of interchangeable ingredients of comparable quality from other suppliers, at lower cost, that motivates this lawsuit. Thus, the relevant market, which is defined to include all reasonably interchangeable products, cannot be restricted solely to those products currently approved by Domino's Pizza, Inc. for use by Domino's franchisees. For that reason, we must reject plaintiffs' proposed relevant market.

Of course, Domino's-approved pizza ingredients and supplies differ from other available ingredients and supplies in one crucial manner. Only Domino's-approved products may be used by Domino's franchisees without violating section 12.2 of Domino's standard franchise agreement. Plaintiffs suggest that this difference is sufficient by itself to create a relevant market in approved products. We disagree. The test for a relevant market is not commodities reasonably interchangeable by a particular plaintiff, but "commodities reasonably interchangeable by consumers for the same purposes." A court making a relevant market determination looks not to the contractual restraints assumed by a particular plaintiff when determining whether a product is interchangeable, but to the uses to which the product is put by consumers in general. Thus, the relevant inquiry here is not whether a Domino's franchisee may reasonably use both approved or nonapproved products interchangeably without triggering liability for breach of contract, but whether pizza makers in general might use such products interchangeably. Clearly, they could. Were we to adopt plaintiffs' position that contractual restraints render otherwise identical products noninterchangeable for purposes of relevant market definition, any exclusive dealing arrangement, output or requirement contract, or franchise tying agreement would support a claim for violation of antitrust laws. Perhaps for this reason; no court has defined a relevant product market with reference to the particular contractual restraints of the plaintiff.

* * * * *

[The plaintiffs alleged that Domino's unlawfully engaged in monopolization, attempted monopolization, exclusive dealing, and predatory pricing. The Court rejected those claims. We turn now to the Court's analysis of the plaintiffs' claim that Domino's imposed unlawful tying arrangements on its franchisees—Ed.]

Plaintiffs allege Domino's Pizza, Inc. imposed an unlawful tying arrangement by requiring franchisees to buy ingredients and supplies from them as a condition of obtaining Domino's Pizza fresh dough, in violation of § 1 of the Sherman Act. "In a tying arrangement, the seller sells one item, known as the tying product, on the condition that the buyer also purchases another item, known as the tied product." "[T]he antitrust concern over tying arrangements is limited to those situations in which the seller can exploit its power in the market for the tying product to force buyers to purchase the tied product when they otherwise would not, thereby restraining competition in the tied product market." "Even if a seller has obtained a monopoly in the tying product legitimately (as by obtaining a patent), courts have seen the expansion of that power to other product markets as illegitimate and competition suppressing." "The first inquiry in any tying case is whether the defendant has sufficient market power over the tying product, which requires a finding that two separate product markets exist and a determination precisely what the tying and tied products markets are."

Here, plaintiffs allege Domino's Pizza, Inc. used its power in the purported market for Domino's-approved dough to force plaintiffs to buy unwanted ingredients and supplies from them. This claim fails because the proposed tying market—the market in Domino's-approved dough—is not a relevant market for antitrust purposes. Domino's dough is reasonably interchangeable with other brands of pizza dough, and does not therefore constitute a relevant market of its own. All that distinguishes this dough from other brands is that a Domino's franchisee must use it or face a suit for breach of contract. As we have noted, the particular contractual restraints assumed by a plaintiff are not sufficient by themselves to render interchangeable commodities noninterchangeable for purposes of relevant market definition. If Domino's had market power in the overall market for pizza dough and forced plaintiffs to purchase other unwanted ingredients to obtain dough, plaintiffs might possess a valid tying claim. But where the defendant's "power" to "force" plaintiffs to purchase the alleged tying product stems not from the market, but from plaintiffs' contractual agreement to purchase the tying product, no claim will lie. For that reason, plaintiffs' claim was properly dismissed.

F

Plaintiffs allege Domino's Pizza, Inc. imposed an unlawful tie-in arrangement by requiring franchisees to buy ingredients and supplies "as a condition of their continued enjoyment of rights and services under their Standard Franchise Agreement," in violation of § 1 of the Sherman Act. This claim is meritless. Though plaintiffs complain of an illegal tie-in arrangement, they have failed to point to any particular tying product or service over which Domino's Pizza, Inc. has market power. Domino's Pizza's control over plaintiffs' "continued enjoyment of rights and services under their Standard Franchise Agreement" is not a "market." Rather, it is a function of Domino's contractual powers under the franchise agreement to terminate the participation of franchisees in the franchise system if they violate the agreement. Because plaintiffs failed to plead any relevant tying market, the claim was properly dismissed.

Affirmed.

Afterword

The plaintiffs in the *Queen City* case filed for a rehearing which was denied. Circuit Judge Becker dissented from that decision:

[The majority] has endorsed the questionable theory that the kind of tying arrangements involved here "are an essential and important aspect of the franchise form of business organization." But these theories are also flawed.

I believe that the approach endorsed by the majority might have been acceptable two decades ago when franchising was in its nascent, or at least its growing stage. But now the food franchisors are leviathans, and I am underwhelmed by the suggestion that they may be permitted with impunity to perpetuate the type of arrangements pled in the complaint. These arrangements are clearly quite onerous to the average franchisee, a relatively small business person whose sunk costs in the franchise represent all or most of his or her assets and who lacks the considerable resources necessary to switch or defranchise. Moreover, the amount of commerce that the franchisors are foreclosing in the tied product market—for the pizza sauce, flour and other supplies (for which nonfranchisor dominated suppliers, be they individual firms or a franchise cooperative, could easily meet quality control specifications) is enormous.[23] [For an explanation of tying law in *Queen City* and similar cases, see **http://www.gcwf.com/articles/interest/interest_21.html**]

Questions

1. Describe the product market as the *Queen City* Court saw it.
2. Explain the potential harm of tying arrangements.
3. Explain why the majority ruled against the plaintiffs' tying claims.
4. Some recent federal court decisions differ with the reasoning in *Queen City Pizza*. Do you think *Queen City* is well reasoned? Explain.
5. Judge Scirica in *Queen City* wrote: "Courts and legal commentators have long recognized that franchise tying contracts are an essential and important aspect of the franchise form of business organization because they . . . prevent franchisees from free-riding . . . " Explain what he meant about free riding.[24]
6. When "Late Night with David Letterman" was an NBC show, the network, for some time, required those wanting to advertise on "Late Night" to also buy spots on the "Tonight Show with Johnny Carson."
   a. Does that packaging constitute a tying arrangement?
   b. Was it lawful? Explain.
7. Chrysler included the price of a sound system in the base price of its cars. Chrysler's share of the auto market was 10 to 12 percent. Chrysler did not reveal the "subprice" for the sound systems. Independent audio dealers objected on antitrust grounds. Explain their claim. Decide. See *Town Sound and Custom Tops, Inc.* v. *Chrysler Motor Corp.*, 959 F.2d 468 (1992), cert. den., 113 S.Ct. 196 (1992).

EXCLUSIVE DEALING AND REQUIREMENTS CONTRACTS

Principal legislation: Clayton Act, Section 3; Sherman Act, Section 1.

An *exclusive dealing* contract is an agreement in which a buyer commits itself to deal only with a specific seller, thus cutting competing sellers out of that share of the market. A *requirements* contract is one in which a seller agrees to supply all of a buyer's needs, or a buyer agrees to purchase all of a seller's output, or both. These arrangements have the competitive disadvantage of closing markets to potential competitors.

After defining the relevant product and geographic markets, the principal issues of interest are: (1) market power and (2) market foreclosure. Exclusive dealing arrangements, such as those noted above involving Victoria's Secret and The Sharper Image are not a primary concern of antitrust authorities unless a supplier or purchaser has market power and unless some undue degree of market foreclosure results. Does the agreement foreclose a source of supply of sufficient magnitude as to substantially lessen competition? Does the agreement foreclose a market for sales of sufficient magnitude as to substantially lessen competition?

Exclusive dealing and requirements contracts do not constitute per se violations of the law. In practice exclusive dealing/requirements analysis reduces to a balancing of the competitive benefits and harms of the arrangement. These arrangements can harm competition by excluding a competitor, raising prices, limiting output, and so on. At the same time, they can have significant virtues such as eliminating the divided loyalties that a dealer may feel in carrying multiple brands, discouraging dealers who might free ride (for example, on a manufacturer's national advertising campaign), ensuring a stable supply, and facilitating long-term planning.

The Ticket Business

In 1994, the rock group Pearl Jam filed a civil complaint with the federal Justice Department claiming that Ticketmaster was violating antitrust laws resulting in unfairly high service charges for tickets. Ticketmaster service fees ranged, generally, from $3 to $15 per ticket. Ticketmaster provides ticket service for more than 50 major sports teams and exclusively controlled ticketing for at least one-half of the major stadiums, amphitheaters, and arenas in America. Experts say Ticketmaster often secures those exclusive deals by providing a payback to the arena; that is, Ticketmaster returns a portion of the service fee it collects on ticket sales to the arena itself. Ticketmaster's clients seem very happy with the company's work. Those clients argue that exclusive ticketing arrangements are necessary to maintain quality control and to prevent customers and advertisers from being confused by multiple ticket sources.

In 1995, the United States Justice Department declined to bring an antitrust action against Ticketmaster. Attorney General Janet Reno explained that "new enterprises were coming into the business," meaning that competition was emerging.[25] Then in 1999, the United States Supreme Court declined to review lower court decisions holding that concert ticketholders did not have standing (see Chapter 4) to bring monopoly and other antitrust claims against Ticketmaster.[26] [For a Federal Trade Commission Brief to the United States Supreme Court in *Alex Campos* v. *Ticketmaster,* see **http://supreme.findlaw.com/Supreme_Court/briefs/98-0127.ami.pet.inv.html**]

Questions

1. Are Ticketmaster's exclusive dealing arrangements unlawful? Explain.
2. Is the Ticketmaster dispute best left to the force of the market? Explain.

PRICE DISCRIMINATION

Principal legislation: Clayton Act, Section 2, as amended by the Robinson-Patman Act:

That it shall be unlawful for any person engaged in commerce . . . to discriminate in price between different purchasers of commodities of like grade and quality, where either or any of the purchases involved in such discrimination are in commerce . . . and where the effect of such discrimination may be substantially to lessen competition or tend to create a monopoly in any line of commerce, or to injure, destroy, or prevent competition with any person who either grants or knowingly receives the benefit of such discrimination, or with customers of either of them . . . Provided that nothing herein contained shall prevent differentials which make only due allowance for differences in the cost of manufacture, sale, or delivery resulting from the differing methods or quantities in which such commodities are to such purchasers sold or delivered . . . And, provided further, that nothing herein contained shall prevent price changes from time to time where in response to changing conditions affecting the market for or the marketability of the goods concerned, such as but not limited to actual or imminent deterioration of perishable goods, obsolescence of seasonal goods, distress sales under court process, or sales in good faith in discontinuance of business in the goods concerned . . . Provided, however, that nothing herein contained shall prevent a seller rebutting the prima facie case thus made by showing that his lower price or the furnishing of services or facilities to any purchaser or purchasers was made in good faith to meet an equally low price of a competitor, or the services or facilities furnished by a competitor.

Discounts/Price Discrimination

Upon graduation from college, suppose you decide to open a "neighborhood" record store in your hometown. Sales go well for a time, but then Best Buy opens a superstore nearby and sells its compact discs and tapes at prices significantly below yours. Because of its enormous volume, Best Buy is able to buy at substantially discounted prices. The result is a big cost saving for Best Buy. You are out of business.

From the early 1990s to the present, drug retailers and small book sellers have brought charges paralleling your hypothetical struggle with Best Buy. Tens of thousands of retail pharmacies have joined together in class actions against drug wholesalers and manufacturers claiming the drug companies have conspired to deny discounts to the plaintiffs while granting those discounts to health maintenance organizations, hospitals, and mail-order drug firms. Similarly, the American Booksellers Association, a trade group representing independent booksellers, has filed suit against Barnes & Noble and Borders accusing those giant retail chains of demanding special wholesale price discounts from book publishers while those discounts were not offered to the small, independent bookstores. Settlements have been reached in some of the drug and book actions, but others continue at this writing. Both of these lines of cases allege *price discrimination* that allows big firms to receive favorable prices not accorded to smaller firms.

As a matter of law, price discrimination involves selling substantially identical goods (not services) at reasonably contemporaneous times to different purchasers at different prices, where the effect may be to substantially lessen competition or tend to create a monopoly. A seller may prevail against such a charge by establishing one of the following defenses: (1) The price differential is attributable to cost savings associated with the least expensive sale. However, in practice, the difficulties in proving cost savings have made successful defenses on that ground quite uncommon. (2) The price differential is attributable to a good faith effort to meet the equally low price of a competitor. (3) Certain transactions are exempt from the act. Of special note is a price change made in response to a changing market. Thus, prices might lawfully be altered for seasonal goods or perishables. Price discrimination is perhaps best understood by reference to diagrams.[27]

The harm in Figure 11.1 falls at the seller's level, the primary line, in that S_1's pricing policy may harm S_2. The specific fear is that S_1 will use its income from sales in New York to subsidize its lower price in Kentucky. S_1 may then be able to drive S_2 from the market. This is precisely the harm that Congress feared would be generated by the advance of chain stores across the nation. Of course, S_1 may be able to offer a defense to explain the pricing differential. For example, the price differential might be permissible if designed to allow S_1 to get a foothold in a new market. Remember that a price discrimination violation requires a showing of competitive injury.

Now turn to the "Secondary Line" problem depicted in Figure 11.2. B_1 and B_2 are direct competitors. Absent a defense, S_1 is clearly engaging in price discrimination. Here, the harm falls at the buyers' level (secondary line).

Harm may also fall on customers of customers, that is, tertiary price discrimination.

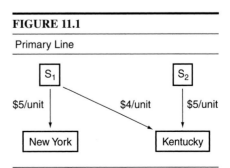

FIGURE 11.1

Primary Line

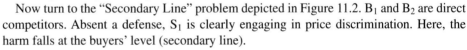

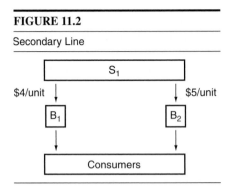

FIGURE 11.2

Secondary Line

Questions

1. Texaco sold gasoline at its retail tank wagon prices to Hasbrouck, an independent Texaco retailer, but granted discounts to distributors Gull and Dompier. Dompier also sold at the retail level. Gull and Dompier both delivered their gas directly to retailers and did not maintain substantial storage facilities. During the period in question, sales at the stations supplied by the two distributors grew dramatically, while Hasbrouck's sales declined. Hasbrouck filed suit against Texaco, claiming that the distributor discount constituted a Robinson-Patman violation. Texaco defended, saying the discount reflected the services the distributors performed for Texaco, and that the arrangement did not harm competition. Decide. Explain. See *Texaco* v. *Ricky Hasbrouck*, 496 U.S. 543 (1990).

2. Utah Pie produced frozen pies in its Salt Lake City plant. Utah's competitors, Carnation, Pet, and Continental, sometimes sold pies in Salt Lake City at prices beneath those charged in other markets. Indeed, Continental's prices in Salt Lake City were beneath its direct costs plus overhead. Pet sold to Safeway using Safeway's private label at a price lower than that at which the same pies were sold under the Pet label. Pet employed an industrial spy to infiltrate Utah Pie and gather information. Utah Pie claimed that Carnation, Pet, and Continental were in violation of Robinson-Patman. Decide. Explain. See *Utah Pie Co.* v. *Continental Baking Co.*, 386 U.S. 685 (1967).

CONCLUSION

Managers must take antitrust seriously. DuPont, for example, distributed a small plastic card (like a credit card) to many of its employees on which was printed the following "Ten Don'ts of Antitrust." These "don'ts," as you can see, are a brief summary of most of the primary issues in this chapter.

---

1. Don't discuss prices with competitors.
2. Don't divide customers, markets, or territories with competitors.
3. Don't agree upon or attempt to control a customer's resale price.
4. Don't attempt to restrict a customer's resale activity.
5. Don't offer a customer prices or terms more favorable than those offered competing customers.
6. Don't require a customer to buy a product only from you.
7. Don't use one product as bait to sell another.
8. Don't disparage a competitor's product unless the statements are true.
9. Don't make sales or purchases conditional on reciprocal purchases or sales.
10. Don't hesitate to consult with your legal counsel.

INTERNET EXERCISE

Using the Federal Trade Commission's "Frequently Asked Questions" page [**http://www.ftc.gov/bc/compguide/question.htm**] answer these questions:

a. Shopping for a stereo loudspeaker made by Sound Corporation, I couldn't find a dealer who would sell it for less than the manufacturer's suggested retail price. Isn't that price fixing?

b. I own a retail clothing store and the Brand Company refuses to sell me any of its line of clothes. These clothes are very popular in my area, so this policy is hurting my business. Isn't it illegal for Brand to refuse to sell to me?

c. I operate two stores that sell recorded music. My business is being ruined by giant discount store chains that sell their products for less than my wholesale cost. I thought there were laws against price discrimination, but I can't afford the legal fees to fight the big corporations. Can you help?

CHAPTER QUESTIONS

1. After reading this entire chapter, what is your judgment about the antitrust system?
   a. Does it work? Explain.
   b. How might it be altered?
   c. Could we place more reliance on the market? Explain.
   d. Do the statutes and case law, as a body, seem to form a rational package? Explain.
2. Scholar and jurist Richard Posner argues:

   [T]he protection of small business whatever its intrinsic merit cannot be attained within the framework of antitrust principles and procedures. The small businessman is, in general, helped rather than hurt by monopoly, so unless the antitrust laws are stood completely on their head they are an inapt vehicle (compared, say, to tax preferences) for assisting small business.[28]

   a. Is antitrust law an inappropriate vehicle for protecting small business? Explain.
   b. Should we protect small business? Explain.
   c. How does the presence of monopolies benefit small business?
   d. If it is not the proper vehicle for protecting small business, what role should antitrust law properly

serve? For example, should social considerations (such as the maintenance of full employment and the dispersal of political power) assume greater importance? Or should antitrust policy hew as closely as possible to economic goals? Explain.

3. Subway sandwich shops required all franchisees to employ a computerized point-of-sale (POS) system. The only approved system was provided by an unrelated company, RBS. Vendors of a competing POS system then sued Subway's parent, Doctor's Associates, alleging, among other things, an unlawful tying arrangement.

   a. Describe the alleged tie.
   b. Defend Doctor's Associates (Subway).
   c. Explain what the plaintiffs would need to demonstrate in order to prevail. See *Subsolutions, Inc.* v. *Doctor's Associates, Inc.,* 62 F. Supp. 2d 616 (D. Conn. 1999).

4. A group of lawyers in private practice in the District of Columbia agreed to decline further appointments to represent indigent criminal defendants until the local government increased their compensation to a level believed satisfactory by the lawyers. That agreement was challenged by the Federal Trade Commission.

   a. What violation(s) was asserted by the FTC?
   b. What defenses were offered by the group of lawyers?
   c. Decide. Explain. See *Federal Trade Commission* v. *Superior Court Trial Lawyers Association,* 493 U.S. 411 (1990).

5. Explain how the apparently competitive practice of guaranteeing to match the prices of any competitor may actually result in price discrimination. See Aaron S. Edlin, "Do Guaranteed-Low-Price Policies Guarantee High Prices, and Can Antitrust Rise to the Challenge?" *Harvard Law Review* 111, no. 2 (December 1997), p. 529.

6. Could Amana, the appliance manufacturer, lawfully refuse to deal with any purchaser who sells the products of a competitor such as Maytag? Explain.

7. Does a businessperson create antitrust problems by joining industry trade associations, promoting common safety standards for the industry, and contributing to industry advertising campaigns such as "take the family to the movies"? Explain. See John H. Shenefield and Irwin M. Stelzer, *The Antitrust Laws—A Primer,* 2d ed. (Washington, D.C.: The AEI Press, 1996), p. 107.

8. SIDA, the State Independent Drivers Association, Inc., was the largest taxi company on Oahu, Hawaii. SIDA's membership was limited to independent taxis. Fleet operators were not admitted. Hawaii's Department of Transportation awarded SIDA the exclusive right to provide taxi service from Honolulu Airport. No restrictions were placed on taxi service to the airport. Charley's Taxi Radio Dispatch Corporation, the largest fleet service on the island, filed suit, challenging, among other things, SIDA's refusal to grant membership to Charley's. At trial, the facts demonstrated that taxi competition was strong on the island of Oahu.

   a. What violation was alleged by Charley's?
   b. Decide. Explain. See *Charley's Taxi Radio Dispatch* v. *SIDA of Hawaii,* 810 F. 2d 869 (9th Cir. 1987).

9. Assume two fertilizer dealerships, Grow Quick and Fertile Fields, hold 70 percent and 30 percent, respectively, of the fertilizer business in the farm community of What Cheer, Iowa. Assume the owner of Fertile Fields learns via inquiry, hearsay, and the like of Grow Quick's price quotes. Then, each growing season the Fertile Fields owner sets her prices exactly equal to those of her competitor. Is that practice unlawful? Explain.

10. Given identical competing products, why is identical pricing virtually inevitable—at least over the long run?

11. The FTC found the Boise Cascade Corporation in violation of Section 5 of the Federal Trade Commission Act (forbidding unfair methods of competition) for using a delivered pricing system for southern plywood, the price for which was based in part on a rail freight charge computed as though the shipping point of origin was the Pacific Northwest. Historically, plywood had originated largely in the Northwest, but technological developments spurred southeastern production. However, southeastern producers continued to quote plywood prices as though the material had been shipped from the West Coast. The commission contended that the practice inhibited price competition. Boise Cascade argued that the freight factor eased price comparisons between southeastern and northwestern plywood. No agreement among southern plywood producers as to West Coast–delivered pricing was proved. In the absence of an agreement, is this practice unlawful? Explain. *Boise Cascade Corp.* v. *FTC,* 637 F. 2d 573 (9th Cir. 1980).

12. Assume firms A, B, C, D, E are charged with price-fixing under Sherman 1 because they have a program of exchanging pricing information among themselves.

a. What element of Robinson-Patman might be used as a defense in that Sherman 1 action?

b. Would the court find that defense persuasive? Explain.

13. Some antitrust experts argue that a firm possessing market power should be challenged by the government with the goal of eradicating the power as quickly as possible while others maintain that the government should be patient with short-term market power. Explain those two points of view.

14. In *Bruce's Juices, Inc.* v. *American Can Co.,* 87 F. Supp. 985 (S.D. Fla. 1949), aff'd 187 F. 2d 919 (5th Cir.), modified 190 F. 2d 73 (5th Cir.), cert. dismissed, 342 U.S. 875 (1951), American Can defended itself against a price discrimination charge by arguing that the cans in question were not of "like grade and quality." The cans sold to Bruce's Juices were 3.14 inches in height, while those sold at a reduced price to Bruce's competitors (but refused to Bruce's) were 3.12 inches in height. Otherwise the cans were functionally identical.

a. Is American Can's defense persuasive? Explain.

b. Why is the presence of price discrimination good evidence of the presence of a monopoly?

c. In what sense does the Robinson-Patman Act conflict with the Sherman Act?

15. A board-certified anesthesiologist was denied admission to the Jefferson Parish Hospital staff because the hospital had an exclusive services contract with a firm of anesthesiologists. The contract required all surgery patients at the hospital to use that firm for their anesthesiology work. Seventy percent of the patients in the parish were served by hospitals other than Jefferson. The anesthesiologist who was denied admission sued the hospital, claiming the contract was unlawful.

a. What antitrust violation was raised by the plaintiff?

b. Decide. Explain. See *Jefferson Parish Hospital District No. 2* v. *Hyde,* 466 U.S. 2 (1984).

16. In 1990, the American Institute of Certified Public Accountants agreed to enforce a change in its ethics rules that allows its members to accept contingent fees and commissions from nonaudit clients. The agreement was the result of a consent order between the AICPA and the Federal Trade Commission. Likewise, in 1990, the American Institute of Architects signed a consent order with the Justice Department that forbids the Institute from adopting policies that would restrain architects from bidding competitively for jobs or offering discounts or doing work without compensation.

a. What antitrust violation was the government seeking to stem in both of these cases?

b. What defenses are offered by the professions for their policies?

17. Starter Sportswear had a license to manufacture and sell satin professional team jackets marketed as "authentic" because they were styled in the manner of jackets actually worn by the members of the various teams. A Starter policy statement provided that it would sell only to retailers that carry a representative amount of Starter's full line of jackets. Starter also had a minimum order policy specifying that it wouldn't deal with retailers who sought quantities beneath that minimum order. Trans Sport, a retailer, began selling Starter jackets to other retailers who did not meet Starter's requirements. At that point, Starter declined to deal further with Trans Sport. Trans Sport then sued Starter.

a. List Trans Sport's claims against Starter.

b. Resolve those claims, raising all the relevant issues. See *Trans Sport, Inc.* v. *Starter Sportswear, Inc.,* 964 F. 2d 186 (2d Cir. 1992).

NOTES

1. *Washington Post,* "Vitamin Giants to Settle Antitrust Suit," *Waterloo–Cedar Falls Courier,* September 8, 1999, p. A9.

2. *Standard Oil Co. of New Jersey* v. *United States,* 221 U.S. 1 (1911).

3. See, for example, John DeQ. Briggs and Stephen Calkins, "Antitrust 1986–87: Power and Access (Part I)," *Antitrust Bulletin* 32, no. 2 (Summer 1987), p. 275.

4. This analysis is drawn from William Kovacic, "The Identification and Proof of Horizontal Agreements under the Antitrust Laws," *Antitrust Bulletin* 38, no. 1 (Spring 1993), p. 5.

5. Associated Press, "Judge Approves $1 Billion Nasdaq Price Fixing Settlement," *Waterloo–Cedar Falls Courier,* November 10, 1998, p. B6.

6. Bruce Ingersoll, "Germany's SGL to Pay $135 Million Fine in Graphite-Electrodes Antitrust Case," *The Wall Street Journal,* May 5, 1999, p. B12.

7. Ian Johnson, "China Fosters Price-Fixing Cartels as Economy Crimps Firms' Profits," *The Wall Street Journal,* December 3, 1998, p. A17.

8. Associated Press, "Infant Formula-Maker Settles State Lawsuits," *Des Moines Register,* May 25, 1996, p. 8S.

9. *California Dental Association* v. *Federal Trade Commission,* 143 L.Ed. 2d 935 (1999).

10. Harry S. David and Todd S. Fishman, "The Proposed Antitrust Guidelines for Competitor Collaborations," *New York Law Journal,* November 9, 1999, p. 1.

11. Anne B. Williams, "Auto Dealerships Settle FTC Charges of Boycott Threat Over Internet Deals," *The Wall Street Journal,* August 6, 1998, p. B7.

12. 359 U.S. 207 (1959).

13. Dominic Bencivenga, "Toy Wars; FTC Introduces Novel Theory on Market Power," *New York Law Journal,* May 30, 1996, p. 5.

14. Ellen Neuborne, "Toys 'R' Us Not Alone in 'Exclusive' Marketing," *Des Moines Register,* May 28, 1996, p. 6S.

15. Amy Westfeldt, "Toys 'R' Us, Toymakers Settle Antitrust Suit with Deal that Includes Free Toys for Kids," *Legal Intelligencer,* May 27, 1999, p. 4.

16. Ellen Neuborne, "Toys 'R' Us Not Alone," p. 6S.

17. *United States* v. *Colgate & Co.,* 250 U.S. 300 (1919).

18. Harold Brown, "The Direction for Antitrust Law," *New York Law Journal,* November 30, 1994, p. 3.

19. *Continental T.V., Inc.* v. *GTE Sylvania, Inc.,* 433 U.S. 36 (1977).

20. *State Oil Co.* v. *Khan,* 522 U.S. 3 (1997).

21. *Albrecht* v. *Herald Co.,* 390 U.S. 145 (1968).

22. Mark Hansen, "It's Not Business As Usual," *ABA Journal* 84 (January 1998), p. 40.

23. *Queen City Pizza, Inc.* v. *Domino's Pizza, Inc.,* 129 F.3d 724 (3d Cir. 1997).

24. *Queen City Pizza, Inc.* v. *Domino's Pizza, Inc.,* 124 F.3d 430, 440 (3d Cir. 1997).

25. "Reno Says No Ticketmaster Case Because Others Entering Business," *Daily Record,* July 7, 1995, p. 1.

26. "No Sup. Ct. Review for Concertgoers Against Ticketmaster," *Antitrust Litigation Reporter* 6, no. 8 (February 1999), p. 18.

27. See Earl Kintner, *A Robinson-Patman Primer* (New York: Macmillan, 1970), p. 93.

28. Richard Posner, *Antitrust Law* (Chicago: University of Chicago Press, 1976), p. 4.

PART IV

Employer–Employee Relations

Chapter 12

Employment Law I: Protecting the Employee

INTRODUCTION

Litigation avoidance is an increasingly important feature of contemporary management practice. Employees are angry, often with good reason, and they are taking their employers to court for alleged wrongs involving wages and hours, job safety, unemployment compensation, workers' compensation, and wrongful dismissal, to name a few. As union strength has declined (see Chapter 14), government rules protecting employees have increased. Those increased legal protections, a volatile economy, downsizing, decreased employer/employee loyalty, and other forces have led to unprecedented levels of employee litigation.

A 1997 national survey found 57 percent of responding employers indicating they had been named as a defendant in at least one employment-related lawsuit in the five years prior to the survey.[1] The primary areas of litigation included discrimination (about 42 percent of the claims), wrongful termination (approximately 33 percent), and sexual harassment (12 percent).[2] Jury awards in 1995, in employment law cases, averaged $204,310.[3] Significantly, however, a 1998 *National Law Journal* study of employment law awards found trial and appellate judges "routinely and radically" reducing or entirely reversing those awards.[4] Indeed, the study found that revisions in jury awards were more likely in employment cases than in any other field of law.[5] Not surprisingly, larger awards were particularly vulnerable to revisions on appeal—80 percent of the $1 million or larger verdicts studied from 1996 and 1997 were reduced or reversed.[6] [For an extensive employment law database, see **http://www.yahoo.com/Government/Law/Employment_Law/**]

Question

Although employers understandably fear lawsuits, employees often are troubled about whether a lawsuit is wise even if they are sure they have been wronged. List some of the considerations that an employee should think about in deciding whether to sue an employer.

Part One—Selection

Managers understand that choosing good employees is often the most critical ingredient in company success. Hence, they seek more and more information before hiring. They may rely on traditional information sources such as resumes, interviews, and references, but increasingly they are turning to state criminal histories, prehire testing, or computer-based screening. For example, Macy's department stores have used an automated interview process where callers to a career hotline use their push-button keypad to answer questions such as: 1. "After meeting someone for the first time, what do you usually know?" and 2. "If you were to overhear a coworker giving a customer incorrect information, what would you do?"[7] Sometimes the questions are considered intrusive or unfair and legal problems result.

In 1993, the Target chain of discount stores, without admitting fault, agreed to pay $1.3 million to settle the claims of an estimated 2,500 applicants for security positions who took the Rodgers Condensed CPI–MMPI "psychscreen" test in California. The true-false questions that follow illustrate those that raised discrimination and privacy concerns:

- I have never been in trouble because of my sex behavior.
- I have not had difficulty starting or holding my bowel movement.
- I am fascinated by fire.
- I believe there is a God.
- I would like to be a florist.[8]

Of course, efforts to combat employment discrimination limit employers' permissible lines of preemployment inquiry. For some time, discrimination concerns have discouraged employers from inquiring into applicants' arrest records, sexual preference, and marital status. Similarly, questions regarding medical history and impairments must be carefully constructed to avoid problems under the Americans with Disabilities Act (ADA). Even such seemingly reasonable questions as how the applicant would meet child care duties or whether the applicant could be available on weekends might raise concerns about discrimination based on gender and religion.[9] (Discrimination issues are addressed in Chapter 13.) Barring civil rights violations, however, job candidates have little protection against preemployment interview and testing methods. If the interview or test is restricted to job-related questions, legal problems for the employer are unlikely.

References.   Expanded testing and questioning of employment applicants is, in part, a response to the declining usefulness of references. Employers fear that providing references may lead to defamation claims (*slander* when spoken; *libel* when written) by former employees. Many state courts, however, recognize what is labeled a *qualified privilege* as a defense in an employment-related defamation suit. The privilege applies where the one communicating the statement and the recipient share a legitimate, business-related interest in the information conveyed. Thus, references, internal employee evaluations, and the like are protected in most states from defamation claims in the absence of malice or extreme recklessness. Similarly, a number of states have passed statutes protecting legitimate reference communications from defamation claims. Nevertheless, some recent court decisions appear to have eroded the qualified privilege a bit, leading many employers to "play it safe" by limiting their references to strictly factual details such as the date of hire, date of departure, and job title.

Broadly, a successful defamation suit requires:

1. A false statement.
2. The statement must be "published" to a third party.
3. The employer must be responsible for the publication.
4. The plaintiff's reputation must be harmed.

Truth is a complete defense in defamation cases, and firms that avoid secondhand information, personal issues, and potential discrimination themes such as age are very likely not to have problems. A mistake, however, can be very expensive.

Paul Calden was fired by Allstate Insurance in 1989 allegedly for carrying a gun in his briefcase. He was then hired by Fireman's Fund in 1990 and was fired in 1992 for being absent without a doctor's note. He returned to his office and allegedly killed three former coworkers and wounded others. Families of those who were harmed sued Allstate. A Florida court allowed the plaintiffs to pursue their claims and to seek punitive damages. The lawsuit alleged that Allstate:

> "(1) provided Calden with a letter of recommendation that stated that his departure was not related to job performance; (2) knew of Calden's mental instability and dangerous propensity for violence but failed to disclose fully and truthfully this information; and (3) was aware of Calden's acts described as devil worship on his personal computer . . . and threatening behavior toward Allstate female staff members."[10]

The case was settled out of court.[11]

Part Two—Employer Liability for Job-Related Harm

Once new employees are selected and on the job, new legal problems may emerge. Employers increasingly bear civil liability both for their employees' job-related mistakes and misconduct and for negligence claims against the employers for their decisions in hiring those employees.

Employee or Independent Contractor?

The impact of much of the law discussed in this chapter depends, initially, on whether the worker in question is considered, as a matter of law, an employee or an *independent contractor.* That is, when an enterprise hires, for example, a trucker, programmer, or service technician, is that person an employee or an independent operator under contract to the organization but not, legally, a part of that organization?

The dominant test in settling the employee–independent contractor question is one of control. Where a worker's performance is controlled by an employer or where the employer has the right or the ability to control that work, the worker is likely to be considered an employee. A business that hires an independent contractor generally is not required to comply with a wide range of employment and labor law standards that would apply were the worker an employee. Thus, a business must provide unemployment insurance, worker's compensation coverage, minimum wages, and so on, to employees, but generally would not need to do so for independent contractors. Similarly, an employer ordinarily will not be liable for the acts of its independent contractors under the doctrine of *respondeat superior* (let the master answer), a form of *vicarious liability* (sometimes called imputed liability). [For a sample of independent contractor agreements, see **http://www. toolkit.cch.com/tools/indcon_m.htm**]

Scope of Employment

Under vicarious liability reasoning, employers have long been held liable for harm to third parties caused by the intentional or negligent acts of their employees. A finding of employer liability, of course, does not excuse the employee from her liability, but the vicarious liability/respondeat superior reasoning does have the potential effect of opening the employer's deeper pockets to the plaintiff. The central inquiry in assigning employer liability lies in the scope of employment question; that is, broadly, did the accident happen while the employee was on the job? The test for answering that question requires proof of all of the following ingredients:

1. The employee was subject to the employer's supervision.
2. The employee was motivated, at least in part, by a desire to serve the employer's business interests.
3. The problem arose substantially within normal working hours and in a work location.
4. The act in question was of the general kind the employee had been hired to perform.

In a 1991 case, *Mary M.* v. *City of Los Angeles,*[12] the City was held liable under the doctrine of respondeat superior for a sexual assault committed by a police officer. At 2:30 AM on October 3, 1981, Sergeant Leigh Schroyer was on duty, in uniform, carrying a gun, and patrolling in his marked police car. He stopped Mary M. for erratic driving. She pleaded not to be arrested. He ordered her to enter his patrol car and took her to her home. He entered her home and said that he expected "payment" for not arresting her. He raped her and was subsequently sentenced to a term in state prison.

Mary M. sued the City of Los Angeles. The general inquiry was whether Schroyer was acting within the scope of his employment during the rape episode. The jury found for Mary M. and awarded $150,000 in damages. The Court of Appeals reversed, saying that Schroyer was not acting within the scope of his employment. The case went to the California Supreme Court. The City argued that Schroyer was acting on behalf of his own interests rather than those of the City, and that the City had not authorized his conduct. Therefore, Schroyer could not have been acting within the scope of employment. However, the Court said that the correct question was not whether the rape was authorized but whether it happened in the course of a series of acts that were authorized. The Court reversed, saying that a jury could find the City vicariously liable (imputed to the principal from the agent) given the unique authority of police officers in our society. [For an employment law overview, see **www.employlaw.com**]

Questions

1. Williams, Hemphill, Dixon, and Osborne, while driving in Chicago, noticed some pizza boxes on top of a car parked in front of the Italian Fiesta Pizzeria. Dixon and Hemphill jumped out, discovered the boxes were empty, dropped them, and reentered their Jeep. Hall, a driver for Italian Fiesta, observed Dixon and Hemphill, yelled at them to return the pizza boxes, and then followed them in his vehicle. Dixon turned the wrong way onto a one-way street and Hall followed. Dixon then collided with another vehicle. Williams died and Hemphill was injured. Italian Fiesta was subsequently sued on negligent hiring and vicarious liability claims. The negligent hiring claim was rejected by the judge, but the vicarious liability theme was allowed to proceed to trial. The defendants provided evidence showing the pizzeria specifically informed employees that they were not to attempt to recover stolen property or punish perpetrators. Rather, the pizzeria's policy was for supervisors to contact police. Further, drivers were not penalized if property was stolen.
   a. What was the central issue in this case?
   b. Decide the case. Explain. See *Williams* v. *Hall,* 681 N.E.2d 1037 (Ill. App. 1997).
2. What policy justifications support the imposition of liability on an employer for the wrongs of an employee operating within the scope of employment?
3. A plaintiff lost one leg and the use of an arm in an accident involving a defendant's employee. The employee had asked his nephew, the plaintiff, to ride on a tractor with him while he disked the defendant's orchard. The plaintiff sat on the toolbox since the tractor had only one seat. The plaintiff was struck by a tree and knocked into the path of the disk. Company rules forbade tractor passengers.
   a. What is the central issue in this lawsuit?
   b. Decide the case. Explain. See *Perez* v. *Van Groningen & Sons, Inc.,* 227 Cal. 719 P.2d 676 (Cal. S.Ct. 1986).

HIRING/RETENTION/TRAINING/SUPERVISION

Negligence

In recent years, employers' potential liability for employee wrong has been significantly expanded by a line of cases finding employers liable for negligence in hiring an employee or retaining an employee who subsequently causes harm to a third party, or for careless training or supervision. Typically, the employer is liable on negligence grounds for hiring or retaining an employee whom the employer knew or should have known to be dangerous, incompetent, dishonest, or the like where that information was directly related to the injury suffered by the plaintiff. Note that under negligence liability an employer may be liable for acts *outside* the scope of employment. The case that follows examines the law of negligent hiring, supervision, and retention.

YUNKER v. HONEYWELL. INC.
496 N.W.2d 419 (Minn.App. 1993)

Judge Lansing

Facts

Honeywell employed Randy Landin from 1977 to 1979 and from 1984 to 1988. From 1979 to 1984 Landin was imprisoned for the strangulation death of Nancy Miller, a Honeywell coemployee. On his release from prison, Landin reapplied at Honeywell. Honeywell rehired Landin as a custodian in Honeywell's General Offices facility in South Minneapolis in August 1984. Because of workplace confrontations Landin was twice transferred, first to the Golden Valley facility in August 1986, and then to the St. Louis Park facility in August 1987.

Kathleen Nesser was assigned to Landin's maintenance crew in April 1988. Landin and Nesser became friends and spent time together away from work. When Landin expressed a romantic interest, Nesser stopped spending time with Landin. Landin began to harass and threaten Nesser both at work and at home. At the end of June, Landin's behavior prompted Nesser to seek help from her supervisor and to request a transfer out of the St. Louis Park facility.

On July 1, 1988, Nesser found a death threat scratched on her locker door. Landin did not come to work on or after July 1, and Honeywell accepted his formal resignation on July 11, 1988. On July 19, approximately six hours after her Honeywell shift ended, Landin killed Nesser in her driveway with a close-range shotgun blast. Landin was convicted of first degree murder and sentenced to life imprisonment.

Jean Yunker, as trustee for the heirs and next-of-kin of Kathleen Nesser, brought this wrongful death action based on theories of negligent hiring, retention, and supervision of a dangerous employee. Honeywell moved for summary judgment and, for purposes of the motion, stipulated that it failed to exercise reasonable care in the hiring and supervision of Landin. The trial court concluded that Honeywell owed no legal duty to Nesser and granted summary judgment for Honeywell.

Issue

Did Honeywell have a duty to Kathleen Nesser to exercise reasonable care in hiring, retaining, or supervising Randy Landin?

Analysis

In determining that Honeywell did not have a legal duty to Kathleen Nesser arising from its employment of Randy Landin, the district court analyzed Honeywell's duty as limited by its ability to control and protect its employees while they are involved in the employer's business or at the employer's place of business. Additionally, the court concluded that Honeywell could not have reasonably foreseen Landin's killing Nesser.

Incorporating a "scope of employment" limitation into an employer's duty borrows from the doctrine of respondeat superior. However, of the three theories advanced for recovery, only negligent supervision derives from the respondeat superior doctrine, which relies on connection to the employer's premises or chattels. We agree that negligent supervision is not a viable theory of recovery because Landin was neither on Honeywell's premises nor using Honeywell's chattels when he shot Nesser.

The remaining theories, negligent hiring and negligent retention, are based on direct, not vicarious, liability. Negligent hiring and negligent retention do not rely on the scope of employment but address risks created by exposing members of the public to a potentially dangerous individual. These theories of recovery impose liability for an employee's intentional tort, an action almost invariably outside the scope of employment, when the employer knew or should have known that the employee was violent or aggressive and might engage in injurious conduct.

I

Minnesota first explicitly recognized a cause of action based on negligent hiring in *Ponticas* in 1983. *Ponticas* involved the employment of an apartment manager who sexually assaulted a tenant. The supreme court upheld a jury verdict finding the apartment operators negligent in failing to make a reasonable investigation into the resident manager's background before providing him with a passkey. The court defined negligent hiring as

predicated on the negligence of an employer in placing a person with known propensities, or propensities which should have been discovered by reasonable investigation, in an employment position in which, *because of the circumstances of the employment,* it should have been foreseeable that the hired individual posed a threat of injury to others.

Honeywell argues that under *Ponticas* it is not liable for negligent hiring because, unlike providing a dangerous resident manager with a passkey, Landin's employment did not enable him to commit the act of violence against Nesser. This argument has merit, and we note that a number of jurisdictions have expressly defined the scope of an employer's duty of reasonable care in hiring as largely dependent on the type of responsibilities associated with the particular job. See *Connes,* 831 P.2d at 1321 (employer's duty in hiring is dependent on anticipated degree of contact between employee and other persons in performing employment duties).

Ponticas rejected the view that employers are required to investigate a prospective employee's criminal background in every job in which the individual has regular contact with the public. Instead, liability is determined by the totality of the circumstances surrounding the hiring and whether the employer exercised reasonable care. The court instructed that

[t]he scope of the investigation is directly related to the severity of the risk third parties are subjected to by an incompetent employee. Although only slight care might suffice in the hiring of a yardman, a worker on a production line, or other types of employment where the employee would not constitute a high risk of injury to third persons, when the prospective employee is to be furnished a passkey permitting admittance to living quarters of tenants, the employer has the duty to use reasonable care to investigate his competency and reliability prior to employment.

Applying these principles, we conclude that Honeywell did not owe a duty to Nesser at the time of Landin's hire. Landin was employed as a maintenance worker whose job responsibilities entailed no exposure to the general public and required only limited contact with co-employees. Unlike the caretaker in *Ponticas,* Landin's duties did not involve inherent dangers to others, and unlike the tenant in *Ponticas,* Nesser was not a reasonably foreseeable victim at the time Landin was hired.

To reverse the district court's determination on duty as it relates to hiring would extend *Ponticas* and essentially hold that ex-felons are inherently dangerous and that any harmful acts they commit against persons encountered through employment will automatically be considered foreseeable. Such a rule would deter employers from hiring workers with a criminal record and "offend our civilized concept that society must make a reasonable effort to rehabilitate those who have erred so they can be assimilated into the community."

Honeywell did not breach a legal duty to Nesser by hiring Landin because the specific nature of his employment did not create a foreseeable risk of harm, and public policy supports a limitation on this cause of action. The district court correctly determined that Honeywell is not liable to Nesser under a theory of negligent hiring.

II

In recognizing the tort of negligent hiring, *Ponticas* extended established Minnesota case law permitting recovery under theories of negligent retention.

* * * * *

The difference between negligent hiring and negligent retention focuses on when the employer was on notice that an employee posed a threat and failed to take steps to insure the safety of third parties. The Florida appellate court has provided a useful definition:

Negligent hiring occurs when, prior to the time the employee is actually hired, the employer knew or should have known of the employee's unfitness, and the issue of liability primarily focuses upon the adequacy of the employer's pre-employment investigation into the employee's background. Negligent retention, on the other hand, occurs when, during the course of employment, the employer becomes aware or should have become aware of problems with an employee that indicated his unfitness, and the employer fails to take further action such as investigating, discharge, or reassignment.

. . . The record contains evidence of a number of episodes in Landin's postimprisonment employment at Honeywell that demonstrate a propensity for abuse and violence towards coemployees.

While at the Golden Valley facility, Landin sexually harassed female employees and challenged a male coworker to fight. After his transfer to St. Louis Park, Landin threatened to kill a coworker during an angry confrontation following a minor car accident. In another employment incident, Landin was hostile and abusive toward a female coworker after problems developed in their friendship. Landin's specific focus on Nesser was demonstrated by several workplace outbursts occurring at the end of June, and on July 1 the words "one more day and you're dead" were scratched on her locker door.

Landin's troubled work history and the escalation of abusive behavior during the summer of 1988 relate directly to the foreseeability prong of duty. The facts . . . show that it was foreseeable that Landin could act violently against a co-employee, and against Nesser in particular.

This foreseeability gives rise to a duty of care to Nesser that is not outweighed by policy considerations of employment opportunity. An ex-felon's "opportunity for gainful employment may spell the difference between recidivism and rehabilitation," but it cannot predominate over the need to maintain a safe workplace when specific actions point to future violence.

Our holding is narrow and limited only to the recognition of a legal duty owed to Nesser arising out of Honeywell's continued employment of Landin. It is important to emphasize that in reversing the summary judgment on negligent retention, we do not reach the remaining significant questions of whether Honeywell breached that duty by failing to terminate or discipline Landin, or whether such a breach was a proximate cause of Nesser's death. These are issues generally decided by a jury after a full presentation of facts . . .

Decision

We affirm the entry of summary judgment on the theories of negligent hiring and supervision, but reverse the summary judgment on the issue of negligent retention.

Afterword

Published reports indicate the *Yunker* case was settled out of court soon after this decision was handed down.

Questions

1. What did the Court mean when it said that "negligent hiring and negligent retention are based on direct, not vicarious, liability"?
2. Why did the Court reject the negligent supervision claim?
3. Why did the Court reject the negligent hiring claim?
4. Why did the Court allow the negligent retention issue to go to trial?
5. A truck driver sexually assaulted a hotel clerk during the driver's course of employment. On his employment application, the driver had stated that he did not have a criminal record. The employer did not conduct a background check of the driver's criminal record. Had the employer done so, it would have discovered the driver's previous convictions for lewd conduct, assault, theft, and other crimes. Was the employer liable for its failure to undertake a more thorough investigation? Explain. See *Connes v. Molalla Transp. Sys. Inc.,* 831 P.2d 1316 (Col. S.Ct. 1992).

Part Three—Fair Labor Standards Act

The Depression of the 1930s shattered many Americans' faith in an unfettered free market and led, among other things, to extensive government regulation of employment relations.

The Fair Labor Standards Act (FLSA), passed in 1938 and later amended, is directed to these major objectives:

1. The establishment of a minimum wage that provides at least a modest standard of living for employees.
2. A flexible ceiling on hours worked weekly, the purpose of which is to increase the number of employed Americans.
3. Child labor protection.
4. Equal pay for equal work regardless of gender. (See Chapter 13).

[For the United States Department of Labor home page, see **http://www.dol.gov/**]

WAGES AND HOURS

The FLSA requires covered hourly employees to be paid a specified minimum wage and to be paid at least "time and a half" for any work in excess of 40 hours per week.

Generally speaking, employees and enterprises are covered by the FLSA if they are engaged in producing goods for interstate commerce. A number of occupations are exempted from some or all of the act. Professional, administrative, and executive employees as well as outside salespersons are exempt from the minimum wage and overtime provisions. About 10 percent of nonsupervisory workers are not covered by the act. The FLSA applies to state and local government workers as well as those in the private sector. And every state has its own wage and hour laws, which often reach workers not covered by the federal act.

Minimum Wage.   At this writing, Congress is considering new legislation that would raise the federal minimum wage from its current $5.15 per hour to $6.15 over a period of three years. Resistance to the increase is led by the service sector of the business community and by Republicans in Congress. The concern is that an increase will unfairly drive up the cost of doing business and reduce the number of entry-level jobs. Federal Reserve Chairman Alan Greenspan told Congress in 1999 that we have "fairly conclusive" evidence that a wage increase would cause job losses among less-skilled workers although that effect might not be felt until the next recession.[13] Some recent studies, however, have found little or no job loss from the 1996–97 minimum wage increase, and one study found that 71 percent of those benefiting from the increase were adults, rather than teenagers, and that the average minimum wage earner was someone who provides more than half of his or her household income.[14] Nonetheless, many business owners report sharp cutbacks in employment with each rise in the minimum wage:

> The last time Congress raised the minimum wage in 1996, Sal Lorenzini couldn't pass the cost on to customers. His string of Wendy's restaurants in the Syracuse, NY area were [sic] locked in a 99-cent burger war with competitors. So to offset the 90-cent-per-hour wage increase, Lorenzini removed the salad bars from eight of his nine restaurants. While popular with health-conscious diners, each salad bar required 49 hours of work each week to stock and clean, a total of 392 hours. Closing them allowed him to fire 16 part-time workers. Now Lorenzini is again looking for cost cuts [because of the proposed increase to $6.15 per hour—Ed.]. Of Lorenzini's 300 workers,

60 make the current minimum wage. He figures the increase would cost him as much as $130,000 a year. The operating profit from his restaurants totaled $470,000 last year, he said. "It's about a 30 percent hit to my bottom line."[15]

Some employers simply ignore the minimum wage laws, in part because those who are caught ordinarily are required only to pay any back wages due—although extreme or repeated violations may produce fines.[16] Violations are particularly common in eating and drinking establishments, the garment industry, and heavy construction.[17] A federal survey released in 1996 of 76 randomly selected Southern California apparel manufacturers found that 43 percent had recently violated the minimum wage law.[18] [For state minimum wage laws, see **http://www.dol.gov/dol/esa/public/minwage/america.htm**]

Overtime.   Workers are losing at least $19 billion annually in pay because of employers' failure to fully comply with overtime laws, according to an employer-supported study.[19] A *Wall Street Journal* analysis of wage and hour cases, pursued by the Labor Department from 1991 to 1995, found that 1 of every 50 workers in the construction and garment industries was illegally denied overtime. Other industries, such as railroads and tobacco, had almost no violations.[20]

In late 1997, Taco Bell agreed to settle a class action lawsuit filed on behalf of some 16,000 nonsalaried workers. A jury found Taco Bell liable for a statewide pattern of wage and hour abuse in Washington. In agreeing to settle, Taco Bell faced claims that lawyers expected to total up to $10 million with individual amounts ranging from $20 to $50,000.[21]

Federal rules in this area are so confusing that employers, federal officials, and judges often have great difficulty in determining who is entitled to overtime. Further, managers feel themselves under such heavy competitive and cost-cutting pressure that they may cheat workers out of pay. Ironically, however, the bigger overtime complaint for many workers is that they don't want it. For many the 40-hour work week is a thing of the past. Indeed, recent studies show that American workers have now passed the Japanese who formerly led the globe in hours worked.[22]

CHILD LABOR AND SWEATSHOPS

Agreeing to pay a $325,000 penalty, Sears, Roebuck & Co. reached a settlement in 1999 of Department of Labor allegations that Sears had violated child labor laws by letting teens operate heavy machinery or work too many hours. Most of the violations allegedly involved 16- and 17-year-olds driving forklifts, operating machines that flatten cardboard, or operating freight elavators.[23] Federal law, in most circumstances, forbids children from operating hazardous equipment. With certain exceptions (principally agriculture), children under 14 years of age may not be employed. Those aged 14 and 15 may engage in sales and certain other jobs outside school hours for a limited time. At age 16, children may engage in nonhazardous work. Then at 18, young adults may enter jobs, such as mining, that the government deems to be hazardous.

Exploitation?   A shrinking labor pool, shifting immigration patterns, and difficult economic conditions for many have led to a concern that young workers may be threatened in

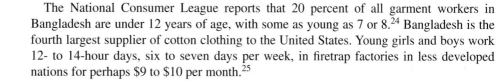

the workplace. In the late 19th century, we were worried about eight-year-old children who were employed for 12-hour days in sweatshops or who lost fingers in textile milling machines. Now, new concerns about safety are being raised, both in underdeveloped nations that export goods to us and in the United States itself.

The National Consumer League reports that 20 percent of all garment workers in Bangladesh are under 12 years of age, with some as young as 7 or 8.[24] Bangladesh is the fourth largest supplier of cotton clothing to the United States. Young girls and boys work 12- to 14-hour days, six to seven days per week, in firetrap factories in less developed nations for perhaps $9 to $10 per month.[25]

We are not surprised to read that child labor is common throughout the underdeveloped world, but a recent report indicates that tens of thousand of children, some as young as eight, work up to 20 hours per week in "sweatshop conditions" and for "token wages" in Australia.[26] Some 1,600 of those children are seriously injured each year.[27]

Reform?   In 1999, the United States announced two initiatives addressing child labor problems, both domestically and abroad. First, President Clinton issued an executive order designed to stop the federal government from buying products made with child labor. The order requires the federal Department of Labor to publish a list of products suspected of being made with abusive child labor or forced labor, whether in the United States or abroad. Contractors who supply those products to the federal government must then certify that they have tried to ensure that no child labor went into the products they buy. Products such as bricks and carpets from India and Pakistan and fireworks from Guatemala are among those identified by the government as being associated with child labor.[28] In the second initiative, the United States became the third nation to approve an international treaty, Convention 182, outlawing the most abusive forms of child labor, such as prostitution and slavery. The treaty requires the nations signing it to take "immediate and effective measures" toward enforcement, but no actual sanctions are included in the largely symbolic treaty.[29] The official United States position in World Trade Organization negotiations favors the development of child labor standards around the world, but less developed nations resist those measures because of the risk to their economies.

In response to governmental and consumer pressure, apparel manufacturers joined with unions, human rights leaders, and others in 1997 to form the Apparel Industry Partnership, which issued a new code of conduct. The code forbids child labor, discrimination, forced labor, and so on in the garment industry while mandating safe working conditions. Joining the Partnership is voluntary, and members agree to external auditing by independent organizations. The agreement does not, however, provide for a "living wage"—progress in that area will, of course, reflect worldwide labor market conditions. Similarly, a cooperative international effort has resulted in moving much of Pakistan's production of soccer balls from children, often working in their homes, to manufacturing centers where inspectors can more easily ensure that children are not being employed. (Most of the world's soccer balls are produced in Pakistan and most formerly were hand stitched by children whose nimble fingers were valued, but who were paid as little as 60 cents per day.) Public and private sources have combined to provide money for schooling for some 3,000 displaced children, while pay for adult stitchers now totals about 60 cents per ball, a good wage for the area.[30] [For a website addressed to abuse of workers, see **http://www.corpwatch.org**]

Part Four—Health and Safety at Work

Deaths and Injuries

- In 1970, deaths in the United States from injuries on the job totaled 14,225.[31] In 1998, that figure was 6,026.[32]
- Occupational illnesses—such as lung diseases and lead poisoning—cause about 137 deaths daily.[33]
- Traffic-related accidents are the biggest cause of death on the job, totaling 1,431 in 1998.[34]
- Occupational injuries and illnesses declined in 1997 for the fifth straight year to a total of 6.1 million or 7.1 cases per 100 full-time workers.[35]
- According to a recent scholarly study, the total cost of work-related deaths, injuries and illnesses is far greater than the cost of dealing with AIDS and at least as much as the cost of cancer or heart disease.[36]

The *New York Times* took a close look at one of those days of occupational death in 1996:

> Every workday Rick Risdal, 29, pedaled his bicycle . . . into the driveway of the Xylen Company. His $6-an-hour job required no special skills. On Oct. 21, he reported to work for the last time. At approximately 10:15 AM, he was operating a forklift when it skidded on gravel, overturned, and pinned him underneath. He died before an ambulance arrived.
>
> Within an hour, a part-time courier was fatally crushed beneath the wheels of a van in Wilmington, Del., [and] a day laborer in El Paso died in a construction accident . . .
>
> By the day's end, at least [10] more people were killed or fatally injured on the job in the United States.
>
> It was an extraordinary day only for the victims, their families, friends, and coworkers. Few of the deaths got more attention than several paragraphs in the local newspaper.[37]

OSHA

In 1970, Congress approved the Occupational Safety and Health Act (OSHA) in response to increasing concerns that workplaces were unnecessarily hazardous. Broadly, OSHA imposes a *general duty* on employers to provide a workplace free of "recognized hazards causing or likely to cause death or serious physical harm to employees." Employers have an absolute duty to remove any serious and preventable workplace hazards that are generally recognized in the industry and are known to the employer or should be known to the employer. That general duty is then supplemented with numerous, detailed, and demanding specific *standards*. A federal agency, the Occupational Safety and Health Administration (OSHA), is responsible for ensuring safe workplaces. [For the OSHA home page, see **www. osha.gov**]

Standards

OSHA, through the secretary of labor, promulgates and enforces health and safety standards that identify and seek to correct specific workplace hazards and problems. These can range from exposure to cancer-causing agents (e.g., the chemical benzine), to the surprisingly commonplace problem of one worker restarting a machine while another is servicing it, to mundane requirements for sanitary toilet facilities in agricultural jobs. These rules are readily available in OSHA publications, and employers must become familiar with them and comply with them.

After proposed OSHA rules are published in the *Federal Register* (see Chapter 8), industry representatives and other interested parties have the opportunity to comment. Most rules are imposed only after some form of cost-effectiveness inquiry. [For OSHA standards, see **http://www.osha.gov/comp-links.html**]

Variances

Employers may seek both permanent and temporary variances (exceptions) from OSHA standards. A permanent variance may be granted only if the workplace will be as safe as if the variance were enforced. A temporary variance permits additional time to put in place the necessary compliance measures. Employees have a right to a hearing to contest variances.

Occupations with the highest fatality rates per 100,000 workers (the national average is five):

Fishers—131

Timber cutters—130

Airline pilots—126

Structural metal workers—98

Taxicab drivers—47

Source: Anne R. Carey and Bob Laird, "The Sea Is Not Forgiving," *USA Today,* September 25, 1997, p. 1A.

Ergonomics—New Standards?   In late 1999, OSHA proposed new ergonomics standards which, if not blocked by Congress, will require some employers to alter workstations, change tools, and engage in other workplace redesign measures. The ergonomic standards are intended to reduce injuries produced by repetitive stress, awkward postures, equipment not designed to the size and strength of workers, and overexertion. The rules would apply to assembly lines, meatpacking, package handling, and other "general industry" jobs, but they might reach to office jobs such as keyboarding, if significant problems are documented at a work site. OSHA data showed 647,000 ergonomic-related injuries in 1996 with a total direct cost of $15 billion.[38] The ergonomic standards consist fundamentally of two parts: (1) all companies with jobs involving manual lifting would have a program to identify ergonomic issues and to train employees in injury avoidance; and (2) any employer who has an employee who reports an ergonomic injury would be required to take steps, such as adjusting workstations, to address the problem.

Much, but not all, of the business community objects to the proposal on the grounds that the scientific evidence is yet unclear about the relationship between injuries and workplace design and because corrective measures could, of course, be expensive. *The Washington Post* provides an example:

> If the proposed standards were implemented, a worker on a poultry processing line, for example, could expect to be protected from having to cut pieces too quickly or to have to reach too far to grab a bird off a conveyor belt. Instead, the company would be required to adjust the speed of the line and adjust the height of the employee's workstation.[39]

The proposal faces stiff opposition from Republicans in Congress. Indeed, repetitive trauma injuries have fallen for the past three reporting years (1995–97), suggesting that employers may be finding it in their best interest to reduce problems where possible.[40] Furthermore, in the most litigated area of repetitive injury problems, juries have repeatedly rejected claims that defectively designed keyboards have contributed to various arm, wrist, and hand problems.[41] At the same time, OSHA says the rules make sense because ergonomic problems account for about one-third of all work time lost to injuries and illness, and the rules would save employers an estimated $9 billion annually while costing only about $4.2 billion annually.[42] Employers dispute those figures.

[For a copy of the Bureau of Labor Statistics illness and injury report, see **http://stats.bls.gov/news.release/osh.toc.htm**]

Question

Dr. David Diamond of the Massachusetts Institute of Technology Medical Center says he has treated over 1,500 repetitive stress injury (RSI) patients in the 1990s. In response, MIT distributes RSI prevention booklets to all incoming freshmen.

a. Do universities, in your judgment, have a duty to help protect students from RSIs?
b. What considerations would be involved in making your decision? [For advice on measures to reduce RSI problems for students, see **http://ergo.human.cornell.edu**]

> Resolving a dispute of many years, OSHA in 1998 issued an interpretation saying that its long-standing regulation on providing toilet facilities in the workplace also requires "timely access" to those facilities. While not considered a widespread problem, workers in some industries, such as poultry processing, have complained that employers did not allow them to leave the processing line for unscheduled bathroom breaks.

Violence.   "Going postal" has, probably unfairly, become a readily recognizable short-hand expression for violence in the workplace. In fact, United States homicides at work fell from 860 in 1997 to 709 in 1998, and only a fraction of those murders involve employees killing each other.[43] Service employees, such as cab drivers, bartenders, and convenience store clerks, face the greatest risk. A 1994 Justice Department report showed that an estimated 8 percent of all rapes, 7 percent of all robberies, and 16 percent of all assaults occurred at work.[44] A 1996 Society for Human Resource Management survey of 5,000 personnel managers found that at least one-half of the companies responding had experienced serious violent incidents in the previous three years and that 17 percent of those incidents involved workers attacking supervisors.[45]

At the same time, workplace violence has actually declined in recent years; falling from its 1994 peak of about 2.2 million victims to about 1.7 million in 1996.[46] That decline mirrors the general reduction in crime in America over the same period. OSHA has initiated efforts to educate managers about workplace violence, including a 1998 recommendation (not a rule) that retail outlets with a history of crime use bulletproof glass and employ at least two clerks during evening hours.[47]

Violence in the workplace has led to many lawsuits, most alleging that employers have failed to properly protect workers or that the hiring process did not involve careful screening. For example, in early 1999, a jury awarded $7.9 million to the families of two men killed on the job by a worker who had recently been fired. The jury apparently felt that the Asheville, North Carolina, company had failed to protect its workers after dismissing the murderer because of a series of violent incidents.[48] Experts say that workplace violence is often a "spillover" from larger societal problems such as domestic abuse, gangs, and sexual harassment.

OSHA INFORMATION REQUIREMENTS

Right to Know

OSHA has adopted an employee *hazard communication standard* to protect employees from the dangers associated with chemicals and other toxins in the workplace. Chemical manufacturers and importers must develop *material safety data sheets* for all chemicals. Employers must then label all chemical containers so that employees will know about the chemical and its dangers, and employers must educate employees about chemical hazards and how to deal with them.

Records

Businesses must maintain records listing and summarizing injuries, illnesses, and deaths on the job. A summary of those records must be posted at the job. Notice of any OSHA citations or of any imminent dangers on the job must also be posted at the job site.

Businesses with 10 or fewer employees and those engaged in nonhazardous activities, such as retailing or insurance, are generally exempt from OSHA record-keeping requirements.

Enforcement

OSHA's most publicized enforcement mechanism is the unannounced on-site inspection. Inspections arise at the initiative of the agency itself or at the request of employees or their representatives. The inspections must be conducted in a reasonable manner during working hours or other reasonable times, and ordinarily they must not be announced in advance. As discussed in Chapter 5, most employers can insist that the inspector produce a warrant prior to undertaking an inspection. Employer and employee representatives may accompany the inspector. Citations may be issued if violations are discovered. Immediate, serious threats can be restrained with a court order.

Citation.   A citation explains the rules that have been violated and the date by which corrective action must be in place. That citation must be posted near the location of the wrong. Following a citation, the employer may request to meet with an area OSHA official to discuss the problem. Often, a settlement emerges from these meetings. Failing a settlement, the employer can appeal to the independent OSHA Review Commission and thereafter to the federal court of appeals. Violations may lead to significant fines and/or imprisonment.

Industrial Fire.   In a justifiably well-publicized example of OSHA enforcement, a North Carolina poultry plant owner pleaded guilty in 1992 to involuntary manslaughter for the deaths of 25 workers in a fire at his processing plant. The plant had no sprinkler system or fire alarms, and inspectors said that many exits were locked or blocked. Some doors allegedly had been locked in order to keep insects out, to keep employees in during breaks, and to prevent theft.[49] The owner was sentenced to nearly 20 years in prison, but he was expected to be released after two to three years. The plant had never been inspected by North Carolina OSHA officials during its 11 years of operation.[50] Indeed, records indicated that only 40 of North Carolina's 83 chicken-processing plants had been inspected in the past 20 years.[51]

REGULATORY ZEAL

OSHA is probably Washington's most criticized agency. The business community and congressional Republicans persistently call for relaxed rules and greater reliance on the market to secure worker safety. Legislation pending in 1999 would, for example, allow overrides of OSHA standards by permitting employers to substitute methods that they take to be effective in achieving worker safety and employers would be protected from penalties as long as they set up a "health and safety program and are certified as 'in compliance' by an employer-selected and paid consultant."[52] Because of budget constraints and a philosophy of cooperation, OSHA, in fact, reduced its inspections by over 40 percent from 1994 to 1997.[53] In 1995, the Clinton Administration initiated an "E-Z Trial" mechanism to expedite employers' appeals of OSHA citations involving no more than $20,000 in proposed fines. The system operates a bit like a small claims court and is directed particularly to small businesses that can least afford a full appeal to the Occupational Safety and Health Review Commission. Similarly, OSHA introduced its Cooperative Compliance Program in 1997 under which over 12,000 companies with a history of injury and illness problems were invited to establish safety programs, correct hazards, involve workers in the process, and report annually to OSHA. In return those companies would face a reduced risk of on-site inspections. Some businesses, including Ford Motor Company, publically supported CCP, but it was challenged in court by the Chamber of Commerce and others on the grounds that it coerced cooperation by threatening inspections for those not agreeing. In 1999, a federal appeals court struck down CCP, saying that the program did not go through the normal rule-making process (see Chapter 8) and thus did not allow industry groups the required opportunity to comment on it.[54]

CCP, at this writing in 1999, is on hold and OSHA has announced a new Site Specific Targeting Plan (SST) for some 2,200 workplaces where lost workday injury and illness rates exceed 16 per 100 full-time employees.[55] Furthermore, nearly 12,500 employers were sent letters in 1999 urging corrections in safety problems with the largest number going to places where a great deal of heavy lifting is required (e.g., nursing homes, warehouses, and trucking firms).[56] Employers receiving the letters noted that they were targeted based on a 1997 OSHA survey and that they had taken steps to correct the problems. UPS, for example, says that it has spent more than $1 billion since 1995 in improving health and safety and that its days lost to disability fell by 7.5 percent in the first quarter of 1999.[57]

WORKERS' COMPENSATION

Historically, when a worker was injured on the job, her recourse was to sue the employer. Typically, the employee would bring a negligence claim, and commonly the employer would assert one of three defenses: (1) *contributory negligence,* meaning the employee was at least partially responsible for her own harm; (2) *assumption of the risk,* meaning the employee recognized or should have recognized a potentially harmful workplace situation but proceeded voluntarily to engage in her duties; and (3) *fellow servant rule,* meaning the harm to the employee was the result of a coworker's conduct. Proof of any of these defenses acted as a complete bar to recovery for the injured employee. The burden of overcoming these defenses and combating the superior resources of the employer meant that employees often could not secure compensation for workplace injuries.

Then, early in this century, the states began enacting workers' compensation laws to provide an administrative remedy for those injured or killed on the job. Now all states provide some form of protection. Rather than filing a lawsuit, workers or their families simply apply for compensation based on illness, injury, or death. Typically, the system is governed by a state board or commission. Most decisions are routine and are accomplished by completing the necessary forms. Often, a claims examiner will check to verify the nature and severity of the injury. Commission decisions can be appealed to the courts.

In most states, employers are compelled to participate in workers' compensation, depending on state law, either by purchasing insurance privately, contributing to a state-managed fund, or by being self-insured (paying claims directly from their own funds). Of course, firms with good safety records are rewarded with lower premium payments.

In 1997, former Texas Christian University running back Kent Waldrep sued the university, claiming that he was entitled to workers' compensation after being paralyzed in a 1974 game. While the National Collegiate Athletic Association now provides catastrophic-injury protection, that insurance was not provided when Waldrep was injured. Waldrep claimed that he was a university employee because he received a full scholarship and helped generate income for the university. The Texas Workers' Compensation Commission agreed with Waldrep and ruled that he would be paid $70 per week for life plus medical bills dating back to the accident. That decision was appealed to the Texas courts. How would you rule?

Benefits

The amount of recovery for injury or death is determined by a benefits schedule, which specifies the sum to be awarded for the injury in question. The amount of the award is normally a percentage of the worker's salary either for a specified period of time or indefinitely, depending on the severity of the injury. Injury benefits normally amount to one-half to two-thirds of regular wages. Death benefits ordinarily are tied to the wages of the deceased. [For state workers' compensation laws, see **http://www.dol.gov/dol/esa/ public/regs/statutes/owcp/stwclaw/stwclaw.htm**]

Coverage

Certain employment classifications such as agriculture may be excluded from workers' compensation, but about 90 percent of the labor force is covered, and some of those not covered are shielded by other statutes such as the Federal Employer's Liability Act.

Legal Requirements

In general, injuries, illnesses, and deaths are compensable where the harm (1) arose out of the employment, and (2) arose in the course of employment. Proof of employer negligence is not required, and the defenses noted above are not available to the employer. Thus, workers' compensation provides a form of no-fault protection in the workplace. Workers give up the right to sue and the burdens that accompany that course, and employers participate in an insurance system that recognizes the inevitability of workplace harm.

Workers' compensation recovery is the exclusive remedy for workplace injury, illness, or death, but some jurisdictions recognize exceptions for intentional torts and/or gross negligence. In those instances, employees are allowed to sue for damages beyond recoveries provided under workers' compensation.

Litigation

Notwithstanding its no-fault character, workers' compensation has generated extensive litigation. For example, a 16-year-old employed as a "gas jockey" was covered by workers' compensation for injuries sustained when, during a slow time at work, he showed a friend a "trick" in which a match might be tossed into oil, gasoline, and grease without causing an explosion. On this occasion, an explosion did result, but the Workers' Compensation Board ruled and the court agreed that this "horseplay" was covered by the New York statute since it was "related to his employment."[58] The case that follows examines the two-part workers' compensation test as well as some other issues that often arise in these cases.

QUAKER OATS CO. v. CIHA
552 N. W. 2d 143 (Iowa S. Ct. 1996)

Chief Justice McGiverin

I. Background Facts

In May 1991, petitioner Bradley Ciha was employed by defendant Quaker Oats Company at its Cedar Rapids plant as an area maintenance supervisor. Quaker Oats employed twenty to twenty-five such supervisors. In that position, he was responsible for the planning, scheduling, and supervising of plant maintenance in a designated area of the plant's operation. By all accounts, Ciha was considered an excellent employee. Ciha's normal work week at Quaker Oats was Monday through Friday. On a typical weekend including Saturday and Sunday, Ciha was not on duty and was not expected to be on call to drive to the plant for emergency maintenance purposes.

For the first forty-eight hours on Memorial Day weekend in 1991, Ciha was assigned as "204 supervisor" for Quaker Oats. In that capacity, he was required to be on call for mechanical emergencies anywhere in the plant.

While preparing dinner at his home on Sunday, May 26, Ciha was contacted at approximately 4:15 PM through a company electronic paging device. He was

informed that several large cooling fans at the plant were malfunctioning. Ciha responded to the breakdown by electing to drive his motorcycle to the plant to remedy the problem himself. To reach the plant, Ciha drove a direct route (of approximately four and a half miles) on Johnson Avenue. After reaching the plant without incident, he personally remedied the problem by cooling the fans with an air hose. At approximately 5:45 PM, Ciha telephoned his wife and informed her that she could resume dinner preparations because he was about to return home.

Ciha drove a different route from the plant to home than he drove earlier from his home to the plant. The return-home route was on Ellis road and was admittedly not the most direct route from the plant to Ciha's home. The Ellis road route (approximately nine miles) was scenic and subject to less traffic and traffic signals than the direct route Ciha commonly drove from home to the plant. Apparently, the Ellis road route took approximately five to seven minutes longer to drive than the direct,

Johnson road route. Ciha chose to drive this route home only during the spring, summer, and fall seasons as the road could become treacherous during the winter months.

On his return trip from the plant to home along Ellis road, Ciha was involved in a serious motor vehicle accident in which he suffered a broken neck and was rendered a quadriplegic. At the time of the accident, Ciha was married and resided in a home in Cedar Rapids with his wife, Kim.

Following the accident, Ciha was admitted to St. Luke's Hospital in Cedar Rapids until June 12, 1991, when he requested transfer to a specialized care facility, Craig Hospital, located in Englewood, Colorado.

In addition to the health care Ciha received while at Craig, the hospital also provided Kim specialized training in order for her to be able to care for Ciha upon his return home.

Ciha was discharged from Craig Hospital on September 14, 1991, to his home in Cedar Rapids. Since his discharge, Kim has performed necessary, extensive home nursing services. Ciha requires assistance in dressing, changing urine bags, and transferring between his wheelchair and his bed. At night, he must be repositioned in bed one to four times in order to prevent him from developing pressure sores.

Ciha first returned to work at Quaker Oats in January 1992 in a new position as materials supervisor. In this position, he works at a computer (with the aid of an adaptive device and telephone headset) in the company's purchasing department. With the aid of a modified computer, Ciha analyzes inventory and makes purchases on behalf of Quaker Oats. Quaker Oats greatly aided in Ciha's return to work by adapting the workplace and position in order for Ciha to be able to perform the job.

In his position as materials supervisor, he receives the same base salary, not including raises, as that of an area maintenance supervisor. Ciha no longer has the same opportunity, however, to earn overtime as he had as an area maintenance supervisor.

In order to return to work, Ciha relied on the county's disabled persons transportation service to and from Quaker Oats. Based on the hours of the transportation service, however, Ciha was not able to return to work full-time.

Ciha was readmitted to Craig for one week in March 1992 for a comprehensive evaluation. At the time of his readmittance, Ciha did not own a van and did not drive. While at Craig, Ciha had his driving potential assessed.

A driving specialist from the hospital concluded Ciha would need to purchase a specially modified van in order to be able to drive independently. At some time thereafter, Ciha purchased the recommended van.

Many of Ciha's medical expenses from the accident were paid for through a group health and accident insurance plan available to Ciha through his employer Quaker Oats. However, there were significant limitations in coverage under the group plan. For example, in addition to a lifetime cap on medical expenses, the group plan did not provide Ciha coverage for necessary home health care services, home modifications, or motor vehicle conversions.

II. Workers' Compensation Litigation

In November 1991, Ciha filed a claim for permanent partial disability benefits with the Iowa industrial commissioner's office against his employer, Quaker Oats.

Ciha's claim proceeded to an arbitration hearing.

* * * * *

[At arbitration, the deputy industrial commissioner reached several conclusions favorable to Ciha. Quaker Oats then appealed to the industrial commissioner who agreed with the deputy. Quaker Oats next took the case to the district court, which affirmed. The Iowa Supreme Court then undertook this review.]

* * * * *

IV. Going and Coming Rule, the "Special Errand" and "Required Vehicle" Exceptions, and Deviation

In Iowa,

[e]very employer, not specifically excepted by the provisions of [Iowa Code chapter 85], shall provide, secure, and pay compensation according to the provisions of this chapter for any and all personal injuries sustained by an employee arising out of and in the course of the employment . . .

Iowa Code § 85.3(1). To obtain such compensation, an injured employee has the burden of proving by a preponderance of the evidence that his injuries arose out of and in the course of his employment. An injury arises "out of" the employment when there is a causal relationship between the employment and the injury. "In the course of" the employment concerns the time, place, and circumstances of the injury. Stated more specifically,

[a]n injury occurs in the course of the employment when it is within the period of employment at a place where the employee reasonably may be in performing his duties, and while he is fulfilling those duties or engaged in doing something incidental thereto. An injury in the course of employment embraces all injuries received while employed in furthering the employer's business and injuries received on the employer's premises, provided that the employee's presence must ordinarily be required at the place of the injury, or, if not so required, employee's departure from the usual place of employment must not amount to an abandonment of employment or be an act wholly foreign to his usual work. An employee does not cease to be in the course of his employment merely because he is not actually engaged in doing some specifically prescribed task, if, in the course of his employment, he does some act which he deems necessary for the benefit or interest of his employer.

First and foremost, Quaker Oats contends Ciha did not sustain his injury in the course of his employment because the injury was sustained away from the employer's premises and while Ciha was on his way home from the plant. The employer relies on the well-established "going and coming" rule, which generally provides: "[A]bsent special circumstances, injuries occurring off the employer's premises while the employee is on the way to or from work are not compensable."

Under the going and coming rule, Ciha admittedly did not sustain an injury in the course of his employment: he was injured while driving his motorcycle home from the Quaker Oats plant.

There are, however, several exceptions to the going and coming rule . . .

The first exception to the going and coming rule relied on by the commissioner is the "special errand" exception.

Under the exception, if an employee is on a special errand or mission for his or her employer at the time of the injury, the injury is held to have arisen in the course of employment.

* * * * *

After considering all arguments raised by the parties, we believe substantial evidence supports the commissioner's conclusion that Ciha was on a special errand at the time of his injury.

[I]n answer to the question "[w]hose business was [the employee] pursuing at the time of the injury?," the answer must be Quaker Oats' business. The fact that Ciha was contacted on Sunday while he was on

204 duty was truly "special:" it was unusual, sudden, and unexpected.

* * * * *

Deviation

Notwithstanding our conclusion that the special errand exception to the going and coming rule applies in the present case, Quaker Oats contends Ciha had "deviated" from his trip home from the plant to such an extent that he abandoned his employment at the time of the accident. The commissioner and district court rejected this argument, and we do the same.

* * * * *

In concluding Ciha did not deviate from his special errand, the commissioner stated:

[Ciha] testified that he often took [the Ellis road] route home because it was more scenic, it had less traffic, it had fewer stop lights, and the actual difference in miles between this route and the more direct route was minimal. [Ciha's] call to his wife from the plant to start the grill for their meal shows that his purpose was to return home, and that he had no other destination other than to return to his residence. The record does not show a deviation from the course of the employment.

V. Claimed Expenses under Iowa Code Section 85.27

Of the expenses awarded by the commissioner under Iowa Code section 85.27, Quaker Oats only challenges the award of costs for home modifications, van conversion, and home nursing services. The commissioner and district court found the home modification and van conversion expenses to be reasonable "appliances" under section 85.27. In addition, the commissioner found the claimed expenses for home nursing services and the claimed value of those services to be reasonable.

Iowa Code section 85.27 provides in pertinent part:

The employer, for all injuries compensable under this chapter or chapter 85A, shall furnish reasonable surgical, medical, dental, osteopathic, chiropractic, podiatric, physical rehabilitation, nursing, ambulance and hospital services and supplies therefor and shall allow reasonably necessary transportation expenses incurred for such services. The employer shall also furnish reasonable and necessary crutches, artificial members and appliances . . .

* * * * *

A. Home Modifications and Van Conversion

In order for Ciha to have been able to access his house in a wheelchair upon his return from Craig Hospital, various home modifications were required. The home modifications included widened doorways, a ramp into the home, a special shower, an elevator, and other items necessitated by Ciha's wheelchair-bound status. He also incurred van conversion expenses in order to be able to return to work full-time.

In his workers' compensation claim, Ciha sought and was awarded $20,788 in home modification expenses and $24,509 in van conversion expenses under Iowa Code section 85.27. The deputy concluded the home modification expenses incurred by Ciha "relate to items designed to substitute for function lost in [his] work injury." Relying on past agency decisions, the commissioner also held Quaker Oats responsible for the van conversion expenses. The commissioner further concluded:

[Ciha's] need for a ramp to enter his home, and for a special shower designed to accommodate a wheelchair, are held to be necessary and reasonable medical expenses. All of the items are related to accommodating [Ciha's] wheelchair. An appliance has been held to be a device that serves to replace a physical function lost by the injury. Just as a wheelchair seeks to replace the lost functions of standing and walking, a wheelchair ramp, a wheelchair shower, etc. also seek to replace physical functions claimant possessed before the work injury but has now lost.

Quaker Oats contends on appeal that the claimed home modification and van conversion costs are not compensable as "appliances" under Iowa Code section 85.27.

*   *   *   *   *

An "appliance" is defined as hearing aids, corrective lenses, orthodontic devices, dentures, orthopedic braces, or any other artificial device used to provide function or for therapeutic purposes.

Appliances which are for the correction of a condition resulting from an injury . . . are compensable under Iowa Code section 85.27.

We begin with the unusually strong medical evidence of necessity and of the record that [the claimant's] family status and past lifestyle reveal no other use for the van. That evidence refutes any contention that the van is a frill or luxury and reveals what can be described as an appliance, not greatly different from crutches or a wheelchair. The point is that a van is necessary in order to make [the claimant's] wheelchair fully useful.

*   *   *   *   *

Under the unique facts of the present case, we conclude substantial evidence supports the commissioner's ruling that the home modifications and van conversion were reasonable appliances under Iowa Code section 85.27.

B. Home Nursing Services

In addition to the claimed home modification and van conversion expenses, Ciha also sought $58,447 in home nursing services performed by his wife after his return home from the hospital in Colorado. At the arbitration hearing, Quaker Oats unsuccessfully contended the claimed home nursing services were not reasonable expenses under section 85.27, and also that the claimed amount of the services set forth in an affidavit prepared by Kim Ciha was unreasonable.

On appeal, Quaker Oats does not dispute that it had a duty under Iowa Code section 85.27 to provide reasonable nursing services to Ciha if his injury was compensable (which we have concluded it is). In addition, Quaker Oats agrees the services performed by Kim were "nursing" services as contemplated by section 85.27. Quaker Oats contends, however, that $58,447 in home nursing expenses claimed by Ciha is unreasonable. The commissioner and district court disagreed and we must affirm this decision if supported by substantial evidence.

In ordering Quaker Oats to pay Ciha's home nursing services, the commissioner stated the following:

The record shows that [Ciha's] wife received special training to perform the functions of a nurse for her husband, including digital manipulation to stimulate a bowel movement.

In the instant case, [Ciha's] spouse, although not a nurse or LPN, did have to receive special training to perform the services. The services themselves are clearly medical nursing services and not general care services such as dressing, bathing, feeding, etc. [Ciha's] spouse's nursing services are held to be compensable under Iowa Code section 85.27.

We believe the affidavit and Kim's testimony establish the reasonableness of the claimed home nursing care expenses . . .

I. Industrial Disability

As a final issue, Quaker Oats contends the commissioner erred in ruling that Ciha had sustained an eighty percent permanent partial industrial disability. Quaker Oats argues Ciha's disability is only fifty to sixty percent because it, Ciha's employer, went to great lengths to accommodate claimant and also that claimant has suffered no loss of earnings.

As we have stated on many occasions, "[i]ndustrial disability measures an injured worker's lost earning capacity." Factors that should be considered include the employee's functional disability, age, education, qualifications, experience, and the ability of the employee to engage in employment for which the employee is fitted.

As a result of the accident and resulting quadriplegia, Ciha is wheelchair-bound, cannot control his bowel functions, and his lifestyle has been severely limited from that prior to the injury. He requires extensive, daily care and attention by his wife, relatives, and coworkers as he no longer has the ability to perform many basic daily living functions. Also, as a thirty-eight year old man, it cannot be reasonably disputed that Ciha's employability outside of the Quaker Oats workforce has been significantly and negatively affected by his injury. Although we applaud the efforts of Quaker Oats in modifying the workplace to accommodate Ciha's disability, such efforts are not determinative of Ciha's industrial disability rating. *See Thilges* v. *Snap–On Tools Corp.,* 528 N.W.2d 614, 617 (Iowa 1995) ("[W]e are satisfied that the commissioner was correct in viewing loss of earning capacity in terms of the injured worker's present ability to earn in the competitive job market without regard to the accommodation furnished by one's present employer.").

In finding eighty percent industrial disability, the commissioner concluded the following:

> [D]efendant [Quaker Oats] has gone to great effort to accommodate claimant's [Ciha's] devastating disability. Defendant has set up a team of five co-employees to assist claimant, installed a special elevator, etc. These efforts are very appropriate, and defendant is to be commended for putting claimant back to work under difficult circumstances. However, defendant also obtains an advantage by doing so in that claimant's disability is reduced from what it otherwise would be. Although claimant's position is not a "make work" job and involves a significant contribution to his employer, nevertheless if claimant were to be suddenly thrust into the job market, his ability to compete with other workers for positions would be limited in the most extreme sense. Clearly, without the accommodation, claimant's disability would be permanent and total. Claimant's industrial disability is found to be [eighty] percent.

We conclude there is substantial evidence to support the commissioner's decision on this issue.
Affirmed.

Questions

1. The Iowa Supreme Court in the *Quaker Oats* (and most courts in workers' compensation cases) required a two-part showing that the injury must have occured both "in the course of" and "arise out of" employment.
   a. Explain those two standards.
   b. Must an employee be engaged in a prescribed task in order to be "in the course of employment?" Explain.
   c. Why did the court conclude that Ciha was on a "special errand?"
2. Why did the court conclude that Ciha had suffered an 80 percent permanent partial industrial disability?
3. Fernandez, an exotic dancer, left her job drunk and was seriously injured in a crash while riding as a passenger in a car driven by another dancer. The crash came within one hour of leaving work. Her intoxication led to her decision to ride with her intoxicated coworker. Fernandez sought workers' compensation. She claimed that her employer, Bottoms Up Lounge in Council Bluffs, Iowa, required her to socialize with male customers when not dancing and to generate at least two drinks per hour from customers. Dancers were not required to drink, but most dancers consumed six to eight drinks per night or more. Did Fernandez's injury arise out of and in the course of employment so that she can recover under workers' compensation? Explain. See *2800 Corp.* v. *Fernandez,* 528 N.W.2d 124 (Iowa 1995).
4. Joseph Smyth, a college mathematics instructor, was killed while driving his personal auto home from work. At the time, Smyth had student papers with him, which he intended to grade that evening. He often worked at home. Many faculty members took work home in the evenings. However, the college did not require that practice. Indeed, the college neither encouraged nor discouraged working at home.

The widely adopted "going and coming rule" provides that employees injured while commuting to and from work, in general, are not covered by workers' compensation.

    a. Should Smyth (and other teachers) be exempted from the going and coming rule, thus permitting recovery by Smyth's family? Explain. See *Santa Rosa Junior College* v. *Workers' Compensation Appeals Board and Joann Smyth,* 708 P.2d 673 (Cal. 1985).

    b. Would you reach a different conclusion had a student been accompanying Smyth? Explain.

5. Casimer Gacioch worked at a Stroh Brewery. The company provided free beer at work. When he began work in 1947 he drank only three to four beers on the weekend. He was fired in 1974, by which time he was drinking 12 bottles of beer daily. After Mr. Gacioch's death, his wife sought workers' compensation benefits. The evidence indicated that Mr. Gacioch had a predisposition to alcoholism but was not an alcoholic at the time he was hired. How would you rule on the widow's workers' compensation claim? Explain. See *Gacioch* v. *Stroh Brewery* 466 N.W. 2d 303 (Mich Ct. of Appeals, 1991).

6. Darnell, a manager for KN Energy, took a company car from his office to make a bank deposit for KN. He then drove toward another bank to conduct personal banking business. Before arriving at the second bank, he was struck from behind and injured. The second, personal banking trip constituted a deviation of about five blocks from Darnell's direct route back to work. Darnell sought workers' compensation. Decide. Explain. See *Darnell* v. *KN Energy, Inc.,* 586 N.W.2d 484 (Neb. Ct. App. 1998).

Part Five—Employee Privacy

Perhaps the most explosive employment issue at the turn of the century is privacy on the job. Increasingly, employers are engaging in an array of testing and monitoring procedures both before and after hiring. Drug testing, integrity tests, personality tests, spying, television and computer monitoring of work performance, and so forth are routine personnel practices in many firms. Employers have a legitimate interest in these strategies not only to hire better employees and improve productivity but to protect coworkers, reduce insurance claims, and protect consumers from poor products and service. On the other hand, job applicants and employees often feel the intrusive presence of "Big Brother" in their lives.

DRUGS AND DRUG TESTING: INTRODUCTION

The business community considers drug and alcohol use to be a serious workplace problem. Nearly 70 percent of Americans using drugs are employed.[59] Ninety-eight percent of *Fortune* 500 companies use some form of drug testing, and over 40 percent of American workers are subject to drug tests.[60] On the other hand, only 5 percent of workers tested positive for illegal substances in 1997; down from 5.8 percent in 1996.[61] Furthermore, those using drugs have been moving away from cocaine and other "hard" drugs to marijuana. A 1994 National Academy of Sciences study found that employees who use drugs off the job were no more likely to be involved in work-related accidents than other employees, and a Postal Service study found that 87 percent of new hires who tested positive for drug use became employees in good standing while 91 percent of those passing drug tests were similarly successful on the job.[62] Regardless of the severity of the risk, many companies feel they must engage in drug testing in order to protect themselves against liability claims should an impaired employee cause harm.

DRUG TESTING IN PRACTICE

Broadly, employment-based alcohol and drug testing occurs in six circumstances: (1) pre-employment screening, (2) routine physical examinations, (3) "reasonable suspicion" testing, (4) post-accident testing, (5) random testing, and (6) follow-up testing.[63]

1. Ordinarily, private sector, preemployment testing is lawful although some state and local laws may impose restrictions. In general, public-sector employers have less drug testing latitude because of constitutional limitations, but when challenged in court, those programs have generally been approved.

2. Drug testing as a part of periodic physical examinations is generally lawful if properly conducted. To avoid legal problems, employers should notify job applicants and current employees of drug testing in association with physicals.

3. Reasonable suspicion is something less than probable cause and means that the employer has evidence, such as lapses in performance, that would justify a drug test. Such tests, given a sound factual foundation and even-handed application, ordinarily are permissible.

4. Post-accident testing involves employees who have been involved in a serious on-the-job accident. Such tests normally are permissible.

5. Selecting employees at random, without notice, for drug testing can be very effective in deterring drug use, but the practice raises significant legal questions. Some states explicitly forbid random testing, except for safety-sensitive jobs such as those in transportation. The Supreme Court has upheld such testing for public-sector employees where public safety is involved and for those having access to particularly sensitive information.[64]

6. Follow-up testing is used for employees who are returning from a drug or alcohol rehabilitation. The testing acts as an incentive for recovering drug users to remain "clean." All states permit follow-up testing, but employers should create contracts with rehabilitating employees to establish testing arrangements.

LEGAL CHALLENGES TO ALCOHOL AND DRUG TESTING

Drug use as a societal problem is undeniable, but critics are concerned that personal rights may be trampled in our zeal to attack substance abuse. Some of the doubts are that the tests (1) are often unreliable, (2) invade employee privacy, and (3) do not measure actual job impairment.

Challenges to drug testing ordinarily spring form the following claims and defenses.

1. Federal Constitution. As explained in Chapter 5, the Fourth Amendment to the United States Constitution forbids unreasonable searches and seizures. Thus, government officials ordinarily cannot conduct a search without individualized suspicion; that is, without probable cause. Certain exceptions, however, have been recognized in cases involving safety, national security, athletic participation, and other special needs. Challenges to testing based on the Fifth Amendment (claiming a due process violation because, for example, the test was inaccurate) and the Fourteenth Amendment (claiming an equal protection violation because certain groups or individuals are treated differently than others) have not often been successful. Remember that the Constitution, in general, protects us from the government, not from private-sector employers.

2. State Constitutions. Many state constitutions offer privacy protection, but court decisions, to date, have generally not extended those protections to private-sector employers. On the other hand, certain states, such as California and Massachusetts, explicitly offer constitutional protection to private-sector employees.

3. Federal Statutes. Drug testing could violate Title VII of the Civil Rights Act of 1964 or the Americans with Disabilities Act (see Chapter 13) if the testing fails to treat all individuals equally. The ADA protects *recovering* drug addicts and those erroneously believed to be drug users.

4. State and Local Statutes. Historically, most state and local drug testing legislation placed limits on that testing, but in recent years, fears about drug use in the workplace and often intense business community lobbying have, in some cases, relaxed those testing restraints. For example, in 1998 the State of Iowa eliminated its ban on random drug and alcohol testing as well as its requirement that employers pay for treatment if a worker tested positive. Now random testing is permissible in all private sector jobs, employees can be fired for testing positive, and companies need not provide drug treatment.

5. Common Law Claims. Some of the more prominent judge-made (common law) claims that might provide a challenge to drug testing include invasion of privacy, defamation (dissemination of erroneous information about an employee), negligence (in testing or in selecting a test provider), intentional infliction of emotional distress, and wrongful discharge (discussed later in this chapter).

The most interesting developments in drug testing in recent years have been at the high school level where, for example, the Rush County, Indiana, High School, in 1996, began testing all students involved in extracurricular activities, and the Miami-Dade County, Florida, schools, in 1998, began a voluntary drug testing program for all students, requiring consent from both students and parents.[65] The U.S. Supreme Court, which had previously approved random drug testing for high school athletes,[66] declined to review a lower court decision supporting the Rush County program.[67] In your view, should students participating in high school extracurricular activities be subjected to random drug testing? All students? Explain.

Privacy. Although most recent decisions have been supportive of properly conducted drug testing, an interesting federal Court of Appeals decision suggests the potential strength of common law privacy considerations.

Sarah Borse, a 15-year employee of Piece Goods Shop of Bethlehem, Pennsylvania, was fired because she refused to take a drug test that was required under a new company policy. She raised various claims and, as outlined in the *Smyth* case, below, the court found that drug testing could constitute an invasion of privacy.[68] [For a critique of workplace drug testing, see **http://www.aclu.org/news/1999/n090199a.html**]

DRUG-FREE WORKPLACE

Congress encouraged the effort against drug abuse by passing the Drug-Free Workplace Act of 1988. The act applies to employers who do business ($25,000 or more) with the federal government or who receive aid from the government. They are required to develop an antidrug policy for employees. They must provide drug-free awareness programs for employees, and they must acquaint employees with available assistance for those with drug problems, while also warning them of the penalties that accompany violation of the policy. The act requires employees to adhere to the company policy and to inform the company within five days if they are convicted of or plead no contest to a drug-related offense in the workplace. Of course, in the event of a violation, company policy might include a mandatory rehabilitation program or termination. Some states, including California, Illinois, Georgia, and South Carolina also have Drug-Free Workplace Acts. [For more drug testing information, see **http://www.courttv.com/legalcafe/work/drug_testing/**]

MONITORING

A McDonald's manager in Elmira, New York, began an affair with a McDonald's employee in another town. They exchanged "steamy" messages by voice mail. An Elmira coworker retrieved the messages and played them for the manager's wife and boss, whereupon the manager was fired. He filed suit claiming violations of a federal wiretapping law and a state eavesdropping statute.[69] The case was settled out of court.

Experts estimate that the conduct of 50 million workers or more is monitored by computer, telephone, and video technologies.[70] Employees are, of course, concerned about privacy, while employers' worries include reduced productivity and company liability, under respondeat superior or negligent supervision reasoning, for criminal or tortious conduct (e.g., sexual harassment or defamation) by employees using company technology. As with drug-testing, an array of constitutional, statutory, and common law protections may shield employees, but the law in this area is unsettled.

The brokerage firm Edward Jones & Co. demanded that workers admit it if they sent pornography or off-color jokes over the company e-mail system—then fired 19 of them for failing to fess up.

Source: Connie Farrow, "Firm Fires 19 Over Risque e-mail," *Des Moines Register,* May 8, 1999, p. 6S.

The principal federal legislation, the 1986 Electronic Communications Privacy Act, prohibits private individuals and organizations from intercepting wire, oral, or electronic communications. However, the act provides for two exceptions: (1) prior consent by one of the parties to the communication, and (2) employer monitoring in the "ordinary course of business" by telephone or other device furnished by a provider of wire or electronic communication service. Thus the law clearly permits employer monitoring and recording of company-related business calls, although that monitoring should stop when it intrudes on purely personal matters. Employers are advised to set out and publicize a clearly defined company policy on monitoring such as the following statement from the Principal Financial Group employee handbook:

> The corporation's electronic mail system is business property and is to be used for business purposes. The corporation reserves the right to monitor all electronic mail messages.[71]

The case that follows is one of the few judicial examinations of privacy and monitoring. The plaintiff, Smyth, was an at-will employee (discussed later in this chapter), meaning that he did not have a contract for a specified period of time. Under the law of Pennsylvania, where the case took place, at-will employees could be fired for any reason unless the discharge violated public policy. The *Smyth* case examines whether an e-mail interception amounts to an invasion of privacy and is thus a violation of public policy. [For more information on e-mail and privacy, see **http://www.hrlawindex.com/email/email.html**]

SMYTH v. PILLSBURY CO.
914 F. Supp. 97 (E.D. Pa. 1996)

District Judge Weiner

[handwritten: Does an employer have a right to terminate an ee from sending inapprop. + unprofessional comments via the company's email system?]

[P]laintiff claims he was wrongfully discharged from his position as a regional operations manager by the defendant. Presently before the court is the motion of the defendant to dismiss . . .

Defendant maintained an electronic mail communication system ("e-mail") in order to promote internal corporate communications between its employees. Defendant repeatedly assured its employees, including plaintiff, that all e-mail communications would remain confidential and privileged. Defendant further assured its employees, including plaintiff, that e-mail communications could not be intercepted and used by defendant against its employees as grounds for termination or reprimand.

In October 1994, plaintiff received certain e-mail communications from his supervisor over defendant's e-mail system on his computer at home. In reliance on defendant's assurances regarding defendant's e-mail system, plaintiff responded and exchanged e-mails with his supervisor. At some later date, contrary to the assurances

of confidentiality . . . defendent, acting through its agents, servants, and employees, intercepted plaintiff's private e-mail messages made in October 1994. On January 17, 1995, defendant notified plaintiff that it was terminating his employment effective February 1, 1995, for transmitting what it deemed to be inappropriate and unprofessional comments* over defendant's e-mail system in October 1994.

* * * * *

Plaintiff claims that his termination was in violation of "public policy which precludes an employer from terminating an employee in violation of the employee's right to privacy as embodied in Pennsylvania common law." In support for this proposition, plaintiff directs our attention

---

*Defendant alleges in its motion to dismiss that the e-mails concerned sales management and contained threats to "kill the backstabbing bastards" and referred to the planned holiday party as the "Jim Jones Koolaid affair."

to a decision by our Court of Appeals in *Borse* v. *Piece Goods Shop, Inc.* 963 F.2d 611 (3d Cir.1992). In *Borse,* the plaintiff sued her employer alleging wrongful discharge as a result of her refusal to submit to urinalysis screening and personal property searches at her workplace pursuant to the employer's drug and alcohol policy. After rejecting plaintiff's argument that the employer's drug and alcohol program violated public policy encompassed in the United States and Pennsylvania Constitutions, our Court of Appeals stated "our review of Pennsylvania law reveals other evidence of a public policy that may, under certain circumstances, give rise to a wrongful discharge action related to urinalysis or to personal property searches. Specifically, we refer to the Pennsylvania common law regarding tortious invasion of privacy."

* * * * *

Although the Court of Appeals in *Borse* observed that "[t]he Pennsylvania courts have not had occasion to consider whether a discharge related to an employer's tortious invasion of an employee's privacy violates public policy," the Court of Appeals predicted that in any claim where the employee claimed that his discharge related to an invasion of his privacy "the Pennsylvania Supreme Court would examine the facts and circumstances surrounding the alleged invasion of privacy. If the court determined that the discharge was related to a substantial and highly offensive invasion of the employee's privacy, [the Court of Appeals] believe[d] that it would conclude that the discharge violated public policy." In determining whether an alleged invasion of privacy is substantial and highly offensive to a reasonable person, the Court of Appeals predicted that Pennsylvania would adopt a balancing test which balances the employee's privacy interest against the employer's interest in maintaining a drug-free workplace. [T]he Court of Appeals in *Borse* remanded the case to the district court with directions to grant Borse leave to allege how the defendant's drug and alcohol program violates her right to privacy.

* * * * *

[In the case before us] we find that plaintiff has failed to state a claim upon which relief can be granted. In the first instance, unlike urinalysis and personal property searches, we do not find a reasonable expectation of privacy in e-mail communications voluntarily made by an employee to his supervisor over the company e-mail system notwithstanding any assurances that such communications would not be intercepted by management. Once plaintiff communicated the alleged unprofessional comments to a second person (his supervisor) over an e-mail system which was apparently utilized by the entire company, any reasonable expectation of privacy was lost. Significantly, the defendant did not require plaintiff, as in the case of a urinalysis or personal property search, to disclose any personal information about himself. Rather, plaintiff voluntarily communicated the alleged unprofessional comments over the company e-mail system. We find no privacy interests in such communications.

In the second instance, even if we found that an employee had a reasonable expectation of privacy in the contents of his e-mail communications over the company e-mail system, we do not find that a reasonable person would consider the defendant's interception of these communications to be a substantial and highly offensive invasion of his privacy. Again, we note that by intercepting such communications, the company is not, as in the case of urinalysis or personal property searches, requiring the employee to disclose any personal information about himself or invading the employee's person or personal effects. Moreover, the company's interest in preventing inappropriate and unprofessional comments or even illegal activity over its e-mail system outweighs any privacy interest the employee may have in those comments.

In sum, we find that the defendant's actions did not tortiously invade the plaintiff's privacy and, therefore, did not violate public policy. As a result, the motion to dismiss is granted.

Questions

1. Why did the Court reject Smyth's invasion of privacy claim?
2. Why did Pillsbury win even though it repeatedly promised employees that the e-mail system would be private and would not be used against employees?
3. In your opinion, should on-the-job e-mail messages be free from employer monitoring? Explain.
4. a. Does an employer have the right to search the office of an employee? Explain.
   b. What if the employer provides a locker for the employee and allows the employee to provide a lock? Explain.

OFFICE ROMANCE

- "When Labor Leads to Love"[72]
- "Cupid's Cubicles"[73]
- "What's Love Got to Do with It? When Passions Spill into the Workplace"[74]

With work consuming ever more space in our lives, we should not be surprised that "passion is spilling into the workplace" and leading to headlines like those noted above. Of course, President Clinton and Monica Lewinsky might well come to mind when thinking of romance at work, but it turns out that their affair was in good company, statistically speaking. A recent survey of 1,000 people found 9 percent of them admitting to making love at work, while another 12 percent say they have walked in on others doing so.[75]

When having so much fun, can legal problems be far behind? Well, sometimes not. Certainly conflict-of-interest issues can emerge from an office romance, but the more highly publicized question today is one of romantic privacy versus sexual harassment. Consider the case of the former president of Staples, Inc., who according to published accounts, resigned in 1997 following an internal investigation that concluded he had violated the company's fraternization policy, which forbids personal relationships between supervisors and subordinates.[76] (He denies having had the alleged romance.)

Most companies consider romance to be a private matter so long as it does not involve superior/subordinate relationships, and fewer than 10 percent of companies maintain fraternization policies, largely because they have proven unworkable.[77] Nonetheless, such policies may prove helpful today as a company defense against sexual harassment claims that sometimes arise out of broken office romances. Court decisions have been generally supportive of the policies,[78] but many states have now approved lifestyle discrimination statutes that forbid job discrimination based on off-the-job conduct (romance as well as smoking, skiing, and other "dangerous" activities). So companies must develop very clear-cut antiharassment policies while recognizing, as one employment lawyer put it, that "The bottom line is, you simply can't legislate love."[79]

Questions

1. In your opinion, should companies be able to fire those who engage in office romances where their work product and the well-being of the company are not at risk? Explain.
2. Wayne Waggoner was Kathey Cyr's supervisor at an Ace Hardware distribution center in the state of Washington. Ace prohibits romantic relationships between supervisors and subordinates and requires employees to disclose conflicts of interest. Ace learned that Waggoner and Cyr were living together, but both denied the relationship and both were fired for dishonesty. Washington law forbids employment discrimination based on marital status. Waggoner and Cyr sued Ace claiming that their social relationship was protected by the statute and that their dismissal was, therefore, unlawful. A state court of appeals ruled in their favor, and Ace appealed. Decide.

Explain. See *Waggoner and Cyr* v. *Ace Hardware Corporation*, 953 P.2d 88 (Wash. 1998).

Part Six—Employee Benefits and Income Maintenance

What were once "fringe benefits"—health insurance, life insurance, pensions, and so forth—are now central to a comfortable, secure life for most employees and central to budgeting decisions for employers. The importance of benefits in contemporary life is evidenced by several pieces of federal legislation designed to increase worker protection. The Consolidated Budget Reconciliation Act of 1985 (COBRA), among other provisions, requires employers with 20 or more employees to permit employees to retain group health coverage at their own expense when they leave the company unless they were fired for gross misconduct. The Health Insurance Portability and Accountability Act of 1996 provides that employees covered by a company health insurance plan who switch jobs must be accorded the same coverage under the new employer's group coverage plan. An employee not covered by a group plan is not guaranteed coverage after a switch, and employers who do not provide health coverage are not required to do so under the law. Finally, the Mental Health Parity Act of 1996 requires that companies employing 50 or more workers and offering group mental health coverage must provide annual and lifetime dollar benefits equal to those provided for medical benefits. Note that the law does not require employers to provide mental health coverage. Rather, mental health benefits, if provided, must be equal to those provided for medical care.

FAMILY LEAVE

The 1993 Family and Medical Leave Act (FMLA) provides up to 12 weeks of unpaid leave in any 12-month period for family needs such as the birth or adoption of a child, caring for a child or parent, or the employee's own serious illness. Employees taking leave are entitled to reinstatement to the same (or equivalent) job. The bill applies to all companies employing 50 or more workers and covers about 50 percent of the workforce. The business community opposed the FMLA, and a 1997 survey found 51 percent of human resources professionals complaining that the costs (paperwork, replacement workers, a "short-changed" feeling on the part of single and childless workers) exceeded the benefits.[80] Further, another survey found only 5 percent of workers taking advantage of the FMLA.[81] On the other hand, in the first 18 months after the bill was enacted 1.5 million to 3 million workers took leave for a median of 10 days and employers reported little difficulty with compliance.[82] So the evidence is mixed, but some members of Congress want to expand the FMLA by, among other options, (1) including businesses with 25 or more workers, and (2) giving employees 24 hours of unpaid leave annually to go to important education-related activities and to take family members to the doctor.[83] Whether the FMLA is burdensome or not, we know that the U.S. standard is quite modest in comparison with those of our competitors abroad, as described in Table 12.1. Have those countries been too generous?

TABLE 12.1   Family Leave Policies around the World

- The International Labour Organization, an arm of the United Nations, reports that maternity benefits to working mothers in the United States are the least generous in the industrial world.
- Eighty percent of countries offer paid maternity leave to working women and, in a third of those countries, leaves last longer than 14 weeks.
- Some paid maternity leave examples: Hungary, 24 weeks; Italy, 5 months; Canada, 17 weeks; and Spain, 16 weeks.
- The ILO reported only two other industrialized nations, Australia and New Zealand, with minimal maternity leave policies comparable to America's FMLA.

Source: Kirsten Grimsley, "Maternity Benefits Lag in U.S.," *Des Moines Register,* February 16, 1998, p. 1A.

Question

A 1998 study by the Families and Work Institute points to gaps between corporate rhetoric supporting family concerns and the actual help offered to workers. The study noted limited maternity leave, work-based child care, and elder care referral services as examples of shortcomings. The Associated Press summarized the study by saying: "Many companies allow workers to slip away for school plays or stay home with a sick child. But Corporate America has far to go before it can be called truly family-friendly."[84]

a. Currently, the United States is the strongest economy in the world. In your view, would our economy be strengthened or weakened if Corporate America were more "family friendly"?

b. The accounting firm, Deloitte & Touche, argues that both men and women seek a "better balance" between work and family life.[85] Do you agree? Explain. [For more on the Family & Medical Leave Act, see **http://www.dol.gov/dol/esa/fmla.htm**]

UNEMPLOYMENT COMPENSATION

The tragedy of the Depression, when up to 25 percent of the workforce was unemployed, led in 1935 to the passage of the Social Security Act, one portion of which provided for an unemployment insurance program. Today, all 50 states and the federal government are engaged in a cooperative system that helps protect the temporarily jobless. The system is financed through a payroll tax paid by employers.

The actual state tax rate for each employer varies, depending on the employer's *experience* ratings—the number of layoffs in its workforce. Thus, employers have an incentive to retain employees.

Rules vary by state but, in general, employees qualify for unemployment benefits by reaching a specified total of annual wages. Those losing their jobs must apply to a state agency for unemployment compensation, which varies by state. Benefits may be collected up to a specified maximum period, usually 26 weeks. During that time, those collecting compensation must be ready to work and must make an effort to find suitable work. Workers may be disqualified from unemployment coverage for a variety of reasons, including quitting work or being fired for *misconduct*. For example, a newly hired police officer in Clarksdale, Mississippi, allegedly made no effort to get in shape and thus was unable to pass the physical test necessary for certification. He was dismissed, whereupon he applied for, and was granted, unemployment compensation. The City appealed and won; the Mississippi Supreme Court ruled that the police officer's "lack of interest" in performing well constituted misconduct.[86]

In 1997, on average, 6.7 million Americans, in a workforce of 129.6 million, were out of work. In any given week, 2.3 million were receiving unemployment benefits averaging over $190 per week for an average duration of nearly 16 weeks.

Source: George C. Leef, "Unemployment Compensation," *Regulation,* Winter 1998, p. 19.

WARN

In 1988, Congress sought to ease some job loss situations by enacting the Worker Adjustment and Retraining Notification Act (WARN), which requires firms with 100 or more employees to provide 60 days notice if they lay off one-third or more of their workers at any site employing at least 150 workers, drop 500 employees at any site, or close a plant employing at least 50 workers. However, a 1993 General Accounting Office study concluded that the law had been ineffectual, with half of plant closings not covered by the law and many firms simply remaining ignorant of the law's requirements. Congress is considering stiffer requirements, although critics fear that any change will simply encourage increased use of contract and part-time employees.

PENSIONS

As early as the late 1800s, some employers began to adopt pension plans for their employees. In 1974, Congress approved the Employee Retirement Income Security Act (ERISA), under which the government regulates pension funds to help ensure their long-term financial security by reducing fraud and mismanagement. ERISA requires that fund managers keep detailed records, engage in prudent investments, and provide an annual report that has been certified by qualified, impartial third parties.

ERISA also establishes strict *vesting* rights (the point at which the employee has a nonforfeitable right to the funds) to ensure that employees actually receive the pensions to which they are entitled. ERISA requires that employee contributions must vest fully and immediately. Employer contributions typically vest after 10 years of work, but other options are available. Furthermore, those vested funds are not lost should the employee change jobs.

ERISA also included provisions for establishing the Pension Benefit Guaranty Corporation to protect retirees in the event of the failure of a pension fund. The PBGC guarantees that vested persons will be paid up to a specified maximum, even if the pension fund does not have sufficient resources to meet its obligations. PBGC funding is provided by company contributions.

Cash-Balance Plans. A big pension battle is currently being waged between what might be thought of as America's old, stable, career-building economy, and the new, fast-moving, mobile economy. Traditional pensions, labled defined-benefit plans, grow slowly until the final 10 years or so of employment when contributions expand dramatically. That approach encourages career loyalty. The high-tech economy, with workers moving from company to company every few years, has led many companies to develop new, cash-balance pensions where employer contributions are spread more evenly over a worker's career rather than being heavily weighted toward the last decade. Since the accumulated money can follow the worker from job to job, the cash-balance system works well for younger employees.

The problems emerge for older workers who believe they are victims of age discrimination. If their company switches to a cash-balance plan prior to the last decade of their career, they ordinarily have accumulated relatively little and probably will not be able to make up the loss under the new approach. Older workers at IBM, AT&T, Duke Energy, and other big companies are flooding the federal Equal Employment Opportunity Commission with complaints. IBM and other employers now allow many older workers to choose either the traditional plan or the cash-balance approach. As of late 1999, the Internal Revenue Service had put a hold on approvals of new cash-balance plans while it determines whether those plans should enjoy the tax deductibility advantages of traditional plans.

Employers note that pensions are not required by law, and that the new approach better serves the needs of younger workers and women (who often move in and out of the job market as they raise children). Of course, the new approach also allows the companies to significantly reduce retirement costs. [For Vermont Congressman Bernie Sanders's materials on cash balance pensions, see **http://www.house.gov/bernie/legislation/ibm/**]

Part Seven—Termination: Protection from Wrongful Discharge

Kurtzman gave up his job, sold his Massachusetts home, and moved his family in order to take a new position in North Carolina. Seven months later he was fired without cause, despite having been told the job was "long term" and "secure." Kurtzman sued claiming the assurances and his move based on those assurances created a contract permitting dismissal only for cause. A jury awarded Kurtzman $350,000, and the court of appeals affirmed, but the North Carolina Supreme Court reversed, holding that an employment relationship without a definite period of time is presumed to be terminable at the will of either party.[87]

That 1997 decision, though seemingly harsh, reflects long-standing legal tradition in the United States. Indeed, most Americans work without benefit of an employment contract for a specified period of time. They are labeled *at-will employees* in that they may be fired at any time, but they may also quit at any time.

Historically, the at-will worker in the United States could be discharged for good reasons, bad reasons, or no reason at all. Employer and employee both freely entered the bargain understanding its terms, and thus the court should, in general, enforce those terms, including the right of dismissal and the right of the employee to quit at any time. Critics argue that the doctrine ignores the historic inequality of bargaining power between employers and employees. In recent decades the at-will rule has been softened in most states by legislative and judicially imposed limitations. Statutory exceptions to the at-will rule include our labor laws protecting union workers and the equal employment opportunity laws that forbid the dismissal of an employee for discriminatory reasons.

Judicial Limitations on At-Will Principles

Many court decisions provide grounds for dismissed at-will employees to claim that they have been wronged. Those judicial decisions were often provoked by transparently unjust dismissals including, for example, whistle-blowers who exposed their employers' misdeeds and employees who declined to commit perjury on behalf of their employers. Those judicial limitations to the at-will doctrine fall into three categories: (1) express or implied contracts, (2) implied covenant of good faith and fair dealing, and (3) public policy. In addition, a number of tort claims may substitute for or supplement wrongful discharge claims.

1. Express or Implied Employment Contracts. A number of states have adopted a contract protection for at-will employees that arises, typically, either from the employee handbook or from employer conduct and oral representations. The notion here is that the courts will recognize a contract based either on language in the handbook or on such assurances of continued employment as routine promotions, no notice of poor performance, longevity, and oral communications.

2. Implied Covenant of Good Faith and Fair Dealing. A few state courts have held that neither party to a contract may *act in bad faith* to deprive the other of the benefits of the contract. For example, a California court recently rejected a bad faith claim in an alleged sexual harassment case. Rollins hired Cotran under an implied contract providing that Cotran would be fired only for good cause. Then when sexual harassment allegations were raised, Cotran was dismissed following an internal investigation. Cotran denied the allegations and sued claiming the dismissal was in bad faith since the company had not gone to court to prove the charges. A jury ruled for Cotran, but an appeals court reversed, and the California Supreme Court affirmed saying that the jury's role in such cases is not to decide whether the harassment actually occurred, but to decide whether the employer acted fairly and in good faith.[88]

3. Public Policy. Most states have now adopted some form of public policy (the general preference of the citizenry) exception providing that a dismissal is wrongful if it results from employee conduct that is consistent with the will of the people as expressed in statutes, constitutions, and so on. Those exceptions are established on a case-by-case basis, and they differ from state to state. In addition to the whistle-blowing and perjury situations noted, the exception often protects, for example, those fired for pursuing a lawful claim (e.g., workers' compensation) and those fired for fulfilling a civic responsibility (e.g., jury duty).

Tort Claims.   In some states, dismissed at-will employees' rights to recover damages in actions for breach of contract and breach of the implied warranty of good faith and fair dealing have been limited to *economic losses* (out-of-pocket costs and lost wages). One of the consequences of that line of reasoning is that dismissed employees are increasingly turning to various kinds of tort actions (often labeled *tag-along torts*) where the potential financial recovery, including punitive damages, is much greater than for contract claims alone. Those tort possibilities include, among others, defamation, intentional infliction of emotional distress, interference with contract, and invasion of privacy.

The following case addresses the public policy limitation on the at-will rule.

DRAY v. NEW MARKET POULTRY PRODUCTS, INC.
518 S. E. 2d 312 (Va. S.Ct. 1999)

Justice Compton

This is another case in which an employee seeks to create an exception to the Commonwealth's established employment-at-will doctrine in order to pursue a common law claim for wrongful discharge.

In August 1997, appellant April L. Dray, the employee, filed a motion for judgment against appellee New Market Poultry Products, Inc., the employer, seeking damages for alleged wrongful termination of her employment. The employer filed a [motion to dismiss] which the trial court sustained in May 1998 . . . The employee appeals.

The employee worked for the employer from August 1994 until she was "fired" on September 11, 1996. For about three months prior to her termination, the employee was a "quality control inspector" on the employer's production lines to assure that no adulterated poultry products were distributed.

Two months prior to her termination, the employee "experienced difficulty" in getting other employees to follow proper sanitary rules. "When management ignored and failed to correct the noted deficiencies," the employee, "in conformance to her training and assigned duties . . ., informed the plant's on-site governmental inspectors."

The inspectors "confirmed the unsanitary conditions," according to the allegations, and "forced" the employer to correct the deficiencies. Subsequently, the employee was told by her supervisor "that she would be fired if she ever again brought plant sanitary deficiencies to the attention of the . . . governmental inspectors."

In the week prior to the employee's termination, she and other quality control inspectors condemned as adulterated some poultry products based on improper work performed on the plant's "wash line." On the day of the employee's termination, a government inspector required the employer to "reprocess a large quantity of poultry product due to contamination by metal-laced ice."

The employer's management believed that the employee had informed the government inspector of this adulterated product. She was discharged for violating the "edict" that she not inform the inspectors of unsanitary conditions and adulterated poultry products. When the employee asked the reason for her discharge, the employer's personnel supervisor informed her that "it was not working out."

In her motion for judgment, the employee says she "states a common law claim for wrongful termination of employment in violation of the public policy of the Commonwealth of Virginia." Elaborating, the employee asserts the public policy relied upon is articulated by the Commonwealth in the "Virginia Meat and Poultry Products Inspection Act," Code §§ 3.1–884.17 through– 884.36 (the Act).

She alleges the employer terminated her in contravention of the public policy she finds set forth in the Act that is applicable to her. As a result, she asserts, she has incurred damages for which she seeks recovery.

In sustaining the [motion to dismiss], the trial court held that the motion for judgment did not set forth a legally cognizable claim for wrongful discharge. The court ruled that the plaintiff had failed "to extrapolate" from the broad declaration found in the Act, of an intent to serve "the public good" generally, a specific public policy intended to benefit the class of individuals to which the plaintiff belonged. Thus, the court decided, the employee's claim did not qualify as an exception to the employment-at-will doctrine.

Virginia adheres to the common law doctrine of employment-at-will. When a contract calls for the rendition of services, but the period of the contract's intended duration cannot be determined from its provisions, either party ordinarily is at liberty to terminate the contract at will upon giving reasonable notice of intention to terminate.

In *Bowman,* we recognized that a number of state courts had applied exceptions to the rule of terminability. By way of illustration, we referred to several decisions from other jurisdictions, that had granted such exceptions, but we did not adopt the rationale for exceptions articulated in those cases.

In *Bowman,* we applied "a narrow exception to the employment-at-will rule." We held that two bank employees, who were also stockholders of the bank corporation, had stated a cause of action in tort against the bank and bank directors when the employees were discharged after failing to heed a threat to vote their stock according to the wishes of their employer. We said that the public policy set forth in former Code § 13.1–32 (now § 13.1–662) conferred upon the plaintiffs as stockholders the right to vote their shares "free of duress and intimidation imposed on individual stockholders by corporate management."

In the present case, the plaintiff seeks to mount a generalized, common law "whistle-blower" retaliatory discharge claim. Such a claim has not been recognized as an exception to Virginia's employment-at-will doctrine, and we refuse to recognize it today. See *Lawrence Chrysler Plymouth Corp.* v. *Brooks,* (motor vehicle repairman unsuccessfully sued employer alleging discharge for his refusal to use method of repair that he believed unsafe); *Miller* v. *SEVAMP, Inc.,* (retaliatory discharge claim rejected when employee alleged she was fired for appearing as witness at co-employee's grievance hearing).

The Act upon which this plaintiff relies does not confer any rights or duties upon her or any other similarly situated employee of the defendant. Instead, the Act's objective is "to provide for meat and poultry products inspection programs that will impose and enforce requirements with respect to intrastate operations and commerce."

The plaintiff identifies two of the Act's provisions that she says articulate a public policy allowing her to evade the employment-at-will doctrine. She relies upon Code § 3.1–884.22, which forbids intrastate distribution of uninspected, adulterated, or misbranded meat and poultry products. She also relies upon Code § 3.1– 884.25(2), which establishes criminal penalties for any person who "resists, . . . impedes, . . . or interferes" with state meat inspectors. These provisions do not secure any rights to this plaintiff, nor do any other provisions of the Act. Rather, the Act establishes a regulatory mechanism directed only to government inspectors and industry management.

In essence, the plaintiff claims she has been wrongfully terminated because she had a right to disregard management's requirements that she report to her company superiors, and not directly to government inspectors, when she believed she was acting to assure the safety of the employer's products. However, the Act affords plaintiff no express statutory right in this regard that is in specific furtherance of the state's public policy regarding inspections of meat and poultry products.

Affirmed.

Questions

1. a. Does the state of Virginia recognize the public policy exception to the employment-at-will doctrine? Explain.

   b. What "public policy" was the plaintiff Dray relying on in her motion for judgment?

2. As a matter of law, why did the plaintiff Dray lose this case?

3. In your view, is this decision in the best interests of the citizens of Virginia?

4. Gilmartin took a job as station manager at a Texas television station. He was hired on a year-to-year basis under an oral agreement providing that his employment would continue so long as his work was satisfactory. Gilmartin was subsequently blamed for declining profits, and he was fired. Gilmartin sued. In his pleadings, Gilmartin said that he was informed of his annual salary, vacation time, and possible future raises, that his contract was to be renewed from year to year contingent on satisfactory performance, and that a commitment by KVTV for one to three years was "very doable." He was also told that a written agreement was not necessary. Was Gilmartin wrongfully discharged? Explain. See *Gilmartin* v. *KVTV-Channel 13,* 985 S.W.2d 553 (Ct. App. Tex. 1998).

5. IBP operates a large hog processing plant in Storm Lake, Iowa. IBP prohibits possession of "look-alike drugs" on company property. An employee, Michael Huegerich, was randomly and lawfully inspected as he was entering the plant. The inspection revealed an asthma medication, Maxalert, which was identical in appearance to an illegal street drug, "speed." Maxalert contained the stimulant ephedrine. The pills actually belonged to his girlfriend and were in his possession by accident. Huegerich was terminated for possessing a look-alike drug in violation of company policy. Huegerich admitted that he was generally aware of IBP drug policies, but since he was a transfer from another IBP division, he had not gone through the company orientation program where new employees are advised of the policy against look-alike drugs. About six months after his dismissal, two IBP employees told Huegerich that they had heard he was fired for possessing speed. Huegerich then sued IBP for, among other claims, wrongful discharge and defamation.

At trial, Huegerich provided no evidence as to how, when, and from whom the IBP employees had heard that he was terminated for possession of speed. The district court found for Huegerich in the amount of $24,000 on the wrongful discharge claim and $20,000 on the defamation claim. The court said that IBP was guilty of negligent discharge in failing to inform Huegerich about its drug policy. IBP appealed to the Iowa Supreme Court. Iowa law recognizes the doctrine of at-will employment with "narrow" exceptions for public policy violations and where a contract is created by an employer's handbook. Decide. Explain. See *Huegerich* v. *IBP,* 547 N.W.2d 216 (Iowa 1996).

6. Freeman, a television anchorperson employed by KSN, gave birth to her second child. On the day she returned from the hospital, she was notified that she had been dismissed. Six weeks later, she became unable to lactate. She sued KSN for wrongful discharge, tortious interference with contract, and negligent infliction of emotional distress. Decide. Explain. See *Freeman* v. *Medevac Midamerica of Kansas, Inc.,* 719 F. Supp. 1014 (D Kan. 1989).

7. An applicant received a job offer, which was confirmed in a letter stating that his annual salary would be $80,000. He was terminated seven months into his first year of work. Was the dismissal a breach of contract? Explain. See *Bernard* v. *IMI Sys. Inc.,* 618 A.2d 338 (N.J. S.Ct. 1993).

Part Eight—The 21st Century

Now that we have looked at the human resources process, we need to look ahead to the challenges of a rapidly changing 21st-century workplace. We will examine two particularly volatile concerns—*contingent workers* and immigration—that received a great deal of attention in the 1990s and promise to play big roles in employment law and human resources practice in years to come. [For emerging human resources issues, see **http://www.shrm.org/issues/**]

CONTINGENT WORKERS

Seeking cost savings and greater flexibility, employers are increasingly replacing traditional, long-term employees with contingent workers (temps, we often call them), including independent contractors, leased or temporary workers from staffing agencies, on-call workers, part-time workers, and company-contract employees. Contingent workers permit employers to rapidly and inexpensively inflate or shrink their workforces as competitive and regulatory conditions change. The bad publicity and bad feelings associated with downsizing can be reduced with greater reliance on temps. Another big impetus for the movement away from full-time, traditional employees lies in cost savings. Employers who choose to provide health and retirement benefits for their traditional employees need not do so for their contingent workers. Employers are not required to withhold income, Social Security, Medicare, and unemployment taxes. With fringe benefits costs reaching 40 percent of total compensation and averaging $15,000 (including payroll taxes) per employee, shrinking benefits has become an important consideration for many firms.[89] Finding ways to reduce benefits has taken on greater importance since a 1997 Supreme Court ruling that employers cannot lawfully fire workers simply for the purpose of cutting benefit costs.[90]

About one-tenth of the 1997 United States workforce of 126.7 million consists of temporary workers: 8.5 million independent contractors, 2 million "on-call," 1.3 million employed by temporary help agencies, and 800,000 employed by contract firms.

Source: Robert J. Grossman, "Short-Term Workers Raise Long-Term Issues," *HRMagazine,* April 1998, pp. 81, 82.

Problems? Of course, reliance on contingent workers does not come without costs, some of which spring from legal disputes. Initially, as discussed early in this chapter, the question often is one of whether a worker is an independent contractor or, in fact, an employee. Microsoft has been engaged in a years-long struggle with thousands of its contract workers who claim they are entitled to participate in Microsoft's pension plan and its stock purchase plan. The latter allows employees to buy Microsoft stock at a discount of about 15 percent off the market price and has been a particularly valuable perk given the dramatic rise in value of Microsoft shares in recent years. The workers had signed contracts acknowledging their status and agreeing that they had no right to participate in the plans, but in 1990 the IRS ruled that the workers were employees. Microsoft agreed and began issuing W-2 forms to the freelance workers. Thereafter, those workers filed a class action claiming a right to the pension and stock option benefits. The United States Ninth Circuit Court of Appeals in 1997 ruled for the workers, finding that they clearly were employees based on the IRS ruling and Microsoft's response, that Microsoft had made a "mistake" in classifying the workers as independent contractors, and that the agreement not to participate in the plans was simply a warning to the workers about their rights had they, in fact, been independent contractors.[91] Basically, the court found that the freelancers did the same work as Microsoft employees and thus had to be treated the same for benefit purposes. The Supreme Court declined to hear an appeal of the Microsoft case,[92] and at this writing, the parties remain in court fighting over how many workers are covered by the ruling.

Joint Employers?   Microsoft turned to using leased or temporary employees from temporary agencies after its independent contractor problems. Many companies do so, of course, because the temporary agency then handles the payroll, workers' compensation, and unemployment compensation. Benefits, if any, would also be provided by the temp agency. A temporary arrangement also sometimes provides a screening or try-out of workers who might later become regular employees. The use of temporary agencies does not, however, free the employer of legal hazards. The Equal Employment Opportunity Commission (see Chapter 13) has made it clear that the government often considers the direct employer and the temporary agency as "joint employers" sharing liability should discrimination problems emerge.[93] The same appears to be true for any problems that might emerge under the Fair Labor Standards Act involving minimum wages, overtime, and the like.[94] In general, workers would be considered joint employees where both the staffing agency and the direct employer exercise substantial control over that worker.

The Wall Street Journal reports that European nations are now relaxing their highly protective labor laws to allow greater use of temporary employees:

> After decades of watching tough labor laws and rigid regulations leave European companies running well behind rivals in the U.S., Europe has adopted the obvious solution: labor flexibility . . . By taking advantage of legal loopholes, temp companies are helping employers by providing "long-term temporary help"—workers who can be fired at will.

Source: Helene Cooper and Thomas Kamm, "Much of Europe Eases Its Rigid Labor Laws, and Temps Proliferate," *The Wall Street Journal,* June 4, 1998, p. A1.

IMMIGRATION

The United States, a nation founded by immigrants and proudly open to the "huddled masses" of the globe for over 200 years, is now clearly divided about embracing those yearning to come here. Much of the unease lies in the numbers. Some 900,000 immigrants legally enter the United States each year, and an estimated 275,000 arrive illegally.[95] Many Americans regard immigrants as a burden on welfare and our schools. Working-class Americans see immigrants as competition in the job market and a drag on wage increases, while small business owners, some farmers, meatpackers, and others regard immigrants as a source of labor for "stoop" jobs that others often will not accept. A broader cultural worry is that we won't be able to assimilate the new immigrants in a manner that respects multiculturalism yet maintains a nation basically of one language, one political tradition, and one will. Some say the current distress is really just another manifestation of racism, as most of the newer immigrants are not European Caucasians. Indeed, a 1993 poll found that 75 percent of Americans believe that Irish immigrants benefit the country; 65 percent feel the same about Poles; but only 19 percent share that sentiment about Haitians.[96]

New Laws.   We have responded to this situation with legislation. Broadly, federal immigration law, including the 1986 Immigration Reform and Control Act, requires employers to verify that each new hire is either a U.S. citizen, a permanent resident, or a foreign national with permission to work in this country. To meet this requirement, employers must complete an employment eligibility verification form (I–9) for each new employee. New employees must present documents (from a list of documents acceptable to the government, including U.S. passports, social security cards, and state drivers licenses) establishing the employee's identity and eligibility to work in the United States. The employer must examine the documents and complete the I–9 if the documents appear legitimate. Both employer and employee must sign the I–9. The employer must retain I–9s for three years after hiring or for one year after dismissal, whichever is later. Of course, employers cannot knowingly hire illegal immigrants, but neither can they discriminate against legal immigrants because of national origin, and similar factors.[97]

In an effort to boost our economy, legislation was approved in 1990 to triple the number of visas allotted to highly skilled workers such as scientists, engineers, artists, athletes, and managers to about 140,000. Additional visas were set aside for investor-immigrants who can create jobs in America.

A 1997 poll of adult Americans asked: "Should immigration be kept at its present level, increased, decreased, or stopped altogether?" The results:

   Kept at present level—39%

   Decreased—36%

   Increased—10%

   Stopped altogether—10%

   Don't know—5%

   Source: Kay Worthington, "Immigration Levels," *USA Today,* October 13, 1997, p. 1A.

The continuing immigration furor led in 1996 to the Illegal Immigration Reform and Immigrant Responsibility Act, which is generally designed to curb illegal immigration and expedite deportation of illegal immigrants by increasing border patrol personnel and equipment and by increasing penalties for offenses such as using phony documents to secure work, visa fraud, illegal entry, and alien smuggling. The act also provides that employers who have made a good faith attempt to comply with the law are protected from sanctions for hiring illegal immigrants.

In 1999, the Immigration and Naturalization Service announced a new policy of reducing work-site raids and focusing on "problem" employers, particularly those who appear to be colluding with smugglers and document forgers. Basically the INS concluded that its old policy of bursting unannounced into workplaces such as meatpacking plants and restaurant kitchens simply had not worked. In 1997, those operations secured 19,000 illegal immigrants out of the 5.5 million estimated to be living in the United States.[98] [For an immigration law database, see **http://www.yahoo.com/Government/Law/Immigration/**]

Questions

1. The evidence suggests that Republicans and the business community are generally somewhat more supportive of immigration than are Democrats and those in the "working class." Why would that be so?
2. In your view, is immigration a serious threat to America's cultural and political cohesiveness? Explain.
3. An excerpt from a *Wall Street Journal* commentary:

   > Just as countries compete in a worldwide market where goods and services are exchanged, they also compete in the market for people . . .
   >
   >   In both Canada and Australia, visas are now allocated through a point system, which grades visa applicants in terms of educational attainment, age, and occupational background. The presence of relatives in the country is only one factor among many. Canada and Australia also "sell" visas to persons who have sufficient financial resources to open businesses and create employment opportunities for natives . . .

   Discrimination?

   > Of course, a visa allocation system based on the applicant's ability to pay discriminates against people who lack these financial resources. Similarly, a point system discriminates against people who lack the favored skill characteristics. Any visa allocation system, however, is bound to lead to inequities, and the inequities that would be created by a merit-oriented immigration policy would be no more egregious than those associated with present or previous immigration policies.[99]

   a. Should we simply sell immigration slots to the highest bidders, as suggested by free market economist Gary Becker?

   b. What are some of the competing policy considerations? See Gary Becker, "An Open Door for Immigrants—the Auction," *The Wall Street Journal,* October 14, 1992, p. A16.

INTERNET EXERCISE

Using the "Frequently Asked Questions" portion of the Occupational Safety and Health Administration (OSHA) website [**www.osha.gov**], answer the following questions:

1. What is ergonomics?
2. Why do women experience high rates of work-related musculoskeletal disorders?
3. Do workplace ergonomics programs actually work?

CHAPTER QUESTIONS

1. In general, employers are forced to bear (or at least share) the legal burden for their employees' negligent conduct on the job.
   a. Why do we force employers to bear that responsibility?
   b. Should we do so? Explain.
2. The government's recent aggressiveness in pursuing child labor violations has been called into question by some scholars and commentators. Some are arguing that jobs and school in combination are the best track for some young people. And Jeff Riggenbach, a freelance writer, argues that the real motivation for aggressive child labor enforcement is to prevent young people from competing with their elders in the job market:

   > This is the real purpose of child labor laws—not the protection of children but the protection of privilege. You aren't "protecting" a 15-year-old by telling him he can't take a part-time job at a burger emporium because the hours are 5–8 PM and it's against the law for kids under 16 to work later than 7 on school nights.
   >
   > That's not protection—it's unfair discrimination.[100]

   Should we vigorously enforce the child labor laws? Explain.
3. Many companies refer to credit reports when investigating job applicants. The Fair Credit Reporting Act requires employers to notify applicants if they are rejected because of information in a credit report.
   a. In your judgment, does evidence of failure to pay debts constitute useful information in the job selection process? Explain.
   b. Is the use of that information an "invasion of privacy" as you understand it? Explain.
4. In some instances, a worker may voluntarily quit a job and still recover unemployment compensation.
   a. How might that happen?
   b. Is that policy fair to the employer? Explain.
5. Dismissing an employee whom the employer believes to have committed a theft at work might lead to a civil suit by the former employee claiming tort violations of the kind discussed in the materials on wrongful discharge.

   a. What tort claims might arise from such a dismissal?
   b. What tort claims might arise if the employer declined to allow the employee to go to the bathroom or to leave the building during questioning about the theft? See, for example, "Warning: Be Cautious in Worker-Theft Cases," *The Wall Street Journal,* May 14, 1990, p. B1.
6. In Iowa, a waitress was dismissed from a Maid-Rite Cafe for misconduct after she told others that the cafe was going to be closed. She had received that information from another employee. She learned that the original source of the story was an individual who was not associated with the cafe. Later, four people asked the waitress if the business was closing and she said that she had heard that to be the case. She lost her job, and she sought unemployment compensation. About 20 people in the community signed a petition saying that she was a good waitress and not the kind to start a rumor. How would you rule on her unemployment compensation claim? Explain. See Gene Raffensperger, "Woman Fired for Passing Rumor," *Des Moines Register,* April 29, 1989, p. 2A.
7. Sharon Kay Riddle sought workers' compensation claiming she had been totally and temporarily disabled by mental stress caused by the implementation of a no-smoking ban in the electronics manufacturing plant of her employer, Ampex. Riddle had smoked one to two packs per day for 24 years. Following the plant-wide ban, Riddle took leave and was diagnosed as suffering from major depression, nicotine dependence, and posttraumatic stress disorder. The administrative law judge found that Riddle had established three of the statutory requirements for her workers' compensation claim, but that she had failed to establish the fourth, which provided that work-related stress disabilities are not compensable if they are based "in whole or in part, upon facts and circumstances that are common to all fields of employment" and that the "facts and circumstances" were "not unique to [claimant's] employment." Riddle appealed the unfavorable ruling to the Colorado Court of Appeals. Is she entitled to

workers' compensation? Explain. See *Riddle* v. *Ampex Corporation,* 839 P. 2d 489 (Colo. App. 1992).

8. As discussed in this chapter, many recent judicial decisions have afforded at-will employees much-improved protection against unfair dismissals. A special area of concern is whether at-will employees can be dismissed for off-duty conduct. The decisions are split, but the trend seems to be toward greater respect and protection for employee privacy. Nonetheless, companies still retain broad latitude to dismiss. For example, an employee convicted of selling drugs would most likely not be protected by the courts from a company dismissal.

Virginia Rulon-Miller, an IBM salesperson, had been dating another IBM employee, Matt Blum, for several years. Her supervisors were aware of the relationship. Blum left IBM to join a competitor, QYX, and he moved from San Francisco to Philadelphia. QYX transferred him back to San Francisco, and he and Rulon-Miller resumed dating. Again, her superiors were aware of the relationship, and one mentioned that he didn't "have any problem" with her romance. Rulon-Miller did well in her sales role and was promoted to a management position, where she continued to do well, as evidenced by a $4,000 raise. Nonetheless, one week after receiving notice of the raise, Rulon-Miller was either dismissed (her version) or "transferred" (the company's version). IBM felt her romance and her concern for the success of Blum created a conflict of interest. Despite being an at-will employee, Rulon-Miller argued that she was protected by IBM's written policies that detail those circumstances under which an employee's private life can become a company issue. She filed suit, claiming wrongful discharge. Decide. Explain. See *Rulon-Miller* v. *IBM,* 1 BNA IER Cases 405, 162 Cal. App. 3d 241 (1984).

9. Illinois state law forbids the retaliatory discharge of employees who file workers' compensation claims. The law provides that the employee must show that he or she was discharged and that the employer's motive for doing so was to deter the employee's exercise of workers' compensation rights.

Assembly-line worker Jonna Lingle, a union member, filed a workers' compensation claim for a wrist injury suffered on her job making washing machine parts for the Norge Division of Magic Chef, Inc. She was fired. The company said her claim was fraudulent. The union filed a grievance on her behalf, claiming a violation of their collective bargaining agreement protecting

employees from discharge in the absense of "just cause." While that action was proceeding, Lingle sued Norge, claiming an unlawful retaliatory discharge. The lower court dismissed her case, saying it was preempted by the Labor-Management Relations Act of 1947 because her claim was "inextricably intertwined" with the union–management agreement prohibiting discharge without just cause. And the court found that allowing the state law case to proceed would undermine the arbitration proceedings provided for under the collective bargaining agreement. The federal court of appeals affirmed, finding that the disposition of the retaliatory discharge claim would require an interpretation of the collective bargaining agreement and that any such interpretation was to employ federal labor law principles, thus assuring uniformity across the country and effectively preempting the application of state laws.

Lingle appealed to the U.S. Supreme Court. A victory for her would significantly expand potential protections for those filing workers' compensation claims, whistle-blowers, victims of discrimination, and others who are parties to contracts but seek the shelter of state statutes providing protection greater than the contracts. The key to the case is whether the resolution of her state-law retaliatory discharge claim requires an interpretation of the meaning of the collective bargaining agreement to which she was a party. Decide. Explain. See *Jonna R. Lingle* v. *Norge Division of Magic Chef, Inc.*, 486 U.S. 399 (1988).

10. American Business Collaboration for Quality Dependent Care, a consortium of 21 major American companies, announced in 1995 that it would spend $100 million over six years to improve and expand child and elder care programs in various communities across the nation. Why would those businesses voluntarily make that commitment?

11. Terrel was employed by Red Giant Foods as a forklift driver. Terrel's supervisor, Rowsey, had received reports from employees that Terrel was drinking on the job. Rowsey later observed Terrel drinking in his car, parked on company property during the noon break. An hour later, Rowsey entered the unoccupied, unlocked car and found beer. Subsequently, Terrel was terminated for violating company policy against drinking on the job. Terrel filed suit.

    a. What claim(s) would Terrel raise?

    b. Decide. Explain. See *Terrel* v. *Rowsey and Red Giant Foods,* 647 N.E.2d 662 (Ind. App. 1995).

12. In most drug testing cases, courts have balanced the employee's privacy interests against the employer's need for information. What business justifications are likely to be most persuasive to a court reviewing the legality of employee drug testing?

13. Some states have approved legislation limiting an employer's right to do genetic testing of employees and applicants.

    a. Why do some employers give such tests?

    b. Should such tests be forbidden? Explain.

14. Perhaps as many as 13 million workers currently might be regarded as telecommuters. As such, they bring new legal problems to the workplace. As a manager, what legal difficulties would you want to anticipate and protect against as more and more of your employees work off-premises and often from their own homes?

15. A reader sent the following story to a newspaper question and answer forum:

    > I was fired recently by my employer, an architecture firm, immediately after serving for one month on a federal grand jury. From the moment I informed my boss. . . I was harassed. . . and told I was not putting the company first. I was told to get out of my jury service, "or else." . . . I was fired exactly one week after my service ended . . .[101]

    Was the dismissal of this at-will employee lawful? Explain.

16. Katherine Born and Rick Gillispie were employed by a Blockbuster Videos store in Iowa. Blockbuster maintained a policy which forbade dating between supervisors and their subordinates. Born and Gillispie were dismissed for violating the policy. They denied that they were romantically involved and filed suit for wrongful dismissal. Under Iowa law, an at-will employee can be discharged at any time for any reason, but Iowa law does recognize the public policy exception. In order to prevail in this lawsuit, what must the plaintiffs show about Iowa law? See *Katherine Born and Rick Gillispie* v. *Blockbuster Videos, Inc.,* 941 F.Supp. 868 (D.Ia. 1996).

17. A pregnant employee was operating a buffing machine when propane gas that powered the machine caused a carbon monoxide buildup at a retail store causing the worker and others to be taken to a hospital. The worker's fetus sustained oxygen deprivation resulting in injuries including abnormal motor functions, cerebral palsy, and a seizure disorder. The worker sued on negligence grounds for her child's injuries. The employer defended by arguing that workers' compensation provides the exclusive remedy in such situations. Does workers' compensation bar the child's suit? Explain. See *Snyder* v. *Michael's Stores, Inc.,* 945 P.2d 781 (Cal. S.Ct. 1997).

18. Lang, a white male, working in a factory, called a black coworker such names as "watermelon" and "buckwheat." The coworker told Lang to stop. Lang continued the racist name-calling and his coworker then called Lang a "cracker" and a "honkey." Later, while Lang was talking with his supervisor, the coworker twice struck Lang, who then filed a workers' compensation claim.

    a. Is Lang entitled to workers' compensation?

    b. What is the key issue? Explain. See *Redman Industries* v. *Lang,* 326 Or. 32 (Sup. Ct. Or. 1997).

19. LaTourette worked for a California college and was attending a conference for work purposes when he suffered a heart attack. He underwent various operations including bypass surgery, subsequent to which he died in the hospital from a bacterial infection. His estate sought workers' compensation claiming that his heart attack was a response to job stress. Is his estate entitled to workers' compensation? Explain. See *LaTourette* v. *Workers' Compensation Appeals Board,* 72 Cal. Rptr. 2d 217 (Sup. Ct. Cal. 1998).

20. Female performers at Cinderella's Castle at Walt Disney World changed into their costumes in a female-only dressing room. In May 1991, Disney found holes in the dressing room walls and told employees that the holes would be repaired and that an employee who had been caught "peeping" had been dismissed. In June 1991, a male costumer set up a peeping and videotaping system using the holes in the wall. In September 1991, Disney learned of the "peeping," inspected the room, did not tell anyone, and allowed the costumer to continue work. In January 1992, Disney carried out a "sting" against the costumer by taping him as he videotaped the women. Disney had not notified the women of the operation. The costumer was discharged, but the women sued Disney.

    a. What were their claims?

    b. How could Disney protect itself from such problems given the vast size of its operations and its many thousands of employees? See *Liberti* v. *Walt Disney World Co.,* 912 F. Supp. 1494 (M.D. Fla. 1995).

NOTES

1. Perkins Cole, "Employment Wars: Who is Suing? And Why Are They Suing?" *Alaska Employment Law Letter* 3, no. 5 (December 1998).

2. Ibid.

3. Maureen Minehan, "Employment Litigation an Ongoing Concern," *HRMagazine* 42, no. 8 (August 1997), p. 144.

4. Margaret Cronin Fisk, "Judges Slash Worker Awards," *National Law Journal,* April 20, 1998, p. A1.

5. Ibid.

6. Ibid.

7. Stephanie Armour, "Firms Key Up PCs for Job Screening," *USA Today,* October 20, 1997, p. 6B.

8. Associated Press, "Strange Questions Cost Target $1.3 Million," *Waterloo–Cedar Falls Courier,* July 11, 1993, p. A3.

9. Junda Woo, "Job Interviews Pose Rising Risk to Employers," *The Wall Street Journal,* March 11, 1992, p. B5.

10. Wayne E. Barlow, D. Diane Hatch, and Betty Southard Murphy, "Misleading Letter of Recommendation May Result in Liability," *Personnel Journal* 74, no. 11 (November 1995), p. 90.

11. Bill Leonard, "Reference-Checking Laws: Now What?" *HRMagazine,* December 1995, p. 57.

12. *Mary M.* v. *City of Los Angeles,* 814 P.2d 1341 (Cal. S.Ct. 1991).

13. Laura Litvan, "Who Pays When Pay Goes Up?—Next Boost in Wages Will Hurt, Employers Say," *Seattle Times,* May 23, 1999, p. E1.

14. Ibid.

15. Ibid.

16. G. Pascal Zachary, "While Congress Jousts Over Minimum Wage, Some People Ignore It," *The Wall Street Journal,* May 20, 1996, p. A1.

17. Ibid.

18. Ibid.

19. G. Pascal Zachary, "Many Firms Refuse to Pay for Overtime, Employees Complain," *The Wall Street Journal,* June 24, 1996, p. A1.

20. Ibid.

21. E. Scott Reckard, "Taco Bell Settles Class-Action Over Pay Abuses," *Los Angeles Times,* December 5, 1997, p. D1.

22. Lynn Hicks, "The Dull Greening of Overtime," *Des Moines Register,* January 27, 1998, p. 8S.

23. John Simons, "Sears Settles Child-Labor Allegations by Paying Fine Totaling $325,000," *The Wall Street Journal,* May 17, 1999, p. B5.

24. Patricia McLaughlin, "Child Labor Issue Causing a Rift in Garment Industry," *Waterloo–Cedar Falls Courier,* May 9, 1993, p. D1.

25. Ibid.

26. "Aussie Sweatshops Using Child Labor," *Straits Times,* October 27, 1998, p. 7.

27. Ibid.

28. Donna Gold, "Maine Merchants Join to Fight Sweatshops," *Boston Globe,* December 6, 1998, p. C24.

29. Ibid.

30. Associated Press, "Officials Crack Down on Soccer's Child Labour," *Ottawa Citizen,* July 3, 1998, p. F7.

31. Department of Labor, "The Cumulative Impact of Congressional Reform on American Working Men and Women," FDCH Federal Department and Agency Documents, August 15, 1996, p. 1.

32. Albert Karr, "Fatal Injuries," *The Wall Street Journal,* September 22, 1998, p. A1.

33. Associated Press, "Cost of Work Injuries Is Far More Than AIDS," *Des Moines Register,* July 28, 1997, p. 1A.

34. Karr, "Fatal Injuries," p. A1.

35. Associated Press, "Fed Reports Job Injuries, Illnesses Down for 1997," *Waterloo–Cedar Falls Courier,* December 18, 1998, p. D6.

36. Associated Press, "Cost of Work Injuries," p. 1A.

37. Jon Nordheimer, "One Day's Death Toll on the Job," *New York Times,* December 22, 1996, section 3, p. 1.

38. *The Washington Post,* "OSHA Ready to Propose Ergonomics Regulations," *Waterloo–Cedar Falls Courier,* February 19, 1999, p. A1.

39. Ibid.

40. "U.S. Repeated Trauma Rates Decline for Third Straight Year," *CTDNEWS Workplace Solutions for Repetitive Stress Injuries* 8, no.1 (January 1999).

41. Saul Hansell, "U.S. Jury Rejects Keyboard Injury Claims," *New York Times,* June 17, 1998, section D, p. 2.

42. "U.S. Repeated Trauma Rates Decline," January 1999.

43. Associated Press, "Homicides Second in Work Deaths," *Waterloo–Cedar Falls Courier,* April 24, 1998, p. B7.

44. Stephanie Armour, "As Pressures Rise at Work, So Do Fears of Violence," *Des Moines Register,* June 24, 1997, p. 8S.

45. Jim Lynch, "Violence at Work Plagues Nation's Businesses," *Albany Times Union,* January 5, 1998, p. C1.

46. Michael J. Sniffen, "Workplace Violence Falls 21 Percent from Peak," *Buffalo News,* July 27, 1998, p. 3A.

47. John Glionna and Joe Mozingo, "OSHA Urges Bulletproof Glass to Protect Clerks," *Los Angeles Times,* April 29, 1998, p. B1.

48. Associated Press, "Jury Awards $7.9 M in Asheville Plant Shooting Case," *Waterloo–Cedar Falls Courier,* May 5, 1999, p. B6.

49. Laurie Grossman, "Owner Sentenced to Nearly 20 Years Over Plant Fire," *The Wall Street Journal,* September 15, 1992, p. C12.

50. Associated Press, "More than Half of Poultry Plants Never Checked in North Carolina," *Waterloo–Cedar Falls Courier,* November 12, 1991, p. B4.

51. Ibid.

52. Robert A. Jordan, "The Battle over Danger in the Workplace," *Boston Globe,* April 25, 1999, p. C4.

53. Carl Quintanilla, "OSHA's Inspections Hit Record Lows," *The Wall Street Journal,* January 7, 1997, p. A1.

54. *Chamber of Commerce of the United States* v. *United States Department of Labor,* 1999 U.S. App. LEXIS 6367 (1999).

55. "With Death of CCP, Fed-OSHA Institutes a New Targeting Plan," *Cal-OSHA Reporter* 26, no. 17 (April 26, 1999).

56. Associated Press, "OSHA Urges Firms to Increase Safety of Lifting Jobs," *The Wall Street Journal,* May 11, 1999, p. B6.

57. Ibid.

58. *Lubrano* v. *Malinet,* 480 N.E.2d 737 (N.Y. 1985).

59. Jillian Lloyd, "Drug Testing Snares Many," *Chicago Sun-Times,* May 2, 1999, p. L48.

60. Ibid.

61. Associated Press, "Study Finds Fewer Workers Testing Positive for Drugs," *Waterloo–Cedar Falls Courier,* April 7, 1998, p. A2.

62. Lewis Maltby, "Another View," *HRMagazine,* March 1998, p. 112.

63. Littler and Mendelson, *The 1996 Employer* (San Francisco: Littler, Mendelson, Fastiff, Tichy & Mathiason, P.C., 1996), p. 860.

64. See, e.g., *National Treasury Employees Union* v. *Von Raab,* 109 S.Ct. 1385 (1989).

65. Steve Rhoades, "Drug-Test the Chess Club?" *USA Weekend,* Nov. 20–22, 1998, p. 14.

66. *Vernonia School District 47J* v. *Acton,* 115 S.Ct. 2386 (1995).

67. *Todd* v. *Rush County Schools,* 133 F.3d 984 (1998). Cert. den., 525 U.S. 824 (1998).

68. *Sarah Borse* v. *Piece Goods Shop, Inc.,* 963 F.2d 611 (3d Cir. 1992). Rehearing denied, 963 F.2d 626 (1992).

69. Frances A. McMorris, "Is Your Office Voice Mail Private? Don't Bet on It," *The Wall Street Journal,* February 28, 1995, p. B1.

70. Samuel Greengard, "Privacy—Entitlement or Illusion?" *Personnel Journal* 75, no. 5 (May 1996), pp. 74, 86.

71. Mark P. Couch, "Eyes Are on Your E-Mail," *Des Moines Register,* January 26, 1997, p. 1G.

72. Stephenie Overman, "When Labor Leads to Love," *HRFocus,* November 1998, p. 1.

73. James Lardner, "Cupid's Cubicles," *U.S. News & World Report,* December 14, 1998, p. 44.

74. Maggie Jackson, "What's Love Got to Do with It?" *Waterloo–Cedar Falls Courier,* February 12, 1999, p. C5.

75. Ibid.

76. William M. Bulkeley, "Staples' President Resigns Following Alleged Incident with Company Worker," *The Wall Street Journal,* October 21, 1997, p. B10.

77. Alex Markels, "Employers' Dilemma: Whether to Regulate Romance," *The Wall Street Journal,* February 14, 1995, p. B1.

78. See Douglas Massengill and Donald J. Petersen, "Legal Challenges to No Fraternization Rules," *Labor Law Journal* 46, no. 7 (July 1995), p. 429.

79. Markels, "Employers' Dilemma," p. B4.

80. "Flack over FMLA," *HRFocus,* June 1997, p. 7.

81. Stephanie Armour, "Unpaid Leave Costly Proposition," *USA Today,* February 9, 1998, p. 4B.

82. Ellen Goodman, "Modified Gloating on Family-Leave Act," *Des Moines Register,* May 10, 1996, p. 9A.

83. Lynn Hicks, "Medical Leave Act Spawns Few Suits," *Des Moines Register,* August 4, 1998, p. 5S.

84. Associated Press, "Report: Family-Friendly Compliance Weak," *Waterloo–Cedar Falls Courier,* July 14, 1998, p. A1.

85. Ibid.

86. *City of Clarksdale* v. *Mississippi Employment Security Commission,* 699 So.2d 578 (Miss. 1997).

87. *Kurtzman* v. *Applied Analytical Industries,* 480 S.E.2d 425 (N.C. 1997).

88. *Cotran* v. *Rollins Hudig Hall International,* 948 P.2d 412 (Cal. 1998).

89. Craig J. Cantoni, "The Case against Employee Benefits," *The Wall Street Journal,* August 18, 1997, p. A14.

90. *Inter-Modal Rail Employees Association* v. *Atchison, Topeka and Santa Fe Railway Company,* 520 U.S. 510 (1997).

91. *Donna Vizcaino* v. *Microsoft Corporation,* 120 F.3d 1006 (9th Cir. 1997).

92. *Microsoft Corporation* v. *Donna Vizcaino,* 522 U.S. 1098 (1998).

93. O'Melveny and Myers, "The Law and Temporary Employees," *New York Employment Law Letter* 5, no. 5 (May 1998).

94. Ibid.

95. Susan Page, "Immigrants New, Goal Old: Brighter Economic Future," *USA Today,* October 13, 1997, p. 1A.

96. Maria Puente, "Sentiment Sours as Rate of Arrival Rises," *USA Today,* July 14, 1993, p. 1A.

97. The materials in this paragraph rely heavily on Moon, Moss, McGill, and Bachelder, P.C., "Employment Verification Under New Immigration Law," *Maine Employment Law Letter* 2, Issue 5 (January 1997).

98. Michelle Mittelstadt, "Work Site INS Raids May Wane," *Des Moines Register,* April 15, 1999, p. 5S.

99. George Borjas, "The U.S. Takes the Wrong Immigrants," *The Wall Street Journal,* April 5, 1990, p. A22.

100. Jeff Riggenbach, "End Labor Laws' Bias Against Teen Workers," *USA Today,* March 19, 1990, p. 10A.

101. *Washington Post,* "The Boss Can't Fire you for Doing Your Civic Duty," *Waterloo–   466-46Cedar Falls Courier,* May 26, 1999, p. C8.

Chapter 13

Employment Law II: Discrimination

PREFACE

In late 1996, Texaco, one of America's largest and most respected companies, agreed to pay $176.1 million to settle a racial discrimination lawsuit filed by nearly 1,400 minority employees. Facing boycotts, threats, and nationwide publicity, Texaco agreed to a plan providing an average of $63,000 to each plaintiff while committing the company to a series of diversity goals for the year 2000:

- Raise minority employment from its 1996 level of 23 percent to 29 percent.
- Raise black managerial representation from its 1996 level of 4 percent to 6.6 percent.
- Base 20 to 25 percent of managers' performance reviews upon their success in minority hiring and promotion.
- Boost the $135 million Texaco annually spends with minority contractors by 48.1 percent.
- Place $200 million of its insurance business with minority firms—up from the 1996 total of $25 million.[1]

The settlement was spurred by public and company outrage over highly publicized media accounts of a conversation secretly taped by a senior Texaco manager. The accounts alleged that high-ranking Texaco officials, in discussing the discrimination lawsuit, had used racial epithets including the words "nigger" and "black jelly bean," mocked Kwanzaa, and discussed destroying documents related to the race discrimination suit. Texaco fired one of the managers and punished the others. While conceding the "categorically unacceptable context and tone of the conversations,"[2] Texaco's own investigation of the conversation concluded that the "black jelly beans" phrase was a reference to a remark in a diversity training session and that the word "nigger" was not used. See Table 13.1.

Since the Settlement. The Texaco story continues to unfold:

- In 1999, Texaco agreed to pay $3.1 million to 186 women employees who were "consistently" underpaid relative to their male counterparts.[3]

TABLE 13.1   How They Interpret the Recording

Transcripts of a taped conversation of Texaco executives, including Richard Lundwall and Robert Ulrich, differ. The one on the left is from an affidavit filed by plaintiffs. The other is from a Texaco investigator.

Plaintiffs' Version:	*Texaco's Version:*
Lundwall: Now we have two friggin' national anthems.	**Lundwall:** We have two friggin' national anthems.
Ulrich: I'm still having trouble with Hanukkah. Now, we have Kwanzaa. . . . (Expletive) niggers, they (expletive) all over us with this.	**Ulrich:** All right. . . . I'm still struggling with Hanukkah, and now we have Kwanzaa, I mean I lost Christmas, poor St. Nicholas, they (expletive) all over his beard.[4]

- In 1998, Richard Lundwall and Robert Ulrich were acquitted of obstruction of justice charges claiming that they plotted to hide or destroy Texaco documents to be used in the race-discrimination suit.

Questions

1. *a.* As a matter of ethics, did Texaco do the right thing in agreeing to set diversity goals for the company? Explain.
    b. Did Texaco do the right thing in settling the case rather than using it as an opportunity for a careful investigation of alleged racism in the company and for a public discussion of institutional racism and the powerful emotions raised by allegations of racism?
2. "When this case was just about African–Americans making serious claims of discrimination at one of the biggest companies in the country, no one paid much attention—not Texaco's executives, not civil rights groups, not the media. Only when the tapes surfaced did the world take notice—and then, only of what was on the tapes."[5] Why did the disputed conversation give this case all of the vigor that it had lacked as a battle over the facts of Texaco's treatment of minorities?
3. Using Texaco's Internet homepage [**www.texaco.com**], explain Texaco's efforts to address its diversity goals and assess Texaco's success in achieving those goals.

Part One—Introduction

Texaco's problems are representative of a tidal wave of discrimination claims, lawsuits, settlements, and affirmative action plans that have taken up an increasingly large space in American management practice. Discrimination in its many forms has been perhaps the most damaging social problem in American history.

EMPLOYMENT DISCRIMINATION: THE FOUNDATION IN LAW

History

In 1941, A. Philip Randolph, president of the predominantly black Brotherhood of Sleeping Car Porters, organized black leaders who threatened a massive march in Washington, D.C. protesting employment discrimination. In response, President Franklin Roosevelt issued Executive Order 8802 (such orders have the force and effect of law), which created a Fair Employment Practice Committee. Congress limited the committee's budget, but Roosevelt's action was a striking first step for the federal government in addressing racial discrimination. Likewise, during the 1940s, several states enacted their own fair employment laws.

The next big step toward racial equality was the landmark *Brown* v. *Board of Education*[6] decision in 1954 in which the Supreme Court forbade "separate but equal" schools. *Brown* repudiated the doctrine enunciated in an 1896 Supreme Court case, *Plessy* v. *Ferguson,*[7] in which the Court held that a Louisiana statute requiring equal but separate accommodations for whites and blacks on trains was not unconstitutional. A period of intense activism followed *Brown,* as citizens engaged in sit-ins, freedom rides, boycotts, and the like to press claims for racial equality in housing, public transportation, employment, and so on. It was a turbulent, sometimes violent, era, but those activities were critical ingredients in subsequent advances for the black population. Then, in 1964, the National Labor Relations Board asserted its jurisdiction over racial discrimination where it constitutes an unfair labor practice. With the passage of the 1964 Civil Rights Act, the campaign against discrimination solidified as one of the most energetic and influential social movements in American history.[8] [For the National Civil Rights Museum, see **http://www.midsouth.rr.com/civilrights/**]

Civil Rights Act of 1964

Title VII of the Civil Rights Act of 1964 changed the course of American life and business practice by forbidding discrimination in employment because of race, color, religion, sex, or national origin. Relying on its authority to regulate commerce, Congress sought to bring civil rights to the workplace. The act applies to private-sector employers with 15 or more employees, employment agencies, labor unions with 15 or more members as well as those operating a hiring hall, state and local governments, and most of the federal government. Private clubs are exempt from the act, and religious organizations may discriminate in employment on the basis of religion. Broadly, the act forbids discrimination in hiring, firing, and general conditions of employment.

Other Legislation and Orders

Title VII is the core of the federal government's authority to attack employment discrimination, but other federal law should be noted:

• The Civil Rights Act of 1866 forbids all forms of racial bias arising out of contract. Employment relationships are, of course, founded in contract. Thus, when a black person is discriminated against by a private employer, the act has been violated.

- The Civil Rights Act of 1991 created some new law and modified or reversed a series of Supreme Court decisions that had increased the burden on plaintiffs in employment discrimination cases. Among other provisions, the 1991 act specifies that Title VII and the Americans with Disabilities Act (ADA) are to apply to United States citizens working abroad for American-owned or American-controlled companies unless compliance with those American laws would require the company to violate the law of its host nation.
- The ADA, the Equal Pay Act, the Age Discrimination in Employment Act, and others are discussed later in this chapter.
- EO 11246 forbids discrimination by firms doing business with the federal government and, in some instances, requires affirmative action to avoid and correct underutilization of minorities and women.

The Constitution

You will remember that the federal Constitution, among other purposes, protects us from wrongful government action. The Fourteenth Amendment to the Constitution provides that no state shall deny to any person life, liberty, or property without *due process of law* or deny him or her the *equal protection of the laws.* Thus, citizens are protected from discrimination via state government action. Similarly, the Supreme Court has interpreted the Due Process Clause of the Fifth Amendment ("nor shall any person . . . be deprived of life, liberty, or property, without due process of law") to forbid discrimination by the federal government.

Civil Rights Enforcement

EEOC.   The Equal Employment Opportunity Commission (EEOC) is the federal agency responsible for enforcing the federal laws forbidding discrimination in employment. The Commission imposes record-keeping requirements on businesses, unions, and employment agencies; issues new regulations and guidelines; investigates discrimination claims; attempts to resolve disputes via conciliation; and, if necessary, engages in litigation. Receiving far more complaints than can be addressed, the commission has established a priority system ranking the complaints in order of importance, and in 1999 a new mediation system was installed under which the EEOC hopes to resolve at least 8,000 cases annually.

Despite its critics' worries, the commission simply does not have the resources to "push business around."[9] While receiving approximatelly 80,000 complaints annually, the commission, in fiscal year 1996, filed only 161 lawsuits.[10] [The EEOC home page is located at **www.eeoc.gov**]

Litigation.   Normally, a private party seeking redress for discrimination in employment cannot immediately file a lawsuit. Rather, a complaint must be filed with the appropriate local or state fair employment practices agency, where provided for by law. After 60 days or upon termination of state or local proceedings, the grievant may turn to the EEOC for aid. Charges must be filed with the EEOC within 180 days of the discriminatory act (or 300 days if preceded by a local or state filing or 30 days after receiving notice that the state/local proceeding was terminated).

Going forward with an EEOC action is often frustrating because the agency is always burdened with a backlog of cases. When a charge is filed, the commission must investigate. The commission may decide that the complaint does not appear to raise a violation, in which case the charges will be dismissed and a "right-to-sue" letter will be issued releasing the grievant to file his or her own lawsuit. If reasonable cause is found to believe that a violation has occurred, the EEOC will attempt to conciliate the dispute. That failing, the commission may file a civil suit or issue a right-to-sue letter to the grievant. Thus, several years may pass before the administrative process and any subsequent lawsuits have run their course.

Financial and emotional incentives to avoid litigation are strong so the parties, as in the Texaco case, often settle. Furthermore, many businesses are now including binding arbitration agreements in job offers requiring job seekers, as a condition of employment, to waive the right to trial and turn any grievance over to arbitration. A recent Supreme Court decision said that such a clause must be a "clear and unmistakable waiver" of the right to sue,[11] but the court has not settled the larger question of the legality of the waivers. In 1999, the Securities and Exchange Commission and the National Association of Securities Dealers agreed to eliminate a rule mandating arbitration for all discrimination complaints in the securities industry.

Remedies

Remedies under Title VII are intended to "make the victim whole" and may include job reinstatement, back pay, and seniority relief, among other possibilities. Additionally, victims of *intentional* discrimination based on race, religion, sex, disability, or national origin can secure other compensatory damages such as pain and suffering, and they can also secure punitive damages in some instances. Combined compensatory and punitive damages, in suits involving religion, sex, disability, or national origin, are capped at $50,000 to $300,000, depending on the size of the employer's workforce. No damage cap is provided for in cases of intentional discrimination based on race. Finally, the EEOC often negotiates consent decrees that may require new procedures to correct wrongful practices. [For the Civil Rights Division of the United States Justice Department, see **http://www.usdoj. gov/crt/crt-home.html**]

Part Two—Discrimination on the Basis of Race, Color, or National Origin

Title VII forbids job discrimination based on race, color, and national origin. Members of those "protected classes" cannot lawfully be denied employment opportunities merely because they are Native Americans, black, of Vietnamese ancestry, or white, for that matter. Therefore, an employment office sign reading "Mexicans need not apply" would clearly be unlawful.

EMPLOYMENT DISCRIMINATION ANALYSIS

Title VII of the 1964 Civil Rights Act provides two primary theories of recovery for individuals—disparate treatment and disparate impact (sometimes labeled *adverse impact*). Those theories are examined below. Title VII also provides for a theory of recovery labeled *pattern or practice* discrimination where a *class* of individuals has been systematically subjected to discriminatory treatment. Normally, a pattern or practice of discrimination is identified by statistical analysis showing a significant "deficiency" in the percentage of minority employees in the employer's workforce, as compared with the percentage of minority employees in the relevant labor pool.

As we turn now to a close look at disparate treatment and disparate impact analysis, the reader should keep in mind the various constitutional, statutory, and executive order protections briefly outlined above.

Disparate Treatment

The basic elements of *disparate treatment* exist where an employer *intentionally* treats some people less favorably than others because of their race, color, religion, sex, or national origin. In a simplified form, a claim under disparate treatment analysis would proceed as follows:

1. Plaintiff's (Employee's) Prima Facie Case (sufficient to be presumed true unless proven otherwise). Optimally the plaintiff would present direct, explicit evidence of intentional disparate treatment. For example, that evidence might take the form of a letter from an employer to an employment agency indicating that "women would not be welcome as applicants for this physically taxing job." Because direct evidence of that nature is ordinarily unavailable, the plaintiff must then build the following prima facie case from which intent and, hence, disparate treatment may be inferred:

a. Plaintiff belongs to a protected class.
b. Plaintiff applied for a job for which the defendant was seeking applicants.
c. Plaintiff was qualified for the job.
d. Plaintiff was denied the job.
e. The position remained open, and the employer continued to seek applications.

2. Defendant's (Employer's) Case. If the plaintiff builds a successful prima facie case, the defendant must "articulate some legitimate, nondiscriminatory reason for the employee's rejection" (for example, greater work experience). However, the defendant need not prove that its decision not to hire the plaintiff was, in fact, based on that legitimate, nondiscriminatory reason. The defendant simply must raise a legitimate issue of fact disputing the plaintiff's discrimination claim.

3. Plaintiff's Response. Assuming the defendant was successful in presenting a legitimate, nondiscriminatory reason for its action, the plaintiff must show that the reason offered by the defendant was not the true reason but was, in fact, merely a *pretext* to hide discrimination. [For an overview of disparate treatment analysis, see **http://www.hr-guide.com/data/G701.htm**]

Question

Rodriguez managed a Wal-Mart store at Fajardo, Puerto Rico. Following an evaluation, his performance was considered unsatisfactory, and he was demoted to assistant manager at another store. Rodriguez filed suit claiming race and national origin discrimination. Rodriguez pointed to two favorable previous performance evaluations, and he argued that he was evaluated in a different manner than non–Puerto Rican managers. Rodriguez was evaluated with the use of an opinion survey given to all of his subordinates. Rodriguez claimed that non–Puerto Rican managers at other stores were not subject to opinion surveys. Assuming that claim is true, would Rodriguez be able to prevail on a disparate treatment cause of action? Explain. See *Rodriguez-Cuervos* v. *Wal-Mart Stores,* 181 F.3d 15 (1st Cir. 1999).

Disparate Impact

Disparate impact analysis arose out of situations in which employers used legitimate employment standards that, despite their apparent neutrality, worked a heavier burden on a protected class than on other employees. For example, a preemployment test, offered with the best of intentions and constructed to be a fair measurement device, may disproportionately exclude members of a protected class and thus be unacceptable (barring an effective defense). Alternatively, an employer surreptitiously seeking to discriminate may establish an apparently neutral, superficially valid employment test that has the effect of achieving the employer's discrimination goal. For example, a tavern might require its "bouncer" to be at least 6 feet 2 inches tall and weigh at least 200 pounds. Such a standard disproportionately excludes women, Asians, and Hispanics from consideration and probably is impermissible (barring an effective defense). Disparate impact analysis is similar to that of disparate treatment, but critical distinctions mark the two approaches. In particular, note that disparate treatment requires proof of intent, while disparate impact does not.

The Test.   Disparate impact analysis requires the following:

1. The plaintiff/employee must identify the *specific employment practice or policy* (e.g., test score, skill, or height) that caused the alleged disparate impact on the protected class.
2. The plaintiff must prove (often with statistical evidence) that the protected class is suffering an adverse or disproportionate impact caused by the employment practice or policy in question. The statistical analysis to establish a disparate impact (against black job applicants, for example) must be based on a comparison of the racial composition of the group of persons actually holding the jobs in question versus the racial composition of the *job-qualified* population in the relevant labor market.
3. Assuming a prima facie case is established in steps 1 and 2, the plaintiff/employee wins unless the defendant/employer demonstrates that the employment practice/policy is (a) *job related* and (b) *consistent with business necessity.*

4. If the defendant/employer succeeds in demonstrating job relatedness and consistency with business necessity, the employer wins unless the plaintiff/employee demonstrates that *an alternative, less discriminatory business practice is available and that the employer refuses to adopt it.* [For brief summaries of some of the leading employment discrimination cases, see **http://www.wapa.gov/CSO/eeo/cases.htm**]

GRIGGS v. DUKE POWER CO.
401 U.S. 424 (1971)

Chief Justice Burger

[Handwritten annotation:] Disparate Impact
- Graduation + testing
→ not business related → previous non hs grad not performing below expectations

We granted the writ in this case to resolve the question whether an employer is prohibited by the Civil Rights Act of 1964, Title VII, from requiring a high school education or passing of a standardized general intelligence test as a condition of employment in or transfer to jobs when (a) neither standard is shown to be significantly related to successful job performance, (b) both requirements operate to disqualify Negroes at a substantially higher rate than white applicants, and (c) the jobs in question formerly had been filled only by white employees as part of a longstanding practice of giving preference to whites.

Congress provided, in Title VII of the Civil Rights Act of 1964, for class actions for enforcement of provisions of the Act and this proceeding was brought by a group of incumbent Negro employees against Duke Power Company . . .

The district court found that prior to July 2, 1965, the effective date of the Civil Rights Act of 1964, the company openly discriminated on the basis of race in the hiring and assigning of employees at its Dan River plant. The plant was organized into five operating departments: (1) Labor, (2) Coal Handling, (3) Operations, (4) Maintenance, and (5) Laboratory and Test. Negroes were employed only in the Labor Department where the highest-paying jobs paid less than the lowest-paying jobs in the other four "operating" departments in which only whites were employed. Promotions were normally made within each department on the basis of job seniority. Transferees into a department usually began in the lowest position.

In 1955 the company instituted a policy of requiring a high school education for initial assignment to any department except Labor, and for transfer from the Coal Handling to any "inside" department (Operations, Maintenance, or Laboratory). When the company abandoned its policy of restricting Negroes to the Labor Department in 1965, completion of high school also was made a prerequisite to transfer from Labor to any other department. From the time the high school requirement was instituted to the time of trial, however, white employees hired before the time of the high school education requirement continued to perform satisfactorily and achieve promotions in the "operating" departments. Findings on this score are not challenged.

The company added a further requirement for new employees on July 2, 1965, the date on which Title VII became effective. To qualify for placement in any but the Labor Department it became necessary to register satisfactory scores on two professionally prepared aptitude tests, as well as to have a high school education. Completion of high school alone continued to render employees eligible for transfer to the four desirable departments from which Negroes had been excluded if the incumbent had been employed prior to the time of the new requirement. In September 1965 the company began to permit incumbent employees who lacked a high school education to qualify for transfer from Labor or Coal Handling to an "inside" job by passing two tests—the Wonderlic Personnel Test, which purports to measure general intelligence, and the Bennett Mechanical Comprehension Test. Neither was directed or intended to measure the ability to learn to perform a particular job or category of jobs. The requisite scores used for both initial hiring and transfer approximated the national median for high school graduates.

The District Court had found that while the company previously followed a policy of overt racial discrimination in a period prior to the Act, such conduct had ceased. The District Court also concluded that Title VII was intended to be prospective only and, consequently, the impact of prior inequities was beyond the reach of corrective action authorized by the Act.

. . . The Court of Appeals concluded there was no violation of the Act.

* * * * *

The objective of Congress in the enactment of Title VII is plain from the language of the statute. It was to achieve equality of employment opportunities and remove barriers that have operated in the past to favor an identifiable group of white employees over other employees. Under the Act, practices, procedures, or tests neutral on their face, and even neutral in terms of intent, cannot be maintained if they operate to "freeze" the status quo of prior discriminatory employment practices.

The Court of Appeals's opinion, and the partial dissent, agreed that, on the record in the present case, "whites register far better on the company's alternative requirements" than Negroes. This consequence would appear to be directly traceable to race. Basic intelligence must have the means of articulation to manifest itself fairly in a testing process. Because they are Negroes, petitioners have long received inferior education in segregated schools.

. . . Congress did not intend by Title VII, however, to guarantee a job to every person regardless of qualifications. In short, the Act does not command that any person be hired simply because he was formerly the subject of discrimination, or because he is a member of a minority group. Discriminatory preference for any group, minority or majority, is precisely and only what Congress has proscribed . . .

. . . The Act proscribes not only overt discrimination but also practices that are fair in form, but discriminatory in operation. The touchstone is business necessity. If an employment practice which operates to exclude Negroes cannot be shown to be related to job performance, the practice is prohibited.

On the record before us, neither the high school completion requirement nor the general intelligence test is shown to bear a demonstrable relationship to successful performance of the jobs for which it was used. Both were adopted, as the Court of Appeals noted, without meaningful study of their relationship to job-performance ability. Rather, a vice president of the company testified, the requirements were instituted on the company's judgment that they generally would improve the overall quality of the work force.

The evidence, however, shows that employees who have not completed high school or taken the tests have continued to perform satisfactorily and make progress in departments for which the high school and test criteria are not used . . .

The Court of Appeals held that the company had adopted the diploma and test requirements without any "intention to discriminate against Negro employees." We do not suggest that either the District Court or the Court of Appeals erred in examining the employer's intent; but good intent or absence of discriminatory intent does not redeem employment procedures or testing mechanisms that operate as "built-in headwinds" for minority groups and are unrelated to measuring job capability.

* * * * *

The facts of this case demonstrate the inadequacy of broad and general testing devices as well as the infirmity of using diplomas or degrees as fixed measures of capability . . .

The company contends that its general intelligence tests are specifically permitted by § 703(h) of the Act. That section authorizes the use of "any professionally developed ability test" that is not "designed, intended *or used* to discriminate because of race . . ." (Emphasis added.)

The Equal Employment Opportunity Commission, having enforcement responsibility, has issued guidelines interpreting § 703(h) to permit only the use of job-related tests. The administrative interpretation of the Act by the enforcing agency is entitled to great deference. Since the Act and its legislative history support the commission's construction, this affords good reason to treat the guidelines as expressing the will of Congress.

. . . From the sum of the legislative history relevant in this case, the conclusion is inescapable that the EEOC's construction of § 703(h) to require that employment tests be job related comports with congressional intent.

Nothing in the Act precludes the use of testing or measuring procedures; obviously they are useful. What Congress has forbidden is giving these devices and mechanisms controlling force unless they are demonstrably a reasonable measure of job performance. Congress has not commanded that the less qualified be preferred over the better qualified simply because of minority origins. Far from disparaging job qualifications as such, Congress has made such qualifications the controlling factor, so that race, religion, nationality, and sex become irrelevant. What Congress has commanded is that any tests used must measure the person for the job and not the person in the abstract.

The judgment of the Court of Appeals is . . . reversed.

Questions

1. According to the Supreme Court, what was Congress's objective in enacting Title VII?
2. Had Duke Power been able to establish that its reasons for adopting the diploma and test standards were entirely without discriminatory intent, would the Supreme Court have ruled differently? Explain.
3. What is the central issue in this case?
4. Why was North Carolina's social and educational history relevant to the outcome of the case?
5. Statistical evidence showed that 35 percent of new hires in grocery and produce at Lucky Stores, a retail grocery chain, were women, while 84 percent of new hires in deli, bakery, and general merchandise were women. Statistical evidence also showed that 31 percent of those promoted into apprentice jobs in grocery and produce were women, while women comprised 75 percent of those promoted into apprentice jobs in deli, bakery, and general merchandise. Grocery and produce jobs generally were higher paying jobs than those in deli, bakery, and general merchandise. Women received significantly fewer overtime hours than men.

   Do these facts regarding Lucky Stores suggest discrimination? Explain. See *Stender* v. *Lucky Stores, Inc.* 803 F. Supp. 259 (DC Cal. 1992).
6. Gregory, a black male, was offered employment by Litton Systems as a sheet metal worker. As part of a standard procedure he completed a form listing a total of 14 nontraffic arrests but no convictions. Thereupon the employment offer was withdrawn. Gregory then brought suit, claiming he was a victim of racial discrimination.
   a. Explain the foundation of his argument.

   b. Decide the case. See *Gregory* v. *Litton,* 412 F.2d 631 (9th Cir. 1972).
7. Eighty-one percent of the hires at Consolidated Service Systems, a small Chicago janitorial company, were of Korean origin. The EEOC brought a disparate treatment claim, saying the firm discriminated in favor of Koreans by relying primarily on word-of-mouth recruiting. Mr. Hwang, the owner, is Korean. Seventy-three percent of the job applicants were Korean. One percent of the Chicago-area workforce is Korean, and not more than 3 percent of the janitorial workforce for the area is Korean. The court found no persuasive evidence of intentional discrimination, although the government claimed that 99 applicants were denied jobs because they were not Koreans.
   a. Does restricting hiring to members of one ethnic group constitute discrimination where hiring is accomplished by word of mouth? Explain.
   b. What if a firm, using the word-of-mouth approach, hired only white applicants? Explain.
   c. In this case, the EEOC brought but dropped a disparate impact claim. Analyze the case using the disparate impact test. See *Equal Employment Opportunity Commission* v. *Consolidated Service Systems,* 989 F.2d 233 (7th Cir. 1993).
8. In *Personnel Administrator of Massachusetts* v. *Feeney,* 442 U.S. 256 (1979), a state policy of absolute hiring preference for veterans was upheld against a charge of gender-based discrimination in that few veterans are women. The disparate impact on women was clear, and Massachusetts's governing authorities can be assumed to have been aware of the "natural and probable consequence" of this preference. The Supreme Court found an absence of discriminatory purpose. Explain and justify that decision.
9. In many Title VII cases, a critical ingredient is identifying the relevant labor market. How would you counter Justice Stevens's argument in dissent in *Hazelwood School District* v. *United States,* 433 U.S. 299 (1976), that as a starting point the relevant labor pool should encompass the geographic area from which incumbent employees come?

10. When disparate impact analysis is applied to *objective* employment selection and promotion methods (such as standardized tests), intent need not be established to build a successful case. Now consider the situation where the employment selection or promotion method in question is *subjective* in character (for example, letters of reference or interviews). Are those situations to be analyzed only under the disparate treatment standard, including its proof of intent requirement, or may the disparate impact analysis be employed, thus eliminating the intent issue? Explain. See *Clara Watson* v. *Fort Worth Bank and Trust,* 108 S.Ct. 2777 (1988).

Statutory Defenses

In a broad sense, business necessity, as explained above, is the principal defense to discrimination charges. However, Title VII also affords four specific exemptions or defenses of particular note: (1) seniority, (2) employee testing, (3) bona fide occupational qualification, and (4) veterans' preferences. Attention is given to veterans' preferences in question 8 following the *Griggs* case. Bona fide occupational qualifications are addressed in the next section as a part of the sex discrimination materials. Seniority issues and employee testing standards are explored here.

Seniority.   Section 703(h) of the Civil Rights Act of 1964 provides that an employer may lawfully apply different standards of compensation or different conditions of employment pursuant to a bona fide (good faith) seniority system, provided such differences are not the product of an intent to discriminate. That is, the seniority system must not have been created for a discriminatory or other illegal purpose, and the seniority provisions must apply equally to all.

Seniority systems are either the product of the employer's initiative or of a collective bargaining agreement. Seniority is important because (1) those with less seniority are ordinarily the first to be laid off in the event of a workforce reduction and (2) benefits—including vacations and such working conditions as a choice of shifts—often depend on seniority.

Many complicated issues have arisen out of Congress's effort to abolish employment discrimination while preserving legitimate seniority plans. In sum, the dilemma is that a seniority system, otherwise entirely legitimate, sometimes has the effect of perpetuating past discriminatory practices. Employees once discriminated against in hiring or promotion suffer the further loss of reduced seniority. However, as established in the *Teamsters*[12] and *American Tobacco*[13] cases, the result of a bona fide seniority system may be to perpetuate discrimination, but such a result is illegal only if discriminatory intent is proven.

Layoffs.   In 1984, the U.S. Supreme Court addressed the difficult issue of whether, in times of employment reductions, employers may lay off workers according to seniority (thereby ordinarily reaching white males after women and minorities) or whether affirmative action requires retaining those low-seniority, protected-class employees while laying off white males of greater seniority. The *Firefighters* case answered the question when the Supreme Court, in effect, held that when layoffs are necessary the legal system may not protect newly hired workers by interfering with legitimate seniority systems.[14] In the *Firefighters* case, a federal district court had approved two affirmative action plans in Memphis, Tennessee, for increasing the number of blacks in the fire department. Soon thereafter, budgetary problems required Memphis to lay off 40 firefighters. The city faced the problem of whether to maintain its affirmative action program by laying off firefighters with greater seniority than the recently hired protected-class employees or to honor the provisions of the collectively bargained agreement on seniority, which, in effect, required laying off those most recently hired. The city decided to follow the collective bargaining agreement, and black firefighters filed suit. In the end, the Supreme Court upheld the seniority system despite its impact on affirmative action. The pursuit of affirmative action goals cannot upset legitimate seniority rights where layoffs are necessary. Thus, affirmative action plans may not "re-allocate jobs currently held."[15]

Employee Testing.   Testing is, of course, central to professional personnel practice and to maximizing employee productivity, but testing has often been, both intentionally and unintentionally, a primary vehicle in perpetuating discrimination. Recall that only job-related tests supported by detailed, statistical evidence as to their scientific validity are lawful.

Four black student–athletes were denied eligibility to participate in college sports because their college entrance exam (SAT) scores fell beneath the level specified by the National Collegiate Athletic Association's (NCAA) Proposition 16, which required, among other things, a minimum SAT score of 820, regardless of the student–athlete's grade point average. The students sued the NCAA and won a federal district court trial in which U.S. District Judge Ronald Buckwalter ruled that the SAT requirement disqualified many more blacks than whites and that the NCAA had failed to show that Proposition 16 was effective in increasing student–athlete graduation rates. The NCAA appealed to the 3rd U.S. Circuit Court of Appeals. How would you rule on that appeal? Explain.

Source: Shannon Duffy, "3rd Circuit Allows . . . ," *The Legal Intelligencer,* March 31, 1999, p. 1.

The Four-Fifths Rule.   The guidelines are rather specific regarding the meaning of adverse impact. An employer will generally be presumed in noncompliance with the guidelines if the selection rate (such as the percentage passing a test, being hired, or being promoted) for any protected class is less than 80 percent of the selection rate for the group with the highest rate. The employer falling below that standard must prove the job relatedness of the employment practice in question and demonstrate that a good faith effort was made to find a selection procedure that lessened the disparate impact on protected classes. [For an extensive employment discrimination database, see **http://www.law.cornell.edu/topics/employment_discrimination.html**]

NATIONAL ORIGIN

Title VII forbids employment discrimination based on national origin. As we continue to struggle with immigration issues and as our culture becomes ever more ethnically diverse, we should not be surprised that allegations of national origin discrimination have increased. These cases typically allege differential treatment based on language, appearance, or both. For example, an economics professor from Trinidad recently claimed he was dismissed from his teaching position at Mary Washington College because of national origin discrimination, but the Fourth Circuit Court of Appeals concluded that the dismissal was based on his poor performance and his failure to secure a Ph.D.[16]

English Only?   National origin claims have recently assumed greater visibility because of conflicts over "English-only" rules in workplaces. Many businesses now forbid employees to speak any language other than English on the job, and 25 states have designated English as their official language. The companies argue that the rules are necessary when dealing with customers, to maintain job safety, and to encourage congenial worker relations. EEOC guidelines say that employers cannot impose a blanket ban on employees speaking their primary language in the workplace, but an English-only rule at certain times is permissible if justified by business necessity and if adequately explained to the employees.

> Many businesses now forbid employees to speak any language other than English on the job

In the leading case to date, the Spun Steak Co. instituted an English-only rule for its bilingual employees in order to enhance safety and product quality and to address allegations that some employees were making rude comments in Spanish to English-speaking employees. The English-only rule applied to work but not to lunch, breaks, or employees' own time. The rule was upheld in court on the grounds that it was narrowly defined and did not create a discriminatory atmosphere.[17]

Question

1. Filipovic was born in Yugoslavia and immigrated to Illinois where he worked as a full-time dockman for K & R Express for about 12 years. He claims to have repeatedly been called names and subjected to vulgar language by coworkers and supervisors. On four occasions over more than one year, he was subjected to comments related to his national origin, such as "dirty Commie," "Russian dick head," and "f . . . ing foreigner." Name-calling of that kind and verbal harassment generally were common on the docks, and Filipovic admits that he too engaged in name-calling. Filipovic was fired for cause. He filed suit claiming national origin discrimination and national origin harassment. Decide. Explain. See *Filipovic* v. *K & R Express Systems,* 176 F.3d 390 (7th Cir. 1999).

RACIAL HARASSMENT

Title VII forbids harassment motivated by race or national origin. Racial harassment claims filed with the EEOC doubled during the 1990s to reach about 10,000 annually. An African–American employee who, among other abuses, allegedly received a threatening note signed by the "KKK," who was subjected to racial epithets and insults in the workplace, and whose lock was cut off his locker, was a victim of racial harassment in violation of Title VII because the behavior was "severe and pervasive," "unreasonably abusive," and adversely affected his ability to do his job.[18] Recent court decisions suggest that the Supreme Court's reasoning in sexual harassment cases (explained below) will probably also apply to cases of racial or national origin harassment. In addition to overt forms of harassment such as racial slurs, some new decisions suggest that the use of more subtle "code words" may constitute racial and/or national origin harassment. In *Aman* v. *Cort Furniture Rental Corporation,*[19] two black employees claimed that they were subjected to a racially hostile work environment in part because black employees were labeled by coworkers and managers with racist "code words" such as "all of you," "one of them," "another one," "that one," and "poor people." The Court, in finding for the employees, ruled that certain phrases in the employment setting cannot be excused as mere rudeness and may, in the totality of the circumstances, add up to discrimination so severe that it creates an abusive work environment. Some companies are now revising their employee handbooks to forbid those expressions at work.

Loaded Words

"You can't expect responsibility from people like that."

"They're all stupid and lazy."

"Your kind of people are just not ambitious."

"Your type."

"You people don't understand how to save money."

"All they're interested in is drugs."

"One of you."

Source: *HRFocus* 74, no. 2 (February 1997), p. 11.

Part Three—Sex Discrimination

EQUALITY FOR WOMEN

By most measures, even after years of struggle, women continue to occupy a secondary role in American professional life. More than 35 years after the passage of the 1963 Equal Pay Act, women earn from 74 to 76 cents (depending on the study) for every dollar earned

> a 25-to 34-year-old, college-educated woman who makes $30,000 per year will lose nearly $900,000 over a lifetime

by men.[20] The result, according to one study, is that a 25- to 34-year-old, college-educated woman who makes $30,000 per year will lose nearly $900,000 over a lifetime.[21] Critics argue, however, that these "gross" comparisons of all employed men and women are misleading. They point to studies that measure *comparably situated* men and women and find a much narrower pay gap. For example, a 1999 study concludes that sex discrimination is no longer "systematic" and that after accounting for experience, education, and the like, women earn about 98 percent of the wages of comparable men.[22] On the other hand:

> [M]en with advanced degrees and one to three years' experience earned 30 percent more than women with similar education and job tenure in the telecommunications industry; and recent female graduates entering the work force earned 16 percent less than male graduates, even though the women had higher grade-point averages."[23]

In any case, we can be encouraged that the pay gap has clearly declined from the 1977 figure of 59 cents on the dollar.[24] [For the AFL-CIO website on equal pay issues, see **www.aflcio.org/women/equalpay.htm**]

"College women are working harder and feeling more stress while their male counterparts are having a good time. In a [1998] nationwide survey of college freshmen . . . , women are five times as likely to be anxious as men. . . . Gender differences in lifestyle seem to contribute to the growing stress gap. During the last year, male students spent considerably more time exercising, partying, watching TV, and playing video games, while female students were juggling more household and child-care chores, studying more and doing more volunteer work."

Source: *Los Angeles Times,* "Study: Female Students Feeling More Stress than Their Male Classmates," *Waterloo–Cedar Falls Courier,* January 25, 1999, p. A1.

Abroad? Other industrial nations, with the exception of Japan, have tended to pay women somewhat better than has been the case in the United States, but for the globe as a whole, women earn only 50 to 80 percent of the wages earned by men.[25] Further, our State Department estimates that women earn only 10 percent of the world's income and own just 1 percent of the world's land.[26]

Globally, the status of women is expected to improve in coming years. In Britain, a record total of 120 women were voted into the House of Commons in 1997 and more than one-third of the world's businesses are now owned by women.[27] In early 1999, Japan revised its Equal Employment Opportunity Law to be much tougher on sex discrimination in hiring and on sexual harassment while also relaxing restrictions on women's work that had, for example, limited overtime and forbade late-night work for women.[28] So gradually, around the world, we are seeing increased gender equality. But mighty struggles remain. In early 1999, the Labor Minister in prosperous Singapore spoke out against proposed legislation outlawing racial, gender, and age discrimination on the grounds that the new rules would hurt economic growth.[29]

Glass Ceiling?   As of 1999, 11.9 percent of the *Fortune* 500 corporate officers were female, up from 8.7 percent in 1995.[30] Just 3.3 percent of those companies' top earners were female, up from 1.2 percent in 1995.[31] Critics see data of this kind as evidence of a "glass ceiling" holding women back from roles of power. Data suggest the problem is particularly severe for minority women who make up 10 percent of the workforce, but hold only 5 percent of managerial jobs while white women hold 35 percent of those jobs.[32] In any case, women increasingly are striking out on their own, starting new businesses in the United States at a faster rate than men.[33] As a result, women-owned businesses increased 42 percent to 9.1 million in 1999, up from 6.4 million in 1992.[34] Polls show the big draw for women in entrepreneurship is personal freedom.[35]

In 1970, 57 percent of the four-year college degrees awarded in the United States went to men; by 1996 women were earning more than 55 percent of those degrees. Men, however, continue to dominate high-paying academic majors such as engineering and business. What might account for the declining ratio of men in college?

Source: *Washington Post,* "Women Outnumber Men on U.S. Campuses," *Waterloor–Cedar Falls Courier,* November 18, 1999, p. A10.

ANALYSIS OF SEX DISCRIMINATION

Under Title VII of the Civil Rights Act of 1964, sex discrimination analysis proceeds in essentially the manner outlined earlier in the chapter: Disparate treatment (intentional discrimination) and disparate impact (discriminatory effect) are the key tests. Intentional discrimination cases are increasingly uncommon as we become better educated both about discriminatory behavior and about the law. Nonetheless, these cases still emerge from time to time. For example, in 1995 a federal court of appeals held that a company president's remarks could constitute direct evidence of intentional sex discrimination when he said that women were simply "not tough enough" to supervise collections and that it was "a man's job" and "I felt that a woman was not competent enough to do this job, but I think maybe you're showing me that you can do it."[36]

According to a 1999 poll, 69 percent of women believe that society continues to treat men better than women. Do you agree?

Source: Karen Thomas, "For Women, a Long Way—But Not Far Enough," *USA Today,* February 17, 1999, p. 7A.

Bona Fide Occupational Qualification

Where intent is not at issue, sex discrimination claims are evaluated via disparate impact analysis. In those cases, the key inquiry usually is the *bona fide occupational qualification (BFOQ)* defense provided by Title VII. Discrimination is lawful where sex, religion, or national origin is a BFOQ reasonably necessary to the normal operation of that business. The exclusion of race and color from the list suggests Congress thought those categories always unacceptable as bona fide occupational qualifications. The judicially created defense of business necessity is applicable to racial classifications. The BFOQ was meant to be a very limited exception applicable to situations where specific inherent characteristics are necessary to the job (e.g., wet nurse) and where authenticity is required (e.g., actors).

The BFOQ defense is lawful only if the following conditions are met:

1. Proof of a *nexus* between the classification and job performance, and
2. "*necessity*" of the classification for successful performance, and
3. that the job performance affected by the classification is the "*essence*" of the employer's business operation.[37]

Nexus.   Will the classification affect job performance? For example, will "maleness" depreciate performance in a job requiring manual dexterity, or will "femaleness" depreciate performance in a laboring job requiring night work and long hours? The courts have thoroughly rejected distinctions based on such stereotypes.

Necessity.   Mere customer preference or, in general, higher costs will not justify an otherwise discriminatory employment practice. Thus, that restaurant customers prefer to be served by women or that hiring women will require the addition of another washroom or that hiring blacks, for example, will anger customers and cause a decline in income are not justifications for discrimination.

A Fourth Grader's Hard Lesson

Beth Peres, 10 years old, figured she deserved a raise in her allowance of 50 cents a week. To make her point, she surveyed the other kids in her fourth-grade class at Whittier School in Oak Park, IL . . .

Lo and behold, she found she was underpaid—and so were the other girls in her class. While boys reaped an average of $3.18 a week, girls averaged only $2.63 a week . . . To top it off, girls reported doing more chores than the boys . . . Ms. Peres wrote a fiery editorial for the latest edition of her classroom newspaper, *Moosepaper:* "Is this fair? I don't think so!" she wrote.

"This is sex disgriminigation," Beth says in an interview, struggling with [the] word . . .

(Continued)

Source: Asra Nomani, "A Fourth Grader's Hard Lesson: Boys Earn More Money Than Girls," *The Wall Street Journal*, July 7, 1995, p. B1.

Question

1. Are women (and girls) simply undervalued throughout life?

Essence.   An employer can lawfully insist on a woman to fill a woman's modeling role because being female goes to the essence of the job. However, airlines, for example, cannot hire only women as flight attendants even if females are shown to perform the "nonmechanical" portions of the job better than most men. Those duties "are tangential to the essence of the business involved."[38]

Many employers have simply assumed that women could not perform certain tasks. Women were thought to be insufficiently aggressive for sales roles, and women were denied employment because they were assumed to have a higher turnover rate due to the desire to marry and have children. Those stereotypes are at the heart of sex discrimination litigation generally and sex as a BFOQ particularly.

The case that follows involves the application of BFOQ analysis to an EEOC charge that a chain of single-sex workout clubs was violating Title VII by engaging in gender-based hiring.

U.S. E.E.O.C. v. SEDITA
816 F.Supp. 1291 (N.D.Ill. 1993)

District Judge Ann Claire Williams

Background

. . . Defendant, Audrey Sedita ("Sedita"), is the President and sole shareholder in defendant clubs, Women's Workout World ("WWW"). WWW consists of approximately fifteen health clubs which have an exclusively female membership. The majority of the clubs employ one Manager, one Assistant Manager, and approximately fifteen to twenty Instructors. Defendants do not employ men in any of the enumerated positions because they claim that the essence of these positions involves a substantial amount of intimate physical contact with members, and exposure to nudity and partial nudity in the showers, locker rooms and exercise rooms. Although a few men have been hired to work as Class

Givers, defendants conclude that employing males as Managers, Assistant Managers, and Instructors would violate club members' legitimate privacy interests . . .

In its January 31, 1991, opinion ("January opinion"), [this] Court entered partial summary judgment in favor of the EEOC. *U.S. EEOC v. Sedita,* 755 F.Supp. 808 (N.D.Ill. 1991) . . .

The Motion to Reconsider

Defendants ask the court to reconsider its January opinion based upon additional evidence in support of their BFOQ defense.

*   *   *   *   *

An employer asserting a privacy-based BFOQ defense must satisfy a three-part test: the employer must establish that (1) there is a factual basis for believing that hiring any members of one sex would undermine the essence of its business, (2) the asserted privacy interest is entitled to protection under the law, and (3) no reasonable alternatives exist to protect the privacy interests other than the gender-based hiring policy. In the instant case, defendants acknowledge that they have employed a hiring policy which discriminates against men on the basis of sex, and that such a policy can only be defended as a BFOQ. Defendants argue that their sex-based hiring policy is a BFOQ because it is based on protecting the legitimate privacy interests of their exclusively female clientele . . .

Privacy Based BFOQ

. . . Defendants argue that these jobs require a substantial amount of intimate touching and exposure to nudity. Although it is not clear whether the EEOC concedes that exposure to nudity implicates a protectible privacy interest, various courts have found that it does. Also, despite the fact that customer preferences do not usually establish a BFOQ, in some situations " [c]ustomer preference may . . . give rise to a BFOQ for one sex where the preference is based upon a desire for sexual privacy." Thus, the privacy right has been recognized in a variety of situations, including disrobing, sleeping, or performing bodily functions in the presence of the opposite sex. Consequently, defendants have articulated a legitimate privacy interest with regard to nudity.

However, the extent to which the privacy interest is implicated given the alleged "intimate" touching involved in this case is unclear. Defendants' evidence indicates that a significant part of defendants' business involves touching clients on their breasts, inner thighs, buttocks, and crotch area when taking measurements and instructing members on the use of equipment and proper exercise form. The EEOC questions the extent of the touching involved and argues that such touching fails to implicate a protectible privacy interest . . .

. . . [N]o court has addressed the issue of whether a protectible privacy interest exists with respect to the sort of touching at issue in this case. However, the court declines the invitation to find that members of a single-sex health club have no legitimate privacy interest in preventing the opposite sex from touching their breasts, buttocks, etc., . . . and for the purposes of this motion, the court will assume that defendants have implicated protectible privacy interests . . .

Since the court assumes that legitimate privacy interests have been implicated, it must determine whether the intrusion on privacy involves the "essence" of the jobs and the Club's business. Defendants have introduced evidence that the nudity and touching concern the essence of the jobs and the business operation. Although the EEOC makes a valid argument that the essence of WWW is providing exercise classes, defendant's evidence allows a reasonable inference that the "essence" of WWW can be more broadly construed as providing personal and individual service to an exclusively female clientele. Thus, defendants have raised a genuine issue of material fact because the essence of the jobs and business might properly include selling memberships, personally instructing clients on exercise form and use of equipment, leading orientation sessions, and taking clients' measurements. The court cannot say, as a matter of law, that the various job duties are not the essence of WWW's business . . .

Factual Basis for Hiring Policy

This court must determine whether there is a factual basis for defendants' hiring policy . . .

Defendants have submitted petitions signed by over 10,000 club members. . . . The petition states:

If Women's Workout World hires males as Instructors, Managers, Assistant Managers or in any other member-servicing capacity, I will no longer patronize Women's Workout World. I joined Women's Workout World to receive personalized exercise instruction and assistance without having my privacy rights violated. I would consider it an invasion of my privacy rights for a man to be present in a locker room, sauna, or shower area when I was nude or partially nude. Additionally, I would not participate in an exercise class or aerobics class which is taught by a male. I would also consider it an invasion of my privacy rights to have a male touch my bust or pelvic area or inner thighs while measuring me or when teaching me how to use equipment or do an exercise properly.

Additionally, Sedita's deposition testimony and the club managers' affidavits all state the belief that Women's Workout World would lose its members if men were employed in any member-servicing capacity. . . . [T]he court finds that these submissions create an inference that women will not patronize Women's Workout World if men are employed there as Instructors, Managers, or Assistant Managers. Thus, defendants have provided a factual basis for their belief that no men can be hired as Managers, Assistant Managers, and Instructors.

Reasonable Alternatives

The EEOC makes a number of suggestions, which it argues would enable the defendants to hire males and still maintain the essence of their business operation. These suggestions include hiring or allowing females to assist clients who object to being touched by males, posting a schedule to inform clients of when male employees would be on duty, or letting clients take themselves through the locker room.

Defendants contend that the club cannot reassign job duties in order to avoid intruding on members' privacy interests, since the conduct which infringes on privacy interests amounts to the essence of the jobs in question, and division of labor would threaten defendants' personal service goals. Defendants also make several cost-related arguments. First, they argue that it would be impossible for Women's Workout World to hire men for the stated positions because their customers would refuse to be served by men, and they would lose their members.

Additionally, defendants insist that hiring men for the clubs is not economically feasible because of the need to substantially restructure their exercise facilities by putting in bathroom facilities for men and doors on the locker room, etc. Although it is unclear that defendants would need to install separate bathroom facilities for men, the court finds that these cost concerns are relevant to the reasonableness of the suggested alternatives, and to the ultimate legitimacy of the BFOQ defense. In sum . . . the court concludes that the issues raised here are more appropriately resolved after a trial on the merits . . .

[handwritten: Ask same judge to reconsider]

Conclusion

For the foregoing reasons, defendants' motion to reconsider is granted and the court vacates its January ruling granting summary judgment in plaintiff's favor.

Afterword

In 1994, the EEOC and WWW settled this case. WWW agreed to hire men, to set aside $30,000 to compensate qualified male job applicants who were denied jobs, and to restructure jobs to minimize invasion of customers' privacy.

Questions

1.
   a. Why is customer preference normally not a justification for gender-based discrimination?
   b. Why did the Court, in this case, give consideration to customer preference?
2. Are cost considerations such as facility remodeling a good justification for maintaining gender-based hiring policies? Explain.
3. WWW owner Audrey Sedita has claimed that up to 70 percent of her customers were obese and did not want to be observed by men while exercising. Do you find that defense persuasive? Explain.
4. Is WWW guilty of sex discrimination in excluding men as customers?
5. Dianne Rawlinson sought employment as a prison guard in Alabama. She was a 22-year-old college graduate with a degree in correctional psychology. She was denied employment because she failed to meet the 120-pound weight requirement for the job. The state also required such employees to be at least 5 feet 2 inches tall. Alabama operated four all-male, maximum security prisons. The district court characterized the Alabama prison system as one of "rampant violence." Rawlinson sued, claiming employment discrimination. Decide. Explain. See *Dothard* v. *Rawlinson*, 97 S.Ct. 2720 (1977).

[handwritten notes: can't have ht & wt requirements — Can have physical test relating to a job — gender - presence of ♀ in all ♂ prison could place all guards under danger.]

Hooters

The article that follows discusses the EEOC claim that the Hooters restaurant chain practices unlawful sex discrimination by its refusal to hire otherwise qualified men to serve food.

HOOTERS GUYS?

Men don't high kick with the Radio City Rockettes or shake pompons with the Dallas Cowboy cheerleaders.

Hooters restaurants, therefore, should be given the same leeway when it comes to gender-based hiring, the chain's parent company argues.

Hooters of America Inc. is fighting to continue hiring only women waitresses, who wear skimpy orange shorts and tight white T-shirts or tank tops while serving up chicken wings and burgers.

The Equal Employment Opportunity Commission said Hooters should hire men to work alongside the women, a recommendation the company said it would ignore.

Hooters bought full-page ads in . . . *USA Today* and *The Washington Post,* featuring a burly mustachioed man wearing a blond wig and Hooters uniform, holding a plate of chicken wings and exclaiming: "Come on, Washington. Get a grip."

Executives of the Atlanta-based chain say their customers expect to see sexy, All-American women at their restaurants, which built a reputation on their perky Hooters Girls.

* * * * *

Duncan Fisher, a manager at the restaurant, said many of the women would lose their jobs if the company were forced to hire male servers. While construction workers who eat at Hooters several times a week guffawed at the ads, waitresses wore orange pins saying "Save Our Jobs."

The EEOC has been investigating the 170-restaurant chain for the past four years and said several months ago that Hooters's policy of hiring only female waitresses amounts to sex discrimination.

Four Chicago men who sued Hooters also filed a complaint with the EEOC, prompting the investigation. Their lawsuit claiming discrimination is pending.

* * * * *

The Rockettes and the Dallas Cowboys are allowed to hire all-female troupes and Playboy is allowed to hire all-female bunnies, Mike McNeil, a Hooters vice president, noted at a news conference in Washington.

David Larson, a professor of labor and employment law at Creighton University in Omaha, Nebraska, said there's no comparison.

"The distinction is that there was never any question that Playboy was selling sex, not in the sense of prostitution, but the image of the club had a very heavy sexual aspect to it," said Larson, a former professor-in-residence at the EEOC. "I don't think Hooters is doing the same thing. They've made it clear publicly that they're selling food."

Source: Associated Press, "Hooters Guys?" *Waterloo–Cedar Falls Courier,* November 16, 1995, p. 36. Reprinted by permission of the Associated Press.

Afterword

Effectively concluding that it has better things to do with its limited resources, the EEOC urged Hooters to hire more men and, in 1996, dropped its Hooters investigation. In 1997, Hooters settled a private litigation by seven men who claimed they were victims of sex discrimination in not being hired to serve food at Hooters. The settlement allows Hooters to hire women only as Hooters Girls, but requires a $3.75 million payment to the plaintiffs and requires Hooters to consider men and women equally for a number of jobs including manager and bartender assistant.[39]

Questions

1. *a.* Explain the EEOC view that Hooters' hiring policy constitutes impermissible sexual discrimination.
    b. Explain Hooters' claim that it does not violate Title VII.
2. Is Hooters' hiring policy better left to the market for resolution? Explain.

Blockbuster established a grooming policy forbidding long hair for men but allowing it for women. Four men, who were fired for refusing to cut their long hair, sued Blockbuster for sex discrimination. Has Blockbuster violated Title VII? Explain.

Source: *Kenneth Harper, Daniel Gomez, Abraham Del Carmen, and Brian Russell* v. *Blockbuster Entertainment Corporation,* 139 F.3d 1385 (11th Cir. 1998).

PARENT AND MANAGER?

Many of the most trying and poignant sex discrimination issues arise out of the conflict (particularly for women, but increasingly for men) between being a parent and pursuing a career. Historically, the employed woman who became pregnant faced a serious threat to her professional future. In 1978, Congress amended the Civil Rights Act of 1964 with the Pregnancy Discrimination Act (PDA), which treats pregnancy discrimination as a form of sex discrimination. The PDA makes it illegal for an employer with 15 or more employees (1) to fire/refuse to hire/demote or refuse to promote/penalize a worker because she is pregnant, or (2) to deny disability leave for pregnancies if leaves are offered for other disabilities, or (3) to deny health insurance for pregnancy if health insurance is provided for other medical conditions, or (4) to deny fringe benefits (e.g., seniority) while an employee is on childbirth leave if other employees continue to accrue benefits when disabled, or (5) to fire a man because his wife is pregnant.

Broadly, the PDA requires that pregnant employees be treated the same as all other employees with temporary disabilities. While the law appears straightforward, complaints are rising. A particular point of dispute is whether pregnant employees must be granted light-duty assignments. The courts are split on the matter, but California has passed a law requiring accommodation wherever reasonably feasible.[40]

Questions

1. A pregnant medical technologist was fired for taking leave because she feared being exposed to on-the-job radiation while working with equipment containing radioactive isotopes. She had sought transfer, but no openings were available so her employer placed her on family and sick leave. When that leave was exhausted, she was fired. Did her termination violate the PDA? Explain. See *Duncan* v. *Children's National Medical Center,* 702 A. 2d 207 (D.C. 1997).
2. Ethel Roskies, a University of Montreal psychologist, reporting the results of a survey of successful professional women: "The woman who gives up marriage and children in order to further her career is making a bad bargain. We found that single childless women are significantly more depressed, report lower self-esteem and lower life satisfaction than married women with children"[41] Comment.

EQUAL PAY

Title VII affords broad protection from discrimination in pay because of sex. The Equal Pay Act of 1963 directly forbids discrimination on the basis of sex by paying wages to employees of one sex at a rate less than the rate paid to employees of the opposite sex for equal work on jobs requiring equal skill, effort, and responsibility and performed under similar working conditions (*equal* has been interpreted to mean "substantially equal"). The act provides for certain exceptions. Unequal wage payments are lawful if paid pursuant to (1) a seniority system, (2) a merit system, (3) a system that measures earnings by quantity or quality of production, or (4) a differential based on "any . . . factor other than sex." The employer seeking to avoid a violation of the Equal Pay Act can adjust its wage structure by raising the pay of the disfavored sex. Lowering the pay of the favored sex violates the act.

Former University of Southern California head women's basketball coach, Marianne Stanley, sued the University for violation of the Equal Pay Act because she was not as well paid as then head men's basketball coach, George Raveling. Both coaches had successful won/lost records. The University defended the pay differential by pointing to Raveling's 14 years of coaching experience beyond Stanley's, his having coached the United States Olympic team, his marketing experience outside of coaching, and his books on basketball. Stanley could not point to similar credentials. Did the University violate the Equal Pay Act? See *Stanley* v. *University of Southern California,* 178 F. 3d 1069 (9th Cir. 1999).

SEXUAL HARASSMENT

The women said they were groped and insulted, and managers did nothing to stop it

Sexual harassment is a form of sex discrimination actionable under Title VII. The EEOC received nearly 16,000 sexual harassment complaints in 1998[42] and, as the following article clearly warns, addressing sexual harassment in the workplace has become an important ingredient in management practice.

RECORD HARASSMENT PACT

Associated Press

Chicago—Mitsubishi Motors agreed to pay a record $34 million Thursday to settle allegations that women on the assembly line at its Illinois factory were groped and insulted and that managers did nothing to stop it.

The payout is the biggest sexual harassment settlement ever obtained by the U.S. government.

The settlement will be shared by 350 women who have worked at the auto plant since 1987. The payout per person will range from a few thousand dollars to $300,000.

Although the settlement contained no admission of wrongdoing, Mitsubishi executive vice president Larry Greene, surrounded by top company executives, said: "We of course apologize to any employee who has been harassed or retaliated against."

The Equal Employment Opportunity Commission sued Mitsubishi's North American division in 1996, alleging the automaker allowed women at its Normal, Ill., plant to be groped and subjected to raunchy insults and pranks.

Mitsubishi women complained that male co-workers and supervisors kissed and fondled women; called them "whores" and "bitches," posted sexual graffiti and pictures, including pornographic drawings of the female workers; demanded sexual favors; and retaliated against women who refused.

Workers also allegedly used company phones to set up parties with strippers. Managers were accused of participating in the parties and doing nothing when others complained.

Bad Publicity

Mitsubishi initially fought the accusations, even organizing an employee protest outside the Equal Employment Opportunity Commission's Chicago office. But it soon reversed its hard-line approach after getting bad publicity.

* * * * *

Mitsubishi said some 20 workers were fired in 1997 for sexual harassment, and several others were disciplined.

Mitsubishi agreed to provide mandatory sexual harassment training to employees, revise its sexual harassment policy as necessary and investigate allegations of harassment within three weeks under a zero-tolerance policy. A three-person independent panel, paid by Mitsubishi, will monitor the automaker's compliance over the consent decree's three-year term.

Source: *Des Moines Register,* June 12, 1998, P.1A. Reprinted by permission of the copyright holder, The Associated Press.

What Is It?   Not surprisingly, a continuing difficulty in dealing with sexual harassment lies in identifying it. At the workplace level, the confusion can be considerable. A 1992 Roper Poll summarized 22 situations and asked the respondents which of them constituted sexual harassment. Clear majorities found sexual harassment in only three of the situations. Those involved direct questions about sexual practices and being required to sleep with the boss in exchange for a raise. Strong majorities rejected a finding of sexual harassment in such situations as these:

- A compliment about a coworker's appearance.
- Asking a coworker for a date.
- A woman looking a man "up and down" as he walks by.
- Referring to women as "girls."

A middle ground of great confusion included such situations as these:

- A male boss calling a female "honey."
- A man looking a woman "up and down" as she walks by.
- Men in the office repeatedly discussing the appearance of female coworkers.[43]

Male Worker Harassed at Domino's

For five months, David Papa's boss at a Domino's Pizza made comments about his body, touched him, and told him she loved him. Six days after he told her to stop she fired him.

A federal judge has ordered the pizza chain to pay Papa $237,000 in damages in the first case the U.S. Equal Employment Opportunity Commission ever took to trial involving a man harassed by a woman.

Source: Associated Press, "Male Worker Harassed at Domino's, Judge Rules," *Des Moines Register,* November 23, 1995, p. 4A.

THE LAW OF SEXUAL HARASSMENT

In brief, sexual harassment, as a matter of law, consists of unwelcome sexual advances, requests for sexual favors, and other verbal or physical conduct of a sexual nature which (1) becomes a condition of employment, or (2) becomes a basis for employment decisions, or (3) unreasonably interferes with work performance or creates a hostile working environment.

Sexual harassment cases have been divided into a pair of categories, *quid pro quo* (this for that; e.g., a sexual experience in exchange for keeping one's job) and *hostile environment* (a workplace rendered offensive and abusive by sexual comments, pictures, jokes, sexual aggression, and the like where no employment benefit is gained or lost). As a result of recent Supreme Court decisions, this two-part division seems to have been reduced in importance, but the phrases remain common in sexual harassment analysis.

The Test.   Once we have some idea of behavior that constitutes sexual harassment, our concern turns to which remedies are available for the victims. Although the question is not settled, most courts to date have ruled that victims of sexual harassment seeking recovery under Title VII cannot sue the person who actually committed the harassment. The victim might be able to sue the wrongdoer under a state statute or by using a tort claim such as assault, but under Title VII, *personal liability* appears not to be available. This result, if the current judicial pattern continues, is not as unfair as might at first appear because well-settled principles of justice hold the employer generally responsible for workplace problems. The victim, therefore, can seek damages from the employer. A pair of 1998 United States Supreme Court decisions in the *Burlington Industries*[44] and *Faragher*[45] cases considerably clarified the circumstances under which an employer is liable for sexual harassment in the workplace. The analysis proceeds as follows:

I. Proof of Sexual Harassment.   The plaintiff/employee/victim must prove items 1–4:

1. Membership in a protected class (male or female, in this instance).
2. Unwanted harassment.
3. Harassment based on sex.
4. Harassment that affected a term, condition, or privilege of employment, and was sufficiently severe and pervasive as to unreasonably interfere with an individual's work performance or create a hostile, abusive working environment.

If the plaintiff is unable to prove items 1–4, her/his claim fails. If the plaintiff proves items 1–4, the inquiry then turns to Part II and the question of employer liability.

II. Employer Liability.

1. If the wrongdoer was a coworker, the plaintiff/employee can bring a negligence claim seeking to prove that the employer unreasonably failed to prevent or remedy the discriminatory harassment of the coworker where management employees knew or should have known about the harassment.
2. If the wrongdoer was a supervisor with authority over the plaintiff/employee, and if the employee suffered a *tangible employment action* (job loss, demotion, etc.) because of the harassment, the employer is vicariously liable (*indirect* liability for employee's misconduct—see Chapter 12) for the employee's losses. That is, the employer is automatically liable for the employee's wrong and cannot offer a defense regardless of lack of knowledge, absence of negligence, or any other factor.
3. If the wrongdoer was a supervisor with authority over the plaintiff/employee, but the employee suffered no tangible employment action, the employer can avoid liability by proving both of the following affirmative defenses: (1) The employer exercised reasonable care to prevent and correct the harassment promptly (by instituting antiharassment training programs, for example), and (2) the employee unreasonably failed to take advantage of those preventive or corrective opportunities. [For an overview of sexual harassment law, see **http://profs.findlaw.com/harassment/harassment_1.html**]

The case that follows illustrates the application of sexual harassment analysis to alleged on-the-job abuse.

[handwritten note: E'er defense - anti harassment program?]

BURRELL v. STAR NURSERY
170 F.3d 951 (9th Cir. 1999)

Circuit Judge Thompson

Overview

Danielle Burrell appeals the district court's summary judgment in favor of Star Nursery, Inc., dismissing her sexual harassment claim under Title VII of the Civil Rights Act of 1964.

With regard to her Title VII claim, Burrell contends the district court erred in concluding there was no genuine issue of material fact as to whether Star Nursery's management knew or should have known of Burrell's alleged sexual harassment.

Background

Burrell worked as a cashier at Star Nursery, first at Star Nursery's Spring Mountain store and then at its Boulder Highway store. Her supervisors at the Boulder Highway store were Glenn Slack, the store manager, and Mark Barita, the assistant store manager.

Burrell alleges that store manager Slack sexually harassed her by making comments that contained sexual references; saying he wanted to take a trip to the mountains with her; and making comments about how Burrell looked and how "well built" she was.

Burrell also alleges that assistant store manager Barita verbally harassed her about being the goddaughter of Donna Noe, the manager of the Spring Mountain store, telling her that she would no longer get any special treatment and treating her unfairly by reprimanding her for minor incidents. In her affidavit in opposition to summary judgment, and in her appeal brief in this court, Burrell also alleges that Barita harassed her because of her sex. In her earlier deposition testimony, however, Burrell explicitly stated that Barita had not sexually harassed her.

Burrell had a confrontation with Barita in front of some store customers. Following that confrontation, Burrell requested a meeting with Star Nursery's corporate management to discuss the conflicts between her and Barita. Burrell admitted in her deposition that she never mentioned at the meeting any of the alleged incidents of sexual harassment by Barita or Slack; she raised only her complaints about Barita's unfair treatment of her. Following the meeting, she received three reprimands, two for cash drawer shortages and one for the incident that led to the confrontation with Barita in front of the customers.

Burrell also alleges sexual harassment by two coworkers, Gerald Brown and Richard Wright. She alleges Brown and Wright made unwanted sexual advances and sexually oriented comments to her, including making frequent comments about her breasts. She also alleges that one time in the parking lot after work, Wright grabbed her breasts.

No one at the management level of Star Nursery witnessed any of the alleged incidents of sexual harassment by Barita, Slack, Brown, or Wright. Burrell also testified in her deposition that she did not complain to management about the alleged harassment. Contrary to her earlier deposition testimony, however, Burrell stated in her affidavit in opposition to summary judgment that she discussed her concerns with her godmother, Donna Noe, the manager of the Spring Mountain store, but that she did not talk to anyone in the corporate office because she feared losing her job.

Around this same time, some of the cashiers, including Burrell, were asked to clean the restrooms, even though cleaning the restrooms was not one of the cashiers' regular job duties. Burrell cleaned the restrooms, but refused to clean the toilets without a toilet brush. At one point Barita suggested that she use the mop or her bare hands to clean the toilets. When she refused, she was reprimanded. Relying on this incident, and two prior reprimands, Star Nursery terminated Burrell.

In her complaint, Burrell alleged sexual harassment in violation of Title VII . . . Summary judgment was entered in favor of Star Nursery, and this appeal followed.

Discussion

A. Sexual Harassment

We first consider whether genuine issues of material fact exist as to whether the alleged behavior of Star Nursery's employees constituted sexual harassment.

Burrell has alleged a hostile work environment. To assert a Title VII claim based on a hostile work environment, a claimant must allege a "pattern of ongoing and persistent harassment severe enough to alter the conditions of employment." The working environment must "both subjectively and objectively be perceived as abusive" because of the sexual harassment.

The district court held that portions of Burrell's affidavit filed in opposition to summary judgment should be disregarded, or at least discounted, because they directly contradicted her earlier deposition testimony and thereby sought to create "sham issues of fact." We agree. Thus, we do not rely on Burrell's allegations of sexual harassment by Barita, which appeared for the first time in Burrell's affidavit and contradicted her earlier deposition testimony. Without these allegations of sexual harassment, there is no evidence that Barita sexually harassed Burrell.

On the other hand, genuine issues of material fact exist as to whether Slack, Brown, and Wright sexually harassed Burrell and whether their conduct created a hostile work environment. The question then becomes whether Star Nursery can be found liable under Title VII based on these alleged acts of sexual harassment.

B. Employer Liability

. . . [W]e first consider whether Burrell has raised a genuine issue of material fact as to whether Star Nursery management knew or should have known of the alleged sexual harassment by Burrell's coworkers Brown and Wright.

With regard to the alleged incidents of sexual harassment by Brown and Wright, there is no indication in the record that anyone withessed those incidents. Moreover, Burrell did not report any alleged harassment by Brown or Wright to Star Nursery's management. Although Burrell says in her affidavit that she reported her concerns to Noe, the manager of the Spring Mountain store, we decline to consider that assertion because it contradicts Burrell's earlier deposition testimony.

We conclude Burrell has failed to come forward with evidence that Star Nursery management knew or should have known about Brown's or Wright's alleged sexual harassment of her. Because she has not raised a genuine issue of material fact on this issue, we affirm the district court's summary adjudication absolving Star Nursery from Title VII liability for the alleged misconduct of these coworkers.

With regard to the alleged sexual harassment by store manager Slack, however, we apply a different standard. Two recent Supreme Court cases have set forth a new test for determining when an employer is vicariously liable for a hostile work environment created by a supervisor. In *Burlington Industries* v. *Ellerth,* and *Faragher* v. *Boca Raton,* the Supreme Court held that "an employer is subject to vicarious liability to a victimized employee for an actionable hostile work environment created by a supervisor with immediate (or successively higher) authority over the employee."

To prevent this rule from imposing automatic liability and to encourage employers to adopt antiharassment policies, the Supreme Court provided employers with an affirmative defense they could assert to avoid vicarious liability for their supervisors' misconduct:

> When no tangible employment action is taken, a defending employer may raise an affirmative defense to liability or damages, subject to proof by a preponderance of the evidence. The defense comprises two necessary elements: (a) that the employer exercised reasonable care to prevent and correct promptly any sexually harassing behavior, and (b) that the plaintiff employee unreasonably failed to take advantage of any preventive or corrective opportunities provided by the employer or to avoid harm otherwise . . . No affirmative defense is available, however, when the supervisor's harassment culminates in a tangible employment action, such as discharge, demotion, or undesirable reassignment.

The Court further explained the requirements of the two necessary elements of the affirmative defense:

> While proof that an employer had promulgated an antiharassment policy with [a] complaint procedure is not necessary in every instance as a matter of law, the need for a stated policy suitable to the employment circumstances may appropriately be addressed in any case when litigating the first element of the defense. And while proof that an employee failed to fulfill the corresponding obligation of reasonable care to avoid harm is not limited to showing any unreasonable failure to use any complaint procedure provided by the employer, a demonstration of such failure will normally suffice to satisfy the employer's burden under the second element of the defense.

This new rule overturns Ninth Circuit precedent as to employer liability for Title VII sexual harassment by supervisory personnel. In such a situation, the new rule focuses on whether the harasser has immediate or successively higher authority over the victim of the harassment, not on whether the employer knew about the harassment. Thus, if the harassment is actionable and the harasser has supervisory authority over the victim, we presume that the employer is vicariously liable for the harassment. This presumption may be overcome only if the alleged harassment has not culminated in a tangible employment action, and then only if the employer can prove both elements of the affirmative defense.

The record establishes that Slack was Burrell's supervisor and that he had immediate or successively higher authority over her, thereby satisfying the first part of the *Burlington Industries* and *Faragher* test. However, the record is not sufficiently developed to allow us to determine the causation question of whether the alleged sexual harassment culminated in a tangible employment action, and if it did not, whether Star Nursery may invoke the affirmative defense described in *Burlington Industries* and *Faragher*.

With regard to the issue of tangible employment action, it is unclear whether Burrell's termination resulted from various instances of her own misconduct, or whether Slack required Burrell to clean toilets and then terminated her because she had resisted his sexual advances.

If the alleged sexual harassment did not culminate in Burrell's termination, or in other "tangible employment action," then Star Nursery may attempt to establish the elements of the affirmative defense discussed in *Burlington Industries* and *Faragher*. In that event, the district court will have to determine whether Star Nursery exercised reasonable care to prevent or promptly correct any sexually harassing behavior (the first element of the affirmative defense). Then, although there appears to be no dispute that Burrell failed to notify management of the alleged sexual harassment, the district court will have to determine whether, if there was no reasonable policy in place, Burrell's failure to complain satisfied the second element of the affirmative defense.

* * * * *

Conclusion

We affirm the district court's summary judgment insofar as it absolves Star Nursery from Title VII liability for the alleged sexual harassment committed by coworkers Brown and Wright, and by assistant store manager Barita.

With regard to the alleged sexual harassment by store manager Slack, however, we reverse the district court's summary judgment absolving Star Nursery from Title VII liability. Slack was Burrell's supervisor with immediate or successively higher authority over her. There is a genuine issue of material fact as to whether he sexually harassed her and whether such conduct created a hostile work environment. If these issues should be resolved against Star Nursery, it would be liable for Burrell's conduct, unless it should prevail on the affirmative defense described in *Burlington Industries* and *Faragher*.

Affirmed in part; Reversed in part; and Remanded.

Questions

1. a. Why did the Court conclude that Barita had not sexually harassed Burrell?
   b. Why did the Court conclude that Star was not legally responsible for the alleged harassment by Brown and Wright?
   c. Why did the Court conclude that Star's knowledge of the alleged harassment by Slack was legally irrelevant to the outcome of the case?

2. Truck driver Lesley Parkins claimed that she was a victim of hostile environment sexual harassment while employed by Civil Constructors beginning in 1994. Parkins alleged that coworkers subjected her to foul language, sexual stories, and touching. Parkins complained to her dispatcher, Tim Spellman, and to one of her purported harassers, Robert Strong. She saw the job superintendent and the company EEO officer almost daily, but she did not complain to either. In 1996, Parkins filed a grievance with her Union-Teamsters Local 325. The Union contacted the company EEO officer, who immediately launched an investigation that led to punishment for the employees. Parkins conceded that she was not harassed following the company punishment. Parkins filed suit charging Civil Constructors with sexual harassment. Parkins claimed that two of her harassers, Strong and Charles Boeke, were foremen who supervised her work. Assuming Parkins can prove that she was, in fact, sexually harassed, what must she prove in order to hold Civil Constructors liable? See *Parkins v. Civil Constructors of Illinois,* 163 F.3d 1027 (7th Cir. 1998).

3. Rena Lockard worked for a Pizza Hut franchise in Atoka, Oklahoma, in September 1993. Two male customers made sexually offensive comments to her such as, "I would like to get in your pants." Lockard told her supervisor she did not like waiting on the men, but she did not mention the sexual comments. In November, 1993, the men returned to the Pizza Hut, and Lockard was instructed to wait on them. One of them asked what kind of cologne she was wearing, and Lockard replied that it was none of his business. The customer then grabbed her by the hair. Lockard told her supervisor what had happened and said that she did not want to wait on the two men. The supervisor ordered her to do so. Lockard returned to the table where one of the men pulled her by the hair, grabbed one of her breasts and put his mouth on her breast. Lockard then quit her job and later sued the local franchise and Pizza Hut. *hostile work environment*

   cust.   a. What do you take to be the central issue(s) in
   treat   this case? *supervisor aware but took*
   same as b. Is the franchise and/or Pizza Hut *no action*
   co-worker   responsible for sexual harassment by a

   customer against an employee? Explain. See *Lockard* v. *Pizza Hut,* 162 F.3d 1062 (10th Cir. 1998).

4. A female Internal Revenue Service agent received a number of love letters from a male coworker. The letters contained some references to sexual activity.

   a. In deciding whether the conduct constituted hostile environment sexual harassment, should the Court evaluate the facts from the point of view of a "reasonable person" or a "reasonable woman"? Explain.
   b. Why does it matter? See *Ellison* v. *Brady,* 924 F. 2d 872 (9th Cir. 1991).

5. If a supervisor makes explicit sexual remarks to both sexes, has made references to sexual conduct, and has called women sexually explicit names, is the supervisor engaging in unlawful sexual harassment? Explain. See *Steiner* v. *Showboat Operating Co.,* 25 F.3d 1459 (9th Cir. 1994), but see *Johnson* v. *Tower Air,* 149 F.R.D. 461 (E.D.N.Y. 1993).

Same Sex?   Joseph Oncale, a heterosexual who worked on an offshore oil rig, charged a supervisor and two coworkers with sexually harassing him, including repeated taunts and several sexual assaults, one with a bar of soap while Oncale was showering. Oncale complained to superiors, but to no avail. He then quit his job and sued his employer for sexual harassment. The case went to the United States Supreme Court, which resolved a split in lower court decisions by unanimously ruling that same-sex harassment is actionable under Title VII.[46] Oncale then settled out of court for an undisclosed amount of money. Justice Scalia, who wrote the Supreme Court opinion, explained that the harassment must be "because of sex;" that is, gender; that harassment can be motivated by hostility as well as by desire; and that common sense and social context count. Thus smacking a football teammate on the rear end, horseplay, roughhousing, or occasional gender-related jokes, teasing, and abusive language ordinarily would not constitute harassment. [For an analysis of the significance of the *Oncale* case for employers, see **http://www.shrm.org/hrmagazine/articles/0698new.htm**]

what if the harasser bothers both genders equally?

Oncale settles the big question of protection against same-sex harassment, but it raises other puzzles. For example, what if the harasser bothers both genders equally?

In the Schools?   Are schools legally and financially responsible when teachers harass students or when students harass each other? In 1998 and 1999 rulings, both by 5–4 votes, the Supreme Court said, "yes" to both questions, but only where school officials know about the harassment and are deliberately indifferent to it.[47] And in the instance of peer sexual harassment the Court raised the bar even further by saying that the harasser must be under the school's disciplinary authority. The Court also ruled that the behavior in question must be so extreme that it denies its victims equal access to education.

No one seems very satisfied with the Court's decisions. On one side, critics think schools are now subject to big financial burdens from claims making federal cases out of school yard teasing. On the other side, critics argue the decisions set such high standards of proof that few schools will bear liability.

The satirical online publication, *The Onion,* writes: "Joey Terzik, a Eugene-area 18-year-old, filed a formal complaint with the Oregon Department of Labor Monday, citing a 'gross lack of sexual harassment' in his workplace . . . 'Not once,' Terzik said, 'have I been made to feel like a sexual object instead of a co-worker.'"

Source: "Area 18-Year-Old Demands Right to be Sexually Harassed in the Workplace." [**http://www.theonion.com/onion3202/area18yearold.html**]

Part Four—Affirmative Action

Frederick Claus, a white man with a degree in electrical engineering and 29 years of experience with Duquesne Light Company, was denied a promotion in favor of a black man who had not earned a bachelor's degree and did not have the required seven years of experience. Only two of 82 managers in that division of Duquesne Light were black. Claus sued, claiming in effect that he was a victim of "reverse discrimination." At trial, both sides conceded that the black candidate was an outstanding employee and that he was qualified to be a manager. A jury awarded Claus $425,000 in damages. The case eventually reached the U.S. Supreme Court where, without comment, the Justices let Claus's victory stand.[48] Duquesne Light was actually responding to governmental affirmative action pressures, in part, when it promoted the black candidate. Twenty years ago that decision almost certainly would have received judicial approval. Today, affirmative action has entered a new, unsettled era. The *Claus* decision at the Supreme Court does not constitute a ruling on the merits and does not constitute precedent in any sense, but it is illustrative of a shift in affirmative action reasoning that we will examine hereafter.

For some 30 years, we have been struggling with *affirmative action* as a means of remedying past discriminatory wrongs and preventing discriminatory wrongs in the future. In following an affirmative action plan, employers consciously take positive steps to seek out minorities and women for hiring and promotion opportunities, and they often employ goals and timetables to measure progress toward a workforce that is representative of the qualified labor pool.

Affirmative action efforts arise in three ways: (1) courts may order the implementation of affirmative action after a finding of wrongful discrimination, (2) employers may voluntarily adopt affirmative action plans, and (3) employers may adopt affirmative action in order to do business with government agencies. All federal contractors with more than $10,000 in annual government business must meet the affirmative action standards of the Office of Federal Contract Compliance Programs.

"Three of the top four NFFL quarterback prospects this year—Akili Smith of Oregon, Dono-van McNabb of Syracuse, and Daunte Culpepper of Central Florida—are black . . . That's as many first-round black quarterbacks as in the entire history of the NFL. In that lies a lesson that extends far beyond the NFL. Like minorities in other fields historically dominated by whites, black quarterbacks been been deprived of opportunities by employers' set notions about what it takes to do a given job . . . The solution to this is outreach . . . Or to use its more common and less popular name, affirmative action . . . Affirmative action isn't charity. Even in one of America's most competitive arenas, it's a matter of self-interest."

Do you agree?

Source: "Affirmative Talent," *USA Today,* April 16, 1999, p.14A.

THE EARLY LAW

For nearly 20 years, judicial decisions were firmly supportive of affirmative action. A massive system of relief emerged at all levels of government and in the private sector. In a 1979 case, *United Steelworkers of America* v. *Weber,*[49] the Court set out perhaps its most detailed "recipe" for those qualities that would allow a voluntary affirmative action plan in the private sector to withstand constitutional scrutiny. Weber, a white male, challenged the legality of an affirmative action plan that set aside for black employees 50 percent of the openings in a training program until the percentage of black craft workers in the plant equaled the percentage of blacks in the local labor market. The plan was the product of a collective bargaining agreement between the Steelworkers and Kaiser Aluminum and Chemical. In Kaiser's Grammercy, Louisiana, plant only 5 of 273 skilled craft workers were black, while the local workforce was approximately 39 percent black. In the first year of the affirmative action plan, seven blacks and six whites were admitted to the craft training program. The most junior black employee accepted for the program had less seniority than several white employees who were not accepted. Weber was among the white males denied entry to the training program.

Weber filed suit, claiming Title VII forbade an affirmative action plan that granted a racial preference to blacks where whites dramatically exceeded blacks in skilled craft positions but there was no proof of discrimination. The federal district court and the federal court of appeals held for Weber, but the U.S. Supreme Court reversed. Several qualities of the Steelworkers' plan were instrumental in the Court's favorable ruling:

1. The affirmative action was part of a *plan.*
2. The plan was designed to "open employment opportunities for Negroes in occupations which have been traditionally closed to them."
3. The plan was temporary.
4. The plan did not unnecessarily harm the rights of white employees. That is,
    a. The plan did not require the discharge of white employees.
    b. The plan did not create an absolute bar to the advancement of white employees.

Then, in an important 1987 decision, *Johnson* v. *Transportation Agency,*[50] the Supreme Court approved the extension of affirmative action to women. The political tides were turning, however. The 1980s were politically conservative years. Appointments to the Supreme Court and to the lower federal courts, by President Ronald Reagan in particular, reflected that mood. Affirmative action was under fire.

[For a wide-ranging *Washington Post* review of affirmative action, see **http://www.washingtonpost.com/wp-srv/politics/special/affirm/affirm.htm**]

RETHINKING AFFIRMATIVE ACTION

From the late 1980s to the present, a series of judicial decisions and increasing public and political skepticism have raised great uncertainty about both the legality and the wisdom of affirmative action. The 1989 *City of Richmond* v. *J.A. Croson Co.*[51] case struck down Richmond, Virginia's minority "set-aside" program that required prime contractors who were doing business with the city to subcontract at least 30 percent of the work to minority businesses. The Court said such race-conscious remedial plans were constitutional only if (1) the city or state could provide specific evidence of discrimination against a particular protected class in the past (rather than relying on proof of general society-wide discrimination) and (2) its remedy was "narrowly tailored" to the needs of the situation.

Then in *Adarand Constructors* v. *Pena,* a landmark 1995 decision, the Supreme Court struck down a federal highway program that extended bidding preferences to "disadvantaged" contractors.[52] The suit was brought by Randy Pech, a white contractor whose low bid on a Colorado guardrail project was rejected in favor of the bid of a minority firm. The Supreme Court ruled that the government's preference program denied Pech his right to equal protection under the law as guaranteed by the Fifth Amendment to the federal Constitution. Ironically, the state of Colorado later declared Pech himself "disadvantaged" (apparently because of the advantages given to minority firms). That "disadvantaged" status put Pech on equal footing with his four main Colorado competitors, all of whom are owned by women or minorities.[53]

The case that follows applies the *Croson/Adarand* reasoning to a public-sector employment law case involving affirmative action for Dallas fire fighters.

DALLAS FIRE FIGHTERS ASS'N v. CITY OF DALLAS, TEX.
150 F. 3d 438 (5th Cir. 1998)

[Firefighters in the Dallas Fire Department (DFD) are promoted according to scores on a promotion examination. Vacancies are filled by those at the top of the promotion list unless there is a countervailing reason such as disciplinary problems.]

Chief Judge Politiz

In 1988 the City Council adopted a five-year affirmative action plan for the DFD, extending same for five years in 1992 with a few modifications. In an effort to increase minority and female representation the DFD promoted black, hispanic, and female firefighters ahead of male, nonminority firefighters who had scored higher on the promotion examinations. Between 1991 and 1995 these promotions occasioned four lawsuits filed by the Dallas Fire Fighters Association on behalf of white and Native American male firefighters who were passed over for promotions. These actions were consolidated by the district court.

The plaintiffs consist of four groups, three of which contend that the DFD impermissibly denied them promotions to the ranks of driver-engineer, lieutenant, and captain respectively. Additionally, a fourth group of plaintiffs challenges the fire chief's appointment of a black male to deputy chief in 1990. The plaintiffs claim that the City and the fire chief, Dodd Miller, acting in his official capacity, violated: (1) the fourteenth amendment of the United States Constitution, (2) the equal rights clause of the Texas Constitution, (3) Title VII of the Civil Rights Act of 1964, and (4) article 5221k of the Texas Civil Statutes.

The district court granted summary judgment in favor of the plaintiffs challenging the out-of-rank promotions, finding violations of their constitutional and statutorily protected rights. The court denied the City's motions for summary judgment, and denied the plaintiffs' motion for summary judgment as to the deputy chief appointment.

Analysis

1. The Out-of-Rank Promotions

A. Race-Conscious Promotions To survive an equal protection challenge under the fourteenth amendment, a racial classification must be tailored narrowly to serve a compelling governmental interest.

A governmental body has a compelling interest in remedying the present effects of past discrimination. In analyzing race conscious remedial measures we essentially are guided by four factors: (1) necessity for the relief and efficacy of alternative remedies; (2) flexibility and duration of the relief; (3) relationship of the numerical goals to the relevant labor market; and (4) impact of the relief on the rights of third parties.

We conclude that on the record before us the race-based, out-of-rank promotions at issue herein violate the equal protection clause of the fourteenth amendment.

The only evidence of discrimination contained in the record is the 1976 consent decree between the City and the United States Department of Justice, precipitated by a DOJ finding that the City engaged in practices inconsistent with Title VII, and a statistical analysis showing an underrepresentation of minorities in the ranks to which the challenged promotions were made. The record is devoid of proof of a history of egregious and pervasive discrimination or resistance to affirmative action that has warranted more serious measures in other cases.

In light of the minimal record of evidence of discrimination in the DFD, we must conclude that the City is not justified in interfering with the legitimate expectations of those warranting promotion based upon their performance in the examinations.

There are other ways to remedy the effects of past discrimination. The City contends, however, that alternative measures employed by the DFD, such as validating promotion exams, recruiting minorities, eliminating the addition of seniority points to promotion exam scores, and initiating a tutoring program, have been unsuccessful, as evidenced by the continuing imbalance in the upper ranks of the DFD. That minorities continue to be underrepresented does not necessarily mean that the alternative remedies have been ineffective, but merely that they apparently do not operate as quickly as out-of-rank promotions.

B. Gender-Conscious Promotions.

Applying the less exacting intermediate scrutiny analysis applicable to gender-based affirmative action, we nonetheless find the gender-based promotions unconstitutional. The record before us contains, as noted above, little evidence of racial discrimination; it contains even less evidence of gender discrimination. Without a showing of discrimination against women in the DFD, or at least in the industry in general, we cannot find that the promotions are related substantially to an important governmental interest.

*   *   *   *   *

2. The Deputy Chief Appointment The City contends that the district court erred in failing to grant its motion for summary judgment on the ground that Chief Miller's

appointment of Robert Bailey, a black male, to deputy chief [did not violate] Title VII. To determine the validity of the appointment we must examine whether it was justified by a manifest imbalance in a traditionally segregated job category and whether the appointment unnecessarily trammeled the rights of nonminorities or created an absolute bar to their advancement. The plaintiffs do not dispute that there is a manifest imbalance in the rank of deputy chief and we therefore limit our discussion to the second prong of the test.

The only summary judgment evidence specific to the Bailey appointment is the affidavit of Chief Miller in which he states:

In 1990, I selected Robert Bailey as Deputy Chief because I believed he was capable of performing the job responsibilities of the position of Deputy Chief, and he was recommended by my executive staff. In addition, the appointment of Chief Bailey was made pursuant to the City of Dallas Affirmative Action Plan.

The City contends that Chief Miller's statement reflects that, in appointing Bailey, he considered race as one factor among many, making the appointment permissible. The plaintiffs concede that Bailey was qualified but insist that the reference to the affirmative action plan, and the failure of Chief Miller to explain how Bailey compared to other candidates, established that Chief Miller based his final decision solely upon race. The plaintiffs also contend that the promotional goals in the affirmative action plan are out of proportion to the percentage of available candidates, demonstrating that the appointment was made to fulfill impermissible goals and, thus, unnecessarily trammeled the rights of nonminorities.

The plaintiffs' position is that any employment decision utilizing the affirmative action plan is illegal. We decline to accept that contention, particularly in light of the fact that the validity of the affirmative action plan is not in question herein. We are persuaded that the mere reference to the affirmative action plan does not create a fact issue concerning whether Chief Miller had an impermissible motive in promoting Bailey. The only relevant summary judgment evidence reflects that Chief Miller chose Bailey based upon substantially

more than just his race, and the opponents have failed to produce any acceptable material evidence to the contrary. We therefore conclude that the appointment did not unnecessarily trammel the rights of nonminorities or pose an absolute bar to their advancement. Accordingly, the appointment was consistent with Title VII.

3. Conclusion

For the foregoing reasons, we AFFIRM the judgment striking down the out-of-rank promotions and we REVERSE and RENDER judgment in favor of the City, upholding the validity of the deputy chief appointment.

Afterword

The United States Supreme Court denied certiorari (declined to review) the *Dallas Fire Fighters* decision, but Justices Breyer and Ginsburg dissented from that denial. (Remember that the Supreme Court decision not to review this case does not set a precedent and does not necessarily mean that the high court would agree with the lower court decision if a full review had been conducted.)

Justice Breyer

The defendants offered the following evidence of past discrimination in support of the plan: (1) The Dallas Fire Department did not hire its first black firefighter until 1969. (2) Blacks and Latinos comprised less than 1 percent of the fire department in 1972. (3) In 1972, the Department of Justice concluded that the fire department had engaged in impermissible racial discrimination. (4) In 1976, the Dallas Fire Department entered into a consent decree with the Department of Justice "to alleviate the effects of any past discrimination that might have occurred." (5) The consent decree and subsequent plans led to advances in the hiring of minorities and women, and, in 1988, 38.7 percent of the entry-level "fire and rescue officers" were black or Latino and 1.9 percent were women. (6) In the upper ranks of the fire department, in 1988, blacks and Latinos made up 14.8 percent of the "driver-engineers," 5.8 percent of the "lieutenants," and 5.2 percent of the "executives/deputy chiefs." Women made up 1.6 percent of the "driver-engineers," but there were no women "lieutenants" or "executives/deputy chiefs."

This Court has held that a government entity's implementation of race-conscious measures that are narrowly tailored to remedy past discrimination by that entity does not violate the Equal Protection Clause. And it has indicated that significant statistical disparities between the pool of those selected for a job and those eligible for the job may be used, among other things, to show past discrimination. In this case, there are both statistics and other evidentiary indicia of past discrimination, including a finding by the Department of Justice of a history of discrimination. Courts of Appeals apparently have upheld affirmative action plans in other cities based on similar records.

In light of the many affirmative action plans in effect throughout the Nation, the question presented, concerning the means of proving past discrimination, is an important one; the lower courts are divided; and the Fifth Circuit's decision may be questionable in light of our precedents. Accordingly, I respectfully dissent from the denial of certiorari in this case.[54]

Questions

1. a. Why did the Court of Appeals support the plaintiffs' challenge to the out-of-rank promotions?

    b. Why did the Court of Appeals reject the plaintiffs' challenge to the appointment of an African–American deputy chief?

2. In your view, was the Supreme Court dissent correct in arguing for a full review of the *Dallas Fire Fighters* decision? Explain.

3. In 1974, Birmingham, Alabama, was accused of unlawfully excluding blacks from management roles in its fire department. After several years of litigation, Birmingham adopted an affirmative action plan that guaranteed black firefighters one of every two available promotions. The city, the Justice Department, and others applauded the arrangement, but a group of 14 white firefighters claimed they were victims of reverse discrimination. After years of wrangling, the white firefighters' claim reached the 11th Circuit Federal Court of Appeals. Was the affirmative action plan lawful? Explain. See *In re Birmingham Reverse Discrimination Employment Litig.,* 20 F.3d 1525 (11th Cir. 1994) cert. den. sub nom., *Martin* v. *Wilks,* 115 S.Ct. 1695 (1995).

SO WHERE ARE WE?

The Law?   Clearly, the boundaries for permissible affirmative action have been narrowed by *Croson, Adarand,* and similar decisions, but remember that those decisions deal with set-aside programs rather than private sector employment, and remember that those decisions are based on constitutional analysis rather than interpretation of Title VII. Nonetheless, we should expect the courts to take a very close look at racial and gender preferences under Title VII. Therefore, affirmative action plans must be much more narrowly drawn and empirically justified than was the case. Affirmative action based broadly on "societal discrimination" is unconstitutional. Diversity as an independent goal for affirmative action apparently is not supported by a majority of the Supreme Court. A permissible affirmative action plan apparently will need to meet all of the following standards:

1. It must be directed to past discrimination as evidenced by specific factual findings in the market in question.
2. If the plan sets goals for hiring, subcontracting, and so on, those goals must be based on a "narrow" set of statistics comparing the percent of employees in the employer's workforce with those in the *qualified* labor pool.
3. The plan would have to be temporary and narrowly tailored while minimizing layoffs and other undue burdens.[55]

Social Policy?   The Clinton Administration has repeatedly asserted its support for affirmative action principles while acknowledging that the *Croson* and *Adarand* decisions required changes in federal policy. While pure set-asides at the federal level are probably a thing of the past, the Transportation Department continues, for example, to maintain an "aspirational goal" of giving minority firms 10 percent of its business.[56] Similarly, the federal government initiated a new program in 1998 that awards a 10 percent pricing preference to small, "disadvantaged" firms in industries with a clear history of discrimination. Thus, those firms would be able to bid as much as 10 percent more than the low bidder and still secure the contract.[57]

So we can most accurately say that affirmative action survives, but in a much more carefully defined form than had been the case. Recent evidence from around the country suggests our continuing struggle to find the most suitable boundaries for permissible affirmative action:

- In 1999, a California jury awarded $2.75 million in damages to a university lecturer who allegedly was denied an improved teaching position at San Francisco State because he was white.[58]
- In 1999, the Ohio Supreme Court upheld that state's set-aside law ruling that the state had demonstrated prior discrimination against minorities.[59]
- In 1998, San Francisco passed an ordinance recognizing Arab–Americans as a legal minority, thus making them eligible for affirmative action contract benefits.[60]
- In 1998, a nationwide poll found that 51 percent of adults favor affirmative action for minorities and women including 82 percent of blacks polled and 45 percent of whites.[61]

A *USA Today* study found that of the 34 law clerks hired by the United States Supreme Court for the 1998–99 term, 22 were white males, 11 were white females and one was an Hispanic female. The study also found that less than 2 percent of the 428 clerks hired by the sitting justices during their time on the Court were black. In your view, should the Supreme Court practice affirmative action in hiring clerks?

Source: Tony Mauro, "Only 1 New High Court Clerk Is a Minority," *USA Today*, September 10, 1998, p. 9A.

In Education?   A 1995 Gallup Poll found 84 percent of the population rejecting an educational admission policy that favors a less-qualified minority over a white applicant.[62] Indeed, 68 percent of blacks oppose such policies.[63] In 1998 a federal appeals court panel struck down an admissions quota system that resulted in denying admission to the prestigious Boston Latin High School to a white student, Sarah Wessmann, even though her record was stronger than that of minority applicants who were admitted.[64] Similarly, a 1996 decision in *Hopwood* v. *Texas* rejected a University of Texas School of Law admission policy that had set diversity goals for admissions (5 percent black and 10 percent Mexican–American) and that employed higher admission standards for whites than for blacks and Mexican–Americans.[65] In 1996, 55 percent of California voters approved Proposition 209, which amended the state constitution to forbid race and gender considerations in college admissions as well as in public hiring and contracting. The long-term effect of Proposition 209 on admissions to the selective University of California system is unclear, but after minority admissions fell significantly in 1998, they rebounded for the class entering in the fall of 1999 to a point just short of minority admissions prior to the change in rules.[66] In any case, the University of California is expected to implement a new plan guaranteeing admission to the top 4 percent of students at each of the state's high schools, thus adding about 700 blacks, Latinos, and Native Americans to those eligible for the freshmen class for 2001.[67]

Diversity.   However one may feel about affirmative action, the reality is that the market now requires respect for diversity. Whites will shrink from 76 percent of the population in 1996 to about 52 percent in 2050.[68] Furthermore, as business journalist Thomas Petzinger notes, "Ideas are everything in a fragmented global marketplace, and great ideas demand a diverse workforce."[69] [For an extensive database on the "dangers in litigation of corporate diversity programs," see **http://www.orrick.com/news/emplaw/diverse/1toc.htm**]

Questions

1. Author and affirmative action critic Dinesh D'Souza says that we should allow "rational discrimination" in the private sector by repealing the Civil Rights Act of 1964 as it applies to the private sector.
   a. What does he mean by "rational discrimination?"
   b. Using the free market reasoning that D'Souza relies upon, explain his argument that the repeal of the Civil Rights Act in the private sector would not lead to racial discrimination in employment.
2. Author Shelby Steele, a black man, does not approve of affirmative action. Rather, he favors treating discrimination by race, gender, or ethnicity as a crime. What do you think of his proposal? Explain.

Part Five—Additional Discrimination Topics

RELIGIOUS DISCRIMINATION

As *The Wall Street Journal* asked, "In a Factory Schedule, Where Does Religion Fit In?"[70] Managers, pushed to the limit by the competitive demands of the global market, must bring all of their wisdom and tact to bear on increasingly common religious conflicts in the workplace. The *Journal* points to the example of a Whirlpool factory near Nashville, Tennessee, where 200 employees, 10 percent of the workforce, are Muslims of six nationalities. In order to maintain their religious principles, many devout Muslim men must wear beards and skull caps while many women must wear loose-fitting clothes and head scarves in public. Muslims pray five times daily and must first wash their hands and feet. The clothing requirements raised safety concerns. Prayers disrupted assembly line schedules. The before-prayer washing left restrooms wet and slippery. Other workers sometimes resented the rituals and worried that production would decline and the factory might not be able to remain competitive in the fierce appliance market. As the law requires, Whirlpool has made efforts to accommodate the religious needs of its workers. Substitutes are available during prayer times. Washrooms are mopped more frequently. Scarves were retained, but had to be tucked in tightly. Sometimes accommodations could not be reached, as in workers' preference for sandals where steel-toed shoes were required. And Muslim men were expected to respectfully take instructions from female managers even though their own culture and religion left the men uncomfortable in that subordinate role.[71]

> "In a Factory Schedule, Where Does Religion Fit In?"

The Law.   Title VII forbids discrimination, such as dismissal, on the basis of religion. That religious faith must be sincere and meaningful, not merely a sham to achieve advantages. Employers must take reasonable steps to prevent and remedy religious harassment. But the much more common problem is that of reasonable accommodation, as described above in the Whirlpool/Muslim situation.

The leading case regarding religious discrimination is *Trans World Airlines, Inc.* v. *Hardison,* in which the plaintiff, who celebrated his religion on Saturdays, was unable to take that day off from his work in a parts warehouse.[72] Efforts to swap shifts or change jobs could not be worked out. The company rejected Hardison's request for a four-day week because the solution would have required the use of another employee at premium pay. The Supreme Court's ruling in the case reduced the employer's duty to a very modest standard: "To require TWA to bear more than a *de minimis cost* in order to give Hardison Saturdays off is an *undue hardship*." Saturdays off for Hardison would have imposed extra costs on TWA and would have constituted religious discrimination against other employees who would have sought Saturday off for reasons not grounded in religion. So any accommodation imposing more than a de minimis cost on the employer represents an undue hardship and is not required by Title VII. Of course, the lower courts have differed considerably on what constitutes a de minimis cost and an undue hardship. For example, a Kentucky court ruled that an employee, a Jehovah's Witness, who objected to answering the phone with the greeting, "Merry Christmas," could have been reasonably accommodated by allowing her to substitute another greeting.[73] On the other hand, the director of information services for Polk County, Iowa, who directed an employee to type his Bible study notes imposed more than a de minimis cost on the county. Similarly, the county had no duty to allow the use of its office before the beginning of the work day in order to accommodate employee prayer meetings. On the other hand, spontaneous prayers, occasional affirmations of Christianity, and isolated references to Bible passages by the director did not amount to an undue hardship in the absence of clear evidence that those religious demonstrations affected personnel decisions.[74] In order to clarify federal workers' religious rights, in 1997 President Clinton issued guidelines describing employees' right to do such things as keep a Bible in the office, wear a yarmulke to work, and discuss religion in the workplace (so long as those with whom they are speaking do not object). Managers also must coordinate work schedules in order to minimize interference with employees' religious observances. [For an overview of religious discrimination, see **http://www.landels.com/working/0999/pres/sld001.htm**]

In 1999, Taco Bell reached a settlement with a Hindu customer who bit into a beef burrito after having ordered a bean burrito. The bite of beef violated the customer's religious views and reportedly required flying to England to perform a religious purification rite and then flying to India to cleanse his soul in the Ganges River.

Source: Hilary MacGregor, "California and the West; Faith and Food," *Los Angeles Times,* January 25, 1998, p. A3 and Ron Lent, "Taco Bell, Customer Settle Burrito Order Dispute," *Journal of Commerce,* February 18, 1999, p. 8A.

Question

Resolving job-related religious conflicts can be among the most emotionally demanding management dilemmas. For example, what, if anything, would you do, as a manager, if one of your subordinates wore to work an antiabortion button displaying a picture of a fetus because of her religious beliefs about abortion? [See *Wilson* v. *U.S. West Communications,* 58 F.3d 1337 (8th Cir. 1995).]

THE AMERICANS WITH DISABILITIES ACT (ADA)

Robert J. Disanto, a salesperson for McGraw-Hill Cos., was awarded $1,280,000 in back pay and damages when a jury concluded, in 1999, that McGraw-Hill had violated the Americans with Disabilities Act (ADA) by firing Disanto after he told his supervisor that he was HIV-positive.[75] Disanto took disability leave after telling his supervisors of his condition and later returned to work. According to Disanto, his work assignments were changed, he was assigned a smaller office, and he was progressively isolated from business decisions and ostracized by his boss. McGraw-Hill argued that Disanto resigned from his job and that nothing in the law or the facts justified the decision, which the employer intends to contest.[76]

That case illustrates the general purpose of the 1990 ADA, which seeks to remove barriers to a full, productive life for disabled Americans. The ADA forbids discrimination in employment, public accommodations, public services, transportation, and telecommunications against the estimated 43 million Americans who are disabled. Small businesses with fewer than 15 employees are exempted from the employment portions of the ADA. The Rehabilitation Act of 1973 protects disabled workers in the public sector from employment discrimination.

Under the ADA, a disabled person (1) has a physical or mental impairment that substantially limits one or more major life activities, (2) has a record of such an impairment, or (3) is regarded as having such an impairment. Major life activities include caring for oneself, seeing, hearing, learning, and working, for example. One who has a history of cancer might "have a record of such an impairment." And one might be regarded by others as impaired because of a physical deformity when, in fact, that condition does not impair job performance in any material way.

Disabilities

Blindness, hearing loss, mental retardation, cosmetic disfigurement, anatomical loss, and disfiguring scars are examples of covered disabilities. Alcoholism, drug abuse, and AIDS are covered. However, the act specifically excludes job applicants and employees who *currently* use illegal drugs when the employer acts on the basis of such use. Thus, the act covers those who are rehabilitated and no longer using illegal drugs, those in rehabilitation and no longer using illegal drugs, and those erroneously regarded as using illegal drugs. Employers may expect the same performance and behavior from alcoholics and drug abusers as from all other employees. In sum, the act treats alcoholism and drug addiction as medical problems and protects those who are overcoming their impairments.

> the act specifically excludes job applicants and employees who *currently* use illegal drugs

Specifically excluded as disabilities are homosexuality, bisexuality, exhibitionism, gambling, kleptomania, and pyromania, among others. Questions regarding which conditions constitute disabilities will continue to require litigation. For example, in interpreting the federal Rehabilitation Act and state disability laws, some courts have treated obesity as a disability while others have not.

Accommodation.   An employer may not discriminate in hiring or employment against a *qualified person with a disability*. A qualified person is one who can perform the *essential functions* of the job. The act requires employers to make *reasonable accommodations* for disabled employees and applicants. Reasonable accommodations might include such things as structural changes in the workplace, job reassignment, job restructuring, or new equipment.

Hardship.   The employer's primary defense is that of *undue hardship*. The employer need not make an accommodation to a disabled person if that adjustment would be unduly expensive, substantial, or disruptive. The employer can call on the hardship defense only after an appropriate accommodation has been identified. All new facilities must be accessible to disabled parties unless structurally impractical, but Congress appears to have intended that changes to existing facilities should not be required if they would involve large expense.

The ADA does not require affirmative action plans or quotas. Unqualified applicants need not be hired, and one who cannot perform the essential functions of the job after reasonable accommodations may be discharged.

Question

Doren, a registered nurse for Battle Creek Health System, worked regular eight-hour shifts but suffered various medical problems. Nurses were allowed to change to 12-hour shifts on a voluntary basis and all did so except Doren. At that point, the 12-hour shift was made mandatory. Doren's doctor said that she was unable to work 12-hour shifts. Doren sought accommodations from Battle Creek, but the hospital refused. Doren eventually lost her job and sued, claiming an ADA violation.

a. Is Doren disabled?

b. Must she be accommodated by Battle Creek? Explain. See *Doren* v. *Battle Creek Health System,* 187 F. 3d 595 (6th Cir. 1999).

The ADA in Practice

Nearly 109,000 ADA claims were filed with the EEOC from 1992 through 1998.[77] In 1997 for the first time, emotional/psychiatric impairments, which constituted 15.3 percent of the claims cited, passed back injuries (14.9 percent) as the leading ADA problem.[78] Almost 90 percent of all ADA cases brought to the EEOC are thrown out,[79] and an American Bar Association (ABA) study found plaintiffs winning only about 2 percent of the cases that are actually litigated.[80] But critics argue the ABA study seriously understates plaintiffs' success.[81] [For a highly rated database on the ADA, see **http://janweb.icdi.wvu.edu/kinder/index.htm**]

Compliance Costs.   A Harris poll of 400 executives found that the median cost of accommodating disabilities was $233 per employee.[82] One study of Sears, Roebuck found that company spending an average of $121 to accommodate disabled employees.[83] On the other hand, a reader complained in a letter to *The Wall Street Journal* that compliance can impose an ADA "tax" on some small businesses:

> I am personally familiar with this "tax" on two small retail establishments. The first is a sandwich shop that has just been established in a 90-year-old building in downtown Milwaukee. It will cost approximately $12,000 to construct a new bathroom of appropriate size for nonexisting wheelchair-bound employees (the owners are the only employees). In the second, a nonprofit group is reopening a restaurant tavern that has been closed for several years. Before the doors can open, the bathrooms must be reconstructed and reconfigured to ADA standards (and correspondingly reduce the restaurant size) to the tune of $25,000.[84]

Success?   ADA criticism is commonplace and fierce. Author Walter Olsen says, "Under the ADA, we may all be disabled."[85] He points to a *Hartford Courant* report that "nearly one in three high schoolers in affluent Greenwich, Conn., are now officially regarded as disabled, entitling them to various benefits ranging from individualized tutoring to laptop computers."[86] Olsen also notes that workforce participation among the disabled has actually fallen from 33 percent in 1986 to 29 percent in the late 1990s.[87] Furthermore, a 1997 study found that disabled workers are 36 percent more likely to be injured on the job than are their able-bodied coworkers.[88]

> nearly one in three high schoolers in affluent Greenwich, Conn., are now officially regarded as disabled

So in some ways, the ADA results to date are not encouraging, but early fears that employers would be inundated with claims and that accommodation costs would soar out of sight have been significantly deflated. And we can be heartened that from 1991 to 1994, an additional 800,000 severely disabled people found a role in the workplace.[89] Perhaps more importantly in the long term, we seem increasingly at ease with those who are disabled. Seventy-one percent of working Americans responding to a 1998 survey said they would be "very comfortable" working with someone with a disability.[90] [For the President's Committee on Employment of People with Disabilities and an extensive ADA database, see **http://www.pcepd.gov/contents.htm**]

What Is a Disability?

The case that follows examines the critical question of whether correctable impairments, such as high blood pressure, constitute disabilities. The case also shows us that the ADA need not be as worrisome to the business community as its critics have suggested.

SUTTON AND HINTON v. UNITED AIR LINES
119 S.Ct. 2139 (1999)

Justice O'Connor

I

Petitioners are twin sisters, both of whom have severe myopia. Each petitioner's uncorrected visual acuity is 20/200 or worse in her right eye and 20/400 or worse in her left eye, but "with the use of corrective lenses, each . . . has vision that is 20/20 or better." Consequently, without corrective lenses, each "effectively cannot see to conduct numerous activities such as driving a vehicle, watching television or shopping in public stores," but with corrective measures, such as glasses or contact lenses, both "function identically to individuals without a similar impairment."

In 1992, petitioners applied to respondent for employment as commercial airline pilots. They met respondent's basic age, education, experience, and FAA certification qualifications. After submitting their applications for employment, both petitioners were invited by respondent to an interview and to flight simulator tests. Both were told during their interviews, however, that a mistake had been made in inviting them to interview because petitioners did not meet respondent's minimum vision requirement, which was uncorrected visual acuity of 20/100 or better. Due to their failure to meet this requirement, petitioners' interviews were terminated, and neither was offered a pilot position.

*   *   *   *   *

[Petitioners filed suit under the Americans with Disabilities Act.]

The District Court dismissed petitioners' complaint for failure to state a claim upon which relief could be granted . . . The Court of Appeals for the Tenth Circuit affirmed.

III [II omitted.]

[W]e turn first to the question whether petitioners have stated a claim under subsection (A) of the disability definition, that is, whether they have alleged that they possess a physical impairment that substantially limits them in one or more major life activities. Because petitioners allege that with corrective measures their vision "is 20/20 or better," they are not actually disabled within the meaning of the Act if the "disability" determination is made with reference to these measures. Consequently, with respect to subsection (A) of the disability definition, our decision turns on whether disability is to be determined with or without reference to corrective measures.

Petitioners maintain that whether an impairment is substantially limiting should be determined without regard to corrective measures. They argue that, because the ADA does not directly address the question at hand, the Court should defer to the agency interpretations of the statute, which are embodied in the agency guidelines issued by the EEOC and the Department of Justice. These guidelines specifically direct that the determination of whether an individual is substantially limited in a major life activity be made without regard to mitigating measures.

Respondent, in turn, maintains that an impairment does not substantially limit a major life activity if it is corrected. It argues that the Court should not defer to the agency guidelines cited by petitioners because the guidelines conflict with the plain meaning of the ADA. The phrase "substantially limits one or more major life activities," it explains, requires that the substantial limitations actually and presently exist.

We conclude that respondent is correct that the approach adopted by the agency guidelines—that persons are to be evaluated in their hypothetical uncorrected state—is an impermissible interpretation of the ADA.

The Act defines a "disability" as "a physical or mental impairment that *substantially limits* one or more of the major life activities" of an individual. Because the phrase "substantially limits" appears in the Act in the present indicative verb form, we think the language is properly read as requiring that a person be presently—not potentially or hypothetically—substantially limited in order to demonstrate a disability. A "disability" exists only where an impairment "substantially limits" a major life activity, not where it "might," "could," or "would" be substantially limiting if mitigating measures were not taken. A person whose physical or mental impairment is corrected by medication or other measures does not have an impairment that presently "substantially limits" a major life activity. To be sure, a person whose physical or mental impairment is corrected by mitigating measures still has an impairment, but if the impairment is corrected it does not "substantially limit" a major life activity.

The definition of disability also requires that disabilities be evaluated "with respect to an individual" and be determined based on whether an impairment substantially limits the "major life activities of such individual." Thus, whether a person has a disability under the ADA is an individualized inquiry.

The agency guidelines' directive that persons be judged in their uncorrected or unmitigated state runs directly counter to the individualized inquiry mandated by the ADA. The agency approach would often require courts and employers to speculate about a person's condition and would, in many cases, force them to make a disability determination based on general information about how an uncorrected impairment usually affects individuals, rather than on the individual's actual condition. For instance, under this view, courts would almost certainly find all diabetics to be disabled, because if they failed to monitor their blood sugar levels and administer insulin, they would almost certainly be substantially limited in one or more major life activities. A diabetic whose illness does not impair his or her daily activities would therefore be considered disabled simply because he or she has diabetes. Thus the guidelines approach would create a system in which persons often must be treated as members of a group of people with similar impairments, rather than as individuals. This is contrary to both the letter and the spirit of the ADA.

*   *   *   *   *

Finally, and critically, findings enacted as part of the ADA require the conclusion that Congress did not intend to bring under the statute's protection all those whose uncorrected conditions amount to disabilities. Congress found that "some 43,000,000 Americans have one or more physical or mental disabilities, and this number is increasing as the population as a whole is growing older." This figure is inconsistent with the definition of disability pressed by petitioners . . .

[The National Council on Disability] explained that the estimates or the number of disabled Americans ranged from an overinclusive 160 million under a "health conditions approach," which looks at all conditions that impair the health or normal functional abilities of an individual, to an underinclusive 22.7 million under a "work disability approach," which focuses on individuals' reported ability to work. It noted that "a figure of 35 or 36 million [was] the most commonly quoted estimate." The 36 million number included in the 1988 bill's findings thus clearly reflects an approach to defining disabilities that is closer to the work disabilities approach than the health conditions approach.

*   *   *   *   *

Because it is included in the ADA's text, the finding that 43 million individuals are disabled gives content to the ADA's terms, specifically the term "disability." Had Congress intended to include all persons with corrected physical limitations among those covered by the Act, it undoubtedly would have cited a much higher number of disabled persons in the findings. That it did not is evidence that the ADA's coverage is restricted to only those whose impairments are not mitigated by corrective measures.

The dissents suggest that viewing individuals in their corrected state will exclude from the definition of "disabled" those who use prosthetic limbs or take medicine for epilepsy or high blood pressure. This suggestion is incorrect. The use of a corrective device does not, by itself, relieve one's disability. Rather, one has a disability under subsection A if, notwithstanding the use of a corrective device, that individual is substantially limited in a major life activity. For example, individuals who use prosthetic limbs or wheelchairs may be mobile and capable of functioning in society but still be disabled because of a substantial limitation on their ability to walk or run. The use or nonuse of a corrective device does not determine whether an individual is disabled; that determination depends on whether the limitations an

individual with an impairment *actually* faces are in fact substantially limiting.

As noted above, petitioners allege that with corrective measures, their visual acuity is 20/20, and that they "function identically to individuals without a similar impairment." Accordingly, because we decide that disability under the Act is to be determined with reference to corrective measures, we agree with the courts below that petitioners have not stated a claim that they are substantially limited in any major life activity.

IV

Our conclusion that petitioners have failed to state a claim that they are actually disabled under subsection (A) of the disability definition does not end our inquiry. Under subsection (C), individuals who are "regarded as" having a disability are disabled within the meaning of the ADA . . . There are two apparent ways in which individuals may fall within this statutory definition: (1) a covered entity mistakenly believes that a person has a physical impairment that substantially limits one or more major life activities, or (2) a covered entity mistakenly believes that an actual, nonlimiting impairment substantially limits one or more major life activities.

Standing alone, the allegation that respondent has a vision requirement in place does not establish a claim that respondent regards petitioners as substantially limited in the major life activity of working. By its terms, the ADA allows employers to prefer some physical attributes over others and to establish physical criteria. An employer runs afoul of the ADA when it makes an employment decision based on a physical or mental impairment, real or imagined, that is regarded as substantially limiting a major life activity. Accordingly, an employer is free to decide that physical characteristics or medical conditions that do not rise to the level of an impairment—such as one's height, build, or singing voice—are preferable to others, just as it is free to decide that some limiting, but not *substantially* limiting, impairments make individuals less than ideally suited for a job.

Considering the allegations of the amended complaint in tandem, petitioners have not stated a claim that respondent regards their impairment as *substantially limiting* their ability to work. When the major life activity under consideration is that of working, the statutory phrase "substantially limits" requires, at a minimum, that plaintiffs allege they are unable to work in a broad class of jobs . . . To be substantially limited in the major life activity of working, one must be precluded from more than one type of job, a specialized job, or a particular job of choice. If jobs utilizing an individual's skills (but perhaps not his or her unique talents) are available, one is not precluded from a substantial class of jobs. Similarly, if a host of different types of jobs are available, one is not precluded from a broad range of jobs.

Assuming without deciding that working is a major life activity and that the EEOC regulations interpreting the term "substantially limits" are reasonable, petitioners have failed to allege adequately that their poor eyesight is regarded as an impairment that substantially limits them in the major life activity of working. They allege only that respondent regards their poor vision as precluding them from holding positions as a "global airline pilot." Because the position of global airline pilot is a single job, this allegation does not support the claim that respondent regards petitioners as having a *substantially limiting* impairment. ("The inability to perform a single, particular job does not constitute a substantial limitation in the major life activity or working"). Indeed, there are a number of other positions utilizing petitioners' skills, such as regional pilot and pilot instructor to name a few, that are available to them.

Affirmed.

Questions

1. Identify and answer the two central questions in the *Sutton* case.
2. As you understand this decision, can employers now lawfully fire or decline to hire those with correctable disabilities who cannot meet legitimate job requirements without the use of those corrective measures, such as glasses or hearing aids? Explain.
3. Immediately after the Court handed down the *Sutton* decision, disabilities advocates and some politicians announced their intention to ask Congress to change the ADA to make it clear that the act covers those with correctable disabilities. How would you vote on such a measure? Explain.
4. John Rossi, a former manager at Northern Automotive Corporation, had weighed 250 pounds when he began work. When terminated, he weighed 400 pounds. He claimed he was dismissed because of his weight. Northern said his dismissal was prompted by a poor performance review. California's Fair Employment and Housing Act prohibits discrimination on the basis of physical disability. At trial, Rossi showed that his weight interfered with his major life functions, including walking, standing, and sitting. He also provided expert testimony that 80 percent of obesity is attributable to genetics and 20 percent to environmental forces. Rossi also provided evidence of abusive comments by his supervisor about his weight. Was Rossi a victim of disability discrimination? Explain. See *Rossi* v. *Northern Automotive Corp.,* Alameda County Superior Court No. 702424–1 (Sept. 1, 1995).
5. Delta Airlines declined to hire 10 former Pan Am flight attendants and pursers because they were overweight. The 10 sued Delta. Are employers legally entitled to impose rules and regulations governing the appearance of their employees? See *Delta Air Lines* v. *New York State Division of Human Rights,* 652 N.Y.S.2d 253 (1996).

AGE DISCRIMINATION

Michael Marks, an accountant, was so good and experienced at his work for Loral Corp. that he earned a substantially higher salary than other younger workers around him. When Loral decided to close its Newport Beach, California, office, Marks lost his job because of his high salary. Marks, then 49 years of age, sued, claiming his dismissal was a violation of the Age Discrimination in Employment Act (ADEA). The question in the *Marks* case and perhaps the biggest ADEA issue in this era of downsizing, mergers, and an aging workforce is whether an employee *40 years of age or older* can lawfully be dismissed simply and exclusively to save money. The answer in *Marks* and some similar cases to date is "yes"[91] so far as age discrimination is concerned although these efforts at cost savings might violate other laws such as the Employee Retirement Income Security Act (ERISA).[92] The Supreme Court has yet to directly address the cost saving issue although in the 1993 *Biggins* case, the Court found no ADEA wrong when an employer fired Biggins a few weeks before he would have qualified for costly pension benefits.[93]

Eighty-eight percent of CEOs surveyed anonymously report that they see a connection between a worker's age and productivity. In a poll of 773 chief executives in 23 countries, consultants Watson Wyatt Worldwide found that most think productivity peaks around age 43.

Source: Glenn Burkins, "Aging Work Force: Issues Companies Would Rather Not Talk About," *The Wall Street Journal,* March 24, 1998, p. A1.

The Law.   Age discrimination under the ADEA is established under disparate treatment analysis (intentional discrimination) similar to that for race and sex, but to date the federal courts are split on the question of applying disparate impact reasoning (employment policies that are neutral on their face but, in practice, disqualify older workers at a disproportionate rate) to age cases. Basically, an ADEA plaintiff must show that she or he is 40 years of age or older, qualified for the position in question, and was not hired or was terminated or demoted while a younger person received more favorable treatment.

Defenses.   The employer ordinarily defends by showing that the termination was based on a legitimate, nondiscriminatory reason (such as poor performance) or that age is a bona fide occupational qualification (BFOQ). To establish age as a BFOQ an employer must demonstrate that only employees of a certain age can safely and/or efficiently complete the work in question. [For an age discrimination database, see **http://www.aarp.org/ wwwstand/agediscm.html**]

Management Practice.   Beyond treating all workers fairly, managers can best avoid age discrimination problems simply by keeping their mouths shut. Age discrimination claims very often arise from ill-advised remarks:

> Claims vary from allegations that managers spoke of getting "new blood" or told older people they were "slowing down" to charges that workers were coerced into retirement.[94]

Language of that kind led directly to an important 1996 Supreme Court decision.[95] James O'Conner alleged that his boss remarked that O'Conner was "too old" to play 18 holes of golf for five days straight, "too damn old for this work,"

> it was time to get "some young blood in the company"

and that it was time to get "some young blood in the company." Two days later, the 56-year-old O'Conner was fired and replaced by a 40-year-old employee. When the case reached the Supreme Court, the central question was whether O'Conner's claim was barred because he was replaced by another employee who was also within the protected age group. A unanimous Court ruled that O'Conner's claim was not barred, thus making it easier for employees to pursue ADEA claims. The Court went on to say that the replacement of the plaintiff by someone substantially younger would be more compelling evidence of age discrimination than whether the replacement was outside the 40-and-over protected class. [For some questions and answers on the law of age discrimination, see **http://www.nolo.com/ChunkEMP/emp2.html**]

The Future. White, male, middle-class managers now frequently see themselves as victims of bias that historically touched only minorities and women. Recent research suggests that older workers are discrimination victims in about the same proportions as blacks and Hispanics of all ages. The research also finds that in job seeking one of the worst strategies an older applicant can employ is to emphasize loyalty, experience, and maturity.[96]

Since the median age of American workers is projected to reach 40.6 years by 2005 (from 34.6 in 1980),[97] we might expect increased pressure for protection against age discrimination, although a healthy economy may make older workers increasingly valuable. And in recent years age discrimination complaints filed with the EEOC have fallen by more than one-fifth.[98] Nonetheless, age claims can become quite expensive as Kmart Corp. recently learned when it agreed to pay $7.5 million to settle the charges of about 80 former managers. Kmart admitted no wrongdoing in reaching the settlement.[99]

Questions

1. Metz alleged that he was fired in violation of the ADEA. He had been a plant manager for a company, Transit Mix, that was experiencing financial problems. His employer notified him that the plant would be closed and he would be laid off. The company then sent the assistant manager of another plant, Burzloff, to Metz's plant to inspect it and make repairs. Burzloff requested that he be allowed to manage Metz's plant; the employer approved this request and discharged Metz. At the time of his layoff, the 54-year-old Metz had a salary of $15.75 an hour; when the 43-year-old Burzloff replaced Metz, his salary was $8.05 per hour.[100]

   Metz had worked for Transit for 27 years. He had received raises each year, even though the company was not profitable during some of those years. The company decided its poor financial performance did not justify retaining Metz, whose salary was comparatively high. Metz was not asked to take a pay cut before he was dismissed. The court framed the issue in the case in this manner:

   > The sole issue on appeal is whether the salary savings that can be realized by replacing a single employee in the ADEA age-protected range with a younger, lower-salaried employee constitutes a permissible, nondiscriminatory justification for the replacement.[101]

   Resolve that issue. Explain. See *Metz* v. *Transit Mix, Inc.,* 828 F.2d 1202 (7th Cir. 1987).

2. The Insurance Company of North America (ICNA) sought to hire a "loss control representative." The ad called for a B.S. degree, two years of experience, and other qualities. The plaintiff, who had 30 years of loss control experience, applied for the job but was not interviewed. ICNA hired a 28-year-old woman with no loss control

experience. The plaintiff sued claiming age discrimination. ICNA said the plaintiff was overqualified.

    a. Explain the plaintiff's argument.

    b. Decide the case. Explain. See *EEOC* v. *Insurance Co. of N. Am.,* 49 F.3d 1418 (9th Cir. 1995).

3. Under its collective bargaining agreement, Trans World Airlines maintained a policy of automatically transferring flight captains to positions as flight engineers when they were disqualified from their pilot's role for reasons other than age (for example, medical disability or a labor force reduction). Under the agreement, the captains were entitled to "bump" any less-senior flight engineer. However, pilots who were retired on reaching age 60 were not automatically entitled to move into a flight engineer position. Rather, they were allowed to remain with TWA only if they had secured a flight engineer position prior to their 60th birthday. They could do so only by submitting a bid in the hope that a vacancy would arise prior to their 60th birthday. Three pilots, forced to retire by TWA, filed suit, claiming a violation of the Age Discrimination in Employment Act, which forbids differential treatment of older workers "with respect to a privilege of employment." Does the ADEA *require* TWA to grant transfer privileges to disqualified pilots? Explain. See *Trans World Airlines, Inc.* v. *Thurston,* 469 U.S. 111 (1985).

SEXUAL ORIENTATION

A Davenport, Iowa, care center manager allegedly fired six employees because they were homosexual and, in his view, did not exhibit acceptable "moral character."[102] The manager explained:

> When I first came here, there was probably at least three—excuse my French—faggots working here and I had at least three dykes working here.[103]

Are those dismissed employees protected by our expansive network of antidiscrimination law? Almost certainly not. Neither federal law nor the law of most states (including Iowa) offers protection against discrimination on the basis of the employee's sexual orientation. The courts have consistently ruled that Title VII's prohibition of discrimination based on sex refers to gender only and thus does not offer protection to gays. Ten states and a number of cities do provide that protection, and 22 states have laws forbidding hate crimes based on sexual orientation.[104] Public sector employees can call on the equal protection provisions of the federal and state constitutions for protection although the courts have often allowed governments to discriminate against homosexuals and lesbians if officials can establish some employment necessity, such as security concerns. In 1998, President Clinton signed an executive order adding sexual orientation to the list of categories for which discrimination against federal workers is illegal. [For a database on the law and ethics of sexual orientation discrimination, see **http://ethics.acusd.edu/ sexual_orientation.html**]

A Louisville, Kentucky, gynecologist, Dr. Barrett Hyman, filed suit in 1999 claiming that Louisville's new "fairness ordinance" violated his constitutional right to religious liberty. The lawsuit argues that gay, bisexual, and transgendered people are "unfit for employment" in his private practice. The fairness ordinance extends antidiscrimination protection to those groups. Dr. Hyman quotes the Old Testament to support his position.

Source: Frederic Biddle, "A Challenge to a Workplace Antidiscrimination Ordinance May Set a Precedent," *The Wall Street Journal,* December 21, 1999, p. A1.

RETALIATION

In the *Blockbuster* sex discrimination case, noted earlier in the chapter, the four male plaintiffs/employees sued claiming they were the victims of sex discrimination because they were required to cut their long hair in order to retain their jobs while female coworkers did not need to do so.[105] They attempted to strengthen their claim against Blockbuster by accusing the video chain of *retaliation;* that is, they argued that they were fired because they protested Blockbuster's grooming code. The four men lost both their sex discrimination and retaliation claims, but their retaliation strategy has become a familiar workplace complaint. Retaliation claims filed with the EEOC rose from approximately 7,500 in 1990 to over 18,000 in 1997.[106]

Retaliation is forbidden by Title VII, the ADA, the ADEA, and other federal and state laws. Retaliation is established by proof that (1) the plaintiff engaged in a statutorily protected activity (opposing an unlawful practice, filing a charge, participating in an investigation, etc.), (2) the plaintiff suffered an adverse employment action (established on a case-by-case basis and ranging from dismissal to emotional abuse), and (3) the adverse employment action was causally related to the protected activity.[107] In addressing a discrimination claim, an employer must take special care not to mistreat the complaining employee because even if the discrimination charge is rejected in court, the employee could still win a retaliation judgment.

Expert advice on reducing retaliation risks:

- Make sure that complaining employees are not shunned by supervisors and coworkers.
- Maintain an effective complaint process.
- Thoroughly investigate all charges.
- Take appropriate disciplinary action.
- Make it clear that you appreciate employees who come forward with complaints.

Source: Perkins Cole, "Retaliation Claims Are on the Rise," *Oregon Employment Law Letter* 5, no. 7 (March 1999), p. 1.

INTERNET EXERCISE

Using UCLA law professor Eugene Volokh's website [**http://www.law.ucla.edu/ faculty/ volokh/harass/**], explain how sexual harassment law is regarded by some as a threat to freedom of speech.

CHAPTER QUESTIONS

1. Can an employer lawfully request age-related information on employment applications? Explain.
2. Christine McKennon, age 62, had worked at the Nashville Banner Publishing Company for 30 years when she was fired. She sued, claiming age discrimination. Subsequently, she admitted that during her final year of employment, she had copied confidential company documents and shown them to her husband. After learning of that misconduct, the Banner argued that McKennon's lawsuit should not be allowed to proceed because, even if she had been a victim of age discrimination, her prior misconduct barred her from recovery. Does an employer's after-the-fact discovery of a dismissed employee's employment-related misconduct negate any discriminatory injury the employee may have suffered on the theory that the employee would have been dismissed anyway when the misconduct was discovered? Explain. See *McKennon* v. *Nashville Banner Publishing Co.,* 513 U.S. 352 (1995).
3. California and the District of Columbia have laws forbidding gender bias in pricing; that is, businesses cannot charge one gender more than the other for services such as haircuts, dry cleaning, and car repairs.
   a. Are those laws a good idea, as you see it? Explain.
   b. The California law allows a higher price where more time and/or cost are required to deliver performance. The Washington, D.C., law has no such exception. Which is the wiser law as you see it? Explain.
4. Title VII disparate impact cases do not require a showing of purposefulness or intent to establish unlawful discrimination. A finding of discrimination under the Fifth and Fourteenth Amendments does require such a showing. Would you favor amending Title VII to require direct, explicit proof of actual discriminatory purpose? Explain.

5. Pan American Airways, Inc., maintained a policy of excluding men from positions as flight attendants. The policy was challenged on sex discrimination grounds. Pan American defended its policy with a survey showing that 79 percent of all passengers preferred being served by females. Then Pan Am offered expert testimony to show that the passenger preference was attributable to "feminine" qualities possessed by few males. The district court ruled for Pan Am on the grounds that "all or substantially all" [the test articulated in *Weeks* v. *Southern Bell Telephone,* 408 F.2d 228 (5th Cir. 1969)] men were unable to successfully fulfill the duties of flight attendants. The decision was appealed. Decide. Explain. See *Diaz* v. *Pan American Airways, Inc.,* 311 F. Supp. 559 (S.D. Fla. 1970), 442 F.2d 385 (5th Cir. 1971), cert. denied, 404 U.S. 950 (1971).
6. Can a Polynesian restaurant lawfully limit employment to "brown-skinned persons" in those jobs visible to the public? Explain.
7. Would a readily visible office wall display of nude and seminude female figures located in a common work area (for example, one poster, on display for eight years, depicted a "woman with a golf ball on her breasts and a man standing over her, golf club in hand, yelling 'fore.'") in combination with obscene comments about women on a routine basis (for example, "whores," "All that bitch needs is a good lay") give rise to an intimidating, hostile, or offensive working environment within the meaning of the sexual harassment law? Explain. See *Rabidue* v. *Osceola Refining Co.,* 805 F.2d 611 (6th Cir. 1986). But see *Robinson* v. *Jacksonville Shipyards,* 760 F. Supp. 1486 (M.D. Fla. 1991).
8. Ali Boureslan, a naturalized United States citizen who was born in Lebanon and was working in Saudi Arabia, was discharged by his employer, Arabian American Oil Company, a Delaware corporation. Boureslan sued ARAMCO under Title VII of the Civil Rights Act of

1964, claiming that he was discriminated against because of his race, religion, and national origin. The lower court ruled that Title VII does not reach U.S. citizens employed abroad by American firms. Boureslan appealed to the U.S. Supreme Court. Decide. Explain. See *Equal Employment Opportunity Commission* v. *Arabian American Oil Company,* 111 S.Ct. 1227 (1991).

9.   *a.*   Assume your employer is hosting a conference at a local hotel to examine the latest insights in total quality management. Further assume that one of the participants is hearing impaired, a fact that was unknown both to your employer and to the hotel. If an interpreter is not provided, can your employer and/or the hotel be sued under the ADA? Explain.

   b.   A physician recommended that the New York board of bar examiners accord a visually impaired bar applicant four days rather than the standard two in which to complete the bar examination. Must the board comply with that recommendation in order to provide "reasonable accommodation" as required under the ADA? See *D'Amico* v. *New York State Board of Law Examiners,* 813 F. Supp. 217 (W.D.N.Y. 1993).

10.   Define *affirmative action.*

11.   Diane Piantanida went on maternity leave. While absent her employer discovered tasks that she had not completed. Before her return, Piantanida was informed that she was being reassigned to a lesser job because of her inability to keep up in her former job. Upon objecting to the change, Piantanida claims she was told that she was being given a position "for a new mom to handle." Piantanida admits that her demotion was not based on her pregnancy or her maternity leave. Piantanida declined the offer and sued claiming a violation of the Pregnancy Discrimination Act stemming from her status as a new mother. Decide. Explain. See *Piantanida* v. *Wyman Center,* 116 F. 3d 340 (8th Cir. 1997).

12.   Blacks employed at the Georgia Power Company were concentrated in the four lowest job classifications, which were maintained as separate seniority units under a collective bargaining agreement. Workers moving to higher classifications were required to forfeit all accumulated seniority. All other classifications were overwhelmingly composed of whites. Movement from those classifications did not require seniority forfeiture. A consent decree in 1979 settled a Title VII lawsuit. The company agreed to count blacks' total time for seniority. Then, with the Supreme Court's *Teamsters* decision, the union that was a party to the consent decree argued that the law had been altered and the old seniority system was bona fide. Thus, the union sought to have the consent decree rescinded. Decide. Explain. See *U.S.* v. *Georgia Power Co.,* 634 F.2d 929 (5th Cir. 1981).

13.   Thornton worked as a manager at a Connecticut retail store. In accordance with his religious beliefs, Thornton notified his manager that he could no longer work on Sundays as required by company (Caldor, Inc.) policy. A Connecticut statute provided that "No person who states that a particular day of the week is observed as his Sabbath may be required by his employer to work on such day. An employee's refusal to work on his Sabbath shall not constitute grounds for his dismissal." Management offered Thornton the options of transferring to a Massachusetts store where Sunday work was not required or transferring to a lower-paying supervisory job in the Connecticut store. Thornton refused both, and he was transferred to a lower-paying clerical job in the Connecticut store. Thornton claimed a violation of the Connecticut statute. The store argued that the statute violated the Establishment Clause (see Chapter 5) of the First Amendment, which forbids establishing an official state religion and giving preference to one religion over another or over none at all. Ultimately the case reached the U.S. Supreme Court.

   a.   Decide. Explain.

   b.   Do the religious accommodation provisions of Title VII of the Civil Rights Act violate the Establishment Clause? See *Estate of Thornton* v. *Caldor, Inc.,* 472 U.S. 703 (1985).

14.   A heterosexual male employee complained that he was sexually harassed by his homosexual male coworkers who placed condoms in his food, exposed themselves to him, and asked him about his sex life. Is he a victim of sexual harassment? Explain. See *McWilliams* v. *Fairfax County Bd. of Supervisors,* 72 F.3d 1191 (4th Cir. 1996).

15.   Must your local country club admit qualified applicants regardless of race, religion, sex, and so on? Explain.

16. A new Texas airline, flying out of Dallas's Love Field, was in a precarious financial posture. A campaign was mounted to sell itself as "the airline personification of feminine youth and vitality." In commercials, its customers, who were primarily businessmen, were promised "in-flight love," including "love potions" (cocktails), "love bites" (toasted almonds), and a ticketing process (labeled a "quickie machine") that delivered "instant gratification." A male was denied a job with the airline because of his sex. He filed a Title VII action. The airline argued that attractive females were necessary to maintain its public image under the "love campaign," a marketing approach that the company claimed had been responsible for its improved financial condition. Decide. Explain. See *Wilson* v. *Southwest Airlines Co.,* 517 F. Supp. 292 (ND Tex. 1981).

17. Should obesity be treated as a *disability* as that term is defined in the Americans with Disabilities Act? Explain.

18. On balance, have the feminist movement and accompanying legal victories improved the quality of life for American women? For American men? Explain.

19. In the late 1980s and 1990s, one in four young black men was in prison, on parole, or on probation. Witnesses testifying before a Senate committee looking into the condition of black males in America called for government and business to cooperate in providing more jobs and better education for young black males. And they suggested that government should provide more assistance to black children in order to reduce problems later in their lives.

    a. Do you approve of those suggestions? Explain.

    b. What role would you assign to the business community in addressing the problems of young black males? Explain.

20. In general, women pay smaller life insurance premiums than men, but women's health insurance premiums substantially exceed those of men. Insurance companies point to differences in risks and subsequent claims patterns to explain the rate differentials. Should all states pass legislation requiring insurance companies to charge equal insurance fees for equal coverage regardless of sex? Explain.

21. Taylor, a black woman, worked for the Burlington County, New Jersey sheriff's office. She heard the sheriff, in speaking to another supervisor, refer to her as a "jungle bunny." She complained to her superiors. She suffered mental distress. She discussed the matter with the media. She was shunned at work. Was Taylor a victim of a hostile working environment? Explain. See *Taylor* v. *Metzger,* 706 A.2d 685 (N.J. 1998).

22. Linda Tarr-Whelan at the Center for Policy Alternatives says, "In this economy we have a diminished sense that the work women do with people is worth the same amount as the work men do with machines and dollars."

    a. Why are "women's jobs" "worth less" than men's?

    b. Should we insist on pay equity by requiring equal pay for work of comparable value? Explain. See Ellen Goodman, "Gender Pay Gap Is Real: $200 Billion," *Des Moines Register,* March 17, 1999, p. 9A.

23. The author of a *Harvard Law Review* article argues for discrimination claims based on appearance:

    The most physically unattractive members of our society face severe discrimination . . . The unattractive ("those individuals who depart so significantly from the most commonly held notions of beauty that they incur employment discrimination") are poorly treated in such diverse contexts as employment decisions, criminal sentencing, and apartment renting. Although appearance discrimination can have a devastating economic, psychological, and social impact on individuals, its victims have not yet found a legal recourse.

    Should we treat some aspects of appearance (for example, shortness, obesity, and unattractive facial characteristics) as disabilities, thus forbidding discrimination based on those characteristics? Explain. See Note, "Facial Discrimination: Extending Handicap Law to Employment Discrimination on the Basis of Physical Appearance," *Harvard Law Review* 100, no. 8 (June 1987), p. 2035.

24. The accompanying ad for foreign exchange dealers appeared in the December 11, 1987, issue (p. 22) of *The Nation,* an English-language newspaper published in Bangkok, Thailand.

    a. Analyze the legality of the ad based on American law.

An American Bank
invites applications for
**CORPORATE FOREIGN EXCHANGE
DEALERS**
for its Bangkok branch

Qualifications:

- Thai national
- Age 23–30 years, preferably male
- University graduate in Finance, Economics, or related field
- 1–2 years' dealing experience
- Good command of both spoken and written English

Salary is negotiable and attractive benefits will be provided for the successful candidates. The bank offers excellent opportunities for career advancement.

Send application stating details of qualifications and experience, present salary, and a recent photo to

**The Nation
Class 1191
GPO Box 594
Bangkok 10501**

---

b. Should American firms abroad adhere to American antidiscrimination policies even if those policies might put the American firms at a competitive disadvantage or offend the values and mores of the host country? Explain.

25. Blacks make up 12.8 percent of the U.S. population, and that share is growing slowly. Four percent of the population is Asian, while 11 percent is Hispanic, and both are growing rapidly. Asians and Hispanics combined outnumber blacks on college campuses. Asians have surpassed all other groups of Americans, including whites, in median income. Commentator Stephen Buckley:

> Today blacks are faced with a somber choice. We can go it alone, fighting against the swelling tide of Asian and Hispanic power, or we can forge coalitions with those groups—and with whites who are sympathetic to minority concerns. We can admit, at least tacitly, that blacks can't maintain or expand our power without their help.[108]

Comment.

26. As discussed in this chapter, American law forbids a variety of forms of discrimination. At the same time, we revere personal freedom. For example, we protect the First Amendment rights of neo-Nazi groups and the Ku Klux Klan, notwithstanding their racist goals. Do you favor legislation banning "hate speech"? Should we pass laws forbidding "group defamation"—malicious and degrading remarks directed to a racial or ethnic group? Explain.

27. John D. Archbold Memorial Hospital excluded all job applicants whose weight exceeded the maximum desirable weight (based on Metropolitan Life's actuarial survey) for large-framed men and women plus 30 percent of that weight. Sandra Murray claimed she was denied a job as a respiratory therapist because her height-to-weight ratio did not meet the guidelines. Murray did not claim to be morbidly obese.

a. Explain the plaintiff's argument.

b. Did the hospital violate the ADA? Explain. See *Murray* v. *John D. Archbold Memorial Hospital,* 50 F. Supp. 2d 1368 (M.D. Ga. 1999).

NOTES

1. Allana Sullivan, "Texaco to Unveil Plan for Diversity in the Workplace," *The Wall Street Journal,* December 18, 1996, p. B9.

2. Dottie Enrico, "Charges of Racism, Sexism Cut Deep," *USA Today,* November 12, 1996, pp. 1B, 2B.

3. Staff Reporter, "Texaco Agrees to Pay $3.1 Million to Women Who Were Underpaid," *The Wall Street Journal,* January 7, 1999, p. A15.

4. Enrico, "Charges of Racism . . . ," pp. 1B, 2B.

5. Alison Frankel, "Tale of the Tapes," *The American Lawyer,* March 1997, p. 64.

6. 347 U.S. 483 (1954).

7. 163 U.S. 537 (1896).

8. A portion of the material in this paragraph is drawn from William P. Murphy, Julius G. Getman, and James E. Jones, Jr., *Discrimination in Employment* 4th ed. (Washington: Bureau of National Affairs, 1979), pp. 1–4.

9. Barbara Rosewicz, "EEOC Flexes New Muscles in Mitsubishi Case, But It Lacks the Bulk to Push Business Around," *The Wall Street Journal,* April 29, 1996, p. A24.

10. Glenn Burkins, "EEOC Sues Fewer Companies but Gets More Money for Victims," *The Wall Street Journal,* June 17, 1997, p. A1.

11. *Wright* v. *Universal Service Corp.,* 119 S.Ct. 391 (1998).

12. *International Brotherhood of Teamsters* v. *United States,* 97 S.Ct. 1843 (1977).

13. *American Tobacco* v. *Patterson,* 456 U.S. 63 (1982).

14. *Firefighters Local Union No. 1784* v. *Stotts,* 467 U.S. 561 (1984).

15. See Malcolm H. Liggett, "Recent Supreme Court Affirmative Action Decisions and a Reexamination of the *Weber* Case," *Labor Law Journal* 38, no. 7 (July 1987), p. 415.

16. *Jiminez* v. *Mary Washington College,* 57 F.3d 369 (4th Cir. 1995), cert. den., 116 S.Ct. 380 (1995).

17. *Garcia* v. *Spun Steak Co.,* 998 F.2d 1480, reh'g den., 13 F.3d 296 (9th Cir. 1993), cert, den., 114 S.Ct. 2726 (1994).

18. Susan Hartmus Hiser, "Supreme Court's Standards for Sexual Harassment Cases Applied to Race Claims," *Michigan Employment Law Letter* 10, no. 2 (April 1999).

19. *Aman* v. *Cort Furniture Rental Corp.,* 85 F.3d 1074 (3d Cir. 1996).

20. See, e.g., "It's Still a Man's World When It Comes to Pay," *Waterloo–Cedar Falls Courier,* April 23, 1998, p. B6, and Associated Press, "Pay Gap Between Men and Women Narrows Slightly," *Waterloo–Cedar Falls Courier,* June 9, 1998, p. A1.

21. Lynn Hicks, "Women, Wages: 26 Cents Adds Up," November 3, 1998, p. 5S.

22. Diana Furchgott-Roth and Christine Stolba, "Women's Figures: An Illustrated Guide to the Economic Progress of Women in America," as reported in "Authors: Women's Pay Nearly Equal to Men's," *Waterloo–Cedar Falls Courier,* June 1, 1999, p. A5.

23. Marilyn Lihs, "Wage Gap: 'Where's My 26 Cents?'" *Des Moines Register,* April 3, 1998, p. 7A.

24. Joan Rigdon, "Three Decades after the Equal Pay Act, Women's Wages Remain Far from Parity," *The Wall Street Journal,* June 9, 1993, p. B1.

25. Associated Press, "Across Globe, Women Earn Less," *Des Moines Register,* July 30, 1996, p. 8S.

26. Sharon Bond, "For Businesswomen, the Climb Seems Even More Steep," *Waterloo–Cedar Falls Courier,* September 26, 1995, p. C7.

27. Maureen Minehan, "Worldwide Progress on Removing Gender Barriers," *HRMagazine,* May 1998, p. 168.

28. Emily Thornton, "Make Way for Women with Welding Guns," *Business Week,* April 19, 1999, p. 54.

29. Associated Press, "Singapore Minister Opposes Bias Law," *Des Moines Register,* February 14, 1999, p. 6AA.

30. Associated Press, "Study: American Women's Corporate Climb Continues," *Waterloo–Cedar Falls Courier,* November 12, 1999, p. B6.

31. Ibid.

32. Associated Press, "Study: Minority Women See Little Advancement," *Des Moines Register,* February 10, 1998, p. 7S.

33. Stacy Kravetz, "Women Launch Businesses for Freedom and Flexibility, Not Money," *The Wall Street Journal,* June 8, 1999, p. A1.

34. Ibid.

35. Ibid.

36. *Haynes* v. *W.C. Caye & Co.,* 52 F.3d 928 (11th Cir. 1995).

37. Mack A. Player, *Federal Law of Employment Discrimination in a Nutshell,* 2d ed. (St. Paul, MN: West Publishing, 1981), p. 202.

38. See, generally, *Diaz* v. *Pan American World Airways, Inc.,* 442 F.2d 385 (5th Cir.), cert. denied, 404 U.S. 950 (1971).

39. Adam Zagorin, "Sexism Will Be Served," *Time,* October 13, 1997, p. 65.

40. Sue Shellenbarger, "Pregnant Workers Clash with Employers over Job Inflexibility," *The Wall Street Journal,* February 10, 1999, p. B1.

41. Associated Press, "Study of Career Women Finds Children Add to Satisfied Lives," *Des Moines Register,* November 22, 1992, p. 5A.

42. "Sexual Harassment Charges; EEOC & FEPAs Combined: FY 1992–FY 1998" **[http://www.eeoc.gov/stats/harass.html]**.

43. Alan Otten, "Uncertainty Persists on Sexual Harassment," *The Wall Street Journal,* July 29, 1992, p. B1.

44. *Burlington Industries* v. *Ellerth,* 524 U.S. 742 (1998).

45. *Faragher* v. *Boca Raton,* 524 U.S. 775 (1998).

46. *Oncale* v. *Sundowner Offshore Services,* 523 U.S. 75 (1998).

47. *Gebser* v. *Lago Vista Independent School District,* 52 U.S. 274 (1998) addresses teacher/student sexual harassment. *Davis* v. *Monroe County Board of Education,* 119 S.Ct. 1661 (1999), addresses student-on-student sexual harassment.

48. *Claus* v. *Duquesne Light Co.,* 46 F.3d 1115 (1994), cert. den., 115 S.Ct. 1700 (1995).

49. 443 U.S. 193 (1979).

50. 480 U.S. 616 (1987).

51. 488 U.S. 469 (1989).

52. *Adarand Constructors, Inc.* v. *Pena,* 115 S.Ct. 2097 (1995).

53. Karen Abbott, "Reverse-Bias Case Officially Moot," *Denver Rocky Mountain News,* March 5, 1999, p. 6A.

54. *City of Dallas* v. *Dallas Fire Fighters Association,* 119 S.Ct. 1349 (1999).

55. This summary of affirmative action law is based, in part, on Littler and Mendelson, *The 1996 Employer,* p. 285.

56. David S. Cloud and Katherine Ackley, "As Nomination for Civil-Rights Chief Sputters, Lee Quietly Scores Victories on Affirmative Action," *The Wall Street Journal,* March 31, 1999, p. A24.

57. Mimi Hall, "Rules Eased for Minority Businesses," *USA Today,* June 25, 1998, p. 1A.

58. Jim Carlton, "Award in Reverse-Discrimination Case to Further Stir Academic-Hiring Debate," *The Wall Street Journal,* April 1, 1999, p. B11.

59. *Ritchey Produce Company* v. *State of Ohio, Department of Administrative Services,* 707 N.E.2d 871 (O. S.Ct. 1999).

60. Glenn Burkins, "The Checkoff," *The Wall Street Journal,* November 3, 1998, p. A1.

61. Dorothy J. Gaiter, "Blacks Mobilize Politically to Defeat Enemies of Affirmative Action," *The Wall Street Journal,* June 8, 1998, p. A24.

62. Paul Craig Roberts, "The Rise of the New Inequality," *The Wall Street Journal,* December 6, 1995, p. A18.

63. Ibid.

64. *Wessmann* v. *Gittens,* 160 F.3d 790 (1st Cir. 1998).

65. 78 F.3d 932 (5th Cir. 1996), cert. den. 116 S.Ct. 2581 (1996).

66. Associated Press, "Minority Admissions Rebound at University of California," *Waterloo–Cedar Falls Courier,* April 4, 1999, p. A4.

67. Martin Kasindorf, "UC Expected to Approve 4 Percent Plan," *USA Today,* March 18, 1999, p. 4A.

68. Del Jones, "Setting Diversity's Foundation in the Bottom Line," *USA Today,* October 15, 1996, p. 4B.

69. Thomas Petzinger, "Finding New Ways to Meet Challenges from Debt to Diversity," *The Wall Street Journal,* January 5, 1996, p. B1.

70. Timothy Schellhardt, "In a Factory Schedule, Where Does Religion Fit In?" *The Wall Street Journal,* March 4, 1999, p. B1.

71. Ibid.

72. 423 U.S. 63 (1977).

73. *Kentucky Commission on Human Rights* v. *Lesco Manufacturing and Design Co.,* 736 S.W.2d 361 (Ky. App. 1987).

74. *Brown* v. *Polk County,* 61 F.3d 650 (8th Cir. 1995), cert. den., *Polk County* v. *Brown,* 516 U.S. 1158 (1996).

75. Francis A. McMorris, "Ex-McGraw-Hill Salesman Is Awarded Over $1 Million in Back Pay, Damages," *The Wall Street Journal,* March 16, 1999, p. B4.

76. Ibid.

77. "Americans with Disabilities Act of 1990 (ADA) Charges FY 1992–FY 1998," **[http://www.eeoc.gov/stats/ada.html]**

78. Ibid.

79. Albert Hunt, "The Disabilities Act Is Creating a Better Society," *The Wall Street Journal,* March 11, 1999, p. A23.

80. Walter Olson, "Under the ADA, We May All Be Disabled," *The Wall Street Journal,* May 17, 1999, p. A27.

81. Ibid.

82. Francine Schwadel, "Sears Sets Model for Employing Disabled," *The Wall Street Journal,* March 4, 1996, p. B6.

83. Lisa J. Stansky, "Opening Doors," *ABA Journal* 82 (March 1996), p. 66.

84. John P. Savage, "The ADA Tax on Small Business," *The Wall Street Journal,* August 18, 1995, p. A9.

85. Olson, "Under the ADA," p. A27.

86. Ibid.

87. Ibid.

88. Associated Press, "Study: Workers with Disabilities at Higher Risk for On-the-Job Injuries," *Waterloo–Cedar Falls Courier,* December 24, 1997, p. B8.

89. Stephanie Armour, "Disabilities Act Abused?" *USA Today* September 25, 1998, p. 1B.

90. Albert Karr, "Comfort Zone: Most Workers Would not Be Uneasy with a Disabled Colleague," *The Wall Street Journal,* October 20, 1998, p. A1.

91. *Marks* v. *Loral Corp.,* 66 Cal. Rptr. 2d 46 (4th District 1997).

92. See "High Court's Ruling Means Companies Must Use Care When Trimming Workforce," *Human Resources Management—Ideas & Trends* 406 (May 21, 1997). p. 1.

93. *Hazen Paper Co.* v. *Biggins,* 507 U.S. 604 (1993).

94. Junda Woo, "Ex-Workers Hit Back with Age-Bias Suits," *The Wall Street Journal,* December 8, 1992, p. B1.

95. *O'Conner* v. *Consolidated Coin Caterers Corp.,* 116 S.Ct. 1307 (1996).

96. Marianne Lavelle, "The Age Boom: Aging in the Workplace: On the Edge of Age Discrimination," *New York Times,* March 9, 1997, section 6, p. 66.

97. Christopher Cameron, "Courts, Companies Killing Job Security," *USA Today,* November 6, 1997, p. 19A.

98. Thomas Fogarty, "Age Bias Cases Hard to Prove," *Des Moines Register,* April 6, 1999, p. 8S.

99. "Settlement of $7.5 Million Reached in Age-Bias Case," *The Wall Street Journal,* September 23, 1997, p. B4.

100. "Age Discrimination," 56 *U.S.L.W.* 2155 (1987), summarizing *Metz* v. *Transit Mix, Inc.*

101. *Metz* v. *Transit Mix, Inc.,* 828 F. 2d 1202, 1205 (7th Cir. 1987).

102. John Carlson, "Six Care Center Workers Are Fired," *Des Moines Register,* June 8, 1997, p. 1B.

103. Ibid.

104. Deborah Mathis, "America Grapples Over Rights for Gays," *Des Moines Register,* June 28, 1998, p. 1A.

105. *Kenneth Harper, Daniel Gomez, Abraham Del Carmen, and Brian Russell* v. *Blockbuster Entertainment Corporation,* 139 F.3d 1385 (11th Cir. 1998).

106. Garry G. Mathiason and Brian L. Johnsrud, "Introduction," *The 1998 National Employer,* p. 2.

107. *Kenneth Harper* v. *Blockbuster,* 139 F.3d 1385 (11th Cir. 1998).

108. Stephen Buckley, "Minorities Compete for Status," *Waterloo–Cedar Falls Courier,* August 8, 1993, p. E2.

Chapter 14

Employment Law III:
Labor–Management Relations

INTRODUCTION

AFL-CIO president John Sweeney recently remarked:

> America needs a raise, and one of the most effective solutions is a bigger and stronger labor movement, one capable of acting as a counterweight to the corporate forces now dominating our economy.[1]

A startling affirmation of Sweeney's advice arrived in 1999 when the politically conservative American Medical Association voted to support doctors who decide to build unions as a counterweight to giant insurance companies and health maintenance organizations (HMOs). Historically, doctors have been fiercely independent, but they have grown frustrated and angry. Dr. Randolph Smoak, Jr., chair of the AMA's Board of Trustees explained: "Our objective here is to give America's physicians the leverage they now lack to guarantee that patient care is not compromised or neglected for the sake of profits."[2] Of course, managed care organizations and insurers argue that they are simply struggling to keep medical costs under control.

Historically, only those doctors who were either salaried employees or doctors-in-training (residents, interns, and fellows) at public hospitals could gain the protections of state and federal labor law. Then in late 1999, the National Labor Relations Board added strength to the growing doctor-union movement by overruling longstanding precedent and concluding by a 3–2 vote that doctors-in-training at private hospitals are "employees" protected by federal labor law in the same manner as other union members.[3] Previously, the doctors-in-training had been considered students and were not able to call upon the protections of federal labor law such as the right to bargain collectively. Immediately after the NLRB ruling, the residents and interns at Boston Medical Center voted 177–1 to be represented by a federally protected union. Their major concern was with work time, which can exceed 100 hours per week. (In addition to labor law questions, doctors' unions also raise troublesome antitrust issues [see Chapter 11] regarding price fixing, refusals to deal, and the like). [For the pros and cons of doctors' unions, see **http://www.aans.org/library/bulletin/winter99/features/articles.html**]

Congress is considering federal law to allow collective bargaining by doctors in independent practice, and Texas passed such legislation in 1999. A small number of doctors and dentists who practice as employees have already joined bargaining units such as the Union of American Physicians and Dentists, a division of the American Federation of State, County and Municipal Employees. The AMA made it clear that strikes by doctors would not be sanctioned by that organization.

Negative attitudes toward unions—1997: 31 percent
1999: 23 percent

Source: Albert R. Karr, "The Checkoff," *The Wall Street Journal*, August 24, 1999, p. A1.

Union Membership.   Notwithstanding the interesting developments in the medical community, union membership and influence have fallen sharply. As recently as 1983, unions represented over 20 percent of our nonfarm labor force.[4] In 1999, that figure was 13.9, although the raw number of union members actually increased from 1998 by 265,000 to 16.5 million people.[5] A marked union resurgence, even in tough economic times, seems unlikely, but the service and government sectors of the economy are showing some signs of restlessness. Child-care workers; "Generation Xers" at Starbucks, Borders Books and the like; immigrants; women; graduate teaching assistants; bike messengers; and even strippers are among the groups that have engaged in union organizing. Unions, headed by the AFL-CIO, are evidencing some signs of the political activism that marked their earlier history. And student attention to union causes grew considerably in the late 1990s. Students on more than 25 campuses held sit-ins, teach-ins, and the like during the spring 1999 term to protest sweatshops, and from 1996 to 1999, 1,700 undergraduates trained in the AFL-CIO's intern program in labor and organizing.[6]

> Students on more than 25 campuses held sit-ins to protest sweatshops

Questions

1. *a.* Would you support doctors in their union organizing plans?
    b. Are working people so disadvantaged in contemporary America that you feel a *personal duty* to support a strengthened, renewed union movement?
    c. Would such a movement benefit working-class people? Explain.
2. Do we need labor unions to counterbalance the power of big corporations?
3. Harvard economics professor Richard Freeman commenting on America's "apartheid economy":

   From all points on the political map comes the message that something is wrong with the U.S. economy. Indeed, income inequality has jumped in the past two decades in almost every category: College graduates have gained in comparison with high school graduates, older workers in comparison with younger ones, professionals in comparison with laborers. The list goes on.

Is the declining power of labor unions a factor in the growing income inequality in America? Explain. See Richard Freeman, "Toward an Apartheid Economy," *Harvard Business Review,* September/October, 1996, p. 114. [For the federal Bureau of Labor Statistics, see **http://stats.bls.gov/**].

Part One—History

As the United States moved from an agrarian to an industrial society in the late 1880s, business competition was fierce.[7] Costs had to be cut. By paying workers as little as possible and making them work 14- to 18-hour days, employers could prosper. Farmers began moving to the city to be near their jobs and thus left their safety net of gardens, chickens, and cows. Similarly, immigrants streamed into the big cities, and competition for jobs became heated. Wages fell and deplorable working conditions were the norm.[8] Some of those immigrants brought with them ideas and experiences in labor conflict and class struggle that would soon contribute to dramatic struggles in the American workplace.

A Grim Picture

To say that working conditions for many people at this time were unpleasant or even dismal would be a vast understatement. The term *desperate* better describes the problem. Children were impressed into service as soon as they were big enough to do a job and then made to work 12- and 14-hour days.[9] In fact, small children were employed in coal mines for 10–12 hours each day, and at a rate of $1–3 per week, because they were small enough to fit in the confined spaces.[10] Textile companies would send men called *slavers* to New England and southern farm communities to gather young women to work in the mills.[11]

The following first-hand report from the early 20th century reveals the grim picture:

> When I moved from the North to the South in my search for work, I entered a mill village to work in a cotton mill as a spinner. There I worked 11 hours a day, five and a half days a week, for $7 a week. In a northern mill I had done the same kind of work for $22 a week, and less hours. I worked terribly hard . . .
>
> The sanitary conditions were ghastly. When I desired a drink of water, I had to dip my cup into a pail of water that had been brought into the mill from a spring in the fields. It tasted horrible to me. Often I saw lint from the cotton in the room floating on top of the lukewarm water. All of the men chewed tobacco, and most of the women used snuff. Little imagination is needed to judge the condition of the water which I had to drink, for working in that close, hot spinning room made me thirsty. Toilet facilities were provided three stories down in the basement of the mill in a room without any ventilation. Nowhere was there any running water . . .
>
> Everything in the village is company owned. The houses look like barns on stilts, and appear to have been thrown together. When I would go inside one of them, I could see outside through the cracks in the walls. The workers do all of their trading at the company store and bank, and use the company school and library for they have no means of leaving the village . . .[12]
>
> [For a history of women in the labor movement, see **http://www.thehistorynet.com/ WomensHistory/articles/19967_cover.html**]

Compare these working-class conditions with those of John D. Rockefeller, the great tycoon of the same era. Although Rockefeller was notoriously frugal, his estate at Pocantico Hills contained

> more than 75 buildings . . . Within his estate were 75 miles of private roads on which he could take his afternoon drive; a private golf links on which he could play his morning game; and anywhere from 1,000 to 1,500 employees, depending on the season.
>   . . . Rockefeller also owned an estate at Lakewood, which he occupied in the spring; an estate at Ormond Beach in Florida for his winter use; a townhouse . . . in New York; an estate at Forest Hill, Cleveland, which he did not visit; and a house on Euclid Avenue in Cleveland, likewise unused by him.[13]

These conditions enable us to better understand the sense of injustice felt by many workers and the belief of many that a redistribution of wealth might provide the only solution to the class conflict.

ORGANIZING LABOR

The Knights of Labor, the first major labor organization in the United States, had a large following during the 1870s and 1880s.[14] The order admitted any workers to its ranks, regardless of occupation, gender, or nationality; in fact, the only people excluded from the group were gamblers, bankers, stockbrokers, and liquor dealers.[15] The Knights of Labor dedicated itself to principles of social reform including the protection of wage and hour laws, improved health care systems, and mandatory education.[16] However, the goals of the Knights of Labor were perhaps too broad and far-reaching to bring workers any relief from their immediate problems. Great philosophical divisions within the Knights of Labor brought about its rapid decline.[17]

Skilled Workers

Samuel Gompers, who built and developed the American Federation of Labor (AFL), had more practical, attainable goals in mind for his organization. Gompers, a worker in the cigar industry, saw the need to organize workers along craft lines (e.g., plumbers, electricians, and machinists) so that each craft group could seek higher wages and better working conditions for its own workers, all of whom had the same type of skills and, presumably, shared the same occupational goals.[18] This approach, a national association of local unions directed to workers' pragmatic needs rather than the more politically motivated activities of the Knights of Labor, proved to be a successful formula for union organization.

Laborers

The Congress of Industrial Organizations (CIO) was organized in response to the needs of ordinary laborers not working in the skilled trades to which the AFL was devoted. The CIO was organized in 1935 and served assembly-line workers and others who often performed repetitive, physically demanding tasks. The AFL and CIO were fierce competitors, but after years of bitter conflict, the organizations agreed to stop raiding one another for members and, in 1955, the two groups united forces. They function together today as the AFL–CIO. [For the AFL-CIO home page, see **http://www.aflcio.org**]

UNIONS AND THE DEVELOPING LAW

Through the late 19th and early 20th centuries, employers had been very successful in discouraging union organizing. Three devices used by employers to inhibit union formations were "yellow dog" contracts, blacklists, and the American Plan. A *yellow dog contract* was an employment agreement under which the employee was bound by the contract's terms not to become a member of a union. *Blacklists* were simply lists of union organizers or sometimes even participants in labor activities circulated among all the companies in an industry or geographic locale; employers were told not to hire the people named on the lists because they were union instigators.[19] The third strategy, the American Plan, associated the union movement with foreign subversives and involved the use of company unions, organizations ostensibly representing employees but controlled and dominated by the employers themselves.[20]

The most effective legal means to halt a union in its incipiency was a court injunction. If a group of workers began picketing a factory, for example, an employer could easily obtain from a state or federal court an order (injunction) forbidding the workers to continue such activities because such efforts were considered either a civil or criminal conspiracy.

Responding to mounting public pressure, Congress passed the Norris–LaGuardia Act in 1932. Designed primarily to prevent antitrust problems, the act withdrew from the federal courts the right to issue injunctions against labor activities and made clear that the terminology "restraint of trade," which was the heart of the 1890 Sherman Antitrust Act, was not meant to include the organization or activities of labor. The Norris–LaGuardia Act also specifically outlawed the use of yellow dog contracts. Even Norris–LaGuardia was not fully effective, however, because employers were still able to go into state courts to obtain injunctive relief.[21]

Labor Protection

From 1932 to 1935, labor tensions continued to mount. The nation was still caught in the Great Depression. Believing that one element essential to economic recovery was stability in the workforce, Congress addressed the labor question with the Wagner Act of 1935. This legislation gave workers for the first time the unequivocal right to organize and engage in concerted activities for their mutual aid and benefit. To protect this right, Congress identified and made illegal a number of unfair labor practices. These unfair labor practices were all activities that Congress feared employers might use to thwart workers' attempts to unionize and to undermine the economic power that would come from workers' new-found

---

FIGURE 14.1   United Steelworkers: Membership

- **Current:** Over 700,000
- **Peak:** 1.2 million, in 1981
- **Recent low:** 540,000, in 1983
- **Industries it represents:** Steel, rubber, plastic, chemicals, nickel, copper and aluminum refining, health care. Members in the manufacturing sector make products ranging from Louisville Slugger baseball bats to M-1 tanks.
- **Union wage:** Ranges from the minimum wage at some companies where the union has yet to negotiate a contract to $15 to $16 an hour.

Source: *Los Angeles Times,* July 28, 1995, p. D1.

rights.[22] Through the Wagner Act, Congress also established the National Labor Relations Board, an administrative agency charged with the responsibility of overseeing and ensuring fair union representation elections and investigating, prosecuting, and trying employers accused of unfair labor practices. [For the NLRB home page, see **http://www.nlrb.gov**]

Management Protection

Unions grew rapidly with the passage of the Wagner Act and, by 1947, Congress decided labor no longer needed such a protective watchdog.[23] In fact, Congress thought management might need a little help in coping with ever-growing labor organizations.[24] Thus, Congress decided to neutralize its position vis-à-vis labor organizations by imposing some responsibilities on these organizations. Congress did so by enacting the Taft-Hartley Act, a series of amendments to the Wagner Act that identified as unfair labor practices certain activities unions used to exercise economic leverage over employers as part of the collective bargaining process. The Taft-Hartley Act also added a provision to the existing labor legislation that ensured employers' right to speak out in opposition to union organizing—in effect, protecting their First Amendment right to freedom of speech. Thus, the Taft-Hartley Act signaled a move by the government away from unconditional support for labor toward a balance of rights between labor and management.[25]

Corrupt Union Leaders

Congressional hearings in the 1950s focused attention on union leaders who were abusing their power. Once in power, some union leaders had prevented others from challenging that power by not holding meetings, not scheduling elections, and using union funds to promote their own election campaigns. Stories came to light accusing some union officials of accepting collective bargaining agreements with terms that were against the interest of their constituencies, in exchange for bribes paid to them by corporate management. These agreements were aptly called *sweetheart deals*. Evidence indicated certain union officials had looted their unions' treasuries.[26]

In response to the growing evidence that union leaders were benefiting at the expense of the membership, Congress in 1959 enacted the Labor–Management Reporting and Disclosure Act (LMRDA), also known as the Landrum–Griffin Act. This act contains provisions requiring unions to keep records of their funds, including statements of their assets, liabilities, salaries paid, and all other expenditures. It also prohibits unions from loaning money except under specified circumstances and in conformity with certain procedural rules. These financial statements and transactions must be reported annually to the government.

Members' Rights

The Landrum–Griffin Act also contains a set of provisions often referred to as the "Bill of Rights" for the individual union members. These provisions are designed to protect union members by requiring that union meetings be held, that members be permitted to speak and vote at these meetings, that every employee covered by a collective bargaining agreement have the right to see a copy of that agreement, and that a union member be informed of the reasons and given a chance for a hearing if the union wishes to suspend or take disciplinary action against that member, unless he or she is being suspended for nonpayment of dues.[27] Although these provisions had the potential for eliminating internal union problems, court decisions have done much to emasculate the protections provided in Landrum–Griffin.

The law has also regulated the manner in which unions represent employees in the collective bargaining process. Because a union serves as employees' exclusive bargaining representative, the courts have devised a *duty of fair representation*.[28] To fulfill this duty, a union must represent employees, both in negotiating and enforcing the collective bargaining agreement, "without hostility or discrimination . . . [and] . . . with complete good faith and honesty [so as to] avoid arbitrary conduct."[29]

Part Two—Labor Legislation Today

THE STATUTORY SCHEME OF LABOR LAW AND ITS GOALS

Today, labor–management relations are governed by the National Labor Relations Act (NLRA), as enforced by the NLRB.[30] This act includes within it the Wagner Act, the Taft–Hartley Act, and portions of the Landrum–Griffin Act. The remaining provisions of the Landrum–Griffin Act make up the Labor–Management Reporting and Disclosure Act (mentioned earlier) and the Bill of Rights of Members of Labor Organizations. [For a glossary (dictionary) of labor law terms, see **http://www.opm.gov/cplmr/html/glossary/index.htm**]

Given its constitutional authority to regulate interstate commerce, the congressional basis for labor legislation is the elimination of obstructions to the free flow of commerce caused by labor conflicts. Congress contends that labor conflict is due, in large part, to a lack of bargaining power on the part of individual employees and, thus, sets out to correct the problem by protecting union and concerted activity by employees and by regulating collective bargaining between labor organizations and management. Keep these ideas in mind as you examine the choices made by Congress in regulating labor–management relations and the decisions made by the NLRB and the courts in interpreting and applying these statutory mandates.[31] [For a vast database of federal labor law statutes, regulations, state codes, and so on, see **http://www.law.cornell.edu/topics/labor.html**]

Right to Organize

First, the NLRA gives employees the right to engage in concerted activity, known for the most part as strikes and collective bargaining. Section 7 of the NLRA states:

> Employees shall have the right to self-organization, to form, join or assist labor organizations, to bargain collectively through representatives of their own choosing, and to engage in other concerted activities for the purpose of collective bargaining or other mutual aid or protection, and shall also have the right to refrain from any and all of such activities except to the extent that such right may be affected by an agreement requiring membership in a labor organization as a condition of employment.

Unfair Labor Practices by Management

Second, as previously mentioned, the act describes and outlaws certain activities by employers that would hamper or discourage employees from exercising the rights granted to them in Section 7. Thus, Section 8(a) of the act makes it an unfair labor practice for an employer to

1. Interfere with, restrain, or coerce employees in the exercise of the rights given to them by Section 7.
2. Dominate, interfere, or assist with the formation of any labor organization, including contributing financial support to it.
3. Encourage or discourage membership in any labor organization by discrimination in regard to hiring, tenure of employment, promotion, salary, or any other term of employment.
4. Discharge or take any other action against an employee because he or she has filed charges or given testimony under the act.
5. Refuse to bargain collectively with a duly certified representative of the employees.

These five provisions are designed to allow employees to organize in an atmosphere free from intimidation by the employer. In addition, if employees have chosen a union as their exclusive collective bargaining representative, Section 8(a) regulates the bargaining between the employer and the union. The provisions also ensure that the employer will not be able to interfere with union activities by either seizing control of the union or rendering it impotent by refusing to bargain collectively.

Unfair Labor Practices by Unions

Section 8(b) lists activities constituting unfair labor practices by a labor organization. Some of these provisions mirror some of the activities prohibited to employers. Moreover, at least since the enactment of the Taft-Hartley Act, the law is not sympathetic to labor organizations that try to use certain coercive tactics, threats of the loss of livelihood, or any other strong-arm methods. Finally, Section 8(b) also regulates the union's collective bargaining practices, including economic action. Thus, a labor organization is not permitted to:

1. Restrain or coerce any employee in the exercise of his or her rights as granted by Section 7.
2. Cause or attempt to cause an employer to discriminate against an employee who has chosen not to join a particular labor organization or has been denied membership in such an organization.
3. Refuse to bargain collectively with an employer on behalf of the bargaining unit it is certified to represent.
4. Induce or attempt to induce an employer to engage in secondary boycott activities.
5. Require employees to become union members and then charge them excessive or discriminatory dues.
6. Try to make an employer compensate workers for services not performed.
7. Picket or threaten to picket an employer in an attempt to force the employer to recognize or bargain with a labor organization that is not the duly certified representative of a bargaining unit.

Representation Matters.   Section 9 of the act also sets forth the procedures by which employees may choose, usually through a secret ballot election, whether to be represented by a particular union or no union at all.

Workers at the Asbestos, Lead and Hazardous Waste Laborers Local 78 in New York put a 30-foot inflatable rat on a flatbed truck and stuck its nose in the third-story windows of CBS Television's Manhattan office to protest against the network's use of nonunion labor on a construction project. Police deflated and confiscated the rat. CBS had no comment.

Source: Stacy Kravetz "Ratted Out," *The Wall Street Journal,* May 11, 1999, p. A1.

NATIONAL LABOR RELATIONS BOARD (NLRB)

The NLRB is an administrative agency instrumental in regulating labor–management relations. Its primary tasks are designating appropriate bargaining units of workers (deciding which workers have a sufficient community of interest so that their needs can best be acknowledged and so that collective bargaining is efficient for the employer and the union); conducting elections for union representation within the chosen bargaining unit; certifying the results of such elections; and investigating, prosecuting, and adjudicating charges of unfair labor practices.[32]

Although the congressional mandate by which the NLRB was formed gives the agency jurisdiction theoretically to the full extent of the interstate commerce powers vested in Congress, the agency has neither the funding nor the staff to administer its duties to all of American industry. Moreover, the act and the NLRB recognize that certain categories of employees should be excluded from the act, either because they play no role in commerce or because they are more closely aligned with management.

These restrictions on jurisdiction take two basic forms. (1) Employers: The NLRB itself requires the portion of an employer's business involved in interstate commerce to exceed certain dollar amounts, which differ depending on the nature of the industry. Labor disputes involving firms falling beneath the minimum are assumed not to significantly affect commerce. (2) Employees: Entire groups of employees are excluded from coverage. For example, government employees, railroad and airline workers covered by the Railway Labor Act, agricultural workers, domestic workers, independent contractors, and supervisors and other managerial employees are not protected by the board.[33]

Part Three—Elections

CHOOSING A BARGAINING REPRESENTATIVE

Representation elections are the process by which the NLRB achieves the first of the two statutory goals under the act—employee freedom of choice. However, as we shall see, in doing so there is sometimes a conflict between that goal and the other statutory goal—stable collective bargaining. The NLRB has devised certain rules to resolve such conflicts. [For the AFL-CIO view of why workers should join unions, see **http://www.aflcio.org/front/joinunions.htm**]

Election Petition

A union, employee, or employer initiates the formal organizing process by filing an election petition with the NLRB. The petition is sent to the employer, thus providing notice of union activity. Also, the employer must post notices supplied by the NLRB so that employees are aware of the petition. The NLRB then assumes its authority to closely oversee the conduct of employer and union. Of course at that point, the employer is free to simply recognize its employees' interest in joining a particular union and to engage in bargaining with that union, normally called *voluntary recognition.* However, this process is uncommon. Failing voluntary recognition, the process proceeds through the NLRB. To conserve its resources for serious matters, the NLRB will accept only those petitions supported by a substantial showing of interest, which has been interpreted to mean the signatures of at least 30 percent of the employees in the bargaining unit the union seeks to represent. (In practice today, most unions will not proceed toward an election without 50 to 65 percent of the employees' signatures.) Those signatures accompany the petition, or they may appear on *authorization cards,* which unions may provide to workers to affirm their interest in an election or in union representation.

Procedure

The NLRB ordinarily will first attempt to settle certain issues such as whether a union contract already covers the employees or whether the election should be delayed either by agreement or by order of the board after a hearing. In determining the timing of the election, the two statutory goals of employee free choice and stable collective bargaining may conflict. For example, if the employees are already covered by a collective bargaining agreement, should they be able to choose again during the term of the agreement? Surely, to do so would provide for employee free choice. But what of stable collective bargaining? Should not the collective bargaining agreement be recognized? Similarly, if the employees have rejected a union in an election, can they be prohibited from voting again in the name of stable collective bargaining? If so, what of their right to freedom of choice? Alternatively, what if the employees choose to unionize in an election, but reconsider before a collective bargaining agreement is reached? Can they have another election?

To resolve these conflicts the NLRB has devised bars to an election. In the first instance set forth above, the board will prohibit an election during the term of a collective bargaining agreement, but only for a period not to exceed three years. This is known as the contract bar rule. An election year or certification year bar prohibits an election for 12 months following a prior election so that the employer can enjoy stable collective bargaining without negating the employees' freedom of choice.

However, the crucial issue to be addressed at this point is normally whether the proposed bargaining unit (the designated employee group, for example, all hourly workers, all welders, or all craftspersons) is appropriate for the election.

Appropriate Bargaining Unit

The key consideration in establishing an appropriate employee bargaining unit is the community of interest among the employees. The NLRB searches for an appropriate bargaining unit because collective bargaining will not be stable and efficient (the second statutory goal) if it involves employees with diverse interests. Therefore, the bargaining unit may range from a portion of a plant to multiple employers in multiple plants. Plants may have more than one appropriate bargaining unit, depending on the composition of the workforce. The NLRB makes the decision regarding the appropriate bargaining unit on the basis of such considerations as physical location of the plants, physical contact among employees, similarity of wages, benefits, working conditions, differences in skill requirements among job categories, and common supervision.

Certain classes of employees, such as supervisors, are excluded from the bargaining unit. Obviously, supervisors are excluded because they act on behalf of the employer and, through their power to direct and assign work and to discipline and discharge employees, exert control over their subordinates who are or may be in the bargaining unit. However, the treatment of other types of employees may not be so clear.

Some employees determine and implement employer policies without assigning work or disciplining other employees. For example, fiscal officers allocate financial resources on behalf of employers. Should these people be permitted to join other employees in an appropriate bargaining unit? [See *NLRB* v. *Bell Aerospace Co.,* 416 U.S. 267 (1974).]

The case that follows examines the practice of "salting" and the question of whether a union organizer who goes to work for a company for the purpose of organizing the company from the inside is an "employee" under the NLRA and thus protected by law.

NATIONAL LABOR RELATIONS BOARD v. TOWN & COUNTRY ELECTRIC, INC. 516 U.S. 85 (1995)

Justice Breyer

Town & Country Electric, Inc., a nonunion electrical contractor, wanted to hire several licensed Minnesota electricians for construction work in Minnesota. Town & Country . . . advertised for job applicants, but it refused to interview 10 of 11 union applicants (including two professional union staff) who responded to the advertisement. Its employment agency hired the one union applicant whom Town & Country interviewed, but he was dismissed after only a few days on the job.

The members of the union (the International Brotherhood of Electrical Workers, Locals 292 and 343) filed a complaint with the National Labor Relations Board claiming that Town & Country and the employment agency had refused to interview (or retain) them because of their union membership. An administrative law judge ruled in favor of the union members, and the Board affirmed that ruling.

In the course of its decision, the Board determined that all 11 job applicants (including the two union officials and the one member briefly hired) were "employees" as the Act defines that word. The Board recognized that under well-established law, it made no difference that the 10 members who were simply applicants were never hired. . . . Neither, in the Board's view, did it matter (with respect to the meaning of the word "employee") that the union members intended to try to organize the company if they secured the advertised jobs, nor that the union would pay them while they set about their organizing. The Board then rejected the company's fact-based

explanations for its refusals to interview or to retain these 11 "employees," and held that the company had committed "unfair labor practices" by discriminating on the basis of union membership.

The United States Court of Appeals for the Eighth Circuit reversed the Board. It held that the Board had incorrectly interpreted the statutory word "employee." In the court's view, that key word does not cover (and therefore the Act does not protect from antiunion discrimination) those who work for a company while a union simultaneously pays them to organize that company. For this . . . reason, the court refused to enforce the Board's order.

*   *   *   *   *

We granted certiorari to decide only that part of the controversy that focuses upon the meaning of the word "employee," a key term in the statute, since these rights belong only to those workers who qualify as "employees" as that term is defined in the Act. . . .

We must specifically decide whether the Board may lawfully interpret [the act] to include company workers who are also paid union organizers . . .

Several strong general arguments favor the Board's position. For one thing, the Board's decision is consistent with the broad language of the Act itself—language that is broad enough to include those company workers whom a union also pays for organizing. The ordinary dictionary definition of "employee" includes any "person who works for another in return for financial or other compensation. . . ." The phrasing of the Act seems to reiterate the breadth of the ordinary dictionary definition, for it says, "[t]he term 'employee' shall include any employee." [§ 2(3)]

For another thing, the Board's broad, literal interpretation of the word "employee" is consistent with several of the Act's purposes, such as protecting "the right of employees to organize for mutual aid without employer interference," and "encouraging and protecting the collective bargaining process."

Finally, at least one other provision of the 1947 Labor Management Relations Act seems specifically to contemplate the possibility that a company's employee might also work for a union. This provision forbids an employer (say, the company) from making payments to a person employed by a union, but simultaneously exempts from that ban wages paid by the company to "any . . . employee of a labor organization, who is also an employee" of the company. [§ 302(c)(1)] If Town & Country is right, there would not seem to be many (or any) human beings to which this last phrase could apply.

* * * * *

Town & Country goes on to argue that application of common law agency principles requires an interpretation of "employee" that excludes paid union organizers . . . It argues that, when the paid union organizer serves the union—at least at certain times in certain ways—the organizer is acting adversely to the company. Indeed, it says, the organizer may stand ready to desert the company upon request by the union, in which case, the union, not the company, would have "the right . . . to control the conduct of the servant." Thus, it concludes, the worker must be the servant (i.e., the "employee") of the union alone . . .

* * * * *

Town & Country's common law argument fails, quite simply, because, in our view, the Board correctly found that it lacks sufficient support in common law . . . The Board . . . concluded that service to the union for pay does not "involve abandonment of . . . service" to the company.

And that conclusion seems correct. Common sense suggests that as a worker goes about his ordinary tasks during a working day, say, wiring sockets or laying cable, he or she is subject to the control of the company employer, whether or not the union also pays the worker.

The company, the worker, the union, all would expect that to be so. And, that being so, that union and company interests or control might sometimes differ should make no difference. . . . Moreover, union organizers may limit their organizing to nonwork hours. If so, union organizing, when done for pay but during nonwork hours, would seem equivalent to simple moonlighting, a practice wholly consistent with a company's control over its workers as to their assigned duties.

Town & Country's "abandonment" argument is yet weaker insofar as the activity that constitutes an "abandonment," i.e., ordinary union organizing activity, is itself specifically protected by the Act. This is true even if a company perceives those protected activities as disloyal. After all, the employer has no legal right to require that, as part of his or her service to the company, a worker refrain from engaging in protected activity.

Neither are we convinced by the practical considerations that Town & Country adds to its agency law argument. The company refers to a union resolution permitting members to work for nonunion firms, which, the company says, reflects a union effort to "salt" nonunion companies with union members seeking to organize them . . . It argues that "salts" might try to harm the company, perhaps quitting when the company needs them, perhaps disparaging the company to others, perhaps even sabotaging the firm or its products. Therefore, the company concludes, Congress could not have meant paid union organizers to have been included as "employees" under the Act.

This practical argument suffers from several serious problems. For one thing, nothing in this record suggests that such acts of disloyalty were present, in kind or degree, to the point where the company might lose control over the worker's normal workplace tasks. Certainly the union's resolution contains nothing that suggests, requires, encourages, or condones impermissible or unlawful activity. For another thing, the argument proves too much. If a paid union organizer might quit, leaving a company employer in the lurch, so too might an unpaid organizer, or a worker who has found a better job, or one whose family wants to move elsewhere. And if an overly zealous union organizer might hurt the company through unlawful acts, so might another unpaid zealot (who may know less about the law), or a dissatisfied worker (who may lack an outlet for his grievances). This does not mean they are not "employees."

Further, the law offers alternative remedies for Town & Country's concerns, short of excluding paid or unpaid union organizers from all protection under the Act. For example, a company disturbed by legal but undesirable activity, such as quitting without notice, can offer its employees fixed-term contracts, rather than hiring them "at will" as in the case before us; or it can negotiate with its workers for a notice period. A company faced with unlawful (or possibly unlawful) activity can discipline or dismiss the worker, file a complaint with the Board, or notify law enforcement authorities . . .

. . . We hold only that the Board's construction of the word "employee" is lawful; that term does not exclude paid union organizers.

Vacated and remanded.

Questions

1. a. Explain the Court's reasoning in supporting the NLRB's determination that the 11 job applicants were "employees."
   b. Explain Town & Country's agency law argument.
2. The Court noted that Town & Country could address its concerns in other ways. What remedies, in the Court's view, were available to Town & Country to protect its interests?
3. What does the Court mean by the term *salt?*

The Election for Union Representative

After the parties have agreed to conduct an election, or alternatively, the NLRB has directed that an election be conducted following a hearing, the board will require that the employer post notices and conduct the election. The union representative may be selected only by a majority of the votes cast by the employees. The NLRB oversees the election to ensure the process is carried on under "laboratory conditions."[34] In other words, elections must be held under circumstances that, to the extent possible, are free from undue or unfair influence by either the employer or by unions vying for the right to represent the bargaining unit.

The NLRB has the power to review the conduct of the employer or the union during the period between the filing of the election petition and the election itself. The board will also, if called upon, monitor the polling place itself. If the NLRB determines that objectionable conduct has taken place, it will invalidate the results of the election and another will be held.

For both employers and employees, the circulation of racist propaganda is grounds for setting aside an election. Historically, the NLRB took a similarly firm stance regarding all manner of propaganda and misrepresentation. Frequently, the board has set aside elections tainted by trickery such as falsehoods, allegations, misstatements, and the like. However, its position in this area has changed; its current position is that misrepresentation alone will not constitute grounds for overturning an election. The burden is on the parties to correct misrepresentations and sort out the truth via the marketplace of ideas. The board would intervene only if the deceptive manner of the misrepresentation (e.g., a forged document) made it impossible for the parties themselves to discern the truth. Some courts have endorsed the NLRB view; others have not.

Protection of Free Speech

Employers also have the right to speak out against unions in the form of ads, speeches, and the like. Section 8(c) of the Taft-Hartley Act is designed to ensure employers' and labor organizations' traditional First Amendment rights so long as they do not overstep certain bounds:

> The expressing of any views, argument, or opinion, or the dissemination thereof, whether in written, printed, graphic, or visual form, shall not constitute or be evidence of an unfair labor practice . . . if such expression contains no threat of reprisal or force or promise of benefit.

Threats of Reprisal or Force

Employers cannot lawfully discriminate in employment in order to encourage or discourage union membership. Clearly, an employer who tells employees that, for example, they will all be discharged if they engage in union activity, has interfered with their rights. Similarly, an employer who interrogates employees about their activities or spies on them while they attend union meetings has engaged in unlawful interference. However, problems often arise in determining whether antiunion arguments put forth by an employer are legitimate or whether they contain veiled threats. Suppose, for instance, that a company owner warns her employees that if she has to pay higher wages, she will be forced to go out of business and the employees will all lose their jobs. Such statements of economic forecast by employers are more likely to be lawful if based on objective facts not under management's control.

Promise of Benefit

Although threats of force or reprisal are clearly unlawful in union campaigns, the rationale behind the prohibition against promises of benefit is not as intuitively obvious. In the case of *NLRB* v. *Exchange Parts Co.,* 375 U.S. 409 (1964), Exchange Parts sent its employees a letter shortly before a representation election that spoke of "the empty promises of the union" and "the fact that it is the company that puts things in your envelope." After mentioning a number of benefits, the letter said: "The Union can't put any of those things in your envelope—only the company can do that." Further on, the letter stated, "It didn't take a Union to get any of those things and . . . it won't take a Union to get additional improvements in the future." Accompanying the letter was a detailed statement of the benefits granted by the company since 1949 and an estimate of the monetary value of such benefits to the employees.

In addition, the letter outlined further benefits, such as additional vacation days and overtime pay, that the company had recently decided to institute. In the representation election two weeks later, the union lost. The Court of Appeals did not think the employer's actions constituted an unfair labor practice. The Supreme Court disagreed, reversing the decision. Justice Harlan stated:

> We think the Court of Appeals was mistaken in concluding that the conferral of employee benefits while a representation election is pending, for the purpose of inducing employees to vote against the union, does not "interfere with" the protected right to organize.
>
> The broad purpose of § 8(a)(1) is to establish "the right of employees to organize for mutual aid without employer interference." We have no doubt that it prohibits not only intrusive threats and promises but also conduct immediately favorable to employees which is undertaken with the

express purpose of impinging upon their freedom of choice for or against unionization and is reasonably calculated to have that effect. In *Medo Photo Supply Corp.* v. *NLRB,* this Court said: "The action of employees with respect to the choice of their bargaining agents may be induced by favors bestowed by the employer as well as by his threats or domination" . . . The danger inherent in well-timed increases in benefits is the suggestion of a *fist inside the velvet glove* [emphasis added]. Employees are not likely to miss the inference that the source of benefits now conferred is also the source from which future benefits must flow and which may dry up if it is not obliged.

Union Persuasion

Employers, of course, are not the only parties affected by Section 8(c). Unions are also restricted in the type of preelection persuasion they employ. In cases involving promises of benefits made by the union, the board has been more reluctant to set aside elections than it

> "the biggest party in the history of Texas"

has when such promises have been made by management. The board's reasoning is that employees realize that union preelection promises are merely expressions of a union platform, so to speak. Employees recognize that these are benefits for which the union intends to fight. Employers, on the other hand, really do hold within their power the ability to confer or withdraw benefits. The case that follows examines a union promise for "the biggest party in the history of Texas," along with alleged misrepresentations and other conduct that arguably tainted a union representation election.

TRENCOR, INC. v. NATIONAL LABOR RELATIONS BOARD
110 F. 3d 268 (5th Cir. 1997)

Circuit Judge Edith H. Jones

I. Background

On August 3, 1995, Trencor's [a heavy construction equipment manufacturer] maintenance and production employees voted on whether the Union would serve as their exclusive collective-bargaining representative. Of 99 eligible voters, 70 voted for representation and 26 voted against. Trencor filed objections to the election, but the NLRB Regional Director issued a report recommending that Trencor's objections be overruled and that the Union be certified. The Board adopted the Regional Director's recommendations and certified the Union as the exclusive collective bargaining agent for the employees.

After certification, Trencor refused to bargain with the Union. In November 1995, the Union filed an unfair labor practice charge and the Regional Director subsequently issued an unfair labor practice complaint. Trencor's answer admitted its refusal to bargain, but alleged that Union misconduct tainted the election and that the Union's certification was invalid.

On appeal, Trencor concedes that it has refused to bargain, but challenges the Board decision to certify the Union. Trencor's challenge centers on three alleged improprieties committed by the Union on the eve of the election.

* * * * *

III. Alleged Union Improprieties

A. Promise of the "Biggest Party in Texas"

The day before the election, Union agent Bill Fears told employees that if the Union won the election, it would host "the biggest party in the history of Texas," and that the Union would buy "all the food and beer."

* * * * *

The Board argues on appeal that a promise to hold a party is qualitatively different from a promise to give a monetary benefit [and] asserts that offering a victory party is not necessarily "inimical to an atmosphere in which free choice can be made." Promising a party which only lasts one night, the Board alleges, would not "substantially influence employees in a decision having a major effect on their working lives."

The Board's reasoning on appeal might be persuasive if it comported with the facts administratively found. But the Regional Director's recommendations, adopted in full by the Board, admitted that the Union's party invitation "may have served as a possible inducement to get employees to vote for the Union."

* * * * *

Furthermore, Trencor contends that the monetary/nonmonetary distinction drawn by the Board is not meaningful, since the benefits promised by the Union have some monetary value.

* * * * *

There is no indication in the record that the offered "biggest party in the history of Texas" had anything to do with laying the "groundwork for a productive employee-union relationship" or, indeed, was anything more than an inducement to vote for the Union.

* * * * *

Trencor has presented prima facie evidence that the Union conditioned "the receipt of benefits on favorable election results," which "is impermissible conduct for parties engaged in the election." We must set aside the order of the Board and remand for an evidentiary hearing and analysis.

B. Union "Guarantees"

On August 2, 1995, the day before the election was to be held, the Union distributed flyers that listed numerous "guarantees" by the Union. The purported guarantees included several matters related to Union membership, such as Union dues payments, the right of employees to resign from the Union, the right of employees to file unfair labor practice charges against the Union, and a pledge to seek employee approval of any negotiated collective bargaining agreement. The Union also "guaranteed" that upon its victory, employees' wages, benefits and working [conditions] would not suffer, and that the Union had negotiated improved terms for employees in every prior first contract negotiation. . . .

Trencor alleges that by making the guarantees, the Union offered employees "a financial benefit to which they would otherwise not be entitled" in the critical period prior to the election, thereby violating Board rules governing elections.

The Board decision to overrule this objection was reasonable. Unions are permitted to promise the extension of existing membership benefits to employees. [T]his is merely an unremarkable promise to extend Union benefits to employees after the Union's election. Unions may also promise to obtain better terms in the future. Trencor's objection to the Union "guarantees" is without merit.

C. Union's "Catch 22" Tactics

Trencor's better argument relates to the Union's challenge to Trencor executives to make guarantees similar to those offered by the Union. Companies are not allowed to make such promises in the period immediately preceding an election, and Trencor argues this challenge put the company in the untenable position of either making illegal promises or appearing to back down from the Union.

Trencor responded to the challenge by printing its own leaflet disputing the Union's guarantees and pointing out that it was prohibited by law from making any type of similar promises. Trencor alleged that Union agent Bill Fears wrote handwritten responses on the face of Trencor's leaflets. Trencor produced one such altered leaflet on which someone had handwritten in the margins that: "THE COMPANY CAN GIVE IT'S [sic] EMPLOYEES A CONTRACT WITHOUT A UNION BEING INVOLVED. IF IT CARED ABOUT ITS WORKERS & WANTED THEM TREATED FAIRLY." (emphasis in original). Trencor alleges that this alteration of its leaflet occurred on the morning of the election, denying Trencor the opportunity to respond to this misrepresentation and putting Trencor in a "false light" because it followed the law. Thus, Trencor argues, the "laboratory conditions" necessary for the employees' free choice were destroyed.

The Board counters that Trencor's responsive leaflet apprised the employees of its views on the Union guarantees and the legal restrictions keeping the company from making similar promises, thereby rebutting the notion that it was backing down from the Union challenge. The Board also argues that there is no evidence that the handwritten message on Trencor's leaflet came from a Union agent or was widely distributed. Ultimately, the Board relies on *Midland Nat'l Life Ins. Co.,* 263 NLRB 127, 131–33, 1982 WL 23832 (1982), in which the Board decided that it would "no longer probe into the truth or falsity of the parties' campaign statements and [would not] set elections aside on the basis of misleading campaign statements." The Board contends that because the thrust of Trencor's complaint about the Union challenge is that it was misleading, the *Midland* doctrine applies and the Board will not invalidate the election on this basis.

* * * * *

The Union's attempt to challenge Trencor to do something that the Union surely knew the company could not do, on the eve of the election, is not an honest tactic and certainly not one that should be condoned. However, in this case, Trencor was able to respond to the Union's challenge with its own leaflets outlining the company's position. The fact that the Union placed handwritten messages on some or all of the company's leaflets did not prevent employees from reading the claims of both sides and making their own determinations. We cannot conclude that "the misrepresentation is so pervasive and the deception so artful that employees will be unable to separate truth from untruth and . . . their right to a free and fair choice will be affected."

Enforcement of Board order denied. Case remanded.

Questions

1. *a.* Why was the Union promise of "the biggest party in Texas" a violation of the NLRB rules?
    b. Why could the Union lawfully promise that wages, benefits, etc. would not suffer and would be extended?
    c. The Union issued an election-eve challenge to Trencor to make guarantees to the workers similar to those offered by the Union. Why was that challenge not considered a misrepresentation in violation of NLRB rules?
2. During an election campaign, the general manager's office was used to interview employees in small groups of five or six. The employees had previously visited that office to discuss grievances and obtain loans. That office was the only space available for the conversations. The general manager's remarks were temperate and noncoercive. The union lost the election. Should that result be set aside for unlawful campaigning? Explain. See *NVF Company, Hartwell Division,* 210 NLRB 663 (1974).
3. Suppose the employees of Steno Office Supply, Inc., a large manufacturing firm, have petitioned the NLRB for an election. Company management personnel begin inviting workers to lunch to discuss the upcoming election and the likely consequences of unionization. These lunches are held at the local country club. During these discussions, at which employee comments are encouraged although not forced, managers make allusions to the union organizer's sexual orientation. The comments, made in the form of jokes, suggest that homosexual favors may be required in lieu of dues.
    a. If the union loses the election, should the NLRB set the election aside because of the tactics used? Explain.
    b. Which, if any, of these tactics seem problematic?
    c. Would any one of the tactics by itself be enough to set aside the election? Explain.
    d. What standard should the board use in making its determination?
    e. What additional information might you want to have before making a decision in this particular case?

[See *General Knit of California,* 239 NLRB 619 (1978), 99 LRRM 1687, for a discussion of the historical standard. But see *Midland National Life Insurance,* 263 NLRB No. 24 (1982) for the current view.]

Remedies for Election Misconduct

Unfair labor practices during a representation election can result in the imposition of penalties and remedies. If the Union loses the election and the employer engaged in wrongful behavior, a new election may be ordered. Under the Supreme Court's *Gissel Packing* decision,[35] the NLRB could order a company to recognize and bargain with a union even if the union had no proof of majority support, but the union could show that the employer had committed "outrageous" and "pervasive" unfair labor practices making impossible an election under "laboratory conditions." Where the employer engaged in a lesser degree of misconduct, the NLRB can also order the employer to bargain if the union can demonstrate that at some point it had enjoyed majority support (e.g., a majority of the employees had signed authorization cards) that was undermined by the employer's misconduct.

More broadly, the NLRB has authority to issue appropriate orders, sometimes including affirmative action steps, to correct unfair labor practices, by either management or labor, during elections and thereafter during the period of the union's relationship with the employer.

Decertification

After a union has been certified or recognized, an employee or group of employees may continue to resist the union or may lose confidence in it. After one year has passed, they can file a *decertification* petition with the NLRB. The employees must be able to demonstrate at least 30 percent support for their petition. Employers cannot initiate the decertification process. Once a decertification petition is properly filed with the board the usual election rules are followed to determine whether the union does enjoy continuing majority support. If not, the union is decertified and at least one year must pass before a new representation election can be conducted.

Escape the Union?

If a union clearly is about to win a representation election or already has done so thus establishing its right to collective bargaining, management sometimes continues to resist. One strategy is to declare bankruptcy. That tactic may be lawful but only after bargaining sincerely with the union and only after convincing the bankruptcy court that fairness requires modification or rejection of the collective bargaining agreement. Similarly, a company may simply choose to shut down its business rather than engage in collective bargaining. Going out of business is fully lawful unless the reason for doing so was to discourage union efforts at plants in other locations. Likewise, companies sometimes employ the *runaway shop* strategy in which the about-to-be-unionized plant is simply shut down and replaced by another in a location less responsive to union interests. If that move was made for the purpose of thrwarting union interests, it is an unfair labor practice, but if the move

> companies sometimes employ the *runaway shop* strategy

reflected legitimate economic goals such as reduced wages or taxes, the move is probably lawful. Finally, companies sometimes use what might be labeled a "partial runaway" tactic. The Dubuque (Iowa) Packing company was suffering financial losses and asked its union to accept a wage freeze. The union asked the company to disclose relevant financial data. The company refused, and the union voted against the wage freeze. At that point Dubuque moved a portion of its work to a nonunion plant in Illinois and laid off 350 workers in Dubuque. The union sued claiming an unfair labor practice, and the NLRB agreed that Dubuque Packing had violated its duty to bargain before moving the work. Basically, the question in such cases is whether the relocation of work involved a fundamental change in the nature of the employer's business. If not, the employer is required to bargain over the move unless it is able to show that the work in the new location is significantly different than that at the old or that labor costs did not prompt the move or, if labor costs were a factor, that the union could not have offered concessions sufficient to prevent the move.[36]

The Union as Exclusive Bargaining Agent

Once a union has been elected and certified as the representative of a bargaining unit, it becomes the exclusive agent for all of the employees within that bargaining unit, whether they voted for the union or not. The exclusivity of the union's authority has a number of implications, but one is particularly relevant in determining whether an employer has failed to demonstrate good faith at the bargaining table. Specifically, the employer must deal with the certified representative who acts on behalf of all employees in the bargaining unit. The employer commits an unfair labor practice if she or he attempts to deal directly with the employees or recognizes someone other than the workers' chosen representative. In both instances, the issue is fairly straightforward. The employer is undermining the position of the representative by ignoring him or her.

Part Four—Collective Bargaining

Section 8(a)(5) of the NLRA requires an employer to engage in good faith collective bargaining with a representative of the employees, and Section 8(b)(3) imposes the same duty on labor organizations. Failure to bargain by either an employer or representative of the employees constitutes an unfair labor practice.

What is collective bargaining? What must one do to discharge the duty imposed? According to Section 8(d) of the NRLA:

> To bargain collectively is the performance of the mutual obligation of the employer and the representatives of the employees to meet at reasonable times and confer in good faith with respect to wages, hours, and other terms and conditions of employment . . . but such obligation does not compel either party to agree to a proposal or require the making of a concession.

Note what is *not* included. The duty to bargain in good faith does not require that the parties reach agreement. The NLRB and the courts recognize that collective bargaining, like any negotiation, is consensual. Thus, the act governs only the process, not the result, of collective bargaining. Three distinct questions are raised by Sections 8(a)(5), 8(b)(3), and 8(d):

1. What constitutes good faith?
2. About which subjects must the parties bargain?
3. What conduct constitutes bargaining in good faith?

BARGAINING IN GOOD FAITH

Good faith is a murky area with no definitive answers. The NLRB and the courts look at the totality of the objective evidence in the negotiations to secure a sense of whether the parties intend to engage in serious negotiations. Over the years, various factors (none of which is conclusive in and of itself) have been identified by the board and the courts as being suggestive of good faith bargaining. Some of these include the following:[37]

1. The employer must make a serious attempt to adjust differences and to reach an acceptable common ground; that is, one must bargain with an open mind and a sincere desire to reach agreement.
2. Counterproposals must be offered when another party's proposal is rejected. This must involve the give and take of an auction system.[38]
3. A position with regard to contract terms may not be constantly changed.[39]
4. The employee must be willing to incorporate oral agreements into a written contract.[40]

Mandatory Bargaining Subjects.   Although employers and labor representatives are free to discuss whatever lawful subjects they mutually choose to discuss, Section 8(d) of the NLRA clearly sets out some mandatory subjects over which the parties must bargain. These are wages, hours, and "other terms and conditions of employment." Although these topics for mandatory bargaining seem simple enough, questions still arise frequently. For example, suppose the union and employer bargain over wages and agree to institute merit increases for employees. Must the employer also bargain over which employees are entitled to receive these increases or who will make the decision at the time they are to be given? Does the question of bringing in subcontractors to perform certain jobs fall within the scope of wages, hours, and terms and conditions of employment since the use of subcontractors may reduce the amount of work available to regular employees? Or does that subject belong more directly to the management of the firm? What about a decision to close a plant?

Generally, the board and the courts will balance three factors. First, they look to the effect of a particular decision on the workers—how direct is it and to what extent is the effect felt? Second, they consider the degree to which bargaining would constitute an intrusion into entrepreneurial interest or, from the opposite side, an intrusion into union affairs. Third, they examine the practice historically in the industry or the company itself.[41]

Permissive and Prohibited Bargaining Subjects.   In the *Borg-Warner* case,[42] the Supreme Court approved and clarified the distinction between mandatory and permissive bargaining subjects. Those matters not directly related to wages, hours, and terms and conditions of employment and not falling within the category of prohibited subjects are considered permissive. Either party may raise permissive subjects during the bargaining process, but neither may pursue them to the point of a bargaining impasse. Refusal to bargain over a permissive subject does not constitute an NLRA violation, and permissive subjects must simply be dropped if the parties do not reach agreement. Permissive subjects ordinarily would include such items as alteration of a defined bargaining unit, internal union affairs, and strike settlement agreements. Prohibited bargaining subjects are those that are illegal under the NLRA or other laws.

> whether a union has a right to bargain over management's placement of hidden surveillance cameras in the workplace

In the case that follows the NLRB had to decide whether a union has a right to bargain over management's placement of hidden surveillance cameras in the workplace. (Note that this decision has not been reviewed by the courts and presumably will not be the "last word" in this highly contentious area.)

COLGATE–PALMOLIVE CO.
323 NLRB No. 82 (1997)

Facts

Colgate–Palmolive's Jeffersonville, Indiana, plant employed approximately 750 workers. Colgate and the employees had a collective bargaining arrangement for over 20 years. In 1994, an employee discovered a surveillance camera in a restroom air vent. The union president later discussed the matter with Colgate's human resources officer who indicated that the camera had been placed in the vent because of theft concerns and that the camera had been removed after employees objected to it. The Union filed a grievance over the matter, and the parties met for discussion where Colgate argued that it had the absolute right to install internal surveillance cameras. Later, the Union sent a letter to Colgate demanding to bargain over the subject of cameras within the plant. Colgate did not respond, and the Union filed an unfair labor practice charge. The case was heard by

an administrative law judge. Evidence indicated that Colgate had installed 11 secret cameras over four years to address problems of theft and misconduct, including sleeping on the job. The cameras were placed in several offices, a fitness center, a restroom and as a monitor for an overhead door that was not a proper exit from the building. The Union and some employees were aware of various "unhidden" cameras in the workplace and in some instances, fortuitously discovered some of the hidden cameras.

The Administrative Law Judge (ALJ) concluded that the use of hidden surveillance cameras is a mandatory subject of bargaining and by failing to do so, Colgate–Palmolive violated the National Labor Relations Act. The ALJ's ruling was then appealed to the National Labor Relations Board. The NLRB decision follows:

Chairman Gould and Members Fox and Higgins

In *Ford Motor Co.* v. *NLRB,* the Supreme Court described mandatory subjects of bargaining as such matters that are "plainly germane to the 'working environment'" and "not among those 'managerial decisions, which lie at the core of entrepreneurial control.'" As the judge found, the installation of surveillance cameras is both germane to the working environment, and outside the scope of managerial decisions lying at the core of entrepreneurial control.

As to the first factor—germane to the working environment—the installation of surveillance cameras is analogous to physical examinations, drug/alcohol testing requirements, and polygraph testing, all of which the Board has found to be mandatory subjects of bargaining. They are all investigatory tools or methods used by an employer to ascertain whether any of its employees has engaged in misconduct.

The Respondent [Colgate–Palmolive] acknowledges that employees caught involved in theft and/or other misconduct are subject to discipline, including discharge. Accordingly, the installation and use of surveillance cameras has the potential to affect the continued employment of employees whose actions are being monitored.

Further, as the judge finds, the use of surveillance cameras in the restroom and fitness center raises privacy concerns which add to the potential effect upon employees. We agree that these areas are part of the work environment and that the use of hidden cameras in these areas raises privacy concerns which impinged upon the employees' working conditions. The use of cameras in these or similar circumstances is unquestionably germane to the working environment.

With regard to the second criterion, we agree with the judge that the decision is not a managerial decision that lies at the core of entrepreneurial control.

* * * * *

The use of surveillance cameras is not entrepreneurial in character, is not fundamental to the basic direction of the enterprise, and impinges directly upon employment security. It is a change in the Respondent's methods used to reduce workplace theft or detect other suspected employee misconduct with serious implications for its employees' job security, which in no way touches on the discretionary "core of entrepreneurial control."

The Respondent urges that bargaining before a hidden camera is actually installed would defeat the very purpose of the camera. The very existence of secret cameras, however, is a term and condition of employment, and is thus a legitimate concern for the employees' bargaining representative. Thus, the placing of cameras, and the extent to which they will be secret or hidden, if at all, is a proper subject of negotiations between the Respondent and the Union. Concededly, the Respondent also has a legitimate concern. However, bargaining about hidden cameras can embrace a host of matters other than mere location. And, even as to location, mutual accommodations can and should be negotiated. The vice in the instant case was the Respondent's refusal to bargain.

* * * * *

Accordingly, we affirm the judge's finding that the Union has the statutory right to engage in collective bargaining over the installation and continued use of surveillance cameras, including the circumstances under which the cameras will be activated, the general areas in which they may be placed, and how affected employees will be disciplined if improper conduct is observed.

Order

The National Labor Relations Board adopts the recommended Order of the administrative law judge as modified and set forth in full below and orders that the Respondent, its officers, agents, successors, and assigns, shall

1. Cease and desist from
   a. Failing and refusing to bargain with Local 15, International Chemical Workers Union, AFL-CIO with respect to the installation and use of surveillance cameras and other mandatory subjects of bargaining.
2. Take the following affirmative action necessary to effectuate the policies of the Act.
   a. On request, bargain collectively with the Union as the exclusive bargaining representative of the Respondent's employees with respect to the installation and use of surveillance cameras and other mandatory subjects of bargaining.
   b. Within 14 days after the service by the Region, post at its facility in Jeffersonville, Indiana, copies of the attached notice.

**Notice to Employees
Posted by Order of the
National Labor Relations Board
An Agency of the United States Government**

The National Labor Relations Board has found that we violated the National Labor Relations Act and has ordered us to post and abide by this notice. Section 7 of the Act gives employees these rights.

To organize
To form, join, or assist any union
To bargain collectively through representatives of their own choice
To act together for other mutual aid or protection
To choose not to engage in any of these protected concerted activities.

We will not fail and refuse to bargain with Local 15, International Chemical Workers Union, AFL-CIO over the installation and use of surveillance cameras within our facility and other mandatory subjects of bargaining.

We will not in any like or related manner interfere with, restrain, or coerce you in the exercise of the rights guaranteed you by Section 7 of the Act.

We will, on request, bargain collectively with the Union as the exclusive bargaining representative of our employees with respect to the installation and use of surveillance cameras within our facility and other mandatory subjects of bargaining.

Colgate–Palmolive Company.

Questions

1. What test did the ALJ and the NLRB employ to determine whether the placement of hidden surveillance cameras was a mandatory subject of bargaining?

2. Why did the union win this case?

3. If you were managing a workplace where theft, sleeping on the job, and other misconduct were at a worrisome level, would you employ hidden, secret cameras to monitor restrooms, fitness areas, and the like? Explain.

Reasonable Doubt?   Must bargaining continue if the employer reasonably believes a majority of employees no longer supports the union? The Supreme Court addressed that question in the 1996 *Auciello Iron Works*[43] and 1998 *Allentown Mack Sales*[44] cases. Basically, a union is presumed to have majority support for one year after a certification election and during the term of a collective bargaining agreement up to three years. After that year has passed or the collective bargaining agreement has expired, the presumption of majority status can be challenged but only if the employer has a "good faith doubt" founded upon sufficient objective evidence that the union no longer enjoys majority support. At that point, the employer can lawfully decline to bargain further with the union, which can then take the question to the NLRB and the courts for resolution. [For the Bureau of Labor Statistics and frequently asked questions about collective bargaining, see **http://stats.bls.gov/cbahome.htm**]

Successors and the Duty to Bargain.   What bargaining duties does a firm have when it acquires or merges with another firm that has a collective bargaining agreement? Is the successor firm legally required to accept the bargained-for contractual arrangements of its predecessors? Does the successor have a duty to bargain with the union? While these questions must be settled on a case-by-case basis, we can safely say that a successor normally has no duty to accept the terms of the labor agreement negotiated by the previous employer, but the successor may well have to bargain with the union. The key considerations in the duty to bargain question include whether a "substantial continuity of identity" was maintained between the original firm and the successor and whether the successor retained a majority of the employees from the unionized labor force. If the general nature of the firm and a majority of its workforce are retained, the successor will be bound to recognize the union and bargain. Furthermore, if the successor deliberately avoids hiring union members from the original firm in order to escape bargaining duties, a bargaining order probably will be imposed.

ADMINISTERING THE AGREEMENT

Union–management bargaining does not end with the negotiation of a labor agreement. Rather, bargaining continues on a day-to-day basis as the parties work out the disputes and confusions and conflicting interpretations that are bound to arise and that cannot be entirely provided for in the labor agreement. Often, this process of contract maintenance takes the form of resolving *grievances,* as in the *Colgate–Palmolive* case. Those problems are addressed through the grievance procedure that is included in all collective bargaining agreements. Often the grievance procedure involves a series of steps beginning with infor-mal discussion mechanisms. Failing there, the dissatisfied employee typically files a writ-ten complaint (the grievance). Normally, grievances are presented to management by a union representative, often with the worker also present.

Arbitration

If, after negotiation, the parties cannot reach a resolution of their dispute, the collective bargaining agreement ordinarily provides for *final and binding arbitration.* Many court decisions have vigorously supported the arbitration process as the means of settling labor–management contract maintenance disputes and tend to find disputes arbitrable unless the labor agreement explicitly and unambiguously exempts the subject at issue from the arbitration process. Further, except for some exceptions including arbitrator miscon-duct or a violation of public policy, neither the company nor the union can turn to the courts to set aside arbitration decisions.

Supreme Court decisions have likewise approved of final, binding arbitration, but some uncertainty remains for discrimination claims arising in a collective bargaining setting. In 1998, the court ruled that a union member could proceed to litigate his disability discrimi-nation claim even though his union contract required arbitration. In this instance, the court said the lawsuit could proceed because of the absence of a "clear and unmistakable waiver" of the employee's right to sue.[45]

Fair Representation

Since grievance processing is part of a union's bargaining responsibility, the union might breach its duty if it declined to represent an employer's grievance. Similarly, unions have a legal duty to represent the grievance interests of nonunion employees just as they would for union members. An employee who feels wronged when a union does not process his or her grievance has the option of appealing to the NLRB or to the courts.

Part Five—Work Stoppages

Strikes.   For many, the initial image of labor conflict is one of employees on strike, picketing a store or factory. Striking is, however, an extremely drastic measure under which employees must bear an immediate loss of wages and, in many instances, risk job loss. Similarly, employers bear the loss of a disruption to continued operations.

Led by a four-week, 152,000 worker dispute between General Motors and the United Auto Workers, major United States work stoppages (strikes and lockouts involving 1,000 workers or more) actually rose a bit in 1998 from 1997 levels, but as Figure 14.2 shows, work stoppages have declined dramatically since World War II.

We will address two kinds of strikes:

1. Those instituted by workers in response to the employer's commission of an unfair labor practice such as interfering with legitimate union activities or failure to bargain in good faith. These are known as unfair labor practice strikes.
2. Those used purely as economic weapons to persuade an employer to provide more favorable employee benefits or better working conditions. These are known as economic strikes.

Economic Strikes.   All strikes not involving unfair labor practices fall into this category. With some exceptions, economic strikers cannot be fired, but they can be permanently replaced. In what has been labeled "the most significant change in collective bargaining to occur since the passage of the Wagner Act in 1934," employers are now increasingly willing to permanently replace economic strikers.[46] Employers had enjoyed that right where necessary "in an effort to carry on the business" since a 1938 Supreme Court decision, but for practical reasons they had rarely exercised it.[47] Later decisions had imposed some limitations on that right. For example, any striker who is permanently replaced is put on a preferential hiring list and will have priority to be selected to fill subsequent vacancies. However, President Reagan's 1981 dismissal of 11,300 striking air traffic controllers effectively crushed their union (PATCO) and caused private-sector employers to reassess

FIGURE 14.2   U.S. Work Stoppages Involving 1,000 Workers or More

Year	Number	Workers	Days Idle	Percent of Estimated
		(thousands)		*Working Time*
1948	245	1,435	26,127	.22
1958	332	1,587	17,900	.13
1968	392	1,855	35,367	.20
1978	219	1,006	23,774	.11
1988	40	387	4,381	.02
1998	34	387	5,116	.02

Source: [**http://stats.bls.gov/news.release/wkstp.t01.htm**].

their long-standing reluctance to use replacements during and after strikes.[48] Thus, recent years have seen some major employers like Hormel, Caterpillar, Greyhound Bus Lines, Firestone/Bridgestone, the National Football League, and Major League Baseball use, or threaten to use, strike replacements.

The following case examines when employers can legitimately decline to reinstate strikers.

DIAMOND WALNUT GROWERS, INC. v. NLRB
113 F.3d 1259 (D.C. Cir. 1997)

Circuit Judge Silberman

I

Diamond Walnut processes and packages walnuts for national and international distribution. The company operates with a year-round workforce, supplemented by additional seasonal hires during the fall harvesting season. Diamond's employees have for years been represented by Cannery Workers, Processors, Warehousemen and Helpers Local 601 of the International Brotherhood of Teamsters, AFL–CIO (the union). In September of 1991, following expiration of the most recent collective bargaining agreement between Diamond and the union, nearly 500 of Diamond's permanent and seasonal employees went on strike. Diamond hired replacement workers to allow it to continue operations.

By all accounts, the strikes was, and remains, a bitter affair. The strikers are alleged to have engaged in various acts of violence against the replacement workers, especially at the outset of the strike, and restraining orders issued against both strikers and replacements. In addition, as part of its effort to exert economic pressure on Diamond, the union undertook an international boycott of its product. The boycott included a well-publicized national bus tour during which union members distributed to the public leaflets which described Diamond's workforce as composed of "scabs" who packaged walnuts contaminated with "mold, dirt, oil, worms and debris."

Approximately one year into the strike, the Board held a representation election. The union lost the election, but its objections prompted the Board to order a rerun to be held in October of 1993. Just over two weeks prior to the new election, a group of four striking employees, represented by a union official, approached Diamond with an unconditional offer to return to work. According to the letter presented to the company at that time by their representative, the employees were convinced that "a fair election [was] simply impossible." Nonetheless, the employees "fe[lt] that it [was] important that the replacement workers . . . have an opportunity to hear from Union sympathizers." Thus, the group of strikers was "available and willing to return to immediate active employment." The following day, the union notified Diamond that pursuant to the above-quoted letter, two additional strikers were willing to return to work.

It is undisputed that for three of the returning strikers, neither the permanent jobs they held before the strike, nor substantially equivalent ones, were available at the time of their return. Diamond placed these three in various seasonal jobs. Prior to the strike, Willa Miller was a quality control supervisor; she was placed in a seasonal packing position even though a seasonal inspection job was available. Alfonsina Munoz had been employed as a lift truck operator and, despite the availability of a seasonal forklift job, was given a seasonal job cracking and inspecting nuts in the growers' inspection department at the front end of the production process. Mohammed Kussair, formerly an air separator machine operator, was, like

Munoz, placed in a seasonal cracking and inspecting position in the growers' inspection department . . .

The rerun election took place as scheduled, and the union lost. Following that election, the General Counsel filed a complaint alleging that Diamond had violated sections 8(a)(3) and 8(a)(1) of the National Labor Relations Act, by unlawfully discriminating against Miller, Munoz, and Kussair. The General Counsel alleged that because of their protected activity, Diamond declined to put them in certain available seasonal positions for which they were qualified and that were preferable to the positions in which they were actually placed. After a hearing, an administrative law judge recommended that the charges be dismissed. He found that Diamond had "discriminated" insofar as it had placed the employees at least in part because of their protected activity, but he did not think that discrimination "unlawful."

* * * * *

[The NLRB reversed saying] "although [Diamond] was under no legal obligation . . . to reinstate the strikers . . . , once it voluntarily decided to reinstate them, it was required to act in a nondiscriminatory fashion toward the strikers." Diamond had discriminated against Miller, Munoz, and Kussair, in the Board's view, by declining "to place them in the [seasonal] positions of quality control assistant, lift truck operator, and loader, respectively, because of their union status and/or because of certain protected union activity they engaged in while on strike." . . . The Board rejected the contention that the placements were warranted by the employer's concern that the replacement workers might instigate violence against the three and thus justified placement in well-supervised jobs, since "there [was] no evidence that Miller, Munoz, or Kussair were involved" in the strike-related violence allegedly causing Diamond's concern. The Board also dismissed the notion that the placements of Miller and Munoz were justified by their participation in the boycott and the circulation of disparaging leaflets: "[T]he strikers' conduct constituted protected . . . activity and there is no evidence indicating that such protection was lost because of threats made by Miller and Munoz to damage or sabotage [Diamond's] equipment or products." Since Diamond had failed to justify its discrimination, the Board found unfair labor practices.

* * * * *

[Diamond sought judicial review of the NLRB ruling.]

II

Diamond Walnut challenges the Board's determination that it lacked substantial business justification for refusing to place the three employees in the specific jobs they sought—quality control assistant, lift truck operator, and loader. It is undisputed that the *Fleetwood* framework governs this case. The General Counsel under *Fleetwood* must make out a *prima facie* case that the employer discriminated within the meaning of the Act, which means the employer's decision as to how to treat the three returning strikers was attributable to their protected activity. *Rose Printing* establishes that a struck employer faced with an unconditional offer to return to work is obliged to treat the returning employee like any other applicant for work (unless the employee's former job or its substantial equivalent is available, in which case the employee is preferred to any other applicant). But Miller and Munoz were not treated like any other applicant for work. Miller was qualified for a seasonal position in quality control that paid 32 cents per hour more than the packing job to which she was assigned. And Munoz was qualified to fill a forklift operating job, a position that paid between $2.75 and $5.00 per hour more than the walnut cracking and inspecting job she received. Diamond admits that it took into account Miller's and Munoz's protected activity in choosing to place them in jobs that were objectively less desirable than those for which they were qualified. Petitioner [Diamond] although it contended that the discrimination was comparatively slight, does not dispute that its action discriminated against Munoz and Miller within the meaning of the Act.

* * * * *

Under *Fleetwood,* after discrimination is shown, the burden shifts to the employer to establish that its treatment of the employees has a legitimate and substantial business justification. Petitioner declined to give Munoz the forklift driver job because of its concern that driving that piece of equipment throughout the plant would be unduly risky in two respects. First, because of the bad feeling between strikers and replacements, Munoz would be endangered if confronted by hostile replacement workers in an isolated area. Second, since Munoz had participated in the bus tour during which the union had accused the company of producing tainted walnuts, Munoz would be tempted to engage in sabotage by using the 11,000 pound vehicle to cause unspecified damage. As for Miller, who was also on the bus tour, the company declined to put her in the "sensitive position of quality control assistant" where "the final visual inspection of walnuts is made prior to leaving the plant." In that position, she would have "an easy opportunity to let defective nuts go by undetected . . . or to place a foreign object into the final product, thereby legitimizing the Union's claim of tainted walnuts."

* * * * *

A. Munoz

The Board rejected petitioner's proffered justifications for its placement of Munoz on the same ground as did the ALJ. As to Diamond's purported fear for her safety, no evidence had been produced that Munoz was thought to be responsible for any violence, so there was no reason to believe she would have been a special target. The Board said, "[T]here is no specific evidence that any replacements harbored hostility toward these three strikers, and, if such evidence did exist as [Diamond] claims, we fail to see how placing them in the positions to which they were assigned would lessen the perceived danger of retaliatory acts being committed against them." The Board discounted Diamond Walnut's contention that Munoz would be under greater protection if closely supervised, noting that petitioner had admitted that "Munoz freely roamed the plant unsupervised during her breaks."

* * * * *

As for the possibility that Munoz would engage in fork-lift sabotage, the Board was more terse, stating only that "the strikers' conduct [referring to the bus tour] constituted protected . . . activity," and there was no evidence indicating that such protection was lost because of threats made by Miller and Munoz. If Munoz had uttered specific threats of sabotage, however, she would have lost her protected status. . . . [T]he Board necessarily concluded that the possibility of Munoz engaging in future sabotage by misuse of her forklift was simply not a sufficient risk to constitute a substantial business justification for her treatment.

* * * * *

Similarly, the Board was reasonable in its determination that the risk of Munoz engaging in sabotage while riding around on her 11,000 pound forklift—the petitioner seems to most fear her crashing the forklift into machinery—is not a substantial business justification for her disadvantageous placement in another job. Strikes tend

to be hard struggles, and although this one may have been more bitter than most, there is always a potential danger of returning strikers engaging in some form of sabotage. There is therefore undeniably some risk in employing returning strikers during a strike. But it could not be seriously argued that an employer cannot be forced to assume *any* risk of sabotage, because that would be equivalent to holding that an employer need not take back strikers during an ongoing strike at all . . .

* * * * *

B. Miller

The Miller case is another matter. It will be recalled that petitioner declined to assign her to the post of quality control assistant, the job responsible for the final inspection of walnuts leaving the plant (she received a job paying 32 cents an hour less). The Board rejected the employer's justification, which was based on Miller's participation in the product boycott and bus tour leafleting, saying only "the strikers' conduct constituted protected . . . activity and there is no evidence indicating that such protection was lost because of threats made by Miller and Munoz to damage or sabotage . . . equipment or products." With respect to Miller, we think the Board's determination that petitioner's business justification is insubstantial is flatly unreasonable.

All strikes are a form of economic warfare, but when a union claims that a food product produced by a struck company is actually tainted it can be thought to be using the strike equivalent of a nuclear bomb; the unpleasant effects will long survive the battle . . . The company's ability to sell the product . . . could well be destroyed.

* * * * *

The Board's counsel argues that it is unfair to assume that an employee would behave in a disloyal and improper fashion. It is unnecessary, however, for us to make that assumption to decide the Board was unreasonable. The Board accepted petitioner's contention that Miller would have been placed "in the sensitive position . . . where final visual inspection of walnuts is made prior to leaving the plant." Miller would therefore have been put in a rather acute and unusual conflict of interest in which her job for her employer could be thought to have as a function the rebutting of her union's claim. A similar conflict would be raised if she wished a bargaining unit job in the company's public relations department. This conflict makes all too likely the possibility that Miller would be *at least* inattentive to her product quality duties . . . To make matters worse, any "mistake" by Miller on the product quality control line would not be easily attributable to her unless petitioner paid someone to stand all day looking over Miller's shoulder . . . If Munoz ran her forklift into valuable machinery, she would run a risk of being discovered and would therefore be deterred. But Miller, as a quality control assistant, could simply avert her eye and cause the damage with apparently little risk of discovery . . .

In short, she would have had a special motive, a unique opportunity and little risk of detection to cause severe harm. Both the risk Diamond faced in its placement of Miller was qualitatively different than a normal risk of sabotage, and the deterrence to Miller's possible misbehavior was peculiarly inadequate.

* * * * *

[W]e are obliged to ask in the last analysis whether the Board's decision, as to whether the employer's action was substantially justified by business reasons, falls within the broad stretch of reasonableness. In this case, at least with respect to one part of the Board's decision, we conclude the Board exceeded the reasonableness limits.

So ordered.

[The Supreme Court declined to review the *Diamond Walnut* decision.][49]

Questions

1. Set out the two-part test the court employed to determine whether Diamond Walnut violated the National Labor Relations Act by discriminating against its employees because of their participation in protected union activities.

2. Explain why the court found that Munoz had been wronged by Diamond but Miller had not.

3. *a.* How would you vote on the proposed federal legislation banning the practice of permanently replacing economic strikers? Explain.

   b. Is there any reason to distinguish between economic strikers and unfair labor practice strikers? Any reason not to do so?

4. Assume Mary Wills, a bottle inspector for Pop Soda Inc. and a member of a certified bargaining unit, struck along with other bottle inspectors to protest an allegedly unfair labor practice committed by the employer. The bottle inspectors offered to return to work after a one-week strike, and, although their positions were not filled, Pop Soda offered them entirely different positions as bottle sorters, telling the employees that they would shortly thereafter be returned to their regular inspector jobs. Wills was the only one who accepted this offer; the other employees insisted that they were legally entitled to their former jobs. Wills made subsequent inquiries, attempting to get her inspecting job back, but the company at no time made a proper offer for that position. After three and a half months of working as a bottle sorter, Wills resigned because of physical problems with her hand. She then made a claim to the NLRB that Pop Soda had committed an unfair labor practice by not reinstating her to her inspecting position. She asked for reinstatement and back pay.

   Do you think she is entitled to either or both of these remedies? [See *The Coca-Cola Bottling Company of Memphis and International Brotherhood of Teamsters, et al.,* 269 NLRB No. 160 (1983–84 CCH NLRB ¶ 16,259), decided April 23, 1984.]

"Sickouts."   The pilots union at American Airlines was fined more than $45.5 million in 1999 for briefly ignoring a federal judge's order to return to work during a "sickout." After 2,500 pilots were off work for five days, the judge ordered their return, but the pilots did not comply until three days thereafter, causing an estimated $200 million in damages for American arising from the cancellation of more than 6,700 flights over the eight-day period. The pilots had called in sick as part of their union's dispute over pay scales involving American's absorption of Reno Air.[50] The pilots union is appealing the fine at this writing.

Fearing full-scale strikes may cost them their jobs, an increasing but still small number of union workers are employing sickouts as leverage against management. A sickout might be thought of as an "illegal, partial strike,"[51] which management ordinarily can stop with a court order. For skilled, not easily replaced workers, however, the sickouts can be effective because they can be long enough to significantly pressure the company, yet short enough to avoid replacement.

Lockouts.   Sometimes management takes the initiative in labor disputes by locking its doors to some or all of its employees. Both the NLRB and the courts allow lockouts as defensive acts to protect businesses against sudden strikes and to prevent sabotage or violence. Some court decisions have also expanded lawful lockouts to include those of an offensive nature designed to improve management's bargaining position. Lockouts, however, are clearly not lawful if designed to interfere with bargaining rights and other legitimate union activity.

The power of the lockout was well illustrated to sports fans in 1998 when the National Basketball Association owners locked out their players after failing to reach an accord with the National Basketball Players Association (the players' union) over a firmer cap on salaries. The dispute was resolved in early 1999, and the league completed an abbreviated 50-game schedule. [For a database of law cases about sports, see **http://www.marquette.edu/law/sports/calldex.html#top**]

PICKETING AND BOYCOTTS

Primary Picketing.   In addition to striking, unions often engage in picketing or boycotting in an effort to pressure an employer with which it is negotiating and to broadly publicize their concerns. Picketing is the familiar process of union members gathering and sometimes marching, placards in hand, at a place of business. Peaceful, informational picketing for a lawful purpose is protected by the NLRA. However, some kinds of picketing are forbidden, and all picketing can be regulated by the government to ensure the public safety. Primary picketing is expressed directly to the employer with whom the picketers have a dispute. Primary picketing enjoys broad constitutional and statutory protection, but it may be unlawful if violent or coercive.

Secondary Picketing/Boycotts.   Secondary picketing or boycotting is directed to a business other than the primary employer, and ordinarily it is unlawful. That is, unions are engaging in an unfair labor practice if they threaten or coerce a third party with whom they are not engaged in a dispute in order to cause that third party to put any indirect pressure on the firm that is the real target of the union's concern. Assume union A has a dispute with company B. Direct, primary picketing, a strike, and the like against company B would normally be permissible. But if A were to impose pressure via picketing, for example, on company C, a supplier of company B, that pressure would ordinarily constitute unlawful behavior. Thus, secondary picketing, secondary boycotts, and other forms of coercion against parties not the principals in a labor dispute are, with some exceptions, unlawful labor practices.

Questions

1. George A. Hormel & Co. and the United Food and Commercial Workers Union settled a long labor dispute. Thereafter, an unhappy employee drove his car in a parade and attended a rally, both of which were designed to encourage a nationwide boycott of Hormel Products. The employee did nothing to signal his feelings beyond his presence at the two events.

   Employees may lawfully be dismissed for disloyalty to their employer. Supporting a boycott of an employer's products ordinarily constitutes disloyalty except where (1) the boycott is related to an ongoing labor dispute and (2) the support does not amount to disparagement of the employer's product.

   Was this Hormel employee engaged in protected activity such that his dismissal was unlawful? Explain. See *George A. Hormel and Company* v. *National Labor Relations Board,* 962 F.2d 1061 (D.C. Cir. 1992).

2. Two stevedoring companies in Fort Pierce and Port Canaveral, Florida, loaded Florida citrus fruit on ships bound for Japan. The International Longshoremen's Association (ILA) had a dispute with the two stevedoring companies and asked for the support of Japanese dockworkers' unions. The Japanese unions agreed and notified their membership and several Japanese stevedoring companies of that support. Concerned that their fruit might not be unloaded upon arrival in Japan, several American shipping companies diverted their ships for citrus loading from Fort Pierce and Port Canaveral to Tampa, Florida. The ILA thanked the Japanese unions for their help and asked that they continue. The result was that the Fort Pierce and Port Canaveral stevedoring companies were injured financially.

   Does the ILA conduct in this case constitute a violation of the National Labor Relations Act? Explain. See *Coastal Stevedoring Co.,* 313 NLRB 53 (1993).

Part Six—Employees' Rights within or against the Union

The Union's Duty of Fair Representation

As you have seen in previous sections of this chapter, the union is given statutory authority to be the exclusive bargaining agent for the employees in the designated bargaining unit. This means that even if an individual employee in the bargaining unit does not agree with the union policies or is not a member of the union, he or she cannot bargain individually with the employer. Such an employee will still be bound by the terms of the collective bargaining agreement.

Hence, unions have a duty to fairly represent all members of the bargaining unit, whether or not they become members of the union. Sometimes the task is difficult because of divergent interests within the unit. For example, if a company is in difficult financial circumstances, it may tell union negotiators that the company must do one of two things to stay viable—lay off workers or give all employees a cut in salary. The workers who have seniority and would not lose their jobs in a layoff are likely to push for the former;

workers with less seniority, who would normally be let go during a layoff, will prefer in most instances to retain their jobs even if they are forced to take a cut in wages.

That situation, however, is a far cry from the routine, institutionalized racial and sexual discrimination of the past. Unions were notorious for negotiating contracts in which women were excluded from certain jobs and paid lower wages for performing work identical to their male counterparts. In recognition of that discrimination, Congress built special provisions into the Equal Pay Act of 1963 and the Civil Rights Act of 1964, making it illegal for unions to discriminate on the basis of race, color, creed, national origin, or sex.

The Bill of Rights of Labor Organization Members

The Bill of Rights for members of labor organizations is contained in Title 1, Section 101 of the Labor–Management Reporting and Disclosure Act (LMRDA or Landrum–Griffin Act). The Bill of Rights was designed to ensure equal voting rights, the right to sue the union, and the rights of free speech and assembly. These rights of union members are tempered by the union's right to enact and enforce "reasonable rules governing the responsibilities of its members."[52]

Even though union members are guaranteed the rights of free speech and assembly, federal court cases, at both the district and circuit court levels, have made clear that unions are not obligated to provide space in union newspapers for articles containing viewpoints opposed to those of union leadership, nor are they obligated to hold meetings at the behest of their membership even when the union constitution provides a procedural means for calling such a meeting. Moreover, the union meeting agenda can be set by the union leadership in such a way as to preclude discussion of particular issues. The union is permitted to establish reasonable rules to govern such situations.

Other federal court decisions have come down equally firmly in interpreting other rights guaranteed by the workers' Bill of Rights. Thus, although union members are entitled to vote in union elections, they do not have the right to demand a vote on a decision of whether to strike. Likewise, the union is not required to submit a proposed collective bargaining agreement to the membership for ratification or approval, although the Bill of Rights gives members the right to see a copy of the agreement under which they are working.[53]

The NLRB and Worker Participation

Spurred by Japanese success and methods, American companies have been experimenting with a variety of strategies to improve productivity. Among them is increased worker participation in management decision making as a part of the more general effort at total quality management (TQM). However, as we have seen, the NLRA, Sections 2(5) and 8(a)(2), provides that employer domination or interference with the formation or administration of any labor organization is an unfair labor practice. Broadly, the law is designed to prevent sham unions that, in fact, are dominated by management. Hence, in 1992 and 1993 the

NLRB was called on to decide two cases involving the legality of some company-created labor–management committees designed to strengthen production quality.

In *E.I. Dupont de Nemours,* the NLRB unanimously concluded that six joint safety committees and one joint fitness committee were "labor organizations" under the terms of the National Labor Relations Act.[54] The committees, designed to discuss safety, incentive awards, jogging tracks, and the like, existed for the purpose of "dealing with" the employer. Further, management dominated the committees in that determinations were subject to management approval, management had the right to establish or disband the groups at will, and management set the size of the groups. Finally, the work of the committees, such as improving working conditions and deciding on worker incentives, was often identical to that of the employees' union, the Chemical Workers Association. Similarly, in the 1992 *Electromation* decision, the NLRB ruled that so-called "action committees" created by an employer were, in practice, illegal sham unions.[55] The action committees were an attempt to respond to employee concerns about working conditions and were considered "communication devices" by management. The NLRB concluded that the purpose of the committees was to reach bilateral solutions to employee concerns, and since employees acted in representational capacities on the committees, they were in effect labor unions created by management in violation of labor law. [For an analysis of *Dupont* and *Electromation,* see **http://www.orrick.com./news/emplaw/diverse/5.htm**]

UNION SECURITY AGREEMENTS AND RIGHT-TO-WORK LAWS

To maintain their membership, unions typically seek a collective bargaining clause requiring all employees to become union members after they have been employed for some period of time—generally 30 days (union shop agreements)—or, at the least, requiring them to pay union dues and fees (agency shop agreements). These union security arrangements are lawful under the NLRA.

In either a union shop or an agency shop, the union has a duty of fair representation for all members of the bargaining unit, whether those employees join the union or not. Furthermore, under the 1988 Supreme Court decision in *Communications Workers of America* v. *Beck*[56] nonunion employees can be compelled to pay union dues and fees only for core collective bargaining activities. Thus, nonunion employees' agency shop dues and fees must be reduced by an amount equal to that applied to such noncore purposes as lobbying and political campaigning. [For the Communications Workers of America home page, see **http://www.cwa-union.org/**]

Right-to-Work.   At least 21 states, primarily in the South and West, have enacted right-to-work laws that prohibit union security arrangements in collective bargaining agreements. In these states, nonmembers do not pay dues or fees but, as members of the bargaining unit, must be represented by the union. Unions regard those employees as free riders, but right-to-work supporters see the matter as one of personal freedom. [For questions and answers on right-to-work laws, see **http://www.nrtw.org/a/a_prime.htm**]

Closed Shop.   At one time, powerful unions insisted on closed-shop arrangements wherein employers could hire only individuals who already belonged to unions, but those arrangements are now forbidden by the NLRA.

"Medicine Ball."   The ongoing "union security" war is well illustrated by a 1998 skirmish between part-time actress Naomi Marquez and the Screen Actors Guild (SAG, a union). Marquez received a one-line part in a television show, "Medicine Ball," but she declined to pay the $500 required to become a member of SAG. Marquez sued SAG, claiming that its standard contract misled her and others into believing that they must become full union members and pay full union dues in order to work. SAG, and unions generally, won a significant victory when the Supreme Court ruled that union contracts need not spell out employees' legal right to decline to become full union members. The court unanimously allowed unions to negotiate contracts that include a clause saying that "union membership in good standing" is a requirement for new employees even though those employees, as explained above, can lawfully decline to join the union and simply pay agency dues and fees. The court upheld the union membership language because it faithfully tracks the language of the National Labor Relations Act, but the Court also ruled that if the clause was used to deceive employees about their membership obligations, the NLRA may have been violated.[57]

> Marquez received a one-line part in a television show, "Medicine Ball"

Part Seven—Other Unions

Public-Sector Unions

The public sector is a growth area for union membership. Legal regulation of public-sector labor–management relations begins with state law. Although the specific provisions of those laws therefore vary, many of the concepts discussed earlier arising under the NLRA are applicable. However, some fundamental policies and doctrines are quite different. Two of these doctrines that apply uniquely to the public sector are the nondelegability doctrine, which bears on the constitutionality of public-sector labor laws, and the ability of public-sector employees to strike.

The nondelegability doctrine is based on the fact that public-sector employees are, either directly or indirectly, held accountable to the electorate via the ballot box. Thus, a mayor or governor, or his or her employees as their representatives, have certain powers and responsibilities that cannot be given to, or delegated to, an individual or entity, such as a union or an arbitrator, that is not accountable to the voters.[58]

With regard to public employee strikes, some states prohibit them and others permit them only under restricted conditions. In either case, the rationale for treating public employees differently than private-sector employees is the role of public employees as servants of the voters. In the minds of many, public servants have a higher duty than private employees. In addition, certain public employees, including police officers and fire fighters, work in positions that clearly involve public safety, and to permit them to strike might endanger the citizenry.

Private sector, nonagricultural workers in unions: 9.5 percent. Government employees in unions: 37.5 percent.

Source: "Unionization Rates High in Government," *USA Today,* September 1, 1999, p. 1A.

INTERNET EXERCISE

1. Using the United Auto Workers' frequently asked questions [**http://uaw.org/faqs.html**]
   a. Explain "how union pay compares to nonunion pay."
   b. Explain why union dues are "a great bargain."

CHAPTER QUESTIONS

1. *a.* In your opinion, what are the average blue-collar worker's biggest sources of job dissatisfaction? Can they be eliminated through collective bargaining? Explain.
   b. In your opinion, what are the average white-collar worker's biggest sources of job dissatisfaction? What means do such workers have for eliminating those sources of dissatisfaction? Explain.
2. *a.* Imagine what the world will be like 50 years from now. In what ways do you picture the work life of the average American to have changed? Explain.
   b. Imagine the ideal work world. How close does that picture come to the one you conjured up in response to the previous question? What types, if any, of labor or other legislation would bring society closer to that ideal? Explain.
3. You are the human resources manager for a manufacturing firm that is presently the subject of an organizing campaign by a union that has filed an election petition with the NLRB just 30 days ago. Your plant manager has come to you and said that she wishes to discharge one of her employees. She further explains that the employee in question has worked for the company for three years and throughout that time has had a terrible attendance record. She adds that up to this point the employee has not received any discipline for his attendance. Upon inquiry, the plant manager tells you that the employee has been seen on the plant floor wearing a button that says "Union Yes!" In addition, the plant manager tells you that she knows that the employee is an outspoken union activist. What would you advise the plant manager to do? Why?

4. A union representing a bargaining unit comprising both men and women and multiple racial and ethnic groups demands to see detailed information that the employer keeps on wages paid to women and minorities, as well as hiring statistics about these members of the workforce.
   a. Should the employer be required to let employees see these data? Explain.
   b. What circumstances might affect your decision? [See *Westinghouse Electric Corp.,* 239 NLRB No. 18 (1978).]
   c. Suppose that, instead of asking for wage information, the union asked to see the questions, answers, and individual scores achieved by employees on psychological aptitude tests that the employer requires them to take. If the employer refuses to turn these scores over, has it committed an unfair labor practice? Explain.
   d. Does this situation differ significantly from the previous situation? [See *Detroit Edison Co.* v. *NLRB,* 440 U.S. 301 (1979).]
5. United Plant Guard Workers of America (UPGWA) sought union certification at Arbitron Services, Inc. The union and the company stipulated certain election procedures to be followed, including, among other things, the hours, date, and location at which balloting would be held and the posting of notices of the election. Several days before the election, the company posted notices of the election in several conspicuous locations. Two days before the election, the union mailed notices to employees listed on sheets supplied to the union by the company. The election was held on a regular payday. Out of 314 employees eligible to vote, a total

of only 64 valid votes (26 of them for the union) were cast. The UPGWA petitioned the NLRB following the union's defeat, claiming that the low voter turnout resulted in the defeat, which led to the inference that notice of the election to the employees had been inadequate and that the election results should be set aside. What do you think the NLRB's response is likely to be? Explain. [See *Iona Security Services, Inc.,* and *National Union, United Plant Guard Workers of America,* 269 NLRB No. 53 (1983–84 CCH NLRB ¶ 16,145), March 21, 1984.]

6. A bargaining unit, consisting of 56 employees at the time of a union representation election, voted in favor of unionization by a vote of 29 to 23. The employer sought to have the election results nullified, alleging that six days prior to the election, a union official meeting with 20 employees had referred to a company vice president as a "stingy Jew." The company had witnesses to substantiate this claim, and the union did not deny it.

    a. Do you think the election results should be set aside? Explain. [See *NLRB* v. *Silverman's Men's Wear, Inc.,* 656 F.2d 53 (3d Cir. 1981).]

    b. Suppose, instead, union officers came to campaign meetings for a Japanese-owned company wearing T-shirts that said, "Remember Pearl Harbor" and "Japs speak with forked tongue and slant eyes." Do you think the result would be any different? Explain. [See *YKK (USA) Inc.* and *Sandra M. Collins et al.,* 296 NLRB No. 8 (1983–84 CCH NLRB ¶ 16,158), March 8, 1984.]

7. The Clayton Act exempts union wage negotiations from the antitrust laws. Workers in many different and competing companies may lawfully join together to form a single bargaining unit (for example, the Teamsters' union). Of course, the antitrust laws forbid competing companies from joining together in the manner workers are allowed to do. Economist Gary Becker of the University of Chicago argued that the time had come to treat union conspiracies in the same manner as those of management. He argued for replacing traditional trade unions with company unions (unions limited in membership to a single company), such as those used in Japan. He said union shop laws and other protections could be strengthened so that management could not dominate the union. He noted the general decline of union membership in the United States. Becker argued that the decline was largely due to the growth of such protections as unemployment compensation, social security, medicare, and new barriers against unfair dismissals. Should labor unions be fully subject to the antitrust laws? Explain. [See Gary Becker, "It's Time to Scrap a Few Outmoded Labor Laws," *Business Week,* March 7, 1988, p. 18.]

8. Lechmere owns a store in a shopping plaza in Newington, Connecticut, and Lechmere is also part owner of the plaza's parking lot. A 46-foot wide strip of grass, most of which is public property, separates the parking lot from the street. Union members, trying to organize Lechmere's employees, placed handbills on the windshields of parked cars. Lechmere then denied the Union access to the parking lot, at which point organizers picketed from the grassy street and personally contacted about 20 percent of the employees. The union filed an unfair labor practice charge with the NLRB claiming that denying them access to the parking lot was a violation of the NLRA. Was the union correct? See *Lechmere, Inc.* v. *NLRB,* 502 U.S. 527 (1992).

9. Ryder Trucking laid off employees represented by the Teamsters Local 243 after Sears Roebuck canceled a contract with Ryder and entered a contract with a trucking company that did not have a union contract. The replacement company hired only a few of those laid off from Ryder. In response, the union mounted a handbilling campaign against Sears in which the handbillers stood on Sears' private property at the entrances to a pair of Sears stores in Michigan malls. The handbills urged customers not to shop at Sears. Sears compelled the removal of the handbillers.

    Do nonemployees have the right to pass out handbills on an employers' property where the handbills urge a boycott of the employer's products and services? Explain. See *Oakland Mall Ltd.,* 316 NLRB 173 [1995].

10. A union–management dispute led to an economic strike, at which point the employer hired replacement workers. At the end of the strike, the workforce consisted of 25 former strikers and 69 replacement workers. The agreement settling the strike provided that strikers would be recalled as vacancies arose. However, the employer did not follow the agreement when it recalled four workers (three of whom were replacements) and failed to consider any of 28 strikers who remained out of work.

    Well-settled labor law provides that "economic strikers who have been permanently replaced but who have unconditionally offered to return to work are entitled to reinstatement upon the departure of the replacements." The NLRB found a violation of the National Labor Relations Act, and framed the issue as follows: "How should the layoff of the permanent replacement worker—who has a contractual right to recall—affect the reinstatement rights of unreinstated strikers?" The NLRB ruled that it would require a showing that the laid-off replacements had no "reasonable expectancy of recall." Then the burden of proof would shift to the employer to justify its failure to recall strikers when vacancies arose. The NLRB decision was appealed. Decide. Explain. [See *Aqua-Chem, Inc.* v. *NLRB,* 910 F.2d 1487 (7th Cir., 1990), cert. denied., 111 S.Ct. 2871 (1991).]

11. Some employees were transferred from a unionized plant to a new location.
    a. Are the employees who were transferred to the new location still members of their original bargaining unit? Explain.
    b. What test should the National Labor Relations Board employ in deciding whether the employer must recognize and bargain with the union in the new location? [See *Gitano Group, Inc.,* 308 NLRB No. 173 (1992).]

12. A field organizer for the International Brotherhood of Electrical Workers sought work with a nonunion electrical firm. In applying for a job as an electrician, the organizer told the company that he would use his time during lunch and after work in an effort to organize employees. Indeed, while his application was being processed, he organized a picket line at the company to protest low wages. The foreman then told the organizer that he would not be hired because "it's kind of hard to hire you when you're out there on the other side picketing." Had he been hired, the organizer acknowledged that he would have maintained some relationship with the union, and he would likely have later returned to full-time employment with the union. Was the organizer unlawfully denied employment? Explain. [See *Willmar Electric Service, Inc.* v. *National Labor Relations Board,* 968 F.2d 1327 (D.C. Cir. 1992), cert. denied, 113 S.Ct. 1252 (1993).]

NOTES

1. Associated Press, "Flow of Workers from Unions Stanched," *Des Moines Register,* February 18, 1997, p. 4A.

2. *Boston Medical Center,* 330 NLRB 30 (1999).

3. Ibid.

4. Glenn Burkins, "Number of Workers in Labor Unions Grew Last Year," *The Wall Street Journal,* January 26, 1999, p. B12.

5. "Unions Celebrate Biggest Membership Gain in Years," *Waterloo–Cedar Falls Courier,* January 20, 2000, p. C6.

6. Mary Beth Marklein, "Students Laboring at More Than Studies," *USA Today,* May 6, 1999, p. 1D.

7. The historical and political background information used in this chapter was drawn from a number of sources and amalgamated in such a way that precise footnoting was difficult. For example, many of the sociological trends described are discussed in three or four sources. We would, therefore, like to acknowledge the works of the following people, whose research and insights proved to be invaluable resources: Richard S. Belous, Hyman Berman, Angela Y. Davis, Richard Edwards, John J. Flagler, Eli Ginzberg, J. David Greenstone, Isaac A. Hourwich, and Sar A. Levitan.

   Amy Gershenfeld Donnella, the author of this chapter (first edition), would like especially to acknowledge and thank Professor Archibald Cox, from whom she took a course in labor law in 1978, and whose textbook and class lectures provided the cornerstone of her understanding of the subject. She hopes that her own good fortune at having had the opportunity to study labor law under Professor Cox will translate into a richer educational experience for students using this textbook.

8. Isaac A. Hourwich, *Immigration and Labor* (New York: Arno Press, 1969), pp. 125–45.

9. John J. Flagler, *The Labor Movement in the United States,* (Minneapolis: Lerner Publications, 1972), pp. 26–28.

10. Alan Glassman, Naomi Berger Davidson, and Thomas Cummings, *Labor Relations: Reports from the Firing Line* (New York: Business Publications, Inc., 1988), pp. 5–6.

11. Flagler, *Labor Movement,* pp. 26–28.

12. Eli Ginzberg and Hyman Berman, *The American Worker in the Twentieth Century: A History through Autobiographies* (New York: Free Press, 1963), pp. 193–95, in *I Am a Woman Worker,* ed. Andria Taylor Hourwich and Gladys L. Palmer, Affiliated Schools for Workers, 1936, pp. 17 ff.

13. Flagler, *Labor Movement,* pp. 33 and 36, quoting Frederick Lewis Allen, *The Big Change . . .* 1900–1950.

14. Flagler, *Labor Movement,* p. 47.

15. J. David Greenstone, *Labor in American Politics* (New York: Alfred A. Knopf, 1969), p. 21.

16. Archibald Cox, with Derek Bok and Robert A. Gorman, *Cases and Materials on Labor Law,* 8th ed. (Mineola, NY: Foundation Press, 1977), pp. 7–8.

17. Greenstone, *Labor in American Politics,* p. 22.

18. Ibid., p. 23.

19. Flagler, *Labor Movement,* pp. 54–56.

20. John Fossum, *Labor Relations—Development, Structure, Process,* 6th ed. (Burr Ridge, IL: Richard D. Irwin, 1995), p. 36.

21. Cox, *Labor Law,* pp. 60–66.

22. Greenstone, *Labor in American Politics,* p. 83.

23. Cox, *Labor Law,* p. 91.

24. Patrick Hardin, *The Developing Labor Law* (Washington, DC: Bureau of National Affairs, 1992), pp. 31–32.

25. Ibid., p. 94.

26. Ibid., pp. 1, 107–8.

27. Ibid., pp. 1, 108.

28. *Steele* v. *Louisville and Nashville Railroad,* 323 U.S. 192 (1944).

29. *Vaca* v. *Sipes,* 386 U.S. 171 (1967); *Miranda Fuel Co.,* 140 NLRB 181 (1962).

30. The National Labor Relations Act is found in Title 29 U.S.C. § 151 et seq.

31. *U.S.* v. *Lopez,* 115 S.Ct. 1624 (1995).

32. Cox, *Labor Law,* pp. 113–22.

33. Ibid., pp. 99–101.

34. See *Sewell Mfg. Co.,* 138 NLRB 66 (1962), stating that the board's goal is to conduct elections "in a laboratory under conditions as nearly ideal as possible to determine the uninhibited desires of employees" and "to provide an atmosphere conducive to the sober and informed exercise of the franchise free from . . . elements which prevent or impede reasonable choice."

35. *NLRB* v. *Gissel Packing,* 395 U.S. 575 (1969).

36. *Dubuque Packing Co., Inc.* v. *UFCWIU, Local 150A,* 303 NLRB No. 66 (1991).

37. Benjamin J. Taylor and Fred Whitney, *Labor Relations Law,* 4th ed. (Englewood Cliffs, NJ: Prentice Hall, 1983), p. 406.

38. *Majure Transport Co.* v. *NLRB,* 199 F.2d 735 (1952).

39. *NLRB* v. *Norfolk Shipbuilding & Drydock Corp.,* 172 F.2d 813 (4th Cir. 1949).

40. *Southern Saddlery Co.,* 90 NLRB 1205 (1950).

41. See *First National Maintenance Corporation* v. *NLRB,* 101 S.Ct. 2573 (1981).

42. 356 U.S. 342 (1958).

43. *Auciello Iron Works* v. *NLRB,* 517 U.S. 281 (1996).

44. *Allentown Mack Sales & Service, Inc.* v. *NLRB,* 118 S.Ct. 818 (1998).

45. *Wright* v. *Universal Maritime Services,* 119 S.Ct. 391 (1998).

46. Littler et al., *The 1990 Employer,* p. V6.

47. *NLRB* v. *Mackay Radio & Tel. Co.,* 304 U.S. 333 (1938).

48. Littler et al., *The 1990 Employer,* p. V6.

49. *Diamond Walnut Growers, Inc.* v. *National Labor Relations Board,* 118 S.Ct. 1299 (1998).

50. Scott McCartney, "American Airlines Union Is Fined $45.5 Million," *The Wall Street Journal,* April 16, 1999, p. A2.

51. Emily Nelson and J.C. Conklin, "Leery of Strikes, More Workers Stage Sickouts," *The Wall Street Journal,* February 12, 1999, p. B1.

52. *United Steelworkers of America* v. *Sadlowski,* 457 U.S. 102 (1982).

53. Zech and Khun, "National Labor Policy: Is It Truly Designed to Protect the Worker?" *Selected Papers of the American Business Law Association: National Proceedings,* 1982, pp. 442–43.

54. 311 NLRB No. 88 (1993).

55. 309 NLRB No. 163 (1992).

56. 487 U.S. 735 (1988).

57. *Marquez* v. *Screen Actors Guild,* 119 S.Ct 292 (1998).

58. Robert Perkovich and Mark Stein, "Challenges to Arbitration Under Illinois Public Sector Labor Relations Statutes," *Hofstra Labor Law Journal* 7, no. 1 (Fall 1989), p. 197.

PART V

Business and Selected Social Issues

Chapter 15

Consumer Protection

INTRODUCTION

Consumer activists argue that wrongs against buyers are commonplace. Clearly, fraud, misleading advertising, faulty products, privacy invasions, and the like exact a heavy price in personal injuries, deaths, and dollars. Furthermore, wrongdoing or even the mishandling of allegations of wrongdoing can be extremely expensive for American business. [For the Consumer Federation of America, see **http://www.consumerfed.org/**]

In recent years, we have witnessed two of the most stunning consumer protection/product liability settlements in United States history.

- In 1998, the tobacco industry and 46 states agreed on a $206 billion settlement of claims brought by the states to recover the public costs, via Medicaid, of providing health care for people with smoking-related illnesses. Four states had earlier settled for $40 billion, and President Clinton has suggested that the federal government should continue to pursue the tobacco industry. (See Chapters 8 and 16 for further details.)

- In late 1999, a federal bankruptcy judge approved a $4.5 billion bankruptcy reorganization of Dow Corning Corp. as a step toward resolving the decade-long, global legal battle over illnesses linked to silicone breast implants. Some 170,000 women are expected to share $3.2 billion in the settlement, with the remaining $1.3 billion going to other Dow Corning creditors. Recoveries for "diseased" women will range from $12,000 to $300,000 depending on the severity of the illness suffered, but many women may take a quick $2,000, "no questions asked" settlement. The plan may yet be appealed and some individuals may yet sue. The implant settlement plan is particularly interesting in that, to date, little credible scientific evidence supports a connection between the implants and the various illnesses the plaintiffs claim to have suffered. In the case of tobacco, on the other hand, evidence both of the hazards and of the industry's knowledge of those hazards is generally considered persuasive. (See Chapter 16 for further details.)

> plaintiffs are suing the paint industry over claims of lead-poisoning injuries and death

Now the success in those two enormous consumer protection settlements, predictably enough, is raising other even more inventive strategies for curbing alleged business abuse and compensating victims. Borrowing from the tobacco litigation and settlement, plaintiffs are suing the paint industry over claims of lead-poisoning injuries and death from the use of lead-based paint. Broadly, the suits accuse the industry of misleading the public about the safety of lead-based paints. Children who sometimes ingest paint chips or powder have been most troubled by lead poisoning. Lead paint is now banned for residential use and was being phased out 50 years ago, according to the industry.

Part One—Common Law Consumer Protection

Later in this chapter, we will explore government efforts to protect consumers from dangerous products, unfair lending practices, and the like. Before turning to that legislation, we need to appreciate the common law (judge-made law) that preceded and, in some respects, provided the foundation for the many federal, state, and local initiatives of recent years. In addition to the product liability protection (negligence, warranties, and strict liability) discussed in Chapter 16, injured consumers can look to several common law protections, including actions for fraud, misrepresentation, and unconscionability. [For an extensive menu of consumer law sites, see **http://seamless.com/talf/txt/ resource/legal.shtml**] [or see **http://www.lectlaw.com/files/cos19.htm**]

Fraud and Innocent Misrepresentation

If the market is to operate efficiently, the buyer must be able to rely on the truth of the seller's affirmations regarding a product. Regrettably, willful untruths appear common in American commerce. A victim of fraud is entitled to rescind the contract in question and to seek damages, including, in cases of malice, a punitive recovery. Although fraud arises in countless situations and thus is difficult to define, the legal community has generally adopted the following elements, each of which must be proven:

1. There was a misrepresentation of a material fact.
2. The misrepresentation was intentional.
3. The injured party justifiably relied on the misrepresentation.
4. Injury resulted.

In identifying a fraudulent expression, the law distinguishes between statements of objective, verifiable facts and simple expressions of opinion. The latter ordinarily are not fraudulent even though they are erroneous. Thus, normal sales puffing ("This baby is the greatest little car you're ever gonna drive") is fully lawful, and consumers are expected to exercise good judgment in responding to such claims. However, if a misleading expression of opinion comes from an expert, and the other party does not share that expertise (e.g., the sale of a diamond engagement ring), a court probably would offer a remedy. (See Chapter 16 for further examination of puffing.)

Silence.   In limited circumstances, silence may constitute fraud. Typically, that problem may emerge where party A misunderstands the facts of the situation and party B both knows the true facts and knows that A does not know those facts and cannot reasonably be expected to discover them. An example would be a cracked engine block, where the cracks were filled with a sealer and covered with a compound such that the crack is unlikely to be discovered even by capable inspection.[1] In such situations, the knowledgeable party may be under a duty to speak. Nonetheless, the general rule is that silence is fully permissible.

Of course, fraud can involve false conduct as well as false expression. A familiar example is the car seller who rolls back an odometer with the result that the buyer is misled.

A variation on the general theme of fraud is innocent misrepresentation, which differs from fraud only in that the falsehood was unintentional. The wrongdoer believed the statement or conduct in question to be true, but he or she was mistaken. In such cases, the wronged party may secure rescission of the contract, but ordinarily damages are not awarded.

An Alabama jury shocked judicial observers in 1999 when they awarded Barbara Carlisle and her parents, George and Velma Merriweather, $581 million in damages in a dispute over financing for a pair of $1,100 satellite dishes. The plaintiffs claimed that they and thousands of Alabama citizens had been cheated out of $8 million by tricking them into signing credit-card deals requiring 300 percent interest when the advertised rate was 22 percent. The plaintiffs further claimed that they had been targeted for those fraudulent practices because of their race, age, lack of education, and financial status. The trial judge allowed the $975,000 judgment for compensatory damages to stand, but reduced the punitive damages to $300 million. Transamerica Bank, the defendant, intends to appeal the decision.

Source: Associated Press, "Alabama Judge Halves Verdict in Case Involving Charges for Satellite Dishes," *The Wall Street Journal*, August 30, 1999, p. B7.

Unconscionable Contracts

The doctrine of unconscionability emerged from court decisions where jurists concluded that some contracts are so unfair or oppressive as to demand intervention. (Unconscionability is also included in state statutory laws via the Uniform Commercial Code 2–302.) The legal system intrudes on contracts only with the greatest reluctance. Mere foolishness or want of knowledge does not constitute grounds for unconscionability, nor is a contract unconscionable and hence unenforceable merely because one party is spectacularly clever and the other is not. Unconscionability takes two forms:

1. *Procedural unconscionability* is a situation where the bargaining power of the parties was so unequal that the agreement, as a practical matter, was not freely entered. Procedural unconscionability usually arises from lack of knowledge or lack of choice. A consumer may not be reasonably knowledgeable about a contract because of the use of fine print, inconspicuously displayed contract terms, or complex legalese. A consumer may not have voluntarily entered a contract because of lack of time, pressing circumstances, or market conditions.

2. *Substantive unconscionability* is a situation where the clause or contract in question was so manifestly one-sided, oppressive, or unfair as to "shock the conscience of the court." A contract price dramatically exceeding the market price, a contract that does not provide a remedy for a breach, or contract terms completely out of line with the relative risks assumed by the parties are among the conditions that might lead to a finding of substantive unconscionability.

Unconscionability claims normally require proof on both procedural and substantive grounds, but exceptions are sometimes recognized, as illustrated in the *Brower* case below. In situations where one party's bargaining power is dramatically superior to the other and a "take it or leave it" situation emerges, some courts evaluate the resulting arrangement as a *contract of adhesion* which, in practice, is much like the more modern notion of procedural unconscionability.

Suppose you own a furniture store, and you find that your customers all too frequently are unable to make their required payments. One method you employ to better protect yourself is to provide in your standard installment sales contract that the balance due on each item purchased by a particular buyer will remain due until payments have been made on *all* items purchased by that buyer. Thus, everything an individual customer buys from you serves as collateral for all other purchases by that buyer. From a business point of view, this extra protection makes good sense; but from the consumer's point of view, is it so unfair as to be unconscionable?[2]

The *Brower* case that follows involves both adhesion and unconscionability reasoning in a mail order computer sale.

BROWER v. GATEWAY 2000, INC.
246 A.D. 2d 246 (App. Div. 1st N.Y. 1998)

Judge Milonas

Appellants are among the many consumers who purchased computers and software products from defendant Gateway 2000 through a direct-sales system, by mail or telephone order. As of July 3, 1995, it was Gateway's practice to include with the materials shipped to the purchaser along with the merchandise a copy of its "Standard Terms and Conditions Agreement" and any relevant warranties for the products in the shipment. The Agreement begins with a "Note to the Customer," which provides, in slightly larger print than the remainder of the document, in a box that spans the width of the page: "This document contains Gateway 2000's Standard Terms and Conditions. By keeping your Gateway 2000 computer system beyond thirty (30) days after the date of delivery, you accept these Terms and Conditions." The document consists of 16 paragraphs, and, as is relevant to this appeal, paragraph 10 of the agreement, entitled "dispute resolution," reads as follows: "Any dispute or controversy arising out of or relating to this Agreement or its interpretation shall be settled exclusively and finally by arbitration. The arbitration shall be conducted in accordance with the Rules of Conciliation and Arbitration of the International Chamber of Commerce. The arbitration shall be conducted in Chicago, Illinois, U.S.A. before a sole arbitrator. Any award rendered in any such arbitration proceeding shall be final and binding on each of the parties, and judgment may be entered thereon in a court of competent jurisdiction."

Plaintiffs commenced this action on behalf of themselves and others similarly situated for compensatory and punitive damages, alleging deceptive sales practices in seven causes of action, including breach of warranty, breach of contract, fraud and unfair trade practices. In particular, the allegations focused on Gateway's representations and advertising that promised "service when you need it," including around-the-clock free technical support, free software technical support and certain on-site services. According to plaintiffs, not only were they unable to avail themselves of this offer because it was virtually impossible to get through to a technician, but also Gateway continued to advertise this claim notwithstanding numerous complaints and reports about the problem.

Insofar as is relevant to appellants, who purchased their computers after July 3, 1995, Gateway moved to dismiss the complaint based on the arbitration clause in the Agreement. Appellants argued that the arbitration clause is invalid under UCC 2–207, unconscionable under UCC 2–302 and an unenforceable contract of adhesion. Specifically, they claimed that the provision was obscure; that a customer could not reasonably be expected to appreciate or investigate its meaning and effect; that the International Chamber of Commerce (ICC) was not a forum commonly used for consumer matters; and that because ICC headquarters were in France, it was particularly difficult to locate the organization and its rules. To illustrate just how inaccessible the forum was, appellants advised the court that the ICC was not registered with the Secretary of State, that efforts to locate and contact the ICC had been unsuccessful and that apparently the only way to attempt to contact the ICC was through the United States Council for International Business, with which the ICC maintained some sort of relationship.

In support of their arguments, appellants submitted a copy of the ICC's Rules of Conciliation and Arbitration and contended that the cost of ICC arbitration was prohibitive, particularly given the amount of the typical consumer claim involved. For example, a claim of less than $50,000 required advance fees of $4,000 (more than the cost of most Gateway products), of which the $2,000 registration fee was nonrefundable even if the consumer prevailed at the arbitration. Consumers would also incur travel expenses disproportionate to the damages sought, which appellants' counsel estimated would not exceed $1,000 per customer in this action, as well as bear the cost of Gateway's legal fees if the consumer did not prevail at the arbitration; in this respect, the ICC Rules follow the "loser pays" rule used in England. Also, although Chicago was designated as the site of the actual arbitration, all correspondence must be sent to ICC headquarters in France.

The IAS Court dismissed the complaint as to appellants based on the arbitration clause in the Agreements delivered with their computers. We agree with the court's decision and reasoning in all respects but for the issue of the unconscionability of the designation of the ICC as the arbitration body.

* * * * *

[W]ith respect to appellants' claim that the arbitration clause is unenforceable as a contract of adhesion, in that it involved no choice or negotiation on the part of the consumer but was a "take it or leave it" proposition, we find that this argument was properly rejected by the IAS Court. Although the parties clearly do not possess equal bargaining power, this factor alone does not invalidate the contract as one of adhesion. As the IAS Court observed, with the ability to make the purchase elsewhere and the express option to return the goods, the consumer is not in a "take it or leave it" position at all; if any term of the agreement is unacceptable to the consumer, he or she can easily buy a competitor's product instead—either from a retailer or directly from the manufacturer—and reject Gateway's agreement by returning the merchandise. The consumer has 30 days to make that decision . . .

While returning the goods to avoid the formation of the contract entails affirmative action on the part of the consumer, and even some expense, this may be seen as a trade-off for the convenience and savings for which the consumer presumably opted when he or she chose to make a purchase of such consequence by phone or mail as an alternative to on-site retail shopping. That a consumer does not read the agreement or thereafter claims he or she failed to understand or appreciate some term therein does not invalidate the contract any more than such claim would undo a contract formed under other circumstances.

* * * * *

Finally, we turn to appellant's argument that the IAS Court should have declared the contract unenforceable, pursuant to UCC 2–302, on the ground that the arbitration clause is unconscionable due to the unduly burdensome procedure and cost for the individual consumer. The IAS Court found that while a class action lawsuit, such as the one herein, may be a less costly alternative to the arbitration (which is generally less costly than litigation), that does not alter the binding effect of the valid arbitration clause contained in the agreement.

As a general matter, under New York law, unconscionability requires a showing that a contract is "both procedurally and substantively unconscionable when made." That is, there must be "some showing of 'an absence of meaningful choice on the part of one of the parties together with contract terms which are unreasonably favorable to the other party.'" The *Avco* Court took pains to note, however, that the purpose of this doctrine is not to redress the inequality between the parties but simply to ensure that the more powerful party cannot "'surprise'" the other party with some overly oppressive term.

As to the procedural element, a court will look to the contract formation process to determine if in fact one party lacked any meaningful choice in entering into the contract, taking into consideration such factors as the setting of the transaction, the experience and education of the party claiming unconscionability, whether the contract contained "fine print," whether the seller used "high-pressured tactics" and any disparity in the parties' bargaining power. None of these factors supports appellants' claim here. Any purchaser has 30 days within which to thoroughly examine the contents of their shipment, including the terms of the Agreement, and seek clarification of any term therein. The Agreement itself, which is entitled in large print "Standard Terms and Conditions Agreement," consists of only four pages and 16 paragraphs, all of which appear in the same size print. Moreover, despite appellants' claims to the contrary, the arbitration clause is in no way "hidden" or "tucked away" within a complex document of inordinate length, nor is the option of returning the merchandise, to avoid the contract, somehow a "precarious" one . . .

With respect to the substantive element, which entails an examination of the substance of the Agreement in order to determine whether the terms unreasonably favor one party we do not find that the possible inconvenience of the chosen site (Chicago) alone rises to the level of unconscionability. We do find, however, that the excessive cost factor that is necessarily entailed in arbitrating before the ICC is unreasonable and surely serves to deter the individual consumer from invoking the process. Barred from resorting to the courts by the arbitration clause in the first instance, the designation of a financially prohibitive forum effectively bars consumers from this forum as well; consumers are thus left with no forum at all in which to resolve a dispute.

While it is true that, under New York law, unconscionability is generally predicated on the presence of both the procedural and substantive elements, the substantive element alone may be sufficient to render the terms of the provision at issue unenforceable. Excessive fees, such as those incurred under the ICC procedure, have been grounds for finding an arbitration provision unenforceable or commercially unreasonable.

* * * * *

Thus, we modify the order on appeal to the extent of finding that portion of the arbitration provision requiring arbitration before the ICC to be unconscionable and remand to Supreme Court so that the parties have the opportunity to seek appropriate substitution of an arbitrator pursuant to the Federal Arbitration Act.

Modified and remanded.

Questions

1. a. Why was the Gateway contract not treated as a wrongful adhesion arrangement?
    b. Why was the Gateway contract substantively unconscionable?
2. What does the court mean by its statement that a contract must be "both procedurally and substantively unconscionable"?
3. Annette Phillips worked as a bartender at a Hooters restaurant in Myrtle Beach, South Carolina (HOMB), beginning in 1989. She claims Gerald Brooks, a Hooters official sexually harassed her in 1996 by grabbing and slapping her buttocks. After appealing to her manager for help and being told to "let it go," she quit her job. Her attorney then contacted Hooters about the alleged harassment and was told that Phillips would be required to submit the claim to arbitration under an agreement Phillips had signed in 1994. Phillips refused to arbitrate and Hooters sued to compel arbitration. Phillips claimed the agreement was unenforceable. She pointed to some of the conditions of the agreement:

   - The employee must supply a list of witnesses; Hooters need not.
   - Arbitrators were chosen from a list supplied by Hooters.
   - Hooters may punish arbitrators by removing them from the list.
   - Hooters may modify the rules without notice to the employee.

     a. Is the arbitration agreement unconscionable and therefore unenforceable? Explain.
     b. Did Hooters breach its contract with Phillips? Explain.

4. Plaintiff Willie had listed his business in the Wichita, Kansas, Yellow Pages for 13 years. The plaintiff was expanding his business, and he entered into an agreement with the defendant phone company to include additional telephone numbers in the directory. The defendant inadvertently failed to include one of the numbers in the directory. The contract signed by the parties included a conspicuous exculpatory clause limiting the phone company's liability for errors and omissions to an amount equal to the cost of the ad. On discovering the omission, the plaintiff had begun advertising the number on television at a cost of approximately $5,000. Plaintiff contends the exculpatory clause is unconscionable, and, therefore, unenforceable. Decide. Explain. [See *Willie* v. *Southwestern Bell Telephone Company,* 549 P.2d 903 (Kan. 1976).]

Part Two—The Consumer and Government Regulation of Business

STATE LAWS

Having looked at the common law foundation of consumer protection, we now turn to some of the many governmental measures that provide shelter in the marketplace. Many states have enacted comprehensive consumer protection statutes, such as Pennsylvania's Unfair Practices and Consumer Protection Law. States also have specific statutes addressing such problems as door-to-door sales, debtor protection, telemarketing fraud, and so forth. We will look at only one of those, the so-called lemon laws, which address the particularly frustrating problem of a hopelessly defective vehicle. [For links to state and local consumer interest organizations, see **http://www.stateandlocal.org/**]

Lemon Laws.   Of course, new car purchases are covered by warranty laws (see Chapter 16 for a discussion of UCC warranty provisions and the federal Magnuson Moss Warranty Act); in addition, all 50 states have some form of law designed to provide recourse for consumers whose new vehicles turn out to be defective such that they cannot be repaired after a reasonable effort. The quarrel, of course, is about when a car is truly a lemon. Lemon laws typically cover new cars for one to two years or 12,000 to 18,000 miles after purchase. Typically, state laws provide that the vehicle must have been returned to the manufacturer or dealer three or four times to repair the same defect and that defect must substantially impair the value or safety of the vehicle, *or* the vehicle must have been unavailable to the consumer for a total of at least 30 days in a 12-month period. Such a vehicle is a lemon, and the purchaser is entitled to a replacement vehicle or full refund of the purchase price. In some states, used cars may also be treated as lemons. In almost all states, the determination about whether a car is a lemon is handled by an arbitration panel, which in certain states is arranged by the automobile manufacturers; other arrangements, such as a panel provided by the American Arbitration Association, are available in many states. If dissatisfied with the ruling, the consumer may then bring suit.

> The quarrel, of course, is about when a car is truly a lemon

The case that follows examines Connecticut's lemon law requirements. [For "The Lemon Car Page," see **http://www.mindspring.com/~wf1/**]

GENERAL MOTORS CORPORATION v. DOHMANN
722 A.2d 1205 (S.Ct. Conn. 1998)

Chief Justice Callahan

The sole issue in this appeal is whether the Connecticut "lemon law" requires the plaintiff, General Motors Corporation, to provide the defendant, Eugene Dohmann, with a replacement vehicle.

* * * * *

The arbitration panel to which the matter had been referred subsequent to the defendant having instituted an arbitration proceeding reasonably could have found the following facts. On October 26, 1996, the defendant purchased a new Chevrolet S-10 pickup truck (truck) from Maritime Motors (Maritime), a General Motors dealership located in South Norwalk. The following day, the defendant noticed defects in the paint on the truck's hood, roof and bumpers. The defendant promptly notified Maritime of the defects and requested that the dealership provide him with a replacement vehicle. Maritime agreed to inspect the truck for defects, but refused the defendant's request for a replacement vehicle.

After inspecting the truck, Maritime agreed that the truck's paint was defective, but again refused to provide a different vehicle. Instead, the dealership offered to replace the truck's hood, the part of the truck on which the paint defects were most visible, with a hood taken from another vehicle of the same color. The defendant allowed Maritime to undertake that repair attempt. The replacement hood, however, did not fit properly and the paint was not an exact match. Dissatisfied with the repair attempt, the defendant told Maritime to reinstall the original hood, and Maritime complied.

Maritime subsequently suggested two other possible methods of curing the defects in the paint: (1) wet sanding and (2) repainting the affected areas of the truck. The defendant, however, rejected these suggestions because he believed that both wet sanding and repainting would remove the truck's original factory finish. In the defendant's view, the factory process produces a paint finish superior to that of a body shop. As a result, he informed Maritime that he would not accept any

repairs that would remove or alter the factory finish of the truck. Because both of the suggested repairs involved processes that would alter the truck's original factory finish, the defendant refused to authorize additional repair attempts.

Thereafter, the defendant initiated an arbitration proceeding against the plaintiff. After a hearing, a three member arbitration panel determined that: (1) the truck had been subject to a reasonable number of unsuccessful repair attempts, and (2) the defective paint substantially impaired the truck's value to the defendant. Consequently, the panel concluded that the defendant was entitled to a new, comparably equipped replacement vehicle.

On appeal, the plaintiff claims that the trial court improperly affirmed the decision of the arbitration panel. Specifically, the plaintiff maintains that the record does not contain substantial evidence to support the arbitrators' findings that: (1) the truck had been subject to a reasonable number of repair attempts, and (2) the defects in the paint substantially impaired the value of the truck to the defendant.

Our analysis begins with a brief overview of Connecticut's lemon law legislation. "In 1982, the Connecticut legislature enacted Public Acts 1982, No. 82–287 (Lemon Law I). For consumer buyers of new motor vehicles, the act provides supplemental remedies of repair, replacement and refund to facilitate the enforcement of express warranties made by the manufacturers of such vehicles. These supplemental remedies come into play whenever a manufacturer or authorized dealer, after a reasonable number of repair attempts, is unable substantially to conform a new vehicle to the terms of the express warranty. . . .

"In 1984, the legislature enacted Public Acts 1984, No. 84–338 (Lemon Law II). The purpose of Lemon Law II is to provide, for consumer purchasers of new motor vehicles, an alternative to civil litigation. The key provision authorizes the department of consumer protection to establish 'an independent arbitration procedure for the settlement of disputes between consumers and manufacturers of motor vehicles which do not conform to all applicable warranties.'"

* * * * *

II

The plaintiff first claims that the record does not contain substantial evidence to support the arbitrators' finding that the defendant's truck had been subjected to a reasonable number of unsuccessful attempts to repair its paint. Specifically, the plaintiff maintains that, because the additional repairs suggested by the dealership were capable of producing a paint finish that met factory standards, the single attempt to cure the defect by replacing the truck's hood was insufficient to constitute the requisite reasonable number of repair attempts. We disagree.

Section 42–179 provides in relevant part: "(d) If the manufacturer, or its agents or authorized dealers are unable to conform the motor vehicle to any applicable express warranty by repairing or correcting any defect or condition which substantially impairs the use, safety or value of the motor vehicle to the consumer *after a reasonable number of [repair] attempts,* the manufacturer shall replace the motor vehicle with a new motor vehicle acceptable to the consumer . . . (e) It shall be presumed that a reasonable number of [repair] attempts have been undertaken . . . if . . . the same nonconformity has been subject to repair four or more times . . . No claim shall be made under this section unless at least one attempt to repair a nonconformity has been made . . ."

* * * * *

[T]he legislative program and review committee's report read in relevant part: "Generally a reasonable number of repair attempts is defined as four attempts during the first 18,000 miles or two years and the problem continues to exist . . . In some instances, less than four repair attempts is allowed if the problem is one for which evidence exists that no repair will bring the vehicle back into conformance." The report further states: "In cases involving problems with the paint on a vehicle, a determination may be made that it is impossible for any dealer to repaint the vehicle in a manner that would match the type of finish originally achieved at the manufacturer's plant when the car was built." Consequently, if the record contains substantial evidence to support a

finding that proposed additional repair attempts would not have produced a paint finish that satisfied factory paint specifications, arbitrators reasonably may find that a single repair attempt is sufficient.

The record before us reveals the following regarding the utility of additional repair attempts. The plaintiff presented affidavits of two automobile body experts who stated that body shop paint processes are capable of producing results equal to, and in some cases superior to, those produced by the original factory paint process. The state's technical expert, Gregory Carver, however, testified that the conditions under which the factory originally paints a vehicle are superior to those that exist in a body shop. Specifically Carver stated that paint bonds to the surface of a vehicle most successfully the first time it is applied, and that, therefore, it is impossible for a body shop to duplicate the bond achieved at the factory. Carver further stated that the finish of a repainted vehicle is less durable than the finish applied at the factory.

The arbitration panel acted within its discretion as a fact finder by crediting Carver's testimony over that of the plaintiff. Moreover, on the basis of Carver's testimony, the arbitration panel reasonably could have concluded that the suggested additional repair attempts would not have produced a finish that met factory paint specifications. We conclude, therefore, that the record contains substantial evidence to support the panel's conclusion that, under the circumstances, Maritime's attempt to replace the truck's hood constituted a reasonable number of repair attempts.

III

The plaintiff next claims that the arbitrators improperly concluded that the paint defects substantially impaired the value of the truck to the defendant.

* * * * *

A

Our analysis begins with the language of [the statute]. Section 42–179 (d) provides in relevant part: "If the manufacturer, or its agents or authorized dealers are unable to conform the motor vehicle to any applicable express warranty by repairing or correcting any defect or condition which *substantially impairs the . . . value of the motor vehicle to the consumer* . . . the manufacturer shall replace the motor vehicle . . ." The phrase "to the consumer" in § 42–179 (d) suggests that the needs and expectations of the individual consumer should be considered in a determination of whether a defect has substantially impaired the value of a vehicle. That language, therefore, suggests that the legislature intended to incorporate a subjective component into the determination of "substantial impairment" under § 42–179 (d).

Other language contained in § 42–179 (d), however, indicates that the standard for "substantial impairment" was intended to incorporate an objective component as well as a subjective component. Specifically, § 42–179 (d) provides that "*it shall be an affirmative defense to any claim under this section . . . that an alleged nonconformity does not substantially impair such . . . value . . .*" The statutory provision that permits a manufacturer to show that the value of a vehicle has not, in fact, been substantially impaired, suggests that the subjective opinion of the consumer is not dispositive. If the standard were completely subjective, the manufacturer would almost never be able to prove lack of "substantial impairment," and thus, the right to prove that the value of the vehicle had not been substantially impaired would be meaningless.

* * * * *

We conclude, therefore, that under the lemon law the standard for determining whether a defect substantially impairs the use, safety or value of a motor vehicle to the consumer is both subjective and objective. The standard is subjective in that the fact finder first must examine the subjective desires, needs and circumstances of the particular consumer. In light of those desires, needs and circumstances, the fact finder then must make an objective determination as to whether the value of the motor vehicle to the consumer has, in fact, been substantially impaired. In making this determination, the fact finder must determine that the consumer's subjective desires, needs and circumstances are reasonable.

B

Having articulated the standard for substantial impairment under the lemon law, we address the plaintiff's claim that the record does not contain substantial evidence to support a finding that the evident defects in the paint substantially impaired the truck's value to the defendant.

During the arbitration hearing, the defendant testified that he takes great pride in the appearance of the vehicles that he owns and maintains the finish of those vehicles in factory condition. Moreover, he stated that appearance was a major factor in his decision to purchase a new truck rather than a used one. On the basis of that testimony, the arbitrators reasonably could have concluded that, had the defendant known of the defects in the paint before accepting delivery, he would not have purchased the truck, and that the statutory requirement of subjective substantial impairment had been satisfied.

Carver, the state's technical expert, testified that, on a scale of one to ten, with ten representing the worst amount of damage, the damage to the truck constituted a three. Carver further stated that the paint defects could not be removed easily. Moreover, Carver corroborated the defendant's contention that wet sanding and repainting the truck would remove its finish. Finally, Carver stated that the paint defects possibly could affect the resale value of the vehicle and that if the vehicle was not maintained meticulously, the affected areas could deteriorate further. Thus, on the basis of Carver's testimony, the arbitrators reasonably could have concluded that the statutory requirement of objective substantial impairment had been satisfied.

We conclude, therefore, that the record contains substantial evidence to support a finding that the defects in the truck's paint substantially impaired its value to the defendant.

Affirmed.

Questions

1. How did the court determine when a "reasonable" number of repair attempts had been undertaken?
2. *a.* What did the court mean in saying that "the standard for determining whether a defect substantially impairs the use, safety or value of a motor vehicle to the consumer is both subjective and objective?"
   b. What was the significance of that dual standard to the outcome of the case?
3. Dieter and Hermes agreed to buy a new 1996 Dodge Ram pick-up truck from Fascona Chrysler-Plymouth-Dodge Trucks on December 12, 1995. They requested the installation of some after-market accessories—a tonneau cover, a bug shield, and rustproofing. When Dieter and Hermes returned to take delivery of the truck, they noticed it had been scratched during the installation of the accessories. The salesperson told them the scratches would be repaired. Four months later the dealership sent the truck to a body shop for repairs.

After repair, Dieter and Hermes noticed swirl marks in the truck's finish. Dieter then demanded that Frascona repurchase the truck. Eight months later Dieter and Hermes sued Chrysler Corporation under Wisconsin's lemon law.

a. Make the argument that the lemon law does not apply to the facts of this case.
b. Decide the case. Explain. See *Dieter and Hermes* v. *Chrysler Corporation,* 600 N.W. 2d 201 (Wis. 1999).

FEDERAL LAWS

The Federal Trade Commission (FTC)

The Federal Trade Commission was created in 1914 to prevent "unfair methods of competition and unfair or deceptive acts or practices in and affecting commerce." In conducting its business, the FTC performs as a miniature government with extensive and powerful quasi-legislative and quasi-judicial roles. [For the FTC's Bureau of Consumer Protection home page, see **http://www.ftc.gov/bcp/bcp.htm**]

Rule Making.   The FTC's primary legislative direction is in issuing trade regulation rules to enforce the intent of broadly drawn congressional legislation. That is, the rules specify those particular acts or practices that the commission deems deceptive.

In the same vein, the FTC issued industry guides, which are the commission's interpretations of laws it enforces. The guides provide advice to industry and the public about the likely legality of specific marketing practices. For example, in 1998, the FTC revised its Environmental Marketing or "Green Guides" to expand the definitions of "recyclable" and "recycled content," specifying instructions for when those words can lawfully be used in advertising. The guides do not have the force of law, but a failure to observe them might result in adjudication. [For a free copy of "Eco-Speak: A User's Guide to the Language of Recycling" and 150 other consumer publications, see the Federal Trade Commission website at **www.ftc.gov**]

The FTC's quasi-legislative or rule-making power is extensive as evidenced by the following examples:

> **Tommy Hilfiger USA agreed to pay a $300,000 civil penalty**

• In 1999, the FTC announced that clothing manufacturer Tommy Hilfiger USA agreed to pay a $300,000 civil penalty for allegedly violating the FTC's Care Labeling Rule for clothing. The FTC says that the Hilfiger garment care instructions, if followed, led to significant bleeding and fading.[3]
• At this writing in 1999, the FTC is considering expanding its rules governing funeral marketing and sales practices. The rules require providing consumers with price information and "unbundling" services so that embalming or an expensive limousine is not imposed on the consumer as part of a package. The FTC is also concerned that the rules

may need to be expanded and applied to cemeteries that are now extensively involved in funeral marketing.

- The FTC's Telemarketing Sales Rule is designed to prevent fraud and reduce a little of the aggravation in life. The rule (1) requires callers to quickly reveal the name of the business, the nature of the product, and so on; (2) limits calls to between 8 AM and 9 PM, local time; (3) bans calls to those who have indicated that they do not want to be called; and (4) bans threats, profanity, and repeated calling.[4]

A 1999 survey asked adult Americans how they feel about telemarketing calls:

- "Always intrusion, never opportunity"—47 percent.
- "Mostly intrusion, occasionally opportunity"—32 percent.
- "Sometimes intrusion, sometimes opportunity"—14 percent.
- "Always opportunity, never intrusion"—3 percent.
- "Mostly opportunity, never intrusion"—3 percent.
- "Don't know"—1 percent.

Source: Anne R. Carey and Bob Laird, *USA Today,* May 3, 1999, p. 1A.

Adjudication.   On its own initiative or as a result of a citizen complaint, the FTC may conduct investigations into suspect trade practices. At that point, the FTC may drop the proceeding, settle the matter informally, or issue a formal complaint. An informal settlement normally takes the form of a consent agreement in which the party under investigation voluntarily discontinues the practice in question but is not required to admit guilt.

Where an agreement cannot be reached, the FTC may proceed with a formal complaint. In that case, the matter proceeds essentially as a trial conducted before an administrative law judge (see Chapter 8).

The FTC has no authority to impose criminal sanctions. Although it can impose fines, the commission often engages in more creative remedies—for example, ordering corrective advertising to counteract previous misleading ads or requiring contracts to be altered.

In 1999, the FTC sent a report to Congress urging new laws regulating cigars in the same manner as cigarettes and smokeless tobacco. The rules would require health warnings and would prohibit cigar ads on television and radio.

Fraud and Deception

Unfair and deceptive trade practices, including those in advertising, are forbidden under Section 5 of the Federal Trade Commission Act. An unfair trade practice (1) must be likely to cause substantial injury to consumers, (2) must not be reasonably avoidable by consumers themselves, and (3) must not be outweighed by countervailing benefits to consumers or to competition. In specifying its intentions about deception, Congress indicated that the FTC need not do a rigorous cost/benefit analysis in each case, but that it must weigh all of the evidence. The FTC test for deception requires that the claim is (1) false or likely to mislead the reasonable consumer and (2) material to the consumer's decision making. Proof of actual deception is not necessary; rather, a showing of some probability of deception is sufficient. The words in an ad must be examined in their total context, and the FTC may consider evidence regarding consumers' actual interpretations. Reasonable consumers are something like "ordinary people." "Materiality" refers to whether the claim actually affects consumer choice.

Deception can take many forms, including, for example, testimonials by celebrities who do not use the endorsed product or do not have sufficient expertise to evaluate its quality. The primary areas of dispute involve quality and price.

Quality Claims.   "Fewer calories," "faster acting," "more effective" are the kinds of claims that may lead to allegations of deception unless they are factually supportable. Under the FTC's ad substantiation program, advertisers are engaging in unfair and deceptive practices if they make product claims without some reasonable foundation for those claims. For example, credible survey evidence must be in hand if an advertiser says, "Consumers prefer our brand two to one." Indeed, in recent years the FTC has settled many such claims, including the following:

- In 1999, the FTC announced that R.J. Reynolds agreed to settle charges that its Winston ads claiming "no additives" led some consumers to think they were buying a healthier cigarette when no evidence supported that conclusion.[5]
- In 1997, Exxon agreed to run "educational" ads to contradict its earlier claims about the importance of high-octane gasoline. The new ads must tell consumers that most cars run just as well on cheaper, regular-octane gasoline.[6]
- In 1999, the FTC announced lawsuits against 25 companies accused of initially offering free or discounted trips to students before changing those terms after signups.[7]

[For an advertising law database, see **http://www.webcom.com/~lewrose/home.html**]

Pricing.   Deception in price advertising sometimes takes the form of the so-called bait and switch practice, where a product is advertised at a very low price to attract customers although the seller actually has no intention of selling at that price. Once the customer is in the door (having taken the bait), the strategy is to switch the customer's attention to another, higher-priced product.

Sale pricing also sometimes leads to claims of deception. When is a sale not truly a sale?

When is a sale not truly a sale?

Do some retailers offer phony markdowns based on inflated "original" or "regular" prices? The FTC has long maintained guidelines for proving that a former price was genuine, but the problem is one that has been left largely to the states.

Question

1. A recent 11-state survey found that the majority of car dealers are not fully complying with a Federal Trade Commission used car rule requiring that dealers post a "Buyer's Guide" in each car saying, among other things, whether the car is to be sold "as is," and spelling out warranty terms, if any.[8]
    a. Is the buyer's guide a good rule? Explain.
    b. Should the FTC have required used car dealers to disclose known defects as part of the buyer's guide? Explain.

THE CONSUMER PRODUCT SAFETY COMMISSION (CPSC)

Imagine yourself to be the parent of a daughter whose hair is eaten by the doll you gave her for Christmas. After extracting her hair from the doll's mouth, she heads for the ballpark and is hit in the head playing Little League baseball. Has she simply had a bad day, or are these episodes evidence that your child needs greater government protection from dangerous products? During and after the 1996 Christmas season, parents across America were amazed when the hair or fingers of about 100 children were chomped by Cabbage Patch Snacktime Kids dolls. The battery-powered dolls were designed to "eat" play versions of carrots and french fries. The manufacturer, Mattel, put warning labels on the doll boxes and offered $40 to all buyers who would turn in a doll, but only about 1,000 of the 500,000 in circulation were returned. The Consumer Product Safety Commission (CPSC), the government agency with oversight in this area, investigated the toy but did not find serious safety hazards.[9]

CPSC Chairwoman Ann Brown argued in late 1996 that baseballs and softballs need softer, spongier cores.[10] Is baseball dangerous? A recent study of 2,800 ball players, ages 7 to 18, found 81 injuries over the course of a season. Eleven of those injuries were severe, resulting in a severe-injury rate of 0.008 per 100 hours played.[11] Each year 19 million kids play baseball; injuries treated in emergency rooms totaled 162,100 in 1995.[12] [For the CPSC home page, see **http://www.cpsc.gov/**]

Questions

1. Do we need government rules to protect children from hair-gobbling dolls and from baseballs? Explain.
2. CPSC official Ken Giles said, "Even one death is one death too many if it can be prevented." Comment.

Reducing Risk

The CPSC, created in 1972, is responsible for reducing the risks in using some 15,000 consumer products, including toys, lawn mowers, washing machines, bicycles, portable heaters, and household chemicals. Each year, about 22,000 deaths and 29.5 million injuries are associated with these products.[13] For example, each year 74 people are killed and 20,000 more injured on or near riding lawn mowers and garden tractors.[14]

Duties. The CPSC's duties may be summarized as follows:

1. Data collection. The commission conducts research and collects information as a foundation for regulating product safety. Its National Electronic Injury Surveillance System (NEISS) collects data from many hospital emergency rooms across the country.

2. Rule making. The commission, via its rule-making authority, promulgates mandatory consumer product safety, performance, and labeling standards. It invites public comments and suggestions. Industry trade associations have been more active in submitting offers to set standards, but consumers and consumer groups have been encouraged to participate. Standards are reviewed under traditional due process requirements, including publication in the *Federal Register,* notice to the affected parties, and hearings. Affected parties may petition for a judicial reversal of the rules.

Successful rule building is a challenge, as evidenced by the CPSC's near 30-year battle over fire standards for children's sleepwear. The original standard, dating from the 1970s, required all children's sleepwear to be flame resistant.[15] The effect of that standard was to largely remove children's cotton sleepwear from the market since it is highly flammable. The result was that polyester, which tends to melt rather than burn, became the material of choice for children's sleepwear. Then in 1996 the CPSC, by a 2–1 vote modified its rules to allow nontreated cotton clothing to be sold as sleepwear so long as it was tight fitting. The Commission said that it changed the rules because they were difficult to enforce and unnecessary.[16] The evidence the commission considered partially explains its reasoning and illustrates the difficulty of writing and enforcing rules of any kind. Long underwear and comfortable cotton clothing, such as highly flammable sweat shirts, were routinely being sold near store's sleepwear departments in order to avoid the CPSC standard.[17] The commission was powerless to act since the garments were not labeled sleepwear. Clothing-related thermal burn deaths declined sharply after the initial rule was approved in the 1970s. Among children under age 15, such deaths totaled 70 in 1970, 15 in 1975, and 3 or fewer in each year from 1993 to 1996.[18] At this writing in 1999, legislation has been introduced in Congress to restore the original standards, a move strenuously resisted by the cotton industry.[19]

> Clothing-related thermal burn deaths declined sharply after the initial rule was approved in the 1970s

3. Compliance. The CPSC is empowered to use a variety of strategies in securing compliance. Manufacturers must certify before distribution that products meet federal safety standards. Agents of the commission may inspect manufacturing sites. The commission can mandate specific product safety testing procedures, and businesses other than retailers are required to keep safety records.

Compliance is often complicated by consumer indifference or resistance to product recalls. Excluding some more expensive items, fewer than 5 percent of recalled toys, for example, are actually returned for repairs or replacements.[20]

4. Enforcement. In cases of severe and imminent hazards, the CPSC may seek an immediate court order to remove a product from the market. In less urgent circumstances, the commission may proceed with its own administrative remedy. Because it prefers to secure voluntary compliance, the commission may urge the company to issue public or private notices of a defect, or it may seek the repair or replacement of defective parts. For example, some 10 million playpens were recalled in 1998 by the CPSC because loose clothing and strings might get caught on protruding rivets, leading to strangulations.[21] Eight children have died since 1982 in that manner.[22]

Where voluntary negotiations fail, the CPSC may proceed with an adjudicative hearing, conducted in the manner of a trial, before an administrative law judge or members of the commission. The decision may be appealed to the full commission and thereafter to the U.S. Court of Appeals. Failure to comply with safety provisions may result in civil or criminal penalties.

In 1999 the CPSC fined McDonald's $4 million for allegedly failing to notify the CPSC about injuries at its playgrounds.[23] Some 400 children had suffered injuries on the "Big Mac Climber," but that device and others have since been removed. All of the injuries occurred prior to 1995. The company now employs cushioned surfaces, rounded corners and nonpinch surfaces, and CPSC chair, Anne Brown, pronounced McDonald's playgrounds safe in 1999.[24]

Only a few products have actually been banned from the market. For example, in 1988 Congress required the CPSC to ban most lawn darts. The play items had resulted in at least three deaths and several thousand injuries. Most lawn-dart injuries have been suffered by children.

CONSUMER PRIVACY

Privacy was never a big deal to Larry Levin. Then, without warning, pornographic marketers began stuffing his mailbox with kinky catalogs.

After months of efforts, Levin was unable to track down how they got his name. But the Cherry Hill, N.J., resident has since had his name removed from hundreds of mailing lists. He even had a rubber stamp made that he stamps across every bill he pays: DO NOT SELL OUR NAMES WITHOUT A COURT ORDER.

"I give the same warning to every company I do business with," Levin says. "If you sell my name, you're done." His campaign has significantly slowed, but not stopped, the flow of junk mail.[25]

Quickly and rather quietly, privacy protection has become one of the biggest consumer concerns in America. Of course, much of the new unease springs from dramatic technology advances that make intrusions and information selling easier and more profitable. Those computer-based privacy concerns are addressed in Chapter 18, but here we will take a more generic look at the ways in which marketers are invading consumer privacy and the methods for curbing that abuse. These privacy invasions take many forms. Phone companies, for example, can legally sell information regarding a consumer's phone calls, such as those to a shopping service, to other companies who might use that information to market their own products. That practice is legal at this writing, following a 1999 federal court ruling striking down Federal Communications Commission rules forbidding such sales.[26] The court found the rules violated the First Amendment and that the government had failed to provide proof of harm to privacy or competition.[27] Similarly, retail stores, banks, mortgage companies, and credit-card companies sell information regarding credit balances, buying patterns, and the like to marketers or information brokers. At this writing in 1999, Congress is debating legislation to reduce or prevent the sale of information taken from medical records. Direct-mail companies, for example, are very interested in selling lists of individuals with continuing illnesses such as diabetes, while drug companies and others are very interested in buying that information.

Of course, smoothly flowing information is vital to efficiency in a free-market economy. Better service and lower prices are both, at least in part, a function of good information. Nonetheless, consumer advocates are lobbying for strong state and federal laws to maintain privacy. Some businesses have voluntarily taken steps to protect consumer rights. In 1998, American Express killed a deal it had struck with a database marketing firm, KnowledgeBase, under which AmEx would have sold detailed data about consumers' purchasing habits. The change in plans appeared to be in response to an intense consumer outcry, although AmEx said the deal simply was not going to be as profitable as anticipated.[28]

Question

1. Mark Johnson of the *Tampa Tribune:*

    Comfort Inn has your number—your credit card number, that is.

    It only takes spending one night at a hotel or motel to put a customer and his or her credit card information into that company's database file. That dossier, however, can grow to include details such as what movies guests ordered, if they used the health club and whether they golf.

    More sophisticated computer systems also can cull information from outside sources such as mailing lists, online public records and census data to assemble a customer profile. The hotel may know the value of your house or whether you own a dog.[29]

    What benefits come to customers and marketers from these intrusions on consumer privacy?

Part Three—Debtor/Creditor Law

CREDIT REGULATIONS

Perhaps you are operating a business selling furniture, appliances, cars, or other consumer goods, and your customers ordinarily do not pay in cash. You may have strong faith in the free market; however, Congress, the state legislatures, and most American people have decided that credit arrangements are so important, so confusing, and so potentially hurtful that they have supplemented the market's powerful messages with specific government rules. We will take an abbreviated look at several particularly important pieces of federal consumer credit legislation. [For a debtor/creditor law database, see **http://www.law.cornell.edu/topics/debtor–creditor. html**]

Truth in Lending Act (TILA)

As we increasingly turned to credit financing, consumers often did not understand the full cost of buying on credit. The TILA is part of the Consumer Credit Protection Act of 1968. Having been designed for consumer protection, it does not cover all loans. The following standards determine the TILA's applicability:

1. The debtor must be a "natural person" rather than an organization.
2. The creditor must be regularly engaged in extending credit and must be the person to whom the debt is initially payable.
3. The purpose of the credit must be "primarily for personal, family, or household purposes" not in excess of $25,000. However, "consumer real property transactions" are covered by the act. Hence, home purchases fall within TILA provisions.
4. The credit must be subject to a finance charge or payable in more than four installments.

Following the enactment of the TILA, the Federal Reserve Board developed Regulation Z detailing the specific requirements of the act. The TILA was designed both to protect consumers from credit abuse and to assist them in becoming more informed regarding credit terms and costs so they could engage in comparison shopping. Congress presumed the increased information would stimulate competition in the finance industry. The heart of the act is the required conspicuous disclosure of the amount financed, the finance charge (the actual dollar sum to be paid for credit) the annual percentage rate (APR) (the total cost of the credit expressed at an annual rate), and the number of payments. The finance charge includes not just interest but service charges, points, loan fees, carrying charges, and others. TILA disclosure requirements apply to both open-end (for example, VISA and MasterCard) and closed-end loans (those of a fixed amount for a definite time), and include special rules for certain home loans. [For TILA protections when using your home as collateral for a loan, see **http://www.ftc.gov/bcp/conline/pubs/homes/getloan.htm**]

The case that follows examines the application of TILA to car sales.

GREEN v. LEVIS MOTORS, INC.
179 F.3d 286 (5th Cir. 1999)

Circuit Judge E. Grady Jolly

Wilmore and Marsha Green have sued their car dealer and the bank that holds their retail installment contract for a violation of the Truth in Lending Act. The district court granted summary judgment for both Levis Motors, Inc. (the car dealer) and Hancock Bank of Louisiana (the holder of the installment contract) . . .
[The Hancock Bank portion of the opinion is omitted.]

I

The core facts in this case are not in dispute. On or about August 31, 1995, Wilmore and Marsha Green purchased a used car from Levis Motors. To finance this purchase, the Greens entered a retail installment contract ("RIC") with Levis Motors. As required by the Truth in Lending Act ("TILA"), the contract disclosed the "amount financed" and, in conjunction with the disclosure of this amount, purported to itemize an amount paid to the state of Louisiana for licensing fees. The relevant portion of the contract reads as follows:

Itemization of Amount Financed

---

(1) Cash Price $11,332.34
(2)   (a) Cash Downpayment $700.00
         (b) Net Trade–In Allowance $n/a
(3) Unpaid Balance $10,632.34

*   *   *

(4) Amount Paid to Public Officials For:

*   *   *

         (c) License Fee $40.00

The issues in this case surround the amount listed as "Paid to Public Officials For License Fee." Although the RIC lists the amount paid to Louisiana as $40, the state only charged $22 for licensing involved with the Greens' car. Levis Motors retained the $18 balance. Apparently, the practice of tacking on dealer charges to amounts paid to third parties is common in the automotive sales industry, and the balance retained is referred to as an "upcharge."

According to Levis Motors, the $40 amount was a standard licensing fee that it applied to the sale of all its cars. In some of the sales, the actual amount charged by Louisiana exceeded the $40 listed, and in others (such as the sale to the Greens) the state charged less than $40. (Louisiana bases its licensing fee on the sale price of the automobile and the length of time the license remains valid.) The Greens have alleged that Levis Motors violated the TILA because of the RIC's inaccuracy in disclosing the amount paid to third parties.

*   *   *   *   *

II

A

The statutory text upon which the Greens base their claim is found in 15 U.S.C. § 1638(a)(2)(B)(iii).
  (a) Required disclosures by creditor.
  For each consumer credit transaction other than under an open end credit plan, the creditor shall

disclose each of the following items, to the extent applicable:

*   *   *   *   *

2(B) In conjunction with the disclosure of the amount financed, a creditor shall provide a statement of the consumer's right to obtain, upon a written request, a written itemization of the amount financed . . . Upon receiving an affirmative indication, the creditor shall provide, at the time other disclosures are required to be furnished, a written itemization of the amount financed. For the purposes of this subparagraph, "itemization of the amount financed" means a disclosure of the following items, to the extent applicable:

*   *   *   *   *

(iii) each amount that is or will be paid to third persons by the creditor on the consumer's behalf, together with an identification of or reference to the third person;

Instead of giving the Greens the option of requesting a written itemization of the amount financed, Levis Motors decided to supply this itemization automatically. An underlying issue in the Greens' case is whether Levis Motors's retention of an upcharge, without notification to the Greens that the upcharge was included in the amount listed as paid to a third party, violates this statutory provision.

At the time the Greens and Levis Motors executed the RIC, the only relevant regulatory provisions offering any guidance were 12 C.F.R. 226.18(c)(iii) (a section within "Regulation Z," 12 C.F.R. 226), and 12 C.F.R. Part 226, App. H–3 ("model form"). These two regulatory enactments have not changed since the time of the RIC's execution (August 31, 1995).

For each transaction, the creditor shall disclose the following information as applicable:

*   *   *   *   *

(c) *Itemization of amount financed.* (1) A separate written itemization of the amount financed, including:

*   *   *   *   *

(iii) Any amounts paid to other persons by the creditor on the consumer's behalf. The creditor shall identify those persons.

12 C.F.R. § 226.18(c)(iii) (1999). Model form H–3 appears as follows:

Itemization of the Amount Financed of $_____
$_____Amount given to you directly
$_____Amount paid on your account
Amount paid to others on your behalf
$_____to [public officials] [credit bureau]
                    [appraiser][insurance company]
$_____to [name of another creditor]
$_____to [other]
$_____Prepaid finance charge

These were the only relevant materials promulgated by the Federal Reserve Board (FRB) (which is charged with elaborating on the TILA's text) at the time the Greens entered the RIC. Nevertheless, some of Levis Motors's and Hancock's arguments rely on FRB interpretations proposed and issued *after* execution of the RIÇ. A description of these materials follows.

B

In [April 1996] the FRB staff [adopted] an official interpretation of § 1638(a)(2)(B)(iii). This proposed interpretation provides the following:

* * * * *

Charges added to amounts paid to others. A sum is sometimes added to the amount of a fee charged to a consumer for a service provided by a third party (such as for an extended warranty or a service contract) that is payable in the same amount in comparable cash and credit transactions. In the credit transaction, the amount is retained by the creditor. Given the flexibility permitted in meeting the requirements of the amount financed itemization, the creditor in such cases may reflect that the creditor has retained a portion of the amount paid to others. For example, the creditor could add to the category "amount paid to others" language such as "(we may be retaining a portion of this amount)."

* * * * *

After the April 1996 adoption of the official interpretation, a handful of district courts (most within the state of Illinois) disagreed as to whether the FRB interpretation would allow creditors to lump the upcharge in with the fees paid to third parties—without informing the buyers that the creditor included an upcharge. Subsequently, the Seventh Circuit settled the intra-circuit controversy by reading the FRB's interpretation as requiring creditors either to itemize the upcharge separately or to include some language indicating that it may have listed the upcharge and the actual amount paid to third parties as one numerical value. *Gibson* v. *Bob Watson Chevrolet–Geo, Inc.,* 112 F.3d 283, 285–86 (7th Cir. 1997) (Posner, C.J.).

III

The Greens filed their TILA claims against Levis Motors and Hancock in May 1996. The Greens filed their action as a putative class action, but the district court granted summary judgment before reaching a decision as to class certification.

* * * * *

IV

A

Levis Motors argues that, irrespective of whether it has technically violated the TILA, the good faith safe harbor provision of that act, 15 U.S.C. § 1640(f), shields it from liability. Section 1640(f) states:

No provision of this section . . . imposing any liability shall apply to any act done or omitted in good faith in conformity with any rule, regulation, or interpretation thereof by the Board . . . , notwithstanding that after such act or omission has occurred, such rule, regulation, interpretation, or approval is amended, rescinded, or determined by judicial or other authority to be invalid for any reason.

* * * * *

(2)

Levis Motors [argues that it] acted in good faith conformity with the official FRB interpretation issued in April 1996. Although this interpretation was not adopted until after execution of the Greens contract, Levis Motors maintains that it must have been acting in good faith because multiple courts split over how to read that interpretation: roughly half of the courts ruled that the FRB interpretation allowed creditors to combine upcharges with amounts paid to third parties without indicating to buyers that they were doing so; the other half of the courts ruled that the buyers must be informed. Levis Motors argues that with half of the courts going one way, and half going the other way, it should be entitled to the good faith safe harbor. Because the FRB adopted its interpretation *after* execution of the Greens' RIC, Levis Motors necessarily argues that one need not actually *rely upon* a regulatory interpretation in order to act "in good faith in conformity with" that interpretation.

(3)

Levis Motors cannot overcome a serious obstacle to its good faith argument: Binding Fifth Circuit precedent holds that a party cannot act "in good faith in conformity with" a regulation or interpretation that does not exist at the time of the disputed act (or omission).

*   *   *   *   *

In the alternative, Levis Motors argues that it acted in conformity with the model form (H–3) and FRB commentary existing at the time the parties executed the RIC . . . [M]odel form H–3, however, does not indicate— in any way—that creditors can lump in upcharges with amounts paid to third parties without telling the buyers that they are doing so.

*   *   *   *   *

Neither the model form nor [the] FRB comments could be read as offsetting the plain language of § 1638(a)(2)(B)(iii) or 12 C.F.R. § 226.18(c)(iii). That plain language requires the itemization of amounts paid to third parties. By lumping the creditors' own charges in with the amounts actually paid to third parties, and failing to denote the conflation, the creditor fails to itemize or disclose (under any ordinary understanding of those terms) the "amount that is or will be paid to third persons."

We will reverse the district court's decision to shield Levis Motors from TILA liability under § 1640(f). A complete reading of the statutory text, regulations, and commentary existing at the time of the relevant transaction mandates the conclusion that Levis Motors failed to conform in good faith with those authorities. Furthermore, Levis Motors cannot rely on subsequently issued FRB interpretations to support its defense.

B

[T]he district court did not go on to decide whether the RIC actually violated the TILA. Notwithstanding this fact, we have discretionary authority to decide the issue on this appeal.

*   *   *   *   *

The issue here is one of pure law: Does a lender violate the TILA by retaining an upcharge and failing to denote this fact in its itemization of the amount paid to third parties.

C

The Seventh Circuit has addressed this identical issue in *Gibson.* That court concluded that the retention of an undisclosed upcharge does violate the TILA. The reasoning in that opinion is convincing, and we will follow it.

The strongest argument against finding a violation is made by narrowly focusing on two sentences of the FRB's official interpretation.

> Given the flexibility permitted in meeting the requirements of the amount financed itemization the creditor in such cases *may* reflect that the creditor has retained a portion of the amount paid to others. For example, the creditor *could* add to the category "amount paid to others" language such as "(we may be retaining a portion of this amount)."

By focusing on the permissive words "may" and "could," some district courts read this interpretation to mean that a creditor could choose to disclose neither the actual amount of any upcharge nor the possible existence of an upcharge.

But read in the context of the interpretation's entire paragraph and the accompanying explanation, it is clear that the inclusion of permissive terms was not intended to leave open the option of saying absolutely nothing at all about the existence of an upcharge. Instead, the FRB undoubtedly meant to give the creditors the option of either separately itemizing the actual amount paid to third parties or reporting one lump sum (made up of the actual amount paid to a third party and the upcharge) with an accompanying notation that the creditor might have included an upcharge.

This is the way that the Seventh Circuit has read the FRB's official interpretation. To read it any other way, the court said, would be to

> read the commentary to say: "You may conceal the fact that you are pocketing part of the fee that is ostensibly for a third party, but if you are a commercial saint and would prefer to tell the truth, you may

do that too." So interpreted, however, the commentary not only would be preposterous; it would contradict the statute. The only sensible reading of the commentary is as authorizing the dealer to disclose only the fact that he is retaining a portion of the charge, rather than the exact amount of the retention. Even this is a considerable stretch of the statute; and it is as far as, if not farther than, the statute will stretch.

In this case, Levis Motors neither itemized the upcharge separately nor indicated that an upcharge might be included. This failure constitutes a clear violation of the Truth In Lending Act.

* * * * *

V

In sum, we have concluded that the good faith safe harbor provision of the TILA does not shield Levis Motors from liability in this case. Furthermore, Levis Motors's RIC did violate the TILA. Therefore, we will remand for further proceedings with regard to Levis Motors.

Questions

1. a. What is an "upcharge?"
   b. Why did Levis lose its "good faith" argument?
   c. Did Levis actually violate the TILA? Explain.
2. What is the practical significance, if any, of the "putative class action" filed by the Greens?
3. A health spa sells some memberships for cash and some on an installment basis. The price is the same whether the buyer pays cash or buys on the installment plan. The spa has an arrangement to sell the installment contracts to a financing agency at a discount (a price lower than the face value of the contract).
   a. How would you argue that the installment contract sales are in violation of TILA and Regulation Z?
   b. How would you rule on such a case? See *Joseph* v. *Norman's Health Club, Inc.,* 532 F.2d 86 (8th Cir. 1976).

Credit and Charge Cards

As an aggressive marketer, you may want to hand out credit cards in your student union, but the TILA provides that credit cards cannot be issued to a consumer unless requested. Cardholder liability for unauthorized use (lost or stolen card) cannot exceed $50, and the cardholder bears no liability after notifying the issuer of the missing card.

The Fair Credit and Charge Card Disclosure Act of 1988 creates extensive disclosure requirements for card issuers. The act requires notification of various cost factors when card issuers solicit applications. Details vary, depending on whether the card application was solicited by mail, telephone, or "take ones" (e.g., a magazine insert). In general, issuers must disclose key cost features, including APR, annual membership fees, minimum finance charges, late payment charges, and so on.

In 1996, the United States Supreme Court unanimously ruled that federally regulated banks can impose nationwide late-payment fees on credit card holders even if the fees are forbidden by the laws of the state where the credit card holder resides. Credit card operations have increasingly been set up in business-friendly states that impose only minimal regulatory demands. Thus, the effect of the Supreme Court decision is to overrule consumer protection measures in some states with the more permissive standards of states where the credit cards were issued.[30]

Sean Moyer, a University of Oklahoma junior, had earned the minimum wage as a part-time salesman and gift wrapper in a department store. Yet by the time he hanged himself in his bedroom closet, he had 12 credit cards and had amassed $10,000 in debt on them.

Mitzi Pool had only three cards, but they were maxed out and $2,500 is a heavy debt load for an 18-year-old. Pool, a freshman at the University of Central Oklahoma, also hanged herself, her checkbook and credit card bills spread out on her dorm bed.

Consumer groups are citing the deaths in 1997 and 1998 to underscore their criticism of credit card companies, who they say are aggressively trying to get college students hooked on credit.

Source: Associated Press, "Hooked on Credit," *Waterloo–Cedar Falls Courier*, June 9, 1999, p. C7.

Consumer Credit Reports

Having a favorable credit rating is an increasingly important part of consumer life, and having reliable credit information is essential to efficient business practice. Thus, the three national credit information giants, Equifax, Experian, and Trans Union, as well as local credit bureaus, provide retailers, employers, insurance companies, and so on, with consumers' detailed credit histories. Effective October 1997, Congress amended the earlier Fair Credit Reporting Act (FCRA) to enhance protection for consumers with credit problems. As a consumer, you are afforded the following protections, among others:

- Anyone using information from a credit reporting agency (CRA), such as Equifax, to take "adverse action" against you (e.g., denying you credit, a job, insurance) must notify you and tell you where it secured the information.
- At your request, a CRA must give you the information in your file and a list of all those who have recently sought information about you.
- If you claim that your credit file contains inaccurate information, the CRA must investigate your complaint and give you a written report. If you remain unsatisfied, you can include a brief statement in your credit file. Notice of the dispute and a summary of your statement normally must accompany future reports.
- All inaccurate information must be corrected or removed from the file, usually within 30 days.
- In most cases, negative information more than seven years old must not be reported.
- You must provide written consent before a CRA can provide information to your employer or prospective employer.
- You can sue for damages if your rights under the act have been violated.[31]

[For an extensive set of practical questions and answers about consumer rights under the Fair Credit Reporting Act, see **http://www.ftc.gov/bcp/conline/pubs/credit/fcra.htm**]

Question

1. Provide some free market reasoning supporting the credit industry position that ever more detailed government regulation of credit providers is not in the public's best interest.

Fair Credit Billing Act (FCBA)

The FCBA, passed in 1974, provides a mechanism to deal with the billing errors that accompany credit card and certain other "open-end" credit transactions. A cardholder who receives an erroneous bill must complain in writing to the creditor within 60 days of the time the bill was mailed. The creditor must acknowledge receipt of the complaint within 30 days. Then, within two billing cycles but not more than 90 days, the creditor must issue a response either by correcting the account or by forwarding a written statement to the consumer explaining why the bill is accurate. The creditor cannot threaten the consumer's credit rating or report the consumer as delinquent while the bill is in dispute although the creditor can report that the bill is being challenged. Where a "reasonable investigation" determines the bill was correct but the consumer continues to contest it, the consumer may refuse to pay and the creditor will then be free to commence collection procedures after giving the consumer 10 days to pay the disputed amount. If the bill is then reported to a credit bureau as delinquent, that report must also indicate the consumer's belief that the money is not owed, and the consumer must be told who received the report. Penalties for a creditor in violation of the act are quite modest. The creditor forfeits the right to collect the amount in question and any accompanying finance charges, but the forfeiture cannot exceed $50 for each charge in dispute.

ELECTRONIC FUND TRANSFERS

With ATMs, point-of-sale machines, electronic deposits, and the like we are deeply immersed in an era of "electronic money." The Electronic Fund Transfer Act provides remedies for consumers confronting electronic banking problems such as liability for lost or stolen cards and billing errors. [Space constraints preclude examining this topic, but the Federal Trade Commission has provided a detailed and readable summary of those protections at **http://www.ftc.gov/bcp/conline/pubs/credit/elbank.htm**]

EQUAL CREDIT OPPORTUNITY

> ECOA was in large part a response to anger over differing treatment of women and men in the financial marketplace

The Equal Credit Opportunity Act is designed to combat bias in lending. Credit must be extended to all creditworthy applicants regardless of sex, marital status, age, race, color, religion, national origin, good faith exercise of rights under the Consumer Credit Protection Act, and receipt of public assistance (e.g., food stamps). ECOA was in large part a response to anger over differing treatment of women and men in the financial marketplace. Creditors often would not loan money to married women under the women's own names and single, divorced, and widowed women were similarly disadvantaged in securing credit. [For more details about ECOA, see **http://www.ftc.gov/ bcp/conline/pubs/credit/ecoa.htm**]

DEBTOR PROTECTION

To a merchant, a nonpaying debtor may be a "lazy bum" who fails to meet his or her contractual obligations, but from the government's point of view the debtor is often the victim of excessively zealous collection measures. In 1995, a jury in El Paso, Texas, awarded $11 million to Marianne Driscol, a victim of a heavy-handed collection agency:

> Collection agents made numerous profanity-laced phone calls to Driscol's home and office

Collection agents made numerous profanity-laced phone calls to Driscol's home and office . . . making at least one death threat and phoning in a bomb threat to her workplace, according to the lawsuit.[32]

Driscol owed $2,000 on a credit card.

Such overzealous practices in company with the humane recognition that many good consumers inevitably suffer economic reverses, particularly in times of recession, caused the government to create protective legislation.

Debt Collection

The Fair Debt Collection Practices Act (FDCPA) is designed to shield debtors from unfair debt collection tactics by debt collection agencies and attorneys who routinely operate as debt collectors. The act does not extend to creditors who are themselves trying to recover money owed to them. Several thousand debt collection agencies nationwide pursue those who are delinquent in their debts. The agencies are normally paid on a commission basis and are often exceedingly aggressive and imaginative in their efforts. As amended in 1996, the FDCPA requires the collector to include a warning in the first communication with the debtor that the communication is an attempt to collect a debt, and any information obtained will be used for that purpose. In any subsequent communication except a court pleading, the collector must always disclose his or her role as a collector.

The FDCPA forbids, among others, the following practices:

- Use of obscene language.
- Contact with third parties other than for the purpose of locating the debtor. (This provision is an attempt to prevent harm to the debtor's reputation.)
- Use of or threats to use physical force.
- Contact with the debtor during "inconvenient" hours. For debtors who are employed during "normal" working hours, the period from 9 PM to 8 AM would probably be considered inconvenient.
- Repeated phone calls with the intent to harass.
- Contacting the debtor in an unfair, abusive, or deceptive manner.

The Federal Trade Commission is responsible for administering the FDCPA. A wronged debtor may also file a civil action to recover all actual damages (for example, payment for job loss occasioned by wrongful debt collection practices as well as damages for associated embarrassment and suffering). [For more details about the FDCPA, see **http://www.ftc.gov/bcp/conline/pubs/credit/fdc.htm**]

The case that follows suggests some of the problems in debt collection practices.

U.S. v. NATIONAL FINANCIAL SERVICES, INC.
98 F.3d 131 (4th Cir. 1996)

Circuit Judge Ervin

National Financial Services, Inc. (NFS), Robert J. Smith, and N. Frank Lanocha are debt collectors who, primarily on behalf of companies selling magazine subscriptions, send out computer-generated dunning letters en masse. They appeal the imposition of civil penalties for violations of the Fair Debt Collection Practices Act (FDCPA). The appellants object to the grant of summary judgment against them, contending that they raised material issues of fact for trial . . .

I. Background

NFS is a collection agency primarily serving magazine subscription clearinghouses. According to Robert J. Smith, the owner and president of NFS, the company handled about 2,200,000 accounts each year in 1986 and 1987. About half of NFS's accounts were placed by American Family Publishers (AFP). Every few weeks, AFP would provide NFS with magnetic tapes containing the names, addresses, and unpaid balances—averaging about $20.00—for 5,000 to 70,000 delinquent accounts. NFS fed that data into its computer, which merged the customer information onto preprinted collection notices, or "dunning letters."

The text of the letters, prepared by Smith, varied over time. A representative letter examined by the district court specified a deadline for payment, and then stated:

[I]t is now being processed by our NATIONWIDE COLLECTION AGENCY DIVISION to enforce IMMEDIATE PAYMENT from you. Notification is hereby given that the date assigned above is your DEADLINE.

If you fail to pay your bill by the DEADLINE, we will then take the appropriate action. Remember your attorney will also want to be paid. An envelope is enclosed for your payment.

Our AUDIOTEX telecommunications system remains on-line to answer your inquiry, twenty-four hours per day, seven days per week. Call anytime (301) 366-3217.

YOUR ACCOUNT WILL BE TRANSFERRED TO AN ATTORNEY IF IT IS UNPAID AFTER THE DEADLINE DATE!!! . . .

Those consumers who contested the amount owed were removed from the NFS system.

Customers who did not pay after receiving a series of the NFS "deadline notices"—about 85 percent of the accounts—received one or more form letters on the letterhead of "N. Frank Lanocha, Attorney at Law." Lanocha was selected by Smith in response to AFP's suggestion that attorney letterhead notices would increase collection rates. Lanocha, who had no separate agreement with AFP relating to collection letters, prepared the text and gave a copy to Smith. Smith would feed the "attorney at law" dunning text into the NFS computer, merge it with the AFP data, and mail out the letters. Several versions of these letters were sent on AFP accounts between 1983 and 1991. Four "Attorney at Law" letters contained in the record included the following text:

PLEASE NOTE I AM THE COLLECTION ATTORNEY WHO REPRESENTS AMERICAN FAMILY PUBLISHERS. I HAVE THE AUTHORITY TO SEE THAT SUIT

IS FILED AGAINST YOU IN THIS MATTER . . . UNLESS THIS PAYMENT IS RECEIVED IN THIS OFFICE WITHIN FIVE DAYS OF THE DATE OF THIS NOTICE, I WILL BE COMPELLED TO CONSIDER THE USE OF THE LEGAL REMEDIES THAT MAY BE AVAILABLE TO EFFECT COLLECTION . . .

* * * * *

I am the collection attorney hired by American Family Publishers to protect their interests in the United States. I have filed suits and obtained judgments on small balance accounts just like yours. My authority to collect these accounts includes the enforcement of judgments . . .

* * * * *

LAW OFFICES—DEMAND NOTICE. YOU HAVE TEN DAYS TO PAY YOUR BILL IN FULL. CONTIN-UED FAILURE TO PAY WILL RESULT IN FURTHER COLLECTION ACTIVITY. ONLY YOUR IMMEDIATE PAYMENT WILL STOP FURTHER LEGAL ACTION.

* * * * *

YOUR ACCOUNT MAY NOW BE FOR SALE . . . ACCOUNTS, LIKE YOURS, THAT ARE SOLD . . . RUN THE RISK THAT THE BUYER WILL FILE SUIT AGAINST THEM. JUDGMENT CAN RESULT IN ASSETS BEING SEIZED. INSTRUCTIONS HAVE BEEN GIVEN TO TAKE ANY ACTION, THAT IS LEGAL, TO ENFORCE PAYMENT.

The notices were not signed by Lanocha. Nor did he receive or review the information on the AFP computer tapes—either in general or in relation to any particular account. Lanocha did not read or review the letters prepared by the NFS computers under his name. He did not have a list of customers who received his letters. According to AFP's Vice President of Finance, Stephen F. McCarthy, Lanocha did not confer with AFP regarding the text of the letters and, in fact, had no contact with AFP regarding any aspect of the collection activities from 1983 until 1990. McCarthy declared that AFP never paid Lanocha any money for any purpose. Lanocha did not forward payments or reports on collections to AFP. Rather, NFS paid AFP half of each account collected and, in its monthly performance reports to AFP, made no distinction between payments received from the NFS letters and payments from the "attorney at law" collections.

Although Lanocha filed fifteen lawsuits in 1984, he did not file any lawsuits during the 1989 to 1991 period of time covered by this prosecution.

* * * * *

On January 25, 1991, the Government filed an action for civil penalties and injunctive relief against NFS, Smith, and Lanocha, alleging violations of 15 U.S.C. §§ 1692e(5) [and] 1692e (10) . . .

* * * * *

II. Summary Judgment

The defendants contend that they were entitled to a jury trial to resolve disputed issues of material fact regarding whether their notices improperly threatened debtors. We review the district court's grant of summary judgment.

* * * * *

A. 15 U.S.C. §§ 1692e(5), (10)

The FDCPA protects consumers from abusive and deceptive practices by debt collectors. . . . Section 1692e forbids the use of "any false, deceptive, or mis-leading representation or means" in debt collection, and provides a nonexhaustive list of prohibited conduct, including:

(5) The threat to take any action that cannot legally be taken or that is not intended to be taken.

* * * * *

(10) The use of any false representation or deceptive means to collect or attempt to collect any debt or to obtain information concerning a consumer.

Thus, collection notices violate § 1692e(5) if (1) a debtor would reasonably believe that the notices threaten legal action; and (2) the debt collector does not intend to take legal action. Most courts that have considered the issue have applied a "least sophisti-cated debtor" standard in evaluating violations of §1692e(5).

* * * * *

As the Second Circuit has explained, evaluating debt collection practices with an eye to the "least sophisti-cated consumer" comports with basic consumer-protec-tion principles:

The basic purpose of the least-sophisticated con-sumer standard is to ensure that the FDCPA protects all consumers, the gullible as well as the shrewd.

This standard is consistent with the norms that courts have traditionally applied in consumer-protection law.

*   *   *   *   *

While protecting naive consumers, the standard also prevents liability for bizarre or idiosyncratic interpretations of collection notices by preserving a quotient of reasonableness and presuming a basic level of understanding and willingness to read with care.

The district court first examined the collection notices to assess whether they threatened legal action. Looking at the NFS notices, the district court found that both a reasonable and the "least sophisticated" debtor would perceive the language, "YOUR ACCOUNT WILL BE TRANSFERRED TO AN ATTORNEY IF IT IS UNPAID AFTER THE DEADLINE DATE," to mean that the account would receive different treatment from an attorney than it did from NFS. Because to most consumers, the relevant distinction between a collection agency and an attorney is the ability to sue, the court reasoned that the debtor would understand the disparate treatment to be the institution of suit. Similarly, the court found that the language, "remember your attorney will want to be paid," implies that the consumer will need a lawyer to defend himself or herself against a debt collection lawsuit.

Turning to the Lanocha letterhead notices, the district court concluded that they also threatened legal action.

The court further found that NFS and Smith had no intention of taking legal action at the time the notices were sent, because NFS had no internal procedure to get authorization to file suit. "In fact," the court found, based on Smith's testimony, "NFS repeatedly conveyed its belief in the impracticality of filing suit when pressed by AFP to do so" . . .

Similarly, the court further found that Lanocha did not intend to take legal action against any debtor who received one of his letters. Lanocha had filed no lawsuits during the period of time covered by this lawsuit. Although Lanocha had had discussions with AFP regarding the mechanics of suing on a large scale, and actually investigated various state small-claims procedures, Lanocha admitted that he had concluded that such an endeavor was not feasible . . .

On appeal, the defendants argue that their notices did not threaten legal action because they never state that a suit "will be" filed, or "is going to be" filed. All of their statements were open to interpretation, they contend. With regard to the NFS notices, they argue, for example,

that referring a matter to an attorney does not necessarily imply that a legal action will be filed, but merely implies that the lawyer will consider whether to institute a proceeding against a consumer. The defendants aver that a reasonable consumer might conclude that he would not be sued because of the small balance involved. Concerning the statement, "remember your attorney will want to be paid," the defendants assert that they simply stated an irrefutable fact: A debtor weighing the risks of nonpayment may need to consult counsel, who will charge a fee. And if the debtor is sued, he or she will incur legal fees . . .

With regard to the Lanocha letters, the defendants argue that they never say that a suit "will be" filed, or "is going to be" filed, but simply that Lanocha had the authority to do so.

*   *   *   *   *

We disagree. The letters connote that a real attorney, acting like an attorney, has considered the debtor's file and concluded in his professional judgment that the debtor is a candidate for legal action. Using the attorney language conveys authority, instills fear in the debtor, and escalates the consequences.

*   *   *   *   *

[T]he defendants ask this court to adopt a hyper-literal approach which ignores the ordinary connotations and implications of language as it is used in the real world. We decline to do so. We concur with the district court's analysis of the notices, and conclude that the defendants' notices threatened to take legal action which they had no intention of taking, in violation of § 1692e(5). No reasonable juror could conclude that those statements were not meant to make debtors fear that they would be sued. To find otherwise would undermine the consumer protection goals of the statute and permit debt collectors to get away with accomplishing the threat under the flimsy disguise of "statements of fact." . . .

Because we concur with the district court's finding that the notices falsely threatened legal action, we concur with the court's conclusion that the defendants also violated § 1692e(10), which prohibits "the use of any false representation or deceptive means to collect or attempt to collect any debt . . . "

*   *   *   *   *

Affirmed.

Questions

1. In what ways did the defendants violate the Fair Debt Collection Practices Act?
2. In your judgment, are we wise to tie debt collection rules to the capabilities of the "least sophisticated consumer"? Explain.
3. Miller owed $2,501.61 to the Star Bank of Cincinnati. Payco attempted to collect the debt by sending a one-page collection form to Miller. The front side of the form included, among other words, in very large capital letters a demand for IMMEDIATE FULL PAYMENT, the words PHONE US TODAY, and the word NOW in white letters nearly two inches tall against a red background. At the bottom of the page in the smallest print on the form was the message: NOTICE: SEE REVERSE SIDE FOR IMPORTANT INFORMATION. The reverse side contained the validation notice required under the FDCPA. Does the form conform to FDCPA requirements? Explain. [See *Miller* v. *Payco-General American Credits, Inc.*, 943 F. 2d 482 (4th Cir. 1991).]
4. Why shouldn't debt collectors be able to use aggressive tactics to encourage payment of legitimate bills?

Part Four—Bankruptcy

This entrepreneurial, unpredictable, and highly competitive economic era forces us to consider the possibility that we may fail. Perhaps you open your own business only to see it collapse around you. Perhaps you begin what looks to be a secure and promising management career when your employer merges with a competitor and your job vanishes. Perhaps you simply run up an insurmountable credit card debt. In each of these instances, you may be faced with the humiliation of personal bankruptcy. Our culture encourages indebtedness. In 1998, a record 1.4 million Americans declared bankruptcy, nearly triple the number in 1988.[33] In 1999, however, the gloom lifted a little when bankruptcy declarations fell to 1,285,000.[34] Consumers have also begun to resist new credit cards and to pay off card debts more quickly, although total personal debt in the United States in 1998 reached a record $1.27 trillion.[35] More women than men or married couples now declare bankruptcy.[36] Experts blame that condition on divorce and the low income of elderly women, along with their susceptibility to fraud.[37]

Critics argue that we have simply made borrowing too easy. In 1998, credit card companies mailed a reported 3.45 billion solicitations.[38] Lawyers aggressively advertise bankruptcy services. Economics reporter Robert Samuelson says those ads and word of mouth may have something to do with increasing bankruptcy because, while easy credit is uniformly available across the United States, bankruptcy rates vary dramatically from state to state. For example, Virginia's bankruptcy rate of 6 per thousand is nearly twice that of nearby Delaware.[39]

Other bankruptcy critics say that an increasing number of Americans simply choose not to pay their debts:

America's bankruptcy problem is not a consumer-debt problem, and it is not a credit-card problem. America's bankruptcy problem is a bankruptcy problem: It's too many people abusing the bankruptcy system to shirk their financial responsibilities and to walk away from debts they can repay but simply choose not to.

In the end, the rest of us are stuck with the bill.[40] Bankruptcy does carry a practical penalty, of course, in that a Chapter 7 filing (see below) remains on the consumer's credit record for up to 10 years, but credit often remains readily available. In any case, some debtors clearly become encumbered beyond reasonable hope of recovery. To help debtors make a fresh start and to help their creditors recover as much as possible, federal bankruptcy laws provide for the possibility of "forgiveness."

The Law

Bankruptcy in the United States is governed exclusively by federal law; the states do not have the constitutional authority to enact bankruptcy legislation, but they do set their own rules within the limits provided by Congress. Our attention will be limited to the principal federal statute, the Bankruptcy Reform Act of 1978, as amended by the Bankruptcy Reform Act of 1994.

Bankruptcy is an adjudication relieving a debtor of all or part of his or her liabilities (see Figure 15.1). Any person, partnership, or corporation may seek debtor relief. Three forms of bankruptcy action are important to us:

1. **Liquidation** (**Chapter 7** of the Bankruptcy Act), in which all assets except exemptions are distributed to creditors.
2. **Reorganization (Chapter 11),** in which creditors are kept from the debtor's assets while the debtor, under the supervision of the court, works out a plan to continue in business while paying creditors.
3. **Adjustment of debts** of an individual with regular income **(Chapter 13),** in which individuals with limited debts are protected from creditors while paying their debts in installments. [For "The Bankruptcy LawFinder," see **http://www.agin.com/lawfind/**]

Liquidation.   A Chapter 7 liquidation petition can be *voluntarily* filed in federal court by the debtor (individual, partnership, or corporation), or creditors can seek an *involuntary* bankruptcy judgment. A Chapter 7 liquidation is commonly called a "straight" bankruptcy.

In a voluntary action, the debtor files a petition with the appropriate federal court. The court then has jurisdiction to proceed with the liquidation, and the petition becomes the *order for relief*. The debtor need not be insolvent to seek bankruptcy. Creditors often can compel an involuntary bankruptcy.

The debtor may challenge that bankruptcy action. The court will enter an order for relief if it finds the debtor has not been paying his or her debts when due or if most of the debtor's property is under the control of a custodian for the purpose of enforcing a lien against that property.

After the order for relief is granted, voluntary and involuntary actions proceed in a similar manner. Creditors are restrained from reaching the debtor's assets. An interim bankruptcy trustee is appointed by the court. The creditors then hold a meeting, and a permanent trustee is elected. The trustee collects the debtor's property and converts it to money, protects the interests of the debtor and creditors, may manage the debtor's business, and ultimately distributes the estate proceeds to the creditors. Both federal and state laws permit the debtor to keep exempt property, which typically includes a car, a homestead, some household or personal items, life insurance, and other "necessities." Normally, a dollar maximum is attached to each.

FIGURE 15.1   The Bankruptcy Option

Though it is considered the measure of last resort, overwhelmed debtors can turn to bankruptcy as a way out of their debt binds. Below is a primer on personal bankruptcy:

Advantages

- Prevents financial ruin.
- Prevents foreclosure on your house.
- Prevents IRS seizure of property for back taxes.
- Provides fresh start.

Disadvantages

- Harms credit rating.
- Possible loss of assets.
- Certain debts cannot be discharged.
- Social stigma.
- Loss of privacy.

Long-Term Effects

- Credit reporting agencies list bankruptcies on personal credit records for up to 10 years.
- Those who have filed bankruptcy may be turned down or have to pay higher interest rates for credit cards and loans.
- Landlords often refuse to rent to those with credit problems.
- Some employers consider an applicant's credit history as a criterion for hiring.

Personal Bankruptcy Options

Chapter 13

- Allows debtors to consolidate debts and pay creditors back in full or in part over three to five years.
- Interest on unsecured debt such as credit card borrowing is waived—payment goes entirely to principal.
- Lump-sum payments are made to a court-appointed trustee who supervises the payment plan.
- Protects homeowners from foreclosure by allowing them to make up missed mortgage payments over time.
- $160 filing fee.
- No time limit on repeat filings.
- Typical attorney fee: $800–$1,600.

Chapter 7

- Also called straight bankruptcy.
- Wipes out unsecured debt.
- Debtor has option to return items bought with secured loans, such as a car, and owe nothing, or keep belongings and continue making payments.
- May keep homes and automobiles with a limited amount of equity.
- $175 filing fee.
- Can be filed once every six years.
- Typical attorney fee: $500–$1,000.

The Process

- Debtor files petition in federal court claiming insolvency.
- Within 15 days, debtor must file papers listing all debts, assets, income, living expenses, and personal information.
- Case is reviewed by a court-appointed trustee. A notice is sent to each of the filer's creditors.
- Within six weeks of initial filing, an administrative hearing is held by the trustee, the debtor, and the debtor's attorney. Creditors may also attend.
- Case is finalized within 90 days of hearing.

Source: *Los Angeles Times*, December 11, 1995, p. D4. Reprinted by permission of the copyright holder, *The Los Angeles Times*.

The debtor's nonexempt property is then divided among the creditors according to the priorities prescribed by statute. Secured creditors are paid first. If funds remain, "priority" claims, such as employees' wages and alimony/child support, are paid. Then, funds permitting, general creditors are paid. Each class must be paid in full before a class of lower priority will be compensated. Any remaining funds will return to the debtor.

When distribution is complete, the bankruptcy judge may issue an order discharging (relieving) the debtor of any remaining debts except for certain statutorily specified claims. Those include, for example, taxes and educational loans. The debtor might fail to receive a *discharge* if he or she had received one in the previous six years, if property was concealed from the court, or if good faith in the bankruptcy process was lacking in other respects.

> While the volume of government student loans tripled in the 1990s, the default rate reached an all-time low of 8.8 percent in fiscal 1997, down from the 1990 peak of 22.4 percent.
>
> Source: Associated Press, "Student Loan Default Rate Dips," *Waterloo–Cedar Falls Courier,* October 6, 1999, p. A9.

Reorganization.   Chapter 11 is available to individuals and most businesses. The basic thrust of this type of bankruptcy is to allow financially troubled enterprises to continue in operation while debtor adjustments are arranged. Thus, both debtor and creditor may ultimately benefit more than from a straight liquidation. The debtor may voluntarily seek reorganization, or the creditors may petition for an involuntary action. When a reorganization petition is filed with the court and relief is ordered, one or more committees of creditors are appointed to participate in bankruptcy procedures. Typically, the debtor continues to operate the business, although the court may appoint a trustee to replace the debtor if required because of dishonesty, fraud, or extreme mismanagement. The company, its bankers, and suppliers will meet to work out a method for continuing operations. A plan must be developed that will satisfy the creditors that their interests are being served by the reorganization. Perhaps new capital is secured, or perhaps creditors receive some shares in the company. The plan must be approved by the creditors and confirmed by the court. The company is then required to carry out the plan.

> Proving that even wealthy celebrities can have financial problems and use the law to abate those problems, the Planet Hollywood restaurant chain declared Chapter 11 bankruptcy in October 1999 but was able to quickly restructure and emerge from bankruptcy in January 2000.
>
> Source: Greg Hernandez, "Judge Clears Planet Hollywood to Emerge from Bankruptcy," *Los Angeles Times,* January 22, 2000, p.C3.

Adjustment of Debts.   Under Chapter 13, individuals (not partnerships or corporations) can seek the protection of the court to arrange a debt adjustment plan. Chapter13 permits only voluntary bankruptcies and is restricted to those with steady incomes and somewhat limited debts. The process can begin only with a voluntary petition from the debtor. Creditors are restrained from reaching the debtor's assets. The debtor develops a repayment plan. If creditors' interests are sufficiently satisfied by the plan, the court may confirm it and appoint a trustee to oversee the plan. The debtor may then have three to five years to make the necessary payments. [For an extensive bankruptcy law database, see **http://www.law.cornell.edu/topics/bankruptcy.html**]

Reform?   At this writing in early 2000, Congress is considering some important adjustments in bankruptcy rules, but the aforementioned 1999 decline in bankruptcies might take some of the steam out of that effort. The key ingredient would be a means test applying to those seeking personal bankruptcy protection under Chapter 7. While unsettled at this writing, the likelihood is that debtors whose income exceeds the median American family income and who can afford to pay 20 to 30 percent of their debts over 3 to 5 years would be barred from Chapter 7 and would be left to take the more demanding Chapter 13 route.

Part Five—Consumer Protection Abroad

Internet commerce is booming, but as the following article explains, the European Union and most nations around the world do not have rules in place to provide the protection for on-line consumers that we have come to expect in conventional transactions. [For an overview of global consumer protection legal issues, see **http://www.ascusc.org/jcmc/vol2/issue2/goldring.html**]

ISSUES MUST BE RESOLVED TO BOOST BUYERS' CONFIDENCE

Nuala Moran

What happens if you buy something and it does not work? The usual procedure would be to take the item back to the shop. But if the purchase was made via the internet, the supplier could be based anywhere in the world.

Apart from the bother and logistical difficulty of returning goods bought on the internet, the consumer laws relating to the replacement or repair of goods in one country may not apply in another. And which is the relevant law—that in the country of the purchaser or the supplier?

These questions give just a taste of the potential for abuse of rights in e-commerce. They must be addressed before consumers gain the confidence to embrace the new medium and before it becomes a suitable channel for the full range of goods and services which most of us currently go shopping for.

"It is not a legal vacuum, but it is unclear as to which laws apply, particularly if the supplier of goods or services is in one jurisdiction and the consumer is in another," says David Wilkinson, a specialist in IT at the law firm of Bristows in London. "At the moment, there is no clear guidance from the courts or national legislatures as to which rules apply."

Mr. Wilkinson says that in internet matters, it is useful to look at the US. "There is a rule of thumb in the US that if you are based in one state and are selling via a website into another, the laws of the latter apply." Europe is less advanced in terms of case law, although in one UK case the judge indicated that by trading on the internet a vendor would take the risk of falling foul of the laws of any jurisdiction if it sold into that territory.

There are various moves to create an appropriate framework for e-commerce. In the European Union, an E-commerce Directive is scheduled to be approved this year, giving member states until the end of 2000 to enshrine it in national law. In addition, the Consumer Policy Committee of the Organisation for Economic Co-operation and Development (OECD) is currently developing consumer protection guidelines which should [soon] be ready for approval. And the International Chamber of Commerce, a world business organization with more than 7,000 member companies, is developing guidelines on advertising and marketing on the internet.

The uncertainty surrounding e-commerce can also cause problems for traders. Michael Arnold, a partner at Eversheds, the international law firm, says that while they are concentrating on security aspects, many companies are overlooking the contractual risks associated with online trading. "Unsuspecting organisations could find themselves breaking the law of other countries or contractually exposed."

He says existing law can be applied to e-commerce and in that sense, there is no difference between trading over the net or in a corner shop.

"This means you must take the usual care about things which may constitute an offer, so if you have 20,000 Spice Girls T-shirts to sell at £9.99 each, you must say 'while stocks last.'" However, he notes that some countries do not allow disclaimers in contracts.

There may be problems for traders because products which are legal in one country are not in another, or the product—for example, women's magazines—could be acceptable in the US or Europe but might offend religious or moral sensibilities in other countries.

"If you advertise a product on a website, what is not clear is the extent to which disclaimers could be applied," says Mr Arnold.

Such difficulties are likely to cause more of a problem to international companies that currently recognise

they cannot supply all their products in particular countries than to more modest national operators who would be harder to pursue.

Despite the problems, there is an explosion in buying over the internet. But much of this growth is in commodities such as books, music, airline tickets, software and financial services where there is little continuing service commitment and issues such as right size or right colour do not apply.

Mr. Arnold says that at present, consumers must treat shopping via the internet with the same circumspection they apply to shopping by mail order.

But this is not good enough for retailers who recognise they need to go beyond faith in the brand if they are to build a broad e-commerce marketplace. James Roper of IMRG, the interactive media in a retail group which represents 250 retailers in 20 countries, says; "Laws, rules and regulations are thick on the ground. The problem is, there is no one to police it. A consumer with a complaint does not know where to take it."

In the UK, IMRG and bodies including the Office of Fair Trading, the Department of Trade and Industry, the Consumers' Association, the Direct Marketing Association, and the Advertising Standards Authority, are working on a supra-organisation to become responsible for consumer protection. "This would act as a first port of call for consumers who could then be directed to the appropriate body within the organisation," Mr. Roper says.

"Merchants urgently need a 'trust framework' because the non-face-to-face nature of the channel dictates that trust, high standards, international accountability, redress, and an ethical approach to privacy are of paramount importance."

He argues that governments cannot provide such a framework because the internet is "frontier land." "They start from a base of existing laws and protocols which often just don't fit."

He adds: "What is needed to tame this wild frontier is a no-nonsense e-commerce marshal dedicated to the task and with the authority and the tools to sort out the bad guys and nip trouble in the bud. We can't afford to have a big bureaucracy with things grinding through the courts."

Source: *Financial Times (London)*, July 7, 1999, Section: "Survey—FT IT Review," p. 5. Reprinted by permission.

Sixty consumer groups from the United States and Europe in 1999 initiated a coordinated, international consumer protection movement by forming a new organization called the Trans-Atlantic Consumer Dialogue. The new group wants health, safety, and fairness considerations to have the same visibility in global trade discussions as the Trans-Atlantic Business Dialogue has achieved for reduced trade barriers and other pro-business goals.

INTERNET EXERCISE

1. Federal law, including the Electronic Fund Transfer Act, provides significant protection for consumers who encounter electronic banking problems. [To answer the following questions, go to the Internet at **http://www.ftc.gov/bcp/conline/pubs/credit/elbank.htm**]

    a. How can you best protect yourself in the event of an error in a bank or credit card statement or in the event of a lost credit card?

    b. If your credit card is lost or stolen, to what extent are you personally responsible for the unauthorized use of that card?

    c. Under federal law, to what extent can you stop payment on a credit card purchase when you are, for some reason, dissatisfied with the transaction?

2. Go to the Center for Auto Safety website [**http://www.autosafety.org/**] and find your way to your state's lemon law. Read the law of your state. Read the law for the states of Texas, Virginia, and West Virginia.

    a. Explain the differences in the law of each of the four states (three if you reside in one of the four).

    b. Which of those three or four states, in your view, provides the "fairest" protection considering the viewpoints of both consumers and dealers?

CHAPTER QUESTIONS

1. A consumer wrote to a newspaper's legal questions and answers column with the following inquiry: "I keep getting harassing phone calls from a bill collector. Is that legal?" Answer the question. See Gregg Jarrett, " . . . Govern Bill Collectors' Calls," *Waterloo–Cedar Falls Courier,* December 20, 1998, p. C4.

2. Jenny Craig, Inc., reached a 1997 agreement with the Federal Trade Commission providing that the company must include the following statement in most ads: "For many dieters, weight loss is temporary." In your view, is that requirement a wise use of FTC authority? Explain.

3. Under 1998 federal rules, golf carts with a maximum speed of 25 miles per hour are exempt from most federal safety regulations and are allowed to use some public roads. The carts must be equipped with seat belts,

windshields, headlight, and turn signals. The carts are widely used in retirement communities. The rules have been heavily criticized.

    a. What factors would you consider in deciding on the wisdom of this golf cart rule?

    b. How would you vote? Explain.

4. Recent studies suggest that consumer bankruptcies are much more common in some states than others. Aside from income levels, what socioeconomic factors would you expect to be closely correlated with high bankruptcy rates?

5. Playtex manufactures the market-leading spillproof cup for children, which is used by sucking on a spout to cause a valve to open. Gerber introduced its own version and ran ads showing an unnamed competitor's product

and claiming that "Gerber's patented valve makes our cup more than 50 percent easier to drink from than the leading cup." Gerber's claims for the superiority of its cup were backed by tests from an independent laboratory. Playtex said the unnamed cup obviously was its brand and that the superiority claims were false and misleading. Playtex sought an injunction to block the Gerber ads. Would you grant that injunction? Explain. See *Playtex Products* v. *Gerber Products,* 981 F. Supp. 827 (S.D.N.Y. 1997).

6. Maguire, a credit card holder at Bradlees Department Store, fell behind in her payments. She received a series of dunning letters from Citicorp, which managed Bradlees' accounts, demanding that she pay the overdue amount. Later Maguire received a letter from "Debtor Assistance," which said that "your Bradlees account has recently [been] charged off." Debtor Assistance is a unit of Citicorp, but was not identified as such in the letter, beyond the phrase, "a unit of CRS." The back of each Bradlees' account statement includes a notice that Citicorp Retail Services was the creditor that handled Bradlees' accounts. In general, creditors are not subject to the requirements of the Fair Debt Collections Practices Act, but Maguire sued claiming the Debtor Assistance letter violated the FDCPA. Is she correct? Explain. [See *Maguire* v. *Citicorp Retail Services, Inc.,* 147 F.3d 232 (2d Cir. 1998).]

7. A door-to-door salesman representing Your Shop at Home Services, Inc., called on Clifton and Cora Jones, who were welfare recipients. The Jones couple decided to buy a freezer from the salesman for $900. Credit charges, insurance, and so on were added to that $900 base so that the total purchase price was $1,439.69. Mr. and Mrs. Jones signed a sales agreement that accurately stipulated the price and its ingredients. The Joneses sued to reform the contract on unconscionability grounds. They had paid $619.88 toward the total purchase price. At trial, the retail value of the new freezer at the time of purchase was set at approximately $300.
    a. What is the issue in this case?
    b. Decide. Explain.
       [See *Jones* v. *Star Credit Corp.,* 298 N.Y.S. 2d 264 (1969).]

8. The plaintiff, a wholesaler, reached an agreement with Philco, a manufacturer, to distribute Philco appliances to retailers. The plaintiff agreed to carry an adequate inventory of Philco parts. The agreement provided that either party could terminate the contract with 90 days' written notice. In the event of termination, the wholesaler agreed on demand to resell and deliver its remaining Philco stock to Philco. The resale price was to be agreed. The agreement was terminated, but Philco declined to exercise its option to repurchase. The wholesaler was unable to sell most of the remaining Philco inventory and demanded that Philco repurchase, but Philco declined. The plaintiff brought suit, claiming the contract was unconscionable. Decide. Explain. [See *W. L. May Co., Inc.* v. *Philco–Ford Corporation,* 543 P.2d 283 (Or. 1975).]

9. Roseman resigned from the John Hancock Insurance Company following allegations of misuse of his expense account. He reimbursed the account. Subsequently, he was denied employment by another insurance firm after that firm read a Retail Credit Company credit report on him. The credit report included accurate information regarding Roseman's resignation. Was Retail Credit in violation of the Fair Credit Reporting Act in circulating information regarding the resignation? Explain. [See *Roseman* v. *Retail Credit Co., Inc.,* 428 F. Supp. 643 (Pa. 1977).]

10. Dun & Bradstreet, Inc., a credit reporting agency, erroneously reported to five subscribers that Greenmoss Builders had filed for voluntary bankruptcy. A correction was subsequently issued. Greenmoss, remaining dissatisfied, filed suit for defamation. The Supreme Court has held—in *New York Times* v. *Sullivan,* 376 U.S. 254 (1964)—that a public official cannot recover damages for defamation in the absence of a showing that the statement was made with "actual malice"—knowledge that it was false or with reckless disregard for whether it was false. Here, the credit report in question was not a matter of public importance. Must the plaintiff, Greenmoss, show actual malice by Dun & Bradstreet? Explain. [See *Dun & Bradstreet, Inc.* v. *Greenmoss Builders, Inc.,* 472 U.S. 749 (1985).]

11. The Fair Debt Collection Practices Act forbids debt collectors from making false or misleading representations or engaging in unfair or abusive practices. The act defines a "debt collector" as one who "regularly collects or attempts to collect [consumer] debts owed to another." In 1986, Congress removed language in the act that had excluded lawyers who, through litigation, engage in collecting consumer debts. Congress did not replace that language.

Heintz is a lawyer representing a bank that sued Jenkins to recover the balance due on a defaulted loan. Heintz wrote to Jenkins listing the amount owed, including over $4,000 for insurance. Jenkins argued that she did not owe the insurance money, as specified. Then Jenkins sued Heintz, claiming that his letter violated the act in making a "false representation of the amount of any debt." The district court dismissed Jenkins's suit for failure to state a claim in that, the court ruled, the act does not apply to lawyers collecting debts through litigation. The court of appeals reversed, saying the act does reach litigating lawyers who are acting as debt collectors. The Supreme Court granted certiorari. Does the FDCPA apply to lawyers who are litigating to collect debts? Explain. [See *Heintz* v. *Jenkins,* 514 U.S. 291 (1995).]

12. Once the government decided to intervene in the free market on behalf of consumers, two broad product safety options presented themselves: (*a*) the government could have limited its effort to generating and distributing information to consumers, or (*b*) the government could have set safety standards for all products. Assuming the government were forced to choose one or the other but not elements of both, which option should it choose? Explain.

13. Consumers sometimes abuse sellers. One familiar technique is shoplifting. Of course, shoplifting is a crime. However, the criminal process is cumbersome and often does not result in monetary recoveries for sellers. As a result, at least 43 states now have laws permitting store owners to impose civil fines, the collection of which is usually turned over to a lawyer or collection agency with a threat to sue in civil court, file criminal charges, or both if payment is not forthcoming. Fines may range from $50 to $5,000 or more, depending on the value of the item stolen.

 a. Defense lawyers say this civil fine system is unfair. Why?

 b. On balance, is the civil fine approach to shoplifting a good idea? Explain.

14. Cite some examples of consumers abusing businesspeople.

15. Attorney Gary Klein: "The notion that our bankruptcy system is in need of major reform is a myth generated by the consumer credit industry. With few exceptions, people who file bankruptcy are honest and hard-working Americans experiencing real financial hardship . . . Responsibility for the increase in filings should be placed where it belongs—on a system that pushes people to use more credit than they can afford." Comment. [See Gary Klein, "Blame the Credit Pushers," *USA Today,* October 4, 1996, p.12A.]

16. The Consumer Product Safety Commission reported that in 1992, 39,000 people were injured while using chain saws.[41] Based on these figures, should chain saw sales be banned until a safer product is produced? Would such a ban be effective? Explain.

NOTES

1. *Lindberg Cadillac Co.* v. *Aron,* 371 S.W.2d 651 (Mo. App. 1963).

2. See *Williams* v. *Walker–Thomas Furniture Company,* 350 F.2d 445 (C.A.D.C. 1965).

3. "Tommy Hilfiger Penalized for Care Labels," *Times-Picayune,* March 23, 1999, p. F5.

4. Laura Hansen, "A Short List of Telemarketing No-No's," *Marketing Tools,* January–February 1997, p. 50.

5. Katherine Ackley, "R.J. Reynolds to Settle Charges Over Ads," *The Wall Street Journal,* March 4, 1999, p. B4.

6. Staff Reporter, "Exxon, FTC Reach Settlement on Ads for High-Octane Gas," *The Wall Street Journal,* June 25, 1997, p. B2.

7. Bruce Ingersoll, "Jenny Craig Settles FTC Charges that Ads Made Deceptive Claims," *The Wall Street Journal,* May 30, 1997, p. B4.

8. "Many Used Car Dealers Violate Federal Used Car Rule; Consumer Group Calls for More Enforcement," *National Association of Attorneys General Consumer Protection Report,* January 1998, p. 18.

9. Associated Press, "About 1,000 Hair-Eating Dolls Returned to Mattel," *Waterloo–Cedar Falls Courier,* January 16, 1997, p. B6.

10. John Omicinski, "Kids' Baseball Going Soft," *USA Today,* October 1, 1996, p. 13A.

11. "New Study Says Baseball Safe," *USA Today,* October 1, 1996, p. 13A.

12. John Omicinski, "Kids' Baseball Going Soft," p. 13A.

13. Ann Brown, Chair, Consumer Product Safety Commission, Testimony Before the VA, HUD, and Independent Agencies Subcommittee of the House Appropriations Committee, February 23, 1999.

14. Angela Curry, "Lawn Care: Don't Trim the Precautions," *Kansas City Star,* May 9, 1999, p. G4.

15. Robert Cohen, "Battle Resumes Over Strict Fire Standards for Kids' Sleepwear," *San Diego Union-Tribune,* September 2, 1999, p. A1.

16. Ibid.

17. Ibid.

18. Ibid.

19. Ibid.

20. Jayne O'Donnell, "Consumers Harbor Lethal Toys," *USA Today,* December 22, 1998, p. 3B.

21. Associated Press, "10 Million Playpens Recalled," *Waterloo–Cedar Falls Courier,* November 24, 1998, p. A2.

22. Ibid.

23. John R. Wilke, "McDonald's Is Fined for Not Reporting Injuries," *The Wall Street Journal,* June 29, 1999, p. A2.

24. Ibid.

25. Bruce Horovitz, "Hot Commodity: Privacy," *USA Today,* July 20, 1998, p. 3B.

26. *U.S. West, Inc.* v. *Federal Communications Commission,* 182 F. 3d 1224 (10th Cir. 1999).

27. Paul Davidson, "FCC to Appeal Ruling Allowing Sale of Phone Customers' Info," *USA Today,* August 26, 1999, p. 1B.

28. Associated Press, "Telemarketers Announce Privacy Plan," *Waterloo–Cedar Falls Courier,* July 7, 1999, p. A2.

29. Mark Johnson, "Credit Card Use Helps Businesses Sell Personal Data," *Tampa Tribune,* August 5, 1999, Section: Business and Finance, p. 7.

30. *Smiley* v. *Citibank,* 517 U.S. 735 (1996).

31. This summary of FCRA requirements was drawn largely from the Federal Trade Commission document, "A Summary of Your Rights Under the Fair Credit Reporting Act," [**http://www.ftc.gov/bcp/conline/ edcams/fcra/summary.htm**].

32. Associated Press, "Credit Company Must Pay Harassment Tab," *Des Moines Register,* August 25, 1995, p. 4A.

33. Robert J. Samuelson, "Once Rarity, This Boom Gaining Congress' Attention; Bankruptcy's Acceptance," *Boston Globe,* August 31, 1999, p. D4.

34. Associated Press, "Consumers Pay Off Debt More Quickly; Bankruptcy Rates Down," *Waterloo–Cedar Falls Courier,* January 19, 2000, p. A8.

35. Christine Dugas, "Bankruptcy Debate Could Change the Face of Debt," *USA Today,* September 24, 1998, p. 1A.

36. Christine Dugas, "Women Rank 1st in Bankruptcy Filings," *USA Today,* June 21, 1999, p. 1A.

37. Ibid.

38. Robert J. Samuelson, "Once Rarity," p. D4.

39. Ibid.

40. Todd J. Zywicki, Assistant Professor of Law, George Mason University, "Bankruptcy Reform Needed," *USA Today,* June 8, 1999, p. 24A.

41. Joanne Ball Artis, "Pattern of Injuries Cited in Wood-Chipper Case," *Boston Globe,* August 19, 1993, p. 34.

Chapter 16

Product Liability

INTRODUCTION

The business of making small airplanes is all but dead in this country, wiped out mainly by product liability lawsuits.[1]

Business Practice. That 1991 pronouncement by *The Wall Street Journal* powerfully depicts the influence of product liability laws in the practice of American business. Today a key ingredient in a successful business is a plan for dealing with litigation costs. Product liability law addresses all those situations in which injuries result from defective products.

In the early 1990s, as *The Wall Street Journal* observed, the single-engine plane industry in the United States was largely dead. The major American manufacturer, Cessna Aircraft of Wichita, Kansas, stopped making small planes in 1986. Its chief rival, Piper Aircraft, struggled with bankruptcy. Single-engine aircraft production in the United States fell from a peak of 13,000 units in 1977 to 444 in 1994.[2] For Cessna, employment fell from approximately 14,000 in the early 80s to fewer than 4,000 in 1986 when the company quit making single-engine planes and focused its attention on the business-plane market.[3] The problems were, in part, attributable to overproduction, high fuel costs, and recession, but the *Journal* argued that the chief cause was the legal system:

> [W]hat is happening now, according to practically every constituency except the lawyers, is a clear case of products-liability law eating a sick industry alive.[4]

Particularly troublesome for the small-plane companies is the so-called liability tail that accompanies their products. Airplanes must be built to last for many years, but because product liability claims ordinarily have no time limit, a manufacturer can be sued decades after the plane has left its control. The result is that insurance fees skyrocket, driving up airplane prices and frightening lenders and investors.[5]

The American Trial Lawyers Association blamed the small-plane industry's problems on poor management. Clearly, poor management did play a role, but ultimately Congress landed on the side of the plane companies by passing, in 1994, the General Aviation Revitalization Act, which offers protection against serious liability claims and limits claims involving planes that are more than 18 years old.[6] Cessna and Piper have now achieved strong recoveries, which they attribute to the new legislation. [For a general database on defective products, see **http://consumerlawpage.com/resource/defect.shtml**]

Justice.   While product liability law can sometimes be devastating to a company or industry, as was the case with small planes, it is often the only recourse for those wronged by defective products. The following story reminds us that product liability litigation compensates those who are harmed while applying important pressure to improve product quality.

LAW STUDENT SPEAKS TO CLASS ABOUT RECOVERY FROM 3RD-DEGREE BURNS

James Kramer

After a chemical explosion nearly took his life, University of Iowa law student Rich Webster has recovered.

The explosion, which was caused by a solvent called acetone, occurred in an Iowa City apartment managed by Webster. The accident left him with third-degree burns that covered 65 percent of his body.

Five years later, thick red scars cover Webster's cheeks and lower lip. His arms, which he said feel like they're covered in Saran Wrap, look like leather due to extensive skin grafting.

*   *   *   *   *

Webster, an Iowa City native, was removing carpet from the apartment, which is located on the east side of the city. After reading the acetone container's warning label and applying the chemical, he opened the apartment's windows and doors and left for 15 minutes.

When he came back, the chemical's fumes ignited from the pilot light in a water heater. He jumped out a first-floor window and got help from a neighbor.

"My immediate reaction was disbelief, then panic," Webster said. "When I got to the the hospital, I didn't hurt that bad because it had burned through the nerves. I thought I was going to be able to go home."

Webster spent seven weeks in the burn unit at the UI Hospitals and Clinics, where he underwent four surgical operations to graft new skin. When he first arrived there, doctors told him he had a "50–50" chance of surviving.

Several months after the incident, Webster filed a negligence lawsuit against Sunnyside, Inc., which produced the acetone; State Industries, the producer of the water heater; and Lenoch & Cilek True Value Hardware, the store from which Webster bought the product.

The case was settled out of court in 1994. Part of the settlement required Webster not to disclose monetary figures, but he said he received "a very, very substantial amount." The money covered all of his hospital bills, which amounted to over $250,000.

*   *   *   *   *

Webster's life has changed in a number of ways since his road to recovery started. Because the chemical, acetone, was in a container without an extensive warning label, he has grown more skeptical of companies.

Since the Webster case was settled, Sunnyside increased the warning on its acetone containers. In general, Webster said he feels warning labels need to be taken more seriously.

"If I read a label that has a warning on it, I automatically think it's a watered-down version," Webster said. "I think there's a problem with people not reading labels, period."

Source: *The Daily Iowan*, March 5, 1997.

Part One—Negligence

The three major product liability causes of action are negligence, breach of warranty, and strict liability. In dangerously simplified terms, negligence is a breach of the duty of due care. A negligent act is the failure to do what a reasonable person would do or doing what a reasonable person would not do. Thus, a producer or distributor has a duty to exercise reasonable care in the entire stream of events associated with the development and sale of a product. In designing, manufacturing, testing, repairing, and warning of potential dangers, those in the chain of production and distribution must meet the standard of the reasonably prudent person. Failure to do so constitutes negligence. Some decisions also extend potential liability to those situations in which a product is being put to an unintended but reasonably foreseeable *misuse*.

Historically, consumers dealt face to face with producers and could bring breach of contract claims if injured by a defective product. However, the development in the modern era of multilayered production and distribution systems eliminated that contractual relationship between producer and consumer, making it difficult for consumers to sue producers. Then in a famous 1916 decision (*McPherson* v. *Buick Motor Co.*),[7] brilliant jurist Benjamin Cardozo and the New York high court ruled that a consumer could bring a negligence claim against the manufacturer of a defective automobile even though the consumer did not purchase the car directly from that manufacturer. Cardozo's view has since been broadly adopted, thus permitting victims of negligence to bring actions against all careless parties in the chain of production and distribution.

To establish a successful negligence claim, the plaintiff must meet each of the following requirements:

1. *Duty*—The plaintiff must establish that the defendant owed a duty of due care to the plaintiff. In general, the standard applied is that of the fictitious reasonable man or woman. That reasonable person acts prudently, sensibly, and responsibly. The standard of reasonableness depends, of course, on the circumstances of the situation.
2. *Breach of duty*—The plaintiff must demonstrate that the defendant breached the duty of due care by engaging in conduct that did not conform to the reasonable person standard. Breach of the duty of due care may result from either the commission of a careless act or the omission of a reasonable, prudent act. Would a reasonable man or woman discharge a firearm in a public park? Would a reasonable person foresee that failure to illuminate one's front entry steps might lead to a broken bone? More formally, we might think of reasonable behavior as that which weighs the costs and benefits of acting or not acting. The reasonable person "takes precautions against harms when doing so costs less than the discounted value of the harms risked."[8]
3. *Causation*
    a. *Actual cause*—Did the defendant's breach of the duty of due care <u>in fact</u> cause the harm in question? Commonly, the "but for" test is applied to determine cause in fact. For example, but for the defendant's failure to stop at the red light, the plaintiff pedestrian would not have been struck down in the crosswalk.
    b. *Proximate cause*—The plaintiff must establish that the defendant's actions were the proximate cause of the injury. As a matter of policy, is the defendant's conduct <u>sufficiently connected</u> to the plaintiff's injury as to justify imposing liability?

Many injuries arise from a series of events—some of them wildly improbable. Did the defendant's negligence lead directly to the plaintiff's harm, or did some intervening act break the causal link between the defendant's negligence and the harm? For example, the community's allegedly negligent maintenance resulted in a blocked road, forcing the plaintiff to detour. While on the detour route, the plaintiff's vehicle was struck by a plane that fell from the sky when attempting to land at a nearby airport. Was the community's negligence the proximate cause of the plaintiff's injury?[9]

4. *Injury*—The plaintiff must have sustained injury, and, due to problems of proof, that injury often must be physical. The case that follows examines negligence analysis. [For a tort law library, see **http://www.findlaw.com/01topics/22tort/**]

KNIGHT v. WAL-MART STORES, INC.
889 F. Supp. 1532 (S.D. Ga. 1995)

Chief Judge Edenfield

Before the Court is Defendant Wal-Mart's motion for summary judgment on Plaintiff Knight's claim that Wal-Mart is liable for selling a firearm to a mentally incompetent customer who later killed himself with it . . .

I. Summary Judgment Standard

Summary judgment is appropriate only when the pleadings, depositions and affidavits submitted by the parties show that there is no genuine issue of material fact and that the moving party is entitled to judgment as a matter of law.

II. Facts

On March 25, 1992, Eric Brown entered the Wal-Mart in Eastman, Georgia. Lisa Edwards, an employee at the store, testified that after noticing Brown, she announced a security code to all departments. Apparently this was standard procedure every time Brown entered the establishment. Another employee, April Wilcox, testified that Brown

walked to the front of the store and stood in front of my register. He looked like he was in a rage. He also appeared rushed, upset and in a hurry and he was talking to himself. Then he turned and rushed back to the back of the store again. When he looked at me, I was afraid of him and I knew he was crazy.

The accuracy of these accounts is not disputed by Wal-Mart, which argues only that they are not relevant.

Brown eventually went to the sporting goods department, in which Patricia Nutt was working that day, and asked to look at a rifle. A different employee showed Brown a weapon that he decided to purchase, and Nutt was asked to assist in completion of the sale. Nutt gave Brown Treasury Form 4473 (U.S. Firearms Transaction Record), a federal form that must be completed by the customer before a firearm may be sold. Brown was told the purpose of the form and how to complete it. With regard to question 8(a)–(h) of section A of the form, he was told to initial each to show that he understood the questions posed. Brown completed section A, answering "no" to all questions, including question 8(e), which asked whether the purchaser had ever been adjudicated mentally defective or committed to a mental institution. This was a lie—Brown had previously been institutionalized.

After completing the form, Brown had not initialed his answers. Nutt once again asked him to do so, and he complied. He then signed the form. Nutt then completed section B of the form. Part B(9) required the seller to state the type of identification used by the purchaser, usually a driver's license. Brown indicated that he did not drive, and produced a valid Georgia State Identification Card. A manager, Anisa Berry, was finally called to approve the sale, as required by Wal-Mart policy. She did so.

At this point Brown tried to buy ammunition for the rifle, but Ms. Nutt explained that it was Wal-Mart policy not to allow the purchase of ammunition with a new firearm. Nutt says Brown remained calm, acknowledged that he understood the policy, and paid for the rifle. After the sale, again according to store policy, Nutt escorted Brown to the front of the store, where she gave him his purchase as he exited the establishment.

On the way out, Nutt gave the gun to Ms. Edwards, stationed at the service desk, who removed the security tape from it. Brown then asked for a bag for the package. At this moment, Nutt claims that she got a bag, walked him out, and gave him the bag with the rifle in it. As she reentered Wal-Mart she claims that Ms. Edwards said to her, "Was that Eric Brown?" to which Nutt replied, "Yes." Edwards then responded, "He's crazy," and laughed. Nutt asserts that Edwards used this term often and loosely, and so Nutt thought nothing of it. She further claims that she was unaware of the storewide security alert, and even if she had been aware of it, such alerts usually related to a known shoplifter. Employees usually became more watchful in response, but did not necessarily know which individual was implicated.

Ms. Edwards remembers Mr. Brown's exit from the store differently. She testified that *before* she removed the security tape from the weapon and gave it to Ms. Nutt, she said to Ms. Nutt, "He's crazy. Y'all sold him a gun?" Nutt replied that "he had an ID [sic] and that she had to follow company policy and sell the rifle to him." Ms. Nutt *then* walked Brown out of the store. Edwards then testified that Ms. Nutt reentered the Wal-Mart after Brown left, found a manager, and both of them went outside to look for Brown. Brown had already pedaled away on his bicycle, however, and the two employees returned to the store.

Brown then proceeded to Horn's Bait & Tackle Shop, which is not named in this suit, and bought bullets. He then pedaled home, assembled his new rifle, loaded it, and shot himself in the head. He died from the wound.

The mother of Mr. Brown's only child filed suit . . . claiming that Wal-Mart breached its common law duty of care and the statutory requirements of the Gun Control Act of 1968, 18 U.S.C. 922(d)(4). This act makes it unlawful for "any person to sell . . . any firearm . . . to any person knowing or having reasonable cause to believe that such person . . . has been adjudicated as a mental defective or has been committed to any mental institution." . . .

III. Law

A. Legal Bases for Recovery

The two potential avenues to establishing liability in this case are the Gun Control Act and negligence, the latter via the Georgia wrongful death statute.

B. [The Court Concluded That Wal-Mart Did Not Violate the Gun Control Act]

C. Wrongful Death

The Georgia wrongful death statute authorizes recovery by children of decedents where the death "results from . . . criminal or other negligence [.]" . . . The Court follows the traditional framework for negligence claims. The Plaintiff must demonstrate: (1) a duty owed by the defendant to the plaintiff; (2) a breach of that duty; and (3) that the breach was the proximate cause of injury to the Plaintiff; and (4) actual injury to the Plaintiff. Actual injury is proven; Mr. Brown, Bridgett Brown's father, is obviously deceased.

1. Duty

As for Wal-Mart's duty in this case, numerous prior cases have clearly established it. With regard to the sale of a rifle to a mentally defective person, a firearm dealer should foresee that such a sale could easily result in irresponsible use of the firearm and thus injury to the buyer or third parties. The dealer clearly has a duty of care to the public to avoid such sales . . .

More specifically to cases of negligent entrustment, Georgia cases follow § 390 of the Second Restatement of Torts (emphasis added):

One who supplies directly or through a third person a chattel for the use of another *whom the supplier knows or has reason to know to be likely because of his youth, inexperience, or otherwise, to use it in a manner involving unreasonable risk of physical harm to himself and others* whom the supplier should expect to share in or be endangered by its use, is subject to liability for physical harm resulting to them.

2. Issues of Fact

In this case there is a genuine issue of fact as to whether Nutt and Edwards knew enough to foresee that selling a gun to Brown could result in harm. It is crucial to note the correct parameters of foreseeability. To be legally negligent, Nutt and Edwards need not have foreseen the exact events that later transpired. They need only have suspected that Brown "would take the [rifle] and commit an act with generally injurious consequences."

First, Lisa Edwards testified that a security alert had been issued in response to Eric Brown's entry numerous times in the past. This fact, along with the fact that an alert was issued when Brown entered the store on March 25, 1994, implies that Ms. Nutt, who had worked at Wal-Mart for seven years, may have been aware that Brown was not a normal customer. Nutt protests to the contrary.

Second, there is a factual issue concerning Brown's physical appearance and demeanor that day. Roosevelt Bray testified that he saw Brown on his bicycle around 11:00–12:00 PM, and that Brown was "looking real wild." He looked so "wild," in fact, that Mr. Bray asked Brown if he was still "taking [his] medicine." Brown responded that "it wasn't doing him no good." April Wilcox, a Wal-Mart cashier, testified that just before purchasing the rifle Brown looked "rushed, upset, and . . . was talking to himself." The Court finds it unlikely that Brown looked deranged that morning, was in a "rage" just before the purchase, but looked completely normal while buying the gun.

Third, there is no doubt that Lisa Edwards firmly believed that Brown was mentally disturbed, but it appears she assisted the sale anyway, by removing security tape from the rifle and returning it to Ms. Nutt with full knowledge that Brown had just purchased it. Edwards testified that before Brown was given his purchase, she told Ms. Nutt that the man was "crazy." Edwards says she questioned Nutt as to whether he should be sold a firearm. Ms. Nutt disputed this in her affidavit, stating that the exchange occurred *after* she returned from walking Brown out of the store. Nutt also testified that she did not "take [Ms. Edwards' comments] to mean [Brown] was unfit to purchase a firearm."

Fourth, Lisa Edwards testified that after Nutt reentered Wal-Mart, she sought out a manager and left the building to look for Brown. Wal-Mart omits mention of this in its statement of facts or Nutt's affidavit, but later asserts that if in fact Ms. Nutt did exit the building a second time, there is no evidence that she did so to look for Brown. If Nutt did leave the building to pursue Brown, this could easily imply to a reasonable trier of fact that she knew the sale was improper. This finding would be even more appropriate if a jury found that Ms. Edwards questioned Ms. Nutt about the sale before Nutt handed over the rifle to Brown. Neither Edwards nor Nutt took any further steps to retrieve the weapon, and they did not notify the police.

These four factual issues alone warrant denying Wal-Mart's motion for summary judgment. . . .

3. Proximate Causation

In cases such as this, "the more difficult question" is always whether the . . . defendant is a proximate cause of the decedent's suicide.

At first glance it appears that the link between Wal-Mart's alleged negligent entrustment and Brown's suicide is tenuous—Brown lied on the federal form about his history of mental illness, bought the rifle, bought ammunition at another establishment, went home, assembled the rifle, and then shot himself. Wal-Mart argues that the criminal act of lying on the form, the purchase of ammunition at another store, and the suicide itself are all intervening acts cutting off liability for Wal-Mart. Indeed, independent illegal acts of third persons are generally deemed unforeseeable and therefore the *sole* proximate cause of any injury. This then relieves other, prior negligent actors of liability.

Several events did occur between the sale to Brown and his death, but they are not intervening acts absolving Wal-Mart of liability as a matter of law. The reason for this is simply that if Brown's misuse of the weapon was foreseeable by the seller, so then (implicitly) were the intervening causes leading to that misuse, and so the seller can be held liable. It is basic common law that defendants remain liable where intervening acts between the negligence and the ultimate harm were foreseeable. In *Milton Bradley Co.* v. *Cooper* it was held that

> [I]n order to hold the defendant liable, the petition must show . . . that [the act complained of] put in operation other causal forces, such as were the direct, natural, and probable consequences of the original

act, or that the intervening agency could have reasonably been anticipated or foreseen by the original wrongdoer.

Foreseeable intervening forces are within the scope of the original risk created by the seller in transferring a firearm to a mentally imbalanced person, and they do not excuse him from liability.

Cases dealing with gun purchasers who then harm third parties hold that the gun seller may be held liable for foreseeable harm resulting from the sale, despite several intervening acts.

The legal analysis is no different in cases of suicide. If anticipated, it matters not whether the intervening act is negligent, intentional, or criminal.

As discussed, purveyors of firearms have a duty to anticipate certain kinds of intervening misconduct, like murder or suicide.

Finally, the fact that another store sold Brown ammunition after the purchase at Wal-Mart does not relieve Wal-Mart of liability. The court in *Milton Bradley* observed that

> [t]here may be more than one proximate cause of an injury. The proximate cause of an injury may be two separate and distinct acts of negligence of different persons acting concurrently. Where two concurrent acts of negligence operated in bringing about an injury the person injured may recover from either or both of the persons responsible.

Plaintiff simply chose to sue Wal-Mart instead of Horn's Bait & Tackle Shop.

There is an issue of fact as to whether Brown's suicide was foreseeable to a reasonably careful gun dealer. If so, the acts of lying on the federal form, buying ammunition, assembling the gun, and shooting himself in the head were all logical, foreseeable steps to that goal. Consequently, there is an issue of fact as to whether Wal-Mart's alleged negligence legally caused Brown's death . . .

IV. Conclusion

Issues of proximate cause—and negligence generally—are properly left to triers of fact "unless the movant can demonstrate plainly and palpably that he did not contribute to the proximate cause of injury . . . and that reasonable minds could not disagree."

. . . [B]ecause there remain questions of fact about what Wal-Mart's employees should have reasonably foreseen as a result of the sale of a rifle to Brown, Wal-Mart's motion for summary judgment on the state law of wrongful death is denied.

Questions

1. What is the central issue in this case?
2. Did the Court find Wal-Mart negligent and thus in violation of Georgia's wrongful death statute? Explain.
3. In order to be found negligent in this case, must the Wal-Mart workers have foreseen that Brown would commit suicide? Explain.
4. Why weren't the intervening acts of purchasing ammunition at another store and the suicide itself sufficient to absolve Wal-Mart of liability as a matter of law?
5. How would you vote on Wal-Mart's liability if you were a member of the jury panel? Explain.
6. Johnny Burnett, described by his mother, Sheila Watters, as a "devoted" Dungeons & Dragons player, killed himself. (The record did not disclose his age at the time of death.) Mrs. Watters blamed the death on her son's absorption in the game. She claimed that "he lost control of his own independent will and was driven to self-destruction."

   Dungeons & Dragons is an adventure game set in an imaginary ancient world; the players assume the roles of various characters as suggested by illustrated booklets. The play is orchestrated by a player labeled the "Dungeon Master." The outcome of the play is determined by using dice in conjunction with tables provided with the game. The game's materials do not mention suicide or guns. More than one million copies of the game have been sold, many to schools where it is used as a learning tool. ~~TSR - no prior knowledge - no warning~~

   In federal district court, Mrs. Watters brought a ~~req.~~ wrongful death claim against TSR, the manufacturer of Dungeons & Dragons. The plaintiff's complaint ~~→ not liable~~ alleged that TSR violated its duty of care in two ways: It disseminated Dungeons & Dragons literature to "mentally fragile persons," and it failed to warn that the "possible consequences" of playing the game might include "loss of control of the mental processes." Decide. Explain. See *Watters* v. *TSR, Inc.,* 904 F.2d 378 (6th Cir. 1990).
7. Plaintiff was seven months pregnant and the mother of 17-month-old James. She was standing on the sidewalk, and James was in the street. A truck being

negligently driven bore down on the boy, running him over. The shock caused the mother to miscarry and suffer actual physical and emotional injury. She brought suit against the driver for harm to herself and the infant child.

    a. What is the issue in this case?

    b. Decide the case. Explain.

[See *Amaya* v. *Home Ice, Fuel & Supply Co.*, 379 P.2d 513 (Cal. S. Ct. 1963). But also see *Dillon* v. *Legg,* 441 P.2d 912 (Cal. S. Ct. 1968).]

8. Is a fireworks manufacturer liable for harm to children who ignited an explosive that had failed to detonate in the town public display the previous day? Explain.

9. The mother of a 12-year-old boy who died in a shooting accident when a gun he was playing with accidentally discharged sued *Boys Life,* a magazine published by the Boy Scouts of America. The mother claimed that the boy was influenced to experiment with a rifle after reading a 16-page firearms advertising section in the magazine.

    a. What product liability claims would the mother raise?

    b. What constitutional defense would the Boy Scouts raise?

    c. Decide. Explain.

[See *Jan Way* v. *Boy Scouts of America,* 856 S.W.2d 230 (Tex. 1993).]

CLASSES OF NEGLIGENCE CLAIMS

Negligence claims emerging from defective products fall into three categories of analysis: (1) manufacturing defects, (2) design defects, and (3) inadequate warnings.

Manufacturing Defects

In building a business, it goes without saying that customers must be satisfied. McDonald's sells a billion cups of coffee each year, in part, because its coffee is extremely hot—180 to 190 degrees—which is exactly what its customers prefer and which, McDonald's believes, produces tastier coffee than the 140–145 degrees normally achieved at home. In 1992, then 79-year-old grandmother, Stella Liebeck, ordered breakfast at an Albuquerque, New Mexico, McDonald's and subsequently caused a sensation that made headlines around the world. While trying to get the top off the container, she spilled the coffee on her lap, resulting in severe burns. She was hospitalized and required skin grafts. She sought a settlement with McDonald's, but according to her family, McDonald's offered only $800.[10] Ms. Liebeck sued, accusing McDonald's of gross negligence for selling coffee that was "unreasonably dangerous" and "defectively manufactured."[11]

> In 1992, then 79-year-old grandmother, Stella Liebeck, ordered breakfast at an Albuquerque, New Mexico, McDonald's and subsequently caused a sensation that made headlines around the world

A jury awarded Ms. Liebeck $160,000 in compensatory and $2.7 million in punitive damages. The jury found Ms. Liebeck 20 percent responsible for her own injury. The judge subsequently reduced the award to $640,000. The parties then settled out of court for an undisclosed amount. According to news reports, the jury awarded Ms. Liebeck

$2.7 million in punitive damages because of what it perceived to be McDonald's callous attitude toward the accident and because of the many previous coffee-burn claims that had been filed against McDonald's.[12] The fallout from the case has been enormous. For example, Wendy's said it would temporarily halt the sale of hot chocolate because it might be too hot for children.[13] And, as *Newsweek* expressed it, Ms. Liebeck became a "poster lady" for the tort reform movement.[14] [For the "actual facts" on the Liebeck/McDonald's episode, see **http://www.lectlaw.com/files/cur78.htm**]

Recent hot coffee decisions have provided some comfort to the *Liebeck* critics, but the issue is far from settled. An Iowa jury, for example, required only 75 minutes to find that McDonald's bore no responsibility for the serious burns suffered by an 18-month-old child who apparently tipped his parents' 185 degree coffee on himself.[15] Similarly, a federal district court dismissed a product liability claim by a woman who suffered second-degree burns when a cup of McDonald's coffee spilled in her lap. The coffee was in a Styrofoam cup covered by a lid and was being held in a beverage carrier in the woman's lap when it tipped over as her husband drove down a steep incline leaving the restaurant. The cup and lid displayed warnings stating "HOT!" and "CAUTION: CONTENTS HOT."[16] On the other hand, the Ohio Supreme Court allowed a hot coffee case to go to the jury because "genuine issues of material fact remain whether the coffee was so hot that its risks outweighed its benefits; whether the coffee was so hot that it was not as safe as an ordinary consumer would expect; and whether the risk of second-degree burns was an unforeseen danger that required a warning."[17]

Res Ipsa.   As we see then with the coffee cases, *improper manufacturing* of products often gives rise to negligence claims. However, the extremely complex process of producing, distributing, and using a product sometimes so obscures the root of the injury in question that proof of fault is nearly impossible to establish. In those circumstances, many courts have adopted the doctrine of *res ipsa loquitur* (the thing speaks for itself), which in some cases permits the court to infer the defendant's negligence even though that negligence cannot be proven—that is, the facts suggest that the plaintiff's injury <u>must</u> have resulted from the defendant's negligence, but the circumstances are such that the plaintiff is unable to prove negligence. A showing of *res ipsa loquitur* requires that (1) the injury was caused by an instrumentality under the control of the defendant, (2) the accident ordinarily would not happen absent the defendant's negligence, and (3) there is no evidence of other causes for the accident.[18]

Design Defects

From Cessna's single-engine airplanes to five-gallon buckets (which may hold liquid sufficient to drown a child) to automobile seat belts and on across the spectrum of American products, manufacturers must think about designing products in such a way as to anticipate and avoid consumer injury that might be attributable to defective design. In recent years, the Ford Motor Company has paid more than $113 million to settle hundreds of injury and

> More than 260 people have died in Bronco II accidents

death claims springing from accidents involving one of its sport utility vehicles, the Bronco II. More than 260 people have died in Bronco II accidents, a number several times higher than in similar vehicles. Ford blames the accidents on bad driving or unsafe modifications. The claimants have argued that the Bronco II's high, short, and narrow design makes it unusually susceptible to rolling over. Ford argues that the Bronco II, which was produced from 1983 to 1990, is safe, and Ford has won several litigations. Critics say that Ford knew the vehicle was dangerous before it went into production but proceeded without proper adjustments because it was in a race with General Motors for the sport utility market.[19]

In 1999, the federal Fifth Circuit Court of Appeals threw out a long-running class action litigation designed to represent all Bronco II owners, saying the class was too large and unwieldy and the claims were too individualized.[20] Then, later in 1999, the National Highway Traffic Safety Administration declined to conduct further investigation of the Bronco II because its rollover rate was no worse than those of comparable vehicles.[21] Meanwhile, the lawsuits continue. For example, the Indiana Court of Appeals, in 1999, affirmed an $18.2 million verdict in a Bronco rollover.[22]

Design issues often lead to serious and convincing claims against manufacturers. Two principal lines of analysis have emerged in these cases: (1) The *risk/utility test* holds that a product is negligently designed if the benefits of a product's design are outweighed by the risks that accompany that design. (2) The consumer *expectations test* imposes on the manufacturer a duty to design its products so that they are safe not only for their intended use but for any reasonably foreseeable use.

In 1997, members of the American Law Institute, a group of legal experts, approved the *Restatement (Third) of Torts,* which does not constitute law but represents those experts' best judgment about what the law <u>should</u> be. They have recommended a design defect standard that supports the risk/utility model and gives much less attention to consumer expectations. Further, a product would be considered defective in design only if its foreseeable risks could have been reduced or avoided by a reasonable alternative design and if failure to include that design makes the product not reasonably safe. That is, plaintiffs apparently would need to show that some better design was available and was not incorporated in the product in question. Whether court decisions embrace the new standard remains to be seen.

Question

1. The *Restatement (Third) of Torts* effectively calls for a free market approach to defective design questions. In theory, with perfectly informed manufacturers and consumers, the price mechanism will produce optimal levels of care by all parties. *The Harvard Law Review,* however, recently argued that "producers generally are much better informed about product risks and the likelihood of liability than are consumers."[23] Thus, the implication is that the market will not work to satisfactorily protect consumers from

defective products. Explain why producers generally are much better informed than are consumers.

Inadequate Warnings

> "PARENT: Please exercise caution. FOR PLAY ONLY: Mask and chest plate are not protective: cape does not enable user to fly"

Small, plastic signs reading something like "Warning! Coffee is hot!" seem to be popping up all over America in the wake of the aforementioned McDonald's case. A parent buying a Batman costume might see the following: "PARENT: Please exercise caution. FOR PLAY ONLY: Mask and chest plate are not protective: cape does not enable user to fly."[24] Warnings are everywhere, but are they of value other than in fending off lawsuits? Some experts think so, but others differ:

> Rower McCarthy, a "human factors" engineer who studies the relationship between people and products, said that warnings simply [do] not work.
>
> He said he [has] collected more than 3,500 articles about the effectiveness of warning labels and [has] found not a single reliable study that documented a reduction in accidents resulting from a warning on a product:
>
> "Consumers who pay attention to warnings don't get hurt in the first place, and consumers who get hurt typically aren't the ones who read warnings," said McCarthy.[25]

Certainly the law provides that a negligence claim may arise from a supplier's failure to warn of a danger associated with the product. The question is whether the supplier knew or should have known that the product could be dangerous in its foreseeable use. Courts would also consider the feasibility of an effective warning and the probable seriousness of the injury.

[For California's failure-to-warn law, see **http://consumerlawpage.com/article/failure.shtml**].

BROWN FORMAN CORP. v. BRUNE
893 S.W.2d 640 (Tex. App. 1994)

In 1983, Marie Brinkmeyer and a friend went to a bar to drink. Brinkmeyer was an 18-year-old, first-year college student. The legal drinking age in Texas at the time was 19. Apparently, she was not asked for identification. She drank a 32-ounce pitcher of Hurricanes and an unknown number of White Russians. After leaving the bar, Brinkmeyer illegally bought a bottle of Pepe Lopez tequila, which was produced by Brown-Forman. At a party that evening, Brinkmeyer drank one-half of a glass of tequila unmixed with nonalcoholic beverages; then she began drinking straight from the tequila bottle. After drinking heavily and rapidly, Brinkmeyer lost consciousness. Friends took her to her room, placed her on her bed, and left her. The next morning she was found in her bed having died from ingesting large amounts of ethanol.

In 1983, no warning labels were required on liquor containers, but in 1988 a federal law was approved requiring warnings about the general health risks associated with drinking and specific warnings about drinking and driving and drinking while pregnant. That statute expressly precluded state warning laws.

Brinkmeyer's mother, Joyce Brune, sued Brown-Forman on grounds of negligence and strict liability (explained later in this chapter). Brune argued that alcohol is unreasonably dangerous in the absence of a warning. A jury found Brown-Forman guilty of negligence and 35 percent responsible for Brinkmeyer's death. Brune was awarded $535,000. Brown-Forman appealed.

Justice Yanez

* * * * *

It is fundamental that the existence of a legally cognizable duty is a prerequisite to all tort liability. Whether a legal duty exists under a set of facts is a question of law. Therefore, regardless of whether the theory of liability is based upon strict liability or negligence, the threshold question is whether Brown-Forman had a duty to warn of the risk of death from overconsumption of alcohol in a short period of time. We note that because there existed no federal or state legislation in 1983 regarding warnings on alcoholic beverage containers does not mean that distillers may not be found liable for a failure to warn should courts find such a duty exists . . . [C]onsidering "the creation of new concepts of duty in tort is historically the province of the judiciary."

Therefore, we consider whether a common law duty existed in 1983 for distillers to warn that overconsumption of tequila within a short amount of time may cause death and whether there existed a duty to provide instructions about the safe use of tequila . . . Determining whether a legal duty exists necessarily entails the interpretation and application of legal precedent as well as policy considerations. We consider social, economic, and political questions and their applicability to the facts at hand. Other factors to be considered include the extent of the risk involved, "the foreseeability and likelihood of injury weighed against the social utility of the actor's conduct, the magnitude of the burden of guarding against the injury, and the consequences of placing the

burden on the defendant." We note that foreseeability alone is not a sufficient basis for creating a new duty. In a failure to warn case, we consider the extent to which the tort system is capable of devising an adequate warning.

In assessing whether a legal duty exists under the facts before us, we find Justice Kilgarlin's words distinguishing moral and legal duties particularly instructive:

> In spite of a societal dynamic to expand duty, Texas still follows a general rule that Texans do not owe others general amorphous legal duties. The rule in Texas still distinguishes between moral and legal duty. Although one may have a moral duty to prevent a blind person from crossing a busy street against a light, a person has no legal duty to do so unless additional factors exist. These other factors include the existence of familial or voluntary relationships which impose a duty, statutes or ordinances which may legally require action, or special circumstances, such as having placed the blind man in his precarious position in the first place . . .

The common law has long recognized that the alcoholic beverage drinker maintains the ultimate power and thus the obligation to control his own drinking behavior. We believe that the common law should remain focused on the drinker as the person primarily responsible for his behavior.

Though no Texas court has had to decide whether a distiller has a duty to warn of the risk of death from overconsuming alcohol in a short period of time, Texas courts have addressed whether alcoholic beverage manufacturers must warn of other risks and dangers associated with alcoholic beverages. All concluded that the alcoholic beverage manufacturer had no duty to warn of whatever risk or danger was asserted.

* * * * *

When choosing to enter the business of manufacturing alcoholic beverages, a manufacturer should make an effort to inform its users about risks and dangers associated with its product. That effort may include a larger public education campaign rather than simply labeling a bottle. In fact, education may be the only remedy we have in preventing binge drinking. Despite education, however, there will always be individuals who, though informed about the dangers associated with the use of alcoholic beverages, choose to misuse the product. The circumstances behind an individual's choice to misuse beverage alcohol are profoundly complex and will not be addressed by placing a few warning words on the outside of a bottle . . . Holding an alcoholic beverage manufacturer financially responsible for the death of an individual who consumed a large quantity of alcohol in a short amount of time does not answer the more direct question about why the individual would consume a known dangerous product in such a quantity.

* * * * *

The standard for common knowledge is the overall knowledge common to the community that is a basis for determining a duty to warn, not what individual users may or may not know. Many products cannot possibly be made entirely safe for all consumption. The product sold must be dangerous to an extent beyond that which would be contemplated by the ordinary consumer who purchases it, with the ordinary knowledge common to the community as to its characteristics . . . While morally it might appear prudent to require manufacturers of alcoholic beverages to place a warning on alcoholic beverages about the danger of death after ingesting large amounts of alcohol over a short period of time, we find no legal duty to do so.

Considering the extensive involvement of the federal and state government in regulating alcoholic beverages, we conclude that the subject of warnings on alcoholic beverages and placing instructions for use on an alcoholic beverage container should be left to the legislative process. The issues relevant to this case have for so long been political issues we conclude that courts are ill-equipped to develop effective and feasible warnings and instructions . . .

In light of this political judgment, it would seem arbitrary for courts to hold a whiskey distiller liable for the foreseeable injurious effects to some people of whiskey which has standard ingredients and qualities. The political judgment would seem to foreclose a judicial holding that the recognized dangers of whiskey render it unreasonably dangerous . . .

We understand that binge drinking and underage drinking is a problem. However, merely because it is foreseeable that an underage drinker may gain access to alcoholic beverages and misuse them is not a reason to impose a duty to warn about death from overconsumption and impose liability for the drinker's death upon the distiller . . .

Additionally, because of the inability to fashion effective instructions about the proper use of tequila, we conclude that no legal duty exists on the part of Brown-Forman to place instructions for proper use on its containers of tequila.

* * * * *

Even if a warning could be fashioned, there existed no evidence that Marie would have heeded the warning. The evidence was that Marie had received and disregarded warnings about the abuse of alcoholic beverages generally.

* * * * *

Finding that Brown-Forman had no legal duty to warn Marie about the dangers of consuming a large amount of tequila over a short time period and no duty to provide instructions about the proper use of tequila, we reverse the trial court's judgment, render judgment for Brown-Forman, and render that Brune take nothing.

Reversed.

Questions

1. What was the issue in this case?
2. Why did the court reverse the jury's judgment?
3. George Hacker, director of the alcohol policies project for the Center for Science in the Public Interest: "In terms of acute intoxication, I don't think it's widely known that this is a highly toxic substance when consumed too rapidly—especially among young people who are inexperienced in drinking." Comment. [See Wendy Bounds, "Liquor Firm Liability Verdict Reversed," *The Wall Street Journal,* January 6, 1995, p. B2.]
4. The Court in the *Brown-Forman* case favorably cites Justice Kilgarlin's view that legal and moral duties are often not one and the same. In your view, if an act (or a failure to act) is immoral, should it also be illegal? Explain.
5. Bresnahan, age 50 and 5'8" tall, was driving her Chrysler LeBaron, equipped with a driver's side air bag, at between 25 and 30 miles per hour. She was seated less than one foot from the air bag cover. Bresnahan was distracted by police lights and rear-ended a Jaguar, triggering the LeBaron air bag, which broke Bresnahan's arm and caused various abrasions. The vehicle did not include a warning about the danger of sitting too close to the air bag. Was the vehicle defective because of the absence of a warning? Explain. [See *Bresnahan* v. *Chrysler Corp.*, 65 Cal. App. 4th 1149 (1998).]

6. Laaperi installed a smoke detector in his bedroom, properly connecting it to his home's electrical system. Six months later, Laaperi's house burned and three of his children were killed. A short circuit, which caused the fire, also deprived the A.C.-powered smoke detector of electricity. Thus the detector did not sound a warning. Laaperi then claimed that Sears, Roebuck, where he purchased the detector, was guilty of negligence for failing to warn him that a fire might disable his smoke detector such that no warning would issue. How would you rule in this case? [See *Laaperi* v. *Sears, Roebuck & Co.,* 787 F.2d 726 (1st Cir. 1986).]

NEGLIGENCE DEFENSES

Even if the plaintiff has established all of the necessary ingredients in a negligence claim, the defendant may still prevail by asserting a good defense. The two most prominent legal defenses in these cases are (1) comparative or contributory negligence and (2) assumption of the risk.

> A trampoline at the Beta Theta Pi fraternity house at the University of Denver led to a broken neck and paralysis when a 20-year-old fraternity member, Oscar Whitlock, unsuccessfully attempted a flip at 10 PM in the dark

A trampoline at the Beta Theta Pi fraternity house at the University of Denver led to a broken neck and paralysis when a 20-year-old fraternity member, Oscar Whitlock, unsuccessfully attempted a flip at 10 PM in the dark. Whitlock had extensive experience with trampolines. The day of the accident he had slept until 2 PM after drinking that morning until 2 AM. The trampoline was located in front of the house on university land that was leased by the fraternity. The trampoline had been used over a 10-year period by students and community members. A number of injuries had resulted. The university kept its own trampoline under lock and key because of safety concerns.

At trial, the jury found the university 72 percent at fault, with the remainder of the blame lying with the plaintiff/student. He recovered 72 percent of $7,300,000 ($5,256,000). On appeal, the judgment was upheld, but the dissent argued that the university had no duty to warn against obvious risks, saying that "no reasonable person could conclude that the plaintiff was not at least as negligent as the defendant." Hence, the dissent was saying, in effect, that the plaintiff had *assumed the risk* and, in any case, was himself arguably more *negligent* than the university.[26]

The Colorado State Supreme Court then reviewed the appeals court decision and reversed on the grounds that the university did not maintain a "special relationship" with the plaintiff that would have justified imposing a duty of due care on the university to assure safe use of the trampoline.[27]

Questions

1. Assume you own an amusement park.
   Would the dissent's reasoning in the court of appeals decision apply to the trampoline in your amusement park business? Explain.

2. Would a warning and close supervision protect you from liability under the court of appeals decision? Explain.
3. Would you have the duty of due care for your customers that the Supreme Court said the University of Denver did not have for Whitlock? Explain.

THE RULES OF NEGLIGENCE DEFENSES

Let's look more closely now at the central defenses in negligence cases.

Comparative Negligence

Most states have adopted comparative negligence as a defense. It involves weighing the relative negligence of the parties. Though the formula varies from state to state, typically the plaintiff's recovery is reduced by a percentage equal to the percentage of the plaintiff's fault in the case. Assume a plaintiff sustained $10,000 in injuries in an accident. If the plaintiff's own negligence is found to be 20 percent responsible for the injuries, then the plaintiff's recovery will be reduced to $8,000. When the plaintiff's fault actually exceeds that of the defendant, the plaintiff may be barred from recovery.

Contributory Negligence

Rather than employing the comparative negligence doctrine, a few states continue to follow the historic rule that any contribution by the plaintiff to his or her own harm constitutes a *complete bar to recovery.* This is called contributory negligence. If the plaintiff is found to have contributed in any way to his or her injury, even if that contribution is minuscule, he or she is unable to recover.

Assumption of Risk

A plaintiff who willingly enters a dangerous situation and is injured, in many states, will be barred from recovery. For example, if a driver sees that the road ahead is flooded, he will not be compensated for the injuries sustained when he loses control as he attempts to drive through the water. His recovery is barred even though the road was flooded due to operator error in opening a floodgate. The requirements for use of the assumption of risk defense are (1) knowledge of the risk and (2) voluntary assumption of the risk. Assumption of the risk and contributory negligence are distinguishable in that the former is based on consent while the latter is rooted in carelessness. Increasingly, states that have adopted the comparative negligence doctrine do not treat assumption of the risk as a complete bar to recovery, but rather as a factor in negligence balancing.

The case that follows examines the allocation of fault in an automobile accident, including the special complications of (1) *enhanced injuries* allegedly resulting from a defective door latch and (2) *mitigation* of punitive damages.

NORWEST BANK N.A. v. CHRYSLER CORPORATION AND HUFFINES CHRYSLER PLYMOUTH, INC.
981 P.2d 1215 (N.M. App. Ct. 1999) Cert. Den., 981 P.2d. 1207 (N.M. S.Ct. 1999)

Judge Bosson

This crashworthiness case arises from a tragic accident in which several occupants were ejected from a Chrysler minivan and suffered severe injuries. The occupants sued Chrysler Corporation (Chrysler) and Huffines Chrysler Plymouth, Inc. (Huffines), the automobile dealership, alleging that a defective latch on the rear door caused them to be thrown from the minivan and suffer enhanced injuries. After trial, the jury agreed that the rear door latch was defective, but found that the defect was not a proximate cause of Plaintiffs' injuries, and therefore, the jury determined that Chrysler was not liable in damages to Plaintiffs. Plaintiffs ask us on appeal to reverse the jury verdict and remand for a new trial. They allege two principal points: (1) that in a crashworthiness case alleging enhanced injuries, it was error to instruct the jury in the special verdict form to compare the negligence of the driver with the negligence of Chrysler in making the defective rear door latch; and (2) that it was error to allow Chrysler to seek to mitigate punitive damages by introducing evidence of a corporate policy that encouraged the use of seat belts.

Background

On July 21, 1995, Plaintiff Minh Lien Jones was driving a 1990 Plymouth Grand Voyager minivan owned by her fiance, David Abercrombie, which was headed west on Interstate 40 near Santa Rosa, New Mexico. Her fiance was in the front seat; her son, mother, two sisters, two nieces, and grandson were passengers in the rear seats. The vehicle suddenly veered sharply to the left and then over-corrected to the right, at which point it hit the guardrail on the north side of the highway, became unstable, and rolled several times. At some point in the crash, five of the seven rear seat occupants were ejected from the minivan. Of those ejected, one died, one lost an arm, and the others were injured more seriously than the four who remained inside the minivan.

The initial cause of the accident was unclear. Plaintiffs contended that a gust of wind caused Ms. Jones to lose control of the vehicle, whereas Defendants suggested that she either fell asleep or was distracted by one of the passengers. At some point in the accident, the rear door of the minivan opened. Plaintiffs contended they were forcefully ejected through the rear door because of a defective latch that caused the door to open. Plaintiffs maintained that Chrysler knew about its defective latch but failed to provide Mr. Abercrombie with a safe latch and led him to believe that the existing, defective latch was safe. Plaintiffs sued Chrysler and its dealer, Huffines, for the torts of strict products liability, negligence, negligent infliction of emotional distress, and negligent misrepresentation, and for a statutory violation of the Texas Deceptive Trade Practices Act (DTPA).

Chrysler attacked Plaintiffs' case on causation. Chrysler presented evidence to the jury suggesting that the passengers were ejected out the side windows, not the rear door, and that the rear door latch, even if defective, was not a proximate cause of Plaintiffs' injuries. Defendants also presented evidence that the force of the minivan striking the guardrail was so great that no latch could have withstood such an impact, no matter how safe the design, and thus, this particular latch, no matter how defective, did not cause Plaintiffs' injuries.

Of all the passengers in the minivan, only those in the front seat were wearing seat belts. Before trial, the court granted Plaintiffs' motion to exclude any seat belt evidence. The court prohibited any reference to the seat belts installed in this minivan and their use or nonuse by any of its occupants. During trial, however, Chrysler persuaded the court to allow it to introduce nonspecific seat belt evidence for the limited purpose of showing the jury that it was not recklessly indifferent to consumer safety and therefore should not suffer an award of punitive damages. Without being allowed to refer specifically to the seat belts in this minivan or to their use at the time of the crash, Chrysler was permitted to offer evidence that it encouraged the public to use seat belts as a matter of safety.

After a lengthy trial, the jury was asked to answer a series of written interrogatories included in special verdict forms. After only four hours of deliberation, the jury returned a verdict in favor of Chrysler and Huffines on all claims brought by all Plaintiffs. Although the jury found that the rear door latch was defective as alleged, the jury also found that Chrysler's tortious conduct in regard to that latch was not a proximate cause of Plaintiffs' injuries, and therefore Defendants were not liable for damages. The special verdict form also instructed the jury to apportion damages by comparing the fault of Ms. Jones, the driver, with any fault of Chrysler and Huffines. The jury concluded that Ms. Jones bore 100% of the fault for Plaintiffs' injuries and that neither Chrysler nor Huffines bore any fault. The jury also indicated that Plaintiffs suffered no compensable injuries and were therefore not entitled to punitive damages.

Discussion

Comparing Fault of the Driver

Plaintiffs argue that the special verdict form erroneously allowed the jury to compare the fault of the driver, Ms. Jones, with the fault of Chrysler as part of the process of apportioning liability. Plaintiffs contend that Chrysler was solely responsible for the defective rear door latch, and Chrysler should be solely responsible for all injuries proximately caused by the failure of the latch; that is, those additional "enhanced" injuries caused by being ejected from the minivan through the rear door.

* * * * *

Under *Lujan* v. *Healthsouth Rehabilitation Corp.,* it appears to be settled in New Mexico crashworthiness cases that the cause of the original accident and the cause of a divisible, enchanced injury are successive, not concurrent torts . . .

According to the rule suggested in Lujan, juries would complete a two-step calculation in determining liability for enhanced injury in crashworthiness cases. Assuming the evidence shows a divisible injury, the enhanced portion of the injury proximately caused by the fault of the successive tortfeasor would be separated from the lesser injury that would have resulted from the original accident if there had been no crashworthiness defect in

the vehicle. The successive tortfeasor would then become liable for the enhanced injury that is proximately caused by that defect. The original tortfeasor who caused the accident would remain liable for the entire injury, but with the prospect of indemnification against the successive tortfeasor for that portion of the judgment reflecting the enhanced injury.

In the matter before us, the special verdict form presented to the jury did not complete this two-step process, but instead instructed the jury as if this were a case of concurrent tortfeasors, like any garden-variety, two-party traffic accident. The jury was instructed:

> Compare the negligence of the following persons and find a percentage for each. The total of the percentages must equal 100%, but the percentage for any one or more of the persons named may be zero if you find that such a person was not negligent or that any negligence on the part of that person was not a proximate cause of Plaintiffs' damages.

Chrysler Corporation
__%
Huffiness Chrysler Plymouth, Inc.
—%
Lien Jones
__%
__%Total 100%

The jury completed the special verdict form by allocating 100% of the fault to Lien Jones and 0% to the two Defendants.

In another context, giving this instruction might require reversal. However, before reaching the point of allocating fault, the jury found that the defective latch did not cause any injuries to Plaintiffs. Thus, Plaintiffs were not prejudiced by the jury's fault allocation exercise.

We know from the instructions within the verdict form that by the time the jury arrived at allocating comparative fault, its members had already determined that Chrysler's defective rear door latch was not a proximate cause of Plaintiffs' injuries. According to the special verdict instructions, if the jurors found that Chrysler's negligence was not a proximate cause of Plaintiffs' injuries, they were to stop and go no further; they were instructed not to proceed to damages or apportionment of fault. Consideration of divisible injury and responsibility for enhanced injury is only material if the successive tort, here the crashworthiness defect, is established as a proximate cause of the enhanced injury.[1]

* * * * *

Chrysler's accident reconstructionist testified at length, with the aid of an animated video, that the occupants of the minivan were ejected through the side windows and not the rear door. In particular, there was evidence that the force of the rollover threw all the occupants forward rather than backward. There was testimony that the centrifugal force of the accident threw the passengers against the windows and roof of the minivan. Defendants' witness testified that the rear end of the vehicle was elevated on the guardrail as it rolled, so that the ground did not block ejection through the side windows.

There were no independent eyewitnesses to verify the ejection theories of either side, and the jury was free to choose whichever theory it found most persuasive. Chrysler's theory had other support as well. For example, the animated video apparently showed that one of the occupants may have been pinned against the right side of the vehicle by other passengers, and that her arm was severed by a guardrail post as she was ejected through the right side window. Another passenger may have been thrown out the same window at about the same time. Three more occupants may have been ejected out the left side window as the minivan continued to roll.

In addition, Chrysler presented a second theory from which the jury could have concluded that the defective

latch did not proximately cause Plaintiffs' injuries. An expert testified that the force of the accident subjected the latch to over 4,000 pounds of force. Chrysler presented evidence that such force would break even a nondefective latch because either the latch or another part of the liftgate structure would not withstand that degree of stress.

In short, the graphic nature of the evidence allowed the jury reasonably to infer that the defective latch did not proximately cause Plaintiffs' injuries. The evidence allowed the jury to conclude that either Plaintiffs were ejected through the side windows and not the rear door, or the latch would have succumbed to the forces of the accident in any event . . .

Seat Belt Evidence in Mitigation of Punitive Damages

Plaintiffs argue that the trial court's admission of seat belt evidence, even when limited to mitigation of punitive damages, violated New Mexico law.

The historical development of New Mexico's policy regarding seat belt evidence derives from both the judicial and legislative branches of government. In *Thomas v. Henson,* this Court attempted to create a common-law duty requiring an occupant of an automobile to fasten the seat belt "as part of the continuing duty to exercise reasonable care for his or her own safety . . . unless the circumstances dictate otherwise." We reasoned that the creation of such a duty would allow for "the apportionment of damages" between the negligent tortfeasor who caused the accident, and the negligent occupant of the vehicle who aggravated his or her own injuries by not wearing a seat belt.

The New Mexico Supreme Court responded swiftly. On its own motion, the Court issued a writ of certiorari and reversed our opinion on the ground that "the creation of a 'seat belt defense' is a matter for the Legislature, not for the judiciary." Reacting almost simultaneously, the 1985 legislative session took up the issue and enacted the Safety Belt Use Act. The Act created a statutory duty for front seat passengers to wear seat belts, but it specifically provided that the failure of those passengers to wear seat belts as required by the Act "shall not in any instance constitute fault or negligence and shall not limit or apportion damages." The Act imposed no duty on rear seat passengers.

The use of seat belt evidence was recently clarified in *Mott,* in which we stated that the language of [the

---

[1] The special verdict form for almost every Plaintiff began with the question:

Question No. 1: Was the minivan rear door latch manufactured and designed by Chrysler Corporation defective?

The jury's answer was uniformly, "Yes." Immediately following, the jury was asked:

Question No. 2: Was the Defendant Chrysler Corporation's defective latch a proximate cause of the damages to . . . ?

The answer in each case was "No." The jury was later instructed that if it answered "No" to either of these two questions, as well as to similarly paired questions relating to other torts and proximate cause, then "you are to stop and your foreperson should sign the verdict." Only if the jury answered affirmatively to both questions, including proximate cause, could it proceed to the questions on damages and comparative fault.

Safety Belt Use Act] does not "indicate any intent to allow the introduction of evidence of failure to use seat belts for any purpose in a negligence action." As we noted in *Mott,* the actions of both the Supreme Court and the Legislature have spoken clearly against the admission of such evidence . . . [O]ur analysis begins with the question whether Chrysler's general policy of encouraging seat belt use is relevant to the issue of punitive damages.

In support of their claim for punitive damages, Plaintiffs presented expert testimony attempting to show that Chrysler exhibited a corporate policy of utter disregard for the safety of its customers. One particular expert, Mr. Flanagan, testified about Chrysler's policy of indifference towards consumer safety. He charged Chrysler with behaving irresponsibly based on the manner in which Chrysler developed its rear door latch and then failed to respond to safety problems as they arose. Mr. Flanagan summarized his critique of Chrysler by referring to what was called "twenty points of corporate misconduct" regarding the latch. In directing Mr. Flanagan's testimony, Plaintiffs' counsel repeatedly asked him questions about whether Chrysler had exhibited good corporate conduct or conduct typical of a "good corporation doing good things for good people." Not surprisingly, Mr. Flanagan answered that Chrysler had not, and that its conduct was bad. Thus, during their own case in chief, Plaintiffs made Chrysler's corporate policy towards consumer safety an issue for the jury.

Chrysler chose to rebut the charge of indifference and bad corporate character, among other ways, by showing that it encouraged the public to use seat belts . . . Chrysler's witnesses were allowed to testify that the corporation had a policy of encouraging the use of seat belts, and that this policy was an example of Chrysler being a "good manufacturer" and a "responsibly acting manufacturer."

* * * * *

We cannot say the court abused its discretion in concluding that such evidence was relevant to mitigating a demand for punitive damages. Arguably, it was fairly related to rebutting Plaintiffs' evidence to Chrysler's bad corporate character . . .

In the context of this case, we are impressed with the trial court's expressions of concern for fairness and what it called an "uneven playing field." The court felt compelled to permit Chrysler some latitude on this subject precisely because of the Flanagan testimony about

"twenty points of corporate misconduct." The trial judge is uniquely situated, at ground zero, to balance the benefits and burdens from such evidence. Under this very limited circumstance, when the court displays such concern and proceeds in such a measured manner, the sound exercise of judicial discretion should not lightly be disturbed.

* * * * *

Although we do not reverse on the seat belt issue, we emphasize the very narrow scope of our ruling. Our decision in this case should in no way be construed as permitting the introduction of case-specific evidence about the use or nonuse of seat belts for any purpose. There has never been, and there still is no "seat belt defense" in New Mexico. Furthermore, it is not our intention to invite even nonspecific seat belt evidence every time punitive damages are at stake. We hold no more than that there may be circumstances when nonspecific evidence of a general corporate policy encouraging seat belt use, like any other potentially mitigating evidence, may be appropriate to rebut a charge of reckless indifference to safety.

Affirmed.

* * * * *

Questions

1. *a.* What are "enhanced injuries?"
   b. What does the court mean by saying that the cause of the original accident and the cause of an enhanced injury are successive, not concurrent torts?
2. *a.* Explain Chrysler's defense.
   b. Why did the jury find for Chrysler?
   c. Why did the appeals court conclude that the introduction of seat belt evidence by Chrysler was permissible?
3. Tidwell was working at an Exxon service station and was shot during a robbery attempt. Tidwell had an eighth-grade education, and his work experience consisted primarily of manual labor. Tidwell sued Exxon, which argued that Tidwell knew the job was dangerous. Decide. See *Exxon Corporation* v. *Tidwell,* 816 S.W.2d 455 (Ct. App. Tx. 1991).
4. David Clapham lost an eye when he was hit by a foul ball at Yankee Stadium in New York City. He sued the Yankees and the city, which owns the stadium, contending they were negligent in failing to

extend the protective screen to reach the box seat he was occupying behind the Yankee dugout.

    a. What defense would you raise on behalf of the Yankees?

    b. Decide the case. Explain.

5. During an unsupervised volleyball team warmup, Jose Barretto, a high school senior, tried to dive over a volleyball net to a mat he had placed on the other side. Catching his wrist in the net, Barretto landed on his head and suffered paralysis. The coach had left the gym to get some equipment and had told the students to avoid horseplay. Barretto sued the school for negligence and the jury apportioned 20 percent of the fault to Barretto and 80 percent to the school. Barretto was awarded $18.8 million, and the school appealed. How would you rule on that appeal? Explain. See *Barretto* v. *City of New York,* 655 N.Y.S. 2d 484 (S.Ct., App. Div., 1st Dept., 1997).

Part Two—Warranties

As explained previously, negligence claims are often difficult to prove. For that reason and others, a wronged consumer may wish to raise a breach of warranty claim in addition to or in place of a negligence action. A warranty is simply a guarantee arising out of a contract. If the product does not conform to the standards of the warranty, the contract is violated (breached), and the wronged party is entitled to recovery. Note that a negligence claim arises from breach of the duty of due care, whereas a warranty claim arises from a breach of contract.

At this writing, the National Conference of Commissioners on State Laws is building a proposed major revision in the statutory language governing warranty laws. The Conference recommendations would eventually be considered by the state legislatures as revisions of existing state law. For now, however, the principles expressed in this chapter represent the law across America. [For the text of the Uniform Commercial Code, Article II, Sales, see **http://www.law.cornell.edu/ucc/2/overview.html**]

EXPRESS WARRANTIES

An express warranty exists if a seller of goods affirms a fact or makes a promise regarding the character or quality of the goods. Warranties are governed primarily by the terms of the Uniform Commercial Code. The UCC is designed to codify and standardize the law of commercial practice throughout the United States. Forty-nine states have adopted all or the bulk of the UCC. Louisiana has adopted only portions.

UCC 2–313. Express Warranties by Affirmation, Promise, Description, Sample

1. Express warranties by the seller are created as follows:

    a. Any affirmation of fact or promise made by the seller to the buyer which relates to the goods and becomes part of the basis of the bargain creates an express warranty that the goods shall conform to the affirmation or promise.

    b. Any description of the goods which is made part of the basis of the bargain creates an express warranty that the goods shall conform to the description.

    c. Any sample or model which is made part of the basis of the bargain creates an express warranty that the whole of the goods shall conform to the sample or model.

The philosophy undergirding UCC 2–313 is straightforward. The seller who seeks to enhance the attractiveness of his or her product by offering representations as to the nature or quality of the product must fulfill those representations or fall in breach of contract and be subject to the payment of damages.

Puffing

Perhaps the area of greatest confusion in determining the existence and coverage of an express warranty is distinguishing a seller's promise from a mere expression of opinion. The latter, often referred to as sales talk or puffing, does not create an express warranty. The UCC requires an affirmation of fact or promise. Hence, a statement of opinion is not covered by the code. For example, the sales clerk who says, "This is the best TV around," would not be guaranteeing that the television in question is the best available. The salesperson is expressing a view. We, as consumers, seem to be quite patient with sellers' exaggerations. If, on the other hand, the clerk said, "This TV has a solid walnut cabinet," when in fact it was a pine veneer stained to a walnut tone, a breach of warranty action might ultimately be in order. The test to be applied in such situations is one of reasonable expectations. An expression of opinion coming from an expert may well create an express warranty because the buyer should reasonably be able to rely on the expert's affirmations. That would particularly be the case if the buyer is not knowledgeable about the product.

IMPLIED WARRANTIES

A seller enters into a contract for the sale of goods and, as a consequence, an implied warranty arises by operation of law. That is, an implied warranty automatically attaches to the sale of goods unless the warranty is disclaimed (disavowed) by the seller.

Two types of implied warranties are provided for:

UCC 2–314. Implied Warranty: Merchantability; Usage of Trade

(1) Unless excluded or modified (Section 2–316), a warranty that the goods shall be merchantable is implied in a contract for their sale if the seller is a merchant with respect to goods of that kind. Under this section the serving for value of food or drink to be consumed either on the premises or elsewhere is a sale.

UCC 2–315. Implied Warranty: Fitness for Particular Purpose

Where the seller at the time of contracting has reason to know any particular purpose for which the goods are required and that the buyer is relying on the seller's skill or judgment to select or furnish suitable goods, there is unless excluded or modified under the next section an implied warranty that the goods shall be fit for such purpose.

The implied warranty of merchantability is a powerful tool for the wronged consumer in that the warranty arises automatically by operation of law. If the seller is a merchant regularly selling goods of the kind in question, the warranty of merchantability simply accompanies the sale unless the warranty is excluded via a disclaimer (explained below). The warranty arises even if the seller made no certification as to the nature or quality of the goods. UCC 2–314 enshrines the consumer's reasonable expectation that only safe goods of at least ordinary quality will appear on the market.

The implied warranty of fitness for a particular purpose likewise arises by operation of law, but only when the seller (merchant or not) knows (or has reason to know) that the goods are to be used for a specific purpose, and the seller further knows that the buyer is relying on the seller's judgment. If those conditions obtain, the warranty exists automatically unless disclaimed. For example, Chris Snapp engages an audio products clerk in a discussion regarding the proper stereo system for Chris's classic Austin Healey sports car. Chris explains the joy he expects to receive in driving his car along the winding Kentucky roads with the convertible top down and the stereo booming. Unfortunately, the stereo selected on the clerk's advice proves insufficiently powerful to be heard clearly above the rushing wind. Should Chris recover for breach of the implied warranty of fitness for a particular purpose? Merchantability?

DISCLAIMERS

Express warranties may be disclaimed (excluded) or modified only with great difficulty. In any contract displaying both an express warranty and language disclaiming that warranty (for example, sold "as is" or "with all faults"), the warranty will remain effective unless the warranty and the disclaimer can reasonably be read as consistent.

Implied warranties may be excluded or modified by following either of the two patterns explained in UCC sections 2–316(2) and (3)(a).

2. Subject to subjection (3), to exclude or modify the implied warranty of merchantability or any part of it the language must mention merchantability and in case of a writing must be conspicuous, and to exclude or modify any implied warranty of fitness the exclusion must be by a writing and conspicuous.
3. Notwithstanding subsection (2)
   a. unless the circumstances indicate otherwise, all implied warranties are excluded by expressions like as is, with all faults or other language which in common understanding calls the buyer's attention to the exclusion of warranties and makes plain that there is no implied warranty.

Finally, when a buyer, before entering a contract, inspects the goods (or a sample thereof), or declines to inspect, no implied warranty exists with regard to defects that should have been apparent on inspection UCC 2–316(3)(b).

MAGNUSON–MOSS WARRANTY ACT

Although the Uniform Commercial Code embodies our primary expression of warranty rules, Congress has extended and clarified those rules by passing the Magnuson–Moss Warranty Act. Congress approved the act following a study that found widespread abuse of consumers. Warranties were often vague, deceptive, or simply incomprehensible to the average purchaser. The act, administered by the FTC, applies only to consumer products and only to written warranties. It does not require offering an express written warranty, but where such a warranty is offered and the cost of the goods is more than $10, the warranty must be labeled *full* or *limited*. A full warranty requires free repair of any defect. If repair is not achieved within a reasonable time, the buyer may elect either a refund or replacement without charge. If a limited warranty is offered, the limitation must be conspicuously displayed.

If a warranty is offered on goods costing more than $15, the warrantor must "fully and conspicuously disclose in simple and readily understandable language the terms and conditions of the warranty." The FTC has developed various rules to implement the intent of the disclosure requirement. For example, if the warrantor requires return of the completed warranty registration card in order to activate the warranty, that return requirement must be clearly disclosed in the warranty.

The effect of the Magnuson–Moss Act has not been entirely consistent with Congress's hopes. In practice, many sellers may have either offered limited warranties or eliminated them entirely.

Part Three—Strict Liability

Imagine you are operating a clothing store. A customer enters and decides to try on a pair of slacks. You show her to the dressing room. Soon after, you hear a scream from the room. As it turns out, your customer has been bitten by a spider.

Sometimes things happen that businesses can neither prevent nor even explain and yet liability may attach. For example, imagine you are operating a clothing store. A customer enters and decides to try on a pair of slacks. You show her to the dressing room. Soon after, you hear a scream from the room. As it turns out, your customer has been bitten by a spider. Not surprisingly, she thinks the blame lies with your store. She sues, but her negligence and breach of warranty claims are rejected by the court. (Can you explain why she loses?) Finally, she raises a strict liability in tort argument, but the court denies that claim also. Read the overview of strict liability that follows and think about why the court denied her claim. [See *Flippo* v. *Mode O'Day Frock Shops of Hollywood,* 248 Ark. 1, 449 S.W.2d 692 (1970).]

STRICT LIABILITY OVERVIEW

Negligence and warranty actions are helpful to the harmed consumer. However, rapid changes in the nature of commercial practice, as well as an increasing societal concern for consumer protection, led the legal community to gradually embrace yet another cause of action. *Strict liability in tort* offers the prospect of holding all of those in the chain of distribution liable for damages from a defective product, rather than imposing the entire burden on the injured consumer. Manufacturers and sellers are best positioned to prevent the distribution of defective products, and they are best able to bear the cost of injury by spreading the loss via pricing policies and insurance coverage.

Strict liability as an independent tort emerged in 1963 in the famous California case of *Greenman* v. *Yuba Power Products, Inc.*[28] In the ensuing quarter century, most states, via either their judiciaries or their legislatures, have adopted strict liability in concept. The essence of the strict liability notion is expressed in Section 402A of the *Restatement*

(Second) of Torts. In brief, 402A imposes liability where a product is sold in a *defective condition, unreasonably dangerous*[29] to the user. The 402A test:

1. One who sells any product in a defective condition, unreasonably dangerous to the user or consumer or to his property, is subject to liability for physical harm thereby caused to the ultimate user or consumer, or to his property, if

    a. the seller is engaged in the business of selling such a product, and,

    b. it is expected to and does reach the user or consumer without substantial change in the condition in which it is sold.

2. The rule stated in Subsection (1) applies although

    a. the seller has exercised all possible care in the preparation and sale of his product, and

    b. the user or consumer has not bought the product from or entered into any contractual relation with the seller.

[handwritten: excl. flea mkt or yard sales]

[handwritten: applies even w/o privity of contract]

The *BIC* lighter case that follows considers those conditions under which a strict liability claim may be raised.

PRICE v. BIC CORPORATION
702 A.2d 330 (N.H. S.Ct. 1997)

Justice Horton

[T]he United States District Court for the District of New Hampshire certified to us the following question of law:

Can the legal representative of a minor child injured as a result of the misuse of a product by another minor child maintain a defective design product liability claim against the product's manufacturer if the product was intended to be used only by adults and the risk that children might misuse the product was open and obvious to the product's manufacturer and its intended users?

We respond in the affirmative.

In November 1991, three-year-old Douglas Moore used a BIC model J-6 lighter to start a fire that severely burned his seventeen-month-old brother, Matthew Ryan Moore. The lighter had been purchased by the boys' mother, Mary Moore.

The packaging on BIC lighters provided the warnings "Keep out of Reach of Children" and "Keep Away From Children." The defendant, BIC Corporation (BIC), was aware that the lighters could be used by children to ignite fires. BIC did not incorporate known and available child resistant features into the design of the J-6 lighter even though it was possible to do so without significantly affecting the lighter's cost or effectiveness.

The plaintiff, Kathleen Price, the guardian over the estate of Matthew Ryan Moore, contends that BIC should be strictly liable because the lighter was defectively designed in that it lacked child resistant features and adequate warnings. The plaintiff produced no evidence in response to BIC's claims that its lighters were intended to be used only by adults and that the risk that minor children might use the lighters to start fires was open and obvious to the intended users of the lighters.

BIC moved for summary judgment, asserting that New Hampshire does not permit a plaintiff to maintain a strict product liability defective design claim if the injuries complained of result from a risk that is open and obvious to the product's intended users. The federal district court asks us to clarify whether we would limit strict liability defective design claims in the manner that BIC suggests.

Nearly thirty years ago this court adopted the doctrine of strict liability of manufacturers for product defects as stated in section 402A (1) of the Restatement (Second) of Torts.

*   *   *   *   *

To maintain a defective design products liability claim, a plaintiff must first prove "that the design of the product created a defective condition unreasonably dangerous to the user . . . " Whether a product is dangerous to an extent beyond that which would be contemplated by the ordinary consumer is determined by the jury using a risk-utility balancing test. A product's design should meet risk-utility balancing standards as seen from the point of view of the public as a whole.

Determining whether a product's design is unreasonably dangerous implicates "a multifaceted balancing process involving evaluation of many conflicting factors." These factors include the social utility and desirability of the product, as "evaluated from the point of view of the public as a whole," weighed against the risk of danger posed by its use, whether the risk of danger could have been reduced without significantly affecting either the product's effectiveness or cost, and the presence and efficacy of a warning to avoid an unreasonable risk of harm from hidden dangers or from foreseeable uses.

Manufacturer liability may still attach even if the danger is obvious to a reasonable consumer or if the user employs the product in an unintended but foreseeable manner. "The obviousness of the danger should be evaluated against the reasonableness of the steps which the manufacturer must take to reduce the danger." Further, a manufacturer's duty to warn is not limited to intended uses of its product, but also extends to all reasonably foreseeable uses to which the product may be put. "When an unreasonable danger could have been eliminated without excessive cost or loss of product efficiency, liability may attach even though the danger was obvious or there was adequate warning."

In undertaking this analysis, we caution that the term "unreasonably dangerous" should not be interpreted so broadly as to impose absolute liability on manufacturers or make them insurers of their products. In certain cases, the court may be able to keep the issue of liability from the jury if, as a matter of law, the utility of the product to the public as a whole completely outweighs the risk posed to consumers or the risk posed by use of the product is extremely remote. If the district court concludes that either of these circumstances are met, the plaintiff's defective design claims will fail.

For these reasons, we respond to the district court that barring a determination that the utility of the product completely outweighs the risk associated with its use or that the risk of harm is so remote as to be negligible, the legal representative of a minor child injured as a result of the misuse of a product by another minor child can maintain a defective design product liability claim against the product's manufacturer, even though the product was intended to be used only by adults, when the risk that children might misuse the product was open and obvious to the product's manufacturer and its intended users.

Remanded.

Questions

1. *a.* Explain the plaintiff's claim.
    b. Explain the defendant's claim.
2. What evidence must a plaintiff provide to maintain a successful defective design product liability claim?
3. Is the manufacturer excused from liability if the product's danger is obvious or if the product is used in an unintended but foreseeable fashion?
4. In a similar BIC case [*Griggs* v. *Bic Corp.,* 981 F.2d 1429 (3rd Cir. 1992)] the court, employing a negligence analysis, found that the central question was whether the foreseeable risk was unreasonable. The court noted that residential fires started by children playing with lighters are estimated to take an average of 120 lives each year and total damages amount to $300–$375 million or 60–75 cents per lighter sold.
    a. Is the foreseeable risk unreasonable, in your judgment?
    b. How did you reach your conclusion?
    c. In your view, are the parents the responsible parties in this episode? Explain.
5. Alison Nowak, a 14-year-old girl, tried to spray her hair with Aqua Net. As the spray valve on the

recently purchased aerosol can would not work properly, she punctured the can with an opener. She was standing in her kitchen near a gas stove at the time and the cloud of spray that gushed from the can ignited. She was severely burned. Nowak sued Faberge, the maker of the spray, on strict liability grounds. Although the back of the can contained the warnings, "Do not puncture," and "Do not use near fire or flame," the jury determined that Faberge had not adequately warned of the fire hazard and awarded her $1.5 million. Faberge appealed. Decide. Explain. See *Nowak* v. *Faberge USA Inc.,* 32 F.3d 755 (3d Cir. 1994).

COVERAGE

All of those engaged in the preparation and distribution of a defective product may be liable for any harm caused by the defect, regardless of proof of actual fault. Furthermore, the courts have extended strict liability coverage to reach injured bystanders. Coverage generally extends to both personal injuries and property damage, but in some states the latter is excluded. Some states limit strict liability recovery to new goods, and some have limited liability to a designated period (for example, 15 years) after the manufacture or sale of the product.

Furthermore, the new *Restatement (Third) of Torts* recommends applying strict liability claims to manufacturing defects but not to design and warning defect cases. Thus, in effect, the new *Restatement* calls for greater reliance on negligence law and its fault requirements. Of course, the courts may choose to stick with the current expansive use of the strict liability doctrine. [For a brief critique of portions of the new *Restatement,* see **http://www.cliffordlaw.com/media/articles/1272.html**]

DEFENSES

Assumption of risk and product misuse are both good defenses and, if factually supported, in many states can act as a complete bar to strict liability recovery. Assumption of the risk involves the plaintiff's decision to proceed to use the product despite obvious dangers associated with that use. Thus, if a pilot decided to fly knowing that the plane's wing flaps were not operating properly, she may well have assumed the risk if she subsequently crashed. When the product is used improperly, or its directions are ignored or it is used in an unforeseeable way, the defendant would raise the misuse defense. Presumably, crop dusting with a plane not designed for that purpose would constitute misuse. Some courts, however, hold those in the chain of distribution liable for foreseeable misuses. Since strict liability is a no-fault theory, contributory negligence ordinarily is not a recognized defense. [For advice on "avoiding the product liability minefield" see **http://www.nfm-online.com/nfm–backs/Oct–99/product–liability.html**]

The case that follows examines strict liability defenses.

CHARLTON v. TOYOTA INDUSTRIAL EQUIPMENT
714 A.2d 1043 (Superior Ct. Penn. 1998)

Judge Joyce

Appellant, Michael Charlton, and his father, Edward Charlton were both employees of Crown Cork & Seal Co., Inc. (CCS). On February 11, 1991, Michael approached his father, who was operating a forklift truck, and asked him to take a break. Edward declined and indicated that he intended to continue working. Appellant, not hearing his father's response, began walking away. While Appellant's attention was focused on activities occurring in another department, Edward put the forklift truck into reverse and ran over his son's left foot. Appellant has become permanently disabled due to the excruciating pain and other symptoms . . .

In February, 1993, Appellant instituted suit against Toyota Industrial Equipment . . . Recovery was sought solely on the basis of strict products liability, i.e., Appellant alleged that the forklift was defective because it contained a gas tank that obstructed the driver's rearward view and lacked rearview mirrors and/or an alarm system that was activated when the forklift was operated in reverse. A jury trial was held in 1996, following which the jury found in favor of Appellant and awarded him $100,000.00 in damages. Appellant appealed [arguing] the trial court erred or abused its discretion by permitting Appellee to introduce evidence of Appellant's and his father's negligence . . .

The instant case is a strict liability action. The concept of strict liability allows a plaintiff to recover where a product in a defective condition unreasonably dangerous to the consumer or user causes harm to the plaintiff. In a design defect case, the question is whether the product should have been designed more safely. Pennsylvania law requires that a plaintiff prove two elements in a products liability action: (1) that the product was defective; and (2) that the defect was a substantial factor in causing the injury.

Mindful of these concepts, the appellate courts have struggled with the issue of whether to admit or exclude evidence which bears on the element of causation. The Pennsylvania Supreme Court has declined to extend negligence concepts into the area of strict products liability and has held that comparative negligence may not be asserted as a defense in a strict products liability action. The Supreme Court nonetheless has observed that evidence which is inadmissible for one purpose may be admissible for another.

[T]his Court has acknowledged that a plaintiff's comparative negligence is irrelevant in a strict products liability action and may not be used to reduce a strictly liable defendant's responsibility for the entire damage award . . . However, this Court has noted certain limited exceptions to this rule. Specifically, this Court has permitted a defendant to introduce evidence that a plaintiff voluntarily assumed the risk or misused a product. This Court has further permitted evidence of reckless conduct to be admitted where such conduct was the sole cause of the accident.

Evidence that a plaintiff engaged in highly reckless conduct also has been deemed admissible in a strict liability action. To demonstrate that a plaintiff's actions are highly reckless, it must be shown that he knew or had reason to know of facts which created a high degree of risk of physical harm to himself or that he deliberately proceeded to act, or failed to act, in conscious disregard of that risk.

Evidence that a plaintiff acted in a highly reckless fashion is akin to evidence that a plaintiff misused a product. The issue of causation is raised when the plaintiff's action is so reckless that the plaintiff would have been injured despite the curing of any alleged defect, or is so extraordinary and unforeseeable as to constitute a superceding cause.

[T]hus evidence of a plaintiff's voluntary assumption of the risk, misuse of a product, or highly reckless conduct is admissible insofar as it relates to the element of causation. However, evidence of a plaintiff's ordinary negligence may not be admitted in a strict products liability action, unless it is shown that the accident was solely the result of the user's conduct and not related [to] the alleged defect in the product. Application of these principles persuades us that evidence of Appellant's and his father's negligence should not have been admitted in this case.

The evidence elicited by Appellee does not suggest that Appellant or his father misused the forklift truck or that he engaged in highly reckless behavior . . . Nor does it indicate that Appellant voluntarily assumed the risk of encountering a specific defect in the forklift. It instead revealed that Appellant and his father were, at most, guilty of contributory negligence in failing to pay attention to each other's exact location.

Evidence of contributory negligence, standing alone, is insufficient to prove a voluntary assumption of the risk by Appellant . . .

Appellee did not show that Appellant's injuries resulted solely from his and his father's careless conduct rather than the alleged defects in the forklift truck. Because evidence regarding Appellant's and his father's negligent conduct does not fall within any of the recognized exceptions, it should not have been admitted. Upon remand, the trial court should therefore exclude evidence relating to Appellant's or his father's ordinary negligence, unless it is shown that the evidence falls within one of the aforementioned limited exceptions.

Reversed and remanded.

Questions

1. The Pennsylvania Superior Court explains that a plaintiff's comparative negligence is irrelevant in a strict product liability action but for certain "limited exceptions." What are those exceptions?

2. The court indicated that the Appellant, Charlton, and his father may have been guilty of contributory negligence. Nonetheless, those facts should not have been admitted into evidence, the court ruled. Why did the court take that position?

3. The deceased had rented an auto from the Hertz Corporation. A tire blew out, and a fatal crash resulted. The tire was manufactured by Firestone. The estate of the deceased filed suit against Hertz and Firestone. Evidence presented at trial caused the jury to believe that the dangerous condition of the tire arose after its manufacture.
   a. Can the plaintiff successfully raise a strict liability claim against Hertz? Explain.
   b. Against Firestone? Explain.
   [See *Stang* v. *Hertz Corp.,* 83 N.M. 730, 497 P.2d 732 (1972).] But see *Livingstone* v. *Begay,* 652 P.2d 734 (N.M. 1982.)

4. Nancy Denny was driving her Ford Bronco II. She swerved to avoid a deer and suffered serious injuries when the Bronco tipped over. She sued on strict liability, negligence, and breach of implied warranty grounds. The jury found for Denny on warranty grounds but rejected the strict liability and negligence claims, finding that the Bronco was not defective. Denny was awarded $3 million. Ford appealed, saying that the jury's findings were inconsistent.
   a. Explain Ford's argument.
   b. Decide. Explain.
   c. The jury found Denny 60 percent responsible for her own harm. Does that finding change the results? Explain.
   [See *Nancy Denny and Robert Denny* v. *Ford Motor Company,* 88-CV-1180, U.S. District Court, Binghamton, New York (1993).] Also see *Denny* v. *Ford Motor Company,* 79 F.3d 12 (2d Cir. 1996).

5. How can we justify holding a company strictly liable without proof that its behavior was negligent in some respect?

6. Does a no-fault policy like strict liability, in any sense, undermine or depreciate our sense of personal responsibility or our conception of right and wrong? Explain.

LIMITS OF STRICT LIABILITY—MARKET SHARE LIABILITY?

The great test now for the courts in the strict liability area is to determine just how far this powerful doctrine should be expanded in providing recoveries for those injured by the multitude of products that are so central to our consumer society.

The next case summarizes the continuing judicial debate over extending negligence and/or strict liability reasoning to what has become a long line of cases in which plaintiff/daughters, while yet fetuses, were exposed to an allegedly defective drug (DES). DES, which was marketed from the early 1940s until 1971, was administered to prevent miscarriages. The drug received FDA marketing approval, but a warning was required indicating that the drug was experimental. Then, in 1971, FDA marketing approval was withdrawn, as evidence emerged linking DES to cancer in the daughters of those who took it. The California Supreme Court, in the groundbreaking DES case *Sindell* v. *Abbott Laboratories* (discussed below), condemned the defendant drug manufacturer:

> During the period defendants marketed DES, they knew or should have known that it was a carcinogenic substance, that there was a grave danger after varying periods of latency it would cause cancerous and precancerous growths in the daughters of the mothers who took it, and that it was ineffective to prevent miscarriage. Nevertheless, defendants continued to advertise and market the drug as a miscarriage preventative. They failed to test DES for efficacy and safety; the tests performed by others, upon which they relied, indicated that it was not safe or effective. In violation of the authorization of the Food and Drug Administration, defendants marketed DES on an unlimited basis rather than as an experimental drug, and they failed to warn of its potential danger.[30]

Some jurisdictions have followed the *Sindell* reasoning, some have modified it, and others have rejected the doctrine entirely.[31] In recent years, courts have ruled that third-generation DES claimants, that is, granddaughters, may not recover on market share grounds.[32]

Because of the passage of time, the loss of records, the large number of manufacturers, and other factors, the plaintiff/daughters ordinarily cannot identify the *specific* manufacturer responsible for the defective drug ingested by their mothers. The *Sutowski* case explores the legal implications of that problem.

SUTOWSKI v. ELI LILLY & COMPANY
696 N.E.2d 187 (S.Ct. Ohio 1998)

Facts

Sutowski claims to have suffered damage to her reproductive system due to her in utero exposure to diethylstilbestrol (DES). Sutowski asserts that each of the named defendants is either a manufacturer, a distributor, or a parent or successor corporation to a manufacturer or distributor, of DES. Her complaint includes counts consisting of strict liability under products liability, negligence under products liability, breach of warranty and market share liability.

"In response, defendant/respondent Eli Lilly and Company ("Eli Lilly") filed a motion for judgment on the pleadings. Among other things, Eli Lilly argues that judgment must be entered against Sutowski on her claim for relief under the market share theory of liability since Ohio has not recognized market share.

Justice Cook

The United States District Court certified the following question of law to this court:

"Whether market share exists in Ohio as a viable theory of liability in a DES products liability action[?]"

Market-Share Liability

DES is a form of synthetic estrogen that gained widespread use in the early 1940s.

* * * * *

Because DES was not patented, some two hundred to three hundred different drug companies produced DES in the years it was widely prescribed for use during pregnancy. Due to the long interval between DES use and manifestation of its effects a generation later, the great number of possible manufacturer–defendants, and the primarily generic form of the drug, many DES plaintiffs experienced difficulty identifying the particular manufacturer of the drug taken by their mothers years earlier. Many manufacturers were no longer in business, medical and pharmacy records were lost or destroyed, and memories had dulled over time.

In response to the DES plaintiff's inability to establish causation, the California Supreme Court fashioned the market-share theory of liability in its benchmark decision *Sindell* v. *Abbott Laboratories* (1980). In *Sindell,* the trial court dismissed a DES plaintiff's complaint because she was unable to identify the particular manufacturer of the drug prescribed for her mother. The supreme court reversed, resolving in the plaintiff's favor the conflict between the traditional causation requirement of tort law and the desire to insulate an innocent plaintiff from bearing the cost of injury.

The California Supreme Court determined that the theory of alternative liability was inapplicable in light of the plaintiff's inability to join all DES manufacturers in the action. The court also rejected the theories of concert of action and enterprise liability. Rather than affirming dismissal of the action, the *Sindell* majority adopted the novel theory of market-share liability proposed in a *Fordham Law Review* student comment. The court cited the following three policy considerations in favor of relieving the plaintiff of the burden of proving causation: (1) the manufacturer should bear the cost of injury as between it and an innocent plaintiff, (2) manufacturers are better able to bear the cost of injury resulting from defective products, and (3) because manufacturers are in a better position to discover and prevent product

defects and to warn consumers of harmful effects, imposing liability would further ensure product safety.

Recognizing that "there is a possibility that none of the five defendants in this case produced the offending substance," the California Supreme Court nonetheless justified shifting the burden of proof of causation to the defendant. To this end, the market-share plaintiff need only (1) identify an injury caused by a fungible product, and (2) join in the action a substantial share of the manufacturers of that product. The burden then shifts to each defendant–manufacturer to prove it did not make the particular injurious product. Market-share liability thus enables a plaintiff who cannot identify a particular tortfeasor to sustain a tort cause of action despite an inability to show proximate causation.

Any manufacturer unable to prove it did not produce the product at issue is held severally liable for the proportion of the plaintiff's awarded damages that reflects the manufacturer's total share of the product market. In support of this unique method of damage allocation, the court reasoned that a defendant–manufacturer's percentage share of the total market for a product is proportional to the likelihood that the defendant–manufacturer produced the specific product that injured the plaintiff. The only causation a plaintiff need prove in order to recover under a market-share theory is the causal connection between exposure to, or use of; the product at issue and the injury sustained.

This atypical theory of tort recovery has not gained wide acceptance outside California. Of the courts that have examined market-share liability in the DES context, most have not considered it a plausible theory of recovery.

Ohio Tort Law

Ohio common law has long required a plaintiff to prove that a particular defendant caused his or her injury through negligence . . . The plaintiff must establish a causal connection between the defendant's actions and the plaintiff's injuries . . .

Under the market-share theory, the plaintiff is discharged from proving this important causal link. The defendant actually responsible for the plaintiff's injuries may not be before the court. Such a result collides with traditional tort notions of liability by virtue of responsibility, and imposes a judicially created form of industrywide insurance upon those manufacturers subject to market-share liability.

In *Minnich* v. *Ashland Oil Co.* (1984), 473 N.E.2d 1199, this court adopted the doctrine of alternative liability where the plaintiff "alleged two negligent defendants and a single proximate cause." John Minnich was injured in an ethyl acetate explosion while at work. He alleged the chemical was delivered to his employer in a defective condition, and that both the Ashland Oil Co. and the M.J. Daly Co. supplied all the ethyl acetate used by his employer. Minnich was unable, however, to identify which of the two companies supplied the particular ethyl acetate that exploded the morning of his injury.

In applying alternative liability to the facts in *Minnich*, this court did not relieve he plaintiff of the burden of identifying the tortfeasors. Rather, Minnich had to show that both companies were negligent and that his injuries were caused by the negligence of one of the two. Alternative liability relieved Minnich only from proving which of the two identified tortfeasors caused his injuries.

* * * * *

Codified in 1988, the Ohio Products Liability Act, R.C. 2307.71 *et seq.,* provided:

> Any recovery of compensatory damages based on a product liability claim is subject to sections 2307.71 to 2307.79 of the Revised Code.

* * * * *

[T]he General Assembly specifically stated that its purpose in enacting current R.C. 2307.79 was "to codify an essential requirement for the use of the alternative liability theory in actions brought under Ohio law:"

> A manufacturer shall not be held liable for damages based on a product liability claim that asserts any of the following theories:
> (A) Industrywide or enterprise liability.
> (B) Alternative liability, except when all possible tortfeasors are named and subject to the jurisdiction of the court.

Statutory language that is plain and unambiguous, and conveys a clear and definite meaning, needs no interpretation. In this instance, the 1988 version of the Products Liability Act applicable to Sutowski's claim unmistakably required identification of a particular tortfeasor: the successful plaintiff had to establish that the harmful product was defective when it left the manufacturer's control.

* * * * *

The Ohio Products Liability Act does not provide for market-share liability. Furthermore, based on the foregoing analysis, the market-share theory is not a part of Ohio common law.

Accordingly, we hold that in Ohio, market-share liability is not an available theory of recovery in a products liability action.

Conclusion

We recognize that the DES plaintiff who, without fault, is unable to identify the manufacturer responsible for her injury engenders sympathy. It is, however, the role of the court to interpret the law, not to legislate. We believe the General Assembly should decide the policy question of whether Sutowski's claims, or others like hers, warrant substantially altering Ohio's tort law.

Judgment accordingly.

Questions

1. Explain the general notion of market-share liability.
2. Do you agree with the judgment of the Ohio Supreme Court in the *Smith* case? Explain.
3. How can a defendant avoid liability under the *Sindell* decision alluded to in the opinion?
4. A victim of asbestosis could not identify all of the manufacturers of the asbestos to which he was exposed. Should the court apply the market share theory of liability to this case? Explain. See *Celotex Corporation* v. *Copeland,* 471 So.2d 533 (Fla. 1985).
5. The City of Philadelphia and the Philadelphia Housing Authority sued various manufacturers of lead-based paints and their trade association seeking in excess of $100 million to help pay the cost of programs to reduce health problems associated with lead-based paint. The federal Department of Health and Human Services has concluded that lead poisoning is a serious threat to children's health in the United States. Some children ingest lead either by chewing on walls and other surfaces coated with lead-based paint or by breathing air containing dust from crumbling paint. Plaintiffs claimed that the defendants had known of these dangers for decades, and plaintiffs conceded that they had known of those dangers for a number of years. Plaintiffs sued on a variety of product liability grounds, among them the theory of market share liability. Only one trial court opinion in Pennsylvania has recognized the market share theory. Should the federal court of appeals apply market share reasoning to this case? Explain. See *City of Philadelphia* v. *Lead Industries Assn,* 994 F.2d 112 (3d Cir. 1993).

Part Four—Product Liability and Public Policy

Giant tort awards have made headlines in recent years while encouraging calls for liability reforms. For example, in 1999, a California jury awarded $290 million in punitive damages to Juan Ramon Romo, who lost three family members in a 1993 Bronco II rollover.[33] These stunning sums are almost always dramatically reduced,[34] but the risk remains a potent factor in business strategy. Imagine yourself in the place of Bruce Hoegger, the president and owner of a small Minneapolis hydraulic-components company. In one three-month period of 1994, he spent 50 tough hours in depositions and meetings with his lawyers as they dealt with a product liability suit. Hoegger feared that he might lose his business if a large penalty were awarded in the case. Not surprisingly, his 15-year marriage to his wife, Linda, was strained. The case eventually was settled for $25,000, and all of the costs were borne by his insurer.[35]

Bigger firms, too, shape their business strategy to cope with liability risks. Consider the discount retailer, Duckwall-Alco Stores:

> Alco won't sell exercise equipment or child car seats unless the supplier carries as much as $5 million in liability insurance. And the retailer won't buy property unless the owner certifies that any environmental mess has been cleaned up. That is necessary, Alco executives say, because under U.S. law retailers can be sued for problems arising from the goods they sell or the property they buy even it they didn't create the problems.[36]

[For materials on "an American legal system that often turns litigation into a weapon," see **http://overlawyered.com/index.html**].

REFORM?

Do we need to reform our liability system? We have examined the economic and even emotional pressures that product liability imposes on the business community. Now let's look at the empirical evidence. Our total annual product liability bill (insurance, legal fees, and actual damages) is about $4 billion.[37] As journalist Robert Kuttner remarks, "$4 billion is less than what Americans spend annually on dog food. It is one-fifth of one percent of retail sales."[38] Jury awards in product liability cases rose 44 percent in 1996 to a median of $733,500 in awards against manufacturers, up from $536,419 one year earlier, but the number of awards fell 9 percent during the year.[39] At a practical level, product liability was estimated to represent about $100 of the cost of a $200 football helmet, $500 of the cost of a new car, and $20 of the cost of a $100 ladder.[40]

> $4 billion is less than what Americans spend annually on dog food

A study by the well-regarded Rand Institute suggests that product liability laws sometimes work well in protecting consumers and sometimes result in curbing innovation and harming business. Some good products have been withheld from the market, but some unacceptably risky products have departed quickly because of liability pressure. In most cases, liability laws have had negligible effects on pricing. Rand senior economist Steven Garber summed up the situation: "One of the important messages here is that liability is very complex, and it has good and bad effects."[41]

Other Countries?

The Tillinghast international consulting firm has provided an interesting perspective on the tort reform debate by comparing tort costs in the United States with those in other industrial countries (Denmark, the United Kingdom, Japan, Canada, France, Switzerland, Spain, Belgium, West Germany, and Italy). Our total tort system costs were estimated at $132 billion or 2.3 percent of our gross domestic product while the estimated average cost for the other nations was 0.9 percent of GDP with a high of 1.3 percent of GDP in Italy.[42] Using that data, Professor Paul Rubin of Emory University then estimated how much of our tort system costs might legitimately be labeled "waste."

> How much of the $132 billion spent on tort liability in the United States is waste? Suppose that the other countries on average provide about the right amount of insurance and deterrence through the tort system; then the difference between U.S. tort costs and this average would be a measure of waste in the system. U.S. tort costs in 1990 were 1.4 percent of GDP higher than costs in the rest of the developed world. Based on a U.S. GDP of $5.546 trillion, the waste in the system was then $82 billion in 1990. That comes to about $900 for each household in the United States. That $900 is paid in higher prices for goods and services and in higher insurance premiums. In other words, if we could only make the U.S. system approximate the tort systems in the rest of the developed world, then the average real income of Americans would increase by 1.4 percent, and each household would have about $900 more to spend on valuable goods and services.[43]

[For a brief overview of Japanese product liability law, see **http://www.faegre.com/areas/area–ib3.html**]

The Punitive Damages Debate

a California state court jury awarded $4.8 billion in punitive damages

In July 1999, a California state court jury awarded $4.8 billion in punitive damages and $107 million in compensatory damages to six people who were badly burned when the gas tank on their 1979 Chevrolet Malibu exploded. That punitive award was later reduced to about $1.09 billion, but the compensatory award was unchanged. (The full story in this Malibu case is set out below.) Enormous awards generate equally enormous publicity, but punitive awards are statistically unlikely. In fact, punitive damages were awarded in only 6 percent of civil cases won by plaintiffs according to a 1995 survey, and awards exceeded $50,000 in only half of those cases.[44]

Further, a 1996 study found that, on average, juries are not simply pulling numbers out of the air in awarding punitive damages, but rather that punitive and compensatory awards are closely related:

> Where compensatory damages were $10,000, punitives averaged around $10,860. Where compensatory damages were $100,000, punitives averaged around $65,720. And where compensatory damages were $1 million, punitives averaged $397,810.[45]

Legislation?   The majority of the states have passed some kind of tort reform, but achieving federal action has been difficult.

As described in Chapter 5, the Supreme Court provided some encouragement to the reformers in a 1996 decision striking down a $2 million punitive damages award as "grossly excessive" and thus a violation of the Constitution's due process requirements.[46] In that case, an Alabama jury had awarded $4,000 in compensatory damages to Ira Gore, whose $40,000 BMW 535i had suffered modest paint damage and been repainted before sale without notification to Gore. The jury then awarded Gore $4 million in punitive damages to penalize BMW for the roughly 1,000 new cars it had refinished and sold as new throughout the United States under its policy of notifying buyers of repairs only when the cost exceeded 3 percent of the suggested retail price of the car. The Alabama Supreme Court reduced that award to $2 million.

After the United States Supreme Court struck down that $2 million award, the Alabama Supreme Court reduced Gore's award to $50,000. In striking down Gore's punitive damage recovery, the U.S. Supreme Court did not set a "bright line" by which to identify unconstitutional punitive damages. Rather, the justices pointed to three factors that should be used, on a case-by-case basis, to resolve that question:

1. The "degree of reprehensibility" of the defendant's conduct.
2. The ratio between the punitive award and the actual harm suffered by the plaintiff.
3. The difference between the punitive award and penalties in "comparable cases."

Although the *Gore* standards are imprecise, the case, lawyers say, has had a significant impact such that big awards now are likely to be reduced on appeal.[47] The story in the aforementioned Chevrolet Malibu tragedy, and its unprecedented punitive award, are set out in the article that follows. As you read this account, think about whether the Malibu case best symbolizes the ideals of justice or the concerns of tort reformers. This case also provides the opportunity to think about the power of both the free market and ethics in resolving product liability cases. Remember that the $4.8 billion punitive award has been reduced to $1.09 billion. The case is on appeal at this writing.

PAPER TRAIL HAUNTS G.M. AFTER IT LOSES INJURY SUIT

Andrew Pollack

The $4.9 billion verdict in a personal-injury lawsuit against General Motors might be only the start of the company's problems. Lawyers and safety consultants pursuing similar cases say corporate documents used as evidence in the case, many for the first time, could be troublesome for General Motors in the future.

The jury here awarded the record-setting damages to six people who were badly burned when the gas tank of their 1979 Chevrolet Malibu exploded after the car was rammed from behind by another vehicle. The plaintiffs have pledged to donate half of any punitive damages they collect after taxes to the state of California to pay for the care and treatment of burn victims, their lawyer, Brian J. Panish, said today.

Central to the case was a 1973 "value analysis" written by an Edward C. Ivey, an Oldsmobile engineer still employed by G.M., who calculated that fuel-tank fires after accidents were costing the company $2.40 per vehicle. Plaintiffs in the Los Angeles case had argued that General Motors did not design cars more safely because it would have cost the company more than it was losing in settlements with accident victims. [The Ivey memo estimated the cost of fixing the problem at $4 to $12 per vehicle—Ed.]

"The Ivey memo is an economic blueprint for lawyers," said Clarence M. Ditlow, executive director of the Center for Auto Safety in Washington, a group co-founded by Ralph Nader that is involved in similar cases. "It set a cost constraint on how much G.M. was willing to put into hardware to prevent a fire that was otherwise preventable."

General Motors argued that its vehicles were safe and that the Ivey memo was the work of a junior engineer and was never used in design.

"There was no evidence that any engineer who worked on this vehicle or any other vehicle at General Motors used the information in the Ivey document or used that approach in making decisions on design," said Richard W. Shapiro, a Phoenix lawyer who represented General Motors in the case . . .

Still, the company has long worried about the document and how it might be perceived. "Obviously, Ivey is not an individual whom we would ever, in any conceivable situation, want to be identified to the plaintiffs," in a lawsuit, a lawyer hired by General Motors wrote after interviewing Mr. Ivey in 1981. "The documents he generated are undoubtedly some of the potentially most harmful and most damaging were they ever to be produced."

General Motors has mainly succeeded in keeping the Ivey memo from being introduced as evidence since it first became known to plaintiffs' lawyers in the early 1980s. Last year a judge in Florida threatened General Motors with "very severe sanctions" if it did not provide the memo and related documents. Some of

that evidence was in turn used in the Los Angeles case.

The "cumulative effect" of documents released in successive trials allows plaintiffs to "lose less and win more," said Sheldon J. Schlesinger, a Fort Lauderdale lawyer who represented the plaintiffs in the Florida case.

In that case, a jury ordered General Motors to pay $60 million to the family of a boy killed in a fuel-tank fire after a trailer struck the 1983 Oldsmobile Cutlass station wagon in which he was riding. The award was later reduced to $33 million.

In the Los Angeles case, the jury in Superior Court of Los Angeles County awarded Patricia Anderson, her four children and a family friend, Jo Tigner, $107.6 million in compensatory damages and $4.8 billion in punitive damages after their Malibu, stopping for a red light, was rammed by a drunken driver on Christmas Eve 1993.

The award is the largest ever in a personal-injury lawsuit, said Thomas F. Harrison, publisher of *Lawyers Weekly USA,* a newspaper published in Boston that tracks such awards. He said the previous largest was $1.24 billion awarded in January by a jury in Wisconsin to the estate of a woman who had died from a fuel-related fire after a go-cart accident at a Florida amusement park.

General Motors said it was confident that Friday's decision would be overturned on appeal, and legal experts said it was highly likely that the award would, at the least, be significantly reduced.

Mr. Shapiro, the lawyer for General Motors, said the Los Angeles case might not have that much influence on other cases because other judges could have different views on what evidence is admissible. He contended that the Los Angeles judge, Ernest G. Williams, did not allow the company to present evidence showing that cars with the same body as the 1979 Malibu had explosions only once in every 23.5 billion miles.

Mr. Panish, the main lawyer for the plaintiffs in Los Angeles, said there were dozens of other cases involving General Motors cars with designs similar to the 1979 Malibu's, with the fuel tank close to the rear bumper, an estimate General Motors called exceedingly high. The company said that the Los Angeles and Florida cases were the only ones it had lost involving such cars and that the Florida plaintiffs were not awarded punitive damages.

Terry Rhadigan, a company spokesman, said the fuel tank had been moved forward around 1984. He said that the placement of the fuel tank behind the rear axle had been common in the industry before that time and that the change was made for overall design reasons, not because the design had been unsafe.

There are about 50 cases pending against the company resulting from fires in pre-1988 G.M. pickup trucks in which the fuel tanks were mounted outside the frame on the side of the vehicles, said Mr. Ditlow of the Center for Auto Safety.

News of the huge Los Angeles verdict could prompt more people to sue for older accidents. One is Linda McOscar, who said she and her three children were sitting in a 1980 Malibu beside a highway in South Texas in June 1980, when their car was rammed from behind by a truck driven by a drunken driver. The Malibu spun around and caught fire. Mrs. McOscar managed to crawl through a window, pulling her 10-year-old son, Spencer, who was in the front passenger seat, out with her. But 13-year-old Joey and 13-month-old Hillary, who were in the back seat, were killed.

Mrs. McOscar, of Monroe, Mich., said that when she heard about the Los Angeles verdict on the news, "It just blew my mind."

"I kept waking up in the night thinking in 1973 they knew there was a defect," she said. Although she and her husband received about $55,000 from General Motors in a settlement, they say they are thinking about suing based on the new evidence.

General Motors in the early 1980s hired six law firms to scour its records to find documents that could be damaging in such cases. These lawyers have been nicknamed the "fire babies" by plaintiffs' lawyers.

One such document is the Ivey memo, only one and a half pages long. It estimated how many fatalities there were from post-accident fuel-related fires and assumed a value of $200,000 per fatality. By dividing by the number of G.M. cars on the road, Mr. Ivey came up with an estimate of the cost to G.M. of $2.40 per vehicle. But Mr. Ivey also cautioned that "it is really impossible to

put a value on human life" and that "a human fatality is beyond value, subjectively."

The memo does not say why the analysis was done. In depositions in this and previous cases, Mr. Ivey said that he could not remember anyone asking him to do the study and did not believe it was distributed.

But the lawyer's interview with Mr. Ivey in 1981 seems to contradict that position. According to the report by the lawyer, who worked for an outside firm hired by G.M., Mr. Ivey did not specifically recall being asked to do the analysis but said he thought he had been asked by a superior to help in "trying to figure out how much Olds could spend on fuel systems." Mr. Ivey said it was probably distributed to several people, though he did not know if it had ever been used.

Some other G.M. memos presented at the trial also showed that cost-benefit analysis was used on safety questions. In a 1974 memo, a G.M. official named R. G. Fischer performed a calculation similar to Mr. Ivey's and concluded that G.M. could spend $2 a car "effectively for rear impact protection." A Jan. 1, 1973, memo said that "cost/safety benefit is to be evaluated before releasing components" for performance that exceeds Federal requirements for fuel system integrity.

"This was literally an 18-year cover-up, and the jurors were outraged," said Mark Robinson Jr., one of the lawyers for the plaintiffs, who said the Los Angeles case was stronger than one two decades ago in which he won a big award for fuel-tank fire in a Ford Pinto—$128 million in punitive and compensatory damages, which was later reduced to $7 million.

Coleman Thorton, the foreman of the Los Angeles jury, said in an interview that the Ivey memo had been just one factor in the verdict. More important, he said, was that Mr. Ivey, who testified through a videotaped deposition, and other General Motors officials appeared to be evasive.

"People who were well-qualified are not supposed to have instant amnesia," Mr. Thorton, a retired custodian, said. "That is the way that most of the witnesses for the defendant reacted."

Source: *New York Times*, July 12, 1999, sec. A, p. 12. Reprinted by permission of the copyright holder, *The New York Times*.

T. P. Rhadigan, Manager, Safety Communications, General Motors Corporation:

The real story of the Anderson trial isn't what the jurors thought about the evidence they heard; the real story is the evidence they were never permitted to hear . . .

For example, evidence proving that the Malibu has a safety record better than most other cars built around the same time was kept from the jury. The court declined to permit jurors to learn that since 1978, GM A/G cars like the Malibu have been involved in only one fuel-fed, fire-related accident for every 23.9 billion miles traveled; that's the equivalent of almost one million trips around the globe.

Source: "Case Against GM: A Judicial Travesty," (Letter to the Editor) *The Wall Street Journal,* October 26, 1999, p. A27.

Questions

1. Do you regard a cost-benefit analysis involving the value of a human life as an immoral/unethical inquiry? Explain.
2. In urging a large recovery, the plaintiff's lawyer pointed to GM's $3.7 billion advertising budget for 1998, $10.8 billion cash on hand, and $13.7 billion in available credit.[48] Is a large punitive award necessary in cases of this kind in order to "get the attention" of the corporate defendant? Explain.
3. Law professor Peter Choharis laments the many inefficiencies of our tort system, including the likelihood that tort victims will need to hire a lawyer on a contingency fee arrangement (thus often paying one-third of any judgment to that lawyer) while waiting years for litigation to be complete. In an imaginative use of free market reasoning, Choharis suggests creating a market for torts. Plaintiffs would be allowed to sell their claims to the highest bidder. Presumably, law firms or perhaps the defendants themselves would buy the claims with the price depending on the likely value to the purchaser. Lawyers as purchasers could then litigate the claim and keep the damages or, in the case of defendants, the purchase would "settle" the claim out of court.
   a. Explain the advantages of such a system.
   b. Would you favor a market in tort claims as an option to litigation? Explain. See Peter Charles Choharis, "Creating a Market for Tort Claims," *Regulation* 18, no. 4 (1995), p. 38.

SOME EXAMPLES

We turn now to some highly publicized examples summarizing much of the product liability debate.

Tobacco

For more than a decade now, we have witnessed a brutal litigation war between the tobacco industry on the one hand and consumers, plaintiffs' lawyers, and government on the other. The results are remarkable and far-reaching.

• As explained in Chapters 8 and 15, the states have reached settlements with the tobacco companies totaling $246 billion to be paid in installments over 25 years. The money compensates the states for the public health costs associated with tobacco use. Then in 1999, the federal government filed its own lawsuit claiming broadly that the tobacco industry has engaged in decades of fraud regarding the risks of smoking thereby driving up federal health care costs dramatically.

• In 1999, Philip Morris conceded at its website [**www.philipmorris.com**] that "there is no 'safe' cigarette" and "cigarette smoking is addictive, as that term is most commonly used today." Those remarkable concessions by a corporate goliath that has resisted all such allegations for half a century indicates a new public relations direction and perhaps an effort to reduce future legal liability. Of course, the Philip Morris acknowledgement only confirms what has been revealed in recent years as the tobacco companies have been forced to produce secret documents indicating that executives have long known of tobacco dangers.

> In 1999, Philip Morris conceded that "there is no 'safe' cigarette"

• Of course, both individual and class action civil suits against tobacco companies continue, with some juries finding the defendants legally blameless and others handing down massive awards to plaintiffs. At this writing in 1999, however, the tobacco companies have yet to pay a penny in damages.

A 1978 Liggett tobacco company memorandum depicts executives' struggles with the morality of producing a safer form of cigarettes:

"Is it morally permissible to develop a safe method for administering a habit-forming drug when, in so doing, the number of addicts will increase?"

The memo then resolved the issue:

"We may conclude that there is nothing unethical in the concept of a safer cigarette; that the use of artificial means to control mood is a very human characteristic; that we should not seek to expand but cannot dispel the habit; and that our real duty lies in diminishing the adverse consequences."

Do you agree with Ligget's moral analysis?

Source: Knight-Ridder Newspapers, "Liggett Documents Reveal Company Knew Cigarettes Addictive, Deadly," *Waterloo–Cedar Falls Courier*, April 4, 1997, p. A5.

[To search for the latest developments in the tobacco wars, see **http://headlines.yahoo.com/headlines/business**].

Breast Implants

Dow Corning introduced silicone breast implants in the 1960s, and by 1997 1.5 to 1.8 million women had received the implants.[49] Multimillion-dollar lawsuits followed quickly in which women claimed that they suffered from cancer, immunological diseases, and other systemic diseases. The FDA suspended silicone implant use in 1992. In 1995 Baxter International, Bristol-Myers Squibb, and Minnesota Mining & Manufacturing reached a $4 billion settlement with many plaintiffs.[50] Approximately 700,000 claims against all implant makers were filed, and each litigation cost the industry about $1 million to defend.[51] Those lawsuits forced Dow Corning to declare Chapter 11 bankruptcy in 1995.[52]

> **The company proposed a $3.2 billion settlement involving some 170,000 women**

The company then proposed a $3.2 billion settlement involving some 170,000 women. As noted in Chapter 15, in late 1999 a federal judge approved a $4.5 billion bankruptcy reorganization of Dow Corning. Assuming that settlement withstands possible appeals, claimants are expected to receive $2,000 to $300,000, depending on the severity of their symptoms. The industry consistently denied that the implants were responsible for any form of systemic illness, but the weight of jury sentiment caused the companies to decide that the settlements were the best strategy for resolving the decades-long disputes. Then in 1999, a report completed at the request of Congress concluded that the available scientific evidence, including some 3,000 publications, failed to establish a link between the implants and systemic diseases.[53] Nonetheless, Dow intended to go forward with its settlement arrangements, and those not entering the settlements presumably will continue to litigate their claims. The Dow Corning bankruptcy and billions of dollars in settlements and legal costs, despite the lack of convincing scientific evidence, have made the case something of a rallying point for tort reformers. *Business Week,* reflecting on those concerns, cautioned against radical restructuring of our tort system:

> Would-be tort reformers have embraced the [implant] report as an indictment of plaintiffs' lawyers everywhere. Just as the implant cases were bogus, they argue, so are most of the other suits brought by contingency-fee attorneys. Now, they're renewing calls for major changes in the American legal system, such as the adoption of rules forcing losers of lawsuits to pay winners' expenses. No question, the breast-implant debacle raises serious questions about the U.S. justice system. And nobody argues that lawyers should be able to use questionable science to launch a class action on behalf of thousands of plaintiffs just to threaten companies with the possibility of multibillion-dollar verdicts. But the way to fix this problem is by fine-tuning the rules for mass litigation, not by reinventing tort law.
>
> Harsh reforms like "loser pays" would render impossible much of the good work plaintiffs' attorneys do. Remember: Tort suits have led manufacturers to recall dangerous or defective birth-control devices, car parts, and children's pajamas. They also play a role in spurring companies to make better products.[54]

Table 16.1 highlights some consumer protections that have resulted from product liability lawsuits.

Guns

> **at least 27 of America's most populous cities and counties are suing gun makers**

Inspired by the remarkable tobacco litigation successes, at least 27 of America's most populous cities and counties are suing gun makers to recover the public sector costs of injuries and deaths associated with handgun violence. In the first of the cases, a Cincinnati trial judge dismissed the plaintiffs' claims in September 1999, but a month later a trial judge in Atlanta ruled that the city could continue its negligence action. The Atlanta decision was

---

TABLE 16.1   Keeping Companies on Their Toes

DALKON SHIELD After a series of punitive-damage awards. A.H. Robins recalled the harmful birth-control device.

KIDS' PRODUCTS Dangerous cribs and flammable pajamas have been taken off the market largely because of tort suits.

TYLENOL After a big personal-injury verdict, the FDA required warnings about the dangers of consuming Tylenol with alcohol.

AUTOMOBILES Windshields, gas tanks, and other car components have been redesigned largely because of product-liability suits.

Source: Mike France, "Class Actions: Fine-Tune the Law, Don't Trash It," *Business Week,* July 12, 1999, p. 45.

the first requiring the gun industry to reveal internal information and answer pretrial questions. If the process of peering into the gun industry's behavior proves as revealing as delving into the tobacco industry history, we may see marked changes in gun production, marketing, and distribution in the United States. The stakes are quite high. Chicago's police department spent more than $75 million in 1997 in addressing gun violations, and Wayne County (Detroit) estimates it spends $20 million annually in paying for prosecutors, courts, jails, and the morgue.[55] The claims basically allege irresponsible marketing and design deficiencies (see Table 16.2). One of the more interesting of the specific claims is the argument that the gun makers flood the legal gun market with more guns than it can absorb in the knowledge that those guns will then reach the illegal underground market.

Further pressure on the gun makers emerged in September 1999 when a California Court of Appeals allowed the families of the victims in a shooting to sue Navegar Inc., the manufacturer of the semiautomatic gun, a TEC-DC9, used in the shooting.[56] The suit sprang from a 1993 rampage in a San Francisco law office when a mentally disturbed man, Gian Luigi Ferri, killed eight people and wounded six before killing himself at the now-defunct firm.[57]

> a mentally disturbed man, Gian Luigi Ferri, killed eight people

---

TABLE 16.2   Cities Filing Suit Against Gun Makers in 1999

- New Orleans: Filed Oct. 30. Argues that guns are unreasonably dangerous in design and are defective products because they lack adequate safety devices.

- Chicago: Filed Nov. 12. Argues that the influx of guns from the suburbs is a public nuisance to the city's residents. Seeks $433 million in damages.

- Bridgeport, Conn.: Filed Jan. 27. Argues that guns are dangerous by design, lack adequate safety devices, are public nuisance, and are marketed falsely by gun makers.

- Cleveland: Filed April 9. Argues that guns are dangerous by design and lack adequate safety devices. Seeks up to $150 million in damages.

Source: Mark Schlinkmann, "St. Louis Files Lawsuit Against 27 Defendants in Gun Industry," *St. Louis Post-Dispatch,* May 1, 1999, p. 8.

The dissenting judge in the 2–1 decision argued that Ferri was solely responsible for the deaths, but the majority said the case should go to trial on the claim that the gun was negligently marketed because the company's ads, including one that promoted the gun's fingerprint resistance, were designed to appeal to criminals.[58] [For an extensive database favoring gun litigation, see **http://www.vpc.org/litigate.htm**]

More Regulation?

Not surprisingly, many Americans are furious with this latest legal campaign against guns. Consider the following excerpt from a letter to the *Buffalo News:*

> I can no longer keep quiet about the failure in our society and government regarding individual responsibility. Currently, law-abiding gun owners and gun manufacturers are under attack. It's "Let's see who has the deepest pockets and file suit."[59]

But as suggested by the following editorial, the burst of lawsuits against gun makers is, at least in part, a consequence of American resistance to gun-control regulation in an industrial world increasingly interested in curbing arms.

DUMPING GROUND FOR GUNS

Editorial

The global flow of guns offers some sad commentary about this country's increasingly gross national arsenal. [T]he United States has become the darling of foreign gun makers, as other major industrialized countries enact increasingly restrictive gun laws for themselves. If you can't market those deadly weapons at home, you can always dump them on gun-happy America.

To rub it in, many of those gun makers with familiar names—Smith & Wesson, Winchester, Beretta, Browning—are owned by foreign companies based in the countries that have cracked down on gun ownership. Smith & Wesson, for example, is owned by a company in Britain—where handgun ownership is prohibited. While people there seem to be surviving without any guns in their homes, on their persons or in their cars, Smith & Wesson is the largest maker of handguns in the United States.

Taurus International Manufacturing Inc., owned by a company in Brazil, produces guns in Miami and imports as well. Brazilian companies export about 90 percent of the guns made in that country. Its exports to the United States began in 1968, after the Brazilian government enacted restrictions on sales there. Now Brazil is considering even tougher restrictions; the state of Rio de Janeiro recently approved one of the toughest gun laws in the world, and a similar law is under consideration for the whole country.

The list goes on: Beretta's parent company is in Italy, where hunters must show membership in a hunting club where they have been trained, and individuals seeking to buy handguns must prove they need them for self-defense. Still other gun makers are subsidiaries of companies in countries with solid controls on firearms.

What is the United States doing to control the furious flow of firearms? The House is doing nothing, having flailed around after the Senate sent over a skimpy control bill. Other countries have found little constructive use for handguns; the United States has no ban on concealable weapons. As foreign countries pour out their lethal exports, gun pushers in the United States welcome them with open arms.

Questions

1. *a.* Do you think America is "gun happy?"
    b. Should handgun purchases in the United States be limited to those who can show the guns are needed for self-defense?

    c. In your view, are guns negligently marketed and/or defectively designed?
2. Should questions about the availability and safety of guns be left to state and federal legislation?

Source: *Washington Post*, July 2, 1999, p. A26. Copyright 1999 *Washington Post*. Reprinted by permission.

TOO MUCH LAW?

Perhaps, as suggested by the following analysis, the key to tort reform is simply to reduce our reliance on the law, thus providing more room for treating risk management as a matter of contractual arrangements in the free market.

FUNDAMENTAL REFORM OF TORT LAW

Paul H. Rubin

[T]he high costs of many goods and services can be traced to misguided attempts by federal regulators and courts to protect the public health and safety. The problems with the courts are especially serious, since they undermine more cost-effective means of achieving that goal.

A principal function of tort law is to deter manufacturers from causing excess harms, or, in the case of medical services, to deter malpractice. But this system has been undermined by unreasonable standards—imposed by the courts—defining parties' liability for damages.

Further, the best alternative means for securing low-cost protection has also been undermined. Before 1960, when parties agreed on an exchange of goods or services, they implicitly, if not explicitly, also agreed on the rules

and limitations that would govern any liability for possible injuries. But over the past three and a half decades courts have voided such contracts, reserving for themselves the power to make determinations of liability.

* * * * *

Government intervention in the market is justified only in circumstances where the market can be expected to "fail." The most common source of market failure is the existence of some externality. An externality is said to exist when a third party, one not directly involved in a transaction, is nonetheless affected by the transaction. The classic example of a negative externality is pollution, where bystanders are harmed by the actions of polluters. Some effort at correction—by establishing or redefining property rights, by internalizing the costs of the externality, or, if all else fails, by direct government regulation—is justified by such externalities.

By this standard, much of modern tort law and much of modern government regulation purporting to protect safety and health cannot be justified, since no externalities exist that must be dealt with. Both forms of government intervention—by the courts and by regulatory agencies—stem from the fact that policymakers are unwilling to rely on private transactions to achieve efficient outcomes.

Undermining Contracts

Much tort law governs accidents between "strangers"—those who have no legal relationship with each other before an accident occurs. Examples include a car striking a pedestrian; two cars colliding; a passerby on the public domain being struck by a baseball flying from a stadium; a drunk punching someone for no reason in a bar. All of the above are classic tort situations, and all are cases in which there is no prior relation between the parties. In each case there is an externality, and therefore some government intervention, through regulation or through the court system, may be proper.

But many activities now governed by tort law are not of that sort. Instead, in many cases, the parties *do* have prior relations with each other, and therefore there is no externality and no need for government intervention. The major examples are product liability, where a purchaser of a product may be harmed by that product, and medical malpractice, where a patient may be harmed by some action of a physician that the patient has hired.

* * * * *

Since about 1960, as a result of a New Jersey Supreme Court case, *Henningsen* v. *Bloomfield Motors,* involving General Motors (GM), courts have generally been unwilling to enforce contracts between buyers and sellers involving compensation for harms caused by accidents. No matter what terms the parties may want to govern the results of an accident, the court will decide and impose its own terms. For example, the parties may want to agree that if there is an accident, the producer of the product will pay only for lost earnings and medical costs, and will not pay anything for "pain and suffering." But if there is an injury, this voluntary agreement will have no effect. The courts will decide what level and type of damage payments from the manufacturer to the consumer are appropriate.

Questions

1. Explain Rubin's argument.
2. Why have the courts, as in the *Henningsen* case, intervened to overturn privately contracted risk and remedy arrangements?
3. Why would we want to reduce our reliance on tort law?

Source: *Regulation* 18, no. 4 (1995), p. 26. Reprinted by permission.

INTERNET EXERCISE

1. At its website, The American Tort Reform Association (ATRA) quotes from portions of an American Bar Association (ABA) document addressing a number of tort reform issues. ATRA then responds to the ABA's positions. Using ATRA's website [**http://www.atra.org/factfict.htm**], summarize the competing views of the ATRA and the ABA on the following issues:
    a. The impact of tort litigation on America's international trade.
    b. The need for punitive damages reforms.

CHAPTER QUESTIONS

1. A bartender, Parrillo, was opening a bottle of grenadine when it exploded, causing injury. Parrillo sued Giroux Company, the producer of the liquor. Giroux packaged the liquor itself after buying bottles from a manufacturer. Giroux visually inspected the bottles and ordinarily found defects in one of every 400 to 500 bottles. The evidence showed that Parrillo did not mishandle the bottle. Decide. Explain. [See *Parrillo* v. *Giroux Co.,* 426 A.2d 1313 (R.I. 1981).]

2. Alejandro Phillips, a young California man, was shot four times in the back at the opening of the movie *Boyz N the Hood,* a depiction of growing up in a dangerous Los Angeles neighborhood dominated by gangs. Phillips was shot during a scuffle involving alleged gang members. According to his lawyers, Phillips himself was not a member of a gang. Dozens of similar violent episodes accompanied the opening of the movie. Phillips's lawyers accused Columbia Pictures of negligence in marketing the film. They claimed that the movie's advertising concentrated on the relatively minor episodes of violence in the movie and largely ignored the affirmative and pacifist ingredients at the core of the movie. They contended that Columbia should have anticipated violence as a consequence of that advertising approach. Phillips filed suit.
    a. Explain Phillips's legal claims.
    b. Defend Columbia.
    c. Decide. Explain.
   [For journalistic accounts, see Joanne Lipman, "Issue of Ads Leading to Violence Is Raised in Suit Tied to Movie," *The Wall Street Journal,* April 27, 1992, p. B10; and "Film Patron Injury," *Entertainment Law Reporter* 15, no. 1, p. 22.]

3. Embs, the plaintiff, was shopping in a self-serve grocery store. A carton of 7UP was on the floor about one foot from where she was standing. She was unaware of the carton. Several of the bottles exploded, severely injuring Embs's leg. Embs brought a strict liability action against the bottler.
    a. Raise a defense against the strict liability claim.
    b. Decide. Explain.
   [See *Embs* v. *Pepsi-Cola Bottling Co. of Lexington, Kentucky, Inc.,* 528 S.W.2d 703 (Ky. Ct. App. 1975).]

4. Plaintiffs Dr. Arthur Weisz and David and Irene Schwartz bought two paintings at auctions conducted by the defendant, Parke-Bernet Galleries, Inc. The paintings were listed in the auction catalog as those of Raoul Dufy. It was later discovered that the paintings were forgeries. The plaintiffs took legal action to recover their losses. Parke-Bernet defended itself by, among other arguments, asserting that the conditions of sale included a disclaimer providing that all properties were sold "as is." The conditions of sale were 15 numbered paragraphs embracing several pages in the auction catalogue. The bulk of the auction catalogue was devoted to descriptions of the works of art to be sold, including artists' names, dates of birth and death, and, in some instances, black-and-white reproductions of the paintings. It was established at trial that plaintiff Weisz had not previously entered bids at Parke-Bernet, and he had no awareness of the conditions of sale. Plaintiffs David and Irene Schwartz, however, were generally aware of the conditions of sale. Is the Parke-Bernet disclaimer legally binding on the plaintiffs? Explain. [See *Weisz* v. *Parke-Bernet,* 325 N.Y.S.2d 576 (Civ. Ct. N.Y.C. 1971), but see *Schwartz* v. *Parke-Bernet,* 351 N.Y.S. 2d 911 (1974).]

5. Lisa Mazur, a Philadelphia girl, received a measles vaccination at school in 1982 as part of a mass immunization program. The vaccination caused a fatal neurological disorder. Her parents sued the manufacturer, Merck & Co. Assume the vaccine was produced according to all applicable safety standards but that all such vaccines carry a small degree of risk of side effects or of mimicking the disease itself.
    a. Explain the Mazur family's legal claim.
    b. Decide.
    c. Assume Merck sold the drug through the federal Centers for Disease Control, which was required by contract with Merck to ensure that all patients received information about the potential risks of the vaccine. Would that arrangement change the outcome of the case? Explain.
   [See *Mazur* v. *Merck,* 964 F.2d 1348 (3d Cir. 1992).]

6. A child contracted Reye's syndrome after being given aspirin. The aspirin package contained an English-language warning regarding a connection between Reye's syndrome and aspirin, but the child's Hispanic mother could not read the warning. Does the manufacturer have a duty to warn in a foreign language? Explain. [See *Ramirez* v. *Plough,* 863 P.2d 167 (Cal 1993).]

7. The plaintiff, born and raised in New England, was eating fish chowder at a restaurant when a fish bone lodged in

her throat. The bone was removed, and the plaintiff sued the restaurant, claiming a breach of implied warranty under the UCC. Evidence was offered at trial to show that fish chowder recipes commonly did not provide for removal of bones. Decide. Explain. See *Webster* v. *Blue Ship Tea Room,* 198 N.E.2d 309 (Mass. 1964).

8. On December 29, 1980, a .38 caliber Saturday night special handgun was used in the attempted robbery of a 7-Eleven store in Dallas, Texas. During the crime, the handgun was used to shoot and kill James Patterson, a clerk at the store. Patterson's mother filed a product liability action against Rohm, the manufacturer of the handgun; R.G. Industries, the distributor of the gun, and R.G. Industries' officers. The plaintiff claimed the gun was defective in design and that it was defectively marketed and distributed. How would you rule on the plaintiff's claim? Explain. [See *Patterson* v. *Rohm Gesellschaft,* 608 F.Supp. 1206 (N.D. Tex. 1985).]

9. Tort claims sometimes arise out of accidents involving strangers, but often those episodes involve people who have some kind of relationship (e.g., buyer–seller or doctor–patient). In the latter set of circumstances, Professor Paul Rubin, among others, suggested that we should allow the parties to establish, in advance, a contract that would resolve the claims if an accident should happen. Thus, a physician and a patient might enter into an agreement in advance of treatment providing that the patient would sue only for limited damages (such as out-of-pocket medical expense and lost wages) in the event of malpractice.
   a. What benefits would consumers derive from such agreements?
   b. Why do the courts ordinarily refuse to enforce such agreements?
   c. Would you favor Rubin's approach to tort reform? Explain.
   [See Paul Rubin, *Tort Reform by Contract* (Washington, DC: The AEI Press, 1993).]

10. In the mid-1980s, the state of Colorado began enacting a series of tort reform measures in hopes of increasing insurance availability, reducing insurance rates, giving business a respite from litigation, and curbing what were believed to be unjustified jury awards. *The Wall Street Journal* summarized some of the measures and their results:

    > State laws here protect ski resorts and dude ranches from lawsuits over accidental injuries. Bars are virtu-ally immune from legal blame for the acts of drunk

patrons. Jury awards for pain and suffering top out at $250,000. And defendants can't be forced to ante up more in damages just because they have the deepest pockets.[44]

After a few years of experience with the Colorado reforms, *The Wall Street Journal* observed that the results have been "quite mixed." Explain that judgment; that is, how is tort reform likely to affect consumers, insurance firms, businesses, and lawyers?

11. A passenger ran after a train as it was leaving a station. Two railroad employees boosted the passenger aboard, but in doing so a package carried by the passenger fell beneath the wheels of the train and exploded. The package, unbeknownst to the employees, contained fireworks. The force of that explosion caused a scale many feet away to topple over, injuring the plaintiff, Mrs. Palsgraf. Mrs. Palsgraf sued the railroad on negligence grounds.
   a. Defend the railroad.
   b. Decide. Explain. [See *Palsgraf* v. *Long Island R.R.,* 162 N.E. 99 (N.Y. 1928).]

12. Pat Stalter was injured when a bottle fell through the bottom of a soft drink carton and broke while she was shopping at Food City, a Little Rock, Arkansas, grocery store. A piece of glass went through her slacks, cutting her. A store employee said the carton was "mushy" and appeared to have been wet for some time. The Coca-Colas were in a display maintained by Coca-Cola Bottling Company. Two or three times a week the company cleaned the shelves and rotated the stock. Coca-Cola said that this process insures that only minimal moisture is on bottles when they are placed in cartons. Most cartons are reused only once. Stalter sued Food City and Coca-Cola Bottling Company for damages.
   a. Explain the plaintiff's claims.
   b. Decide. [See *Pat Stalter* v. *Coca-Cola Bottling Company of Arkansas and Geyer Springs Food City, Inc.,* 669 S.W.2d 460 (Ark. 1984).]

13. Diane Elsroth was visiting her boyfriend, Michael Notarnicola, in the home of his parents. Diane complained of a headache and Michael provided a Tylenol that his mother had bought earlier that week. Michael noted nothing unusual about the Tylenol packaging. After consuming two Tylenol capsules, Diane went to bed. She died during the night. The medical examiner concluded that the Tylenol had been contaminated with potassium cyanide. The murder was

not solved. The evidence established that the tampering with the Tylenol occurred after the product left the manufacturer's control. The packaging included a foil seal glued to the mouth of the container, a "shrink seal" around the neck and cap of the container, and a box with its ends glued shut. The manufacturer, McNeil, a wholly owned subsidiary of Johnson & Johnson, knew through its research that a determined, sophisticated tamperer could breach the packaging and reseal it in a manner that would not be visible to the average consumer. John Elsroth sued McNeil on behalf of Diane's estate. Was the Tylenol packaging defective in design? Explain. [See *Elsroth* v. *Johnson & Johnson,* 700 F. Supp. 151 (S.D.N.Y. 1988).]

14. In 1985, two young adult males (18 and 20 years of age) shot themselves with a 12-gauge shotgun after drinking beer and listening to the "Stained Glass" album by the "heavy metal" band, Judas Priest. One man died immediately and the other three years later. The families of the two men sued the band and CBS Records on the grounds that subliminal messages in the music caused the men to shoot themselves. After listening to the evidence, the trial judge concluded that the subliminal message, "Do It," could be heard throughout the album, but he also concluded that the message was the result of a chance combination of sounds. The judge found for the defendants.

    Do you agree with the judge's decision? Explain. For a journalistic account of the case, see Amy Dockser Marcus and Arthur S. Hayes, "CBS Is Found Blameless in Music Suicides," *The Wall Street Journal,* August 27, 1990, p. B3.

15. In 1984, a woman was killed in an aerial tramway car at Palm Springs, California, when a piece of the tram machinery crashed through the Plexiglas roof of the car. The victim's blood splashed on two nearby passengers. Those passengers sued, seeking monetary damages for the emotional trauma of the episode. The passengers suffered nightmares, flashbacks, claustrophobia, and other complaints that they linked to the anguish of the tramway accident. So-called horror suits of this kind, where bystanders seek to recover for emotional injury from witnessing accidents, have become increasingly common in recent years.

    a. Raise the policy arguments against extending legal protection to those not themselves physically harmed in an accident such as that at Palm Springs.

    b. How would you rule on their claim? Explain. [For a journalistic account of the case, see Philip Hager, "State High Court . . . Suit by 'Horror' Witnesses," *Los Angeles Times,* August 21, 1990, p. A3.]

16. In an attempt to commit suicide, Connie Daniell locked herself in the trunk of her 1973 Ford LTD automobile, where she remained for nine days before being freed. During the nine days, Daniell changed her mind and sought to escape, but she was unable to do so. She sued the Ford Motor Company for the injuries she sustained from her entrapment.

    a. What claims would she bring?

    b. Decide those claims. Explain.

    [See *Daniell* v. *Ford Motor Company,* 581 F. Supp. 728 (N.Mex. 1984).]

17. Plaintiff James L. Maguire was seriously injured when the motor vehicle in which he was a passenger was struck by another motor vehicle. Plaintiff alleges that Vikki Paulson, the driver of the other vehicle, was intoxicated at the time of the accident. Following the accident, Paulson entered guilty pleas to (1) operating a motor vehicle while under the influence of alcohol, (2) involuntary manslaughter as a consequence of the death of another passenger riding with Maguire, and (3) failure to stop at a stop sign. During the time in question in the case, Pabst Brewing Company had engaged in an advertising campaign promoting the sale of its products. Plaintiff claims the defendant Pabst was liable for his injuries because (among other claims) its advertising promoting the consumption of alcohol by those who drove to taverns constituted a danger to highway safety and because the brewer had failed to warn consumers of the dangers of alcohol consumption. Decide. Explain. [See *Maguire* v. *Pabst Brewing Company,* 387 N.W.2d 565 (Iowa 1986).]

18. Twenty-year-old Stephen Pavlik died from inhaling Zeus-brand butane while trying to "get high." His estate sued the Zeus maker, Lane. The fuel came in a small can with a printed warning reading, "DO NOT BREATHE SPRAY." The plaintiff argued that the can was defective because the warning inadequately expressed the hazard. A federal district court ruled that Pavlik was aware of the danger so the warning was adequate, and in any case, a warning would have had no effect so proximate cause could not exist. That decision was appealed. How would you rule on that appeal? Explain. [See *Pavlik* v. *Lane Limited,* 135 F.3d 876 (3d Cir. 1998).]

19. A man drowned on a family outing while using equipment rented from a canoe and inner-tube outfitter.

His family sued, claiming the outfitter was negligent in failing to properly patrol the river and provide emergency assistance. The family won an $800,000 jury award. The parties later agreed to settle the case out of court. According to expert opinion, a six-mile canoe trip costing $12 per person would cost more than $87 if lifeguards were to be required along rivers. In addition to the lack of safety equipment and personnel, what other claims are plaintiffs likely to raise in such situations? Explain.

NOTES

1. Timothy K. Smith, "Liability Costs Drive Small-Plane Business Back into Pilots, Barns," *The Wall Street Journal,* December 11, 1991, p. A1.

2. Mike Clancy, "Cessna Will Once Again Make Small Aircraft," *Des Moines Register,* March 15, 1995, p. 8S.

3. Barbara Carton, "Cessna Says It Will Make More Small Airplanes," *The Wall Street Journal,* March 14, 1995, p. B1.

4. Smith, "Liability Costs," p. A8.

5. Ibid.

6. Carton, "Cessna Says," p. B1.

7. 111 N.E. 1050 (N.Y. 1916).

8. Heidi Hurd, "The Deontology of Negligence," *Boston University Law Review* 76 (April 1996), p. 249.

9. *Doss* v. *Town of Big Stone Gap,* 134 S.E. 563 (Va. 5.Ct. 1926).

10. Aric Press, Ginny Carrol, and Steven Waldman, "Are Lawyers Burning America?" *Newsweek,* March 20, 1995, p. 30.

11. Ibid., p. 34.

12. "McDonald's Settles Lawsuit over Burn from Coffee," *The Wall Street Journal,* December 2, 1994, p. A14.

13. "Wendy's to Interrupt Hot Chocolate Sales to Cool Temperature," *The Wall Street Journal,* November 23, 1994, p. A4.

14. Press, "Are Lawyers Burning America?" p. 30.

15. Associated Press, "Jury Sides with McDonald's in Burn Suit," *Waterloo–Cedar Falls Courier,* November 19, 1998, p. A3.

16. *Holowaty* v. *McDonald's,* 10 F. Supp.2d 1078 (Minn. D.Ct. 1998).

17. *Nadel* v. *Burger King,* 684 N.E.2d 706 (Ohio S.Ct. 1997).

18. *Pat Stalter* v. *Coca-Cola Bottling Company of Arkansas and Geyer Springs Food City, Inc.,* 669 S.W.2d 460 (Ark. 1984).

19. Milo Geyelin, "Second Ford Pact to End Bronco Suit Is Thrown Out," *The Wall Street Journal,* February 6, 1997, p. B5.

20. "5th Circuit Rejects Revival of Class Actions Over Bronco II," *Associated Press State & Local Wire,* March 1, 1999.

21. *Automotive News,* "NHTSA Officials Still Bent on Rating Vehicles' Tendencies to Roll Over," *San Diego Union-Tribune,* July 3, 1999, Wheels p. NC-6.

22. "IN App. Ct. Affirms $18.2 Million Verdict in Bronco II Case," *Automotive Litigation Reporter* 18, no. 10 (March 16, 1999), p. 3.

23. Note, "Just What You'd Expect: Professor Henderson's Redesign of Products Liability," *Harvard Law Review* 111 (June 1998), p. 2366.

24. John M. Broder, "Warning Labels for Every Danger," *Des Moines Register,* March 9, 1997, p. G1.

25. Ibid.

26. *Whitlock* v. *University of Denver,* 712 P.2d 1072 (Col. Ct. App. 1985).

27. *University of Denver* v. *Whitlock,* 744 P.2d 54 (Col. S. Ct. 1987).

28. 27 Cal. Rptr. 697, 377 P.2d 897 (1963).

29. Some states have eliminated the "unreasonably dangerous" standard from their strict liability tests.

30. 163 Cal. Rptr. 132, 607 P.2d 924 (1980), cert. denied, 449 U.S. 912 (1980).

31. See, e.g., *Smith* v. *Eli Lilly & Co.,* 560 N.E.2d 324 (Ill. 1990).

32. For a journalistic account, see Amy Stevens and Christi Harlan, "Third-Generation DES Lawsuit Dismissed by State Appeals Court," *The Wall Street Journal,* February 21, 1991, p. B7.

33. Jay Reeves, "'Jackpot Justice' in Alabama," *Atlanta Journal and Constitution,* May 11, 1999, p. 1A.

34. Associated Press, "Huge Awards Aside, Few Companies Forced to Write Big Checks," *Waterloo–Cedar Falls Courier,* October 12, 1997, p. C5.

35. Michael Selz and Jeffrey A. Tannenbaum, "Scared of Lawsuits, Small Businesses Applaud Reform," *The Wall Street Journal,* March 13, 1995, p. B1.

36. Bob Davis, Peter Gumbel, and David Hamilton, "To All U.S. Managers Upset by Regulations: Try Germany or Japan," *The Wall Street Journal,* December 14, 1995, p. A1.

37. Robert Kuttner, "Product Liability Reform: You Lose," *Des Moines Register,* June 26, 1994, p. 3C.

38. Ibid.

39. "Product-Liability Awards Increased 44% Last Year," *The Wall Street Journal,* June 27, 1997, p. B17.

40. Dick Thornburgh, "Fourth Down in Super Bowl of Civil Justice," *Waterloo–Cedar Falls Courier,* December 28, 1995, p. A6.

41. Junda Woo and Milo Geyelin, "Rand Liability Study," *The Wall Street Journal,* September 24, 1993, p. B6.

42. Paul H. Rubin, "Fundamental Reform of Tort Law," *Regulation* 18, no. 4 (1995), p. 26.

43. Ibid., p. 31.

44. Richard C. Reuben, "Plaintiffs Rarely Win Punitives, Study Says," *ABA Journal* 81 (October 1995), p. 26.

45. Edward Felsenthal, "Punitive-Damage Awards Found to Be Generally Modest and Rare," *The Wall Street Journal,* June 17, 1996, p. B7.

46. *BMW of North America* v. *Gore,* 116 S.Ct. 1589 (1996).

47. Margaret A. Jacobs, "BMW Decision Used to Whittle Punitive Awards," *The Wall Street Journal,* September 17, 1999, p. B2.

48. Milo Geyelin, "How an Internal Memo Written 26 Years Ago Is Costing GM Dearly," *The Wall Street Journal,* September 29, 1999, p. A1.

49. Milo Geyelin and Laurie McGinley, "Panel Concludes There Is No Connection Between Implants and Major Diseases," *The Wall Street Journal,* June 22, 1999, p. B15.

50. Ibid.

51. Editorial, "The Big Lie Exposed," *Detroit News,* June 23, 1999, p. A8.

52. Ibid.

53. Geyelin and McGinley, "Panel Concludes There Is No Connection," p. B15.

54. Mike France, "Class Actions: Fine-Tune the Law, Don't Trash It," *Business Week,* July 12, 1999, p. 45.

55. "Why Stop Cities from Suing?" *USA Today,* October 21, 1999, p. 18A.

56. Associated Press, "California Appellate Court Allows Gun Maker to Be Sued," *New York Times,* September 30, 1999, sec. A, p. 24.

57. Ibid.

58. Ibid.

59. Jay Glendenning, "Don't Target Gun Makers with Unfair Lawsuits," *Buffalo News,* October 16, 1999, p. 3C.

Chapter 17

Environmental Protection

Part One—Environmental Concerns of Business

From the moment a firm begins to produce, service, manufacture, or create, its operations affect the environment. Imagine the small decisions made by a company: Does it pack its glassware in plastic bubbles or corrugated wrapping? Does it publish a catalogue once a month or once a year? Is that catalogue published on paper or only through the Internet? Does it meet with the community before choosing a disposal system? Each of these decisions will have an impact on our physical world; hence it is critical to understand the law as it relates to the environment and to be aware of the ethical component of each decision.

From local issues such as routing a new highway around a wetland or allowing leaf burning to colossal fears such as global warming and the loss of tropical rainforests, environmental issues mark our lives in a manner that was unimaginable a few decades ago. At this writing, 10 years have passed since the most highly publicized ecological disaster in American history—the Exxon Valdez oil spill. The editorial that follows gives us a chance to see how the Earth, with our help, is able to cope with a massive wound. [For an environmental database, see **http://ecosys.drdr.virginia.edu/Environment.html.** Also see **http://seamless.com/alexanderlaw/txt/resource/environ.shtml**]

10 YEARS AFTER THE SPILL

Editorial

A DECADE after the supertanker Exxon Valdez ran aground and dumped 11 million gallons of gooey crude oil into Alaska's Prince William Sound, the ecology is recovering but oil remains a threat to America's northern wilds.

Even now, oil damage to the Gulf of Alaska's coastline, marine life, fishing industry and social fabric is still being measured, analyzed and bitterly debated.

Exxon Corp., which poured nearly $3 billion into the largest and most costly oil-spill cleanup ever, says the sound has been restored and is "healthy, robust and thriving."

Local residents angrily disagree. They say their once-thriving fishing industry has crashed, their way of life is ruined and many doubt the sound will ever return to normal.

Chronicle Staff Writer Glen Martin visited the spill scene recently to report on the condition of the sound and how the people and ecology are recovering.

"Today," he wrote, "local waters are blue and pellucid and the air is as crisp and sweet as an autumn apple. Oil? There's no visible sign of it over the 15,000 square miles of open water, tidal flats, islands and forested littoral that constitute the sound."

But, Martin said, the spill's sour after-effects linger among the people there, "whose economic and spiritual connection with the sound is irretrievably lost."

A few minutes after midnight on March 24, 1989, a Good Friday, the 987-foot, oil-laden Exxon Valdez struck a rock called Bligh Reef and hemorrhaged a gusher of thick North Slope crude into the cold, crystalline waters of Prince William Sound.

"We've fetched up—ah—hard aground north of Goose Island off Bligh Reef, and—ah—evidently leaking some oil," Joseph Hazelwood, the ship's captain radioed the Coast Guard in Valdez.

It was the worst oil disaster in U.S. history. The deadly slick blackened 1,500 miles of the spectacular Gulf of Alaska coastline and poisoned the food chain from top to bottom.

[Hazelwood was cleared of piloting a tanker while drunk, but he was convicted of a misdemeanor count of spilling oil and sentenced to 1,000 hours of picking up trash in Anchorage. He (started in the summer of 1999).]

Although the debate continues about the continuing impact of the spill, there is no dispute that the harm done to the sound and its marine life was catastrophic.

About 300,000 seabirds, 2,650 sea otters, 300 harbor seals, 250 bald eagles, 400 loons, and 1,000 cormorants were killed, according to the Exxon Valdez Oil Spill Trustee Council, the federal–state agency appointed to monitor the cleanup.

The council says that of 23 species affected by the spill, only two—the bald eagle and the river otter—are fully recovered. The future is uncertain for the rest. Killer whales, harbor seals and Pacific herring show little indication they are making a comeback at all.

Experts on both sides disagree on the current health of Prince William Sound and its marine life, but one thing is clear: the Exxon Valdez oil spill galvanized the environmental movement and caused legislative reforms that have changed how big oil companies ship their product and do business.

It is too much to suggest the spill had a silver lining, but it did focus public attention on the serious environmental dangers posed by oil-industry operations on land and sea, and goosed Congress into action.

The most important congressional reaction was passage of the landmark Oil Pollution Act of 1990 that toughened penalties and liability for oil spillers; ordered double-hulling of tankers by 2015; created a clean-up fund; required drug and alcohol tests for tanker crews; expanded Coast Guard monitoring of tanker traffic and established spill-response equipment along tanker routes.

Yet the ominous question remains: Could another major spill happen again? With an armada of escort tugs and clean-up vessels as well as increased monitoring of tankers in Prince William Sound, an Exxon Valdez-size spill is unlikely to repeat there.

But environmentalists insist oil companies pose an equally dangerous threat to Alaska's fragile wilderness and wildlife by seeking to expand oil leases in Northeast Alaska's pristine Arctic National Wildlife Refuge.

Last week Congressman Bruce Vento, D-Minn., introduced a praiseworthy bill that would declare 1.5 million acres of the refuge as a wilderness area, placing it forever off-limits to commercial exploitation.

*　*　*　*　*

Source: *San Francisco Chronicle,* March 28, 1999, p. 6. Copyright *San Francisco Chronicle.* Reprinted by permission of the *San Francisco Chronicle.*

Afterword

At this writing in late 1999, Exxon is still appealing a 1994 jury decision awarding $5 billion in punitive damages to 14,000 fishermen and women, native Alaskans, and other property owners. With the Alaskan plaintiffs earning only a 5.9 percent postjudgment interest rate, critics say Exxon has no incentive to settle because the company is earning more than twice that amount (close to $1 million per day) by investing the money.[1] [For the "online environmental community," see **http://envirolink.org**]

Questions

1.   *a.*   Have you declined to buy Exxon products because of the oil spill?
      b.   Should we do so?
      c.   Would you expect that the oil spill, its bad publicity, and the lawsuits have imposed a heavy financial penalty on Exxon? Explain.

MARKET FAILURE?

Without regulation, a firm may consider that dumping its garbage into a nearby canal is no big deal. In fact, perhaps the slight amount of garbage the firm dumps *is* no big deal. However, if every firm were allowed to dump that amount, the canal might become thoroughly polluted. Or consider the possibility that we may all prefer less costly cars that pollute more. Would future generations concur?

As discussed in Chapter 7, pollution in these cases would be categorized by economists as a negative "externality." Wilfred Beckerman described the economic analysis as follows:

> [T]he costs of pollution are not always borne fully, if at all, by the polluter . . . Naturally, he has no incentive to economize in the use [of the environment] in the same way that he has for other factors of production that carry a cost, such as labor or capital . . . This defect of the price mechanism needs to be corrected by governmental action in order to eliminate excessive pollution.[2]

Thus, environmentalists claim the market has failed to protect us from pollution and rules are necessary. Polling data suggests the public agrees. A 1999 CNN/*USA Today*/Gallup Poll found 85 percent of Americans saying that they personally worry about the pollution of rivers, lakes, and reservoirs.[3] Primary concerns are air and water pollution, destroying the rain forests, and global warming.[4] Sixty-five percent of Americans favor protection of the environment even at the risk of curbing economic growth.[5] The nonpartisan Pew Research Center found that over 80 percent of Americans want stricter laws to protect the environment although those willing to make economic sacrifices to accomplish that goal fell from 67 to 57 percent from 1992 to 1994.[6] According to a 1997 study, 20 percent of the customers in six pilot projects around the country are paying up to 10 percent more than the market price for "green" electricity.[7] Environmental interventions appear to be paying off at least in psychic rewards, since two-thirds of Americans polled in 1999 said they were generally satisfied with the state of environmental protection in America.[8]

> Sixty-five percent of Americans favor protection of the environment even at the risk of curbing economic growth

FIGURE 17.1

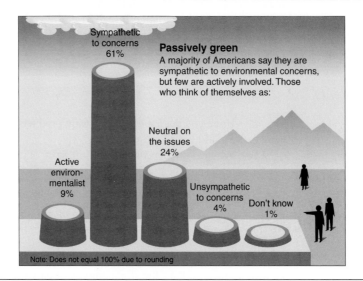

Source: "USA SNAPSHOTS," *USA Today,* January 30, 1997, p. 1A. Copyright 1997, *USA Today.* Reprinted by permission.

BUSINESS TO BLAME?

Nearly three-quarters of Americans polled in 1999 said that business and industry are "not worried enough" about environmental issues, a decline from 85 percent in 1990.[9] In blaming business, however, we may forget our own role in pollution. Individual citizens are primarily responsible for particulate matter discharged by wood-burning stoves, indoor pollution from cigarette smoking, and air pollution caused by our national one-worker-per-car commuting habits. Most forms of pollution, however, probably do have some business connection—whether direct or indirect. Thus, this chapter provides an opportunity to review the ethical considerations of business decision making and the overall social responsibility of business.

Part Two—The Global Picture

Greenies. Tree huggers. Granolas. Greenpeacemakers. Whatever they are called, individuals who support the protection of the environment often find themselves in the minority. Critics claim that the problems aren't that bad or that the solutions cost more than the harm. To be sure, hearing that there is a hole in the ozone layer is much akin to hearing that the sky is falling. Yet, there is a difference. Environmentalists in America and around the world have something to be worrying about. Consider the following.

- "Asia Stinks." So says *Fortune* magazine.[10] Many Asians agree:

[N]ow an increasingly affluent, well-educated middle class is starting to realize that deadly pollution is a high price to pay for the ability to buy Toyotas and Big Macs. In burgeoning democracies across the region, they are raising their voices and prodding their leaders to focus on quality of life and not just growth. "Living here is like living in hell by American standards," says mechanical engineering professor Jeff Chiang as he looks out over Taiwan's smoky landscape studded with refinery smokestacks and riddled with oily black steams.[11]

> **About 20 percent of the Amazon rain forest has already been lost**

- About 20 percent of the Amazon rain forest has already been lost to logging, mining, farming, and other development activities.[12] Greenpeace claims that the forest will be gone in 80 years if deforestation continues at the current pace, which is estimated to be approximately equal to the loss of an area the size of Connecticut each year.[13]

- "The Aral Sea is going, gone. Once the world's fourth-largest inland body of water, the Aral has shriveled to half its former area and a third of its volume. As for the region's drinking water, even the local vodka has a salty tang."[14] The Aral is the victim of the former Soviet Union's central planners who decreed that the area would be the nation's main source of cotton. In order to achieve that goal, intense irrigation was required with the result that only a trickle of fresh water was left to feed the Aral. Refilling the Aral would require tremendous dislocations in the agriculture of the vast region.

- The Earth is getting warmer—about 1 degree Farenheit over the 20th century.[15] One hundred and sixty nations have signed the 1997 Kyoto Protocol to address the problem.[16] Critics argue, however, that we don't know how much of the warming is actually attributable to human behavior, and they fear that the United States will bear more than its share of corrective costs.

U.S. SIGNS INTERNATIONAL GLOBAL WARNING TREATY

Traci Watson

In a largely symbolic gesture, the USA has signed an international treaty to slow global warming.

[The] signing does not commit the USA to abide by the treaty, written in 1997 at a historic meeting in Kyoto, Japan. Before its provisions can take effect in the USA, the treaty must be ratified by the Senate, an action seen as highly unlikely in the next few years.

"This was an important decision. Many countries doubted we would sign the (treaty)," Stuart Eizenstat,

lead U.S. negotiator at a global warming summit in Buenos Aires, Argentina, said.

* * * * *

Opponents in the USA insist that humans are not responsible for global warming.

Most scientists agree that global warming is caused in part by greenhouse gases, created by burning fossil fuels. The gases trap heat in the atmosphere, and the resultant warming might lead to more droughts and floods.

To prevent such disasters, the Kyoto treaty calls for wealthy nations to cut greenhouse-gas emissions. It does not require poorer nations to limit their emissions.

The White House stance on the treaty has faced major opposition in Congress and from some businesses. Critics say the treaty would damage the U.S. economy, and they object to the lack of restrictions on developing nations.

* * * * *

With a solid Republican majority in the Senate, there is little chance for ratification of the treaty, particularly because some Democrats, such as those from coal-producing states, are against it.

Over the past year, the USA has tried repeatedly to get developing countries to voluntarily limit their greenhouse gases as Congress and industry have demanded. But the developing nations that emit the most greenhouse gases—China and India—refuse to consider limits, saying rich nations should clean up first.

The USA has also angered its allies by insisting on unlimited use of emissions trading, a complex system that would allow a country to exceed its emission quota by paying a country that emits less than its quota.

European and developing nations say there should be limits on such trading. But others say limits would make the Kyoto treaty too expensive and awkward to implement.

However, there has been some progress since Kyoto:

- Several dozen companies have agreed to try to lower their emissions of greenhouse gases. The group includes corporations such as Monsanto and Shell.
- Argentina and Kazakhstan agreed to limit their greenhouse-gas emissions, though the Kyoto treaty does not require them to do so.

* * * * *

Until countries can agree on topics such as how to monitor progress and how to punish nations that don't comply, there can be no action against global warming.

Still, lurking in the background is the widespread acceptance that the treaty is too weak to keep the globe from warming. That is no excuse to abandon the Kyoto treaty, scientists say. But it does mean the Earth probably will warm several degrees—with the accompanying catastrophes—unless the world agrees to even stricter limits than those in the Kyoto treaty.

Source: *USA Today,* November 13, 1998, p. 19A. Copyright 1998, *USA Today.* Reprinted by permission.

Afterword

Critics argue that global warming fears have been dramatically overstated, and that in some respects, warming will be beneficial. The most recent evidence suggests that warming will increase temperatures 1 to 3.5 degree Celsius, about half of earlier projections, and crop productivity may increase by about 30 percent due to higher levels of carbon dioxide.[17] Furthermore, greenhouse conditions appear to be improving:

> There's good news concerning economic growth and fears about global warming. During the boom years of 1997 and 1998, the economy grew by 4 percent annually, but greenhouse gas emissions stayed nearly static.
>
> According to the nonprofit Center for Energy and Climate Solutions, which has worked with the World Wildlife Fund to help businesses reduce greenhouse gas emissions, the energy required to produce a dollar of gross national product fell by 3 percent in 1997 and 1998, compared to a 1 percent annual decline in the prior decade.
>
> One factor may be the Internet, which has reduced energy use in transportation. However, the report also cites more energy-efficient businesses.[18]

[For the United Nations Environment Programme, see **http://www.unep.ch/**]

A variety of factors can take days off your life:

Toxic waste sites:	0–4 days
Pesticide residue:	0–4
Driving:	182
25 percent overweight:	303
Smoking:	2,580
Poverty:	3,600

Source: Bernard Cohen, University of Pittsburg, reported in John Stossel, "Overcoming Junk Science," *The Wall Street Journal,* January 9, 1997, p. A10.

Part Three—Laws and Regulations

The United States has developed a wide variety of environmental protection laws and remedies, some of which are discussed in this section. Throughout this discussion, keep in mind the central problem in environmental law—how much are we willing to pay? This is not an easy question to answer. As a society, do we want clean air at any cost? How do we value human life? Must we sacrifice short-term economic development to achieve long-term environmental goals? And, if so, who should pay for achieving these goals? [For environmental law searches and links, see **http://www.yahoo.com/ Society–and–Culture/Environment–and–Nature/Law/**]

THE FEDERAL ROLE

The federal government has long maintained a role in the protection of the environment; some would argue too great a role. As early as 1899, Congress enacted a law that required a permit to discharge refuse into navigable waters. As it became apparent that private, state, and local environmental efforts were not adequate to the burgeoning problems, in the early 1970s Congress began to take more aggressive legislative initiatives.

National Environmental Policy Act (NEPA)

The 1970 National Environmental Policy Act (NEPA) established a strong federal presence in the promotion of a clean and healthy environment. NEPA represents a general commitment by the federal government to "use all practicable means" to conduct federal affairs in a fashion that both promotes "the general welfare" and operates in "harmony" with the environment. A portion reads:

Public Law 91-190, 42 U.S.C. § 4331 *et seq.*
PURPOSE
The purposes of this Act are: To declare a national policy which will encourage productive and enjoyable harmony between man and his environment; to promote efforts which will prevent or

eliminate damage to the environment and biosphere and stimulate the health and welfare of man; to enrich the understanding of the ecological systems and natural resources important to the Nation; and to establish a Council on Environmental Quality.

The **Council on Environmental Quality** (CEQ) serves as an advisor to the president. Specifically, the CEQ must "assist and advise the president in the preparation of the [annual] Environmental Quality Report." The CEQ is a watchdog of sorts. It is required to conduct studies and collect information regarding the state of the environment. The council then develops policy and legislative proposals for the president and Congress.

But NEPA's primary influence results from its environmental impact statement (EIS) requirements. With few exceptions, "proposals for legislation and other major federal action significantly affecting the quality of the human environment" must be accompanied by an EIS explaining the impact on the environment and detailing reasonable alternatives. Major federal construction projects (highways, dams, and nuclear reactors) would normally require an EIS; but less visible federal programs (ongoing timber management or the abandonment of a lengthy railway) may also require EIS treatment. Although the focus here is on *federal* actions, thus exempting solely private acts from this scrutiny, a major private-sector action supported by federal funding or by one of several varieties of federal permission may also require an EIS. Hence, private companies receiving federal contracts, funding, licenses, and the like may be parties to the completion of an EIS.

Environmental Protection Agency (EPA)

The private sector was not left without regulation or constraint. The Environmental Protection Agency (EPA) was created in 1970 to mount a coordinated attack on environmental problems. EPA duties include, among other things, (1) information gathering, particularly in surveying pollution problems, (2) conducting research on pollution problems, (3) assisting state and local pollution control efforts, and (4) administering many of the federal laws directed to environmental concerns.

An encouraging EPA program labeled the "Common Sense Initiative" holds out the promise of a less expensive, less bureaucratic approach to environmental oversight. Basically, the plan approaches pollution problems on an industry-by-industry basis rather than the pollutant-by-pollutant approach that has been the norm. The Common Sense Initiative Council, composed of business, government, and public interest representatives, is looking for industry-specific strategies that provide better protection with fewer headaches. The initiative is designed, in part, to move away from the sometimes heavy-handed and often inconsistent, "command and control" policies of the past. [For the EPA home page, see **www.epa.gov/**]

New Rules and Programs

Under the NEPA and EPA umbrellas, the federal government has, of course, erected a massive array of rules and programs to deal with environmental problems. The job, however, is far from complete and the EPA is busy on many fronts:

- In 1999, the EPA ordered 12 states in the Midwest and East to reduce their "export" of smog to other states. The new rules replace a set struck down in court and are designed to curb air pollution that travels on prevailing winds. Characteristically, that problem involves pollution from Midwest power plants being blown eastward to states such as Massachusetts.[19]

- The EPA has proposed new emission rules, effective in 2004, for sport utility vehicles, minivans, and pickup trucks that would impose on them the same standards as those applying to passenger cars. The new standards would require those vehicles to be about 77 percent cleaner than they are today.[20]

> rules imposing the first emission standards for snowmobiles and all-terrain vehicles

- By September 2000, the EPA expects to issue rules imposing the first emission standards for snowmobiles and all-terrain vehicles. An EPA study found that those machines emit 25 percent as much hydrocarbon pollution as all of our cars and trucks put together. New standards for outboard motors and personal watercraft (jet skis) are scheduled to go into effect in 2006.[21]

- The EPA recognizes the burdens associated with its rules and processes and has indicated that it intends to "develop a system that works better and costs less" by focusing on five areas: "Greater public access to information; more regulatory flexibility to obtain better results; stronger partnerships with states and industries; more compliance assistance; and less paperwork and red tape."[22] The EPA has announced that it intends to bring together "stakeholders" from business, interest groups, state and local government, and similar entities so that "all interested parties can participate in the design of innovative, less costly approaches to environmental and public health protection."[23]

- An interesting example of the new EPA enforcement approach is its Sector Facility Indexing Project, which purports to provide "public access to more environmental information than has ever before been available to the public in one location."[24] The project, covering such industries as auto assembly and petroleum refining, puts detailed records of environmental violations, inspections, and enforcement actions on the Internet for all to see. [For the SFIP Fact Sheet, see **http://es.epa.gov/oeca/sfi/factsht.htm**]

REGULATION OF AIR POLLUTION

We depend on (indeed, we emotionally embrace) the automobile. In doing so, we have opened vistas of opportunity not previously imagined. However, for the present at least, we also have eliminated clean air. Motor vehicles discharge carbon monoxide, nitrogen oxide, and hydrocarbons as by-products of the combustion of fuel.

Motor vehicles are the major source of air pollution, but industrial production and the combustion of fossil fuels in homes and industry are also significant contributors to the dilemma of dirty air. For most Americans, air pollution is simply an unpleasant fact of life.

Clean Air Act of 1990 (CAA)

Early clean air legislation in 1963 and 1965 afforded the government limited authority. The Clean Air Act amendments of 1970 and 1977 gave the EPA the power to set air-quality standards and to ensure that those standards were achieved according to a timetable prescribed by the agency. Politics brought clean air to the fore in 1990, and a new Clean Air Act followed. The Clean Air Act of 1990, which is being phased in over a period of years, generally requires tougher auto emission controls, cleaner burning gasoline, and new equipment to capture industrial and business pollution, all of which work toward the general goal of reducing airborne pollutants by about 50 percent.

Not satisfied with air-quality progress, the EPA in the late 1990s took an increasingly aggressive stance. As noted above, midwestern and eastern states were ordered to curb "exports" of airborne pollution, and in late 1999 the EPA vigorously signaled its growing frustration by taking legal action against 32 coal-fired power plants operating in 10 states (Alabama, Florida, Georgia, Illinois, Indiana, Kentucky, Mississippi, Ohio, Tennessee, and West Virginia). Some of the plants were given administrative citations and warnings, but seven utilities and 17 of their plants were sued for violating EPA rules. Most of the plants were built before the enactment of the Clean Air Act of 1970 and were allowed, under "grandfather" clauses, to meet less-stringent air-quality requirements unless they undertook major modifications in their plants. The supposition was that the old plants would soon be phased out. The phaseouts did not happen, and the EPA claims that major renovations have been made in order to extend the plants' useful lives without making the required EPA upgrades.[25]

Our societal commitment to clean air seems to be growing ever more zealous. The market (that is, us) appears to be demanding clean air as evidenced, for example, by Ford Motor Company's 1999 announcement that all of its pickups, sport utilities, and minivans will meet or exceed California's strict air-quality standards by 2001.[26] Honda agreed in 1998 to pay $17 million and extend warranties on 1.6 million vehicles to settle government claims that it disabled emission control systems.[27] In 1999, New York Governor George Pataki announced that New York will adopt auto emission standards tougher than those required by the federal government.[28] Those stronger standards were already in place in California and are expected to be adopted in Massachusetts. The standards may add several hundred dollars to the cost of each new vehicle, but by 2010, new cars, on average, would be permitted to produce less than half of today's new vehicle pollution.[29] New York, California, and Massachusetts account for about one-fourth of the national vehicle market. Some experts believe the state action will effectively require a new national standard at the more stringent level because auto manufacturers are reluctant to build different cars for different states.

> Honda agreed in 1998 to pay $17 million and extend warranties on 1.6 million vehicles to settle government claims that it disabled emission control systems

Trucks. As noted above, the EPA announced new rules requiring sport utility vehicles, pickups, and minivans to meet the same air pollution standards as cars. By 2007, 85 percent of cars and trucks must meet the rules and the biggest SUVs and pickups must meet those standards by 2009.[30] The EPA says the new standards will cost about $100 per car and $200 per truck. The new rules will also require petroleum refiners to produce low-sulfur gas that, according to EPA estimates, will raise fuel prices by one to two cents per gallon.[31] Those standards, while burdensome, appear to be paying off in cleaner air. For example, hydrocarbon emissions from cars fell from 4.1 grams per mile in 1968, when the federal rules were introduced, to an anticipated 0.25 in 1997–2003.[32] Cleaner air is expected to produce improved health and other benefits that will exceed the additional costs from the new rules.

Particulates and Ozone. In 1997, the EPA announced new, more demanding clean-air standards to reduce particulate matter and ozone coming from many sources, such as refineries, factories, and utilities. The new standards were expected to cost at least $2.5 billion more annually, but the EPA expected savings of at least $70 billion annually in health-care costs and productivity.[33] The case that follows involves a challenge by a number of industry groups to those new standards. The core of the challenge was the constitutional *nondelegation doctrine,* which provides that Congress cannot cede its power to make laws to another branch of the federal government.

AMERICAN TRUCKING ASSOCIATIONS v. U.S. E.P.A.
175 F.3d 1027 (D.C. Cir. 1999)

Circuit Judges Williams, Ginsburg, and Tatel PER CURIUM

Introduction

The Clean Air Act requires EPA to promulgate and periodically revise national ambient air-quality standards ("NAAQS") for each air pollutant identified by the agency as meeting certain statutory criteria. For each pollutant, EPA sets a "primary standard"—a concentration level "requisite to protect the public health" with an "adequate margin of safety"—and a "secondary standard"—a level "requisite to protect the public welfare."

In July 1997 EPA issued final rules revising the primary and secondary NAAQS for particulate matter ("PM") and ozone.

I. Delegation

Certain "Small Business Petitioners" argue in each case that EPA has construed §§ 108 & 109 of the Clean Air Act so loosely as to render them unconstitutional delegations of legislative power. We agree. Although the factors EPA uses in determining the degree of public health concern associated with different levels of ozone and PM are reasonable, EPA appears to have articulated no "intelligible principle" to channel its application of these factors; nor is one apparent from the statute. The nondelegation doctrine requires such a principle. Here it is as though Congress commanded EPA to select "big guys," and EPA announced that it would evaluate candidates based on height and weight, but revealed no cut-off point. The announcement, though sensible in what it does say, is fatally incomplete. The reasonable person responds, "How tall? How heavy?"

EPA regards ozone definitely, and PM likely, as nonthreshold pollutants, i.e., ones that have some possibility of some adverse health impact (however slight) at any exposure level above zero.

* * * * *

Thus the only concentration for ozone and PM that is utterly risk-free, in the sense of direct health impacts, is zero. Section 109(b)(1) says that EPA must set each standard at the level "requisite to protect the public health" with an "adequate margin of safety." These are also the criteria by which EPA must determine whether a revision to existing NAAQS is appropriate. For EPA to pick any nonzero level it must explain the degree of imperfection permitted. The factors that EPA has elected to examine for this purpose in themselves pose no inherent nondelegation problem. But what EPA lacks is any determinate criterion for drawing lines. It has failed to state intelligibly how much is too much.

We begin with the criteria EPA has announced for assessing health effects in setting the NAAQS for nonthreshold pollutants. They are "the nature and severity of the health effects involved, the size of the sensitive population(s) at risk, the types of health information available, and the kind and degree of uncertainties that must be addressed." Although these criteria, so stated, are a bit vague, they do focus the inquiry on pollution's effects on public health. And most of the vagueness in the abstract formulation melts away as EPA applies the criteria: EPA basically considers severity of effect, certainty of effect, and size of population affected. These criteria, long ago approved by the judiciary, do not themselves speak to the issue of degree.

Read in light of these factors, EPA's explanations for its decisions amount to assertions that a less stringent standard would allow the relevant pollutant to inflict a greater quantum of harm on public health, and that a more stringent standard would result in less harm. Such arguments only support the intuitive proposition that more pollution will not benefit public health, not that keeping pollution at or below any particular level is "requisite" or not requisite to "protect the public health" with an "adequate margin of safety," the formula set out by § 109(b)(1).

*   *   *   *   *

In other words, effects are less certain and less severe at lower levels of exposure. This seems to be nothing more than a statement that lower exposure levels are associated with lower risk to public health.

In addition . . . EPA cited the consensus of the Clean Air Scientific Advisory Committee ("CASAC") that the standard should not be set below 0.08. That body gave no specific reasons for its recommendations, so the appeal to its authority, adds no enlightenment . . . Nothing in what CASAC says helps us discern an intelligible principle derived by EPA from the Clean Air Act.

II. Other General Claims

The petitioners contend that the EPA erroneously failed to consider a host of factors in revising the PM and ozone NAAQS. We reject each of these claims in turn.

A. Consideration of Cost in Revising Standards

As this court long ago made clear, in setting NAAQS under § 109(b) of the Clean Air Act, the EPA is not permitted to consider the cost of implementing those standards.

See *NRDC*, 902 F.2d at 973 ("Consideration of costs . . . would be flatly inconsistent with the statute, legislative history and case law on this point"); *NRDC* v. *EPA*, 824 F.2d 1146, 1158–59 (D.C.Cir.1987) ("*Vinyl Chloride*") ("[S]tatute on its face does not allow consideration of technological or economic feasibility . . . Congress considered the alternatives and chose to close down sources or even industries rather than to allow risks to health").

[Petitioners' additional claims are omitted.] Remanded to the EPA.

Afterword

In a split decision, the full District of Columbia U.S. Court of Appeals declined to rehear the *American Trucking* decision, and an EPA appeal to the United States Supreme Court was expected.

Questions

1. Why did the court strike down the new EPA standards?

2. *a.* Why did the court rule that cost could not be a consideration in evaluating the legality of the new clean-air rules?

   b. Do you agree that cost should not be a consideration in achieving clean air? Explain.

3. The new clean-air rules were expected to save about 2,800 lives annually. Would 2,800 lives saved each year be worth the additional costs, which, as noted above, were expected to total at least $2.5 billion? Explain.

America's Deadliest Cities
(Annual Deaths Attributable to Particulate Pollution)

Los Angeles	5,873
New York	4,024
Chicago	3,479
Philadelphia	2,599
Detroit	2,123

Source: Dick Thompson, "Smog Alert," *Time*, December 9, 1996, p. 71. [For an environmental law database and search engine, see **http://www.law.indiana.edu/law/v-lib/envlaw.html**].

REGULATION OF WATER POLLUTION

As with the air, we often treat our water resources as free goods. Rather than paying the full cost of producing goods and services, we have simply dumped a portion of that cost into the nearest body of water. The waste from production—indeed from the totality of our life experience—has commonly been disposed of in the water at a cost beneath that required to dispose of the waste in an ecologically sound fashion. The results range from smelly to dangerous to tragic.

• *Rivers.* Around the globe, we are destroying our great river systems—sources of so much of our food, drinking water, fun, and beauty. More than half of the world's 500 major rivers are either going dry from overuse or are seriously polluted. China's giant Yellow River actually dried up for 226 days in 1997, and more than 90 percent of the Nile's natural flow either evaporates in reservoirs or is diverted for irrigation. Only four major rivers (the Amazon in South America, the Congo in Africa, the St. Lawrence in North America, and the Mekong in Southeast Asia) are considered "healthy."[34] While we have achieved great progress, 40 percent of America's waterways remain too polluted for fishing and swimming.[35] [For more information about threatened bodies of water in the United States, see **http://www.epa.gov/owow/tmdl**]

> More than half of the world's 500 major rivers are either going dry from overuse or are seriously polluted

• *Gulf of Mexico.* Farm fertilizer, industrial wastes, lawn chemicals, decaying plants, and household wastes from all over the vast Mississippi River watershed flow relentlessly past New Orleans and into the Gulf of Mexico. One of the results is a great "dead zone," a band of water perhaps 20 meters thick and about the size of New Jersey, in which nothing of value lives during the summer months. Nitrates from farm fertilizers encourage massive algae growth that sinks to the Gulf floor, decays, and consumes the available oxygen with the result that no crab, shrimp, or fish are found there.[36]

• *Runoff.* Much of America's water pollution is directly attributable to our personal habits. Surface water runoff is polluted with lawn fertilizer, pet waste, grease and oil from vehicles, and all the other sludge from our modern lives. That runoff, of course, eventually debases our waterways.

Federal Policy

The Clean Water Act (CWA), designed to "restore and maintain the chemical, physical, and biological integrity of the nation's waters," establishes two national goals: (1) achieving water quality sufficient for the protection and propagation of fish, shellfish, and wildlife and for recreation in and on the water; and (2) eliminating the discharge of pollutants into navigable waters. The states have primary responsibility for enforcing the CWA, but the federal government, via the Environmental Protection Agency, is empowered to assume enforcement authority if necessary.

The goals of the Clean Water Act are to be implemented primarily by imposing limits on the amount of pollutants that may lawfully enter the water of the United States from any "point source" (typically a pipe). The National Pollutant Discharge Elimination System (NPDES) requires all pollutant dischargers to secure an EPA permit before pouring effluent into a navigable stream. The permit specifies maximum permissible levels of effluent. Typically, the permit also mandates the use of a particular pollution control process or device and requires the permit holder to monitor its own performance and report on that performance to the state or the EPA, as appropriate.

The federal government has recently taken a number of steps to aggressively address our clean water problems. In 1999, under the terms of the Safe Drinking Water Act, higher water filtration standards were imposed on systems serving tens of millions of Americans. Likewise in 1999, the federal government announced tight new rules to reduce runoff from large hog, cattle, and poultry farms. Ten years after imposing the 1988 groundwater rules, 45 percent of America's underground storage tanks—the most common source of groundwater contamination—do not meet EPA safety standards, which require tanks to be equipped with spill, overfill, and corrosion protection.[37]

Clean Water Case

The case that follows involves a constitutional challenge to the federal government's power under the Commerce Clause (see Chapter 7) to regulate some kinds of wetland development. Wetlands are valuable as wildlife habitat, for their capacity to filter pollutants before they reach streams, and for their natural beauty. Basically, the wetlands conflict is between property owners and developers, on the one hand, and environmental/governmental interests on the other. The former argue that they have the constitutional right to do generally as they wish with their property, that the government has unnecessarily restricted the development of land that is actually dry for much of the year, and that the government's wetland protection rules are a bureaucratic nightmare.

U.S. v. WILSON
133 F.3d 251 (4th. Cir. 1997)

Circuit Judge Niemeyer

The defendants in this case were convicted of felony violations of the Clean Water Act for knowingly discharging fill and excavated material into wetlands of the United States without a permit. On this appeal they challenge: (1) the validity of federal regulations purporting to regulate activities that "could affect" interstate commerce; (2) the district court's application of the Clean Water Act to wetlands that do not have a "direct or indirect surface connection to other waters of the United States" . . .

*   *   *   *   *

I

In February 1996, after a seven-week trial, a jury convicted James J. Wilson, Interstate General Co., L.P., and St. Charles Associates, L.P., on four felony counts charging them with knowingly discharging fill material and excavated dirt into wetlands on four separate parcels without a permit, in violation of the Clean Water Act, 33 U.S.C. §§ 1319(c)(2)(A) & 1311(a). The district court sentenced Wilson to 21 months imprisonment and 1 year supervised release and fined him $1 million. It fined the other two defendants $3 million and placed them on 5 years probation. The court also ordered the defendants to implement a wetlands restoration and mitigation plan proposed by the government.

Wilson, a land developer with more than 30 years of experience, was the chief executive officer and chairman of the board of directors of Interstate General. He was personally responsible for various decisions relevant to the defendants' convictions in this case. Interstate

General was a publicly traded land development company with 340 employees, 2,000 shareholders, and assets of over $100 million. It was the general partner of St. Charles Associates, a limited partnership that owned the land being developed within the planned community of St. Charles, which lies between the Potomac River and the Chesapeake Bay in Charles County, Maryland. The convictions involve discharges onto four parcels that are part of St. Charles.

St. Charles currently consists of approximately 4,000 developed acres and 10,000 housing units with 33,000 residents. At completion, it is expected to be a 9,100 acre planned community of some 80,000 residents. The community was created under the New Communities Act of 1968 and developed initially in partnership between Interstate General and the United States Department of Housing and Urban Development ("HUD"). The project agreement provides for the creation of schools, parks, and recreational areas and designates at least 20% of the community to be reserved as "open space." It also provides for the preservation of 75 acres of wetlands near Zekiah Swamp . . .

At trial, the government introduced evidence that during the period from 1988 to 1993, the defendants attempted to drain at least three of the four parcels of land involved in this case by digging ditches. The government also introduced evidence that the defendants transported a substantial amount of fill dirt and gravel and deposited it on three of the parcels . . . The government presented evidence that all four of these parcels contained wetlands and that the defendants failed to obtain permits from the Army Corps of Engineers, the agency charged with issuing permits under the relevant section of the Act, 33 U.S.C. § 1344, prior to making efforts to drain and fill the parcels.

Although the parcels in question were not, because of neighboring development, located in pristine wilderness areas, the government presented substantial evidence about the physical characteristics which identified them as wetlands, including testimonial and photographic evidence of significant standing water, reports of vegetation typical to hydrologic soils, and infrared aerial photographs showing a pattern of stream courses visible under the vegetation. Evidence also showed that the properties were identified as containing wetlands on public documents including the National Wetlands Inventory Map and topographical maps of Charles County and the State of Maryland. The government demonstrated that water from these lands flowed in a drainage pattern through ditches, intermittent streams, and creeks, ultimately joining the Potomac River, a tributary of the Chesapeake Bay.

* * * * *

II

The defendants challenge the authority of regulation 33 C.F.R. § 328.3(a)(3) (1993) (defining waters of the United States to include those waters whose degradation "could affect" interstate commerce) to extend jurisdiction of the Clean Water Act to the four parcels in question. They argue that the regulation and instructions exceed not only the authority of the Clean Water Act (which regulates "waters of the United States" without defining them), but also the Commerce Clause, U.S. Const. art, I, § 8, cl. 3. They maintain that in allowing the jury to find a nexus with interstate commerce based on whether activities "could affect" interstate commerce, the court authorized a "limitless view of federal jurisdiction," far more expansive than the standard recently summarized in *United States.* v. *Lopez,* 514 U.S. 549 (1995).

* * * * *

The Clean Water Act prohibits the discharge, without a permit, of pollutants into "navigable waters." 33 U.S.C. §§ 1311(a), 1362(12)(A). While the regulatory power of Congress over waters that are navigable in fact is well established, the Clean Water Act defines "navigable waters" as "the waters of the United States," 33 U.S.C.

§ 1362(7). Construing the Clean Water Act, the Supreme Court has indicated that in defining "navigable waters" as "waters of the United States," Congress intended "to exercise its powers under the Commerce Clause to regulate at least some waters that would not be deemed 'navigable' under the classical understanding of that term." Accordingly, the power of Congress to regulate the discharge of pollutants into at least some nonnavigable waters is indisputable, but the limits of this power are far from clear.

* * * * *

However, we need not resolve these difficult questions about the extent and limits of congressional power to regulate nonnavigable waters to resolve the issue before us. The regulation challenged here, 33 C.F.R. § 328.3(a)(3) (1993), defines "waters of the United States" to include:

All other waters such as intrastate lakes, rivers, streams (including intermittent streams), mud flats, sand flats, wetlands, sloughs, prairie potholes, wet meadows, playa lakes, or natural ponds, the use, degradation or destruction of which *could affect* interstate or foreign commerce . . .

(Emphasis added). This regulation purports to extend the coverage of the Clean Water Act to a variety of waters that are intrastate, nonnavigable, or both, solely on the basis that the use, degradation, or destruction of such waters *could* affect interstate commerce. The regulation requires neither that the regulated activity have a *substantial* effect on interstate commerce, nor that the covered waters have any sort of nexus with navigable, or even interstate, waters.

* * * * *

Absent a clear indication to the contrary, we should not lightly presume that merely by defining "navigable waters" as "the waters of the United States," 33 U.S.C. § 1362(7), Congress authorized the Army Corps of Engineers to assert its jurisdiction in such a sweeping and constitutionally troubling manner. Even as a matter of statutory construction, one would expect that the phrase "waters of the United States" when used to define the phrase "navigable waters" refers to waters which, if not navigable in fact, are at least interstate or closely related to navigable or interstate waters. When viewed in light of its statutory authority, 33 C.F.R. § 328.3(a)(3) (1993), which defines "waters of the United States" to include intrastate waters that need have nothing to do with navigable or interstate waters, expands the statutory phrase "waters of the United States" beyond its definitional limit.

Accordingly, we believe that in promulgating 33 C.F.R. § 328.3(a)(3) (1993), the Army Corps of Engineers exceeded its congressional authorization under the Clean Water Act, and that, for this reason, 33 C.F.R. § 328.3(a)(3) (1993) is invalid.

III

The defendants also contend that the district court, in instructing the jury on the relationship between wetlands and interstate waters, gratuitously and improperly extended the jurisdiction of the Clean Water Act beyond its stated limits to any wetland "even without a direct or indirect surface connection" with interstate waters. They claim that their property was not adjacent to waters of the United States and that any wetlands that may have been involved were too remote from navigable waters to be under the jurisdiction of the Clean Water Act. They observe that the wetlands involved here were "more than ten miles from the Chesapeake Bay, more than six miles from the Potomac River, and hundreds of yards from the nearest creeks." They add that the district court's interpretation of the nexus between wetlands and interstate waters also exceeds the Commerce Clause's limitation of governmental power.

The government argues, without addressing the district court's instruction, that the wetlands involved in this case "were [as a factual matter] clearly adjacent to streams which flow into the Chesapeake Bay" and therefore "were properly regulated pursuant to the Commerce Clause." Although the Clean Water Act itself authorizes the regulation of only "navigable waters," which are defined as "waters of the United States," the Army Corps of Engineers has defined "waters of the United States" to include wetlands *adjacent* to waters that otherwise constitute waters of the United States. 33 C.F.R. § 328.3(7)(1993). Although the Supreme Court has upheld the validity of 33 C.F.R. § 328.3(7) as a reasonable construction of the Clean Water Act, it did so explicitly in the context of a wetland "that *actually abuts* on a

navigable waterway." *Riverside Bayview Homes,* 474 U.S. at 135, 106 S.Ct. at 463 (emphasis added).

In instructing the jury in this case, the district court extended the application of the Clean Water Act substantially beyond the regulations that had been approved in *Riverside Bayview Homes,* instructing the jury that waters of the United States included adjacent wetlands "*even without a direct or indirect surface connection to other waters of the United States.*" (Emphasis added). This instruction intolerably stretches the ordinary meaning of the word "adjacent" and the phrase "waters of the United States" to include wetlands remote from any interstate or navigable waters. Furthermore, as noted above, we should interpret the Clean Water Act in light of the constitutional difficulties that would arise by extending the Act's coverage to *waters* that are connected closely to neither interstate nor navigable waters, and which do not otherwise substantially affect interstate commerce. It was thus error for the district court to have instructed the jury to extend the jurisdiction of the Clean Water Act to wetlands that lack any "direct or indirect surface connection" to interstate waters, navigable waters, or interstate commerce.

* * * * *

Reversed and remanded for a new trial.

Afterword

Following the *Wilson* decision, the Corps of Engineers announced that it would implement the court's ruling in the five affected states, but that it would continue its former policy elsewhere in the United States, pending future judicial clarification. Furthermore, the Corps indicated that it would continue to regulate isolated wetlands within the states covered by the Fourth Circuit Court when it could establish a link between those wetlands and interstate or foreign commerce and it could show that the use of the wetland would have a substantial effect on that commerce.

The *Wilson* case was settled out of court in 1999 when Interstate General agreed to pay $1.5 million in fines and to restore and protect 155 acres of wetlands and buffer property. Charges against James J. Wilson were dropped. [For the Sierra Club home page, see **http://www.sierraclub.org/**]

Questions

1. Summarize the holding in *Wilson*.
2. Explain why the court struck down the Corps of Engineers' regulation.
3. In your view, is the *Wilson* decision in the public's best interest? Explain.
4. Polluted waterways around the world contributed to 25 million environmental refugees, which for the first time exceeded the world's total of 21 million war-related refugees.[38]

   a. Do the American people contribute in any substantial way to those environmental refugee conditions around the globe? Explain.
   b. Do you personally contribute in any substantial way to environmental pollution in the United States or abroad? Explain.

REGULATION OF LAND POLLUTION

Pollution does not fit tidily into the three compartments (air, water, land) used for convenience in this text. Acid rain debases air and water as well as the fruits of the water and land, such as fish and trees. Similarly, the problems of land pollution addressed in this section often do damage to the fullness of the natural world. For most of recorded history, we felt safe and comfortable in using the Earth as a garbage dump.

Garbage

Basically, the problem is that our lifestyles result in mountains of solid waste that grow higher every year. Indeed, New York City's Fresh Kills Landfill is one of the world's largest man-made structures and one of the highest points of land on the East Coast. Each of us, on average, produces about 4.4 pounds of garbage daily, nearly 40 percent of which comes in the form of paper and paperboard.[39] Of course, we pay a great immediate price to dispose of all of the leftovers of our lives, but the long-term concern is that the waste will come back to haunt us. Even state-of-the-art landfills will leak with the result that toxic elements will enter our groundwater. We had long assumed that much of the waste will simply decompose, but studies show that does not happen. The leading "garbologist," Professor William Rathje, explains: "The thought that after 30 or so years newspapers and food would disintegrate is off-track. Things become mummified. We found hot dogs that could be recooked and perfectly legible newspapers."[40] We do burn about 16 percent of our waste, in the process killing germs and creating steam and electricity, but the resulting fly ash, some of which escapes into the air, can be highly toxic.[41] The suggested solution, of course, is to "reduce, reuse, recycle."[42]

Recycling. From the mid-1980s to the present, the EPA, environmental activists, and the garbage industry have warned about an impending trash-disposal crisis. We are rapidly running out of dumping space, they have said. *The Wall Street Journal,* however, reports that both industry and EPA officials knew that we had ample waste disposal space, even as we were being warned to recycle (and, not surprisingly, as waste companies were pushing up prices):

> "I've always wondered where that crap about a landfill-capacity crisis came from," says Allen Geswein, an EPA solid-waste official . . . The EPA, when asked, now agrees that there isn't any capacity shortage. Yet materials the agency continues to distribute warn of a shortage and cite it as one of the reasons for recycling.[43]

Whatever the current truth of the matter, the EPA reported that the number of solid waste landfills fell to 3,581 in 1995 from 5,300 in 1992, while the national goal of recycling 25 percent of municipal garbage was reached in 1995. The agency is targeting a 35 percent standard for 2005.[44]

Western European nations have generally been much more aggressive than the United States in demanding recycling. In 1999, the European Union created new rules, which if approved by the European Parliament, will require manufacturers to take back used cars for recycling starting in 2006. Studies indicate the recycling bill may reach $200 per car for collecting, transporting, dismantling, separating plastics and metals for recycling, and shredding the remainder.

Source: "EU Wants Automakers to Recycle All Old Cars," *Ottawa Citizen,* July 30, 1999, p. C5.

Solid Waste Disposal Act

To attack the massive garbage problem, Congress approved the Solid Waste Disposal Act of 1965. The act, in brief, leaves solid waste problems to states and localities, but the federal government offers research and financial support.

Toxic Substances Control Act (TSCA)

In 1976, Congress approved the Toxic Substances Control Act (TSCA) to identify toxic chemicals, assess their risks, and control dangerous chemicals. Under the terms of the TSCA, the Environmental Protection Agency requires the chemical industry to report any information it may have suggesting that a chemical poses a "substantial risk." The EPA is empowered to review and limit or stop the introduction of new chemicals.

Surprisingly, toxic pollution provided the central theme in a 1998 John Travolta/Disney movie, *A Civil Action,* based on a true story about some middle class families who sued two corporate giants, Beatrice Foods and W.R. Grace & Co., for allegedly polluting the groundwater in East Woburn, Massachusetts, where eight children had died of leukemia. [For more information about the movie, see (from an environmentalist perspective) **http:// www.civilactive.com** (from the corporate perspective) **http://www.civil-action.com** (from the perspective of one of the lawyers in the case) **http://oasis.bellevue.k12.wa.us/cheeseb/ photos/ACivilAction.html** and (from the Disney perspective) **http://www. civilaction.com**].

Resource Conservation and Recovery Act (RCRA)

By 1976, the dangers of hazardous substances were becoming apparent to all, and Congress complemented the TSCA with the Resource Conservation and Recovery Act (RCRA). The act addresses both solid and hazardous wastes. Its solid waste provisions are more supportive than punitive in tone and approach. The federal government is authorized, among other strategies, to provide technical and financial assistance to states and localities; to prohibit future open dumping; and to establish cooperative federal, state, local, and private-enterprise programs to recover energy and valuable materials from solid waste.

Subtitle C of the RCRA is designed to ensure the safe movement and disposal of hazardous wastes. The generator of the waste must determine if that waste is hazardous under EPA guidelines and, if so, report the waste site and waste activities to the government. The waste generator must then create a manifest to be used in tracking the waste from its creation to its disposal. Along the cradle-to-grave path of the waste, all those with responsibility for it must sign the manifest and safely store and transport the waste. Once the waste reaches a licensed disposal facility, the owner or manager of that site signs the manifest and returns a copy of it to the generator.

Disposal Sites.   Owners and operators of hazardous waste disposal sites must obtain government permits to begin operation. Those sites must be operated according to EPA standards, and remedial action must be taken should hazardous wastes escape from the sites.

Superfund—Comprehensive Environmental Response, Compensation, and Liability Act of 1980 (CERCLA)

CERCLA, known as Superfund, is designed to help clean up hazardous dumps and spills. In many instances, those responsible for hazardous dumps and spills cannot afford to pay for cleanup. Other hazardous sites have been abandoned. In both cases, the threat to the public is such that the government created the Superfund to attack those sites that are so dangerous that they have been included on the National Priorities List (NPL). The bulk of the fund had been drawn from taxes on chemicals and petroleum, but that taxing authority lapsed in 1995 and, subsequently, the Superfund program has been running on annual appropriations and reserve funds. Private citizens injured by hazardous wastes do not receive relief under CERCLA. They may sue, however. [For a hazardous waste clean-up database, see **http://www.clu-in.com/**]

Superfund's Future.   At this writing in 2000, Congress is considering bills to revise Superfund. Dissatisfaction is widespread, but finding common ground for reform has been very difficult. The criticisms include the following:

- In 20 years, fewer than 200 sites have been fully cleaned, and the cost for doing so was some $17 billion. Nearly 1,200 high priority sites remain.[45]
- The General Accounting Office reports that less than one-half of the annual $1.5 billion spent on Superfund actually goes into cleaning up sites. The balance supports bureaucratic expenses.[46]
- About $10 billion, one-third of the total expenditures associated with Superfund, has gone to litigation.[47]
- The Superfund law draws a very broad liability brush: "The law declared that not only firms or organizations that illegally polluted the land had to pay for the cleanup. It also made companies that stayed within the law and did what they were told to do liable, too. For instance, a report in *The Washington Times* indicated that earlier this year, 165 small businesses in Quincy, Illinois, were asked to pay $3 million for having legally disposed of trash in a licensed landfill (now a Superfund site) more than 20 years ago."[48]
- "Brownfields" are hundreds of thousands of less-contaminated former industrial and commercial sites that are not on the Superfund priority list, but that need attention if the land, much of it urban, is to be recycled for productive use. The major problem is that potential developers fear being held responsible for contamination caused by previous owners.

Reform?   Congress has been quarreling over Superfund for a number of years. Almost everyone agrees some adjustments are necessary. The competing proposals address the problems noted above: allocation of cleanup costs, assignment of liability, brownfields, and so on. One Republican-backed bill calls for reducing the Superfund budget by 35 percent over an eight-year period, but the future of the program is simply unclear at this point. Most agree, however, that continued cleanup is a necessity for both health and economic reasons.

Part Three—Penalties and Enforcement under Federal Law

Civil/Criminal Actions.   Because of the risks associated with pollution, environmental protection bodies have been given strong enforcement authority. Very often, violators initially are warned and a compliance schedule is set out. If corrective action is not forthcoming, sterner measures are followed, including an administrative order to comply. Where problems persist or the difficulties are more serious, the government may initiate civil or criminal actions against both firms and managers. Penalties vary with the act in question, but civil and criminal fines are provided for. Individuals may be jailed for one year or more. In some instances, an entire operation may be shut down.

In the largest civil environmental enforcement in American history, the seven largest makers of heavy diesel engines agreed to pay $1 billion in fines and corrective actions to settle EPA claims that the manufacturers cheated on tests to measure whether their engines met federal emission standards. The manufacturers deny any wrongdoing.[49] Fines have long been the standard remedy in governmental pollution enforcement, but in recent years, both federal and state regulators have increasingly turned to Supplemental Environmental Projects (SEPs) to settle wrongs. Normally, the SEP will involve some environmental "good work" in place of a fine. Thus, 11 Los Angeles–area corporations, accused of responsibility for polluting the drinking supply of the San Gabriel Valley, agreed in principle in 1999 to pay $85 million for the construction of a water-treatment plant to remove dangerous chemicals from the aquifer running beneath the valley floor. The companies will also pay $10 million annually for 30 years to operate the plant. The aquifer was designated a Superfund site in 1984.[50]

Additional Enforcement Mechanisms.   Many environmental statutes require companies to monitor their own environmental performance and report that information, including violations, to the government. Government agencies generally have broad authority to conduct environmental inspections of both plants and records as necessary, although they will need to seek search warrants if criminal prosecutions are anticipated. Finally, many environmental statutes provide for the possibility of *citizen suits,* wherein an individual is empowered to challenge government environmental decisions such as the granting of a permit and generally to demand both governmental and private-sector compliance with the law.

The following case is a 1997 Supreme Court analysis of citizens' authority to sue under the Endangered Species Act (ESA) (requiring the government to take steps to protect fish, wildlife, and plant species that are "threatened" or "endangered"). Two ranch operators and two irrigation districts wanted to challenge the government's decision to reduce irrigation water during a drought. The government's goal was to protect two endangered species of fish in a pair of reservoirs in southern Oregon and northern California. The plaintiffs, however, claimed that the water policy was unnecessary and caused economic loss when crops died in the fields, forcing farmers to sell cattle they could no longer feed. Their claims eventually reached the United States Supreme Court where the justices had to decide whether the ESA allows citizen suits where the plaintiffs seek to protect economic rather than environmental interests; that is, the plaintiffs claim the right to sue when they seek reduced—rather than strengthened—environmental protection. The Court's unanimous decision follows.

BENNETT v. SPEAR
117 S.Ct. 1154 (1997)

Justice Scalia

This is a challenge to a biological opinion issued by the Fish and Wildlife Service in accordance with the Endangered Species Act of 1973 (ESA).

* * * * *

I

The ESA requires the Secretary of the Interior to promulgate regulations listing those species of animals that are "threatened" or "endangered" under specified criteria, and to designate their "critical habitat." [16 U.S.C. 1533] The ESA further requires each federal agency to "insure that any action authorized, funded, or carried out by such agency . . . is not likely to jeopardize the continued existence of any endangered species or threatened species or result in the destruction or adverse modification of habitat of such species which is determined by the Secretary . . . to be critical." [16 U.S.C. 1536]

* * * * *

The Klamath Project, one of the oldest federal reclamation schemes, is a series of lakes, rivers, dams, and irrigation canals in northern California and southern Oregon. The project was undertaken by the Secretary of the Interior pursuant to the Reclamation Act of 1902, and is administered by the Bureau of Reclamation. In 1992, the Bureau notified the Service that operation of the project might affect the Lost River Sucker and Shortnose Sucker, species of fish that were listed as endangered in 1988. After formal consultation with the Bureau, the Service issued a Biological Opinion which concluded that the " 'long-term operation of the Klamath Project was likely to jeopardize the continued existence of the Lost River and shortnose suckers.' " The Biological Opinion identified "reasonable and prudent alternatives" the Service believed would avoid jeopardy, which included the maintenance of minimum water levels on Clear Lake and Gerber reservoirs. The Bureau later notified the

Service that it intended to operate the project in compliance with the Biological Opinion.

Petitioners, two Oregon irrigation districts that receive Klamath Project water and the operators of two ranches within those districts, filed the present action against the director and regional director of the Service and the Secretary of the Interior . . . The complaint asserts that the Bureau "has been following essentially the same procedures for storing and releasing water from Clear Lake and Gerber reservoirs throughout the twentieth century," that "[t]here is no scientifically or commercially available evidence indicating that the populations of endangered suckers in Clear Lake and Gerber reservoirs have declined, are declining, or will decline as a result" of the Bureau's operation of the Klamath Project, that "[t]here is no commercially or scientifically available evidence indicating that the restrictions on lake levels imposed in the Biological Opinion will have any beneficial effect on the . . . populations of suckers in Clear Lake and Gerber reservoirs," and that the Bureau nonetheless "will abide by the restrictions imposed by the Biological Opinion."

* * * * *

The complaint asserts that petitioners' use of the reservoirs and related waterways for "recreational, aesthetic, and commercial purposes, as well as for their primary sources of irrigation water" will be "irreparably damaged" by the actions complained of, and that the restrictions on water delivery "recommended" by the Biological Opinion "adversely affect plaintiffs by substantially reducing the quantity of available irrigation water." In essence, petitioners claim a competing interest in the water the Biological Opinion declares necessary for the preservation of the suckers.

The District Court dismissed the complaint for lack of jurisdiction. It concluded that petitioners did not have standing because their "recreational, aesthetic, and commercial interests . . . do not fall within the zone of interests sought to be protected by ESA." The Court of Appeals for the Ninth Circuit affirmed. *Bennett* v. *Plenert,* 63 F.3d 915 (1995). It held that the "zone of interests" test limits the class of persons who may obtain judicial review under the citizen-suit provision of the ESA, and that "only plaintiffs who allege an interest in the *preservation* of endangered species fall within the zone of interests protected by the ESA." We granted certiorari.

In this Court, petitioners raise two questions: first, whether the prudential standing rule known as the "zone of interests" test applies to claims brought under the citizen-suit provision of the ESA; and second, if so, whether petitioners have standing under that test notwithstanding that the interests they seek to vindicate are economic rather than environmental . . .

II

We first turn to the question the Court of Appeals found dispositive: whether petitioners lack standing by virtue of the zone-of-interests test . . . To satisfy the "case" or "controversy" requirement of Article III, which is the "irreducible constitutional minimum" of standing, a plaintiff must, generally speaking, demonstrate that he has suffered "injury in fact," that the injury is "fairly traceable" to the actions of the defendant, and that the injury will likely be redressed by a favorable decision. In addition to the immutable requirements of Article III, "the federal judiciary has also adhered to a set of prudential principles that bear on the question of standing." Like their constitutional counterparts, these "judicially self-imposed limits on the exercise of federal jurisdiction," are "founded in concern about the proper—and properly limited—role of the courts in a democratic society," but unlike their constitutional counterparts, they can be modified or abrogated by Congress. Numbered among these prudential requirements is the doctrine of particular concern in this case: that a plaintiff's grievance must arguably fall within the zone of interests protected or regulated by the statutory provision or constitutional guarantee invoked in the suit.

* * * * *

The first question in the present case is whether the ESA's citizen-suit provision negates the zone-of-interests test (or, perhaps more accurately, expands the zone of interests). We think it does. The first operative portion of the provision says that "any person may commence a civil suit"—an authorization of remarkable breadth when compared with the language Congress ordinarily uses. Even in some other environmental statutes, Congress has used more restrictive formulations, such as "[any person] having an interest which is or may be adversely affected."

Our readiness to take the term "any person" at face value is greatly augmented by two interrelated considerations: that the overall subject matter of this legislation is the environment (a matter in which it is common to think all persons have an interest) and that the obvious purpose of the particular provision in question is to encourage enforcement by so-called "private attorneys general."

* * * * *

It is true that the plaintiffs here are seeking to prevent application of environmental restrictions rather than to implement them. But the "any person" formulation applies to all the causes of action authorized by § 1540(g)—not only to actions against private violators of environmental restrictions, and not only to actions against the Secretary asserting underenforcement under § 1533, but also to actions against the Secretary asserting overenforcement under § 1533.

* * * * *

[Part III, including the Court's analysis of 16 USC 1536 is omitted.]

IV

The foregoing analysis establishes that the principal statute invoked by petitioners, the ESA, does authorize review of their § 1533 claim, but does not support their claims based upon the Secretary's alleged failure to comply with § 1536. To complete our task, we must therefore inquire whether these § 1536 claims may nonetheless be brought under the Administrative Procedure Act (APA), which authorizes a court to "set aside agency action, findings, and conclusions found to be . . . arbitrary, capricious, an abuse of discretion, or otherwise not in accordance with law."

A

In determining whether the petitioners have standing under the zone-of-interests test to bring their APA claims, we look not to the terms of the ESA's citizen-suit provision, but to the substantive provisions of the ESA . . . 16 U.S.C. § 1536 requires, *inter alia,* that each agency "use the best scientific and commercial data available." Petitioners contend that the available scientific and commercial data show that the continued operation of the Klamath Project will not have a detrimental impact on the endangered suckers, that the imposition of minimum lake levels is not necessary to protect the fish, and that by issuing a Biological Opinion which makes unsubstantiated findings to the contrary the defendants have acted arbitrarily and in violation of § 1536(a)(2). The obvious purpose of the requirement that each agency "use the best scientific and commercial data available" is to ensure that the ESA not be implemented haphazardly . . . While this no doubt serves to advance the ESA's overall goal of species preservation, we think it readily apparent that another objective (if not indeed the primary one) is to avoid needless economic dislocation produced by agency officials zealously but unintelligently pursuing their environmental objectives. That economic consequences are an explicit concern of the Act is evidenced by § 1536(h), which provides exemption from § 1536(a)(2)'s no-jeopardy mandate where there are no reasonable and prudent alternatives to the agency action and the benefits of the agency action clearly outweigh the benefits of any alternatives. We believe the "best

scientific and commercial data" provision is similarly intended, at least in part, to prevent uneconomic (because erroneous) jeopardy determinations. Petitioners' claim that they are victims of such a mistake is plainly within the zone of interests that the provision protects.

[Reversed and remanded.]

Questions

1. Explain the Court's decision and the reasons for it.
2. The Clinton administration had sought a "one-way" interpretation of the law. What did they mean?
3. In your opinion, *should* economic considerations play a role in deciding what measures are taken to preserve endangered species?
4. The ESA forbids "harm" to protected species. In 1995, the Supreme Court ruled that the forbidden harm to protected species includes changes in habitat that injure wildlife. A lower court had ruled that harm involves only those situations where force is directly applied to animals. As a matter of public policy, which standard do you favor? Explain. See *Babbitt* v. *Sweet Home Chapter, Etc.,* 115 S.Ct. 2407 (1995).

Spotted Owls or Jobs?   The *Bennett* decision and the Endangered Species Act (ESA) are at the heart of one of the most interesting and poignant disputes of the long struggle between environmentalists and business. Should we save the Grizzly bear, nine populations of Pacific Northwest salmon, the Delhi Sands flower-loving fly? Each is among the nearly 1,200 species officially protected by the Endangered Species Act. Most Americans don't want to lose those creatures but as usual the question is, who pays? As written, the act effectively forces landowners to bear the cost because they must do what the government requires and the ESA forbids any practice, such as cutting trees, that results in the "taking" of any creature that is part of an endangered species. The ESA also forbids the degradation of the habitat of those species. As a result affected communities face a dramatic decline in the economic use of the property: no building, no logging, no pesticides, for example.

> Should we save the
> Grizzly bear?

The struggle was front-page news in the mid-1990s as tens of thousands of Pacific Northwest loggers struggled to retain their jobs while environmentalists fought to protect the habitat of the northern spotted owl. A compromise led to allowing logging on about one-third of the contested timberland under President Clinton's Northwest Forest Plan, but the issue reemerged in late 1999 when federal judge William Dwyer halted almost all cutting in the affected areas because federal agents were not, he believed, fulfilling their duty under the plan to conduct thorough surveys for rare plants and wildlife before logging could proceed. At this writing, a tentative settlement has been reached that would allow logging to resume.

Salmon or Jobs?   The remarkable spotted owl fight may pale before the struggle emerging over preserving salmon. A general scientific consensus has emerged that four lower Snake River dams have played a major role in the well-documented decline of the salmon population in the Pacific Northwest.[51] Federal officials are considering removing the earthen portions of those dams to allow 140 miles of the river to flow freely, thus greatly enhancing salmon migration. The $1 billion plan will probably end up in Congress where decisions must be made about balancing salmon-preservation with economic losses to eastern Washington and Idaho. Five percent of the region's hydroelectric power comes from the dams. Farmers depend on the dams for irrigation pools and for shipping their grain and fruit to market. Ralph Broetje's 4,000-acre apple and cherry orchard in eastern Washington, for example, employs 700 people full time and 600 part time.[52]

Perhaps Congress will find a more comfortable middle ground. Rules proposed in late 1999 for addressing the salmon-run problem suggest some flexibility on both sides of the debate. The rules provide a long list of exceptions to the "takings" standard noted above so that, for example, irrigation could continue if approved fish screens are used to keep young salmon out of canals and loggers could operate if they follow careful guidelines.

This debate, in the larger sense, is about what we want America to be. *Boston Globe* writer, Derrick Z. Jackson, better understood Judge Dwyer's order temporarily halting some Northwest logging after Jackson's summer 1999 hike through an old-growth forest in Oregon:

> Having the hike fresh in my mind, it was easy to understand the judge's caution as timber companies complained about big government. It is not just feeling so small and insignificant among Douglas firs that are 800 to 1,000 years old and nearly as tall as redwoods.
>
> It is the completeness of the forest, from the moss and lichens hanging from the trees to the dense carpet of ferns and underbrush at your feet. It is the deepest kind of green, a green that yielded to sunlight in only the most miserly, scant beams, obscuring the details that mark the little brown wrens that hopped along the branches.
>
> Alongside the trail the Salmon River gurgled, as clear as tap water. The answer to its clarity lay beneath my feet. The forest floor of packed-down leaves and needles, ancient root systems, and massive piles of decayed rubble from previous generations of Douglas firs and Western red cedars filters the mountain runoff and allows no soil to erode, even in the heaviest storms.
>
> "Old growth is not essential to the functioning of the earth," Jerry Franklin, the University of Washington ecologist and one of the first environmentalists to study old growth, once said. "I view old growth somewhat like I view museums or libraries or universities. They increase the richness of our life here. The world could survive without them, but it would be a much poorer place."[53]

[For more on the Endangered Species Act, see **http://www.wri.org/wri/biodiv/esa-info.html**] [For the National Wildlife Federation home page, see **http://www.nwf.org/nwf/index.htm**]

Questions

1. Please comment on the following from Forester William Wade Keye:

> Even within the broader vision of ecosystem management, the national forests' use still includes timber, recreation, water and many other benefits both economic and aesthetic. With disproportionate power to extremists, national forest management is being stripped of its ability to optimize comprehensive social benefits.

Blasphemous as it may be to some, there is an appropriate and sustainable level of timber harvest and use of our national forests. We don't need to worship forests or study them to death. We need a forestry program that is inclusive of competing interests but able to forge ahead with a strong, science-based effort. After all, our consumption of forest products hasn't declined. America is currently replacing lost wood supply with imports, despite the fact that we have some of the world's most extensive and productive public forest resources.[54]

2. Reducing lawn fertilizers and retarding development near waterways would be helpful in saving the endangered salmon. In order to save those salmon, should we limit citizens' rights to live as they see fit and as they can afford to live? Explain.

STATE AND LOCAL REGULATION

Under their constitutionally authorized police powers, state and local governments have the right to impose various controls on citizens to protect and maintain the public health, safety, and general welfare. State and local governments have become increasingly aggressive in pursuing environmental concerns. At the same time, they face the same conflicts troubling federal regulators. As a result, a number of states have passed laws to protect companies from penalties and required public disclosures when they discover environmental wrongs at their own plants. The idea is to encourage self-policing, but federal law permits state enforcement under statutes such as the Clean Water Act only so long as that enforcement equals federal standards.[55] Similarly, about half of the states have enacted some form of property rights protection designed to block government regulatory takings (such as restricting logging or limiting development in wetlands) without just compensation. [For more information on regulatory takings and environmental protection, see the Environmental Policy Project at **http://www.envpoly.org/index.htm**]

Part Four—Remedies Other than Legislation

A Modest Proposal

One major component of a federal privatization agenda would be to sell off federal enterprises and assets . . . Not national parks and wilderness areas, but supposedly income-producing "commodity lands" administered by the Bureau of Land Management and the U.S. Forest Service. A 1989 Reason Foundation study estimated their value at $160 billion. Environmentalists would go ballistic, but in fact some of the most successful examples of ecologically sensitive resource development occur in privately owned commercial forests and wilderness areas owned by environmental groups. Given the feds' dismal record in managing grazing and timber lands, enlightened environmentalists might see net gains in some form of privatization.

Source: Robert Poole, "The Asset Test: A Privatization Agenda," *Reason Magazine,* February 1995, p. 34.

THE COMMON LAW

Long before the federal government became actively involved in environmental issues, courts were grappling with the problem. As early as the 1500s, city officials were ordered by a court to keep the streets clean of dung deposited by swine allowed to run loose; the air was said to be "corrupted and infected" by this practice. Legal arguments have typically revolved around the right of a person to use and enjoy private or public property if such usage causes harm to a neighbor's property.

The doctrines of nuisance and trespass are paramount in common law environmental litigation. A private nuisance is a substantial and unreasonable invasion of the private use and enjoyment of one's land; a public nuisance is an unreasonable interference with a right common to the public. Harmful conduct may be both a public and private nuisance simultaneously; the case law distinctions between the two are often blurred. A trespass occurs and liability is imposed with *any* intentional invasion of an individual's right to the exclusive use of his or her own property.

The distinction between trespass and nuisance is fine, and the two may be coextensive. Nuisance and trespass causes of action have been entered for such offenses as fouling a neighbor's water, flooding another's land, or causing excessive noise, smell, or particulate matter on another's property. The remedies available to a successful plaintiff are monetary damages for the harm suffered or an injunction to prevent similar conduct by the defendant in the future, or both.

Negligence and strict liability claims may also arise from pollution cases. For example, a company might well be guilty of negligence if it failed to correct a pollution problem where the technology and necessary resources were available to do so, and that failure caused harm to someone to whom the company owed a duty. In addition, certain activities, such as the use of toxic chemicals, might be so abnormally dangerous as to provoke a strict liability claim.

Common law pollution remedies, although taking a backseat to federal and state laws, remain useful tools in addressing environmental harm.

THE FREE MARKET

Having surveyed our legal mechanisms for addressing environmental problems, let's return to the free market theme raised early in the chapter. Our steady, even spectacular, strides forward in environmental protection have not dispelled the view, particularly among economists and businesspeople, that legislation is sometimes not the best remedy for environmental problems. To them, pollution control is not so much a matter of law as of economics. They believe that with proper incentives, the market will, in many instances, prove superior to legislation in preventing and correcting environmental problems.

Pollution Credits.   Improvements are sometimes achieved when the government itself employs free market tactics. The most prominent and successful such effort is the market in pollution credits. The federal government decided in the early 1990s to cut air pollution from utilities and some big factories without fining them or imposing new technology requirements. Rather, the government set a cap on the number of tons of pollutants to be permitted in the air. Then pollution credits were issued to several hundred of the biggest power plants and certain factories. These "dirty" plants can either buy expensive new equipment to cut emissions or they can buy pollution credits from clean companies that do not need them. The result is that pollution has declined substantially since the total credits available are lower than total emissions before the program began.[56] Electric utilities in 1999 produced about 41 percent more electricity than in 1980, while emitting 25 percent fewer tons of sulfur dioxide.[57] The same principles are expected to be applied worldwide to greenhouse gases, principally carbon dioxide, which are believed to cause global warming.[58] [For more on market-based approaches to environmental problems, see **http://www.free-eco.org/index.html**] [Or see **http://www.reason.org/ environment.html**]

The Globe's Biggest Carbon-Dioxide Producers

Annual Carbon-Dioxide Emissions		
	Total Tons (millions)	*Tons per Capita*
U.S.	5,475	20.52
China	3,196	2.68
Russian Federation	1,820	12.26
Japan	1,126	9.03
India	910	0.90

Source: "The Globe's Dirty Dozen," *The Wall Street Journal,* October 3, 1999, p. A5.

Subsidies.   Even as the United States appears to be making headway on market-based pollution strategies, other government interventions, such as subsidies, often directly harm the environment. A 1996 Worldwatch Institute report estimates that government subsidies cost taxpayers/consumers some $500 billion annually. Most such programs are laudably intended to preserve industries, aid the poor, spur economic growth, and so on. Unfortunately, subsidies often degrade the environment while elevating taxes by perhaps 7 percent annually.[59]

For example, the burden we bear in fouled air and other environmental degradation is increased dramatically because, in the United States, we subsidize the cost of fuel by about 70 cents per gallon, thus encouraging more driving.[60]

Cost-Benefit.   A key ingredient in a market-based approach to environmental protection lies in weighing costs and benefits. In many instances, emotions and politics seem to be the only explanations for some of our environmental expenditures. For example,

> the cost for each otter saved by the cleanup of Alaska's Prince William Sound after the Exxon Valdez oil spill is a reported $80,000

the cost for each otter saved by the cleanup of Alaska's Prince William Sound after the Exxon Valdez oil spill is a reported $80,000.[61] Are they worth the price? Apparently out of fear of lawsuits, we continue to spend about $3 billion per year in removing asbestos from buildings even though "incontrovertible scientific evidence" shows that the cancer-causing risk from cancer in buildings is so low, it is barely measurable.[62] "A person who spends a career inside a building rich with asbestos materials is more likely to die of a lightning bolt, a bee sting or a toothpick lodged in the throat than an asbestos-related cancer."[63]

Questions

1. Suggested free market incentives for pollution control include government taxes or fees on pollution and government rules mandating refundable deposits on hazardous materials. Explain how those incentives would work.
2. A *Wall Street Journal* editorial commenting on a market for pollution rights:

   > The best news about the introduction of a market for rights to avoid compliance is that the public will finally get a precise measure of the cost of environmental rules. Once that is known, voters can decide if the price is worth the result, or if the law should be changed to comply with what the public is willing to pay.[64]

   Are we paying too much for environmental protection? Explain.

Part Five—The Business Response

We complete this chapter by thinking about how the business community should respond to the environmental challenge. Clearly, both legal and market forces must play roles in environmental protection, but likewise the business community has a heavy managerial/ethical burden. Terrible problems remain, especially in less-developed nations around the world, but corporate progress is obvious. Consider just a pair of examples. In 1999, Home Depot announced that it would no longer sell wood or wood products from threatened, "old-growth" forests,[65] and Mobil announced, at a global warming discussion, that within economic limits "a responsible company should reduce its emissions."[66] Interestingly, Mobil's merger partner, Exxon, has long challenged the legitimacy of the global warming theory.[67] Of course, environmental responsiveness from companies like Home Depot and Mobil is often generated by market pressure. Being seen as "green" by consumers—or at least as something other than an environmental predator—is an important ingredient in contemporary business strategy. Nonetheless, the big question remains, does the market reward sound environmental practices? We cannot yet be sure, but an interesting recent study found a strong relationship between environmental high performance and high profitability.[68] Some companies simply comply with the environmental laws while others take affirmative steps to improve their environmental performance. The authors theorize that the latter companies build more skillful workers by expecting them to cope with the complexities of the "clean technologies." Prevention and improvement are more complicated than mere compliance so perhaps the environmentally active firms are actually building their performance "muscles" by their activist approach while the compliance firms are expending their energies on the external world in an effort to fend off new rules.

Certainly we must remain a bit skeptical about Americans' willingness to pay more for products and services in order to meet "green" goals, but at least in the polls, the public is zealous in its commitment to the environment.[69] The combination of an ethical approach by some managers, market forces, and government rules have had a dramatic impact in cleansing America as so vividly evidenced by the renewal of our nation's urban rivers:

Last week the *New York Times* chronicled the extraordinary rebirth of the Hudson River in one of the world's most heavily urbanized areas. Thirty years ago, the Hudson's fish were gone, and the river was called dead. "River trout" was the local term for human feces, and children skipped stones off floating industrial scum.

Today, the Hudson teems with striped bass. Sturgeon, oysters, blue crabs, harbor seals, and porpoises are back. Bald eagles (thanks also to the Endangered Species Act) soar overhead. Long-abandoned waterfronts are hot properties and communities plan boathouses and swimming areas.[70]

In late 1999, the citizens of Libby, Montana, met in the school gymnasium to talk about deaths they believe were caused by decades of exposure to asbestos fibers in the vermiculite ore they had been mining in the nearby mountains:

A newspaper investigation last month revealed that at least 192 people have died of asbestos-related diseases from the mine near Libby, owned for 27 years by the W.R. Grace Co. At least another 375 have been diagnosed with fatal diseases. The articles also detailed how federal, state and local agencies had not stepped forward to help the people of Libby, either denying knowledge of the problem or pointing toward other agencies for solutions.

Source: Andrew Schneider, "Mining Town Bares Its 'Dirty Little Secret' About Death," *Des Moines Register*, December 5, 1999, p. 1AA.

INTERNET EXERCISE

Using the EPA's "Superfund Reforms" webpage [**http://www.epa.gov/oerrpage/superfund/programs/reforms/faqs.htm**] answer the following questions:

1. How have the Superfund reforms changed the Superfund program?
2. Since EPA has improved the program through reforms, does Congress still need to pass a new Superfund law?

CHAPTER QUESTIONS

1. Ott Chemical Co. polluted the ground at its Michigan plant. CPC International created a wholly owned subsidiary to buy Ott, which was accomplished in 1965. CPC retained the original Ott managers. Pollution continued through 1972 when CPC sold Ott. In 1981, the United States EPA began a cleanup of the site. To recover some of the tens of millions in cleanup costs, the EPA sued CPC (now called Bestfoods) among other potentially responsible parties. The Superfund law places responsibility on anyone who "owned or operated" a property when pollution was deposited. The district court held that CPC was liable because of its active participation in Ott's business and its control of Ott's decisions in that it selected the Ott board of directors and placed some CPC managers as executives at Ott.

   a. Was the district court correct in holding CPC liable? Explain.

   b. What test would you employ to determine whether a parent corporation should be liable for a subsidiary's pollution? See *United States* v. *Bestfoods,* 524 U.S. 51 (1998).

2. Economist B. Peter Pashigian:

   It is widely thought that environmental controls are guided by the public-spirited ideal of correcting for "negative externalities"—the pollution costs that spill over from private operations. This view is not wrong by any means. But it is suspiciously incomplete.

   After all, there are numerous studies of regulatory programs in other fields that show how private interests have used public powers for their own enrichment.[71]

   What forces in addition to correcting for negative externalities might be influencing the course of federal pollution control?

3. William Tucker:

   [Environmentalism is] essentially aristocratic in its roots and derives from the land- and nature-based ethic that has been championed by upper classes throughout history. Large landowners and titled aristocracies . . . have usually held a set of ideals that stresses "stewardship" and the husbanding of existing resources over exploration and discovery. This view favors handicrafts over mass production and the inheritance ethic over the business ethic.[72]

   Tucker went on to argue that environmentalism favors the economic and social interests of the well-off. He said people of the upper middle class see their future in universities and the government bureaucracy, with little economic stake in industrial expansion. Indeed, such expansion might threaten their suburban property values. Comment.

4. Professor and business ethics scholar, Norman Bowie:

   Environmentalists frequently argue that business has special obligations to protect the environment. Although I agree with the environmentalists on this point, I do not agree with them as to where the obligations lie. Business does not have an obligation to protect the environment over and above what is required by law; however, business does have a moral obligation to avoid intervening in the political arena in order to defeat or weaken environmental legislation.[73]

   a. Explain Professor Bowie's reasoning.

   b. Do you agree with him? Explain.

5. Economist Robert Crandall:

   [O]ur best chances for regulatory reform in certain environmental areas, particularly in air pollution policy, come from the states. Probably, responsibility for environmental regulation belongs with the states anyway, and most of it ought to be returned there.[74]

   a. What reasoning supports Crandall's notion that responsibility for environmental regulation belongs with the states?

   b. How might one reason to the contrary?

   c. If the power were yours, would environmental regulation rest primarily at the state or the federal level? Explain.

6. Why do plaintiffs typically experience great difficulty in prevailing in negligence actions alleging injury from toxic substances?

7. The doctrine of strict liability—originally applied to extrahazardous activities and more recently to defective products—could be extended to the area of toxic waste. Jeremy Main commented on that possibility in *Fortune* magazine:

   If strict liability were now extended to toxic wastes, then it would do a company no good to plead that it had obeyed the laws and followed approved procedures when it disposed of its wastes. It would still be liable, even if the hazards are seen only in retrospect.[75]

Should the strict liability doctrine routinely be extended to toxic waste cases? Explain.

8. The Pennsylvania Coal Company owned coal land in the drainage basin of the Meadow Brook. The company's mining operation released water into the brook, thus polluting it. Sanderson owned land near the stream, and she had been securing water from it. However, the mining operation rendered the stream useless for Sanderson's purposes. Sanderson filed suit against the coal company. In 1886, a final verdict was rendered in the case. Should Sanderson prevail? [See *Pennsylvania Coal Co.* v. *Sanderson and Wife,* 6 A. 453 (1886).]

9. Gaston operated a metal smelter that functioned under a pollution permit governing how much of the smelter's pollution could lawfully enter a nearby lake. Two environmental groups sued the smelter for allegedly violating its discharge permit. The suit was brought on behalf of downstream water users who feared they were being exposed to dangerous chemicals. The case was dismissed by the Fourth Circuit Court of Appeals. Explain why the case was dismissed. [See *Friends of the Earth, Inc.* v. *Gaston Copper Recycling,* 179 F.3d 107 (4th Cir. 1999).]

10. Americans' commitment to the car obviously raises serious environmental problems. The vast parking areas required to house those cars are themselves a significant environmental hazard. Explain some of the environmental problems created or encouraged by parking lots.

11. The Endangered Species Act provides that all federal agency actions are to be designed such that they do not jeopardize endangered or threatened species. The act had been interpreted to reach to federal agency work or funding in foreign countries, but the federal government changed that interpretation in 1986 to limit the act's reach to the United States and the high seas. A group labeled Defenders of Wildlife filed suit, seeking to reinstate the original interpretation. The case reached the U.S. Supreme Court, where Justice Scalia wrote that Defenders of Wildlife would have to submit evidence showing that at least one of its members would be "directly" affected by the interpretation. In response, one member of Defenders of Wildlife wrote that she had visited Egypt and observed the endangered Nile crocodile and hoped to return to do so again but feared that U.S. aid with the Aswan High Dam would harm the crocodiles.

   a. Why did Scalia call for that evidence?
   b. Decide the case. Explain.
      [See *Lujan* v. *Defenders of Wildlife,* 112 S.Ct. 2130 (1992).]

12. Worldwatch Institute, an environmental group, says: "Food-production subsidies and market controls in Western industrial countries cost consumer–taxpayers $302 billion in 1995, an average of $1,500 a year for a family of four."[76] What *environmental* harm comes from these policies?

13. How might the government's ever-increasing environmental regulations, along with the public's call for a new environmental consciousness, favor big-business interests over those of small-business owners?

14. Some argue that so-called frost belt states will be particularly insistent on maintaining strict air-quality standards for new emission sources.

   a. Other than general concern for air quality, why would the frost belt states have a particular interest in maintaining those standards?
   b. Might the frost belt states be expected to modify that stand over time? Explain.

NOTES

1. Kelly Flaherty, "The Exxon Valdez Spill: 10 Years Later," *The Recorder,* March 24, 1999, News, p. 1.

2. Wilfred Beckerman, cited in Robert Solomon, *The New World of Business* (Lanham, MD: Rowman & Littlefield, 1994), p. 319.

3. Mark Gillespie, "U.S. Public Worries about Toxic Waste, Air and Water Pollution as Key Environment Threats,"

Gallup News Service, March 25, 1999 [**http://www.gallup.com/poll/releases/pr990325.asp**].

4. Ibid.

5. Ibid.

6. John J. Fialka, "Gore Faces Cool Response to Issue of Global Warming," *The Wall Street Journal,* August 26, 1997, p. A18.

7. *Los Angeles Times,* "Many Consumers Will Pay More for 'Green' Energy, Study Shows," *Waterloo–Cedar Falls Courier,* July 13, 1997, p. B2.

8. Lydia Saad, "Environmental Concern Wanes in 1999 Earth Day Poll," Gallup News Service, April 22, 1999 [**http://www.gallup.com/poll/releases/pr990422.asp**].

9. Ibid.

10. Susan Moffat, "Asia Stinks," *Fortune,* December 9, 1996, p. 120.

11. Ibid.

12. Michael Astor, "New Ideas Keep Amazon Alive," *Des Moines Register,* August 21, 1999, p. 4A.

13. Ibid.

14. Hugh Pope, "Uzbeks Manage to Endure Amid Ruins of the Aral Sea," *The Wall Street Journal,* February 5, 1998, p. A18.

15. Bill Corporon, "Product of Politics, Kyoto Pact Sidesteps Science, Economics," *The Lamp,* Summer 1998, p. 8.

16. Ibid.

17. George Will, "Earth Isn't Hanging in a Precarious Balance," *Des Moines Register,* December 4, 1999, p. 9A.

18. Editorial, "Energy Use Static Even with Growth," *Waterloo–Cedar Falls Courier,* December 28, 1999, p. A7.

19. Traci Watson, "EPA Orders 12 States to Cut Pollution," *USA Today,* June 15, 1999, p. 11A.

20. "Proposed 'Tier 2' Emission Standards for Vehicles and Gasoline Sulfur Standards for Refineries," [**http://www.epa.gov/oms/consumer/f99010.htm**].

21. Philip Brasher, "Snowmobiles, ATVs to Fall Under EPA Emission Standards," *Des Moines Register,* February 19, 1999, p. 3A.

22. Environmental Protection Agency Priorities, [**http://ciir.cs.umass.edu/ciirdemo/. . . 8/web_pages/ priority/pfile-14.html**]

23. Ibid.

24. Sector Facility Indexing Project Fact Sheet, [**http://es.epa.gov/oeca/sfi/factsht.htm**].

25. David Stout, "7 Utilities Sued by U.S. on Charges of Polluting Air," *New York Times,* November 4, 1999, p. A1.

26. Micheline Maynard, "Ford Vows Cleaner Trucks," *USA Today,* May 18, 1999, p. 1B.

27. Jayne O'Donnell, "Air Pollution Claim Costs Honda $17M," *USA Today,* June 9, 1998, p. 1B.

28. Richard Perez-Pena, "Pataki to Impose Strict New Limits on Auto Emissions," *New York Times,* November 7, 1999, Sec. 1, p. 1.

29. Ibid.

30. Jayne O'Donnell, "Trucks Will Have to Meet Clean-Air Rule," *USA Today,* December 21, 1999, p. 1B.

31. Campion Walsh, "The Regulatory Toll," *The Wall Street Journal,* September 13, 1999, p. R9.

32. "Emissions Regulations Pay Off," *USA Today,* December 21, 1999, p. 1B.

33. Editorial, "The Cost of Cleaner Air Is Well Worth Paying," *USA Today,* November 29, 1996, p. 12A.

34. Jeff Nesmith, "Most Major Rivers Seriously Degraded, a Commission Finds," *Des Moines Register,* November 30, 1999, p. 4A.

35. Press Release, "President Clinton Announces New Actions to Clean Up Polluted Waters," *Environmental News,* August 16, 1999.

36. Perry Beeman, "Gulf Damage Blamed on Iowa Farmers," *Des Moines Register,* August 16, 1999, p. 1A.

37. Masood Farivar, "EPA Fights Underground-Tank Leaks," *The Wall Street Journal,* November 16, 1998, p. B71.

38. Associated Press, "Study: More Than Half World Rivers in Peril," *Waterloo–Cedar Falls Courier,* November 29, 1999, p. A1.

39. Bernard Gavzer, "Take Out the Trash, and Put It. . . Where?" *Parade Magazine,* June 13, 1999, p. 4.

40. Ibid.

41. Ibid.

42. Ibid.

43. Jeff Bailey, "Curbside Recycling Comforts the Soul, but Benefits Are Scant," *The Wall Street Journal,* January 19, 1995, p. A1.

44. Scripps-Howard News Service, "White House Delays Notice of Welfare Cuts," *Waterloo–Cedar Falls Courier,* September 15, 1996, p. F3.

45. Tom Bliley, "Superfund Law Needs a Cleanup," *Washington Post,* August 16, 1999, p. A15.

46. Ibid.

47. Editorial, "Needed: Superfund Cleanup," *Omaha World-Herald,* November 26, 1999, p. 26.

48. Ibid.

49. John J. Fialka and Carl Quintanilla, "Diesel-Engine Makers Agree to Penalty Over $1 Billion in EPA Pollution Case," *The Wall Street Journal,* October 23, 1998, p. A6.

50. Richard Winton, "Firms to Pay $200 Million to Clean Up Water Supply," *Los Angeles Times,* September 16, 1999, p. B1.

51. Fredreka Schouten, "Dam-Breaking Idea Spawns Fierce Debate About Fish," *USA Today,* November 24, 1999, p. 22A.

52. Ibid.

53. Derrick Z. Jackson, "We Could Live Without the Old-Growth Forest, but Life Would Be Poorer," *Boston Globe,* September 1, 1999, p. A23.

54. William Wade Keye, "Forest Puritans Want It All," *San Francisco Chronicle,* October 15, 1999, p. A27.

55. John H. Cushman, Jr., "Many States Give Polluting Firms New Protections," *New York Times,* April 7, 1996, sec. 1, p. 1.

56. Mark Golden, "Dirty Dealings," *The Wall Street Journal,* September 13, 1999, p. R13.

57. Ibid.

58. Ibid.

59. Associated Press, "Report Urges Smarter Planning of Subsidies to Aid Environment," *Des Moines Register,* December 8, 1996, p. 4A.

60. Ibid.

61. Editorial, "Ignorance Makes Success of Oil Cleanup Hard to Gauge," *USA Today,* March 24, 1999, p. 24A.

62. Dennis Cauchon, "Risk of Cancer in USA Is Barely Measurable," *USA Today,* February 11, 1999, p. 1A.

63. Ibid.

64. "Efficient-Markets Pollution," *The Wall Street Journal,* March 2, 1992, p. A12.

65. Associated Press, "Home Depot Ends Sale of Wood from Endangered Areas," *Waterloo–Cedar Falls Courier,* August 27, 1999, p. D6.

66. Steve Liesman, "Mobil, Exxon Like Oil, Water on Air Pollution," *The Wall Street Journal,* May 24, 1999, p. B1.

67. Ibid.

68. Michael V. Russo and Paul A. Fouts, "A Resource-Based Perspective on Corporate Environmental Performance and Profitability," *Academy of Management Journal* 40, no. 3 (1997), p. 534.

69. Cathy Young, "Property Compensation a Winning Issue," *Detroit News,* December 17, 1996, p. A9.

70. Jessica Mathews, "Results of Environmental Laws Are Clear," *Waterloo–Cedar Falls Courier,* June 19, 1996, p. A6.

71. B. Peter Pashigian, "How Large and Small Plants Fare under Environmental Regulation," *Regulation,* March–April 1983, p. 19.

72. "Tucker Contra Sierra," *Regulation,* March–April 1983, pp. 48–49.

73. Norman Bowie, with Kenneth Goodpaster, "Corporate Conscience, Money and Motorcars," in *Business Ethics Report, Highlights of Bentley College's Eighth National Conference on Business Ethics,* ed. Peter Kent, 1989, pp. 4, 6.

74. Robert Crandall, "The Environment," in "Regulation—The First Year," *Regulation,* January–February 1982, pp. 19, 29, 31.

75. Jeremy Main, "The Hazards of Helping Toxic Waste Victims," *Fortune* 108, no. 9 (October 31, 1983), pp. 158, 166.

76. Associated Press, "Report Urges Smarter Planning of Subsidies to Aid Environment," *Des Moines Register,* December 8, 1996, p. 4A.

Chapter 18

Internet Law and Ethics

INTRODUCTION: LAW AND THE MARKET

The Internet has changed our lives. The extraordinary power of nearly instantaneous communication around the globe promises remarkable advances, but at the same time, new challenges are emerging. Broadly, policy makers are concerned about the degree to which we need to impose the force of law on Internet activities. The question is familiar: Can we count on the free market and ethics to govern Internet conduct or are government rules necessary? Put another way, which model is best for the Internet—no regulation, government regulation, self-regulation, or some combination of the three? [For links to many Internet law websites, see **http://www.willyancey.com/internet–law.htm**]

Certainly the law will play a great role in the future of the Internet. Experience confirms that a framework of law will be necessary for predictability, efficiency, and trust in the new global economy. Many of the problems of law that have become routine in the conventional commercial world must now be revisited in the virtual world. Digital signatures, privacy, trademark infringement, freedom of speech, fraud, and (probably the biggest battleground) taxes are among the big issues that are likely to require attention from the law. The question, of course, is how much law? In general, the United States hopes to rely largely on the market and the immense, innovative power of freedom. Of course, even the firmest free market advocates recognize the necessity for clear contractual principles and effective means to prevent fraud and other criminal behavior. [For a pair of electronic privacy advocates, see **www.epic.org** and **www.eff.org**]

A 1999 *USA Today*/Gallup Poll asked: ". . . [P]lease say whether you think the federal government should do more to regulate violence [on the Internet], whether it should do less or if it is doing the right amount?"

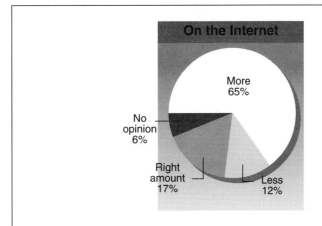

Source: Julie Stacey, "Is the Government Doing Enough?" *USA Today,* May 4, 1999, p. 6D.

The Internet is often referred to as the new Wild West, and American leaders hope to retain all of the creativity and energy that the name implies. The European Union, on the other hand, is somewhat more willing to impose rules on Internet behavior. Thus, for many American business and public sector leaders, the key regulatory question is how to maintain the vigor of the free market while establishing a limited array of binding legal standards that will bring consistency to the global Internet market. Steve Case, CEO of America Online explained: "Without such a new international framework, e-commerce will prove to be destabilizing and conflict inducing, rather than emerging as the new glue that binds nations, and the new fuel that expands world and regional economies."[1] The article that follows examines many of the difficult issues facing policy makers in deciding the future of the Internet.

TAMING THE WILD, WILD WEST

Stephen Baker

It appeared to be an open-and-shut case involving nude pictures of a French model—reprinted without her permission. But these photos were posted on the Internet. No sooner did Estelle Hallyday win a copyright-infringement suit last spring than things got complicated.

A French judge used a 40-year-old publishing law to slap AlternB, the company hosting the offending website, with a $70,000 fine. AlternB promptly responded by shutting down its server, which hosted 4,000 websites. Then it threatened to lead a migration of French e-businesses to friendlier jurisdictions. Soon, "Keep the

Net Free" groups rallied on the Web to AlternB's defense. Sites around the world thumbed their noses at the French courts by plastering the images of Hallyday all over cyberspace.

In the end, Hallyday reached an out-of-court settlement with AlternB, which agreed to give $7,000 to her favorite charity. By that time, her property and privacy were irretrievable, and French law was moot. On the Internet, says cybervisionary Esther Dyson, "Things are moving a lot faster than governments realize."

And how. In the early stages of the Industrial Revolution, coping with the technological and legal issues was a fairly forgiving process. If train tracks were different widths in France and Spain or travelers had to carry electrical converters to deal with different voltages, no big deal. But the Internet zips information across borders with the click of a mouse. The speed and scale are immense challenges for the rule of law. "We're having problems of pornography distribution to minors, violations of intellectual-property rights, potential violations of privacy, and new types of crime," says Ira Magaziner, the architect of the White House Internet strategy. "We've got to move quickly to get them addressed in real time so we don't engender a reaction against the Internet."

Bringing law and order to the Wild West of cyberspace will be a tall order. Without broad international agreements, the sheriffs, judges, regulators, and tax collectors are easily given the slip. That's why the settlers—not just the lawmakers—will have to play a large role in taming this frontier. Business, in particular, has little choice but to come up with its own system of rules if it wants to protect property rights and get customers to feel comfortable online. For better or worse, the Net is spawning two parallel and sometimes contending regimes for regulation.

The success of the two regimes—public and private—will determine how powerful the Net becomes. To develop into the world's largest marketplace, the Net must provide the same guarantees as any marketplace, from the rights of property-holders to the power of short-changed consumers to get refunds. In short, before societies en masse start buying cars and taking out mortgages online, they'll need to ensure customers that their transactions are secure and legally binding. A Forrester Research Inc. study predicts that the global Internet economy will reach

$3.2 trillion in 2003 if it is managed well—but less than half as much if security and regulatory snarls persist.

Hung Up

It's not that regulators aren't trying. Negotiators at the Organization for Economic Cooperation & Development in Paris have been working on the most basic tenets of Internet Law for two years—eons in Internet time. And they continue to get hung up over liability and jurisdiction. If a Japanese website with its server in the U.S. defrauds a customer in Canada, whose laws count? This year it seemed that the European Commission had ironed out an agreement on jurisdiction for its e-commerce directive. Then negotiators allowed for one seemingly small change: Customers would rely on consumer-protection regulations in sellers' home countries. This would force e-merchants to wrestle with dozens of different laws. A business uproar scotched the deal. "It's the exception that ate the rule," laments Microsoft Corp. attorney Peter Fleischer.

For business, the search for solutions starts, not surprisingly, with technology. An entire industry is growing around security, mainly software programs designed to keep hackers, thieves, or even government tax snoops, from infiltrating Web bank accounts, e-mails, or corporate purchasing networks. "It's a terrifying, brave new world," says Peter R. Beverley, managing director of Magex, an e-commerce security company in London. And every time a hacker makes the news, the market for protection programs heats up.

At the same time, e-merchants know that technology alone provides scant comfort against gifted hackers and organized criminals. To allay fears, e-businesses are likely to start certifying safe sites. These would be industry seals of approval for sites meeting standards ranging from privacy to high-tech encryption of customers' or business partners' financial or health data. Eventually, website rating agencies similar to debt-rating agencies are likely to emerge. In such a scheme, a security downgrade on a major e-merchant could prompt investors, customers, or business partners to flee.

Hornet's Nest

It may be a while before governments can mete out such punishments. In the U.S., a national commission on

Internet taxation is studying collection methods—but is deadlocked on whether Net transactions should be taxed at all. And the latest global efforts are faring no better. The nonprofit, quasi-government Internet Corporation for Assigned Names & Numbers (ICANN) has already stirred up a hornet's nest just by trying to manage the Web's addressing system.

Basically, governments are torn because making e-commerce secure seals out police who want to keep an eye on crime. In the U.S., for example, the National Security Agency wants to limit access to the world's top cryptography, and leave open access "keys" to encrypted computer systems; the fear is that cartels and terrorists, protected by a maze of code, will be able to conduct drug deals and plot assassinations with impunity on the Net. Meanwhile, the Japanese government may soon permit police to intercept e-mail. Russia forces Internet service providers to install hotlines to the Federal Security Bureau so agents can keep an eye on traffic.

Cultural differences rankle, too. Take the privacy battle between the U.S. and Europe, which wants strong rules to protect privacy in cyberspace. Europeans still harbor vivid memories of the Gestapo and Stasi amassing files on citizens. But what good is protecting a Dane's privacy in Denmark, if e-merchants in Kuala Lumpur are creating a profile based on her bank statements and video preferences? The European Union is enacting a rule to prohibit export of data, such as airline frequent-flyer information, to countries that don't meet European standards. That would include the U.S., where much of the data flow is protected by the Constitution.

Privacy may be the best example yet of how difficult it is to harness both private and public interests in regulation. For the past year, Europe and the U.S., the two biggest e-economies, have been negotiating a joint standard for protecting privacy. The U.S. proposal would set up a self-regulatory body to create "safe harbors" for e-businesses that adhere to Europe's standards. For now, the result is a regulatory vacuum. "E-companies in Europe are not complying with Europe's law," says Clive Mayhew-Begg, international vice-president at CDNOW.com, a leading online music business.

So Europe's law, like so many other attempts, promises only to disrupt e-commerce until it becomes world law, which is a long way off. Battles like this could rage for decades as the wild frontier of cyberspace gradually grows civilized. "There are no silver bullets, either legislative or technological," says Paul Saffo, director of the Institute for the Future in Menlo Park, Calif. "The way through this swamp is with a lot of small, comparatively weak solutions acting in concert." E-businesses may find out what it was like to run a sagebrush saloon before the law rode into town.

Source: *Business Week*, October 4, 1999, p. 154. Reprinted by permission.

Questions

1. According to the Internet article
   a. Why is speed in putting regulations in place important to the long-term success of the Internet?
   b. Which two guarantees to consumers are necessary before the Internet can begin to realize its full commercial potential?
   c. How is the market reacting to begin providing protection against hackers, fraud, and crime of all kinds on the Internet?
2. a. Germany, France, the Netherlands, and Austria have laws that allow publishing groups to specify the price at which new books are to be sold at retail. That is, anyone selling one of those books at retail in those countries must sell it at the

price specified by publishers or they won't be supplied with the books. Why would those countries support price fixing in book sales?

b.   Germany's *Rabattgesetz* (discount law) requires that all customers pay precisely the same price for a product. Thus an Internet concept like *Priceline.com* where buyers specify a price they are willing to pay for a product is unlawful. Why would Germany insist on identical pricing for products?

c.   How would you expect the Internet to affect those laws forbidding discounts on books and other products? See Neal Boudette, "In Europe, Surfing a Web of Red Tape," *The Wall Street Journal,* October 29, 1999, p. B1.

INTRODUCTION: ETHICS

So we see that market forces and law will blend in some uncertain, emerging formula to provide the security and confidence necessary for effective e-commerce. Now we ask what role ethics, that is, self-regulation, can play in this equation. The anonymity, the speed, the elusiveness, and the global vastness of the Internet all suggest very difficult new ethical problems (or perhaps old problems in a new venue). Some of those problems such as privacy, consumer fraud, and crime of all kinds will be discussed separately later in this chapter. In this introduction, let's take a brief look at a pair of ethics and social responsibility problems (see Chapters 2 and 3) that are raising concerns in virtual commerce much like the concerns we are now addressing in conventional business practice. [For Harvard University's Berkman Center for Internet and Society, see **http://cyber.law.harvard.edu/**]

Selected Ethical Dilemmas

Access.   New data raise the fear that the Internet may further broaden the income/wealth gap that splits not only Americans but the globe. A 1999 United States Department of Commerce study shows that in-home computer availability is highest, at 80 percent, among Americans making $75,000 or more annually and lowest, at 16 percent, among those making $20,000 or less annually.[2] Similarly, in-home Internet use varies dramatically by race with 32.4 percent of white households reporting Internet use as opposed to 11.7 percent of black households.[3] Those gaps, says the Department of Commerce, represent "one of America's leading economic and civil rights issues."[4] Another 1999 study, however, suggests that nearly half of women use the Internet, the same percentage as men, and that use by blacks and Hispanics is expected to reach 40 and 43 percent in 2000. These figures cast doubts on the need for government rules to equalize online access.[5] At the global level, the seriousness of the accessibility problem is indisputable. Obviously, poorer nations do not enjoy widespread Internet access. The result is the likelihood—indeed, the near certainty—that world income/wealth gaps will continue to broaden. As the United Nations put it in 1999: "Developing nations—and parts of Europe—face a very significant threat of being marginalized if they fail to apply information and communication technology to their economies."[6]

Community.   We cannot know what our lives will be like as the Internet begins to assert its full technological potential, but we can be sure that everything will be different. Doubtless, we will be much better off in many ways, but a reservation often raised involves the human need to relate closely to each other. Certainly many argue that the Internet, because of its immense communication efficiencies, is strengthening our sense of community, particularly at the global level. Others, however, are concerned that our increasingly computer-dependent lives will lead to new, previously unimagined levels of alienation. A 1999 poll found 31 percent of men and 34 percent of women saying that the Internet makes having relationships with others more difficult.[7] Journalist Brian McGrory comments on what he takes to be the Internet threat to community in Boston:

> For many people, there is really no compelling reason to buy anything in person ever again . . . Life is great, right? Well, no, not when you walk by the shuttered doors of Waterstone's Booksellers on Exeter Street and see what used to be a community gathering spot reduced to an empty shell . . . Amazon.com, the behemoth Internet bookseller, is scaring too many bookstores to oblivion . . .
>
> So at what cost convenience? Is there no value left to thumbing through a copy of a book in the aisles of a store . . . ? Is there no comfort to sitting in an easy chair and spreading the pages of a newspaper in your lap, as my father used to do each night? . . .
>
> Take it another step. How many opportunities are missed through the computer phenomenon, how many relationships foreclosed before they ever begin? By having all daily chores fulfilled by a UPS driver or deliveryman who slips in and out of your garage each week, you will never get to know the dry cleaner, the pharmacist, the grocer, the townie at the local store.[8]

Virtual Life?   The article that follows suggests the power of the Internet to encourage ever greater distance between ourselves and others, but it also raises very important legal questions about the government's right to restrict access to Internet-provided images of young women in their "home." [For the latest in news affecting the "cyber-world," see **www.wirednews.com**]

VOYEUR DORM SUES OVER ZONING

Larry Dougherty

Can a city zone an Internet business? This dispute in Tampa [Florida] may well break new legal ground on the question.

Tampa's attempt to regulate the Internet business Voyeur Dorm, which uses 30 cameras to record even the most private moments in the lives of five young women inside a Tampa home, has landed the city in federal court.

In a case that lawyers are calling the first of its kind, the owners of Voyeur Dorm filed a lawsuit Friday that claims the city is violating their right to free expression by trying to zone an Internet business.

"The city's attempts to enforce zoning regulations on e-commerce are totally inappropriate," said Luke Lirot, an attorney representing Voyeur Dorm. "They're trying to impose obsolete regulations on technology."

Voyeur Dorm is broadcast from an otherwise innocuous stucco home in the West Tampa neighborhood of Wellswood. Cameras mounted throughout the home are hooked to an Internet website and, for $34 a month, anyone with a computer can watch the women go about their lives, even as they shower, sleep and change their clothes.

Last month, the City Council upheld a zoning decision that outlawed Voyeur Dorm in the residential Wellswood neighborhood.

"The only difference between the smut we see on Dale Mabry (Highway) and this is you're taking the information highway to bring homes into the peep shows," City Council member Bob Buckhorn said at the time.

The owners of Voyeur Dorm have argued that the business attracts no customers to the home and has no impact on the neighborhood. Most neighbors were unaware what was happening in the home until learning about it from news reports.

One of Voyeur Dorm's residents, 19-year-old Autumn Marenger, is a plaintiff in the lawsuit filed Friday. As a silver stud flashed from her tongue, Marenger, who is known to her Internet visitors as "Amber," told reporters that the city was "basically turning a morality issue into a zoning issue."

Legal experts say the suit is without precedent.

A ruling in favor of Voyeur Dorm could show that adult services on the Internet stand beyond the reach of municipal zoning regulations.

"What you've got is a real neighborhood, which is invaded by virtual means, without the accompanying consequences of a red-light district," said Robert O'Neil, who teaches a course in cyberspace issues at the University of Virginia law school. "It would make a wonderful exam question."

Voyeur Dorm's owners dispute it is even an adult-use business.

They say in their lawsuit that its unblinking cameras transmit "documentary, anthropological and sociological information and commentary regarding the lives of the residents."

Voyeur Dorm's lawyers say nudity is relatively rare. And they emphasize how the house presents no harm to its neighbors. "The public is never on the premises," Lirot said.

O'Neil said the lawsuit has the potential to rob local governments of their single most effective means of regulating adult-use businesses—zoning regulations.

While local governments may not outlaw adult businesses per se, the Supreme Court has allowed them to focus on so-called secondary effects of some adult businesses—loss of real estate value and increased crime, for example—to regulate them.

But now that commerce has moved onto the Internet, governments might find themselves without their most effective weapon to date, O'Neil said.

"It's a very difficult issue," O'Neil said. "On one hand the courts are extremely deferential to local governments' exercise of zoning powers and will uphold restrictions that are zoning-based that would not be held up under any other municipal authority.

"On the other hand, the rationale for deference to the zoning function is to protect the value, integrity and ethos of a community," O'Neil said, Voyeur Dorm's operation over the Internet, instead of face-to-face with its customers, "makes it harder to justify the zoning power."

* * * * *

The city has said it won't actually shut down Voyeur Dorm while appeals of its zoning decision are pending.

Source: *St. Petersburg Times*, September 25, 1999, p. 1B. Reprinted by permission.

Questions

1. Are zoning laws "obsolete" vehicles for dealing with today's technology?
2. *a.*   Why are local governments not allowed to simply outlaw all "adult" businesses?

b. Why are local governments allowed to impose zoning restrictions on adult businesses?

3. Would you simply ignore the Voyeur Dorm if you were the mayor of Tampa? Explain.

4. Comment on the following portion of John Perry Barlow's "Cyberspace Declaration of Independence":

> Governments of the Industrial World, you weary giants of flesh and steel, I come from Cyberspace, the new home of Mind. On behalf of the future, I ask you of the past to leave us alone. You are not welcome among us. You have no sovereignty where we gather.
>
> We have no elected government, nor are we likely to have one, so I address you with no greater authority than that with which liberty itself always speaks. I declare the global social space we are building to be naturally independent of the tyrannies you seek to impose on us. You have no moral right to rule us nor do you possess any methods of enforcement we have true reason to fear.[9]

Part One—Jurisdiction

Business in the cyberworld raises puzzling new legal problems. The Internet, after all, is borderless. We can and do communicate and conduct transactions around the world. When a dispute arises from one of those billions of communications and transactions, where will that dispute be litigated? If an American website provides child pornography viewed by a German on the Internet, which nation will have the authority to prosecute the offense? If an Iowa resident uses the Internet to buy a defective computer from a Texas supplier and a lawsuit results, where will it be heard? These are jurisdiction questions. What court has jurisdiction over the issues in dispute (the subject matter), and what court has jurisdiction over the parties? (For a general discussion of jurisdiction, see Chapter 4.) [For an extensive cyberlaw database, including jurisdiction links, see **http://www.gseis.ucla.edu/ iclp/hp.html**]

A party filing suit over an Internet dispute must take that claim to a court that has both *subject-matter jurisdiction* (the authority and power to address the particular kind of legal problem being raised) and *personal jurisdiction* (the power to make the defendant respond to the court). In order to establish that personal jurisdiction, the defendant must either be a resident of the forum state (where the case is being tried) or, by its actions, must have subjected itself to the jurisdiction of the courts in that state.

Where the plaintiff and defendant are both residents of the forum state, jurisdiction ordinarily is not an issue. Broadly and in brief, jurisdiction over nonresidents depends on the constitutional requirement of *due process.* In practice, the test is one of *minimum contacts:* Did the defendant have sufficient contact with the forum state that being sued there would be fair and just? Put another way, was the defendant's contact with the forum state such that he or she should expect to be subject to the state's courts? Thus, the more business a defendant does in a state, the more likely that personal jurisdiction would be found. The Internet, of course, raises special problems because the "contacts" often are electronic and fleeting. Thus, if you order software via the Internet from a California company, but the Internet access provider is located in Florida where you live, will you be able to sue in Florida and secure personal jurisdiction over the software provider? The case that follows illustrates the analysis of these jurisdiction issues.

MINK v. AAAA DEVELOPMENT
190 F.3d 333 (5th Cir. 1999)

Circuit Judge Parker

David Mink appeals the district court's dismissal of his complaint for lack of personal jurisdiction.

I. Facts and Proceedings

David Mink is a Texas resident who works in the retail furniture business. In January 1997, Mink claims that he began to develop a computer program, the Opportunity Tracking Computer System ("OTC"), designed to track information on sales made and opportunities missed on sales not made. On May 13, 1997, Mink submitted a patent application for the computer software and hardware that he developed to the United States Patent and Trademark Office. He also submitted a copyright application for the OTC to the United States Copyright Office.

Mink claims that in June 1997 he was approached by a Colorado resident named Richard Stark at a trade show. Stark allegedly asked Mink if he would be interested in marketing the OTC product with Stark's software at an upcoming computer seminar. Mink gave Stark a full demonstration of the OTC system, including its written material. While Mink initially declined Stark's offer to market the software together, Mink later contacted Stark to discuss the possibility of Stark marketing his product.

Between June 1997 and October 1997, Stark allegedly shared all of Mink's ideas and information on the OTC system with David Middlebrook. According to Mink's complaint, Middlebrook and two companies, AAAA Development and Profitsystems, conspired to copy Mink's copyrighted and patent-pending OTC system and create an identical system of their own for financial gain.

AAAA Development is a Vermont corporation with its principal place of business in Vermont. Middlebrook is a Vermont resident. Neither AAAA Development nor Middlebrook own property in Texas. Mink is silent concerning where his contacts with the defendants occurred. However, we infer that the contacts were not in Texas based on the statement in Middlebrook's affidavit that AAAA has not made any sales in Texas nor has it had any agents or employees travel to Texas or represent it in Texas. The company has advertised in a national furniture trade journal and maintains a website advertising its sales management software on the Internet.

On November 7, 1997, Mink filed his original complaint in the United States District Court for the Southern District of Texas against AAAA Development and David Middlebrook, alleging that they conspired to copy Mink's computer program in violation of federal copyright and patent pending rights. AAAA Development and Middlebrook moved to dismiss for lack of personal jurisdiction. The district court granted their motions. Mink filed a motion for reconsideration of the order dismissing AAAA and Middlebrook, adding allegations that the defendants had been actively targeting customers in Texas with cold calls and asserting for the first time that AAAA's Internet website, accessible from Texas, could fulfill the minimum contacts requirement for the exercise of personal jurisdiction. The district court denied the motion for reconsideration.

II. Discussion

The sole issue on appeal is whether the district court erred in dismissing defendants AAAA and Middlebrook for a lack of personal jurisdiction . . .

A federal court sitting in diversity may exercise personal jurisdiction over a nonresident defendant if (1) the long-arm statute of the forum state confers personal jurisdiction over that defendant; and (2) exercise of such jurisdiction by the forum state is consistent with due process under the United States Constitution. Because Texas's long-arm statute has been interpreted to extend to the limits of due process, we only need to determine whether subjecting AAAA and Middlebrook to suit in Texas would be consistent with the Due Process Clause of the Fourteenth Amendment.

The Due Process Clause of the Fourteenth Amendment permits the exercise of personal jurisdiction over a nonresident defendant when (1) that defendant has purposefully availed himself of the benefits and protections of the forum state by establishing "minimum contacts" with the forum state; and (2) the exercise of jurisdiction over that defendant does not offend "traditional notions of fair play and substantial justice."

The "minimum contacts" aspect of the analysis can be established through "contacts that give rise to 'specific' personal jurisdiction or those that give rise to 'general' personal jurisdiction." Specific jurisdiction exists when the nonresident defendant's contacts with the forum state arise from, or are directly related to, the cause of action. General jurisdiction exists when a defendant's contacts with the forum state are unrelated to the cause of action but are "continuous and systematic." Because we conclude that Mink has not established any contacts directly related to the cause of action required for specific jurisdiction, we turn to the question of whether general jurisdiction has been established.

At the outset, we note that Mink has not met his burden of establishing that the district court had personal jurisdiction over defendant Middlebrook. Mink, however, contends that the district court could exercise personal jurisdiction over AAAA because its World Wide website is accessible by Texas residents . . .

Courts addressing the issue of whether personal jurisdiction can be constitutionally exercised over a defendant look to the "nature and quality of commercial activity that an entity conducts over the Internet." *Zippo Mfg. Co.* v. *Zippo Dot Com, Inc.,* 952 F.Supp. 1119,

1124 (W.D. Pa. 1997). The *Zippo* decision categorized Internet use into a spectrum of three areas. At the one end of the spectrum, there are situations where a defendant clearly does business over the Internet by entering into contracts with residents of other states which "involve the knowing and repeated transmission of computer files over the Internet . . . " In this situation, personal jurisdiction is proper. At the other end of the spectrum, there are situations where a defendant merely establishes a passive website that does nothing more than advertise on the Internet. With passive websites, personal jurisdiction is not appropriate. In the middle of the spectrum, there are situations where a defendant has a website that allows a user to exchange information with a host computer. In this middle ground, "the exercise of jurisdiction is determined by the level of interactivity and commercial nature of the exchange of information that occurs on the website." We find that the reasoning of *Zippo* is persuasive and adopt it in this Circuit.

Applying these principles to this case, we conclude that AAAA's website is insufficient to subject it to personal jurisdiction. Essentially, AAAA maintains a website that posts information about its products and services. While the website provides users with a printable mail-in order form, AAAA's toll-free telephone number, a mailing address and an electronic mail ("e-mail") address, orders are not taken through AAAA's website. This does not classify the website as anything more than passive advertisement which is not grounds for the exercise of personal jurisdiction.

This case does not fall into the spectrum of cases where a defendant clearly conducted business over the Internet nor does it fall into the middle spectrum of interactivity where the defendant and users exchange information through the Internet. There was no evidence that AAAA conducted business over the Internet by engaging in business transactions with forum residents or by entering into contracts over the Internet.

We note that AAAA's website provides an e-mail address that permits consumers to interact with the company. There is no evidence, however, that the website allows AAAA to do anything but reply to e-mail initiated by website visitors. In addition, AAAA's website lacks other forms of interactivity cited by courts as factors to consider in determining questions of personal jurisdiction. For example, AAAA's website does not allow consumers to order or purchase products and services on-line. In fact, potential customers are instructed by the website to remit any completed order forms by regular mail or fax.

In this case, the presence of an electronic mail access, a printable order form, and a toll-free phone number on a website, without more, is insufficient to establish personal jurisdiction. Absent a defendant doing business over the Internet or sufficient interactivity with residents of the forum state, we cannot conclude that personal jurisdiction is appropriate.

Affirmed.

Questions

1. Explain the distinction the court draws between specific personal jurisdiction and general personal jurisdiction.
2. Why was AAAA's website an insufficient basis for finding general personal jurisdiction?
3. Bancroft & Masters, a small California company providing computer support services, owns and uses the Internet domain name MASTERS.COM.

After negotiations failed, Bancroft filed suit in California against Augusta National, Inc. (ANI), a Georgia corporation, which operates the Augusta National Golf Club because ANI likewise used the MASTERS.COM domain name. Bancroft sued for trademark dilution and infringement. ANI moved to dismiss the Bancroft claim on the grounds of lack of personal jurisdiction over the defendant. ANI maintains no employees, offices, property, or inventory in California. ANI is not licensed to do business in California, does not pay taxes there, and is owed no debts by California companies. ANI did, however, ship some $16,507 worth of golf-related merchandise to California each year and sells over $26,000 in tournament tickets to California residents each year. ANI logos are used on goods manufactured in California but sold in ANI's pro shop. Are ANI's contacts with California sufficient to warrant the exercise of general personal jurisdiction over ANI? Explain. See *Bancroft & Masters, Inc.* v. *Augusta National, Inc.,* 45 F.Supp.2d 777 (N.D. Cal. 1998).

Part Two—Constitutional Law: Speech and Privacy

SPEECH

Not surprisingly, the speech conflicts that have routinely marked American life are already common on-line. The Internet's anonymity, ease of use, relatively low costs, and global reach make it a natural vehicle for transporting speech messages from smut to "walmart-sucks.com" [**http://walmartsucks.com/**], where anyone who has a gripe with the retail giant can spout off. As we saw in Chapter 5, the First Amendment protects us from government restraints on the *content* of speech, although reasonable restraints on the context (time, place, and manner) of that speech are sometimes constitutionally permissible. Remember that the First Amendment does not protect us from private-sector restraints on speech although legal claims for defamation and the like are, of course, employed in cases of wrongful speech from private-sector sources. [For many links to cyberlaw free speech materials, see **http://www.jmls.edu/cyber/index/speech.html**]

> an anti-abortion Web site labeled "The Nuremberg Files" was devoted to unlawful threats of violence, including murder

Obviously, the Net is a vast, largely unorganized, largely unpoliced competition of messages. Sometimes those messages step across legal bounds. In 1999, a federal judge upheld a $107 million jury verdict that an anti-abortion website labeled "The Nuremberg Files" was devoted to unlawful threats of violence, including murder.[10] The site published detailed information on "Wanted Posters" about doctors who provide abortions, including their photos, their addresses, and names of their children. Then a doctor's name was chillingly crossed off when he was killed. Similarly, a portion of the federal Communications Decency Act was upheld in court in 1999 against First Amendment challenges. While other portions of the act (see Chapter 5) have been struck down as First Amendment wrongs, this section, which makes it, in brief, a crime to use a "telecommunications device" to transmit obscene messages with intent to harass others, was upheld by the United States Supreme Court.[11] ApolloMedia Corp. had sued to establish that the government had no power to outlaw "indecent" speech on-line. The Supreme Court decision, in effect, agreed by limiting the law's speech restrictions to obscene remarks only. ApolloMedia's website, annoy.com, receives and posts often insulting messages directed against public figures. [For more on the ApolloMedia case and many angry messages, see **http://www.annoy.com**]

The case that follows examines First Amendment questions about on-campus, computer access to sexually explicit material.

UROFSKY v. GILMORE
167 F.3d 191 (4th Cir. 1999)

Circuit Judge Wilkins

Six professors employed by various public colleges and universities in Virginia brought this action challenging the constitutionality of a Virginia law restricting state employees from accessing sexually explicit material on computers that are owned or leased by the state. The district court granted summary judgment in favor of [the] Plaintiffs, holding that the Act unconstitutionally infringed on state employees' First Amendment rights.

I

The central provision of the Act states:

Except to the extent required in conjunction with a bona fide, agency-approved research project or other agency-approved undertaking, no agency employee shall utilize agency-owned or agency-leased computer equipment to access, download, print or store any information infrastructure files or services having sexually explicit content. Such agency approvals

shall be given in writing by agency heads, and any such approvals shall be available to the public under the provisions of the Virginia Freedom of Information Act.

Va. Code Ann. § 2.1-805. Another section of the Act defines "sexually explicit content" to include:

(i) any description of or (ii) any picture, photograph, drawing, motion picture film, digital image or similar visual representation depicting sexual bestiality, a lewd exhibition of nudity, as nudity is defined in § 18.2-390, sexual excitement, sexual conduct or sadomasochistic abuse, as also defined in § 18.2-390, coprophilia, urophilia, or fetishism.

Va. Code Ann. § 2.1-804

As its language makes plain, the Act prohibits state employees from accessing sexually explicit material on computers owned or leased by the Commonwealth. But, the Act does not prohibit all access by state employees to such materials, for a state agency head may give permission for a state employee to access such information on computers owned or leased by the Commonwealth if the agency head deems such access to be required in connection with a bona fide research project or other undertaking. Further, state employees remain free to access sexually explicit materials from their personal or other computers. Thus, the Act prohibits state employees from accessing sexually explicit materials only when the employees are using computers that are owned or leased by the Commonwealth and permission to access the material has not been given by the appropriate agency head.

Plaintiffs maintain that this restriction—the denial of access to sexually explicit materials on computers owned by or leased to the Commonwealth when permission for such access has not been given by the appropriate department head—is violative of their First Amendment right to freedom of expression. Plaintiffs do not assert that they possess a First Amendment right to access this information on stateowned or leased computers for their personal use; rather, Plaintiffs confine their challenge to the denial of access to sexually explicit material for work-related purposes.

II

It is well settled that citizens do not relinquish all of their First Amendment rights by virtue of accepting public employment. Nevertheless, the state, as an employer, undoubtedly possesses greater authority to restrict the speech of its employees than it has as sovereign to restrict the speech of the citizenry as a whole . . . A determination of whether a restriction imposed on a public employee's speech is violative of the First Amendment requires " 'a balance between the interests of the [employee], as a citizen, in commenting upon matters of public concern and the interest of the State, as an employer, in promoting the efficiency of the public services it performs through its employees.' " This balancing involves an inquiry first into whether the speech at issue touches upon a matter of public concern, and, if so, whether the employee's interest in First Amendment expression outweighs the public employer's interest in what the employer has determined to be the appropriate operation of the workplace.

Thus, our threshold inquiry is whether the Act regulates speech by employees of the Commonwealth in their capacity as citizens upon matters of public concern. If a public employee's speech does not touch upon a matter of public concern, the Commonwealth, as employer, may regulate it without infringing any First Amendment protection . . .

Speech involves a matter of public concern when it affects a social, political, or other interest of a community. And, to determine whether speech involves a matter of public concern, we examine the content, context, and form of the speech at issue in light of the entire record. An inquiry into whether a matter is of public concern does not involve a determination of how interesting or important the subject of an employee's speech is. Further, the place where the speech occurs is irrelevant: An employee may speak as a citizen on a matter of public concern at the workplace, and an employee may speak in his capacity as an employee away from the workplace . . .

The challenged aspect of the Act does not regulate the speech of the citizenry in general, but rather the speech of state employees in their capacity as employees. It cannot be doubted that in order to pursue its legitimate goals effectively, the Commonwealth must retain the ability to control the manner in which its employees discharge their duties and to direct its employees to undertake the responsibilities of their positions in a specified way . . . The essence of Plaintiffs' claim is that they are entitled to access sexually explicit material in their capacity as state employees. Because Plaintiffs assert only an infringement on the manner in which they perform their work as state employees, they cannot demonstrate that the speech to which they claim entitlement would be made in their capacity as citizens speaking on matters of public concern.

III

We reject the conclusion of the district court that Va. Code Ann. §§ 2.1-804 to -806, restricting state employees from accessing sexually explicit material on computers that are owned or leased by the Commonwealth unless given permission to do so, infringes upon the First Amendment rights of state employees. The Act regulates the speech of individuals speaking in their capacity as Commonwealth employees, not as citizens, and thus the Act does not touch upon a matter of public concern. Consequently, the speech may be restricted consistent with the First Amendment.

[Reversed.]

Questions

1. The court detailed one domain of speech for public employees that clearly could not be restricted by the state. Explain that branch of speech.
2. Why did the court rule against the professors–appellants?
3. Would an Internet service provider, such as America Online or CompuServe, itself be legally responsible if one of its customers posted on the Internet a defamatory message or if it failed to block access by its customers to obscene, criminal materials such as child pornography? Explain. See, e.g., *Zeran* v. *America Online, Inc.* 129 F.3d 327 (4th Cir. 1997). For an overview of the issue, see Jean Eaglesham, "Screening Out the Net Pornographers," *Financial Times,* December 1, 1999, p. 21.

Commercial Speech. You will remember from Chapter 5 that commercial speech is accorded reduced First Amendment protection. Thus, on-line advertising is subject to the same kinds of government oversight as that in print and on television. One form of on-line commercial message receiving special attention is so-called *spam* (mass e-mailings). This electronic form of junk mail can be considered a legitimate form of commercial message, but it can also be considered an annoyance or, because of its bulk, a threat to the efficiency of the Internet. Spamming has brought pleas for government intervention, but the market and self-regulation (ethics) may satisfactorily address the problem. New technology is emerging to block unwanted advertising, and of course lawsuits claiming trespass, for example, can be used to stop spam.

PRIVACY

Americans cherish the right to privacy, but the Internet opens up previously uncontemplated possibilities for intrusion. The result is that we hear increasingly insistent calls for government intervention. While Congress has developed some protections and is considering others, the federal government's general position has clearly been to allow the market and ethics to work their will. The Federal Trade Commission in 1999 explicitly advised that new rules were "not appropriate at this time," but the agency, using existing legal tools, has become the primary Internet law enforcer.[12] [For an extensive "law and computers" database, see **http://www.kentlaw.edu/clc/lrs/lawlinks/computer.shtml**]

While Internet privacy concerns, for example, involving school and hospital databases, range across society, the real fear, of course, lies with e-commerce where companies are racing to collect as much information as possible about each American consumer. As Sun Microsystems, Inc. CEO, Scott G. McNealy glibly remarked, "You already have zero privacy. Get over it."[13] But Americans are not taking McNealy's advice as evidenced by a 1998 Harris Poll showing that 82 percent of those polled felt they had lost control over how their personal information is used by companies.[14] We fear that we will be victimized by false or out-of-date information, or that we will be bombarded with ads tailored to our history of on-line habits, or we will

"You already have zero privacy. Get over it."

actually be discriminated against because of data collected on-line. Companies already use data collected on-line to decide, for example, which customer-service calls should be answered first, depending upon the customer's value to the company.

"Cookies" and On-Line Profiles

When visiting a website ad, a "cookie" (a snippet of code that identifies each computer) often is automatically placed on a user's hard drive. The cookie allows the user's Internet movements to be tracked so that a profile emerges of ads viewed, whether the user clicked on those ads, and so on. With that information, a user profile is developed and ads can be directed to sites the user visits touting products the user's profile suggests would be of interest. Now some companies are collecting e-mail addresses, ZIP codes, and the like that are used to log into sites and comparing that information with other databases to try to match virtual-world profiles with real-world persons.

In early 2000, the Federal Trade Commission announced a probe of on-line ad giant, DoubleClick, for possible privacy violations. Soon thereafter, DoubleClick voluntarily announced that, pending the development of government privacy rules, it will not tie people's names, addresses, and so on with the data it collects about those people's Internet surfing behaviors.

Sources: See Dave Merrill, "How Marketers 'Profile' Users," *USA Today,* November 8, 1999, p. 2A, and Associated Press, "DoubleClick Retreats on Database Plan," *Waterloo–Cedar Falls Courier,* March 3, 2000, p. C5. [For more information on cookies, see **http://www.cookiecentral.com/com002.htm**].

Consumers are, of course, alarmed about these privacy threats, but the business community is similarly concerned because privacy worries are clearly discouraging some consumers from engaging in e-commerce. As a result, many companies are now trying to address consumer fears. A 1999 survey of the 364 websites that draw 99 percent of Web traffic found that 239 have posted a privacy policy of some sort.[15] Among those 239 sites, 87 percent explain how they collect data and how they use it.[16] Similarly, Microsoft and IBM have announced that they will discontinue buying ads from sites that decline to publish adequate privacy promises to consumers.[17]

New technology, such as self-destructing e-mail, will also help preserve privacy. These developments suggest that the market and ethics may be powerful enough in this area to maintain the FTC's preference for no new rules, although many members of Congress feel that further legislation is necessary.

The Children's Online Privacy Protection Act of 1998 (COPPA) prohibits websites from collecting personal information from children under the age of 13 without parental permission, and parents must be allowed to review and correct any information collected about their children. [See **http://www.ftc.gov/os/1999/9910/childrensprivacy.pdf**].

Europe. The European Union has taken quite a different tack from America's market-driven approach to on-line privacy. The EU's Data Protection Directive basically allows individuals to decide how their collected data can be used. Thus, if a European consumer provides personal information such as an address when buying from an on-line store, that store cannot legally send an ad to the purchaser without first seeking permission.[18] The directive also prohibits the transfer of data to countries outside the 15-nation EU who do not have "adequate" privacy rules.[19] The United States is one of the nations deemed inadequate and, in practice, almost all American companies doing business in Europe probably are violating the directive. In early 2000, European and United States negotiators reached agreement on privacy rules, but they must yet be ratified by each national government. In January 2000, the European Commission announced that it was taking France, Luxembourg, the Netherlands, Germany, and Ireland to the European Court of Justice for failing to fully implement the directive.[20] [For general information regarding on-line privacy, see **http://www0.delphi.com/navnet/privacy.html**]

Case. On-line privacy protection largely resides in the Fourth Amendment prohibition against unlawful searches and seizures (see Chapter 5), and in four common-law (judge-made) tort claims: intrusion upon seclusion, public disclosure of embarrassing private facts, publicity placing a person in a false light, and appropriation of a person's name or likeness without permission. Basically a common law tort claim requires an intentional intrusion that would be highly offensive to a reasonable person. Remember that the federal constitution protects us only from government action, not from private-sector wrongs.

The case that follows involves the Fourth Amendment in a situation of alleged criminal behavior on the Internet. The key inquiry is whether the defendant had a legitimate expectation of privacy in his account with his Internet service provider.

UNITED STATES OF AMERICA v. SCOTT M. HAMBRICK
55 F.2d 504 (W.D.Va. 1999)

Judge Michael

I

Before the court is the defendant's January 27, 1999, "Motion to Suppress." Defendant Scott M. Hambrick seeks the suppression of all evidence obtained from his Internet Service Provider ("ISP"), MindSpring, and seeks the suppression of all evidence seized from his home pursuant to a warrant issued by this court . . .

II

Facts

On March 14, 1998, J. L. McLaughlin, a police officer with the Keene, New Hampshire Police Department, connected to the Internet and entered a chat room called "Gay dads 4 sex." McLaughlin's screen name was

"Rory14." In this chat room, Detective McLaughlin encountered someone using the screen name "Blowuinva." Based on a series of online conversations between "Rory14" (Det. McLaughlin) and "Blowuinva," McLaughlin concluded that "Blowuinva" sought to entice a fourteen-year-old boy to leave New Hampshire and live with "Blowuinva." Because of the anonymity of the Internet, Detective McLaughlin did not know the true identity of the person with whom he was communicating nor did he know where "Blowuinva" lived. "Blowuinva" had only identified himself as "Brad."

To determine Blowuinva's identity and location, McLaughlin obtained a New Hampshire state subpoena that he served on Blowuinva's Internet Service Provider, MindSpring, located in Atlanta, Georgia. The New Hampshire state subpoena requested that MindSpring produce "any records pertaining to the billing and/or user records documenting the subject using your services on March 14th, 1998 at 1210HRS (EST) using Internet Protocol Number 207.69.169.92." MindSpring complied with the subpoena. On March 20, 1998, MindSpring supplied McLaughlin with defendant's name, address, credit card number, e-mail address, home and work telephone numbers, fax number, and the fact that the Defendant's account was connected to the Internet at the Internet Protocol (IP) address.

A justice of the peace, Richard R. Richards, signed the New Hampshire state subpoena. Mr. Richards is not only a New Hampshire justice of the peace, but he is also a detective in the Keene Police Department, Investigation Division. Mr. Richards did not issue the subpoena pursuant to a matter pending before himself, any other judicial officer, or a grand jury. At the hearing on the defendant's motion, the government conceded the invalidity of the warrant. The question before this court, therefore, is whether the court must suppress the information obtained from MindSpring, and all that flowed from it, because the government failed to obtain a proper subpoena.

III

Discussion

A

* * * * *

In *Katz* v. *United States,* the Supreme Court provided an important starting point in defining the scope of the interest that the Fourth Amendment protects. 389 U.S. 347, 353 (1967). The Court held that the capacity to claim the protection of the Fourth Amendment depends on "whether the person who claims the protection of the Amendment has a legitimate expectation of privacy in the invaded place." Since *Katz,* the Court has instructed that the Fourth Amendment applies only where: (1) the citizen has manifested a subjective expectation of privacy, and (2) the expectation is one that society accepts as "objectively reasonable." This is still the appropriate standard of analysis for use in determining whether the Fourth Amendment protects Mr. Hambrick's MindSpring records. In order to determine whether an individual's privacy has been intruded, the *Katz* test must first be applied to assess whether that individual had a reasonable expectation of privacy. Applying the first part of the *Katz* analysis, Mr. Hambrick asserts that he had a subjective expectation of privacy in the information that MindSpring gave to the government. However, resolution of this matter hinges on whether Mr. Hambrick's expectation is one that society accepts as "objectively reasonable."

The objective reasonableness prong of the privacy test is ultimately a value judgment and a determination of how much privacy we should have as a society. In making this constitutional determination, this court must employ a sort of risk analysis, asking whether the individual affected should have expected the material at issue to remain private. The defendant asserts that the Electronic Communications Privacy Act ("ECPA") "legislatively resolves" this question.

The Electronic Communications Privacy Act

Congress enacted the Electronic Communications Privacy Act of 1986 to protect against the unauthorized interception of various forms of electronic communications and to update and elaborate on federal privacy protections and standards in light of changing computer and telecommunications technologies . . .

The government may require that an ISP provide stored communications and transactional records only if (1) it obtains a warrant issued under the Federal Rules of Criminal Procedure or state equivalent, or (2) it gives prior notice to the online subscriber and then issues a subpoena or receives a court order authorizing disclosure of the information in question . . .

Although Congress is willing to recognize that individuals have some degree of privacy in the stored data and transactional records that their ISPs retain, the ECPA is hardly a legislative determination that this expectation of privacy is one that rises to the level of "reasonably objective" for Fourth Amendment purposes. Despite its concern for privacy, Congress did not provide for suppression where a party obtains stored data or transactional records in violation of the Act. Additionally, the ECPA's concern for privacy extends only to government invasions of privacy. ISPs are free to turn stored data and transactional records over to nongovernmental entities. For Fourth Amendment purposes, this court does not find that the ECPA has legislatively determine[d] that an individual has a reasonable expectation of privacy in his name, address, social security number, credit card number, and proof of Internet connection. The fact that the ECPA does not proscribe turning over such information to private entities buttresses the conclusion that the ECPA does not create a reasonable expectation of privacy in that information. This, however, does not end the court's inquiry. This court must determine, within the constitutional framework that the Supreme Court has established, whether Mr. Hambrick's subjective expectation of privacy is one that society is willing to recognize.

Privacy Interests and Internet Service Providers

To have any interest in privacy, there must be some exclusion of others. To have a reasonable expectation of privacy under the Supreme Court's risk-analysis approach to the Fourth Amendment, two conditions must be met: (1) the data must not be knowingly exposed to others, and (2) the Internet service provider's ability to access the data must not constitute a disclosure. In *Katz,* the Supreme Court expressly held that "what a person knowingly exposes to the public, even in his home or office, is not a subject of Fourth Amendment protection." Further, the Court "consistently has held that a person has no legitimate expectation of privacy in information he voluntarily turns over to third parties."

The Supreme Court's risk-analysis approach makes the work of the courts difficult when analyzing previously unadjudicated situations in the world of cyberspace . . .

The court finds the defendant's implicit argument that certain information in cyberspace should be private requires careful consideration. Legal scholars and Congress have noted the ubiquity of cyberspace in the lives of all Americans. The members of our society increasingly live important parts of their lives through the

Internet. Cyberspace is a nonphysical "place" and its very structure, a computer and telephone network that connects millions of users, defies traditional Fourth Amendment analysis. So long as the risk-analysis approach of *Katz* remains valid, however, this court is compelled to apply traditional legal principles to this new and continually evolving technology.

When Scott Hambrick surfed the Internet using the screen name "Blowuinva," he was not a completely anonymous actor. It is true that an average member of the public could not easily determine the true identity of "Blowuinva." Nevertheless, when Mr. Hambrick entered into an agreement to obtain Internet access from MindSpring, he knowingly revealed his name, address, credit card number, and telephone number to MindSpring and its employees. Mr. Hambrick also selected the screen name "Blowuinva." When the defendant selected his screen name it became tied to his true identity in all MindSpring records. MindSpring employees had ready access to these records in the normal course of MindSpring's business, for example in the keeping of its records for billing purposes, and nothing prevented MindSpring from revealing this information to nongovernmental actors. Also, there is nothing in the record to suggest that there was a restrictive agreement between the defendant and MindSpring that would limit the right of MindSpring to reveal the defendant's personal information to nongovernmental entities. Where such dissemination of information to nongovernment entities is not prohibited, there can be no reasonable expectation of privacy in that information.

Although not dispositive to the outcome of this motion, it is important to note that the court's decision does not leave members of cybersociety without privacy protection. Under the ECPA, Internet Service Providers are civilly liable when they reveal subscriber information or the contents of stored communications to the government without first requiring a warrant, court order, or subpoena. Here, nothing suggests that MindSpring had any knowledge that the facially valid subpoena submitted to it was in fact an invalid subpoena. Had MindSpring revealed the information at issue in this case to the government without first requiring a subpoena, apparently valid on its face, Mr. Hambrick could have sued MindSpring. This is a powerful deterrent protecting privacy in the online world and should not be taken lightly.

* * * * *

[Motion to suppress denied.]

Questions

1. What test did the court employ to determine whether Hambrick had a reasonable expectation of privacy in the data and records stored with his Internet service provider, MindSpring?
2. Why did the court conclude that Hambrick had no reasonable expectation of privacy?
3. An FBI agent monitored an AOL chat room suspected of being a site for exchanging child pornography. The agent did not participate in the chat room conversations. Charbonneau allegedly distributed child pornography to the chat room participants including the FBI agent. Charbonneau was arrested.
   a. Did Charbonneau have a First Amendment free speech right to transmit child pornography on-line?
   b. Does the Fourth Amendment's prohibition on unreasonable searches and seizures protect the statements made in the AOL chat room? Explain. See *United States of America* v. *Kenneth Charbonneau,* 979 F.Supp. 1177 (S.D.Ohio, 1997).

Part Three—Crime

Regardless of their philosophical preferences about regulating the Internet, most observers agree that strong criminal law enforcement is essential both to protect consumers and to encourage trust in Internet transactions. In late 1999, United States Deputy Secretary of State Jonathan Winer, addressing an international conference, argued that governments and law enforcement agencies are in danger of losing the fight against economic crime in part, because of "disappearing electronic money," which regulators are often unable to trace.[21] In January 2000, United States Attorney General Janet Reno proposed the creation of a global, around-the-clock, anti-cybercrime network:

> Jonathan Winer argued that governments and law enforcement agencies are in danger of losing the fight against economic crime

The program would include teams of highly skilled computer crime prosecutors and investigators, regional forensic computer laboratories and technology sharing, Reno said.

She also proposed a new interstate compact to ensure enforcement of out-of-state subpoenas and warrants stemming from Internet investigations.

"The Internet is indeed a splendid tool of wonder, but there is a dark side of hacking, crashing networks and viruses that we absolutely must address," she said.

The growth in e-commerce is creating opportunities for cybercrime. An FBI survey of *Fortune* 500 companies found 62 percent reported computer security breaches during the past year, she said.[22]

Cyberstalking.   We have already looked at on-line pornography and noted the increasing concern about "disappearing" electronic money, hackers, and viruses, but on-line crime, of course, can take many forms. For example, law enforcement officials are increasingly concerned about "cyberstalking." At least 16 states have laws forbidding criminal harassment (stalking), and federal law forbids transmitting interstate or foreign communications that include a threat to hurt another, but the Internet is becoming an effective weapon for those who want to threaten, intimidate and harass. False addresses and names make the Internet an easy place to hide.

In 1999, a University of Oregon student pleaded guilty to illegally distributing thousands of pirated movies, music, and software from his Web site

Piracy.   In 1999, a University of Oregon student pleaded guilty to illegally distributing thousands of pirated movies, music, and software from his website.[23] Likewise in 1999, Microsoft won its first court case in China against a pair of companies using pirated software. Experts estimate that 90 percent of China's software is illegal.[24] In January 2000, Hong Kong stiffened its criminal penalties for software piracy and planned new legislation to outlaw bootlegging.[25] These developments highlight an increasing worldwide awareness of the criminal potential of the electronic world. [For the recording industry anti-piracy database, see **http://www.riaa.com/piracy/piracy.htm**]

Encryption.   For years, the United States has enforced strong rules against exporting data-scrambling technology (encryption) designed to prevent piracy, hacking, electronic theft, and the like by making it difficult to discover the electronic "keys" and "locks" that can scramble and unscramble computer data. The computer industry has argued for years that it should be allowed to export encryption technology, but the federal government has been concerned about terrorist access to that information. In January 2000, however, the Clinton administration withdrew its objections, and most software and hardware sold in the United States for encryption purposes can now be sold abroad. Some experts are concerned about the policy change:

> In recent months, hackers, thieves and computer hobbyists have succeeded in purloining credit card numbers from supposedly "secure" Internet transactions. They have unscrambled Hollywood hit movies on digital videodiscs, broken into government websites and cracked the codes on thousands of computer software products.
>
> "We keep seeing product broken after product broken every week, and it's going to get worse as computing technology gets more complex," said Bruce Schneier, an encryption expert and founder of Counterpane Internet Security Inc. of San Jose. Encryption, he added, "is an important tool, but it is not magic security dust that makes your computer impenetrable."
>
> Silicon Valley fought for seven years for permission to export its encryption technology abroad. The industry argued that the spread of strong encryption would fuel electronic commerce and reassure consumers that their credit card numbers and other private communications would not be compromised.
>
> After battling the industry over the politically charged issue, the White House did an about-face and announced new rules that clear the way for the high-tech industry—major contributors to Democratic campaigns—to more freely sell the hardest-to-crack scrambling technology overseas.[26]

Fraud.   With e-commerce thriving, we know that e-fraud cannot be far behind. The Federal Trade Commission, in 1999, said that it had identified 800 websites making deceptive health claims for products such as shark cartilage and magnetic therapy devices.[27] FTC regulators, likewise in 1999, asked Congress for tougher rules to combat on-line pharmacies that, in some instances, do not require doctors' prescriptions before filling drug orders.[28]

Perhaps the biggest fraud concerns are in the securities area where on-line trading of stocks has skyrocketed as the economy has boomed. Reporter John Yaukey recently described a common stock fraud gambit:

> Take the case of Pairgain, a California company that scam artists hyped as being poised for a takeover by Israeli interests.
>
> The perpetrators went onto an Internet message board announcing the pending "takeover" and then hyperlinked the message to a fabricated news story that looked as if it had been written by a well-known financial reporting service . . .
>
> This was an Internet variation on the classic "pump and dump," where sellers artificially drive up a stock price by hyping it with an exaggerated story or a lie, then unload it on investors who think it's on the rise.[29]

The Securities and Exchange Commission receives 200 to 300 fraud complaints (mostly electronic) daily, but the SEC did not create its special unit to coordinate cyberspace enforcement efforts until 1998.[30]

> *USA Today* asked "if online investing ads have crossed the ethics line?" Consider the following E*Trade commercial. It "shows an elderly woman peering outside and waiting expectantly. The punch line: 'The sweepstakes van ain't coming. It's time for E*Trade, the No.1 place to invest on-line.' " Do you find the commercial to be unethical? Explain.
>
> Source: "Have On-Line Investing Ads Crossed the Ethics Line?" *USA Today,* May 10, 1999, p. 3B.

Part Four—Commercial Law

CONTRACTS AND UNIFORM LAWS

Internet sales have grown significantly, but for the Internet to reach its commercial potential a routine, well-settled contracts structure is essential. The basic ingredients of a binding contract, as we saw in Chapter 6, apply generally to Internet deals:

- *Capacity* to enter the contract.
- *Offer and acceptance* of the terms of the contract.
- *Consideration* for the promises in the contract.
- *Legality* of purpose of the contract.

Thus, an exchange of e-mails meeting the traditional contract requirements should result in an enforceable agreement. But what about acceptance by providing an "electronic signature" (a digital code unique to an individual), downloading some information, or opening a shrink-wrap package? [For an overview of electronic commerce, see **http://www.willyancey.com/elec–com.htm**]

E-Signature. Electronic signatures can take a variety of forms (voice prints, distinctive marks, mathematical codes), but the key is that they are electronic symbols, sounds, or processes intended to have the same effect as a signature affixed by hand. Electronic signatures obviously will be central to trust and efficiency in on-line contracting, but at this writing in early 2000, United States law in this area is unclear. Absent enforceable electronic signatures, an agreement would need to be reduced to writing at some point to assure enforceability.

Congress was unable, in 1999, to reach an agreement creating a uniform, national law on electronic signatures. The European Union did so in late 1999 although the law must yet be ratified by each member nation. And in 1999, American legal experts (the National Conference of Commissioners on Uniform State Laws—NCCUSL) developed a suggested model statute, the Uniform Electronic Transactions Act (UETA) to deal generally with electronic communications in contracting. The suggested legislation expressly supports the use of electronic signatures and records. Thus, under UETA if machines controlled by humans actually create an electronic agreement, it will be considered enforceable even if no human being expressly confirms the arrangements. UETA must be approved on a state-by-state basis, and a few have done so. [For more on UETA, see **www.webcom.com/legaled/ETAForum**]

UCITA. In 1999, NCCUSL approved another new model law designed to achieve uniformity across the United States in the law governing software and Internet transactions. The proposed law reaches all deals involving computer information or goods and is designed to address the special problems of the new electronic market including, especially, software licensure (right to use). UCITA addresses the substance of computer information transactions while UETA is procedural in character and governs, as we have noted, the electronic signatures and records relating to transactions.

UCITA will move to each state legislature, but at this writing none of the states have adopted UCITA, and the odds of general approval are not promising. In brief, opponents argue that UCITA favors big software interests at the expense of consumers and business users. [For information and views favoring UCITA, see **www.nccusl.org**. For the other side of the argument, see **www.badsoftware.com**]

Until UCITA or some such legislation is widely approved, the Uniform Commercial Code, other applicable state and federal laws, and the common law of contracts (judge-made law) will govern electronic contractual arrangements. You remember that the UCC, having been approved in 49 of the 50 states, is designed to provide nationwide consistency, predictability, and fairness in contract law where a sale of goods is involved.

Shrink-Wrap Agreements. Software typically arrives in a package with license terms printed on the outside, on a document inside the package, or onscreen during the installation. Those terms often say that in opening the shrink-wrap package or using the software the buyer agrees to the terms. Whether those terms are enforceable or not is the subject of dispute in the courts. The likelihood is that shrink-wrap terms will be enforceable if the buyer has a reasonable opportunity to review those terms, the buyer is clearly told how to accept the terms, and does so voluntarily. Other new forms of contracts such as *click-wraps* (where one agrees to contract terms by clicking in a box on a web page) add to the potential efficiencies of the e-market, but the law dealing with them remains, as yet, unsettled. The case that follows looks at e-commerce contract issues, including whether the contract in question was fully integrated; that is, whether it constituted a complete statement, as intended by the parties, of all the terms of the agreement.

M. A. MORTENSON COMPANY v. TIMBERLINE SOFTWARE CORPORATION
970 P.2d 803 (Wash.Ct.App. 1999)

Judge Webster

Appellant M. A. Mortenson Company licensed specialized software from Respondent Timberline Software Corporation via Respondent Softworks Data Systems ("SDS"), Timberline's local authorized dealer (the Respondents will be referred to collectively as "Timberline"). The software program is used by contractors in preparation of construction bids. Use of the program is generally subject to a form license agreement that is shipped with the diskettes. Mortenson used the program and encountered an error but nevertheless submitted the bid generated by the program. After submitting the bid, Mortenson discovered that it was two million dollars less than it should have been. Mortenson sued Timberline for breach of warranties. The contract issues to be resolved are: (1) whether the purchase order constituted an integrated contract; [and] (2) whether the license terms are part of the contract . . .

Background Facts

A. The Purchase

Prior to early 1993, Mortenson licensed and used the Medallion Version of Timberline's Bid Analysis Software. After upgrading its computer system, Mortenson was forced to upgrade to the then-current version of Timberline's software called Precision.

Mortenson negotiated the price and number of copies of the upgrade with Mr. Reich of SDS. The negotiations concerned a discounted price due to the quantity of copies Mortenson intended to purchase. On May 7,

1993, Reich issued a quote, and on July 12, 1993, Mortenson issued a purchase order confirming the purchase of eight copies of Precision. The purchase order was signed by Nell Ruud of Mortenson and by Reich.

B. The Installation

When the software arrived at SDS, Reich unpacked the cardboard shipping boxes to check the contents against the order but did not unpack the diskettes from the small white product boxes in which they were shipped. Reich delivered the software to Mortenson's Bellevue office in July 1993.

At Mortenson's request, Reich returned to Mortenson at a later date to install the software on Mortenson's machines. Mortenson claims that Reich opened the white boxes in which the diskettes were shipped, installed the software, and obtained the activation codes from Timberline. Mortenson asserts that it never saw any licenses or disclaimers pertaining to liability, warranties, or remedies. Mortenson does not recall receiving any manuals with the software shipment.

C. The License Agreement

Timberline shipped the diskettes in sealed envelopes that were placed inside white product boxes. The full text of the license agreement is printed on the outside of each sealed envelope. The license agreement is also printed on the inside cover of the user manuals and a reference to the license appears on the introductory screen each time the program is executed.

The relevant license agreement provisions appear below:

CAREFULLY READ THE FOLLOWING TERMS AND CONDITIONS BEFORE USING THE PROGRAMS. USE OF THE PROGRAMS INDICATES YOUR AC-KNOWLEDGEMENT THAT YOU HAVE READ THIS LICENSE, UNDERSTAND IT, AND AGREE TO BE BOUND BY ITS TERMS AND CONDITIONS. IF YOU DO NOT AGREE TO THESE TERMS AND CONDI-TIONS, PROMPTLY RETURN THE PROGRAMS AND USER MANUALS TO THE PLACE OF PUR-CHASE AND YOUR PURCHASE PRICE WILL BE REFUNDED. YOU AGREE THAT YOUR USE OF THE PROGRAM ACKNOWLEDGES THAT YOU HAVE READ THIS LICENSE, UNDERSTAND IT, AND AGREE TO BE BOUND BY ITS TERMS AND CONDITIONS.

*   *   *   *   *

D. The Two-Million-Dollar Bug

The Precision program is used by contractors to prepare their final bid the day the bid is due. On December 2, 1993, Mortenson utilized the Precision program in preparing its bid for the Harborview Hospital project. Two employees working with the program on the final bid received an error message that read "Abort: cannot find alternate. Press enter to continue." After the users pressed enter, the program exited to the DOS prompt. Upon reentering the program and returning to the place where they were working, the previously entered data appeared accurate. Mortenson employees assumed they could proceed safely. The program aborted in like fashion five to seven times during bid preparation that day. Mortenson's bid, generated with the help of the Precision program, was two million dollars under what Mortenson later discovered it should have been.

Mortenson and Timberline employees attempted to discover what caused the incorrect bid. The abort was reproduced, but the source of the problem was not determined at that time. After litigation was initiated, Mortenson discovered a Timberline internal memoran-dum dated May 26, 1993, that alerted software devel-opers that a bug had been found in the version of Pre-cision that Mortenson was using. This bug caused an abort with the same message that Mortenson received and occurred only under specific conditions. The memo-randum stated that "[g]iven the unusual criteria for this problem, it does not appear to be a major problem."

Other Timberline customers encountered the problem and a newer version of the program was sent to some of these customers. After further analysis in July 1995, a Timberline programmer came to the conclusion that this bug caused the bad alternate keys in Mortenson's file.

E. The Trial Court's Conclusions

The trial court found that the purchase order is not an integrated contract as a matter of law because it did not contain "many of the terms which are germane to this contractual relationship." The trial court found as a mat-ter of law that the license agreement is conspicuous, not unconscionable, and controlling.

F. Proceedings Below

Mortenson filed its action alleging breach of express and/or implied warranties on December 8, 1995. Timberline moved for summary judgment on July 21, 1997. The trial court granted summary judgment on August 15, 1997. Mortenson moved to vacate the judgment.

Analysis

I. The Contract

The parties apparently agree that Article II of the Uniform Commercial Code ("UCC") applies to the licensing of computer software. We accept, without deciding, this proposition . . .

A. The Purchase Order Is Not an Integrated Contract

The dispute in this appeal is not over the existence of a contract but over the nature of its terms. The parties dis-pute whether the purchase order comprises the entire contract between the parties and whether the license agreement terms are part of the contract.

*   *   *   *   *

The parties take [UCC] § 2–204 as their starting point:

(1) A contract for sale of goods may be made in any manner sufficient to show agreement, including con-duct by both parties which recognizes the existence of such a contract.

(2) An agreement sufficient to constitute a contract for sale may be found even though the moment of its making is undetermined.

(3) Even though one or more terms are left open a contract for sale does not fail for indefiniteness if the parties have intended to make a contract and there is a reasonably certain basis for giving an appropriate remedy.

Mortenson argues that the purchase order reflects an offer, consideration, and acceptance, and that it satisfies the statute of frauds; thus, the purchase order is sufficient under § 2–204 to show agreement between the parties and constitutes the entire contract. Mortenson also asserts that its understanding of a software license is that a license only determines the number of copies purchased. Timberline argues that under § 2–204 the purchase order shows only the *existence* of an agreement, not its extent. Timberline asserts that § 2–204 allows that a contract may be formed in many ways but does not mandate that all terms are defined as soon as there is evidence of an agreement.

Mortenson's arguments ignore the commercial realities of software sales. Mortenson's purchase of the newer version of the Timberline software package was prompted by its need to upgrade an older version of the program that it licensed at the time. Mortenson licensed other software packages, the licenses of which were similar to Timberline's in that they came with the software, disclaimed warranties, limited remedies, and included choice of law and forum selection clauses. Reasonable minds could not differ concerning a corporation's understanding that use of software is governed by licenses containing multiple terms. Even construing the facts in the light most favorable to Mortenson, we find that the facts do not support the conclusion that the purchase order constitutes an integrated contract.

B. The License Terms Are an Enforceable Part of the Contract

"Transactions in which the exchange of money precedes the communication of detailed terms are common." *ProCD, Inc.* v. *Zeidenberg,* 86 F.3d 1447, 1451 (7th Cir. 1996). In *ProCD,* the Seventh Circuit held that shrinkwrap licenses accompanying off-the-shelf computer software are enforceable unless their terms are objectionable under general contract law. The defendant purchased *ProCD* software at a retail outlet and made the database information therein available on the World Wide Web at a cost less than what *ProCD* charged consumers. The district court refused to enforce the license agreement that came with the software because the purchaser did not agree to "hidden terms"—those inside the box—even though a printed notice on the outside of the box referred to the license terms inside. The Seventh Circuit reversed. The court stated: "Notice on the outside, terms on the inside, and a right to return the software for a refund if the terms are unacceptable (a right that the license expressly extends), may be a means of doing business valuable to buyers and sellers alike." The court discussed several examples of "money now, terms later" transactions (the purchase of insurance, airline tickets, electronic goods containing warranties inside the box, and drugs with inserts describing interactions and contraindications). Turning to the software industry, the court noted that software is often ordered over the phone and the Internet and that increasingly the delivery is also over the Internet. The court rejected the defendant's theory that would make these sales "unfettered by terms—so the seller has made a broad warranty and must pay consequential damages for any shortfalls in performance, two 'promises' that if taken seriously would drive prices through the ceiling or return transactions to the horse-and-buggy age."

The Seventh Circuit again upheld license terms in a pay-now-terms-later transaction with an accept-or-return provision in *Hill* v. *Gateway 2000, Inc.,* 105 F.3d 1147, 1150 (7th Cir.), cert. denied, 118 S.Ct. 47, 139 L.Ed.2d 13 (1997). In *Hill,* the customer ordered a computer over the phone, paying with a credit card, and received the computer in the mail accompanied by a list of terms to govern if the customer did not return the computer within 30 days. The court posed this question: "Are these terms effective as the parties' contract, or is the contract term-free because the order-taker did not read any terms over the phone and elicit the customer's assent?" Relying in part on *ProCD,* the court held that the terms were effective, stating: "Practical considerations support allowing vendors to enclose the full legal terms with their products."

ProCD and *Hill* allow a vendor to propose that a sale contract be formed not when the product is requested or the money is paid but after the customer has inspected the item and the terms. We find the Seventh Circuit's reasoning persuasive and see similarities between these cases and the present appeal. Timberline's license agreement, included with the software, is fairly standard and contains an accept-or-return provision. Mortenson argues that the negotiations between it and Timberline distinguishes this case from *ProCD* and *Hill,* cases involving off-the-shelf purchases where no negotiations took place between the buyer and seller. But although the software provided by Timberline is specialized to a specific market, no evidence suggests that the software was customized for Mortenson, and we find that it is analogous to an off-the-shelf package.

* * * * *

We find that Mortenson's installation and use of the software manifested its assent to the terms of the license and that it is bound by all terms of that license that are not found to be illegal or unconscionable.

[Judgment affirmed.]

Questions

1. At this writing in early 2000, the Supreme Court of Washington state has agreed to review the *Mortenson* decision.[31] Based on the portion of the case you have read here, would you reverse the Court of Appeals decision? Explain.

2. Why was the purchase order not considered an integrated contract?

3. According to the court, how did Mortenson manifest its acceptance of the license terms?

4. Enza and Richard Hill ordered a Gateway 2000 computer by telephone and paid by credit card. The computer was delivered in a box that also contained the terms of sale. Those terms were to be effective unless the computer was returned within 30 days. Among those terms was a clause providing for arbitration of any problems. The Hills kept the computer for more than 30 days before complaining about its performance and components. They filed suit, and Gateway argued that the arbitration clause should be enforced. The Hills conceded that they noticed the statement of terms, but they did not read those terms closely enough to notice the arbitration provision. Should the arbitration clause be enforced? Explain. See *Hill* v. *Gateway 2000,* 105 F.3d 1147 (7th Cir. 1997).

INTELLECTUAL PROPERTY

The anticipated explosion of electronic commerce depends to a significant extent on the business community's success in protecting its technology from theft, copying, infringement, and the like. Intellectual property, broadly, is composed of creative ideas that are the products of the human mind. Songs, computer programs, new medicines, a novel, and so on are forms of intellectual property. Recalling our discussion of market failure in Chapter 7, you may recognize that intellectual property, from an economics point of view, is a public good. Clearly, the market alone cannot effectively protect those ideas from theft and exploitation. Intellectual property law preserves the rights to those ideas for those who developed them. In doing so, we hope to provide justice by rewarding those whose ingenuity and hard work developed those ideas and their tangible results (recordings, movies, and the like), and we want to provide an incentive to produce those imaginative advances. Rational creators are less likely to invest the time and resources ordinarily necessary to achieve great innovations if they know that others may immediately appropriate a part of those ideas for their own good. At least that is the American and western view of intellectual property. Some cultures remain reluctant to recognize property rights of this kind, but globalization seems certain to generate relatively consistent intellectual property standards for most of the world. [For the "Intellectual Property Mall at the Franklin Pierce Law Center," see **www.ipmall.fplc.edu**]

Forms of Protection.   Intellectual property can be described in several primary categories, including patents and trade secrets, but we will restrict our discussion to the two areas that are most relevant to the Internet: copyrights and trademarks. [For more on patents, see the United States Patent and Trademark Office at **http://www.uspto.gov/**]

Copyrights.   In America and much of the world, anyone who creates "original works of authorship," whether in print or digital form, is, in most cases, automatically protected by copyright laws if the "works" are original and are "fixed in tangible form" (e.g., written down on paper). Consequently, the author has exclusive rights for a period of years to commercially exploit those works. Virtually all of the information available on-line is protected by the United States Copyright Act and includes such intellectual creations as data, databases, literature, music, software, photos, and multimedia works. While original works of authorship are automatically copyrighted, the full protection of the law can be achieved by placing a copyright notice on the work (e.g., "copyright 2000 Irwin/McGraw-Hill") and registering the copyright with the United States Copyright Office. International protection is provided by the principal copyright treaty, the Berne Convention. [The United States Copyright Office is located at **http://www.lcweb.loc.gov/**]

The copyright holder possesses the exclusive right to (1) reproduce the copyrighted work, (2) prepare adaptations based on the copyrighted material, (3) distribute the material by sale or otherwise, (4) perform or display the material. When anyone other than the copyright holder or one acting with the holder's permission makes use of one of those rights, the copyright has been *infringed* unless the use falls within a series of exceptions. Perhaps the most notable of those exceptions is the *fair use* doctrine, which allows use of copyrighted material without permission under some conditions, such as limited, nonprofit use in a classroom.

Trademarks.   Words, names, symbols, devices, or combinations thereof that are used to distinguish one seller's products from those of another are called *trademarks* when associated with products (e.g., IBM, Coke, Pepsi Cola) and *service marks* when associated with service businesses (e.g., United Airlines).

While states have trademark laws, our concern will be with the federal Lanham Act. Simply using a trademark in commerce can produce legal protection, but that protection is strengthened by federal registration of the mark with the U.S. Patent and Trademark Office. A trademark owner has the exclusive right to use that mark, thus preventing confusion in consumers' minds.

Trademark infringement occurs when that exclusive right is violated and consumer confusion is likely. *Trademark dilution* occurs when the distinctiveness of the mark is gradually whittled away or blurred by a nonconfusing use on an unrelated good or service. Thus, the shape of the Coke bottle was protected from dilution as was the name Polaroid, which was, for a time, being used on heating systems. If you established your own website and labeled it *Mercedes,* that choice would undoubtedly be challenged as a dilution of the mark, even if you were not dealing in cars.

Amazon.com and the tiny, feminist Amazon Bookstore Cooperative of Minneapolis, Minnesota, worked out a deal

An interesting trademark infringement fight was settled out of court in 1999 when Amazon.com and the tiny, feminist Amazon Bookstore Cooperative of Minneapolis, Minnesota, worked out a deal.[32] The Cooperative had sued the on-line book giant for infringement even though the Coop had never registered its name. It had, however, used the name since 1970 and thus claimed a common law right to it. The settlement allows the Coop to continue referring to itself as Amazon Bookstore Cooperative while its common law rights to the name were transferred to Amazon.com.[33] [The Cyberspace Law Institute provides a database on intellectual property at **http://www.cli.org**]

Domain Names.   Zack Exley, clearly a clever guy, noticed that the Internet address, www.gwbush.com, had not been registered so he did so thinking that then–presidential candidate George W. Bush, Jr., might want to buy the site.[34] At this writing, the sale has not

"It's just capitalism," Exley said

happened so Exley is operating gwbush.com as a parody of the official Bush site (www.georgewbush.com). Exley's site received over a million hits in its first nine months. "It's just capitalism," Exley said.[35] Sometimes this "cybersquatting" practice can pay off in a big way. Gateway Computer Co. paid $100,000 to the owner of www.gateway2000.com. That site had been used for posting pornographic pictures.[36]

The Internet address for a webpage is called its domain name. Ordinarily, a business entering electronic commerce will want to use the simplest form of its name as its domain name. Rights to a domain name are secured simply by being the first to request a name and paying a $70 registration fee. Under a license from the federal government, Network Solution, Inc. (NSI), has been the sole registrar of domain names in the United States, but now the market has been expanded so that a number of registrars will be available and domain names will be limited only by our imagination. Disputes about domain names can be resolved with an arbitration process set up by the Internet Corporation for Assigned Names and Numbers (ICANN), a nonprofit organization designed to promote competition in registering commercial domain names.

In January 2000, ICANN issued its first decision under its new arbitration policy. Bosman, the registrant of the domain name worldwrestlingfederation.com, told a World Intellectual Property Organization (WIPO) arbitration panel that he had registered the domain name in order to sell it. He offered the name to the World Wrestling Federation for $1 million. The panel concluded that Bosman had displayed bad faith in registering and using the name and had no legitimate right to it, and the WWF prevailed.

Source: "Lex 8256: Law in Cyberspace—NEW DEVELOPMENTS"
[**http://www.law.wayne.edu/litman/newdeve.html**].

In 1999, Congress approved the Anticybersquatting Consumer Protection Act, which created a cause of action where a trademark has been infringed upon by the registration of a domain name. The trademark holder must show a bad faith intention on the part of the registrant to profit from the registration, traffic in the name or use the name. Harvard University doubtless appreciates the new anticybersquatting weapon in its legal battle with a man (or men) who registered 65 Internet domain names incorporating the words Harvard and Radcliffe with a total asking price of at least $325,000.[37]

Critics argue the new law is premature in that it may hamper the rapid and imaginative development of the Internet. They also regard the Anticybersquatting Act as a club for big business. For example, the makers of Gumbey and Pokey toys threatened a 12-year-old who registered his nickname, Pokey. Similarly Archie Comics went after Little Veronica when she registered her name. How would you respond if you received a note from a corporate attorney reminding you of the potential of $100,000 in fines under the act because your personal webpage arguably infringes on a corporate mark?[38] So domain name disputes involve not only cybersquatting but also those situations where more than one party has a legitimate claim to a name.

> In 1999, the Los Angeles firm, Ecompanies, paid a Houston entrepreneur $7.5 million for the domain name business.com, and the domain name America.com is up for sale at $10 million.
>
> Source: Shelly Murphy, "Harvard Seeks Rights to Own Name in Cyber Suit," *Boston Globe,* December 8, 1999, p. B1.

TAXES?

We close this chapter with perhaps the most interesting public policy question in the remarkable confusion of the Internet. If you buy a CD on the Internet, your neighborhood retailer will not receive your business and your state and local governments often will not receive sales taxes as they would have if you had made the purchase at that local store. To address that issue and others, the federal government has undertaken a study of e-commerce tax policy. Sales taxes have received the most attention, but other taxes, such as a charge for World Wide Web access, have been suggested. Congress and President Clinton imposed a moratorium on Internet taxes that does not expire until October 2001. Not wanting to diminish the inventive energy of the Internet, government officials are proceeding with care. Not only would a tax threaten Internet business growth, but the nature of the Internet makes it comparatively easy for businesses to move around the globe to tax-free havens. On the other hand, equal treatment for all businesses as well as government's requirements for reasonable levels of revenue argue for Internet taxation. Congress must now act on the tax question, which clearly is critical to the long-term development of e-commerce. [For a website devoted to state and local e-commerce taxation, see **http://www.ryanco.com/gateway/electron.html**]

> the Internet makes it comparatively easy for businesses to move around the globe to tax-free havens

Three-quarters of Americans oppose Internet sales taxes according to a 1999 nationwide poll.

Source: Associated Press, "Poll Shows Resistance to E-Commerce Taxation," *Waterloo–Cedar Falls Courier,* September 15, 1999, p. C6.

The editorial that follows examines some of the competing considerations in the Internet taxation debate.

PREMATURE TO PUT SALES TAXES ON E-COMMERCE

One advantage the Internet enjoys over bricks-and-mortar businesses is the lack of sales taxes. That's not unique to e-commerce. Catalog merchants are not required to impose a sales tax if they ship a product out of state and don't have operations in that state.

Consumers, though, are supposed to pay a "use tax," equivalent to their local sales tax and applied to credit cards, but that is typically ignored.

* * * * *

The National Governors' Association, on the other hand, wants an online sales tax so Main Street merchants are not at a competitive disadvantage with online retailers. Their concerns are simple. Communities could see many shops close and jobs disappear without a level playing field on the tax issue, although online consumers do incur shipping fees that often negate any sales tax advantage.

The governors would make the tax voluntary and have it distributed through a third-party clearinghouse.

Arguments against the Internet sales tax range from the fact that retailers have survived the assault of largely tax-free catalog sales to those who believe Internet growth could force states to end sales taxes entirely—wishful thinking considering 46 states impose it as well as hundreds of localities.

* * * * *

It is premature to impose a sales tax on e-commerce (and all catalog retailers) until the effect of the genre can be better assessed. But neither should that option be abandoned forever.

Said George Zodrow of Rice University, speaking on behalf of 49 tax experts nationwide, "Once electronic commerce has been an established retail channel, it should not be treated differently than other commerce."

Source: *Waterloo-Cedar Falls Courier,* December 23, 1999, p. A6. Reprinted by permission. [For the development of cyberspace law through the 1990s, see **http://www.gseis.ucla.edu/iclp/decade.html**].

Question

Would you impose a tax on all Internet sales? Explain.

INTERNET EXERCISE

Using the Cyberspace Law Center at **http://cyber.findlaw.com/index.html**, click on the *defamation* library and make your way to "Reputation on (the) Line: Defamation and the Internet." Summarize the authors' advice about the major issues in dealing with on-line defamation directed at corporations.

CHAPTER QUESTIONS

1. Bensusan Restaurant Corporation owns the famous New York City jazz club "The Blue Note," and in 1985 it registered the name as a federal trademark. Since 1980, King has operated a small club in Columbia, Missouri, also named "The Blue Note." Around 1993, Bensusan wrote to King demanding that he discontinue use of "The Blue Note" name. King's attorney responded by saying that Bensusan had no legal right to make the demand. In 1996 King created, in Missouri, a website for "The Blue Note," which also contained a hyperlink to the New York club's website. Bensusan then sued in the Southern District of New York alleging Lanham Act and trademark violations, among other things. The New York court dismissed the case for lack of personal jurisdiction. Bensusan appealed. Decide. Explain. See *Bensusan Restaurant Corp.* v. *King,* 126 F.3d 25 (2d Cir. 1997).

2. In March 1992, Danish police seized the business records of BAMSE, a computer bulletin board system based in Denmark that sold child pornography over the Internet. The records included information that Mohrbacher, who lived in Paradise, California, had downloaded two graphic interface format (GIF) images from BAMSE in January 1992.

   In March 1993, police executed a search warrant at Mohrbacher's workplace and found, among other images, two files that had been downloaded from BAMSE, one of a nude girl and one of a girl engaged in a sex act with an adult; both girls were under 12. During the execution of the warrant, Mohrbacher was cooperative, confessing that he had downloaded the two images from BAMSE. Mohrbacher was charged with transporting or shipping images by computer as prohibited by 18 U.S.C. 2252(a)(1). Mohrbacher argued that downloading is properly characterized as receiving images by computer, which is proscribed by section 2252(a)(2). He was not charged under (a)(2).

   Mohrbacher made a Rule 29 motion for acquittal on the transporting counts, arguing that downloading images constituted receiving, rather than transporting or shipping, within the commonsense meaning of the statute. The district court denied the motion, reasoning that downloading from a computer bulletin board was analogous to "the seller putting [an item] on his shelf and the buyer being the person who takes it off the shelf. Here, it was Mr. Mohrbacher who pushed the right buttons that caused the images to be sent from Denmark to California." The court also stated that Mohrbacher could be criminally liable for causing the images to be transported, commenting that "it was Mr. Mohrbacher who caused the images or visual depiction to be transported in foreign commerce."

   Does downloading from a computer bulletin board constitute shipping or transporting within the meaning of 18 U.S.C. section 2252(a)(1)? Explain. See *United States of America* v. *Mohrbacher,* 182 F.3d 1041 (9th Cir. 1999).

3. America Online (AOL), an Internet service provider, sued TSF Marketing and Joseph Melle, who founded TSF. AOL claimed that Melle and TSF sent unauthorized bulk e-mail advertisements (spam) to AOL subscribers. The e-mail contained the letters "aol.com" in the headers. AOL claimed that the e-mail totaled some 60 million messages over a 10-month period. Melle allegedly continued the mailings after he was notified in writing by AOL to stop. AOL received over 50,000 complaints from subscribers. AOL claimed, among other things, that Melle had diluted its trademark. Decide. Explain. See *America Online, Inc.* v. *IMS,* 24 F.Supp.2d 548 (E.D.Va. 1998).

4. Plaintiff Marobie-FL, Inc., released software of copyrighted clip art for use in the fire service industry. Robisheaux administered the National Association of Fire Equipment Distributors (NAFED) webpage. He received the clip art from a source that he could not remember. He placed the clip art on NAFED's webpage. At that point, the clip art could be readily accessed and downloaded by any Web user. Marobie claimed copyright infringement. Among other arguments, NAFED claimed that its display of the clip art constituted a fair use, within the meaning of federal copyright law. Decide. Explain. See *Marobie-FL* v. *National Ass'n of Fire Equip. Dist.,* 983 F.Supp. 1167 (N.D.Ill. 1997).

5. McLaren was an employee of Microsoft Corporation. In December 1996, Microsoft suspended McLaren's employment pending an investigation into accusations of sexual harassment and "inventory questions." McLaren requested access to his electronic mail to disprove the allegations against him. According to McLaren, he was told he could access his e-mail only by requesting it through company officials and telling them the location of a particular message. By memorandum, McLaren requested that no one tamper with his Microsoft office workstation or his e-mail. McLaren's employment was terminated on December 11, 1996.

   Following the termination of his employment, McLaren filed suit against the company alleging as his sole cause of action a claim for invasion of privacy. In support of his claim, McLaren alleged that, on information and belief, Microsoft had invaded his privacy by "breaking into" some or all of the personal folders maintained on his office computer and releasing the contents of the folders to third parties. According to McLaren, the personal folders were part of a computer application created by Microsoft in which e-mail messages could be stored. Access to the e-mail system was obtained through a network password. Access to personal folders could be additionally restricted by a "personal store" password created by the individual user. McLaren created and used a personal store password to restrict access to his personal folders.

   McLaren concedes in his petition that it was possible for Microsoft to "decrypt" his personal store password. McLaren alleges, however, that "[b]y allowing [him] to have a personal store password for his personal folders, [McLaren] manifested and [Microsoft] recognized an expectation that the personal folders would be free from intrusion and interference." McLaren characterizes Microsoft's decrypting or otherwise "breaking in" to his personal folders as an intentional, unjustified, and unlawful invasion of privacy.

   Did Microsoft unlawfully invade McLaren's privacy? Explain. See *McLaren* v. *Microsoft,* No. 05–97–00824–CV (Ct. of Appeals, 5th Dist. of Tex. at Dallas, 1999).

6. Increasingly, employers are dismissing employees for improper use of the Internet while at work.
   a. List some of the nonwork uses employees are making of the Internet.
   b. In addition to reduced productivity, why should an employer be concerned about employees' nonwork use of the Internet while on the job?

7. Recently, journalist John Snell remarked, "Not long ago you couldn't turn around in cyberspace without bumping into a tech geek. Now you're no more than a mouse click away from a lawyer. Attorneys are everywhere."[39] What factors account for the dramatic increase in lawyers addressing Internet issues?

8. Psychologists are worried that the Internet will make shopping too easy. Explain their concern.

9. The United Nations recently warned that the worldwide growth of e-commerce may constitute a threat to the well-being of the world's developing nations as well as parts of Europe. Explain the UN concerns.

10. Philosopher Richard De George was recently asked about the "ethics" of employer monitoring of employee e-mail. Respond to that question.

11. Critics of a free market approach to the on-line economy worry about the development of entrenched monopolies and the ease with which digital data can simply be copied, rather than purchased, by consumers. Explain the on-line nature of those two problems and whether the free market can resolve them.

12. Critics argue that even if the United States wanted to impose significant new government regulations on the Internet the effort would fail in the global market. Explain that argument.

NOTES

1. Stuart S. Malawer, "National Governments Should Defer to the Private Sector and Avoid Undue Restrictions on Electronic Commerce," *Legal Times,* February 8, 1999, p. S40.

2. David Lieberman, "Internet Gap Widening," *USA Today,* July 9/11, 1999, p. 1A.

3. Ibid.

4. Ibid.

5. Bloomberg News, "More Women, Minorities Using Internet," *Arizona Republic,* April 13, 1999, p. E3.

6. Ron Corben, "UN to Developing Nations: Start E-Commerce or Else," *Journal of Commerce,* May 5, 1999, p. 9A.

7. Anne R. Carey and Jerry Mosemak, "Clicking with Others," *USA Today,* June 3, 1999, p. 1A.

8. Brian McGrory, "Alienation Finds a Future on Web," *Boston Globe,* July 16, 1999, p. B1.

9. John Perry Barlow, "Cyberspace Declaration of Independence," [**http://hobbes.ncsa.uiuc.edu/sean/declaration.html**].

10. Patrick McMahon, "Judge Agrees Web Site a Threat," *USA Today,* February 26, 1999, p. 2A.

11. *ApolloMedia Corp.* v. *Reno,* 119 S.Ct. 1450 (1999).

12. Associated Press, "FTC: No Net Laws for Privacy," *Atlanta Journal and Constitution,* July 13, 1999, p. 3E.

13. Edward C. Baig, Marcia Stepanek, and Neil Gross, "Privacy," *Business Week,* April 5, 1999, p. 84.

14. Ibid.

15. John Simons, "New Internet Privacy Laws Appear Less Likely with Release of New Survey," *The Wall Street Journal,* May 13, 1999, p. B9.

16. Ibid.

17. Ted Bridis, "Microsoft to Require Privacy Promises on Internet Sites," *Des Moines Register,* June 24, 1999, p. 8S.

18. Noble Sprayberry, "Confronting the Cookie Monster," *San Diego Union-Tribune,* August 22, 1999, p. I–9.

19. Reuters, "EU Takes Five States to Court Over Internet Privacy," January 11, 2000, [**http://legalnews.findlaw.com/legalnews/s/20000111/L1137104.html**].

20. Ibid.

21. Jimmy Burns, "Electronic Crime 'Beating Regulators' " *Financial Times,* September 14, 1999, p. 2.

22. Associated Press, "Attorneys General Consider New Laws to Address Internet Crime," *FindLaw Legal News,* [**http://legalnews.findlaw.com/News/s/20000110/netcrime.html**].

23. "Student Faces Piracy Sentence," *Des Moines Register,* August 21, 1999, p. 6S.

24. Julie Schmit, "Microsoft Makes Inroads on Pirated Software," *USA Today,* March 10, 1999, p. C2.

25. Adam Creed, "Hong Kong's Piracy Laws Come into Effect," *Newsbytes,* [**http://www.technews.com/pubNews/00/142167.html**].

26. Jube Shriver, Jr., "Easing of Rules on Encryption Worries Experts," *Los Angeles Times,* January 14, 2000, p. C1.

27. John Simons, "FTC to Curb Medical Sales Pitches on Web," *The Wall Street Journal,* June 24, 1999, p. A2.

28. Carl T. Hall, "FTC Wants to Regulate Online Pharmacies," *San Francisco Chronicle,* July 31, 1999, p. A2.

29. John Yaukey, "Stock Fraud Proliferates Via the Internet," *Des Moines Register,* March 18, 2000, p. 7C.

30. Ibid.

31. *Mortenson* v. *Timberline,* 1999 Wash. LEXIS 483 (1999).

32. David Phelps, "Amazon Bookstore and Amazon.com Agree to Coexist," *Minneapolis Star Tribune,* November 5, 1999, p. 1D.

33. Ibid.

34. Jessica Lee, "Bill Would Protect Trademarks, Names from Cybersquatters," *USA Today,* August 3, 1999, p. 8A.

35. Ibid.

36. Ibid.

37. Shelley Murphy, "Harvard Seeks Rights to Own Name in Cyber Suit," *Boston Globe,* December 8, 1999, p. B1.

38. Mark Grossman, "New Year, New Laws on Cybersquatting," *Miami Daily Business Review,* January 11, 2000, sec: Cyberlaw, p. A1.

39. John Snell, "Lawyers Drawn to Unsettled Internet; Lots of Legal Issues, Large and Small, Must Be Sorted Out," *Minneapolis Star Tribune,* November 29, 1999, p. 6D.

Appendix A

The Constitution of the United States of America

Preamble

We the People of the United States, in Order to form a more perfect Union, establish Justice, insure domestic Tranquility, provide for the common defence, promote the general Welfare, and secure the Blessings of Liberty to ourselves and our Posterity, do ordain and establish this Constitution for the United States of America.

Article I

Section 1. All legislative Powers herein granted shall be vested in a Congress of the United States, which shall consist of a Senate and House of Representatives.

Section 2. (1) The House of Representatives shall be composed of Members chosen every second Year by the People of the several States, and the Electors in each State shall have the Qualifications requisite for Electors of the most numerous Branch of the State Legislature.

(2) No Person shall be a Representative who shall not have attained to the Age of twenty-five Years, and been seven Years a Citizen of the United States, and who shall not, when elected, be an Inhabitant of that State in which he shall be chosen.

(3) Representatives and direct Taxes shall be apportioned among the several States which may be included within this Union, according to their respective Numbers, which shall be determined by adding to the whole Number of free Persons, including those bound to Service for a Term of Years, and excluding Indians not taxed, three fifths of all other Persons.[1] The actual Enumeration shall be made within three Years after the first Meeting of the Congress of the United States, and within every subsequent Term of ten Years, in such Manner as they shall by Law direct. The Number of Representatives shall not exceed one for every thirty Thousand, but each State shall have at Least one Representative; and until such enumeration shall be made, the State of New Hampshire shall be entitled to chuse three, Massachusetts eight, Rhode Island and Providence Plantations one, Connecticut five, New York six, New Jersey four, Pennsylvania eight, Delaware one, Maryland six, Virginia ten, North Carolina five, South Carolina five, and Georgia three.

---

[1]Refer to the Fourteenth Amendment.

(4) When vacancies happen in the Representation from any State, the Executive Authority thereof shall issue Writs of Election to fill such Vacancies.

(5) The House of Representatives shall chuse their Speaker and other Officers; and shall have the sole Power of Impeachment.

Section 3. (1) The Senate of the United States shall be composed of two Senators from each State, chosen by the Legislature thereof,[2] for six Years; and each Senator shall have one Vote.

(2) Immediately after they shall be assembled in Consequence of the first Election, they shall be divided as equally as may be into three Classes. The Seats of the Senators of the first Class shall be vacated at the Expiration of the Second Year, of the second Class at the Expiration of the fourth Year, and of the third Class at the Expiration of the sixth Year, so that one third may be chosen every second Year; and if Vacancies happen by Resignation, or otherwise, during the Recess of the Legislature of any State, the Executive thereof may make temporary Appointments until the next Meeting of the Legislature, which shall then fill such Vacancies.[3]

(3) No Person shall be a Senator who shall not have attained to the Age of thirty Years, and been nine Years a Citizen of the United States, and who shall not, when elected, be an Inhabitant of that State for which he shall be chosen.

(4) The Vice President of the United States shall be President of the Senate, but shall have no Vote, unless they be equally divided.

(5) The Senate shall chuse their other Officers, and also a President pro tempore, in the Absence of the Vice President, or when he shall exercise the Office of President of the United States.

(6) The Senate shall have the sole Power to try all Impeachments. When sitting for that Purpose, they shall be on Oath or Affirmation. When the President of the United States is tried, the Chief Justice shall preside: And no Person shall be convicted without the Concurrence of two thirds of the Members present.

(7) Judgment in Cases of Impeachment shall not extend further than to removal from Office, and disqualification to hold and enjoy any Office of honor, Trust, or Profit under the United States: but the Party convicted shall nevertheless be liable and subject to Indictment, Trial, Judgment, and Punishment, according to Law.

Section 4. (1) The Times, Places and Manner of holding Elections for Senators and Representatives, shall be prescribed in each State by the Legislature thereof; but the Congress may at any time by Law make or alter such Regulations, except as to the Places of chusing Senators.

(2) The Congress shall assemble at least once in every year, and such Meeting shall be on the first Monday in December, unless they shall by Law appoint a different Day.[4]

Section 5. (1) Each House shall be the Judge of the Elections, Returns, and Qualifications of its own Members, and a Majority of each shall constitute a Quorum to do Business; but a smaller Number may adjourn from day to day, and may be authorized to compel the Attendance of absent Members, in such Manner, and under such Penalties as each House may provide.

(2) Each House may determine the Rules of its Proceedings, punish its Members for disorderly Behavior, and, with the Concurrence of two thirds, expel a Member.

(3) Each House shall keep a Journal of its Proceedings, and from time to time publish the same, excepting such Parts as may in their Judgment require Secrecy; and the Yeas and Nays of the Members of either House on any question shall, at the Desire of one fifth of those Present, be entered on the Journal.

---

[2]Refer to the Seventeenth Amendment.

[3]Ibid.

[4]Refer to the Twentieth Amendment.

(4) Neither House, during the Session of Congress, shall, without the Consent of the other, adjourn for more than three days, nor to any other Place than that in which the two Houses shall be sitting.

Section 6. (1) The Senators and Representatives shall receive a Compensation for their Services, to be ascertained by Law, and paid out of the Treasury of the United States. They shall in all Cases, except Treason, Felony and Breach of the Peace, be privileged from Arrest during their Attendance at the Session of their respective Houses, and in going to and returning from the same; and for any Speech or Debate in either House, they shall not be questioned in any other Place.

(2) No Senator or Representative shall, during the Time for which he was elected, be appointed to any civil Office under the Authority of the United States, which shall have been created, or the Emoluments whereof shall have been encreased during such time; and no Person holding any Office under the United States, shall be a Member of either House during his Continuance in Office.

Section 7. (1) All Bills for raising Revenue shall originate in the House of Representatives; but the Senate may propose or concur with Amendments as on other Bills.

(2) Every Bill which shall have passed the House of Representatives and the Senate, shall, before it becomes a Law, be presented to the President of the United States; If he approve he shall sign it, but if not he shall return it, with his Objections to the House in which it shall have originated, who shall enter the Objections at large on their Journal, and proceed to reconsider it. If after such Reconsideration two thirds of that House shall agree to pass the Bill, it shall be sent together with the Objections, to the other House, by which it shall likewise be reconsidered, and if approved by two thirds of that House, it shall become a Law. But in all such Cases the Votes of both Houses shall be determined by yeas and Nays, and the Names of the Persons voting for and against the Bill shall be entered on the Journal of each House respectively. If any Bill shall not be returned by the President within ten Days (Sundays excepted) after it shall have been presented to him, the Same shall be a Law, in like Manner as if he had signed it, unless the Congress by their Adjournment prevent its Return in which Case it shall not be a Law.

(3) Every Order, Resolution, or Vote, to Which the Concurrence of the Senate and House of Representatives may be necessary (except on a question of Adjournment) shall be presented to the President of the United States; and before the same shall take Effect, shall be approved by him, or being disapproved by him, shall be repassed by two thirds of the Senate and House of Representatives, according to the Rules and Limitations prescribed in the Case of a Bill.

Section 8. (1) The Congress shall have Power To lay and collect Taxes, Duties, Imposts and Excises, to pay the Debts and provide for the common Defence and general Welfare of the United States; but all Duties, Imposts and Excises shall be uniform throughout the United States;

(2) To borrow money on the credit of the United States;

(3) To regulate Commerce with foreign Nations, and among the several States, and with the Indian Tribes;

(4) To establish a uniform Rule of Naturalization, and uniform Laws on the subject of Bankruptcies throughout the United States;

(5) To coin Money, regulate the Value thereof, and of foreign Coin, and fix the Standard of Weights and Measures;

(6) To provide for the Punishment of counterfeiting the Securities and current Coin of the United States;

(7) To Establish Post Offices and Post Roads;

(8) To promote the Progress of Science and useful Arts, by securing for limited Times to Authors and Inventors the exclusive Right to their respective Writings and Discoveries;

(9) To constitute Tribunals inferior to the Supreme Court;

(10) To define and punish Piracies and Felonies committed on the high Seas, and Offenses against the Law of Nations;

(11) To declare War, grant Letters of Marque and Reprisal, and make Rules concerning Captures on Land and Water;

(12) To raise and support Armies, but no Appropriation of Money to that Use shall be for a longer Term than two Years;

(13) To provide and maintain a Navy;

(14) To make Rules for the Government and Regulation of the land and naval Forces;

(15) To provide for calling forth the Militia to execute the Laws of the Union, suppress Insurrections and repel Invasions;

(16) To provide for organizing, arming, and disciplining, the Militia, and for governing such Part of them as may be employed in the Service of the United States, reserving to the States respectively, the Appointment of the Officers, and the Authority of training the Militia according to the discipline prescribed by Congress;

(17) To exercise exclusive Legislation in all Cases whatsoever, over such District (not exceeding ten Miles square) as may, by Cession of particular States, and the Acceptance of Congress, become the Seat of the Government of the United States, and to exercise like Authority over all Places purchased by the Consent of the Legislature of the State in which the Same shall be, for the Election of Forts, Magazines, Arsenals, dock-Yards, and other needful Buildings;—And

(18) To make all Laws which shall be necessary and proper for carrying into Execution the foregoing Powers, and all other Powers vested by this Constitution in the Government of the United States, or in any Department or Officer thereof.

Section 9. (1) The Migration or Importation of Such Persons as any of the States now existing shall think proper to admit, shall not be prohibited by the Congress prior to the Year one thousand eight hundred and eight, but a Tax or duty may be imposed on such Importation, not exceeding ten dollars for each Person.

(2) The privilege of the Writ of Habeas Corpus shall not be suspended, unless when in Cases of Rebellion or Invasion the public Safety may require it.

(3) No Bill of Attainder or ex post facto Law shall be passed.

(4) No Capitation, or other direct, Tax shall be laid, unless in proportion to the Census or Enumeration herein before directed to the taken.[5]

(5) No Tax or Duty shall be laid on Articles exported from any state.

(6) No Preference shall be given by any Regulation of Commerce or Revenue to the Ports of one State over those of another; nor shall Vessels bound to, or from, one State be obliged to enter, clear, or pay Duties in another.

(7) No money shall be drawn from the Treasury, but in Consequence of Appropriations made by Law; and a regular Statement and Account of the Receipts and Expenditures of all public Money shall be published from time to time.

(8) No Title of Nobility shall be granted by the United States; And no person holding any Office of Profit or Trust under them, shall, without the Consent of the Congress, accept of any present, Emolument, Office or Title, of any kind whatever, from any King, Prince, or foreign State.

Section 10. (1) No State shall enter into any Treaty, Alliance, or Confederation; grant Letters of Marque and Reprisal; coin Money; emit Bills of Credit; make any Thing but gold and silver Coin a Tender in Payment of Debts; pass any Bill of Attainder, ex post facto Law, or Law impairing the Obligation of Contracts, or grant any Title of Nobility.

(2) No State shall, without the Consent of the Congress, lay any Imposts or Duties on Imports or Exports, except what may be absolutely necessary for executing its inspection Laws: and the net Produce of all Duties and Imposts, laid by any State on Imports or Exports, shall be for the Use of the

---

[5]Refer to the Sixteenth Amendment.

Treasury of the United States; and all such Laws shall be subject to the Revision and Controul of the Congress.

(3) No State shall, without the Consent of Congress, lay any Duty of Tonnage, keep Troops, or Ships of War in time of Peace, enter into any Agreement or Compact with another State, or with a foreign Power, or engage in War, unless actually invaded, or in such imminent Danger as will not admit of delay.

Article II

Section 1. (1) The executive Power shall be vested in a President of the United States of America. He shall hold his Office during the Term of four Years, and, together with the Vice President, chosen for the same Term, be elected as follows:

(2) Each State shall appoint, in such Manner as the Legislature thereof may direct, a Number of Electors, equal to the whole Number of Senators and Representatives to which the State may be entitled in the Congress; but no Senator or Representative, or Person holding an Office of Trust or Profit under the United States, shall be appointed an Elector.

(3) The Electors shall meet in their respective States, and vote by Ballot for two Persons, of whom one at least shall not be an Inhabitant of the same State with themselves. And they shall make a list of all the Persons voted for, and of the Number of Votes for each; which List they shall sign and certify, and transmit sealed to the Seat of the Government of the United States, directed to the President of the Senate. The President of the Senate shall, in the Presence of the Senate and House of Representatives, open all the Certificates, and the Votes shall then be counted. The Person having the greatest Number of Votes shall be the President, if such Number be a Majority of the whole Number of Electors appointed; and if there be more than one who have such Majority, and have an equal Number of Votes, then the House of Representatives shall immediately chuse by Ballot one of them for President; and if no Person have a Majority, then from the five highest on the List the said House shall in like Manner chuse the President. But in chusing the President, the Votes shall be taken by States, the Representation from each State have one Vote; A quorum for this Purpose shall consist of a Member or Members from two thirds of the States, and a Majority of all the States shall be necessary to a Choice. In every Case, after the Choice of the President, the Person having the greater Number of Votes of the Electors shall be the Vice President. But if there should remain two or more who have equal Votes, the Senate shall chuse from them by Ballot the Vice President.[6]

(4) The Congress may determine the Time of chusing the Electors, and the Day on which they shall give their Votes; which Day shall be the same throughout the United States.

(5) No person except a natural born Citizen, or a Citizen of the United States, at the time of the Adoption of this Constitution, shall be eligible to the Office of President; neither shall any Person be eligible to that Office who shall not have attained to the Age of thirty-five Years, and been fourteen Years a Resident within the United States.

(6) In case of the removal of the President from Office, or of his Death, Resignation or Inability to discharge the Powers and Duties of the said Office, the Same shall devolve on the Vice President, and the Congress may by Law provide for the Case of Removal, Death, Resignation or Inability, both of the President and Vice President, declaring what Officer shall then act as President, and such Officer shall act accordingly, until the Disability be removed, or a President shall be elected.[7]

---

[6]Refer to the Twelfth Amendment.
[7]Refer to the Twenty-Fifth Amendment.

(7) The President shall, at stated Times, receive for his Services, a Compensation, which shall neither be encreased nor diminished during the Period for which he shall have been elected, and he shall not receive within that Period any other Emolument from the United States, or any of them.

(8) Before he enter on the Execution of his Office, he shall take the following Oath or Affirmation: "I do solemnly swear (or affirm) that I will faithfully execute the Office of President of the United States, and will to the best of my Ability, preserve, protect, and defend the Constitution of the United States."

Section 2. (1) The President shall be Commander in Chief of the Army and Navy of the United States, and of the militia of the several States, when called into the actual Service of the United States; he may require the Opinion, in writing, of the principal Officer in each of the executive Departments, upon any Subject relating to the Duties of their respective Offices, and he shall have Power to grant Reprieves and Pardons for Offenses against the United States, except in Cases of Impeachment.

(2) He shall have Power, by and with the Advice and Consent of the Senate, to make Treaties, provided two thirds of the Senators present concur; and he shall nominate, and by and with the Advice and Consent of the Senate, shall appoint Ambassadors, other public Ministers and Consuls, Judges of the supreme Court, and all other Officers of the United States, whose Appointments are not herein otherwise provided for, and which shall be established by Law; but the Congress may by Law vest the Appointment of such inferior Officers, as they think proper, in the President alone, in the Courts of Law, or in the Heads of Departments.

(3) The President shall have Power to fill up all Vacancies that may happen during the Recess of the Senate, by granting Commissions which shall expire at the End of their next Session.

Section 3. He shall from time to time give to the Congress Information of the State of the Union, and recommend to their Consideration such Measures as he shall judge necessary and expedient; he may, on extraordinary Occasions, convene both Houses, or either of them, and in Case of Disagreement between them, with Respect to the Time of Adjournment, he may adjourn them to such Time as he shall think proper; he shall receive Ambassadors and other public Ministers; he shall take Care that the Laws be faithfully executed, and shall Commission all the Officers of the United States.

Section 4. The President, Vice President and all civil Officers of the United States, shall be removed from Office on Impeachment for, and Conviction of, Treason, Bribery, or other high Crimes and Misdemeanors.

Article III

Section 1. The judicial Power of the United States, shall be vested in one supreme Court, and in such inferior Courts as the Congress may from time to time ordain and establish. The Judges, both of the supreme and inferior Courts, shall hold their Offices during good Behaviour, and shall, at stated Times, receive for their Services a Compensation, which shall not be diminished during their Continuance in Office.

Section 2. (1) The judicial Power shall extend to all Cases, in Law and Equity, arising under this Constitution, the Laws of the United States, and Treaties made, or which shall be made, under their Authority;—to all Cases affecting Ambassadors, other public Ministers and Consuls;—to all Cases of admiralty and maritime Jurisdiction;—to Controversies to which the United States shall be a Party;—to Controversies between two or more States;—between a State and Citizens of another State,[8]—between Citizens of different states;—between Citizens of the same State claiming Lands

---

[8]Refer to the Eleventh Amendment.

under the Grants of different States, and between a State, or the Citizens thereof, and foreign States, Citizens or Subjects.

(2) In all Cases affecting Ambassadors, other public Ministers and Consuls, and those in which a State shall be a Party, the supreme Court shall have original Jurisdiction. In all the other Cases before mentioned, the supreme Court shall have appellate Jurisdiction, both as to Law and Fact, with such Exceptions, and under such Regulations as the Congress shall make.

(3) The trial of all Crimes, except in Cases of Impeachment, shall be by Jury; and such Trial shall be held in the State where the said Crimes shall have been committed; but when not committed within any State, the Trial shall be at such Place or Places as the Congress may be Law have directed.

Section 3. (1) Treason against the United States, shall consist only in levying War against them, or, in adhering to their enemies, giving them Aid and Comfort. No Person shall be convicted of Treason unless on the Testimony of two Witnesses to the same overt Act, or on Confession in open Court.

(2) The Congress shall have Power to declare the Punishment of Treason, but no Attainder of Treason shall work Corruption of Blood, or Forfeiture except during the Life of the Person attainted.

Article IV

Section 1. Full Faith and Credit shall be given in each State to the public Acts, Records, and judicial Proceedings of every other State. And the Congress may by general Laws prescribe the Manner in which such Acts, Records and Proceedings shall be proved, and the Effect thereof.

Section 2. (1) The Citizens of each State shall be entitled to all Privileges and Immunities of Citizens in the several States.

(2) A Person charged in any State with Treason, Felony, or other Crime, who shall flee from Justice, and be found in another State, shall on demand of the executive Authority of the State from which he fled, be delivered up, to be removed to the State having Jurisdiction of the Crime.

(3) No Person held to Service or Labour in one State, under the Laws thereof, escaping into another, shall, in Consequence of any Law or Regulation therein, be discharged from such Service or Labour, but shall be delivered up on Claim of the Party to whom such Service or Labour may be due.[9]

Section 3. (1) New States may be admitted by the Congress into this Union; but no new State shall be formed or erected within the Jurisdiction of any other State; nor any State be formed by the Junction of two or more States, or Parts of States without the Consent of the Legislatures of the States concerned as well as of the Congress.

(2) The Congress shall have Power to dispose of and make all needful Rules and Regulations respecting the Territory or other Property belonging to the United States; and nothing in this Constitution shall be so construed as to Prejudice any Claims of the United States, or of any particular State.

Section 4. The United States shall guarantee to every State in this Union a Republican Form of Government, and shall protect each of them against Invasion; and on Application of the Legislature, or of the Executive (when the Legislature cannot be convened) against domestic Violence.

---

[9]Refer to the Thirteenth Amendment.

Article V

The Congress, whenever two thirds of both Houses shall deem it necessary, shall propose Amendments to this Constitution, or, on the Application of the Legislatures of two thirds of the several States, shall call a Convention for proposing Amendments, which, in either Case, shall be valid to all Intents and Purposes, as part of this Constitution, when ratified by the Legislatures of three fourths of the several States, or by Conventions in three fourths thereof, as the one or the other Mode of Ratification may be proposed by the Congress; Provided that no Amendment which may be made prior to the Year One thousand eight hundred and eight shall in any Manner affect the first and fourth Clauses in the Ninth Section of the first Article; and that no State, without its Consent, shall be deprived of its equal Suffrage in the Senate.

Article VI

(1) All Debts contracted and Engagements entered into, before the Adoption of this Constitution shall be as valid against the United States under this Constitution, as under the Confederation.

(2) This Constitution, and the Laws of the United States which shall be made in Pursuance thereof; and all Treaties made, or which shall be made, under the Authority of the United States, shall be the supreme Law of the Land; and the Judges in every State shall be bound thereby, any Thing in the Constitution or Laws of any State to the Contrary notwithstanding.

(3) The Senators and Representatives before mentioned, and the Members of the several State Legislatures, and all executive and judicial Officers, both of the United States and of the several States, shall be bound by Oath or Affirmation, to support this Constitution, but no religious Test shall ever be required as a Qualification to any Office or public Trust under the United States.

Article VII

The Ratification of the Conventions of nine States shall be sufficient for the Establishment of this Constitution between the States so ratifying the Same.

[Amendments 1–10, the Bill of Rights, were ratified in 1791.]

Amendment I

Congress shall make no law respecting an establishment of religion, or prohibiting the free exercise thereof; or abridging the freedom of speech, or of the press; or the right of the people peaceably to assemble, and to petition the Government for a redress of grievances.

Amendment II

A well regulated Militia, being necessary to the security of a free State, the right of the people to keep and bear Arms, shall not be infringed.

Amendment III

No Soldier shall, in time of peace be quartered in any house, without the consent of the Owner, nor in time of war, but in a manner to be prescribed by law.

Amendment IV

The right of the people to be secure in their persons, houses, papers, and effects, against unreasonable searches and seizures, shall not be violated, and no Warrants shall issue, but upon probable cause, supported by Oath or affirmation, and particularly describing the place to be searched, and the persons or things to be seized.

Amendment V

No person shall be held to answer for a capital, or otherwise infamous crime, unless on a presentment or indictment of a Grand Jury, except in cases arising in the land or naval forces, or in the Militia, when in actual service in time of War or public danger; nor shall any person be subject for the same offence to be twice put in jeopardy of life or limb; nor shall be compelled in any criminal case to be a witness against himself, nor be deprived of life, liberty, or property, without due process of law; nor shall private property be taken for public use, without just compensation.

Amendment VI

In all criminal prosecutions, the accused shall enjoy the right to a speedy and public trial, by an impartial jury of the State and district wherein the crime shall have been committed, which district shall have been previously ascertained by law, and to be informed of the nature and cause of the accusation; to be confronted with the witness against him; to have compulsory process for obtaining witnesses in his favor, and to have the Assistance of Counsel for his defence.

Amendment VII

In Suits at common law, where the value in controversy shall exceed twenty dollars, the right of trial by jury shall be preserved, and no fact tried by jury, shall be otherwise re-examined in any Court of the United States, than according to the rules of the common law.

Amendment VIII

Excessive bail shall not be required, nor excessive fines imposed, nor cruel and unusual punishments inflicted.

Amendment IX

The enumeration in the Constitution, of certain rights, shall not be construed to deny or disparage others retained by the people.

Amendment X

The powers not delegated to the United States by the Constitution, nor prohibited by it to the States, are reserved to the States respectively, or to the people.

Amendment XI [1798]

The Judicial power of the United States shall not be construed to extend to any suit in law or equity, commenced or prosecuted against one of the United States by Citizens of another State, or by Citizens or Subjects of any Foreign State.

Amendment XII [1804]

The Electors shall meet in their respective states and vote by ballot for President and Vice-President, one of whom, at least, shall not be an inhabitant of the same state with themselves; they shall name in their ballots the person voted for as President, and in distinct ballots the person voted for as Vice-President, and they shall make distinct lists of all persons voted for as President, and of all persons voted for as Vice-President, and of the number of votes for each, which lists they shall sign and certify, and transmit sealed to the seat of the government of the United States, directed to the President of the Senate;—The President of the Senate shall, in the presence of the Senate and House of Representatives, open all the certificates and the votes shall then be counted;—The person having the greatest number of votes for President, shall be the President, if such number be a majority of the whole number of Electors appointed; and if no person have such majority, then from the persons having the highest numbers not exceeding three on the list of those voted for as President, the House of Representatives shall choose immediately, by ballot, the President. But in choosing the President, the votes shall be taken by states, the representation from each state having one vote; a quorum for this purpose shall consist of a member or members from two-thirds of the states, and a majority of all the states shall be necessary to a choice. And if the House of Representatives shall not choose a President whenever the right of choice shall devolve upon them before the fourth day of March next following, then the Vice-President shall act as President, as in the case of the death or other constitutional disability of the President.[10]—The person having the greatest number of votes as Vice-President, shall be the Vice-President, if such number be a majority of the whole number of Electors appointed, and if no person have a majority, then from the two highest numbers on the list, the

---

[10] Refer to the Twentieth Amendment.

Senate shall choose the Vice-President; a quorum for the purpose shall consist of two-thirds of the whole number of Senators, and a majority of the whole number shall be necessary to a choice. But no person constitutionally ineligible to the office of President shall be eligible to that of Vice-President of the United States.

Amendment XIII [1865]

Section 1. Neither slavery nor involuntary servitude, except as a punishment for crime whereof the party shall have been duly convicted, shall exist within the United States, or any place subject to their jurisdiction.

Section 2. Congress shall have power to enforce this article by appropriate legislation.

Amendment XIV [1868]

Section 1. All persons born or naturalized in the United States, and subject to the jurisdiction thereof, are citizens of the United States and of the State wherein they reside. No State shall make or enforce any law which shall abridge the privileges or immunities of citizens of the United States; nor shall any State deprive any person of life, liberty, or property, without due process of law; nor deny to any person within its jurisdiction the equal protection of the laws.

Section 2. Representatives shall be apportioned among the several States according to their respective numbers, counting the whole number of persons in each State, excluding Indians not taxed. But when the right to vote at any election for the choice of electors for President and Vice President of the United States, Representatives in Congress, the Executive and Judicial officers of a State, or the members of the Legislature thereof, is denied to any of the male inhabitants of such State, being twenty-one years of age,[11] and citizens of the United States, or in any way abridged, except for participation in rebellion, or other crime, the basis of representation therein shall be reduced in the proportion which the number of such male citizens shall bear to the whole number of male citizens twenty-one years of age in such State.

Section 3. No person shall be a Senator or Representative in Congress, or elector of President and Vice President, or hold any office, civil or military, under the United States, or under any State, who having previously taken an oath, as a member of Congress, or as an officer of the United States, or as a member of any State legislature, or as an executive or judicial officer of any State, to support the Constitution of the United States, shall have engaged in insurrection or rebellion against the same, or given aid or comfort to the enemies thereof. But Congress may by a vote of two thirds of each House, remove such disability.

Section 4. The validity of the public debt of the United States, authorized by law, including debts incurred for payment of pensions and bounties for services in suppressing insurrection or rebellion, shall not be questioned. But neither the United States nor any State shall assume or pay any debt or obligation incurred in aid of insurrection or rebellion against the United States, or any claim for the loss or emancipation of any slave; but all such debts, obligations and claims shall be held illegal and void.

---

[11]Refer to the Twenty-Sixth Amendment.

Section 5. The Congress shall have power to enforce, by appropriate legislation, the provisions of this article.

Amendment XV [1870]

Section 1. The right of citizens of the United States to vote shall not be denied or abridged by the United States or by any State on account of race, color, or previous condition of servitude.

Section 2. The Congress shall have power to enforce this article by appropriate legislation.

Amendment XVI [1913]

The Congress shall have power to lay and collect taxes on incomes, from whatever source derived, without apportionment among the several States, and without regard to any census or enumeration.

Amendment XVII [1913]

(1) The Senate of the United States shall be composed of two Senators from each State, elected by the people thereof, for six years; and each Senator shall have one vote. The electors in each State shall have the qualifications requisite for electors of the most numerous branch of the State legislatures.

(2) When vacancies happen in the representation of any State in the Senate, the executive authority of such State shall issue writs of election to fill such vacancies: *Provided,* That the legislature of any State may empower the executive thereof to make temporary appointments until the people fill the vacancies by election as the legislature may direct.

(3) This amendment shall not be so construed as to affect the election or term of any Senator chosen before it becomes valid as part of the Constitution.

Amendment XVIII [1919]

Section 1. After one year from the ratification of this article the manufacture, sale, or transportation of intoxicating liquors within, the importation thereof into, or the exportation thereof from the United States and all territory subject to the jurisdiction thereof for beverage purposes is hereby prohibited.

Section 2. The Congress and the several States shall have concurrent power to enforce this article by appropriate legislation.

Section 3. This article shall be inoperative unless it shall have been ratified as an amendment to the Constitution by the legislatures of the several States, as provided in the Constitution, within seven years from the date of the submission hereof to the States by the Congress.[12]

---

[12]Refer to the Twenty-First Amendment.

Amendment XIX [1920]

(1) The right of citizens of the United States to vote shall not be denied or abridged by the United States or by any State on account of sex.

(2) Congress shall have power to enforce this article by appropriate legislation.

Amendment XX [1933]

Section 1. The terms of the President and Vice President shall end at noon on the 20th day of January, and the terms of Senators and Representatives at noon on the 3rd day of January, of the years in which such terms would have ended if this article had not been ratified; and the terms of their successors shall then begin.

Section 2. The Congress shall assemble at least once in every year, and such meeting shall begin at noon on the 3rd day of January, unless they shall by law appoint a different day.

Section 3. If, at the time fixed for the beginning of the term of the President, the President elect shall have died, the Vice President elect shall become President. If the President shall not have been chosen before the time fixed for the beginning of his term or if the President elect shall have failed to qualify, then the Vice President elect shall act as President until a President shall have qualified; and the Congress may by law provide for the case wherein neither a President elect nor a Vice President elect shall have qualified, declaring who shall then act as President, or the manner in which one is to act shall be selected, and such person shall act accordingly until a President or Vice President shall have qualified.

Section 4. The Congress may by law provide for the case of the death of any of the persons from whom the House of Representatives may choose a President whenever the right of choice shall have devolved upon them, and for the case of the death of any of the persons from whom the Senate may choose a Vice President whenever the right of choice shall have devolved upon them.

Section 5. Sections 1 and 2 shall take effect on the 15th day of October following the ratification of this article.

Section 6. This article shall be inoperative unless it shall have been ratified as an amendment to the Constitution by the legislatures of three-fourths of the several States within seven years from the date of its submission.

Amendment XXI [1933]

Section 1. The eighteenth article of amendment to the Constitution of the United States is hereby repealed.

Section 2. The transportation or importation into any State, Territory, or possession of the United States for delivery or use therein of intoxicating liquors, in violation of the laws thereof, is hereby prohibited.

Section 3. This article shall be inoperative unless it shall have been ratified as an amendment to the Constitution by conventions in the several States, as provided in the Constitution, within seven years from the date of the submission hereof to the States by the Congress.

Amendment XXII [1951]

Section 1. No person shall be elected to the office of the President more than twice, and no person who has held the office of President, or acted as President, for more than two years of a term to which some other person was elected President shall be elected to the office of President more than once. But this Article shall not apply to any person holding the office of President when this Article was proposed by the Congress, and shall not prevent any person who may be holding the office of President, or acting as President, during the term within which this Article becomes operative from holding the office of President or acting as president during the remainder of such term.

Section 2. This article shall be inoperative unless it shall have been ratified as an amendment to the Constitution by the legislatures of three-fourths of the several States within seven years from the date of its submission to the States by the Congress.

Amendment XXIII [1961]

Section 1. The District constituting the seat of Government of the United States shall appoint in such manner as the Congress may direct:

A number of electors of President and Vice President equal to the whole number of Senators and Representatives in Congress to which the District would be entitled if it were a State, but in no event more than the least populous state; they shall be in addition to those appointed by the states, but they shall be considered, for the purposes of the election of President and Vice Prisident, to be electors appointed by a state; and they shall meet in the District and perform such duties as provided by the twelfth article of amendment.

Section 2. The Congress shall have power to enforce this article by appropriate legislation.

Amendment XXIV [1964]

Section 1. The right of citizens of the United States to vote in any primary or other election for President or Vice President, for electors for President or Vice President, or for Senator or Representative in Congress, shall not be denied or abridged by the United States or any State by reason of failure to pay any poll tax or other tax.

Section 2. The Congress shall have power to enforce this article by appropriate legislation.

Amendment XXV [1967]

Section 1. In case of the removal of the President from office or of his death or resignation, the Vice President shall become President.

Section 2. Whenever there is a vacancy in the office of the Vice President, the President shall nominate a Vice President who shall take office upon confirmation by a majority vote of both Houses of Congress.

Section 3. Whenever the President transmits to the President pro tempore of the Senate and the Speaker of the House of Representatives his written declaration that he is unable to discharge the powers and duties of his office, and until he transmits to them a written declaration to the contrary, such powers and duties shall be discharged by the Vice President as Acting President.

Section 4. Whenever the Vice President and a majority of either the principal officers of the executive departments or of such other body as Congress may by law provide, transmit to the President pro tempore of the Senate and the Speaker of the House of Representatives their written declaration that the President is unable to discharge the powers and duties of his office, the Vice President shall immediately assume the powers and duties of the office as Acting President.

Thereafter, when the President transmits to the President pro tempore of the Senate and the Speaker of the House of Representatives his written declaration that no inability exists, he shall resume the powers and duties of his office unless the Vice President and a majority of either the principal officers of the executive departments or of such other body as Congress may by law provide, transmit within four days to the President pro tempore of the Senate and the Speaker of the House of Representatives their written declaration that the President is unable to discharge the powers and duties of his office. Thereupon Congress shall decide the issue, assembling within forty-eight hours for that purpose if not in session. If the Congress, within twenty-one days after receipt of the latter written declaration, or, if Congress is not in session, within twenty-one days after Congress is required to assemble, determines by two-thirds vote of both Houses that the President is unable to discharge the powers and duties of his office, the Vice President shall continue to discharge the same as Acting President; otherwise, the President shall resume the powers and duties of his office.

Amendment XXVI [1971]

Section 1. The right of citizens of the United States, who are eighteen years of age or older, to vote shall not be denied or abridged by the United States or by any State on account of age.

Section 2. The Congress shall have power to enforce this article by appropriate legislation.

Amendment XXVII [1992]

No law, varying the compensation for the services of the Senators and Representatives, shall take effect, until an election of Representatives shall have intervened.

Glossary of Legal Terms

A

absolute privilege   In libel and slander law, situations where a defendant is entirely excused from liability for defamatory statements because of the circumstances under which the statements were made.

acceptance   The actual or implied receipt and retention of that which is tendered or offered.

accord and satisfaction   A legally binding agreement to settle a disputed claim for a definite amount.

accredited investors   Financially sophisticated and/or wealthy individuals and institutions who understand and can withstand the risk associated with securities investments.

act of state doctrine   The view that a judge in the United States or another country does not have the authority to challenge the legality of acts by a foreign government within that foreign government's own borders.

actus reus   Wrongful act or omission.

ad substantiation   Under Federal Trade commission policy, product claims for which reasonable evidentiary support does not exist. Constitute unfair and deceptive trade practices.

ad valorem   According to value. Hence, an ad valorem tax would be based upon the value of the item in question rather than, for example, a fixed rate for all such items.

adjudication   The formal pronouncement of a judgment in a legal proceeding.

adjustment of debts   Individuals with limited debts are protected from creditors while paying their debts in installments (Chapter 13).

administrative agency   An agency of the government charged with administering particular legislation.

administrative law   That branch of public law addressing the operation of the government's various agencies and commissions. Also the rules and regulations established by those agencies and commissions.

administrative law judge   An officer who presides at the initial hearing on matters litigated before an administrative agency. He or she is independent of the agency staff.

Administrative Procedure Act   A federal statute specifying the procedural rules under which the government's agencies and commissions conduct their business.

adverse impact   An employee may make a prima facie case for adverse impact where the employer's facially neutral rule may result in a different impact on one protected group than on another.

adverse possession   Open and notorious possession of real property over a given length of time that denies ownership in any other claimant.

advisory jurisdiction   Power of the ICJ to hear a dispute and to render an advisory opinion on the matter. The opinion is not binding on any party.

affidavit   A written statement sworn to by a person officially empowered to administer an oath.

affirmative action   A government/private sector program, springing from the civil rights movement, designed to *actively promote* the employment or educational opportunities of protected classes rather than merely forbidding discrimination.

affirmative defense   A portion of a defendant's answer to a complaint in which defendant presents contentions that, if proved true, will relieve the defendant of liability even if the assertions in the complaint are correct.

agent   A person entrusted by a principal to act on behalf of that principal; one who is authorized to carry out the business of another.

agreement   A meeting of the minds based upon an offer by one party and acceptance by another.

alternate dispute resolution   The growing practice of employing strategies other than conventional litigation to solve conflicts. Those strategies include negotiation, arbitration, and mediation with variations such as "minitrials" and "rent-a-judge" arrangements.

amicus curiae   A "friend of the court" who, though not a party to the case, files a brief because of a strong interest in the litigation.

annual percentage rate (APR)   The rate of interest charged for borrowing money as expressed in a standardized, yearly manner allowing for comparison among lenders' fees.

annual percentage yield (APY)   The rate of interest paid on a deposit as expressed in a standardized, yearly manner allowing for comparison of returns among institutions.

answer   The defendant's first pleading in a lawsuit, in which the defendant responds to the allegations raised in the plaintiff's complaint.

anticipatory breach   A contracting party's indication before the time for performance that he cannot or will not perform the contract. Same as anticipatory repudiation.

appeal   The judicial process by which a party petitions a higher court to review the decisions of a lower court or agency in order to correct errors.

appellant   The party filing an appeal.

appellee   The party against whom an appeal is filed.

appraisal   Assessment of the value of property by one with appropriate qualifications for the task.

appropriation   Making commercial use of an individual's name or likeness without permission.

arbitrary trademark   A trademark that is a new word or a common word that bears no relation to the product to which it is applied.

arbitration   An extrajudicial process in which a dispute is submitted to a mutually agreeable third party for a decision.

arraignment   A criminal law proceeding in which a defendant is brought before a judge to be informed of the charges and to file a plea.

assault   A show of force that would cause reasonable persons to believe that they are about to receive an intentional, unwanted, harmful physical touching.

assignee   A person to whom an assignment is made.

assignment   A transfer of property, or some right or interest therein, from one person to another.

assignor   The maker of an assignment.

assumption of risk   An affirmative defense in a negligence case in which the defendant seeks to bar recovery by the plaintiff by showing that the plaintiff knowingly exposed himself or herself to the danger that resulted in injury.

attachment   As to secured transactions, the process by which a security interest in the property of another becomes enforceable.

at-will employee   An individual not under contract for a specified term and therefore, under the general rule, subject to discharge by the employer at any time and for any reason.

B

bait-and-switch advertising   An unlawful sales tactic in which the seller attracts buyer interest by insincerely advertising a product at a dramatically reduced price while holding no genuine intent to sell the product at that price. The seller then disparages the "bait" and diverts the buyer's attention to a higher-priced product (the switch), which was the sales goal from the first.

barriers to entry   Economic or technological conditions in a market making entry by a new competitor very difficult.

battery   An intentional, unwanted, harmful physical touching.

beyond a reasonable doubt   The level of proof required for conviction in a criminal case.

bilateral contract   A contract formed by an offer requiring a reciprocal promise.

blacklists   Lists of union organizers or participants in labor activities circulated to companies in order to dissuade the companies from hiring the listed individuals.

blue laws   Laws forbidding certain kinds of business on Sundays.

blue sky laws   Statutes regulating the sale of stocks and other securities to prevent consumer fraud.

bona fide   In good faith; honestly.

bona fide occupational qualification (BFOQ)   A defense in a discrimination claim where the employer argues that a particular religion, sex, or national origin is a necessary qualification for a particular job.

boycott   A confederation or conspiracy involving a refusal to do business with another or an attempt by the confederation to stop others from doing business with the target person or organization.

breach of contract   Failure, without legal excuse, to perform any promise that forms the whole or part of a contract.

breach of warranty   Failure, without legal excuse, to fulfill the terms of the guarantee.

bribe   Anything of value given or taken with the corrupt intent to influence an official in the performance of her or his duties.

brief   A written document setting out for the court the facts, the law, and the argument of a party to the lawsuit.

burden of proof   The party with the burden of proof (normally the plaintiff in a civil suit and the state in a criminal case) is required to prove the truth of a claim or lose on that issue.

business judgment rule   A rule protecting business managers from liability for making bad decisions when they have acted prudently and in good faith.

bylaws   A document that governs the maintenance and operation of an organization.

C

capacity   The ability to incur legal obligations and acquire legal rights.

capitalism   Private ownership of the means of production with a largely unrestricted marketplace in goods and services.

cause in fact   The actual cause of an event. One of the required elements in a negligence claim.

cause of action   The legal theory upon which a lawsuit is based.

caveat emptor   Let the buyer beware.

cease and desist order   An instruction from an agency instructing a party to refrain from a specified goal.

certificate of incorporation   An instrument from the state bestowing the right to do business under the corporate form of organization. Same as charter.

certiorari   A legal procedure affording an appellate court the opportunity to review a lower court decision. Also a writ asking the lower court for the record of the case.

choice of law rule   A rule of law in each jurisdiction that determines which jurisdiction's laws will be applied to a case. For instance, one state may have a choice of law rule that says that the law of the jurisdiction where the contract was signed shall govern any dispute, while another state may apply a different rule.

civil law   The branch of law dealing with private rights. Contrast with criminal law.

class action   A legal action brought by one on behalf of himself or herself and all others similarly situated.

Clean Air Act   Amended in 1990, establishes airquality standards and enforcement procedures for the standards.

Clean Water Act   Establishes standards for water quality relating to the protection of water life as well as for safe recreation, and the enforcement of those standards.

closed-end loan   Credit arrangement where a specified sum is borrowed and a repayment plan usually is established.

closing date   The date on which a transfer of property is made.

Code of Federal Regulations   A compilation of final federal agency rules.

codetermination   German corporate governance and labor law system in which board representation by labor unions is required.

Colgate doctrine   Sellers may lawfully engage in resale price maintenance if they do nothing more than specify prices at which their products are to be resold and unilaterally refuse to deal with anyone who does not adhere to those prices.

collateral   Property pledged as security for satisfaction of a debt.

comity   Courtesy. Nations often recognize the laws of other nations not because they must do so but because of the tradition of comity: that is, goodwill and mutual respect.

Commerce Clause   The portion of the United States Constitution that provides for federal regulation of foreign and interstate trade.

commercial impracticability   The standard used by the UCC to relieve a party of his or her contract obligations because of the occurrence of unforeseeable, external events beyond his or her control.

commercial speech   Speech directed toward a business purpose. Advertising is an example of commercial speech. Such speech is protected by the First Amendment, but not to the degree that we protect other varieties of speech.

Commodity Futures Trading Commission (CFTC)   Federal regulatory agency responsible for overseeing futures trading.

common law   Judge-made law. To be distinguished from statutory law as created by legislative bodies.

common shares   Most universal type of corporate stock.

community property   Property acquired during marriage through the labor or skill of either spouse.

comparable worth   The legal theory that all employees should be paid the same wages for work requiring comparable skills, effort, and responsibility and having comparable worth to the employer.

comparative negligence   Defense in a negligence suit in which the plaintiff's recovery is reduced by an amount equivalent to her contribution to her own injury.

compensatory damages   Damages that will compensate a party for actual losses due to an injury suffered.

complaint   The first pleading filed by the plaintiff in a civil lawsuit.

comp time   Compensatory time. Giving an employee time off from work in place of cash for hours of overtime worked.

concerted activity   Organizing, forming, joining, or assisting labor organizations, bargaining collectively through representatives of the employees' choosing, or other activities taken for the purpose of collective bargaining or other mutual aid or protection.

concurrent conditions   When each party's obligation to perform under a contract is dependent on the other party's performance.

condemning   To appropriate land for public use.

conditions precedent   Conditions that operate to give rise to a contracting party's duty to perform.

conditions subsequent   Conditions that operate to discharge one from an obligation under a contract.

condominium or cooperative ownership   An interest in property where owners retain individual control and specific ownership over a precise segment of real estate, but own common areas as tenants in common.

confession of judgment clause   A clause stipulating that the lessee grants judgment in any action on the contract to the landlord without the formality of an ordinary proceeding.

conglomerate merger   A merger between firms operating in separate markets and having neither buyer–seller nor competitive relationships with each other.

conscious parallelism   Conduct by competitors that is very similar or identical but that is not the product of a conspiracy and thus is not, in and of itself, illegal.

consent decree   A settlement of a lawsuit arrived at by agreement of the parties. Effectively, an admission by the parties that the decree is a just determination of their rights.

consent order   The order administrative agencies issue when approving the settlement of an administrative action against some party.

consequential damages   Damages that do not flow directly and immediately from an act but rather flow from the results of the act.

consideration   A required element in an enforceable contract. The thing of value passing between the parties which results in a benefit to the one making the promise or a detriment to the one receiving the promise.

conspiracy   An agreement between two or more persons to commit an unlawful act.

constructive eviction   A breach of duty by the landlord that makes the property uninhabitable or otherwise deprives the tenant of the benefit of the lease and gives rise to the tenant's right to vacate the property and to terminate the lease.

consumer goods   Under the UCC, goods used or bought primarlily for personal, family, or household purposes.

contentious jurisdiction   Power of the ICJ to hear a dispute and to render a binding opinion on the issue and the parties involved. All parties must give prior consent to contentious jurisdiction.

contingent fee   An arrangement wherein an attorney is compensated for his or her services by receiving a percentage of the award in a lawsuit rather than receiving an hourly wage or specified fee.

contingent workers   Workers that do not have an implicit or explicit contract for ongoing employment.

contract   An agreement that is legally enforceable by the courts.

contract bar rule   The NLRB prohibits an election during the term of a collective bargaining agreement, for a maximum of three years.

contract firm workers   Workers employed by a company that provides them or their services under contract or leases. Usually are assigned to only one customer and work at the customer's worksite.

contract of adhesion   One in which all the bargaining power (and all the contract terms) are unfairly on one side. This often occurs when buyers have no choice among sellers of a particular item, and when the seller uses a preprinted form contract.

contributory negligence   A defense in a negligence action wherein the defendant attempts to demonstrate that the plaintiff contributed to the harm on which the litigation was based. Contrast with comparative negligence.

conversion   Wrongfully exercising control over the personal property of another.

copyright   The creator's (artist, author, etc.) right to control the copying and distribution of his or her work for a period of time specified by statute.

corporate opportunity   A doctrine that prevents corporate officials from personally appropriating an opportunity that belongs to the corporation.

corporation   A form of business organization that is owned by *shareholders* who have no inherent right to manage the business, and is managed by a board of directors elected by the shareholders.

Council on Environmental Quality   Council serves as an advisor to the president in connection with the preparation of the annual Environmental Quality Report.

counterclaim   A cause of action filed by the defendant in a lawsuit against the plaintiff in the same suit.

counteroffer   Response by the offeree that, in its legal effect, constitutes a rejection of the original offer and proposes a new offer to the offeror.

countervailing duties   Duties imposed by a government against the products of another government which has offered subsidies to its own producers.

covered disabilities   A physical or mental impairment that substantially limits one or more major life activities of an individual; a record of such impairment or being regarded as having such impairment.

creditor   A person to whom a debt is owed.

creditor beneficiary   Person who has given consideration, who is an intended beneficiary of a contract though not a party, and thus is entitled to enforce the contract.

crime   A public wrong, an act punishable by the state.

criminal law   Wrongs against society that the state has seen fit to label crimes and that may result in penalties against the perpetrator(s). Contrast with civil law.

cumulative voting   A procedure for voting for directors that permits a shareholder to multiply the number of shares he or she owns by the number of directors to be elected and to cast the resulting total of votes for one or more directors.

curtesy interest   The right of a husband upon the death of his wife to receive all of the wife's real property as long as the two had a child between them.

D

d.b.a.   Doing business as.

de facto   In fact. Actually. As *de facto* school segregation, which is caused by social and economic conditions rather than by government act.

de jure   Legitimate. Lawful. Of right. As *de jure* school segregation, which is caused by government order and thus is legally correct even if morally wrong.

debenture   Any long-term debt instrument, such as a bond, issued by a company or institution, secured only by the general assets of the issuer.

deceit   A tort involving intentional misrepresentation to deceive or trick another.

deception Trade claim which is either false or likely to mislead the reasonable consumer and which is material to the consumer's decision making.

deceptive advertising Advertising practices likely to mislead the reasonable consumer where the practice in question is material in that it affected consumer choice.

decertification petition Election petition stating that a current bargaining representative no longer has the support of a majority of the employees in the bargaining unit.

declaration A document that defines the rights, responsibilities, and powers of property owners in a condominium.

declaratory judgment or order A judicial or agency action expressing an opinion or articulating the rights of the parties without actually requiring that anything be done.

deed An instrument transferring title to property.

deed of trust A three-party instrument used to create a security interest in real property in which the legal title to the real property is placed in one or more trustees to secure the repayment of a sum of money or the performance of other conditions.

defamation A false and intentional verbal or written expression that damages the reputation of another.

default A party fails to pay money when due or when lawfully demanded.

defeasible fee simple A title to property that is open to attack, that might be defeated by the performance of some act, or that is subject to conditions.

defendant The party in a civil suit against whom the cause of action was brought and, in a criminal case, the party against whom charges have been filed.

delegatee The one to whom a duty is delegated.

delegator The one who delegates a duty.

deontological ethics The rightness of an action depends on its conformance with duty, obligation, and moral requirements regardless of outcome.

deposition A discovery procedure wherein a witness's sworn testimony is taken out of court, prior to trial, for subsequent use at trial.

deregulation Returning authority to the free market by shrinking government bureaucracies and reducing government rules.

derivative suit A lawsuit by a stockholder on behalf of the corporation where the corporation declines to act to protect the organization's rights against the conduct of an officer, director, or outsider.

derivatives Specialized trading contracts tied to underlying assets such as bonds or currencies.

descriptive mark A trademark that is merely descriptive of the product or its qualities.

dicta Statements in a judicial opinion that are merely the views of the judge(s) and are not necessary for the resolution of the case.

directed verdict Party to a lawsuit makes a motion asking the judge to instruct the jury to reach a particular decision because reasonable minds could not differ about the correct outcome of the case.

discharged Released from liability.

disclaimer   As to warranties, a contract term wherein a party attempts to relieve itself of potential liability under that contract.

discovery   Legal procedures by which one party to a litigation may obtain information from the other party. Depositions and interrogatories are examples of discovery procedures.

disparate impact   Employment discrimination theory in which a facially neutral employment practice (such as requiring a high school diploma for new hires) results in an unfair and adverse impact on a protected class.

disparate treatment   Theory of employment discrimination wherein an individual or group is intentionally disfavored via actual discriminatory policies and practices.

dissolution   In partnership law, the change in the relation of the partners caused by any partner ceasing to be associated with the carrying on of the business.

diversity of citizenship   One standard by which federal courts may gain jurisdiction over a lawsuit. Plaintiffs and defendants must be from different states and more than $50,000 must be at issue.

divestiture   In antitrust law, a remedy wherein the court orders a defendant to dispose of specified assets.

dividend   A shareholder's earnings from his or her stock in a corporation.

doctrine of sovereign immunity   Principle that a foreign nation may not be sued in American courts, with certain exceptions.

dominant estate   The property accessed through an easement appurtenant or implied easement.

donee beneficiary   Person who has not given consideration, but is an intended beneficiary of a contract, though not a party, and is entitled to enforce the contract.

double jeopardy   The United States Constitution provides that the same individual may not be tried twice in the same tribunal for the same criminal offense.

dower interest   The right of a wife upon the death of her husband to receive a life estate in one-third of her husband's real property.

dramshop law   State laws imposing liability on the seller of intoxicating liquors when a third party is injured as a result of the intoxication of the buyer where the sale has caused or contributed to that intoxication.

due care and diligence   Corporate officers and directors must act in good faith and in a prudent manner.

due diligence   A defense against a securities violation claim where the defendant used ordinary prudence and still failed to find an error or omission in the registration statement.

due process   A constitutional principle requiring fairness in judicial proceedings and that government laws and conduct be free of arbitrariness and capriciousness.

dumping   The commercial practice of selling goods in a foreign market at a price substantially beneath that charged in the domestic market.

duress   Overpowering of the will of a person by force or fear.

duty of due care   Standard of conduct expected of a reasonable, prudent person under the circumstances.

E

easement   The right to use property without taking anything away from the property.

easement or profit appurtenant   The right of an owner of adjacent land to enter or to enter and take away from property next to it.

economies of scale   Expansion of a firm or industry's productive capacity resulting in a decline in long-run average costs of production.

efficiencies   A defense to an otherwise unlawful merger in which costs of production are reduced because of the merger.

election year or certification year bar   NLRB prohibits an election for 12 months following a prior election.

elective share   Legislative mandate that a spouse receive a specific percentage interest in a deceased spouse's estate.

embargo   Government order prohibiting importation of some or all products from a particular country.

embezzlement   The fraudulent and unauthorized taking of the money of another while charged with the care of that money.

Emergency Planning and Community Right-to-Know Act of 1986   Amended Superfund requiring companies to inform the government upon release of any hazardous chemicals into the environment, and to provide to the government an inventory of their hazardous chemicals. The act also requires states to establish emergency procedures for chemical discharges.

eminent domain   The state's power to take private property for public use.

employer identification number   Number issued to employer by federal and state governments for the purpose of record keeping associated with income and social security tax collections.

en banc   All of the judges hearing a case as a group rather than individually or in panels.

enabling legislation   Law that establishes an administrative agency and grants power to that agency.

enjoin   To require. A court issues an injunction requiring a certain act or ordering a party to refrain from a certain act.

enterprise law   Legal doctrine treating all companies in a corporate group as one giant organization rather than a collection of smaller, independent units.

entity law   Legal doctrine treating each company in a corporate group as a separate, independent unit.

environmental impact statement   Statement of the anticipated impact on the environment of legislation or other major federal action, and suggestions for reasonable alternatives.

Environmental Protection Agency   Created in 1970 to gather information relating to pollution and to assist in pollution control efforts and sanctions.

equal protection   The Fourteenth Amendment to the United States Constitution provides that all similarly situated individuals are entitled to the same advantages and must bear the same burdens under the law.

equitable remedies   Injunction, specific performance, restraining orders, and the like, as opposed to money damages.

equity   Fairness; a system of courts that developed in England. A chancellor presided to mete out fairness in cases that were not traditionally assigned to the law courts headed by the king.

essential functions of a position   Those tasks that are fundamental, as opposed to marginal or unnecessary, to the fulfillment of the position's objectives.

establishment clause   The First Amendment to the United States Constitution forbids the United States government from creating a government-supported church or religion.

estate   An interest in land or property owned by a decedent at the time of her or his death.

estate per *autre vie*   A life estate that is measured by the life of someone other than the possessor.

estoppel   A legal doctrine providing that one may not assert facts that are in conflict with one's own previous acts or deeds.

eviction   Depriving the tenant of the possession of the leased premises.

excise taxes   Taxes imposed at both the state and federal levels on the sale of particular commodities, especially alcohol, tobacco, and gasoline.

exclusive dealing   Agreement to deal only with a particular buyer or a particular seller.

exculpatory clause   Portion of a contract that seeks to relieve one of the parties to the contract from any liability for breach of duty under that contract.

executed   In contract law, full performance of the terms of the bargain.

executed contract   Performances are complete.

executory contract   Not yet fully performed, completed.

exemplary damages   Same as punitive damages.

exempt property   Specified classes of property which are unavailable to the creditor upon default of the debtor.

exempt security   Certain kinds of securities and certain transactions involving securities are not required to meet federal registration requirements under the 1933 act.

existentialism   A philosophy emphasizing the individual's responsibility to make herself what she is to become. Existence precedes essence.

express authority   Corporate officers' powers as expressed in the bylaws or conferred by the board of directors.

express authorization   In contract law, offeror specifies a means of communication by which the offeree can accept.

express conditions   Conditions within contracts that are clear from the language.

express contract   Contract whose terms are clear from the language.

express warranty   A guarantee made by affirmation of fact or promise, by description of the goods, or by sample or model.

expropriation   A government's taking of a business's assets, such as a manufacturing facility, usually without just compensation.

extraterritoriality   The application of United States laws on persons, rights, or relations beyond the geographic limits of this country and even though the parties involved are not American citizens.

F

failing company doctrine   A defense to an otherwise unlawful merger in which the acquired firm is going out of business and no other purchaser is available.

fair use   A doctrine that permits the use of copyrighted works for purposes such as criticism, news reporting, training, or research.

false imprisonment   Tort of intentionally restricting the freedom of movement of another.

false light   Falsely and publicly attributing certain characteristics, conduct, or beliefs to another such that a reasonable person would be highly offended.

featherbedding   A labor law term describing the practice where workers were paid even though they did not perform any work. Featherbedding is a violation of federal labor law.

federal question   Litigation involving the federal constitution, statutes, and treaties. The federal courts have jurisdiction over cases involving federal questions.

Federal Register   Daily publication of federal agency regulations and other legal materials coming from the executive branch of government.

Federal Sentencing Guidelines   Standards established by the U.S. Sentencing Commission that rank the seriousness of individual and organizational federal crimes and provide sentences that, with little flexibility, must be applied to those crimes.

Federal Trade Commission   Agency of the federal government responsible for promoting fair trade practices in interstate commerce.

federalism   The division of authority between the federal government and the states to maintain workable cooperation while diffusing political power.

fee simple   A form of land ownership that gives the owner the right to possess and to use the land for an unlimited period of time, subject only to governmental or private restrictions, and unconditional power to dispose of the property during his or her lifetime or upon death.

felony   A crime of a serious nature ordinarily involving punishment by death or imprisonment in a penitentiary.

fiduciary   One who holds a relationship of trust with another and has an obligation to act in the best interests of the other; as one who manages property on behalf of another.

fiduciary duty   The responsibility of one in a position of trust with another to act in the best interests of the other.

financing statement   Document notifying others that the creditor claims an interest in the debtor's collateral. Must be filed as provided for by law in order to perfect a security interest.

firm offer   Under the Uniform Commercial Code, a signed, written offer by a merchant containing assurances that it will be held open, and which is not revocable for the time stated in the offer, or for a reasonable time if no such time is stated.

fixture   A thing that was originally personal property and that has actually or constructively affixed to the soil itself or to some structure legally a part of the land.

foreclose   To terminate the mortgagor's rights in the property covered by the mortgage.

franchise   A marketing arrangement in which the franchisor permits the franchisee to produce, distribute, or sell the franchisor's product using the franchisor's name or trademark.

franchisee   A holder of a franchise.

franchisor   A party granting a franchise.

fraud   An intentional misrepresentation of a material fact with intent to deceive where the misrepresentation is justifiably relied on by another and damages result.

fraud-on-the-market theory   Misleading statements distort the market and thus defraud a securities buyer whether the buyer actually relies on the misstatement or not. Based on the assumption that the price of a stock reflects all of the available information about that stock.

Free Exercise Clause   First Amendment provision guaranteeing all Americans the right to pursue their religious beliefs free of government intervention (with limited exceptions).

free riders   Those who lawfully benefit from goods or services without paying a share of the cost of those goods or services.

Full Faith and Credit Clause   Provision of the United States Constitution requiring each state to recognize the laws and judicial decisions of all other states.

futures   Contracts to deliver or take delivery of specified quantities of commodities at a previously specified price.

G

G7   An association embracing seven of the world's leading industrial powers (Canada, France, Italy, Germany, Japan, the United Kingdom, and the United States) designed to improve worldwide economic and political conditions.

garnishment   Action by a creditor to secure the property of a debtor where that property is held by a third party.

General Agreement on Tariffs and Trade   Establishes and regulates import duties among signatory countries.

general duty   An OSHA provision requiring that employers furnish to each employee a place of employment free from recognized hazards that cause or are likely to cause death or serious physical harm to the employee.

general warranty deed   A deed that carries with it certain warranties or guarantees.

generic mark   A trademark employing a common descriptive name for a product.

genuineness of assent   In contract law, the parties knowingly agreed to the same thing.

going public   Selling shares in a company on the open market.

good faith   Honesty; an absence of intent to take advantage of another.

goods   All things that are movable at the time of identification to the contract for sale except the money in which the price is to be paid, investment securities, and so forth.

grand jury   A body of people convened by the state to determine whether the evidence is sufficient to bring a criminal indictment (formal accusation) against a party.

grant deed   A deed that does not have the warranties contained in a warranty deed.

gray market   Transactions conducted outside the usual supplier-approved channels of distribution. These transactions (unlike *black market* sales) are lawful but are often discouraged by suppliers. The gray market operates parallel to the "officially" authorized chain of distribution.

grease   Payments to low-ranking authorities for the purpose of facilitating business in another nation. Not forbidden by the Foreign Corrupt Practices Act if legal in the host nation.

greenmail   Takeover defense involving the target corporation's repurchase of a takeover raider's stock at a premium not offered to other shareholders.

group boycott   An agreement among traders to refuse to deal with one or more other traders.

guarantor   A person who promises to perform the same obligation as the principal if the principal should default.

H

Herfindahl-Hirschman Index (HHI)   Calculation used by the Justice Department to determine the degree of economic concentration in a particular market and to determine the degree to which a proposed horizontal merger would further concentrate that market. Computed by squaring the market share of each firm in a market and summing those totals.

holdover lease   The tenancy that exists where a tenant subject to a term lease is allowed to remain on the premises after the term has expired.

horizontal divisions of the market   Competitors agree to share their market geographically or to allocate customers or products among themselves.

horizontal merger   Acquisition by one company of another company competing in the same product and geographic markets.

hostile environment   A form of sexual harassment in which sexual conduct, sexual remarks, sexual depictions, and the like render the workplace offensive and intimidating such that performance is affected even though no tangible employment action has occurred.

hostile takeover   The acquisition of a formerly independent business where the acquired business resists the union.

I

Immigration Reform and Control Act (IRCA)   Enacted by Congress, IRCA's purpose is to discourage the entry of illegal aliens to the United States.

implied authority   Corporate officers' powers to take actions that are reasonably necessary to achieve their express duties.

implied authorization   In contract law, where the offeror's behavior or previous dealings with the offeree suggest an agreeable means of communicating an acceptance.

implied easement   Also called easement by prescription or way of necessity. An interest created where someone has openly used an adjoining piece of property for access with no complaint from the owner for a statutorily determined period of time.

implied warranty of fitness for a particular purpose   A warranty that arises by operation of law and promises that the good warranted is reasonably useful for the buyer's purpose where the buyer was relying on the seller's expertise in making the purchase.

implied warranty of habitability   Implied warranty arising in lease or sale of residential real estate that the property will be fit for human habitability.

implied warranty of merchantability   A warranty that arises by operation of law and promises that the good warranted is at least of average, fair, reasonable quality.

implied-in-fact conditions   Conditions derived from the parties' conduct and the circumstances of the bargain.

implied-in-law conditions or constructive conditions   Conditions imposed by the court to avoid unfairness.

implied-in-fact contract   Contract whose terms are implicitly understood based on the behavior of the parties.

in personam jurisdiction   The power of the court over a person.

incidental beneficiary   Person who is not a party to a contract, who benefits indirectly from the contract, who was not contemplated by the parties, and who may not enforce the contract.

incidental damages   Collateral damages that are incurred because of a breach; damages that compensate a person injured by a breach of contract for reasonable costs incurred in an attempt to avoid further loss.

incorporators   Those who initiate a new corporation.

indemnification   Corporate policy to compensate officers and directors for losses sustained in defending themselves against litigation associated with their professional duties where those duties were performed with reasonable business judgment.

indemnify   Reimburse one who has suffered a loss.

indenture   Agreement governing the conditions under which bonds are issued.

indenture trustee   Person or institution holding legal title to trust property and charged with carrying out the terms of the indenture.

independent contractor   A person who contracts with a principal to perform some task according to his or her own methods, and who is not under the principal's control regarding the physical details of the work.

indictment   A grand jury's formal accusation of a crime.

Industry Guides   Published advice to industry and the public providing Federal Trade Commission interpretations of the likely legality of specific marketing practices.

information   A prosecutor's formal accusation of a crime.

initial public offering (IPO)   A security offered for sale to the public for the first time.

injunction   A court order commanding a person or organization to do or not do a specified action.

injurious falsehood   Intentional tort based on a false statement made with malice that disparages the property of another.

innocent misrepresentation   An unintentional misrepresentation of material fact where the misrepresentation is justifiably relied on by another and damages result.

insider   In securities law, anyone with a fiduciary duty who has knowledge of material facts not available to the general public.

insider trading   Trading securities while in possession of material nonpublic information, in violation of a fiduciary duty.

intellectual property   Intangible personal property.

intent   A conscious and purposeful state of mind.

intentional infliction of emotional distress   Intentional tort based on outrageous conduct that causes severe emotional distress in another.

intentional tort   Voluntary civil wrong causing harm to a protected interest.

interference with contractual relations   Improperly causing a third party to breach or fail to perform its contract with another.

interference with prospective advantage   Improperly causing a third party not to enter a prospective contractual relationship.

interpretive rules   In administrative law, an agency's view of the meaning of statutes governing agency action.

interrogatories   An ingredient in the discovery process wherein one party in a lawsuit directs written questions to another party in the lawsuit.

intrastate offerings   Registration exemption for securities sold only to residents of the state in which the issuer is organized and doing business.

intrusion   Wrongfully entering upon or prying into the solitude or property of another.

invasion of privacy   Violation of the right to be left alone.

invitee   One who comes on the premises of another by invitation of the owner, in connection with the owner's business, and for the benefit of the owner or for the mutual benefit of the invitee and the owner.

J

joint and several liability   Liability of a group of persons in which the plaintiff may sue all members of the group collectively or one or more individuals for the entire amount.

joint liability   Liability of a group of persons in which, if one of these persons is sued, he can insist that the other liable parties be joined to the suit as codefendants, so that all must be sued collectively.

joint tenancy   An estate held by two or more jointly with an equal right in all to share in the enjoyment of the land during their lives.

joint venture   A form of business organization essentially identical to a partnership, except that it is engaged in a single project, not carrying on a business.

judgment notwithstanding the verdict (judgment n.o.v.)   A judge's decision overruling the finding of the jury.

judgment proof   Describes those against whom money judgments will have no effect because they are insolvent or their assets are beyond the reach of the court.

judicial review   A court's authority to review statutes and, if appropriate, declare them unconstitutional. Also refers to appeals from administrative agencies.

jurisdiction   The power of a judicial body to adjudicate a dispute. Also the geographical area within which that judicial body has authority to operate.

jurisprudence   The philosophy and science of law.

jury instructions   A judge's directions to the jury explaining the law that must be applied in the case at hand.

K

keiretsu   Japanese cartels of vertically related firms working together in a collaborative fashion.

L

land contract   Typically, an installment contract for the sale of land wherein the purchaser receives the deed from the owner on payment of the final installment.

landlord/lessor   A party to a lease contract who allows a tenant to possess and to use his or her property in return for rent payments.

latent defects   Imperfections that are not readily apparent upon reasonable inspection.

lease   A contract for the possession and use of land or other property, including goods, on one side, and a recompense of rent or other income on the other.

leasehold estate   A right to occupy and to use land pursuant to a lease or contract.

legal detriment   Any act or forbearance by a promisee.

legal impossibility   A party to a contract is relieved of his or her duty to perform when that performance has become objectively impossible because of the occurrence of an event unforeseen at the time of contracting.

legality of purpose   The object of the contract does not violate law or public policy.

legitimate nondiscriminatory reason (LNDR)   An employer's justification for taking adverse action against an employee or applicant where the basis for the action is something other than the individual's membership in a protected class (such as termination for dishonesty or theft).

lemon laws   State statutes providing remedies for those buying vehicles which turn out to be so thoroughly defective that they cannot be repaired after reasonable efforts.

letter of credit   A statement from a financial institution such as a bank guaranteeing that it will pay the financial obligations of a particular party.

libel   Tort of defaming or injuring another's reputation by a published writing.

license   A contractual right to use property in a certain manner.

licensee   A personal lawfully on land in possession of another for purposes unconnected with business interests of the possessor.

licenses   Government-granted privileges to do some act or series of acts. Authorization to do what, without a license, would be unlawful. Same as *permits*.

lien   A claim against a piece of property in satisfaction of a debt; the financial interest of the lien-holder in the property as a result of a debt or other obligation of the landowner.

life estate   A property interest that gives a person the right to possess and to use property for a time that is measured by her or his lifetime or that of another person.

life tenant   The possessor of a life estate interest.

limited liability   Maximum loss normally limited to the amount invested in the firm.

limited liability company (LLC)   Hybrid of limited partnership and corporation receiving partnership tax treatment with the operating advantages of a corporation.

limited liability partnership   A special partnership form providing some of the advantages of limited liability.

limited partnership   A form of business organization that has one or more general partners who manage the business and have unlimited liability for the obligations of the business and one or more limited partners who do not manage and have limited liability.

liquidated damages   Damages made certain by the prior agreement of the parties.

liquidation   "Straight" bankruptcy action in which all assets except exemptions are distributed to creditors (Chapter 7).

lockout defense   Takeover defense where the target company manipulates its assets, shares, and so on, in order to make the company unattractive as a takeover candidate.

lockouts   Where employees are kept from the workplace by the employer. Where the landlord deprives the tenant of the possession of the premises by changing the locks on the property.

long-arm statute   A state enactment that accords the courts of that state the authority to claim jurisdiction over people and property beyond the borders of the state so long as certain "minimum contacts" exist between the state and the people or property.

M

mail box rule   Rule holding that a mailed acceptance is effective upon dispatch when the offeror has used the mail to invite acceptance; the rule has been expanded to include the use of any reasonable manner of acceptance.

malice   A required element of proof in a libel or slander claim by a public figure. Proof of a defamatory statement expressed with actual knowledge of its falsity or with reckless disregard for the truth would establish malice.

malicious prosecution   Criminal prosecution carried on with malice and without probable cause with damages resulting.

malpractice   Improper or negligent conduct in the performance of duties by a professional such as a doctor or lawyer.

market failure   Economic theory arguing that the free market works imperfectly because of certain allegedly inherent defects such as monopoly, public goods, and so forth.

market foreclosure   In vertical mergers, the concern that the newly combined firm will close its doors to potential suppliers and purchasers such that competition will be harmed.

market share liability   Product liability action by which plaintiffs may be able to recover against manufacturers of defective products based on those manufacturers' market shares even though proof of causation cannot be established.

material breach   In contract law, performance that falls beneath substantial performance and does not have a lawful excuse.

mechanic's lien or materialman's lien   A claim created by law for the purpose of securing a priority of payment of the price or value of work performed and materials furnished in erecting or repairing a structure.

mediation   An extrajudicial proceeding in which a third party (the mediator) attempts to assist disputing parties to reach an agreeable, voluntary resolution of their differences.

mens rea   Evil intent.

merger   The union of two or more business organizations wherein all of the assets, rights, and liabilities of one are blended into the other with only one firm remaining.

misappropriation   In securities law, taking material, nonpublic information and engaging in insider trading in violation of a fiduciary duty.

misdemeanor   A criminal offense less serious than a felony normally requiring a fine or less than a year in a jail other than a penitentiary.

misrepresentation   The innocent assertion of a fact that is not in accord with the truth.

mitigation   Obligation of a person who has been injured by a breach of a contract to attempt to reduce the damages.

Model Business Corporation Act (MBCA)   Drafted by legal experts, the MBCA is designed to improve corporate law and to serve as a model for state legislatures in drafting their corporate laws.

mommy track   An employment track, whether formally or informally instituted, in some firms that allows for slower upward mobility for mothers who must divide their attention between their positions and their families.

monopoly   Market power permitting the holder to fix prices or exclude competition.

moot   An issue no longer requiring attention or resolution because it has ceased to be in dispute.

mortgage   An interest in land formalized by a written instrument providing security for the payment of a debt.

mortgagee   One who receives a mortgage to secure repayment of a debt.

mortgagor   One who pledges property for a particular purpose such as security for a debt.

most favored nation status (MFN)   Preferential status offered to certain countries under the GATT, WTO, which allows the MFN country to obtain the lowest applicable tariff on goods.

motion   A request to a court seeking an order or action in favor of the party entering the motion.

motion for a directed verdict   A request by a party to a lawsuit arguing that the other party has failed to prove facts sufficient to establish a claim and that the judge must, therefore, enter a verdict in favor of the moving party.

multinational enterprise   A company that conducts business in more than one country.

mutual mistake   Where both parties to the contract are in error about a material fact.

N

National Environmental Policy Act   Requires that the government "use all practicable means" to conduct federal affairs in harmony with the environment.

National Pollutant Discharge Elimination System   Requires that all who discharge pollutants obtain an EPA permit before adding pollutants to a navigable stream.

National Priorities List   A list of hazardous dump or spill sites scheduled to be cleaned using CERCLA funds.

national treatment   Concept that requires that, once goods have been imported into a country, they must be treated as if they were domestic goods (i.e., no tariff may be imposed other than that at the border).

nationalization   A country taking over a private business often without adequate compensation to the ex-owners.

necessaries   That which is reasonably necessary for a minor's proper and suitable maintenance.

negative externality   A spillover in which all the costs of a good or service are not fully absorbed by the producer and thus fall on others.

negligence   Failure to do something that a reasonable person would do under the circumstances, or an action that a reasonable and prudent person would not take under the circumstances.

negligence per se   Action violating a public duty, particularly where that duty is specified by statute.

negligent tort   Unintentional, civil wrong causing harm to a protected interest. Injury to another resulting from carelessness.

nolo contendere   A no-contest plea in a criminal case in which the defendant does not admit guilt but does submit to such punishment as the court may accord.

nominal damages   Small damages, oftentimes $1, awarded to show that there was a legal wrong even though the damages were very slight or nonexistent.

noncompetition clause   Employee agrees not to go into business in competition with employer.

nonpossessory interest   An interest in real property that is not sufficient to be an ownership or possessory interest.

nonprice restraints   Resale limitations imposed by manufacturers on distributors or retailers in any of several forms (such as territorial or customer restraints) that do not directly affect price.

nonreversionary interest   The interest held by the remainderman. It is called nonreversionary because it does not revert to the original grantor.

nonvoting stock   Owners of nonvoting stock participate in firm profits and dividends but may not vote at shareholder meetings.

novation   A mutual agreement between all parties concerned for the discharge of a valid existing obligation by the substitution of a new valid obligation on the part of the debtor or another, or a like agreement for the discharge of a lessee to a landlord by the substitution of a new lessee.

nuisance   A class of wrongs that arises from the unreasonable, unwarrantable, or unlawful use by a person of his or her property that produces material annoyance, inconvenience, discomfort, or hurt.

O

obligor   A person who is bound by a promise or other obligation; a promisor.

offer   A proposal by one person to another that is intended to create legal relations on acceptance by the person to whom it is made.

oligopoly   An economic condition in which the market for a particular good or service is controlled by a small number of producers or distributors.

on-call workers   Workers who report to work only when called.

open-end loan   Credit arrangement not involving a lump sum but permitting repeated borrowing where payment amounts are not specified.

option contract   A separate contract in which an offeror agrees not to revoke her or his offer for a stated period of time in exchange for some valuable consideration.

ordinance   A law, rule, or regulation enacted by a local unit of government (e.g., a town or city).

output restriction   An agreement to limit production which is a per se violation of the Sherman Act and may have the effect of artificially stabilizing or raising prices.

over-the-counter securities   Those stocks, bonds, and like instruments sold directly from broker to customer rather than passing through a stock exchange.

P

parole evidence   When the written document is intended as the parties' final expression of their contract, oral evidence of prior agreements or representations cannot be used to vary the terms of the document.

partial ownership interest   An interest that may revert back to the original grantor.

partition   A legal proceeding that enables joint tenants or tenants in common to put an end to the tenancy and to vest in each tenant a sole estate in specific property or an allotment of the lands and buildings. If division is impossible, the estate may have to be sold and the proceeds divided.

partnership   An association of two or more persons where they agree to work together in a business designed to earn a profit.

past consideration   Performance that is not bargained for and was not given in exchange for the promise.

patent   A right conferred by the federal government allowing the holder to restrict the manufacture, distribution, and sale of the holder's invention or discovery.

patent defects   Imperfections that are visible and obvious.

per curiam   By the court. Refers to legal opinions offered by the court as a whole rather than those instances where an individual judge authors the opinion.

per se   By itself; inherently.

per se doctrine   Certain antitrust violations are considered so harmful to competition that they are always unlawful and no proof of actual harm is required.

peremptory challenge   At trial, an attorney's authority to dismiss prospective members of the jury without offering any justification for that dismissal.

perfection   Process by which a secured party obtains a priority claim over other possible claimants to certain collateral belonging to a debtor.

periodic tenancy   The tenancy that exists when the landlord and tenant agree that the rent will be paid in regular successive intervals until notice to terminate is given but do not agree on a specific duration of the lease.

personal jurisdiction   The authority of a particular court over the parties to a lawsuit.

personal property   Movable property. All property other than real estate.

piercing the corporate veil   Holding a shareholder responsible for acts of a corporation due to a shareholder's domination and improper use of the corporation.

plaintiff   One who initiates a lawsuit.

pleadings   The formal entry of written statements by which the parties to a lawsuit set out their contentions and thereby formulate the issues on which the litigation will be based.

police power   The government's inherent authority to enact rules to provide for the health, safety, and general welfare of the citizenry.

political action committee   A legally defined lobbying group that uses funds and activities to support certain political views.

possibility of reverter   An interest that is uncertain or may arise only upon the occurrence of a condition.

precedent   A previously decided lawsuit that may be looked to as an authoritative statement for resolving current lawsuits involving similar questions of law.

predatory pricing   Selling of goods below cost for the purpose of harming competition.

preemption doctrine   Constitutional doctrine providing that the federal government "preempts the field" where it passes laws in an area thus denying the states the right to pass conflicting laws or, in some cases, denying the states the right to pass any laws in that area.

preemptive right   A shareholder's option to purchase new issuances of shares in proportion to the shareholder's current ownership of the corporation.

preexisting duty   Prior legal obligation or commitment, performance of which does not constitute consideration for a new agreement.

preferred shares   Shares having dividend and liquidation preferences over other classes of shares.

pretext   After an employee has established a prima facie case of discrimination and the employer has articulated a BFOQ or LNDR, the employee must show that the proffered defense is pretextual, that is, that the BFOQ is not actually bona fide (or not applied in all situations) or that the LNDR has been applied differently to this individual compared to another.

price discrimination   Selling goods of like grade and quality to different buyers at different prices without justification where competitive harm results.

price-fixing   An agreement among competitors to charge a specified price for a particular product or service. Also any agreement that prevents a seller from independently setting a price or from independently establishing the quantity to be produced.

prima facie case   A litigating party may be presumed to have built a prima facie case when the evidence is such that it is legally sufficient unless contradicted or overcome by other evidence.

principal   In agency law, one under whose direction an agent acts and for whose benefit that agent acts.

private law   Individually determined agreement of the parties relating to choice of laws, where disagreements shall be settled, and the language of the transactions.

private placements   Securities sold without a public offering, thus excusing them from SEC registration requirements.

privatization   The many strategies for shifting public-sector activities back to private enterprise. Those strategies include contracting out government work to private parties, raising the user fees charged for public services, selling state-owned property and enterprises, and returning government services such as garbage collection to the private sector.

privity of contract   The legal connection that arises when two or more parties enter a contract.

procedural due process   Constitutional principle requiring that the government assure fundamental fairness to all in the execution of our system of laws.

procedural rules   In administrative law, an agency's internal operating structure and methods.

product liability   Refers to legal responsibility of manufacturers and sellers to compensate buyers, users, and, in some cases, bystanders for harm from defective products.

profit à prendre   The right to enter property and to take something away from it, such as crops.

promisee   The person to whom a promise is made.

promisor   A person who makes a promise to another.

promissory estoppel   An equitable doctrine that protects those who foreseeably and reasonably rely on the promises of others by enforcing such promises when enforcement is necessary to avoid injustice.

promoter   A person who incorporates a business, organizes its initial management, and raises its initial capital.

prospectus   A communication, usually in the form of a pamphlet, offering a security for sale and summarizing the information needed for a prospective buyer to evaluate the security.

proximate cause   Occurrences that in a natural sequence, unbroken by potent intervening forces, produce an injury that would not have resulted in the absence of those occurrences.

proxy   Written permission from a shareholder to others to vote his or her share at a stockholders' meeting.

public disclosure of private facts   Public disclosure of private facts where disclosure of the matter in question would be highly offensive to a reasonable person.

public goods   Goods or services usually provided by government when underproduced by markets.

public law   Rules of national law that regulate transactions between parties, as well as the relationships between nations.

public policy   That which is good for the general public, as gleaned from a state's constitution, statutes, and case law.

puffing   An expression of opinion by a seller not made as a representation of fact.

punitive damages   Damages designed to punish flagrant wrongdoers and to deter them and others from engaging in similar conduct in the future.

purchase money security interest   A security interest that is (1) taken or retained by the seller of collateral to secure all or part of its purchase price or (2) taken by a debtor to acquire rights in or the use of the collateral if the value is so used.

Q

qualified person with a disability   An individual with a covered disability who can perform the essential functions of her or his position, with or without reasonable accommodation.

qualified privilege   In libel and slander law, situations where a defendant is excused from liability for defamatory statements except where the statements were motivated by malice.

quantum meruit   As much as he deserves. Describes a plea for recovery under a contract implied by law. Fair payment for work performed.

quasi-contract   The doctrine by which courts imply, as a matter of law, a promise to pay the reasonable value of goods or services when the party receiving such goods or services has knowingly done so under circumstances that make it unfair to retain them without paying for them.

quid pro quo   Exchanging one thing of value for another. In sexual harassment law, quid pro quo cases are those where employment benefits are conditioned on the subordinate's submission to sexual advances.

quitclaim deed   A deed conveying only the right, title, and interest of the grantor in the property described, as distinguished from a deed conveying the property itself.

R

ratified   The adoption or affirmance by a person of a prior act that did not previously bind her or him.

ratify   Adopting or affirming a prior, nonbinding act.

real property   Land, buildings, and things permanently attached to land or buildings.

real property or real estate   The earth's crust and all things firmly attached to it.

reasonable accommodation   An accommodation to an individual's disability or religion that does not place an undue burden on the employer, which may be determined by looking to the size of the employer, the cost to the employer, the type of employer, and the impact of the accommodation on the employer's operations.

reasonable expectations test   Measure of negligence holding that a product is negligently designed if it is not safe for its intended use and also for any reasonably foreseeable use.

reasonable person   Fictitious being the law constructs to determine whether a person's behavior falls short of what a "reasonable person" would do under the circumstances.

red herring   A preliminary securities prospectus which provides information but does not constitute an offer to sell.

redlining   Most commonly, the practice of refusing to make loans in economically unstable areas with the result that minorities are sometimes discriminated against in securing credit.

reformation   An equitable remedy in which a court effectively rewrites the terms of a contract.

registration statement   Document filed with the SEC upon issuance of a new security detailing the information investors need to evaluate that security.

Regulation Z   Rules of the Federal Reserve Board implementing provisions of the Federal Truth-in-Lending Act.

release   Agreement to relinquish a right or a claim. Sometimes labeled a "waiver" or a "hold harmless" clause.

remainderman   One who is entitled to the remainder of the estate after a particular estate carved out of it has expired.

remand   To send back. For example, a higher court sends a case back to the lower court from which it came.

rent   The consideration paid by a lessee to a lessor in exchange for the right to possess and to use property.

rent-strike statutes   Legislation that allows a tenant to deduct from the rent payment the cost of property repairs that are otherwise the responsibility of the landlord.

reorganization   A bankruptcy action in which creditors are kept from the debtor's assets while the debtor, under court supervision, works out a re-payment plan and continues operations (Chapter 11).

res   A thing, object, or status.

res ipsa loquitur   The thing speaks for itself. Rule of evidence establishing a presumption of negligence if the instrumentality causing the injury was in the exclusive control of the defendant, the injury would not ordinarily occur unless someone was negligent, and there is no evidence of other causes.

res judicata   A thing decided. A doctrine of legal procedure preventing the retrial of issues already conclusively adjudicated.

resale price maintenance   Manufacturer's effort to restrict the price at which its product is resold.

rescission   Cancelling a contract; its effect is to restore the parties to their original position.

Resource Conservation and Recovery Act   Authorizes the federal government to provide assistance to states and localities in connection with solid waste, to prohibit open dumping, and to establish programs to recover energy and valuable materials from solid waste.

respondeat superior   Let the master respond. Doctrine holding the employer liable for negligent acts committed by an employee while in the course of employment.

Restatement of Contracts   A collection of the rules of contract law created by the American Law Institute to provide guidance to lawyers and judges.

restitution   A remedy whereby one is able to obtain the return of that which he has given the other party, or an equivalent amount of money.

restraints of trade   Contracts, combinations, or conspiracies resulting in obstructions of the marketplace, including monopoly, artificially inflated prices, artificially reduced supplies, or other impediments to the natural flow of commerce.

restrictive covenant   An agreement restricting use of real property.

retaliation   Various statutes, including Title VII of the Civil Rights Act of 1964, forbid employers from punishing employees who legitimately exercise their legal rights.

reverse   Overturn the decision of a court.

RICO   Federal organized crime law making it illegal to acquire or operate an enterprise by a pattern of racketeering behavior.

right of survivorship   A feature of a joint tenancy that causes a co-owner's interest in property to be transferred on her or his death to the surviving co-owner(s).

right-of-way   Where an easement appurtenant refers to the right to physically cross property.

right-to-know laws   Federal and state laws and regulations requiring employers to assume the affirmative responsibility of acquainting employees with hazardous substances and conditions in the workplace.

risk/utility test   Measure of negligence holding that a product is negligently designed if the benefits of that product's design are outweighed by the risks that accompany that design.

rule of reason   For antitrust purposes, reviewing an agreement in its specific factual setting, considering its pro- and anticompetitive features, to determine if it is harmful to competition.

runaway shop   An employer closes in one location and opens in another to avoid unionization.

S

scienter   Intent to commit a legal wrong. Guilty knowledge.

scope of employment   Limitation on master's liability to only those torts that a servant commits while "about the master's business."

scorched earth defense   Takeover defense where the target corporation takes on new debt, sells assets, and so on, in an effort to make itself a less attractive target.

secondary boycott   Typically a union strategy that places pressure not on the employer with whom the union has a dispute but rather with a supplier or customer of that employer in the hope that the object of the boycott will persuade the employer to meet the union's expectations.

Securities and Exchange Commission (SEC)   Federal regulatory agency responsible for overseeing the securities markets.

security   A stock, bond, note, or other investment interest in an enterprise designed for profit and operated by one other than the investor.
    As to loans, refers to lien, promise, mortgage, or the like, given by a debtor to assure payment or performance of her debt.

security interest   A lien given by a debtor or his creditor to secure payment or performance of a debt or obligation.

self-employment tax   A social security tax on people who are self-employed.

separate property   Property held by either spouse at the time of marriage or property received by either spouse through a gift or inheritance.

separation of powers   The strategy of dividing government into separate and independent executive, legislative, and judicial branches, each of which acts as a check on the power of the others.

service mark   A word, mark, symbol, design, picture, or combination thereof that identifies a service provider.

servient estate   The property subject to an easement appurtenant or implied easement.

sexual harassment   Unwelcome sexual advances, requests for sexual favors, and other unwanted physical or verbal conduct of a sexual nature.

shareholder   One holding stock in a corporation.

shark repellant   Various kinds of corporate behaviors designed to make a company unattractive to potential acquirers.

shelf registration   IPO registration which permits the issuer to hold the securities for sale until favorable market conditions emerge or the issuer needs the proceeds.

short-swing profits   Profits made by an insider through sale/purchase of company stock within six months of acquisition.

slander   A defamatory statement orally communicated to at least one third party.

slander per se   Category of oral defamation not requiring proof of actual harm in order to recover.

small claims courts   Courts of limited powers designed to hear cases involving modest sums of money (often limited to about $1,000) in hearings free of many of the formalities and burdens associated with the more conventional judicial process.

small issues   Registration exemption for securities issued in small amounts.

sole proprietorship   A form of business under which one person owns and controls the business.

sovereign immunity   The government's right to exclude itself from being sued for damages in all but those situations where it consents to be sued. In international law, sovereign immunity permits a nation to decline to be sued in the courts of other nations.

specific performance   A contract remedy whereby the defendant is ordered to perform precisely according to the terms of his contract.

standing   A stake in a dispute sufficient to afford a party the legal right to bring or join a litigation exploring the subject of the dispute.

stare decisis   Let the decision stand. A doctrine of judicial procedure expecting a court to follow precedent in all cases involving substantially similar issues unless extremely compelling circumstances dictate a change in judicial direction.

state action   Situation of a sufficiently close relationship between the state and the action in question that the action can reasonably be treated as that of the state itself.

statute   A legislative enactment.

statute of frauds   A statute specifying that certain contracts must be in writing to be enforceable.

statute of limitations   A statute requiring that certain classes of lawsuits must be brought within defined limits of time after the right to begin them accrued or the right is lost.

straight voting   A form of voting for directors that ordinarily permits a shareholder to cast a number of votes equal to the number of shares he or she owns for as many nominees as there are directors to be elected.

strict liability   Civil wrong springing from defective and "unreasonably dangerous" products where responsibility automatically attaches without proof of blame or fault.

sub S corporation   A close corporation whose shareholders have elected to be taxed essentially like partners are taxed under federal income tax law.

subject-matter jurisdiction   The authority of a particular court to judge a particular kind of dispute.

sublease   A transfer of some but not all of a tenant's remaining right to possess property under a lease.

subpoena   An order from a court or administrative agency commanding that an individual appear to give testimony or produce specified documents.

substantial performance   Performance with minor, unimportant, and unintentional deviation.

substantive due process   Due Process Clause of the Constitution requires that a statute be fair and reasonably related to a legitimate government purpose so that persons are not improperly deprived of their property rights.

suggestive mark   A trademark that suggests the product or its qualities, more than merely descriptive.

summary judgment   A judicial determination prior to holding that no factual dispute exists between the parties and that, as a matter of law, one of the parties is entitled to a favorable judgment.

summons   A document originating in a court and delivered to a party or organization indicating that a lawsuit has been commenced against him, her, or it. The summons constitutes notice that the defendant is expected to appear in court to answer the plaintiff's allegations.

sunset legislation   A statute providing that a particular government agency will automatically cease to exist as of a specified date unless the legislative body affirmatively acts to extend the life of the agency.

Superfund/CERCLA   Established to help pay for the cleanup of hazardous dumps and spills.

Supremacy Clause   An element of the U.S. Constitution providing that all constitutionally valid federal laws are the paramount law of the land and, as such, are superior to any conflicting state or local laws.

surety   A person who promises to perform the same obligation as the principal and is jointly liable with the principal for that performance.

suretyship   A third party agrees to answer for the debt of another.

T

takeover bid   A tender offer designed to assume control of a corporation.

teleological ethics   The rightness of an action depends on its contribution to an end; often the maximum good.

temporary workers   Workers paid by a temporary help or staffing company.

tenancy at sufferance   The leasehold interest that occurs when a tenant remains in possession of property after the expiration of a lease.

tenancy at will   A leasehold interest that occurs when a property is leased for an indefinite period of time and is terminable at the will of either party to the lease.

tenancy by the entirety   A form of co-ownership of property by a married couple that gives the owners a right of survivorship.

tenancy in partnership   The manner in which partners co-own partnership property, much like tenancy in common, except that partners have a right of survivorship.

tenant/lessee A party to a lease contract who pays rent in return for the right to possess and to use property.

tenants in common Co-owners of real property who have undivided interests in the property and equal rights to possess it.

tender offer A public bid to the shareholders of a firm offering to buy shares at a specified price for a defined period of time.

term tenancy The tenancy that exists where a landlord and tenant have agreed to the terms of the lease period and a specific termination date for the lease.

test of nonobviousness Determines whether the development described in a patent application would have been obvious to an ordinary skilled worker in the art at the time the invention was made.

third-party beneficiaries People who are not parties to a contract but who have the right to enforce it because the contract was made with the intent to benefit them.

thrust upon Company holds a monopoly innocently because of superior performance, the failure of competition, or changing market conditions.

tippee In securities law, one who receives inside information from another.

tipper In securities law, one who conveys inside information to another.

tombstone ad A securities advertisement that does not constitute an offer and that usually appears in the financial press set inside heavy black borders suggestive of a tombstone.

tort A civil wrong, not arising from a contract, for which a court will provide a remedy.

totalitarianism A rigid, undemocratic government according power to a particular political group and excluding all others from access to political influence. The Soviet Union, Nazi Germany, and Fascist Italy were totalitarian states.

Toxic Substances Control Act Requires chemical manufacturers to report information relating to chemicals that pose a "substantial risk" and allows the EPA to review and limit, or to stop, the introduction of new chemicals.

Trade Regulation Rules Directives from the Federal Trade Commission interpreting the will of Congress and specifying those practices that the Commission considers unfair or deceptive.

trademark A word, name, or other distinctive symbol registered with the government and used exclusively by the owner to identify its product.

trademark infringement Unauthorized use of the trademark of another.

treaty or convention A contract between nations.

treble damages An award of damages totaling three times the amount of actual damages, authorized by some statutes in an effort to discourage further wrongful conduct.

trespass Entering the property of another without any right, lawful authority, or invitation.

trespasser A person who enters the property of another without any right, lawful authority, or invitation.

tying arrangement Dealer agrees to sell or lease a product (the tying product) only on the conditions that the buyer also purchases or leases another product (the tied product).

U

ultra vires   Corporate conduct beyond the scope of activities provided for under the terms of incorporation.

unconscionable   A contract so one-sided and oppressive as to be unfair.

underwriter   Professional who helps sell new securities or buys those securities for the purpose of resale.

undivided share   A share of the interest in property that is not subject to division into parts.

undue hardship   A burden imposed on an employer by accommodating an individual's disability or religion that would be too onerous for the employer to bear. [See *reasonable accommodation.*]

undue influence   Dominion that results in a right to rescind a contract.

unemployment taxes   Federal and state (most) taxes paid by employers as a percentage of the total payroll for the purpose of funding benefits for those who have lost their jobs.

unenforceable contract   Meets basic requirements, but remains faulty.

unfair labor practice   Activities identified by Congress that employers might use to thwart workers' attempts to unionize and to undermine the economic power that would come from the workers' right to concerted activities and to unionize.

unfair subsidies   Subsidies offered to producers in a certain industry by a government in order to spur growth in that industry. These subsidies are considered unfair if they are used to promote export trade that harms another country.

Uniform Partnership Act (UPA)   Original uniform act for creation and operation of partnerships.

unilateral contract   A contract wherein the only acceptance of the offer that is necessary is the performance of the act.

unilateral mistake   Where one party to a contract is in error about a material fact.

union shop   In labor law, the situation where all employees of a company must join a union in order to retain employment. Forbidden in right-to-work states.

unjust enrichment   An unearned benefit knowingly accepted.

unsecured   Refers to a loan not backed by some kind of security.

use taxes   Normally, taxes imposed on the use, storage, or consumption of tangible personal property bought outside of the state imposing the taxes.

usury   Charging an interest rate exceeding the legally permissible maximum.

V

venture capital funds   Organizations designed to invest in new and often risky business enterprises.

venue   The specific geographic location in which a court holding jurisdiction should properly hear a case, given the convenience of the parties and other relevant considerations.

verdict   The jury's decision as to who wins the litigation.

vertical merger   A union between two firms at different levels of the same channel of distribution.

vesting rights   The right of an individual to a present or future fixed benefit.

vicarious liability   Legal responsibility for the acts of another person because of some relationship with the person; for example, the liability of an employer for the acts of an employee.

voidable contract   Capable of being made void; enforceable but can be cancelled.

voir dire   The portion of a trial in which prospective jurors are questioned to determine their qualifications, including absence of bias, to sit in judgment in the case.

voting stock   Owners of voting stock have the right to vote at shareholder meetings.

W

waiver   Relinquishing a legal right—as the situation where one agrees not to sue if injured while participating in a particular activity, such as attending a baseball game.

warranty   Any promise, expressed or implied, that the facts are true as specified. For example, in consumer law, the warranty of merchantability is a guaranty that the product is reasonably fit for the general purpose for which it was sold.

watered stock   Inadequate consideration received for stock.

white-collar crime   Law violations by corporations or by managerial and executive personnel in the course of their professional duties.

white knight   In a takeover battle, a friendly company that rescues the target company from a hostile takeover. Often the rescue is accomplished by a merger between the target and the white knight.

winding up   In partnership and corporation law, the orderly liquidation of the business' assets.

without reserve   At an auction advertised as "without reserve," the seller is not free to withdraw an item before the high bid is accepted.

workers' compensation laws   State statutes providing fixed recoveries for injuries and illnesses sustained in the course of employment. Under those statutes, workers need not establish fault on the part of the employer.

wrongful discharge   Tort of dismissing another from employment in violation of public policy.

Y

yellow dog contract   An employment agreement by an employee not to become a member of a union.

Z

zoning   Restriction on the use of land as a result of public land use regulation.

zoning ordinances   Dividing a city or a county into geographical areas of restriction—for example, only residential housing would be permitted in an area zoned R.

Selected Internet References

A

Abuse of Workers
http://www.corpwawtch.org

Accountability and Common Sense, Regulation Demanding
http://www.heritage.org/issues/chap3.html

Advertising Law Database
http://www.webcom.com/~lewrose/home.html

Affirmative Action, Washington Post Review of
http://www.washingtonpost.com/wp-srv/politics/special/affirm/affirm.htm

AFL-CIO, Equal Pay Issues
http://www.aflcio.org/women/equalpay.htm

AFL-CIO Home Page
http://www.aflcio.org

AFL-CIO View of Why Workers Should Join Unions
http://www.aflcio.org/front/joinunions.htm

Age Discrimination Database
http://www.aarp.org/wwwstand/agediscm.html

Age Discrimination Law, Questions and Answers
http://www.nolo.com/ChunkEMP/emp2.html

Alternative Dispute Resolution (ADR), International
http://www.internationaladr.org

American Bar Association Antitrust Section
http://www.abanet.org/antitrust

American Bar Association's Business Law
http://www.abanet.org/buslaw/efss/home.html

American Civil Liberties Union (ACLU)
http://www.aclu.org/

American Civil Liberties Union (ACLU), Drug Testing of Students
http://www.aclu.org/news/1999/no81899a.html

American Tort Reform Association (ATRA)
http://www.atra.org/factfict.html

Americans with Disabilities Act (ADA) Database
http://janweb.icdi.wvu.edu.kinder/index.htm
http://www.pcepd.gov/contents.htm

Antibribery Provisions of the FCPA
http://www.tradecompass.com/library/legal/antibri.htm

Anti-Dumping – United States International Trade Administration
http://www.ita.doc.gov/import_admin/records/

Antitrust Division, Federal Justice Department
http://www.usdoj.gov/atr/index.html

Antitrust Division, Federal Trade Commission (FTC)
http://www.ftc.gov/ftc/antitrust.htm

Antitrust Law, Canadian Overview of
http://www.smithlyons.ca/dbic/com_anti.htm

Antitrust Litigation Page, Toys "R" Us
http://www.toysettlement.com/info.html

Antitrust Overview
http://www.law.cornell.edu/topics/antitrust.html

Antitrust Section, American Bar Association
http://www.abanet.org/antitrust

Antitrust Settlement, Nasdaq
http://www.antitrust.org/cases/pricefixing.html#nasdaq

Antonelli, Angela – "Regulation: Demanding Accountability and Common Sense"
http://www.heritage.org/issues/chap3.html

D

Drug Testing of Students, ACLU Challenge to
http://www.aclu.org/news/1999/no81899a.html

Drug Testing in the Workplace
http://www.aclu.org/news/1999/n090199a.html

Dupont and Electromation, Analysis of
http://www.orrick.com/news/emplaw/diverse/5.htm

E

E-Mail and Privacy
http://www.hrlawindex.com/email/email.html

ECOA, Details About
http://www.ftc.gov/bcp/conline/pubs/credit/ecoa.htm

Electromation, Analysis of Dupont and
http://www.orrick.com/news/emplaw/diverse/5.htm

Electronic Commerce, Overview of
http://www.willyancey.com/ele_com.htm

Electronic Deregulation, Overview of
http://www.stateline.org/

Electronic Piracy Advocates
http://www.epic.org
http://www.eff.org

Employment of People with Disabilities, President's Commission on
http://www.pcepd.gov/contents.htm

Employment Discrimination Cases, Summaries of
http://www.wapa.gov/CSO/eeo/cases.htm

Employment Discrimination Database
http://www.law.cornell.edu/topics/employment_discrimination.html

Employment Law Database
http://www.yahoo.com/Government/Law/Employment_Law/

Employment Law Overview
http://www.employlaw.com

Employment of People with Disabilities, President's Committee
http://www.pcepd.gov/contents.htm

Endangered Species Act (ESA)
http://www.wri/org/wri/biodiv/esa-info.html

Environmental Community
http://envirolink.org

Environmental Law Databases
http://ecosys.drdr.virginia.edu/Environment.html
http://seamless.com/alexanderlaw/txt/resource/environ.s
html http://www.law.indiana.edu/law/v-lib/envlaw.html

Environmental Law Searches and Links
http://www.yahoo.com/Society_and_Culture/Environment_and_Nature/Law

Environmental Policy Project
http://www.envpoly.org/index.htm

Environmental Problems, Market-Based Approaches to
http://www.free-eco.org/index.html
http://www.reason.org/environment.html

Environmental Protection Agency (EPA), "Superfund Reforms" of
http://www.epa.gov/oerrpage/superfund/programs/reforms/faqs.htm

Environmental Protection Agency (EPA) Home Page
http://www.EPA.gov/

Equal Credit Opportunity Act (ECOA)
http://www.ftc.gov/bcp/conline/pubs/credit/ecoa.htm

Equal Employment Opportunity Commission (EEOC) Home Page
http://www.eeoc.gov

Ethics, Josephson Institute of
http://www.jiethics.org/

Ethics Database
http://www.scu.edu/Ethics/

Ethics Links
http://www.depaul.edu/ehtics

Ethics Materials, Business
http://www.depaul.edu/ethics

Ethics Online Project, Codes of
http://216.47.152.67/codes/

Ethics Resource Center
http://www.ethics.org/index.html

European Union Merger Law Database
http://europa.eu.int/en/comm/dg04/dg4home.htm

F

Federal Aviation Administration (FAA)
http://www.faa.gov

Global Corporate Governance and Citizenship
http://www.conference-board.org/

Global Corporate Power
http://www.uaw.org.solidarity/9610/11_2.html

Global Exchange
http://www.globalexchange.org

Globalization, Arguments Supporting
http://www.iccwbo.org/home/menu_case_for_the_global_
economy.asp

Globalization, Critique of
http://www.oneworld.orguides/globalization/index.html

Globalization and World Trade
http://www.oneworld.org/guides/trade/front.shtml

Government Aid to Start-Ups
http://www.sbaonline.sba.gov/

Government Intervention, Public Goods
http://plsc.uark.edu/book/books/budget/marketfail/mar-
ket.htm

Gun Litigation Database
http://www.vpc.org/litigate.htm

H

**Harvard University's Berkman Center for Internet and
Society**
http://cyber.law.harvard.edu

Hate Crimes Legislation
http://www.gallup.com/poll/releases/pr990407.asp

Hazardous Waste Clean-up Database
http://www.clu-in.com/

Hoover's Online
http:http://www.hoovers.com

Human Resources Issues
http://www.shrm.org/issues/

Human Rights Watch
http://www.hrw.org/

I

Illness and Injury Report, Bureau of Labor Statistics
http://stats.bls.gov/news.release/osh.toc.htm

Immigration Law Database
http://www.yahoo.com/Government/Law/Immigration/

Indecency in Broadcasting Litigation
http://www.cba.uni.edu/decencyl

Independent Contractor Agreements
http://www.toolkit.cch.com/tools/indcon_m.htm

Insider Trading Law Explanation
http://encyclo.findlaw.com/lit/5650art.htm

Intellectual Property – Cyberspace Law
http://www.law.wayne.edu/litman/newdeve.html

Intellectual Property Database
http://www.cli.org

**Intellectual Property Mall at the Franklin Pierce Law
Center**
http://www.ipmall.fplc.edu

International Business Law, Current News and Updates
http://www.lawnews.net/papers

International Court of Justice (ICJ)
http://www.icj-cij.org/icjwww/icj002.htm

International Labour Organization (ILO)
http://www.ilo.org

International Trade Law Database
http://lexmercatoria.net/

Internet, Freedom of Speech on (Wal-Mart Comment)
http://walmartsucks.com/

Internet, Legal Research on
http://www.virtualchase.com

Internet Law
http://www.willyancey.com/internet_law.htm

**Internet and Society, Harvard University's Berkman
Center for**
http://cyber.law.harvard.edu

J

Josephson Institute of Ethics
http://www.jiethics.org/

Jurisdiction – in Cyberlaw Database
http://www.gseis.ucla.edu/iclp/hp.html

K

Kohlberg's Theory of Moral Development
http://syncorva.cortland.edu/~ANDERSMD/KOHL/cont
ent.HTML

L

Labor Law, Federal Statutes, Regulations, State Codes, etc.
http://www.law.cornell.edu/topics/labor.html

Labor Law Terms, Glossary of
http://www.opm.gov/cplmr/html/glossary/index.htm

Labor Statistics, Federal Bureau of
http://stats.bls.gov/

Lakota Sioux
http://www.lakota.org/

Law, Catalogue of
http://www.catalaw.com/

Law, Cyberspace
http://cyber.findlaw.com/index.html
http://www.cli.org
http://www.gseis.ucla.edu/iclp/decade.html
http://www.law.wayne.edu/litman/newdeve.html

Law – "Hands-On Practice"
http://www.virtualchase.com/govdoc/handson.shtml

Law and Computers
http://www.kentlaw.edu/lrs/lawlinks/computer.shtml

Law and Policy Related to Vertical Restraints
http://www.antitrust.org/law/vertical.html

Law of Speech Codes Outlines
http://www.fac.org/publicat/warwords/warofwrd.htm

Law Topics Database
http://www.findlaw.com
http://www.yahoo.com/law

Lawyer Jokes Database
http://dir.yahoo.com/Entertainment/Humor/Jokes/Lawyer_Jokes/

Legal News Daily Update
http://www.lawnewsnet.com

Legal Problems, Practical Advice on
http://www.nolo.com

Legal Research on the Internet
http://www.virtualchase.com

Lemon Car Page, The
http://www.mindspring.com/~wfl/

Lieback/McDonald's Episode, "actual facts"
http://www.lectlaw. com/files/cur78.htm

Limited Liability Companies
http://www.llc-usa.com/

Litigation
http://overlawyered.com/index.html

M

Management Practice
http://www.net-impact.org/

Markkula Center for Applied Ethics
http://www.scu.edu/Ethics/

Merger Law Database, European Union
http://europa.eu.int/en/comm/dg04/dg4home.htm

Merger Law and Policy, Overview of
http://www.antitrust.org/mergers.htm

Merger Wave, 1998 Congressional Testimony of Robert Pitofsky
http://www.ftc.gov/opa/1998/9806/chairtes.htm

Minimum Wage Laws
http://www.dol.gov/dol/esa/public/minwage/america.htm

Moral Development, Kohlberg's Theory of
http://syncorva.cortland.edu/~ANDERSMD/KOHL/content.HTML

N

NAFTA, Overview of
http://www.nafta.net

NAFTA, Canada/Mexico Trade
http://www.embamexcan.com/trade.html

"NAFTA Stumbles Short of Expectations"
http://www.latinolink.com/nafecon.html

Nasdaq
http://www.nasdaq.com

Nasdaq, Price-rigging Scheme
http://www.antitrust.org/cases/pricefixing.html#nasdaq

National Association of Securities Dealers (NASD)
http://www.nasdr.com

National Basketball Association Collective Bargaining Agreement, Frequently Asked Questions
http://members.home.net/lmcoon/salarycap.htm

National Center for State Courts
http://www.ncsc.dni.us/

National Civil Rights Museum
http://www.midsouth.rr.com/civilrights/

National Constitution Center
http://www.constitutioncenter.org/

National Labor Relations Board (NLRB) Home Page
http://www.nlrb.gov

National Wildlife Federation
http://www.nwf.org/nwf/index.htm

New York Stock Exchange (NYSE)
http://www.nyse.com

O

Occupational Safety and Health Administration (OSHA) Home Page
http://www.osha.gov

Occupational Safety and Health Administration (OSHA) Standards
http://www.osha.gov/comp-links.html

Oncale, Joseph, Case for Employers
http://www.shrm.org/hrmagazine/articles/0698new.htm

Open Secrets
http://www.opensecrets.org/home/index.asp

P

Pace University CISG Database
http://www.cisgw3.law.pace.edu/

Patent and Trademark Office, U.S.
http://www.uspto.gov/

Pensions, Cash Balance, Bernie Sanders's Materials
http://www.house.gov/bernie/legislation/ibm/

Philip Morris
http://www.philipmorris.com

Piracy Advocates, Electronic
http://www.epic.org
http://www.eff.org

Piracy Database, Anti-
http://www.riaa.com/piracy/piracy.htm

Pitofsky, Robert, 1998 Congressional Testimony, Merger Wave
http://www.ftc.gov/opa/1998/9806/chairtes.htm

Pitofsky, Robert, Explanation of Federal Vertical Merger Policy
http://www.ftc.gov/speeches/pitofsky/fordham7.htm

Political Correctness on Campus Critique
http://www.shadowuniv.com

Politics, Center for Responsive – Database on Money in Politics
http://www.opensecrets.org/home/index.asp

President's Committee on Employment of People with Disabilities Database
http://www.pcepd.gov/contents.htm

Price Fixing Database
http://www.antitrust.org/price.htm

Price Fixing Problems, ADM
http://www.herald-review.com/03/adm0711.9html

Privacy, Children's Online
http://www.ftc.gov/os/1999/9910/childrensprivacy.pdf

Privacy, E-Mail and
http://www.hrlawindex.com/email/email.html

Privacy, Online
http://www0.delphi.com/navnet/privacy.html

Privatization Abroad
http://www.adamsmith.org.uk/policy/publications/world-privatization.html

Privatization Database
http://www.privatization.org/

Product Liability
http://www.nfm-online.com/nfm_backs/Oct_99/product_liability.html

Product Liability, Japanese Overview
http://www.faegre.com/areas/area_ib3.html

Public Citizen
http://www.citizen.org/

Public International Law Database
http://www.law.ecel.uwa.edu.au/intlaw/

R

Racketeer Influenced and Corrupt Organizations Act (RICO) Summary
http://www.lectlaw.com/files/cri18.htm

Rand, Ayn, and Objectivism
http://www.aynrand.org

S

T

Taxes on Electronic Commerce
http://www.ryanco.com/gateway/electron.html

Technology, Center for Democracy and
http://www.cdt.org

Telecom Deregulation, Favorable Views and Information on
http://www.telecompolicy.net/dereg/

Texaco's Internet Homepage
http://www.texaco.com

"Tobacco, Children and" – FDA
http://www.fda.gov/opacom/campaigns/tobacco.html

Tobacco Wars
http://headlines.yahoo.com/headlines/business

Tort Law Library
http://www.findlaw.com/01topics/22tort/

Tort Reform Association, American
http://www.atra.org/factfict.html

Toys "R" Us Antitrust Litigation Page
http://www.toysettlement.com/info.html

Traffic Stop Case of Supreme Court
http://www.fbi.gov/leb/nov965.txt

Trans Atlantic Business Dialogue Database
http://www.tabd.com/index1.html

Transparency International
http://www.transparency.de/

Truth in Lending Act (TILA) Protections in Using Your Home as Collateral
http://www.ftc.gov/bcp/conlilne/pubs/homes/getloan.htm

Tying Law in Queen City, Explanation of
http://www.antitrust.org/law/vertical.html

U

UCITA
http://www.nccusl.org
http://www.badsoftware.com

Uniform Commercial Code (UCC), Article II, Sales Text
http://www.law.cornell.edu/ucc/2/overview.html

Uniform Electronic Transactions Act (UETA)
http://www.webcom.com/legaled/ETAForum

Unions, AFL-CIO View of Why Workers Should Join
http://www.aflcio/front/joinunions.htm

Drug Testing of Students, ACLU Challenge to
http://www.aclu.org/news/1999/no81899a.html

Unions, Pros and Cons of Doctors'
http://www.aans.org/library/bulletin/winter99/features/articles.html

UNITE
http://www.uniteunion.org/sweatshops

UNITE – Statement on White House Apparel Industry Partnership
http://www.sweatshopwatch.org/swatch/headlines/1998/aip_nov98.html

United Auto Workers Union, Frequently Asked Questions
http://uaw.org/fags.html

United Nations Environment Programme
http://www.unep.ch/

United States, Poverty in
http://www.census.gov/hhes/www/poverty.html

United States, Water Pollution in
http://www.epa.gov/owow/tmdl

United States, Work Stoppages Involving 1,000 Workers or More in
http://stats.bls.gov/news.release/wkstp.101.htm

United States Copyright Office
http://www.lcweb.loc.gov/

United States Customs Service
http://www.customs.ustreas.gov

United States Department of Labor Home Page
http://www.dol.gov/

United States International Trade Administration, Anti-Dumping
http://www.ita.doc.gov/import_admin/records/

United States Patent and Trademark Office
http://www.uspto.gov/

United Students Against Sweatshops
http://www.asm.wisc.edu/usas/

Utilitarianism Database
http://www.hedweb.com/philsoph/utillink.htm

V

Vertical Restraints, Law and Policy Related to
http://www.antitrust.org/vertical.htm
http://www.antitrust.org/law/vertical.html

Violence Against Women Act (VAWA), executive summary
http://www.usdoj.gov/vawo/cycle.htm

Violence Against Women Office
http://www.usdoj.gov/vawo/

Virtual Chase
http://www.virtualchase.com/govdoc/handson/shtml

Vitamin Civil Case Settlement Documents
http://www.ded.uscourts.gov/99ms197d.pdf

Volokh, Eugene – Sexual Harassment and Freedom of Speech
http://www.law.ucla.edu/faculty/volokh/harass/

W

Wal-Mart, Internet Free Speech and
http://walmartsucks.com/

Washington Post Review of Affirmative Action
http://www.washingtonpost.com/wp-srv/politics/special/affirm/affirm.htm

Water Pollution in the United States
http://www.epa.gov/owow/tmdl

Wellstone, Paul – Critique of the Financial Services Modernization Act
http://www.senate.gov/~wollstone/What_s_New/financeflr.htm

Whistle-blowers
http://www.whistle-blowers.com

White House Apparel Industry Partnership, UNITE Statement
http://www.sweatshopwawtch.org/swatch/headlines/1998/aip_nov98.html#UNITE

Women in Labor Movement, History of
http://www.thehistorynet.com/WomensHistory/articles/19967_cover.html

Work Stoppages Involving 1,000 Workers or More in the U.S.
Http://stats.bls.gov/news.release/wkstp.101.htm

Workers, Abuse of
http://www.corpwawtch.org

Workers' Compensation Laws
http://www.dol.gov/dol/esa/public/regs/statutes/owcp/stwclaw/stwclaw.htm

Workplace Code of Conduct and Principles of Monitoring
http://www.dol.gov/dol/esa/public/nosweat/partnership/report.htm

World Trade Organization (WTO)
http://www.wto.org

Worldwide Regulatory Reform Database
http://www.oecd.org/puma/regref/index.htm

WT0-GATT, Overview of
http://www.wto.org/wto/dispute

Table of Cases

Subject Index